NOVELL'S®

CNE® Study Guide for NetWare® 5.1

NOVELL'S®

CNE® Study Guide for NetWare® 5.1

DAVID JAMES CLARKE, IV

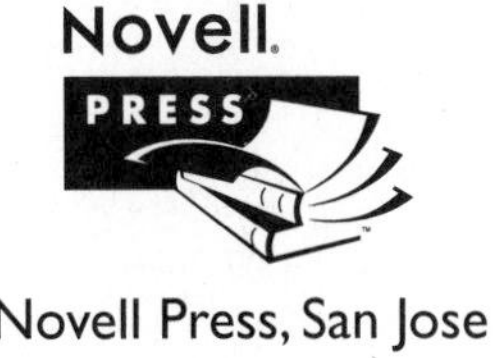

Novell Press, San Jose

Novell's CNE® Study Guide for NetWare® 5.1
Published by
Novell Press
1800 S. Novell Place
Provo, UT 84606

ISBN: 0-7645-4770-4

Printed in the United States of America

10 9 8 7 6 5 4 3 2 1

1P/RV/QT/QR/FC

Distributed in the United States by Hungry Minds, Inc.

Distributed by CDG Books Canada Inc. for Canada; by Transworld Publishers Limited in the United Kingdom; by IDG Norge Books for Norway; by IDG Sweden Books for Sweden; by IDG Books Australia Publishing Corporation Pty. Ltd. for Australia and New Zealand; by TransQuest Publishers Pte Ltd. for Singapore, Malaysia, Thailand, Indonesia, and Hong Kong; by Gotop Information Inc. for Taiwan; by ICG Muse, Inc. for Japan; by Intersoft for South Africa; by Eyrolles for France; by International Thomson Publishing for Germany, Austria, and Switzerland; by Distribuidora Cuspide for Argentina; by LR International for Brazil; by Galileo Libros for Chile; by Ediciones ZETA S.C.R. Ltda. for Peru; by WS Computer Publishing Corporation, Inc., for the Philippines; by Contemporanea de Ediciones for Venezuela; by Express Computer Distributors for the Caribbean and West Indies; by Micronesia Media Distributor, Inc. for Micronesia; by Chips Computadoras S.A. de C.V. for Mexico; by Editorial Norma de Panama S.A. for Panama; by American Bookshops for Finland.

For general information on Hungry Minds' products and services please contact our Customer Care department within the U.S. at 800-762-2974, outside the U.S. at 317-572-3993 or fax 317-572-4002.

For sales inquiries and reseller information, including discounts, premium and bulk quantity sales, and foreign-language translations, please contact our Customer Care department at 800-434-3422, fax 317-572-4002 or write to Hungry Minds, Inc., Attn: Customer Care Department, 10475 Crosspoint Boulevard, Indianapolis, IN 46256.

For information on licensing foreign or domestic rights, please contact our Sub-Rights Customer Care department at 650-653-7098.

For information on using Hungry Minds' products and services in the classroom or for ordering examination copies, please contact our Educational Sales department at 800-434-2086 or fax 317-572-4005.

For press review copies, author interviews, or other publicity information, please contact our Public Relations department at 650-653-7000 or fax 650-653-7500.

For authorization to photocopy items for corporate, personal, or educational use, please contact Copyright Clearance Center, 222 Rosewood Drive, Danvers, MA 01923, or fax 978-750-4470.

Library of Congress Cataloging-in-Publication Data

Clarke, David James, 1964-
Novell's CNE study guide for Netware 5.1 /
David James Clarke, IV.
p. cm.
ISBN 0-7645-4770-4 (alk. paper)
1. Computer networks--Examinations--Study guides.
2. Novell, Inc.--Examinations--Study guides.
3. Telecommunications engineers--Certification.
4. NetWare--Study and teaching. I. Title.

TK5105.8.N65 C532 2001
005.4'4769--dc21 2001016267

John Kilcullen, *CEO, Hungry Minds, Inc.*
Richard K. Swadley, *Senior Vice President, Technology Publishing*

Steve Rife, *Publisher, Novell Press, Novell, Inc.*

Welcome to Novell Press

Novell Press, the world's leading provider of networking books, is the premier source for the most timely and useful information in the networking industry. Novell Press books cover fundamental networking issues as they emerge — from today's Novell and third-party products to the concepts and strategies that will guide the industry's future. The result is a broad spectrum of titles for the benefit of those involved in networking at any level: end user, department administrator, developer, systems manager, or network architect.

Novell Press books are written by experts with the full participation of Novell's technical, managerial, and marketing staff. The books are exhaustively reviewed by Novell's own technicians and are published only on the basis of final released software, never on prereleased versions.

Novell Press at Hungry Minds is an exciting partnership between two companies at the forefront of the knowledge and communications revolution. The Press is implementing an ambitious publishing program to develop new networking titles centered on the current versions of NetWare, GroupWise, BorderManager, ManageWise, and networking integration products.

Novell Press books are translated into several languages and sold throughout the world.

Steve Rife
Publisher
Novell Press, Novell, Inc.

Novell Press

Publisher
Steve Rife

Hungry Minds

Acquisitions Editors
Ed Adams
John Gravener

Project Editors
Julie Smith
Martin V. Minner

Technical Editor
Robb Tracy

Copy Editors
Lane Barnholtz
Jessica Montgomery
KC Hogue

Proof Editor
Cindy Lai

Project Coordinators
Joe Shines
Danette Nurse

Graphics and Production Specialists
Robert Bilhmayer
Rolly Delrosario
Jude Levinson
Michael Lewis
Victor Pérez-Varela
Ramses Ramirez

Quality Control Technician
Dina F. Quan

Permissions Editor
Laura Moss

Media Development Specialist
Travis Silvers

Media Development Coordinator
Marisa Pearman

Illustrator
John Greenough

Proofreading and Indexing
York Production Services

Illustrator
David Puckett

Cartoonist
Norman Felchle

About the Author

David James Clarke, IV is the original creator of the CNE Study Guide phenomenon. He is the author of numerous #1 best-selling books for Novell Press, including *Novell's CNA Study Guide for NetWare 5.1*, *Novell's CNE Update to NetWare 5*, *Novell's CNE Study Guide for NetWare 5*, *Novell's CNA Study Guide for NetWare 5*, *Novell's CNE Study Set for NetWare 5*, and the new *Clarke Notes* series.

Clarke is an online professor for CyberStateU.com (a virtual IT university) and cofounder of the Computer Telephony Institute (home of the CTE certification). He is also the developer of The Clarke Tests v5.0 (an interactive learning system) and producer of the best-selling video series "So You Wanna Be a CNE?!"

Clarke is a Certified Novell Instructor (CNI), a CNE, and a CNA. He speaks at numerous national conferences and currently serves as the president and CEO of Clarke Industries, Inc. He lives and writes in the heart of Silicon Valley.

I dedicate this book in loving memory of Ray Ettelson, a kind and gentle man of character. His light continues to illuminate our path.

Foreword

The author of this comprehensive, if not voluminous, manuscript asked me to write a few words in the form of a brief foreword. It boggles the mind what I could possibly have to say about technology invented five centuries after my birth, but why not? — *I have done crazier things!* As a matter of fact, the evidence against me is overwhelming. So, here we go. . . .

What you are about to experience can best be described as *life changing*. In simpler terms, "the knowledge presented in this guide will significantly alter your perception of network-based communications in such a way that you will permanently modify your behavior toward technology." There you go — life changing.

NetWare 5.1 provides the means for creating a virtual global community. As such, people anywhere can interact with each other instantaneously. While this concept alone boggles even the largest mind, it slowly gains perspective when you place it in the same company as digital watches, microwave cooking, and daytime television. Now, if you are going to be a successful CNE and help us save the world, you will need to expand your understanding of Novell technology beyond the local LAN and into the global Web. When I say "Web" I mean the pervasive worldwide communications network known as the *Internet*.

In order to help expand your understanding of the Novell Internet, the author of this manuscript presents several exciting new technical advancements — many of which dwarf the significance of daytime television. In this guide, you will learn how to build a global Novell Internet and connect to it — using TCP/IP and any client browser. In addition, you will architect a local area network using Ethernet, troubleshoot NDPS printing, optimize the Tree with NDS Manager, and traverse the seven-layer OSI Model. Stunning!

For the record, I still prefer painting, the sundial, and food cooked over an open flame. However, I am sure that I will eventually adapt to the "virtuosity" of 21st century life. After all, we're all in this together, so we might as well make the best of it.

Yours,

Leonardo Da Vinci

Preface

Welcome back!

Leonardo DaVinci once said that inside every stone is a beautiful statue waiting to be exposed. "The trick", he said, "is chiseling away the pieces that don't belong."

Leonardo DaVinci is my inspiration for the *CNE Study Guide* series of Novell certification companions. Through great effort, I have identified the core of NetWare 5.1 design, installation, and management — and it *is* very beautiful. The bottom line is — this book is your guide through the jungle of NetWare 5.1 CNE test objectives. It will help you focus your formal education, study guide lessons, and/or hands-on skills. And to aid you during your quest for "life changing" knowledge, I offer two different types of help at key points during the adventure:

TIP

Highlights time-proven management techniques and action-oriented ideas. These tips are great ways of expanding your horizons beyond just CNEship — they're your ticket to true nerddom.

REAL WORLD

Welcome to the real world. I don't want you to be a two-dimensional CNE in a three-dimensional world. These icons represent the other dimension. In an attempt to bring this book to life, I've included various real-world scenarios, case studies, and situational walk-throughs.

In the first leg of your exciting NetWare 5.1 CNE journey, we explored Novell's CNA certification objectives — also known as NetWare 5.1 Administration. In this first course, we used *Novell's CNA Study Guide for NetWare 5.1* as our road map. We learned about ACME (A Cure for Mother Earth), their mission to save the Net, and how NetWare 5.1 expands local and wide-area networking via Novell Directory Services (NDS).

In this book, *Novell's CNE Study Guide for NetWare 5.1*, we will continue the CNE journey beyond mere Administration tasks, into the realm of "engineer" stuff — such as pure IP, Internet infrastructure, advanced security, optimization,

NDS design, and troubleshooting. We even launch you into the seven-layer OSI model with five comprehensive networking-technologies chapters.

Here's a brief peek forward in time:

- *Part I: NetWare 5.1 Advanced Administration (Novell Course 570)* — In Part I, we will build on NetWare 5.1 Administration with a plethora of advanced CNE tasks, including installation, IP services, and Novell's Internet infrastructure. Then, we'll explore three advanced management arenas — advanced server management, advanced NDS management, and advanced security management. Finally, we'll complete Novell Course 570 with a comprehensive look at NetWare 5.1 optimization.

- *Part II: NDS Design and Implementation (Novell Course 575)* — In Part II, we will expand our NetWare 5.1 LAN into the realm of global NDS connectivity. We will master the first three steps in saving the Net — namely, NDS preparation, NDS design, and NDS implementation. In the first step, we will gather ACME data and build a project team. Then, in Step 2, we will construct ACME's NDS tree with the help of naming standards, tree design guidelines, partitioning, time synchronization, and resource accessibility. Finally, in Step 3, we will execute the plan with a comprehensive NDS implementation schedule.

- *Part III: Service and Support (Novell Course 580)* — In Part III, we will experience NetWare troubleshooting — a boot camp of sorts. In "NetWare Service and Support," you will learn how to troubleshooting NICs, hard drives, workstations, and printing. In addition, we will build a maintenance bag full of troubleshooting tools and learn some preventative medicine with server fitness and network optimization.

- *Part IV: Networking Technologies (Novell Course 565)* — Finally, in Part IV, we will venture into the final frontier of NetWare 5.1 CNEship — networking technologies. This "hands off" conceptual course surveys the entire galaxy of networking, from the OSI model to IP routing to IBM's SNA gateway (and everything in between). First, we will begin with a brief introduction to the OSI model and learn about its three primary functions: communications, networking, and services. Then, we will explore each of these functions in excruciating depth.

As you can see, NetWare 5.1 is much more than a simple file/print server. It includes numerous intranet/Internet solutions for global connectivity. In this book, we will explore the final four nonelective courses for NetWare 5.1 CNEship: Novell Courses 570, 575, 580, and 565.

But you can't do it alone. I'm guessing that at some point, you will want to apply all this "life changing" knowledge to a physical, practical application — a network, perhaps. One assumes that you will act on this book's technical concepts, philosophies, schematics, lab exercise, puzzles, tips, and examples. In the meantime, I'd like to hear from you as I strive to provide the best certification study materials available. Please feel free to e-mail me at `DClarke@iACME.com`. Let me know how you liked this book and/or what features you would like added.

So, get prepared for an adventure through Novell's certification jungle. And don't forget your guide . . . there's no limit to where you can go from here!

Enjoy the show and good luck on the exam!

Acknowledgments

Unless you've lived with a writer, it's hard to understand the divine patience that it takes to accept a writer's crazy hours, strange insights, and constant pitter-patter on the keyboard. Mary, my wife, deserves all the credit in the world for supporting my work and bringing a great deal of happiness into my life. She is my anchor! And, of course, thanks to my two lovely princesses: Leia and Sophie. Somehow they know just when I need to be interrupted — daughter's intuition. Most of all, they both have brought much needed perspective into my otherwise one-dimensional life. For that, I owe my family everything.

Next, I would like to thank the other great architect of this book — my partner Cathryn Ettelson. She has been instrumental in all aspects of this project — research, chiseling away the unneeded stone, testing hands-on exercises in the Mad Scientist's laboratory, building puzzles, and the list goes on. In addition, she has helped me understand that "less is more!" I owe a great deal to this brilliant woman, and I truly couldn't have written this book without her.

Behind every great book is an incredible production team. It all starts with Kevin Shafer — legendary publishing director. His flawless organization, quick wit, and patience were instrumental in bringing this book to life. Kevin did a marvelous job of leading this unique mission from beginning to end. As usual, John Gravener and Ed Adams did their acquisitions duties with aplomb. And, speaking of a great team — how about Julie Smith and Lane Barnholtz. Julie was instrumental in keeping us on our toes and Lane polished the words with a rare craftsman's touch. They are the best one-two punch in the business. Thanks a ton to Robb Tracy for his thorough technical edit of this book. Robb worked very hard to make sure that you receive the latest and greatest infobits from Novell Education. And thanks to Cindy Valdez for opening the gateway to Novell, and Phil Richardson for guidance through the quagmire of Novell course objectives. Also, thanks to Steve Rife for supplying us with what we needed, when we needed it!

Finally, thanks a million to the Hungry Minds' production department, sales staff, marketing wizards, and bookstore buyers for putting this *CNE Study Guide* into your hands. After all, without them I'd be selling books out of the trunk of my car!

I saved the best for last. Thanks to *you* for caring enough about NetWare 5.1, your education, and the world to buy this book. You deserve a great deal of credit for your enthusiasm and dedication. Thanks again, and I hope this education changes your life. Good luck, and enjoy the show!

Contents at a Glance

Contents

PART I

NetWare 5.1 Advanced Administration

CHAPTER 1

NetWare 5.1 Installation

Welcome back!

In the first leg of your exciting NetWare 5.1 CNE journey, we explored Novell's CNA certification objectives — also known as NetWare 5.1 Administration. In this first course, we used *Novell's CNA Study Guide for NetWare 5.1* as our road map. Wasn't that fun?

We learned about ACME (A Cure for Mother Earth), their mission to save the Net, and how NetWare 5.1 expands local- and wide-area networking via Novell Directory Services (NDS). Whether you are a new CNE or just want to manage your network with NetWare 5.1, you need to become intimately familiar with Novell Course 560, "NetWare 5.1 Administration," before you continue this exhaustive CNE journey. See the "Introduction" of this book for a brief review.

In this book, *Novell's CNE Study Guide for NetWare 5.1*, we continue the CNE journey beyond mere administration tasks, into the realm of "engineer" stuff — such as Pure IP, Internet infrastructure, advanced security, optimization, NDS design, and troubleshooting. We even launch you into the seven-layer OSI model with four comprehensive chapters in Part IV of this book, "Networking Technologies." This exhaustive CNE journey all begins with a review of Novell Course 570, "NetWare 5.1 Advanced Administration." In these chapters, we will examine all the cool NetWare 5.1 administrative features that enhance everything we learned in *Novell's CNA Study Guide for NetWare 5.1*. Here's a brief peek:

- **Chapter 1:** *NetWare 5.1 Installation* — We'll start at the beginning. The NetWare 5.1 installation procedure includes a graphical user interface (GUI), NDS integration, improved licensing, and on-the-fly driver support (via Hot Plug PCI and automatic hardware detection).

- **Chapter 2:** *NetWare 5.1 IP Services* — Once we have installed the server, we will discover *Pure IP*! TCP/IP is the pavement of NetWare 5.1's information superhighway. NetWare 5.1 supports native access to TCP/IP networks with the help of DNS/DHCP Services, IPX compatibility, network address translation (NAT), and the Service Location Protocol (SLP).

- **Chapter 3:** *NetWare 5.1 Internet Infrastructure*—So far we have built the NetWare 5.1 server (using NetWare 5.1 installation) and poured the electronic pavement of the Information Superhighway (using TCP/IP and DNS/DHCP services). Now it's time to build a complete Internet infrastructure for access to the World Wide Web. In this chapter, we will learn how to build a complete Internet infrastructure using NetWare 5.1. In preview, we will study the following NetWare World Wide Web components: NetWare Enterprise Web Server, NetWare FTP Server, NetWare News Server, NetWare MultiMedia Server, NetWare Web Search Server, and IBM's WebSphere Application Server.

- **Chapter 4:** *NetWare 5.1 Advanced Server Management*—What about the server? In Chapter 4, we will begin a journey through three key advanced management tasks: server, NDS, and security. It all starts with the NetWare 5.1 server and Java. NetWare 5.1 and Java combine to create native support for the Java Virtual Machine (JVM) and GUI ConsoleOne interface. In addition, we will learn about server management at the console, Novell Storage Services (NSS), and backup/restore via Storage Management Services (SMS).

- **Chapter 5:** *NetWare 5.1 Advanced NDS Management*—Then we will continue our advanced administrative journey with some key NDS maintenance and troubleshooting tasks. As you'll learn in Chapter 5, NDS is the heart of NetWare 5.1's enterprise solution. Keeping it running smoothly should be your #1 priority.

- **Chapter 6:** *NetWare 5.1 Advanced Security Management*—Next, we will explore advanced security management using public key cryptography and the NetWare 5.1 Novell Certificate Server. This server process natively integrates public key authentication and encryption mechanisms into NDS and enables you to mint, issue, and manage both user and server certificates. In this chapter, we will study the basic fundamentals of public key cryptography and learn how the Novell Certificate Server can help you extend communication security within NetWare 5.1. In addition, we will learn how to install the Certificate Server and manage security objects using the Java-based ConsoleOne tool.

- **Chapter 7:** *NetWare 5.1 Optimization* — Finally, we will complete Part I (and our review of Novell Course 570) with the "Final Frontier" of NetWare 5.1 optimization. As a certified network administrator, you will learn how to optimize NetWare using two important tools: monitoring with MONITOR.NLM and optimization with SET commands. Remember, *balance* is the key. Server performance, reliability, and security must live in cohesive harmony.

STOP!

This completes our brief tour of Part I, "NetWare 5.1 Advanced Administration." As you can see, we will soon be managing our network in style. But before we can manage anything, we must build the NetWare 5.1 server. This is where the journey begins.

In this chapter, we will learn what it takes to build a NetWare 5.1 server. We will skip hardware assembly (that's the easy part) and jump straight into software installation. This is where the CNE journey begins.

Have a great trip!

NetWare 5.1 can be installed using a variety of installation, upgrade, and migration methods. Only the Basic installation method is covered in this chapter. With this method, NetWare 5.1 can be installed from scratch. In other words, it assumes that the target computer does not contain any programs osr data that must be retained.

Before You Begin

Unlike earlier versions of NetWare, you no longer need to decide whether to perform a Simple or Custom installation before you begin. Instead, you simply install the NetWare 5.1 operating system, then choose whether or not to customize any parameters at the end of the process.

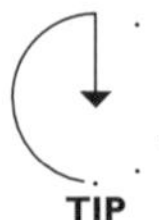
TIP

When performing the lab exercises in this book, it is *imperative* that you use a nonproduction server (that is, a practice server) in an isolated tree. You should use nonproduction workstation(s), as well.

Installation Features

The NetWare 5.1 Installation program provides the following features:

- *The Novell Installation Wizard* — This program uses a Java-based graphical user interface (GUI) during the later stages of server installation. (The earlier stages of the process still use a text-mode interface.)
- *Automatic Hardware Detection and Selection of Drivers* — The Installation program attempts to auto-detect platform support modules, PCI Hot Plug support modules, storage adapters, storage devices (such as hard disks, CD-ROMs, and tape units), and local area network (LAN) adapters.
- *Batch Support* — This feature enables you to install one server and then use the same profile to install other servers.
- *Multiple Protocol Support* — This feature enables you to choose IPX-Only, Pure IP, or both.
- *Version Checking* — This feature ensures that only the latest files are copied to the server.

Before you can install NetWare 5.1, you must ensure that your server satisfies a minimum set of hardware requirements. Keep in mind that these are just minimum requirements — the *recommended* values are considerably higher.

Minimum Hardware Requirements

Here are the minimum and recommended hardware requirements (the recommended requirements are in parentheses) for a NetWare 5.1 server:

- A server-class PC with a Pentium II or higher processor
- A VGA or higher-resolution display adapter (SVGA with VESA support recommended)

- 128MB of RAM for standard products; 256MB if you install both standard NetWare products and WebSphere Application Server for NetWare (with 512MB recommended); 512MB for all products, including Oracle8
- 50MB DOS partition with 35MB of available space (256MB recommended for core dump)
- 750MB free disk space on the SYS: volume for standard NetWare products; 1.3GB on the SYS: volume if you install both standard NetWare 5.1 products and WebSphere Application Server for NetWare
- One or more network boards
- The appropriate network cabling (Ethernet, Token Ring, FDDI, ARCnet, baseband, and so on) and related components (hubs, uninterruptible power supplies, and so on)
- A CD-ROM drive that can read ISO 9660-formatted CD-ROM disks (if NetWare 5.1 is being installed from a CD-ROM). (**Note:** Bootable CD-ROM drives must meet the El Torito specification for booting CD-ROMs from multiple operating systems.)
- (Optional, but recommended) PS/2 or serial mouse

Basic NetWare 5.1 server installation consists of multiple steps in four stages. Following is a brief preview of the four stages:

- *Stage 1*: Getting Started
- *Stage 2*: Text-Based Input Screens
- *Stage 3*: GUI Input Screens
- *Stage 4*: Customization

It all starts in Stage 1, where you perform preinstallation tasks and run INSTALL.BAT. Then in Stage 2, you get to attack the text-mode portion of the installation process, including choosing the type of installation, indicating server settings, selecting regional settings, modifying selected drivers, creating the NetWare partition and SYS: volume, and mounting the SYS: volume.

Once you've built the foundation of the NetWare 5.1 server, it's time to plug in the key functional components. Next, in Stage 3, you build on the text-based platform with some GUI-mode tasks, including naming the server, configuring the file system, selecting networking protocols, indicating DNS settings, choosing the server time zone, installing NDS, and installing NLS. Finally, in Stage 4, you finish the installation by selecting additional products and services (in the case of a Custom installation) and customizing server parameters (if desired).

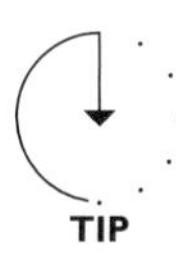
TIP

In this chapter, we'll use the local CD-ROM method for all installation options, because it's the most common method.

NetWare 5.1 Installation

To install NetWare 5.1, you'll need to complete the tasks listed in the following sections that discuss Stages 1 through 4.

Stage 1: Getting Started

In the first installation stage, you'll prepare the server for installation and execute the main Installation program — INSTALL.BAT.

Step 1: Complete Preinstallation Tasks

You'll need to perform a number of tasks before you can install your NetWare 5.1 server, such as the following:

- Determine if your "computer room" meets recommended power and operating environment requirements.
- Verify that your server meets the minimum NetWare 5.1 hardware requirements and that all hardware is compatible. (**Note:** See the "Minimum Hardware Requirements" section earlier in this chapter.) Be sure that you install and configure any necessary hardware (such as network interface cards, hubs, cabling, uninterruptible power supplies, and so on).

- Confirm that you have all the appropriate DOS, NetWare 5.1, application software, and application documentation that you need.
- Be sure you that that you have performed all of the planning required for the installation and that you have any required information handy. (Obviously, the best time to make installation-related decisions is *before* you begin the actual installation.) For example, a few of the numerous decisions you'll want to make before you start are whether to use the CD-ROM or network installation method, which protocol(s) to use (that is, IPX and/or IP), whether to install the server in a new or existing tree, how big to make the DOS partition, and so on.
- Back up your existing system. Create at least two full server backups on tape or other storage media. Remember that all data on the server will be destroyed during preinstallation.
- Boot the server using the DOS version supplied by your computer manufacturer. (**Note:** NetWare requires DOS 3.3 or higher, with DOS 6.22 or higher recommended. Do *not* use the version of DOS that comes with Windows 95/98 or Windows NT/2000!)
- Create a boot disk. To format a disk and make it bootable, insert the disk in the floppy drive (or drive A:) and type the following:

  ```
  FORMAT A: /S
  ```

  After the disk is formatted, you'll need to use the DOS COPY command to copy two important utilities to the disk: FDISK.EXE and FORMAT.COM. You may also want to include copies of your AUTOEXEC.BAT and CONFIG.SYS files, DOS CD-ROM drivers (plus MSCDEX.EXE), and utilities such as EDIT.COM (to edit ASCII files), XCOPY.EXE (to copy files), and MEM.EXE (to display information about available RAM).

- Create the DOS partition. The DOS partition is required because NetWare 5.1 does not have its own cold-boot loader. This means that in order to start the server, you must load the NetWare 5.1 operating system via SERVER.EXE from a DOS prompt (or AUTOEXEC.BAT file). When determining the appropriate size for your DOS partition, make sure that it's large enough to support disk drivers, LAN drivers, name space modules, the SERVER.EXE boot file, and repair utilities. Once you've determined the appropriate DOS partition size, use the DOS FDISK utility to delete existing partitions and to create a new, active DOS partition of 50MB or more — leaving the rest of the hard disk space unpartitioned. (**Note:** When determining how large a DOS partition to create, don't forget to ensure that you end up with at least 35MB of available disk space *after* you've loaded any nonnetwork-related files.)
- Format the DOS partition. Use the DOS FORMAT utility contained on the boot disk that you made to format the new partition and make it bootable. In other words, type the following at the DOS prompt:

  ```
  FORMAT C: /S
  ```

  Note: Be sure to copy all DOS CD-ROM drivers from your computer *before* you run FDISK or FORMAT. Doing so afterward won't help, because you will have wiped out the files.
- Install the CD-ROM drive as a DOS device, following the instructions provided by the drive manufacturer.
- Use the DOS DATE and TIME commands to verify the computer's date and time, and then modify them, if necessary.

REAL WORLD

With newer PCs that can boot off a CD-ROM, it is much easier to simply boot off of the *NetWare 5.1 Operating System* CD-ROM. It will clean off the hard disk, create a DOS partition, and make the DOS partition bootable, automatically.

Step 2: Run INSTALL.BAT

At the server console, insert the *NetWare 5.1 Operating System* CD-ROM into the CD-ROM drive, switch to the drive letter assigned to the drive, and type the following:

```
INSTALL
```

Note: The INSTALL.BAT file is located in the root directory of the CD-ROM. If you have a bootable CD-ROM drive that meets the El Torito specification, the Installation program will boot automatically when the CD-ROM is inserted in the CD-ROM drive.

Stage 2: Text-Based Input Screens

In the second stage, we'll build the foundation of the server using a text-based interface. This early server foundation consists of regional configurations, disk drivers, LAN drivers, one or more NetWare 5.1 partitions, and the SYS: volume.

Step 3: Choose the Type of Installation

As the Installation program begins to load, a colorful NetWare title screen eventually appears. (It may take a while.) Wait for a few minutes until the next screen appears. If you have an international version of the program, a NetWare Installation screen eventually appears, giving you the opportunity to select the language to be used during installation. Next, the "NetWare 5.1 Software License" screen appears. Press F10 to accept the terms of the License Agreement.

When the "Welcome to the NetWare Server Installation" screen appears (see Figure 1.1), indicate the type of installation you are interested in (that is, New Server or Upgrade) and the startup directory (that is, the destination for the NetWare 5.1 server boot files). You'll notice that the defaults are Upgrade (installation type) and C:\NWSERVER (startup directory). (**Note:** For the purposes of the lab exercises in this book, you will need to create a new server. Therefore, in the "Is This a New Server or an Upgrade?" field, press Enter to toggle the value from Upgrade to New Server. Also, in the Startup Directory field, verify that C:\NWSERVER is selected.)

FIGURE 1.1

Choosing the type of server installation

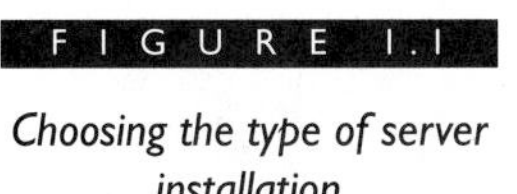

NetWare Installation

Welcome to the NetWare server installation.

Select the type of installation. A new installation will destroy existing data on NetWare partitions. To keep data, select Upgrade.

IMPORTANT: You must run NetWare Deployment Manager before installing into an existing network. If you have not, insert the NetWare 5 CD into a Windows workstation and run NWDEPLOY.EXE.

Use the Tab or arrow keys to move between windows.

Is this a new server or an upgrade? Upgrade
Startup directory C:\NWSERVER

Options
Continue
Modify

Alt+F10=Exit Enter=Select/View F1=Help

Step 4: Select Server Settings

The Server Settings screen appears next, listing the following default values:

- NDS Version: NDS 8
- CD-ROM Driver to Access Install: NetWare
- Server ID Number: (random number)
- Load Server at Reboot: Yes
- Server Set Parameters: Edit

Review the default settings and modify them as necessary. You'll probably find that most of the defaults are fine. (You may want to change the server ID number, however, to one that you will recognize. In Lab Exercise 1.1, for example, we will use 1001 as the server ID number.)

Step 5: Select Regional Settings

The Regional Settings screen appears next, as shown in Figure 1.2. Regional settings are used to customize server language and keyboard settings. If you are located in the United States, the default values are as follows:

- Country: 001 (USA)
- Code Page: 437 (United States English)
- Keyboard: United States

Review the default settings and modify them as necessary.

FIGURE 1.2

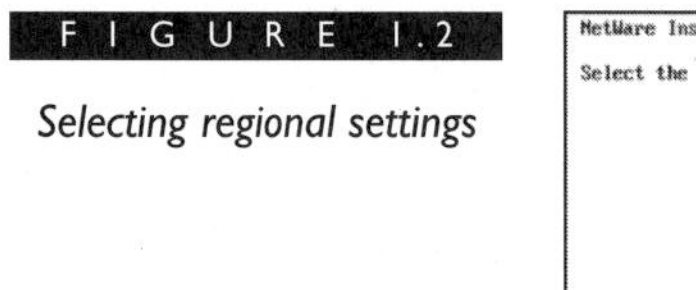

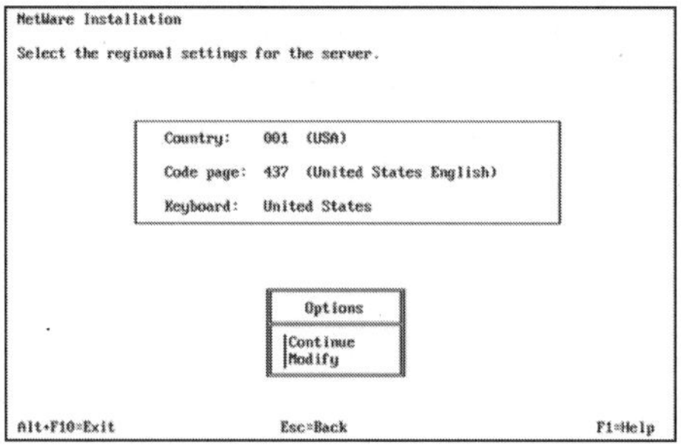

Selecting regional settings

```
NetWare Installation

Select the regional settings for the server.

        Country:    001  (USA)
        Code page:  437  (United States English)
        Keyboard:   United States

                    Options
                    Continue
                    Modify

Alt+F10=Exit              Esc=Back              F1=Help
```

Step 6: Modify Selected Drivers

During Step 6, the Installation Wizard attempts to automatically detect certain types of hardware and determine the appropriate drivers. Other drivers must be selected manually.

As you can see in Figure 1.3, the first driver screen lists mouse type and video mode parameters. Because the Installation program does not attempt to auto-detect these parameters, you will need to select the appropriate settings manually.

- *Mouse Type* — Although the Installation program supports PS/2 and serial mouse types, a mouse is not required (although it is recommended). Optionally, you can use the keyboard's arrow keys to control pointer movement.

- *Video Mode* — The Installation program is optimized to use Super VGA resolution and work with display hardware that is VESA 2 complaint. You should only choose Standard VGA if your video card does not support 256 colors.

Review the values listed on this screen and modify them as necessary.

The Installation program then automatically copies a number of server boot files from the CD-ROM to the startup directory you indicated earlier (the default is C:\NWSERVER). These include files such as SERVER.EXE, disk drivers, LAN drivers, NWCONFIG.NLM, NWSNUT.NLM, VREPAIR.NLM, and other NetWare Loadable Modules (NLMs).

FIGURE 1.3

Selecting mouse type and video mode

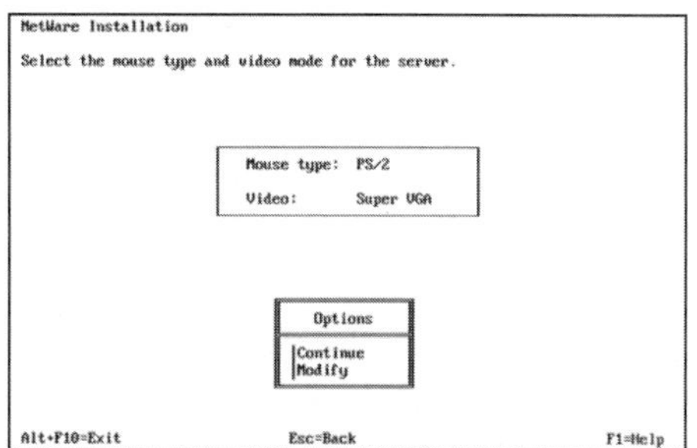

The second driver screen lists the following types of drivers (which have been auto-detected, wherever possible):

- *Platform Support Module* — The performance of servers with multiple processors and other configurations can be optimized by loading a platform support module driver. (Platform support modules typically have a .PSM filename extension.)

- *HotPlug Support Module* — Computers that provide support for PCI Hot Plug technology allow storage adapters and network boards to be inserted and removed while the computer is powered on. (Hot Plug modules typically have an .NLM extension.)

- *Storage Adapters* — Storage adapters require a software driver called a *Host Adapter Module* (HAM) to communicate with the computer (host). Because a single storage adapter can control more than one type of storage device, only one HAM may be required. Various types of storage adapters, such as Integrated Drive Electronics (IDE) and Small Computer System Interface (SCSI), may be auto-detected. If a particular storage adapter is not detected, choose the appropriate driver from the list, or load it from a manufacturer-specific disk.

Review the values listed on this screen and modify them as necessary.

As you can see in the example in Figure 1.4, the third driver screen lists the following types of drivers:

- *Storage Devices* — Storage devices require a software driver, called a *Custom Device Module* (CDM) to communicate with the storage adapter that controls it. Each type of storage device requires a separate CDM. The Installation Wizard auto-detects many types of storage devices, such as SCSI/IDE drives, CD-ROM drives, and tape drives.
- *Network Boards* — Network boards require a software driver called a *LAN driver* to communicate with the network. The Installation program auto-detects many types of network boards. If a particular network board is not detected, choose the appropriate driver from the list provided, or load it from a manufacturer-specific disk.
- *NetWare Loadable Modules* — Some servers and network configurations require that you load a NetWare Loadable Module (NLM) before completing the server installation. For example, if you are installing the server in a Token Ring environment, you may need to load ROUTE.NLM. If so, add it to the NetWare Loadable Modules field.

Review the values listed on this screen and modify them as necessary.

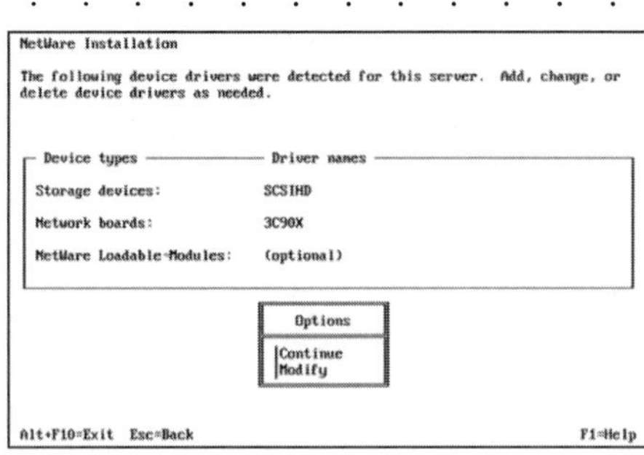

FIGURE 1.4

Reviewing selected drivers and specifying NLMs

Step 7: Create the NetWare Partition and Mount the SYS: Volume

To complete the NetWare 5.1 server foundation, you'll need to create internal disk partitions and volumes. In Step 7, the "Volume SYS and Partition Properties" screen appears, as in Figure 1.5. This text-mode screen displays the default parameters for creating NetWare partitions and the SYS: volume. If a server contains only one hard disk, the installation utility creates a single NetWare 5.1 partition consisting of all free disk space beyond the DOS partition.

FIGURE 1.5

Creating the NetWare partition

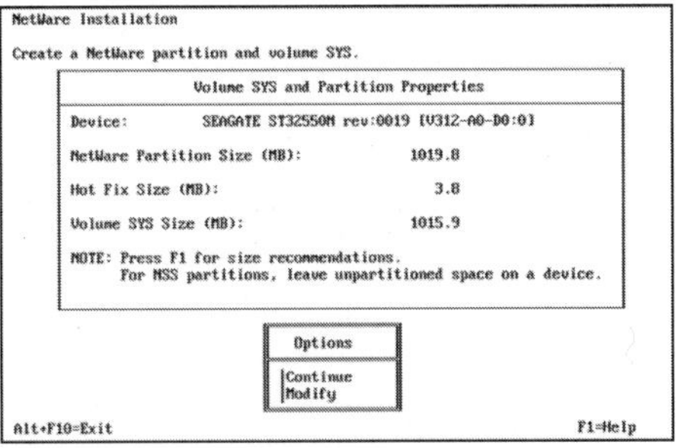

If you plan to have additional volumes on this partition, you must decrease the size of the SYS: volume to leave room for the other volume(s). It's probably a good idea to create one or more additional volumes for your data, to keep it separate from your NetWare operating system files. It also makes it easier to restrict access to specific directories or files. Also, don't forget that if you plan to use Novell Storage Services (NSS), you must leave additional unpartitioned space on each hard disk that will contain an NSS partition, rather than using all of the free space on each disk for a NetWare partition.

Although the basic NetWare operating system requires only about 750MB, it's important to make sure that the SYS: volume is large enough to handle any additional NetWare products and services, online documentation, and applications that may be installed. (**Note:** Novell recommends that the SYS: volume has at least 1.3GB for NetWare 5.1 if you install both standard NetWare products and the WebSphere Application Server for NetWare.)

TIP

Don't forget that if you plan to use NSS, you'll need to leave additional unpartitioned space on the hard disk for the NSS partition, rather than using all of the free space for the NetWare volume. Also, you can create additional partitions and volumes after installation by loading NWCONFIG.NLM at the server console.

Stage 3: GUI Input Screens

In Stage 3, we will establish networking protocols, an NDS context, and licensing authentication. In this stage, we will leave the boring text-mode world and switch to a Java interface. Although a mouse is recommended, you can use keystrokes to navigate through the Installation program.

Step 8: Name the NetWare 5.1 Server

At this point, the Installation Wizard copies a number of files to the server hard drive (called the *preparatory file copy* process). A Java Virtual Machine (JVM) is then created on the server and the GUI portion of the Installation Wizard is loaded. This step may take a while.

When the Server Properties dialog box appears (see Figure 1.6), type the server name in the Server Name field. The name should consist of 2 to 47 characters (including letters, numbers, hyphens, and/or underscores — but no spaces). The first character cannot be a period. Don't forget that each server in your NDS tree must have a unique name. (**Note:** For the lab exercises in this book, you'll need to use the following server name: WHITE-SRV1.)

FIGURE 1.6

Naming the server

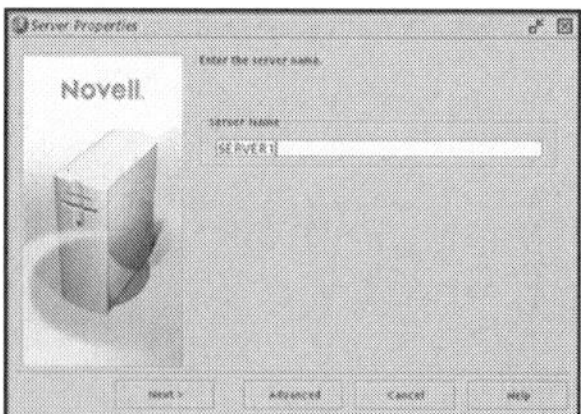

You'll notice this screen also has an Advanced button, which will let you modify your server's AUTOEXEC.BAT file, CONFIG.SYS file, your server ID number (which we set to 1001 earlier in the installation process), as well as language information.

Step 9: Configure the File System

If a Configure File System dialog box appears (like the one in Figure 1.7), review the information listed. If you modified the size of the SYS: volume in an earlier step, you can create additional volumes at this point using available free space. To create additional volumes, click the Free Space icon and then click Create.

FIGURE 1.7

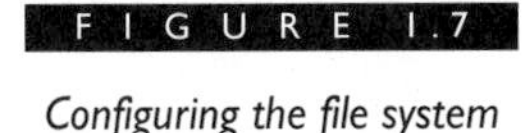

Configuring the file system

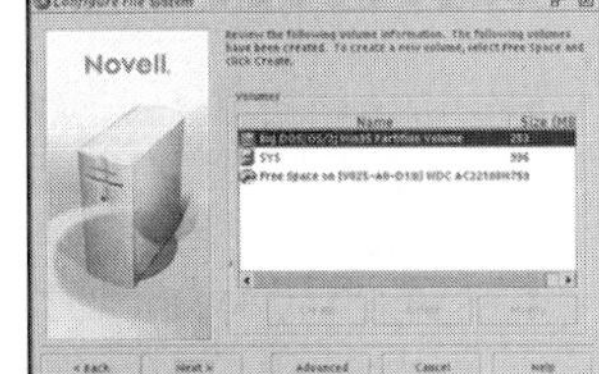

When the New Volume dialog box appears (see Figure 1.8), type the name of the new volume in the Volume Name field and click OK. The new volume should then be listed on the Configure File System screen.

FIGURE 1.8

Creating a new volume

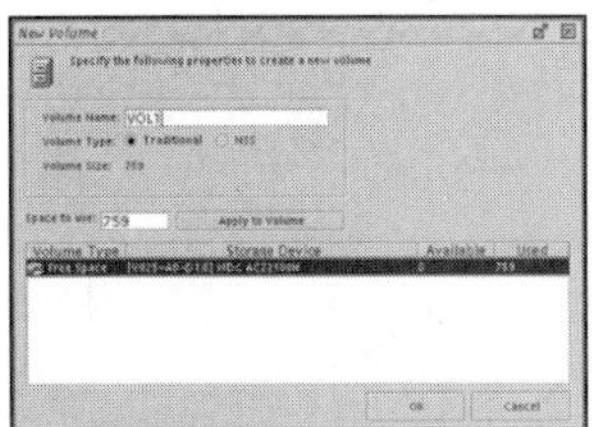

If the Mount Volumes dialog box appears, you are asked whether you want to mount all volumes when the server reboots or whether you want to mount all volumes now, as indicated in Figure 1.9. Verify that Yes is selected, so that all volumes will be mounted when the server reboots.

FIGURE 1.9

Mounting server volumes

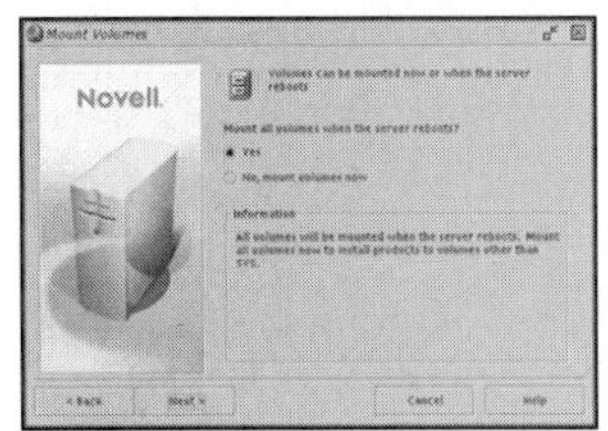

Step 10: Select Networking Protocols

At this point, the Protocols dialog box should appear, as shown in Figure 1.10. It asks you to specify the network protocol(s) for each internal server network interface card (NIC).

To configure the IP protocol, follow these simple steps:

1. In the Network Boards pane on the left, verify that your network board is highlighted. (If not, click it to highlight it.)

2. In the Protocols section on the right, mark the IP checkbox.

3. In the IP Address field, enter the IP address. (If your server is *not* connected to the Internet, use 187.165.182.18.)

4. In the Subnet Mask field, enter the subnet mask. (If your server is *not* connected to the Internet, use 255.255.0.0.)

5. (Optional) In the Router (Gateway) field, enter the router (gateway) address.

6. In the Protocols section on the right, mark the IPX checkbox.

FIGURE 1.10

Selecting protocols

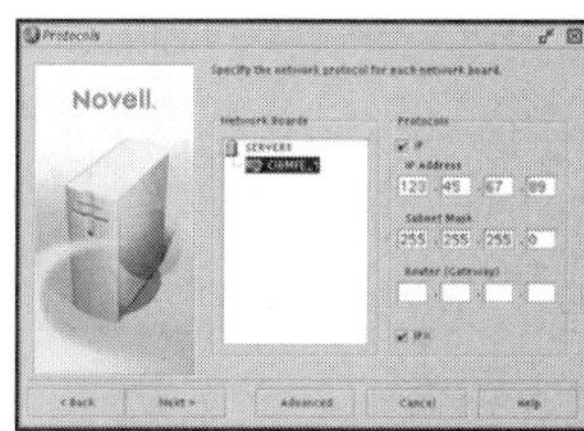

You'll notice that there's also an Advanced button, which enables you to configure a number of protocol-related parameters, such as IPX frame types, IPX Compatibility settings, and SNMP information.

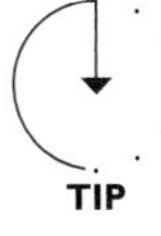

TIP

In order to configure the IP protocol, you must be familiar with and know the IP address, the subnet address, and the router (gateway) address. (Note: The Installation utility uses default frame types of Ethernet_802.2 [for Ethernet] and Ethernet_II [for TCP/IP].)

Step 11: Domain Name Service (DNS)

When the Domain Name Service screen appears (see Figure 1.11), you would normally fill in the required information. Leave all of these fields blank for now, however. When you click Next, a message will appear warning you that because you have not configured Domain Name Service, you will obtain limited functionality from products that require this service. Click OK to acknowledge the message.

FIGURE 1.11

Configuring DNS information

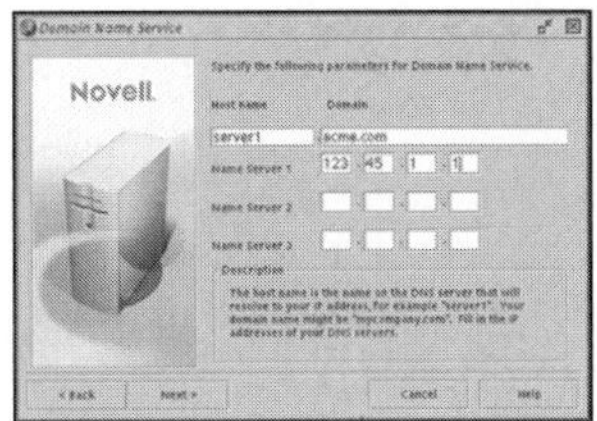

Step 12: Choose the Server Time Zone

In Step 12, the Time Zone dialog box appears, as shown in Figure 1.12. Choose the correct time zone for your server and make sure that the "Allow System to Adjust for Daylight Saving Time" checkbox is marked, if appropriate.

FIGURE 1.12

Choosing the server time zone

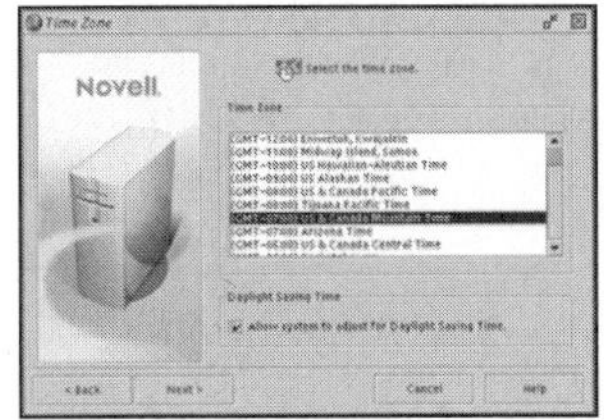

Step 13: Install Novell Directory Services (NDS)

This is probably one of the most important steps in the installation process. At the beginning of Step 13, the first NDS Install dialog box appears, as displayed in Figure 1.13. If this is the first NetWare server in your NDS tree, select New NDS Tree. (**Note:** For the lab exercises in this book, you need to select New NDS Tree because you need to work in an isolated tree. Be aware that the resources available in the new tree will *not* be available to users who are logged into a different tree.)

FIGURE 1.13

Selecting the NDS tree

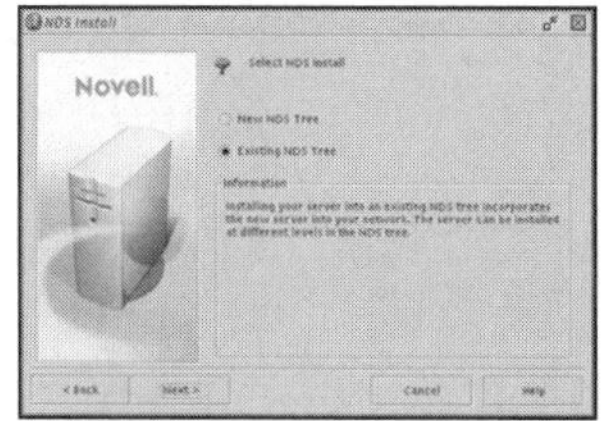

A second NDS Install screen will appear, like the example in Figure 1.14. If this is a new tree (which it should be, because you are using a nonproduction server for the lab exercises in this book), follow these steps:

1. Enter the tree name in the Tree Name field. This is usually the [Root] name of your tree followed by the term TREE. (**Note:** For the lab exercises in this book, you need to use the following tree name: ACME-TREE.)

2. **Warning:** Do *not* type the server location in the "Context for Server Object" field. Instead, you need to "build" the context by using the browse button to the right of the "Context for Server Object" field. (**Note:** For the lab exercises in this book, you need to build the following server context: OU=WHITE.OU=CRIME.OU=TOKYO.O=ACME.)

   In order to build this server context, follow these steps:

   a. Create the ACME Organization. Click the browse button to the right of the "Context for Server Object" field. On the NDS Context Browser screen, click ACME-TREE and then click Add. When the New Container dialog box appears, enter ACME in the Container Name field, verify that the Organization radio button is selected in the Container Type field and then click OK.

b. Create the TOKYO Organizational Unit. When the NDS Context Browser screen reappears, verify that ACME is highlighted and then click Add. When the New Container dialog box appears, enter TOKYO in the Container Name field, verify that the Organizational Unit radio button is selected in the Container Type field, and then click OK.

c. Create the CRIME Organizational Unit. When the NDS Context Browser screen reappears, verify that TOKYO is highlighted, then click Add. When the New Container dialog box appears, enter CRIME in the Container Name field, verify that the Organizational Unit radio button is selected in the Container Type field, then click OK.

d. Create the WHITE Organizational Unit. When the NDS Context Browser screen reappears, verify that CRIME is highlighted and then click Add. When the New Container dialog box appears, enter WHITE in the Container Name field, verify that the Organizational Unit radio button is selected in the Container Type field, and then click OK. Finally, click OK to return to the NDS Install screen.

3. In the Administrator Information section, enter the leaf name of the Admin User object in the Admin Name field, if you want it to be something other than "admin." (**Note:** For the lab exercises in this book, you need to leave it as "admin.")

4. Enter the context for the Admin User object in the Admin Context field, if you want it to be different than the context of the Server object. (**Note:** For the lab exercises in this book, you need to leave the default name and context.)

5. Enter the password for the Admin User object in the "Password" and "Retype Password" fields. Keep track of this information for future reference. If you lose any of the Admin configuration details, your life will get much more complicated. (**Note:** For the lab exercises in this book, you need to enter ACME.)

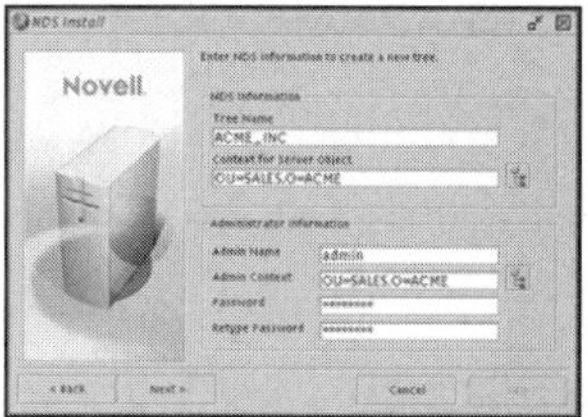

FIGURE 1.14

Installing Novell Directory Services (NDS)

If you had chosen to install the server in an existing tree (rather than creating a new tree), you would have been asked to provide the tree name (if there's more than one tree), the Admin username, and the Admin password.

At this point, the Installation Wizard checks for duplicate tree names and installs NDS. When the NDS Summary screen appears (see Figure 1.15), write down the following information and store it in a safe place for future reference:

- NDS Tree Name: ACME-TREE
- Server Context: OU=WHITE.OU=CRIME.OU=TOKYO.O=ACME
- Administrator name: CN=Admin.OU=WHITE.OU=CRIME.OU=TOKYO.O=ACME
- Administrator Password You Entered on Previous Screen: ACME+

REAL WORLD

Remember that the Admin User object is the one NDS User object created by default during installation of the first NDS tree. A non-NDS (bindery) Supervisor User object is created, which can be used to log into the tree in Bindery Emulation mode (LOGIN /B). Because Supervisor is not an NDS object, it is not displayed in the NDS tree.

FIGURE 1.15

NDS installation summary screen

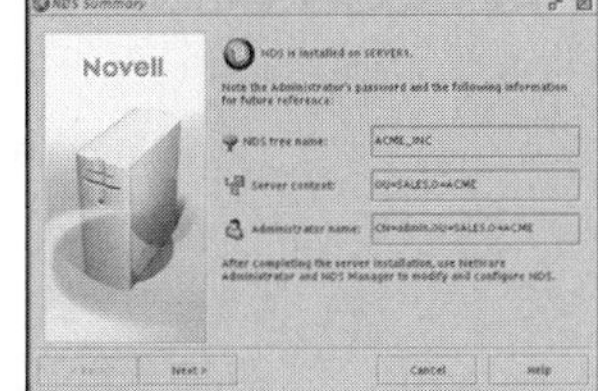

Step 14: Install Novell Licensing Services (NLS)

Now it's time to license the NetWare 5.1 server, as indicated in Figure 1.16. Normally, you would insert the NetWare license disk in the floppy drive and select the appropriate license file. (Be sure to use a unique license disk.) If using a license disk, make sure you actually browse to and select the license file, instead of just listing the drive letter (a common mistake). When you click the file, you'll notice that the type of license appears in the Description section, such as "NetWare 5.1 Server, Plus Fifty User Connections."

FIGURE 1.16

Licensing the server

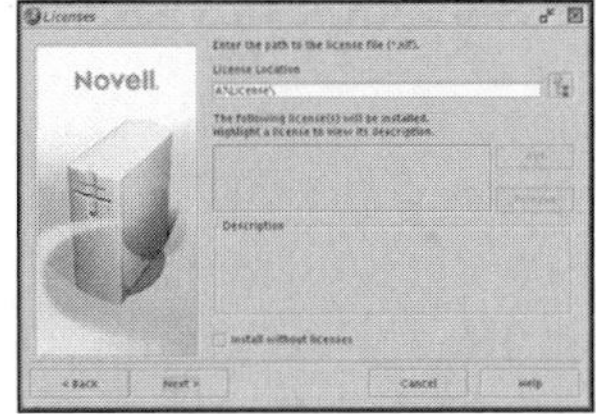

Note: If you are using a "demo version" of the *NetWare 5.1 Operating System* CD-ROM (that is, one that does not have an associated license disk), use the license file in the LICENSE/DEMO directory on the CD-ROM. If you can't locate the license file, mark the "Install without Licenses" checkbox, although you may experience problems with features such as NDPS, which use multiple connections.

Stage 4: Customization

In the fourth and final stage, you are given the choice to install additional products and services and/or to customize numerous operating system parameters.

Step 15: Install Additional Products and Services

Toward the end of the NetWare 5.1 installation process, the Installation Options dialog box appears, allowing you to select from the following list (see Figure 1.17):

- Install Standard NetWare Products
- Install Standard NetWare Products Plus WebSphere App Serv
- Custom

FIGURE 1.17

Select the products to install

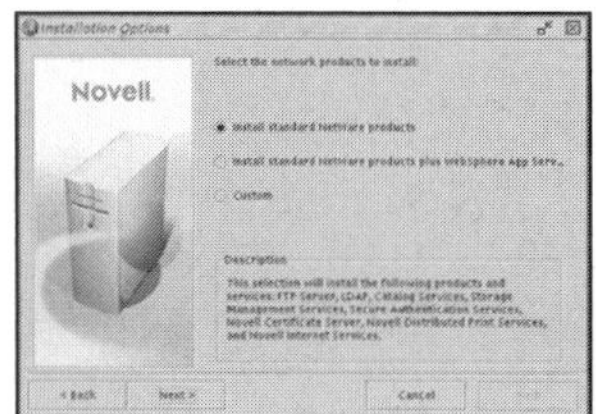

If you click each radio button, it lists the products to be installed in the Description section. For instance, if you select Install Standard NetWare Products, you would install the following products and services: FTP Server, LDAP, Catalog Services, Storage Management Services, Secure Authentication Services, Novell Certificate Server, Novell Distributed Print Services, and Novell Internet Services. If you select the Custom option, you will need to indicate the products you wish to install. (**Note:** For the purposes of the lab exercises in this book, you need to use the Install Standard NetWare Products option.)

The screens that display next will be determined by which option you previously chose. If you selected Install Standard NetWare Products, you will see the screens described in the next three paragraphs.

When the Novell Certificate Server 2.0 Objects screen appears, as shown in Figure 1.18, review the onscreen information. When the Organizational CA Warning dialog box appears, read the information and then click OK to acknowledge the warning. The Novell Certification Server 2.0 Objects screen then briefly reappears. Ignore this screen and wait until the next screen appears.

FIGURE 1.18

Installing Novell Certificate Server

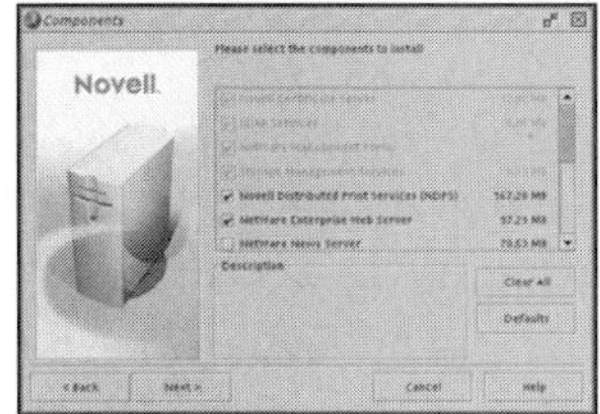

When the NetWare Enterprise Web Server Settings screen appears, make note of the onscreen information. You'll notice an optional setting that enables you to optimize WebBench performance, if desired. When the NetWare Web Manager Settings screen appears, make note of the onscreen information.

When the Summary screen appears (as in Figure 1.19), review the additional NetWare 5.1 products to be installed. When you are satisfied with the list of products, click Customize to be allowed to customize various installation parameters.

FIGURE 1.19

Summary of products to install

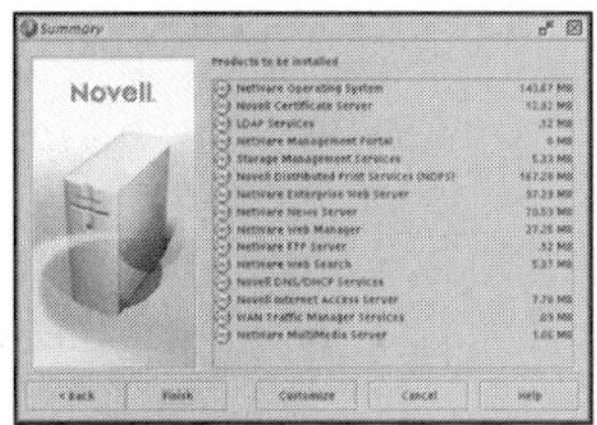

Step 16: Customize the Server

You can enhance the basic NetWare 5.1 installation with some additional configurations using the Product Customization dialog box. Categories of customizable options include the core operating system, file system, protocols, time synchronization, Novell Directory Services, and additional products and services. Browse the tree to find the first NetWare 5.1 component you want to modify, select the component, and then click Configure. When you have finished customizing your selections, click OK to return to the Summary screen.

Step 17: Complete the Installation

On the Summary screen, click Finish to complete the installation process.

The Installation Wizard then performs the main file copy. (This step may take a while.) When the final copy is complete, the Installation Complete window appears. Select View Log or View Readme, if desired. Next, remove the NetWare 5.1 License disk from the floppy drive (if you actually used one) and the CD-ROM from the CD-ROM drive, and then click Yes to restart your computer.

Congratulations — you've done it! You have successfully traversed the four stages and 17 steps of NetWare 5.1 installation! Now it's time to use your new server to help *save the Net!*

LAB EXERCISE 1.1: INSTALLING THE WHITE-SRV1 SERVER

To install the NetWare 5.1 operating system on a server, you'll need the following components:

- A server-class computer that meets (or exceeds) the minimum requirements for running the NetWare 5.1 operating system. (**Note:** See the "Minimum Hardware Requirements" section earlier in this chapter for additional details.)
- A *NetWare 5.1 Operating System* CD-ROM.

In this lab exercise, you will build the WHITE-SRV1 server from scratch. The basic stages involved in NetWare 5.1 installation are as follows:

- *Stage 1:* Getting Started
- *Stage 2:* Text-Based Input Screens
- *Stage 3:* GUI Input Screens
- *Stage 4:* Customization

It all starts in Stage 1, where you perform preinstallation tasks and run INSTALL.BAT. Then in Stage 2, you get to attack the text-mode portion of the installation process, including choosing the type of installation, indicating server settings, selecting regional settings, modifying selected drivers, creating the NetWare partition and SYS: volume, and mounting the SYS: volume.

Once you've built the foundation of the NetWare 5.1 server, it's time to plug in the key functional components. In Stage 3, you build on the text-based platform with some GUI-mode tasks, including naming the server, configuring the file system, selecting networking protocols, indicating DNS settings, choosing the server time zone, installing NDS, and installing NLS. Finally, in Stage 4, you finish the installation by customizing server parameters (if desired).

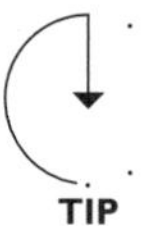

You must complete this exercise before performing any other exercises in the remainder of the book. Make sure you use a *nonproduction* server (that is, a practice server) in an *isolated* tree for all exercises in this book!

The following tasks must be completed before you install NetWare 5.1 on your server:

1. Ensure that the computer you will use as a NetWare 5.1 server *exceeds* the minimum hardware requirements listed in the "Minimum Hardware Requirements" section near the beginning of this chapter. For example, make sure the computer exceeds the following requirements:

    a. Even though the NetWare 5.1 courseware suggests a minimum of 50MB for the DOS partition and 750MB for the SYS: volume, you'll probably find that you'll want to have a minimum of 256MB or more for the DOS partition and at least 1.3GB for the SYS: volume. Typically, the more hard disk space you have, the better.

    b. Although the NetWare 5.1 courseware lists the minimum server RAM required as 128MB for the standard NetWare products, you need 512MB, for example, if you install the WebSphere Application Server for NetWare at a later time.

Stage 1: Getting Started

Step 1: Complete Preinstallation Tasks

1. Select the computer to be used as a server. Then create at least two verified backup copies of all data on tape or on other storage media. Remember that all data on this computer will be destroyed during installation. If this computer is currently being used as a server, be sure to back up the network security information (such as the bindery or NDS), as well as the file system.

2. Install and configure network board(s) in the server. Refer to the network board manufacturer's documentation for configuration instructions.

3. Boot the server using the version of DOS supplied by your computer manufacturer. (NetWare requires DOS 3.3 or higher, with DOS 6.2 or higher recommended.)

4. Create a temporary boot disk. To format a disk and make it bootable, insert a disk in Drive A, type **FORMAT A: /S**, and press Enter.

   After the disk is formatted, use the DOS COPY command to copy the FDISK.EXE and FORMAT.COM utilities to the disk. You may also want to copy the AUTOEXEC.BAT and CONFIG.SYS files, DOS CD-ROM drivers, and utilities such as EDIT.COM (to edit ASCII files), XCOPY.EXE (to copy files), and MEM.EXE (to display information about available RAM).

5. Use the DOS FDISK utility to delete existing hard disk partitions and to create a new, active DOS partition of 50MB or more, leaving the rest of the hard disk space free.

6. After you've created the DOS partition, use the DOS FORMAT utility on the boot disk you made to format the new partition and make it bootable. To do this, type **FORMAT C: /S** and press Enter.

7. On the server, install the CD-ROM drive as a DOS device, following the instructions provided by the drive manufacturer.

8. Use the DOS DATE and TIME commands to verify the computer's date and time, and then modify them, if necessary.

Step 2: Run INSTALL.BAT

1. Insert the *NetWare 5.1 Operating System* CD-ROM in the server's CD-ROM drive.

2. Switch to the drive letter assigned to the CD-ROM drive. For example, if the drive letter for your CD-ROM drive is D, type **D:** and press Enter.

3. Run the INSTALL.BAT batch file located in the root directory of the CD-ROM by typing **INSTALL** and then pressing Enter.

Stage 2: Text-Based Input Screens

Step 3: Choose the Type of Installation

1. While the Installation program is loading, the NetWare 5 title screen appears. Wait while the Installation program continues to load.

2. If the NetWare Installation screen appears, select the language to be used during installation and press Enter. (This screen only appears if you have an international version of the software.)

3. When the NetWare 5.1 Software License screen appears, read the agreement and then press F10 to continue.

4. Follow these steps on the "Welcome to the NetWare Server Installation" screen:

   a. In the "Is This a New Server or an Upgrade?" field, press Enter to toggle the value from "Upgrade" to "New Server."

   b. In the Startup Directory field, confirm that C:\NWSERVER is selected.

   c. When the values are correct, select Continue from the Options menu and press Enter. (In order to do this, press Tab to move to the Options menu. In the Options menu, verify that Continue is highlighted and then press Enter to select it.)

Step 4: Select Server Settings

When the Server Settings screen appears, you'll notice that the following default values are listed:

- NDS Version: NDS 8
- CD-ROM Driver to Access Install: NetWare
- Server ID Number: (random number)
- Load Server at Reboot: Yes
- Server Set Parameters: Edit

1. Press Tab to move to the Server Settings menu and then press the down arrow twice to move to the Server ID Number field.

2. In the Server ID Number field, type **1001** and press Enter.

3. Review the remaining settings and modify them, if necessary. (You'll probably find that the remaining default values are fine.)

4. When the values are correct, select Continue from the Options menu and press Enter.

Step 5: Select Regional Settings

When the Regional Settings screen appears, you'll notice that default values are listed for the country code, code page, and keyboard type. If you are located in the United States, the default values are the following:

- Country: 001 (USA)
- Code Page: 437 (United States English)
- Keyboard: United States

Review the default settings and modify them, if necessary. When the values are correct, select Continue from the Options menu and press Enter.

Step 6: Modify Selected Drivers

The NetWare 5.1 Installation program automatically attempts to detect the following types of hardware and select the appropriate driver(s): platform support module, Hot Plug PCI support module, storage adapters, storage devices (such as hard disks, CD-ROMs, and tape drives), and LAN adapters. The mouse type and video driver, however, are not auto-detected. Therefore, they must be selected manually. The drivers will be listed on a series of three screens.

1. The first driver screen lists mouse type and video mode parameters. Because the Installation program does not attempt to auto-detect these parameters, you need to select the appropriate settings manually:

   - *Mouse Type* — Although the Installation program supports PS/2 and serial mouse types, a mouse is not required (although it is recommended). Optionally, you can use the keyboard's arrow keys to control pointer movement.

   - *Video Mode* — The Installation program is optimized to use Super VGA resolution and to work with display hardware that is VESA 2 compliant. You should choose Standard VGA only if your video card does not support 256 colors.

   Review the values listed on this screen and modify them if necessary. When the values are correct, select Continue from the Options menu and press Enter.

2. The Installation program then automatically copies a number of server boot files from the CD-ROM to the startup directory that you indicated earlier (that is, C:\NWSERVER). These include files such as SERVER.EXE, disk drivers, LAN drivers, NWCONFIG.NLM, NWSNUT.NLM, VREPAIR.NLM, and other NetWare Loadable Modules (NLMs).

3. The second driver screen lists the following types of drivers:

   - *Platform Support Module* — Servers with multiple processors and other specific configurations can be optimized by loading a platform support module driver. Platform support modules typically have a .PSM filename extension. If no platform support module driver is detected, the server probably doesn't need one.

   - *HotPlug Support Module* — Computers that provide support for PCI Hot Plug technology allow storage adapters and network boards to be inserted and removed while the computer is powered on. Hot Plug modules typically have an.NLM extension. If no Hot Plug PCI support driver is auto-detected, your computer probably does not support Hot Plug PCI technology.

   - *Storage Adapters* — Storage adapters require a software driver called a *Host Adapter Module* (HAM) to communicate with the computer (host).

Because a single storage adapter can control more than one type of storage device, only one HAM may be required. The Installation program attempts to automatically detect storage adapters (such as those using IDE or SCSI technology) and then select the appropriate HAM driver. If a particular storage adapter is not detected, choose the appropriate HAM driver from the list, or load it from a disk or CD-ROM provided by the storage adapter manufacturer.

Review the values listed on this screen and modify them if necessary. When the values are correct, select Continue from the Options menu and press Enter.

4. The third driver screen lists the following types of drivers:

- *Storage Devices* — Storage devices require a software driver, called a *Custom Device Module* (CDM), to communicate with the storage adapter that controls it. Each type of storage device requires a separate CDM. The Installation program attempts to automatically detect devices such as hard disks, CD-ROMs, and tape drives, and then it attempts to select the appropriate CDM driver. If your storage device is not detected, choose the appropriate driver from the list provided or load it from a disk or CD-ROM provided by the storage device manufacturer.
- *Network Boards* — Network boards require a software driver called a *LAN driver* to communicate with the network. The Installation program attempts to automatically detect network adapters and then select the appropriate driver. If your LAN adapter is not detected, choose the appropriate driver from the list provided, or load it from a disk or CD-ROM provided by the LAN adapter manufacturer.
- *NetWare Loadable Modules* — Some servers and network configurations require that you load an NLM before completing the server installation. If this is the case, add the NLM in the NetWare Loadable Modules field.

Review the values listed on this screen and modify them if necessary. When the values are correct, select Continue from the Options menu and press Enter.

Step 7: Create the NetWare Partition and Mount the SYS: Volume

1. Follow these steps if your server has less than 1.3GB of available disk space:
   a. Select Continue from the Options menu and press Enter.
   b. Skip to Step 8.
2. Otherwise, select Modify from the Options menu and press Enter. Next, press F3 to view the volume parameters for the SYS: volume.
   - On this screen, you'll notice a variety of interesting information regarding the SYS: volume, such as the volume block size and the status of the following features: file compression (on), block suballocation (on), data migration (off).
   - Do *not* modify any of the parameters on this screen. Instead, press Esc to return to the previous screen.
3. Follow these steps when the Volume SYS and Partition Properties screen reappears:
   a. Press the down-arrow key twice to move to the Volume SYS: Size (MB) field.
   b. In the Volume SYS: Size (MB) field, modify the value to a number that is up to half the size of the existing SYS: volume, but in no case less than 1.3GB. Be sure to press Enter after you key in the new value.
   c. If the values on the Volume SYS and Partition Properties screen are correct, Press F10 to save them. Next, select Continue from the Options menu and press Enter.

Stage 3: GUI Input Screens

Step 8: Name the NetWare 5.1 Server.

1. Next, the Installation program copies a number of files to the server (called the *preparatory file copy* process).

2. The Installation program then loads the GUI-based Installation Wizard, at which point the installation interface switches from being text based to graphic based.

3. Follow these steps when the Server Properties screen appears:

   a. In the Server Name field, enter the following:

      ```
      WHITE-SRV1
      ```

   b. Click Next to continue.

Step 9: Configure the File System

1. Follow these steps if the Configure File system screen appears:

   a. Review the information listed.

   b. If you modified the size of the SYS: volume in an earlier step, click the Free Space icon and then click Create. If you did not modify the size of the SYS: volume in an earlier step, click Next and then skip to Step 10.

2. When the New Volume screen appears, in the Volume Name field type **VOL1** and then click OK. This action assigns all of the remaining free space to the VOL1 volume.

3. When the Configure File System screen reappears, ensure that the new volume (VOL1) is listed and then click Next to continue.

4. If a Mount Volumes screen appears, ensure that Yes is selected, indicating that all volumes should be mounted when the server reboots (rather than be mounted immediately). Then click Next to continue.

Step 10: Select Networking Protocols

Configure your server for both the IP and IPX protocols:

1. Follow these steps to configure the IP protocol:

   a. In Network Boards pane on the left, verify that your network board is highlighted. (If not, click it to highlight it.)

   b. In the Protocols section on the right, mark the IP checkbox.

c. In the IP Address field, enter the IP address. (If your server is *not* connected to the Internet, use 187.165.182.18.)

d. In the Subnet Mask field, enter the subnet mask. (If your server is *not* connected to the Internet, use the default of 255.255.0.0.)

e. (Optional) In the Router (Gateway) field, enter the router (gateway) address.

2. Perform the following in order to bind IPX:

a. In the Protocols section on the right, mark the IPX checkbox.

3. When the values are correct, click Next.

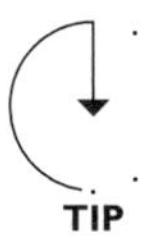

If your server will be connected to the Internet, you must register with the Internet Network Information Center (InterNIC) and obtain a unique IP address. For information on receiving an IP address, contact your Internet Service Provider (ISP) or the Internetwork Information Center (InterNIC) directly at `hostmaster@internic.net`**.**

Step 11: Domain Name Service (DNS)

1. Follow these steps when the Domain Name Service screen appears:

a. Normally, you would fill in the information required. Leave all of these fields blank for now, however.

b. Click Next to continue.

2. Follow these steps when the Warning screen appears:

a. If you read the warning, you'll find that since you have not configured Domain Name Service, you will obtain limited functionality from products that require this service.

b. Click OK to acknowledge the warning.

Step 12: Choose the Server Time Zone

1. Follow these steps when the Time Zone screen appears:

   a. In the Time Zone list box, click the appropriate time zone for where *you* are currently located. (**Note:** Normally, you'd choose the appropriate time zone for Tokyo, Japan, because that's where this server is theoretically located. In this case, however, choosing your current time zone makes performing the lab exercises in this book less confusing.)

   b. In the Daylight Saving Time section, verify that the "Allow System to Adjust for Daylight Saving Time" checkbox is marked, if appropriate.

   c. Click Next to continue.

Step 13: Install Novell Directory Services (NDS)

1. Follow these steps on the first NDS Install screen:

   a. Select New NDS Tree to install this server into a new NDS tree. Note that the resources available in the new tree will not be available to users who are logged into a different tree.

   b. Click Next to continue.

2. Follow these steps on the second NDS Install screen:

   a. In the Tree Name field, enter the following:

      ```
      ACME-TREE
      ```

   b. Click the browse button to the right of the Context for Server Object field.

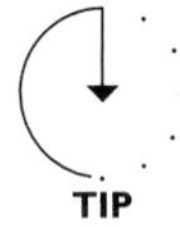
TIP

Do *not* try to save time by keying in the context for the Server object. Instead, "build it" using the browse button. Failure to head this warning may cause undesirable results. (Don't say you weren't warned!)

3. Create the ACME Organization. On the NDS Context Browser screen, click ACME-TREE and then click Add. When the New Container dialog box appears, enter **ACME** in the Container Name field, verify that the Organization radio button is selected in the Container Type field, and then click OK.

4. Create the TOKYO Organizational Unit. When the NDS Context Browser screen reappears, verify that ACME is highlighted and then click Add. When the New Container dialog box appears, enter **TOKYO** in the Container Name field, verify that the Organizational Unit radio button is selected in the Container Type field, and then click OK.

5. Create the CRIME Organizational Unit. When the NDS Context Browser screen reappears, verify that TOKYO is highlighted and then click Add. When the New Container dialog box appears, enter **CRIME** in the Container Name field, verify that the Organizational Unit radio button is selected in the Container Type field, and then click OK.

6. Create the WHITE Organizational Unit. When the NDS Context Browser screen reappears, verify that CRIME is highlighted and then click Add. When the New Container dialog box appears, enter **WHITE** in the Container Name field, verify that the Organizational Unit radio button is selected in the Container Type field, and then click OK. Finally, click OK to return to the NDS Install screen.

7. Follow these steps when the NDS Install screen reappears:

   a. In the Admin Name field, do *not* change the default value (that is, admin).

   b. In the Admin Context field, do *not* change the default value (that is, OU=WHITE.OU=CRIME.OU=TOKYO.O=ACME).

   c. In the Password field, enter the following:

      ```
      ACME
      ```

   d. In the Retype Password field, enter the following:

      ```
      ACME
      ```

   e. When the values on this screen are correct, click Next.

8. At this point, the Installation Wizard checks for duplicate tree names and installs NDS. When the NDS Summary screen appears, write down the following information and store it in a safe place for future reference:

   - NDS Tree Name: ACME-TREE
   - Server Context: OU=WHITE.OU=CRIME.OU=TOKYO.O=ACME
   - Administrator name: CN=admin.OU=WHITE.OU=CRIME.OU=TOKYO.O=ACME
   - Administrator Password You Entered on Previous Screen: ACME

9. Click Next to continue.

Step 14: Install Novell Licensing Services (NLS)

1. Now it's time to license the NetWare 5.1 server. To license it, you would normally insert your NetWare license disk in the floppy drive and select the appropriate license file. (Be sure to use a unique license disk.) If using a license disk, make sure you actually browse to and select the license file, instead of just listing the drive letter (a common mistake). When you click the file, you'll notice that the type of license appears in the Description section, such as "NetWare 5.1 Server, Plus Fifty User Connections."

2. **Note:** If you are using a "demo version" of the *NetWare 5.1 Operating System* CD-ROM (that is, a version that does not have an associated license disk), use the license file in the LICENSE/DEMO directory on the CD-ROM. If you can't locate a license file, mark the "Install without Licenses" checkbox. Unfortunately, you may experience problems with features like NDPS, which use multiple connections.

3. After you make your selection, click Next to continue.

Stage 4: Customization

Step 15: (Optional) Install Additional Products and Services

1. Follow these steps when the Installation Options screen appears:
   a. Mark the "Install Standard NetWare Products Plus WebSphere Application Server" radio button.
   b. Click Next to continue.
2. Follow these steps when the Novell Certificate Server 2.0 Objects screen appears:
   a. Review the onscreen information. (The defaults should be fine.)
   b. Click Next to continue.
3. Follow these steps when the Organizational CA Warning screen appears:
   a. Read the onscreen information.
   b. Click OK to acknowledge the warning.
4. When the Novell Certification Server 2.0 Objects screen reappears, just ignore it and wait until the next screen appears.
5. Follow these steps when the NetWare Enterprise Web Server Settings screen appears:
   a. In the Regular field, enter the appropriate host name and port number. If this server will not be connected to the network, you can use the following:

      ```
      http://WHITE-SRV1.acme.com:80
      ```

   b. In the Secure field, enter the appropriate host name and port number. If this server will not be connected to the network, you can use the following:

      ```
      https://WHITE-SRV1.acme.com:443
      ```

   c. Write down the regular and secure URLs listed above for future reference.

   d. You'll notice an optional setting that enables you to optimize WebBench performance, if desired.
   e. Click Next to continue.

6. Follow these steps when the NetWare Web Manager Settings screen appears:
   a. Enter the appropriate host name and port number. If this server will not be connected to the network, you can use the following:

      ```
      https://WHITE-SRV1.acme.com:2200
      ```

   b. Write down the URL listed above for future reference.
   c. Click Next to continue.

7. Follow these steps when the WebSphere License Agreement screen appears:
   a. Mark the "I Do Accept the Terms of This License" radio button.
   b. Click Next to continue.

8. Follow these steps when the WebSphere Install Options screen appears:
   a. Verify that the Development Kit (Full Installation) radio button is marked. (**Note:** You'll notice that this option installs everything, including the server, Web server, plug-ins, console, help, developer's client files, documentation, and samples.)
   b. Verify that the following is listed in the Destination Directory field: SYS:\WebSphere\AppServer.
   c. Click Next to continue.
   d. Wait until the Summary screen appears. (If the WebSphere Install Options screen appears, for example, just ignore it.)

9. Follow these steps when the Summary screen appears:
   a. Review the list of NetWare 5.1 products to be installed.

  b. When you are satisfied with the list of products, click Customize to be allowed to customize various installation parameters.

Step 16: (Optional) Customize the Server

1. Perform these tasks on the Product Customization screen:
   a. Click NetWare Operating System.
   b. Click Configure.
2. When the Advanced screen appears, review the parameters on the various pages. When you're finished, click Cancel to return to the Product Customization screen without making any changes.
3. When the Product Customization screen reappears, click Close to return to the Summary screen.

Step 17: Complete the Installation

1. On the Summary screen, click Finish to complete the installation process.
2. The Installation program then performs the main file copy and displays the server console screen. (This step may take a while.)
3. When the copying is complete, the Installation Complete window appears. Follow these steps:
   a. (Optional) Click View Log to view the installation log.
   b. (Optional) Click View Readme to view the Release Notes.
   c. Remove any CD-ROM or disk from your computer drives.
   d. Click Yes to reboot the computer.

Now that you've successfully built your WHITE-SRV1 NetWare 5.1 server, it's time to shift our focus to the distributed workstations. After all, the server won't have anyone to serve if the clients can't speak NetWare.

In the next two sections, we'll explore the detailed installation steps for two prominent workstation platforms:

- Windows 95/98
- Windows NT/2000

Installing the Novell Client

Both the Novell Client for Windows 95/98 and the Novell Client for Windows NT/2000 were designed to be closely integrated with their respective workstation operating systems. For this reason, you must be intimately familiar with both the Novell Client and the Windows 95/98 and Windows NT/2000 interfaces.

To perform a local installation of the Novell Client for Windows 95/98 or the Novell Client for Windows NT/2000, you'll need to run the WINSETUP.EXE file from the root directory of the *NetWare 5.1 Novell Client Software* CD-ROM. WINSETUP.EXE automatically activates the correct workstation setup file from a platform-specific directory when you insert the CD-ROM (it uses the AutoRun feature of Windows 95/98 and Windows NT/2000).

If you have an international version of the program, you'll need to select the language to be used during the installation process. Next, you'll need to select from a variety of installation options, as shown in Figure 1.20. These options include ZENworks, Windows 95/98 Client, Windows NT/2000 Client, Windows 3.*x* Client, Documentation, and Browse CD-ROM. After you make your selection, a "NetWare 5.1 Software License" screen appears. Press F10 to accept the terms of the License Agreement.

FIGURE 1.20

Selecting a client installation option

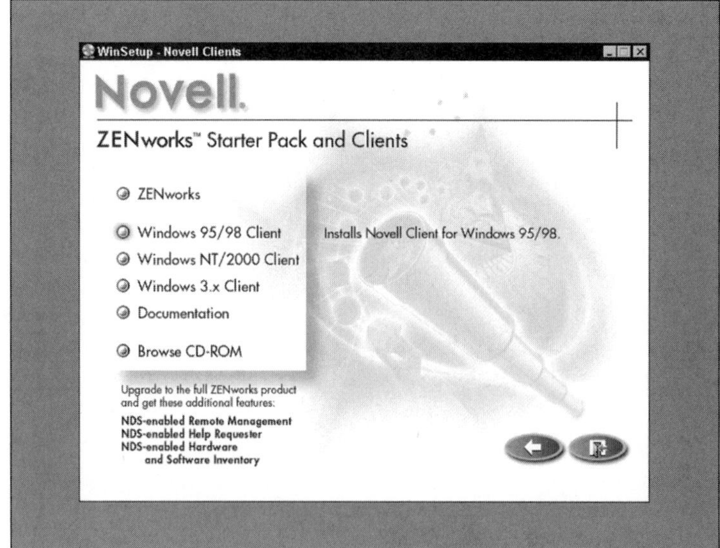

During the installation process, you'll need to determine whether to do a Typical or Custom installation, as shown in Figure 1.21. If you select the Typical option, the Novell Client is automatically installed and configured using detected (or default) protocols. This option is recommended for most computers.

FIGURE 1.21

Select Typical or Custom installation

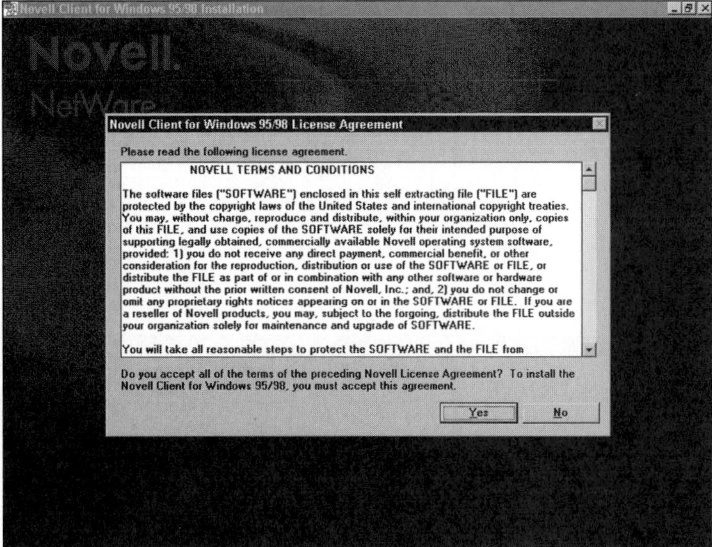

If you select the Custom option, you will need to establish specific protocol and login configurations. In addition, you will be given the opportunity to select optional workstation installation components — such as the Novell Workstation Manager and Novell Distributed Print Services (NDPS).

During a Custom Novell Client installation, you'll need to make the following configuration choices, in this order:

- Protocol preference
- Login authentication
- Custom installation components

Let's take a closer look. Feel free to follow along in the "Lab Exercise 1.2: Novell Client Installation" section.

Protocol Preference

Communication protocols are the common language of the network. The Novell Client for Windows 95/98 and the Novell Client for Windows NT/2000 support both TCP/IP and IPX protocols. TCP/IP is the protocol of the Internet, whereas IPX supports previous versions of NetWare.

As a network administrator, you must decide which protocol to use on each workstation. Many organizations allow both the TCP/IP and IPX protocols on workstations to ensure network compatibility. This allows each workstation to connect to previous versions of NetWare, the Internet, and/or NetWare 5.1 networks using IP-Only.

As you can see in Figure 1.22, the following four options are available in the Protocol Preference configuration screen: IP-Only, IP with IPX Compatibility, IP and IPX, and IPX.

FIGURE 1.22

Selecting protocol(s) during a Custom Novell Client installation

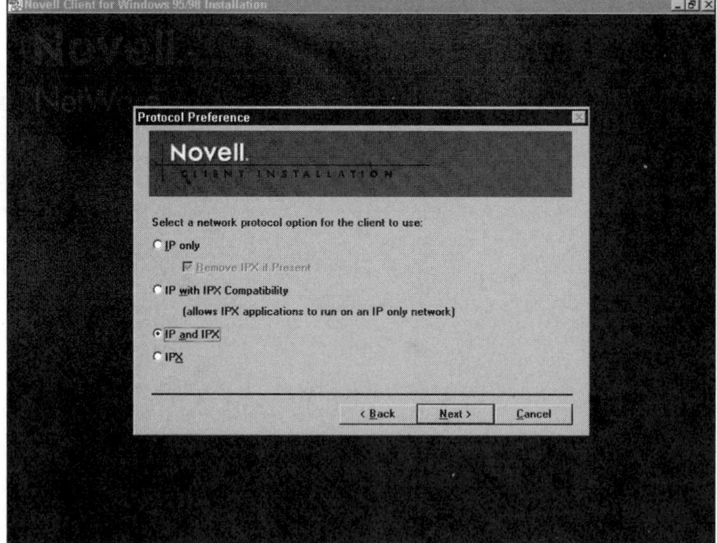

Login Authentication

Authentication is the process of identifying an individual when he or she requests access to the network. This is accomplished when a user enters their username and password in the NetWare 5.1 GUI Login screen.

The Login Authenticator configuration screen shown in Figure 1.23 provides two authentication options: NDS (NetWare 4.*x* or later) and Bindery (NetWare 3.*x*).

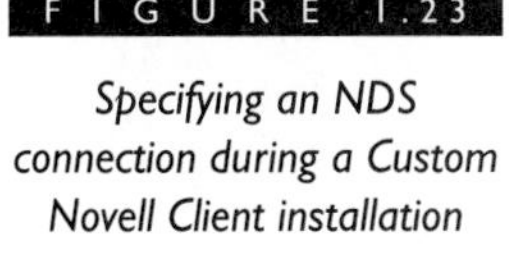

FIGURE 1.23

Specifying an NDS connection during a Custom Novell Client installation

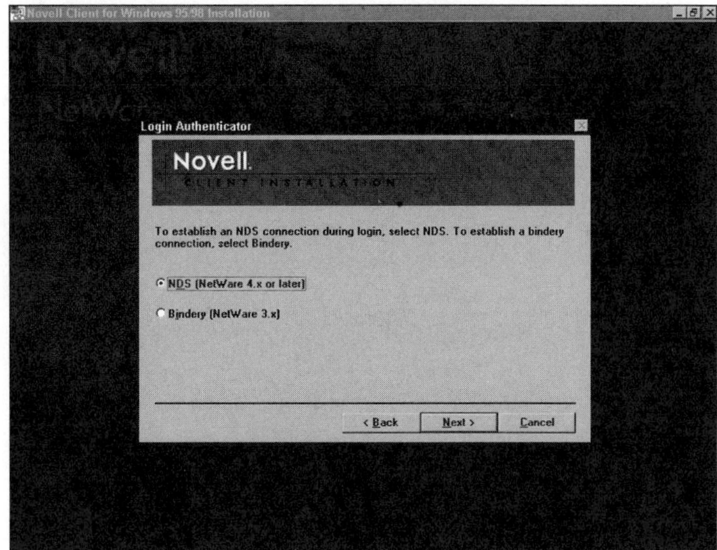

Custom Installation Components

Near the end of the Custom Novell Client installation procedure, the Optional Components screen provides a myriad of optional client components. The specific components available depend on which NetWare 5.1 client is being installed. For example, Figure 1.24 illustrates the optional components that are supported by the Novell Client for Windows 95/98.

FIGURE 1.24

Selecting optional components during a Custom Novell Client installation

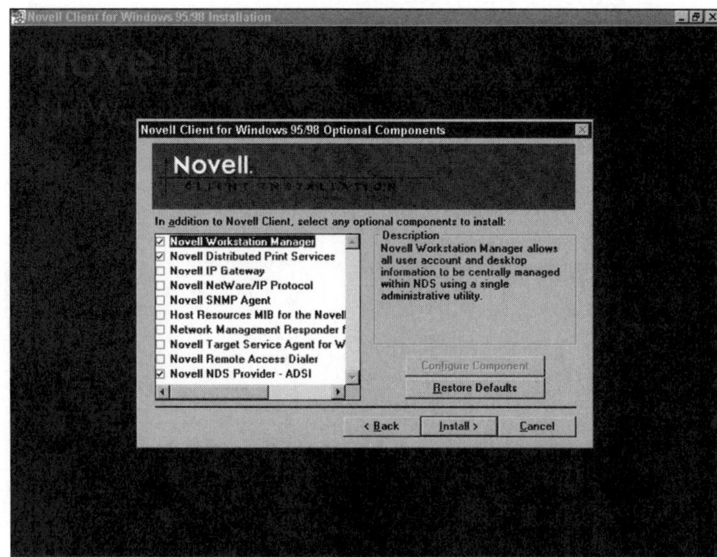

Once you've installed the Novell Client, there's only one task left — logging in. Let's get connected!

Logging In

As a network administrator, you've already accomplished the hard part — automating the workstation connection. Now it's the user's turn. The good news is that both the Novell Client for Windows 95/98 and the Novell Client for Windows NT/2000 provide a friendly GUI login utility for users. As you can see in Figure 1.25, the Novell Login window provides simple Username and Password input boxes within the native MS Windows environment.

FIGURE 1.25

Novell Login window

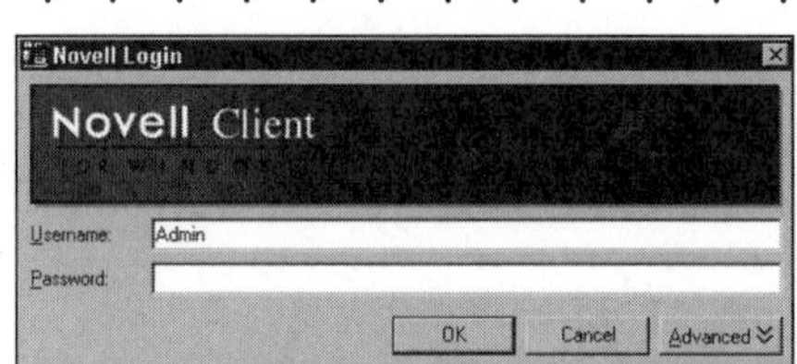

The Novell Login window also contains an Advanced button for login script and NDS configuration, as shown in Figure 1.26. This feature enables you to configure additional information such as tree name, server name, user context, whether to clear current connections, and login script information.

FIGURE 1.26

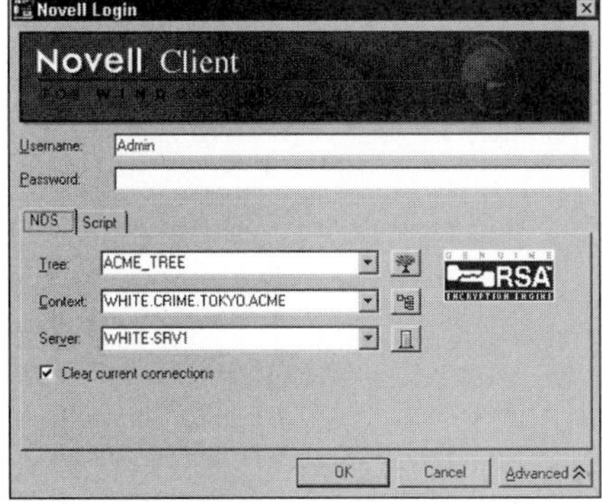

NDS tab on expanded Novell Login window

LAB EXERCISE 1.2: NOVELL CLIENT INSTALLATION

To install the NetWare 5.1 Novell Client on a Windows 95/98 workstation, you will need the following components:

- A workstation that meets the minimum requirements for running the NetWare 5.1 Novell Client for Windows 95/98.
- A *NetWare 5.1 Novell Client Software* CD-ROM.

Complete the following steps to perform a local installation of the NetWare 5.1 Novell Client for Windows 95/98 on a workstation:

1. Exit any applications that you are running.
2. Configure the client's IP address.
   - **a.** Right-click Network Neighborhood.
   - **b.** Select Properties from the pop-up menu that appears.
   - **c.** When the Network dialog box appears, the Configuration tab should be selected by default.
     - Click the TCP/IP protocol. (Two TCP/IP protocols will probably be listed. Select the one that is associated with your network board.)
     - Click Properties.
   - **d.** When the TCP/IP Properties dialog box appears, the IP Address tab should be selected, by default.
     - Mark the "Specify an IP Address" radio button.
     - In the IP Address field, enter the appropriate IP address. (If your computer is not connected to the Internet, you can use 187.165.182.19.)

- In the Subnet Mask field, enter the appropriate subnet mask. (If your workstation is not connected to the Internet, you can use 255.255.0.0.)
- Click OK to return to the Network dialog box.
- Click OK to exit the Network dialog box.

3. Install the NetWare 5.1 Novell Client for Windows 95/98 on your workstation.

a. Insert the *NetWare 5.1 Novell Client Software* CD-ROM in your workstation's CD-ROM drive.

b. If you have an international version of the software, a "WinSetup — Novell Clients" screen appears, requesting that you indicate the language to be used for Novell Client installation. If one appears, click the appropriate language.

c. Next, a "WinSetup — Novell Clients" screen appears. Click Windows 95/98 Client.

d. Follow these steps when the Novell Client for Windows 95/98 License Agreement window appears:

- Read the agreement.
- Click Yes to accept its terms and conditions.

e. Follow these steps when the "Welcome to the Novell Client for Windows 95/98 Install" window appears:

- Click Custom to indicate that you'd like to perform a Custom installation.
- Click Next.

f. Follow these steps when the Protocol Preference window appears:

- Verify that the "IP and IPX" radio button is selected.
- Click Next.

g. Follow these steps when the Login Authenticator window appears:

- Verify that the "NDS (NetWare 4.*x* or Later)" radio button is selected.
- Click Next.

h. Follow these steps when the "Novell Client for Windows 95/98 Optional Components" window appears:

- Ensure that the following checkboxes are marked:

  `Novell Workstation Manager`

  `Novell Distributed Print Services`

  `Novell NDS Provider - ADSI`

- Click Install.

i. Wait while the NetWare 5.1 Novell Client software is installed.

j. When the "Novell Client for Windows 95/98 Installation" window appears, click Reboot to reboot the computer.

4. Log into the network using the Novell Client.

a. When the Novell Login dialog box appears, set default values for the tree name, context, and server fields by following these steps:

- Click Advanced. An expanded Novell Login dialog box will appear. The NDS tab should be selected, by default.
- In the Tree field, enter the following:

  `ACME-TREE`

- In the Context field, enter the following:

  `WHITE.CRIME.TOKYO.ACME`

- In the Server field, enter the following:

  `WHITE-SRV1`

- Verify that the Clear Current Connections checkbox is marked.

b. Log into the tree as the Admin user by following these steps:

- In the Username field, verify that the following is listed:

  `admin`

- In the Password field, enter the following:

  `ACME`

  (You'll notice that asterisks, rather than the actual password, are displayed for security reasons.)

- Click OK to initiate the login process.

NetWare 5.1 Novell Client for Windows NT Installation

To install the NetWare 5.1 Client on a Windows NT workstation, you will need the following components:

- A workstation that meets the minimum requirements for running the NetWare 5.1 Novell Client for Windows NT.

- A *NetWare 5.1 Novell Client Software* CD-ROM.

Complete the following steps to perform a local installation of the NetWare 5.1 Windows NT client on a workstation:

1. Exit any applications that you are running.

2. Configure the Client's IP address.

a. Right-click Network Neighborhood.

b. Select Properties from the pop-up menu that appears.

c. Click Protocols, and choose the TCP/IP protocol. Two TCP/IP protocols will probably be listed. Select the one that is associated with your network board, and click Properties.

d. When the TCP/IP Properties dialog box appears, the IP Address tab should be selected by default. Then go ahead and follow these steps:

- Mark the "Specify an IP Address" radio button.
- In the IP Address field, enter the appropriate IP address. (If your computer is not connected to the Internet, you can use 187.165.182.19.)
- In the Subnet Mask field, enter the appropriate subnet mask. (If your workstation is not connected to the Internet, you can use 255.255.0.0.)
- Click OK to return to the Network dialog box.
- Click OK to exit the Network dialog box.

3. Install the NetWare 5.1 Novell Client for Windows NT on your workstation by following these steps:

a. Insert the *NetWare 5.1 Novell Client Software* CD-ROM in your workstation's CD-ROM drive.

b. If you have an international version of the software, a "WinSetup — Novell Clients" screen appears, requesting that you indicate the language to be used for Client installation. When the screen appears, click the appropriate language.

c. When the next "WinSetup — Novell Clients" screen appears, click Windows NT Client.

d. Follow these steps when the Novell Client Installation window appears:

- Click Custom Installation to indicate that you'd like to perform a Custom installation.
- Click Next.

e. Follow these steps when the Novell Client Installation window appears:

- Ensure that the following checkboxes are marked:

  `Novell Client for Windows NT (Required)`

  `Novell Distributed Print Services`

`Novell Workstation Manager`

`Z.E.N.works Application Launcher NT Serv`

- Click Next.
- Select IP & IPX, and click Next.
- Mark the NDS box, and click Next.
- In the Tree Name field, enter the name of your NDS tree, and click Next.
- Click Finish.
- In the License Agreement screen, click Yes.
- In the Supply Path to NT Files screen, enter the path to your Windows NT installation files, and click Next.
- When prompted, click Reboot.

f. Wait while the NetWare 5.1 Novell Client software is installed.

g. When the Installation Complete window appears, click Reboot to reboot the computer.

4. Log into the network using the Novell Client.

a. When your workstation has rebooted, press CTRL+ALT+DEL.

b. When the Novell Login dialog box appears, set default values for the tree name, context, and server fields by following these steps:

- Click Advanced. An expanded Novell Login dialog box appears. The NDS tab should be selected by default.
- In the Tree field, enter the following:

  `ACME-TREE`

- In the Context field, enter the following:

  `WHITE.CRIME.TOKYO.ACME`

- In the Server field, enter the following:

  `WHITE-SRV1`

- Verify that the Clear Current Connections checkbox is marked.

c. Log into the tree as the Admin user by following these steps:

- In the Username field, verify that the following is listed:

  `admin`

- In the Password field, enter the following:

  `ACME`

  (You'll notice that asterisks, rather than the actual password, are displayed for security reasons.)

- Click OK to initiate the login process.

Novell Licensing Services (NLS)

In order to license NetWare applications, Novell has created a whole new licensing engine called Novell Licensing Services (NLS). NLS helps you monitor and control the use of licensed software on your network. As a matter of fact, NetWare 5.1 itself is a *licensed application*. It requires the number of users connecting to the network to remain within the number of license provided by the NetWare software.

The following steps describe how License Services Providers (LSPs) handle requests from NLS clients by interacting with the NDS database:

- *Step 1*—A licensing-enabled application issues a request for a license to the NLS client. For example, the NetWare 5.1 server can request a license on behalf of a workstation connecting to the server. This request is issued to the NLS client software running on the NetWare 5.1 server.
- *Step 2*—The NLS client packages the request from the application and submits it to a License Service Provider (LSP).
- *Step 3*—The LSP examines the request and determines whether it can respond with a license. The LSP accomplishes this by checking the NDS context of the requesting client for a specific NetWare license unit. If the requested resource is available, the LSP fills the request and delivers a license to the NLS client.
- *Step 4*—However, if the LSP cannot fill the request, it searches for another resource. The LSP resource check begins at the next-higher context in the NDS tree and continues until it reaches the [Root]. In our example, the LSP will begin its licensed search in the host server's NDS context and "walk" up the tree looking for a server-based license certificate. This process is known as *Server Connection Licensing* (SCL).
- *Step 5*—Once the LSP finds a NetWare license unit, it returns a successful *status* to the NLS client. The NLS client then delivers the license to the requesting application and a connection to the server is allowed.

The process described above relies on two main licensing components: License Service Provider (LSP) and NLS clients. An LSP is licensing software that you install and run on NetWare servers. This software is contained in the NLSLSP.NLM program running on a NetWare 4.11 (or later) server.

When you install NLS on a NetWare server, NLS automatically installs the LSP software and creates an LSP object (NLS_LSP_*servername*) in the NDS tree. The host LSP server must have a writeable replica of each partition in order to serve License Certificate objects from NDS. This replica can be a Master or Read/Write replica. You can run LSPs on other servers without replicas as long as they can communicate with the LSP that has a writeable replica. As a result, the server with the writeable replica can make changes to the NDS database on the other server's behalf.

In addition to an LSP, NLS relies on client software as an interface between licensing-enabled applications and the central LSP. An NLS client can run on either a workstation or a server. When you install NLS on a server, all files that enable an application to use NLS are copied to SYS:PUBLIC and SYS:SYSTEM.

Because NLS relies on NDS integration for storing license certificates, the following NDS Licensing objects are required:

- *NLS_LSP Objects* — The LSP object is at the heart of Novell Licensing Services. By default, the NLS_LSP_*servername* object is created automatically when the NDS Schema is extended with SETUPNLS.NLM, or when you run NWCONFIG ⇨ License Options ⇨ Create License Service Provider.

- *License Container Objects* — NetWare 5.1 supports two different types of License Container objects: the *Server* License Container (Novell + NetWare 5 Server + 510) and the *Connection* License Container (Novell + NetWare 5 Conn SCL + 510). Each of these containers stores the license usage information for the previous 15 months. They can be moved up the tree to centralized licensing without moving the server object. By default, these objects are added to the NDS tree in the host server container when NetWare 5.1 is installed on the server. Finally, License Container objects appear as leaf objects in the NDS container, yet they can contain multiple License Certificate objects.

- *License Certificate Objects* — License Certificate objects are also created in NDS when the NetWare 5.1 server is installed. From a security perspective, License Certificates can either be *secure* or *unsecure*. Secure License Certificates are digitally signed and cannot be modified. These License Certificates usually come from a software vendor. On the other hand, Metering Certificates are unsecure and are usually created by network administrators. For example, ZENworks functions as the NLS client and requests Metering Certificates on behalf of applications.

NLS supports the following three Server License types:

- *Master License Agreement (MLA)* — A nonrestricted generic license that can be installed on many servers. All MLA servers report the same serial number and you can install this License Certificate for as many connections as the license agreement allows. MLA licenses are ideal for global organizations.

- *Corporate License Agreement (CLA)* — A restricted license, meaning that each server must have a unique base server license. In addition, one or more connection licenses can be installed per server. With this license, network administrators cannot change the name of the server in AUTOEXEC.NCF without causing licensing problems. CLA licenses are ideal for medium-to-large- size organizations.

- *Volume License Agreement (VLA)* — A restricted license just like CLA. VLA licenses are ideal for small-to-medium-size organizations.

REAL WORLD

If MLA License Containers are moved down the NDS tree and the Server object is not moved with them, licensing will not function. On the other hand, CLA and VLA licenses do support this type of NDS object relocation because licensing is attached directly to the Server object.

In this discussion, we will delve into much more detail regarding NLS installation and management. The following licensing responsibilities will have a dramatic impact on the functionality of your NetWare 5.1 server.

Installing NLS

The details of NLS installation depend entirely on the version of NLS and the version of NetWare you are running. Refer to Table 1.1 for an NLS installation comparison. In this section, we will study NLS v5.02, which was released with NetWare 5.1.

Before you install NLS, consider the following guidelines:

- For fault tolerance purposes, make sure to have at least two servers running NLS v5.02 in each partition of the NDS tree. Remember, each NLS server must have a Read/Write replica of the partition holding its home container. Finally, it's best if one of these servers holds the Master replica.
- NLS v5.02 does not run on NetWare 3 or NetWare 4.10 servers. Make sure that you use NetWare Deployment Management to install NLS on any of the following NetWare servers: NetWare 4.11, NetWare 4.12, NetWare 5.0, or NetWare 5.1.
- You don't need special software installed on workstations to take advantage of NLS. Licensing-enabled software communicates with NetWare LSPs by using DLL or NLM files that are automatically installed on NetWare servers.

TABLE 1.1

NLS Installation Comparison

NLS VERSION	NETWARE VERSION	INSTALLATION DETAILS	FEATURES	LICENSING FOR NETWARE
NLS v3.0	NetWare 4.11	By default, not installed during NetWare 4.11 installation.	Basic licensing features. Also used by NetWare for Small Business.	Stored licensed units in SERVER.EXE.
NLS v4.0	NetWare 5	By default, installed during NetWare 5 installation.	Added reporting capabilities and tools. Also used by BorderManager.	Stored license certificates in NDS.
NLS v5.0	Novell Licensing Tool Kit 1.0	Uses SETUPNLS.EXE to easily install NLS on an entire NDS tree, in a partition, or on selected servers.	Supports event notification, enhanced NLS snap-in for NetWare administrator. Also used by NetWare Cluster Services.	Supports object licensing using the User Access Licensing (UAL) model.
NLS v5.01	NetWare Cluster Services	Uses SETUPNLS.EXE to easily install NLS on an entire NDS tree, in a partition, or on selected servers.	Supports event notification, enhanced NLS snap-in for NetWare administrator. Also used by NetWare Cluster Services.	Supports object licensing using the User Access Licensing (UAL) model.
NLS v5.02	NetWare 5.1	By default, installed during NetWare 5.1 installation. Uses Deployment Manager to install NLS on an entire NDS tree, in a partition, or on selected servers.	Only used by NetWare 5.1 servers.	Supports SCL and UAL licensing models.

When you install a NetWare 5.1 server, NLS 5.02 is automatically installed on that server. No other action concerning Novell Licensing Services is required. However, if you want to install NLS into an existing network, you must perform the following steps:

- *Step 1:* Prepare the existing network using Deployment Manager.
- *Step 2:* Upgrade NetWare 4 and NetWare 5 servers.
- *Step 3:* Verify that NLS is installed.

Let's take a closer look.

Step 1: Prepare the Existing Network Using Deployment Manager

If you install NLS v5.02 on an existing NetWare 4 or NetWare 5 network, you need to use Deployment Manager (NWDEPLOY.EXE) from a Windows workstation. By installing from a workstation, you do not have to access the individual NetWare servers. NWDEPLOY.EXE is located at the root of the NetWare 5.1 operating system CD-ROM.

To prepare an existing network for NLS installation, perform the following steps:

1. Launch NWDEPLOY.EXE on a Windows workstation from the [Root] directory of the NetWare 5.1 operating system CD-ROM. Next, accept the License Agreement and select Network Preparation ➪ Step 4: Novell Licensing Services. This step assumes that you have already completed Deployment Manager Steps 1–3.

2. Double-click View, and then choose Update Novell Licensing Services. At the Welcome screen, click Next and accept the software license agreement.

3. The "Where to Install NLS" screen displays a default tree. If the currently selected partition is not correct, use the Browse button to navigate and select the Server's Host Partition. Click OK.

4. Mark the box to update NLS on the desired servers and click Next. Click Finish to completed the Deployment Manager update.

Deployment Manager performs the following five tasks: it extends the NDS Schema, installs NLSLSP.NLM on selected servers, creates the appropriate NLS_LSP_*servername* objects, configures NLS, and modifies AUTOEXEC.NCF on NetWare 4.11 and NetWare 4.2 servers with the appropriate NLS commands. In addition, Deployment Manager checks NDS partitioning information on each host server to make sure that at least two servers are running NLS v5.02 in each NDS partition. Remember, this is required for fault tolerance.

Step 2: Upgrade NetWare 4 and 5 Servers

Once you have used Deployment Manager to prepare the existing network for NLS v5.02, you must upgrade NetWare 4 and 5 servers and activate the appropriate version of NLS.

As shown earlier in Table 1.1, NetWare 5 servers run NLS v4.0 by default. When you install NetWare 5.1 on an existing NetWare 5 server, the Installation program replaces these files with NLS 5.02 by default. Because both NLS v4.0 and v5.02 support NDS integration, this upgrade process is seamless.

Furthermore, NetWare 4.11 servers run NLS v3.0 by default (as shown in Table 1.1). Because NLS v3.0 is not NDS integrated, you will need to perform the following steps during a NetWare 4.11 upgrade:

- Use Deployment Manager to modify AUTOEXEC.NCF to include the following line:

  ```
  LOAD NLSLSP
  ```

- Use Deployment Manager to copy a new NLSAPI.NLM to the server. This file isn't available until the server is rebooted or the program is manually reloaded.

- Use the NetWare 5.1 Installation program to extend the NDS Schema to support NLS.

- Use the NetWare 5.1 Installation program to create an NLS_LSP_*servername* object for this server.

- Use the NetWare 5.1 Installation program to install NLS 5.02 files on the server.

- Use SETUPNLS.NLM to convert NLS 3.0 objects to NLS 4.0 objects and then use Deployment Manager to convert the NLS 4.0 to NLS 5.02 objects.

Step 3: Verify That NLS Is Installed

To verify whether NLS is installed on any server, you can use either of the following two options:

- At the server console, type **NWCONFIG** and select Product Options ➪ View/Configure/Remove Installed Products. Then scroll through the list of currently installed products to find NLS 5.0.2 Novell Licensing Services.
- At the server console, enter **MODULES NLS***. This will verify that NLSLSP.NLM is running on the server.

Once you have installed NLS, your NetWare 5.1 server is ready to accept user connections. However, it is not ready to license client applications. At this point, you must perform some or all of the management tasks described in the next section. Let's take a closer look.

Managing NLS

NLS license management relies on NDS-integrated License Certificates. These certificates include the license resources NLS needs to successfully respond to client requests. In this section, we will explore the following NLS management tasks:

- *Installing License Certificates* — First, we will learn a little bit more about the Server Connection Licensing (SCL) model and how license units are contained within License Certificates and/or licensing envelopes. In addition, we will learn how to use NetWare Administrator to install License Certificates.
- *Managing License Certificates* — Next, we will learn how to create Metering Certificates for non-NLS-enabled applications. In addition, we will learn how to move License Certificates and make Server Assignments using NetWare Administrator.

- *Configure Notifications and Reports*—When NLS generates notifications, they are sent by default to the User object that installed the certificate. Using NetWare Administrator, you can change this designated person by modifying the License Container object's Notify property page. In addition, you can use NetWare Administrator to create reports for all licensed units in a specific License Container.
- *Troubleshooting Server Connection Licensing*—Finally, we will explore some guidelines for troubleshooting a variety of SCL licensing problems.

Let's take a closer look at Novell Licensing Services management.

Installing License Certificates

In the Server Connection Licensing (SCL) model, you must install license units within a single License Certificate or within an NLS envelope. Furthermore, the SCL model requires each server to use a server-based license unit and for each user that connects to the server to use a connection-based license unit. If you select Install without Licenses during a NetWare 5.1 installation or upgrade, License Certificates are not installed and the server automatically supports three "grace" server connections. These connections are used in the following way: one grace connection for the server and two grace connections for users and/or server-based applications (such as SAS or the NDPS Broker).

After a NetWare 5.1 installation or upgrade, you can use NWCONFIG.NLM or NetWare Administrator to manually install License Certificates. In either case, you can install License Certificates one at a time (using Single Certificates), or you can add multiple License Certificates in an envelope:

- *Single Certificates*—When a Certificate for an NLS-aware application is installed, NLS adds a License Container object to the NDS tree and a Single License Certificate object within that container. A License Container can include multiple License Certificates, but they must be installed one at a time. Install these License Certificates by accessing NLS and KEY files.

- *Envelopes* — An envelope is an.NLF file containing one or more License Certificates. Envelopes also reside within License Container objects but enable you to install more than one License Certificate at a time. For example, if you purchased a suite of four different NLS-aware applications, you can use an envelope to simultaneously install License Certificates for all four products.

When you add License Certificate objects to the NDS tree, you should plan their distribution intelligently. For example, some NetWare policies require that certificates be placed close to the requesting entity. This means you must place License Certificate objects in or above the same NDS context as the server you are licensing (that is, the server running NLSLSP.NLM).

Companies with complex NDS trees should place License Certificates at the Organizational Unit level beneath [Root]. On the other hand, smaller companies can place License Certificates at the topmost container of the tree. Finally, if you are using a remote site and a WAN link, place a License Certificate in the Remote Sites context so that users and server-based applications can authenticate locally without crossing the WAN link.

After a NetWare 5.1 installation or upgrade, you can use NWCONFIG.NLM or NetWare Administrator to install License Certificates. In NetWare Administrator, click Tools ➪ Novell Licensing Services ➪ Add Licenses ➪ License File, and follow the onscreen prompts. If an Activation Key window appears, use the online help facility to access the information you need. Once the License Certificates have been installed using NetWare Administrator, you must manually assign them to an LSP server.

In addition, you can perform the following steps in NWCONFIG.NLM to install License Certificates on an existing NetWare 5.1 server:

1. At the server console, enter **NWCONFIG** and press Enter.

2. From the NWCONFIG main console screen, select License Options ➪ Install Licenses. Then select a path to the NLS file that has the License Certificate. For example, select A:\LICENSE.

3. Enter the full context name and password of the NDS tree Administrator in order to authenticate. NLS License Certificates cannot be added to an NDS tree without administrative rights to the target container.

4. From the Installable Licenses screen, select an envelope file. This NLF file contains one or more License Certificates. Once the License Certificate has been added to the NDS tree, exit NWCONFIG.NLM. You can now view the installed License Certificate objects within NetWare Administrator's NDS tree browser.

REAL WORLD

License Certificates with a nine-digit serial number cannot be installed while upgrading an existing server to NetWare 5.1. If the serial number printed on your license disk has nine digits, you must select Install Without Licenses on the License Installation screen during server installation or upgrade and manually install the License Certificates using NWCONFIG or NetWare Administrator.

License Certificates for Master License Agreements (MLA) do not contain a server or a connection limit. When the first NetWare 5.1 server is installed into an NDS tree, the server-based license and connection license certificates are created in the same container as the NetWare 5.1 server. You can install and reinstall these certificates for as many connections as the terms and conditions of the License Agreement allow. For best performance, install the MLA License Certificate in each partition that contains a NetWare 5.1 server. These multiple installations speed authentication by allowing users and servers to access local partitions of the NDS database.

During a typical NetWare 5.1 installation, the NICI Foundation Keys (.NFK) are automatically copied from the MLA license disk to the server. If you choose Install without Licenses, you must manually copy the NFK files from the MLA license disk to each server. This cryptographic foundation key is stored on the MLA disk as a file named "*serial_number*.NFK." In order to manually activate NICI features on an MLA server, copy this file from the MLA disk to the SYS:SYSTEM directory and rename it to "NICIFK." Remember to reboot the server in order for these changes to take effect.

Managing License Certificates

Once you have installed distributed License Certificate objects into your NDS tree, NLS-aware applications will be able to use them for user and service authentication. In addition, you may need to perform any or all of the following License Certificate management tasks:

- *Creating a Metering Certificate* — Metering Certificates enable you to track usage of applications even though they are not NLS-enabled. By using Metering Certificates, you can enable users to continue using these applications while you track and manage the software licenses associated with them. For example, you can configure ZENworks as an NLS client for applications that are not NLS-enabled, and it can request NLS units on behalf of those applications. To create Metering Certificates within NetWare Administrator, use the following menu options: Tools ➪ Novell Licensing Services ➪ Add Licenses ➪ License Metering.

- *Moving a License Certificate* — You can move License Certificate objects from one context to another in the NDS tree by using the following NetWare Administrator menu options: Tools ➪ Novell Licensing Services ➪ Move Selected License Certificates. Once you have moved the License Certificate, you must collapse and expand the browse view to see the objects in their new container.

- *Configuring Server Assignments* — Through the Assignments property page in NetWare Administrator, you can allow only designated servers to grant requests for license units. This is known as a *Server Assignment*. As a matter of fact, some NLS-aware applications require that a License Certificate have a Server Assignment before it can be used. On the other hand, not all certificates require a Server Assignment. For example, the License Certificate in off-the-shelf NetWare 5.1 requires a Server Assignment, but certificates for MLAs do not. To configure Server Assignments for License Certificates in NetWare Administrator, right-click the License Certificate object you want to assign to a server and activate the following menu options: Details ➪ Assignments ➪ Add. When you are configuring Server Assignments, remember that only one assignment can be made for each License Certificate, and no other server is allowed to use the units from an assigned Certificate.

Configuring Notifications and Reports

When NLS generates notifications, they are sent by default to the User object that installed the Certificate. Using NetWare Administrator, you can change this designated person by modifying the License Container object's Notify property page.

License Certificate notifications are used to identify when a company is out of compliance concerning an NLS-aware application. The designated NLS administrator receives a notification when an application assigned to a License Certificate attempts to exceed the available number of licenses. Once notified, the administrator can then purchase and install more License Certificates or resolve the issues that are related to the License Agreement and its usage.

In addition to License Certificate notifications, NLS includes a variety of license reports that track data about licensed and metering products. As an NLS administrator, you can create, use, and save these reports to help you monitor the usage of NLS-aware applications.

First, you can create NLS license reports for all license units used in a given context, a specific container, or within a single License Certificate. The default reports provide data for the past 15 months. NetWare Administrator provides a license generation capability at the container level. Simply click a License Container object and access the Report Wizard by using the following menu options: Tools ➪ Novell Licensing Services ➪ Generate License Reports.

Next, you can save license reports in any of the following formats:

- *Save Graph as Bitmap* — This option enables you to save the data as a bitmap file with the .BMP extension. The Graph tab on the report enables you to view this data.
- *Save Summary as Text* — This option enables you to save the data as a text file with the .TXT extension. The Summary tab on the report enables you to view this data.
- *Save Reloadable Data* — You can use this option to save the data as a .DAT file. This provides a 15-month snapshot of the product's usage on the network.

- *Save Tab-Delimited Data* — This option enables you to save the data in a two-column tabbed format for import into a database or a spreadsheet application.

Troubleshooting Server Connection Licensing

Once you have installed and configured Novell Licensing Services, you attention should turn to keeping it running. Following are troubleshooting tips that help maintain longevity and continuity in your Server Connection Licensing system:

- *LSP Placement* — Some NLS clients might not have access to licensing services if LSP objects are not well-placed in the NDS tree. Make sure to place the central LSP and its License Certificates as close as practical to users but high enough in the NDS tree so that they are accessible to everyone who needs them. Also, make sure that NLS servers do not have to traverse slow WAN links in order to access license units.

- *Server Beeps Frequently* — If your server beeps frequently, the server-based license may not be consuming a license unit. This can be caused by two problems: the License Certificate is not installed or the server-based License Certificate is not assigned to the Server object.

- *Error When You Move a Server Object in the NDS Tree* — When you move a server in the NDS tree, you may need to move the License Certificates along with it.

- *Error When You Use NWCONFIG.NLM to Uninstall and Reinstall NDS* — If you uninstall NDS from a server and then reinstall it, you must run NWCONFIG.NLM to reinstall or move the License Certificates. This is accomplished by using the following menu options: License Options ➪ Set Up Licensing Services.

- *Error When You Rename a Server That Is Using a Server +5 License Certificate* — When you rename a server, you need to make sure to change the Server Assignment on the License Certificate object so that it matches the new name of the server.

- *NLS Error Code C0001005* — This NLS error code is typically caused by a License Certificate object that requires a Server Assignment but doesn't have a Server Assignment. Simply make a Server Assignment as described in the "Managing License Certificates" section in order to solve the problem.

- *NLS Error Code C0001002* — This NLS error code typically occurs when you remove or reinstall NDS or the Server and [Public] objects don't have enough rights. Furthermore, the following two NetWare partitioning problems can cause this NLS error code: (1) you remove the Read/Write replica from the NLS server that is running NLSLSP.NLM; or (2) two NetWare 5.1 servers contain a replica of the [Root] partition.

This completes our comprehensive discussion of Novell Licensing Services. As you have learned, this NetWare 5.1 security feature is flexible, comprehensive, and secure. In addition, it provides numerous configuration and management options via NDS integration and the NetWare Administrator tool. Now that your new NetWare 5.1 server has been installed, configured, and licensed, it's time for the real fun . . . advanced administration.

LAB EXERCISE 1.3: GETTING STARTED

Use the hints provided to find the 20 installation, upgrade, and migration terms hidden in this word search puzzle. Omit any punctuation characters (such as blank spaces, hyphens, and so on) and spell out any numbers.

N	O	N	P	R	O	D	U	C	T	I	O	N	N	R	I
S	F	N	L	S	E	N	V	E	L	O	P	E	N	M	B
S	E	C	U	R	E	R	M	L	A	A	T	A	N	E	A
E	Y	X	S	D	I	S	O	L	A	T	E	D	S	T	T
R	S	E	Z	I	M	O	T	S	U	C	D	Y	H	V	C
V	D	O	S	P	A	R	T	I	T	I	O	N	B	K	H
E	M	A	N	G	K	D	R	Q	O	W	V	G	Y	E	N
R	E	G	I	O	N	A	L	S	E	T	T	I	N	G	S
I	B	F	O	E	W	S	K	V	X	J	B	F	F	I	J
D	X	I	G	R	S	W	D	T	E	T	I	J	V	M	M
N	C	C	U	P	R	U	Z	B	C	Q	K	I	Z	H	D
U	J	U	L	H	I	V	P	V	N	R	T	X	A	E	O
M	C	G	T	I	P	J	D	Z	C	N	F	I	N	V	B
B	R	B	T	U	V	Q	B	C	F	F	C	E	S	S	V
E	K	K	L	O	V	S	Z	N	J	I	V	L	N	H	V
R	S	Z	B	H	Q	V	B	X	X	P	F	L	Q	W	G

Hints

1. DOS configuration boot file that is typically used to execute the SERVER.EXE file.
2. Type of NetWare 5.1 installation method covered in this chapter.
3. A restricted license agreement designed for medium-to-large-sized organizations.
4. During the NetWare 5.1 installation process, click this button before clicking the Finish button to be allowed to make changes.
5. Home of the NWSERVER directory.
6. Type of tree to use for lab exercises in this book.

7. A non-restricted license agreement that reports the same serial number to all NetWare servers in a given network.
8. An .NLF file that contains one or more License Certificates.
9. Type of server to use for lab exercises in this book.
10. Optional enhanced storage management system in NetWare 5.1.
11. Refers to country, code page, and keyboard settings.
12. A type of License Certificate that contains a digital signature and cannot be modified.
13. A random, automatically generated identification number that uniquely distinguishes each NetWare server.
14. A transactional tracking system that protects NetWare servers from data corruption during a "crash."
15. A restricted license agreement designed for small-to-medium-sized organizations.

See Appendix C for answers.

LAB EXERCISE 1.4: NETWARE 5.1 INSTALLATION

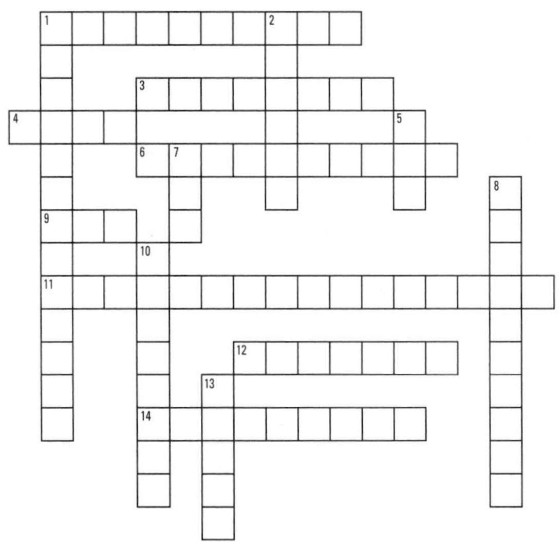

Across

1. Administrator for bindery-based servers
3. CD-ROM standard, not a restaurant
4. Recommended for ConsoleOne
6. NetWare 5.1 installation utility
9. Storage device driver
11. Contains NetWare volumes
12. Better to be safe than sorry
14. VESA 2 compliance is recommended

Down

1. Installation messages displayed here
2. Mouse type supported on server
5. Storage adapter driver
7. Secure licensing in NetWare 5.1
8. Automatically loads SERVER.EXE
10. Disk drivers are stored here
13. Typical NetWare 5.1 installation media

See Appendix C for answers.

CHAPTER 2

NetWare 5.1 IP Services

Now that you have constructed the NetWare 5.1 server, it's time to pour the electronic pavement of our information superhighway — also known as TCP/IP.

The Internet's main protocol suite is called *TCP/IP*. It consists primarily of the Internet Protocol (IP), which provides Network Layer routing, and the Transmission Control Protocol (TCP), which operates at the Transport Layer. Today TCP/IP is *the* industry protocol standard for global communications.

In the past, NetWare only supported native NetWare Core Protocol (NCP) requests over the Internetwork Packet Exchange (IPX) protocol. This protocol required little administrative intervention to configure and maintain. With the release of NetWare 5.*x*, Novell has added native NCP support for TCP/IP, thus eliminating the need to encapsulate. Following are some critical TCP/IP administrative features included with NetWare 5.1:

- *IP* — All NetWare 5.1 core protocols can use the benefits of TCP/IP's open connectivity. This provides the capability to run in a "Pure IP" environment — *pure* in the sense that NetWare 5.1 can be configured to offer NCP services natively over the TCP/IP stack. This eliminates the need for IPX-based encapsulation (or, in the case of NT server, a NetBIOS encapsulation). In other words, a NetWare 5.1 server configured for IP-Only uses TCP/IP rather than IPX/SPX as the transport mechanism for all NCP calls. This eliminates multiple protocols on the wire and frees valuable network bandwidth. Of course, IP doesn't come without its fair share of management costs. Fortunately, NetWare 5.1 offers some relief in the form of Compatibility Mode and Novell DNS/DHCP Services.

- *Compatibility Mode* — NetWare 5.1 also includes significant backward compatibility with older IPX-based networks via its *Compatibility Mode*. With Compatibility Mode enabled, you can execute IPX-based applications on special IP-based Compatibility Mode network segments and ensure compatibility between IP and IPX networks.

- *Service Location Protocol (SLP)* — In the past, NetWare used the Service Advertising Protocol (SAP) method of discovering network services. In NetWare 5.1, you have three main choices: Service Location Protocol (SLP), Dynamic Host Configuration Protocol (DHCP), and Static Configuration. In addition, NDS and DNS offer service location capabilities. The first (and most popular) service-discovery method is SLP. This IP Migration component provides automatic resource discovery and registration on a TCP/IP network. SLP is particularly advantageous, because it provides full backward compatibility with IPX-based network services and with applications that rely on SAP discovery.

- *Novell DNS/DHCP Services* — To help ease the IP management burden, NetWare 5.1 includes two TCP/IP administration services for IP address allocation and host configuration. First, Domain Name System (DNS) offers a distributed name/address database to translate numerical IP addresses into alphanumeric names. Second, the Dynamic Host Configuration Protocol (DHCP) provides a framework for dynamically passing configuration information to TCP/IP clients.

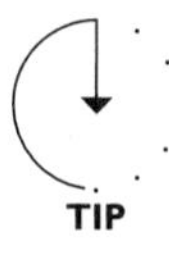
TIP

Study the four TCP/IP administration features discussed in this section. These topics are precursors to the Novell DNS/DHCP lessons. Specifically, learn that IP-Only allows clients to access a NetWare 5.1 server without IPX-based encapsulation. Also, remember that Compatibility Mode enables you to execute IPX-based applications on IP-based network segments.

The challenges of migrating to IP are offset by its benefits. A Novell IP network increases the throughput on taxed network segments and improves overall interoperability. The overhead required to configure and to administer a TCP/IP network, however, can be time-consuming. For this reason, you should study this chapter carefully.

Now let's start our TCP/IP discussion with a detailed look at the challenge of migrating to IP.

Migrating to IP

As we just learned, NetWare 5.1 allows you to access NetWare services through the use of *Pure IP*. Although many network administrators may use both TCP/IP and IPX on their current networks, an IP-Only system is more easily integrated with other operating systems, such as UNIX and Windows NT.

Because of the complexity of migrating an IPX-based network to an IP-based network, the migration components have been integrated into NetWare 5.1 instead of being placed in a separate migration tool. These migration components are used by the server only when required. Because an IPX stack is loaded on the server, some IPX symbols may persist. This does not mean, though, that the system is using IPX on the wire — only that the system is compatible with IPX if it needs to be.

The good news is that the challenges of migrating to IP-Only are more than offset by the benefits of a single protocol network. In short, an IP-Only network increases the throughput on taxed network segments and improves overall interoperability. In this overview section, we will begin with three different protocol configurations:IP-Only, IPX-Only, and IP and IPX together. Then we will discover some exciting IP migration scenarios, and offer some simple steps for configuring Compatibility Mode servers/clients. Next, we will learn how to expand IP addresses within private and public networks using Network Address Translation (NAT). Finally, we will explore service discovery and SAP redirection using the Service Location Protocol (SLP).

Now let's take a look at the three different protocol configurations offered by NetWare 5.1. Then we can use this information to explore a variety of IP migration scenarios.

NetWare 5.1 Protocol Configurations

Your ability to support IP-Only and/or IPX-Only connectivity within your WAN relies entirely on how the clients and servers are configured during installation. In NetWare 5.1, you have three different protocol configuration options:

- *IP-Only* — Server A in Figure 2.1
- *IPX-Only* — Server C in Figure 2.1
- *IP and IPX together* — Servers B, D, and E in Figure 2.1

FIGURE 2.1

NetWare 5.1 protocol configurations

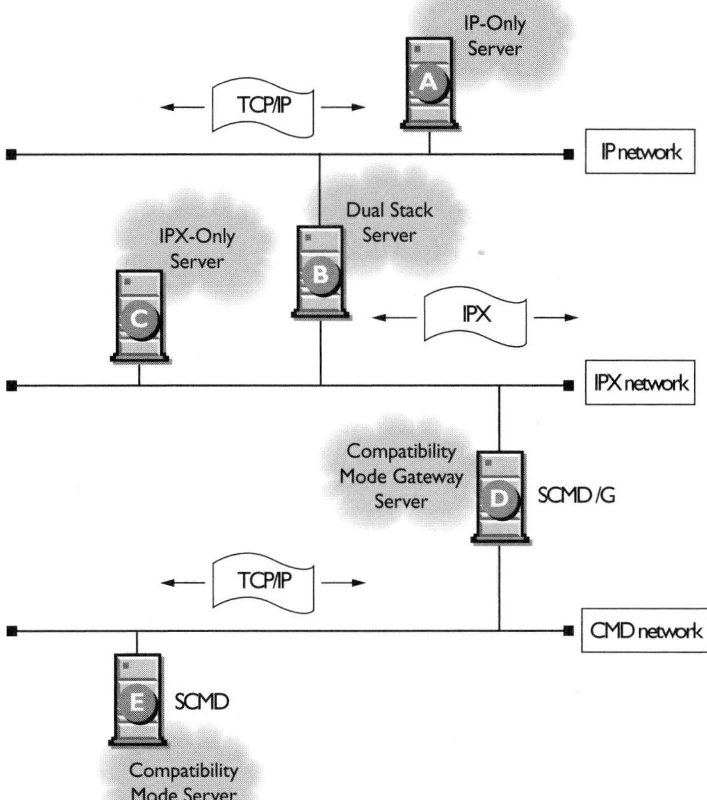

The protocol configuration you choose determines the binding between protocol stacks and network adapters. It does not determine which protocol stacks are loaded in the system. For example, if you select the IP-Only install option, both the TCP/IP and IPX stacks are loaded, but only the TCP/IP stack is bound to the network adapter.

Figure 2.1 has three network configurations (IP, IPX, and Compatibility Mode) servicing four server configurations (IP-Only, IPX-Only, Dual Stack, and Compatibility Mode).

Now let's take a closer look at each of these protocol configurations, because you will probably come across each of them during your migration from an IPX to an IP network.

IP-Only

If you install your NetWare 5.1 clients and servers using the IP-Only install option, you'll end up with a Pure IP network (see Figure 2.1). Interestingly, though, IP-Only servers *do* load both the TCP/IP and IPX protocol stacks, but only the TCP/IP stack is bound to the internal network adapter. The IPX protocol stack is loaded on IP systems to give them the capability to execute IPX applications and to connect to IPX LANs through a Migration Agent.

IPX-Only

If you install your NetWare 5.1 clients and servers using the IPX-Only install option, you'll end up with a "Pure IPX" network (see Figure 2.1 earlier). As with the IP-Only configuration, servers installed using the IPX-Only option load both the TCP/IP and IPX stacks. However, the IPX stack is the only stack attached to the internal network adapter.

IP and IPX Together

If you configure your NetWare 5.1 servers and clients for IP and IPX, you'll end up with a mixed network (see Figure 2.1).This third protocol configuration option can be accomplished at the NetWare 5.1 client/server in one of two ways:

- *Dual Stacks* — The server and client are configured with both protocol stacks (refer to Server B in Figure 2.1). This means each machine supports both the IP and IPX protocols. While this creates overhead on the network wire, it does ensure multiprotocol connectivity.

- *Compatibility Mode* — This second option occurs automatically if you select the IP-Only option when you install your server. In this case, the IPX Compatibility Mode Driver (CMD) creates a virtual IPX network within the IP-Only WAN (refer to Server E in Figure 2.1). This is the preferred option because it doesn't cause any network bandwidth overhead. As you'll learn in just a moment, a CMD Network requires a Migration Agent for connection to IPX-Only networks (refer to Server D in Figure 2.1).

This completes our brief discussion of NetWare 5.1 client/server protocol configurations. As you can see, the choices you make during installation dramatically impact your ability to communicate in a mixed IP and IPX environment. Choose wisely. Now let's continue our discussion of IP migration with a detailed look at some interesting migration scenarios.

IP Migration Scenarios

The strategy that you choose to migrate your existing network to IP-Only depends on a number of important criteria, such as the migration path that you're using (IPX to IP, for example), the size of your network, your company's Internet access requirements, and your users' IPX compatibility needs.

Some small networks (with minimal legacy considerations) might consider an *immediate* rollover to the IP protocol. This is possible with a little planning and a good understanding of how to build an IP infrastructure. However, most large installations will require some time for the transition to an IP-Only network. NetWare 5.1 provides the tools that you can use to first "clear the wire" (create IP-Only network traffic) and then "clean the applications" (replacing legacy IPX applications with versions that support IP).

The gradual *phased* transition from IPX to IP is made possible because of NetWare 5.1's Compatibility Mode and Migration Agent features. In this section, we're going to explore three basic approaches to a phased migration to IP (see Figure 2.2):

- *Network Segments First* — This approach focuses on the migration and the immediate rollover of a specific segment of your network to IP-Only. Once that segment has resolved any application-support problems, the next segment is attacked. This way you can gradually roll over your network one piece (segment) at a time.
- *Leaf Networks First* — This approach is similar to the previous approach; however, it focuses on distributed WAN networks instead of segments. These "leaf networks" can be immediately rolled over to IP-Only and eventually connected to the WAN backbone using IPX/IP Migration Agents.

- *Backbone First* — Finally, you may consider replacing IPX on the network backbone with IP-Only first. This approach focuses on the cost savings that can be realized by a routing infrastructure that supports only one protocol. By allowing IPX and IP compatibility on leaf networks, you can minimize risk and disruption to overall operations.

FIGURE 2.2

Three IP migration scenarios

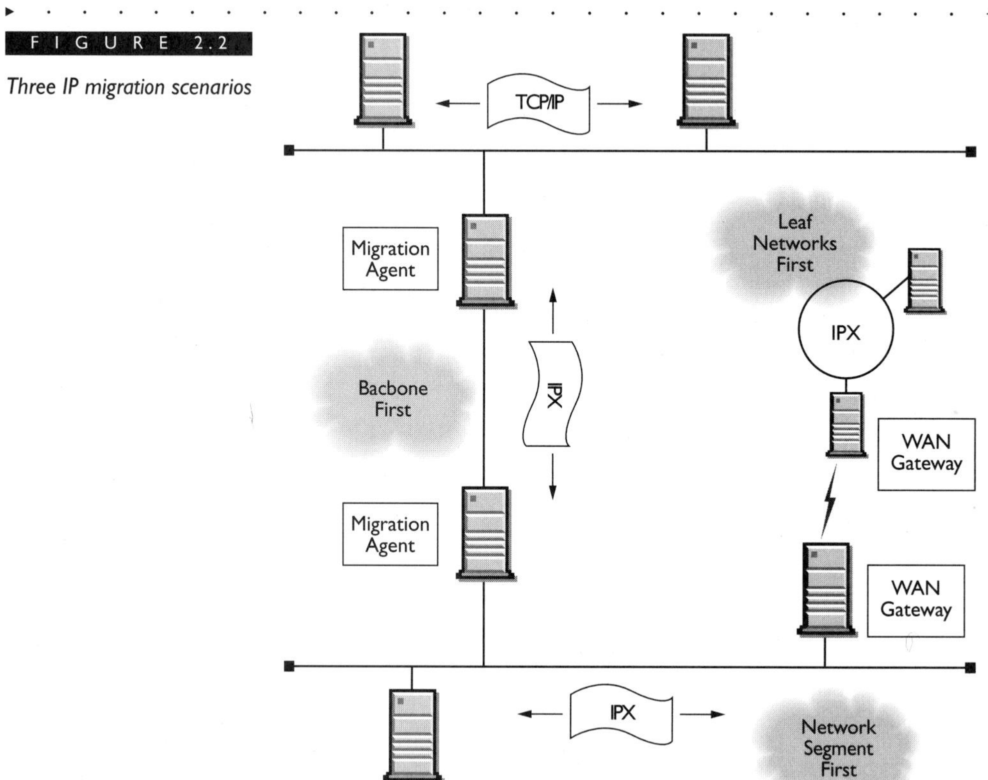

Let's take a closer look at each of these three IP migration scenarios.

Migrating a Network Segment First

The first option for a phased IP migration is to identify specific segments of the WAN and roll them over first (see Figure 2.2). For this scenario to work successfully, the network segment that you choose must not be used to interconnect any other sections of the network using IPX. The following five steps enable you to upgrade or to install IP servers/clients in a phased manner without losing connectivity:

- *Step 1*—Select and upgrade/install a specific number of servers in the network segment to act as Migration Agents.
- *Step 2*—Upgrade/install all servers in the network segment using the "IP and IPX" option.
- *Step 3*—Upgrade/install all clients in the network segment using the IP-Only option.
- *Step 4*—Modify the configuration of the servers and services in the network segment so that they resolve requests using IP-Only. This can be accomplished by unbinding IPX from all server adapters and loading the SCMD.NLM.
- *Step 5*—Turn off IPX networking between the selected segment and the rest of your WAN.

Migrating Leaf Networks First

Migrating leaf networks first reduces the impact of the migration on the IPX routing infrastructure. It also allows you to focus efforts on specific geographically separated sites (see Figure 2.2). Keep in mind, however, that because the backbone is the last portion of the network that migrates, administrative costs may not be reduced as quickly.

Following are the steps necessary to migrate a network from IPX to IP starting with the leaf networks:

- *Step 1*—Identify the nodes and links that form the backbone of the network.
- *Step 2*—Select and upgrade/install specific servers in the backbone to act as Migration Agents.

- *Step 3* — Select the leaf portion of the network that will be migrated. This may be, for instance, a group of segments connected to the backbone via a WAN link. Then migrate the selected segment of the network following the steps outlined previously in the section, "Migrating a Network Segment First."

- *Step 4* — Repeat Step 3 until all networks connected to the backbone have been migrated.

- *Step 5* — Migrate the network backbone to IP-Only using the tasks described in Step 3.

Migrating the Backbone First

Migrating the network backbone first alleviates administrative costs associated with supporting multiple protocols over the backbone. This migration path requires a Migration Agent (with the Backbone Support feature enabled) on each of the segments that are connected to the backbone. Once both of these features have been installed, you can disable IPX routing on the backbone. (See Figure 2.2).

The following steps describe the process of migrating a network from IPX to IP, starting with the backbone:

- *Step 1* — Identify the nodes and links that form the backbone of your network.

- *Step 2* — Select and upgrade/install specific servers in each of the distributed network segments as Migration Agents. Be sure to use the Backbone Support option when you install the Migration Agents.

- *Step 3* — Migrate the network backbone using the steps outlined previously in the section, "Migrating a Network Segment First."

- *Step 4* — Identify the leaf portions of the network that you would like to migrate once the backbone is routing IP-Only. Migrate each leaf network one-by-one using the steps previously outlined in the section, "Migrating Network Segments First."

- *Step 5*—Repeat Step 4 until all networks connected to the backbone are migrated and you're living in an IP world.

This completes our discussion of IP migration in NetWare 5.1. As you can see, there's much more to Pure IP than meets the eye. So far, we've discovered three different protocol configurations and explored some sample migration scenarios. The centerpiece of IP migration is a well-configured Compatibility Mode server. So, now's an excellent time to explore NetWare 5's IPX Compatibility Mode configuration.

Configuring Compatibility Mode

As you just learned, it is crucial to maintain IP and IPX compatibility during migration to IP. Novell created the Compatibility Mode feature to facilitate migration to IP and maintain backward compatibility for IPX-based applications. This technology provides on-demand support for existing IPX applications, while maintaining full support for IP-based and NCP-based applications. Also, Compatibility Mode provides backbone support, which in turn facilitates connecting two disconnected IPX networks across an IP-Only backbone.

Compatibility Mode technology consists of two components working together: *Compatibility Mode Server* (the CMD NLM running on the server) and *Compatibility Mode Client* (the CMD service running on the client). Furthermore, the CMD NLM can be run in one of three modes: CMD (providing backward compatibility for legacy IPX applications), Migration Agent (enabling IP and IPX segments or networks to be connected), and Backbone Support (enabling IPX segments to connect over an IP backbone).

In this section, we will discuss the following Compatibility Mode topics in greater depth :

- *Compatibility Mode Server*—The Compatibility Mode server is configured in such a way that all basic OS applications behave both as IP-Only applications and as IPX-Only applications (and advertise themselves accordingly). For example, the Compatibility Mode server (Node E in Figure 2.1) enables NDS synchronization between an IP-Only server (Node A) and an IPX-based server (Node C) via the Migration Agent. Similarly, if Network Print Services behave as IPX-based queues in an IP environment, then an IPX client can use the queues by accessing the Compatibility Mode driver.

- *Migration Agent* — The Migration Agent resides on a CMD server and acts as a gateway between the existing network and the IP-Only network. Figure 2.1 shows a Compatibility Mode Gateway (Server D) connecting two dissimilar networks: a CMD network and an IPX network. This node should be accessible to all clients/servers from both networks. In short, the Migration Agent provides IPX-based services to IP segments and IP-based services to IPX segments. In addition, the Migration Agent provides service visibility and accessibility between IPX networks that are connected through an IP-Only backbone — using the MA (Migration Agent) tag.
- *Compatibility Mode Client* — a Compatibility Mode IP-Only client can access the services being provided by a Compatibility Mode server and can also access the services being provided by an IPX-Only server through the Migration Agent component.

Now let's take a closer look at how we configure Compatibility Mode Servers and Migration Agents.

Compatibility Mode Server Configuration

The Compatibility Mode Server and Migration Agent capabilities are integrated into a single module called SCMD.NLM. This module is called the Compatibility Mode Driver (CMD), and it's bundled with NetWare 5.1. The functionality of SCMD.NLM depends on the options you use when the module is loaded:

- Compatibility Mode Server — LOAD SCMD
- Migration Agent — LOAD SCMD /MA
- Migration Agent with Backbone Support — LOAD SCMD /MA

The Compatibility Mode driver is the centerpiece of IP migration. Fortunately, it is loaded automatically in NetWare 5.1 when the IP-Only option is used. Another key point is the presence or absence of IPX in the Compatibility Mode Server. You must bind IPX to all server NICs if the CMD server is acting as a Migration Agent or offering Backbone Support. On the other hand, you *cannot* bind IPX to any server NICs if the CMD server is operating in standard Compatibility mode.

REAL WORLD

In earlier versions of NetWare, the Migration Agent (MA) was loaded with the/G parameter to act as a gateway and the /BS parameter to offer backbone support. In NetWare 5.1, all of this functionality has been incorporated into the /MA parameter. SCMD.NLM is smart enough to determine how to behave based on the protocols that are loaded and the configurations of the Compatibility Mode Server.

The Compatibility Mode driver treats the IP network as a virtual IPX network segment — called a CMD Network Segment (see Figure 2.1). The default virtual IPX network number used by CMD is FFFFFFFD. As I'm sure you've guessed, SLP must be enabled across the network in order for IPX applications to work on IP networks. Additionally, at least one Migration Agent (shown in Figure 2.1) must be used on the network if you interconnect IPX and IP segments.

The good news is that the services of the CMD drivers are only utilized when the system needs to process an IPX-based application. Also, these drivers kick in automatically when an IP-Only client tries to establish a connection with an IPX-based resource (such as a printer or bindery-based server). When not in use, the IPX compatibility drivers are dormant and do not affect network communications.

In this section, we learned that CMD servers enable IPX connectivity in an IP-Only WAN by creating a virtual IPX network segment. However, if you need to communicate with a "real" IPX network, you should configure your CMD server as a Migration Agent. Let's take a closer look.

Migration Agent Configuration

Migration Agents are Compatibility Mode servers that act as gateways between IP-Only segments and IPX segments. As we learned previously, a CMD server can become a Migration Agent simply by loading the SCMD module with the following switch (see Figure 2.1):

```
LOAD SCMD /MA
```

This option enables the Migration Agent capabilities of your Compatibility Mode server. But that's not all. In addition to the /MA option, you will need to make sure that both IP and IPX are bound to the internal server NIC.

Once you activate the Migration Agent, you can test it by typing DISPLAY SERVERS on both your IP and IPX servers. On the IP servers, you should see a list of IPX-based services. Similarly, on your IPX servers, you should see a list of available CMD servers.

In addition to their typical gateway function, you may also consider using Migration Agents to create an IP-Only backbone. In this configuration, a Migration Agent is placed at each connection portal to IPX-based segments. This way, you can use the efficiency and speed of IP over your Internet backbone and still support IPX-based local communication. To load your Migration Agents with IP-Only backbone support, type the following at the CMD server console and press Enter:

```
LOAD SCMD /MA
```

Congratulations—now you have Compatibility Mode servers acting as Migration Agents at either end of an IP-Only backbone.

Now let's learn how to expand IP networking into the realm of private and public networks using Network Address Translation (NAT).

Network Address Translation (NAT)

With the growth of the Internet and corporate use of IP addresses, you may run out of registered IP addresses for your organization. Fortunately, NetWare 5.1 provides a feature called Network Address Translation (NAT) as a strategy to create a private network and, thus, conserve valuable IP addresses. Simply stated, NAT enables private IP intranetworks to use nonregistered IP addresses internally and registered IP addresses externally (via the Internet).

NAT operates on a router connecting two networks together. It translates the local private IP addresses into registered external IP addresses before packets are forwarded onto the Internet. In addition, NAT serves as a firewall by keeping individual IP addresses on your local network hidden from the outside world. In this configuration, NAT advertises only one address for the entire network to the public Internet. (**Note:** NAT only provides protection at the Network layer of the OSI model and, therefore, should not be considered a total firewall solution.)

REAL WORLD

To determine which IP address to assign to private hosts when NAT is used, Novell recommends that you follow the addressing guidelines presented in RFC 1918. RFC 1918 explains that the Internet-Assigned Numbers Authority (IANA) has reserved the following three blocks of IP addresses for private networks:

- 10.0.0.0 – 10.255.255.255 (a single Class A network number)
- 172.16.0.0 – 172.31.255.255 (a set of 16 continuous Class B network numbers)
- 192.168.0.0 – 192.168.255.255 (a set of 256 continuous Class C network numbers)

Any private network can use these addresses without coordination with IANA. These addresses are often referred to as *nonroutable* addresses because backbone routers on the Internet have filters that prevent them from being forwarded.

For smaller companies, the entire network can be configured as a private network connecting to the Internet through a single NAT router. This enables you to provide Internet access to your entire network using only one registered IP address. For larger companies, individual intranets should be configured as private networks connected by multiple NAT routers and a registered IP backbone.

In either case, you must consider the following NAT limitations before you begin configuring your NAT routers: (1) NAT does not support applications that embed an IP address in the "data" portion of the TCP/IP packet, and (2) multicast and broadcast packets are not translated.

NAT can be configured to operate in one of three modes:

- *Dynamic Only* — In this mode, NAT enables IP hosts on a private network to access the public network (such as the Internet) without requiring an administrator to assign a globally unique IP address to each system. Instead, the NAT interface is configured with one public address. Hosts accessing the Internet are then dynamically assigned the Internet address bound to the NAT interface and a port from a pool of available ports that are constantly reused.

NAT provides a pool of 5,000 ports for TCP connections, a pool of 5,000 ports for UDP mappings, and a pool of 5,000 ports for ICMP mappings. In Dynamic Mode, no connections can be initiated from the public network into your private network. This means host resources inside your private network are unavailable to hosts on the Internet.

- *Static Only* — In this mode, a permanent one-to-one mapping of public registered IP addresses to unregistered IP addresses is established inside a private network. Static address translations are recommended when internal hosts (such as FTP or Web servers) must be made available to the public Internet. In Static Only mode, NAT is configured with a table of IP address pairs. Each table entry contains a pair of addresses for each host that the public is allowed to access. Keep in mind that Static Only NAT routers drop packets addressed to hosts that do not have an address mapping entry in the static table.
- *Static and Dynamic* — The combination of static and dynamic NAT strategies is used if some hosts on your network require dynamic address translation and others require static availability to the public Internet. With the combined Static and Dynamic Mode, you can use the methods simultaneously. In order to use this NAT mode, you must configure one public address for dynamic translations and one public address for each private host that is to be accessible from the public Internet. Because the Static and Dynamic Mode requires more than one public address bound to the same NAT interface, secondary IP addresses (multihoming) must be configured. When secondary IP addresses are bound to the NAT interface, and the Static and Dynamic Mode of operation is selected, NAT uses the primary IP address for Dynamic Mode. Secondary IP addresses should be mapped to private host IP addresses in the Static Network Address Translation Table.

To configure NAT on a NetWare 5.1 server, you must use the INETCFG console utility. First, enable the LAN drivers on the public and private networks and bind the TCP/IP protocol to each. Next, select an NAT mode on the NetWare 5.1 server that is acting as an NAT router. In INETCFG, select Bindings and choose the LAN driver binding of your public network board. Then select Expert TCP/IP Bind

Options and choose Network Address Translation. Finally, change the status to the desired NAT mode and reinitialize the system for the changes to take effect.

To troubleshoot NAT, check the following configurations:

- Verify that you can PING the private interface in the NAT router from a private client. If this fails, check the local hardware and cabling and verify that the TCP/IP stacks on the client and server are correctly configured and enabled. Finally, make sure the default route on the clients point to the NAT router.
- Verify that you can PING the NAT-enabled public interface in the NAT router from a private client. If this fails, make sure that the NAT router is the default gateway when accessing the public network. Also, make sure IP routing is enabled. To verify, load TCPCON and make sure the following field is set to "Router": Protocol Information ➪ IP ➪ IP Packet Forwarding.
- Verify that you can PING all remote public servers from the private client. If this fails, make sure the IP routing table on the NAT router contains either an entry for the remote network you are trying to PING or a default route entry pointing to a next hop router that contains an entry for the remote network you are trying to access. Also, use "SET TCPIP DEBUG=1" to verify that the conversion is taking place. Finally, make sure NAT is *not* enabled on more than one interface for access to the public host.

Now that you have your IP addresses in check, let's complete our IP migration adventure with the Service Location Protocol (SLP).

Service Location Protocol (SLP)

SLP is an Internet Standard protocol (RFC2165) used for the discovery of network services. Services on the network register themselves with an SLP agent running on a NetWare server. When a client needs to locate a service on the network, it queries the SLP agent, which in turn provides the client with the address of the service. In addition, SLP performs some SAP redirection duties when Compatibility Mode is enabled. As you may remember, SAP is the service discovery protocol used by IPX-based networks.

In this section, we will learn how SLP performs the following two critical IP functions:

- Service Discovery with SLP
- SAP Redirection in Compatibility Mode

Let's get started.

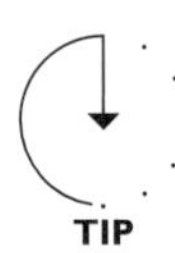
TIP

When moving from IPX to IP, Novell chose not to rewrite SAP for IP. Instead, Novell integrated SLP with NetWare 5.x IP networks.

Service Discovery with SLP

Over the past five years, developers have had plenty of time to integrate NDS system calls into their software. Consequently, many applications are already prepared to register themselves directly into the NDS database. IPX-based applications that use SAP are already registered into the Bindery Context of NDS and are made accessible through the existing Bindery calls. And if that's not good enough, any service may be manually registered into the NDS database.

SLP works with NDS to help bring together the IP infrastructure services, such as NDS trees, DNS servers, NCP servers, NDPS service registries, and some network protocol gateways. This allows NetWare 5.1 clients to discover services by querying one database rather than the whole network. The client then uses this information to gain access to infrastructure services.

SLP uses the following software agents to store information about services available on the TCP/IP network:

- *User Agent (UA)* — A UA is used on every SLP client and server. The UA queries Service Agents and Directory Agents for information about the location of network services.
- *Service Agent (SA)* — An SA is found on every network device that hosts a service. When a service is started or stopped, it communicates with the SA to register and deregister itself. SAs are primarily used on smaller networks.

- *Directory Agent (DA)* — A DA creates a catalog of available services by collecting information from multiple SAs. DAs avoid most of the multicast traffic associated with SAs by using unicasts. DAs are primarily used on larger, enterprise networks.

In previous IPX-based versions of NetWare, this kind of global distribution of infrastructure knowledge was accomplished using the SAP/Bindery architecture. SAP was global and each machine had a Bindery. Consequently, any service that could place an SAP packet on the wire could be globally known. Unfortunately, this global distribution had a price. Bandwidth was consumed and network administrators had to engage in significant filtering to regulate line congestion and service visibility.

With the advent of NDS, these problems began to fade away. Newer applications were able to forego SAP, register themselves directly with NDS, and take advantage of the NDS replication strategy to attain global visibility.

Furthermore, SAP was created in the early days of networking with a worst case scenario in mind. The system refreshed itself every 60 seconds, whether anything had changed or not. This was advantageous for plug-and-play in the LAN but impractical across WAN links. Services are registered in SLP with a lifetime that defines the amount of time the service will be available. If the service goes away or deregisters before the lifetime has elapsed, a request to the service fails. If a service goes down, it automatically deregisters.

The bottom line is SLP dramatically improves the performance and global visibility of network resources in a Pure IP WAN. However, if you need backward compatibility to SAP services, SLP offers that, as well. This is accomplished using the SAP Redirector feature built into Compatibility Mode.

Let's take a closer look.

SAP Redirector in Compatibility Mode

SLP also functions as a compatibility facilitator in NetWare 5.1. In the Compatibility Mode architecture, SLP provides connectivity for IPX-based applications in a Pure IP world. SLP helps make this happen by allowing the Compatibility Mode drivers to translate SAP packets into SLP data that can be delivered to other CMD servers. Additionally, the SLP packets are translated into SAP packets and placed in the router tables.

A small network will not need SLP configuration. The User and Service Agents on both client and server are automatically loaded and require no configuration. In a small network (up to 30 servers), there's probably no need to implement a Directory Agent. For larger networks, however, a Directory Agent will be needed to provide scaling and enterprise visibility of services. Placement and frequency of Directory Agents in the network depends upon several factors, including the following factors:

- *Organizational Considerations*—There is no typical network infrastructure. The network can exist in a single building, in several buildings on a single campus, or in many campuses located around the globe. Within buildings, high-performance LAN segments make IP Multicast and NDS replication attractive technologies. However, when the WAN is based on leased line technology, NDS replication with WAN management synchronization or on-demand location of services through DHCP and DNS might be more appropriate. Another example involves a remote office consideration. If you have a remote office that connects through a modem link, it would not be appropriate to implement IP Multicast, nor would you likely want to replicate NDS information across the WAN. However, several possible solutions exist for this connection. First, the network administrator could configure the local SLP User and Service Agents to use DHCP to locate one of the corporate SLP Directory Agents. The administrator could also use a static configuration to point the clients directly to a specific SLP Directory Agent or directly to a specific NDS tree.
- *IP Multicast*—The advent of IP Multicast technology creates an additional factor that network administrators must consider when implementing SLP as a SAP Redirector. On a local segment, Multicast is manageable. But when routers are configured to enable Multicast, the Multicast packet enters the router and begins "listening" to the network. Upon finding a registered listener, the router moves the Multicast packet into another segment. With the wrong configuration, Multicast takes on characteristics of broadcast—thus, consuming bandwidth. Properly configured, however, IP Multicast can provide a global distribution of critical information. In its default mode in a local network segment environment, the SLP User Agent uses IP Multicast to access SLP Service Agents.

Additionally, IP Multicast can be configured and made available across the networks. Then SLP will utilize the available bandwidth to continue seeking Service Agents. If you decide to restrict Multicast traffic, you can implement DHCP to help the User Agents find Service and Directory Agents that are not local and that cannot be discovered through Multicast.

- *NDS Replication* — NDS Replication can be used to synchronize the data in numerous SLP Directory Agents across the network. Synchronization traffic across a WAN link can be expensive, though, and it can consume bandwidth. Within the LAN, however, this replication service is a viable alternative. System Administrators should consult the existing literature on NDS deployment to understand the administrative requirements and the network impacts of NDS replication.
- *Fault Tolerance* — While a single SLP Directory Agent could provide service for a fairly large company, it would create a single point of failure. The pressure of multiple Directory Agents provides a degree of fault tolerance so that the failure of a single Agent will not impact the network. Once again, there exists the issue of synchronizing the multiple Directory Agents. Each of the alternatives previously presented carries both costs and benefits.
- *Service Visibility* — Services do not necessarily have to be provided to the whole network. For many years, network administrators have been regulating network congestion and service visibility through IPX packet filtering at the router level. Not every user on the network would see every service that SAP advertised in the network. A similar situation could also be achieved by disabling IP Multicast. A network could then be configured to use multiple SLP Directory Agents, each containing different data and servicing a different region of the WAN.
- *Administration* — In a large network, network administrators will likely have to use the SLP Directory Agent to achieve scalability across the network. The Directory Agent may be installed with system defaults that make it immediately useable. On installation, the Directory Agent extends the NDS NCP object schema and creates an SLP/DA record within the NCP server object.

It also creates a default container in the NDS database to SLP entries. This container may be replicated at the discretion of you, the network administrator.

SLP administration is such an important aspect of managing a TCP/IP network that we should explore it in a little more depth.

SLP Administration

As we just learned, SLP administration works best when SLP is integrated with NDS. In the largest networks, however, the use of a "flat" SLP implementation may prove inadequate for scalability and traffic management. Fortunately, SLP does support certain levels of hierarchy. This support is accomplished by creating subdivided *scopes*. For example, some services may be regularly registered on machines in the engineering department and have no use to anyone outside that department. Thus, you could configure the DA on a server in the engineering department with a scope of ENG. Clients in the engineering department would then be configured with the IP address of the DA for that area..

Such subdividing of SLP services provides a kind of filtering that administrators can use in both IP and IPX environments. By the way, SLP implementations that don't utilize scopes are said to be *unscoped*.

Now let's take a quick look at how SLP implementations differ for each of the following network sizes:

- *Small Network* — A small network with less than 25 servers gains negligible advantage from an SLP Directory Agent. All SLP communication can be handled by the SLP Service and User Agents with local segment IP Multicast. With this simple system, the network client is able to have dynamic discovery of NDS trees, NCP servers, NDPS service registry, and other infrastructure services (such as gateways). In addition, NDS-aware services can register themselves with NDS.

- *Medium to Large Networks* — In a medium- to large-sized network, the SLP requires SLP Directory Agents to provide scaling and WAN support. If the network is architected to be a rather flat system, then a single Directory Agent may be sufficient. Unlike the smaller systems, there will be little IP Multicast in this network. In that case, DHCP can be used to configure the client User Agents with the IP address of the Directory Agent. Also, with the Directory Agent, information can be stored in an NDS container that can be replicated through the corporate network and which also has information that can be made available to other Directory Agents.

- *Enterprise Networks* — Large-scale implementation of SLP will most likely require a combination of SLP Directory Agents and NDS replication. The SLP Directory Agent collects service information from the local Service Agents. That information is then loaded to a container in NDS. That container then replicates as necessary with other SLP Directory Agents that are feeding information from different parts of the network. Thus, the local service receives global distribution at the administrator's discretion.

All of the Server SLP configuration options discussed in the preceding list can be configured from the server console using the SET command with the parameters (included in the STARTUP.NCF file) in Table 2.1.

TABLE 2.1

SLP Server Configuration Settings

PARAMETER	FUNCTION
SLP DA Discovery options = *value*	Use Multicast DA advertisements. Bit 0x01 = Use Multicast Directory Agent advertisements Bit 0x02 = Use DHCP discovery Bit 0x04 = Use static file SYS:ETC\\SLP.CFG (you must first change the set parameter to something else, then back to static to reread SLP.CFG) Bit 0x08 = Scopes Required These bits can be ordered together for Multiple values. **Supported values**: 0 to 8 **Default**: 3
SLP TCP = *value*	Use TCP packets instead of UDP packets when possible. **Supported values**: OFF, ON **Default**: OFF

Continued

TABLE 2.1

SLP Server Configuration Settings (continued)

PARAMETER	FUNCTION
SLP Debug = *value*	Enable SLP debug mode. Bit 0 x 01 = COMM Bit 0 x 02 = TRAN Bit 0 x 04 = API Bit 0 x 08 = DA Bit 0 x 10 = ERR Bit 0 x 20 = SA **Supported values**: 0 to 4294967255 **Default**: 0
SLP Multicast Radius = *value*	Specify an integer describing the Multicast radius. **Supported values**: 0 to 32 **Default**: 32
SLP Broadcast = *value*	Use broadcast packets instead of Multicast packets. **Supported values**: OFF, ON **Default**: OFF
SLP MTU Size = *value*	Specify an integer describing the maximum transfer unit size. **Supported values**: 0 to 4294967255 **Default**: 1472
SLP Rediscover Inactive Directory Agents = *value*	Specify the minimum time period in seconds that SLP will wait to issue service requests to rediscover inactive Directory Agents. **Supported values**: 0 to 4294967255 **Default**: 60
SLP Retry Count = *value*	Specify an integer value describing the maximum number of retries. **Supported values**: 0 to 128 **Default**: 3
SLP Scope List = *value*	Specify a comma-delimited scope policy list. **Supported values**: 1023 **Default**: 1023
SLP SA Default Lifetime = *value*	Specify an integer value describing the default lifetime in seconds of service registers. **Supported values**: 0 to 4294967255 **Default**: 900

TABLE 2.1

SLP Server Configuration Settings (continued)

PARAMETER	FUNCTION
SLP Event Timeout = *value*	Specify an integer value describing the number of seconds to wait before timing utility Multicast packet requests. **Supported values**: 0 to 4294967255 **Default**: 53
SLP DA Heart Beat Time = *value*	Specify an integer value describing the number of seconds before sending the next Directory Agent heartbeat packet. **Supported values**: 0 to 4294967255 **Default**: 10800
SLP Close Idle TCP Connections Time = *value*	Specify an integer value describing the number of seconds before idle TCP connections should be terminated. **Supported values**: 0 to 4294967255 **Default**: 300
SLP DA Event Timeout = *value*	Specify an integer value describing the number of seconds to wait before timing out Directory Agent packet requests. **Supported values**: 0 to 429 **Default**: 5

In addition to Server SLP configuration, the NetWare Client SLP interaction can be configured from the Novell Client Configuration Property Page under Advanced Settings. The client settings are listed in Table 2.2.

TABLE 2.2

SLP Client Configuration Settings

SETTING	PARAMETER GROUP	FUNCTION
SLP Active Discovery	SLP General	This parameter specifies that SLP is required to look up services from a Directory Agent and that SLP is not to use IP Multicast directly to SLP Service Agents for services. SLP's normal operation is to first check Directory Agents. If no Directory Agent is found, SLP Multicasts to Service Agents. **Default**: ON

Continued

TABLE 2.2

SLP Client Configuration Settings (continued)

SETTING	PARAMETER GROUP	FUNCTION
SLP Cache Replies	SLP Times	When SLP receives a service request from a User Agent, the SLP reply is saved for the amount of time specified by the SLP Cache Replies parameter. If SLP receives a duplicate of this request, the cached reply is sent, so the same reply does not have to be generated again. The default value is one minute. Setting this value higher will consume more memory to retain replies longer. It is recommended that you do not change this default, because any duplicate requests should occur within the first minute. **Range**: 1 to 60 (minutes) **Default**: 1
SLP Default Registration Lifetime	SLP Times	This parameter specifies the lifetime of a service registration, which is registered by a service provider requesting the default lifetime value. If the service provider specifies a lifetime value when the service is registered, this value is not used. The Directory Agent deletes the service when the lifetime expires if it hasn't been specifically renewed or unregistered before then. This prevents the Directory Agent's information from becoming too stale if the Server Agent registering the service goes down. The Server Agent automatically renews the service so that the application doesn't need to. The default value is 10800 seconds, which is 3 hours. Using a smaller value will make the Directory Agent's information less stale, but this results inmore network traffic, which is needed to renew services more frequently. This parameter does not affect how long the service is registered by the Server Agent. **Range**: 60 to 60000 (seconds) **Default**: 10800

TABLE 2.2

SLP Client Configuration Settings (continued)

SETTING	PARAMETER GROUP	FUNCTION
SLP Maximum Transmission Unit	SLP General	This parameter specifies the maximum transmission unit (UDP packet size) for the Link Layer used. Setting this parameter either too large or too small will adversely affect performance of SLP. **Range**: 576 to 4096 **Default**: 1400
SLP Multicast Radius	SLP General	SLP uses IP Multicast to dynamically discover other SLP Service Agents and Directory Agents. This parameter is a number specifying the maximum number of subnets (number of routers plus 1) that SLP's Multicast should traverse. A value of 1 confines Multicasting to the local segment (no routers). **Range**: 1 to 32 (number of routers plus 1) **Default**: 32

Wow, you have come a long way since we embarked on this IP journey together. Amazingly, this is only the beginning. So far, we have learned how to migrate your network to IP, we have enabled Compatibility Mode drivers, built Migration Agents, and created an IP-Only backbone. Congratulations! Your IP-Only network is in place.

Now it's time to explore a whole new world of IP management. Once you have successfully migrated your network to IP, you must build a system for automated configuration of IP options. That is, you will need to learn everything there is to know about DNS/DHCP Services.

In the remainder of this chapter, we will show you how to overcome the configuration pain of TCP/IP with detailed lessons in Novell DNS/DHCP Services, which is the single most powerful tool NetWare 5.1 offers IP administrators.

So, without any further ado, let's explore NetWare 5.1 DNS/DHCP administration.

DNS/DHCP Overview

NetWare 5.1 includes a product called *Novell DNS/DHCP Services*, which is designed to help alleviate many of the administrative requirements associated with TCP/IP. This product integrates the following two IP services into the NDS database:

- *Dynamic Host Configuration Protocol (DHCP)* — DHCP provides a framework for dynamically passing configuration information to clients or service-providing resources on a TCP/IP network.
- *Domain Name System (DNS)* — DNS is a distributed name/address database used to translate numerical IP addresses into alphanumeric names, and vice versa.

Together, DNS and DHCP can greatly simplify TCP/IP administrative complexity. Furthermore, by integrating these services into NDS, you can achieve centralized administration and enterprise-wide management of Internet Protocol (IP) network addresses and host names.

Specifically, DNS/DHCP Services provides the following benefits:

- DNS/DHCP significantly reduces the time needed for administering IP names and addresses.
- DNS/DHCP completely automates IP address assignment and host name updates.
- DNS/DHCP increases security when updating addresses and host names.
- DNS/DHCP eliminates network problems associated with duplicate IP addresses because cataloging is controlled by a central database.

DNS/DHCP is a powerful IP management tool. Let's begin our journey through NetWare 5.1 DNS and DHCP with a few brief introductions, starting with DHCP.

DHCP Overview

This elegant IP management tool begins with *communication.* If you want a computer (or some other device) to function on a TCP/IP network, you must first configure it with a number of IP options. These "options" are small, but important, tidbits of data that help network devices communicate — such as a client's own domain name, a client's IP address, the DNS server's IP address, the subnet mask, and so on. All computers must be aware of these facts in order to coexist peacefully on a Pure IP WAN.

In the past, IP addresses have been assigned through a service called the Bootstrap Protocol (BOOTP), which stored host information in a flat-file server database. Now TCP/IP networks have moved to DHCP. This dynamic protocol relies on servers that automatically hand out addresses and other parameters to TCP/IP workstations.

As you can see in Figure 2.3, DHCP is built on the client/server model. In this model, the server is a host that provides initialization parameters to clients using the DHCP protocol. Similarly, the client is an Internet host that requests parameters from the DHCP server. In this scenario, the DHCP server delivers host-specific configuration parameters and assigns network addresses.

As you can see in Figure 2.3, the DHCP client initiates a broadcast request to the network which says, "I need DHCP info!" In response, the DHCP server examines the request broadcast to determine which network segment it came from. If the DHCP server is configured to respond to that segment, it sends IP configuration data to the client, such as an IP address, the location of a DNS server, subnet mask info, and so on. This process is illustrated in Figure 2.3.

FIGURE 2.3

The DHCP client/server communication model

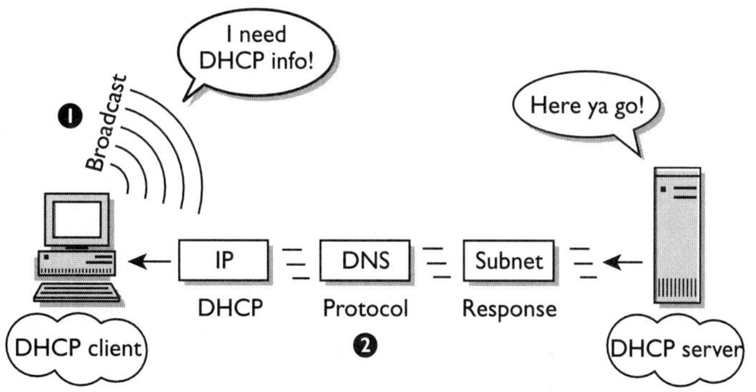

In this model, IP addresses can be allocated to DHCP clients in one of three ways:

- *Automatic Allocation* — DHCP assigns a permanent IP address to every host. Using this method, the server always assigns the same address to each host.
- *Dynamic Allocation* — DHCP assigns a temporary IP address to each host from an internal pool. This address is valid for a defined period of time (*lease time*), and it expires if the client doesn't renew the address or the server decides to let it expire. At this point, the client's IP address then goes back into the pool for reassignment. This capability enables more efficient use of scarce IP addresses.
- *Manual Allocation* — This requires that you (the CNE) assign IP addresses manually. With this method, DHCP simply delivers the address to the host upon connection. However, *you* have to do all the hard work.

In addition to IP address allocation, you must be aware of how broadcast requests are routed — or, more accurately, how they're *not* routed. By default, routers do not route broadcast requests. Therefore, if a client does not physically reside on the same segment as the DHCP server, the request will never be answered. To solve this problem, you must use a *Relay Agent*. The Relay Agent is software that runs on a router to forward DHCP requests to servers on remote segments. Novell's implementation of a Relay Agent is BOOTPFWD.NLM. If you have DHCP clients on remote segments from their host server, you must load BOOTPFWD.NLM on each NetWare 5.1 server.

Finally, you must understand how Novell DHCP Services integrates with Novell Directory Services (NDS). NetWare 5.1 uses NDS to help automate DHCP activities by storing IP addresses in the central database. In this way, when users log into the network, the DHCP server can consult NDS and provide an appropriate IP address to each machine automatically. This eliminates the older methods of manually tracking and assigning IP addresses. Thanks to NetWare 5.1, NDS ensures that DHCP provides managed IP addresses throughout the enterprise. Even more importantly, you can administer DHCP configurations as objects in the NDS tree. We'll explore this feature later in this chapter.

This completes our brief introduction to Novell's DHCP. Now let's learn how DNS translates complex IP addresses into more user-friendly Internet names.

DNS Overview

Host names have been part of the Internet and its predecessors since the earliest days. For years, Internet computers located each other by looking up host names in a database that was downloaded to each server and/or router manually or automatically from the Network Information Center (NIC). But before too long, the flat-file host name database became unwieldy and replicating it around the network became too cumbersome. But then, DNS was born.

DNS is simply a fancy database that matches user-friendly computer names to device IP addresses. To accomplish this impressive task, DNS employs the following two services:

- *DNS Hierarchy* — The DNS Hierarchy (also called the *Domain Name Space*) specifies a host's location in the global Internet tree. This tree consists of top-level *domains* and more precise partitions called *zones*.
- *DNS Name Services* — This is the functional DNS component that actually maps the host's name to a computer's IP address. DNS Name Services uses a client/server model similar to DHCP. In this case, there are *Master* and *Replica* servers and clients called *resolvers*.

Let's take a closer look at how DNS resolves domain names using a logical hierarchy and functional name services.

DNS Hierarchy

The DNS Hierarchy organizes IP hosts into a logical upside-down tree — much like the file system directory structure (as shown in Figure 2.4). In Figure 2.4, the first three levels of the tree represent domains. The end leaves of the tree are individual host machines on the Internet. When you build an IP network, each resource must maintain a unique host name. In theory, DNS Hierarchy follows the same architectural rules as another Novell logical tree — Novell Directory Services (NDS). Even though the acronyms are similar (simply reverse the first two consonants), don't confuse the DNS and NDS logical trees. DNS is a distributed database for IP addressing of physical Internet resources. NDS, on the other hand, is an intranetwork solution for logically identifying distributed network resources.

In theory, DNS naming operates similarly to fully distinguished naming in NDS. In the IP world, an absolute (or *fully qualified*) DNS domain name is constructed by listing all domains on the path from the end device to the root. Just like NDS, a period is used to delimit the labels in the domain name. For example, in Figure 2.4, the absolute domain name for the host SRV1 in NORAD is represented as

```
SRV1.NORAD.ACME.COM.
```

In this case, the interior nodes of the DNS tree (such as .COM and .ACME) do not represent network devices. Instead, they represent logical divisions of the DNS name space — analogous to logical containers in the Novell NDS tree.

FIGURE 2.4

The upside-down DNS tree

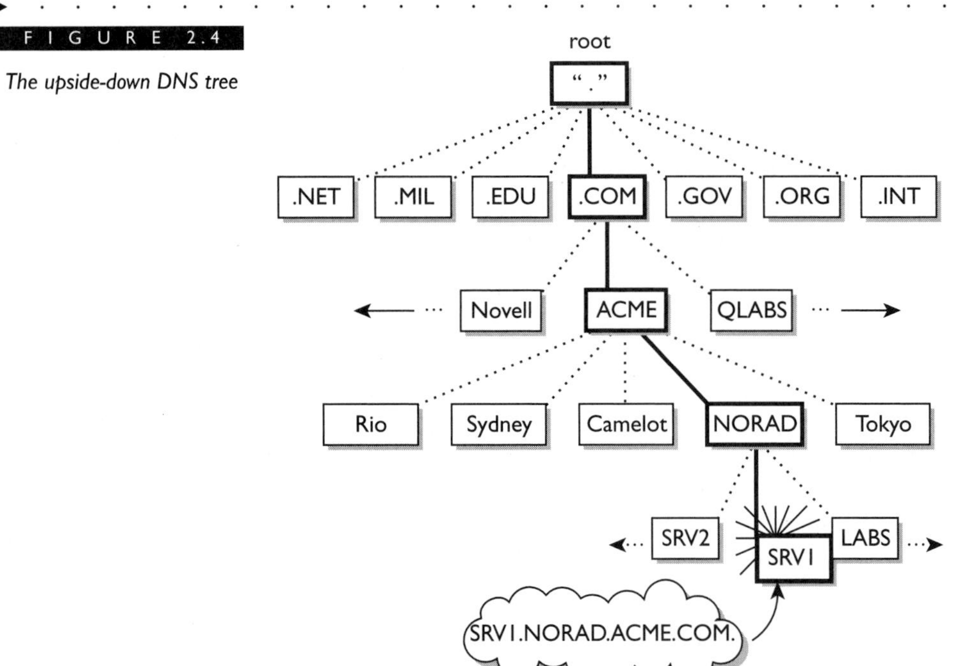

As you can see in Figure 2.4, many of the top-level domains have already been established by the Internet governing body — InterNIC. These predefined domains help organize the vast Internet into functional zones. Check them out in Table 2.3.

The DNS Hierarchy can be further subdivided into partitions called *zones* (or *subdomains*). Zones begin at a specific domain and extend downward until they reach either a terminating leaf object or another subzone.

REAL WORLD

To master the subtle differences between DNS and NDS naming, you should memorize the following rules:

- DNS domain names can be up to 255 characters long.
- Each domain within the absolute name can be up to 63 characters long, provided that the total length doesn't exceed 255 characters.
- DNS domain names are not case sensitive.
- All absolute DNS domain names should end in a trailing period; however, the period can be omitted.
- You can use relative DNS domain naming by specifying the path from your current position to the root. (This naming scheme is analogous to relative NDS naming.)

TABLE 2.3

Predefined Domains at the Top of the DNS Tree

DOMAIN	FUNCTION
.COM	Commercial organizations. This is the most popular domain used by today's high-profile Internet organizations.
.EDU	Educational institutions. Many universities, colleges, schools, educational service organizations, and consortia have registered here. More recently, a decision has been made to limit further registrations to four-year colleges and universities. Primary schools, secondary schools, and two-year colleges are now registered in the Country domains.
.UK	A new two-letter country code. The ISO-3166 Committee has determined that each country should be represented by a specific two-letter country code. For example, .UK represents Great Britain, .AU represents Australia, .US represents the United States, .DE represents Germany, and .CA represents Canada.
.GOV	Government agencies. This domain is reserved for U.S. Federal Government agencies.

Continued

TABLE 2.3

Predefined Domains at the Top of the DNS Tree (continued)

DOMAIN	FUNCTION
.INT	International organizations. This domain is reserved for organizations that have been established by international treaties.
.MIL	United States military. This domain is reserved for branches of the U.S. Armed Forces.
.NET	Networking entities. This domain represents computers of network providers, such as NIC and NOC computers.
.ORG	Miscellaneous organizations. This domain is an open book for organizations that do not fit into any of the previous domain categories.

For example, the shaded area in Figure 2.5 represents the ACME.COM. zone. Furthermore, any private network (such as ACME.COM.) can implement its own domain names within a specific zone. However, you must be sanctioned by the Network Information Center (NIC) to connect your zone to a public network, such as the Internet. For more information on setting up a domain on a public network, consult the accompanying Real World icon.

DNS supports three different zone types:

- *Standard Zones*—A standard DNS zone contains records that resolve domain names into IP addresses. Most of today's Internet devices are addressed using standard DNS zoning rules.
- *IN-ADDR.ARPA Zones*—The IN-ADDR.ARPA. zone type provides mappings of IP addresses to domain names in a specific format—backward. Specifically, IP addresses contained in an IN-ADDR.ARPA. zone are defined backward. For example, if the ACME.COM. domain had an IP address of 187.165.182.18, then the address in the IN-ADDR.ARPA. subdomain would be 18.182.165.187.IN-ADDR.ARPA. Wow, that was fun.
- *IP6.INT Zones*—The ever-increasing use of the Internet, along with the limited number of available IP addresses, is driving the development of a new IP addressing scheme known as IPv6, which provides a greater quantity of unique IP addresses. Devices using this scheme in a subdomain of the Internet are part of an IP6.INT. zone type.

FIGURE 2.5

The ACME.COM. DNS zone

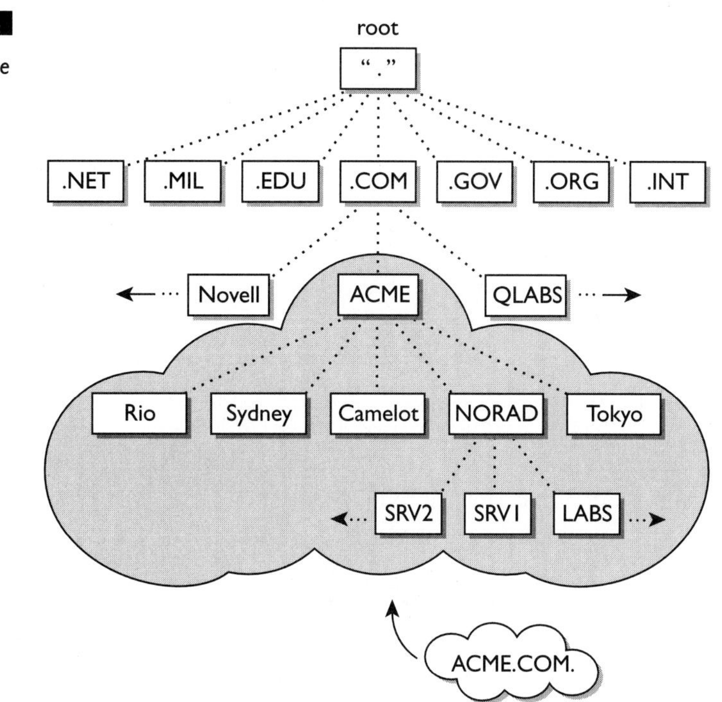

This completes our discussion of the logical DNS Hierarchy. As you can see, the virtual DNS tree resembles our own logical NDS Cloud, but with a strange twist—the DNS tree is upside-down! From an organizational naming perspective, it seems pretty straightforward. Now let's learn how DNS servers and clients implement name services.

DNS Name Services

The second half of the DNS one-two punch is DNS Name Services. This is where the actual work is done. DNS Name Services actually maps user-friendly host names to IP addresses, and this helps computers throughout the Internet locate each other. Similar to DHCP, DNS Name Services relies on a server-client architecture. In this model, clients (resolvers) query one or more servers for host address information. If the DNS server doesn't have the information a client needs, it relays the request to another name server up or down the DNS Hierarchy. As soon as it finds the answer it needs, the original DNS server relays it to the requesting client (resolver).

The names and IP addresses for all hosts in a DNS zone are maintained on a single server called the *Master server.* The information contained on the Master Server is called the *Authoritative Database* for that zone. This database includes the following information:

- Names and addresses of all IP hosts within the zone.
- Names of all subzones and addresses of the DNS servers for these zones.
- Addresses and DNS servers for the *root* domain and all other zones within the tree. These addresses are necessary to link your domain to the existing DNS Hierarchy.

In Figure 2.6, I have set up the SRV1.NORAD.ACME.COM. server as the Master DNS Server for the NORAD.ACME.COM. zone. All updates to the DNS database for the zone are made on this server.

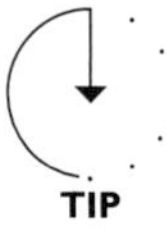
TIP

It's a good idea to keep the Master DNS server within your local zone; however, it's not required. By rule, the DNS server for NORAD. ACME.COM. can be located anywhere in the DNS Hierarchy.

Furthermore, DNS supports a backup naming server called a *Replica server* (also known as the *Secondary server*). Replica DNS servers provide redundancy and load balancing for DNS naming within a zone. This backup periodically downloads a copy of the DNS database from the Master server. It's important to note that updates to the zone database are only made at the Master server and then distributed to the Replica server when it requests a copy. This process is known as a *zone transfer*.

In Figure 2.6, we have configured SRV2.ACME.COM. as the Replica DNS server for the NORAD.ACME.COM. zone. As I'm sure you noticed, the Replica DNS Server is located outside its home zone. Once again, a DNS name server can be located anywhere in the hierarchy. While it's a good idea to keep Master DNS servers inside the zone, you should distribute Replica DNS servers in geographically remote locations. Remember, we're trying to achieve redundancy and load balancing. A remote Replica server can service queries originating from outside the zone and provide a redundancy in case the local link goes down.

FIGURE 2.6

Using Master and Replica DNS servers

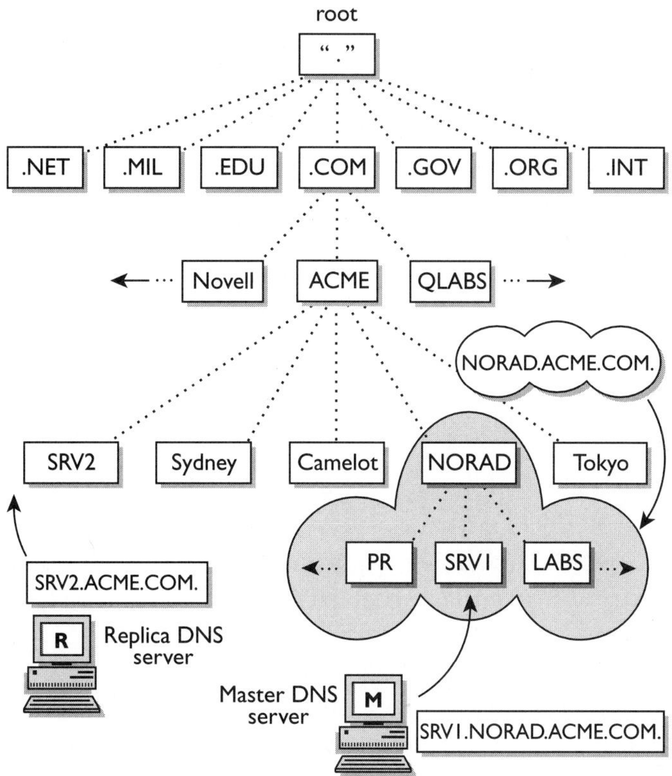

The process of DNS name resolution is actually quite similar to the way you might find a telephone number for someone who lives in a remote city. Let's say, for example, you lived in NORAD and wanted to call somebody in Tokyo. First, you would call your local operator to obtain the country code and the number for directory information in Japan. Then you would call directory information in Japan and get the local number for Tokyo. Then you would call Tokyo and query for your friend by name.

Let's say you reside in the LABS division of NORAD within ACME. From your DNS client (resolver), you want to access a device in the QLABS.COM. zone.

Here's how your local DNS server would resolve the destination IP address (follow along in Figure 2.7):

- *Point 1* — To find a machine named JANE in the QLABS.COM. zone, you must first ask your local DNS server if it has a cached entry for JANE. If not, your local Master server will relay the request to the *root* server.
- *Point 2* — Your local Master DNS server asks the *root* DNS server for the location of the .COM server. At this point, you'll begin resolving JANE's IP address from the top down.
- *Point 3* — Next, the .COM server will find the IP address of the Master server in the QLABS.COM. zone and send it to your local server.
- *Point 4* — Once your request finds its way to the Master DNS server in the QLABS.COM. zone, you'll be able to resolve the specific IP address for JANE. This address will then be relayed back to our local Master DNS server (Point 1) by backtracking through all the servers (or routers) that it took to get there.

As you can see, DNS is a powerful tool for helping users resolve complex IP addresses. This dramatically reduces your TCP/IP management load. Now let's expand our DNS/DHCP journey into the realm of NetWare 5.1. Fortunately, Novell offers a couple of fine administration tools and extended NDS objects for DNS/DHCP management.

REAL WORLD

Master DNS servers can also function as Replica DNS servers for other zones. In this way, if you're short on DNS name servers, you can service local and remote zones from the same machine.

FIGURE 2.7

DNS address resolution for JANE.QLABS.COM.

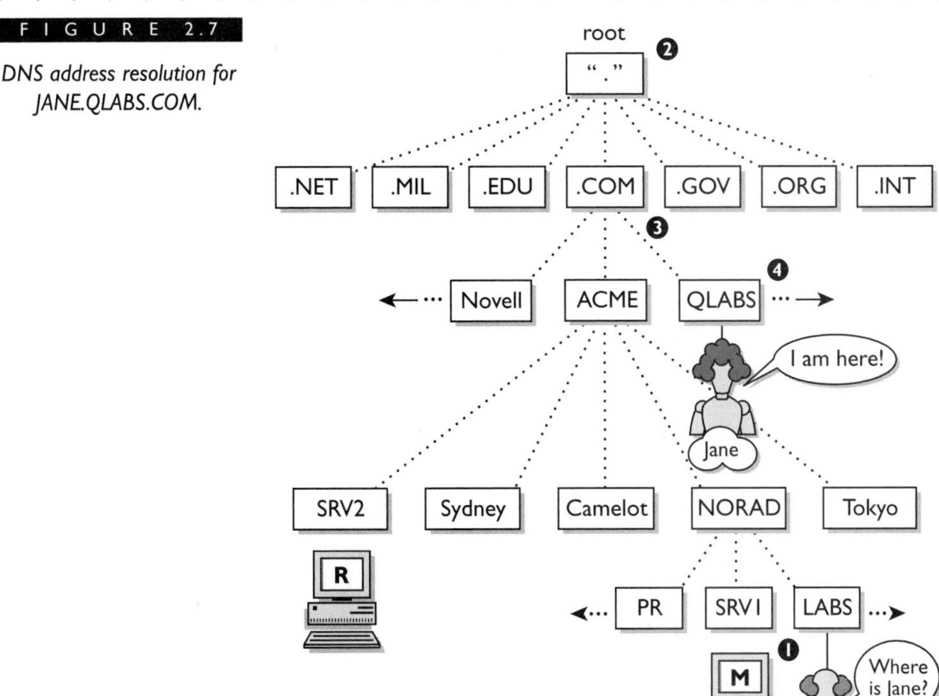

DNS/DHCP Installation

If you selected DNS/DHCP Services when you installed NetWare 5.1, then the key program files for Novell DNS/DHCP Services are copied to the SYS: volume on your server. These files include program NLMs (which are copied to SYS:SYSTEM) and the DNS/DHCP Management Console setup program (which is copied to SYS:PUBLIC\DNSDHCP).

Once these program files are copied to the server, you must complete the following three DNS/DHCP installation steps:

- *Step 1:* Extend the NDS Schema

- *Step 2:* Install the NetWare 5.1 Novell Client
- *Step 3:* Install the DNS/DHCP Management Console

It all begins by extending the NDS Schema. This is necessary to integrate the new DNS/DHCP management objects with NDS. Once you have extended the schema, you will switch over to the workstation. In Step 2, you will install the new Novell Client for NetWare 5.1. This prepares you for the final step—installation and configuration of the DNS/DHCP Management Console. This console allows you to create and to configure IP management objects in the extended NDS tree.

That's all there is to it—so let's not waste another moment. It's time to get started.

Step 1: Extend the NDS Schema

In the first DNS/DHCP installation step, you must extend the NDS schema to support twelve new DNS and DHCP objects. To be more precise, three NDS objects are created automatically (a DNSDHCP-GROUP Group object, a DNS-DHCP Locator object, and a RootServerInfo Zone object), and nine objects are created manually. We will study these new NDS objects in more detail later in the chapter.

You can extend the NDS Schema and automatically create the three default DNS/DHCP objects in one of three ways:

- Install Novell DNS/DHCP Services during initial NetWare 5.1 server installation.
- Install Novell DNS/DHCP Services by running the NetWare installation program from the NetWare GUI.
- Run the DNIPINST.NLM installation program at the server console.

Before you extend the NDS Schema for DNS/DHCP support, review the NDS considerations in Table 2.4. If you follow these simple planning guidelines, you will improve the productivity of IP and NDS integration. Furthermore, review your general NDS design considerations before ever extending the tree.

TABLE 2.4

NDS Considerations for DNS/DHCP Installation

NDS CONSIDERATION	RECOMMENDATION
Where should I place the DNSDHCP-Group and DNS-DHCP Locator objects?	You should place the DNSDHCP-Group and DNS-DHCP Locator objects within a container that can be accessed from and replicated to all points in the enterprise. Although changes to these objects occur infrequently, DNS and DHCP servers need access to copies of these objects at all times. In addition, plan to create an Administrator Group object under this DNS/DHCP container. The Administrator Group should have Read and Write access to all DNS-DHCP Locator object attributes, except the Global Data and Options fields. Members of this Group can then use the DNS/DHCP Management Console to create and to modify DNS/DHCP objects throughout the tree.
Where should I place DNS and DHCP servers?	You should place your DNS and DHCP servers geographically close to the hosts that require their services. Plan to have one DHCP server in each partition of your network to minimize any WAN communication problems caused by normal load, configuration changes, or replication.
What replication strategy should I use?	You should replicate the partition that contains the DNSDHCP-Group and DNS-DHCP Locator objects to all servers in the network that need access to IP Services. This ensures access to IP in the event that a specific part of the network becomes unavailable.
How can I achieve DNS/DHCP fault tolerance?	When planning your NDS replication strategy, consider that replication accomplishes two things: load balancing and fault tolerance. A well-planned replication strategy (like the one here) is the best way to provide fault tolerance for DNS/DHCP objects.

To extend the NDS Schema using the NetWare 5.1 GUI or DNIPINST.NLM, follow these simple steps:

1. First, determine which DNS/DHCP installation method you want to use:

   a. To use the NetWare installation program, activate the NetWare GUI (if it isn't already activated) and select Novell ➪ Install. In the Installed Products window, click Add and browse to the NetWare 5.1 installation directory. In the "Additional Products and Services" window, mark the Novell DNS/DHCP Services checkbox and click Next to continue to the NDS authentication screen.

   b. To use the special DNS/DHCP installation program, type **DNIPINST** at the server console and press Enter. Once you activate this program, you will be greeted with an NDS authentication screen.

2. Next, you must authenticate yourself as an NDS Administrator who has rights to extend the schema (specifically, Supervisor object rights to the [Root] of the tree). The DNS/DHCP Authentication screen prompts you for two pieces of information: administrator username and password. In the Username field, type the fully distinguished name of the Admin user. In the Password field, type the Admin password and click OK.

3. Next, you must provide an NDS context for the new DNS/DHCP objects. By default, the installation program will use Admin's home container as the DNS/DHCP context. Click Finish to extend the NDS schema and automatically create the three default DNS/DHCP objects.

The following three global NDS objects are created automatically during Step 1 of the DNS/DHCP Installation process. (**Note:** Only one instance of each can exist in a given NDS tree.)

- *DNSDHCP-GROUP Group Object*—The DNSDHCP-GROUP object offers an easy method for providing the rights granted to new DNS/DHCP objects to other objects in the tree. By default, the DNSDHCP-GROUP object is given the Browse object right and the Supervisor property right to all new DNS and DHCP objects you create. This way, you can guarantee access to DNS/DHCP information for any NDS object by simply assigning it as a member of the DNSDHCP-GROUP object. NetWare servers that you designate as DNS and/or DHCP servers are automatically made members of the DNSDHCP-GROUP.

- *DNS-DHCP Locator Object* — The DNS-DHCP Locator object contains global defaults and DHCP options. It also contains a list of all of the DNS/DHCP entities in the tree, including servers, subnets, and zones. The purpose of the DNS-DHCP Locator object is simply object location. This object enables the DNS/DHCP Management Console to display DNS/DHCP objects without having to search the tree. (**Note:** The DNS-DHCP Locator object is unconfigurable and, therefore, not displayed in the Management Console.)
- *RootServerInfo Zone Object* — The RootServerInfo Zone object contains the IP addresses of the Root servers on the Internet. It enables you to resolve domain names that belong to zones outside your current zone. Root servers are DNS servers that are maintained on the Internet as top-level phone books. The RootServerInfo Zone object provides your DNS server with the IP addresses of the root-level servers when it needs to resolve an address outside your zone.

Step 2: Install the NetWare 5.1 Novell Client

Before you can use the DNS/DHCP Management Console to configure your new extended NDS objects, you must upgrade your workstation to the NetWare 5.1 Client. In addition, you can further enhance the Novell Client by adding ZENworks.

To install the new-and-improved NetWare 5.1 Client, follow these simple steps:

- *Getting Started* — First, find your way over to the workstation and insert the *NetWare 5.1 Novell Client* CD-ROM. Normally, WINSETUP.EXE will autoload. If not, you can activate the client installation program by running WINSETUP.EXE from the root directory of the CD-ROM. Next, click the language you're interested in and platform (such as Windows 95/98). Finally, click Install Novell Client. WINSETUP.EXE will launch SETUP.EXE from the E:PRODUCTS\WIN95\IBM_ENU folder (assuming that drive E: is the CD-ROM drive in this example). Accept the Novell License Agreement by clicking Yes.

- *Installation Type* — At this point, the client installation program asks you to choose between a Typical and Custom installation type. With the Typical option, SETUP.EXE installs default settings, such as native IP protocol, but no additional client services. The Custom option, on the other hand, gives you a plethora of choices, including addition of the IPX protocol, Novell Distributed Print Services (NDPS), ZENworks, Novell Workstation Manager, and a Novell Target Service Agent (TSA) for local backup. Highlight the installation type you are interested in and click Install to continue.

- *Customize* — If you choose a Typical installation type, the client installation program will attempt to auto-detect your local hardware and copy the appropriate drivers to your internal drive. It will also make numerous network-centric changes to your local Windows 95/98 Registry. Once the installation program finishes, it will give you the option to Customize your client configuration options. These options include Preferred Server, Preferred Tree, Name Context, and First Network Drive. In addition, Figure 2.8 illustrates a number of Configuration tabs presented by your new Novell Client for NetWare 5.1. Make any required changes and finish the client installation.

FIGURE 2.8

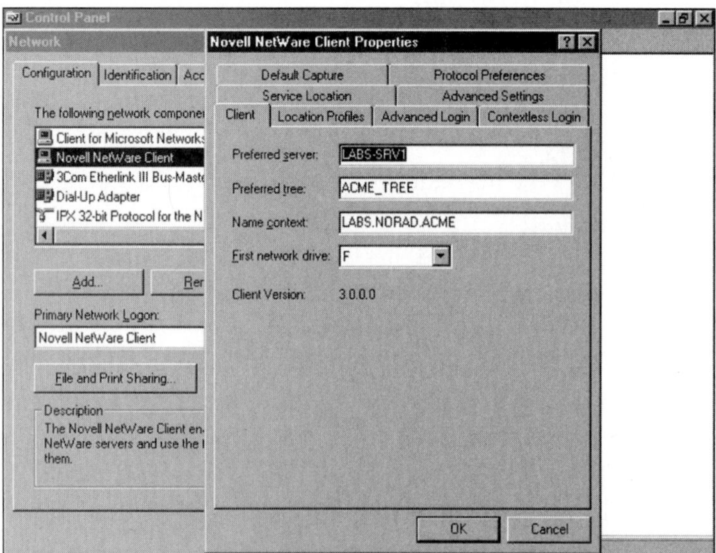

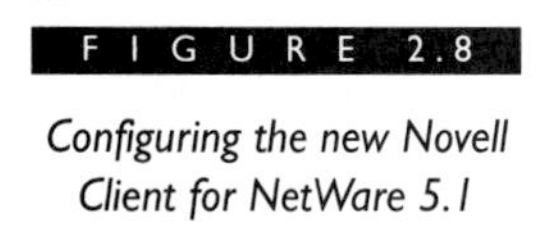

Configuring the new Novell Client for NetWare 5.1

Once you have installed the Novell Client, it's time to finish the workstation portion of our DNS/DHCP installation process.

Step 3: Install the DNS/DHCP Management Console

Once the NDS Schema has been extended and Novell DNS/DHCP Services has been integrated into the tree, you will have two graphical tools available for managing your IP network:

- DNS/DHCP Management Console
- NetWare Administrator

To create and configure new DNS/DHCP objects in an extended NDS tree, you will need to use the new Java-based *DNS/DHCP Management Console*. The DNS/DHCP Management Console is a graphical Java-based application that enables you to configure and to manage IP addresses and name services through NDS-based DNS and DHCP objects.

The DNS/DHCP Management Console can either be launched from the Tools menu of NetWare Administrator or as a standalone utility on a Windows 95/98 or Windows NT client (through the DNSDHCP desktop shortcut). Your administrative workstation needs to meet certain minimum requirements in order to gain access to the DNS/DHCP Management Console, such as having a current version of the NetWare 5.1 Novell Client, a minimum of 48MB of RAM (64MB is recommended), and approximately 8.5MB of available disk space.

The DNS/DHCP Management Console setup program is copied to a NetWare 5.1 server during initial NetWare 5.1 installation. To access this program, simply log into the host NetWare 5.1 server and run the SETUP.EXE program from the SYS:PUBLIC\DNSDHCP subdirectory. After reading the Welcome screen, click Next. The setup program then asks you to define a destination path for the DNS/DHCP Management Console program files. Choose a directory on your local drive and click Next. The program files will then be copied to your administrative workstation.

REAL WORLD

Know how to install the DNS/DHCP Management Console as both a standalone application using SYS:PUBLIC\DNSDHCP\SETUP.EXE and as a NetWare Administrator 32 snap-in

Also, remember that snap-in files can be found in the SYS:PUBLIC\WIN32 directory. Finally, know the difference between the NetWare Administrator 32 snap-in and the SYS:PUBLIC\DNSDHCP\SETUP.EXE utilities—namely, that DNS/DHCP objects can be created and fully managed using the DNS/DHCP Management Console, but only viewed and deleted using NetWare Administrator 32.

To view DNS/DHCP objects in *NetWare Administrator*, you must install the appropriate snap-in files to the Z:\PUBLIC\WIN32 directory (where the NetWare Administrator utility resides). Make sure the Copy Snap-In File radio button is marked and click Next. When prompted for a destination directory for the snap-in files, click Browse and navigate to the Z:\PUBLIC\WIN32 subdirectory. Click OK, Next, and Finish to complete the installation. Reboot your computer in order for the changes to take effect.

After the DNS/DHCP snap-in files have been installed, you can view DNS/DHCP objects in the main NetWare Administrator browser window. (Otherwise, they appear as Unknown objects.) The DNS/DHCP snap-in files do not enable you to view or to configure the details of DNS/DHCP objects in NetWare Administrator. You can, however, perform basic NDS operations, such as viewing and deleting DNS/DHCP objects.

To launch the DNS/DHCP Management Console from NetWare Administrator, use the Tools menu in the main NDS browser window. To launch the DNS/DHCP Management Console as a standalone executable, simply double-click the DNS/DHCP shortcut created on your Windows 95/98 or Windows NT/2000 desktop during DNS/DHCP client installation.

If you launch the DNS/DHCP Management Console from a Windows 95/98 or Windows NT/2000 desktop, you will be prompted for the target NDS tree. Then, when the main DNS/DHCP Management Console screen appears, you'll notice that it contains two tabs: a DNS Service tab and a DHCP Service tab. In Figure 2.9, the DHCP Service tab is activated. As you can see in the figure, each tab page contains three panes:

- *Left Pane* — This pane displays the managed DNS/DHCP objects in tree form. The DHCP Service tab lists all IP addresses in ascending numeric order. The DNS Service tab displays all zones or resource records in alphanumeric order. By double-clicking a logical container object in the left pane (such as a Subnet or a Subnet Address Range), you can expand the view to display subordinate objects or collapse it to see a concise view of the DNS/DHCP database structure.
- *Bottom Pane* — This pane identifies the DNS servers or DHCP servers that have been configured for the selected tree. Remember, the DNS/DHCP Locator object enables you to view all IP management resources without having to search the NDS Hierarchy. In addition to the DNS/DHCP server icons, the bottom pane includes a status bar. The status bar (shown below the DHCP server icon at the bottom of Figure 2.9) displays two fields: the current database operation in progress and the operational status of the selected object.
- *Right Pane* — This pane displays detailed information about the highlighted IP address or zone (in the left pane) or DNS/DHCP server (in the bottom pane). In Figure 2.9, the main window displays configuration information for a specific DHCP subnet.

The DNS/DHCP Management Console offers no menu items. Instead, this Java-based interface provides a context-sensitive toolbar. As you can see in Figure 2.9, the toolbar appears near the top of the window, under the DNS/DHCP Service tabs. To simplify your life, the context-sensitive toolbar only highlights the functions that are relevant for the selected item. In addition, each graphical button on the toolbar has a rollover help tag associated with it. It is important to learn which toolbar functions are active for any given DNS/DHCP object. Study the toolbar in Figure 2.10 and Table 2.5.

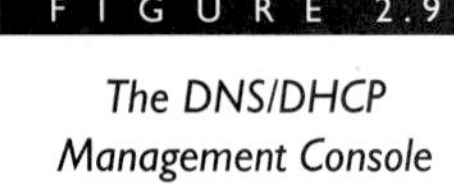

FIGURE 2.9

The DNS/DHCP Management Console

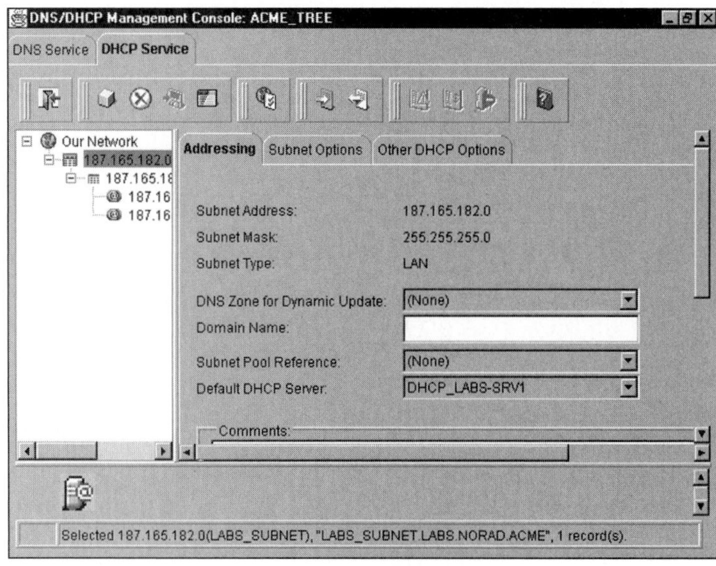

FIGURE 2.10

The DNS/DHCP Management Console toolbar

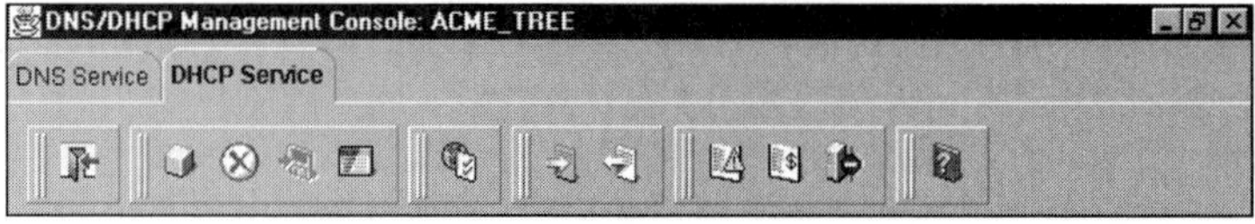

Once you've mastered the graphical Java-based DNS/DHCP Management Console, you should consider performing your first IP configuration — *Create*.

When you click the Create button in the toolbar, a dialog box appears that enables you to choose the type of object you want to create. All DNS and DHCP objects are built as NDS entities. Therefore, they are subject to NetWare Administrator conventions. As a result, whenever you create a new object, you should always name the object first in each Create dialog box. Also, some objects can be created in any context, while others are a little more picky about where they live. In either case, the Create dialog box will display a Browse button enabling you to choose any context for which you have Write or Supervisor rights.

TABLE 2.5

Understanding the Buttons in the DNS/DHCP Management Console Toolbar

TOOLBAR BUTTON	ENABLED FOR . . .
Exit	Always enabled
Create	Enabled for the following DNS/DHCP objects: Network, Subnet, Free Addresses, Subnet Address Range, All Zones, Zone, and/or RRSet
Delete	Enabled for the following DNS/DHCP objects: Subnet, Free Addresses, Subnet Address Range, All Zones, Zone, RRSet, Resource Record, DHCP Server, and/or DNS Server
Save	Enabled when fields have been changed or updated
Tree Refresh	Always enabled
Global Preferences	Enabled for all DHCP objects
Import	Enabled for the following DNS/DHCP objects: Network and/or All Zones
Export	Enabled for the DNS Zone object
View Events/Alerts	Enabled for the following DNS/DHCP objects: DNS Server and/or DHCP Server
View Audit Log	Enabled for the following DNS/DHCP objects: DNS Server and/or DHCP Server
Help	Always enabled

REAL WORLD

When you create a new DNS/DHCP object, the Management Console grants the Read and Write object rights to the DNS-DHCP Locator object. This causes the new objects to automatically appear in the Management Console interface. Once they appear, you can configure them all you want.

Congratulations! You have successfully constructed a DNS/DHCP IP management system. Furthermore, you have extended the NDS Schema, activated the new Novell Client, and built a Management Console for DNS/DHCP objects.

Now comes the fun part — configuration. Once you have mastered DNS/DHCP architecture and installed the server-client components, it's time to build customized functionality into our new IP management objects. In the remainder of this chapter, we will focus on IP object configuration from both the DHCP and DNS perspective.

LAB EXERCISE 2.1: INSTALLING DNS/DHCP SERVICES IN TOKYO

Now it's time to test your true mettle as a DNS/DHCP administrator. In this first lab exercise, we will use everything we have learned about DNS/DHCP installation to actually create a DNS/DHCP system for the Crime Fighting division of ACME.

Specifically, you will learn to install the DNS/DHCP Management Console and the NetWare Administrator snap-in files that are required to administer DNS and DHCP Services through NDS. Here's a brief peek forward in time:

- *Stage 1:* Extend the NetWare 5.1 Schema
- *Stage 2:* Install the DNS/DHCP Management Console and NetWare Administrator snap-in files

The following hardware is required for this exercise:

- A NetWare 5.1 server
- A workstation running the NetWare 5.1 Novell Client for Windows 95 or Novell Client Windows NT (Version 3.00 or better)

Stage 1: Extend the NetWare 5.1 Schema

It all begins by extending the NDS Schema. This is necessary to integrate the new DNS/DHCP management objects with NDS.

The files required to install DNS/DHCP Services are copied to the server during NetWare 5.1 installation. These files include Management Console setup files (which are copied to the SYS:\PUBLIC\DNSDHCP directory) and various NLMs (which are copied to the SYS:SYSTEM directory).

To extend the schema, complete the following tasks at the server console prompt:

1. If the NetWare 5.1 GUI screen is displayed, press Alt+Esc to toggle to the console prompt.

2. Execute the DNIPINST utility.

   a. Type the following and then press Enter:

      ```
      DNIPINST
      ```

   b. If a message appears advising you that the Novell DNS/DHCP Services NDS Schema extensions already exist, skip to Stage 2 of this exercise.

   c. When the Novell DNS/DHCP Services Login to NDS screen appears, authenticate yourself to NDS as Admin. (Remember that the User object you use to authenticate must have Supervisor object rights to the [Root] of the tree.)

      - Ensure that the following full distinguished name of the Admin User object is listed in the Username field:

        ```
        CN=Admin.CRIME.TOKYO.ACME
        ```

      - Type the following Admin User object password in the Password field:

        ```
        ACME
        ```

      - Ensure that "Press <Enter> to log into NDS" is highlighted and then press Enter.

   d. When the DNS Context Query Form screen appears, indicate the NDS context where you want to create the DNS/DHCP Locator, DNSDHCP-GROUP Group, and RootServerInfo Zone objects.

      - Ensure that the following context is listed for each object:

        ```
        OU=CRIME.OU=TOKYO.O=ACME
        ```

      - Highlight "Press <Enter> to create the objects" and then press Enter.

   e. When the Novell DNS/DHCP Services Setup screen appears advising you that the Novell DNS/DHCP Services Schema extensions were added successfully, press Enter to acknowledge the message.

Stage 2: Install the DNS/DHCP Management Console and NetWare Administrator Snap-in Files

Once you've extended the NDS schema and found an active Novell Client, you're ready for Step 2—installation and configuration of the DNS/DHCP Management Console. This Console enables you to create and to configure IP management objects in the extended NDS tree . . . all from the comfort of your very own workstation.

1. If you haven't already, log into your NetWare server as the Admin user.

2. Exit any applications that are currently running.

3. Run the DNS/DHCP installation utility.

   a. Execute the SYS:PUBLIC\DNSDHCP\SETUP.EXE file:

   - Click Start in the Windows taskbar.
   - Click Run.
   - When the Run dialog box appears, type the following in the Open field and then click OK:

     `Z:\PUBLIC\DNSDHCP\SETUP.EXE`

   b. When the Welcome screen appears, read the onscreen information and then click Next.

   c. When the Choose Destination Location dialog box appears, click Next to accept the following default destination path:

   `C:\Program Files\Novell\DNSDHCP\`

   d. Wait while the program files are copied to the directory indicated in the previous step.

   e. When the Select Components dialog box appears, indicate that you want the setup program to copy the NWADMIN snap-in files for the DNS/DHCP Management Console to the workstation. To do this, ensure that the "Copy the Snap-in Files" checkbox is marked and then click Next.

f. When the Choose Destination Location dialog box appears, click Browse.

g. Navigate to the Z:\PUBLIC\WIN32 directory and then click OK.

h. When the Choose Destination Location dialog box reappears, click Next.

i. When the Question dialog box appears asking if you want to view the Readme file, click No.

j. When the Information dialog box appears advising you that the DNS/DHCP Management Console setup is complete, click OK.

4. A DNS/DHCP shortcut should appear on your desktop.

Dynamic Host Configuration Protocol (DHCP) Configuration

DHCP is built on a client/server model. In this model, the DHCP server provides initialization parameters to IP clients using the Dynamic Host Configuration Protocol. Novell's DHCP solution hinges on integration with NDS. NetWare 5.1 uses NDS to help automate DHCP activities by storing IP addresses in the central Directory. To activate DHCP Services on a Novell network, perform the following five simple configuration steps:

- *Step 1: Create a DHCP Server*—First, you must create and configure a DHCP server for dynamic or manual IP address assignment. This is where DHCP clients get their IP address information. The DHCP Server object contains all supported subnet address ranges, server-specific configuration information, and DHCP policies. You can create a DHCP Server object in an Organization, Organizational Unit, Country, or Locality container.
- *Step 2: Configure Subnet Addresses*—Second, you must configure the IP address information that you want the server to hand out via the Subnet object. The DHCP Subnet is a container that holds Subnet Address Range and IP Address objects. A subnet's specific DHCP options and configuration parameters apply to the entire subnet and override global options. You can create a DHCP Subnet and/or Subnet Pool object in an Organization, Organizational Unit, Country, or Locality container.
- *Step 3: Assign Addresses with SAR or IP Address Objects*—Third, you must configure the IP address information for dynamic assignment (using a Subnet Address Range, or SAR) or for manual assignment (using an IP Address object). The SAR object identifies a range of addresses available for dynamic assignment. Conversely, the IP Address object represents a single IP address on the network. This object can provide specific IP configurations to a workstation that override global or subnet settings.

- *Step 4: Activate the DHCP Server*—Fourth, you must activate the DHCP server as a parallel process on the NetWare 5.1 server console by typing **DHCPSRVR**.
- *Step 5: Configure DHCP Workstations*—Finally, you must configure distributed IP workstations so that they can request IP address information from the DHCP server upon initialization.

Step 1: Create a DHCP Server

To create a DHCP Server object, follow these instructions:

1. Start the DNS/DHCP Management Console. Click the Create button on the DHCP Service tab page (as shown in Figure 2.11).
2. The Create New DHCP Object dialog box appears. It enables you to create a DHCP Server, Subnet, or Subnet Pool object. Select DHCP Server and click OK.
3. Click the Browse button to select a host NetWare Server object for DHCP activity. The default DHCP server name will be the same as the selected NDS Server object, except with the following prefix: "DHCP_". You can modify the name of the DHCP Server object later using NetWare Administrator. Click Create to complete the process.

When you add a DHCP Server object to your NDS tree, it will appear as an icon in the bottom pane of the DNS/DHCP Management Console (see Figure 2.11). The DHCP Server object will be nonoperational (with a red diagonal line through the icon) until you activate the DHCP server from the NetWare 5.1 server console (during "Step 4: Activate the DHCP Server").

To configure the DHCP Server object, click the icon at the bottom of the DNS/DHCP Management Console. The DHCP Server detailed information window displays two tab pages: Server and Options. On the *Server* page, you can view the Subnets and SARs serviced by this server. In addition, you can view the current DHCP version and enter any comments chronicling the server's activities (up to 256 characters).

FIGURE 2.11

The DHCP Server Configuration screen in DNS/DHCP Management Console

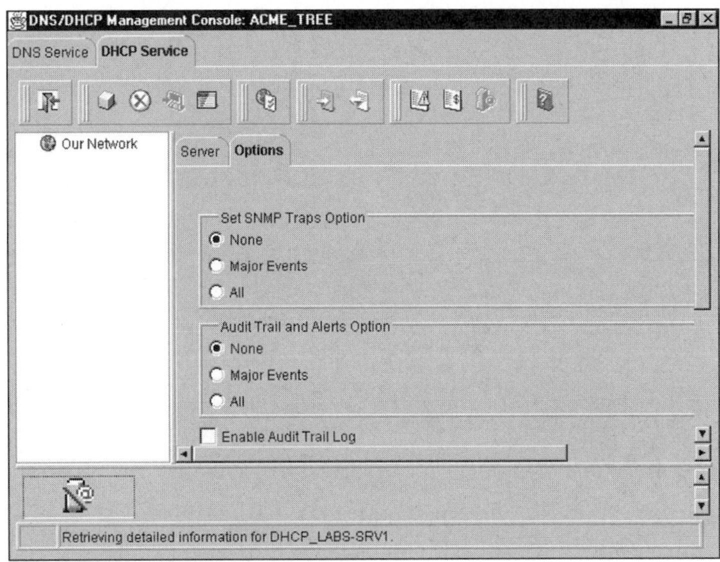

On the Options page (shown in Figure 2.11), you can configure specific policies relating to the operation of this DHCP server. Here's a quick list:

- *SNMP Traps* — This option determines the type of information that can be monitored using network management software (such as Novell ManageWise).
- *Audit Trails and Alerts* — This choice controls the level of event and audit logging the DHCP Server will generate. The auditing and alert logs can be viewed by selecting the View Events/Alerts button and the View Audit Trail Log button on the toolbar.
- *Mobile Users* — This option enables you to configure how the DHCP Server will treat a workstation that moves from one subnet to another.
- *PING Enabled* — If you mark the PING Enabled box, the DHCP Server will PING an IP address before making an IP assignment. If something responds to the PING, the server does not assign the IP address. This prevents IP addressing conflicts on your network.

Once your DHCP Server object is alive, you must configure IP addresses for automatic, dynamic, and manual distribution. Let's start with a Subnet container where we can store our SAR and IP Address objects.

Step 2: Configure Subnet Addresses

The DHCP Subnet object is a container that holds all of the SAR and IP Address objects for a physical network segment. To create a DHCP Subnet object, simply follow the same initial instructions as you did when creating the DHCP server: click the Create button in the DNS/DHCP Management Console toolbar and double-click Subnet. Once you do this, you'll be greeted with the Create Subnet dialog box (as shown in Figure 2.12):

- *Subnet Name*—Each Subnet object must have a unique NDS name. The Subnet creation process will fail if you name the object the same as any other NDS object in the same container.
- *Select NDS Context*—This is the full, distinguished name of the NDS container where the Subnet object resides. Typically, it's the same container that holds the new DHCP server. You can accept the default context or browse to another container using the Browse button to the right of this input field.
- *Subnet Address*—This identifies the actual IP address of the subnet's logical network segment. Remember, the purpose of a Subnet object is to group SAR and IP Address objects according to the physical segmentation of your network. Make sure you input the appropriate physical IP address in dotted-decimal notation.
- *Subnet Mask*—This is a filter that is used to determine which subnet an IP address belongs to. The Subnet Mask determines the IP Address class and subnetting strategy.
- *Default DHCP Server*—Finally, you'll need to specify a default DHCP server for subnet address assignment. You can accept the default server or choose from a pull-down list. Click Create to complete the creation process.

FIGURE 2.12

The Create Subnet dialog box in DNS/DHCP Management Console

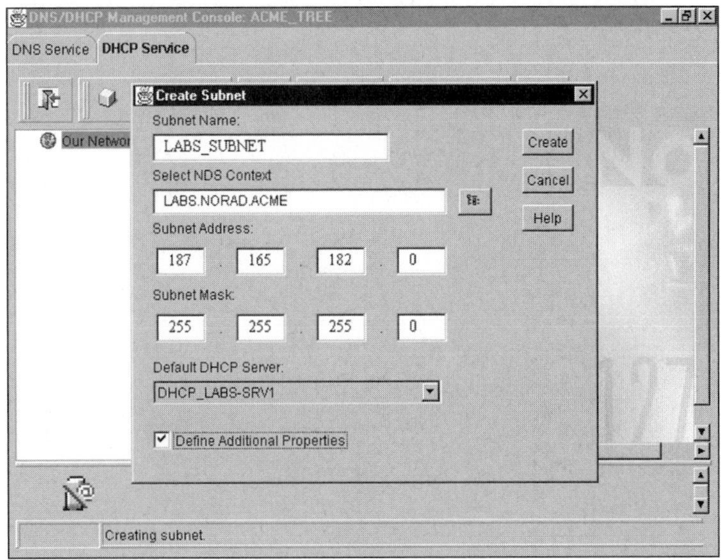

Once you create the DHCP Subnet object, you can further customize it using the Details information window. This window appears in the right pane of the DNS/DHCP Management Console if you either mark the Define Additional Properties checkbox in the Create Subnet screen, or if you double-click the Subnet icon in the left pane. The Subnet details window enables you to customize the subnet's domain name, DNS zone for dynamic update, subnet pool reference, and/or make comments about the object.

If you are already using DHCP on an IP-based Novell network (such as Novell DHCP Services 2.0), you don't have to re-create the IP configuration information when you move to NetWare 5.1 (Novell DHCP Services 3.0). Instead, you can use the Import DHCP Database button in the DNS/DHCP Management Console to import a DHCP 2.0 or 3.0 file into NDS. During this process, you will specify two DHCP objects: Server and Subnet.

Finally, Novell supports the configuration of multiple IP subnet addresses for a single physical network segment. This is accomplished using the DHCP Subnet Pool object. First, create multiple Subnet objects within a single NDS context. Then use the DNS/DHCP Management Console to create a Subnet Pool object and add multiple Subnet objects to the pool.

Step 3: Assign Addresses with SAR or IP Address Objects

Once you have created the DHCP server and subnet, you must prepare the IP addresses for assignment. This can be accomplished using either of the following two DHCP objects:

- *SAR* — For dynamic address assignment to a group of workstations or a specific machine
- *IP Address* — For manual address assignment to a specific machine

Dynamic Address Assignment Using the SAR Object

The SAR object identifies a range of IP addresses available for dynamic assignment. It can also be configured to exclude a range of addresses from the automatic pool or to assign the start of a client's host name.

When creating a new SAR object, you must first select a Subnet object in the left pane of the DNS/DHCP Management Console (the SAR must be contained within a Subnet). Initially, all available network address blocks within the subnet are available for selection, except addresses 0 and 255. After you highlight the Subnet object, click the Create button in the toolbar and choose Subnet Address Range. Next, the Create Subnet Address Range dialog box appears (see Figure 2.13):

- *Subnet Address Range Name* — Each subnet range must have a unique name to identify it within the physical subnet segment. If you define multiple SARs within a single subnet, you may need to determine a distinguishing characteristic for each name.
- *Start Address* — This identifies the specific IP address that starts the SAR.
- *End Address* — Similarly, you must define an ending IP address for the second boundary of your SAR. The address ranges of SAR objects cannot overlap with each other. Furthermore, you must use contiguous and unassigned network addresses for each SAR within a subnet.

FIGURE 2.13

The Create Subnet Address Range dialog box in DNS/DHCP Management Console

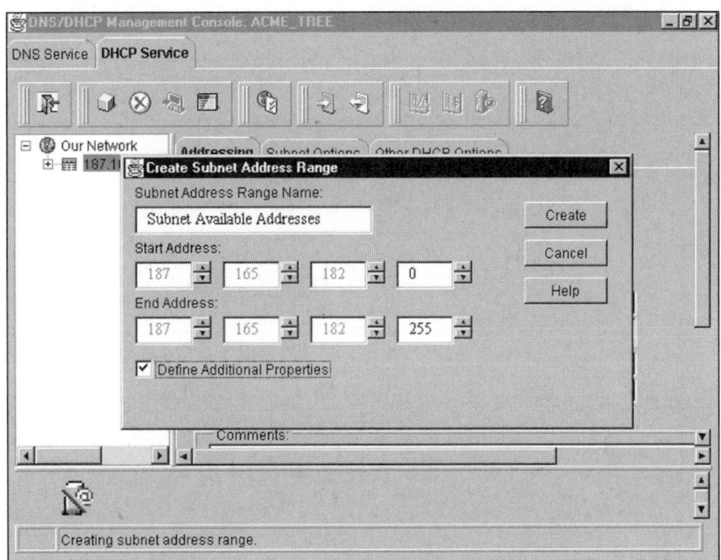

Once the DHCP SAR object has been created, you can access the details information window by marking the Define Additional Properties checkbox during creation or by double-clicking the object once it appears in the left pane of the DNS/DHCP Management Console. In this configuration screen, you can customize SAR properties (such as Range Type, DNS Update Option, and Default DHCP Server Assignment). You can also record comments about the SAR object.

Manual Address Assignment Using IP Address Objects

The IP Address object enables you to override dynamic SAR addresses and manually assign (or exclude) a specific IP address to (or from) a specific machine on the network. This is accomplished in two steps. First, create an IP Address object within an existing subnet using the Create button in the DNS/DHCP Management Console. Then associate the IP Address object with a specific machine's MAC address using the Addressing tab in the IP Address Details window.

For every Subnet object you create, two IP Address objects are automatically created. These two objects are exclusions for the IP addresses of "0" and "255." These exclusions are created because most TCP/IP stacks do not support the assignment of either of these two addresses to hosts (0 is usually reserved for the network address and 255 is usually used as a broadcast address).

REAL WORLD

The following DHCP Server debug switch provides helpful onscreen information:

```
DHCP SRVR -D3
```

Step 4: Activate the DHCP Server

After you create the DHCP server and configure its IP information via Subnet, SAR, and IP Address objects, you must *activate* the DHCP server. This is accomplished by typing the following command at the NetWare 5.1 server console prompt:

```
DHCPSRVR
```

When the DHCPSRVR NLM is loaded, it reads IP address configuration data from NDS and loads the information into the server's cache. Now the server is ready to hand out IP addresses to DNS/DHCP clients. The clients will not be ready to request the IP address information, however, until they have been properly configured.

Step 5: Configure DHCP Workstations

Once the DHCP server is running, you must configure the DHCP workstations to automatically accept IP configuration information. This is accomplished by customizing the TCP/IP Protocol property using Network Neighborhood on Windows 95/98 and Windows NT clients:

1. Right-click the Network Neighborhood icon on a Windows 95/98 or Windows NT/2000 desktop. Then click Properties in the pop-up menu that appears.

2. The Network window should appear, with the Configuration tab activated (refer to Figure 2.14). Highlight the TCP/IP protocol and click Properties. If you are using a Windows NT/2000 machine, the TCP/IP properties can be found under the Protocols tab.

FIGURE 2.14

The Network Configuration tab of Windows 95 Network Neighborhood

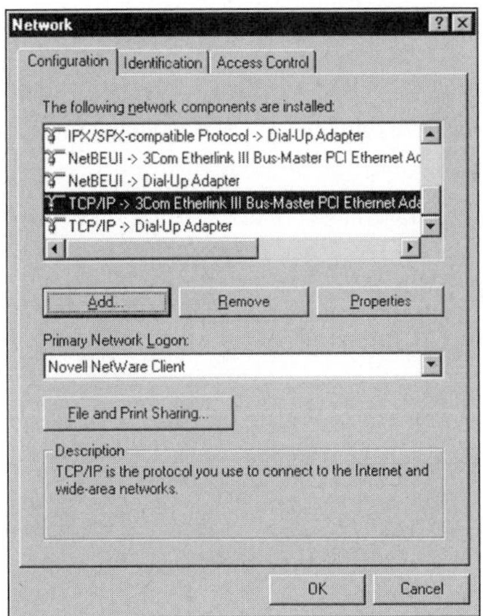

3. A TCP/IP Properties window will appear with seven tabs (as shown in Figure 2.15). When you click the IP Address tab, you will be greeted with two radio buttons that enable you to specify whether the client will obtain an IP address automatically or will use a manually assigned address.

FIGURE 2.15

The TCP/IP Properties screen in Windows 95 Network Neighborhood

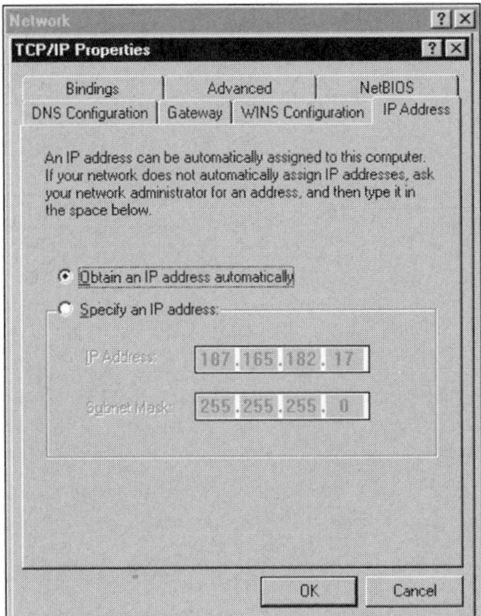

4. To configure a Windows 95/98 workstation for automatic address assignment, mark the "Obtain an IP Address Automatically" radio button. To configure a Windows NT/2000 workstation, mark the "Obtain an IP Address from a DHCP Server" radio button. If the workstation previously had an IP address that was configured manually, you'll be asked if you want to enable DHCP at this point. If so, click Yes.

5. To close the Network Neighborhood window and save your new settings, simply click OK a few times and reboot the workstation.

All finished! Your NetWare 5.1 Novell Clients are all ready to accept IP addressing information from your new DHCP Server. And, more importantly, your life as an IP administrator is getting much easier. Now let's shift gears and install DNS services for NetWare 5.1.

LAB EXERCISE 2.2: CONFIGURING DHCP SERVICES FOR BLUE-COLLAR CRIME FIGHTING IN TOKYO

Welcome back to Tokyo!

Today, we are going to configure ACME's NetWare 5.1 enterprise to manage IP address configurations automatically using DHCP—the Dynamic Host Configuration Protocol. In this exercise, we explored the many facets of DHCP configuration, including the DNS/DHCP Management Console, DHCP server configuration, the value of DHCP subnets, and automatic IP address assignment at the NetWare 5.1 workstation.

Now it's time to prove that you haven't been sleeping through the critical IP management lessons in this section. In this exercise, you will learn how to do the following:

- *Stage 1:* Configure DHCP Using the DNS/DHCP Management Console Utility
- *Stage 2:* Start the DHCP Server
- *Stage 3:* Configure Workstations to Use DHCP Services

The following hardware is required for this exercise:

- A NetWare 5.1 server (preferably CRIME-SRV1 in CRIME.TOKYO.ACME)
- A workstation running the NetWare 5.1 Novell Client for Windows 95 or Novell Client Windows NT (Version 3.0 or better)

Also, ensure that you have activated DNS/DHCP Services as outlined in "Lab Exercise 2.1: Installing DNS/DHCP Services in TOKYO."

Stage 1: Configure DHCP Using the DNS/DHCP Management Console Utility

First, we must create and configure DHCP Services (and all the corresponding NDS objects) using the DNS/DHCP Management Console utility. Follow these steps at the client workstation:

1. If you haven't already done so, log into the NDS tree as Admin.

2. Start the DNS/DHCP Management Console.

   a. Double-click the DNS/DHCP shortcut on your Windows desktop.

   b. When the Launch Novell DNS/DHCP Management Console dialog box appears, ensure that the following tree name is listed in the "Enter NDS Tree Name" field and then click Launch:

      ```
      ACME_TREE
      ```

3. Create a DHCP Server object.

   a. When the main DNS/DHCP Management Console screen appears, click the DHCP Service tab.

   b. When the main DNS/DHCP Management Console screen reappears, click Create. (The icon looks like a three-dimensional yellow box.)

   c. When the Create New DHCP Record dialog box appears, ensure that DHCP server is listed in the Select DHCP Record field and click OK.

   d. When the Create DHCP Server screen appears, click the Browse button to the right of the Select Server Object field.

   e. When the Select NDS Object dialog box appears, navigate to the CRIME-SRV1 Server object in the right pane. When you find the server, ensure that it is highlighted in the left pane and click OK.

   f. When the Create DHCP Server screen reappears, ensure that the following is listed in the Select Server Object field and then click Create to create the object:

      ```
      CRIME-SRV1.CRIME.TOKYO.ACME
      ```

   g. Wait while the DHCP Server object is created.

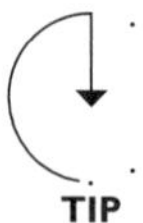
TIP

If you look in the lower-left corner of the screen, you will notice a DHCP Server object icon. This icon will have a diagonal red line through it until the DHCP server is actually running on your NetWare 5.1 server.

4. Create a Subnet object.

   a. When the main DNS/DHCP Management Console screen reappears, click Create. (Remember, it's the icon that looks like a three-dimensional box.)

   b. When the Create New DHCP Record object dialog box appears, click Subnet and then click OK.

   c. Follow these steps when the Create Subnet dialog box appears:

      - Type the following subnet name in the Subnet Name field:

        `CRIME_SUBNET`

      - Ensure that the following container is listed in the Select NDS Context field:

        `CRIME.TOKYO.ACME`

      - Enter the appropriate subnet address in the Subnet Address field. If you're using the subnet address in this book, type the following:

        `187.165.182.0`

      - Enter the appropriate subnet mask in the Subnet Mask field. If you're using the subnet mask in this book, type the following:

        `255.255.255.0`

      - Ensure that the following server name is listed in the Default Server field:

        `DHCP_CRIME-SRV1`

      - When the values listed onscreen are correct, click Create.

5. Create a Subnet Range object that will assign an IP address range of 25 to 100.

   a. Locate your Subnet object:

      - If it does not appear, click Refresh Tree. (The icon looks a bit like a report printed in landscape format.) When the Tree Refresh dialog box appears asking you if you are sure that you want to refresh the tree even though it may take some time, click Yes.

- Click your Subnet object and then click Create. (Remember, it's the icon that looks like a three-dimensional box.)

b. When the Create New DHCP Record dialog box appears, be sure that the Subnet Address Range is highlighted and then click OK.

c. Follow these steps when the Create Subnet Address Range dialog box appears:

- Type the following entry in the Subnet Address Range Name field:

  `Available Addresses`

- (Don't worry if your Caps Lock key doesn't seem to work properly in this field.)

- Type the following in the fourth octet of the Start Address field:

  `25`

- Type the following in the fourth octet of the End Address field:

  `50`

- When the values listed onscreen are correct, click Create.

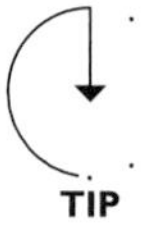

The address ranges of SAR objects cannot overlap. In other words, you must use continuous unspecified and unassigned network addresses within the associated subnet.

6. Configure your DHCP Server to exclude the IP address of 15 on your subnet.

a. Locate your subnet object.

- In the left pane, double-click your Subnet object, if necessary, to expand it.

- Notice that there are two default IP address exclusions for your subnet (that is, 0 and 255).

- Click your Subnet object and then click Create. (Remember, it's the icon that looks like a three-dimensional box.)

b. Follow these steps when the Create New DHCP Record dialog box appears:

- Click IP Address.
- Click OK.

c. Follow these steps when the Create IP Address dialog box appears:

- Use the up-arrow button to set the fourth octet of the IP address to the following:

  ```
  15
  ```

- Ensure that the following entry is listed in the Assignment Type field:

  ```
  Exclusion
  ```

- When the values listed are correct, click Create.

7. Follow these steps to exit the DNS/DHCP Management Console utility:

a. Click Exit. (It's the icon that looks like an open door.)

b. When the Exit dialog box appears, click Yes to indicate you're sure you want to exit.

Stage 2: Start the DHCP Server

Once you've created and configured all of the appropriate DHCP objects, you must activate DHCP Services at the CRIME-SRV1 server. To do this, type the following at the NetWare 5.1 server console prompt and press Enter:

```
DHCPSRVR
```

If the NetWare 5.1 GUI screen is displayed, press Alt+Esc first to get to a console prompt.

Stage 3: Configure Workstations to Use DHCP Services

Finally, we must configure the CRIME workstations to automatically obtain IP addresses from the new DHCP server. Check it out.

1. Configure the TCP/IP protocol stack for DHCP services.

   a. From a Novell Client workstation, right-click Network neighborhood in Windows 95/Windows NT.

   b. Click Properties from the pop-up menu that appears.

   c. Follow these steps when the Network dialog box appears:

      - If you are on a Windows NT machine, click the Protocols tab.
      - Click the TCP/IP protocol. (If you are using a Windows 95 workstation, there may be two TCP/IP protocols listed. Select the one that is associated with your network board.)
      - Click Properties.

   d. When the TCP/IP Properties dialog box appears (in the case of a Windows 95 machine) or the Microsoft TCP/IP Properties dialog box (in the case of a Windows NT machine), set up the client workstation to obtain an IP address automatically from the server.

      - If you are on a Windows 95 machine, click the "Obtain an IP Address Automatically" radio button.
      - If you are on a Windows NT machine, click the "Obtain an IP Address from a DHCP Server" radio button.
      - If you previously had an IP address that was configured manually, you may be asked if you want to enable DHCP. If so, click Yes when asked.
      - Click OK to close the TCP/IP Properties (or Microsoft TCP/IP Properties) dialog box.

   e. Click OK to close the Network dialog box.

   f. Wait while Windows builds a driver information database.

   g. When the System Settings Change dialog box appears, notice that the screen advises you to reboot your computer before the new settings take effect. Click Yes to acknowledge the message and reboot the computer.

2. If your client workstation is running Windows 95, verify that your workstation obtained IP address configuration information from a DHCP server.

   a. Click Start in the Windows taskbar.

   b. Click Run.

   c. When the Run dialog box appears, type the following in the Open field and then click OK:

      ```
      WINIPCFG
      ```

   d. When the IP Configuration dialog box appears, click More Info.

   e. Normally, when the IP Configuration dialog box reappears, it would include information that it obtained from the DHCP server. (The reason that the server does not respond to your workstation's DHCP request in this case is that the DHCP server is not configured for the network segment.)

3. If your client workstation is running Windows NT, verify that your workstation obtained IP address configuration information from a DHCP server.

   a. Click Start in the Windows taskbar.

   b. Click Programs.

   c. Click Command Prompt.

   d. Enter the following command and then press Enter:

      ```
      IPCONFIG /ALL
      ```

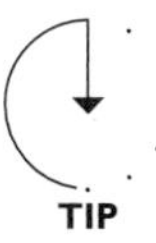

TIP

If you are unable to execute IPCONFIG successfully, try running it from the SYSTEM32 directory.

   e. Normally, IP Address information obtained from the DHCP server would be displayed. If it's not, don't panic. The server may not respond to your workstation's DHCP requests at this point because it hasn't been configured for the specific network segment.

Domain Name System (DNS) Configuration

In the past, DNS was administered by building a large text database including all of a zone's resource records. This database file used a unique format called Berkeley Internet Name Domain (BIND). Master and replica name servers answered client domain naming queries by searching the flat-file BIND database, which could include thousands of entries for different types of resource records. When changes occurred, replica name servers requested configuration updates from a Master name server in what was called a *zone transfer*.

This traditional Master/Slave approach has several disadvantages, the most significant being that all changes must be made at the Master server (a single point of failure and performance bottleneck). Novell has solved many of these problems by integrating DNS into the NDS Directory.

By shifting control away from the Master/Replica servers, Novell enables DNS changes to occur anywhere in the network through NDS. This removes the single point of DNS failure—the traditional Master server. Instead, zone data is stored within NDS and replicated just like any other data in the NDS tree. To activate DNS Services on a Novell network, perform the following five configuration steps:

- *Step 1: Create a DNS Server*—First, create a DNS server that can respond to DNS queries within a given DNS zone (primary or secondary). This is a separate logical entity from the standard NetWare Core Protocol (NCP) Server object and can be created within an Organization, Organizational Unit, Country, or Locality container.

- *Step 2: Configure a DNS Zone*—Next, configure a DNS Zone object to house all the domain naming information contained within resource records. This is an NDS container that holds all the data for a single DNS zone. The DNS Zone object contains data that correlates to a variety of DNS-specific entities, including Start of Authority (SOA), resource records (RRs), a list of all NDS-based servers that support the DNS zone, and associated server information. (**Note:** The hierarchy of DNS appears flat within the NDS tree. A Zone object and its children, for example, might display as peers within the NDS tree, even though they have a parent-child relationship in DNS.)

- *Step 3: Define Resource Records*—Third, define the resource records (RRs) that will contain the actual IP naming data for a given DNS zone. These leaf objects are placed in resource record set (RRSet) containers automatically. DNS Resource Record Set objects contain all the resource records for a specific zone. The RRSet contains the following DNS information: DNS domain name, a DNS address class, and a time-to-live (TTL) record. Finally, the DNS Resource Record object contains the record type and data of its host RR.

- *Step 4: Activate the DNS Server*—Fourth, activate the DNS server on the NetWare 5.1 console by typing **NAMED**.

- *Step 5: Configure DNS Workstations*—Finally, configure distributed IP workstations so that they can resolve host names automatically using DNS.

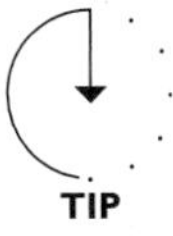
TIP

Carefully study the four DNS objects (DNS Server, DNS Zone, Resource Record, and Resource Record Set) and understand the purpose of each. Specifically, know that the DHCP Zone object contains Resource Record and Resource Record Set objects. Also, be aware that a DNS server can be a primary or secondary designated server.

Step 1: Create a DNS Server

If you want a NetWare 5.1 server to obtain and update DNS data in the NDS tree, you must create a corresponding DNS Server object. Once you create the server, it can be *designated* to service primary or secondary zones. A *designated server* is a NetWare 5.1 server that is assigned to obtain and update DNS data from a DNS Zone object. Novell DNS Services supports two different types of designated DNS servers:

- *Master (or Primary) Designated Server*—If the DNS server services a primary zone, it performs the duties of a Master DNS server. As a result, the DNS server ill be able to query NDS to resolve names into IP addresses, update the zone's serial number, and manage resource records.

- *Replica (or Secondary) Designated Server* — If the DNS server services a secondary zone, it becomes a transition point between NDS and an external Master name server. As a result, the DNS server performs the tasks of a Replica name server. For example, you can improve name resolution performance by creating a DNS Zone object that acts as a secondary to an ISP's Master name server. You can also create a secondary designated server that receives zone transfers from the ISP Master name server and also places IP naming information in your NDS tree. These resource records would then be replicated throughout the network by NDS.

To create a DNS Server object, follow these instructions:

1. Start the DNS/DHCP Management Console. Click the Create button within the DNS Service tab.

2. The Create New DNS Record dialog box appears. It allows you to create a DNS server, zone, or resource record. Select DNS Server and click OK.

3. Click the Browse button to select a host NetWare Server object for DNS activity. In the Host Name field, type a name for the new DNS Server object. The default DNS server name will be the same as the selected NDS Server object, except with the following prefix: "DNS_". You can modify the name of the DNS Server object later from within NetWare Administrator, if desired.

4. In the Domain Name field, type the name of the host domain for this DNS server. The domain may or may not already exist in your NDS tree. Click Create to complete the process.

After you add the DNS Server object to your NDS tree, it will appear as an icon in the bottom pane of the DNS/DHCP Management Console. The Server object will be nonoperational (with a red diagonal line through the icon) until you activate the server from the NetWare 5.1 server console (during "Step 4: Activate the DNS Server").

To configure the DNS Server object, click its icon at the bottom of the DNS/DHCP Management Console screen. The DNS Server object detailed information window enables you to configure a forwarding list, specify that a no-forwarding list will be used, enable event logging for the server, or enter comments chronicling the server's activities.

Step 2: Configure a DNS Zone

After you create a DNS Server object, you must assign it to a primary or secondary DNS zone. At that point, the server becomes a Master or Replica designated server. To create a DNS Zone object, click the DNS Service tab in the DNS/DHCP Management Console. Next, click the All Zones virtual object in the left pane. Then click the Create button in the toolbar and choose Zone. Once you do this, you'll be greeted with the Create Zone dialog box (as shown in Figure 2.16):

- *Create New Zone* — At the top of the Create Zone dialog box, you'll be asked to choose from three different zone types: Standard, IN-ADDR.ARPA, or IP6.INT. Unless you have any special requirements, mark the Create New Zone radio button to define a Standard zone. (**Note:** You can only create one IP6.INT Zone object in a given NDS tree, so the Create IP6.INT box will only be displayed if an IP6.INT Zone object doesn't already exist. All IP Version 6 addresses must be grouped under this object.)

- *NDS Context* — Next, you must specify a valid NDS context for the DNS Zone object. This context should match the highest point in the zone's DNS Hierarchy.

- *Zone Domain Name* — This identifies the specific subdomain for your zone. This name will be used both inside and outside NDS for zone transfers. If you specify a secondary zone type, the domain name must match the name of the domain being replicated from the Master name server.

- *Zone Type* — All DNS Zone objects must be configured as either primary or secondary zones. By default, the Primary radio button is highlighted, and all DNS resource records are distributed through NDS.

However, you also have the option of using an outside (non-NDS) Master server as your primary management point for DNS. If you retain the services of a non-NDS Master server, you must create a secondary DNS Zone object to interface with NDS. In this case, the Zone object name must follow the specifications put forth by the Master server. You will also need to provide the IP address of the Master server in the Create Zone window. This allows the Secondary Zone object to request updates from the non-NDS Master and to distribute them throughout the network.

- *Designated Server* — A DNS server must be assigned to a Zone object during zone creation. It can either be an existing DNS Server object or one that will be created later. To assign a DNS server that is already defined in NDS, select it from the Assign Authoritative DNS Server list. If you haven't created a DNS Server object yet, provide the Host Name and Domain information in the fields provided. Then, when you create the designated DNS server, the Zone object will automatically find it. Finally, click Create to complete the process.

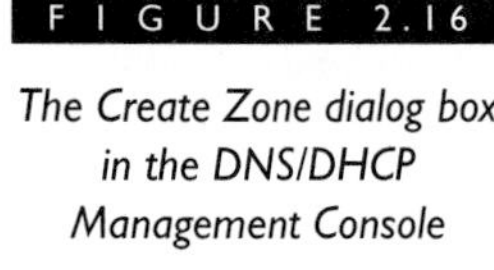

FIGURE 2.16

The Create Zone dialog box in the DNS/DHCP Management Console

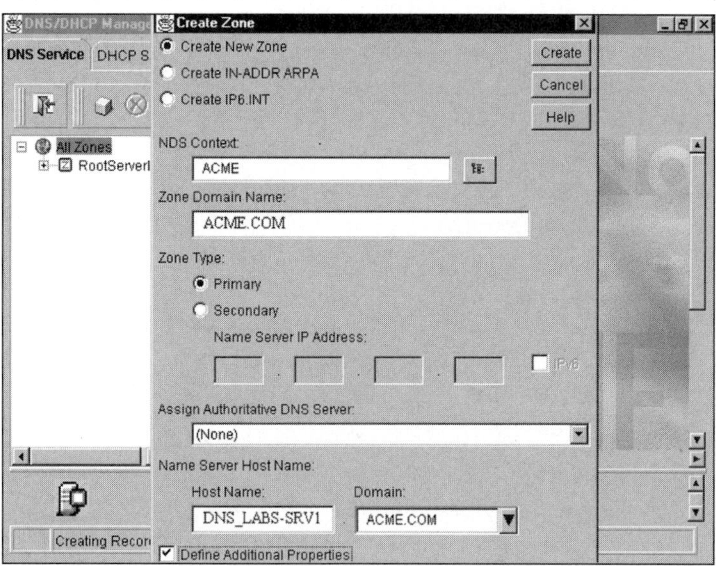

After you create the DNS Zone object, it will appear as an icon in the left pane of the DNS/DHCP Management Console. You can perform additional configuration tasks by simply clicking on the Zone object icon. In its Details window, you will find SOA (Start of Authority) configurations, serial numbers, e-mail addresses, and a comment field.

Step 3: Define Resource Records

Resource records (RRs) are NDS leaf objects that contain the IP-based host information maintained by DNS name servers. In short, these *are* the DNS database. Each DNS zone must contain several types of resource records for DNS to function properly. Following is a list of the most common resource record types:

- *Name Server Record (NS)* — This RR binds a domain name with a host name for a specific DNS server. The Zone object must contain "NS" records for each primary and secondary server in the zone.
- *Canonical Name Record (CNAME)* — This RR maps alias names to DNS names.
- *Address Record (A)* — This RR provides the IP address for the zone. Each IP host uses the "A" record to map host names to IP addresses.
- *Mail eXchange Record (MX)* — This RR maps Simple Mail Transfer Protocol (SMTP) mail addresses to domain names.
- *Pointer Record (PTR)* — This RR maps IP addresses to host names within an IN-ADDR.ARPA zone.

To create a DNS Resource Record object, first highlight an existing DNS zone and then click the Create button on the DNS/DHCP Management Console toolbar. Next, highlight Resource Record and click OK to continue. At this point, you'll be greeted with the Create Resource Record dialog box:

- *Domain Name* — In the Domain Name field, type a unique name for this Resource Record object. Typically, the name should resemble the host object it is servicing and the host object's predetermined function.

For example, an "A" record for your new DNS Server object should be named DNS_SRV1_A.

- *Resource Record Type* — Then select a resource record type and provide the necessary configuration information. By default, the Management Console creates an "A" record. If you want a "CNAME" record, you can highlight that choice or mark the Others checkbox to create an RR from a large list of supported types. The configuration information required for each RR depends on the type you choose. Finally, click Create to build the RR NDS object.

Once you have created a Resource Record object, it will be placed in a corresponding resource record set (RRSet) container. The RRSet object is created automatically for each unique DNS zone. The resource record is designated "Read Only," which means you must delete the object and re-create it to make any modifications.

Novell DNS Services also enables you to import DNS configuration information from a text-based BIND master file into NDS. You can use the Import DNS Database button in the DNS/DHCP Management Console to transfer configuration information from a BIND Master file into a new DNS zone. During this process, you will specify two pieces of information: the NDS context for the new zone and the DNS server to service the new zone.

Step 4: Activate the DNS Server

After you have created the DNS server and associated it with a new DNS zone, you must *activate* the DNS server. This is accomplished by typing the following command at the NetWare 5.1 server console:

```
NAMED
```

If you make any changes to your DNS Server object while NAMED.NLM is loaded, you'll need to unload and reload the module for your changes to take effect.

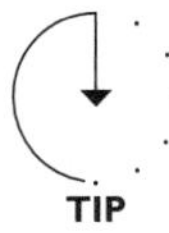

Study the steps for creating DNS Zone objects using the DNS/ DHCP Management Console. Be able to specify all required Zone properties, such as the zone name, the domain name, the zone type, and the designated DNS server. Learn how to import BIND master files into NDS using the Import DNS Database button in the DNS/DHCP Management Console. Also, know that two pieces of information are required during DNS importing: NDS context for the new DNS zone and a DNS server name to service the new zone. Finally, remember how to activate the DNS server at the NetWare server console (that is, by typing NAMED**).**

Step 5: Configure DNS Workstations

Once the DNS server is running, you must configure the workstations to use DNS for automatic name resolution. This is accomplished by customizing the TCP/IP Protocol property using Network Neighborhood on Windows 95/98 and Windows NT/2000 clients:

1. Right-click the Network Neighborhood icon on a Windows 95/98 or Windows NT/2000 desktop. Next, select Properties from the pop-up menu that appears.

2. The Network window should appear, with the Configuration tab activated. If this is a Windows 95/98 workstation, highlight the TCP/IP Protocol and click Properties. If this is a Windows NT/2000 workstation, the TCP/IP properties can be found under the Protocols tab.

3. The TCP/IP Properties window will appear with seven tabs. When you click the DNS Configuration tab, you'll be greeted with two radio buttons: "Disable DNS" and "Enable DNS" (as shown in Figure 2.17).

4. To configure Windows-based DNS, first click the Enable DNS radio button. Next, provide a host and domain name for this client and build a DNS server search order. Finally, in the DNS Server Search Order field, enter the IP address of your DNS server and then click Add.

REAL WORLD

If you're already using DNS in an IP-based Novell network, you've probably already built a pretty impressive BIND database file by now. Fortunately, NetWare 5.1 DNS Services includes an import tool for older BIND Master files. As a matter of fact, this new import tool is built into the DNS/DHCP Management Console. To access it, simply click the Import DNS Database button from within the DNS Service tab in the DNS/DHCP Management Console.

5. To close the Network Neighborhood window and save your new settings, simply click OK a few times and reboot the workstation.

FIGURE 2.17

The DNS Configuration tab in Windows 95/98 Network Neighborhood

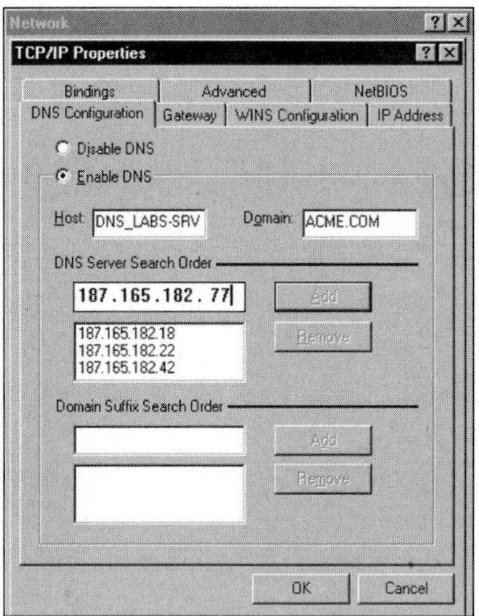

All finished! Now your NetWare 5.1 Novell Clients are all ready to surf the Web. And, more importantly, your life as an IP administrator is a whole lot easier. Let's recap. So far, we have built the NetWare 5.1 server using a GUI installation process and poured the electronic pavement of the network using Pure IP.

Our journey through IP management started with the fundamental architecture of DHCP, and we learned how it facilitates IP address distribution. Then we explored the DNS Hierarchy and DNS Name Service via DNS servers and resolvers. Furthermore, we were introduced to a powerful Java-based tool for IP administration — the DNS/DHCP Management Console. With it, we learned how to extend the NDS Schema, build DNS/DHCP objects, and automate much of the pain usually associated with IP-based networks.

Next we'll extend the new IP network into the realm of the Web using Novell's new Internet infrastructure. I'll see you in the next chapter. But before you go, take a crack at the remaining DNS/DHCP lab exercises.

LAB EXERCISE 2.3: CONFIGURING DNS FOR WHITE-COLLAR CRIME FIGHTING IN TOKYO

Welcome to DNS management!

Earlier in this chapter, we learned that the Domain Name System (DNS) is simply a fancy database that matches "humane" computer names to device IP addresses. To accomplish this impressive task, DNS operates in two different realms: *DNS Hierarchy* and *DNS Name Services.*

In this exercise, we will learn how to build and configure DNS Services for NetWare 5.1. We will explore three new NDS objects and gain experience managing them using the Java-based DNS/DHCP Management Console. Then we'll activate the DNS Server and discover how IP-based workstations resolve naming issues via Windows 95/NT. Here's a quick peek:

- *Stage 1:* Configure DNS Services Using the DNS/DHCP Management Console Utility.
- *Stage 2:* Start DNS Services
- *Stage 3:* Configure Workstations to Use DNS Services

The following hardware is required for this exercise:

- A NetWare 5.1 server
- A workstation running the NetWare 5.1 Novell Client for Windows 95 or Novell Client Windows NT (Version 3.00 or better)

Also, be sure that you have activated DNS/DHCP Services, as outlined earlier in Lab Exercise 2.1.

Stage 1: Configure DNS Services Using the DNS/DHCP Management Console Utility

First, we must create and configure DNS Services (and all the corresponding NDS objects) using the DNS/DHCP Management Console utility. Follow these steps at the client workstation:

1. If you haven't already done so, log into the NDS tree as Admin.

2. Start the DNS/DHCP Management Console.
    a. Double-click the DNS/DHCP shortcut on your Windows desktop.
    b. When the Launch Novell DNS/DHCP Management Console dialog box appears, ensure that the following tree name is listed in the "Enter NDS Tree Name" field and then click Launch:

       `ACME_TREE`
3. Create a DNS Server object.
    a. When the main DNS/DHCP Management Console screen appears, the DNS Service tab will be selected by default. Click Create. (Remember, it's the icon that looks like a three-dimensional yellow box.)
    b. When the Create New DNS Record dialog box appears, ensure that the DNS server is listed in the Selected DNS Record field and then click OK.
    c. When the Create DNS Server dialog box appears, click the Browse button to the right of the Select Server Object field.
    d. When the Select NDS Object dialog box appears, navigate to the CRIME-SRV1 Server object on the right side of the screen and then double-click it. The CRIME-SRV1 server should appear in the left pane. Be sure it is highlighted and then click OK.
    e. When the Create DNS Server dialog box reappears:
        - Ensure that the following is listed in the Select Server Object field:

          `CRIME-SRV1.CRIME.TOKYO.ACME`
        - In the Hostname field, type the following:

          `DNS_CRIME-SRV1`
        - In the Domain field, type the following

          `acme.com`
        - When the values listed onscreen are correct, click Create to create the DNS Server object.

4. Create a DNS Zone object.

   a. With the DNS Service tab still selected, ensure that All Zones is highlighted in the left pane.

   b. Click Create. (Remember, it's the icon that looks like a three-dimensional box.)

   c. When the Create New DNS Record dialog box appears, click Zone and then click OK.

   d. Follow these steps when the Create Zone dialog box appears:

      - Ensure that the radio button in front of Create New Zone is selected.
      - Ensure that the following is listed in the NDS Context field:

        `CRIME.TOKYO.ACME`

      - In the Zone Domain Name field, type the following:

        `crime.tokyo.acme.com`

      - Ensure that the radio button in front of Primary in the Zone Type section is selected.
      - In the Assign Authoritative DNS Server field, identify your NetWare 5.1 server by typing the following:

        `DNS_CRIME-SRV1`

      - When the values in this dialog box are correct, click Create to create the zone.

   e. When the Create Resource Record dialog box appears, read the information onscreen that reminds you to create proper resource records and then click OK.

5. Assign your DNS server to service your DNS zone:

   a. Click your DNS Zone object (`crime.tokyo.acme.com`) in the left pane. (If your DNS Zone object is not displayed, click Refresh Tree. The icon looks a bit like a report printed in landscape format. When the Tree Refresh dialog box appears asking you if you are sure you want to refresh the tree even though it may take some time, click Yes.)

- In the Available DNS Servers field, click your DNS Server object and then click Add. (If the field is empty and the Add button is gray, skip to the next bullet.)
- Ensure that the following server is listed in the Authoritative DNS Servers field:

  `DNS_CRIME-SRV1`

- Ensure that the following server is listed in the Dynamic DNS Server field:

  `DNS_CRIME-SRV1`

- When the values listed in this dialog box are correct, click "Save Data to NDS." (It's the icon to the left of the Tree Refresh button.) If the button is grayed out, indicating you have not made any changes, skip Step 5c and go on to Step 6.

b. When the Save Record dialog box appears, click Yes when prompted to save changes to `crime.tokyo.acme.com`.

6. Create a Resource Record object type for your server in your DNS Zone.

a. Ensure that your DNS Zone object (`crime.tokyo.acme.com`) is selected in the left pane and then click Create. (Remember, it's the icon that looks like a three-dimensional box.)

b. When the Create New DNS Record dialog box appears, click Resource Record and then click OK.

c. Follow these steps when the Create Resource Record dialog box appears:

- Type the following in the Host Name field:

  `CRIME-SRV1`

- Ensure that the following is listed in the Domain field:

  `crime.tokyo.acme.com`

- Type your server's IP address in the Server IP Address field. If you used the IP address in this book, type the following:

  ```
  187.165.182.18
  ```

- When the values listed in this dialog box are correct, click Create.

7. Exit the DNS/DHCP Management Console:

   a. Click Exit. (It's the icon that looks like an open door.)

   b. When the Exit dialog box appears, click Yes to indicate that you're sure you want to exit.

Stage 2: Start DNS Services

Once you've created and configured all of the appropriate DNS objects, you must activate DNS Services at the CRIME-SRV1 server. If the NetWare 5.1 GUI screen is displayed, press Alt+Esc first to get to a console prompt. Then type the following at the NetWare 5.1 server console prompt and press Enter:

```
NAMED
```

Stage 3: Configure Workstations to Use DNS Services

Finally, we'll need to configure the CRIME workstations to automatically obtain IP naming configurations from the new DNS server. Check it out.

1. If you're working on a Windows 95 machine, configure your workstation to use your DNS server for name resolution.

   a. Right-click Network Neighborhood.

   b. Click Properties in the pop-up menu that appears.

   c. When the Network dialog box appears, the Identification tab should be selected by default.

      - Write down the workstation name listed in the Computer Name field. (You'll need it in a minute.)

      - Click the Configuration tab.

d. Follow these steps when the Configuration tab page appears:

- Click the appropriate TCP/IP protocol. (There will be two TCP/IP protocols listed. Select the one that is associated with your network board.)
- Click Properties.

e. When the TCP/IP Properties dialog box appears, click the DNS Configuration tab.

f. Follow these steps when the DNS Configuration tab page appears:

- If not already selected, mark the Enable DNS radio button.
- In the Host Name field, type the workstation name you wrote down earlier.
- In the Domain Name field, type the following domain name that you configured in Stage 1, Step 4d:

  `crime.tokyo.acme.com`
- Under the DNS Search Order window, enter your server IP address. If you're using the server IP address in this book, type the following:

  `187.165.182.18`
- Click Add.

g. Reboot the workstation.

- Click OK to close the TCP/IP Properties dialog box.
- Click OK to close the Network dialog box.
- When the System Settings Change dialog box appears (advising you that you must reboot your computer before the new settings take effect), click Yes to reboot the computer.

2. If you're working on a Windows NT machine, follow the same directions outlined in Step 1, except the Configuration tab in Step 1c is called Protocols.

3. Test your DNS configuration by logging into your NetWare server using its Domain Name.

a. Follow these steps when the Novell Login dialog box appears during the boot process:

- Enter the following in the Username field:

  ```
  Admin
  ```

- Enter the Admin password in the Password field. If you're using the password in this book, type the following:

  ```
  ACME
  ```

- Click Advanced.
- Clear the values in the Tree field and the Context field.
- Type your NetWare 5.1 server's domain name in the Server field. If you're using the domain name in this book, type the following:

  ```
  crime-srv1.crime.tokyo.acme
  ```

- When the values listed in this dialog box are correct, click OK.

b. The Login utility should locate your server by its domain name.

LAB EXERCISE 2.4: MIGRATING TO IP AND DNS/DHCP

Use the hints provided to find the 20 IP terms hidden in this word search puzzle. Omit any punctuation characters (such as blank spaces, hyphens, and so on) and spell out any numbers.

Hints

1. Service previously used to assign IP addresses.
2. Enables you to run IPX-based applications on a Pure IP NetWare 5.1 server and link IPX segments to IP networks with ease.
3. Provides a framework for dynamically passing configuration information to TCP/IP clients.
4. Object that serves as a central repository for IP address information.
5. Is used to extend the NDS Schema to run DNS/DHCP Services.

6. Offers a distributed name/address database to translate numerical IP addresses into alphanumeric names.
7. Object that contains specific configuration parameters, including a zone list, DNS Server IP address, server options, and a forwarding/no-forwarding list.
8. Another name for DNS Hierarchy.
9. Older NetWare protocol that provides connectionless, datagram delivery of messages.
10. One of the four containers under which you can create a DHCP Server.
11. DNS server that contains the Authoritative Database.
12. Required by a CMD network for Pure IP access to IPX-Only networks.
13. Software that runs on a router to forward DHCP requests to servers on remote segments.
14. Backup DNS server that provides services in the event the Master server becomes unreachable, or to reduce the load on the Master server or the network.
15. Object that identifies a range of IP addresses available for dynamic address assignment.
16. Must be extended to integrate DNS/DHCP Services into NDS.
17. Provides automatic resource discovery and registration on a TCP/IP network.
18. Object that provides support for multiple subnets through a DHCP or BOOTP forwarder by identifying a pool of subnet addresses for remote LAN address assignments.
19. Protocol that accepts messages from IP and packages them for Internet-based applications.
20. Process of downloading the authoritative database to a Replica server.

See Appendix C for answers.

LAB EXERCISE 2.5: NETWARE 5.1 IP SERVICES

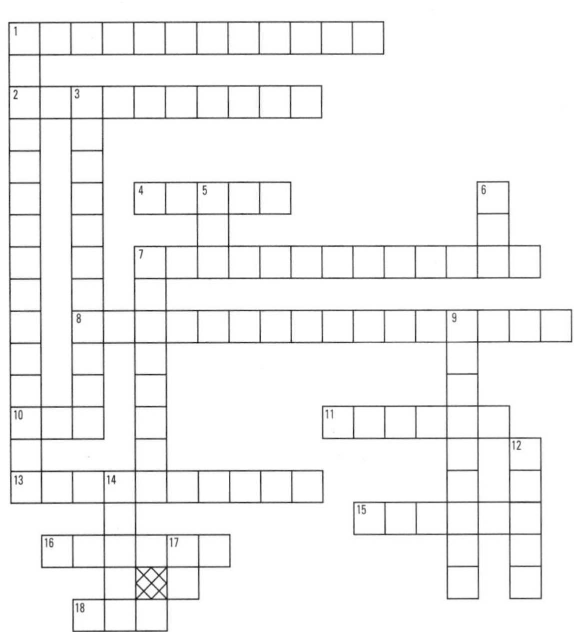

Across

1. Also known as Domain Name Space
2. DNS zones
4. Logical divisions of the DNS hierarchy
7. Database on a Master server
8. Assigned to service a DNS zone
10. Domain name for commercial entities
11. Delimiter used in domain names
13. Typically set to 255.255.255.0
15. Doesn't require encapsulation in NetWare 5.*x* and above
16. Each node in the tree represents one
18. Domain name used for educational institutions

Down

1. "Humane" names for IP addresses
3. Novell's implementation of a Relay Agent
5. Domain name for network providers
6. Domain name for U.S. Federal agencies
7. Fully-qualified DNS domain name
9. DNS clients
12. Main protocol suite used for the Internet
14. NLM for loading the DNS server
17. Network layer routing for the Internet

See Appendix C for answers.

CHAPTER 3

NetWare 5.1 Internet Infrastructure

So you want to be a Webmaster. A noble proposition!

So far we have built the NetWare 5.1 server (using NetWare 5.1 installation) and poured the electronic pavement of the Information Superhighway (using TCP/IP and DNS/DHCP services). Now it's time to build a complete Internet infrastructure for access to the World Wide Web.

The Internet and the World Wide Web can be intimidating at first. But actually, they are simply electronic mechanisms for publishing multimedia documents, either locally (corporate intranets) or to the world at large (the Internet). These multimedia Web pages are published using HyperText Markup Language (HTML) and spread around cyberspace by using the File Transfer Protocol (FTP). In addition, the HyperText Transfer Protocol (HTTP) offers a platform for client/server communications.

In this chapter, we will learn how to build a complete Internet infrastructure using NetWare 5.1. In preview, we will study the following NetWare World Wide Web components:

- *NetWare Enterprise Web Server* — We will begin with the fundamentals of NetWare 5.1's Enterprise Web Server and learn how to customize, configure, and secure it with a Web-based tool called the NetWare Web Manager.

- *NetWare FTP Server* — Next, we will learn how to build a Web-based NetWare file system by using File Transfer Protocol (FTP). FTP is a fast and efficient protocol for routing files on TCP/IP networks, like the Internet. In addition, FTP includes functions to log into the network, to list directories, and to copy files. The NetWare FTP Server enables you to support FTP functionality directly on top of a NetWare 5.1 server.

- *Additional NetWare Internet Components* — Finally, we will explore a variety of additional Web-based components that extend the functionality of NetWare's Enterprise Web Server and FTP Server. These components include the NetWare News Server, the NetWare MultiMedia Server, the NetWare Web Search Server, and the WebSphere Application Server.

As you can see, the NetWare 5.1 Internet infrastructure enables you to serve Web pages, transfer files, and stream multimedia services from a single NetWare server. Be careful . . . this is powerful stuff.

The NetWare Enterprise Web Server

The NetWare Enterprise Web Server is a set of NetWare Loadable Modules (NLMs) that work together to publish multimedia HTML files to local intranets or the global Internet. These files are read using graphical browsers and HTTP protocol. All of this Internet infrastructure runs on the foundation of NetWare 5.1.

Following is a brief glossary of the terms we'll be using in this chapter:

- *World Wide Web* — A wide-area, hypermedia information-retrieval initiative that "humanizes" the Internet. Web servers publish information to client programs called *browsers*.
- *HyperText Markup Language (HTML)* — HTML files are text files with special tags usually enclosed in less-than (<) and greater-than (>) symbols. HTML files tell graphical browsers how to format files on your screen.
- *Browsers* — These are client applications that convert HTML code into formatted text and graphics. Sample Web server files include executable (EXE), video (MOV and AVI), audio (MP3 and WAV), graphics (GIF and JPEG), and compressed (ZIP) formats.
- *HyperText Transfer Protocol (HTTP)* — HTTP enables Web servers and browsers to communicate with each other over the World Wide Web by using TCP/IP.

The NetWare Enterprise Web Server is installed by default during NetWare 5.1 installation. It is configured and managed using a Web-based utility called the NetWare Web Manager. The NetWare Web Manager is a set of NLMs that are automatically loaded from AUTOEXEC.NCF when the NetWare 5.1 server boots. You can manually load the Web Manager at the server console by typing the following:

```
ADMSERV or NSWEB
```

In this chapter, we will gain valuable Web mastering skills with the help of the NetWare Web Manager. Here's a quick preview:

- *Configuring Basic Parameters* — First, we'll learn how to use the NetWare Web Manager to start or to stop the Enterprise Web Server and to configure basic network settings, including server name, port numbers, and IP address.
- *Configuring Directories in the Document Tree* — Next, we'll use the Web Manager to configure Enterprise Server content. This consists of identifying document directories.
- *Configuring Document Preferences* — In addition, we'll learn how to use the Web Manager to configure specific document preferences, including index file name and directory index types.
- *Web Server Security* — Finally, we will learn how to integrate the Web Manager and NDS in order to secure the Enterprise Server via sophisticated NDS authentication methods. In addition, you can control access based on IP addressing.

Okay, that's all it takes to become a NetWare Webmaster. Let's start by exploring the fundamentals of the NetWare Web Manager tool.

Using NetWare Web Manager

The NetWare Web Manager is a central point of control for Enterprise Web Server configuration management and maintenance. From this single Web-based interface, you can configure server preferences, establish access restriction security, and manage Web server documents.

Once the NetWare Web Manager has been activated, you can access it by using any standard Web browser, such as Netscape Navigator or Internet Explorer. Once you have launched the browser at the Novell Client Workstation, enter the following Uniform Resource Locator (URL) in the Location field:

```
https://hostname:2200/
```

The *Hostname* is the IP address (or domain name) that you assigned to the Enterprise Server during NetWare 5.1 installation. Similarly, the port number (*2200* by default) is the Enterprise Server port number assigned during NetWare 5.1 installation. Make sure to document this number during installation. For purposes of security, HTTPS is used. This protocol ensures that your user name and user password are encrypted when you access NetWare Web Manager. When a Web browser uses HTTPS, a small graphic of a lock appears in the bottom of the browser window.

When the NetWare Web Manager loads, you will be presented with a New Site Certificate screen (see Figure 3.1). Click Next on the Certificate home page (Figure 3.1), and an assistant will load with three security options: "Accept This Certificate for a Particular Session," "Accept This Certificate until It Expires," or "Do Not Accept This Certificate." When NetWare 5.1 Web components are installed, a public key certificate and the Secure Socket Layer (SSL) are installed and configured (see Chapter 6 for more information on public key certificates and SSL). Because this certificate originates from your NetWare 5.1 server, accept it until it expires.

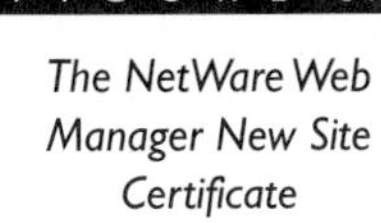

FIGURE 3.1

The NetWare Web Manager New Site Certificate

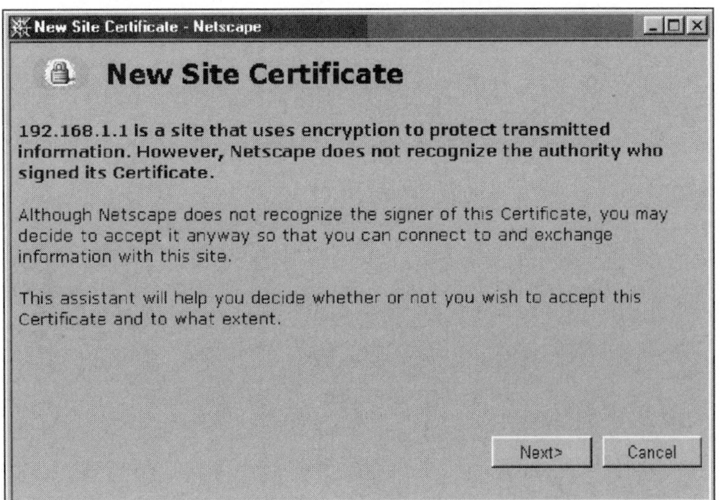

Next, the Enterprise Server returns the NetWare Web Manager Authentication window. As you can see in Figure 3.2, this window includes two input fields: User Name and Password. Make sure to enter the username and password that were designated during NetWare 5.1 installation and click OK.

FIGURE 3.2

The NetWare Web Manager Authentication window

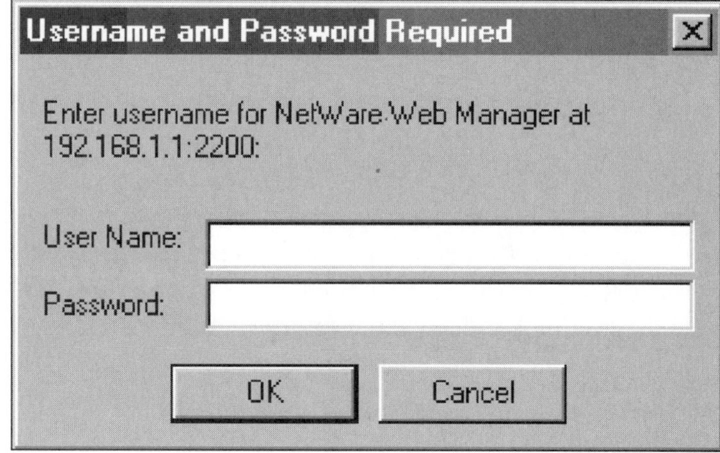

Once you have been authenticated, the NetWare Web Manager home page appears. This home page is a central access point for Enterprise Web Server configuration management and maintenance. As you can see in Figure 3.3, the NetWare Web Manager operates in the following two functional realms:

- *General Administration* — This realm covers global configuration for the Enterprise Server itself, including Admin Preferences, Global Settings, Users and Groups, and Cluster Management.
- *Servers Supporting General Administration* — This realm lists specific Enterprise Servers within your virtual domain. Each of these servers can be individually configured through the Enterprise Server Manager. In addition, you will see buttons for any active NetWare News Servers, NetWare FTP Servers, or NetWare Web Search Servers. Finally, you can use this home page to access the NetWare Management Portal and Novell Directory Services (NDS). See Figure 3.3 for more information.

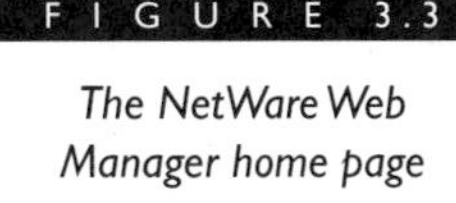

FIGURE 3.3

The NetWare Web Manager home page

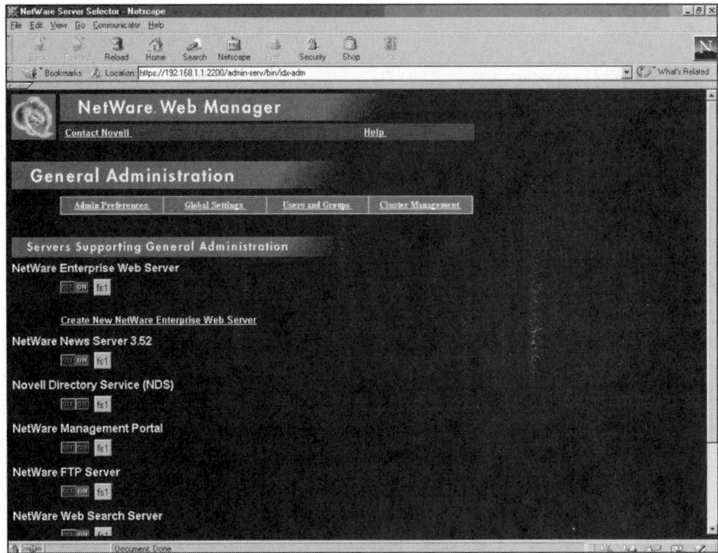

To configure the NetWare Enterprise Web Server within the Web Manager, simply click one of the Enterprise Server buttons shown in Figure 3.3 (in the example, the Enterprise Server is named "fs1"). At this point, you will be greeted with the NetWare Enterprise Server Manager home page, as shown in Figure 3.4. As you can see in the figure, the home page consists of the following three frames:

- *Server Configuration Buttons* — A list of seven configuration buttons is organized horizontally across the top frame. These buttons represent the Server Preferences, Programs, Server Status, Styles, Content Management, Web Publishing, and Agents and Search categories of Enterprise Server configuration. In Figure 3.4, the Server Preferences button has been activated.
- *Server Configuration Links* — Each time you activate a configuration button, a list of configuration links appears in the left-hand frame. These links correspond with specific subtopics under each configuration category. For example, in Figure 3.4, the Server Preferences button has been activated. In this case, the On/Off link has been chosen.

- *Main Frame* — Once you choose a server configuration link from the left-hand frame, the corresponding Java form pops up in the main frame. This Java form is where you will perform all of your Web mastering. In Figure 3.4, for example, the Server On/Off form is displayed. If you need more information about a specific form, you can always click Help for context-sensitive assistance.

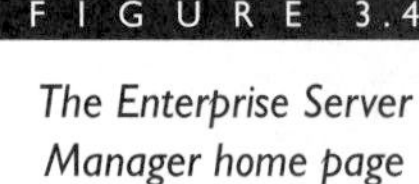

FIGURE 3.4

The Enterprise Server Manager home page

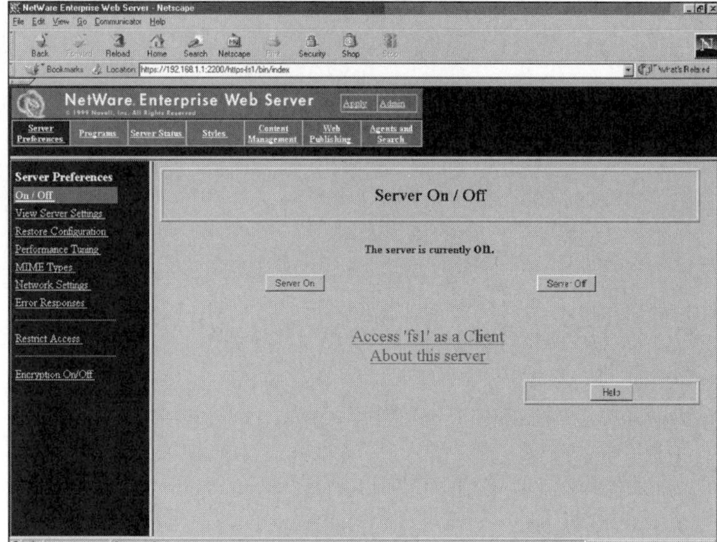

In addition to the three Web Manager frames described, you should be aware of the following two buttons:

- *Apply* — Once you submit a Java form, you will be presented with a Hypertext link that saves and applies your changes. When configuring your Enterprise Server, you must always save and apply your changes. You can also manually apply any changes you have made using the Apply button in the top-right corner of the Enterprise Server home page.

- *Admin* — When you have finished Web mastering with NetWare Manager, you can return to the General Administration home page by clicking the Admin button in the top-right corner of the Enterprise Server home page.

Most of the Enterprise Web Manager Java forms make changes that apply to the entire Enterprise Server. However, some forms can configure either the entire server or specific resources, such as files or directories. Any Web Manager form that supports changes to a subset of the Enterprise Server must use the *Resource Picker* to specify which resources to configure.

That completes our preview of the NetWare Web Manager configuration tool. As you can see, it offers a Web-savvy look and feel with fairly straightforward navigation. Now let's learn how to use this tool to configure basic parameters, documents, and Enterprise Server security.

Configuring Basic Parameters

The two most fundamental Enterprise Server Manager configurations are the following:

- On/Off
- Network Settings

First, we'll learn how to turn the Enterprise Server on and off by using the Enterprise Server Manager. Then we can explore some of the Enterprise Server's more basic network settings, including Server Name, Server Port, and IP Address.

On/Off

Once installed, the Enterprise Server runs constantly. It's always listening for, accepting, and responding to user requests. When your Enterprise Server is running, you will see the On icon and a green light in the Web Manager home page (see Figure 3.3).

Also, you can verify the Enterprise Server's status within the Server Preferences category of the Enterprise Server Manager. Server Preferences include an On/Off link. Simply choose this link and you will see the Server On/Off Java form. Furthermore, you can control the status of your Web Server by using the Server On/Off configuration form. Simply click Server On to activate your Web Server and Server Off to deactivate it.

Now let's move on to a little tougher configuration task — Network Settings.

REAL WORLD

In addition to the Web Manager and the Enterprise Server Manager utilities, you can activate or deactivate the Enterprise Server manually from the NetWare 5.1 server console. To do so, complete the following steps:

- To activate the Enterprise Server, type the following at the NetWare 5.1 console:

  ```
  NSWEB
  ```

- To deactivate the Enterprise Server, type the following at the NetWare 5.1 console:

  ```
  NSWEBDN
  ```

Network Settings

Another key Web mastering form within the Enterprise Server Manager is Network Settings. This Java screen can be found under the Server Preferences button by choosing the Network Settings link on the left-hand side of the screen.

The Network Settings form includes the following two critical pieces of IP connectivity data:

- *Server Name* — This specifies the DNS host name of your Enterprise Server. This is the URL that virtual villagers use to find your city on the Information Superhighway.
- *Server Port* — The Server Port number is the TCP port that the Enterprise Server listens to for HTTP requests. The standard *insecure* Web Server Port number is 80. The standard *secure* Web Server Port number is 443. The Port number you choose can be any number from 1 to 65535. In the example in Figure 3.4, we used the default Port Number of 2200. If you remember correctly, this was the Server Port you defined during the Enterprise Server installation stage.

This completes our discussion of the basic Enterprise Server Manager configurations. Now let's step up the difficulty level a little bit and learn how to Web master Enterprise Server content, starting with directories in the Document tree.

Configuring Directories in the Document Tree

Next, you should shift your Web mastering studies from server preferences to content management. The next two sections focus on the following two key Content Management configurations: Directory Management and Document Preferences.

To get started, click the Content Management configuration button at the top of the Enterprise Server Manager home page. As you can see in Figure 3.5, the Enterprise Server responds with a long list of configuration links in the left-hand frame. In this section, we will focus on the first two links:

- Primary Document Directory
- Additional Document Directories

FIGURE 3.5

The Primary Document Directory configuration form in the Enterprise Server Manager

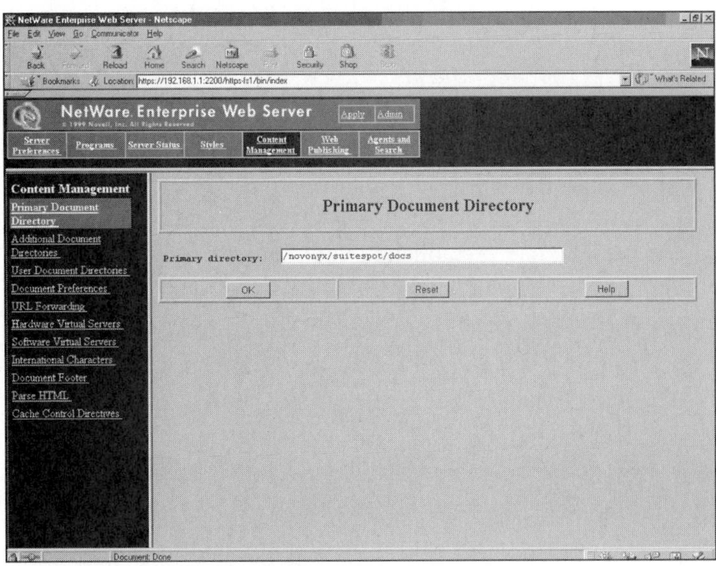

The Primary Document Directory

A Web server is only as good as its content. The Enterprise Server keeps its Web pages in a central location within the NetWare server directory structure. This location is known as the Document Root or *Primary Document Directory*. By default, the Primary Document Directory for your Enterprise Server (see Figure 3.5) is the following:

```
SYS:NOVONYX\SUITESPOT\DOCS
```

By default, the Enterprise Server URL address will map to this Primary Document Directory. Here's an example of the correlation between URL and file system from the world of ACME:

- *URL* — `www.acmelabs.com/pr/info.htm`
- *Document Directory* — sys:novonyx\suitespot\docs\pr\info.html

The Enterprise Server Manager provides the Java form you need to change the Enterprise Server's Primary Document Directory. As you can see in Figure 3.5, the Enterprise Server Manager uses the NOVONYX file system by default.

The beauty of this system is that it enables you to move your Web content anywhere on the NetWare file server without having to remap all of your URLs. All you have to do is simply change the Primary Document Directory. Of course, be sure to save and apply your changes once you are finished.

Additional Document Directories

Once you have established your Primary Document Directory, you may want to configure additional URLs for content outside the default directory structure. The Enterprise Server allows you to serve documents from any directory on the NetWare 5.1 server as long as you establish a unique URL prefix (called *Virtual Directories*). Here's how it works (see Figure 3.6):

- *URL Prefix* — For virtual villagers to find Web content outside the default file system, you will need to give them an extended URL address. For example, users who want a graphical map of ACME distribution sites will have to pull up Web pages from the new Distribution URL. This Distribution prefix is appended to the standard URL.

In our AMCELABS example, any user who points a Web browser to `www.acmelabs.com/distribution/` will retrieve Web pages from the directory specified in the next bullet.

- *Map to Directory* — Next, you must provide the Enterprise Server with the content directory for the new URL. In this field, be sure to type the following absolute directory path: **SYS:NOVONYX\ACMELABS\DISTRIBUTION**. This is where the graphical distribution maps are stored in HTML format. When users access the Distribution URL, their browser now can find the HTML map files.

FIGURE 3.6

The Additional Document Directories configuration form in the Enterprise Server Manager

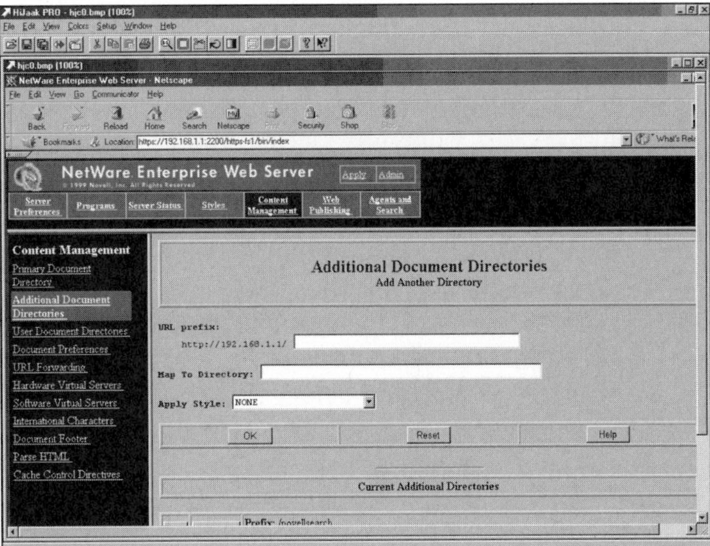

This completes our lesson on *where* Web pages are stored. Now let's shift our focus to *how* virtual villagers access them.

Configuring Document Preferences

Now that you have made it easy for your villagers to find the Web content they need, we need to learn how to customize the way the Web content appears. Document Preferences control *how* virtual villagers access your Web content. As you can see in Figure 3.7, these Web server configurations are accomplished by using three options:

- *Index File Names* — If a user doesn't explicitly request a filename in the URL, the Enterprise Server automatically displays the file you place in the Index Filenames field. As you can see, the defaults are INDEX.HTML and HOME.HTML. If more than one filename is specified, the Enterprise Server scans in the order in which the names appear in this field until one of the indicated filenames is found.

- *Directory Indexing* — In addition to filenames, the Enterprise Server also indexes directories. The Web server first searches the Primary Document Directory or URL-specified directory for one of the listed index files. If an index file is not found, the Enterprise Server generates a list of all files in the Document Root. This directory listing can have one of the following formats: *Fancy* directory indexing, which includes a graphic representing the type of file, the date the file was last modified, and the file size; or *Simple* directory indexing, which simply lists the files available. Finally, the Enterprise Server skips the directory list altogether if you choose *None*.

- *Home Page* — By default, the Enterprise Server finds the specified index file and uses it for the home page. However, you can configure a different home page simply by marking the Home Page radio button and entering a filename in the appropriate field.

Now that you fully understand where virtual villagers go for Web content and how it is displayed for them, it's time to tackle the most important Web mastering topic of all — *what* is available.

Enterprise Server Security

The final Enterprise Server configuration topic is the most important one of all — security. This section focuses on protecting your valuable Web server content. Keep in mind, with one wrong click you can accidentally publish all your internal data to the world . . . this is not a good thing.

FIGURE 3.7

The Document Preferences configuration form in the Enterprise Server Manager

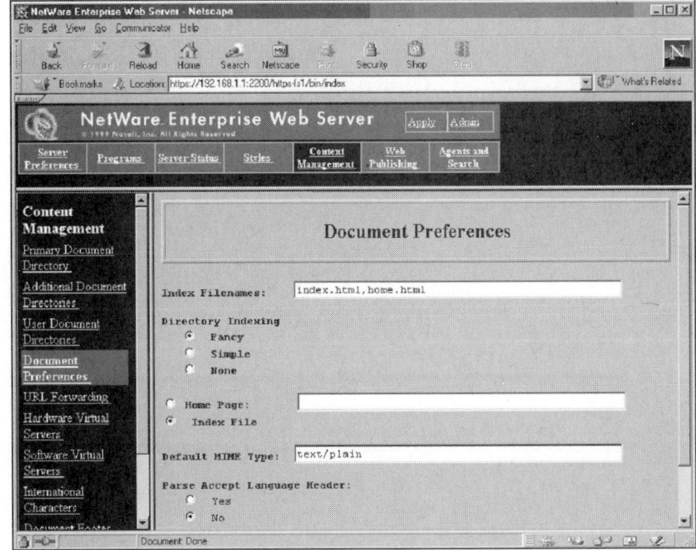

Fortunately, the Enterprise Server allows you to take advantage of the following two powerful access restriction methodologies:

- Public Access
- NDS Authentication

With either of these options, you can control access to the entire Enterprise Server or only to parts of it, such as directories, files, or file types. When the Enterprise Server evaluates an incoming request, it determines access based on a hierarchy of rules called *Access Control Entries* (ACE), which uses the matching entries to determine if the request is allowed or denied. Fortunately, each ACE specifies whether the Enterprise Server should continue to the next ACE in the hierarchy.

The collection of ACEs is called an Access Control List (ACL). Enterprise Server Access Control files are stored in function-specific directories. For example, the Web Manager uses ADMINACL, while the Enterprise Server uses HTTPACL.

When the Enterprise Server receives a request for a Web page, it looks in a specific ACL file to determine access. This file is called OBJ.CONF. By default, this one server-based ACL file contains multiple ACLs. For a more detailed example, check out the accompanying Real World icon.

Now let's explore how the Enterprise Server controls access using NDS Authentication and/or IP address restrictions.

Public Access

Once the Enterprise Server is installed, anyone accessing your Web server with a standard browser can access documents in the primary document directory and in any of its subdirectories.

REAL WORLD

To better understand Enterprise Server access control, consider the following example. Suppose a virtual villager requests the following ACMELABS URL:

```
www.acmelabs.com/pr/info.html
```

Following is the Enterprise Server's response:

- First, the Enterprise Server checks access control for the entire server. If the Entire Server resource is set to *continue*, the Enterprise Server moves on.
- Next, the Enterprise Server looks for an ACL for the file type — in this case, ".html." If this resource is set to *continue*, the Enterprise Server moves on.
- Then the Enterprise Server checks for an ACL for each of the directories in the URL path. In this case, it begins with "PR." If an ACL exists, the Enterprise Server checks the ACE and then moves on to the next directory.
- The Enterprise Server continues traversing the directory path until it reaches an ACL that says *Don't Continue* or until it reaches the final ACL for INFO.HTML.

To set up Access Control for this example by using the Enterprise Server Manager, you could create an ACL only for the "info.html" file or for any resource leading to the file — including the entire server or PR directory.

If you change the Primary Document Directory or add additional document directories, you must provide public access to the directories, as shown in Figure 3.8. To insert a directory for public access, click the Restrict Access link within Server Preferences and choose Insert File. Remember to restart the Enterprise Server in order for the changes to take effect.

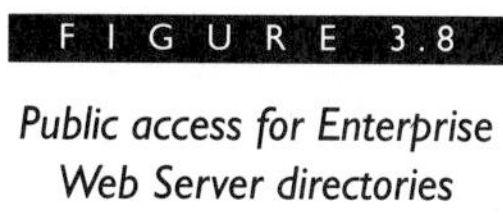

FIGURE 3.8

Public access for Enterprise Web Server directories

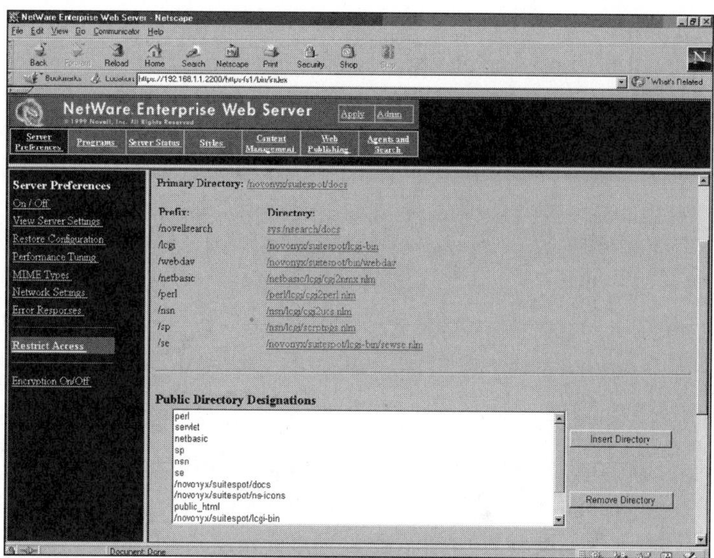

NDS Authentication

If public access is too open for you, consider the security features available via NDS Authentication. Fortunately, the Enterprise Server supports this access control method with a few minor modifications. Once the Enterprise Server's NDS authentication has been activated, users will be prompted to enter their username and password whenever accessing a restricted file or a directory.

This completes our discussion of Enterprise Server configuration and management. As you can see, this Internet component is at the heart of your Web mastering strategy. In review, the NetWare Enterprise Web Server is a set of NLMs that work together to publish multimedia HTML files to local intranets or the global Internet — all on the foundation of NetWare 5.1.

Now let's expand the NetWare 5.1 Internet into the realm of Web-based file system management with the NetWare FTP Server.

The NetWare FTP Server

The NetWare FTP Server enables NetWare 5.1 clients to use File Transfer Protocol (FTP) to work with files within their corporate intranet or on the global Internet via Web-based browsers. FTP is a fast and efficient protocol for routing files on TCP/IP networks, like the Internet. In addition, FTP includes functions to log into the network, to list directories, and to copy files.

All of these Web filing features operate in a client/server relationship — your NetWare 5.1 workstation and browser act as the client and the NetWare FTP Server is the server. FTP transfers can be initiated by entering the URL preceded with "ftp://", rather than with "http://". Corporations typically use FTP servers for archiving and distributing documents, computer programs, pictures, sound, and video.

In the next section, we will learn how to activate a NetWare FTP Server on top of your NetWare 5.1 file server. In addition, we will learn how to use the NetWare FTP Server Manager to configure FTP users and to establish security restrictions.

Using NetWare FTP Server Manager

If NetWare FTP Services is installed on your NetWare 5.1 server, the NetWare FTP Server icon appears on the NetWare Web Manager home page (see Figure 3.3, earlier in this chapter). Once the FTP Server has been installed and loaded, it runs constantly, listening for and responding to FTP requests. To access the NetWare FTP Server Manager (shown in Figure 3.9), click the button displaying the name of the server from the NetWare Web Manager home page.

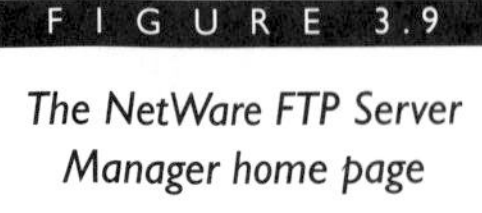

FIGURE 3.9

The NetWare FTP Server Manager home page

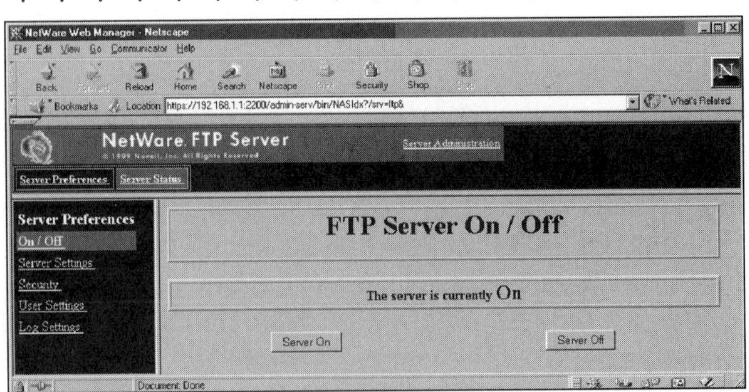

As you can see in Figure 3.9, the FTP Server Manager home page resembles the Enterprise Web Server home page, including configuration buttons, configuration links, and a main frame. In our example, the Server Preferences configuration button has been activated along with the On/Off configuration link. From within this management console, you can start, stop, and restart the NetWare FTP Server. In addition, you can shut down and restart an FTP Server from the NetWare server console with the following commands:

`Unload NWFTPD` *(to shut down the NetWare FTP Server)*

`NWFTPD` *(to restart the NetWare FTP Server)*

Once you have activated the NetWare FTP Server, you can use FTP Server Manager to set the default home directory and/or configure user restrictions. Let's take a closer look.

Configuring the NetWare FTP Server

When an authorized FTP client accesses the NetWare FTP Server, via Netscape Navigator or Internet Explorer, it's placed in the SYS:PUBLIC home directory by default. You can specify a different default home directory by selecting the User Settings link from the Server Preferences configuration button of FTP Server Manager. In the Default Home Directory field, enter the directory path by using the following format:

Volume:/directory/subdirectory

Once you have entered the new default home directory, you will need to click Save and OK to complete the Java form. Then you must restart the FTP Server in order for the changes to take effect.

By default, the NetWare FTP Server allows all NDS users to log in and browse through SYS:PUBLIC and other public directories. In addition, you can specify access restrictions at a variety of different levels using the SYS:ETC/FTPREST.TXT restrictions file. The following levels of access restrictions are supported:

- *Container Level* — Restrictions can be specified for any NDS container. This setting controls all users in that container and its subcontainers.
- *User Level* — Restrictions can be specified for a particular user.

- *Domain Level* — Restrictions can be specified at a domain level. This controls all hosts in that domain and its subdomains.
- *Host Level* — Restrictions can be specified for a particular host.

Refer to Table 3.1 for a description of the access rights permitted by the NetWare FTP Server. When modifying these rights in the FTP Server restriction file, keep in mind that each line should have one entity name and corresponding access rights, and all rights specified on that line are applied to the entity. Also, make sure to assign the rights of the entities according to the order in which they appear in the restriction. If different rights apply to the same entity, those rights that appear last in the restriction file are applied. Finally, if the restrictions file does not exist or is empty, access is given to all users without restrictions.

TABLE 3.1

NetWare FTP Server Access Rights

ACCESS RIGHT	DESCRIPTION
Deny	Denies access to the FTP Server for that client
Read only	Description gives Read-Only access to the client
No remote	Restricts access to remote server navigation
Guest	Gives only Guest access to the user
Allow	Gives the user FTP access to the server

Following is an example of NetWare FTP Server restrictions at ACME:

```
.NORAD.ACME ACCESS=ALLOW
.LABS.NORAD.ACME ACCESS=DENY
.AEinstein.LABS.NORAD.ACME ACCESS=READONLY
```

In the preceding example, AEinstein at LABS is allowed the Read-Only right. Other users in the LABS.NORAD.ACME container are denied access. However, all other Organizational Units in the NORAD location are allowed access to the NetWare FTP Server.

If your NetWare FTP Server has documents or programs that the public needs access to, it is impractical to set up a user account for every individual user on the Internet. Fortunately, the NetWare FTP Server supports an anonymous user account with access to files intended for public use. To enable or disable access to anonymous users, set the following three User Settings parameters in NetWare FTP Server Manager (see Figure 3.10):

- *Allow Anonymous Access* — YES or NO (default is NO)
- *Anonymous Users Home Directory* — *Volume:/directory/subdirectory* (default is SYS:/PUBLIC)
- *Require E-mail Address for Password* — YES or NO (default is YES)

In order to access the FTP Server, the anonymous user must be represented by a valid NDS User object. This object can be created in NetWare Administrator with the login name "Anonymous" and appropriate file system rights to the anonymous user home directory.

FIGURE 3.10

The FTP Server Anonymous User configuration screen

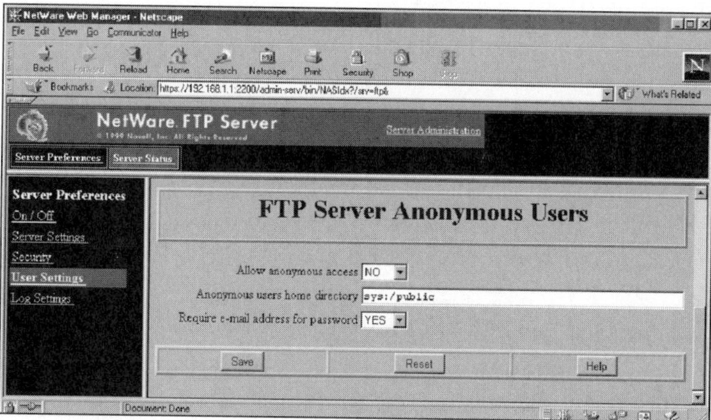

This completes our lesson in NetWare FTP Services. With this Internet infrastructure component activated, files will appear as HyperLink documents inside client browsers. As a matter of fact, the Enterprise Server, FTP, and TCP/IP work in synergy to provide transparent data access to World Wide Web netizens.

Now let's expand our discussion of NetWare 5.1's Internet infrastructure with some additional World Wide Web components — the NetWare News Server, the NetWare MultiMedia Server, the NetWare Web Search Server, and the WebSphere Applications Server.

Additional NetWare Internet Components

In addition to the NetWare Enterprise Web Server and the FTP Server, NetWare 5.1 offers four additional Internet infrastructure components. These components are designed to extend your server's Internet capabilities beyond simple document publishing and file transfer. Following is a brief preview of these four Internet components:

- *NetWare News Server* — The NetWare News Server enables you to create a central location for public and private discussion groups. Client software called a *News Reader* connects to a News Server to retrieve the discussion groups. A discussion group is a collection of articles that reside on one or more News Servers. Each discussion group is related to a particular topic and contains one or more articles of interest to a particular group of people.
- *NetWare MultiMedia Server* — The NetWare MultiMedia Server enables NetWare 5.1 servers to stream multimedia content to client workstations. This service uses Real-Time Streaming Protocol (RTSP) to support streaming audio and video to clients by using the RealPlayer from RealNetworks, Inc. RTSP is a client/server, multimedia-presentation control protocol that addresses the need for efficient delivery and streamed multimedia over IP networks. The NetWare MultiMedia Server supports the following file formats: WAV, MP3, and RM (RealVideo file format).
- *NetWare Web Search Server* — The NetWare Web Search Server is a powerful customizable search and print service that enables you to index information on the Enterprise Web Server. These indexes enable users to effectively search for and print content from multiple collections of information. In addition, you can use the NetWare Web Server to customize the look and feel of search and print results across multilanguage data collections.
- *WebSphere Application Server* — The IBM WebSphere Application Server combines with NetWare 5.1 and NDS to provide a reliable, scaleable, and high-performance platform for development, deployment, and management of Web applications. In addition, the WebSphere Application Server includes two development tools: WebSphere Studio

(for development for Web-based content) and VisualAge for Java (a complete Java IDE environment for application programming).

Hopefully, you can appreciate that the NetWare 5.1 Internet infrastructure offers many more features beyond simple document publishing and file sharing. Now let's learn more about the NetWare News Server.

The NetWare News Server

The NetWare News Server is a NetWare 5.1 Internet component that enables you to create a central depository of public and private discussion groups. These discussion groups consist of a collection of articles residing on the server that are accessed through News Reader clients using the Network News Transport Protocol (NNTP). NNTP supports newsgroup discussions over TCP/IP networks through connectivity between NNTP-compliant clients (News Readers) and NNTP-compliant servers (such as the NetWare News Server).

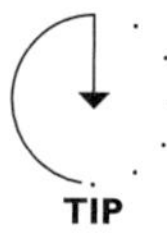

TIP

The public collection of thousands of news groups (organized by topic) is usually referred to on the Internet as *Usenet*. These news groups are sent around the world, and their articles are stored on many news servers.

Once the NetWare News Server is installed and loaded on a NetWare 5.1 server, it runs constantly, listening for and responding to NNTP requests. If your news server is running, the On icon and its green light appear on the Web Manager home page (see Figure 3.3).

To access the NetWare News Server Manager, simply click the button displaying the name of the NetWare News Server, and a screen similar to Figure 3.11 appears. As you can see from the figure, this screen resembles the Enterprise Server Manager — with configuration buttons across the top, configuration links on the left-hand side, and a main frame in the center of the browser window. You can start and stop the NetWare News Server by using one of the following three methods: Off and On icons on the NetWare Web Manager home page, Start/Stop in the Server link within the Preferences button, or from the NetWare server console by typing the following:

```
NVXNEWDN (to shut down the News server)
NSNEWS (to restart the News server)
```

FIGURE 3.11

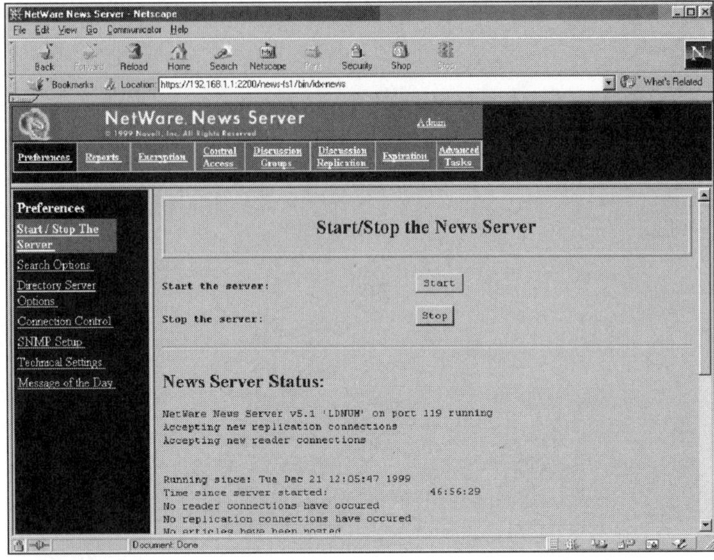

The NetWare News Server Manager

You can use the NetWare News Server Manager to perform the following administrative configurations:

- *Changing the Spool Directory Location* — The Spool Directory indicates where all discussion articles on your server are stored. Articles are stored in subdirectories corresponding to their discussion group names. When you install the NetWare News Server, the Spool Directory is created in the following default directory: SYS:/NOVONYX/SUITESPOT/NEWS-*servername*/SPOOL. If you connect to Usenet or if you have an internal discussion group that is heavily used, your Spool Directory can use a significant amount of disk space. In either case, you may want to change the Spool Directory to a different location. When you do, make sure it has the correct ownership and permissions (Read, Write, and Execute). To change the Spool Directory using the NetWare News Server Manager, simply copy the SPOOL folder to a new location and specify a different Spool Directory Location in the Technical Settings link within the Preferences configuration button.

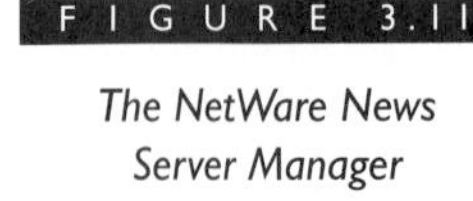

- *Creating a Discussion Group* — You can decide which discussion groups you want your News Server to provide to users. In addition, you can create new discussion groups or receive Usenet news groups from other servers. To create a new discussion group, access the Manage Discussion Groups link from within the Discussion Groups configuration button of the NetWare News Server Manager. Next, select a parent or root-level discussion group and click New. Then enter a name for the discussion group and a topic in the Name and Description fields, respectively. Finally, select either a categorized or standard discussion group and click Submit. With NDS, only the News Server Administrator can manage discussion groups.

- *Setting Control Access for NDS Users* — Instead of creating new NDS objects for access to NetWare News Server discussion groups, you can use NDS objects that already exist and grant them rights to discussion-group directories. First, you must make sure that the NDS users or groups are in the context that is specified in the Configure Directory Service form of the Global Settings button of the NetWare Web Manager home page. If your users or groups are in a subcontext of this container, they must specify the additional context when authenticating to the discussion group. Once you have verified that the users are in the correct context, you can set up discussion-group access control within the Access Control Options link of the Control Access button on the NetWare News Server Manager. Within this form, make sure to set Access Control to On. Finally, you need to ensure that the users and groups have adequate NDS rights to the discussion group's SPOOL directory. You can use NetWare Administrator to ensure that readers have at least File Scan and Read file system rights and that posters have at least File Scan, Read, Create, and Write file system rights.

This completes our discussion of NetWare 5.1's News Server Internet component. Now let's continue extending our Internet infrastructure with a lesson in configuring the NetWare MultiMedia Server.

The NetWare MultiMedia Server

The NetWare MultiMedia Server enables NetWare 5.1 servers to stream multimedia content to client workstations. It uses Real-Time Streaming Protocol (RTSP) to stream audio and video content to NetWare clients who are using the RealPlayer browser plug-in from RealNetworks, Inc. RTSP is a client/server, multimedia-presentation protocol that efficiently delivers streamed multimedia over IP networks.

Currently, the NetWare MultiMedia Server supports the following file formats:

- *WAV* — A digital audio file format for storing WAVFORM data.
- *MP3* — An excellent audio compression format. MP3 is short for MPEG-1 Layer III.
- *RM* — The RealVideo file format for streaming audio and video content over IP networks.

Once the NetWare MultiMedia Server is installed and loaded, it runs continuously, listening for and responding to RTSP protocol requests. When your MultiMedia Server is running, you will notice the On icon and its green light on the NetWare Web Manager home page (see Figure 3.3). To access the NetWare MultiMedia Server Manager, click the button displaying the name of the server, and a screen similar to Figure 3.12 appears.

You can start and stop the NetWare MultiMedia Server by using one of the following three methods: clicking the Off and On icons on the NetWare Manager home page, selecting the On/Off configuration link within the Server Preferences configuration button of NetWare MultiMedia Server Manager, or typing any of the following commands at the NetWare server console:

```
MEDIA (to shut down the NetWare MultiMedia Server)

UMEDIA (to restart the NetWare MultiMedia Server)
```

You can perform the following critical multimedia configurations by using the NetWare MultiMedia Server Manager:

- *Configuring the Media Directory* — First, you should specify where you will store your multimedia files. By default, the path to server-based multimedia files is SYS:\PUBLIC\MEDIACONTENT (as shown in Figure 3.12).

You can specify a different default media directory in the Server Settings form within the Server Preferences configuration button of NetWare Multi-Media Server Manager. Simply specify a new directory in the Multimedia File Path field and click Save to continue. Finally, make sure that users have public access rights to the multimedia directory. Don't forget to restart the MultiMedia Server in order for these changes to take effect.

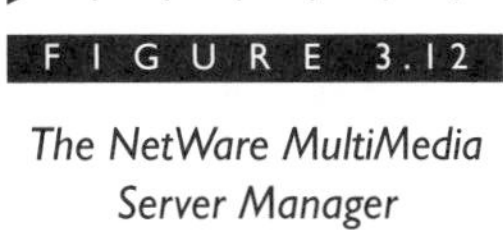

FIGURE 3.12

The NetWare MultiMedia Server Manager

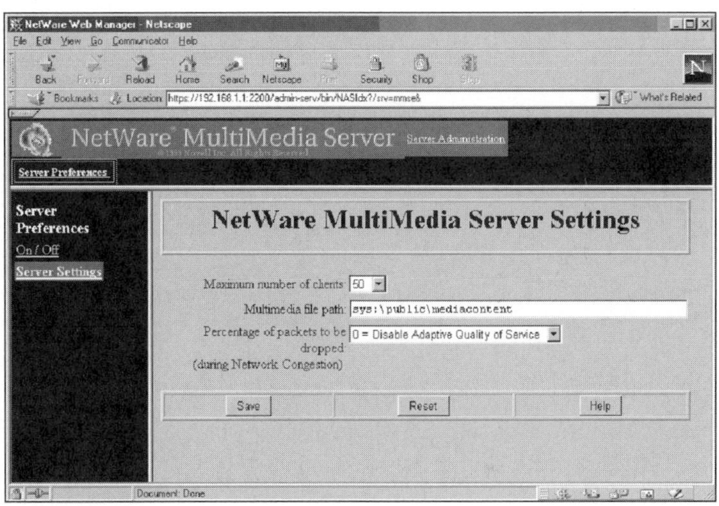

- *Setting Quality of Service* — For optimum performance, the NetWare MultiMedia Server uses a feature called *Adaptive QoS*. The primary function of Adaptive QoS is to adjust the required bandwidth depending on network conditions. If the bandwidth available to a workstation is less than the required bandwidth, QoS regulates the multimedia data being transferred so that congestion minimally affects the performance of the multimedia files being played. The Adaptive QoS value indicates the number of data packets to be dropped while sending files to the clients. A value of 0 disables Adaptive QoS (as shown in Figure 3.12), while a value of 100 indicates that streaming is optimized to maintain the quality of service at the workstation when network traffic is high. Once again, you can configure Adaptive QoS by using the server settings form within Server Preferences. Don't forget to restart the MultiMedia Server in order for your changes to take effect.

That completes our discussion of the NetWare MultiMedia Server. As you can see, this Internet component adds a powerful level of media streaming to the NetWare 5.1 Enterprise Server. Even though this service spices up your Web site with more interactive content, you should be cautious about using the NetWare MultiMedia Server because it places a bandwidth burden on client and server communications.

The NetWare Web Search Server

The NetWare Web Search Server is a powerful customizable search and print service that allows you to index information on your NetWare 5.1 file server or Enterprise Web server. These indexes allow users to effectively search for and print content from multiple collections of information.

With NetWare Web Search Server you can perform the following tasks:

- Print large collections of dispersed but related files as a single, coherently organized document.
- Search across multilanguage data collections within a single interface.
- Customize the look and feel of search and print results.
- Configure searches according to a variety of diverse information, including categories, products, chapters, languages, and files.

When you install NetWare 5.1, the contents of the NetWare 5.1 Enterprise Web Server's root directory is indexed automatically. Then you can access the default search template and run a search query on the contents of this directory by typing the following command into your browser's Location field:

```
HTTP://EnterpriseWebServer/NOVELLSEARCH
```

The NetWare Web Search Server is installed and loaded automatically when you activate your NetWare Enterprise Web Server. You can gain access to the NetWare Web Search Server Manager by clicking on the button that displays the name of your NetWare server on the NetWare Web Manager home page (as shown earlier in Figure 3.3).

You can use any of the following two methods to start and stop your NetWare Web Search Server: clicking the Off and On icons in the NetWare Web Manager home page (see Figure 3.3) or clicking the On/Off link within the Server Preferences configuration button of the NetWare Web Search Server Manager.

The following critical configuration options are available using the NetWare Web Search Manager (follow along in Figure 3.13):

- *Creating a Collection* — A *collection* is a method of referencing how directories, files, and documents will be searched. The beauty of the NetWare Web Search Server is that a collection can include files in one or more directories on one or more file servers or Enterprise Web Servers. To create a collection, select the Configuration link within NetWare Web Search Server Manager to activate the configuration form shown in Figure 3.13. Next select Define New File System Collection and click Define. Enter the collection name and the path to the files that will be searched and click OK. Repeat this process for all the collections you want to add.

- *Building an Index* — After you specify the collection of files that will be searched, you need to index those files for fast, efficient searching. Building an index involves a process known as *crawling*. The NetWare Web Search Server begins indexing files on your Web server at the directory level and then continues to index along Hypertext links until it reaches a dead end. The indexing process ends when the NetWare Web Search Server cannot find a linked file or a defined link. To build an index, select the Maintenance link and click Update. Next, define the name of your collection and click Submit. At this point, the indexing process starts and will continue for as long as is required to index all documents in your collection.

- *Customizing Search Templates* — The NetWare Web Search Server uses templates to generate search and print results, as well as process user feedback. A *template* is an HTML document containing one or more Web Search Server variables. When you perform a search on a given collection, the default Novell Search form is used. You can customize this form and extend its capabilities for your own needs. By default, the SYS:/NSEARCH/TEMPLATES directory contains eight standard templates.

Refer to Table 3.2 for a brief description and purpose of each of these templates. If you are familiar with HTML, you can quickly modify the design of any of these default Web search forms. For example, you can change the background color of the search table or the header text, and/or add graphics. In addition, you can modify the design of the default Search Results template.

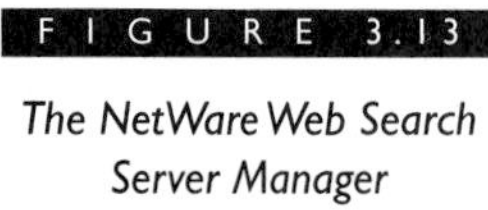

The NetWare Web Search Server Manager

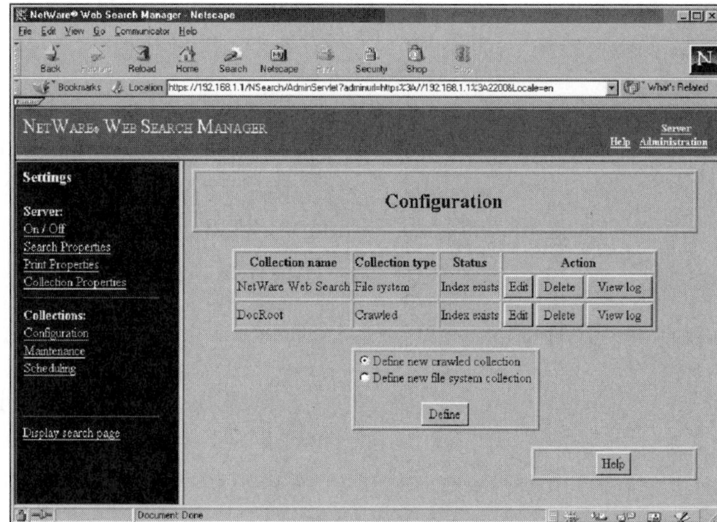

This completes our discussion of the NetWare Web Search Server. As you can see, this integrated Enterprise Server component offers a single interface for searching collections of data in multiple locations. This is a great way to pull together Web documents from all over your network.

This also completes our discussion of all the Internet infrastructure components that are integrated with NetWare 5.1. Now we will finish this chapter with a brief overview of IBM's WebSphere Application Server. This powerful Web suite can be integrated with NetWare 5.1 and NDS to extend the capabilities of your NetWare Internet into the realm of Web-based applications.

TABLE 3.2

Default Templates for the NetWare Web Search Server

TEMPLATE NAME	PURPOSE
SearchTemplate.html	Standard form for specifying what to search for. This form provides selected options used in the output of a search.
ResultListTemplate.html	Formats and organizes search results and offers additional sorting functions to the user.
ResultListNoHitsTemplate.html	Indicates when no hits were found during a search and offers users a chance to refine the search.
ResultListTerseTemplate.html	Similar to ResultListTemplate, but it returns less information, such as headings only instead of headings and text.
ResultListVerboseTemplate.html	Enables users to sort search results by relevance, title, language, date, file size, or URL.
ErrorMessageTemplate.html	Returns error messages invoked during searching.
ResponseMessageTemplate.html	Returns a specific message to the user, such as "Print job exceeds recommended size limits."
PrintResultTemplate.html	Formats and organizes search results optimized for printing. Includes a complete table of contents.

The WebSphere Application Server

The IBM WebSphere Application Server is used to build business logic and e-commerce enabled Web sites for large-scale Enterprise level networks. It incorporates the network infrastructure and foundation services that are necessary for the rapid development and deployment of applications in a network environment. More simply, it provides a run-time environment for Web-based applications.

On the Web Application Server and its internal Java Virtual Machine, applications run as a combination of servlets, server-side scripts, and Enterprise JavaBeans. These server-side components communicate with clients and other application components using HTTP. They also combine with NetWare 5.1 and NDS to provide a single point of management for interoperability with other NDS and LDAP-enabled Web applications.

The WebSphere Application Server supports Java servlets, Java Server pages, XML, Enterprise JavaBeans, transactional processing, and robust database connectivity. NetWare's integrated WebSphere Application Server comes with the following two development tools:

- *WebSphere Studio* — Used for development of Web-based content. It provides wizards, content management, content authoring, and component development.
- *Visual Age for Java* — The Enterprise addition of IBM's complete Java IDE environment for application programming.

You can install the WebSphere Application Server either during or after NetWare 5.1 installation. To install WebSphere during NetWare 5.1 installation, mark the WebSphere Application Server option when prompted for additional products. WebSphere will then be installed and the startup command will be placed in AUTOEXEC.NCF.

To install WebSphere after NetWare 5.1 installation, you can use either NWCONFIG or the NetWare GUI Install option. You can find the WebSphere Application Server product install option on the NetWare 5.1 CD-ROM.

Regardless, when you install the WebSphere Application Server, make sure the host server satisfies the following hardware and software requirements:

- *Hardware Requirements* — 200 MHz Pentium processor or faster (400 MHz recommended), 40MB free disk space, and 256MB of memory (512MB recommended).

REAL WORLD

If your server has less than 256MB of memory, you will receive a warning during installation. You must edit AUTOEXEC.NCF to disable the Web Server Start Server command before restarting the server. Once you add sufficient memory to the server, you can reenable the command and load the WebSphere Application Server.

- *Software Requirements* — NetWare 5.1 operating system, client Web browser that supports HTML 4 and cascading style sheets (such as Netscape Navigator 4.07 or later, or Internet Explorer 4.01 or later), and the NetWare Enterprise Web Server v3.51, v3.6, or later.

Once you complete the WebSphere Application Server installation, you must manually configure the WebSphere Servlet engine. This can be accomplished using the following steps:

1. First, make sure the screen resolution on the server is high enough to run the WebSphere Admin console. Select Novell ➪ Settings ➪ GUI Configuration and change the screen settings to at least 800 × 600. This resolution can also be modified using XSETUP.NCF in the SYS:SYSTEM directory.

2. Launch the WebSphere Administrator Console from the NetWare GUI. This is accomplished by selecting Novell ➪ WebSphere ➪ Administrator's Console. You can also load the console from the NetWare server command line by typing **ADMINCLIENT**. Keep in mind, the WebSphere Administrator's console requires a few minutes to load. When the message at the bottom of the screen displays "Console Ready," the Administrator console is ready.

3. Select the Topology tab and expand the WebSphere Admin Domain. Select Start to activate the WebSphere servlet engine.

4. To verify that the servlet engine is running, enter the following command at the server console:

   ```
   RUN JAVA -SHO.
   ```

   The console should display a message stating that the following servlet is running:

   ```
   COM.IBM.EJS.SM.SERVER.ManagedServer.
   ```

This completes our discussion on activating and configuring IBM's WebSphere Application Server. As we've learned, this is a mission-critical extension of NetWare's Internet infrastructure.

Congratulations! You have successfully built a comprehensive Internet infrastructure for NetWare 5.1. In this chapter, we learned how the NetWare Enterprise Web Server and FTP Server provide document publishing and file sharing over a local intranet or the global Internet. Furthermore, we explored the NetWare News Server, MultiMedia Server, and Web Search Server as extensions of this fundamental World Wide Web platform. Finally, we learned how to deliver Web-based applications using IBM's WebSphere Application Server.

Now that you have built the NetWare 5.1 server, poured the electronic pavement of TCP/IP, and cruised the World Wide Web, it's time to explore the following three advanced management topics:

- *Chapter 4, "NetWare 5.1 Advanced Server Management"* — First, we will supercharge the NetWare 5.1 server with enhanced NLMs, remote console, script files, Java, the NetWare 5.1 server-based GUI, and Storage Management Services (SMS).
- *Chapter 5, "NetWare 5.1 Advanced NDS Management"* — Then we will return to the NDS tree and explore some advanced partitioning, replication, synchronization, and maintenance topics.
- *Chapter 6, "NetWare 5.1 Advanced Security Management"* — Finally, we will experience the Novell Certificate Server firsthand and learn how to secure e-mail, Web servers, and network applications with public key cryptography.

It's time for some advanced fun. I will see you there.

LAB EXERCISE 3.1: THE NETWARE WEB

Use the hints provided to find the 20 Internet infrastructure terms hidden in this word-search puzzle. Omit any punctuation characters (such as blank spaces, hyphens, and so on) and spell out any numbers.

M U L T I M E D I A S E R V E R N

W R R W M C E T G I X S R L U M M

F A N C Y X Y V M H Z P L M W Z L

H T T P R R K P K N O N Y H F D W

R T P Y C A L H S H J F B I H I B

A D M I N E W S S E R V E R J G M

D Y B L J Y H L A S K Q W O W O I

A P P L I C A T I O N S E R V E R

P X Z U K O L Q L N V V W O F S T

T M E R V T W C T M G O I K O R P

I Z M H Q I E H S E F G E Z R E H

V W T Y V E D M M S Q V I Q R S E

E W P J T Q A F P J O H R H D W U

Q O P J U V C C O L L E C T I O N

O I X P Y Q N J F P A T O B X R N

S K O Q T R S F E I M T Y W R B L

Q P H G K B D U X G O J E R S D B

Hints

1. A feature of the NetWare MultiMedia Server that adjusts the required bandwidth of a streaming file, depending on network conditions.
2. Enterprise Server Manager button that returns you to the NetWare Web Manager's home page.
3. IBM's WebSphere and others enable you to serve applications to distributed users from a central location.

4. Client applications that convert HTML code into formatted text and graphics.
5. A group of target directories, files, and documents to be searched using the NetWare Web Search Server.
6. A method of directory-level indexing used by the NetWare Web Search Server.
7. A type of Enterprise Server directory indexing that includes a graphic representing the type of file being indexed.
8. Web-based file transfer and storage over public and private networks.
9. Web-based text files with special tags that inform graphical browsers how to format text and graphics onscreen.
10. Enables Web servers and browsers to communicate with each other over the World Wide Web using TCP/IP.
11. Enables you to stream multimedia content to client workstations by using the Real-Time Streaming Protocol and TCP/IP.
12. A central repository for public and private discussion groups.
13. A type of Enterprise Server directory indexing that only lists the files available.
14. The foundation of a "secure" NetWare Enterprise Web Server.
15. An HTML document that includes one or more searching variables and/or instructions for the NetWare Web Search Server.

See Appendix C for answers.

LAB EXERCISE 3.2: NETWARE 5.1 INTERNET

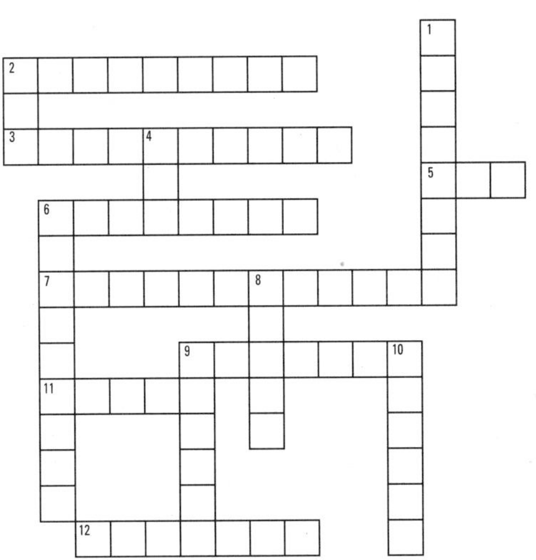

Across

2. IBM's Application Server
3. An "Enterprise" by Novell
5. A collection of ACEs
6. The biggest network on Earth
7. The Primary Document Directory
9. Deactivating the Enterprise Server at the console
11. Secure Web communications
12. Starting the NetWare Web Manager

Down

1. A private, corporate Internet
2. The "humanized" Internet
4. Hierarchy of Enterprise Server security rules
6. Default Enterprise Server index file

8. Booting the Enterprise Server from AUTOEXEC.NCF
9. Restarting the NetWare News Server at the console
10. Starting the NetWare FTP Server

See Appendix C for answers.

CHAPTER 4

NetWare 5.1 Advanced Server Management

While the world is concentrating on the Information Superhighway itself (intranets and the Internet), few people seem to be paying much attention to the vehicles that run on the superhighway. Your *server* is one of the vehicles of 21st-century networking. It provides a platform for the protons and photons as they bounce along in the fast lane at the speed of light.

As a network administrator, it is your responsibility to focus on the NetWare 5.1 server and to make sure it stays fine-tuned and in peak condition. In Chapter 1, we began our advanced administration journey by building the NetWare 5.1 server—this is your first responsibility. Then in Chapters 2 and 3, we poured the IP pavement and constructed a complete Internet infrastructure.

Now that the NetWare 5.1 server is up and running, let's shift our focus from "starting it" to "supercharging" it. It all starts with the core operating system (OS)—also known as the *NetWare kernel*. As you can see in Figure 4.1, the NetWare 5.1 kernel is only the beginning.

FIGURE 4.1

The NetWare 5.1 core OS

In summary, the NetWare 5.1 kernel offers the following features:

- *Multiprocessor Support*—Like previous versions, NetWare 5.1 supports multiple parallel processors in the server. Unlike previous versions, however, NetWare 5.1 supports single and multiple processors through the same kernel. The cool thing is, NetWare automatically detects the number of processors available in the server (the maximum is 32). In addition, the kernel is smart enough to detect and distribute processing load across multiple processors when multiple processors are available—this is known as *load balancing*. With the NetWare 5.1 multiprocessor kernel (MPK), the server can accomplish more tasks in less time.

- *Memory Protection* — NetWare 5.1 segments core OS memory into "protected" areas of server RAM. This enables you to test misbehaving applications at the server without risking a kernel crash. In addition, NetWare 5.1 supports memory protection for Java applications. We'll learn more about this in Chapter 7.

- *Virtual Memory* — NetWare 5.1 further enhances server performance by offering as much memory as you need whenever you need it. This is accomplished by using a new feature called virtual memory. Virtual memory enables NetWare 5.1 to store information temporarily on a hard drive when there is not enough physical RAM to complete a server operation. Although this slows down performance a little, it does avoid that age-old bugaboo — "insufficient memory" — or even worse — "abend." NetWare 5.1 uses an intelligent Least Recently Used (LRU) algorithm to determine which operations get moved into virtual RAM. This approach ensures that memory swapping is completely transparent to server applications. Refer to Chapter 7 for more details.

- *Preemptive Scheduling* — Finally, the NetWare kernel enables you to manage the amount of time each application uses the server processor(s). This gives you total control over high-priority and mission-critical operations. Furthermore, NetWare 5.1 uses preemption to take control of processors instantly — regardless of the state of the currently running application.

NetWare 5.1 administrators have a variety of options when it comes to supercharging the server. In this chapter, we will discover many of the most interesting options — including console commands, NetWare Loadable Modules (NLMs), server configuration files, remote console, server protection, Java, Novell Storage Services (NSS), and Storage Management Services (SMS). Here's a quick preview:

- *Using the Server Console* — Life at the NetWare 5.1 server begins at the colon (:) prompt. This interface is where you begin your supercharging duties. To help you, the colon prompt accepts two different kinds of commands — console commands and NLMs. Most text-based management duties are accomplished by using NLM utilities, such as MONITOR.NLM (shown in Figure 4.2).

As you can see from the figure, the C-worthy text interface offers limited functionality. Fortunately, NetWare 5.1 expands server management with GUI-based Java tools.

FIGURE 4.2

Text-based screen of MONITOR.NLM

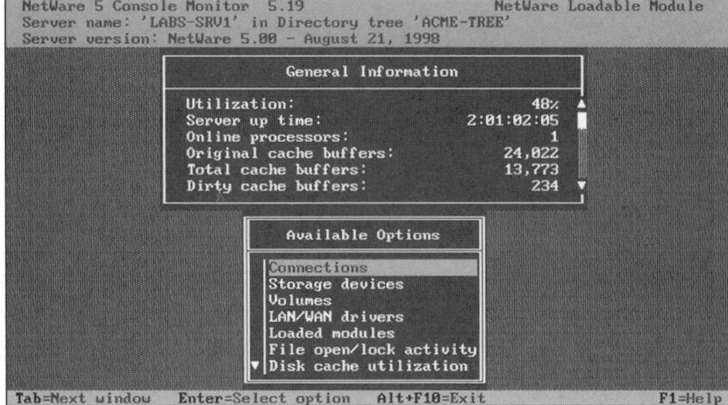

- *Java Support for NetWare 5.1* — Welcome to the world of Java. Java represents a quantum leap in server modularity. It's an exciting new application-building tool that enables developers to create truly portable and modular NetWare 5.1 server applications. Check out the new GUI console management interface offered by ConsoleOne (as shown in Figure 4.3).
- *NetWare 5.1 GUI* — When you load Java and GUI support on the NetWare 5.1 server, the GUI background automatically activates. NetWare 5.1 GUI is a native Novell Java environment that enables you to perform basic server-management tasks at the console. In this chapter, we will learn how to launch applets from a GUI console. We will also explore a native Novell Java application, ConsoleOne, which is a console GUI tool for advanced server-management tasks and NDS administration.
- *Novell Storage Services (NSS)* — The NetWare 5.1 file system includes a powerful new high-performance file storage and access technology known as Novell Storage Services (NSS). NSS is an optional file system that operates independently of, yet is fully compatible with, the default NetWare file system. In this chapter, we will expand your traditional file system management capabilities into the advanced realm of Novell Storage Services.

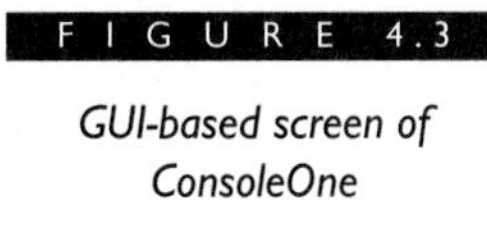

FIGURE 4.3

GUI-based screen of ConsoleOne

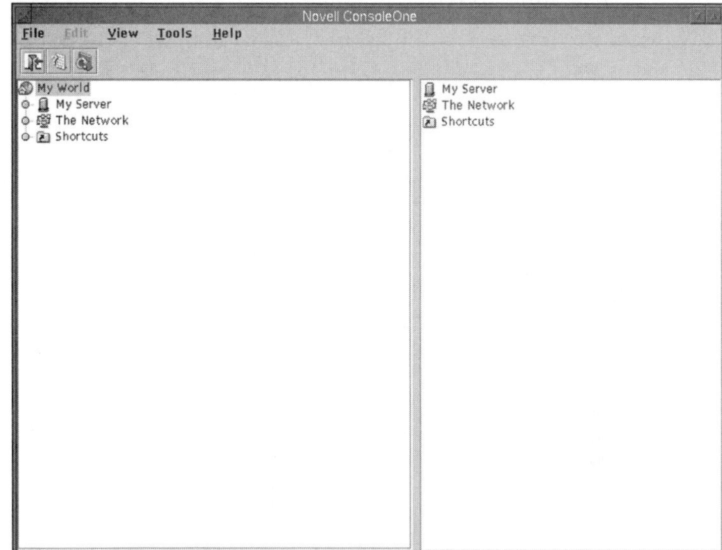

- *Storage Management Services (SMS)* — Finally, we will learn how to back up your NetWare 5.1 server using Storage Management Services (SMS). SMS is a NetWare 5.1 backup engine that provides data storage and retrieval from various front-end applications to numerous back-end storage devices.

So, that's all it takes to supercharge your NetWare 5.1 server. Let's begin with the server console.

Using the Server Console

A *NetWare server* is a computer that is running any version of the NetWare operating system. Typically, NetWare 5.1 runs on a computer containing an Intel Pentium processor. Interestingly, NetWare 5.1 is loaded on a server by executing a file called SERVER.EXE from the server's DOS partition.

The NetWare 5.1 server console provides a rudimentary interface for all of your advanced management duties. In this chapter, we will explore four management features offered by the NetWare 5.1 server console:

- *The NetWare 5.1 Operating System* — It all begins at the colon (:) prompt. The colon (:) prompt is the server console. This is where you'll spend most of your server-management time. The colon prompt accepts two kinds of NetWare 5.1 server commands: console commands and NLM load commands. NetWare 5.1 includes numerous console commands for various server management and maintenance tasks (including NDS management, time synchronization, Bindery Services, sending messages, activating NLMs, server protection, and network optimization). This chapter explores a few of the most interesting NetWare 5.1 console commands and provides some hints on how to use them. In addition, there are four basic types of NLMs: disk drivers, LAN drivers, name space modules, and NLM utilities (including management utilities and server enhancements).

- *Server Configuration Files* — In addition, you can take server console management one step further with server configuration files. These NetWare "batch files" enable you to automate common server tasks, such as loading disk drivers, binding LAN drivers, activating name space, setting time synchronization parameters, and mounting volumes.

- *Remote Console* — The Remote Console feature enables you to manage the server console from anywhere in the world. Remote Console will quickly become the cornerstone of your daily server maintenance schedule. Of course, it's hard to maintain the server when it's chained up and locked away in a hidden closet. Fortunately, Remote Console enables you to access the server from any distributed workstation.

- *Server Protection* — Finally, we will learn how to protect our precious NetWare 5.1 server. Server protection includes locking up the physical server machine, preventing access to the keyboard with SCRSAVER.NLM, using the SECURE CONSOLE command, and adding a password for remote console.

Let's start with an overview of the NetWare 5.1 Operating System.

The NetWare 5.1 Operating System

The NetWare operating system is modular. It is composed of many components that work together to provide network services. In this section, we will discuss the following three components:

- NetWare kernel
- Server console
- NetWare Loadable Modules

The NetWare Kernel

In an operating system, a *kernel* is typically defined as the basis or core of the operating system. In other words, the kernel is the portion of the operating system that is responsible for essential tasks such as allocating system resources; maintaining the date/time; managing memory, files, and peripheral devices; and launching applications.

As you can see in Figure 4.4, the NetWare kernel provides a central platform for running server applications, such as NetWare Loadable Modules (NLMs). Additional functions that are provided by the NetWare kernel include multiprocessor support, virtual memory, memory protection, load balancing, scheduling, and preemption.

The *server console* is the tool that interfaces with the NetWare kernel. It provides a command prompt where console commands can be executed and NLMs can be loaded and unloaded. NetWare 5.1 also provides a Java-based GUI interface, called the NetWare GUI, which is loaded by default. You can toggle between the various console screens, including the command prompt and the NetWare GUI, by pressing Alt+Esc. You can perform the following tasks at the NetWare server console: shut down and restart the server, edit configuration and batch files, set server configuration parameters, add/remove name space from server volumes, load and unload programs, view network traffic, and send messages.

FIGURE 4.4

NetWare 5.1 kernel and NLMs

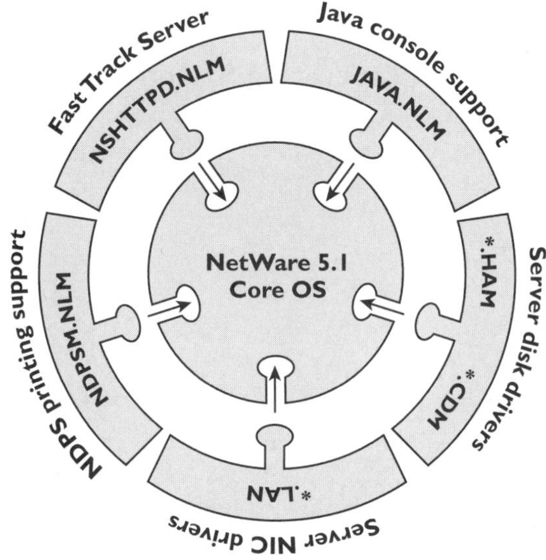

The Server Console

NetWare 5.1 supports a variety of hot-key sequences that enable you to navigate and troubleshoot the server console, such as the following:

- *Ctrl+Esc* — This key sequence displays the Current Screens menu, which lists active NLM screens. To switch to a particular screen, type the corresponding menu number and press Enter.
- *Alt+Esc* — This key sequence enables you to toggle quickly between active NLM screens.
- *Ctrl+Alt+Esc* — This key sequence displays the Hung Console screen, which enables you to safely bring down the server or cancel a volume mount.

Console commands are command line utilities that are built into the NetWare 5.1 kernel and that are executed at the server console. They enable you to perform a variety of server-management maintenance tasks, including NDS management, time synchronization, Bindery Services, NLM activation, server protection, network optimization, and sending messages.

The syntax of console commands is relatively straightforward. To execute a console command, simply type the command at the server console prompt and press Enter. For example, to obtain detailed help for a particular console command, type the following:

```
HELP console_command
```

The following are five important NetWare 5.1 console commands:

- *BIND*—The BIND command is used to link a communications protocol to a network board and its LAN driver. After a LAN driver is loaded, a BIND command must be issued to activate LAN communications. The default NetWare 5.1 communications protocols are TCP/IP and IPX.
- *CONFIG*—The CONFIG command displays general server information, as well as hardware information relating to internal communications components, such as network boards.
- *DOWN*—The DOWN command performs an orderly shutdown of server activity and closes open files. Before DOWN deactivates the server, it performs various tasks, including clearing all cache buffers and writing them to disk, closing open files, updating appropriate directory and file allocation tables, dismounting volumes, clearing connections, and closing the operating system.
- *LOAD/UNLOAD*—The LOAD command is used to activate an NLM and to link it to the operating system. The UNLOAD command is used to terminate an NLM and to free valuable server resources, such as server RAM. (**Note:** In NetWare 5.1, the LOAD command is typically optional, because in most cases you can load an NLM at the server console prompt by simply entering the name of the NLM and pressing Enter.)
- *SET*—The SET command is used to view and customize operating system parameters. To configure a SET parameter, use the following syntax: SET *parameter = value*. Or you can view all available SET categories by simply typing **SET** at the server console. (**Note:** You can also change SET commands with MONITOR.NLM, which provides a menu interface.)

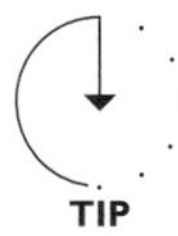
TIP

Console commands are internal operating system tools that are similar to DOS's internal commands. They are built into SERVER. EXE just like CD or CLS is built into COMMAND.COM.

NetWare Loadable Modules (NLMs)

NLMs are modular software programs that provide additional functionality and services to the NetWare server (see Figure 4.4). NLMs have the following advantages: they free up server RAM by enabling network administrators to remove unneeded modules, they can typically be loaded and unloaded without bringing down the server, and they provide an easy method for third-party developers to write their own modules.

NetWare 5.1 supports many different types of NLMs, including the following:

- *Disk Drivers* — Disk drivers control communication between the NetWare 5.1 operating system and storage devices (such as hard disks or CD-ROMs). Typically, you can load and unload disk drivers with the server running. NetWare 5.1 supports disk drivers that meet the Novell Peripheral Architecture (NPA) standard. NPA drivers consist of two types of components: a Host Adapter Module (.HAM) (which controls the host bus adapter), and a Custom Device Module (.CDM) driver (which controls hardware devices that are attached to the host bus adapter). NetWare 5.1 does not support the .DSK drivers found in earlier versions of NetWare.

- *LAN Drivers* — LAN drivers control communication between the NetWare operating system and network boards. Typically, you can load and unload LAN drivers with the server running. When you load a LAN driver, you must specify the appropriate hardware configuration information (such as interrupt, port address, memory address, and frame type).

- *Name Space Modules* — Name space modules allow files that follow non-DOS naming conventions to be stored on a NetWare volume. Name space modules have a .NAM filename extension and are stored in the SYS:SYSTEM directory along with other NLMs. Name space modules supported by NetWare 5.1 include MAC.NAM (Macintosh), LONG.NAM (Windows 95/98, Windows NT/2000, and OS/2), and NFS.NAM (UNIX).

In addition to loading name space NLMs, you must use the following console command to activate the new file system: ADD NAMESPACE.

- *NLM Utilities* — NLM utilities help you install, manage, maintain, troubleshoot, and optimize a NetWare 5.1 server. Some of the most popular NLM utilities are MONITOR, NWCONFIG, PSERVER, and JAVA.

This completes our brief discussion of NetWare 5.1 console commands and NLMs. In this section, we learned about the core NetWare kernel and its powerful built-in console commands. In addition, we further empowered the server engine with some modular NLMs. Now let's learn how to automate server management with server "batch" files.

REAL WORLD

NLMs can be activated at the server console in one of two ways: by simply typing the name of the module (followed by Enter) or by using the LOAD command as described in the previous section. By default, NetWare assumes that you're running NLMs from the SYS:SYSTEM directory. Similarly, you can deactivate server NLMs gracefully (using the Exit command within the NLM menu) or forcefully (using the UNLOAD command). It's nice to have so many choices!

Server Configuration Files

NetWare enables you to automate a variety of server-management tasks using NetWare Configuration Files (.NCFs). These files are similar to DOS batch files, except that they contain commands that are specific to a NetWare server. To activate one, simply type its name at the server console prompt and press Enter.

You can create server configuration files using NWCONFIG.NLM, EDIT.NLM, or an ASCII text editor. By default, EDIT.NLM (1) assumes that server configuration files are stored in SYS:SYSTEM, (2) does not automatically add an extension (which means you will manually need to add .NCF), and (3) can also be used to edit text files on the DOS partition.

During server startup, the following files are executed in the order shown:

1. *AUTOEXEC.BAT* — Executes SERVER.EXE.

2. *SERVER.EXE* — Loads the NetWare operating system and executes the commands in STARTUP.NCF.

3. *STARTUP.NCF* — Executes critical server startup commands (such as loading disk drivers, activating name space modules, and configuring SET parameters). Refer to Figure 4.5 for a sample STARTUP.NCF file. By default, this file is stored in the C:\NWSERVER directory on the server's DOS partition. If you prefer to use an alternate STARTUP.NCF file, use the following command:

   ```
   SERVER -S=<batchfile.NCF>
   ```

   If desired, you can also activate the server without a STARTUP.NCF file with this command:

   ```
   SERVER -NS
   ```

FIGURE 4.5

Editing the server STARTUP.NCF configuration file

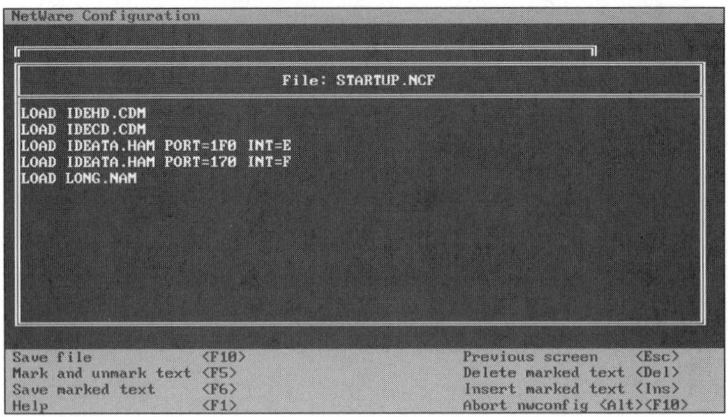

4. *AUTOEXEC.NCF* — Completes the server startup process. This file includes information such as time zone instructions, bindery context information, NetWare server name, Server ID, commands to load and to bind LAN driver(s), calls to other .NCF files, and so on (see Figure 4.6). By default, this file is stored in the SYS:SYSTEM directory on the NetWare partition. You can activate the server without an AUTOEXEC.NCF file using the following command:

```
SERVER -NA
```

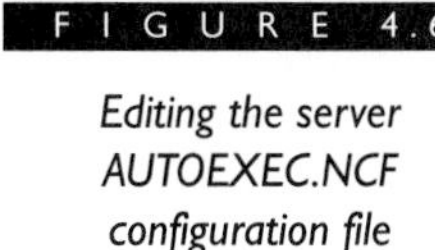

FIGURE 4.6

Editing the server AUTOEXEC.NCF configuration file

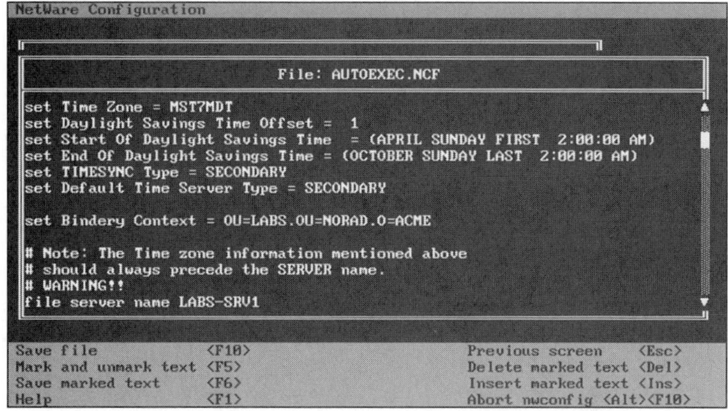

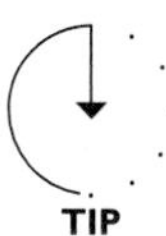

TIP

You'll notice that the STARTUP.NCF and AUTOEXEC.NCF files are stored in two different locations. The STARTUP.NCF file is stored in the C:\NWSERVER directory on the DOS partition, and the AUTOEXEC.NCF file is stored in the SYS:SYSTEM directory on the NetWare 5.1 partition. This is because the NetWare 5.1 partition isn't available until the disk driver is loaded.

This completes our discussion of NetWare 5.1 server batch files. Now let's learn how to manage them remotely.

Using Remote Console

NetWare 5.1 supports remote access to text-based server console screens using the architecture illustrated in Figure 4.7. As you can see in the figure, Remote

Console supports access from both a local workstation and a remote modem. In either case, it consists of two main components:

- *Remote NLMS* — The Remote Console server NLMs are broken into two functions: REMOTE and connection services. The REMOTE.NLM module manages information exchange to and from the workstation and the server. In addition, REMOTE.NLM enables you to specify a Remote Console password. Connection services are a little bit trickier. When you access Remote Console from a direct workstation, connection services are provided by RSPX.NLM. On the other hand, when you access Remote Console from an asynchronous modem, RS232.NLM and AIO.NLM provide connection services.
- *RCONSOLE Programs* — Remote console supports one text-based utility (RCONSOLE.EXE) and one Java-based utility (RConsoleJ).

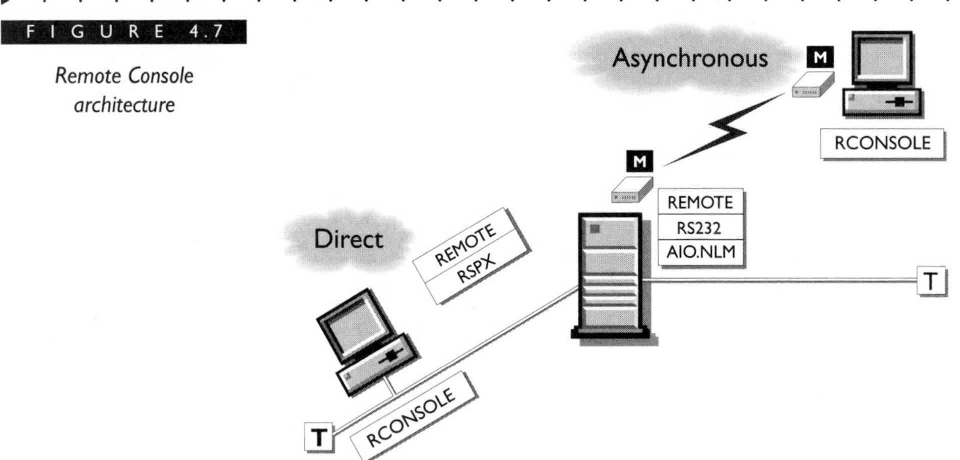

FIGURE 4.7
Remote Console architecture

Let's take a closer look at each of these two Remote Console approaches.

RConsoleJ

RConsoleJ provides remote access to text-based server console screens over an IP connection. You can only access a remote server if it has the RConsole agent (RCONAG6.NLM) loaded. RCONAG6.NLM sets the remote password, TCP port, and SPX port used to gain access to the remote server.

RConsoleJ supports remote access from a NetWare 5.1 server or a Novell Client on a Java, Windows 95/98, or Windows NT workstation using TCP/IP.

- *RConsoleJ at the Server* — Choose "RConsoleJ" from within ConsoleOne.
- *RConsoleJ at the Workstation* — Choose either "Pure IP Remote Console" from the Tools menu in NetWare Administrator or run SYS:PUBLIC\RCONJ.EXE.

Remote Console

This utility can be accessed from a remote workstation using either RCONSOLE.EXE or the Tools menu of NetWare Administrator. It provides remote access to text-based server screens from a Novell Client using SPX (a direct connection) or a modem (an Asynchronous connection). The required NLMs you must load at the target server in each configuration are as follows:

- *SPX Direct Connection* — To establish a direct remote connection, load the following two NLMs on the target server: REMOTE.NLM and RSPX.NLM. REMOTE manages the information exchange between a workstation and the server and enables you to specify a Remote Console password. RSPX provides communications support and advertises the server's availability to the network.
- *Asynchronous Connection* — To establish an asynchronous remote connection, load the following three NLMs at the target server: REMOTE.NLM, RS232.NLM, and AIO.NLM. As we discussed earlier, REMOTE manages the information exchange between a workstation and the server, and it enables you to specify a Remote Console password. RS232 and AIO initialize the server modem port and transfer screen and keystroke information to REMOTE.

Once you establish an RCONSOLE session, you can perform text-based server tasks at the remote workstation as if you were physically seated at the target server. In addition, you can perform various special RCONSOLE tasks, including the following:

- Changing screens
- Scanning server directories
- Transferring files to the server
- Switching to the DOS prompt

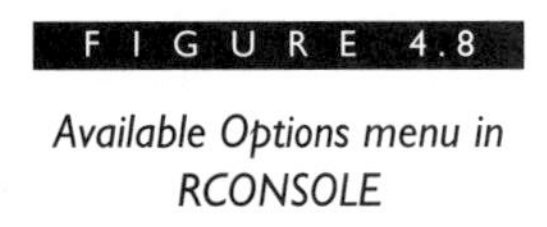

These advanced server-management tasks are accomplished using the Remote Console Available Options menu (which can be activated by pressing Alt+F1). Refer to Figure 4.8 for an illustration of the Available Options menu in RCONSOLE.

FIGURE 4.8

Available Options menu in RCONSOLE

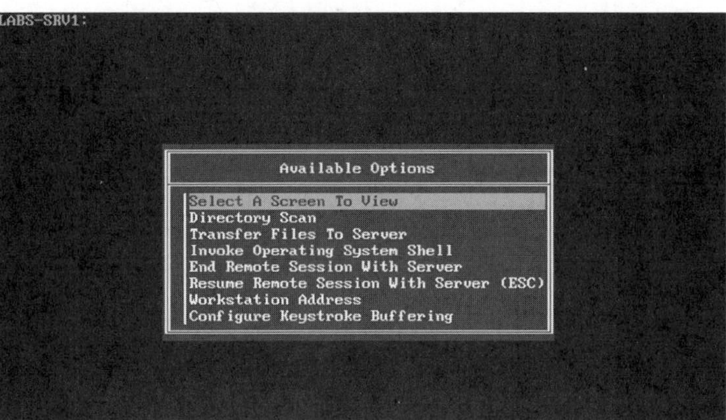

Refer to Table 4.1 for a list of NetWare 5.1 RCONSOLE function keys.

TABLE 4.1
NetWare 5.1 RCONSOLE Function Keys

KEYS	TASK
Alt+F1	View the Remote Console Available Options menu
Alt+F2	Exit RCONSOLE
Alt+F3	Move forward through active server console screens; similar to using Alt+Esc at the server console itself
Alt+F4	Move backward through active server console screens
Alt+F5	Show your workstation address
F1	Display remote console help from within the Available Options menu
Esc	Resume the remote session with the server

REAL WORLD

Understand the capabilities of both remote console connectivity strategies: RConsoleJ (using IP) and RCONSOLE (SPX direct or asynchronous using a modem). Also, know the two methods for executing RConsoleJ (namely, at a server or workstation using ConsoleOne or at a workstation using SYS:PUBLIC\RCONJ.EXE).

Protecting the Server Console

NetWare 5.1 has an elaborate security system that protects NDS and the file system from unauthorized access. This system does nothing, however, to protect the physical server console itself. Following are four strategies that can protect the server console:

- *Limit Physical Access* — The first step in protecting the server console is to physically limit access to the server hardware. This is accomplished in three easy steps: (1) lock the server in a secure, well-ventilated, air-conditioned wiring closet or other restricted room, (2) remove the server keyboard, and (3) remove the server monitor.

- *SCRSAVER.NLM Locking*—You can use the SCRSAVER.NLM screensaver utility to "lock" the server console and prevent unauthorized keyboard entry. When a key is pressed on the server keyboard, the user is prompted to authenticate as an NDS user to gain access to the server console prompt. To view the many security-based features supported by this utility, type: `SCRSAVER HELP`.

- *SECURE CONSOLE*—To further enhance server protection, you can use the SECURE CONSOLE command. This command prevents unauthorized users from loading NLMs outside of the SYS:SYSTEM directory, disables keyboard entry into the NetWare 5.1 operating system debugger, and prevents the server date and time from being changed.

- *REMOTE.NLM*—The final server protection strategy involves restricting access via the Remote Console utility. When you activate REMOTE.NLM at the target server console, you can specify a password by typing the following syntax at the server console (replace "password" with an alphanumeric password):

  ```
  LOAD REMOTE password
  ```

- Furthermore, you can encrypt the REMOTE password using LDREMOTE. (**Note:** You can accomplish this same level of Remote Console security by using the RCONAG6 ENCRYPT command and by placing the newly created LDRCONAG6 command in the server's AUTOEXEC.NCF file.

Well, there you have it—the tools of a great NetWare 5.1 server administrator. Now let's expand the NetWare 5.1 server and embrace the GUI console. This is server management the "warm and fuzzy" way.

Java Support for NetWare 5.1

NetWare 5.1 extends the traditional text-based server console with integrated support for Java applets and applications. In fact, the new Java-based graphical user interface (called the *NetWare GUI*) is loaded at the server console by default. You can also manually load and unload the NetWare GUI, if desired.

Typically, Java applications requiring a GUI are written using the Java Abstract Windowing Toolkit (AWT). NetWare 5.1 also supports Java applications that are developed using the Java Foundation Class.

Java Hardware Requirements

A NetWare 5.1 server must meet the following minimum requirements to run Java applications that use a GUI interface:

- *Memory Requirements* — A NetWare 5.1 server should have at least 128MB of RAM to run Java programs
- *Mouse Support* — During NetWare 5.1 installation, you can configure a server-based pointing device. The NetWare GUI supports either a PS/2 or serial mouse that conforms to the Microsoft standard. If your server does not have a mouse, the GUI interface can also be configured during NetWare 5.1 installation to work with the numerical keypad on the server's keyboard.
- *Video Support* — The NetWare GUI supports Industry Standard Architecture (ISA), Extended Industry Standard Architecture (EISA), and Peripheral Component Interconnect (PCI) video cards. Novell recommends using a PCI video card that conforms to the Video Electronics Standard Association (VESA) 1.2 or greater specification. If your video card conforms to the VESA 1.2 specification, NetWare 5.1 loads a VESA video driver using the default setting of 640 × 480 resolution with 256 colors. If your video card does not meet the VESA 1.2 specification, NetWare 5.1 loads a default video driver that supports 640 × 480 resolution with 16 colors. The VESA video driver also supports greater resolutions, but the resolutions must be configured manually. This is accomplished using the Display Properties tab within the Tools menu of the NetWare GUI.

When you install NetWare 5.1 on your server, NetWare attempts to automatically detect your server mouse and video hardware and loads the appropriate drivers. If you change your video card or mouse, you must execute the SYS:\JAVA\NWGFX\VESA_RSP.NCF configuration file to have NetWare 5.1 attempt to redetect this hardware and load the proper drivers.

Running Java Applications

NetWare 5.1 supports Java applications in one of two forms:

- *Java Classes* — Fully functioning applications written in Java.
- *Java Applets* — Java programs written to run within a Java-compatible browser.

JAVA.NLM is used to provide Java support on a NetWare 5.1 server. This NLM is part of the JavaSoft Java Virtual Machine that provides an interpreter platform for executing Java classes and applets.

By default, a file named STARTX.NCF automatically launches from the AUTOEXEC.NCF file whenever the server is started. This file, in turn, loads JAVA.NLM, mouse and video drivers, and the NetWare GUI.

Java support can be dynamically loaded and unloaded on the server, if desired. To load the Java Virtual Machine (JVM) manually on the NetWare 5.1 server, enter the following at the server console prompt:

```
JAVA
```

To view the runtime options available when running a Java application, enter the following at the console prompt:

```
JAVA -help
```

When you execute a Java application at the server console, remember two important rules: Java class names are case sensitive, and Java classes require LONG name space support (which NetWare 5.1 loads by default on the SYS: volume using LONG.NAM).

If JAVA.NLM is loaded on your server, the APPLET command can be used to launch an applet viewer. You can use this viewer to run Java applets that have been defined as part of a Hypertext Markup Language (HTML) document. Following is the syntax for the APPLET command

```
APPLET [HTTP://URL or HTML_filename]
```

To define an applet in an HTML document, insert the appropriate code between `<applet>` and `</applet>` parameters. For example, the following HTML code would define an applet called Clock2.class with a width of 170 pixels and a height of 150 pixels:

```
<applet codebase="1.0.2" code="Clock2.class" width=170
height=150> </applet>
```

The APPLET console command executes only `<applet>` statements and ignores other HTML code in an HTML document. Therefore, an HTML document viewed by a Java-enabled browser will look different from an HTML document run by using the APPLET console command.

Java GUI Support

NetWare 5.1 Java GUI support can be dynamically loaded and unloaded at the server console. Java GUI support is loaded using the STARTX.NCF configuration file. The STARTX.NCF file loads JAVA.NLM, mouse and video drivers, and the NetWare GUI. When the NetWare GUI is loaded but not active, it consumes minimal system resources, and has no residual effect on the server when it is unloaded.

You can load Java GUI support on a NetWare 5.1 server using one of the following three methods:

- By default, STARTX.NCF launches automatically from the AUTOEXEC.NCF file during server startup.
- You can execute STARTX.NCF manually at the server console prompt by typing the following:

  ```
  STARTX.NCF
  ```

- You can load NetWare GUI support by loading a Java applet or class that requires GUI support. If GUI support is not loaded, STARTX.NCF will be launched automatically.

Java GUI support on a NetWare 5.1 server is accomplished via Novell's implementation of X-Windows. Even though Java GUI support is implemented on top of X-Windows, users and application developers cannot write programs directly to the X-Windows layer. Instead, access to the X-Server must be obtained through the Java AWT. This enables Novell to change the GUI implementation to something other than X-Windows without adversely affecting existing Java AWT applications.

REAL WORLD

The NetWare 5.1 GUI is flexible—so much so that you can customize its menu items to launch your own Java programs or applets. You can also create NetWare GUI menu items that execute NLMs. (**Note:** If an NLM is launched as a NetWare GUI menu item, the NLM runs outside the NetWare GUI and the display switches to the NLM.) To add an NLM as a menu item, simply follow these construction steps:

1. First, you'll need to use an ASCII text editor (such as the Notepad utility in Windows) to create a `menuname.menu` file (such as MONITOR.menu) in the SYS:\Java\Lib\Taskbar subdirectory.

   For example, use the following syntax to add MONITOR to the file you created:

   ```
   #This launches MONITOR

   menu "MONITOR.menu"

         item "MONITOR" command MONITOR

   endmenu
   ```

2. Close the NetWare GUI and then restart it for your changes to take effect. (**Hint:** Type **STARTX.NCF** followed by Enter at the console prompt to restart the NetWare GUI.)
3. Launch MONITOR from the Novell GUI menu.

Server Management with the NetWare 5.1 GUI

When you load Java and GUI support on the NetWare 5.1 server, the NetWare GUI is activated automatically. The NetWare GUI is a native Novell Java environment that enables you to perform basic server-management tasks at the server console. NetWare 5.1 also includes a graphical management tool (called ConsoleOne) that can be accessed via the NetWare GUI.

The NetWare GUI includes a number of integrated server utilities that can be used to perform tasks such as the following:

- Product installation
- Keyboard configuration

- Video configuration
- Background configuration

Installing Additional Products

One of the tasks that can be performed using the NetWare GUI is to install additional NetWare 5.1 products and services. Follow these simple steps:

1. In the NetWare GUI, select Novell ➪ Install. A list of currently installed products appears.
2. Click Add to install additional NetWare products. Enter the source path to the INSTALL directory on the *NetWare 5.1 Operating System* CD-ROM and then click OK.
3. In the "Additional Products and Services" window, select the product(s) that you want to install. When they are all highlighted, click Next. (Some products may prompt you for additional configuration information.)
4. A Summary window appears that lists the products to be installed. Click Customize if you want to update any of the product configuration settings.

Keyboard Configuration

If you have keyboards that support international character sets, you can use the Keyboard Properties utility to specify a unique keyboard type. Here's how it works:

1. In the NetWare GUI, select Novell ➪ Settings ➪ GUI Environment.
2. Click the Input tab.
3. From the list of available keyboards, select the keyboard type desired, click Apply, and then click OK.
4. Click Yes to restart the NetWare GUI with the new settings.

Video Configuration

If your server's video card and monitor support video resolutions greater than 640×480, you can manually configure higher resolutions with the Display Properties configuration tool. Novell recommends a video resolution of 800×600 for the NetWare GUI. Follow these steps to change the video configuration:

1. In the NetWare GUI, select Novell ➪ Settings ➪ GUI Environment.
2. When the XSetup dialog box appears, the Video Board tab should be selected by default. Click the Probe button.
3. When the Probe Warning dialog box appears, read the warning message and click Yes to continue. When the Video Card Probe Results window appears, note the video card information indicated (including manufacturer, model number, and amount of RAM) and then click OK.
4. The XSetup dialog box reappears. In the Video Board list box, click your video card. In the Resolution section, select the desired resolution from the list of available resolutions and click Test. When the first Test Mode dialog box appears, read the warning and then click OK. When the second Test Mode dialog box appears, read the warning and then click Test. If your monitor passes the test, click OK to finish.
5. When the Save Confirmation dialog box appears, click Yes to save your change. Then, when the Restart GUI dialog box appears, click Yes to restart the GUI.

Background Configuration

The NetWare GUI includes a variety of available backgrounds. In fact, you can add your own custom backgrounds to the NetWare GUI by placing the corresponding .XPM graphic files in the SYS:JAVA\NWGFX\PIXMAPS directory. These new graphics will then appear the next time you run the Background Configuration applet. To change the server GUI background, follow these simple steps:

1. In the NetWare GUI, select Novell ➪ Settings ➪ Backgrounds.

2. When the Background Configuration dialog box appears, select the desired background and then click Test. If you like what you see, click OK to finish. Otherwise, click Cancel.

So, that's everything you need to know about NetWare 5.1 support for Java applications at the server. Okay, now that you're a Java configuration pro, let's take a close look at NetWare 5.1's hottest Java GUI environment — ConsoleOne.

But before you start reading the next section, be sure to take a java break — you deserve it.

LAB EXERCISE 4.1: RUNNING JAVA APPLICATIONS ON THE NETWARE 5.1 SERVER

Welcome to the world of Java! In this exercise, you will get a chance to explore the GUI world of NetWare 5.1 server modularity.

First we'll practice some simple configuration options, such as GUI background and video resolution. Then we'll learn how to activate the NetWare 5.1 GUI environment using STARTX. Next, we'll see how to install additional products and services using Java. Finally, we'll add a menu item to the NetWare GUI Tools menu.

Here's a quick preview of the tasks you'll perform in this exercise:

- *Step 1:* Change the NetWare GUI background
- *Step 2:* Modify the server video resolution
- *Step 3:* Install additional products and services
- *Step 4:* Add a menu option to the NetWare GUI menu

The following hardware is required for this exercise:

- A NetWare 5.1 server
- A mouse (the electronic kind)

To run Java, you'll need a Video Graphics Array (VGA) compatible video card and a server-attached mouse. Assuming that you're all set, let's get started.

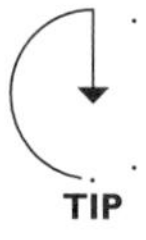
TIP

You may find that Java programs run more slowly on your server than other programs, such as NLMs. Therefore, if you select a menu option in a NetWare GUI menu and nothing seems to happen—just wait a moment, and the desired screen should appear. Don't forget that Novell recommends 128MB of server RAM if you plan to run Java programs on the server.

Perform the following steps at your NetWare 5.1 server console:

1. Change the NetWare GUI background.

a. On your server console, ensure that the NetWare GUI screen is displayed. (It's the screen with the Novell button in the lower-left corner.) If the NetWare GUI screen is not displayed, press Alt+Esc until it is.

b. On the NetWare GUI screen, click Novell ➪ Settings ➪ Backgrounds.

c. Follow these steps when the Background Configuration dialog box appears:

- Click PEBBLES.XPM and then click Test.
- Click RICEPAPER.XPM and then click Test.
- Scroll down, click MINI-NOVELL.XPM, and then click Test.
- Click Cancel to retain the original background and exit the Background Configuration window.

2. Modify the server video resolution.

a. On the NetWare GUI screen, click Novell ➪ Settings ➪ GUI Environment.

b. When the XSetup dialog box appears, the Video Board tab should be selected by default. Click Probe.

c. When the Probe Warning dialog box appears, read the warning message and click Yes to continue.

d. When the Video Card Probe Results window appears, note the video card information indicated (including manufacturer, model number, and amount of RAM) and then click OK.

e. Follow these steps when the XSetup dialog box reappears:

- In the Video Board list box, click your video card.
- In the Resolution section, select the highest resolution supported on your server from the list of available resolutions. Click Test to display the test pattern at the new resolution for ten seconds.

f. When the first Test Mode dialog box appears, read the warning and then click OK.

g. When the second Test Mode dialog box appears, read the warning and then click Test.

h. **Note:** Normally, if your monitor passed the test, you would click OK and then Yes to save your changes, and then click Yes to restart the GUI. In this case, however, click Cancel to revert to the previous resolution setting.

3. Install additional products and services.

   a. On the NetWare GUI screen, click Novell ⇨ Install.

   b. When the Installed Products dialog box appears, a list of installed products, including version numbers, will be displayed. Note that you can click Add to install additional NetWare 5.1 products and services. However, do *not* install any additional products or services at this time.

   c. Click Close to exit the Installed Products dialog box.

4. Add a menu option to the NetWare GUI menu.

   a. Create a menu file.

      - On your workstation, launch the Windows Notepad utility by selecting Start ⇨ Programs ⇨ Accessories ⇨ Notepad.
      - When the Notepad window appears, enter the following:

```
#This launches MONITOR

menu "MONITOR.MENU"

item "MONITOR" command MONITOR

endmenu
```

      - Save the file as SYS:\JAVA\LIB\TASKBAR\MONITOR.MENU. (**Note:** If you can't locate the TASKBAR subdirectory, it's probably because you are accidentally looking in C:\JAVA\LIB instead of SYS:\JAVA\LIB.)

   b. Restart the NetWare GUI.

      - On the NetWare GUI screen, click Novell ⇨ Close.
      - When the Close GUI dialog box appears, click Yes.

- At the server console prompt, type the following and then press Enter:

```
STARTX
```

c. Launch MONITOR.

- When the NetWare GUI screen reappears, click Novell ➪ MONITOR to launch MONITOR.
- **Note:** If MONITOR does not appear in the menu, check to see if you accidentally saved the MONITOR.MENU file with a .TXT filename extension.

Server and NDS Management with ConsoleOne

ConsoleOne is a Java-based graphical utility that enables you to perform basic server management and NDS administration tasks. ConsoleOne can be activated at the NetWare 5.1 server in one of three ways:

1. Load the C1START.NCF file from a server console prompt.

2. Load the C1START.NCF file from an NCF file (such as AUTOEXEC.NCF).

3. Launch ConsoleOne from the NetWare GUI.

If you execute the C1START.NCF file, it loads Java and GUI support prior to launching the ConsoleOne utility. Once ConsoleOne has been activated, it displays a GUI browser screen similar to the one in Figure 4.9. As you can see, ConsoleOne resembles a typical workstation-based GUI Explorer utility. The left window pane enables you to browse objects, while the right sidedisplays the contents of the object being browsed.

The ConsoleOne interface enables developers to add custom object types that can be browsed or managed from the server. To expand or collapse a container in the object tree, simply double-click a container object on the left side of the screen or click the dot next to the container object.

The ConsoleOne GUI browser relies on a variety of different object types:

- *My World* — The highest-level object in the ConsoleOne browser screen. By default, the My World object contains The Network object.

- *Container Objects* — NDS container objects (such as Organization and Organizational Unit objects) appear as browsable container objects in ConsoleOne. File system volumes and subdirectories are also browsable.

- *Leaf Objects* — These NDS objects represent physical or logical network resources.

Let's get GUI with ConsoleOne.

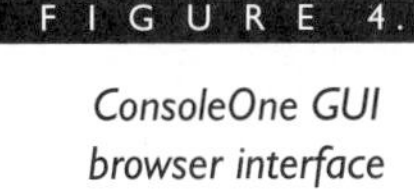

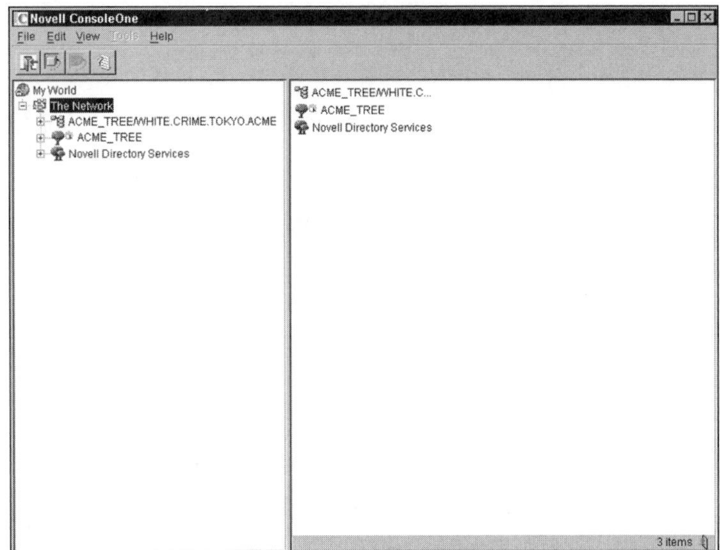

ConsoleOne GUI browser interface

Accessing Local and Remote Server Consoles

The RConsoleJ utility can be accessed via the Tools menu in ConsoleOne. RConsoleJ enables you to access text-based server console screens on *remote* NetWare servers. You can also use RConsoleJ to access server console screens on your *local* server.

Interestingly, although this utility is GUI-based, it only allows you to access text-based (that is, nongraphical) server console screens, such as the server console prompt and NLM screens.

Loading the Remote Console Agent (RCONAG6.NLM)

The RConsoleJ utility can only be used to access text-based server console screens on a server that has the RCONAG6.NLM Remote Console Agent loaded. This agent sets the server password, TCP port, and SPX port using the following syntax (default values are shown):

```
LOAD RCONAG6 <password> 2034 16800
```

This statement is automatically added to a server's AUTOEXEC.NCF file during NetWare 5.1 installation. However, by default, it is commented out with a semicolon (;). To activate a target server for local or remote access, you must remove the semicolon from the beginning of this statement in the server's AUTOEXEC.NCF file and reboot the server. Don't forget to change the password in the statement from `<password>` to a *real* password. (Alternately, you could also execute the command manually if you don't want to restart the server.)

Accessing Remote Server Consoles Using RConsoleJ

To launch RConsoleJ, perform the following steps:

1. In ConsoleOne, highlight the server you want to access.
2. Select Tools ➪ Remote Console.
3. In the Novell RConsoleJ window, connect to the target server either directly or through a proxy. To authenticate to a server, you must know the target server's IP address and password. The password is the one that was defined when you loaded RCONAG6.NLM on that server. (**Note:** The password is case sensitive.)

For security reasons, the remote server does not display RConsoleJ navigation screens unless both server screens are synchronized. This is accomplished by switching the remote server to the local screen or by clicking the synchronize button in RConsoleJ.

Managing the Server File System

ConsoleOne enables you to manage your local server's file system under The Network object. Some of the tasks you can perform include navigating the file system, creating a file, renaming a file, deleting a file, and copying a file. You can also view and change volume statistics, modify file attributes, and control disk-space allocation.

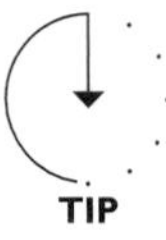

Remember that the Tools menu provides access to a Java program called RConsoleJ for accessing remote text-based server console screens. Also, remember that RCONAG6.NLM must be loaded on a server before its server console can be accessed by RConsoleJ.

Administering NDS

In addition to server management, ConsoleOne also enables you to administer NDS from your server console. The Network object displays all NDS trees discovered on your network. This enables you to administer all the NDS trees listed from a single GUI screen. When you expand an NDS tree, ConsoleOne provides you with an authentication login window if you are not already authenticated to that tree (see Figure 4.10).

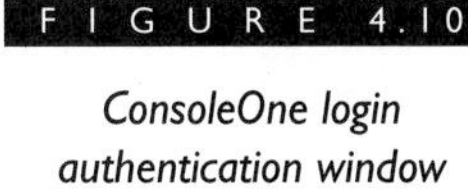

FIGURE 4.10

ConsoleOne login authentication window

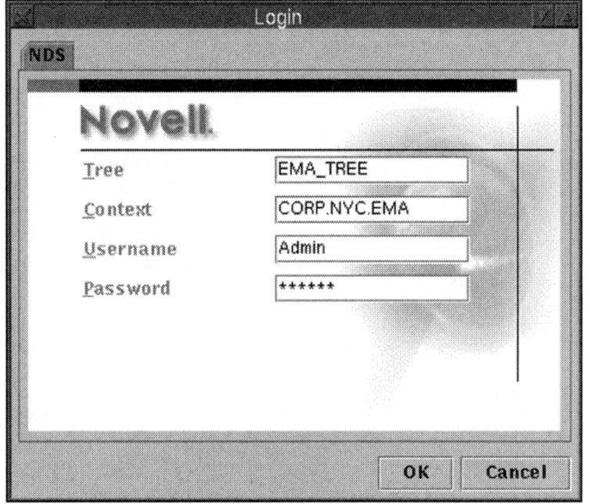

After you have been authenticated, you can create and manage NDS objects for that tree using ConsoleOne:

- *Creating NDS Objects* — ConsoleOne supports the creation of most types of NDS container and leaf objects. You can create any of these objects using the File menu. Simply click New and highlight the NDS object type desired. This Java utility was designed to partially duplicate the functionality of your favorite workstation-based tool: NetWare Administrator.
- *Managing NDS Objects* — ConsoleOne also enables you to manage existing NDS objects from the server console. To do this, simply browse to the object's home container in the left window pane and then right-click the object you want to administer in the right window pane. When you do this, a pop-up menu appears. Click Properties to display details for the NDS object selected.

For example, in Figure 4.11, we're managing the Identification property tab of the Admin User object. Once you've made your modifications, click Apply to save your changes.

FIGURE 4.11

Managing the Admin User object in ConsoleOne

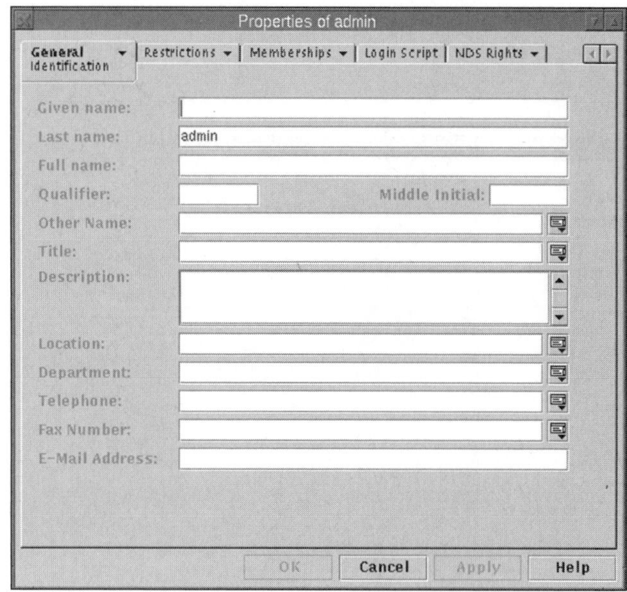

This completes our romp through NetWare 5.1's sophisticated server-based GUI tool, ConsoleOne. This advanced utility enables you to execute most of your NetWare server and NDS management tasks . . . all from the comfort of your very own Java-based console.

Now let's continue our advanced server-management studies with a look at NetWare 5.1's new-and-improved file system: Novell Storage Services (NSS).

LAB EXERCISE 4.2: SERVER AND NDS MANAGEMENT WITH CONSOLEONE

As you've learned in this chapter, Java is a GUI environment for launching server-based applications. One of the most powerful NetWare 5.1 Java applications is ConsoleOne. ConsoleOne is an advanced server-management tool for console-based access to ACME's NDS tree.

Once ConsoleOne is alive, you'll notice that it resembles a typical workstation-based GUI Explorer tool. The left window pane enables you to browse objects, and the right pane displays the contents of the highlighted icon.

In this exercise, you will learn to use ConsoleOne to perform the following types of tasks:

- Server administration tasks
- NDS administration tasks

The hardware required for this exercise is a NetWare 5.1 server.

Now let's explore Java-based GUI management at the CRIME-SRV1 server in TOKYO. Remember, ConsoleOne is your friend.

Ready, set, click!

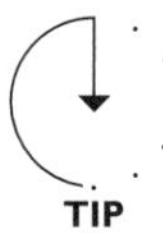
TIP

You may find that Java programs run more slowly on your server than other programs, such as NLMs. Therefore, if you click an object in ConsoleOne and nothing seems to happen, just wait a moment, and the desired screen should appear. If not, try scrolling or resizing the window.

Part I: Server Administration Tasks

First, let's see what ConsoleOne can do for us at the server front. In this section, we will learn how to launch ConsoleOne, edit configuration files, use the Console Manager, and activate remote server management. (**Note:** For best performance, the server version of ConsoleOne should be run on a server with a fast processor and much RAM.)

Perform the following tasks on your server console. Follow the bouncing ball.

1. Launch ConsoleOne.

   a. On the NetWare GUI screen, click Novell ⇨ ConsoleOne.

   b. Log into the network as Admin.

   c. Follow these steps when the ConsoleOne screen appears:

      - Click the Maximize button in the upper-right corner of the window to maximize the window.

      - Use the mouse cursor to resize the left pane by dragging the vertical bar (which separates the left pane and right pane) to the right a bit. This provides a better view of the objects in the left pane.

Part II: NDS Administration Tasks

Now that you're a ConsoleOne pro with the CRIME-SRV1 server in TOKYO, let's increase the stakes a little and attack the large ACME tree. In this section, we'll expand our management scope beyond the single server and learn how to create NDS users and to modify user configurations using ConsoleOne.

Here's how it works:

1. Create an NDS User object using ConsoleOne.

   a. Follow these steps to navigate to the WHITE container:

      - In the left pane, click the dot to the left of The Network.

      - In the left pane, click the dot to the left of ACME-TREE.

      - In the left pane, click the dot to the left of ACME.

      - In the left pane, click the dot to the left of TOKYO.

      - In the left pane, click CRIME.

      - In the right pane, click WHITE.

   b. Click File ⇨ New ⇨ User.

   c. Follow these steps when the New User dialog box appears:

      - Type the following in the Name field:

        `SHolmes`

- Type the following in the Surname field:

  `Holmes`

- Click OK.

d. When the Create Authenticate Secrets window appears, provide a new password for the SHolmes User object:

- Type the following in the New Password field:

  `ACME`

- Type the following in the Confirm New Password field:

  `ACME`

- Click OK.

2. Modify an NDS User object using ConsoleOne.

a. In the right pane, double-click WHITE to expand it.

b. Scroll to find the SHolmes object and then right-click it.

c. Select Properties from the pop-up menu that appears.

d. When the "Properties of SHolmes" window appears, click the triangle on the Restrictions tab and then select Login Restrictions from the drop-down list.

e. Follow these steps when the Login Restrictions window appears:

- Mark the "Account Has Expiration Date" checkbox.
- Click the Date/Time icon to the right of the "Expiration Date and Time" field.

f. When the "Date and Time" window appears, change the expiration date to 12:01 a.m. of today's date one year from now. (In other words, if today is May 3, 2010, you would change the expiration date to May 3, 2011, at 12:01 a.m.) Follow these steps to change the expiration date:

- Select the appropriate year using the up arrow and down arrow to the right of the Year field.

- Use the single arrows and double arrows to the left and right of the Time field to change the time to 12:01 AM. (Double arrows change the hour; single arrows change the minutes.)
- Click OK to exit the "Select Date and Time" window.

g. Follow these steps when the SHolmes Properties dialog box reappears:

- Click Apply.
- Click Close.

h. Follow these steps to exit ConsoleOne:

- Click ConsoleOne in the taskbar to return to the main ConsoleOne screen.
- Click File to display the File menu; then click Exit.

Bingo! You're a ConsoleOne pro. Now run out there and attack the Java-based NetWare 5.1 server with new confidence and vigor.

Novell Storage Services (NSS)

The NetWare 5.1 file system includes a powerful new high-performance file storage and access technology knows as Novell Storage Services (NSS). As a network administrator, you need to be well versed in both traditional and NSS file system management. In *Novell's CNA Study Guide for NetWare 5.1*, we explored the fundamental architecture of Novell's traditional file system. In this chapter, we expand those management capabilities into the advanced realm of Novell Storage Services.

NSS is an optional file system that operates independently of, yet is fully compatible with, the default NetWare file system. As you can see in Table 4.2, NSS was developed to meet the anticipated storage needs of the next decade. Table 4.2 compares the key NSS improvements to NetWare 5.1's traditional default file system. Take a quick look.

TABLE 4.2

Comparing NetWare 5.1's Two File Systems: Traditional Versus NSS

SPECIFICATION	TRADITIONAL FILE SYSTEM	NSS FILE SYSTEM
Maximum file size	2GB	8TB
Directory entries	16 million	Trillions
Volume mounting performance	Several minutes	Several seconds
NetWare partitions per disk	One	Four
Volumes per partition	Eight	Unlimited
CD-ROM Support	Additional drivers	Integrated

Unfortunately, there's a downside to this wonderful story. With all its power, NSS cannot fully replace the traditional NetWare 5.1 file system. Here are a few reasons why:

- NSS cannot currently create its own SYS: volume.
- NSS does not support the Transaction-Tracking System (TTS), software-based disk striping, disk mirroring, Hierarchical Storage Management (HSM), or Real Time Data Migration (RTDM).

- NSS does not support file compression.
- NSS does not support VREPAIR (it uses REBUILD and VERIFY instead).

Future versions of NSS will address many of these limitations. Despite these current limitations, you may want to create one or more NSS volumes on your NetWare 5.1 server in addition to the traditional file system. This will provide you with the advantage of high storage capacity and increased data-access performance.

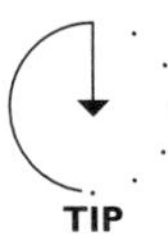
TIP

Although CD-ROMs are automatically mounted as NSS volumes, they're not automatically added to the NDS tree. CD-ROM volumes can be created easily as Volume objects in the NDS tree by using NetWare Administrator or ConsoleOne.

In this section, we will study NSS installation, configuration, and management in depth. But first, let's study the fundamental architecture of NSS Storage Groups and NSS volumes.

Understanding NSS Architecture

NSS was designed to make use of storage space regardless of its location. To accomplish this, Novell has added additional abstraction layers to file system management. Fundamentally, the NSS architecture consists of the following two objects:

- *NSS Storage Groups* — NSS scans for free space on all devices attached to a server. Free space is deposited in a pool called an *NSS Object Bank*. The Object Bank is an overall term for all available file system components that can be mapped to an NSS volume. Within the Object Bank are a variety of hard drive (or other media) partitions called *storage deposits*. Storage deposits are effectively free space. NSS gathers free space from unpartitioned areas of a hard disk or available free space inside an existing NetWare volume. When NSS takes free space out of a NetWare volume, the traditional file system acknowledges the reduction in free space and identifies the NSS volume as a file. When NSS claims ownership of a storage deposit in the NSS Object Bank, that deposit becomes a *managed object*.

These managed objects are then organized into one or more Storage Groups. An NSS Storage Group is a single object representing all logical storage space residing on one or more storage devices.

- *NSS Volumes* — Free space organized into Storage Groups resides in many physical locations. NSS combines one or more Storage Groups and organizes them into an NSS volume. Even though all available free space represented by Storage Groups does not physically reside on a given server, the NSS volume organizes this free space to behave as if it did. In other words, NSS volumes aggregate storage deposits from multiple media and from devices to behave as a traditional volume.

The NSS architecture is made up of five interface layers that work together to present multiple storage media as a single, cohesive file system to clients. The five layers are as follows (starting at the storage device and working their way to the client):

- Layer 1: Media Access Layer (MAL)
- Layer 2: Loadable Storage Subsystem (LSS)
- Layer 3: Object Engine Layer (OEL)
- Layer 4: Common Layer Interface (CLI)
- Layer 5: Semantic Agent (SA) Layer

Let's take a closer look at this NSS architecture.

Layer 1: Media Access Layer (MAL)

The MAL interface connects to and communicates with storage devices, such as hard disks and CD-ROMs. This communication enables the MAL to identify free space on storage devices. When the MAL identifies free space, the NSS Object Storage

Bank registers it as either usable or unusable. Usable free space is deposited in the Object Bank, and unusable space is ignored.

In addition, the MAL manages the storage of free space by relying on two types of storage managers:

- *Providers* — Installed with NSS and scan the server's storage devices for free space. In addition, providers locate partitions on NetWare volumes, determine whether those partitions and volumes are in use, construct storage objects, and ultimately deposit the storage objects in the Object Bank.
- *Consumers* — Configure and take ownership of the storage deposits in the Object Bank. Consumers register themselves with the bank so that they can manage any deposited storage object they own. NSS consumers cannot own NetWare partition space, but they can consume free space inside a NetWare volume.

Layer 2: Loadable Storage Subsystem (LSS)

The LSS gathers information from the MAL interface about the storage devices it scans and recognizes as usable. After LSS obtains device information from MAL, the MAL registers an existing NSS volume on those storage devices with NSS. LSS can then obtain information from MAL about the NSS volume on which data resides.

In addition, the LSS interface provides the following benefits:

- *Rapid Recovery* — The LSS maintains a log that records all volume transactions that have been written and that are waiting to be written to a disk. From that log, the LSS implements the management recovery system. This means that if a server crashes, NSS locates the disk error by referencing the log, noting the incomplete transaction, and correcting the error by reprocessing the incomplete transaction (by backing it out).
- *Modularity* — The LSS enables you to define new storage devices and plug them into the storage system whenever they are needed and without affecting other pieces of the software.

Layer 3: Object Engine Layer (OEL)

The OEL is where the Object Storage Bank is located. Because the OEL uses sophisticated and efficient mechanisms to manage the objects it stores, it provides the following benefits:

- *Performance* — Storage objects are stored on disks in balanced trees called *B-Trees*. This compact structure enables NSS to locate a storage object anywhere without loading the entire directory into memory. As a result, access time is decreased.
- *Scalability* — The OEL enables you to create larger storage objects and more of them than the traditional NetWare file system.

Layer 4: Semantic Agent (SA) Layer

The SA Layer contains loadable software modules that define how specific clients communicate with stored NSS objects. These modules can be the NetWare Operating System, Internet services, traditional file system, and so on. This means that you no longer need separate storage solutions for the various storage systems used by different platforms.

Layer 5: Common Layer Interface (CLI)

The CLI contains a set of APIs that define how the SA Layer accesses the object engine for the following NSS services:

- *Naming Services* — Include basic object naming and lookup operations, as well as name space and context management services.
- *Object Services* — Provide the creation, deletion, storage, and definition of objects.
- *Management Services* — Provide other underlying types of NSS management, such as registration, file locking, and transactions and management of storage pools as NSS volumes.

Clearly the NSS solution is much more complex than your traditional tree-based file system. The good news is that most of this architecture is transparent to users. The bad news is that network administrators need to learn much more about how to install and manage this architecture. Let's continue with a lesson in installing NSS volumes.

Installing NSS Volumes

NSS installation is much simpler than its architecture would suggest. All you have to do is design the NSS volume to identify its intended purpose and then create it.

You can load and configure NSS when installing NetWare 5.1. If you choose this option, NSS creates one NSS volume, using all or a portion of your existing unpartitioned free space. On the other hand, if you do not load and configure NSS during NetWare 5.1 installation, you will need to execute the following two steps manually:

- *Step 1:* Load and Configure NSS
- *Step 2:* Create an NSS Volume

Let's start at the beginning.

Step 1: Load and Configure NSS

You should follow the same general planning strategies for NSS volumes that apply to creating new NetWare volumes. For example, you must first determine your data size requirements. Will data files be large or small? Then you should determine if your NSS volumes will be used for long-term or short-term storage. Next, you will need to plan the scale of your NSS implementation. If you want most of your volumes in NSS, consider setting up a small SYS: volume (500MB to 1GB) on your NetWare server then create one or more NSS volumes to hold the rest of your data.

Next, consider how NSS will be integrated with your backup procedure and whether your NSS volumes will span several devices. And finally, how will your NSS volumes be organized—that is, according to department, organization, types of users, groups, and so on?

After you plan your NSS setup and are ready to load and configure NSS, you must have the following:

- A server running NetWare 5.*x*
- A minimum of 10MB of free space to create an NSS volume
- 1.5MB of RAM (300 cache buffers) for loading the modules
- 2MB of RAM (500 cache buffers) for running NSS

When you install NetWare 5.1, the NSS NLMs are copied to the SYS:SYSTEM directory by default. To load NSS, type the following command at the server console:

```
LOAD NSS
```

NSS then displays all command line options available for managing NSS at the server console. In addition, you can configure and manage NSS using one of the following two utilities:

- *NWCONFIG* — NWCONFIG offers a convenient, text-based menu system for creating and managing NetWare and NSS volumes. This functionality can be found in the Storage menu of NSS Disk Options. The Storage menu enables you to view and to prepare free space for NSS configuration. To take advantage of the NWCONFIG tools, you must authenticate to NDS with Administrator rights.
- *NSS Administration Menus* — The NSS Administration menus are presented at the server console when you load NSS with the /MENU command line option. This tool provides the following three NSS Administration menus: Configure (used to configure NSS Storage Groups and NSS volumes), View (used to view free space, NSS Storage Groups, and NSS volumes), and Utilities (used to access the REBUILD utility and a verification utility to check system integrity).

Step 2: Creating an NSS Volume

When you get ready to create an NSS volume from existing server disk space, you'll have to watch out for one particular caveat: physical hard disk space might already be allocated to existing DOS or NetWare partitions. If your server's hard disk is already fully partitioned, you have three options if you wish to use NSS:

- *In-Place Upgrade*—You may use the NSS In-Place Upgrade utility to convert existing traditional NetWare file system volumes (except SYS:) to NSS. Make sure not to convert traditional volumes that contain files using features that NSS cannot support, such as file compression, TTS-enabled files, or disk-mirrored drives.

- *RePartition*—You may repartition your server's hard drive to allow for free space. This free space will become part or all of an NSS Storage Group and NSS volume.

- *New Install*—You can always install a new hard drive into the server and devote it to NSS.

Once you have gained access to the free space you need, you can create an NSS volume using either NWCONFIG or the NSS Administration menus. However, before you can create the volume, you must identify the available free space, assign ownership of all or a portion of that free space to NSS, and then create the NSS volume.

To identify the free space available on your server and to attach devices and assign ownership of that space to NSS, use the Storage Menu within the NSS Disk Options of NWCONFIG. Then choose Update Provider Information and begin to scan for available free space by selecting MMPRV NSS Media Mgr. Provider.

To create an NSS volume using NWCONFIG, select the NSS Volume Options tool within the NSS Disk Options tool. Next, authenticate to NDS and select Create ➪ NSS Volume.

If you want to use the NSS Administration menus to create a Storage Group and one NSS volume, you can use the one-step configuration method. This choice is available by selecting the Configure ➪ Create option and then choosing One Step Configuration.

Once you have installed NSS and created one of more NSS volumes, users can take advantage of the exciting new NSS file system. Of course, this also means that you will have to learn more about how to perform some basic NSS management tasks. Let's take a closer look.

Managing Storage Groups and NSS Volumes

To manage Storage Groups and NSS volumes effectively, you must perform the following tasks in NWCONFIG or the NSS Administration menus:

- *View NSS Volumes*—You can view Storage Groups and NSS volumes in both NWCONFIG and NSS Administration menus. To view NSS components in NWCONFIG, select NSS Volume Options from the NSS Disk Options menu. Next, authenticate as Admin and choose View Volumes. This option displays the volume ID, size, and NSS volume name. To view NSS components in the NSS Administration menus, select View and choose one of the following options: Free Space or NSS Volume Information.

- *Combine Storage Groups and NSS Volumes*—You can increase the data capacity of any of your existing NSS volumes by combining a Storage Group with an existing volume. In NWCONFIG, select Modify ➪ Increase NSS Volume Size and choose an existing NSS volume. Then select an available Storage Group and confirm your decision with Yes. In the NSS Administration menus, perform the exact same procedure from the Configure menu.

- *Repair an NSS Volume*—You cannot use VREPAIR to repair an NSS volume. Instead, you must use REBUILD to salvage data and repair a broken NSS volume. REBUILD has the following advantages: it recovers data that is not corrupted, it operates much faster than VREPAIR, and it leverages the existing leaves of an object tree to rebuild all other trees in the system. It is important to note that while NSS volumes are being verified and rebuilt, they are placed in maintenance mode and must be remounted once the repair process is completed (using "NSS/VERIFY" and "MOUNT" at the server console). You can use two utilities to repair NSS volumes: the NSS Administration menus (under the Utilities option) and the "NSS/REBUILD" command at the server console.

- *Add and Remove NSS Volume Objects*—If you create an NSS volume using the NSS Administration menus, NSS won't automatically create a corresponding Volume object in NDS. You will need to use the Directory Options menu in NWCONFIG to add the new Volume object to NDS. You can use NetWare Administrator, as well. NWCONFIG, on the other hand, will automatically create an NDS Volume object during NSS volume creation as long as NDS is running at the time. Finally, you can remove NSS volumes from NDS by using NWCONFIG, NetWare Administrator, or the NSS Administration menus.

- *Release NSS Ownership*—You can return NSS-owned data objects to free space at any time using NWCONFIG or the NSS Administration menus. Deleting unneeded NSS volumes returns storage space to NetWare 5.1's traditional file system. However, the process does destroy the following NSS components: Storage Group, NSS volume, data, and NSS ownership.

This completes our jaunt through NetWare 5.1's second directory structure—Novell Storage Services (NSS). This strange new file system is different from the traditional directory structure, but once you get past its rough exterior, you will see that the nontraditional NSS file system performs most of the same data-sharing tasks as NetWare 5.1's default structure.

Now we have arrived at the final NetWare 5.1 server administration task—backup. Fortunately, you have the power of Storage Management Services (SMS) at your fingertips.

Storage Management Services

Storage Management Services (SMS) is a combination of related services that facilitate the storage and retrieval of data to and from NetWare 5.1 servers and workstations. The SMS backup process involves a host server, a target file system or NDS Directory, and a controlling workstation (see Figure 4.12):

- *Host Server*—The SMS host server is where the backup program and storage device reside. (**Note:** SMS is a *backup engine* rather than an *application*. This means that it requires a front-end backup/restore application on the host server to communicate with modules on target devices.)

You can either use the NetWare Backup/Restore software that is included with NetWare 5.1, or any third-party backup software that is SMS-compliant.

- *Target* — The SMS target is a NetWare workstation or server that contains a file system or NDS Directory that needs to be backed up. Target Service Agents (TSAs) are resident programs that run on each target server or workstation. In conjunction with an SMS-compliant backup engine, such as NetWare Backup/Restore, these agents enable data from a specific workstation or server to be backed up and restored.
- *Workstation* — The SMS workstation is a NetWare 5.1 client that provides a GUI interface for configuring the backup sessions and for submitting instructions to the host server. This workstation is normally a Windows 95/98 or Windows NT machine running the NWBACK32.EXE program.

FIGURE 4.12

NetWare 5.1 SMS architecture

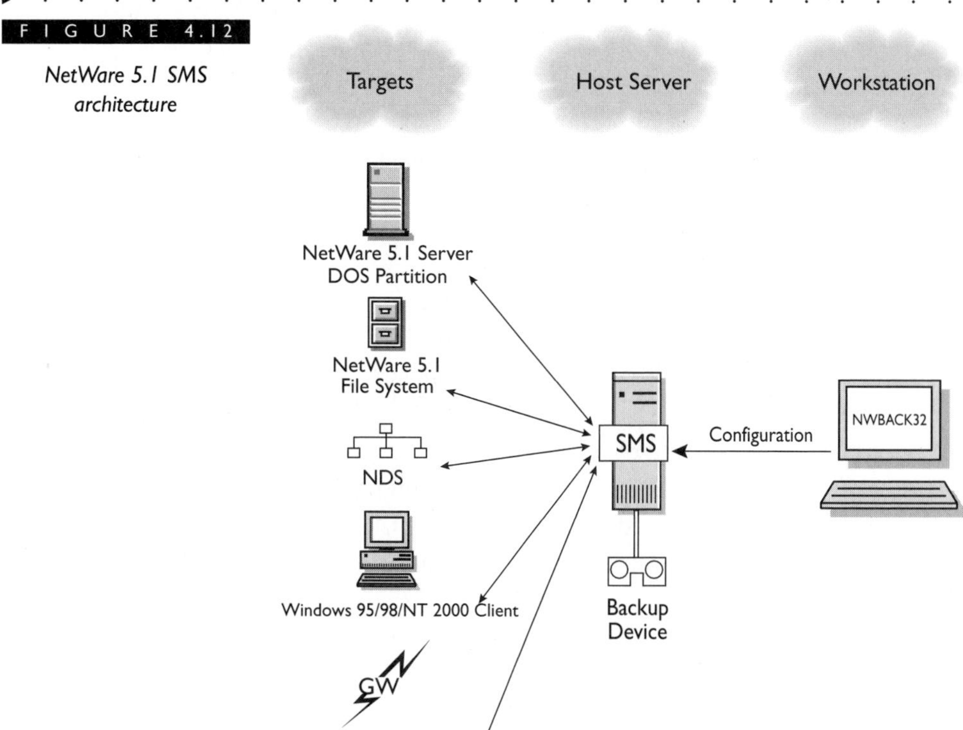

The SMS server application reads the file system or NDS Directory data from the target device (using TSA instructions) and sends it to a storage medium (such as a DOS read/write disk, tape, or optical drive). SMS supports the following types of information: NetWare 5.1 file system, NetWare 5.1 server DOS partition, NDS, Windows 95/98 and Windows NT workstation file systems, and GroupWise databases.

Choosing a Backup Strategy

NetWare Backup/Restore provides four basic strategies for backing up and restoring data (follow along in Figure 4.13):

- *Full* — The full backup option is the most thorough. During a full backup, all data is copied, regardless of when, or if, it was previously backed up. While this option is the most time-consuming, it provides fast and easy restores because you only have to restore the latest full backup. (**Note:** During a full backup, the Modify bit of each file is cleared.)

- *Incremental* — The incremental option backs up only those files that have changed since the last backup. To restore all system data, you must restore the last full backup and every incremental backup since then, in chronological order. (**Note:** During an incremental backup, the Modify bit of each file is cleared.)

- *Differential* — The differential backup strategy backs up all data that has been modified since the last full backup. This strategy often provides the best balance of efficiency and performance because it minimizes the number of restore sessions. The main improvement with the differential strategy is in the state of the Modify bit — it is not cleared. As a result, all the files that have changed since the last full backup are copied each time. (**Note:** Because the Modify bit is cleared during an incremental backup, be sure you never perform an incremental backup between differential backups.)

- *Custom* — The Custom strategy enables you to specify which files are backed up and to designate whether or not the Modify bit of each file is cleared.

FIGURE 4.13

Understanding the three main NetWare Backup/Restore strategies

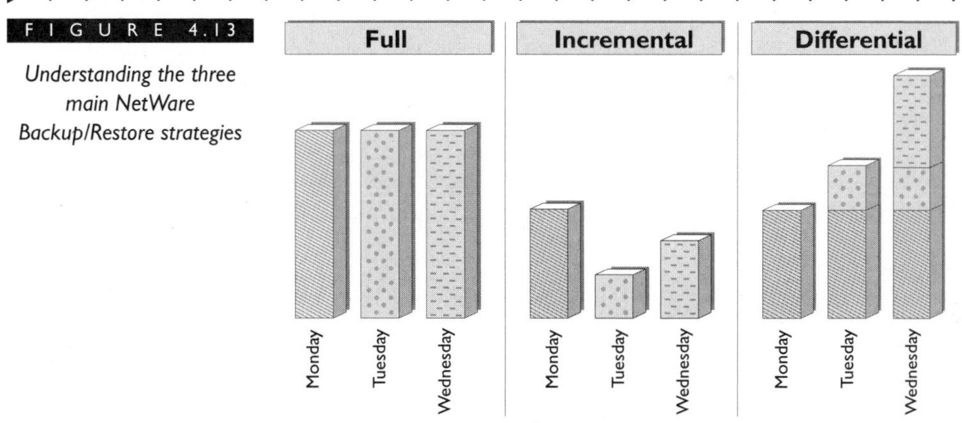

Table 4.3 shows a comparison of the three NetWare Backup/Restore strategies. You might find one of the following three combinations useful:

- Every day — Differential
- Once a week on Friday — Full
- Once a month — Custom

TABLE 4.3

Getting to Know the NWBACK32 SMS Workstation Application

BACKUP STRATEGY	BACKUP	RESTORE	MODIFY BIT
Full	Slow	Easy	Cleared
Incremental	Quick	Hard	Cleared
Differential	Kind of quick	Relatively easy	Not cleared
Custom	Whatever	Your choice	Doesn't matter

You can combine these three backup strategies into a *custom* SMS plan for your organization. Here are a few ideas:

- Full backup during every backup session
- Full backup combined with incremental backups
- Full backup combined with differential backups

When you are choosing a backup strategy, consider the time required by each method to back up the data and the time required by each method to restore the data. An efficient balance of backup and restore duration provides you with an excellent solution to NetWare 5.1 workstation and server fault tolerance.

Now that we have learned the fundamental architecture of SMS and chosen our ideal backup strategy, it's time for *action!* Let's take a closer look at SMS backup/restore procedures.

SMS Backup/Restore Procedures

To back up and restore NetWare servers and workstations, you can either use the backup software that comes with NetWare 5.1 (NetWare Backup/Restore and NWBACK32) or use a third-party program that is SMS-compliant.

NetWare Backup/Restore is a series of NLMs that run on the host NetWare server. This program processes the job, creates a session, establishes communications with distributed targets, and conducts the data backup or restore. *NWBACK32* is a Windows-based program that runs on the administrative backup/restore workstation (see Figure 4.14). NWBACK32 configures backup/restore jobs and submits them to the NetWare Backup/Restore application.

Following are some backup/restore terms you should be familiar with. A *host* is a NetWare 5.1 server that is running both the NetWare Backup/Restore software and has the backup device attached. A *target* is any NetWare 5.1 server, workstation, or service that has a TSA loaded. This is where the backup source material resides. A *TSA,* or Target Service Agent, is a program that processes data moving between a specific target and the NetWare Backup/Restore application. A *parent* is a data set that may have subordinate data sets; that is, other parents or children. In NetWare 5.1, for example, a parent would be a directory, subdirectory, or container. A *child* is a data set that has no subordinates. In NetWare 5.1, a child would be a file or a leaf object.

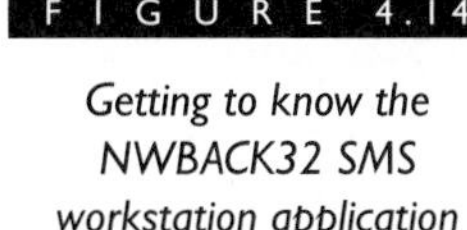

FIGURE 4.14

Getting to know the NWBACK32 SMS workstation application

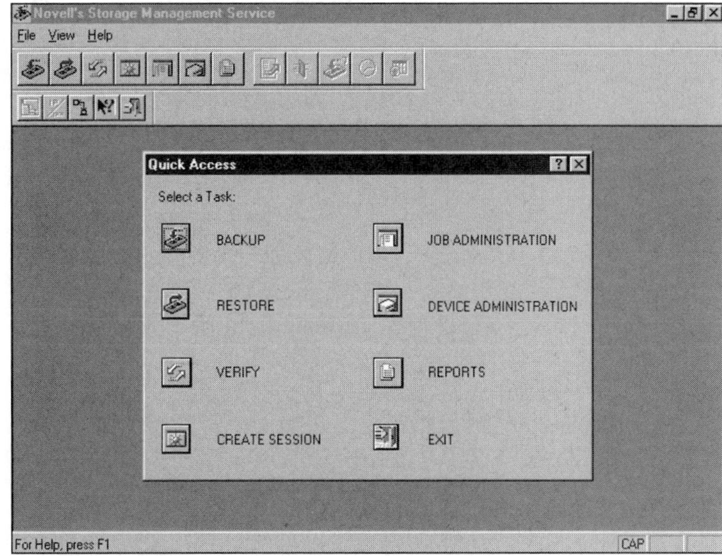

SMS Guidelines

Before performing a backup or a restore, ensure that you meet the following guidelines:

- Load the NetWare Backup/Restore software on the NetWare server on which the backup device is attached (that is, the *host*).
- Verify that you have enough disk space on the host server's SYS: volume for temporary files and log files. (1MB should be sufficient.)
- Confirm that the designated media has enough storage space. Be aware that security can be compromised if the scheduled backup session does not fit on the media. If the data does not fit, you will be prompted to insert another tape (or other medium) when the first one is full. If another medium is not inserted, the backup will not finish and the program will not terminate. To reduce this risk, set Append to "No," attend the backup so that you can insert the next tape, or use a tape loader backup device.
- Limit access to the NetWare Backup/Restore NLMs to maintain the security of your NetWare 5.1 server and to ensure data integrity.

- Remember that the error and backup log files display both the DOS-equivalent name and the name space (such as LONG, Macintosh, NFS, or OS/2) used to create the directory or file.
- Monitor the size of NetWare Backup/Restore temporary files. These temporary files may become quite large if there are extended attributes or linked UNIX files.
- Do not mount or dismount volumes or unload drivers during a backup session. You may corrupt data or abend the host server.
- The backup administrator will need Read and File Scan [RF] access rights to the directories and files that he or she plans to back up. The administrator will also need additional rights (that is, [RWCEMF]) for restoring data.
- The backup administrator will need the Browse [B] object right and Read [R] property right to the entire tree for backing up NDS information. He or she will also need the Create [C] NDS right to the tree for restoring NDS data.
- The backup administrator must know the password on all servers that act as hosts and targets. In addition, the backup administrator must know the password to a workstation if a password has been used with the target software.

TIP

Study the SMS guidelines carefully. Pay particular attention to the management of log files, name space, and SMS volumes. Also, remember the backup administrator security requirements for NDS backup ([BR]), NDS restore ([BCR]), file system backup ([RF]), and file system restore ([RWCEMF]).

NetWare 5.1 Server Backup Steps

Following are the detailed steps to back up file system or NDS data on a NetWare 5.1 server:

1. Load the tape device driver or driver interface on the host server. Make sure that a Print Queue object exists that is dedicated to and configured for backup operations.

2. Load the appropriate TSAs: *TSA500* (on the host server, to back up the host server), *TSA500* (on each target server), and/or *TSANDS* (on each NetWare 5.1 server that holds a replica of the NDS tree, to back up NDS). Keep in mind that TSAs can be loaded and unloaded as needed to conserve server RAM. If the TSAs remain on the system, SMDR is loaded when NetWare Backup/Restore is activated.

3. Load the NetWare Backup/Restore NLMs on the host server.

4. On your administrative workstation, run NWBACK32.EXE (located in SYS:\PUBLIC).

5. In NWBACK32, specify the information that will be backed up from the target server and the location where the information will be backed up. Also, select the type of backup you will perform (full, incremental, differential, or custom).

6. Set the schedule and rerun interval. Finally, complete the configuration by providing a description for the session.

7. Submit the job, insert the media, and proceed with the backup. Add tapes (or other media) as required.

Windows 95/98/NT Workstation Backup Steps

The NetWare Backup/Restore utility can also be used to back up distributed NetWare workstations. Follow these detailed steps to back up a target Windows 95/98 or Windows NT/2000 workstation:

1. At the host server, load TSAPROXY.

2. On any target Windows 95/98 workstation, load the Novell Target Service Agent for Windows 95/98. On any target Windows NT/2000 workstation, load the Novell Target Service Agent for Windows NT.

3. Load the NetWare Backup/Restore NLMs on the host server.

4. On your administrative workstation, run NWBACK32.EXE (located in SYS:\PUBLIC).

5. In NWBACK32, specify the information that will be backed up from the target server and the location where the information will be backed up. Also, select the type of backup you will perform (full, incremental, differential, or custom).

6. Set the schedule and rerun interval. Finally, complete the configuration by providing a description for the session.

7. Submit the job, insert the media, and proceed with the backup. Add tapes (or other media) as required.

Restoring Data

Follow these detailed steps to restore NDS or file system data onto target NetWare servers or workstations:

1. Load the tape device driver or driver interface on the host server.

2. Load the appropriate TSAs: *TSA500* (on the host server, to restore the host server), *TSA500* (on each target server), or *TSANDS* (on each NetWare 5.1 server that holds a replica of the NDS tree, to restore NDS). Keep in mind that TSAs can be loaded and unloaded as needed to conserve server RAM. If the TSAs remain on the system, SMDR is loaded when NetWare Backup/Restore is activated.

3. Load the NetWare Backup/Restore NLMs on the host server.

4. On your administrative workstation, run NWBACK32.EXE (located in SYS:\PUBLIC).

5. In NWBACK32, select a target server or workstation. If necessary, log in as a user with appropriate restore security (file system and NDS access rights). Keep in mind that NDS must be restored before the file system is restored.

6. Insert the media, select a restore device, and select a specific session to be restored. Next, specify the data that you want restored to the target server or workstation. Finally, set the schedule and rerun interval for the restore session.

7. Submit the job.

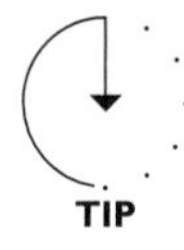

If you are restoring both NDS and the file system, NDS must be restored first.

There you have it! That wasn't so hard, was it? In this section, we explored the fundamental architecture, backup strategies, and detailed steps of NetWare 5.1 SMS backup and restore. After you have completed these procedures, you will find a certain peace of mind in knowing that your server and workstations are protected.

Vro-o-o-o-m!

In this chapter, we focused on the NetWare 5.1 server as a vehicle for cruising the Information Superhighway. We learned a little about server console management, and a lot about how to supercharge the server using Java GUI support and ConsoleOne. In addition, we explored two powerful file system and backup strategies: Novell Storage Services (NSS) and Storage Management Services (SMS).

Now what? Like I said earlier, "this is only the beginning." In the next chapter, we will continue this advanced management journey with a discussion of advanced NDS management. It's time for NDS partitioning, synchronization, and maintenance.

LAB EXERCISE 4.3: THE NETWARE 5.1 SERVER

Use the hints provided to find the 20 server-management terms hidden in this word-search puzzle. Omit any punctuation characters (such as blank spaces, hyphens, and so on) and spell out any numbers.

```
Q D D C D H C T U C T R O H S H Q
R H N M L O A D B A L A N C I N G
T S U G Y T R E F R E S H R S G W
Q A P P L E T V I E W E R F R T E
D L L T Q Q C E V E D P Q H E H J
Y P F I J M B Q C U K G I M M E G
N J A V A A P P L I C A T I O N T
A A A U M O N I T O R N L M T E G
M V M V W Y N P J M Q H D U E T X
I A D E A G S N H G G F L K C W O
C C K K S A S E V P S H R D O O T
A L J P H P P T R I T D O K N R I
L A H T M L A P B V P J W O S K F
L S R N X W R C L P E E Y E O F B
Y S X S W V F U E E F R M T L S N
O E M J P R E E M P T I O N E V E
```

Hints

1. Type of software needed to run a Java applet that has been defined as part of an HTML document.
2. Java support can be loaded and unloaded in this manner on a NetWare 5.1 server.
3. A Java applet can be defined as part of this type of document.
4. Name for Java application written to run within a Java browser.
5. Generic term for a Java applet or class.
6. Generic name for a fully functioning application written in Java.

7. NetWare 5.1 capability to detect and intelligently distribute processing across multiple processors.
8. Algorithm used for determining which operations get moved into virtual RAM.
9. Server menu utility that can be used to change set parameters.
10. NetWare 5.1 operating system software that provides support for both single and parallel processors.
11. Most server-management tasks supported by ConsoleOne are located under this object.
12. By default, this ConsoleOne object contains the My Server, The Network, and Shortcuts objects.
13. Type of module that supports the storage of non-DOS files on a NetWare 5.1 server.
14. Capability of the operating system to take control of the processor at any point, regardless of the state of applications that are currently running.
15. Click this icon to view any server consoles that have become available after Console Manager has started.
16. Feature that enables you to manage a NetWare 5.1 server console from anywhere in the world.
17. NetWare 5.1 feature that provides the ability to manage the amount of processor time used by each application.
18. Text file that defines a file, folder, or applet to be added to the ConsoleOne interface.
19. You can access NDS objects through this container object in ConsoleOne.
20. Novell recommends that you use PCI video cards that conform to Version 1.2 of this specification when using the NetWare 5.1 GUI.

See Appendix C for answers.

LAB EXERCISE 4.4: NETWARE 5.1 ADVANCED SERVER MANAGEMENT

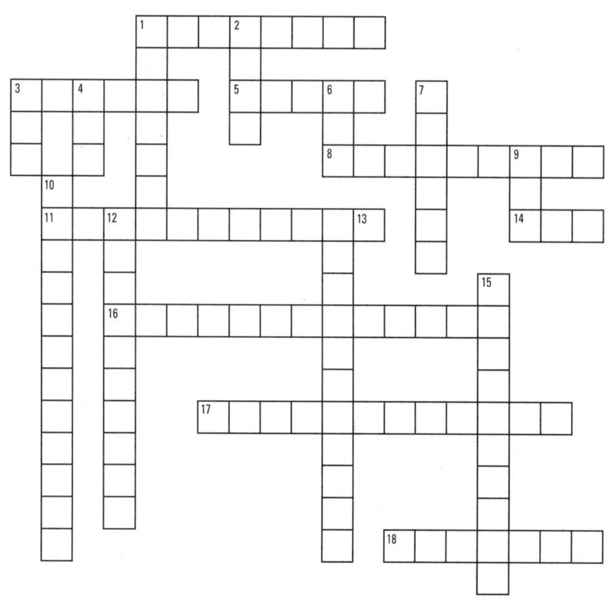

Across

1. Basis for NetWare 5.1 GUI support
3. Console command for loading Java applet viewer
5. NetWare 5.1 GUI pointing device
8. Server configuration file that loads GUI support
11. Backup technique that resets the archive bit
14. Optimization at the server console
16. Prevents server console date/time changes
17. You must do this before accessing ConsoleOne features
18. ConsoleOne file system management object

Down

1. Accessible only through Java AWT
2. Non-Java server programs
3. Development tool for Java applications
4. Recommended server video bus

6. NetWare 5.1 backup/restore engine
7. NetWare 5.1 operating system core
9. High-performance file storage technology
10. Backup technique that doesn't reset the archive bit
12. GUI-based server administrative utility
13. Contains commented-out RCONAG6.NLM line
15. NetWare 5.1 server graphical user interface

See Appendix C for answers.

CHAPTER 5

NetWare 5.1 Advanced NDS Management

Welcome back to the NDS eDirectory!

Novell's CNA Study Guide for NetWare 5.1 introduced you to a beautiful, powerful NDS eDirectory. Now you are back for more. In this chapter, we are going to build on your fundamental eDirectory skills and explore advanced NDS management. This involves the following two topics:

1. *NDS Partitioning and Replication* — The first step in building an NDS maintenance plan is partitioning fundamentals. In addition, you must understand how to scatter partitions throughout the WAN using replication. NDS replication serves two purposes: fault tolerance and resource accessibility. Finally, you must learn how NDS replicas communicate, also known as NDS synchronization management.

2. *NDS Maintenance* — In the "NDS Maintenance" section of this chapter, we will explore the heart of your NDS maintenance plan, including NDS preventative maintenance, troubleshooting NDS inconsistencies, repairing NDS, removing a server from the network, and recovering from a database crash.

So, there you have it — your future as an advanced eDirectory engineer. Advanced NDS management is important business, and today we're going to learn all about it.

Understanding NDS Partitioning and Replication

NetWare 5.1's NDS eDirectory is the world's leading directory service. It provides a unifying, cross-platform infrastructure for managing, securing, accessing, and developing all major components of your network. In fact, NDS scales to the largest network environment, including the Internet. And, because it is based on the X.500 standard, NDS supports LDAP, HTTP, and the Java programming environment.

Following is a brief description of the key network benefits offered by NetWare 5.1's NDS eDirectory:

- *Network Administration* — NDS simplifies network administration by using objects to represent any network resource, including physical devices, such as routers, switches, printers, and fax machines; software, such as databases and applications; and volumes in the network file system. Furthermore, you can move individual objects, groups, or entire branches of the NDS tree to different locations by using a simple drag-and-drop method. Finally, NDS network administration supports both centralized and distributed network control.
- *Network Performance* — NDS integrates entire enterprise network systems, consolidating company data into a single database. In addition, NDS enables multiple operating systems to run as if they were designed to work together.
- *Network Security* — With NDS authorization, authentication, and access control services, you can manage and secure the relationships and interactions between objects. In addition, NDS supports RSA encryption.
- *Network Availability* — NDS has a reliable track record spanning over 7 years and well over 30 million users. NDS is renowned for its ability to prevent downtime by allowing network information to be stored and to be updated on multiple systems, including the 24 × 7 requirements of today's large telecommunications and government agencies.
- *Scalability* — In NDS, User objects have the same network view and login procedure, whether they are logging in from their location workstation or from a different country. In addition, the NDS Schema is extensible, so you can add any resource you need for network management or user accessibility. Finally, NDS supports rapid network growth through server migration, tree merging, and container scalability.

The NetWare 5.1 NDS eDirectory includes a segmentation strategy known as NDS partitioning. *Partitioning* breaks up an NDS tree into two or more logical divisions that can be separated and distributed, which makes dealing with NDS objects more manageable. Furthermore, copies of partitions can be distributed on multiple file servers in a strategy known as *replication*. NDS replicas increase network performance (by decreasing the size of database files and by placing them closest to the users who need them) and increase fault tolerance (because extra copies of the database are distributed throughout the network).

In this lesson, we will review the fundamentals of NDS partitioning, replication, and synchronization in preparation for the five main tasks of NDS maintenance. Remember, a well-maintained NDS tree leads to a well-functioning network.

NDS Partitioning Overview

To fully understand partitioning and replication, you need to be aware of the following Directory characteristics:

- The database contains data on all objects in the Directory tree, including object names, object security rights, and object property values. All network information, except server file systems, is stored in the Directory.
- NDS uses the Directory for access control to other objects in the network. NDS checks the Directory to make sure that you can view, manipulate, create, or delete resource objects.
- NDS uses the Directory for authentication (an important part of logging in).
- Except for Server and Volume objects, the Directory does not contain information about the file system.

As you can see in Figure 5.1, NDS partitioning has been used to break up the ACME organization into three pieces:

- *Partition A* — Known as the *[Root] partition* because it is the only one that contains the [Root] object.

- *Partition B* — Known as the *LABS partition* because OU=LABS is the highest container object in the partition. In addition, Partition B is termed a *parent* of Partition C because the LABS Organizational Unit contains the R&D Organizational Unit.
- *Partition C* — Known as the *R&D partition* because OU=R&D is the highest container object in the partition. In addition, Partition C is termed a *child* of Partition B because the R&D Organizational Unit is located in the LABS container.

FIGURE 5.1

ACME partitioning and replication

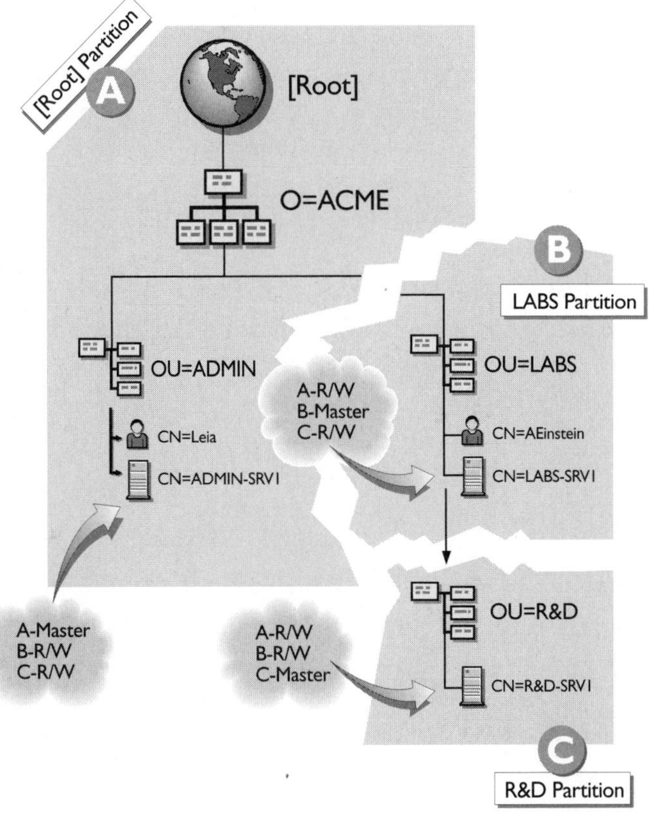

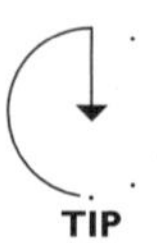

Keep in mind, though, that size and number of partitions can significantly affect the synchronization and responsiveness of your network. Avoid creating partitions that are too large (greater than 3,500 objects) or with too many copies (more than 10) because host servers can take too long to synchronize, and managing replicas becomes more complex. On the other hand, avoid partitions that are too small (fewer than 100 objects). If a partition contains only a few objects, the access and fault-tolerance benefits may not be worth the time you invest in managing the partition.

NDS Replication Overview

Partitioning has many advantages, because it enables you to separate the NDS tree into smaller segments. You can also increase network fault tolerance by placing copies of other partitions on local servers. This is known as *replication,* and network administrators can increase efficiency by placing a replica of the partition most frequently needed by users on a server that is geographically close to the users.

NetWare 5.1 supports four types of NDS replicas:

- *Master*—A Master replica is the original read/write copy of a partition that is created by default when you define the partition. A Master replica contains a complete copy of the object data for the partition. Each partition may have only one Master replica. A Master replica can perform original requests for partition and object changes. If you want to redefine a partition boundary or join it with another, you must have access to the server that holds the Master replica.

- *Read/Write*—A Read/Write replica is a read/write copy of a partition that contains a complete copy of the object data for the partition. Each partition can have multiple Read/Write replicas. When you modify objects in a Read/Write or Master replica, those changes are propagated to all other replicas of the same partition. This process, known as *replica synchronization*, creates background traffic over network communication lines. Finally, a Read/Write replica can fill original requests for object changes, but it passes all partition change requests to the Master replica. It cannot handle changes to partition boundaries—that requires a Master replica.

- *Read-Only* — A Read-Only replica is a read-only copy of a partition that contains a complete copy of the object data for the partition. These replicas are only used for searching the NDS tree and viewing objects. They cannot handle original change requests, which means they cannot be used for login authentication. Instead, they pass on all such requests to Read/Write and Master replicas.
- *Subordinate References* — Subordinate References are a special type of replica that are created and maintained by NDS. They do not contain object data — they point to replicas that do, which facilitates tree connectivity.

Read/Write replicas are the most popular replicas. Master replicas are created automatically during partitioning, and Subordinate References flourish throughout the tree as needed. Read-Only replicas, however, can be effective if you have many servers and few containers.

NDS Synchronization Management

Because NDS is a distributed, replicated database, NetWare 5.1 servers continually share information and synchronize changes with each other. In addition, the NDS database is loosely consistent. Therefore, it requires time for replication and synchronization when major changes occur. The amount of time required for a change to be replicated and synchronized depends on the type of change, the size of the partition, and the number of servers the partition is replicated on. Therefore, you should not assume that delays in replication and synchronization or that an occasional Unknown object necessarily indicate problems in the database.

Figure 5.1 illustrates a simple, saturated replication scheme. As you can see, each server has a copy of each partition. This provides exceptional fault tolerance and accessibility, but synchronization may be a problem. In large environments, this scheme would not be practical because of synchronization delays. Replica updates take place automatically at specific intervals.

Some updates (such as changing a user's password) are immediate (within ten seconds). Other updates (such as login updates) are synchronized every five minutes. Changes made to Figure 5.1, for example, would generate 27 replica updates — that's 3^3. This is manageable. But consider what background traffic would look like with 50 servers and 20 different partitions — that is 9,536,743, 164,062,000,000,000,000,000,000,000 updates every few minutes.

NDS synchronization is accomplished within a group of servers known as a *replica ring*. A replica ring is an internal system group that includes all servers that contain replicas of a given partition. In Figure 5.1, the replica ring for Partition A includes the following:

- *Master*: CN=ADMIN-SRV1
- *R/W*: CN=LABS-SRV1
- *R/W*: CN=R&D-SRV1

NDS synchronization works differently for simple and complex changes. *Simple* changes, such as changing a user's phone number, occur almost instantaneously because the replica information already exists on the affected servers, and only the modified information is sent to servers containing a replica that includes the User object.

Creating a partition is another example of a simple NDS change. When you create a partition, the system uses partition attributes to "draw" the new boundary of the partition. In this case, the replica information needed already exists on the affected servers.

Complex changes take more time. For example, joining two partitions on different servers will take time to synchronize throughout the network. During this process, NDS initiates a chain reaction of three synchronization events:

1. NDS determines where all the replicas of each partition (called the *replica ring*) are stored.

2. NDS replicates the data of both partitions to all servers in the replica ring.

3. NDS completes the merge, at which point the affected servers have the composite information of both partitions.

NDS may have a problem synchronizing between IP-Only and IPX-Only networks because direct communications between servers is not normally allowed.

To resolve this, NetWare 5.1 includes *transitive synchronization*. Transitive synchronization eliminates the requirement that all servers in a replica ring have to communicate and have to synchronize directly. Instead, target servers receive NDS updates through an intermediary server that uses both IP and IPX. Also, if the source server's replica is more recent than the target server's replica, the source server does not need to receive synchronization updates from the target server. This reduces synchronization traffic.

As NDS synchronizes partition replicas, it creates network traffic. If this traffic crosses WAN links unmanaged, it can increase costs and it can overload slow WAN links during high-use periods. Fortunately, NetWare 5.1 includes the WAN Traffic Manager (WTM) to help you manage synchronization traffic across WAN links (refer to Chapter 11 for more WTM details). Following is a list of the tasks that WTM performs, as well as tasks that it does not perform:

- WTM controls server-to-server traffic generated by NDS.
- WTM can restrict traffic based on cost, time of day, and/or type of traffic.
- WTM controls periodic events initiated by NDS, such as replica synchronization.
- WTM does *not* control events initiated by network administrators or users.
- WTM does *not* control non-NDS server-to-server traffic, such as time synchronization. Fortunately, we have Network Time Protocol (NTP) to solve that problem.

TIP

Transitive synchronization is not necessary if you configure your IP-Only network with IPX Compatibility Mode. Refer to Chapter 2 for more information on migrating to dual-protocol stack support.

That completes our NDS partitioning, replication, and synchronization overview. Now let's use this new-found knowledge to build an NDS maintenance plan.

NDS Maintenance

As we discussed earlier, NDS is a distributed, replicated database. Therefore, you should build an NDS maintenance plan to help maintain the health of the Directory. If these measures don't work, you will need a plan for identifying and for dealing with database inconsistencies. Finally, you will want to make sure that you are familiar with the procedures used to repair NDS, recover from a crash, and remove a server from the network.

In this final advanced NDS management lesson, we will learn some time-proven strategies for dealing with unwanted NDS realities:

- Preventative maintenance
- Troubleshooting NDS inconsistencies
- Repairing NDS
- Removing a server from the network
- Recovering from a crash

Let's take a closer look.

Preventative Maintenance

NDS maintenance begins with prevention. The following strategies will help you prevent NDS database inconsistencies (defined as dropped object links, Unknown objects, or general replica unavailability):

- *Plan Replica Placement* — You should always maintain at least three replicas of each partition for fault tolerance purposes. Having too many replicas, however, can cause excessive synchronization traffic and can increase the risk of database inconsistencies. Also, you will probably want to distribute most replicas locally, with only a few distributed over WAN links.

- *Regulate Partition Management Rights* — Partition operations (such as splitting and joining) can have a dramatic impact on NDS synchronization. For this reason, you will probably want to regulate who performs these operations and where they are performed. One method of regulation is to limit who has Supervisor [S] NDS rights to the partition root object, which means granting only [BCDRI] privileges to container administrators. Another strategy is to limit partition operations to a single workstation at a time. This is useful because partitions lock as they are split and joined. As a result, you can only perform one such operation on a partition at a time.

- *Back Up the Directory* — Backing up a server's file system does not back up the NDS Directory. Therefore, you will need to design an effective strategy for backing up NDS data. Also, be sure to test your backups to make sure the data can be restored properly. You should consider backing up the Directory every day (or at least every week). You should also back up the Directory before creating or merging a partition. Finally, you should only consider restoring an NDS backup if all other options have been exhausted (such as recreating a damaged replica from another replica in its replica ring).

- *Maintain a Standard NDS Version* — Each update of DS.NLM (the NDS module) fixes problems and increases functionality. When a new version of NDS is released, the new features are not available until all servers in a replica ring are updated. You can use NDS Manager to view the NDS version by selecting Object ➪ NDS Version ➪ View (as shown in Figure 5.2). Similarly, you can update a server's DS.NLM version by choosing Object ➪ NDS Version ➪ Update. The source server is the one with the newest version, and the target is the one being updated. (**Note:** The Version Update feature of NDS Manager can be used to upgrade DS.NLM within operating system versions, but not across them.)

- *Monitor SYS: Volume Space* — The NDS database is stored in a hidden directory on the SYS: volume, and it is protected by the Transactional Tracking System (TTS) feature. If the SYS: volume fills up, TTS shuts down, and the NDS database is closed to future changes. To avoid running out of disk space on the SYS: volume, consider the following guidelines: set minimum space requirements to receive a warning before SYS: runs out of space, store print queues and user files on other volumes, move the default virtual memory SWAP file off of the SYS: volume, and control the size of audit data files. Also, don't add replicas to full volumes, don't disable TTS, and for NetWare 4.*x* servers, consider removing CD-ROM drives from replica servers (because they create huge index files on the SYS: volume).

- *Prepare a Server for Downtime* — If you must shut down a server for more than a few hours, use NDS Manager to move replicas to other servers. If you want to shut down the server or WAN link for more than a few days, you should remove NDS from the server using NWCONFIG. Fortunately, the Directory is designed to withstand these problems, and replicas are resynchronized when the servers come back online and DS is reinstalled.

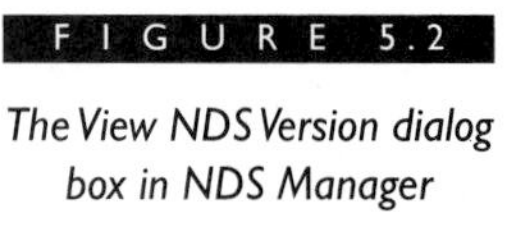

FIGURE 5.2

The View NDS Version dialog box in NDS Manager

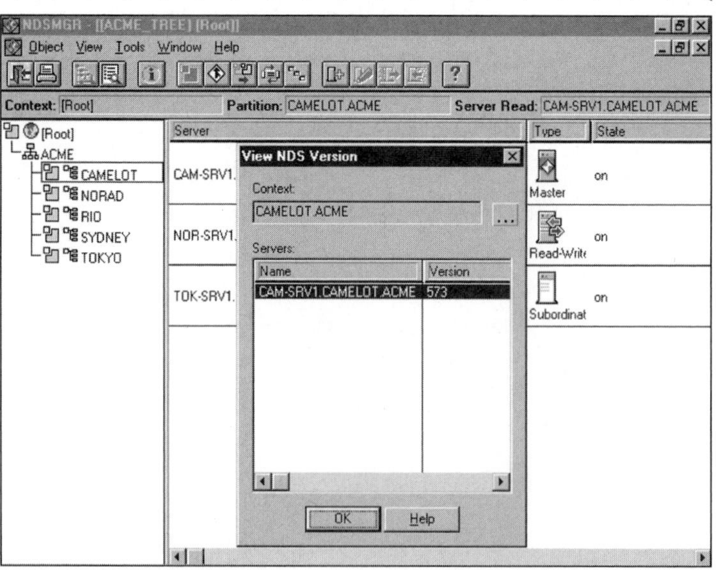

Troubleshooting NDS Inconsistencies

The first sign of NDS trouble is often an "inconsistent database." This occurs when replicas of a partition cannot be synchronized, and the shared information becomes dissimilar and/or corrupted. Sometimes, the inconsistency is temporary—for instance, when splitting or joining multiple partitions. Most of the time, however, the inconsistency represents a symptom of a larger problem.

Use the following signs to identify NDS inconsistencies:

- *Client Symptoms*—The following client problems may indicate that replicas are out of sync: the client prompts for a password when none exists, client logins take much longer than they should, modifications to the Directory disappear, previously assigned NDS rights disappear, and client problems are inconsistent and cannot be duplicated.

- *Unknown Objects*—The presence of Unknown objects in the tree can indicate problems with synchronization. Unknown objects don't always point to a problem, however. For example, objects can become Unknown during partition creation and merge operations. This is normal, because the partition root is changing. Volume and Alias objects also become Unknown when their host objects are deleted.

- *NDS Error Codes*—The NetWare 5.1 server console displays NDS error messages whenever the server is unable to complete a synchronization process. These messages can be viewed in the File Server Error Log, in NDS Manager, or at the server console prompt by using the SET DSTRACE = ON command.

Repairing NDS

If you identify an NDS database inconsistency, you can attempt to repair it by using NDS Manager. In this section, we will discuss the following topics:

- Partition Synchronization

- Partition Continuity

- NDS Manager Help
- General Guidelines

Let's learn a little more about how to repair NDS database inconsistencies.

Partition Synchronization

To view partition synchronization information in NDS Manager, highlight the appropriate partition. Then choose Object ⇨ Check Synchronization (see Figure 5.3).

A synchronization problem is indicated when the "All Processed = No" line has a value greater than 0. One word of warning: Check Synchronization may provide incomplete information because it only checks for synchronization errors on the first server in the replica ring. If you want to check all servers in the ring, use the Partition Continuity option, instead.

FIGURE 5.3

The Partition Synchronization window in NDS Manager

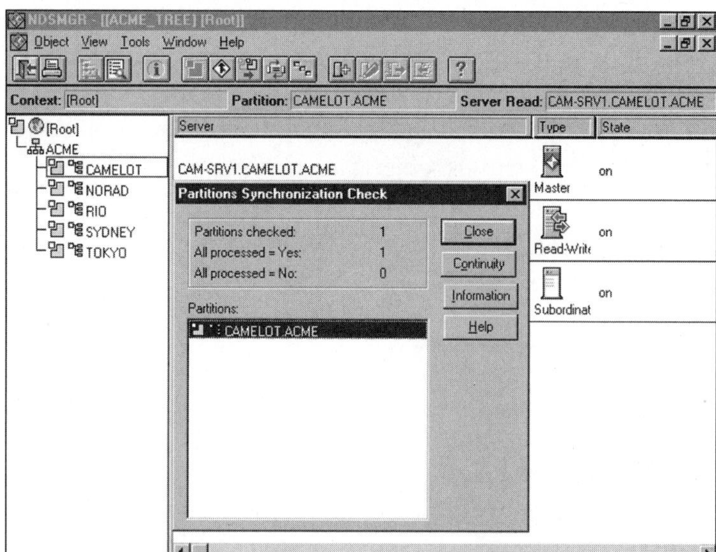

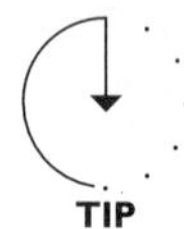
TIP

The Partition Synchronization option in NDS Manager doesn't work on NDS versions earlier than Version 489.

Partition Continuity

To check for synchronization errors on all servers in a replica ring, choose Object ➪ Partition Continuity in NDS Manager (see Figure 5.4).

The Partition Continuity window includes a matrix showing each server in a partition's replica ring (row) and the different types of replicas it supports (column). A replica icon containing an exclamation point (!) indicates a server with synchronization errors (see CAM-SRV1 in the figure). Also, you can track replica ring inconsistencies in this window by matching row and column icons (they should match).

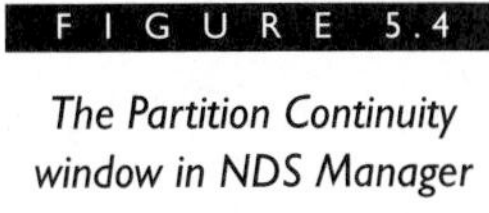

FIGURE 5.4

The Partition Continuity window in NDS Manager

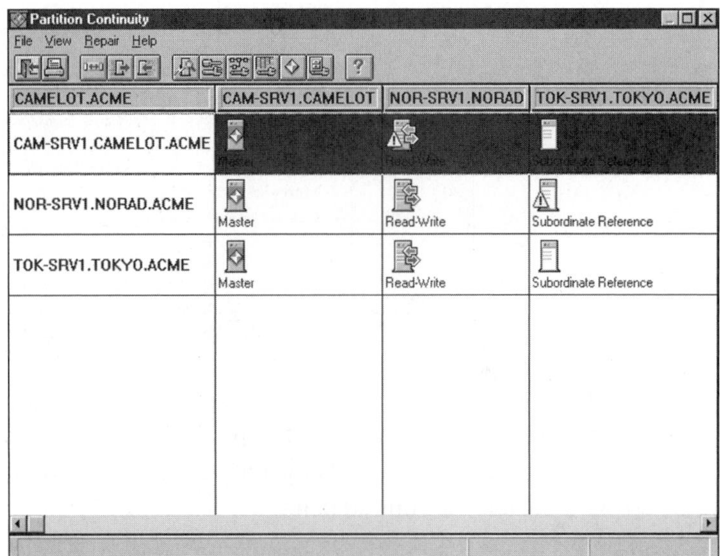

NDS Manager Help

Once you identify a database inconsistency, you can consult the NDS Manager Help system for a list of possible solutions. First, double-click the problem icon to display an error code. To view more information and a list of solutions, click the "?" (Help) button or select List of Codes and Server Codes in the Contents window of Help. You can also obtain Help information by consulting NetWare 5.1 documentation.

Refer to Figure 5.5 for an illustration of the NDS Error Codes Help window in NDS Manager. In this example, we are viewing the explanation screen for an NDS transport failure.

FIGURE 5.5

An NDS error code help in NDS Manager

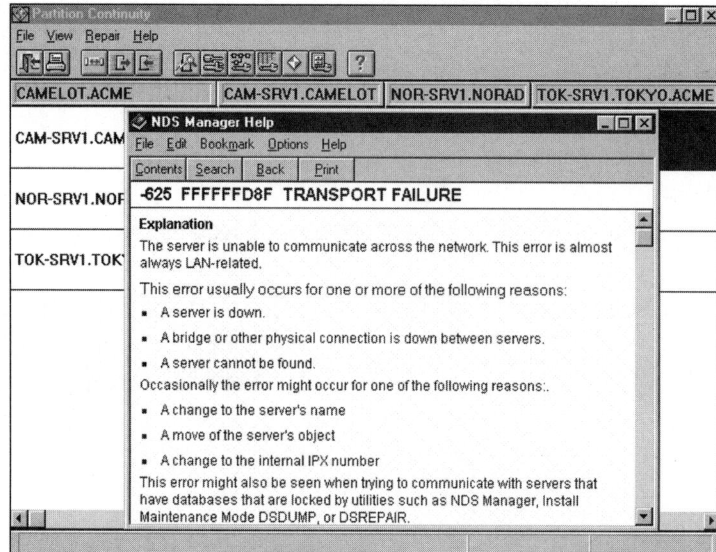

General Guidelines

The type of action you take to resolve NDS database inconsistencies depends entirely on the specific error being reported. Follow these simple guidelines to repair NDS database inconsistencies:

1. Let the system run for a few hours (it might synchronize itself).
2. Do not shut down the server because this will prevent self-healing.
3. Follow error-code repair guidelines carefully.
4. Do not attempt any partition management operations on a partition that is already experiencing problems.

REAL WORLD

You should be able to identify the symptoms of an out-of-sync NDS database, namely client problems, Unknown objects, and NDS error messages displayed on the server console. Also, learn how to use NDS Manager to check partition synchronization for a given server, check partition continuity throughout an entire replica ring, and view repair solutions using the Help button.

Note: For more information on advanced NDS troubleshooting techniques, refer to Novell Course 991, "Advanced NDS Tools and Diagnostics."

Most NDS repair procedures can be performed using options found in the Repair menu located in the Partition Continuity window in NDS Manager (see Figure 5.6). Some of the most powerful procedures include the following (refer to Table 5.1 for a complete list):

- *Synchronize Immediately* — Forces all servers in a replica ring to synchronize immediately.
- *Receive Updates* — Deletes a replica on a specific server and replaces it with a copy of the object data from the Master replica for that partition.
- *Send Updates* — Forces a specific server to immediately synchronize with all servers in its replica ring.
- *Repair Replica* — Confirms and corrects the replica ring and server IDs for a given replica.
- *Remove Server* — Removes a specific server from a selected replica ring.

FIGURE 5.6

The Repair menu in NDS Manager

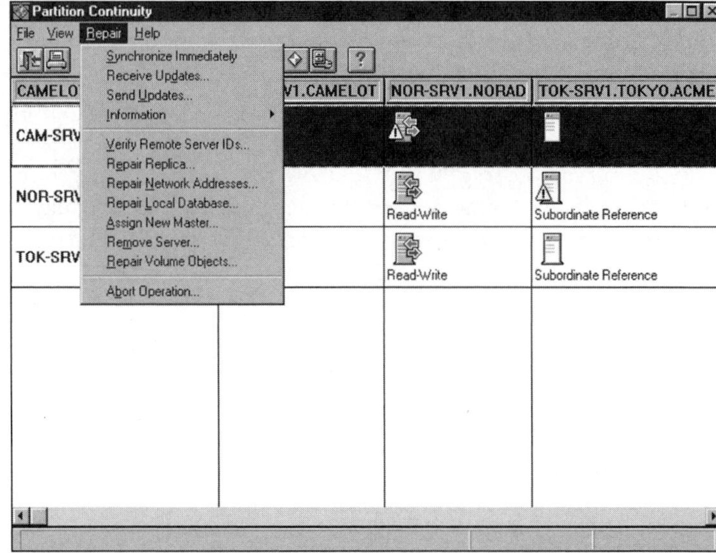

TABLE 5.1

Exploring the NDS Repair Menu in NDS Manager

MENU CHOICE	ACTION
Synchronize Immediately	Forces all servers in the replica ring to synchronize immediately.
Receive Updates	Deletes a replica on a server and replaces it with a copy from the Master replica. This is performed on a target server when the target server's replicas are known to be corrupted. (**Note:** This operation can cause excessive traffic on the WAN because the entire replica is sent.)
Send Updates	Selected server. Forces the server to synchronize immediately with all servers in its replica ring.
Information	Displays information about the selected partition, server, or replica.
Verify Remote Server IDs	Selected server. Confirms and corrects the replica ring and server IDs for all replicas stored on this server. This ensures that the server can communicate with all servers containing the same replicas.

TABLE 5.1

Exploring the NDS Repair Menu in NDS Manager (continued)

MENU CHOICE	ACTION
Repair Replica	Confirms and corrects the replica ring and server IDs for the replica. This ensures that the server can communicate with all servers containing this replica (also known as a replica ring).
Repair Network Addresses	Corrects inconsistencies in network address information between servers in a replica ring. Incorrect network address information can result in communication failure between servers (NDS Error code -625).
Repair Local Database	Selected server. Corrects specific inconsistencies within all replicas on this server. This action is similar to the repair performed by VREPAIR on local volumes found in earlier versions of NetWare.
Assign New Master	Selected replica. Changes a Read/ Write or Read-Only replica into a Master replica. Performed when the Master replica becomes corrupted or unavailable.
Remove Server	Selected server. Removes a server from the selected replica ring. Performed when a server becomes corrupted or unavailable. (**Note:** This operation is performed in the Partition Continuity window of NDS Manager.)
Repair Volume Objects	Selected server. Confirms that NDS Volume objects exist for all physical volumes on this server. In addition, this operation will create Volume objects if they are missing. Finally, this operation can also confirm that all Trustees are, in fact, NDS objects in the Directory.
Abort Operation	Selected partition. Cancels the current partitioning operation.

Removing a Server from the Network

If the previously described repair procedures don't solve your NDS inconsistency problems, then you may need to remove the server from the Directory tree. Removing a server requires careful consideration because the server probably contains replicas and other essential references to NDS. In this situation, these references must be deleted so that the rest of the servers in the replica ring can synchronize properly.

In order to remove a server from NDS, you must first remove the Directory from the server's SYS: volume. This accomplishes several auxiliary tasks, including deleting associated Volume objects, solving replica placement problems, informing other servers in the replica ring that the server is being removed, and removing all essential NDS references from the server.

Follow these simple steps to remove a server from the NDS Directory:

1. Load NWCONFIG at the server console. Alternatively, you can load NWCONFIG with the DSREMOVE option to remove the Directory from the server unconditionally.

2. Select Directory Options.

3. Select "Remove Directory Services from This Server." A warning message will appear. Press Enter to close the window and continue.

4. Select Yes to confirm.

5. Log into the server as Admin (or any user with Supervisor rights to all replicas). You will receive a message that Master replicas exist on this server. Press Enter to close the window.

6. If this is the only server in the NDS tree, then you're finished. You will receive a message confirming that NDS has been removed.

7. If this is not the only server in the NDS tree, you need to send the Master replica to another server. Choose Do It Automatically if you want NWCONFIG to find an appropriate Read/Write replica and upgrade it. Otherwise, choose Designate Which Servers Yourself and choose the Read/Write replica manually.

Recovering from a Crash

Because the Directory is stored on the SYS: volume, a hard disk crash involving a server's SYS: volume is equivalent to losing NDS and the entire operating system. Recovering from this kind of crash can be tricky because the Directory was not properly removed from the server prior to the failure.

Follow these procedures to recover from a server hard disk crash:

1. *Determine Replica Status* — Use NDS Manager to document the replicas that were stored on this server. To do this, highlight the Server object from another server and document the replica list. If any of the replicas were Masters, you will need to upgrade another Read/Write to Master status in each case by using NDS Manager.

2. *Delete the Server Object* — Use NDS Manager to delete the Server object from NDS that corresponds to this server.

3. *Delete Volume Objects* — Use NetWare Administrator to delete any Volume objects associated with this server.

4. *Resolve NDS Problems* — Use NDS Manager to resolve any outstanding NDS problems caused by the crash. Highlight the server's home partition and activate Partition Continuity. If you receive a "-625" NDS error, use the Remove Server option in the Repair menu.

5. *Install NetWare 5.1* — Install the new hard disk and NetWare 5.1 Operating System. When the NDS Server Context screen appears, install the server in its original context.

6. *Restore the Replicas* — Use NDS Manager and your replica list from Step 1 to replace all replicas (including Masters) on the new server. This step may take a while, particularly in the case of extensive updates across WAN links.

7. *Restore the File System* — Use Storage Management Services (SMS) to restore the file system from tape (or optical) backup media.

8. *Confirm the Correct Bindery Context* — Use MONITOR.NLM to restore the server's bindery context. Alternately, you can use the SET BINDERY CONTEXT = *context_name* command at the console prompt.

REAL WORLD

Practice repairing NDS inconsistencies by following the steps outlined in this chapter. Also, make sure you are intimately familiar with the Tools menu in NDS Manager and the Repair menu in Partition Continuity within NDS Manager.

Congratulations! Your NDS server has been restored. Fortunately, there are few disasters you can't recover from with eDirectory. All you need is a quick wit and a really heavy book (preferably *Novell's CNE Study Guide for NetWare 5.1*).

This completes our lesson in advanced NDS management. These strategies should help you sleep better at night by decreasing the chances that something horrible will happen to your NDS Directory. Now let's continue our Advanced NetWare 5.1 Administration lessons with advanced security management — also known as the Novell Certificate Server.

LAB EXERCISE 5.1: MAINTAINING THE NDS TREE

Use the hints provided to find the 20 Advanced NDS Management terms hidden in this word search puzzle. Omit any punctuation characters (such as blank spaces, hyphens, and so on) and spell out any numbers.

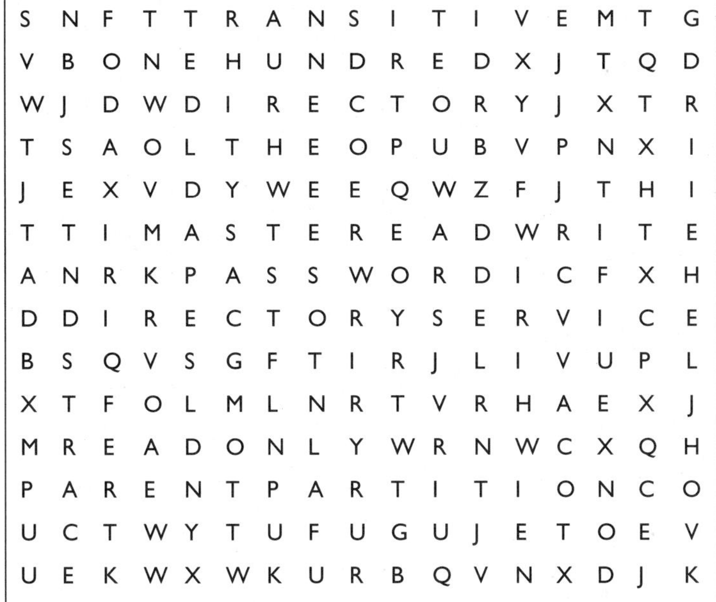

S	N	F	T	T	R	A	N	S	I	T	I	V	E	M	T	G
V	B	O	N	E	H	U	N	D	R	E	D	X	J	T	Q	D
W	J	D	W	D	I	R	E	C	T	O	R	Y	J	X	T	R
T	S	A	O	L	T	H	E	O	P	U	B	V	P	N	X	I
J	E	X	V	D	Y	W	E	E	Q	W	Z	F	J	T	H	I
T	T	I	M	A	S	T	E	R	E	A	D	W	R	I	T	E
A	N	R	K	P	A	S	S	W	O	R	D	I	C	F	X	H
D	D	I	R	E	C	T	O	R	Y	S	E	R	V	I	C	E
B	S	Q	V	S	G	F	T	I	R	J	L	I	V	U	P	L
X	T	F	O	L	M	L	N	R	T	V	R	H	A	E	X	J
M	R	E	A	D	O	N	L	Y	W	R	N	W	C	X	Q	H
P	A	R	E	N	T	P	A	R	T	I	T	I	O	N	C	O
U	C	T	W	Y	T	U	F	U	G	U	J	E	T	O	E	V
U	E	K	W	X	W	K	U	R	B	Q	V	N	X	D	J	K

Hints

1. A distributed, replicated database of physical and logical network resource information.
2. Novell's is called NDS. It is a distributed mechanism for representing network resources as objects.
3. The primary communications mechanism for HTML files over TCP/IP intranets and the Internet.
4. A graphical, Web-based programming environment. Supported by NDS.
5. A Directory protocol standard supported by NDS.
6. Only one of these per partition. It is the administrative replica.
7. Novell's distributed directory service based on the X.500 standard.

8. Fewer objects than this and you probably are not going to benefit from the fault tolerance benefits of NDS partitioning.
9. When partition boundaries meet, the partition that is closer to the [Root].
10. Provides security during login authentication.
11. The most popular type of NDS replica. It contains a complete copy of the object data for a partition.
12. These replicas are used for searching the NDS tree and viewing objects only.
13. NDS synchronization error messages can be viewed at the server console prompt using this command.
14. Always maintain at least this many replicas of every partition for fault tolerance purposes.
15. This type of NDS synchronization eliminates the requirement that all servers in a replica ring have to communicate and synchronize directly.

See Appendix C for answers.

LAB EXERCISE 5.2: NETWARE 5.1 ADVANCED NDS MANAGEMENT

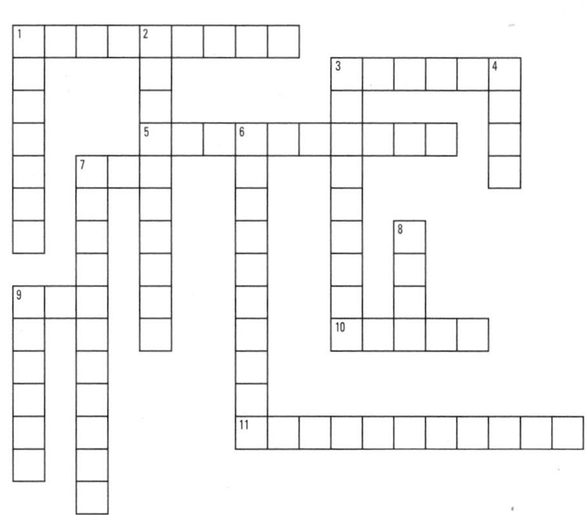

Across

1. Consider moving these off SYS:
3. Use NDS Manager to delete this object
5. NDS Version 8
7. NetWare 5.1 backup engine
9. Secure authentication scheme
10. NDS core file
11. The NDS database is "spread out"

Down

1. Mysterious object
2. Not stored in NDS
3. Expensive replication scheme
4. Automatically created partition
6. NDS is distributed and _________

7. One benefit of NDS
8. Traumatic NDS event
9. Important NDS Manager menu

See Appendix C for answers.

CHAPTER 6

NetWare 5.1 Advanced Security Management

Security in the information age poses an interesting challenge. Computers and communications have made it possible to collect volumes of data about you and me — from our last Internet purchase to our most detailed medical records. As a network administrator, it is your responsibility to design, install, and manage the NetWare 5.1 network. But most importantly, you must protect it. Think of this chapter as your impenetrable network armor.

Existing NetWare 5.1 NDS and file system security are, in general, very good. However, for a few of today's most sophisticated network architects, they are not good enough. Fortunately, NetWare 5.1 extends the existing security model into the realm of Internet communications through support for public key cryptography and the Novell Certificate Server.

Public key cryptography is a security standard for using digital codes, called *keys*, to facilitate secure transmissions. At the most fundamental level, public key cryptography prevents Internet communications from being monitored by using authentication and encryption tools. Following is a brief overview of how public key cryptography extends the basic NetWare 5.1 security model:

- *NDS Security* — This access-oriented security scheme forms the "front line" of NetWare 5.1 security. It uses a system of granting and withholding rights to containers and objects in the NDS tree.
- *File System Security* — This access-oriented security scheme forms the next line of security. It relies on a system of granting and withholding rights to directories and files in the file system.
- *Public Key Cryptography* — This communications-oriented security scheme forms the final line of defense. It relies on authentication and encryption processes to secure communication transmissions between senders and receivers over local and global networks.

Public key cryptography is implemented in NetWare 5.1 by using the Novell Certificate Server. This server process natively integrates public key authentication and encryption mechanisms into NDS and enables you to mint, issue, and manage both user and server certificates. In this chapter, we will study the basic fundamentals of public key cryptography and learn how the Novell Certificate Server can help you extend communication security within NetWare 5.1. In addition, we will learn how to install the Certificate Server and manage security objects using the Java-based ConsoleOne tool.

Now let's start our advanced security management studies with a brief lesson in public-key-cryptography fundamentals.

Understanding Public Key Cryptography

Public key cryptography is a standard security system for using digital codes, called *keys,* to facilitate secure transmissions over the Internet. At the most basic level, it prevents the content of most Internet communications, such as web page browsing or public chat forums, from being monitored by anyone equipped to do so. In addition, public key cryptography enables the content of other data transmissions, such as credit card purchases, to be kept private.

Public key cryptography is built on a pair of mathematical related digital codes, or keys. One key in each pair is publicly distributed; the other key is kept strictly private. Each data originator (person, place, or software system) is issued a key pair by a public-key-cryptography system. Following is a summary of the basic principles and functions of each key in the key pair:

1. Digital keys in the key pair are generated by a cryptography system and used in combination only with each other.

2. The cryptography system openly publishes a public key to any party needing to validate a signature or encrypt a private communication.

3. The key pair owner, or a cryptography system acting on the owner's behalf, closely guards the private key. The owner uses the private key to create digital signatures and to decrypt data that is encrypted with a specific matching public key.

4. Parties requiring private communication with a key pair owner use the public key to validate signatures and to encrypt data.

In this chapter, we will explore the fundamentals of public key cryptography and learn more about its two main functions: authentication and encryption/decryption. Let's start with public and private key authentication.

Authentication

Authentication in the public key cryptography sense is a little different from what you might expect—it has nothing to do with logging in (as in NDS). Authentication in this case assures data receivers that the sender is exactly who or what he, she, or it claims to be.

In public key cryptography, the sender of a message can be authenticated through a certified public key that the sender makes available in the form of a public key certificate. Furthermore, public key certificates are certified by a Certificate Authority (CA). Normally, this process involves some due diligence on the part of the CA to verify that the individual or entity is indeed whom they claim to be.

For example, if Marie Curie and Albert Einstein want to exchange secure e-mail messages, they need to exchange public keys that enable them to decrypt each other's messages. The trick is finding a secure way to exchange these keys. Albert needs to be assured that the public key he gets from Marie is indeed her key, and vice versa. They could meet somewhere face to face and exchange floppy disks with their public keys, but this type of exchange would be highly inconvenient.

Instead, Albert and Marie can use a Certificate Authority (CA) to mediate the exchange of public keys. After this verification takes place, the CA issues a public key certificate for each of them. This CA authentication is accomplished using a *digital signature*.

To create a digital signature, the CA combines the data being signed with the private key of the signer. As a result, no one else can duplicate the signature because no one else has the signer's private key. In addition, the signer cannot deny having signed the data. This is known as *nonrepudiation*. When a CA signs a public key certificate with a digital signature, the CA guarantees that it has verified the identity of the public key owner according to the CA's established and published policies.

After signed data is received, software verifies data authenticity by applying the same computation to the data that the signing software used originally. If the data is unaltered, both computations produce identical results. It can then be safely assumed that neither the data nor the signature were modified in transit.

In summary, Certificate Authority authentication is accomplished using the following four steps:

- *Step 1*—Party A (the one requesting certification) sends a data packet and Party A's public key to a Certificate Authority (CA). This is called a certificate signing request.
- *Step 2*—The CA creates a public key certificate containing the required information and then runs a computation on the information in the certificate to produce a small data string (usually 16 to 20 bytes).
- *Step 3*—The CA encrypts the small data string using the CA's private key. This generates a unique CA digital signature for the certificate packet.
- *Step 4*—The CA sends the public key certificate containing the requesting party's public key and the CA digital signature to Party A.

That's how public key cryptography uses Certificate Authorities and digital signatures to authenticate network communications. Now let's learn how encryption extends Internet security into the realm of data authentication.

Encryption and Decryption

Earlier, we learned that authentication ensures that two communicating parties are who they say they are. The next level of public key security (encryption and decryption) ensures that the data being exchanged can only be read by the communicating parties.

When data is encrypted using a public key, it can be decrypted only by the private key. Conversely, when data is encrypted using a private key, it can only be decrypted using the corresponding public key. This system relies on a verified pair of public and private keys.

Suppose, for example, you want to order a book from an Internet vendor and need to use your credit card to pay for it. Obviously, you don't want your credit card number read by anyone other than the intended recipient. When you place your order and enter your credit card number into the bookstore's Web application, the secured Java script in your browser uses the bookstore's public key to encrypt the message that contains your credit card number. The application then sends the encrypted message over the Internet to the bookstore server, where the bookstore's private key decrypts the encrypted message. The only way anyone could view your credit card number is if they had both the bookstore's public and private keys.

Encryption and authentication in the public-key-cryptography system rely on the following two critical components:

- *Public Key Certificates* — A public key certificate is a digital message signed with a private key that provides a cryptographic binding between the public key and a given subject. This certificate is generated by a trusted entity called a Certificate Authority (CA). Public key certificates are also referred to as digital public key certificates, digital IDs, digital passports, and, simply, certificates. Public key certificates contain, at a minimum, a public key, a subject name, and a CA-generated digital signature. All certificates generated by commercial CAs and/or the Organizational CA are encoded in the X.509 v3 format.

- *Certificate Authorities* — The Certificate Authority verifies and certifies the identity of a person or an organization. A CA can be a commercial entity, such as VeriSign, or an internal organization, such as your corporate MIS department. The CA's chief functions are to verify the identity of senders and receivers and to issue public key certificates. In addition, CAs may offer additional security services, including key pair generation, key pair archival, public-key-certificate revocation services, public-key-certificate publishing services, and insurance against public-key-certificate errors.

This completes our fundamental discussion about public key cryptography. By now, you should have an appreciation for the difficulty of securing Internet communications. Now let's learn how NetWare 5.1 implements public key cryptography using the Novell Certificate Server.

REAL WORLD

The Organizational CA signs public key certificates for Server Certificate objects. Only users with Supervisor rights to the Organizational CA object can administer the Organizational CA.

Novell Certificate Server Architecture

The Novell Certificate Server provides public-key-cryptography services to NetWare 5.1 clients. The server integrates with NDS to enable you to mint, issue, and manage both user and server certificates. Novell Certificate Server provides the following advanced security functions to network administrators:

- It provides public key cryptography services on the network. This is accomplished by creating an Organizational CA within your NDS tree that issues user and server certificates. You can also use the services of an external CA or a combination of both an Organizational CA and an external CA, if needed.
- It controls the costs associated with obtaining key pairs and with managing public key certificates by handling these services internally in the NetWare 5.1 server.
- It allows public keys and certificates to be openly available while also protecting them against tampering. Because key pairs are stored in NDS, they can leverage the access control features and fault tolerance of Novell Directory Services.
- It uses Novell International Cryptography Infrastructure (NICI) to encrypt private keys and to make private keys available only to requesting entities.
- It securely backs up private keys via NDS backup utilities.

- It enables central administration of certificates by using a ConsoleOne snap-in.
- It enables users to manage their own user certificates via the Novell Certificate Console utility.
- It supports popular e-mail clients and browsers, such as GroupWise 5.5, Microsoft Outlook, and Netscape Messenger.

In this chapter, we will study the fundamental architecture of the Novell Certificate Server and briefly outline the components that offer these comprehensive security features. Let's start by learning how the Novell Certificate Server integrates with NDS.

REAL WORLD

The cryptography services available in Novell Certificate Server depend on the country in which your network is located. This product will not function if cryptography services are not fully installed. For example, the mass-market exportable version of NICI is limited to 512-bit RSA keys for data encryption. The American and Canadian version of NICI, on the other hand, supports key sizes up to 2,048 bits for all types of keys. To ensure that you have the highest level of cryptography services available in your area, contact the nearest Novell-authorized reseller.

Understanding NDS Certificate Objects

The Novell Certificate Server consists of two parts: a snap-in module for ConsoleOne, which is the administration point for Novell Certificate Server; and PKI.NLM, which must be loaded on the Certificate Server. (**Note:** You must use the client version of ConsoleOne, rather than the server version, to manage the Novell Certificate Server.)

Using ConsoleOne, the Novell Certificate Server enables you to request, manage, and store public key certificates and their associated key pairs in the NDS tree. In addition, you can establish an Organizational CA that is specific to your tree and your organization. The following NDS objects create the foundation of Novell Certificate Server functionality:

- *Security Container* — The Security container holds security-related objects for the NDS tree, including the Organizational CA object. This container physically resides at the top of the NDS tree. The Security container is created when Novell Secure Authentication Services (SAS) is installed during NetWare 5.1 installation.
- *Organizational CA* — During NetWare 5.1 installation, you can elect to create an Organizational CA if one does not exist in the NDS tree. Using ConsoleOne, you can also create or recreate the Organizational CA after installation. This object contains the public key, private key, certificate, certificate chain, and other configuration information for the Novell Certificate Server. The Organizational CA object resides in the Security container in NDS. **Note:** There can only be one Organizational CA per NDS tree.
- *Server Certificate* — During NetWare 5.1 installation, you can also elect to create a Server Certificate object. This NDS object contains the public key, private key, certificate, and certificate chain that enables Secure Sockets Layer (SSL) security services for server applications. In addition, you can use ConsoleOne to create Server Certificate objects after installation. In either case, Server Certificate objects can only be created in a container where the server resides. If the Server object is moved, all Server Certificate objects belonging to that server must be moved, as well. Finally, a server can have many Server Certificate objects associated with it; however, a Server Certificate object cannot be shared between different servers.
- *User Certificate* — A user certificate allows users to send and receive digitally signed and encrypted e-mail by using the S/MIME standard. Generally, only the CA administrator has sufficient rights to create User Certificates. However, only the user has rights to export or download the private key from NDS. The User Certificate is created from the Security tab of the user's Property page and is signed by an Organizational CA. Finally, multiple certificates can be stored in the user's NDS object.

- *Trusted Root Container* — A *trusted root* provides the basis for trust in public key cryptography. Trusted roots are used to validate certificates signed by CAs. Trusted roots enable security for SSL, secure e-mail, and certificate-based authentication. A Trusted Root container is an NDS object that contains one or more Trusted Root objects. You must create the Trusted Root container in the Security container.

- *Trusted Root* — A Trusted Root object contains a trusted root certificate from a CA that is trusted (in other words, that is known to be authentic and valid). A trusted root certificate is used to validate certificates signed by the CA, and can be exported and used as needed.

This completes the list of new NDS Certificate objects offered by NetWare 5.1. Now let's learn a little more about how we can use these NDS objects to configure the Novell Certificate Server.

Configuring Novell Certificate Server

The first step in setting up Novell Certificate Server is to configure the Organizational CA object. The CA service runs on a single NetWare server. Therefore, you should select a server within the NDS tree that will always be available for digital signing and, therefore, resides in a physically secure location.

During the CA creation process, you will be prompted to name the Certificate Authority object and to choose the server on which it will reside. Once the Organizational CA is configured, you can create Server Certificate objects in the container that holds the host server.

During the server-certificate creation process, you are prompted to name the key pair and choose the server that the key pair is to be associated with. By default, the Server Certificate object name is generated by Novell Certificate Server and is based on the key pair name you choose. Finally, you must also specify whether the Server Certificate object will sign certificates using the internal Organizational CA or an external CA. If you use an external CA to sign certificates, the host will generate a Certificate Signing Request (CSR) that you must submit to the external Certificate Authority.

Following is a summary of how the Novell Certificate Server CA process works:

1. From the client you send a request to the host server to generate a server certificate object using ConsoleOne.

2. The server generates a key pair and stores it in a new Server Certificate object (which resides in the host server's home container). If the server is signing certificates based on an external CA, it then creates a CSR and sends it back to the client.

3. The CSR is routed to an internal or external CA by e-mail or http for validation.

4. The external or internal CA validates the requests, signs the certificate, and returns the certificate and the CA's trusted root to the user by e-mail, HTTP, or other mechanism.

5. The trusted root and public key certificate are stored in the Server Certificate object using ConsoleOne.

After the Server Certificate objects are created, you can configure your applications to use them. Keys are referenced in a given Application's configuration by the key pair name you entered when the Server Certificate object was created. For example, suppose you create a Server Certificate object for a server running LDAP Services, and the server's name is "Payroll." If the name given to the key pair is "LDAPKeys," the Server Certificate object would be named "LDAPKeys-Payroll."

In order to configure LDAP Services to use the LDAPKeys key pair, simply launch ConsoleOne, select the LDAP Application object, and then choose LDAPKeys from a list of key pair names. Finally, keep in mind that you can use both internal and external CAs simultaneously within Novell Certificate Server.

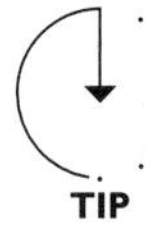

Remember, a key pair is restricted in its use to only one server. You can have multiple applications running on a given server that reference the same Server Certificate object, but you cannot use a Server Certificate object on multiple servers. Finally, all Server Certificate objects must belong to a server, and their ownership cannot be changed or transferred.

Public key certificates contain a life span specification to control the damage that might be caused by an undiscovered key compromise. The default life span for the Organizational CA's public key certificate is two years. For externally signed public key certificates, the external CA determines the life span (normally one year). If you suspect that an attacker has your private key, discontinue using it by deleting the Server Certificate object from the NDS tree. Then generate a new key pair and obtain a new public key certificate from the Organizational CA or an external CA.

The life cycle of a key pair follows these seven phases:

- Key pair generation
- Issuance of public key certificates by a CA
- Key distribution: public key to public repository and private key to owner
- Key pair activation
- Use of the key pair
- Public-key-certificate suspension, revocation, or expiration
- Key pair termination

In certain instances, it might be sufficient to renew the public key certificate for an existing key pair. However, do not renew an existing certificate if you suspect that your private key has been compromised. Instead, obtain a new key pair.

That completes our brief lesson in Novell Certificate Server architecture. As you can see, public key cryptography at the NetWare 5.1 server relies heavily on unique security-based NDS objects and secure communications with external CAs. Now let's learn a little more about how to set up and manage the Novell Certificate Server.

REAL WORLD

The Novell Certificate Server relies on the following two advanced security standards for cryptography and secure communications:

- *Novell International Cryptographic Infrastructure (NICI)*—NICI is the underlying cryptographic infrastructure that provides the cryptography for Novell Certificate Server, Novell Authentication Service, and other applications. NICI must be installed on the host server for the Novell Certificate Server to work properly. This process is accomplished during NetWare 5.1 server installation. The NICI license is tied to the server-based license, so you must make sure that the server has a sufficient license count to support multiple CA requests.
- *Secure Sockets Layer (SSL)*—SSL is a protocol that establishes and maintains secure communications between SSL-enabled servers and clients. Through a process called *SSL handshake*, SSL enables a client and any server to establish a communication channel that prevents eavesdropping, tampering, and forgery. This secure communication channel is the foundation of key exchange in the public key cryptography model.

Novell Certificate Server Management

At the heart of Novell Certificate Server management are two utilities and the Certificate Authority. NetWare 5.1 enables you to manage most Certificate Server administration tasks using the client version of ConsoleOne. You can use ConsoleOne to manage public key certificates, Server Certificate objects, and their associated components. In addition, the user-oriented Novell Certificate Console utility enables users to access their own user certificates and keys without having to use the administrative capabilities of ConsoleOne.

During the Novell Certificate Server setup process, you are asked which type of Certificate Authority (CA) will sign specific Server Certificate objects. As you learned earlier, the Novell Certificate Server gives you two CA options: Organizational CA (internal) and external CA (such as VeriSign).

The benefits of using an Organizational CA as opposed to an external CA are compatibility (an Organizational CA is compatible with applications that share a common trusted root in NDS), cost savings (you can create an unlimited number of public key certificates at no cost), NDS integration, content control (through critical public key certificate attributes, such as certificate life span, key size, and signature algorithm), and simplified management.

On the other hand, the benefits of using an external CA are liability (an external CA might offer some liability protection in case any private keys are exposed) and availability (an external CA might be more widely available and more compatible with applications outside of NDS).

In this chapter, we will study the critical management tasks associated with the following four Novell Certificate Server components:

- Certificate Authorities
- Server Certificate objects
- User certificates
- Trusted Root objects

Now let's begin your transformation from NDS guru to certificate server expert.

Managing Certificate Authorities

By default, the Novell Certificate Server installation process creates a single Organizational CA for you. At that time, you are prompted to specify a unique name for the internal CA. When you click Finish, the Organizational CA object is created with default parameters and placed in the Security container.

If you want more control over the creation of the Organizational CA or need to create one manually, you must first log into the NDS tree as an Administrator with Supervisor rights to the Security container. Next, start ConsoleOne, right-click the Security container object, and then select New ➪ Object. In the list provided, double-click NDSPKI:CertificateAuthority. This launches the CA creation wizard. Remember, you can only have one Organizational CA in an NDS tree.

During the Organizational CA creation process, you are prompted to name the CA and to choose a host server. It is important that you select a server that is physically secure, supports all protocols running on your network (including both IP and IPX), and only run software that you trust.

Once you have created the Organizational CA, you can use ConsoleOne to perform any of the following Certificate Authority management tasks:

- *Issuing a Public Key Certificate* — ConsoleOne enables you to generate certificates for cryptography-enabled applications that do not recognize Server Certificate objects. The public key certificate signed by the Organizational CA is automatically installed when you create a Server Certificate object that uses the NDS tree. Public key certificates are processed and imported directly into cryptography-enabled applications in the same way that clients authenticate via external CAs — via Certificate Signing Requests (CSRs). To issue a public key certificate using ConsoleOne, click the hosting container object and select Tools ➪ Issue Certificate. Next, paste a CSR into the dialog box or use the browse button to locate a CSR file, and then click Next. Then, select the CA that will sign the certificate, and click Next. Finally, you must specify how the key will be used, and you must configure specific properties, including subject name, validity period, and expiration dates. When you click Finish, a dialog box explains that a certificate has been created and that data about the certificate can be found on the Details page.

- *Viewing Certificate Authority Properties* — ConsoleOne enables you to view the Organizational CA's properties, including information about the public key certificate and the self-signed certificate associated with it. In order to view the Organizational CA's properties, simply double-click the Organizational CA object in the ConsoleOne browser. This activates the following property pages: General, Certificates, and other NDS-related property pages. In the Organizational CA's Certificates page, you can view properties relating to two types of CA-owned certificates: public key and self-signed certificates. Both certificate-oriented property pages display the subject name, issuer's full name, and the validity date of the corresponding certificate.

- *Exporting the Organizational CA's self-signed public key certificate*—From the Self-Signed Certificate property page described in the preceding paragraph, you can export the integrated public key certificate to a file for use in cryptography-enabled applications. The self-signed certificate that resides in the Organizational CA provides the same verification of the CA's identity as the trusted root certificate that is exported from a server certificate. Any service that recognizes the Organizational CA as a trusted root will accept the self-signed or trusted root certificate as valid. Click Export from the Self-Signed Certificate Property page to open a wizard that help you export the Organizational CA certificate to a file.

Now that you have installed and configured the Organizational CA, let's take a closer look at managing Server Certificate objects.

Managing Server Certificate Objects

Server Certificate objects are created in the container that holds the host server's NDS object. Depending on your needs, you may want to create a separate Server Certificate object for each cryptography-enabled application on the server or to create one Server Certificate object for all applications used on the server.

The terms *Server Certificate object* and *Key Material object* are synonymous. The schema name of the NDS object is "NDSPKI:KeyMaterial." By default, the Novell Certificate Server installation process creates a Server Certificate object and allows you to give it a unique name. If you want to create a Server Certificate object manually, use the New ➪ Object tool in ConsoleOne. From the list in the New Objects dialog box, select "NDSPKI:KeyMaterial" and click OK in order to start the server certificate creation wizard.

During the Server Certificate object creation process, you are prompted to name the key pair and to choose the server that the key pair will be associated with. In addition, you will have to determine whether the server certificate will be signed by your internal Organizational CA or an external CA. If you use the internal Organizational CA, the host certificate server must be able to communicate with the server that is running the Organizational CA process (they must be running the same protocol). If you use an external CA to sign the server certificate, then the object will automatically generate a CSR that you must submit to the external CA. Once the certificate is signed and returned to you, you will need to install the externally authenticated certificate and trusted root into the Server Certificate object using ConsoleOne.

Once you have installed the Server Certificate object, you can use ConsoleOne to perform any of the following management tasks:

- *Importing a Public Key Certificate* — If your server certificate chooses to sign with an external CA, you must use ConsoleOne to import the public key and trusted root certificates that are returned. These certificates are then imported and stored in the Server Certificate object within the NDS tree. Ultimately, the cryptography-enabled applications that link to this Server Certificate object use this information to perform secure transactions. In order to import these two certificates into a Server Certificate object, double-click the Server Certificate object in ConsoleOne. Next, from the General or Certificates tab, click Import Certificates. At this point, you can either install the trusted root certificate from a file or paste the certificate information using a text editor. Remember, the trusted root must be installed first, before the public key certificate. Next, the server certificate can be imported either by installing it from a file or pasting the certificate information using a text editor. Finally, when you click Finish, the Certificate Property page displays the distinguished names of the subject and the issuer of the public key and trusted root certificates.

REAL WORLD

In order to paste an external trusted-root certificate into a Server Certificate object, you must open the authenticated certificate using any text editor and then copy the information between the following two lines:

-------BEGIN CERTIFICATE-------

-------END CERTIFICATE-------

Note: Don't forget to include the BEGIN CERTIFICATE and END CERTIFICATE lines as well (a common mistake).

- *Exporting a Trusted Root Certificate* — ConsoleOne also enables you to export a trusted root certificate to a file so that your browser can use it to verify the certificate chain sent by a cryptography-enabled application. (**Note:** A certificate chain is an ordered list of public key certificates indicating all the certificates that chain back to the root authority. In a certificate chain, the top-most public key certificate is known as the trusted root certificate of the certificate chain.) If you export a trusted root certificate to a file, you can specify one of two formats: DER (.DER) and Base64 (.B64). Otherwise, you can export the trusted root certificate to the system clipboard and then paste it directly into a cryptography-enabled application. In order to export a trusted root certificate that is enabled in the Server Certificate object of NDS, simply double-click the Server Certificate object and choose the Certificates tab. Next, select Trusted Root Certificate and click Export.

- *Deleting a Server Certificate Object* — ConsoleOne enables you to delete a Server Certificate object if you suspect that its private key has been compromised. Once a Server Certificate object has been deleted, you cannot recover it. Before you delete this object, make sure that no cryptography-enabled applications still need to use it. Once it has been deleted, you can re-create a Server Certificate object and assign a new key pair. All of this functionality is provided by ConsoleOne by using the same steps you would use to delete any other NDS object.

- *Viewing a Server Certificate Object's Properties* — ConsoleOne enables you to view typical Server Certificate object properties, as well as public key and trusted root certificate properties that are unique to the server certificate. When you double-click the Server Certificate object in ConsoleOne, it brings up a General page, a Certificates page, and typical NDS-related properties pages. In the Certificates page, you can view details regarding embedded public key and trusted root certificates, including the subject's name, the issuer's full name, and the validity dates of the certificates.

That completes our lessons in configuring and managing the Novell Certificate Server's two most important components — Organizational CA and server certificate. Now let's complete this chapter with a quick look at user certificates.

Managing User Certificates

User certificates are authenticated, user-owned keys that enable secure e-mail and other communications. User certificates are embedded into User objects in the NDS tree. In order to create a user certificate in ConsoleOne, double-click a host User object and click Create in the Security window. Select the type of Certificate Authority to use and click Next. Then select a key type and size. Make sure the following radio button is selected: "Allow Private Key to Be Used for Secure Email and Authentication."

Finally, view the certificate parameters and make sure the user's e-mail address is present. Click Finish to complete the process.

Once you have created a user certificate and attached it to a User object, you can use ConsoleOne to export this certificate for use in secure e-mail. This process can be accomplished with or without the private key. Keep in mind, the network administrator or any user with sufficient rights can export a user certificate, but only the user who owns the certificate can export it with the private key.

In addition to ConsoleOne, the Novell Certificate Console utility enables users to export a given user certificate for use in secure e-mail. Once the Novell Certificate Console has been installed, you can access it by double-clicking the corresponding icon on your desktop. If you are logged in as more than one user, select the appropriate user from the Current Connections pull-down menu. Keep in mind that you must be logged in as the user who owns the user certificate and must have Browse rights to the User object if you are exporting the certificate and the private key. Once you log in, you will be presented with a list of user certificates. Select the correct one and click Export.

Once you have established an Organizational CA, embedded server certificates into your NDS Server objects, and activated user certificates, the Novell Certificate Server is ready to go.

In this chapter, we have learned how public key cryptography and the Novell Certificate Server can dramatically improve the security of network communications. In addition to authentication and encryption, these services help you create a complete *trusted* network using NetWare 5.1. In creating a trusted network, it is your job to identify network threats and implement appropriate security countermeasures to eliminate them. This isn't easy. You have many factors working against you — including open communications, hackers, and high data sensitivity. Fortunately, NetWare 5.1 has a dramatically improved security model for extending NDS network armor beyond the LAN and WAN and into the realm of a global Internet.

Now that you have learned everything you need to know about advanced server, NDS, and security management, let's complete our "NetWare 5.1 Advanced Administration" studies with a few great lessons in server and network optimization.

Full speed ahead!

REAL WORLD

You can install the Novell Certificate Console utility by running SETUP.EXE from the SYS:PUBLIC/MGMT/CERTCONSOLE directory.

You can also configure ZENworks to automate the distribution of the Novell Certificate Console by using the following ZENworks file that ships with the Novell Certificate Server: CERTCNSL ZENWORKS.EXE (a self-extracting file that contains everything you need to distribute Novell Certificate Server by using ZENworks).

LAB EXERCISE 6.1: NOVELL CERTIFICATE SERVER

Use the hints provided to find the 20 security-management terms hidden in this word search puzzle. Omit any punctuation characters (such as blank spaces, hyphens, and so on) and spell out any numbers.

C E N C R Y P T I O N S H E M
O G B I S X B F T H U U X W N
N N M L C R E D F R O P I N N
S P U B L I C K E Y O E A I Y
O R C R Y P T O G R A P H Y S
L I F E S P A N T X Y D M H P
E V G T F J J G K E Y P A I R
O A U T H E N T I C A T I O N
N T R U S T E D R O O T J K F
E E K A H S D N A H B E V S M
H K G J B I J I J W B J F T L
J E Y N L X W F K H J K D K N
N Y Y K D H L E M K T I X T X

Hints

1. Assures data receivers that the sender is exactly who or what he, she, or it claims to be.
2. Novell Certificate Server is a snap-in module for this utility.
3. A standard security system for using digital codes called "keys" to facilitate secure transmissions over the Internet.
4. If you use an external CA to sign license certificates, the host will generate this for submission to an external Certificate Authority.
5. One of two formats for an exported trusted root certificate file.
6. One half of the process that ensures data can only be read by the communicating parties during an exchange.
7. ConsoleOne allows you to do this to trusted root certificates so your browser can use a file to verify the certificate chain sent by cryptography-enabled applications.

8. Using this process, SSL allows a client and any server to establish a communications channel that prevents eavesdropping, tampering, and forgery.
9. If your server certificate chooses to sign with an external CA, you must use ConsoleOne to do this to the public key and trusted root certificates that are returned.
10. One key is publicly distributed; the other is kept strictly private.
11. The default for the Organizational CA's public key certificate is two years.
12. The Novell Certificate Server uses this to encrypt private keys and make them available only to requesting entities.
13. The owner uses this key to create digital signatures and decrypt data that is encrypted with a specific matching public key.
14. The cryptography system openly publishes this key to any party needing to validate a signature or encrypt a private communication.
15. A special NDS object that contains a CA's main certificate. Applications that are configured to use this certificate consider it valid if it has been signed by one of the CAs in the parent container.

See Appendix C for answers.

LAB EXERCISE 6.2: NETWARE 5.1 ADVANCED SECURITY MANAGEMENT

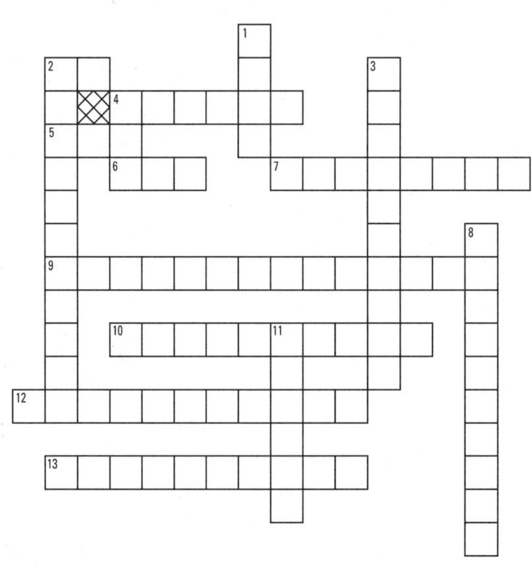

Across

2. The authenticating heart of public key cryptography
4. Where Novell public key cryptography happens
5. Data encryption key for NICI
6. Ensures secure network communications
7. Most popular External CA
9. Signers cannot deny having signed the data
10. The other half of data validation
12. Also known as server certificate
13. Gathering digital certificate signatures outside NDS

Down

1. The benefactor of security
2. Novell Certificate Console setup directory
3. Each public key certificate must do this eventually

4. Creates the Security container
8. Signing by NDS
11. Novell Certificate Server module

See Appendix C for answers.

CHAPTER 7

NetWare 5.1 Optimization

Optimization . . . the final frontier. Welcome to NetWare 5.1 server and network optimization.

In this chapter, we will learn how to fine-tune the server and network for peak performance. This is required in order to handle the demands of NetWare 5.1 users. NetWare 5.1 performance optimization involves the following three network components:

- *Server Memory* — This has the most dramatic impact on server performance. Memory optimization involves memory allocation, virtual memory, and memory protection.
- *Server Disk* — Blocks and buffers affect server memory and disk utilization and, therefore, overall network performance. Check out the architecture in Figure 7.1. Disk optimization starts with MONITOR.NLM and leads to block suballocation and file compression. In addition, you can further optimize the server by prioritizing applications.
- *Network Packets* — The fundamental building blocks of network communication. Network optimization involves MONITOR.NLM, Packet Receive Buffers, packet bursting, and Large Internet Packets (LIPs).

Now that you understand the big picture, let's start our journey with a discussion of memory management.

Memory Management

Server memory obviously has a dramatic impact on NetWare 5.1 server performance. Thus, NetWare 5.1 memory management architecture is designed to achieve the following goals:

- Allocate memory to the processes that need it
- Utilize memory deallocation
- Achieve efficient performance

FIGURE 7.1

Blocks and buffers in NetWare 5.1

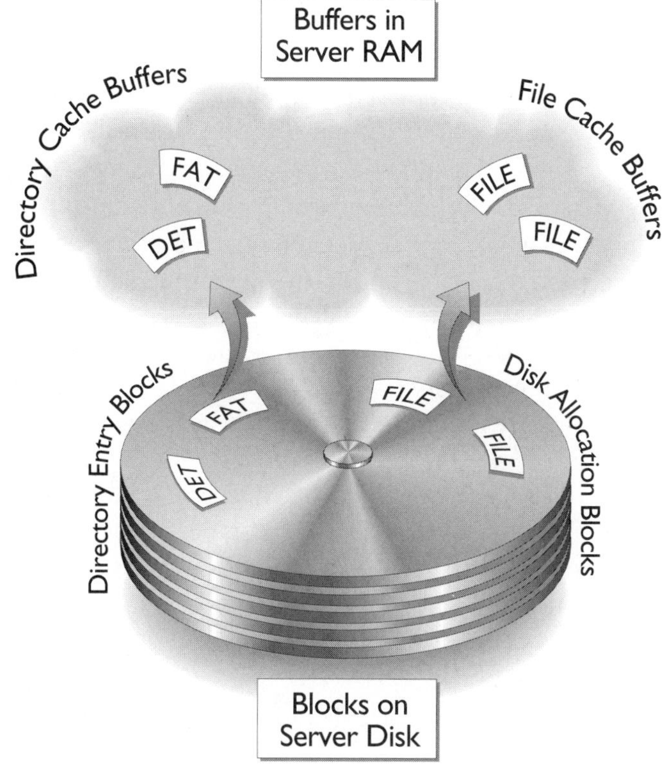

- Create a secure server environment
- Provide a simple, straightforward environment for NLM developers

In this first section on optimization, we will explore three important aspects of NetWare 5.1 memory management: memory allocation, virtual memory, and memory protection.

Memory Allocation

NetWare 5.1 includes a highly efficient memory allocation strategy called *paging*. Each memory "page" consists of a 4K block of RAM. With paging, the server can assign physically noncontiguous pages of memory in a logically contiguous (adjacent) range, resulting in efficient memory allocation and utilization.

As a network administrator, you must be aware of how memory allocation affects server performance. Specifically, the paging memory allocation scheme reserves a special memory location in RAM for processes, instructions, and data. NetWare then assigns each process to its own allocation pool. A process requests memory from its own allocation pool and returns memory to the same pool. This minimizes fragmentation and maximizes efficiency. It also enables third-party developers to easily create and optimize applications.

In addition, NetWare 5.1 includes the following two server processes for recovering unused segments of memory and returning them to a common memory pool:

- *Memory Deallocation* — NLM programmers can tell NetWare that a particular buffer of memory is no longer needed by using an application program interface (API) called *Free,* which labels the memory as deallocated.
- *Garbage Collection* — Once freed, these deallocated memory buffers are ready for collection. This is accomplished using a sophisticated internal *garbage collection* process, which automatically occurs every five minutes (by default). If virtual memory is heavily used, then garbage collection is activated immediately. You can optimize garbage collection by using the SET GARBAGE COLLECTION INTERVAL command (the range is from 1 to 60 minutes; the default is 5).

Periodic garbage collection is necessary to ensure that deallocated memory is recovered by NetWare. Furthermore, garbage collection can be accelerated by other memory management features, such as virtual memory. By default, NetWare checks virtual memory usage every ten seconds. If virtual memory is being used heavily, then garbage collection is immediately activated.

If virtual memory usage is low, then garbage collection occurs according to a variety of server-based parameters. For example, you can use the SET GARBAGE COLLECTION INTERVAL command to optimize the garbage collection process. This parameter sets the interval for collection. The range is from 1 to 60 minutes; the default is 5 minutes. You can set this parameter using MONITOR or SET.

We'll explore SET commands later in the chapter. But here's a quick preview. SET is a NetWare 5.1 console command. The great news about SET is that when you select a category, the current values for each parameter display onscreen. In addition, the range of parameters is also displayed, so you know how high or low you can go. It sure beats looking it up in a manual.

In addition to SET, MONITOR.NLM provides numerous memory utilization statistics. Most of them are found under the Resource Utilization option. Figure 7.2 illustrates the NetWare 5.1 memory utilization statistics. Later in this chapter, we'll use this screen to determine how our server resources utilize available RAM.

FIGURE 7.2

Memory utilization in MONITOR.NLM

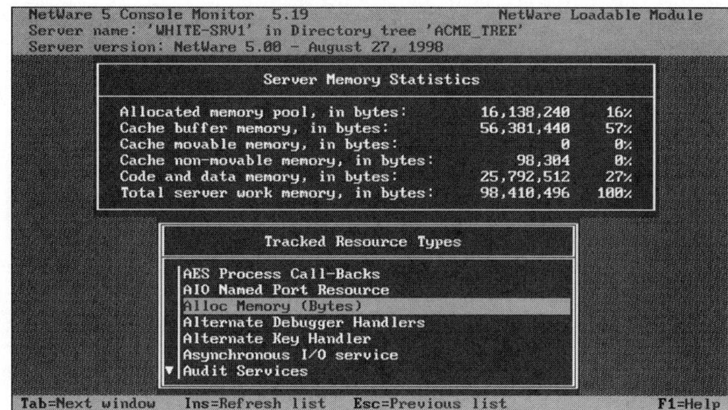

Memory deallocation and garbage collection go a long way in helping you optimize physical server RAM. However, they can't solve one critical problem: *running out of memory!* Fortunately, NetWare 5.1 offers virtual memory to solve this problem. Let's take a closer look.

Virtual Memory

NetWare 5.1 *virtual memory* increases server-based application performance by supporting as much memory as applications require, whenever they require it. This is accomplished by temporarily storing memory files on the hard drive when there is not enough RAM to complete an operation.

NetWare 5.1 monitors available server memory using the Least Recently Used (LRU) algorithm. Data that has not been used for some time is moved from memory to disk, thus freeing memory for other uses. When the data on disk is needed again, it is moved back into available memory. Because data is swapped on and off the disk, the available memory supports more operations than its physical capacity would usually allow.

When data is moved from memory to disk, it is stored in a *swap file*. By default, NetWare 5.1 automatically creates a swap file on the SYS: volume. You can create swap files on any NetWare 5.1 volume, although only one swap file can exist per volume.

Java applications and server modules that are loaded into protected address spaces automatically use virtual memory. Although swapping data between memory and disk requires additional system resources, it increases the memory available for applications — ultimately improving overall server performance, if managed correctly.

Following are some important considerations for using NetWare 5.1 virtual memory:

- You can only create one swap file per volume. The swap file on the SYS: volume is created by default. It is named _SWAP_MEM and occupies 2MB in the root directory. You can delete this swap file and move it to another volume if desired. Swap file management tasks must be performed using the NetWare SWAP utility. These operations cannot be performed using Windows or DOS file management utilities. (**Note:** You can also view, but not modify, swap file statistics using MONITOR.NLM.)

- Data moved to virtual memory will be stored in any available swap file on any available volume. To avoid running out of space on SYS:, you should consider moving the swap file on SYS: to a different volume. The best choices for swap file placement are fast volumes with large amounts of available disk space.

- You can add a swap file to a volume even if the volume is not mounted. The file will then be created automatically when the volume is mounted.

- When you down a server, all swap files on host volumes are deleted. The exception is the SYS: volume, which automatically re-creates its swap file each time the server is started. In addition, swap files are deactivated when host volumes are dismounted. Swap files are then automatically reactivated when host volumes are mounted.

- Swap files are dynamic. They change in size as data is swapped in and out of memory.

You can use the SWAP console command to manage NetWare 5.1 virtual memory at the server. For more information, type **HELP SWAP** at the server console. With this utility, you can display information about swap files currently in use, create swap files on specific volumes, delete a swap file, or change swap file parameter values. Refer to Table 7.1 for some quick tips on virtual memory management using SWAP.

TABLE 7.1

Managing Virtual Memory

TO DO THIS	TYPE THIS AT THE SERVER CONSOLE
Display information about swap files	**SWAP** Alternatively, from the MONITOR Available Options menu, select Virtual Memory ➪ Swap Files.
Create a swap file on a designated volume.	**SWAP ADD *volume_name [parameter=value]*** Optional parameters are MIN=, MAX=, and MIN FREE=. These parameters specify the minimum and maximum size of the swap file and the minimum free space that must be left on the volume. Values are in millions of bytes. If parameters are not included, the following default values are used: (c)MIN = 2 (c)Max = Free volume space (c)MIN FREE = 5
Delete a swap file from a designated volume.	**SWAP DEL *volume_name*** If the swap file is being used when it is deleted, then the swapped data is moved to another swap file.
Change the parameter values for a swap file on a designated volume.	**SWAP PARAMETER *volume_name parameter=value*** Parameters are MIN=, MAX=, and MIN FREE=.

If the overall supply of server memory is low, swapping occurs more frequently. If memory is extremely low, however, the server may spend numerous processor cycles swapping memory to and from the disk and then have no time left to accomplish useful work. This is called *disk thrashing*.

If disk thrashing occurs, you should immediately add more RAM to the server. Virtual memory cannot compensate for an overall lack of server memory, although it can prevent processes from failing, and it can enable the server to continue to function. The real value of virtual memory is that it enables a server to use a sufficient supply of memory more efficiently, thus improving server performance. Running server applications in virtual memory also protects the application and improves server reliability.

Memory Protection

Any NLM that you load from the server console is always loaded into the OS address space unless you explicitly specify that it be loaded in a protected space. NetWare 5.1 also includes a memory protection scheme that enables you to load server programs into the following two different types of memory space:

- *Protected Address Space* — Also known as *protected memory*. Protected address space is a portion of memory that is allowed only carefully controlled communication with the NetWare operating system. NetWare creates a boundary around the protected address space so that any programs running in the space are prohibited from referencing areas of memory outside the boundary. Therefore, the protected address space provides a safe place to run programs because modules loaded into a protected address space can't corrupt the operating system or cause server abends.
- *OS Address Space* — Also known as *kernel address space*. The NetWare operating system itself cannot run in a protected address space. Instead, it is loaded outside the boundary of protected memory. This "unprotected" space offers better performance and direct connections to critical server programs.

NetWare 5.1 memory protection is accomplished using SYSCALLS.NLM. This server-based utility works in conjunction with the memory protection subsystem to prevent modules in a protected address space from having direct contact with anything outside the boundary.

By default, modules that are loaded into protected address spaces use virtual memory. Both the module and the data it accesses can be swapped to disk. Modules that are loaded outside of protected address space can also use virtual memory, but the modules themselves cannot be swapped to disk.

Follow these guidelines when using NetWare 5.1 memory protection:

- Because modules loaded into a protected address space have controlled communication with the operating system, all modules that must communicate with each other should be loaded into the same protected address space. NetWare automatically loads all dependent modules of an NLM in the same space as the host program.
- If the same module is loaded into more than one address space, the module's code will be shared among the address spaces. Therefore, loading a module into multiple address spaces does not require additional memory for the module itself (because only the data for the required module is unique in each space).
- Even if an NLM is designed to be loaded only once, you can load multiple copies of the NLM if you load them into different protected spaces.
- When you load modules into a protected address space, NetWare assigns whatever amount of memory the loaded modules need (up to a maximum of 512MB). The maximum size of a protected address space is fixed, but within that maximum limit, the memory size of the space grows and shrinks as needed by the loaded modules.
- If you want the server to clean up an abended address space, enter the following command at the server console: **SET Memory Protection Fault Cleanup=On**. If an address space abends, the server removes the space and its modules and returns the resources to the system. If the Memory Protection Fault Cleanup parameter is set to OFF, the situation is left to the abend recovery mechanism.

Network administrators can create a protected address space, load modules into a protected address space, unload modules from a protected address space, remove a protected address space, or kill a protected address space by using the commands in Table 7.2.

TABLE 7.2

Managing Protected Address Spaces

TO DO THIS	ENTER THIS COMMAND AT THE SERVER CONSOLE
Display a list of loaded modules with their address space names. This command displays the name of each loaded NLM and the name of the address space it resides in.	**MODULES**
Display a list of all address spaces. This command displays each address space on the system and a list of modules in that space.	**PROTECTION**
Load one module into a new protected address space. A new address space named ADDRESS_SPACE*n* (where *n* is a number) is created and the module is loaded into it.	**LOAD PROTECTED *module_name***
Load one module into a new protectedspace with Restart enabled. A new address space named ADDRESS_SPACE*n* (where *n* is a number) is created and the module is loaded into it. If the module in the protected space abends, the system shuts down and restarts the space, and then the system reloads the module into the space.	**RESTART *module_name***
Load more than one module into the same protected space. The specified module is loaded into the specified address space.	**LOAD ADDRESS SPACE=*address_space_name module_name***
Load multiple modules into a new protected space. A new protected space named the same as the .NCF file is loaded into the address space.	**PROTECT *NCF_file_name***
Unload a module from an address space. The specified module is unloaded from the specified address space, but the address space itself remains intact.	**UNLOAD ADDRESS SPACE=*address_space_name module_name***
Unload all modules from an address space and remove the address space. All the modules are unloaded from the specified address space, the address space is closed, and the resources are returned to the system.	**UNLOAD ADDRESS SPACE=*address_space_name***

TABLE 7.2

Managing Protected Address Spaces (continued)

TO DO THIS	ENTER THIS COMMAND AT THE SERVER CONSOLE
Remove the address space without unloading modules. The specified address space is removed, but the modules in it are not unloaded first. The resources are then returned to the system.	**UNLOAD KILL ADDRESS SPACE=** ***address_space_name***

That's it. A great overview of NetWare 5.1 memory management. Wasn't that fun? Now it's time to begin our monitoring and optimization expedition with a detailed look at MONITOR.NLM. This comprehensive server-based tool helps you isolate performance bottlenecks in the server disk or network packets. Then you can optimize them in the second half of this chapter.

Monitoring with MONITOR.NLM

The real journey begins with MONITOR.NLM.

I know that you are a great network administrator, but nobody can fix problems that he or she doesn't know about. Monitoring is important because it enables you to create an *Optimization Plan*. NetWare 5.1 server and network optimization is a two-step process:

- *Step 1: Monitoring* — Involves periodic interrogation of key server and network performance components, including file cache buffers, service processes, PacketReceive Buffers (PRBs), and disk allocation blocks. This is accomplished using the MONITOR.NLM server-based utility.
- *Step 2: Optimization* — Involves a variety of server and network solutions aimed at solving the problems identified in Step 1. Optimization is accomplished by using MONITOR.NLM, SET parameters, packet bursting, and Large Internet Packets (LIP).

The main screen of MONITOR.NLM is displayed in Figure 7.3. It consists of two text-based windows (General Information and Available Options) surrounded by two status bars (top and bottom). The General Information window offers a snapshot of performance statistics and can be further expanded by pressing the Tab key.

FIGURE 7.3

The main screen of MONITOR.NLM

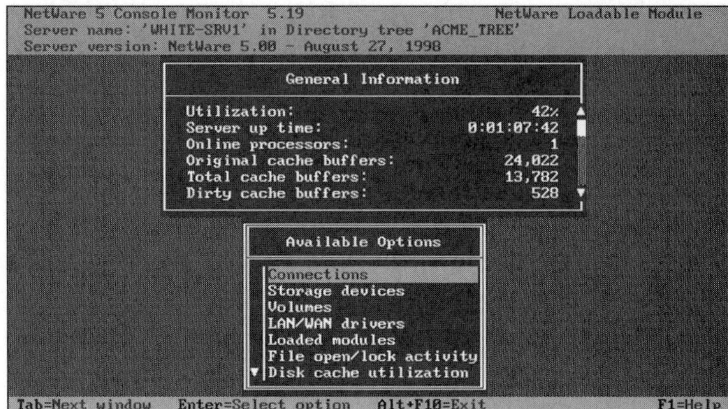

The Available Options window in MONITOR.NLM provides access to several performance-based subscreens. In this section, we will study the following four critical options:

- Memory Utilization
- Cache Utilization
- Processor Utilization
- Network Board Statistics

You'll spend most of your monitoring time in these four areas. But MONITOR doesn't stop there. Refer to Table 7.3 for an expanded list of all the choices in the Available Options menu in MONITOR.NLM.

TABLE 7.3

Monitoring Parameters on the Main Screen of MONITOR.NLM

ITEM	MEANING
Server Name	Server name and tree (see upper-left corner of screen).
Server Version	Operating system version and release date (see upper-left corner of screen).
Utilization	Percentage of time the CPU is working (versus idle).
Server Up Time	Days, hours, minutes, and seconds since the server was last started.
Online Processors	Number of processors enabled.
Original Cache Buffers	Number of cache buffers measured just after the OS Kernel (SERVER.NLM) is loaded.
Total Cache Buffers	Number of buffers currently available for file caching. This number decreases as modules are loaded into memory.
Dirty Cache Buffers	Number of buffers that have updated data not yet written to disk.
Long-Term Cache Hits	Number of times requested data was found in RAM rather than having to access data on the hard disk.
Current Disk Requests	Number of disk I/O requests currently pending.
Packet Receive Buffers	Pool of buffers set aside for incoming network packets.
Directory Cache Buffers	Pool of buffers set aside for volume directory tables.
Maximum Service Processes	Maximum number of task handlers or threads that can be allocated for station requests. When the number of station requests exceeds what is currently allocated, the operating system uses extra task handlers to execute the requests. Once memory is allocated for a service process, it remains allocated. The only way to remove this memory allocation is to bring down the servers.
Current Service Processes	Number of task handlers or threads currently allocated for station requests.
Current Connections	Number of licensed and unlicensed connections currently attached to the NetWare server.
Open Files	Number of files currently being accessed by the server itself and by any connected workstations.

Memory Utilization

The System Resource information screen in MONITOR.NLM provides a method of tracking memory utilization for specific NLMs. You should be proactive about tracking NLM usage because some NLMs may not immediately return unused memory to the main OS pool. This decreases server performance because it limits available cache buffers.

Consider the following points with respect to NLM memory utilization:

- Many NLMs rely on prerequisite NLMs. Memory needed for loading an NLM is approximately the same as the file size of the NLM, plus the file sizes of all prerequisite NLMs.
- Some NLMs allocate additional memory while they are running.

Furthermore, the Loaded Modules screen of MONITOR.NLM allows you to choose any of the NLMs loaded on your system and to view how each is using server memory. If you add a new NLM, perhaps as a result of purchasing a new server-based program (SMS Backup, for example), you might want to track its supporting resources through the Loaded Modules screen.

A well-behaved NLM will take the memory it needs and then free it after use. The Remote Console is a good example. Figure 7.4 shows the Memory Utilization screen for REMOTE.NLM when it's being used. As you can see in Figure 7.4, ten 4K pages have been allocated for use by REMOTE.NLM, of which about two-thirds are being used. Garbage collection will pick up these free blocks the next time it is activated.

Cache Utilization

The Cache Utilization Statistics screen in MONITOR.NLM displays numerous server cache utilization statistics (see Figure 7.5). NetWare uses caching to speed up reads and writes to and from server disks. A *cache* is a temporary, quickly accessible area in RAM that stores frequently used hard disk files. As long as data stays in RAM, NetWare can access it much faster.

FIGURE 7.4

Memory utilization for REMOTE.NLM

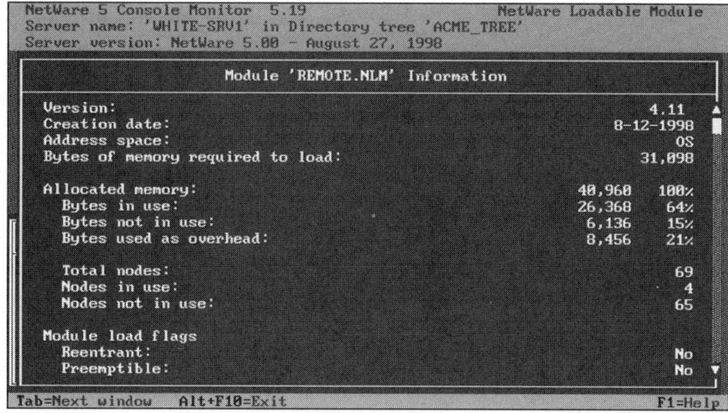

FIGURE 7.5

Cache utilization in MONITOR.NLM

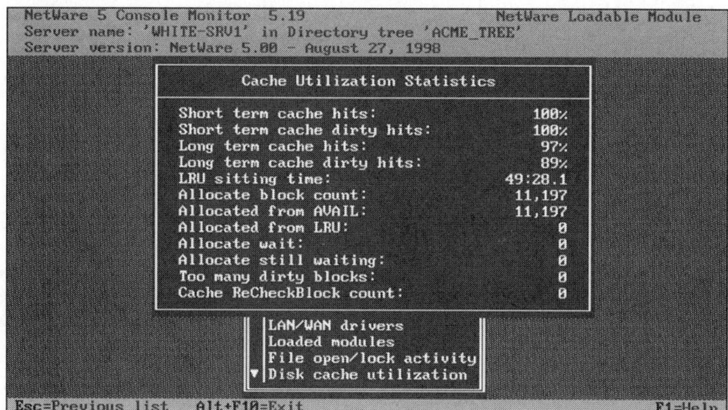

Caching is the converse of virtual memory in that it holds frequently used disk files in memory for faster access. The more memory that you have available for caching, the more "cache hits" you will get. Furthermore, a large number of cache hits improves server performance. On the other hand, the more server NLMs that you load, the less RAM the server has available for caching data. This lowers your cache hit percentage and slows network performance.

Cache hits are organized into the following two groups:

- *Short-Term Cache Hits* — Data that has been accessed from the server cache within the last second. Your server should not fall below 98 percent short-term cache hits (see Figure 7.5).
- *Long-Term Cache Hits* — Includes all cache requests since the server was last booted. Your server should not fall below 90 percent long-term cache hits (see Figure 7.5).

Use the Cache Utilization Statistics screen, shown in Figure 7.5, to track short-term and long-term cache hits. If the number of hits falls below the targets listed above, you have two options: add more RAM to the server (most effective) or unload noncritical NLMs (least effective).

NetWare 5.1 also includes some cache-related SET parameters that enable you to manage file reads and writes. You can improve server performance by optimizing caching for reads or writes (follow the guidelines presented in Table 7.4).

TABLE 7.4

SET Parameters for Write-Intensive and Read-Intensive Servers

PARAMETER	WRITE SETTING	READ SETTING	DEFAULT	MEANING
Maximum Concurrent Disk Cache Writes	750	150	750	Maximum number of disk cache writes that will be scheduled on one pass of the read/write head.
Maximum Concurrent Directory Cache Writes	185	40	75	Maximum number of directory cache writes that will be scheduled on one pass of the read/write head.
Dirty Disk Cache Delay Time	7 seconds	N/A	3.3 seconds	Minimum amount of time the system waits before writing a not-completely dirty disk cache buffer.

TABLE 7.4

SET Parameters for Write-Intensive and Read-Intensive Servers (continued)

PARAMETER	WRITE SETTING	READ SETTING	DEFAULT	MEANING
Dirty Directory Cache Delay Time	2 seconds	N/A	0.5 seconds	Minimum amount of time the system waits before writing a not-completely dirty directory cache buffer.
Directory Cache Buffer Non-referenced Delay	N/A	60 seconds	5.5 seconds	Minimum time a directory block will be held in cache after it was last accessed.

Processor Utilization

The third critical element affecting server performance is the CPU. Fortunately, a high processor-utilization percentage by itself is not always a problem. Processes that make efficient use of the server CPU can cause utilization to stay at 100 percent for short periods. For example, processes such as compression and decompression make efficient use of the processor, but may cause 100 percent utilization.

On the other hand, you might have a problem if a process monopolizes the server CPU at 100 percent for several minutes or so. This can cause dropped connections or degraded server performance. If you have a server with a significant CPU load, you should find the monopolizing process or task and move it to another machine.

Refer to Figure 7.6 for a snapshot of the Processor Information screen in MONITOR.NLM. To display this screen, choose Kernel from the Available Options menu and then select Processors from the Kernel Options menu.

Here are a few tips to consider for lowering your server's processor utilization:

- Compile baseline data to determine your server's typical utilization and then take action when it gets high.
- Place some services (printing, database, application, gateway, and communications) on other dedicated servers. Also, consider upgrading the hardware in this server.

- Set low-priority threads to remain low priority. Refer to the "Application Management" section later in the chapter for further details.
- Manage compression and backup activity during off-hours.

FIGURE 7.6

Processor utilization in MONITOR.NLM

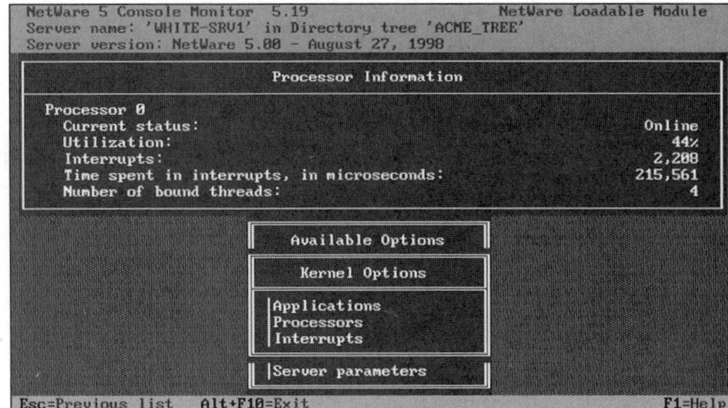

Network Board Statistics

The LAN/WAN statistics screen in MONITOR.NLM provides a snapshot of network communication performance (see Figure 7.7). These network board statistics are important for performance optimization because they reveal trends in network communication or problem areas that must be addressed.

FIGURE 7.7

Network board statistics in MONITOR.NLM

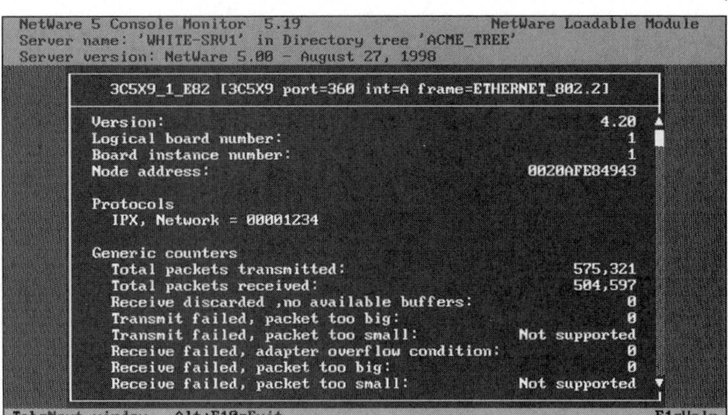

Following are two vital network board statistics you should monitor:

- *Receive Discarded, No Available Buffers* — This statistic is updated whenever an incoming packet must be rejected because there is no available Packet Receive Buffer (PRB) for it. If this statistic climbs above 2 percent of the total packets received, then the server is not handling processes fast enough for the network board. To solve this problem, you should increase the maximum and minimum PRB settings and/or upgrade the server processor or RAM.
- *Packets Queued for Transmission* — Tracks the packets that the server has not yet processed. If this statistic climbs above 2 percent of the total packets received, then the network board is not handling processes fast enough for the server. In this case, you should consider upgrading the server network board.

REAL WORLD

Study the four MONITOR.NLM screens covered in "Monitoring with MONITOR.NLM" section carefully. You should be able to determine which items need attention if given a sample statistics screen. For example, remember that short-term cache hits should not fall below 98 percent and long-term cache hits should not fall below 90 percent. Also, remember that server utilization should not operate at 100 percent for more than a few minutes. Finally, remember that neither of the following two network board statistics should exceed 2 percent of the total packets received: "Receive discarded, no available buffers" and "Packets queued for transmission."

NetWare Management Portal

In addition to MONITOR.NLM, NetWare 5.1 includes a new GUI-based browser resource management and optimization tool called the *NetWare Management Portal.* This tool enables you to remotely manage NetWare servers through any 32-bit version of Windows running an appropriate Web browser — such as Netscape Navigator (version 4.5 or later) or Internet Explorer (version 4 or later).

In addition, the browsing workstation must have at least a 28.8 Kbps connection to an intranet or the Internet.

The secure NetWare Management Portal homepage requires an https connection and NDS authentication. It includes a "traffic light" indicator on the top-left corner of the page that displays the general health of the target server. Below the traffic-light graphic is the following series of tabs:

- *Volume Management* — This tab allows you to view a list of volumes, individual files, and volume statistics. In addition, it enables you to manage volumes and files, including mounting volumes, dismounting volumes, uploading files, and renaming and deleting files.
- *Server Management* — This tab allows you to view SET parameters, debugging information, system statistics, and console screens. In addition, it enables you to manage server resources, including memory, connections, and SET parameters. Finally, you can use the Server Management tab to bring down the server, but the NetWare Management Portal will not allow you to remotely restart it.
- *Application Management* — This tab enables you to view and load modules, manage address spaces, configure memory protection, view the entire Registry tree structure, and manage Winsock 2.0.
- *NDS Management* — This tab allows you to walk the NDS tree and view NDS partitioning information.
- *Remote Server Access* — This tab enables you to jump to any other server's Management Portal homepage and to list other NetWare Remote Server Access (NWRSA) activated server consoles.
- *Hardware Management* — This tab allows you to view hardware adapters in the server, processor information, hardware resources, and detailed PCI device information.

- *Health Monitors*—This tab is linked to the Traffic Light indicator. It provides detailed statistics regarding a variety of server health conditions: green (good), yellow (suspect), and red (bad). The Health Monitor tab enables you to track DS thread usage, allocated and available server processes, abend /debug information, CPU usage, connection availability, buffers availability, and virtual memory (VM) performance.

Well, that does it for monitoring. Now that you are comfortable with the first phase of NetWare 5.1 optimization, let's move on to the second phase—optimizing the server and network. In the next two sections, we will explore the details of proactive optimization using a variety of server and network tools, including block suballocation, file compression, PRBs, packet bursting, and LIP.

Optimizing the Server

While NetWare servers have been optimized for LAN services, recent advancements in the Internet, high-capacity multimedia files, and complex digital printing have placed a tremendous load on the NetWare 5.1 file server. As a result, you must spend more time tuning and optimizing it.

In this section, we will study three NetWare 5.1 optimization solutions aimed at solving server performance problems:

- *Application Management*—Enables you to prioritize server-based applications by intelligently allocating processor cycles.
- *Block Suballocation*—Enables you to avoid inefficient server disk storage by suballocating multiple pieces of data into a single block.
- *File Compression*—Enhances server disk performance by automatically compressing infrequently used files.

Let's get busy . . . starting with server applications.

Application Management

The first server optimization strategy involves internal CPU utilization by server-based applications. NetWare 5.1 allows you to allocate shares of CPU time to each application running on your server. This helps you prioritize server application performance.

NetWare 5.1 application management relies on the following two important components:

- *Threads* — NLM code is composed of routines that can travel various potential paths. When an NLM runs, it chooses a particular path, called a *thread*. If one thread encounters a delay, other threads are forced to wait in line. In this case, the thread causing the delay is said to have "gone to sleep" or is guilty of being a "CPU hog." To avoid these delays, NetWare can suspend a thread that is hogging the CPU and then reactivate it at a later time at the exact point where the thread went to sleep. NetWare can then give CPU time to process another thread while the first thread is suspended.

- *Application* — Sometimes referred to as a *virtual machine*. An *application* consists of a group of threads within a given application space that are treated as a unit when processing resources are assigned. The physical resources in the computer can be used to share the CPU and to make each application appear to have its own processor. This enables you to specify the amount of CPU time that threads in the application are allowed to use when competing with other applications.

When a NetWare 5.1 server is started, one application is created by default — the *NetWare Application*. All traditional file, print, and connectivity services are provided by the NetWare Application. The NetWare Application is loaded with a default share value of 100. All the threads run by startup NLMs are assigned to the NetWare Application.

You can customize application prioritization when you load new NLMs by using the following syntax:

```
LOAD -A=application NLM
```

In this example, *application* refers to your new process tag and *NLM* refers to the full NLM name. For example, if you want to load MONITOR and create an application named "LABS-Monitor" for it, you would enter the following command at the server console: **LOAD -A=LABS-Monitor MONITOR.NLM.**

Once an application is loaded, you can adjust the share value assigned to it. *Share value* is the proportional amount of CPU time that threads in the application are allowed to use when competing with other applications on the server. For example, if you assign one application 70 shares and another application 10 shares, the first application will receive seven times more CPU time than the second application.

To adjust the share value assigned to an application, perform the following tasks in MONITOR.NLM: First, select Kernel from the Available Options menu. Then select Applications and choose the process you're interested in from the Applications menu. Finally, press F3 and enter the new share value in the New Share Value window.

REAL WORLD

Some server programs will create their own application tags when the host NLM is loaded. Programs that cannot create their own applications can either be (1) manually assigned to a user-created application or (2) loaded into the NetWare Application (by not assigning it to an application).

Now that you have mastered NetWare 5.1 application prioritization, let's continue our server optimization discussion with block suballocation.

Block Suballocation

Block suballocation is a disk optimization feature that increases the efficiency of file storage on internal server disks. In NetWare 5.1, data files are stored on hard drives in units called *blocks*. Each volume has a predefined block size, ranging from 4K to 64K.

Problems arise when you combine large block sizes and numerous small files. For example, without suballocation, a 64K block would be fully occupied by a 5K or 63K file. In either case, the unused space (59K or 1K, respectively) is wasted and unavailable for other files. See Figure 7.8.

FIGURE 7.8

NetWare 5.1 disk storage without block suballocation

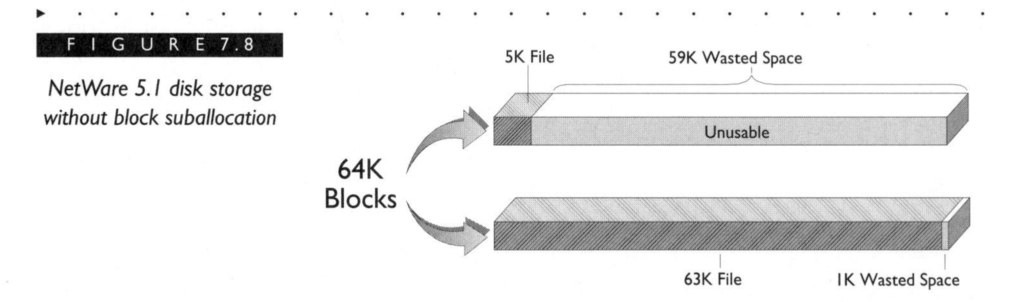

Block suballocation solves this problem by dividing partially used disk blocks into 512-byte suballocation blocks. These suballocation blocks can then be used by multiple files. In the first example in Figure 7.8, we would be able to allocate the remaining 59K to other files. A second 100K file, for example, would take up another 64K block and send the remaining 36K over to the first block (as shown in Figure 7.9).

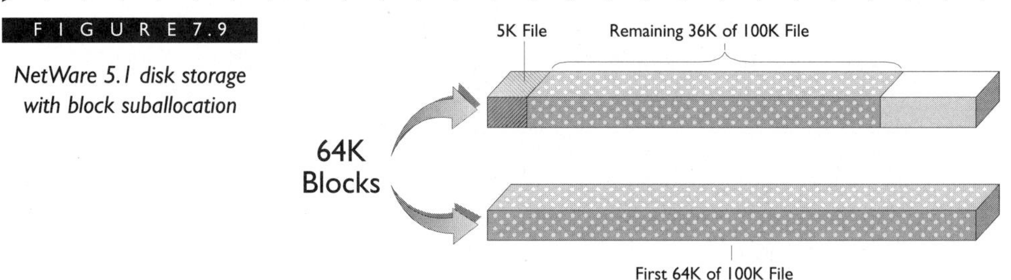

FIGURE 7.9

NetWare 5.1 disk storage with block suballocation

It is important to remember that files always start at the beginning of a new block. You cannot start a new file within an already occupied suballocation block. You can, however, store the remainder of a large file within the suballocation area. Here's the bottom line:

- *Without Block Suballocation*—The two files totaling 105K would occupy three 64K blocks and waste 87K of server disk space.

- *With Block Suballocation*—The two files totaling 105K would occupy two suballocated blocks, leaving 23K of server disk space to be used by one or more other files.

Because block suballocation saves so much disk space, NetWare automatically activates it during volume creation.

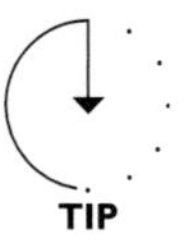

You cannot disable block suballocation once a volume has been created. Your only option is to re-create the volume from scratch.

File Compression

File compression enables NetWare 5.1 volumes to hold more online data by automatically compressing inactive files. Users can save up to 63 percent of a server's disk space by activating file compression—that's 1GB of files in 370MB of space. This is called the *compression ratio*. It's important to note that NetWare sacrifices speed to optimize the compression ratio.

File compression is turned on automatically during volume creation. It cannot be turned off without re-creating the volume. Once file compression has been turned on, it can be activated in one of the following two ways:

- You can activate file compression by flagging directories and files as IC (Immediate Compress). The files will then be compressed immediately. However, if the SET ENABLE FILE COMPRESSION parameter is set to OFF, NetWare will queue IC files until compression is turned on again. Incidentally, you can use NetWare Administrator, FILER, FLAG, or Windows Explorer to set these file/directory attributes.

- You can also activate file compression by using either file compression SET commands at the server console or MONITOR.NLM to configure volume-based inactivity delay parameters. These settings should be stored in the server's AUTOEXEC.NCF file to ensure automatic activation when the server starts. To configure file compression parameters using MONITOR.NLM as shown in Figure 7.10, select Server Parameters ⇨ File System.

FIGURE 7.10

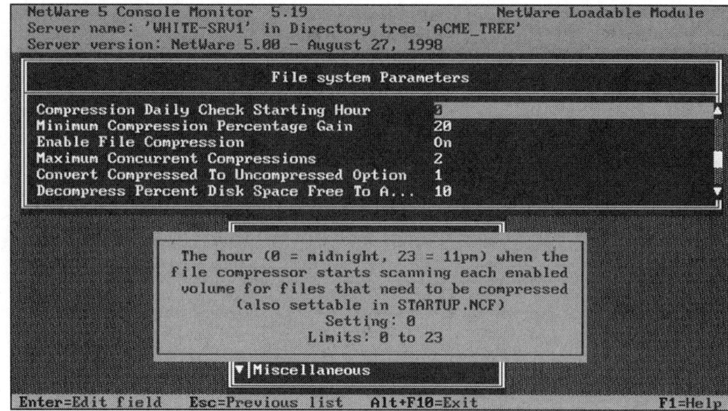

File compression parameters in MONITOR.NLM

By default, the file compression inactivity delay is set to seven days. If a file is not accessed within seven days, it will automatically be compressed. Users can avoid having their files compressed by flagging specific files or directories as DC (Don't Compress). Files are automatically decompressed when users access them. Decompression occurs in server RAM before the file is delivered to the workstation. This process happens much faster than compression.

The NetWare 5.1 file compression process occurs in a series of five steps:

1. A timer goes off, and file compression begins. Once file compression is activated, NetWare 5.1 reads and analyzes each file.

2. NetWare 5.1 builds a temporary file describing the original file. This feature ensures that the original file is not at risk if data is corrupted during the compression process.

3. NetWare 5.1 determines whether any disk sectors can be saved by compressing the file. A gain of at least 20 percent (by default) is required before a file is compressed. This parameter is configurable using the SET console command.

4. NetWare 5.1 begins creation of the compressed file.

5. NetWare 5.1 replaces the original with the compressed file after an error-free compressed version has been created.

Although file compression is set at the volume level, you can control specific file compression parameters with SET commands or MONITOR. These settings should be stored in the AUTOEXEC.NCF file to ensure automatic activation when the server starts. Check out Table 7.5 for a list of all the SET commands you can use to manage file compression. These settings affect all files and directories on the server.

TABLE 7.5

Understanding File Compression SET Commands

COMMAND	DEFAULT	MIN.	MAX.	MEANING
Compression Daily Check Stop Hour	6:00 a.m.	0	23	When system should stop scanning for compression candidates. Automatic searching for unopened files stops until the starting hour on the next day. If equal to start hour, then run until finished.
Compression Daily Check Start Hour	0	0	23	Time when system should start scanning for candidates to com-press. Hours are specified in military time. Default is 0 (midnight).
Minimum Compression Percentage Gain	20	0	50	If a file compresses less than this percent, then leave it expanded.
Enable File Compression	ON			If OFF, then don't scan for compression and queue all IC flag requests. If you enter **SET ENABLE FILE COMPRESSON=OFF**, file compression is still enabled for the volume, but files will not be compressed. The setting applies to the entire server.
Maximum Concurrent Compressions	2	1	8	Number of volumes that can be scanned for compression at one time. Novell does not recommend increasing the default.

Continued

TABLE 7.5

Understanding File Compression SET Commands (continued)

COMMAND	DEFAULT	MIN.	MAX.	MEANING
Convert Compressed to Uncompressed option	1	0	2	0 = leave it compressed; 1 = store uncompressed after a single access in "untouched" period; 2 = always change to an uncompressed version.
Decompress Percent Disk Space Free to Allow Commit	10	0	75	This option specifies the percentage of free disk space required on a volume before an uncompressed file can be committed to disk. This prevents newly uncompressed files from filling up the volume.
Decompress Free Space Warning Interval	31 minutes, 18.5 seconds	0	29 days, 15 hours, 50 minutes, 3.8 seconds	This number specifies the interval for displaying warning alerts when the volume has insufficient free disk space for uncompressed files. To turn off the alerts, set it to 0.
Deleted Files Compression Option	1	0	2	0 = don't; 1 = compress next day; 2 = compress immediately.
Days Untouched Before Compression	14	0	100,000	Number of days to wait before an unmodified file becomes a candidate for compression.

Once you have activated file compression, you can monitor disk space savings in NetWare Administrator. Figure 7.11 illustrates the File Compression statistics available in the Statistics page of a Volume object. As you can see, the volume has 1,658.87MB of disk space, of which 1,333.31MB are free. Yet, there are more than 430.13MB of data already stored on it. Fortunately, the compressed size is 177.00MB. Apparently, you can get seven pounds of sand into a two-pound bag, if you have a good compression program. NetWare 5.1 has an average compression ratio of 63 percent.

FIGURE 7.11

File compression statistics in NetWare Administrator

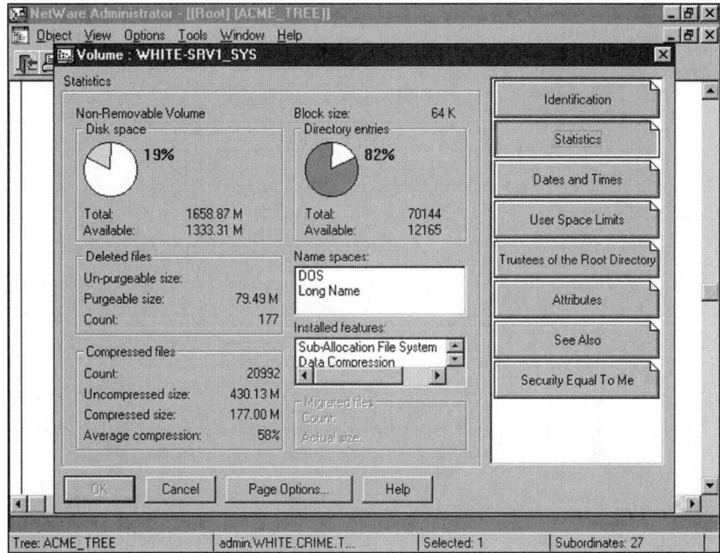

REAL WORLD

During file compression, NetWare 5.1 builds a temporary file describing the contents of the original file. It compresses the temporary file and eventually replaces the original file. If the server fails during compression, the original (uncompressed) file is left intact.

That completes our brief, but informative, journey through NetWare 5.1 server optimization. In summary, your server performs best when you activate the following options:

- Critical applications are prioritized with a Share value approaching 100.
- Block Suballocation is enabled.
- File Compression is enabled with a short inactivity threshold.
- Volumes are defined with large disk allocation blocks (16K or larger).

Now that the server is optimized, let's turn our attention toward network optimization. Full speed ahead.

Optimizing the Network

Data is transferred across the network in small chunks known as *packets*. As you might imagine, the server sends and receives far more of these packets than do normal workstations. As an advanced network administrator, you need to employ as many packet-optimization strategies as you can.

In this section, we will study the following three NetWare 5.1 optimization solutions aimed at solving network performance problems:

- *Packet Receive Buffers* — The Packet Receive Buffer pool (sometimes called the PRB pool) is a holding tank for incoming packets as they wait for available service processes. You must achieve a balance between small pools (poor network performance) and large pools (wasted server RAM).
- *Packet Burst Protocol* — This network feature bunches packets into a bursting group and sends them together, effectively decreasing communications overhead and improving network performance.
- *Large Internet Packets* — NetWare 5.1 further enhances network throughput by allowing large packet sizes on router-controlled WAN links.

Let's take a closer look at network optimization — our way!

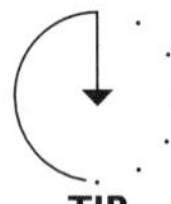
TIP

The Packet Burst feature and the Large Internet Packets feature only work with the IPX protocol.

Packet Receive Buffers

Packets are discrete allocation units of data organized into messages, which travel from one device to another over a network. When a packet arrives at a

NetWare server, it has to wait in a "holding tank" called the *Packet Receive Buffer pool* until a *service process* becomes available to handle it.

In order to optimize network communications, you must achieve a balance between the size of the PRB pool and the number of service processes available to handle incoming requests. This is accomplished using the following five SET parameters:

- *Maximum Packet Receive Buffers* — Determines the maximum number of PRBs that the server can allocate. The default setting (500) is too low for busy servers. Consider increasing it to 700 or 1,000.
- *Minimum Packet Receive Buffers* — Determines the minimum number of PRBs allocated at server startup. This parameter must be set in STARTUP.NCF.
- *Maximum Service Processes* — The maximum number of service processes available to handle incoming user requests. If the number of allocated processes is at its maximum (in the General Information window of MONITOR.NLM), then you should consider increasing this parameter to decrease the need for more PRBs.
- *Minimum Service Processes* — The minimum number of service processes allocated at server startup. If a large number of users are accessing the server, then you should increase this parameter to improve network performance. Both service process parameters can be configured using the Server Parameters ➪ Miscellaneous menu in MONITOR.NLM.
- *Maximum Physical Receive Packet Size* — The largest client packet size supported on the server. You should configure the server LAN driver for the largest packet size it will support so that you don't artificially limit the size of packets on the network. This parameter must be set in STARTUP.NCF.

Refer to Table 7.6 for a summary.

TABLE 7.6

Packet-Related SET Parameters

COMMAND	MIN.	MAX.	MEANING
Maximum Packet Receive Buffers	50	4,294,967,295	Maximum number of PRBs supported on the server for incoming packets. The default is 500.
Minimum Packet Receive Buffers	10	4,294,967,295	Minimum number of PRBs allocated at server startup. The default is 128. Must be set in STARTUP.NCF.
Maximum Service Processes	50	1,000	Maximum number of service processes available for handling incoming user requests. Displayed in the General Information screen of MONITOR.NLM.
Minimum Service Processes	10	500	Number of service processes automatically available when the server boots. Allocated processes are dynamically added until they reach the maximum.
Maximum Physical Receive Packet Size	618	24,682	Largest client packet size supported at the server, as determined by the LAN driver. Must be set in STARTUP.NCF. Default: Token Ring (4202), Ethernet (1514), and ARCNet (not supported).

REAL WORLD

Study the two packet-related SET parameters that must be activated from STARTUP.NCF during server startup (Minimum Packet Receive Buffers and Maximum Physical Receive Packet Size). Also, remember that each of the three main topology standards supports a different default Maximum Physical Receive Packet Size: Token Ring (4202), Ethernet (1514), and ARCNet (not supported). Specifically, know that ARCNet can only route 512-byte packets. Therefore, it doesn't support Large Internet Packets (LIP) or the Maximum Physical Receive Packet Size parameter.

Packet Burst Protocol

The Packet Burst Protocol (PBP) is an integrated NetWare Core Protocol (NCP) feature that improves the performance of large reads and writes. It accomplishes this by sending multiple packets in a "burst" with a single acknowledgment. With packet bursting enabled, NetWare 5.1 clients can issue a single read or write request for blocks of data of up to 64K. The data is partitioned into packets and these packets are transmitted back-to-back without requiring individual acknowledgments. This boosts network performance from 10 to 300 percent, depending on available memory, bandwidth, and message sizes.

NetWare 5.1 packet bursting relies on the following two key performance components:

- *Burst Gap Time*—A time delay requested by the client before individual packets are placed back-to-back on the media. This gap time is used to prevent fast servers from overrunning the client's buffers.
- *Burst Window Size*—The number of frames or packets contained in a single burst. With Packet Burst Protocol, the number of packets in the window is variable, up to a theoretical maximum value of 128 (64K divided by 512-byte packets). The window size is also variable by workstation, depending on how many buffers the workstation has available. The client renegotiates these parameters without user intervention. This is one area in which the PBP's window technology differs from traditional sliding window protocols, such as Synchronous Data-Link Control (SDLC).

When network traffic is heavy enough that packets are being dropped in transmission, the Novell Client decreases the window size to minimize packet loss. Any packets that are lost are retransmitted individually—the entire burst does not need to be retransmitted.

In previous versions of NetWare, Packet Burst had to be enabled both at the workstation and at the server. In NetWare 5.1, Packet Burst is automatically enabled. It cannot be disabled at the server, but it can be disabled on individual workstations. Follow these steps to enable packet bursting on Windows 95/98 workstations:

1. Select Start ➪ Settings ➪ Control Panel and then double-click Network. This provides access to the Windows 95/98 Network Settings dialog box.
2. On the Configuration tab, select Novell NetWare 5.1 Client 32 and then click Properties.

3. Select the Advanced Settings tab. Scroll down the choices until you find the following three packet bursting parameters: Packet Burst, Packet Burst Read Window Size, and Packet Burst Write Window Size.

Each workstation establishes a Packet Burst connection with a NetWare server at login. Once established, the connection remains for the duration of the attachment. Packet Burst is established individually for each connection to different servers. As a result, a workstation running the Novell Client can be attached to a NetWare 5.1 server using Packet Burst and to a NetWare 3.12 server using a standard NCP connection.

Large Internet Packets (LIP)

Novell's Large Internet Packet (LIP) feature enhances throughput on routed networks by allowing workstations and servers to communicate using large packets. Earlier, we learned how the Maximum Physical Receive Packet Size parameter increases packet sizes on NetWare servers. Unfortunately, this number automatically drops to 512 bytes if the server detects a router on the network.

In NetWare 5.1, LIP is automatically enabled at both the workstation and the server. In this configuration, the server ignores the router check during packet-size negotiation and allows data packets larger than 512 bytes. You can configure NetWare routers for larger packet sizes by placing the appropriate Maximum Physical Receive Packet Size SET parameter in each server's STARTUP.NCF file and rebooting the servers.

When LIP is used in conjunction with the Packet Burst Protocol, several large packets can be sent consecutively without having to wait for the standard request/response dialog box. This increases data transmission speed, while reducing the number of packets exchanged.

One of your most challenging and rewarding responsibilities is optimizing performance on the server and network. You should consider several areas when you assess the efficiency of your network or encounter a performance problem:

- Review performance statistics provided through MONITOR to determine the efficiency of your network.

- Enable server performance features, such as application prioritization, block suballocation, and file compression.
- Consider upgrading key network components, such as Packet Receive Buffers, packet bursting, and LIP.

Congratulations! You survived NetWare 5.1 optimization.

As you can see, it's definitely the new frontier of NetWare 5.1 networking. Optimization is more important now than ever—mostly because NDS taxes the server so much. In this chapter, we have learned much about server memory management, monitoring with MONITOR, server optimization, and network communications.

What's next?!!

Believe it or not, this completes another NetWare 5.1 CNE course—Novell Course 570, "NetWare 5.1 Advanced Administration." In Part I of this book, we expanded NetWare 5.1 Administration with a plethora of advanced CNE tasks, including installation, migrating to IP, and exploring the Novell Internet Infrastructure. Then we explored three advanced management arenas: advanced server management, advanced NDS management, and advanced security management. Finally, we topped it all off with a comprehensive look at NetWare 5.1 optimization.

I'm ready to help save the Net . . . how about you?!

LAB EXERCISE 7.1: MONITORING AND OPTIMIZING THE SERVER

Use the hints provided to find the 20 optimization terms hidden in this word search puzzle. Omit any punctuation characters (such as blank spaces, hyphens, and so on) and spell out any numbers.

F	R	E	E	G	C	Q	L	P	E	H	V	T	V	E	U	J	X	Q
I	G	J	N	A	U	T	O	E	X	E	C	N	C	F	W	Q	Q	I
L	B	Q	C	O	M	P	R	E	S	S	I	O	N	R	A	T	I	O
E	D	H	O	F	Q	D	N	G	P	K	K	I	Z	C	E	X	X	M
C	E	I	P	W	J	B	Z	A	M	A	X	I	M	U	M	V	S	D
A	S	E	R	V	I	C	E	P	R	O	C	E	S	S	E	S	W	X
C	V	B	B	T	W	E	N	T	Y	M	Y	K	R	B	H	Q	A	S
H	R	C	H	B	Y	N	T	S	R	U	B	T	E	K	C	A	P	Q
I	Q	W	D	N	H	S	W	V	O	Y	W	S	N	T	N	E	F	J
N	N	C	D	V	J	A	G	Z	Q	I	C	M	J	X	K	I	I	B
G	A	R	B	A	G	E	C	O	L	L	E	C	T	I	O	N	L	P
E	S	I	V	Q	W	H	C	D	D	S	M	W	F	Q	H	O	E	E
Y	Z	Q	Y	W	O	J	S	T	A	R	T	U	P	N	C	F	C	D
D	Z	K	T	W	B	H	C	D	X	M	O	X	D	K	B	M	O	C
Q	K	E	R	N	E	L	A	D	D	R	E	S	S	L	S	U	C	O
F	Z	A	L	T	K	C	T	G	I	A	X	I	E	Q	G	E	C	O
R	H	P	I	Q	W	P	M	G	F	L	Z	V	V	U	T	N	T	G
J	L	V	I	R	T	U	A	L	M	E	M	O	R	Y	J	X	F	N

Hints

1. SWAP commands should be placed in this server configuration file.
2. This is automatically set during server installation and is based on volume size.
3. A quickly accessible area of server RAM that is used to temporarily store frequently used data from the hard disk.
4. Relative comparison of file size before and after compression.
5. Type of cache buffers that contain data that has not yet been written to disk.
6. Process of storing files in server RAM to improve access time.
7. API used to label server RAM as deallocated.
8. Process of recovering unused server RAM.
9. Another name for OS address space. [Note: Omit the word "space" in your answer.]
10. Type of Packet Receive Buffer setting where the default of 500 might be too low for busy servers.
11. Maximum number of swap files allowed per NetWare 5 volume.
12. Unit of information used in network communications.
13. Protocol used to increase the transfer speed of multiple-packet NCP file reads and writes.
14. Consists of a 4K unit of server RAM that can be used by NetWare to assign physically noncontiguous portions of memory in a logically contiguous range.
15. An area of memory that is used to temporarily store incoming data packets until the server is able to process them.
16. Task handlers that process station requests.
17. To change the Maximum Physical Packet Receive Size setting, you should place the appropriate SET command in this configuration file.
18. Contains information that was moved from server RAM to hard disk because of the virtual memory feature.
19. By default, a gain of at least this percentage is required before NetWare 5.1 will compress a file.
20. Memory-management technique in which information in server RAM is swapped to and from a hard disk, when necessary, to provide more efficient use of physical memory.

See Appendix C for answers.

LAB EXERCISE 7.2: NETWARE 5.1 OPTIMIZATION

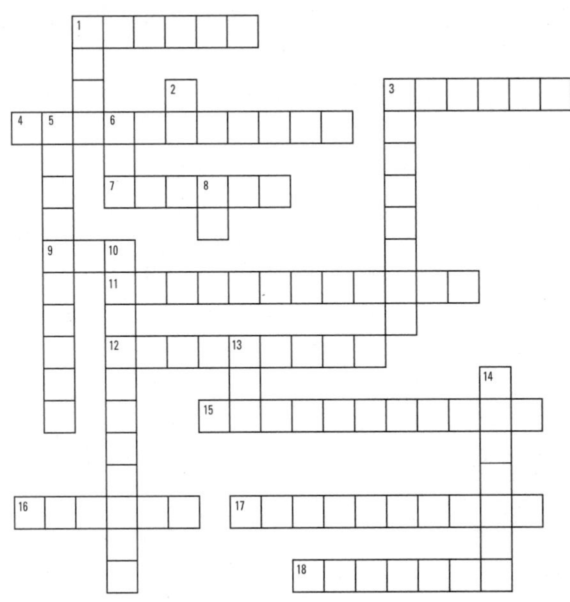

Across

1. Units of CPU time
3. Impolite thread behavior
4. Also known as virtual machine
7. Server RAM allocation strategy
9. Also known as Packet Receive Buffers
11. Fine-tuning for peak performance
12. Excessive disk activity
15. CPU load percentage
16. Units of disk space
17. Server optimization utility
18. Units of RAM

Down

1. Swap file management command
2. Compression prevention attribute
3. Better than a miss

5. Displays list of server RAM address spaces
6. Allows use of larger packet sizes
8. Compression activation attribute
10. These inhibit performance
13. Optimization console command
14. Displays list of NLMs in server RAM

See Appendix C for answers.

PART II

NDS Design and Implementation

CHAPTER 8

NDS Preparation

Novell Directory Services (NDS) is a fundamental network service that all NetWare 5.1 servers supply. As a matter of fact, it's the most fundamental network service offered by NetWare 5.1, after network communications. As a result, NDS design is one of the key responsibilities of a network administrator.

In fact, NDS design can have a profound impact on the success or failure of your net. To illustrate this point, we have created an organization called ACME (A Cure for Mother Earth), which is staffed by the greatest heroes from our unspoiled history. These heroes are the founding mothers and fathers of Earth's Golden Age — before instant popcorn, talking cars, and daytime television.

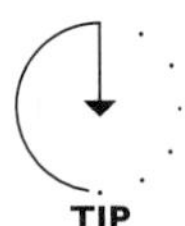
TIP

For more information about ACME, consult the "ACME Mission Briefing" in Appendix E.

As a NetWare 5.1 CNE, you come highly recommended. Your mission — *should you choose to accept it* — is to build the ACME WAN and NDS tree. You will need courage, design experience, NDS know-how, and this book.

Actually, you have a daunting task ahead of you. A project of this magnitude requires sharp thinking and an organized approach. All the fancy footwork in the world isn't going to help you if you don't have a game plan. This is where Figure 8.1 comes in — it's your ACME game plan. As you can see, NDS design and management falls into four simple steps:

- *Step 1: NDS Preparation* — In Step 1, the project starts rolling with NDS preparation. The primary focus of this phase is the project team. The project team consists of many networking experts, including management, server specialists, NDS experts, and connectivity specialists. These are the men and women who will carry you through the triumphs and pitfalls of NDS design and management. The team's first task is systems analysis and data gathering.
- *Step 2: NDS Design* — Step 2 is the first of the three main project phases: design, implementation, and management. NDS design begins with the formation of a tree framework. This framework is further refined with the help of three important NDS concepts: partitioning, time synchronization, and resource accessibility. These design components have a dramatic effect on the success or failure of your WAN.

- *Step 3: NDS Implementation* — The goal of NDS implementation is NetWare 5.1 installation and migration. This typically involves fresh NetWare server installations and complex tree migrations. The centerpiece of NDS implementation is the implementation schedule.

FIGURE 8.1

How to save the Net in four easy steps!

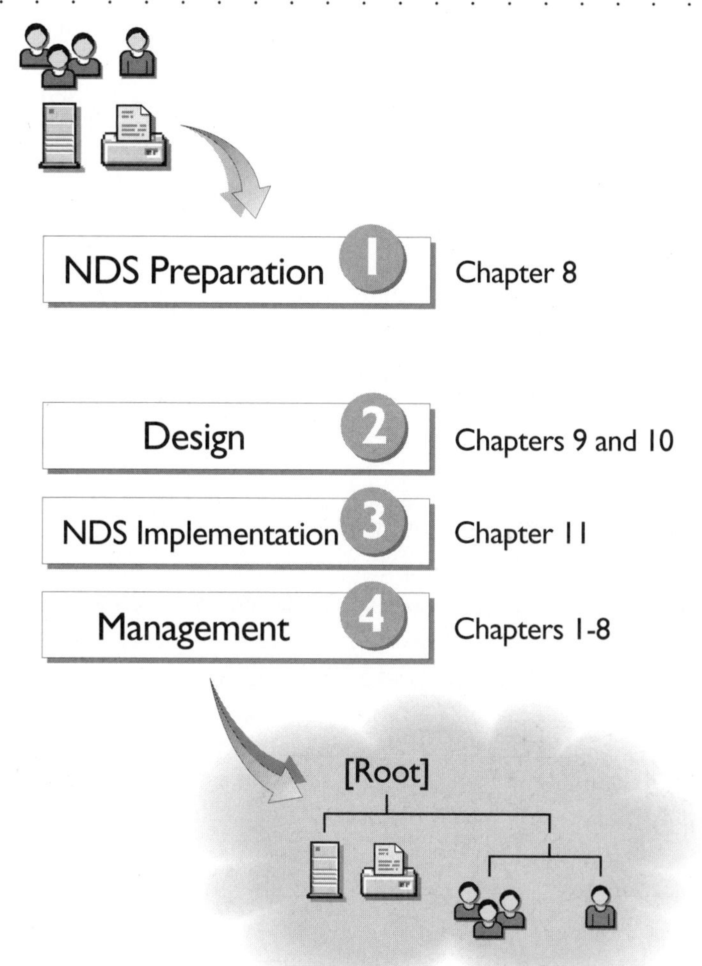

- *Step 4: Management*—Welcome to Step 4. Management is the ongoing process of optimizing and maintaining your NetWare 5.1 network. NetWare 5.1 management hinges on four main topics: advanced server management, advanced NDS management, advanced Internet infrastructure management, and advanced security management. This is where you'll spend most of your time as a CNE. Fortunately, we have already devoted one third of this book to NetWare 5.1 Management (Chapters 1 through 7).

This is all it takes to save the Net and become a NetWare 5.1 CNE. Don't hyperventilate—I am here to walk you through every step . . . one at a time. But be careful not to let this information fall into the wrong hands. Let's start our exciting NDS design journey with a closer look at the *Process*.

Good luck; and by the way, thanks for saving the Net!

The Process

Novell Directory Services (NDS) is one of the most important services built into the NetWare 5.1 operating system infrastructure. It provides a central database for network resource security, management, and reliability. In order to take full advantage of NDS, it is important to carefully plan, implement, and manage a detailed NDS design. In short, a good NDS design can enhance the performance and value of your entire network by making it more efficient, fault tolerant, and secure.

Furthermore, a successful NDS implementation provides the following benefits:

- Enables users to have an efficient, predictable structure, supporting easy location of, and access to, network services
- Enables network administrators to easily name, locate, and manage network resources
- Permits network administrators to easily prevent access to network resources by unauthorized users
- Supports high-performance network access for all users

- Provides a high degree of fault tolerance to minimize the impact of network equipment failure
- Simplifies the scalability of the network as users and services grow or change

No single design is perfect for every network. Therefore, you will want to create a design and implementation process that is customized for your network. The process that you choose should be structured with the following four steps in mind: NDS preparation, NDS design, NDS implementation, and NDS management.

Having a systematic approach like this reduces the time it takes to design the network, which gives you a head start on implementation and management. It also ensures that the needs of the project manager are met and all critical requirements are addressed. This ultimately results in an efficient NetWare 5.1 WAN for today and tomorrow.

REAL WORLD

Programmers and Information Services (IS) professionals sometimes call the Process a System Design Life Cycle (SDLC); others call it an Information Systems Development Methodology; or better yet, a Software Engineering Process Model. Regardless of what you call it, the Process is a structured approach toward designing, implementing, and managing an information system.

Following are different approaches to the Process:

- *Linear* — The linear approach handles each step one at a time in a first-to-last order. It is used in traditional bottom-up software and in systems development efforts.
- *Structured* — The structured model, on the other hand, enables all activities to take place simultaneously. This approach is used in top-down development that involves nonlinear efforts.
- *Incremental* — The incremental approach is a variation on the structured model with a focus on rapid prototyping.

- *Spiral* — Finally, the spiral model enables you to modify certain requirements during the life of the project. This approach is used in inherently risky, costly, or unstable environments — kind of like saving the world.

Let's take a closer look at the Process and learn a little more about saving the Net.

Step 1: NDS Preparation

The first NDS design phase focuses on gathering the necessary people and data for your network design and implementation project. This is also called the "Project Approach" phase.

Following are the tasks and responsibilities you should perform during NDS Preparation. Refer to Figure 8.2 as you study.

- *Creating the Project Team* — First, poll the network personnel who will be impacted by the NDS design and create a project team. At a minimum, the team should consist of a project manager, an NDS expert, a server administrator, and a connectivity specialist.

- *Gathering Data* — Next, gather organizational and technical information related to the network design. The project team members can use a variety of methods for data gathering, including observation, conversation, research, questionnaires, and random sampling. Eventually they will settle on a few key design inputs: the company's organizational chart, a physical WAN layout map, network resource lists, a world location map, background information, and a workflow diagram. Later in this chapter, we will explore data gathering for ACME. We will discover each of these design inputs and learn the role they play in the Process and in NDS design.

- *Determining the Project Scope* — Establishing the scope of a project is critical for keeping things under control. It is important to accomplish this task early in the design process. The project scope provides physical boundaries for the network, as well as financial and personnel limitations. The following two tasks help establish the project scope: determining project complexity (simple or complex) and developing an implementation schedule.

FIGURE 8.2

Step 1: NDS Preparation

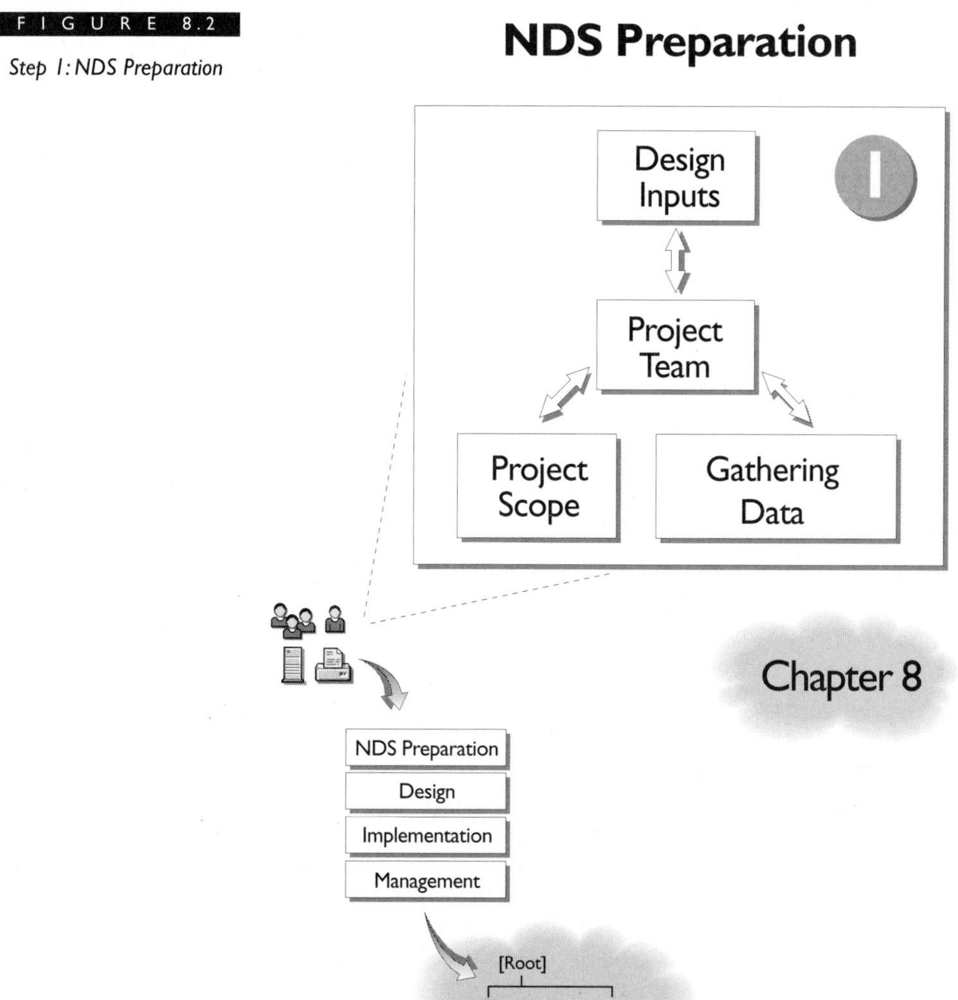

Step 2: NDS Design

NDS design impacts virtually every network user and resource. Therefore, you should create your design in synergy with organizational operations, NDS functionality, and network layout.

To achieve an effective NDS design, you should use a dual-strategy approach: organizational and technical. You should pursue both of these strategies simultaneously during the NDS design process.

Organizational design focuses on the organizational structure of the company. First, you need to determine the organizational chart and functional operation of the company. Next, you need to determine the skills that are needed to accomplish the design and locate the personnel with the appropriate skills. Finally, you need to make sure that you understand what it takes to manage this type of organizational process.

Technical design, on the other hand, is based on the network layout of the company. In this model, you will need to design NDS so that it adheres to all the recommended design requirements in this book. Then you can optimize NDS to meet your company's specific needs.

The best NDS design is a synergy between the following four network components (see Figure 8.3):

- *Tree Design* — When you design the upper and lower layers of the Directory tree, you will want to focus on optimizing NDS so that it is both productive for users and easy to manage. This is accomplished by using a naming standards document and by following specific guidelines for designing location-based upper layers and organization-based lower layers. These tasks are important because a well-designed tree lays the foundation for partitioning and time synchronization.

- *Partition Design* — Next, your design should include partition boundaries and replica placement. This helps provide scalability, fault tolerance, and resource access. (**Note:** This step is conditional. A simple network — less than 15 servers — does not require a customized partitioning strategy.)

- *Time Synchronization* — The design should also include guidelines for either a default or customized time-synchronization strategy, depending on the size of your organization. If a customized strategy is used, it should contain efficient guidelines for time-server placement. This helps provide accurate synchronized time to all servers on the network. (**Note:** This step is conditional. A simple network — less than 30 servers, with no WAN link — will not require a customized time-synchronization strategy.)

- *Accessibility Design* — Finally, the system should be designed so that both physical and logical resources are easily accessible to users. An effective NDS accessibility plan helps you set login script and NDS security standards, determine standardized file system structures, adopt strategies for travelling users, and create guidelines for the use of Alias, Directory Map, and Profile objects.

FIGURE 8.3

Step 2: NDS Design

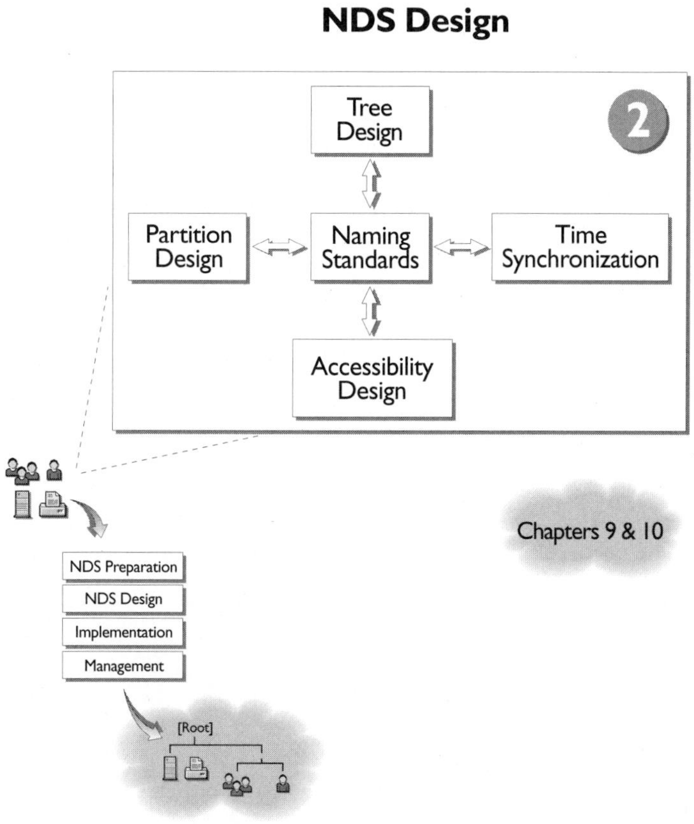

Step 3: NDS Implementation

After your NDS design has been completed, you will need to implement it by using a detailed implementation schedule and pilot program. Refer to Figure 8.4 for an overview.

- *Implementation Schedule*—This schedule outlines the rollout of NetWare 5.1 installation and migration procedures. You should begin in an offline testing lab, where you can test partitioning, replication, time synchronization, and common network applications. You can also test user compatibility with NDS and Bindery Services without affecting the production network. (**Note:** You may need to perform an NDS merge in order to integrate resources from multiple trees.)

- *Pilot Program*—Once you are comfortable with the results of the testing lab, you can begin implementing your NDS design in a controlled pilot program. A pilot program involves installing your first production NetWare 5.1 server and associated production applications.

FIGURE 8.4

Step 3: NDS Implementation

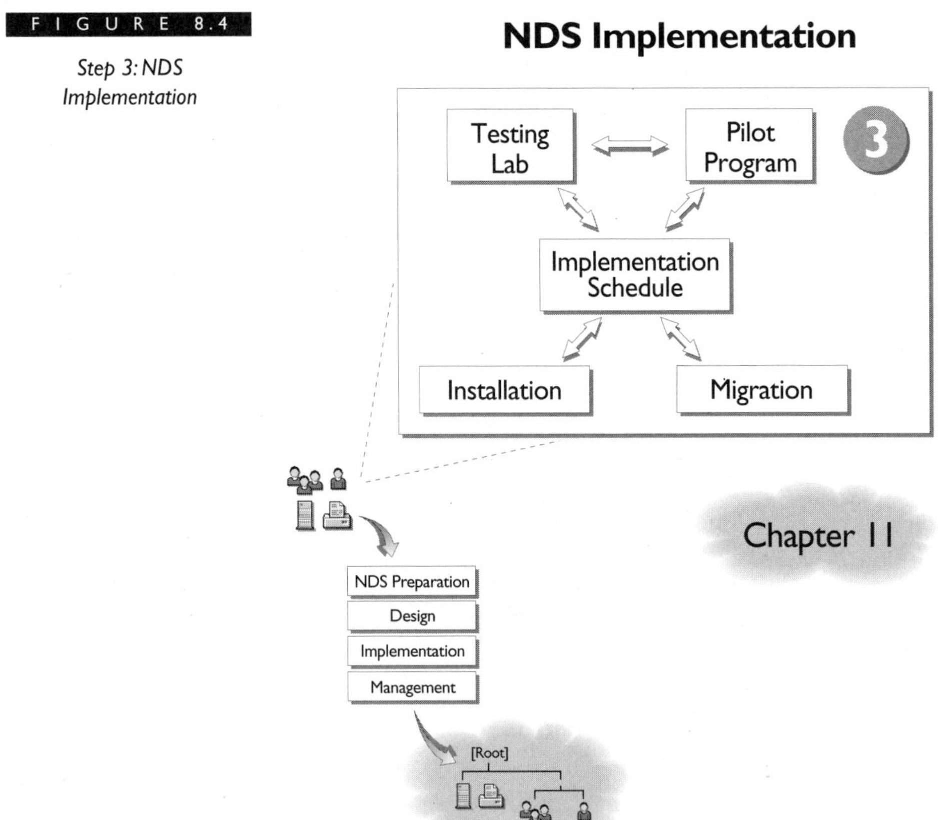

Step 4: Management

In the final phase of NDS design, you will want to continually analyze the impact of your NDS implementation and take measures to optimize it. This is also called the "Analysis of the Current NDS Design" phase.

Step 4 is dominated by regular network administration responsibilities, including building an Internet infrastructure, managing servers, determining security, and optimizing performance. Refer to Figure 8.5 for more information. (**Note:** Network administration concepts are covered in detail in Novell Course 560, "NetWare 5.1 Administration," and Novell Course 570, "NetWare 5.1 Advanced Administration.")

FIGURE 8.5

Step 4: Management

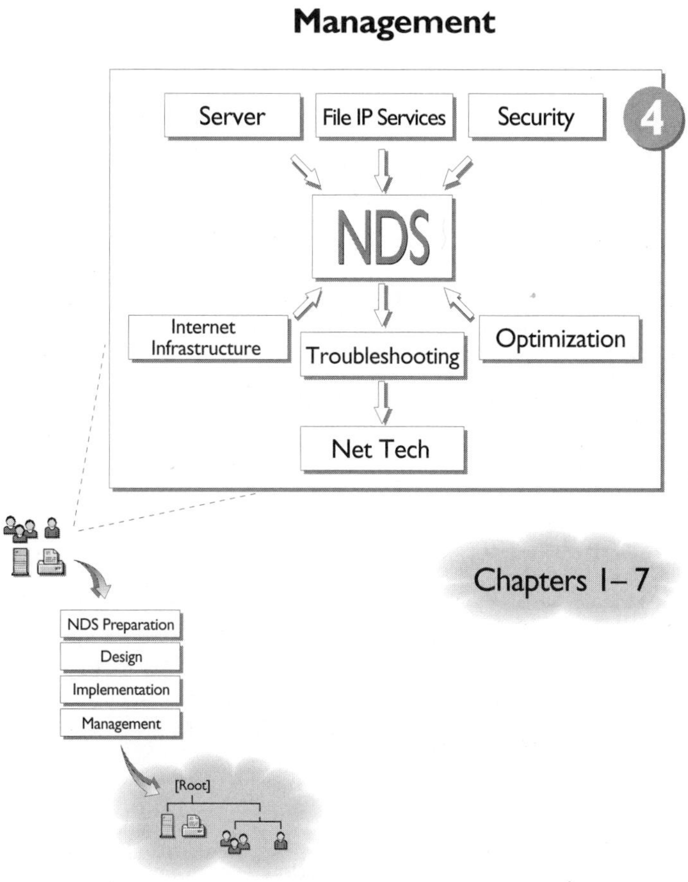

NetWare 5.1 management dominates the majority of your life as a network administrator. The first three phases—NDS preparation, design, and implementation—typically occur once. Management occurs every day. Refer to Table 8.1 for more details.

TABLE 8.1

A Road Map for Saving the Net

PHASE	TASK	NOVELL'S CNE STUDY GUIDE FOR NETWARE 5.1
Step 1: NDS Preparation	Project team	Chapter 8
	Understand roles	Chapter 8
	Design inputs	Chapter 8
	Project scope	Chapter 8
Step 2: NDS Design	Naming standards	Chapter 9
	Tree design	Chapter 9
	Partition design	Chapter 10
	Time synchronization	Chapter 10
	NDS accessibility design	Chapter 9
Step 3: NDS Implementation	Testing lab	Chapter 11
	Pilot program	Chapter 11
	Implementation schedule	Chapter 11
	Installation	Chapter 1
Step 4: Management	NDS	Chapter 5
	Server	Chapter 4
	IP services	Chapter 2
	Security	Chapter 6
	Internet infrastructure	Chapter 3
	Optimization	Chapter 7
	Troubleshooting	Chapters 12–17
	Networking technologies	Chapters 18–22

Now that you understand the overall process, let's get started with Step 1: NDS Preparation. Fortunately, you don't have to do it alone. Let's get some help. Let's build a project team.

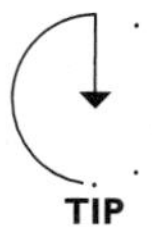

You should match each of the four NDS design phases to a particular task. For example, data gathering occurs in the Project Approach phase, time synchronization and partitioning design take place in the NDS Design phase, and implementation evaluation takes place in the Analysis of Current NDS Design phase.

The Project Team

As we discussed earlier, in order to create an effective NDS design, you need to identify the required skills, tasks, and personnel. Then you need to organize these roles into a *project team*. Project team members can perform single roles, multiple roles, or specific subtasks within a role. It all depends on the size of your organization and the complexity of your network. In a large network, the most efficient balance is typically a one-to-one relationship—that is, one team member for each design role.

The following four roles are required in most NDS design projects:

- Project manager
- NDS expert
- Server administrator
- Connectivity specialist

In addition, you may want to consider adding a printing expert, a workstation expert, and an application specialist to the team. Once you have established a project team, you should make sure all members have a clear understanding of their responsibilities and priorities.

Project Manager

The *project manager* is the central contact person for your project team. This member, who must understand the various ramifications of the NDS design process, is often the head of the IS department. Following is a list of the project manager's responsibilities:

- Coordinate with the NDS expert to ensure an efficient transition to NetWare 5.1.
- Coordinate and manage the implementation.
- Acquire the appropriate resources and funding to proceed with all phases of the process.
- Know the organization and act as a liaison between the project team and senior management.
- Give direction to the project and ensure that the design integrates with the organization's layout.
- Manage costs and estimates.
- Organize and schedule management meetings.
- Create an efficient and effective network design.
- Coordinate the evaluation of software and licensing issues, cost of implementation, and operation.
- Coordinate design, implementation, and management timelines.
- Ensure user productivity and adequate training.
- Oversee the testing lab, pilot implementation, and NDS design rollout.
- Educate the organization on the changes and impacts of the new design.
- Promote post-implementation coordination and support.
- Ensure acceptance and rollout of the newly designed NDS tree.

NDS Expert

The *NDS expert* should have a firm grasp of the sophisticated nature of NetWare 5.1 and NDS, along with specialized training. An outside consultant can fill this role, if necessary. Following is a list of the NDS expert's responsibilities:

- Lead the project team through most of the NDS design phase, including creating the Directory tree design and organizing the upper and lower portions of the tree.
- Design and implement NDS security.
- Design and implement NDS management components, including partitions, replica placement, time synchronization, and accessibility.
- Participate in choosing the team members. Also, communicate NDS concerns of the team members to the project manager.
- Ensure that the design is thorough and meets all department needs at key points throughout the process. Also, ensure that each project team member participates in data gathering, and that the design phase meets established timelines.
- Coordinate System, Profile, and User login scripts with other team members.
- Oversee the creation and maintenance of detailed design documentation.
- Manage the expectations of each department and of management.

Server Administrator

The *server administrator* is responsible for choosing the correct network hardware and keeping it running. Following is a list of the server administrator's responsibilities:

- Determine and plan the pilot implementation.
- Maintain network performance levels.

- Install, upgrade, and migrate all NetWare 5.1 servers.
- Ensure effective time-synchronization strategies.
- Plan server placement in the NDS tree and determine how to add and remove servers.
- Calculate needed disk space and memory for new and existing servers.
- Establish a disaster recovery strategy based on the NDS design.
- Determine backward compatibility.

Connectivity Specialist

The *connectivity specialist* works with the physical network, Internet backbone, telecommunications, WAN design, and router placement. Therefore, this person needs to understand the technical aspects of internetworking. In addition, a connectivity specialist must understand traffic concerns caused by replicas, time synchronization, and NDS overhead. For this reason, he or she must work closely with the other project team members to optimize router placement. Following is a list of the connectivity specialist's responsibilities:

- Determine the effect of routing, protocols, telecommunications, and WAN structure on the NDS tree design.
- Make decisions regarding single or multiple protocols on the network. Also, coordinate with the server administrator to ensure protocol compatibility.
- Deliver optimal internetwork traffic throughput and assist in overall NDS design with respect to WAN traffic.
- Advise the project team about routing, protocols, and WAN structure.

- Determine the efficiency of LAN/WAN bandwidth.
- Establish the use of single or multiple protocols and determine which protocol(s) to use on the LAN and which protocols to use on the WAN.
- Identify current utilization figures.
- Maintain seamless connectivity to host computers and other non–NetWare 5.1 operating systems.

Now it's your turn. . . .

You are the final piece in our globe-trotting puzzle. You will become ACME's Management Information System (MIS) department and the architect of its communications strategy. As a NetWare 5.1 network administrator, you come highly recommended. Your mission—*should you choose to accept it*—is to build the ACME WAN. You will need courage, design experience, NDS know-how, and this book. If you succeed, you will save the Net and become a CNE! All in a day's work.

Following is a brief synopsis of the ACME case study and some crucial details regarding NDS data gathering. For more details concerning ACME, please read the comprehensive mission briefing in Appendix E, "ACME Mission Briefing."

Good luck; and by the way, thanks for saving the Net!

REAL WORLD

Throughout this book, we will use ACME as a global case study for key NetWare 5.1 advanced management, NDS design, and troubleshooting tasks. (See Appendix E, "ACME Mission Briefing," for more details.) You will design and build ACME's enterprise NDS tree, construct an advanced internet strategy, optimize ACME servers, and troubleshooting a variety of network components (including NICs, hard drives, workstations, and printers). Pay attention! ACME may just change your life . . . and help you become a NetWare 5.1 CNE.

Gathering NDS Information at ACME

The process of gathering data for NDS design is interesting. You have a specific purpose — building a WAN infrastructure using NetWare 5.1 and NDS. With this purpose in mind, when you approach ACME, view the data from two unique points of view:

- *Organizational* — How does the company operate and what is its purpose?
- *Technical* — What technical devices are in place to facilitate the exchange of information?

This is a pretty tricky balancing act. Organizational design inputs are more subjective. They deal with the company as a business unit and ignore the means for exchanging information. Technical design inputs, on the other hand, are objective. They involve the physical WAN infrastructure and ignore the content of the message. Obviously, both are equally important, but because we are designing an NDS infrastructure, we may want to give more weight to the technical inputs (see Figure 8.6).

FIGURE 8.6

Balancing organizational and technical design inputs

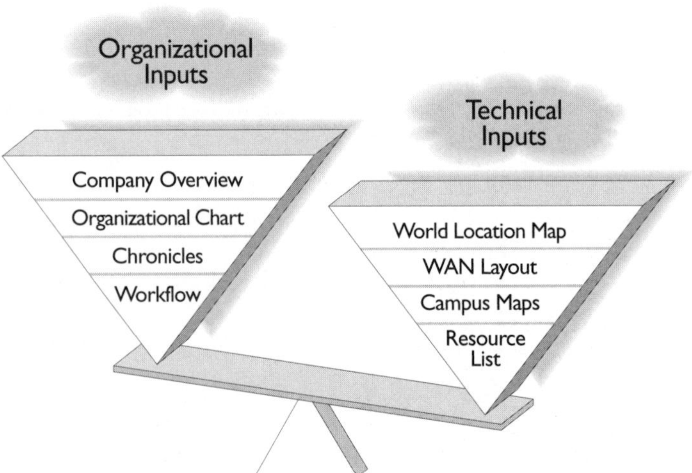

There are four organizational design inputs. They are represented as a reverse pyramid in Figure 8.6, because information narrows as you move down the model:

- *Company Overview* — Organizational design inputs start with a company overview and a snapshot of the company's mission statement.
- *Organizational Chart* — More detail is normally contained in the organizational chart than in the organizational overview. These details help you identify the players and their relationships to each other.
- *Chronicles* — The Chronicles is a detailed study of each division and its key players.
- *Workflow* — Finally, a careful study of the in-depth Chronicles will help you to create a workflow diagram. The workflow document and its accompanying diagram describe the daily operations of the company and each key player's task-oriented responsibilities. It also describes the daily or weekly movement of data from one location to another. Along with the organizational chart, the workflow document is probably the most important organizational design input.

There are also four technical design inputs. These inputs concentrate more on the delivery of information than on the information's content. Technical inputs typically are already in place and must be redesigned to accommodate NetWare 5.1 and NDS:

- *World Location Map* — Technical design inputs start with the world location map — a global view of the company's geography.
- *WAN Layout* — From a connectivity point of view, the world location map quickly becomes a WAN layout. The WAN layout is one of the most important technical design inputs because it summarizes the movement of data between company locations.
- *Campus Maps* — Next, you should zero in on each location and create detailed campus maps. Each campus map identifies the distribution of buildings, LANs, routers, and existing WAN backbones.

- *Resource List* — Finally, the resource list, which is the most nerdy technical design input, breaks out each campus into its physical network resources — users, file servers, print servers, print queues, and printers.

Each of these organizational and technical design inputs will play a key role in building ACME's network. As you'll learn in following chapters, technical design inputs help define the upper layers of the NDS tree. They also play an important role in NDS naming, partitioning, replica distribution, and time synchronization. It's important to note that object placement plays a key role in resource accessibility and WAN productivity.

The organizational design inputs, on the other hand, define the bottom layers of the NDS tree. With them, we can add flexibility and purpose to the WAN infrastructure. Organizational inputs play an important role in security, configuration, management, and application design. They also help us refine our NDS objects and ensure their productive placement in the tree.

Let's learn more about NDS data gathering at ACME.

ACME Design Inputs

You will find various design inputs in this book. They are for your eyes only. Once you have read the inputs, eat them! Following is a list of our eight ACME design inputs and the respective roles of each project team member.

ACME Overview

- *Project Manager* — Provide an in-depth tour of the ACME facilities.
- *All Project Team Members* — Absorb ACME's mission and integrate it into everything the team does.

ACME Organizational Chart

- *Project Manager* — Identify upper management.
- *NDS Expert* — Identify major divisions and potential ACME workgroups.

ACME Chronicles

- *Project Manager* — Identify ACME management tasks and the relationships between employees.
- *All Project Team Members* — Grasp the daily routine of ACME and identify communications paths.

ACME Workflow

- *Project Manager* — Learn how ACME's workflow affects the big picture. Determine better communications paths.
- *NDS Expert* — Learn how information flows throughout the company. Isolate data flow to help design the bottom layers of the NDS tree. Finally, associate workflow tasks with new NDS objects.
- *Connectivity Specialist* — Follow the flow of data over the existing network communications path. Determine whether to include remote sites in the NDS tree.

ACME World Location Map

- *Server Administrator* — Determine how many servers are at each location. Track which version of NetWare each of the servers is running and then document these servers in a global location map to help the NDS expert build the top levels of the tree.
- *NDS Expert* — Use server information to plan the upper layers of the NDS tree. Begin to sketch partitioning and replication strategies. Finally, decide whether regional containers are necessary.
- *Connectivity Specialist* — Determine how information is flowing throughout the main ACME locations.

ACME WAN Layout

- *Server Administrator*—Identify key servers performing routing functions in the ACME WAN topology.
- *Connectivity Specialist*—Identify the fastest and slowest WAN links. Determine a need for remote dial-in.
- *NDS Expert*—Count the WAN sites and measure throughput across all WAN links. This helps define the upper layers of the NDS tree. It also impacts replication and time synchronization.

ACME Campus Maps

- *Server Administrator*—Determine how many servers are in each LAN segment. Identify requirements for special services, such as NetWare for Macintosh and supplemental protocols.
- *NDS Expert*—Determine the major resources in each LAN. Discover how they are grouped and build appropriate NDS objects.
- *Connectivity Specialist*—Learn how data is routed within LAN segments. Discover more efficient alternatives.

ACME Resource List

- *Project Manager*—Identify the resources that will require special management. Budget for upgrading existing hardware and buying new equipment.
- *Server Administrator*—Track NetWare 3, NetWare 4, and NetWare 5 servers in each location. Determine the diversity of clients and the diversity of special networking products, such as Systems Application Architecture (SAA), Network File System (NFS), Macintosh, and Transmission Control Protocol/ Internet Protocol (TCP/IP). Plan for expansion.

- *NDS Expert* — Convert existing and new resources to the new NDS naming standard, and then use this list to create and to place NDS objects in the tree.
- *Connectivity Specialist* — Identify existing protocols and plan for the addition of new ones. Propose a strategy for connecting these physical resources in local- and wide-area environments.

There you have it. The eight ACME design inputs and how they map to each of your four project team members. Now let's take a closer look at the three key technical design inputs — also known as ACME WAN maps.

ACME WAN Maps

Now we must shift our focus to the three most critical NDS design inputs — the WAN Maps. These documents play an important role in designing the upper layers of the NDS tree. In addition, they affect NDS naming, partitioning, replica distribution, time synchronization, and object placement. In this section, we will explore the first three technical design inputs:

- ACME world location map
- ACME WAN layout
- ACME campus maps

ACME World Location Map

ACME's global structure is shown in Figure 8.7. This structure includes the five main divisional headquarters and five more distribution/World Health Index (WHI) data-collection centers. (See Appendix E, "ACME Mission Briefing," for a thorough explanation of the World Health Index.) The ACME organization has been distributed to all four corners of the globe to ensure cultural diversity. Five different continents are represented, as well as most of the world's major countries. ACME is truly an organization for the world.

FIGURE 8.7

ACME world location map

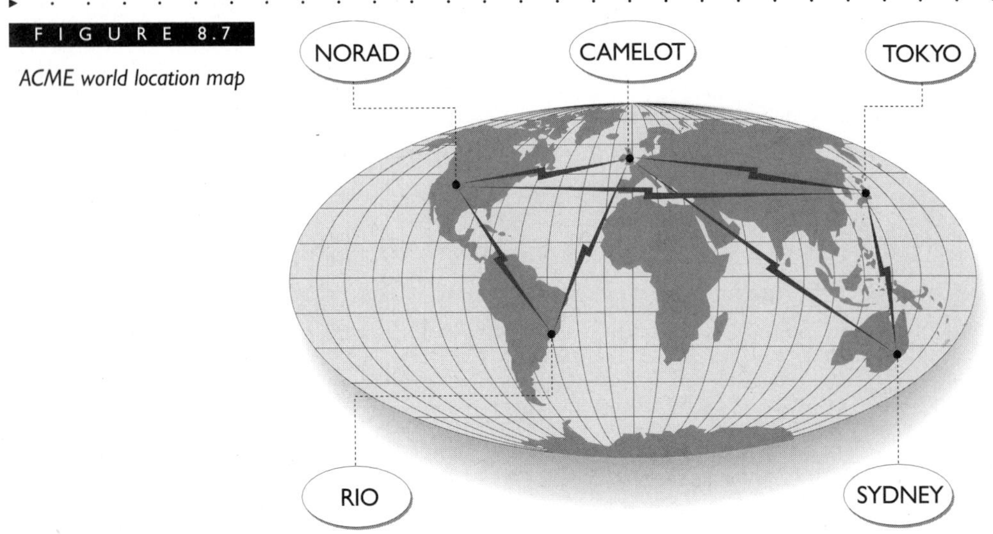

ACME WAN Layout

As you can see in Figure 8.8, ACME organizes its five main hubs in a ring/star redundant design. This structure provides multiple redundant paths from each location. Even if the center of the star (Camelot) goes down, all other sites remain connected. This is accomplished with the help of sophisticated WAN hubs (via advanced routing equipment) and high-bandwidth lines.

Note the bandwidth measurements on each WAN link. These values are important to an NDS expert when he or she is attempting to design the upper layers of the tree. These values also affect replica placement and the distribution of time providers. Refer to Chapter 9 for a more detailed discussion.

In addition to the ACME organizational chart, WAN layout is probably one of the most important design inputs. The WAN layout represents how ACME shares network resources. Your NDS tree should model it closely.

FIGURE 8.8

ACME WAN layout

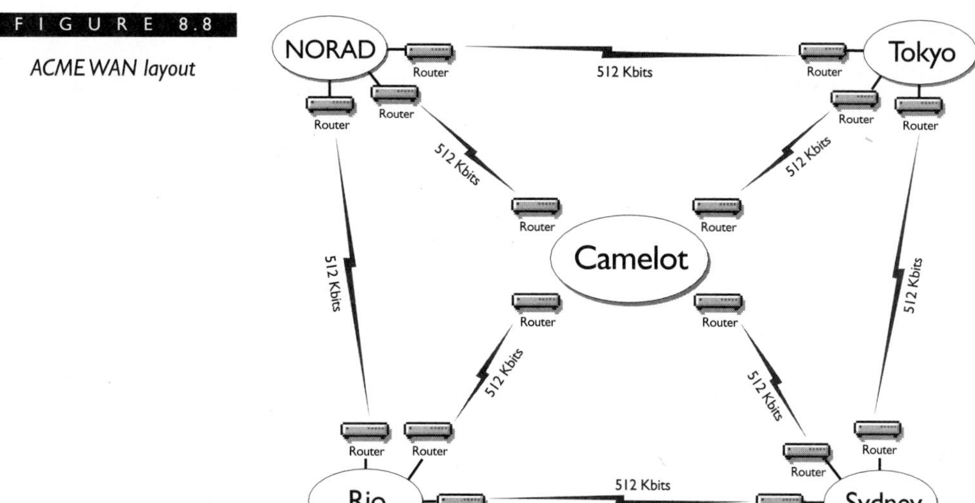

ACME Campus Maps

The ACME campus maps enable you to zero in on specific details about primary WAN hubs. You will need to better understand ACME's local area networks in order to refine the NDS tree. The campus maps show server distribution, router placement, remote access points, and the backbone topology. Each location within the hub provides more insight into how ACME uses its existing network resources. Adding newer technology can further enhance these campus maps.

In this case, we've identified three important campuses:

- *Tokyo*—Headquarters for the Crime Fighting division (see Figure 8.9)
- *Camelot*—Headquarters for ACME Operations (see Figure 8.10)
- *NORAD*—Headquarters for ACME Labs and technical wizardry (see Figure 8.11)

FIGURE 8.9

ACME campus map for Tokyo

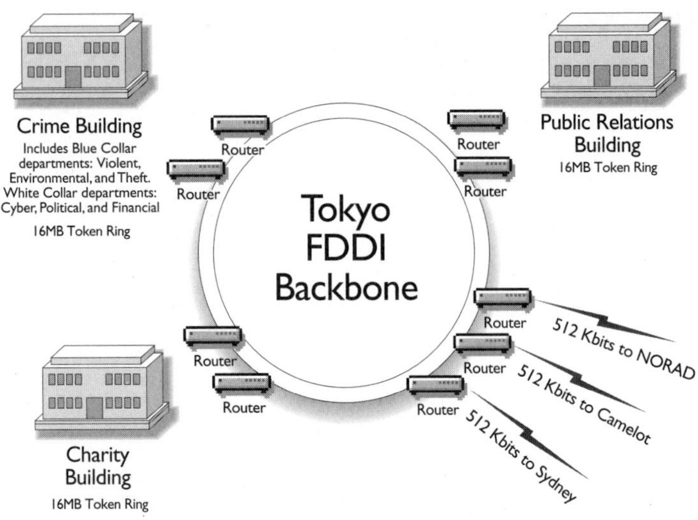

FIGURE 8.10

ACME campus map for Camelot

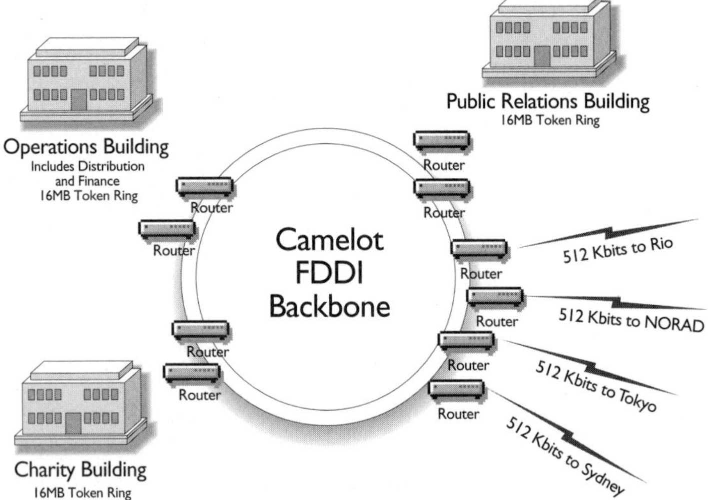

FIGURE 8.11

ACME campus map for NORAD

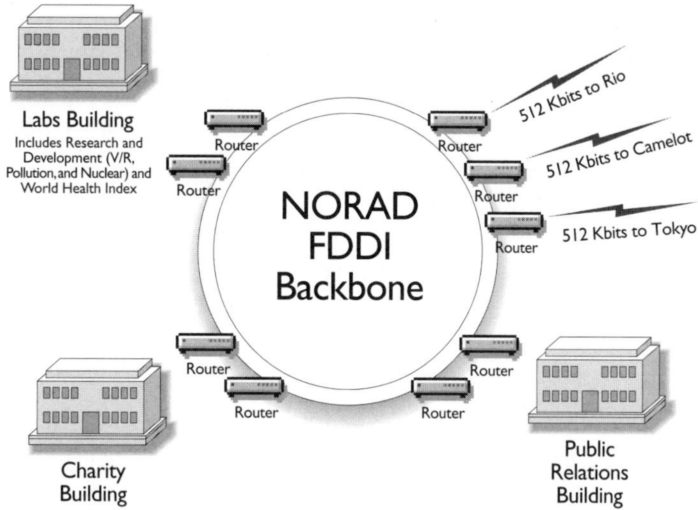

Study these campus maps closely, because they represent a graphical organization of ACME's network resources. These campus maps should help you better understand the final technical design input — ACME's resource list.

ACME Resource List

Resources are the lifeblood of your network. Before you connect the resources, you must bring them all up to the same level. This process involves upgrading NetWare 3 and NetWare 4 servers to NetWare 5.1, installing the Novell Client software, testing and upgrading network applications, and improving printer hardware. In addition to upgrading, you will need to buy some new equipment.

The migration process should be reflected in your resource lists. The first list you should create is a "wish list" of existing and new equipment. This list includes all the equipment (old and new) that you will need to accomplish your goal. When you are creating ACME's wish list, focus on these key resources:

- Administrators
- File servers
- Print servers

- Print queues
- Printers

Now let's take a look at the resources you will need in each ACME division.

Human Rights Division

The Human Rights division has one main user (Gandhi) and three department heads. The main division has two file servers, a global print server, and one HP4SI printer. Albert Schweitzer runs the Medical department. He also has two file servers and one HP4SI printer. Next, the Food department relies on Mother Teresa and her network resources: one file server and one HP4SI printer. The Shelter department has Florence Nightingale at the helm and uses two file servers and an HP4SI printer. Finally, the Peace department is managed by Buddha, who has one file server and an HPIII printer.

Labs Division

The Labs division is under the quality tutelage of Albert Einstein. He relies on one main division-oriented file server. In the Research and Development (R&D) department, Leonardo da Vinci shares one file server with his three departments. The main print server is also located in the R&D building. Charles Darwin (Pollution), Sir Isaac Newton (Virtual Reality), and Marie Curie (Nuclear) each have their own HP4SI printers.

Charles Babbage and Ada run the WHI department. They need three file servers for index calculations and data storage. They also rely on a print server for output to their Canon BubbleJet printer.

Operations Division

King Arthur runs the Operations division with one file server and a lot of guile. He uses a single print server to service his Canon BubbleJet printer. The Financial department, however, is much more technically demanding than the other departments. Guinevere needs three file servers, two print servers, and two HP4SI printers. In addition, Merlin runs the Distribution department with the help of two file servers, a print server, and an HP III LaserJet printer.

Network resources for the Charity department are much more difficult to track because they are spread across the five global hubs.

Each charity center is different, depending on the needs of its network administrator:

- *NORAD* — Sir Gawain uses one file server, a print server, and one HP4SI printer.
- *Rio* — Sir Percival also uses one file server, one print server, and an HP4SI printer.
- *Camelot* — Sir Galahad relies on one file server, a print server, and a new HP5 LaserJet printer.
- *Sydney* — Sir Lancelot needs one file server, a print server, and one HP4SI printer.
- *Tokyo* — Sir Kay is a little busier than his counterparts at the other locations. He needs two file servers, a print server, and an HP4SI LaserJet printer.

Crime Fighting Division

Sherlock Holmes and Dr. Watson rely on the latest technology to help their crime-fighting efforts. They use two file servers, a print server, and an HP5 LaserJet printer. Each of their Crime Fighting departments follows suit and takes advantage of new technology.

Wyatt Earp runs the Blue Collar department. He needs one file server, a print server, and a single HP III LaserJet printer. In addition, each of his crime-fighting units needs its own file server and HP4SI printer. As a matter of fact, Bat Masterson needs two file servers for the Violent Crimes unit.

Robin Hood runs the White Collar Crime Fighting department. His criminals are a little more sophisticated than the criminals that Wyatt Earp faces. Therefore, he needs two file servers, a print server, and a Canon BubbleJet printer. In addition, each of his crime-fighting units requires its own file server and LaserJet printer. Friar Tuck uses an HP LaserJet III, Maid Marion has an HP4SI, and Little John needs two HP4SI printers to fight financial crime.

Admin Division

George Washington heads up the Admin division. He uses two file servers, a print server, and a Canon BubbleJet printer. Each of his department heads uses a similar configuration. James Madison of Facilities uses one file server, a print server, and an HP4SI printer. Abraham Lincoln has a file server and an HP4SI printer for the Auditing department, and Thomas Jefferson uses a file server and two HP III LaserJet printers.

Network resource tracking for the PR department is a bit trickier because the department is spread across all five ACME locations. Here's a quick breakdown:

- *NORAD* — David James Clarke, IV, uses one file server, a print server, and two printers: an HP4SI and a Canon BubbleJet.
- *Rio* — Jeff Hughes uses one file server and two printers: an HP4SI and a Canon BubbleJet.
- *Camelot* — Cathy Ettelson doesn't print as much as David and Jeff. She uses a file server, a print server, and one HP4SI printer.
- *Sydney* — Mary Clarke requires the same configuration as Cathy, that is, a single file server, a print server, and an HP4SI printer.
- *Tokyo* — Blair Thomas follows suit with a single file server, a print server, and an HP4SI printer.

In addition to these resources, ACME has a special NDS file server in each of its five main locations: NORAD, Tokyo, Sydney, Rio, and Camelot.

This completes our detailed discussion of the ACME resource wish list. For a complete summary, refer to Table 8.2. In Chapter 9, "NDS Tree Design," we will develop a naming standards document and rename these resources.

TABLE 8.2

The Acme Resource Wish List

DIVISION	DEPARTMENT	RESOURCES
Human Rights	Headquarters	Gandhi Two file servers One print server One HP4SI printer

TABLE 8.2

The Acme Resource Wish List (continued)

DIVISION	DEPARTMENT	RESOURCES
Human Rights *(continued)*	Medical	Albert Schweitzer Two file servers One HP4SI printer
	Food	Mother Teresa One file server One HP4SI printer
	Shelter	Florence Nightingale Two file servers One HP4SI printer
	Peace	Buddha One file server One HPIII printer
Labs	Headquarters	Albert Einstein One file server
	R&D	Leonardo Da Vinci Charles Darwin Sir Isaac Newton Marie Curie One file server One print server Three HP4SI printers
	WHI	Charles Babbage Ada Three file servers One print server One Canon BubbleJet printer
Operations	Headquarters	King Arthur One file server One print server One Canon BubbleJet printer
	Distribution	Merlin Two file servers One print server One HPIII LaserJet printer

Continued

TABLE 8.2

The Acme Resource Wish List (continued)

DIVISION	DEPARTMENT	RESOURCES
Operations *(continued)*	Financial	Guinevere Three file servers Two print servers Two HP4SI printers
	Charity	Sir Percival Sir Lancelot Sir Gawain Sir Galahad Sir Kay Six file servers Five print servers Three HP4SI printers Two HP5 printers
Crime Fighting	Headquarters	Sherlock Holmes Dr. Watson Two file servers One print server One HP5 printer
	Blue Collar	Wyatt Earp Bat Masterson Wild Bill Hickok Doc Holliday Five file servers One print server
	Blue Collar	Three HP4SI printers One HPIII LaserJet printer
	White Collar	Robin Hood Friar Tuck Maid Marion Little John Five file servers One print server Three HP4SI printers One HPIII LaserJet printer One Canon BubbleJet printer

TABLE 8.2 *The Acme Resource Wish List (continued)*

DIVISION	DEPARTMENT	RESOURCES
Admin	Headquarters	George Washington Franklin Delano Roosevelt Two file servers One print server One Canon BubbleJet printer
	Facilities	James Madison One file server One print server One HP4SI printer
	Auditing	Abraham Lincoln One file server One HP4SI printer
	Marketing	Thomas Jefferson One file server Two HPIII LaserJet printers
	Public Relations	Mary Clarke David James Clarke, IV Cathy Ettelson Jeff Hughes Blair Thomas Five file servers Five print servers Five HP4SI printers Two Canon BubbleJet printers

This completes our discussion of gathering NDS information. In this section, we put ACME under the NDS microscope. This is a critical part of Step 1. All the information that you gather here will act as raw material for ACME design, installation, and management.

In Step 1, we created the project team and gathered filing cabinets full of ACME information. This information will become the foundation of Steps 2, 3, and 4. Study the information in this chapter carefully, and when you are ready, move on to Step 2 — NDS design.

Good luck; and by the way, thanks for saving the Net!

LAB EXERCISE 8.1: BUILDING THE ACME TEAM

Use the hints provided to find the 20 NDS-preparation terms hidden in this word-search puzzle. Omit any punctuation characters (such as blank spaces, hyphens, and so on) and spell out any numbers.

P	R	O	J	E	C	T	S	C	O	P	E	O	M	D	X	S	L
I	E	R	N	Y	U	O	B	F	B	G	D	V	S	I	S	A	T
L	S	G	D	A	T	A	G	A	T	H	E	R	I	N	G	Z	Q
O	O	A	S	L	U	H	B	H	P	R	S	H	O	A	D	Z	R
T	U	N	D	S	P	R	E	P	A	R	A	T	I	O	N	X	R
P	R	I	V	C	F	T	A	P	M	P	Z	J	N	K	G	U	X
R	C	Z	I	C	L	D	S	T	R	U	C	T	U	R	E	D	I
O	E	A	N	W	O	R	K	F	L	O	W	K	M	P	U	H	S
G	L	T	E	B	V	C	O	N	N	E	C	T	I	V	I	T	Y
R	I	I	L	P	R	O	J	E	C	T	T	E	A	M	B	U	Q
A	S	O	A	Q	K	D	F	O	M	N	H	R	S	D	A	V	H
M	T	N	D	E	S	I	G	N	I	N	P	U	T	S	X	D	H
R	S	A	L	J	H	L	A	C	I	N	H	C	E	T	A	B	C
S	C	L	S	Q	Q	V	H	U	U	R	X	J	W	M	V	B	T

Hints

1. Type of specialist who works with the physical network, Internet backbone, telecommunications, WAN design, and router placement.
2. The main task of Step 1 in our plan to save the Net.
3. The two main types are organizational and technical.
4. Fundamental network service that is supplied by all NetWare 5.1 servers.
5. In this step, you will build the Project Team and gather data.
6. Design inputs include Company Overview and Organizational Chart.
7. Controlled rollout of first production systems.
8. This determines the physical boundaries for the network, as well as financial and personnel limitations.

9. Group that consists of networking experts, including management, server specialists, NDS experts, and connectivity specialists.
10. Technical input that breaks out each campus into its physical network resources—such as users, file servers, printer servers, and so on.
11. What programmers call the "The Process."
12. Model that allows all activities to take place simultaneously.
13. Design inputs include WAN Layout and Resource Lists.
14. A systematic methodology for designing, implementing, and managing NetWare systems.
15. Describes the daily operations of ACME staff and their task-oriented responsibilities.

See Appendix C for answers.

LAB EXERCISE 8.2: NDS PREPARATION

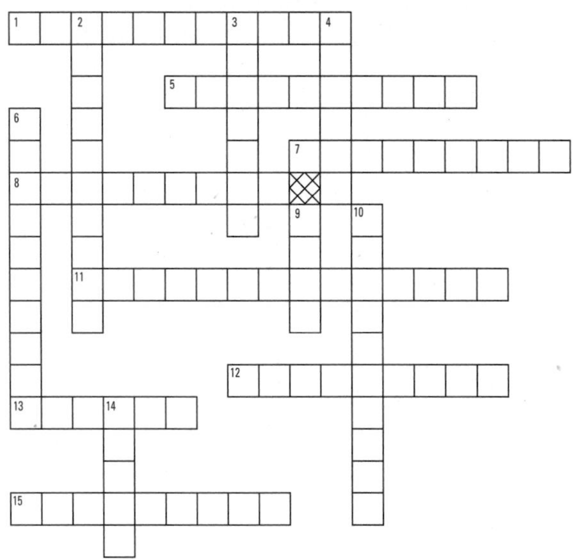

Across

1. Approach used with rapid prototyping
5. Best place for experimentation
7. Design input for geographic leaf objects
8. Examples include people, equipment, and money
11. In charge of the project team
12. Step 2 in our plan to save the Net
13. Approach used in risky environments
15. Person who truly understands the "Cloud"

Down

2. A more granular version of ACME's WAN layout
3. Focus of design efforts
4. Approach that handles steps in order
6. "A day in the life of ACME"
9. Heroes from our unspoiled history
10. Step 4 in our plan to save the Net
14. Every team member should understand theirs

See Appendix C for answers.

CHAPTER 9

NDS Tree Design

NDS design is the most critical phase of the NetWare design and implementation process. It impacts virtually every network user and/or resource. As you can see in Figure 9.1, the NDS design phase consists of five interrelated tasks:

- *NDS Naming Standards* — A complete Naming Standards Document is important because it enables you to design an NDS database that is flexible, easy to use, and meets your business needs.
- *NDS Tree Design* — Next, you should convert your design inputs into a preliminary design of your NDS tree. The top layers should be location based and the bottom layers should be function based. The design of the container structure should resemble the shape of a pyramid, with most of the containers at the bottom and fewer containers at the top.
- *Partition and Replica Design* — Once the tree design is in place, you need to divide the new tree into smaller pieces *(partitioning)* and strategically place copies of the pieces on particular servers in the network *(replica placement)*. This task is important because it directly affects your network's performance, accessibility, and fault tolerance. (**Note:** This task is covered in Chapter 10.)
- *Time Synchronization Design* — Next, you must build a time synchronization system that ensures consistent time stamps throughout the network. You can choose to accept the NetWare 5.1 defaults, or you can institute a customized time synchronization strategy, for instance, that mixes IPX and IP protocol segments. (**Note:** This task is covered in Chapter 10.)
- *NDS Accessibility Design* — Finally, you should create a User Environment Plan that addresses special NDS accessibility considerations, including mobile users, remote users, login scripts, Bindery Services, connections, and non-DOS workstations.

So much to learn, and so little time. Let's start with a closer look at the fundamentals of object naming, and explore a Naming Standards Document for ACME.

FIGURE 9.1

Step 2: NDS Design

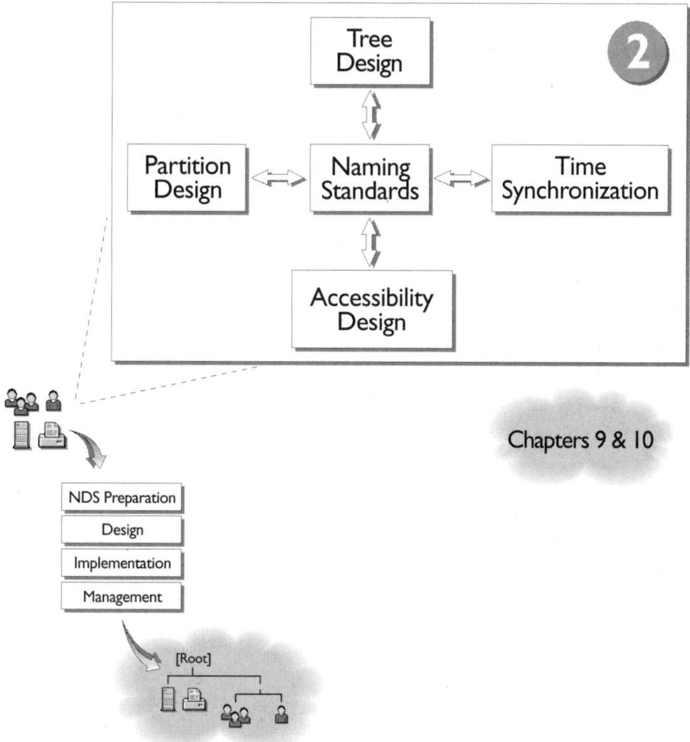

REAL WORLD

Throughout this book, we will use ACME as a global case study for key NetWare 5.1 advanced management, NDS design, and troubleshooting tasks. See Appendix E, "ACME Mission Briefing," for more details regarding the ACME organization and its purpose.

NDS Naming Standards

The NDS design phase begins with an NDS Naming Standards Document. This document provides guidelines for naming key container and leaf objects (including Users, Printers, Servers, Volumes, Print Queues, and Organizational Units). In addition, it identifies standard properties and value formats.

NDS uses a mechanism called the *schema* to define the NDS naming structure for all network resources. The schema is distributed to all NDS servers and follows specific rules. Unlike the NetWare 3.12 Bindery, NDS is a special-purpose naming service that stores objects in a hierarchical format and services up to billions of objects per server (assuming NDS Version 8 and above). Your understanding of the schema will help you manage the internal structure of NDS naming. Also, it will help you plan for the future through supplemental object types, add-on products, or third-party applications.

Let's start our discussion of NDS naming standards with a brief overview of NDS object types. Then we will explore NDS naming rules, including distinguished names, relative distinguished names, context, typeful, and finally, typeless naming.

NDS Objects

The NDS Directory consists of objects, properties, and values.

An *object* is similar to a record or row of information in a database table. It contains information about a particular network entity. NDS represents each network resource as an object in the Directory. For example, a User object represents a particular user on the network.

An object *property* is similar to a field in a database record. It is a category of information you can store about an object. For example, properties of a User object include such things as Login Name, Password, and Telephone Number. Each type of object has a specific set of properties associated with it; this defines its "class." Properties are predefined by NDS and determine how a given object can be used. For example, Server properties differ from Printer properties because they are different NDS objects with different functions.

Finally, a property *value* is similar to a data string in a field of a database record. In other words, it's a data item associated with a property. For example, the value associated with the Password property of a User object would be the actual password for that User object.

Refer to Table 9.1 for an illustration of the relationship between NDS objects, properties, and values.

TABLE 9.1

Understanding NDS Objects, Properties, and Values

OBJECT	PROPERTY	VALUE
User	Login Name	AEinstein (also known as AEinstein.LABS.NORAD.ACME)
	Title	Super Smart Scientist
	Location	NORAD
	Password	Relativity
Printer (Non NDPS)	Name	WHITE-P1.WHITE.CRIME.TOKYO.ACME
	Default Print Queue	WHITE-PQ1.WHITE.CRIME.TOKYO.ACME
	Print Server	WHITE-PS1.WHITE.CRIME.TOKYO.ACME
NetWare Server	Other Name	LABS-SRV1
	Version	Novell NetWare 5.00h[DS]
	Operators	Admin
	Status	Up

Understanding NDS Objects

The NDS Directory is an object-oriented database that is organized in a hierarchical structure called the NDS tree. It provides a way to view the logical organization of network resources stored in the Directory database. As you can see in Figure 9.2, the tree is similar to the DOS file system. It contains the following three main classes of objects:

- [Root]
- Container objects (such as Organization and Organizational Unit objects)
- Leaf objects

FIGURE 9.2

Understanding NDS objects

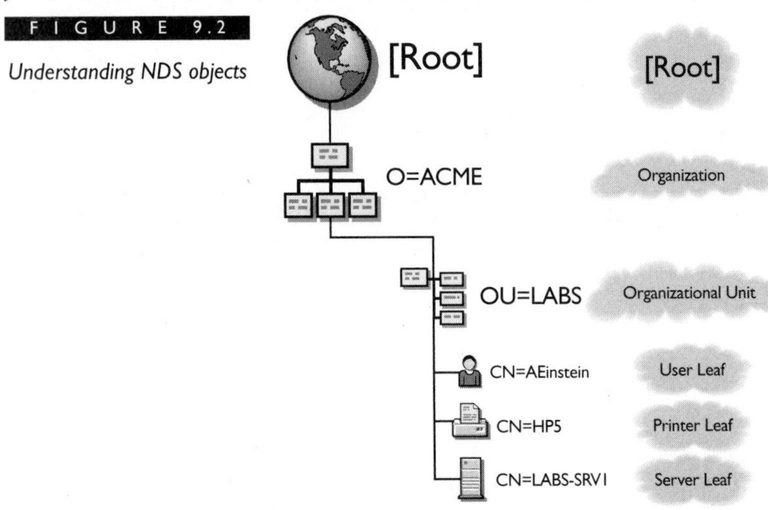

The top of the tree is called the *[Root]*. *Container objects*, which are analogous to folders, define the organizational boundaries of the Directory and are used to store other container objects and/or leaf objects, depending on which type of container they are. (A container object is called a *parent object* if it contains other objects.) *Leaf objects*, which are analogous to files, are typically stored in container objects. They are the physical or logical network resources that provide technical services and WAN functionality. Leaf objects define the lowest level of the NDS structure and, thus, cannot contain other objects.

The main difference between NDS and DOS architecture is that NDS containers have restrictions on where they can be placed and what can be placed in them. Typically, each NetWare 5.1 network will only have one NDS tree. If a network has more than one tree, each will function as separate, independent databases. In other words, resources cannot be shared between them.

In the Directory, each network resource is defined as a logical object. There are a number of different types of objects. For example, an object can represent a person (such as a user), a physical resource (such as a printer), an NDS resource (such as a group), or an organizational resource (such as an Organizational Unit container).

Now that you've mastered the subtle differences between NDS objects, properties, and values, let's explore some of the most interesting objects in detail, starting with [Root].

[Root]

The [Root] is a required object that defines the top of the NDS organizational structure. Because it represents the opening porthole to our NDS world, its icon is appropriately a picture of the earth. Each Directory tree can only have one [Root], which is created during installation of the first server in that tree. The only objects that can be created directly under the [Root] are Country, Organization, and Alias. (In this case, the Alias object can only point to a Country or Organization.) The square brackets ([ ]) are mandatory when referring to this object.

Although some people think of the [Root] as a container object (because it contains all the objects in the Directory), it differs from other container objects in the following ways:

- The [Root] cannot be created except during installation of the first NetWare 5.1 server on a network.
- It is essentially a placeholder; it does not have properties.
- It cannot be moved, deleted, or renamed.
- The NDS tree name is sometimes confused with the [Root] object. Unlike the [Root] object, however, the tree name can be changed.

Country

The *Country* object is an optional container that is used to organize a Directory tree by country. This type of object can only be defined directly under the [Root] and must be named using a two-character abbreviation. Novell states that you must use a *valid* two-character country abbreviation. Presumably, this is to ensure that your network is in compliance with the two-character abbreviations defined in the ISO X.500 standard.

Interestingly, if you create a Country object using the NetWare Administrator utility, it allows you to use any two-character name. To determine which two-character names are compliant with the ISO X.500 standard, click Help when creating the Country object, and NetWare 5.1 will tell you. The only objects that can exist in a Country container are an Organization or Alias object pointing to an Organization.

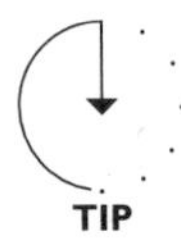

If you don't have any compelling reasons to use the Country object, stay away from it. It only adds an unnecessary level of complexity to your network. As a matter of fact, Novell doesn't even use the Country object in its own multidimensional, worldwide NDS tree.

Organization

If you don't use a Country object, the next layer in the tree is typically an Organization. As you can see in Figure 9.2, ACME is represented as an *O*. You can use an Organization object to designate a company, a division of a company, a university or a college with various departments, and so on. Every Directory tree must contain at least one Organization object. Therefore, it is required. Many small implementations use only the Organization object and place all their resources directly underneath it. Organization objects must be placed directly below the [Root], unless a Country object is used. Finally, Organization objects can contain all objects except [Root], Country, and Organization.

Earlier, we defined the Organization as a one-dimensional object. This means the tree can only support one layer of Organization objects. If you look closer at the icon, you'll see a box with multiple horizontal boxes underneath. Additional vertical hierarchy is defined by Organizational Unit objects, which are multidimensional. We'll describe them in just a moment.

Organizational Unit

The Organizational Unit object is a "natural group." It enables you to organize users with the leaf objects that they use. You can create group login scripts, a user template for security, trustee assignments, security equivalences, and distributed administrators.

Organizational Units can represent a division, business unit, project team, or department. In Figure 9.2, the LABS Organizational Unit represents a division within the ACME organization. In this container, AEinstein works with his printers and servers. Organizational Units are multidimensional, in that you can have many hierarchical levels of containers within containers. Remember, Organization objects can only exist at one level in the NDS tree.

Organizational Units are the most flexible containers because they can contain other Organizational Unit objects or leaf objects. As a matter of fact, Organizational

Units can contain most of the NDS object types, except the [Root], Country, or Organization containers (or Aliases of any of these).

Now let's take a look at the real stars of our NDS world — leaf objects.

Leaf Objects

Leaf objects represent logical or physical network resources. Because leaf objects reside at the end of the structural NDS tree, they cannot be used to store other objects. In other words, they represent the proverbial "end of the road." As we learned earlier, each class of leaf object has certain properties associated with it. This collection of properties differentiates the various leaf object classes from each other. For example, User objects contain different properties than Printer objects.

The following are some of the key leaf objects covered in Part II, "NDS Design and Implementation":

Alias — An Alias object points to another object that exists in a different location in the NDS tree. It enables a user to access an object outside of the user's normal working context (that is, outside of the container where their User object is located).

Application — An Application object enables network administrators to manage applications as objects in the NDS tree. The advantage of this object is that users don't have to worry about drive mappings, paths, or rights when they want to execute an application. This information is defined by Application object properties.

Auditing File (AFO) — An Auditing File object represents an audit trail's log of events associated with a container, workstation, or volume. This object enables you to manage auditing file logs as objects in the NDS tree.

Directory Map — A Directory Map object represents a logical pointer to a physical directory in the NetWare 5.1 file system. This object is useful in mapping statements because it enables you to map a drive to a resource without knowing its physical location. If the path to the resource changes, you only need to change the path designated in the Directory Map object, rather than login script mapping statements that refer to the path.

 *Group* — A Group object defines a list of users for the purpose of assigning access rights or other configuration parameters. The members of a group can be a subset of users in the same container or spread across multiple containers. The difference between containers and groups is that container objects store actual objects (such as Users and Printers), whereas Group objects store a list of associated leaf objects (such as related Users).

 *License Certificate* — A License Certificate object is used by NetWare Licensing Services (NLS) to monitor and to control the use of licensed applications on the network.

 *NetWare Server* — A NetWare Server object represents a server on your network that is running any version of the NetWare operating system. This object is used by various leaf objects (such as Volume objects) to identify a physical server that provides particular network services.

 *Organizational Role* — An Organizational Role object defines a position or role within the organization that can be filled by any designated user. The Organizational Role is particularly useful for rotating positions that support multiple employees where the responsibilities of the job and the network access required are static. If a User object is assigned as an occupant of an organizational role, the user "absorbs" all trustee rights assigned to it. Some organizational role examples include PostMaster, Network Administrator, Silicon Valley CEO, or Receptionist.

 *Printer (Non NDPS)* — A Printer (Non NDPS) object represents a queue-based physical printing device on the network, such as a printer or plotter.

 *Print Queue* — A Print Queue object represents a print queue used to store print jobs sent from client workstations. In NetWare 5.1, each print queue is stored as a subdirectory under the QUEUES directory at the root of a NetWare volume.

 *Print Server (Non NDPS)* — A Print Server (Non NDPS) object represents a network print server used for monitoring queue-based print queues and printers.

 *Profile* — A Profile object defines a login script for a subset of users in the same container or spread across multiple containers. (If all of the users in a container need the same login script, you should use a Container login script instead.)

 *Template* — A Template object can be used to create User objects with similar properties.

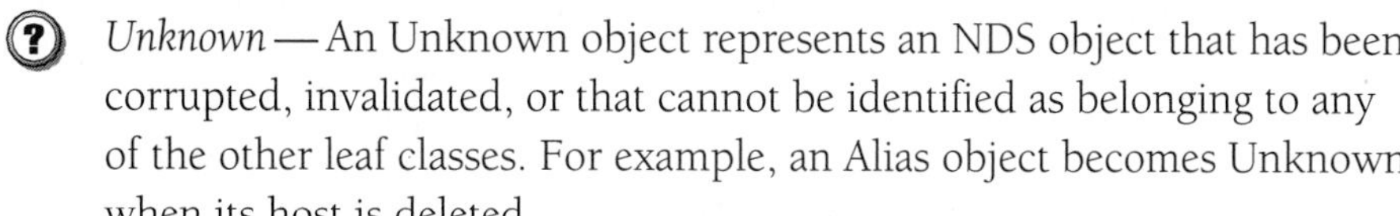 *Unknown* — An Unknown object represents an NDS object that has been corrupted, invalidated, or that cannot be identified as belonging to any of the other leaf classes. For example, an Alias object becomes Unknown when its host is deleted.

 *User* — A User object represents a person who uses the network (for example, you, me, or Fred). For security reasons, you should create a separate User object for each user on the network. A User object contains a plethora of interesting properties, including Login Name, Password, Full Name, Login Restrictions, and so on.

 *Volume* — A Volume object represents a physical volume on the network. Typically, volumes are created during the server installation process. Remember that a Volume object is a leaf object rather than a container object — even though the NetWare Administrator utility may give you the opposite impression. It is used to store information about a volume including server name, physical volume mapping, and volume use statistics.

 *Workstation* — A Workstation object enables you to manage network workstations through NDS. This leaf object is automatically created when a workstation is registered and imported into the NDS tree.

 *Workstation Group* — A Workstation Group object lets you manage or maintain a group of Workstation objects. This leaf allows you to apply a change to a Workstation Group object, instead of to each individual Workstation object.

Table 9.2 summarizes some important NDS object characteristics.

TABLE 9.2

NDS Object Characteristics

OBJECT	CAN EXIST IN	CAN CONTAIN	EXAMPLES
[Root]	Top of the tree	Country	[Root]
		Organization	
		Alias *(of Country or Organization only)*	
Country	[Root]	Organization	US
		Alias *(of Organization only)*	UK
Organization	[Root] Country	Organizational Units	Novell
		All leaf objects	MIT
Organizational Unit	Organization	Organizational Unit	Sales
	Organizational Units	All leaf objects	Finance
Leaf Objects	[Root] *(Alias of Country or Organization only)*	Cannot contain other NDS objects	CRIME-SRV1 DClarkeIV CEttelson
	Country *(Alias of Organization only)*		
	Organization		
	Organizational Unit		

This completes our discussion of NDS objects. You'll want to get to know all these leaf objects because future discussions center around how to design and manage them. Once you understand the relationships between NDS objects, you can start building an NDS Naming Standards Document.

LAB EXERCISE 9.1: UNDERSTANDING NDS OBJECTS (MATCHING)

Part I

Write C for *container* or L for *leaf* next to each of the following objects:

1. ___ Volume
2. ___ Country
3. ___ User
4. ___ Group
5. ___ Organizational Unit
6. ___ NetWare Server
7. ___ Print Queue
8. ___ Organizational Role
9. ___ Computer
10. ___ Organization

See Appendix C for answers.

PART II

Indicate whether you think each item below would be a container or a leaf object. If you think it would be a container object, indicate what type of container (that is, Country, Organization, or Organizational Unit).

1. ________ The Human Resources department
2. ________ David IV

3. ________ A database server

4. ________ The PAYCHECK print queue

5. ________ ACME, Inc.

6. ________ The Administrator Organizational Role

7. ________ UK (that is, United Kingdom)

8. ________ A dot matrix printer

9. ________ The Tokyo office

10. ________ The SYS: volume

See Appendix C for answers.

NDS Naming Rules

The name of an NDS object identifies its location in the hierarchical tree. Therefore, each object name must be unique. NDS naming impacts two important NetWare 5.1 tasks:

- *Login* — Typically, you need to identify the location of your User object in the NDS tree in order for NetWare 5.1 to authenticate you during login.
- *Resource Access* — NDS naming exactly identifies the type and location of NetWare 5.1 resources, including file servers, printers, login scripts, and files.

The NDS tree affects resource access because the organization of objects in the tree dictates how they can be found and used. In fact, the whole NDS naming strategy hinges on the concept of *context*.

There are two main types of context: current context and object context.

Context

Current context is sometimes referred to as *name context*. It defines *where you are* in the NDS tree at any given time, not *where you live*. This is an important distinction. For example, if you are using a NetWare 5.1 utility, it's important to know what the utility considers as the current context (that is, the default container) in the NDS tree. This concept is somewhat similar to knowing your current default drive and current default directory when using a DOS or Windows utility on your workstation.

In addition, current context affects how much of an object's distinguished name you must provide to find it. (See the next section, "Distinguished Names," for more information.) Current context also allows you to refer to an object in your current container by its common name because the object's context is the same. Note that current context always points to a container object, rather than a leaf object. Typically, at login, you'll want a workstation's current context set to the container that holds the user's most frequently used resources.

Object context (sometimes referred to as *context*) defines where a particular object is located in the NDS tree structure. It is a list of container objects leading from the object to the [Root]. Locating an object through context is similar to locating a file using the directory path. As we learned earlier, object context is used for two important purposes: logging in and accessing resources. Unfortunately,

NDS does not have a search path feature (such as the way the NetWare SEARCH drives or the DOS PATH commands are used in the file system). This means that when you request a particular network resource, you (or your workstation) must provide NDS with enough information to locate the object in the tree.

Each NDS object has a naming type associated with it. This naming type is identified by a one- or two-character abbreviation, for example, the following abbreviations:

- *C* = Country container
- *O* = Organization container
- *OU* = Organizational Unit container
- *CN* = Common name (specifies a leaf object)

Also, notice the syntax used to create an object's context. In Figure 9.3, Fred's context is created by identifying each of his containers in reverse order, leading to the [Root]. Note that each container is separated by a period. In Figure 9.3, Fred's context is .OU=ADMIN.O=ACME. This context identifies where the Fred User object lives in the NDS tree structure. In addition to context, his common name specifically identifies his User object as Fred.

FIGURE 9.3

Getting to know the real Fred

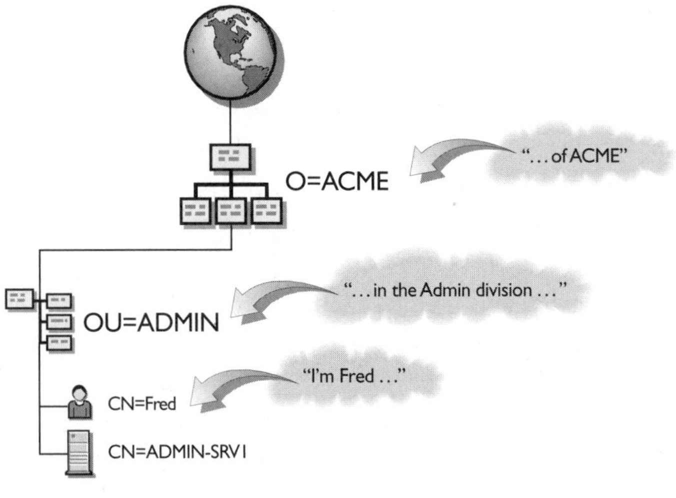

What if you have two users named Fred? Two objects in the same NDS tree can have the same common name — provided, however, that they have different contexts. In other words, that they are located in different containers. This is why naming is so important.

Now that you understand how NDS context works, let's review the naming rules associated with it:

- Current context defines your workstation's current position in the Directory tree.
- An object's context defines its location in the NDS tree.
- Each object has an identifier abbreviation that defines it for naming purposes, namely C = Country, O = Organization, OU = Organizational Unit, and CN = common name (of leaf object).
- Context is defined by listing all containers from the object to the [Root], in that order. Each object is separated by a period.
- Context is important for logging in and accessing NDS resources.

So, there you have it. That's how context works. With this in mind, it's time to explore the two main types of NDS names: distinguished names and typeful names.

Distinguished Names

An object's *distinguished name* is its complete NDS path. It is a combination of common name and object context. Each object in the NDS tree has a distinguished name that uniquely identifies it in the tree. In other words, two objects cannot have the same distinguished name.

In Figure 9.4, AEinstein's context is .OU=R&D.OU=LABS.O=ACME, and his common name is CN=AEinstein. Therefore, Einstein's distinguished name is a simple mathematical addition of the two:

```
.CN=AEinstein.OU=R&D.OU=LABS.O=ACME
```

FIGURE 9.4

Building AEinstein's distinguished name

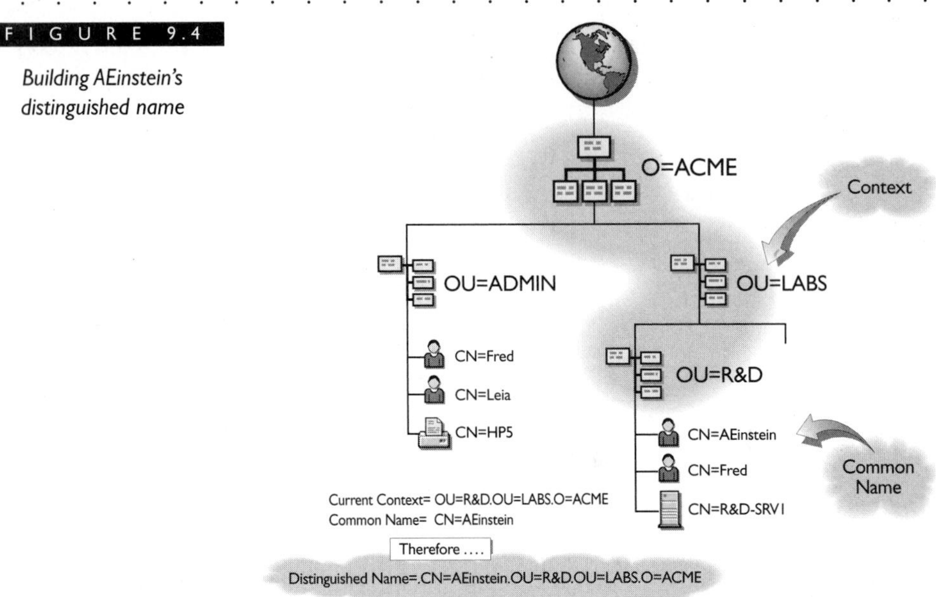

Notice the use of periods. A distinguished name always starts with a leading period—trailing periods aren't allowed. The leading period identifies the name as distinguished (that is, complete). Otherwise, it is assumed to be incomplete—in other words, a relative distinguished name.

Relative Distinguished Names

A *relative distinguished name* lists an object's path to the current context—not to the [Root]. The relativity part refers to how NDS builds the distinguished name when you supply a *relative* name. By definition, for example, the common name of a leaf object is a relative distinguished name. When you use a relative distinguished name, NDS builds a distinguished name by appending the current context to the end of the relative distinguished name:

Relative distinguished name + current context = distinguished name

For example, if the current context is .OU=LABS.O=ACME and you submit a relative distinguished name of CN=AEinstein.OU=R&D, the distinguished name would be resolved as the following:

```
.CN=AEinstein.OU=R&D.OU=LABS.O=ACME
```

To distinguish a relative name, you must not lead with a period. Instead, you can use trailing periods to change the current context used to resolve the name (as if naming wasn't hard enough already). The bottom line is that each trailing period tells NDS to remove one object name from the left side of the current context being used. This concept is somewhat similar to the trailing dot feature used in the DOS CD command.

For example, assume that .OU=R&D.OU=LABS.O=ACME is your current context and that CN=LEIA.OU=ADMIN.. is your relative distinguished name. In this case, the distinguished name would resolve as follows:

```
.CN=LEIA.OU=ADMIN.O=ACME
```

As you can see, it's important where you place your dots! Here's a quick summary:

- All objects in an NDS name are separated by dots.
- Distinguished names are preceded by a dot. This identifies them as complete.
- Relative distinguished names are not preceded by a dot. This identifies them as incomplete.
- Trailing dots can only be used in relative distinguished names because they modify the current context to be used. Each dot moves the context up one container as the distinguished name is resolved.

For a complete summary of NDS distinguished naming rules, refer to Table 9.3. Now let's step back in reality for a moment and explore the other NDS naming category — typeful names.

TABLE 9.3

Distinguished and Relative Naming

	DISTINGUISHED NAMES	RELATIVE NAMES
What it is	Complete unique name	Incomplete name based on current context
How it works	Lists the complete path from the object to the [Root]	Lists the relative path from the object to the current context

Continued

TABLE 9.3
Distinguished and Relative Naming (continued)

	DISTINGUISHED NAMES	RELATIVE NAMES
Abbreviation	DN	RDN
Leading period	Leading periods required	No leading periods allowed
Trailing periods	No trailing periods allowed	Trailing periods optional

Typeful versus Typeless Names

Typeful names use attribute type abbreviations to differentiate between the different container types and to distinguish container objects from leaf objects in NDS names. In all the examples up to this point, we've used these abbreviations to help clarify context, distinguished names, and relative distinguished names. As we discussed earlier, the most popular attribute type abbreviations are *C*=Country, *O*=Organization, *OU*=Organizational Unit, and *CN*=Common name (leaf objects only).

Although these attribute types are not mandatory, they help to avoid confusion that can occur when creating complex distinguished names and relative distinguished names. I highly recommend that you use them. Of course, like most things in life — they are optional!

Typeless names operate the same as typeful names, but they don't include the object attribute type for each object. In such cases, NDS has to "guess" what object types you're using. For example, AEinstein's distinguished typeless name is the following:

```
.Einstein.R&D.LABS.ACME
```

Now that you have learned the fundamentals of NDS naming and discovered some name-related design caveats, it's time to dive into the real star of naming design — the NDS Naming Standards Document. I promise that we will put all of your naming knowledge to good use.

NDS Naming Standards Document

Following are some guidelines you should consider when creating your NDS Naming Standards Document:

- Make browsing and navigation of the NDS tree easier for users.

- Make maintenance of the NDS tree easier for network administrators.
- Make merging separate NDS trees easier.
- Keep NDS object names unique.
- Avoid special characters reserved by operating systems.

The NDS Naming Standards Document consists of two NDS components: objects and properties. The *NDS Object Naming Standard* contains a list of the object types present in your NDS tree, as well as a consistent naming scheme for each object type (see Table 9.4). The *NDS Property Naming Standard* defines required properties for each object type, a consistent property-naming scheme, and examples of each property type (see Table 9.5).

NDS Object Naming Standard

NDS tree design begins with an object naming standard. Begin by taking a long, hard look at ACME and the network resources it uses. Consider the impact of naming on these resources and come up with some simple guidelines for standardizing the names. The good news is that most of your effort is focused on a few leaf and container objects, namely the following:

- *Users* — When creating a naming standard, the first step is to decide what to do with the users. NDS allows usernames up to 64 characters long. However, a 64-character username is ridiculous. Consider limiting it to eight characters or less. This is appropriate in many cases, but not ACME. The eight-character rule makes file system management much easier, but it hinders the identity and exclusivity of key users. It is important to ensure that each username is unique throughout a company. Even though NDS doesn't require it, exclusivity aids messaging management.
- *Organization* — Your Organization name should reflect your company name. In our case, "A Cure for Mother Earth" becomes "ACME," and the Organization name becomes O=ACME. With the Organization restricted to the company's name, it frees up the Organizational Units to become the true Tupperware containers of NDS logic. In addition, you may consider adding a location to the Organization name and accommodate future tree merging.

- *Organizational Units* — Organizational Units can span multiple container depths. With this flexibility, they can be used for "geography" and "organization." As you'll learn in the next section, geography defines the upper layers of the NDS tree. So, the first few layers of Organizational Units should be reserved for locations, such as OU=SYDNEY and OU=TOKYO. They could have been abbreviated to SYD and TOK, but their names are already short. Remember, the names must be both short and descriptive (SYD isn't very descriptive). The next OU layers are dedicated to divisions and departments, such as OU=R&D for the Research and Development department and OU=MRKT for Marketing. Remember, be short, but descriptive. This allows for much easier tree searching and navigation.

- *Servers* — Server names must be unique across the entire WAN because of Service Advertising Protocol (SAP) and Routing Information Protocol (RIP) broadcasting. You may wish to consider a server name that incorporates both its location and department. For ACME, a NetWare 5.1 server in the CHARITY department of NORAD is called NOR-CHR-SRV1, and a print server is called NOR-CHR-PS1. On the other hand, a file server in the R&D department of NORAD is called R&D-SRV1 because R&D is a unique department within the ACME tree and, therefore, it doesn't need any special location designator. However, the CHARITY and PR departments are not unique departments — they exist in each location throughout the ACME tree. Therefore, the servers in those containers should use the location designator to uniquely identify them.

- *Printers and Print Queues* — Unlike servers, printers and print queues don't require naming exclusivity. The department and location information is obtained through the object's NDS context. This means that an HP LaserJet 4SI in R&D can share the same name as an HP LaserJet 4SI in WHITE — they have different distinguished names because they have different parent containers. In summary, a printer's distinguished name identifies its location and department. Therefore, printer and print queue names should reflect functionality, not location.

This completes our discussion of the main NDS object classes. In addition, you might want to consider naming standards for Group, Organizational Role, Directory Map Object, and Profile objects. Refer to Table 9.4 for a detailed summary of ACME's NDS object naming standard.

TABLE 9.4

NDS Object Naming Standard

NDS OBJECTS	STANDARD	EXAMPLES
NDS Tree	Name of the company or network location.	ACME-TREE
Users	First character of the first name, plus the entire last name. All titles are spelled out. Eight characters maximum.	GWashing, SirGawai
Organization	Abbreviation of the company name, which is "A Cure for Mother Earth." Alternatively, you can append multiple locations to the company abbreviation for multiple Organization objects.	ACME or ACME_TOKYO
Organizational Unit	Location, division, or department name. Abbreviate the name if there are over eight characters.	NORAD, R&D, ADMIN
Server	*Department*-SRV#. Exception for the CHARITY and PR departments, which is Location-Department-SRV#.	LABS-SRV1, NOR-CHR-SRV1
Volumes	*ServerName_VolumeName*	LABS-SRV1_SYS, NOR-CHR-SRV1_SYS
Print Server	*Department*-PS#. Exception for the CHARITY and PR departments, which is Location-Department-PS#.	FAC-PS1, TOK-PR-PS1
Printer	*PrinterType*-P#	HP4SI-P1, CANONBJ-P2
Print Queue	*PrinterType*-PQ#	HP4SI-PQ1, CANONBJ-PQ2
All Common Names	Avoid spaces and special characters, such as +, =, /, |, *, ^, %, and #.	

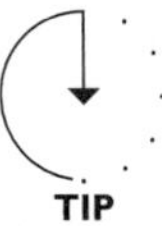
TIP

NDS supports single object names up to 64 characters in length. However, a limitation of the DOS command-line utilities imposes a maximum context length of 255 characters. Finally, remember that bindery rules restrict object names to 47 characters for previous versions of NetWare.

NDS Property Naming Standard

The final step is to put your naming guidelines under the microscope. Now you must focus in on each object class and provide rules for Required, Optional, and System properties.

First, determine which properties should be *required*. Start with the mandatory NDS properties and expand from there. For example, NDS won't allow you to create a User object without the Login Name and Last Name properties. In ACME's case, we're also requiring Given Name, Full Name, Middle Initial, Title, Location, Telephone Number, Fax Number, Home Directory, and Require Password.

Next, determine which properties will be *optional*. Finally, identify *system* properties (such as Network Address and so on). In addition, you'll want to provide naming rules for how the properties look. Refer to Table 9.5 for a detailed summary of ACME's NDS property naming standard.

TABLE 9.5

NDS Property Naming Standard

PROPERTY	REQ/OPT/ SYSTEM	STANDARD
Login Name	Required	First character of the first name, plus the entire last name. Add a middle initial to resolve name conflicts. First initial, middle initial (if applicable), and last name (all lowercase) Eight characters maximum Common names unique throughout the company
Given Name	Required	First name of the user Initial capitalization

TABLE 9.5

NDS Property Naming Standard (continued)

PROPERTY	REQ/OPT/ SYSTEM	STANDARD
Last Name	Required	Last name of the user Initial capitalization
Full Name	Required	First and last name of the user
Generational Qualifier	Optional	For example, IV or Jr.
Middle Initial	Optional	Middle initial of the user, if known Capitalized
Other Name	Optional	Other name that the user may go by Initial capitalization
Title	Required	Job title
Description	Optional	Brief description of the physical characteristics of the user
Location	Required	City or site location (NORAD, RIO)
Department	Optional	Name of the organization the user belongs to
Telephone Number	Required	Business phone number with area code Numbers separated by dashes Avoid parentheses, commas, or the long-distance prefix number "1-"
Fax Number	Required	Fax phone number with area code Numbers separated by dashes Avoid parentheses, commas, or the long-distance prefix number "1-"
Language	Optional	Preferred language of the user
Network Address	System	N/A
Home Directory	Required	Enter the volume:subdirectory\user path
Require Password	Required	Require the user to have a password

Continued

TABLE 9.5

NDS Property Naming Standard (continued)

PROPERTY	REQ/OPT/ SYSTEM	STANDARD
Require Password *(continued)*		Have the user create a password upon first login Minimum seven characters
Login Script	Optional	Determined by site administrators
Print Job Configuration	Optional	Determined by site administrators
Post Office Box	Optional	Precede the mail stop number with MS and a colon
Street	Optional	The address of the building where the user conducts business
City	Optional	The name of the city in which the building is located where the user conducts business
State or Province	Optional	The two-character abbreviation of the state or province in which the building is located where the user conducts business Capitalized
Zip Code	Optional	The ZIP or postal code for the building where the user conducts business
See Also	Optional	The fully qualified name of an NDS object that the user is aliased to

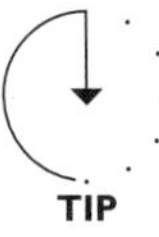

Currently, NetWare 5.1 utilities can't be configured to enforce additional required properties.The User object, for example, is only required to have a Login Name and Last Name.Your standard, however, may be different.You will need to enforce required user properties at the management level — in your naming guidelines. Also, it helps if you explain the reasoning for including the property. This helps distributed administrators buy into it. Finally, you may want to consider extending the NDS schema to support additional required properties using the NDS Schema Manager.

Once you have completed the naming guidelines and examples, there's only one more set of rules to complete your Naming Standards Document — Syntax. Table 9.6 shows a simple, but effective, syntax standard. Notice that we have also included examples. In the most basic sense, this is a summary of the entire Naming Standards Document. As a matter of fact, small organizations could probably get away with just the naming syntax guidelines.

TABLE 9.6

ACME's Naming Standard Syntax

OBJECT TYPE	SYNTAX	EXAMPLE
[Root] or Tree Name	AAAA-TREE	ACME-TREE
Organization	AAAA	O=ACME
Organizational Units	XXXXX or YYYYY	OU=NORAD, OU=LABS
Servers	XXX-YYYYY-SRV#	LABS-SRV1
Print Servers	XXX-YYYYY-PS#	NOR-CHR-PS4
Printers	<Prn Type>-P#	HP4SI-P1
Print Queues	<Prn Type>-PQ#	HP4SI-PQ1
Volume Names	<Server>_<Volume>	LABS-SRV1_SYS

Here's the legend for Table 9.6:

- *AAAA* — Company Name
- *XXX* — Location (NOR, RIO, CAM, TOK, SYD)
- *YYYYY* — Department (LABS, CHR, PR, ADM, OPS, FIN)
- *SRV* — File Server
- *PS* — Print Server
- *#* — Quantity (1, 2, 3, . . ., 9)
- *Volumes* — SYS, VOL1, DATA, USERS, SHARE

Congratulations! You have completed the ACME Naming Standards Document. What an accomplishment. It wasn't easy, but now you should feel much more comfortable about the future of ACME's design. At the very least, we know what to call NDS objects and their properties.

The next step is *NDS tree design*. This is when you get a chance to establish rules for tree design, just as you did for naming standards. Have fun.

NDS Tree Design

NDS tree design is the most important phase in the design and implementation process. Most general NDS design benefits stem from a well-planned Directory tree, including the following benefits:

- Partitioning and replication can be successfully designed.
- The network can accommodate growth without complicating revisions.
- Directory trees can be merged more easily.
- Other network services and network accessibility can be designed more easily.
- The Directory tree can be navigated more intuitively.

You should take extra caution in designing the top layers of the tree because changes here can have a large impact on the placement of resources lower in the tree. Furthermore, this importance is amplified when the network spans WAN links.

In order to build an efficient NDS tree design, you should follow these three steps:

- *Step 1: Use a Pyramid Design*—Design the NDS tree in the shape of a pyramid.
- *Step 2: Design the Top Layers*—Use a single Organization object and design the top layers of the tree according to location and network infrastructure.

- *Step 3: Design the Bottom Layers* — Design the bottom layers of the tree according to organization and function.

Before you can begin building your NDS tree design, you must pull together the required design inputs. In Chapter 8, "NDS Preparation," we discovered eight different design inputs in two different categories (organizational and technical). In this section, "NDS Tree Design," we're very interested in the following five ACME inputs:

- *ACME WAN Layout* — The WAN layout consists of all your major hub locations and their interconnected routers and bridges (see Figure 9.5). Notice in ACME's WAN layout map that all five main sites are shown with their router connections and the speed of these links in kilobits (Kbits) per second. Your WAN layout map may look similar, and it may additionally include the link speeds of your satellite offices (or distribution centers in our case). This document is necessary for the upper-layer design of your tree, as we will explain in Step 2. Most companies have some sort of WAN map, but you may have to draw a new one. Try to consolidate all of the important interconnectivity information in a single overview.

FIGURE 9.5

ACME WAN layout map

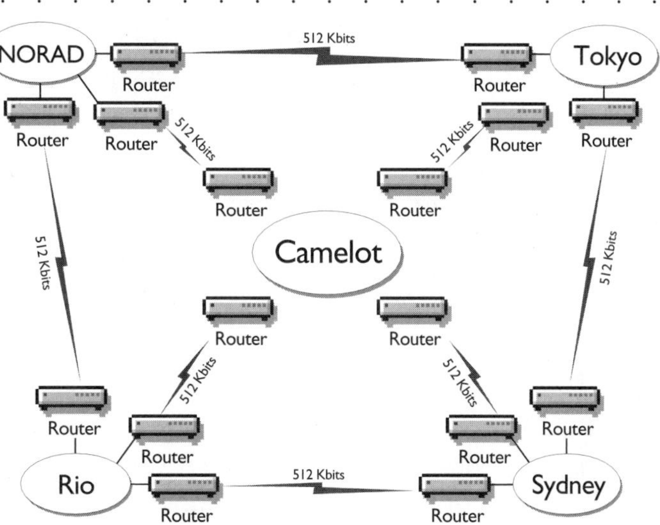

- *ACME Campus Maps* — The WAN layout provides a great interconnectivity overview, but it's not enough. You'll need campus maps for each major hub site. The campus maps should show the type of information illustrated in Figure 9.6. This is ACME's campus map for the CAMELOT hub. The ACME campus map for CAMELOT shows a Fiber Distributed Data Interface (FDDI) ring and routers connecting the distributed buildings. The ACME WAN layout shows a network in CAMELOT and a list of sites within the Camelot area, such as an operations center (OPS) located at the northwest end of the city and a public relations office (PR) located in the downtown district. An office for charitable contributions (CHR) is also found at the southwest end of the city. Campus maps are important because they refine ACME's WAN/LAN infrastructure. We need the campus maps to organize the second tier of ACME's top layers.

FIGURE 9.6

ACME campus map for CAMELOT

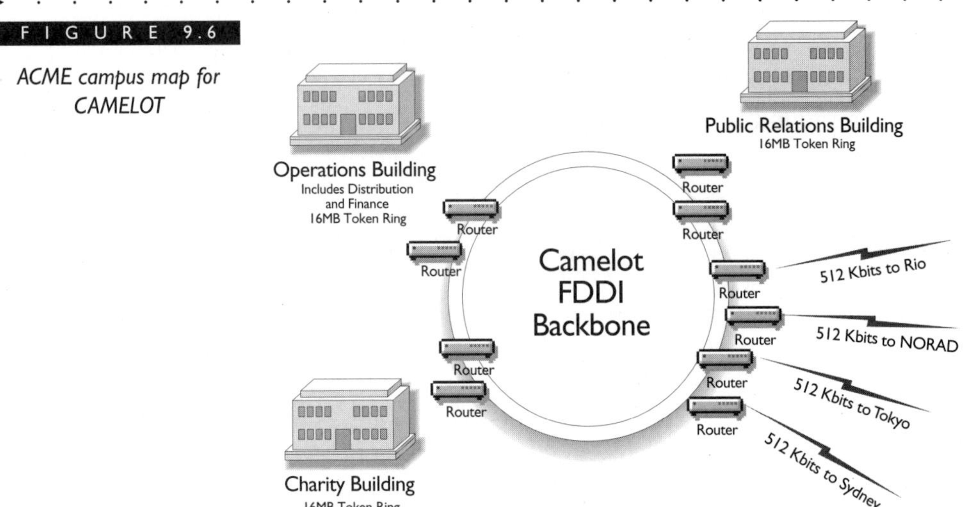

- *ACME World Location Map* — The last map is a big one. It provides a global view of ACME and its distributed locations. Each hub site, building, and distribution center should be integrated into one ACME world location map. This provides a snapshot of the ACME geography and becomes the foundation of the top layers of ACME's tree.

In addition, this information combines with the ACME WAN layout to determine if regional containers are necessary. Refer to Figure 8.7 in Chapter 8 for a picture of ACME's world location map.

- *ACME Resource List* — The final technical input is the ACME resource list. This list gives valuable information about the servers and printers found in each region, site, building, or department. Table 8.2 in Chapter 8 shows the original ACME resource wish list. The updated ACME resource list in Table 9.7 has been rewritten to include the naming standards discussed previously. Additionally, appropriate administrator, servers, and printers have been distributed to their proper locations, as per the WAN layout and campus maps. Study this list carefully, because everything we do from now on will center around these critical resources. This is the foundation of Step 3.
- *ACME Organizational Chart* — This brings us to the final design input — ACME's organizational chart (see Figure E.1 in Appendix E, "ACME Mission Briefing"). Some companies have pages of organizational charts. Try not to get too wrapped up in them. Your main purpose here is to identify divisions, departments, or other organizational workgroups. Also, use the Work Flow Diagram (see Figure E.7 in Appendix E) to identify auxiliary workgroups throughout the WAN. These divisions, departments, and workgroups will become the foundation of ACME's bottom layers — Step 3.

TABLE 9.7

ACME's Resource List

LOC	ORG	ADMIN	SERVERS	PRINTER/QUEUES
NORAD			NOR-SRV1	
	CHARITY	SirGawain	NOR-CHR-SRV1 NOR-CHR-PS1	HP4SI-P1/PQ1
	PR	DClarke	NOR-PR-SRV1 NOR-PR-PS1	HP4SI-P1/PQ1 CANONBJ-P1/PQ1
	LABS	AEinstein	LABS-SRV1	
	WHI.LABS	CBabbage	WHI-SRV1	CANONBJ-P1/PQ1

(Continued)

TABLE 9.7

ACME's Resource List (continued)

LOC	ORG	ADMIN	SERVERS	PRINTER/QUEUES
NORAD *(continued)*	*WHI.LABS*	Ada	WHI-SRV2 WHI-SRV3 WHI-PS1	
	R&D.LABS	LDaVinci	R&D-SRV1 R&D-PS1	
	POLL.R&D.LABS	CDarwin		HP4SI-P1/PQ1
	NUC.R&D.LABS	MCurie		HP4SI-P2/PQ2
	VR.R&D.LABS	INewton		HP4SI-P3/PQ3
RIO			RIO-SRV1	
	CHARITY	SirPercival	RIO-CHR-SRV1 RIO-CHR-PS1	HP4SI-P1/PQ1
	PR	JHughes	RIO-PR-SRV1 RIO-PR-PS1	HP4SI-P1/PQ1 CANONBJ-P1/PQ1
	ADMIN	GWashington FDR	ADMIN-SRV1 ADMIN-SRV2 ADMIN-PS1	CANONBJ-P1/PQ1
	FAC.ADMIN	JMadison	FAC-SRV1 FAC-PS1	HP4SI-P1/PQ1
	AUDIT.ADMIN	ALincoln	AUD-SRV1	HP4SI-P2/PQ2
	MRKT.ADMIN	TJefferson	MRKT-SRV1	HPIII-P1/PQ1 HPIII-P2/PQ2
CAMELOT			CAM-SRV1	
	CHARITY	SirGalahad	CAM-CHR-SRV1 CAM-CHR-PS1	HP5-P1/PQ1
	PR	CEttelson	CAM-PR-SRV1 CAM-PR-PS1	HP4SI-P1/PQ1
	OPS	KingArthur	OPS-SRV1 OPS-PS1	CANONBJ-P1/PQ1
	FIN.OPS	Guinevere	CAM-FIN-SRV1 CAM-FIN-SRV2	HP4SI-P1/PQ1 HP4SI-P2/PQ2

TABLE 9.7

ACME's Resource List (continued)

LOC	ORG	ADMIN	SERVERS	PRINTER/QUEUES
CAMELOT *(continued)*	*FIN.OPS*		CAM-FIN-SRV3 CAM-FIN-PS1 CAM-FIN-PS2	
	DIST.OPS	Merlin	DIST-SRV1 DIST-SRV2 DIST-PS1	HPIII-P1/PQ1
SYDNEY			SYD-SRV1	
	CHARITY	SirLancelot	SYD-CHR-SRV1	HP5-P1/PQ1
	PR	MClarke	SYD-PR-SRV1 SYD-PR-PS1 SYD-CHR-PS1	HP4SI-P1/PQ1
	HR	Gandhi	HR-SRV1 HR-SRV2 HR-PS1	HP4SI-P1/PQ1
	MEDICAL.HR	ASchweitzer	MED-SRV1 MED-SRV2	HP4SI-P2/PQ2
	FOOD.HR	MTeresa	FOOD-SRV1	HP4SI-P3/PQ3
	SHELTER.HR	FNightengale	SHELT-SRV1 SHELT-SRV2	HP4SI-P4/PQ4
	PEACE.HR	Buddha	PEACE-SRV1	HPIII-P1/PQ1
TOKYO			TOK-SRV1	
	CHARITY	SirKay	TOK-CHR-SRV1 TOK-CHR-SRV2 TOK-CHR-PS1	HP4SI-P1/PQ1
	PR	BThomas	TOK-PR-SRV1 TOK-PR-PS1	HP4SIP1/PQ1
	CRIME	SHolmes	CRIME-SRV1	HP5-P1/PQ1
		DrWatson	CRIME-SRV2 CRIME-PS1	
	BLUE.CRIME	WEarp	BLUE-SRV1 BLUE-PS1	HPIII-P1/PQ1

(Continued)

TABLE 9.7

ACME's Resource List (continued)

LOC	ORG	ADMIN	SERVERS	PRINTER/QUEUES
TOKYO *(continued)*	VIO.BLUE.CRIME	BMasterson	VIO-SRV1 VIO-SRV2	HP4SI-P1/PQ1
	ENV.BLUE.CRIME	WBHickok	ENV-SRV1	HP4SI-P2/PQ2
	THEFT.BLUE.CRIME	DHoliday	THEFT-SRV1	HP4SI-P3/PQ3
	WHITE.CRIME	RHood	WHITE-SRV1 WHITE-SRV2 WHITE-PS1	CANONBJ-P1/PQ1
	CYBER.WHITE.CRIME	FrTuck	CYBER-SRV1	HPIII-P1/PQ1
	POL.WHITE.CRIME	MMarion	POL-SRV1	HP4SI-P1/PQ1
	FIN.WHITE.CRIME	LJohn	TOK-FIN-SRV1	HP4SI-P2/PQ2 HP4SIP3/PQ3

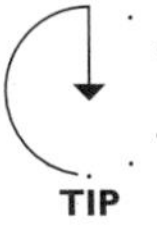
TIP

Resist the temptation to design your tree around the organizational chart. This mistake is more common than you think, mostly because the chart is the only design input people understand. It's also the only design input available in many cases. I know it's more work, but develop technical inputs for your organization and use them for your tree design. You'll thank me in the long run, especially when it comes time to design partitions and replica placement.

Keep in mind that few companies document their WAN to this extent. You might even have to create a few design inputs yourself. But it's worth it. Nothing's harder than trying to design the tree without them. These documents are the driving forces of the entire NDS design process.

Speaking of the process, let's start with Step 1—the pyramid.

Step 1: Use a Pyramid Design

The overall NDS tree design should form the shape of a *pyramid* (or inverted tree). This type of design places most of the objects at the bottom of the structure and the fewest containers at the top (see Figure 9.7). The pyramid design should be split into two sections:

- *Top* — The top of the tree should reflect the physical structure of the network because it builds a solid foundation for the bottom layers. This is the static section of the design where few changes are made. Another advantage of static top layers is "natural partitioning." This means that partition boundaries can flow naturally and Subordinate Reference replicas are minimized.
- *Bottom* — The bottom of the tree is defined by the local area network (LAN) structure and is based on the functional organization of the company. This can be accomplished by planning around divisions, departments, and company workgroups. The bottom layer containers will hold the majority of the company's NDS objects, including users, file servers, printers, print queues, and other network resources. Finally, using this strategy, the bottom layers of the tree will be more dynamic and will give you the flexibility to change the tree, when necessary.

FIGURE 9.7

Use a pyramid design

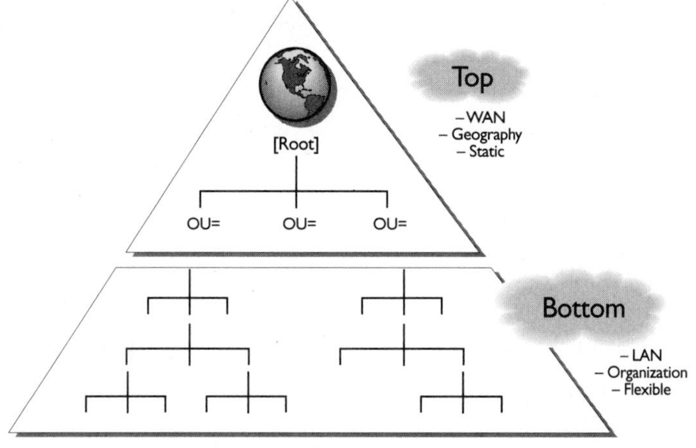

An alternative to the pyramid design is a *flat tree* that places all NDS objects in the top layers (refer to Figure 9.8). With all NDS objects at the top of the tree, your

Directory tree will become inefficient. A flat tree is not recommended because of the way it must be partitioned and replicated. This type of design tends to create increased synchronization traffic. A large number of Subordinate Reference replicas may also occur.

FIGURE 9.8

The flat design of ACME's tree

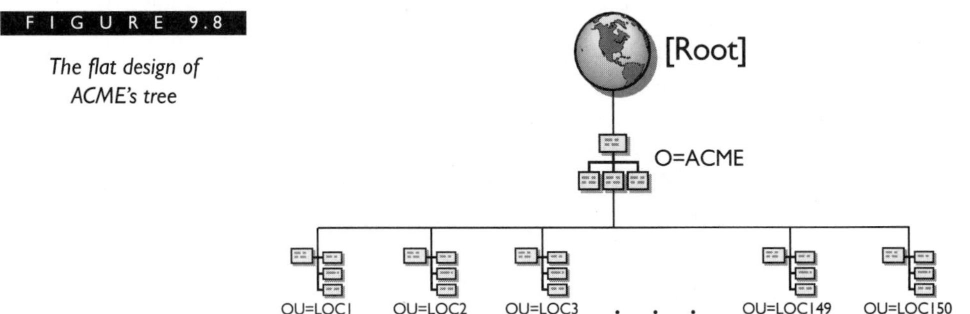

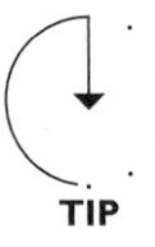

TIP

Study the benefits of a well-designed NDS tree, specifically that partitioning and replication can be designed successfully, the network can accommodate growth without complicating revisions, and Directory trees can be merged more easily. In addition, learn the purpose of each of the two halves of the pyramid tree design: physical (top) and functional (bottom).

Now that we understand the rough pyramid shape of ACME's tree, let's take a closer look at the top and bottom layers. Remember, each half serves a unique and special purpose.

Step 2: Design the Top Layers

As in most things, the top is the most important half. It is the foundation of ACME's NDS tree design . . . the rest of the tree branches downward from there. The top layers of the NDS tree typically include the following three container types (see Figure 9.9):

- *[Root]* — The [Root] is the top of the NDS tree and defines the tree itself. Therefore, you cannot have duplicate tree names within the same network.

- *O=Organization* — An Organization object is used to define a corporation, association, university, operating division, and so on. Generally, you should only create one Organization object per NDS tree. There are, however, instances when the use of multiple Organization objects is justified.
- *OU=Organizational Units* — Organizational Unit objects provide structure to the top of the NDS tree. OUs can be designed according to location, function, or region.

FIGURE 9.9

Top layers of the ACME tree

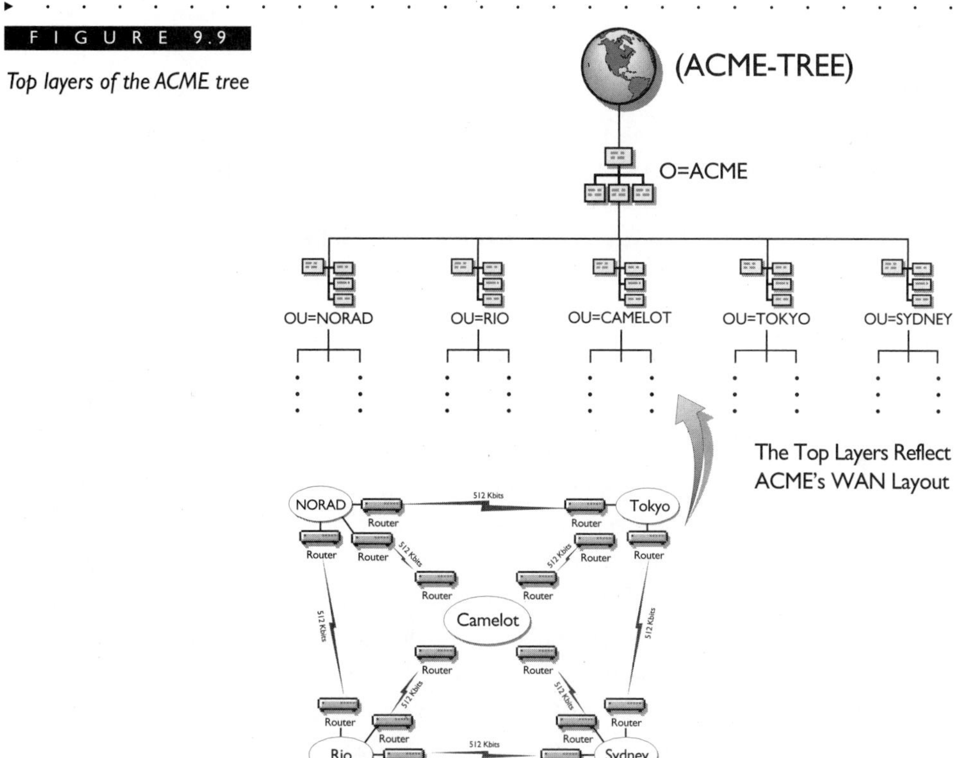

[Root] Object

First, you must name the tree itself. The tree name is represented by the [Root] object, which is placed at the top of the NDS pyramid. A good strategy is to create a tree name that consists of the name of your organization name plus "-TREE." For example, our company is called ACME, so we named the tree "ACME-TREE" (see Figure 9.9).

The tree name must be unique. If you need to install more than one logical tree on the same physical network, be sure that the trees have different names. You can change the name of the tree after initial NDS installation, if necessary, using the DSMERGE utility. Changing the tree name has a greater impact on larger networks because it requires a great deal of effort to reconfigure clients to use the new tree name.

TIP

It is not recommended that you name the O=Organization the same as the [Root]. The ACME tree, for example, uses the company name plus -TREE for the tree name. Our corporation would therefore be named O=ACME, with a tree name of ACME-TREE.

O=Organization Layer

The Organization layer defines the company and its purpose. All other geographic and organizational functions are provided by lower Organizational Unit layers. A good strategy is to use an abbreviation of your organization's name as the name of the Organization object. For example, our company is named "A Cure for Mother Earth," which is abbreviated to "ACME" (see Figure 9.9).

Using a single Organization container provides an excellent tool for distributing management policies throughout the entire company. For example, you can implement a workstation-naming convention from your NDS Naming Standards Document by creating ZENworks Workstation Import Policy objects and placing them at the Organization level. In this policy, you can define how Workstation objects are named when they are created in NDS. In this case, the policy would affect the whole company. See Figure 9.10 for an example of a single O=ACME Organization tree design.

FIGURE 9.10

A single O=Organization at ACME

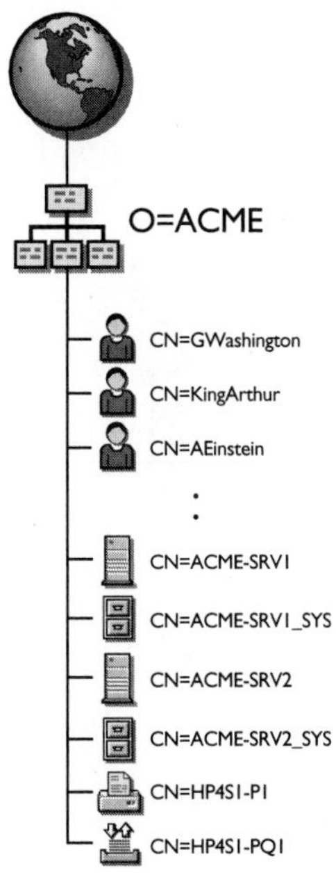

Limiting your NDS tree to a single Organization object is not a requirement. Following are a few exceptions that may justify the use of multiple Organization containers:

- Some multinational conglomerates consist of different companies that operate independently. In this case, you may want to create an Organization container for each company.
- Some companies track financial performance according to business units or divisions. In this case, multiple Organizations allow administrators to track network resources separately.
- Some companies have other business reasons or internal guidelines that force divisions to operate independently.

In Figure 9.11, we have combined ACME and the UN into a single NDS tree. In this example, the two multinational conglomerates (ACME and UN) include many different locations, each of which operate independently from each other. As you can see in the figure, we have created an O=Organization for each corporation.

FIGURE 9.11

ACME and the UN share an NDS tree

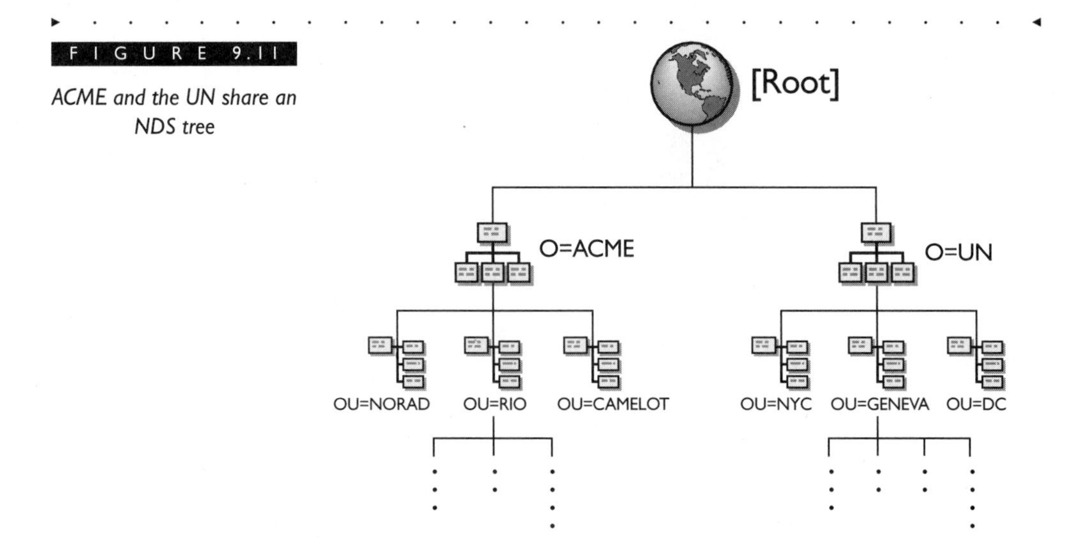

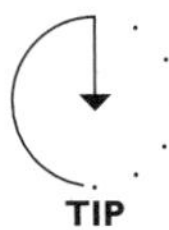

TIP

In Chapter 11, "NDS Implementation," we will learn how to merge separate NDS trees into a single Directory at the Organization level. Remember the example in Figure 9.11, because we will return to the ACME versus UN scenario later in Chapter 11.

OU=Geographic Top Layers

The final top layers are defined by Organizational Unit containers. These are the most important layers in the tree because they represent a transition point between the inflexible upper layers and the flexible bottom layers. These OU layers also define the layout of the rest of the tree. In summary, this is where your tree begins to take shape.

You can choose one of three approaches for the final tier of the top layers:

- *Geographic* — Organize the upper layers according to ACME's WAN layout map and distributed sites. This is the preferred NDS architecture.

- *Regional* — Insert regional containers to further organize numerous distributed sites.
- *Functional* — Organize the upper layers according to ACME's organizational chart and departmental workgroups.

The first approach is based on the *geographic* boundaries of your WAN. Remember, the sole purpose of the NDS tree is to productively organize network resources. These resources are geographically distributed and rely on slow WAN links for interconnectivity. To optimize partitioning, replica placement, and time synchronization, you should design the first layer of OUs along these WAN boundaries.

As a matter of fact, the dynamic nature of NDS essentially forces you to design the top layers of the tree according to geography: Some reasons include the following:

- A design based on geography reflects the WAN infrastructure.
- It minimizes WAN traffic and related costs.
- It facilitates partitioning because the WAN design provides a structure for partitions.
- It reduces significant future changes to the Directory tree because locations are fairly permanent.
- It places the physical network resources near the users and groups that need them.

The geographic approach relies on your WAN layout map. As you could see earlier in Figure 9.5, ACME is organized around five main hubs: CAMELOT, RIO, SYDNEY, TOKYO, and NORAD. These hubs become the foundation of ACME's OU structure, as shown earlier in Figure 9.9. Once you have established the geographic top of the tree, you can zero in on each location with an organizational design — at the bottom layers.

Of course, life is full of exceptions. And the geographic approach is not always the answer. Following are two exceptions:

- *Exception 1* — Companies with a single site or local campus network are not dependent upon the geographic design approach. Because there's little geography with which to work, you should skip the geographic layers and go straight to organization. Some companies with few servers and users may not need to create additional containers at all. Rather, they can place all the NDS objects under a single O=Organization (see Figure 9.10).
- *Exception 2* — Companies with WAN sites or local campuses connected with very high-speed links (such as T-3 or greater). In this type of environment, the location of OU layers is less important because the limiting, slow WAN links have been removed. In this case, the very high bandwidths nullify geographic considerations.

If you are using a campus layout (such as a research park or university), first consider the speed of the links between buildings or floors. The geographic approach could still be used with buildings representing minor OU sites within the network infrastructure. Even in ACME's case, the distributed campus buildings could be useful second-tier container objects — as long as they help organize the network resources.

REAL WORLD

Many companies still choose to use geographic designators, even though they have very high-speed WAN links. One such company, for example, has a metropolitan area network (MAN) running FDDI between 12 buildings across a city. The basis of their decision to stick with geographic sites was twofold. First, for administrative purposes, they wanted to have each building supported by a single administrator. The geographic orientation of NDS made security distribution very natural. Second, certain local applications worked best with the geographic design at the top of the tree.

OU=Regional Top Layers

The second approach relies on the introduction of *regional* containers above the geographic OU layers. This is necessary if the total number of locations is high—60 to 80 subcontainers per location, for example. Adding an intermediate regional layer helps to ensure a balanced pyramid design.

Consider what happens when ACME decides to expand. Let's say it decides to integrate more offices throughout the world. In this example only, ACME's WAN infrastructure would look something like Figure 9.12. Notice that the distributed offices connect together via 56-Kbit links, while the hubs still use 512-Kbit lines. Also, each city is added to the WAN layout through their appropriate regional hub.

FIGURE 9.12

ACME'S new WAN layout with expanded cities

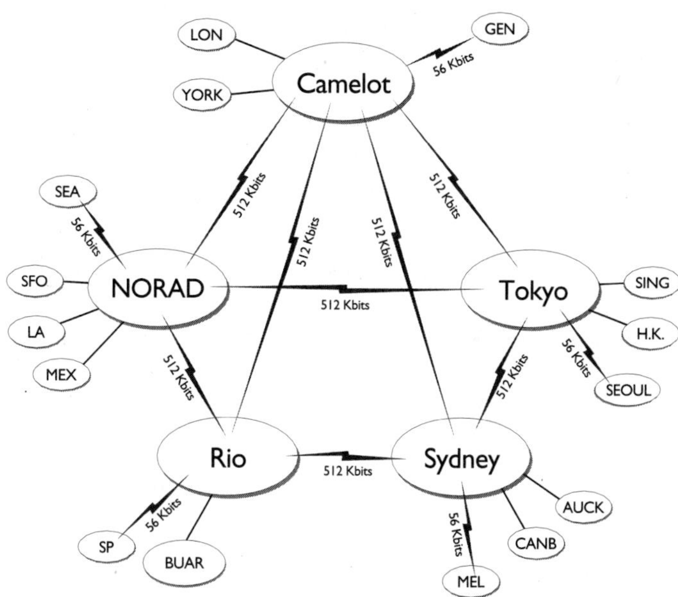

Using the WAN infrastructure, we have designed a new tree that includes regional OUs named North America (NA), South America (SA), Europe (EUR), Asia (ASIA), and Australia (AUST). These regional OU layers group the appropriate cities and help keep the NDS tree design looking like a pyramid (see Figure 9.13).

FIGURE 9.13

Regional top layers for ACME

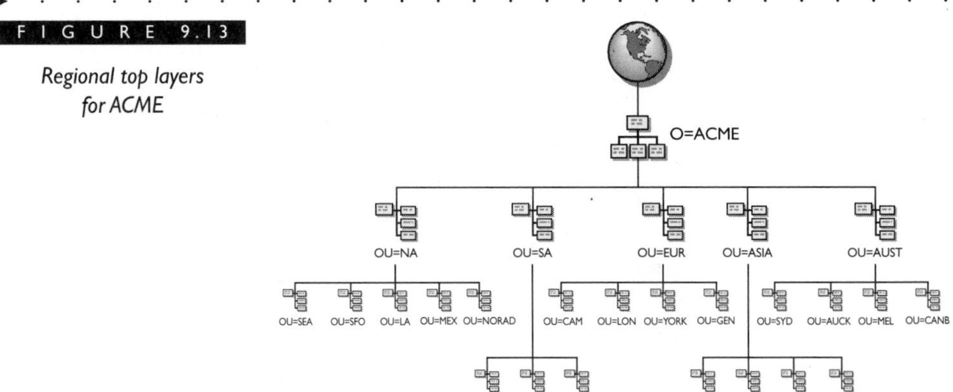

OU=Functional Top Layers

The final option is based on *functional* workgroups throughout your company. This functional approach should only be used in the following two cases:

- *Case 1*—Your company doesn't have a WAN infrastructure or other locations to worry about. If your company operates over a LAN or high-speed WAN, then you can skip the geographic design and go directly to the organizational bottom-layer design. This approach is based solely on the organizational chart.
- *Case 2*—You are a rebel, and you really want to design your tree according to the company's organizational chart. This approach is justified if there is something "very special" about your company—like you have fewer than 250 users in your entire organization.

In either of these cases, you can place your departments, divisions, and workgroups at the top of the tree and physical locations at the bottom. This is a little less efficient because any change to the organizational structure ripples down the entire NDS tree design.

Consider the example in Figure 9.14. We have reversed the ACME design and put their workgroups at the top. Remember, most network changes occur at the organizational level. Therefore, this functional design will cause numerous changes to the top of the tree. Remember this design strategy: flexibility at the bottom, rigidity at the top. Also, when considering other design requirements (such as administration, partitions, replicas, and Bindery Services), it is apparent that the functional design causes much more management overhead because of the inflexibility of the top layers of the tree.

FIGURE 9.14

Functional top layers for ACME

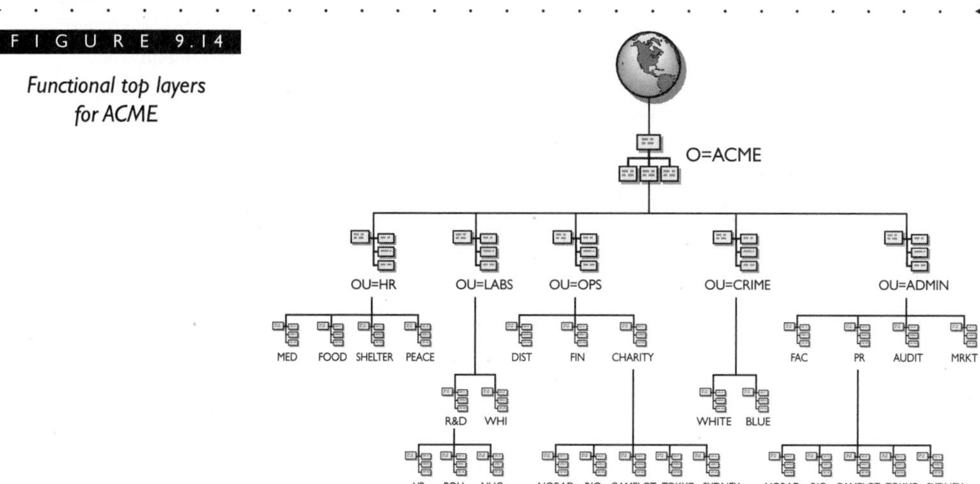

Refer to Table 9.8 for a critical comparison of the two most popular tree-design approaches: geographic and functional.

TABLE 9.8

Comparison of Geographic and Functional Design Approaches

FEATURE	GEOGRAPHIC	FUNCTIONAL
Location of objects in a partition	All objects in a partition exist at the same location.	Objects in a partition exist at multiple locations separated by WAN links.
Authentication	All users log in and are authenticated locally, not across the WAN link.	Authentication takes longer and ties up the WAN links for those who must log in to a remote partition.

Continued

TABLE 9.8

Comparison of Geographic and Functional Design Approaches (continued)

FEATURE	GEOGRAPHIC	FUNCTIONAL
Administration	Changes to objects are generally made by local administrators, so updates to the Directory are faster.	An administrator of functional Organizational Units must manage objects long distance, which increases cost and complexity.
Replication	All replicas can be stored on local servers, reducing the synchronization costs of updating events.	To make authentication and administration faster, Read/Write replicas of all partitions must be stored throughout the WAN. Because of this, replica synchronization consumes the WAN link bandwidth, and Directory updates are slow.
Sharing of network resources	Users tend to share resources locally. Administration of security and access is easier because rights can be granted at a higher level in the Directory tree.	Users tend to share resources locally. However, access to those resources is complicated because separate branches of the Directory tree contain those resources.

This completes Step 2: Design the Top Layers—Yeah! We are well on our way to completing ACME's NDS tree design. There's only one step left, and it involves thousands of resources. Good luck.

REAL WORLD

Given an exhibit containing a sample NDS tree, you should be able to recognize the OU design approach being used: location, regional, or functional. Also, know the benefits of a location-based OU design strategy (namely, it minimizes WAN traffic and related costs, facilitates NDS partitioning, and supports distributed administration and security). Finally, remember that a single Organization container offers a simple design alternative for small offices with few servers.

Step 3: Design the Bottom Layers

The bottom layers of the NDS tree should be designed according to the organizational boundaries of your company. In other words, the bottom Organizational Units should be built along the lines of company divisions, departments, and workgroups (see Figure 9.15).

FIGURE 9.15

Bottom layers of the ACME tree

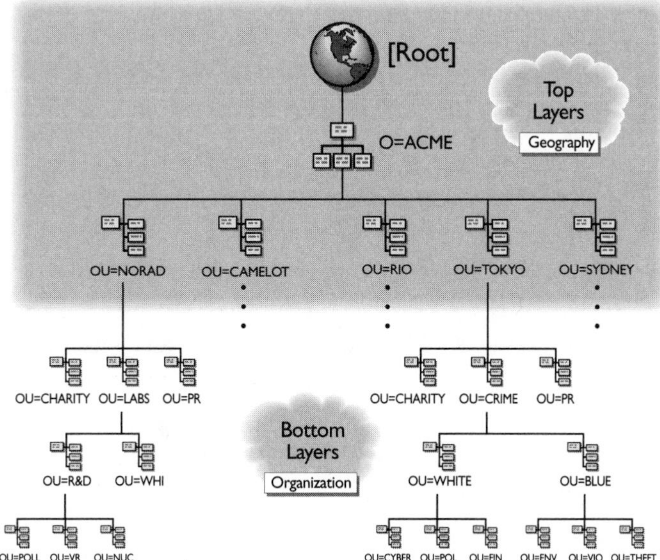

During the design of the bottom layers, you will need to ensure that there is a place for every user and network resource. Shared resources should be distributed near the users who need them. For example, ACME's Charity and PR departments have an office in each major location. Each office has at least one server and shares information with a central database in CAMELOT. For this reason, we have decided to create an OU=CHARITY and OU=PR container in every location (see Figure 9.15).

Resource placement considerations will also affect how you design the bottom layers of your Directory tree. If network resources are organized according to workgroups, they should be placed in the same container where users have been placed. However, if network resources offer services to multiple departments, you should place the resources higher in the tree, possibly at the location-based OU container.

Congratulations!

You're the proud owner of a new NDS tree design. Let's review: pyramid, geography, organization—all done. Well, at least with the rough draft. Next, you should consider a few external design factors before finalizing the design. It's time for some fine-tuning.

NDS Tree Design Considerations

Once you have completed the NDS tree design, you will need to fine-tune it by using a variety of special NDS design considerations. Fortunately, these considerations affect only the bottom layers of the tree because they only impact user accessibility and resources. Following is a list of the four most critical NDS tree design considerations:

- *Administration*—Impacts the primary methods of network administration: centralized and/or decentralized.
- *Container Size*—Impacts NDS partitioning, replication, fault tolerance, and synchronization traffic efficiency.
- *Login Scripts*—Impacts user access to network resources.
- *Bindery Services*—Impacts backward compatibility to NetWare 2 and NetWare 3 clients.

Fortunately, the bottom layers of the tree represent the flexible half. Let's explore these four external design pressures in a little more depth.

Administration

Tree administration is a key NDS design consideration because it impacts how you and your distributed network administrators manage Directory objects, partitioning, time synchronization, and security.

To manage NDS effectively, Novell suggests you consider the following two main types of network administration:

- *Centralized* — Relies on one or more Information Services (IS) Admin(s) for all portions of the NDS tree. The User object for this type of administrator is typically stored at the Organization level.
- *Decentralized* — Distributes branch control to container administrators, typically at the functional or location OU level.

Centralized Administration

A *centralized administration* strategy depends on a single network administrator or IS group for management of NDS objects, partitioning, replication, and security. Central administrators (including Admin) are typically placed at the Organization level and must have Supervisor and Inheritable [SI] rights to the [Root] object.

If the NDS tree is to be managed centrally, the IS staff will build the entire tree and have control over all NDS objects. This approach helps standardize naming, simplifies object placement, and improves administrator navigation.

Another unique centralized administration strategy is to place all servers in a single NDS container (called the *Server Container* approach). The Server Container approach provides easier server access for users and simpler tracking of server activity. Refer to Table 9.9 for a summary of the advantages and disadvantages of the Server Container centralized administration strategy.

TABLE 9.9

Understanding the Server Container Strategy

ADVANTAGES	DISADVANTAGES
Works for local area network (LAN) or metropolitan area network (MAN) environment	Inefficient for WAN environment
Simpler administration	One partition for all servers
Levels of security for server administrators	More setup and design considerations
More centralized control of server administration	Requires a fault-tolerance strategy for the partitions held by servers in the container

Decentralized Administration

A *decentralized administration* strategy relies on various distributed individuals or groups who have managerial control over decentralized branches of the NDS tree. These individuals may be departmental administrators, or they may be responsible for all the network resources in a particular location.

In the decentralized administration model, you still need a centralized IS administrator to handle the top layers of the tree. However, you can block Admin from sensitive local information by placing an Inherited Rights Filter (IRF) at the department or location level.

Container Size

The next NDS design consideration involves container size and NDS partitioning. The total number of NDS objects in a container can negatively impact network performance if it rises above 3,500 objects. This is because very large containers are unwieldy to manage and can have an adverse effect on NDS partitioning and replication. (**Note:** This limitation only applies to NDS Version 7 and below. NDS Version 8 and above is much less susceptible to container sizing problems.)

For example, consider a university whose network consists of a LAN spanning a single campus, with a fiber-optic backbone between buildings. The NDS tree contains 37,500 User objects representing students, each of whom need approximately the same access to resources. In this scenario, utilizing a single Organizational Unit with 37,500 User objects would be difficult to manage. It also means that all of the objects would be in the same partition. A better strategy would be to consider using five to ten functional OU containers for the User objects instead of just one.

It is also important to note that the number of objects in a given container can impact the effectiveness of Novell products that require the use of NDS, such as ZENworks, NDS for NT, and DNS/DHCP Services.

Login Scripts

Login scripts impact the bottom layers of the tree and indirectly control how users access certain NDS resources. In general, users need login scripts to map network drives, capture print queues, and set environmental variables.

Typically, users who share login scripts should be grouped together in the same OU container. In this way, you can create a single Container login script for all users with similar needs. Figure 9.16 shows two Container login scripts — one for OU=FIN (shared by Guinevere and other users) and one for OU=DIST (shared by Merlin and other users). You should separate the users who need different login scripts for the same reason into groups. As you design the login scripts for your users, you are, in fact, designing the organizational structure for the bottom level of the tree.

FIGURE 9.16

Understanding Container login scripts

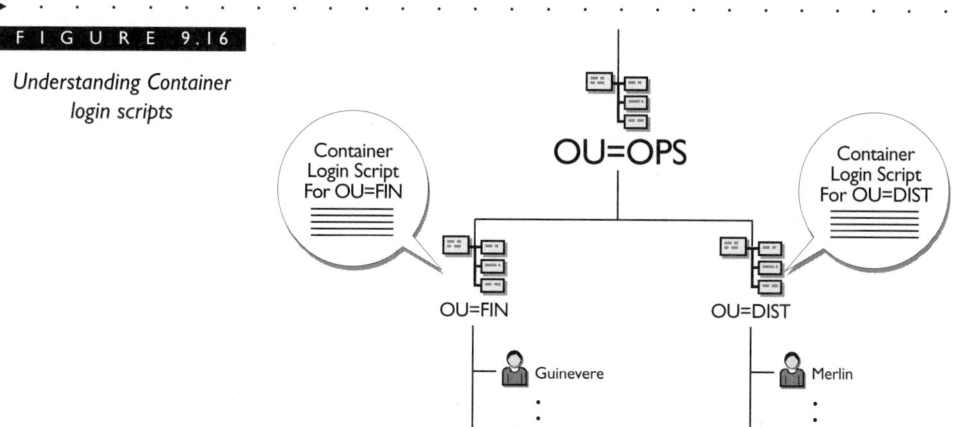

Consider the following login script components as you organize users at the bottom layers of the NDS tree:

- Menus
- Applications
- Drive mappings
- Printer capture statements
- Environment variable settings

Bindery Services

Bindery Services provides NDS backward compatibility for NetWare 2 and NetWare 3 users. This feature enables bindery clients and other third-party software to access the NDS database as if it were a flat-file bindery. From an NDS design perspective, it often makes sense to group bindery users and bindery resources in the same OU container.

Bindery Services can be enabled on any NetWare 5.1 server using either the SET BINDERY CONTEXT console command or the NWCONFIG menu utility. You can select from 1 to 16 OU containers as the bindery context(s). When searching for bindery resources, NDS will follow the list of bindery contexts in order (from 1 to 16).

From a partitioning perspective, it is important to note that a bindery server requires a Master or Read/Write replica of any partition that includes a container in the server's bindery context(s). Because you can set up to 16 bindery contexts per server, the server could contain up to 16 corresponding replicas. This, in turn, will affect tree design because you may be forced to split a partition to reduce the number of replicas. Bindery Services is one of the main reasons you would want to maintain more than a few replicas of a partition.

Note: To support Bindery Services in NetWare 5.1, you must use IPX-Only or the IPX Compatibility Mode gateway. Then users within the bindery context of the server will be able to view and execute services on that server.

TIP

Remember that NDS Version 7 containers should never hold more than 3,500 objects. Also, learn which replicas are required to enable Bindery Services on a NetWare 5.1 server (Master or Read/Write). Finally, study the NDS search order for bindery resources; it follows the server's bindery context list in order (1 through 16).

Well, this completes our discussion of NDS tree design, but it doesn't end this chapter. There's one related topic remaining, and it almost always gets overlooked — NDS accessibility design. NDS accessibility transcends everything you do in NetWare 5.1. If you ignore accessibility during the NDS design phase, some users will invariably get left out in the cold.

NDS Accessibility Design

The goal of NDS accessibility design is to simplify user access to network resources. This is accomplished using client software, NDS objects, and login scripts. The client software provides initial access to the network, while NDS objects and login scripts build a productive user environment.

In this final section, we will learn how to build a User Environment Plan (UEP) that outlines how client configuration, NDS objects, and login scripts provide access to network resources. This is accomplished in three simple steps:

- *Step 1: Perform a Needs Analysis for User Accessibility* — First, you must determine your users' physical network, legacy, and application needs. The result of this step is a Needs Analysis Document.
- *Step 2: Develop Accessibility Guidelines* — Once you fully understand the needs of your users, you will need to develop accessibility guidelines to meet such needs. The guidelines you develop should address how NDS objects are used to create the user environment.
- *Step 3: Create an Administrative Strategies Document for User Accessibility* — Finally, you will apply the accessibility guidelines to four distinct accessibility portals: ZENworks and client configurations, login scripts, file system and security, and mobile users.

So, you wanna be a CNE? Okay, let's see what kind of Accessibility Engineer (AE) you are.

Step 1: Perform a Needs Analysis for User Accessibility

The first step in developing a User Environment Plan is to perform a needs analysis for user accessibility. This is accomplished by gathering key information about the users in your organization and their network needs. The following topics are included when analyzing users' needs:

- *Physical Resource Needs* — First, you must gather user information related to physical network resource needs. This analysis includes network peripherals (such as printers, scanners, plotters, and so on) and network storage requirements.
- *Legacy Network Services Needs* — If NetWare 3 resources exist anywhere on the network, consider creating guidelines for using Bindery Services. During your analysis, consider which applications and resources are bindery-based, and who uses them. In addition, you should evaluate how many groups need bindery-based network resources and indicate specific contexts for bindery-based resources in your accessibility guidelines.
- *Application Needs* — Finally, you must gather information about the types of applications and data files your users need. This includes shared applications, shared data needs, group application configurations, and client OS requirements (including Macintosh, DOS, Windows, OS/2, and Unix).

Step 2: Develop Accessibility Guidelines

After you have developed a Needs Analysis Document, you should create accessibility guidelines. These guidelines should address how NDS objects are used to create a productive user environment. The guidelines should also address how you will implement network security for restricting user access and how you plan on controlling user access through the manipulation of NDS objects.

Following are suggested NDS accessibility guidelines:

- *Container and User Policy Package Objects* — Specify where Container Policy Package and User Policy Package objects should be used. Place Container Policy packages at the highest possible level of the tree without spanning a WAN and make sure there is no more than one Container Policy Package for each geographic location. User Policy Packages, on the other hand, should be placed lower in the NDS tree, so they are closer to the users who need them.

- *Application Objects* — Place Application objects close to the users who access them. If your network has multiple geographic locations connected by a WAN, create Application objects in the containers that represent the physical locations. If you have multiple application servers at one location, create Application objects for each application on each server.

- *Groups* — Use Group objects for accessibility only when all the group members exist in the same physical location. If you use global groups that span a WAN link, you will create considerable background synchronization traffic. Finally, ensure that Group objects never contain more than 1,500 members.

- *Alias Objects* — Identify which objects can (and cannot) use an Alias object.

- *Profile and User Login Scripts* — If users with similar needs exist in separate containers, consider linking them with a Profile login script. These scripts create an additional level of maintenance over Container scripts, but they are easier to manage than User login scripts. Consider using User login scripts only in special cases (such as mobile users).

- *Organizational Roles* — Use Organizational Role objects (ORs) for administrative fault tolerance. Whenever you create a container administrator, use an OR and assign two members: the centralized Administrator User object and a backup administrator.

- *Directory Map Objects and Drive Mappings* — Identify the names of Directory Map objects to be used throughout the organization and the data they represent. Also, implement drive-mapping naming conventions and standards for company-wide applications.

- *Security Precautions* — Identify company-wide security practices and educate distributed administrators. For example, make sure users always authenticate to a local replica and avoid granting users the [S] Supervisor object right to Server objects. Finally, use IRFs to create exclusive container administrators, when appropriate.

Step 3: Create an Administrative Strategies Document for User Accessibility

NDS accessibility is important because it defines all access points to network resources. In order to balance user accessibility and security, you will need to create an Administrative Strategies Document for user accessibility.

The following four administrative strategies will help you create a productive, secure user environment:

- ZENworks and client configurations
- Login scripts
- File system and security
- Mobile users

ZENworks and Client Configurations

NDS accessibility design begins with the client. You should include administrative strategies for each of these strategic ZENworks objects. The strategies should answer the questions that follow each of the listed objects:

- *Container Policy Package Objects* — Where should Container Policy Package objects be placed in the NDS tree? Which containers should they be associated with? Where should the search level be set? What should the search order be set to?
- *User Policy Package Objects* — Which operating systems will User Policy Package objects need to be created for? Where should they be placed in the NDS tree? Which NDS objects should User Policy Package objects be associated with? Will Desktop Preferences be enabled? Will User System Policies be enabled?
- *Application Objects* — Which applications will be run from servers and which will be run from local hard disks? Where will Application objects be placed in the NDS tree? Which NDS objects will be associated with each application? What are the operating system and hardware requirements for each application?

In addition to ZENworks administration, Novell Client configuration can have an impact on your Administrative Strategies Document. Consider including administrative strategies for determining name context, preferred servers and trees, and the first network drive.

Login Scripts

The second step of user accessibility design involves login scripts. Traditionally, login scripts provide network and search drive-mapping capabilities, application support, and printer capturing. In addition, NDS login scripts enable you to set important environmental parameters for large groups of users. Four NDS objects contain a Login Script property: Organization, Organizational Unit, Profile, and User.

You should use your Needs Analysis Document and accessibility guidelines to build an NDS login script strategy that automates the user environment and minimizes network administration.

File System and Security

To ease file system administration across the network, you should specify a standard file system structure that defines the following: number of volumes per server, application and data storage requirements, user data storage needs, and drive mapping guidelines.

You should also build a distributed team of security roles to support NDS and file system administration. Following is a list of the security roles that may be an integral part of your Administrative Strategies Document:

- *Enterprise-Wide Administrator*—Typically, an NDS tree has only one or two enterprise-wide administrators with all object and file system rights starting at [Root]. Furthermore, Admin should be controlled by another Organizational Role object in a hidden NDS container for fault-tolerance purposes.

- *Container Administrator*—To divide management of the NDS tree among network administrators, consider using an Organizational Role object with the name *Container Admin* for each secure container. Grant this Organizational Role object right to manage the container where it is located. The appropriate administrative user(s) can then be made occupants of the new role.

- *Backup Administrator* — In addition, you should create a backup administrator user who has all the rights of the Container Admin Organization Role object discussed in the preceding paragraph, except that this administrator can't change users of, add users to, or remove users from the role. The administrator should be able to install servers but should not be able perform any partitioning operations. The backup administrator should also have all file system rights to all volumes and servers within the container.

- *Server Administrator* — Next, you should create a server administrator for each distributed server. This manager should have all object rights within the server's home container, except Create [C] and Rename [R]. Also, make sure the administrator can modify existing objects, passwords, group memberships, and login scripts. The server administrator should not be able to partition or install servers, however. Instead, give the server administrator file system rights to the SYSTEM, PUBLIC, and application directories.

- *Password Administrator* — One of the most troublesome user-management tasks is password administration. Consider creating distributed password administrators with limited property rights for User objects, passwords, groups, login scripts, and so on. Make sure these managers do not have object rights to create objects, rename objects, install servers, or create partitions. In addition, password administrators do not require any file system rights.

- *Special Use Administrator* — Special use administrator Organizational Role objects can be created for department-specific servers not controlled by IS. These administrators should only have minimal rights to NDS objects (that is, they should only be able to assign group membership rights and should be able to modify passwords and login scripts). Make sure these administrators do not have object rights to create objects, add or remove users from the role, install servers, or create partitions. They should, however, have all rights to the server file system(s) they manage.

Mobile Users

Mobile users offer the greatest challenge to accessibility design. As users wander throughout the network, they access the NDS tree and its resources in different ways. Knowing the types of access each user requires will help you set up specific user environments.

Essentially, the definition of a traveling user can be broken into two types:

- *Remote Users* — Remote users require network access from a laptop computer through dial-in lines. Remote users are normally self-contained (that is, all activity is restricted to their home container). Remote users require less accessibility design considerations than mobile users because they only access the tree for login authentication and access to resources in their home container. In other words, they simply dial into specific predetermined access points in the WAN and use their normal NDS context.
- *Mobile Users* — If a remote user travels to another office and plugs a laptop computer into the network, the user suddenly becomes a *mobile user.* Mobile users are more challenging because they travel from computer to computer and demand full access to local resources, as well as requiring access to their home server. In addition, some mobile users may maintain a separate computer at each network location. (**Note:** Users who carry laptop computers to a new location are not considered mobile users if they do not need to access local network resources. If such users are content to access their home resources across the network, then they are simply considered remote users.)

To support mobile users, you must solve one challenging problem: How do mobile users determine their context during login? Following are the four most popular solutions:

- *Knowledgeable User Login* — This option requires user intervention. In this case, each mobile user can manually enter his/her name context into the computer before logging in. This implies that the user understands the complexities of NDS naming and context during login. If logging in from a DOS client, the user must know how to specify his/her context with LOGIN; or if logging in from a Windows client, the user must know how to enter his/her context in the Context field of the GUI login window.

- *Alias Object*—This option does not require user intervention. In this case, a mobile user's current context can be changed automatically with the help of an Alias object. If you have a small number of mobile users, you can create an Alias object in the Organization container for each mobile user that points to the user's User object in his/her parent container. The value of this strategy is that it creates a simple context for each mobile user. All they need to remember is their login name and the company abbreviation (that is, the name of the Organization object).
- *Client Configuration*—This option also does not require any user intervention. It simply involves setting the user's Name Context and Preferred Server settings in the client properties screen of Windows 95/98 and Windows NT workstations or in the NET.CFG file of DOS/Windows 3.1 workstations.
- *Login Scripts*—In addition to name context challenges, you must find a way to simultaneously point mobile users to local applications (on a local server) and remote data (on their home server). One strategy for accomplishing these tasks is to use sophisticated login script variables and a special environment variable called "NW_SITE". Below is an example of a special mobile login script created for JMadison. This Container script exists in the .OU=FAC.OU=ADMIN.OU=RIO.O=ACME context:

```
;*****************************************************
; MOBILE CONTAINER LOGIN SCRIPT
;   for OU=FAC.OU=ADMIN.OU=RIO.O=ACME
; Creation Date: 11/8/03
; Revisions:
;*****************************************************
REM Do not execute default script
NO_DEFAULT
Write "Good %GREETING_TIME, %LOGIN_NAME"
REM Map PUBLIC drive to local server
```

```
MAP S16:=SYS:PUBLIC
REM Map F: drive to the user's home server
MAP F:="HOME_DIRECTORY"
REM Map NetWare Drives according to the NW_SITE variable
IF <NW_SITE> == "NORAD" THEN BEGIN
   MAP ROOT M:= NOR-SRV1\SYS:MAIL
   MAP ROOT W:= NOR-SRV1\SYS:APPS\WP
   MAP ROOT Q:= NOR-SRV1\SYS:APPS\MSOFFICE
   END
IF <NW_SITE> == "RIO" THEN BEGIN
   MAP ROOT M:= RIO-SRV1\SYS:MAIL
   MAP ROOT W:= RIO-SRV1\SYS:APPS\WP
   MAP ROOT Q:= RIO-SRV1\SYS:APPS\ MSOFFICE
   END
IF <NW_SITE> == "CAMELOT" THEN BEGIN
   MAP ROOT M:= CAM-SRV1\SYS:MAIL
   MAP ROOT W:= CAM-SRV1\SYS:APPS\WP
   MAP ROOT Q:= CAM-SRV1\SYS:APPS\ MSOFFICE
   END
IF <NW_SITE> == "TOKYO" THEN
   BEGIN MAP ROOT M:= TOK-SRV1\SYS:MAIL
   MAP ROOT W:= TOK-SRV1\SYS:APPS\WP
   MAP ROOT Q:= TOK-SRV1\SYS:APPS\ MSOFFICE
   END
```

```
IF <NW_SITE> == "SYDNEY" THEN BEGIN
   MAP ROOT M:= SYD-SRV1\SYS:MAIL
   MAP ROOT W:= SYD-SRV1\SYS:APPS\WP
   MAP ROOT Q:= SYD-SRV1\SYS:APPS\ MSOFFICE
   END
EXIT
```

TIP

Study the differences between remote and mobile users carefully. Specifically, remember that remote users access the network through dial-up lines, and they restrict their activity to resources in their own home container. Mobile users, on the other hand, are more challenging because they demand simultaneous access to both local applications and remote data.

Wow, what a chapter! No matter how you slice it, NDS tree design is complex and rewarding. And just think, this is just the first part of NDS design. There is more gut-wrenching, spine-tingling, hair-tugging fun to come. In Chapter 10, we will explore the impact of partitioning and time synchronization on our NDS design.

Hold on tight!!

LAB EXERCISE 9.2: DESIGNING THE ACME NDS TREE

Use the hints provided to find the 20 NDS design terms hidden in this word search puzzle. Omit any punctuation characters (such as blank spaces, hyphens, and so on) and spell out any numbers.

R	M	R	J	P	I	I	U	E	F	L	M	K	D	F
D	A	O	B	J	E	C	T	C	O	N	T	E	X	T
S	C	R	B	T	Y	P	E	L	E	S	S	N	U	Q
X	P	G	B	I	W	A	N	L	I	N	K	S	O	Z
T	P	A	B	O	L	R	E	M	O	T	E	P	T	V
N	T	N	Q	K	R	E	G	I	O	N	A	L	I	B
W	D	I	S	T	I	N	G	U	I	S	H	E	D	U
H	W	Z	C	O	N	T	E	X	T	L	E	S	S	G
J	A	A	H	W	W	K	Y	Z	V	R	J	Q	T	P
V	N	T	E	G	P	R	O	P	E	R	T	I	E	S
U	J	I	M	U	H	O	Y	U	E	Y	N	H	G	R
N	V	O	A	D	Q	F	N	K	I	F	D	H	O	K
C	E	N	T	R	A	L	I	Z	E	D	U	F	J	T
Z	E	H	F	U	N	C	T	I	O	N	A	L	S	B

Hints

1. Type of management where the entire NDS tree is controlled by one individual or group in the company.
2. This type of NDS login allows users to log into the network from anywhere, without having to specify their NDS context.
3. A "full" NDS name, including object context.
4. An OU top-layer design strategy that builds containers based on a company's organizational chart and departmental workgroups.
5. A type of user who travels from one location to another and plugs a laptop into the destination network.
6. An object's location in the NDS tree structure.
7. Foundation of the top layers of the NDS tree.

8. The NDS partition that includes subordinate pieces of the NDS tree structure.
9. These should be specified for each object class selected in your NDS Naming Standards Document.
10. A compromise design for the upper layers of your tree. This layer normally slips in between the upper and lower layers.
11. A type of user who requires network access from a laptop computer through dial-in lines.
12. Used to define the NDS naming structure for the entire NetWare 5.1 network.
13. Naming strategy that uses attribute abbreviations to differentiate between different objects types.
14. Naming strategy that "assumes" attribute abbreviations by their location in the name.
15. You should avoid spanning these when building an NDS replica design.

See Appendix C for answers.

LAB EXERCISE 9.3: NDS TREE DESIGN

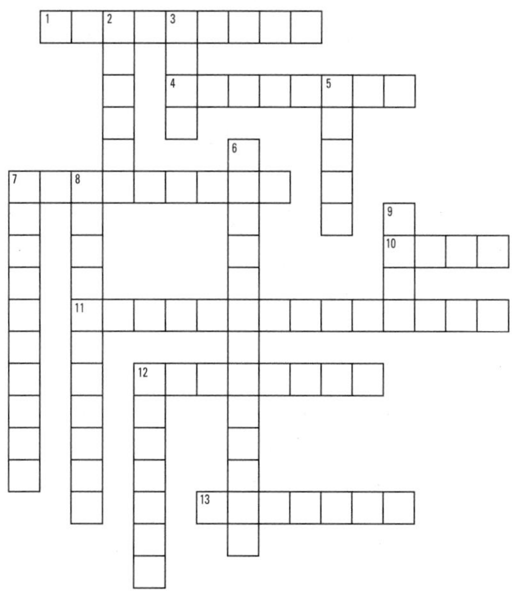

Across

1. Foundation for top layers of the NDS tree
4. Design input for bottom layers of the NDS tree
7. Logical NDS branch
10. An NDS resource object
11. Where you are
12. Details of each logical network entity
13. Optional geographic container

Down

2. Logical network entity
3. Top of the NDS tree
5. An object's "clone" in another location
6. Required for distinguished naming
7. "Partial" NDS name
8. A user's current context

9. The wrong shape for your NDS tree design
12. Typical shape of an NDS tree design

See Appendix C for answers.

CHAPTER 10

NDS Partitioning and Time Synchronization Design

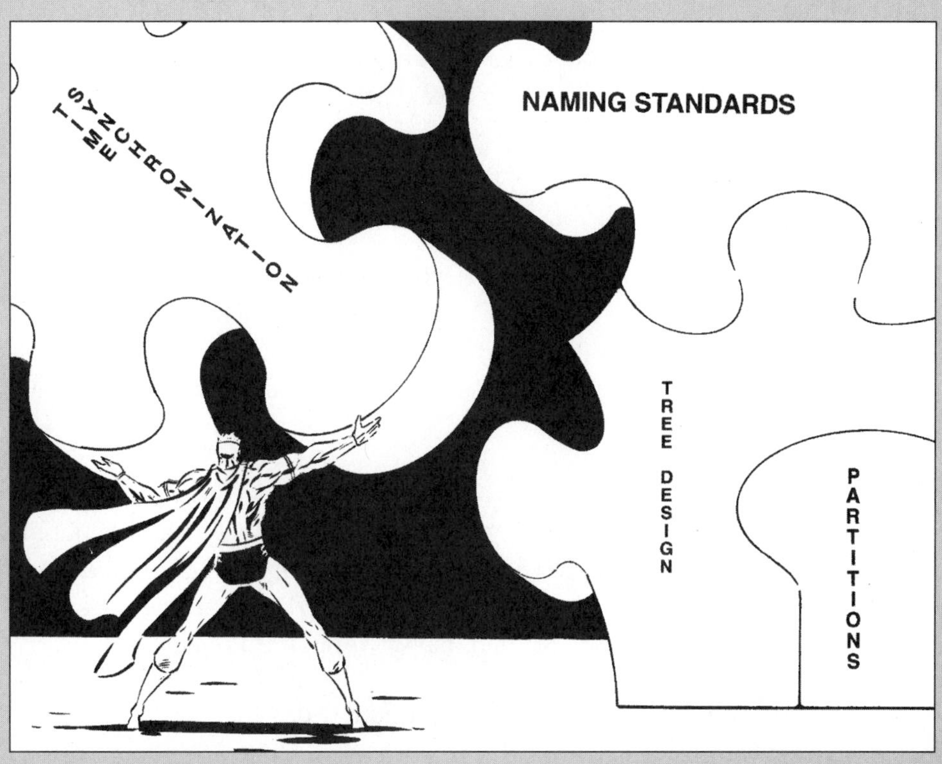

Our next stop along the NDS design tour is partitioning and time synchronization design. Once the tree has been designed, we must break it into small little pieces *(partitioning)* and scatter them around the WAN *(replica placement)*. Then we need to focus on time synchronization design and coordinate a consistent time stamp for all of the servers in the NDS tree.

In this chapter, we will explore ACME's partition boundaries, replica placement, and time design. Here's what's in store for us:

- *Designing NDS Partitions* — We'll start our partition design discussion with a brief review of NDS partitioning rules. Then we will learn various partition design guidelines and building boundaries for the top and bottom layers of our ACME tree. In the "Designing NDS Partitions" section, we will discover seven important guidelines that impact the bottom layers of our partition strategy.

- *Placing ACME's Replicas* — Then we'll move on to replica design with a brief review of NDS's four different replica types: Master, Read/Write, Read-Only, and Subordinate Reference. Next, we'll discover a variety of different reasons for placing ACME's replicas intelligently, including fault tolerance, local distribution, Bindery Services, and improved name resolution.

- *Managing NDS Partitions and Replicas* — In this section, we will explore partition and replica management with the following hands-on topics: managing NDS partitions with NDS Manager, adding NDS replicas, changing replica types, and managing replica synchronization with WAN Traffic Manager.

- *Designing Time Synchronization* — Finally, we will explore the following two time design environments: IPX-Only and IP/IPX time synchronization. IPX-Only time synchronization relies on four different time server types and the TIMESYNC.NLM utility. On the other hand, IP/IPX mixed networks negotiate time using TCP/IP and the Network Time Protocol (NTP).

Let's start at the beginning with NDS partitioning design.

Designing NDS Partitions

The beauty of NDS is its scalability and flexibility. NDS is *scalable* because it allows you to make the database as small, medium, or large as you want. NDS is *flexible* because it allows you to store the database (or pieces of it) anywhere you want. Of course, all of these benefits require design, implementation, and management.

Once the NDS tree has been properly designed, you can divide the Directory into small pieces *(partitioning)* and intelligently distribute them over the network *(replica placement)*. NDS partitioning and replica design is one of the most important aspects of NDS design because it directly affects your network's performance, accessibility, and fault tolerance.

Understanding NDS Partitions

NDS partitions are logical divisions of the NDS tree (see Figure 10.1). Partitioning effectively splits the NDS database into sections that can be distributed to NetWare 5.1 servers throughout the network. Furthermore, NDS partitioning enables you to selectively distribute NDS information near the users who need it.

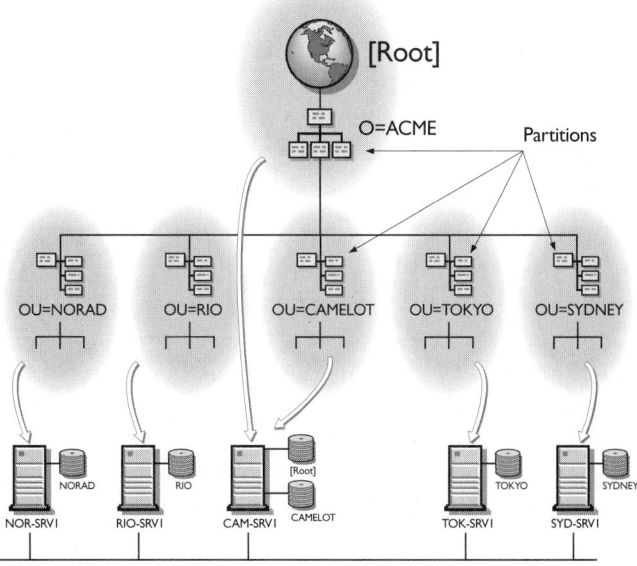

FIGURE 10.1

Understanding ACME partitioning

The purpose of partitioning is to scale the NDS database across the NetWare 5.1 servers in your network. For example, in Figure 10.1, the NORAD partition and its object information is placed on the NOR-SRV1 server in NORAD. The same is true for all other location-based partitions. This enables you to keep local NDS information in each geographically separated location. In our example, Camelot is a special partition because it includes the [Root].

NDS partitioning follows these simple rules:

- Partitioning is *hierarchical*, meaning that the root-most partition is a "parent" to its subordinate "children." When all the partitions in a tree are taken together, they form a hierarchical map back to the [Root] object. Figure 10.1 illustrates the hierarchical partition map formed by ACME's distributed locations. It also shows the parent-child relationship between O=ACME and its subcontainers.

- During installation of the initial NetWare 5.1 server in your Directory tree, the [Root] partition is created and a Master copy (replica) of it is placed on the new server. In NetWare 5.1, the [Root] partition is the only partition created automatically by the Installation program. No default partitioning occurs beyond this.

- Each partition must be named and requires a single container object as the top (or root) of the partition (not to be confused with the [Root] partition). The container object that is used as the start of the partition is called the *partition root object*. Only one partition root object can exist for each partition, and it is, by definition, the topmost container object. Refer to Figure 10.2 for an example of what you should *not* do. (**Note:** The reason that a partition could not be created containing only the NORAD and RIO containers is that the partition would not be a partition root because both of these containers exist at the same level in the NDS tree.)

- Partitioning occurs along the boundaries of container objects. A partition can include more than one container, but it cannot overlap another partition. An NDS object can only exist in one partition, and all leaf objects in a container are in the same partition as the container. Also, only NDS information (not file system data) can be stored in partitions.

FIGURE 10.2

Peer partitions must have parental supervision

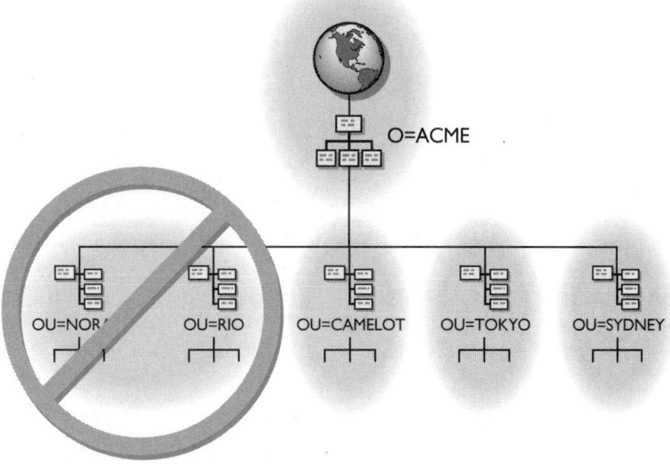

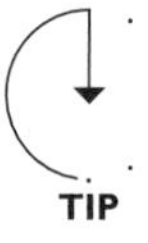
TIP

Make sure that you understand the definition of a partition (that is, a logical division of the NDS Directory). Study the hierarchical nature of NDS partitions and remember that only one partition is created automatically (during initial server installation). Also, know that the top-level container of a partition is called the *partition root object*. Finally, study the rules of partition construction (that is, partitions cannot overlap each other, and partitions store NDS information but not file system data).

Partitioning the NDS Tree

The primary reason for partitioning and replicating the Directory is to increase user resource access and improve fault tolerance. In most cases, you should partition containers along the physical layout of the network. This coincides with the approach used in designing the upper layers of the NDS tree (refer to Figure 10.1, shown earlier in this chapter).

By default, no new partitions are created automatically beyond the first (that is, [Root]) partition. This single partition strategy is recommended if your network has no WAN links, 15 or fewer servers holding replicas, and less than 3,500 objects. (**Note:** NDS Version 8 and above can support more than 3,500 objects per partition.) See Figure 10.3 for an illustration of ACME's default partition strategy.

FIGURE 10.3

The default [Root] partition for ACME

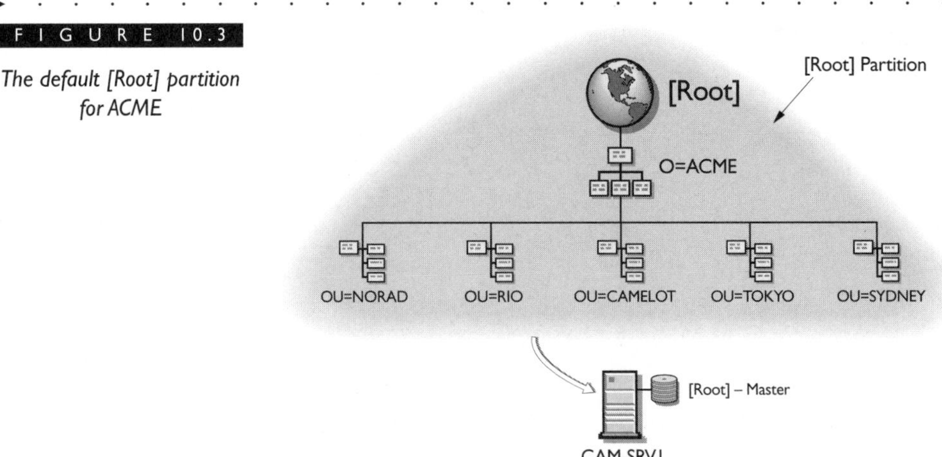

In many cases, your network will grow beyond the recommended limits discussed above. As a result, you will need to create and to implement a partitioning design. Creating a new partition under an existing "parent" is sometimes referred to as a *partition split* because the child simply splits away from underneath the parent's control. In Figure 10.4, the NORAD child simply splits away from the [Root] partition. This operation is extremely fast because it doesn't generate any traffic on your WAN. We are simply dividing one database into two with all the information staying on the same server that contained the original partition. This split operation will create a new child Subordinate Reference pointer on all the servers that had a copy of the parent partition.

The number one design consideration for partitioning is the physical layout of your network infrastructure—mostly the location of network servers. Keeping this in mind, your main task is to partition the NDS database so that it localizes NDS information. The bottom line is keep the NORAD information in NORAD, the RIO information in RIO, and so on. Figure 10.1 showed how the ACME tree has been partitioned along the lines of WAN communications. Note that in our example the [Root] partition is small and includes only the [Root] and O=ACME. This recommendation will be discussed later when we address replication.

The primary reason for partitioning and replicating the NDS database is to increase efficiency for users and to create fault tolerance. In most cases, you should design partition boundaries around the physical layout of your network infrastructure. This coincides with the approach used in designing the upper and lower layers of the NDS tree. If your tree design is structured correctly, your partition strategy is generally easy to implement and maintain.

FIGURE 10.4

Creating the new NORAD partition

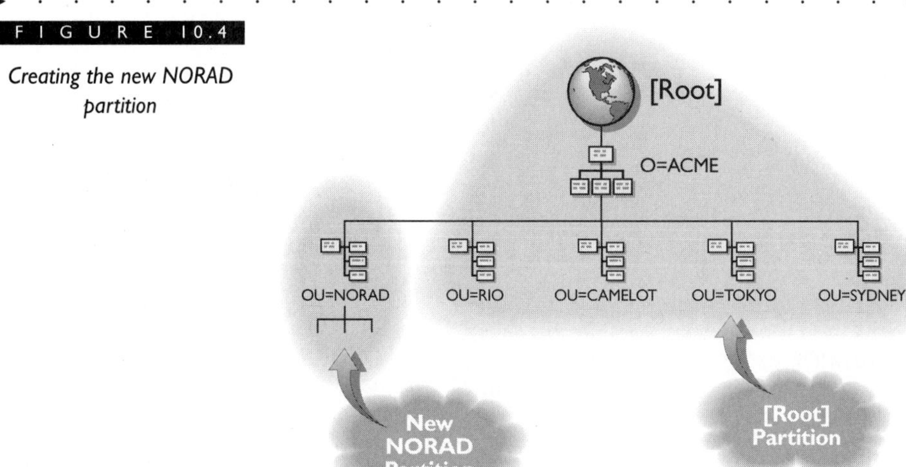

Follow these guidelines when partitioning the NDS tree:

1. *Don't span a WAN link or physical locations with a partition* — This design guideline is important and should not be ignored. If you span a WAN link, it creates unnecessary NDS synchronization traffic between two or more locations. This is why you should partition the top layers according to location. See Figure 10.5 for an example of how *not* to partition the ACME tree.

2. *Keep the [Root] partition small* — Typically, the first partition should only include the [Root] object and the O=Organization container. Do not include any other subordinate containers in the partition with the [Root] object, because it will create unnecessary subordinate references.

3. *Use the Pyramid design for partitioning* — You should design a small number of partitions at the top layers of the tree and more partitions as you move toward the bottom. If you have designed the tree based on a pyramid shape, as recommended, then your partition design will naturally follow the tree design.

FIGURE 10.5

Don't span WAN links with a partition

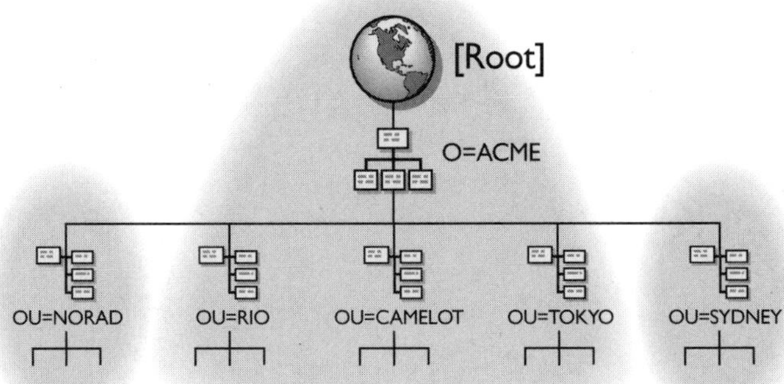

4. *Partition the top layers according to location* — Partition locally, whenever possible. The topmost parent partitions should follow the location-based Organizational Units of your tree design.

5. *Partition the bottom layers according to organization* — The bottom layers of the tree should only be partitioned if there is a special requirement, such as if the partition is too large (the total number of objects is greater than 3,500), if there are too many replicas of the same partition (beyond 10–15), or if there is a need to break out an administrative container.

6. *Do not create a partition unless there is a local server* — Do not create a partition (even if it includes a WAN link) if there is no local server on which to store the replica. This type of situation is common, for instance, if you have small, remote offices that do not have servers on site. Refer to Figure 10.6 for an example.

7. *Smaller is better* — Typically, a partition should have fewer than 3,500 objects. Maintain as few child partitions as possible (less than 35 child partitions per parent). Because most partition operations affect child partitions, minimize the number of children linked across unreliable WAN connections. Table 10.1 explains the advantages and disadvantages of creating smaller NDS partitions.

FIGURE 10.6

Don't create a partition unless there is a local server.

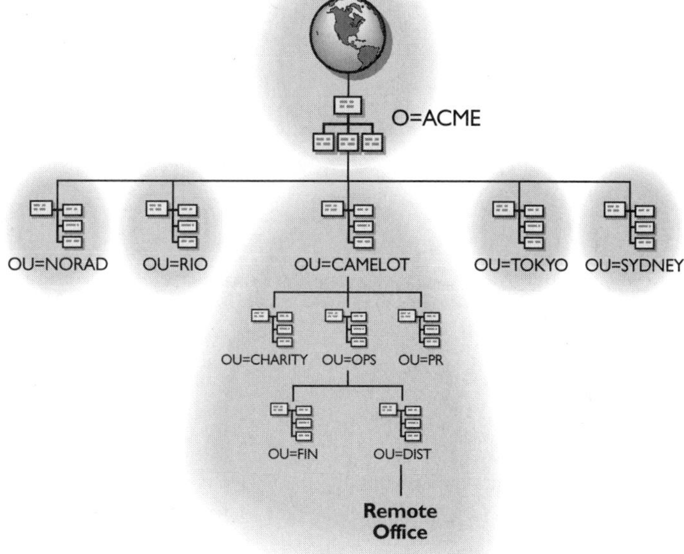

TABLE 10.1

Smaller Is Better in Partitioning Design

ADVANTAGES OF MORE SMALL PARTITIONS	DISADVANTAGES OF MORE SMALL PARTITIONS
Decreases the size of individual partitions	Causes administrative overhead
Reduces the size of the database for any single server	Creates additional Subordinate References for the child and parent partitions
Improves performance by placing resources near users	Increases network complexity
Reduces network wire traffic caused by user access	Increases the time needed to navigate the NDS tree
Reduces the size of partitions, which also reduces network traffic	Increases the need for synchronization among partitions
Reduces dependency on a single network server	

This completes our partition design for ACME. If you follow these partitioning guidelines at both the top and bottom layers, the NDS information always will remain close to the user and other leaf objects. Remember, location is the key when creating partition boundaries. Review Table 10.2 for a complete picture of NDS partition design.

TABLE 10.2

When to Create an NDS Partition

WHY CREATE MORE PARTITIONS	WHY CREATE FEWER PARTITIONS
They decrease administrative overhead.	They create additional Subordinate References for the child and parent partitions.
They reduce the size of the NDS database for a given server.	They increase network complexity.
They improve performance by placing resources near users.	They increase the time needed to navigate the Directory tree.
They reduce network traffic caused by user access over WAN lines.	They increase traffic over WAN links caused by synchronization.
They distribute and replicate important information and reduce dependency on a single server.	

Very good. Now that we have ACME's partition design in place, it's time to spread them across the network — *replica placement*. This is the fun part. We get to distribute all the little pieces to ACME servers everywhere.

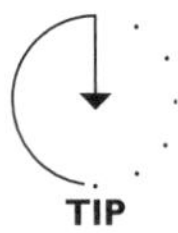

These guidelines do not suggest that you partition every Organizational Unit in your tree. There is also such a thing as *overpartitioning*. Partition locally, and further partition at remote sites only if necessary.

Placing NDS Replicas

Once you have designed an NDS partitioning strategy, the next step is to distribute replicas for fault tolerance, network performance, and name resolution:

- *Fault Tolerance* — Replication increases the availability of partitions by spreading multiple copies of various pieces of the Directory to distributed servers. This also increases reliability. For example, if a server holding a replica of a given partition goes down, you can simply use another copy (that is, a replica) for authentication and updates.
- *Network Performance* — Distributed replicas increase NDS and client performance by ensuring that users access NDS resource information locally. This level of NDS scalability is particular important during authentication, NDS changes, Directory searches, and NDS database access.
- *Name Resolution* — Replication enhances name resolution by ensuring that users can "walk the tree" from child to parent replicas. To facilitate this process, NDS automatically creates Subordinate Reference replicas on every server that contains a parent replica, but not all of the parent replica's child replicas.

Now let's start our replica placement lesson with a brief review of the four NDS replica types.

Understanding NDS Replicas

NDS supports the following four different types of replicas:

- *Master* — Created automatically when you define a partition. Each partition can have only one Master replica.
- *Read/Write* — Placed automatically on the second and third server in a partition and manually on all subsequent servers that you specify.
- *Read-Only* — Rarely used. Read-Only replicas must be created manually.

- *Subordinate References* — Automatically placed on servers that contain a parent replica, but not all of the parent replica's child replicas.

Refer to Table 10.3 for a detailed overview of these four NDS replica types and their corresponding characteristics.

TABLE 10.3

Understanding NDS Replicas

CHARACTERISTICS	MASTER	READ/ WRITE	READ ONLY	SUBORDINATE REFERENCES
Maintains a list of all other replicas	X	X	X	X
Contains a complete copy of all object information in the partition	X	X	X	
Controls partition boundary changes (such as merging, splitting, moving, creating, deleting, and repairing)	X			
Controls object changes (such as creating, moving, deleting, and modifying objects and object property values)	X	X		
Supports authentication	X	X		
Supports viewing of objects	X	X	X	
Can have multiple replicas per partition		X	X	X
Can be changed into a Master replica		X	X	
Can be changed into a Read/Write replica			X	
Can be used on a server where Bindery Services is required	X	X		
Contains only the partition root object				X

TABLE 10.3

Understanding NDS Replicas (continued)

CHARACTERISTICS	MASTER	READ/ WRITE	READ ONLY	SUBORDINATE REFERENCES
Is automatically removed if you add a replica of that child partition to the server				X
May be created automatically when NetWare servers are installed (conditional)	X	X		X
Can be created by the network administrator	X	X	X	
Cannot be created by the network administrator (created automatically by the system)				X

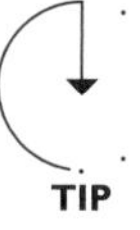
TIP

Carefully study the characteristics of the four NDS replica types in Table 10.3. Specifically, learn which replica types match the following characteristics: contains a complete copy of all NDS information for a partition (Master, Read/Write, and Read-Only); is required for Bindery Services (Master or Read/Write); and is not created automatically when servers are installed (Read-Only).

NDS replication relies on the following basic rules:

- *Replica List*—When a partition is created, the partition root object receives a *replica list*. When changes are made to objects within a partition, those changes are sent to the other replicas on the list. The replica list (also called the *replica ring*) includes a list of all servers containing the replicas, the type of replica they hold, and each replica's current state. All replicas, including Subordinate References, contain a copy of the replica list. Furthermore, the replica list of a Subordinate Reference is used by the server to locate replicas of a child partition.

- *Replica Synchronization* — The NDS Directory is a loosely consistent database. As changes occur, all replicas of a partition do not always contain exactly the same information at every instant. For this reason, it's imperative that each replica server *synchronize* with the other servers in the replica list every few minutes. For instance, some changes (such as changes to a user's password) are immediately sent to all servers on the list. Other less-critical changes (such as a user's last login time) are collected locally for a short period of time before being sent to other servers on the replica list. Each type of replica participates in the synchronization process differently: Master and Read/Write replicas initiate and receive updates, while Read-Only replicas only receive updates.

- *Transitive Synchronization* — NDS includes an additional level of synchronization complexity by supporting simultaneous access to IP-Only and IPX-Only networks. The problem with this scenario is that IP-Only servers can't synchronize directly with IPX-Only servers. Fortunately, NDS includes a feature called *transitive synchronization*, which eliminates the requirement that all servers in a replica list be capable of directly synchronizing with each other. Instead, they communicate indirectly by using intermediary servers or IPX Compatibility Mode gateways.

Well, that completes our quick lesson in the basics of NDS replication. The rules we've learned in this section are important because they describe the way servers replicate and synchronize. You must understand how replicas behave before you start copying ACME's partitions throughout the network.

Now it's your turn. Ready, set, *replicate!*

Design Considerations for Replica Placement

The first step in building an NDS replica placement plan is to explore the following two design considerations and their related issues:

- *Installing NetWare Servers* — What happens to your replica plan when you install the first NDS server? More importantly, what happens when you install subsequent servers?

- *Merging NDS Trees* — How does an NDS merge affect the replica plan of your source and target trees?

Installing NetWare Servers

The initial NDS partition in a tree is called the *[Root] partition* because it is the only one that includes the [Root] (see Figure 10.7). This special partition is created when the initial NetWare 5.1 server is installed in an NDS tree. The Master replica of the [Root] partition is placed on that server. The Master replica of the [Root] can be removed at any time or changed to a Read/Write replica after other servers have been placed in the NDS tree. However, you must first upgrade an existing Read/Write replica to Master status because there must always be a Master replica of every partition.

FIGURE 10.7

Replica placement during server installation

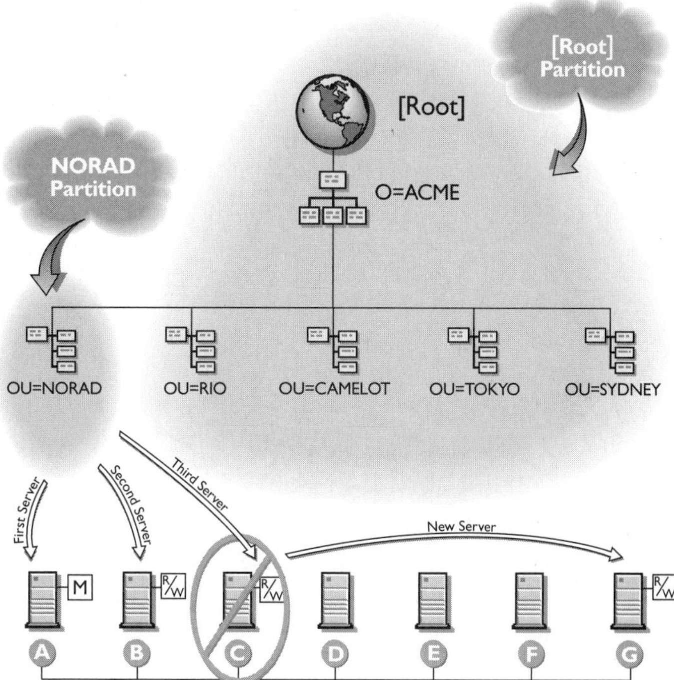

The following NDS partitioning and replication rules apply to all subsequent servers installed in the same NDS tree (follow along in Figure 10.7):

- When you install a new NetWare 5.1 server in an existing NDS tree, the server is automatically added to an existing partition. In other words, no new partition is created.

- The second and third new servers installed in an existing partition receive Read/Write replicas of the host partition. The fourth and subsequent servers *do not* receive replicas. As you can see in Figure 10.7, new Servers B and C receive Read/Write replicas, but D, E, and F don't.

- When a new NetWare 5.1 server is added to an existing partition, NDS determines whether there are enough replicas for fault tolerance. If there are not at least one Master and two Read/Write replicas of the partition, NDS places a Read/Write replica on the new server (see the example in Figure 10.7). For instance, suppose the NORAD partition automatically places the Master replica of itself on Server A and Read/Write replicas on Servers B and C. Assume that Servers D through F hold no replicas. Next, suppose that you remove Server C from the network. When you install Server G, NDS discovers that there are not enough replicas for fault tolerance and automatically places a Read/Write replica on Server G. Although Server G isn't the third server installed in the partition, it is the third server required for fault-tolerance purposes.

- In all other cases, if you want a replica created on a server, you must add it manually using NDS Manager.

Merging NDS Trees

NDS merging has a dramatic impact on NDS partitioning and replication. During an NDS merge, you identify a *source* tree and a *target* tree. It is imperative that each of these servers contains a Master replica of its host tree's [Root] partition. In Chapter 11, "NDS Implementation," we will cover NDS merging in much greater depth. In summary, the following partitioning and replication changes occur during an NDS merge:

- During an NDS merge, the Master replica of the target [Root] partition becomes the Master replica of the new, combined [Root] partition. Any servers in the target tree that held replicas of the old [Root] partition are given replicas of the new [Root] partition.

- Only the source server (that held a Master replica of the source [Root] partition) is given a Read/Write replica of the new [Root] partition. Any other servers in the source server's original tree that held replicas of the old source [Root] lose their copies and do not receive copies of the new [Root] partition.
- All first-level containers in the source tree [Root] partition become independent *partition roots* in the new, combined tree. All other servers in the source server's original tree that held a replica of the source [Root] lose the [Root] replica, but they maintain replicas of the new first-level partitions—except, of course, the source server itself, which receives a Read/Write replica of the new [Root] partition.
- Any server containing a replica of the new [Root] partition receives Subordinate References to child partitions of the new [Root] partition. The name of the new NDS tree is the name of the target server's NDS tree.
- The Access Control List (ACL) of the source tree [Root] is discarded, and the ACL of the target tree [Root] is kept. The only source [Root] trustee assignments that survive are those that belong to the source User object that performed the merge (typically, Admin). This administrative user gains Supervisor rights to the new, combined [Root].

Now that wasn't so hard—was it?! Of course, we've only just begun. In the remainder of this chapter, we are going to build on these design considerations and discover some valuable design strategies for placing NDS replicas.

Placing NDS Replicas

Welcome to phase two of partition design—replica placement. The partitions we created in the previous section aren't going to do us any good until we clone them. As a matter of fact, replica placement is one of your most important design responsibilities—for the many reasons outlined previously.

Your NDS replica placement plan should accomplish the following four goals:

- *Fault Tolerance*—Attempt to eliminate any single point of failure in your NDS tree.

- *Local Distribution* — Place replicas on local servers for efficiency and speed.
- *Bindery Services* — Bindery users and applications need access to a Master or Read/Write replica of each container in a server's bindery context.
- *Tree Walking with Subordinate References* — Distribute replicas strategically to create "bridges" between separated containers for tree-walking purposes. Also, use a replica table to track automatic Subordinate Reference placement.

Let's take a closer look at replica placement for ACME.

Fault Tolerance

The primary goal of replication is to eliminate any single point of failure in the entire NDS tree. Distributing multiple replicas of a partition increases the availability of object information if one of the servers should become unavailable. In Figure 10.8, the NORAD and CAMELOT partitions have been replicated to multiple servers within their locations. This provides fault tolerance for each partition. If one of the servers in the partition goes down, the information isn't lost — it's available from the other server.

The NetWare 5.1 server Installation program automatically creates up to three NDS replicas for each partition for fault tolerance. When you install additional servers into the NDS tree, NDS places a replica of the server's home partition on the first three servers, a Master and two Read/Write replicas. After that, you're on your own.

For example, in Figure 10.9, the NORAD partition is automatically replicated as new servers are added. It starts with NOR-SRV1, then NOR-CHR-SRV1, and finally LABS-SRV1. Also, notice that NOR-SRV1 gets a Master replica. That's because it was the first server installed into the NORAD partition. The others receive Read/Write replicas.

FIGURE 10.8

Replication for NORAD and CAMELOT

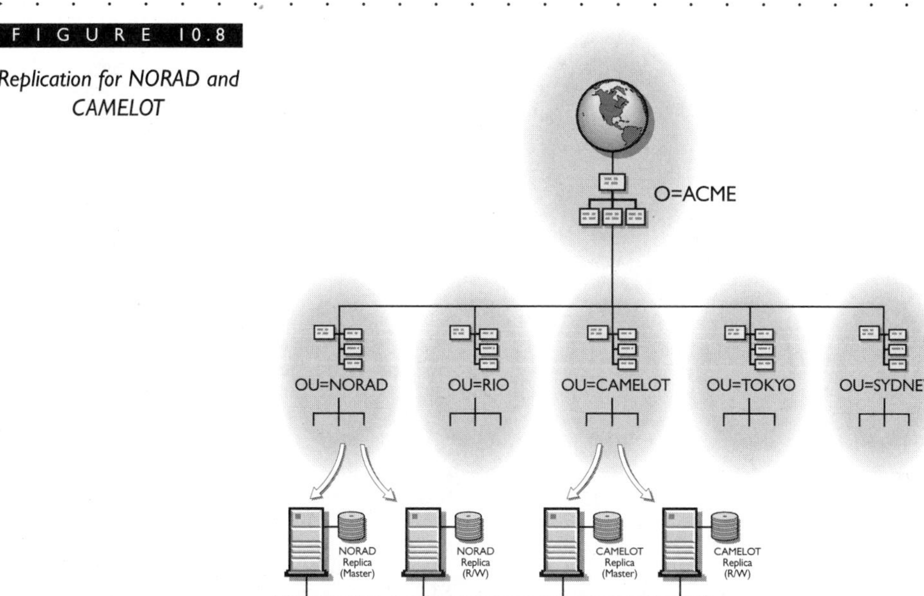

So, what happens when you decide to install a fourth server (R&D-SRV1) into the NORAD partition — nothing! Remember, by default, NDS only replicates the partition on the first three servers. The first thing you should do is place a Read/Write NORAD replica on the new R&D-SRV1 server. This strategy only applies to the new server's home partition. It doesn't have any effect on other partitions in the tree. This is done for one simple purpose — fault tolerance of the NDS database. If you are comfortable with where the three automatic replicas are placed, then you don't need to place any of your own.

As a general guideline, you should have at least a Master and two Read/Write replicas of every partition, but never more than ten replicas of any partition, except the [Root]. If you don't have three servers in the same site, replicate the partition elsewhere. Just make sure the NDS information is available somewhere, but never more than ten replicas of any partitions, except the [Root].

FIGURE 10.9

Default replication at NORAD

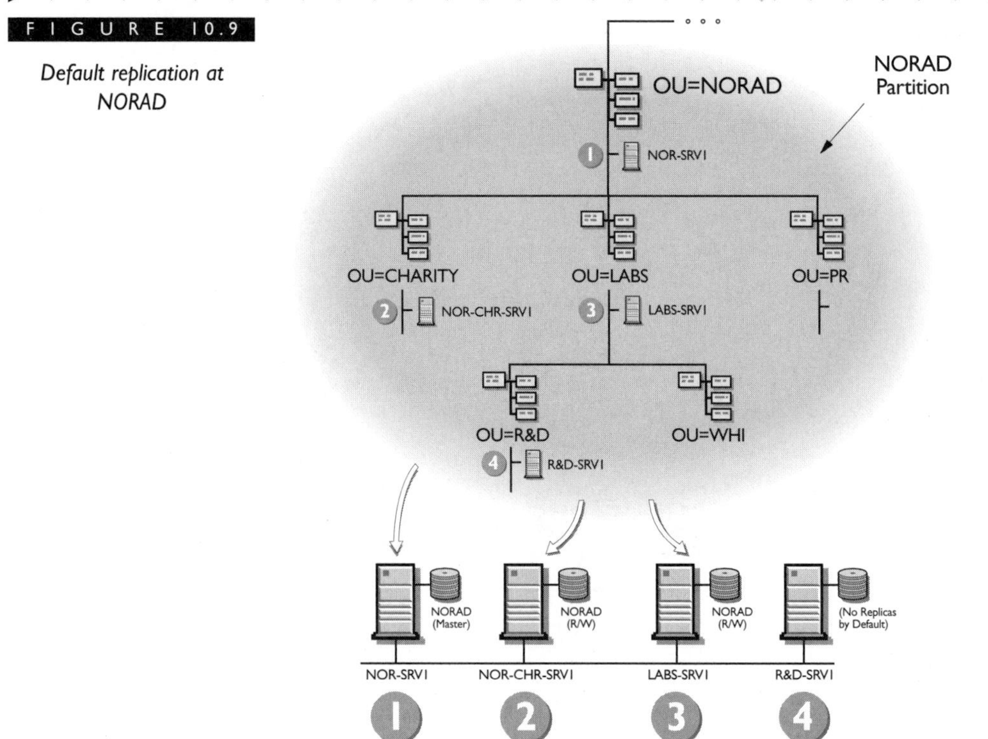

Local Distribution

Always replicate a partition locally, near the users who need the resources defined in the partition. Do not place replicas on servers across a WAN if a local server is available. If you follow these guidelines, the users will be able to retrieve their personal information from the nearest available server. Benefits of using this strategy are that it is faster, more efficient, and more reliable than spanning partitions across a WAN link.

Figure 10.10 illustrates how a small remote office should be replicated. For this example only, assume that there is a small remote site called OU=SLC connected to the NORAD hub. There is only one server in the remote site, and it's called SLC-SRV1. You should create a small partition and Master replicate it to SLC-SRV1. You should also place a Read/Write replica of OU=SLC in the NORAD location, possibly on the Master NOR-SRV1 server.

FIGURE 10.10

Replicating a remote site for NORAD

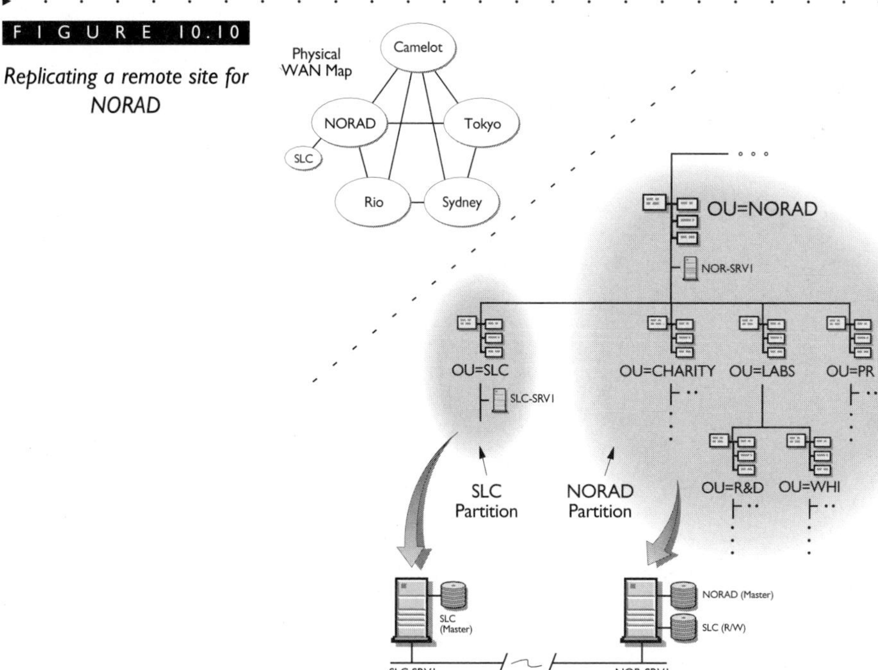

Ideally, you should place the replica that contains a user's NDS information on the same server that stores the user's home directory. This may not always be possible, but it does improve the user's access to NDS objects and the speed of login authentication (a Master or Read/Write replica is required).

You should also pay attention to WAN synchronization when placing replicas locally. As NDS synchronizes replica updates, it creates network traffic. If this traffic crosses WAN links unmanaged, it can increase costs and overload slow WAN links during high-use periods. Fortunately, NetWare 5.1 includes a synchronization management tool called *WAN Traffic Manager* (WTM), which we will discuss in the next section.

Finally, be sure to manage the number of replicas you create for any partition. The time cost of synchronization is greater when the servers in a replica ring are separated by relatively slow WAN links. Therefore, the limiting factor in creating multiple replicas is the amount of processing time and traffic required to synchronize them. As a general rule, you should never create more than ten replicas for any partition or place more than 20 replicas on any server.

Bindery Services

Bindery Services has a big impact on replica placement. Each bindery user or application requires a Master or Read/Write replica of its server's bindery context in order to access NDS resources. Following is an example of the console command that can be used to set a server's bindery context:

```
SET BINDERY CONTEXT=OU=PR.OU=NORAD.O=ACME
```

In Figure 10.11, the bindery users attached to NOR-PR-SRV1 can only see the NDS objects in the OU=PR.OU=NORAD.O=ACME container. Actually, they can't see all the NDS objects, just the bindery-equivalent objects (such as servers, users, groups, printers, print queues, print servers, and profiles). In case you were wondering, the Profile NDS object was added to NetWare 5.1 as a bindery-equivalent object. Unfortunately, NDS-dependent NDS objects aren't available to bindery users (such as Directory Maps, Organizational Roles, Computers, and Aliases).

FIGURE 10.11

Bindery Services in the NORAD container

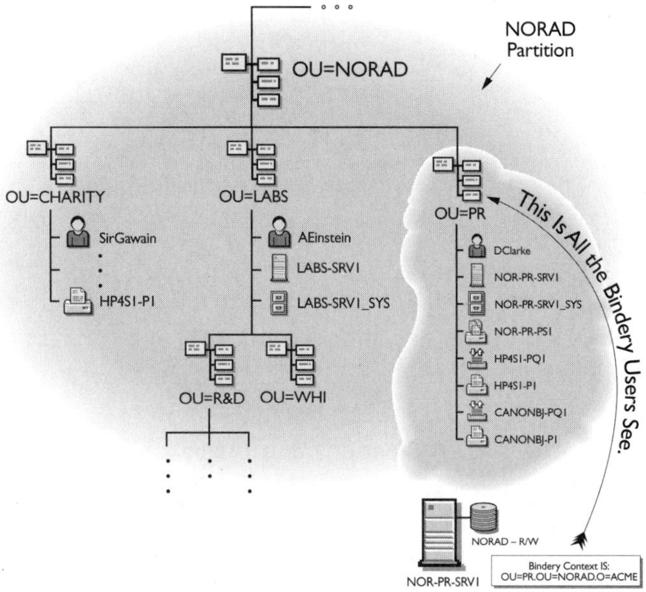

Bindery Services is also required during a NetWare 3.12 to NetWare 5.1 server upgrade. For example, when you upgrade a NetWare 3.12 server, a Read/Write replica of its home partition is placed on the new NetWare 5.1 server. This happens regardless of whether there are already three replicas of the partition.

Tree Walking with Subordinate References

Tree walking (also referred to as *name resolution*) is the mechanism used by NDS to find object information that is not stored on local servers. If the NDS information you need is not stored locally, the server must "walk" the Directory tree to find a server containing an appropriate replica. Every replica maintains a list of the other servers holding replicas of the same partition (called the *replica ring*).

The [Root] is probably the most troublesome name resolution replica because it stores information about every resource. Initially, replicas of the [Root] partition include the containers at the top of the NDS tree. For this reason, you should replicate the [Root] partition to all major hub sites in your network. Also, keep the [Root] partition small to avoid unnecessary Subordinate Reference replicas.

As we discussed earlier, you should use a replica table to track the automatic placement of Subordinate References throughout the network. These pointers are automatically placed on servers that hold a parent replica, but not all of the parent replica's child replicas. A replica table consists of a matrix containing partition columns and server rows. To determine the location of Subordinate References, simply compare the matrix in the replica table to a representation of the graphical NDS tree structure. If a server box holds a parent replica but not all of the parent's child replicas, it is an indication that Subordinate References have been created automatically.

This completes our discussion of NDS partition and replica design. In review, we can organize most network designs into two different classifications:

- *Quick Design* — Most networks have few special needs. As a result, they can use a conservative approach to replica design.
- *Advanced Design* — Some networks have special needs that require complex design strategies.

Now let's learn how to manage NDS partitions and replicas using NDS Manager and WTM.

Managing NDS Partitions and Replicas

NDS partition and replica management involves the daily tasks required to scale the NDS Directory. Once you have created an NDS partitioning and replication design, you must master the following three partition management skills:

- *Managing NDS Partitions* — Involves creating, merging, and moving NDS partitions using NDS Manager.
- *Managing NDS Replicas* — Involves adding NDS replicas and changing the replica type using NDS Manager.
- *Managing WAN Traffic* — Involves managing replica synchronization traffic across WAN links using WAN Traffic Manager.

NDS Manager is a graphical Windows-based tool that enables you to manage all NDS partitions in the tree. It can be launched from the Tools menu of NetWare Administrator. NetWare 5.1 supports the following two versions of NDS Manager:

- SYS:PUBLIC\NDSMGR16 for Windows 3.1
- SYS:PUBLIC\WIN32\NDSMGR32.EXE for Windows 95/98 and Windows NT

As you can see in Figure 10.12, NDS Manager splits the screen vertically into two sections, with partitions (on the left side) and servers (on the right side). It uses a "replica table" concept that enables you to mange partitions, replicas, and servers within a single window.

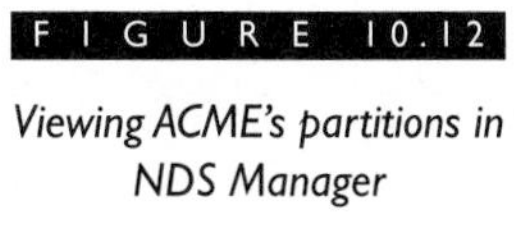
FIGURE 10.12

Viewing ACME's partitions in NDS Manager

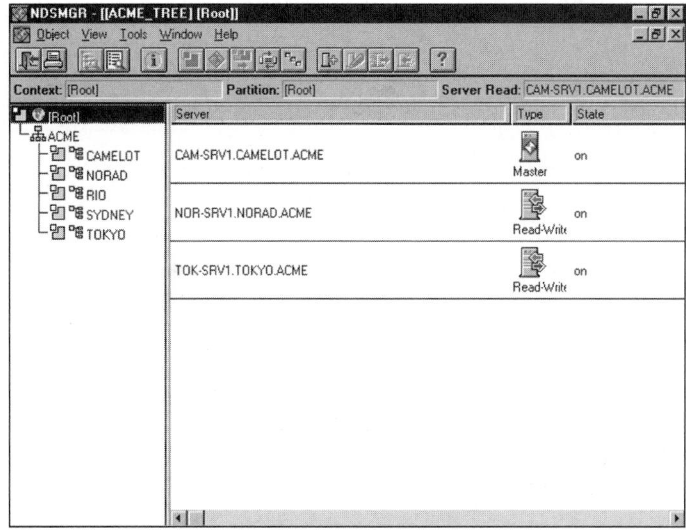

Managing NDS Partitions

NDS partition management involves the following three tasks:

- *Creating Partitions* — Creating a new partition actually involves "splitting" a child partition from its parent. Normally, partition splits occur on a single server because the parent partition already resides there. Therefore, splitting such a partition doesn't generate any traffic and happens quickly. For example, in Figure 10.13, you can see that partitions have already been created for OU=CAMELOT and OU=NORAD. We are currently in the process of creating a partition for OU=TOKYO. This is accomplished by using the Object ➪ Create Partition menu in NDS Manager.

- *Merging Partitions* — Merging is the opposite of splitting. Typically, merging takes longer than splitting and generates a great deal of WAN traffic, depending on the physical location of all servers in both partitions' replica rings. This is especially important if a Wide Area Network is involved. To merge partitions, each server holding a replica of the parent partition must have a copy of the child partition. In return, each server holding a copy of the child partition must have a copy of the parent partition. The merge operation attempts to move copies of either the parent or child partitions to the appropriate servers, as needed.

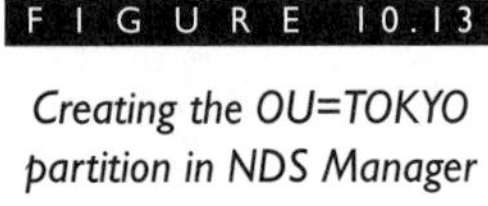

Creating the OU=TOKYO partition in NDS Manager

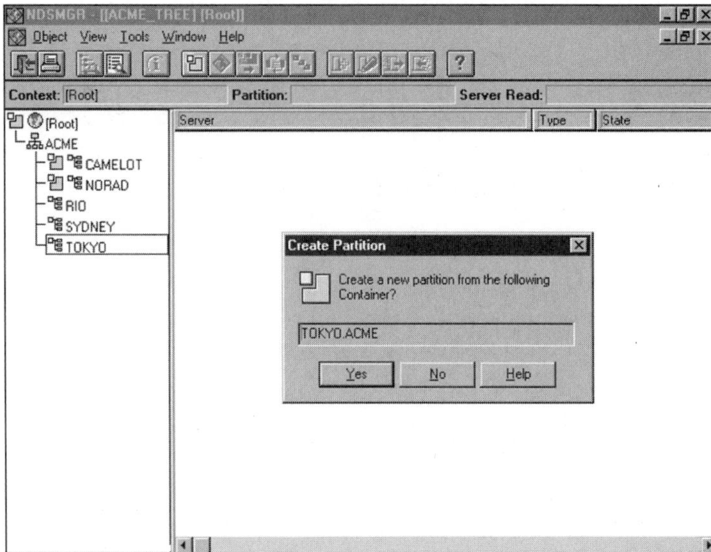

- *Moving Partitions* — NDS allows you to move entire subtrees from one location to another. This is accomplished by moving a container (which must be a partition root) along with its contents. Once you move a container and its contents, all users in the old container must perform the following two tasks to adapt to their new home context: (1) Log in using his/her new distinguished name, and (2) Change the Name Context field in the Login window of their Novell Client workstation. To perform a partition move operation, use the Object ➪ Partition ➪ Move menu in NDS Manager.

REAL WORLD

Practice using NDS Manager to view, create, merge, and move NDS partitions. Specifically, know how to access NDS Manager from the Tools menu of NetWare Administrator. Also, be familiar with the replica table format that NDS Manager uses to display partitions (on the left side) and servers (on the right side).

Managing NDS Replicas

NDS replica management involves the following two operations:

- *Adding Replicas* — Adding replicas is the method used to distribute partition copies throughout the network. When you add replicas to distributed servers, all the NDS data for that partition is copied from one server to another over the network. This operation causes significant network traffic. Figure 10.14 shows the NDS Manager screen for adding NDS replicas. To add a replica, choose a partition (CAMELOT.ACME, in this case), select Object ➪ Add Replica, and then choose a server (NOR-SRV1.NORAD.ACME in this case).

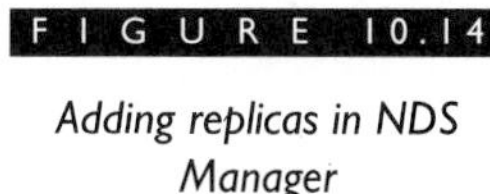
FIGURE 10.14

Adding replicas in NDS Manager

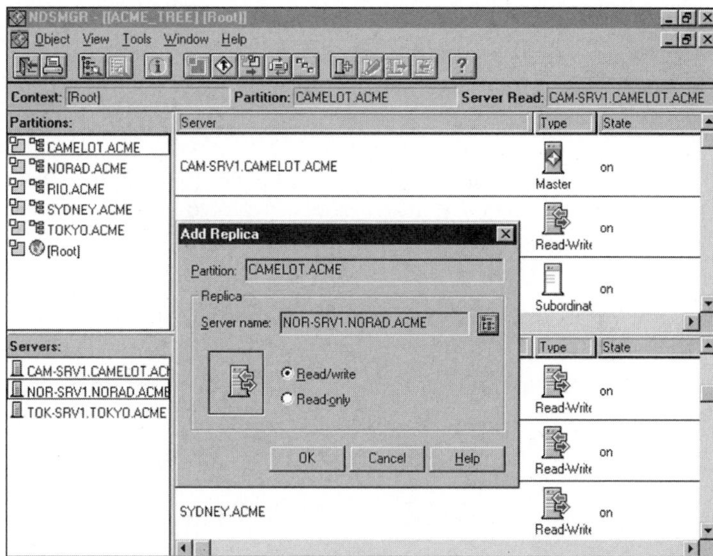

- *Changing Replica Type* — NDS also allows you to change a replica's type. This is particularly important when you want to manage NDS partitions or authenticate to a local Master or Read/Write replica of your home container. NDS allows you to upgrade or downgrade Master, Read/Write, and Read-Only replicas.

Managing WAN Traffic

When NDS synchronizes partition replicas, it creates network traffic. If this traffic crosses WAN links unmanaged, it can increase costs and overload slow WAN links during high-use periods. NetWare 5.1 includes the WAN Traffic Manager (WTM) to help you manage synchronization traffic across WAN links in the following ways:

- WTM controls server-to-server traffic generated by NDS.
- WTM controls periodic events initiated by NDS (such as replica synchronization).
- WTM can restrict traffic based on cost, time of day, type of traffic, or a combination of these criteria.

However, WAN Traffic Manager does *not* perform the following tasks:

- WTM does *not* control events initiated by network administrators or users.
- WTM does *not* control non-NDS server-to-server traffic, such as time synchronization. Fortunately, we have Network Time Protocol (NTP) to solve that problem.

WAN Traffic Manager consists of the following three components:

- *WTM.NLM*—This resides in the SYS:SYSTEM directory on each server. Before NDS initiates server-to-server traffic, WTM.NLM reads a WAN Traffic Policy and determines whether that traffic will be sent.
- *NetWare Administrator Snap-in Files*—These files create an interface to the WAN Traffic Manager from within NetWare Administrator (see Figure 10.15). NetWare Administrator enables you to create or to modify policies, to create LAN Area objects, and to apply policies to LAN Area objects or to servers. When WAN Traffic Manager is installed, the schema is extended to include a LAN Area object and three new detail pages: LAN Area Membership, WAN Policies, and Cost. A LAN Area object enables you to administer WAN Traffic Policies for a group of servers. If you do not create a LAN Area object, you can still manage each server's WAN traffic individually.

- *WAN Traffic Policies* — These are rules that control the generation of NDS synchronization traffic. They are stored as an NDS property value of each NetWare server or LAN Area object. For example, you might restrict NDS traffic over a WAN link during high-use times. This shifts high-bandwidth activities to off-hours. You might also limit replica synchronization traffic to times when telecommunication rates are low (thereby, reducing costs). WAN Traffic Manager provides a number of policies that allow you to restrict traffic according to a variety of criteria, including time of day, cost, protocol, geographic area, spoofing, and traffic type.

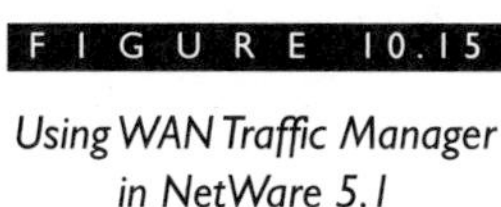

FIGURE 10.15

Using WAN Traffic Manager in NetWare 5.1

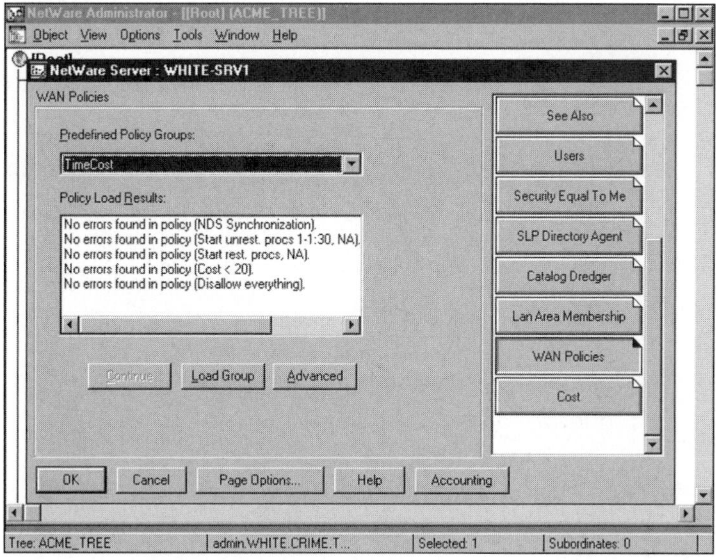

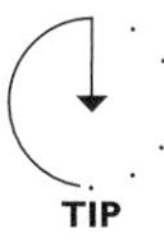

TIP

Study WAN Traffic Manager carefully. Learn what it can do for you (such as restrict NDS traffic based on cost, time of day, type of traffic, or a combination of these criteria) and define its three components (WTM.NLM, NetWare Administrator snap-in files, and WAN Traffic Policies).

That's it. You have taken another step toward completing ACME's NDS design. So far, you have created a Naming Standards Document, designed the top and bottom layers of the tree, and outlined partition boundaries.

In this chapter's final section, "Designing Time Synchronization," you will learn how to coordinate network-wide time synchronization via distributed time servers and the Network Time Protocol (NTP). Are you ready?!

Designing Time Synchronization

The final step in NDS design focuses on time synchronization. The time synchronization process attempts to coordinate and maintain consistent time for all servers in your NDS tree. No matter how you look at it, *time* controls everything. This is especially true in NDS. Time impacts almost every aspect of NetWare 5.1:

- *NDS Operations* — Time synchronization sorts changes in the NDS database.
- *File System* — Time synchronization applies time stamps to file and directory operations.
- *Messaging* — Time synchronization applies time stamps to electronic messages.
- *Printing* — Time synchronization controls print job flow and queue priorities.
- *Resource Access and Security* — Time synchronization manages network authentication, auditing, and access to NDS resources.
- *Network Applications* — Time synchronization tracks when application files and data files are created, modified, archived, and deleted.

In this lesson, we will learn how to design a time synchronization strategy in two environments:

- *IPX Network* — To build an IPX-Only time synchronization system, you will need to become intimately familiar with the four different time server types, learn a little more about time configuration, and master the subtleties of TIMESYNC.NLM.

- *IP and Mixed IP/IPX Networks* — In IP-Only and mixed IP/IPX networks, NetWare 5.1 servers negotiate time with each other using TCP/IP. This is accomplished using two time synchronization components: *Network Time Protocol* (NTP), which is an open IP standard that provides time stamps for synchronizing time servers by using external time sources; and *TIMESYNC.NLM,* a protocol-independent time-synchronization management tool.

The good news is — once NetWare 5.1 time synchronization has been configured, there's little left to do . . . it just runs! Now let's begin our interactive temporal journey with a detailed look at IPX time synchronization.

Understanding IPX Time Synchronization

Time synchronization provides NetWare 5.1 servers with a mechanism for coordinating NDS time stamps. NetWare 5.1 uses TIMESYNC.NLM to coordinate time stamps between all servers on the network. TIMESYNC.NLM maintains each server's Universal Time Coordinated (UTC) time stamp, also known as Greenwich Mean Time (GMT).

Local time for each server is calculated by applying (adding) the time zone and daylight-saving-time settings to the server's UTC value. For example, if a server is located in the Mountain Standard time zone (NORAD), its UTC offset would be +7. This value is applied (as well as subtracting one hour for daylight saving time, if it is in effect) as an offset to standardize the server's time to UTC. Therefore, each server, regardless of its geographic location, can be standardized to UTC time with the following command:

```
Local time +/- time zone offset from UTC - Daylight Savings
Time offset
```

The TIME server console command displays the time zone string, status of daylight saving time (DST), activation status, time synchronization status (synchronized or not), and the current server time (in both UTC and local format). You should use this command periodically to check the status of your time servers (see Figure 10.16).

FIGURE 10.16

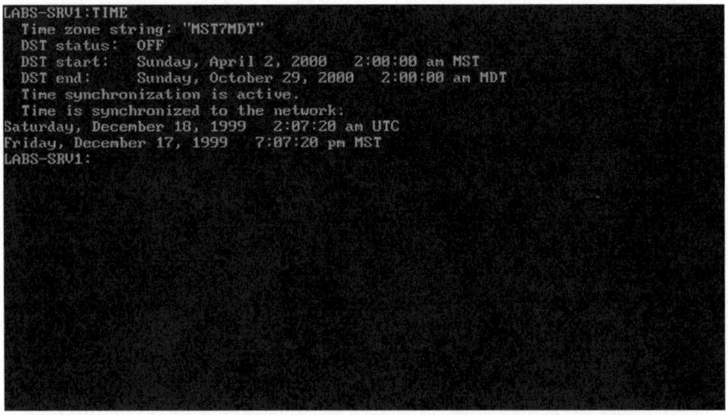

The NetWare TIME command

```
LABS-SRV1:TIME
  Time zone string: "MST7MDT"
  DST status:  OFF
  DST start:    Sunday, April 2, 2000    2:00:00 am MST
  DST end:      Sunday, October 29, 2000    2:00:00 am MDT
  Time synchronization is active.
  Time is synchronized to the network.
Saturday, December 18, 1999   2:07:20 am UTC
Friday, December 17, 1999   7:07:20 pm MST
LABS-SRV1:
```

IPX Time Server Types

All NetWare servers are time servers of some type—either providers or consumers. *Time providers* provide time to *time consumers* (who simply accept time stamps from providers at regular intervals). IPX time synchronization supports the following four types of time servers (see Table 10.4 for complete descriptions):

- *Single Reference*—A stand-alone time provider for the entire network. This is the default configuration for the first NetWare 5.1 server in an NDS tree, and it requires no intervention during installation. The main difference between a Reference server and a Single Reference server is that the Single Reference server can raise its synchronization flag without confirming its time with any other time source. A Single Reference server should only be used at small sites with less than 30 servers and no WAN connections. In a Single Reference time configuration, all other servers are Secondary time servers (that is, time consumers).

- *Reference*—Adds important stability to a Primary time provider group. Both Primary and Reference time providers vote on network time—with Reference servers getting 16 votes and Primary servers getting only one vote. During each polling interval, all Primary time servers converge 50 percent of the gap between their internal clocks and the network time, which is published by the Reference time server.

Although a Reference time server participates in the voting process, it never adjusts its clocks. Because a Reference server is the only server that does not adjust its internal clock, you should connect it to an *external* time source. Finally, you can define multiple Reference servers on the same network, but they must be connected to the same external source.

- *Primary* — Primary time servers are the principal time providers because they distribute time to requesting Secondary servers. Primary servers contact all other time providers and identify any discrepancies between the Primary server's local clock and the calculated network time. If there is a difference, then the Primary server adjusts its clock to 50 percent of the discrepancy during each polling loop.
- *Secondary* — Secondary time servers rely on other sources to provide them with network time. A Secondary server must contact a Single Reference, Reference, or Primary provider for the network time. A Secondary server is the most prevalent type of time server on your network because most servers do not need to participate in time providing. By default, all servers except the initial server installed in an NDS tree are designated as Secondary servers when they are installed. The first server in an NDS tree is defined as a Single Reference time provider.

Refer to Table 10.4 for a summary of these four IPX time-server types and their capabilities.

IPX Time Synchronization Management

In order to transform a file server into an IPX time provider, you must use the SET console command or MONITOR.NLM menu utility. Following is an example of a time server SET command:

```
SET TIMESYNC TYPE = SINGLE REFERENCE
```

If your time servers become unsynchronized (that is, if server time is more than two seconds different from network time), the polling interval switches from every ten minutes to every ten seconds, until time is synchronized again.

TABLE 10.4

IPX Time-Server Types and Functions

SERVER TYPE	DESCRIPTION	GETS TIME FROM	ADJUST CLOCK	GIVES TIME TO
Single Reference	Default configuration for the first server in a tree. Does not poll any other server for the time. Same as a Reference server, but always claims to be synchronized with network time. Cannot coexist with Primary or Reference time servers.	Hardware clock or external source	No	Secondary time servers and clients
Reference	Participates in the voting process with Primary time servers, but does not adjust its internal clock. Provides a central point of time control for the entire network. A higher-priority time source than a Primary time server, because it is considered more reliable. For fault tolerance purposes, you should have at least two Primary time servers for each Reference time server.	Hardware clock or external source	No	Primary and Secondary time servers and clients
Primary	Polls Reference and other Primary time sources.	Network time determined by time provider group	Yes (50% correction per polling interval)	Secondary time servers and clients

TABLE 10.4

IPX Time-Server Types and Functions (continued)

SERVER TYPE	DESCRIPTION	GETS TIME FROM	ADJUST CLOCK	GIVES TIME TO
Primary *(continued)*	Votes to determine correct network time by calculating the weighted average of the time of each server in the group and changes its time to half of the difference between its time and the time-provider group time. Sets synchronization status based on its deviation from calculated network time without regard to status of other time sources polled.	Network time determined by time provider group	Yes (50% correction per polling interval)	Secondary time servers and clients
Secondary	Default configuration for the second or subsequent servers in a tree. Attempts to remain synchronized with only one time source. Does not participate in voting.	Single Reference, Reference, Primary, or Secondary	Yes (100% correction per polling interval)	Secondary and client workstations

However, if a Single Reference server is brought up with the wrong time, it won't get synchronized because it doesn't change its own time. Follow these simple steps to synchronize an erroneous Single Reference time server:

1. First, determine if replica time stamps are ahead of actual time (causing an error in synchronization). To determine this, load DSREPAIR and choose Advanced Options ➪ Replica and Partition Operations. Then highlight a particular replica, select Display Replica Information, and review the Timestamp value.

2. Next, type the following command at the server console: **TIME**. If the time on a Single Reference server is earlier than the actual time, set the time forward to the correct time. If the time on your Single Reference server is less than one week ahead of actual time, try one of the following two options: (1) Shut down the servers during off-business hours to allow actual time to catch up with the future time stamps, or (2) Avoid replica or partitioning operations until actual time catches up with the future time stamps.

3. If the server time stamp is more than one week ahead of the partition time, do not set the server time backward. This will generate *synthetic time*. Synthetic time occurs when the partition time stamp is in the future as compared to the server time. Because replica synchronization depends on time stamps, synthetic time can cause serious problems with NDS.

IPX Time Synchronization Communication

Time communication occurs in the following two instances: (1) When time providers "vote" with each other, and (2) When Secondary time servers "poll" time providers for the correct time. IPX time servers can share synchronization information in one of two ways:

- Default: SAP method
- Custom: Configured Lists method

The *SAP method* is the default time communication design and, thus, requires no intervention. Both time providers and time consumers communicate using the Service Advertising Protocol (SAP), by default. You should be aware that SAP causes a small amount of additional network traffic during time synchronization polling cycles. Also, SAP is self-configuring. This means there's no protection against a misconfigured time server. In summary, time servers use SAP for the following reasons:

- Reference, Primary, and Single Reference time servers use SAP to announce their presence on the network.

- Reference and Primary servers use SAP to poll each other to determine the network time.
- Secondary time servers use SAP to request temporal guidance (also known as *time*).

You can configure SAP in such a way that it filters intratree and intertree time polling by setting the Directory Tree parameter to ON. To allow time servers to find *any* server regardless of its tree, set the Directory Tree mode to OFF and SAP to ON.

The *Configured Lists method* provides much more flexibility for IPX time-synchronization communications than the default method. A configured list allows you to specify which time server a server should contact. When you set SAP mode to OFF (or when you remove a time server from a tree that is using the Configured Lists method), you must update the configured lists on all IPX time servers accordingly.

The Configured Lists time communication design provides you with complete control of the time synchronization hierarchy. It also reduces SAP traffic on your network and provides direct server-to-server contact. In addition to MONITOR, you can also configure TIMESYNC.CFG by using SET commands at the server console.

If desired, you can use a configured list and activate SAP at the same time. While this combination increases network traffic slightly, it does provide fault tolerance in case the Configured List method fails.

Understanding IP and IP/IPX Time Synchronization

In IP and mixed IP/IPX networks, NetWare servers synchronize time with each other using TCP/IP. This is accomplished by using the following two time synchronization components:

- *Network Time Protocol (NTP)* — This is an open IP standard that provides time stamps for time synchronization by using external time sources. When TIMESYNC.NLM is loaded on an IP server, NTP becomes the time source for both IP and IPX servers. In this configuration, IPX servers must be configured as Secondary servers.
- *TIMESYNC.NLM* — This is the NetWare 5.1 time synchronization management tool, regardless of server protocol. TIMESYNC.NLM loads automatically when the server is installed.

NTP supports the following two types of time servers:

- *Servers* — Allow local servers to be synchronized to remote servers. Remote servers, however, cannot be synchronized to the local server. This NTP time server performs a similar function to Single Reference or Reference servers in the IPX time synchronization model.
- *Peers* — Allow the local server to synchronize its time with a remote server and vice versa. This is an ideal model for distributed time synchronization fault tolerance (such as IPX Primary servers).

If you use TIMESYNC.NLM to sync with an NTP time source, configuration information is saved in the NetWare registry with other SET parameters.

When NTP is installed using the older NTP.NLM utility, however, the NTP.CFG configuration file is created. This file specifies the IP time-server type and indicates where the server should go to find local time. By default, NTP.CFG specifies the local clock as 127.127.1.0. This means the local clock timer kicks in when all outside sources become unavailable.

You can change the NTP.CFG configuration of any of these sources by replacing the term "server" with "peer." Also, note that NTP does not negotiate time the way Primary servers do in the IPX model. Instead, the Network Time Protocol operates under the assumption that the time any NTP time server receives from an Internet time source is the correct time. As such, the NTP time server is forced to change its own time according to the time it receives, and all Secondary servers in the NTP server's replica list must change their time to match.

Designing an IPX Time Synchronization Strategy

The first step in building an IPX time-synchronization design strategy is to determine whether or not the default settings are adequate. Following are your two design choices:

- Default: Single Reference time server
- Custom: time provider group

Default: Single Reference Time Server

The first NetWare 5.1 server installed in an NDS tree is automatically configured as a Single Reference time server. By default, all subsequent servers are designated as Secondary time servers. This design strategy is adequate as long as your network satisfies the following conditions:

- Single site
- Less than 30 servers
- No IP servers or segments

One benefit of the default strategy is that it is simple and requires absolutely no advanced planning. Additionally, no configuration files are needed, and thus the possibility of encountering errors during time synchronization is considerably minimized.

The default design strategy relies on a central file server with a trusted hardware clock (see Figure 10.17). Because it is the sole time provider, you should monitor its time frequently. If you are unhappy with your first time provider, you can always redesignate another server as the Single Reference time server using the MONITOR utility.

FIGURE 10.17

Default time configuration design

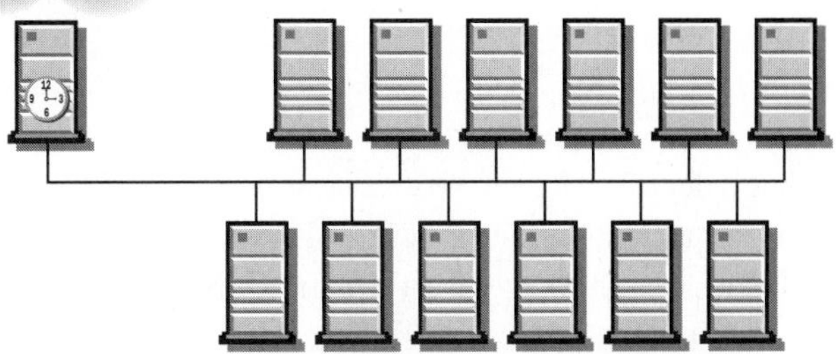

In summary, following is a list of design considerations you should keep in mind when using the Single Reference time synchronization design strategy:

- The time server must be contacted by all network servers.
- A misconfigured server can disrupt the network, especially if you overcompensate for the error by repeatedly changing the server's time.
- Some Secondary servers might synchronize to an unsynchronized server, rather than to the authorized Single Reference time server.
- One time source means a single point of failure. However, if a Single Reference time server goes down, a Secondary time server can be set as the Single Reference time server using a SET parameter.
- The Single Reference method might not be ideal for implementations with many sites connected by WAN links. The SAP process might involve more network traffic than is acceptable.

Custom: Time Provider Group

The custom time design strategy provides more fault tolerance, efficiency, and flexibility for large interconnected networks. In this type of scenario, the time provider group requires one Reference time server and a minimum of two Primary time servers. These three (or more) time providers form a time provider group that in turn provides time to Secondary servers and clients.

The best custom approach is to organize your time providers according to geography, placing one time provider group in each WAN hub. This configuration requires simple adjustments to the servers in the time provider group. In this case, one server will be designated as a Reference time server and two to seven servers can be designated as Primary time servers.

The selection of your Reference server should be based on a centralized location within your WAN infrastructure. For example, the ACME WAN uses a hub-and-spoke design. CAMELOT is the central hub, so it will be the home of the Reference server (refer to Figure 10.18). The Primary servers are then distributed across the WAN links to each of the spoke locations.

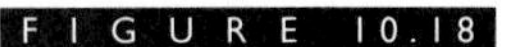

FIGURE 10.18

ACME's custom time-configuration design

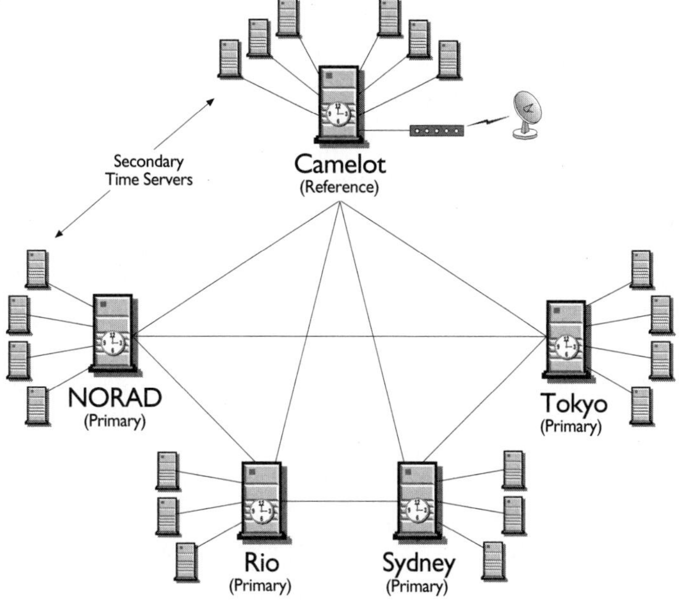

In addition, you should connect the Reference Server to an external time source to ensure highly accurate time. In summary, following is a list of design considerations you should keep in mind when using the time-provider-group design strategy:

- Customization requires careful planning, especially on a large network.
- Adding time sources usually requires that configuration files on several servers be updated.
- If you use a time provider group, at least one server must be designated as a Reference time server and two servers must be designated as Primary time servers.
- These servers will poll assigned time providers in their time provider group to vote on the correct time.
- Whenever Primary and Reference time servers exist on a network, they must be able to contact each other for polling and voting.

- If you use more than one Reference time server, you must synchronize each Reference time server with the same external time source (such as a radio clock, atomic clock, or Internet time).
- A server designated as a Reference time server should be placed in a central location.
- You should spread the other servers in your time provider group around the network to control the flow of traffic that is generated when the Secondary time servers request the time from their designated time source.
- A time provider group should include a Reference time server and a small number of Primary time servers. All other time servers should be Secondary time servers.
- Place each Primary time server close to the Secondary time servers that rely on it for network time. Also, make sure the Primary time server has a reliable link to the appropriate Reference time server.
- If your WAN infrastructure forces you to have more than seven Primary time servers in a time provider group, implement additional time provider groups, as necessary. Ensure that each Reference time server, however, is synchronized to the same external time source. In this case, designate all other servers as Secondary time servers.
- Limit the number of time providers. The amount of traffic involved in time synchronization is small.

In addition, you may want to consider using multiple time provider groups. This increases redundancy in worldwide operations. For example, ACME could implement this approach by creating three independent time provider groups and locating one independent time provider group each in NORAD, CAMELOT, and RIO (see Figure 10.18). This way, time is determined locally, instead of traversing WAN links during every polling interval.

If you decide to use multiple time provider groups, make sure that the Reference server in each group uses the same external clock. This will ensure a single (yet external) source of time convergence.

Your time is up! Congratulations, you have really finished ACME's NDS design. Wow, it's been a long and tough journey, but we made it to the end. Let's review:

- *Naming Standards Document* — It all started with ACME's Naming Standards Document. A complete naming standard is important so that you design an NDS database that is flexible, easy to use, and meets your business needs. As a matter of fact, ACME's naming standard is the center of the NDS design.
- *NDS Tree Design* — After we created the Naming Standards Document, we moved on to the real action — NDS tree design. We started with a rough pyramid design outlining the geographic top and organizational bottom layers of the tree. Then we further refined the design with respect to administration, partitioning, login scripts, and Bindery Services.
- *Partition and Replica Design* — With the tree in place, we moved on to partitioning and replication. We started by breaking the tree into small little pieces (NDS partitioning). This occurred along the geographic boundaries of ACME. Then we scattered the pieces around the network (replica placement). Replica placement is one of the most important aspects of NDS design because it directly affects your network's performance, accessibility, and fault tolerance.
- *Time Synchronization Design* — Finally, Time Synchronization Design ensured that all our servers agreed on the time. We explored the four different IPX time server types and learned how to design them according to two important factors: time configuration and time communication. Then we explored IP time synchronization with NTP and TIMESYNC. NLM. We determined that ACME needs five Time Providers (one in each location) with a Reference server in CAMELOT.

Now that the ACME NDS design is complete, it is time for the next step in network construction — NDS implementation. In Chapter 11, we will discover ACME's implementation schedule and learn how to merge two separate NDS trees into a single, cohesive WAN. *It's time for action!*

LAB EXERCISE 10.1: DESIGNING ACME'S NDS

Use the hints provided to find the 20 NDS partitioning and time synchronization design terms hidden in this word search puzzle. Omit any punctuation characters (such as blank spaces, hyphens, and so on) and spell out any numbers.

T	I	M	E	S	Y	N	C	N	L	M	U	E	P	O
N	E	T	W	O	R	K	T	I	M	E	M	M	A	V
A	X	N	W	T	M	N	L	M	E	V	T	L	R	E
M	N	X	R	E	P	L	I	C	A	L	I	S	T	R
E	E	Q	G	E	N	L	V	U	K	I	U	L	I	L
R	E	E	F	Q	L	T	C	N	S	M	I	V	T	A
E	W	B	U	G	J	Q	Y	X	I	Y	I	Q	I	P
S	Y	N	C	H	R	O	N	I	Z	A	T	I	O	N
O	A	Q	M	W	K	N	B	Z	E	D	S	L	N	R
L	E	C	N	A	R	E	L	O	T	T	L	U	A	F
U	T	S	I	L	D	E	R	U	G	I	F	N	O	C
T	C	T	R	E	F	E	R	E	N	C	E	W	A	R
I	I	I	U	K	D	I	D	G	U	D	D	G	X	N
O	R	N	O	I	T	A	C	I	L	P	E	R	O	J
N	I	I	B	B	F	B	T	O	B	V	S	Q	Y	L

Hints

1. Allows you to specify exactly which servers should be contacted for a time provider group and allows you to make requests for time consumers.
2. A benefit of replica distribution that increases the availability of partitions throughout the NDS tree.
3. A benefit of replica distribution that enhances user access to resources by allowing them to "walk the tree."
4. Time maintained by all servers in a NetWare 5.1 network.
5. Something that partitions cannot do.
6. Logical division of the NDS database.

7. Time server voting process.
8. Time server that votes, but does not change its time.
9 A list of all servers containing a replica of a given NDS partition.
10. Process of creating copies of partitions for fault-tolerance purposes.
11. A partitioning process that updates all replicas of a given partition when changes are made to the NDS database.
12. The maximum number of replicas you should maintain per partition.
13. A protocol-independent time-synchronization management tool.
14. The maximum number of replicas you should place on a single server.
15. A tool used for managing replica synchronization traffic across WAN links.

See Appendix C for answers.

LAB EXERCISE 10.2: NDS PARTITIONING AND TIME

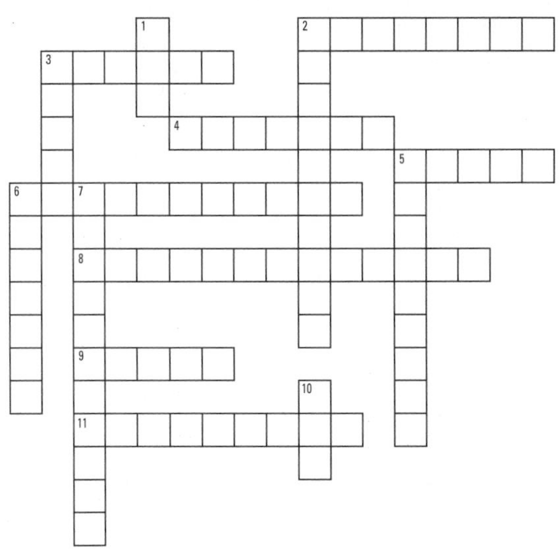

Across

2. Replicas that must be created manually
3. The king of the replica hill
4. NDS partition "copy"
5. Creating more child partitions
6. One of three reasons to replicate
8. The topmost object in a partition
9. "Young" subordinate partitions
11. Most common replica type

Down

1. Time synchronization in an IP-Only network
2. Type of external time source
3. Building a bigger parent partition
5. Most popular type of time server

6. Time server that "haggles" for time
7. A list of all replicas in a given partition
10. Also known as GMT

See Appendix C for answers.

CHAPTER 11

NDS Implementation

Welcome to Step 3 — NDS implementation. This is prime time!

If you are feeling a little restless from all the preparing, planning, and designing in the preceding three chapters, then this chapter is for you. As you can see in Figure 11.1, all the initial action of Step 3 centers on the implementation schedule. This schedule outlines the rollout of NetWare 5.1 installation, upgrade, and migration. But before you can implement NetWare 5.1 for ACME in a production environment, you should test it in a more controlled pilot program.

FIGURE 11.1

Step 3: NDS Implementation

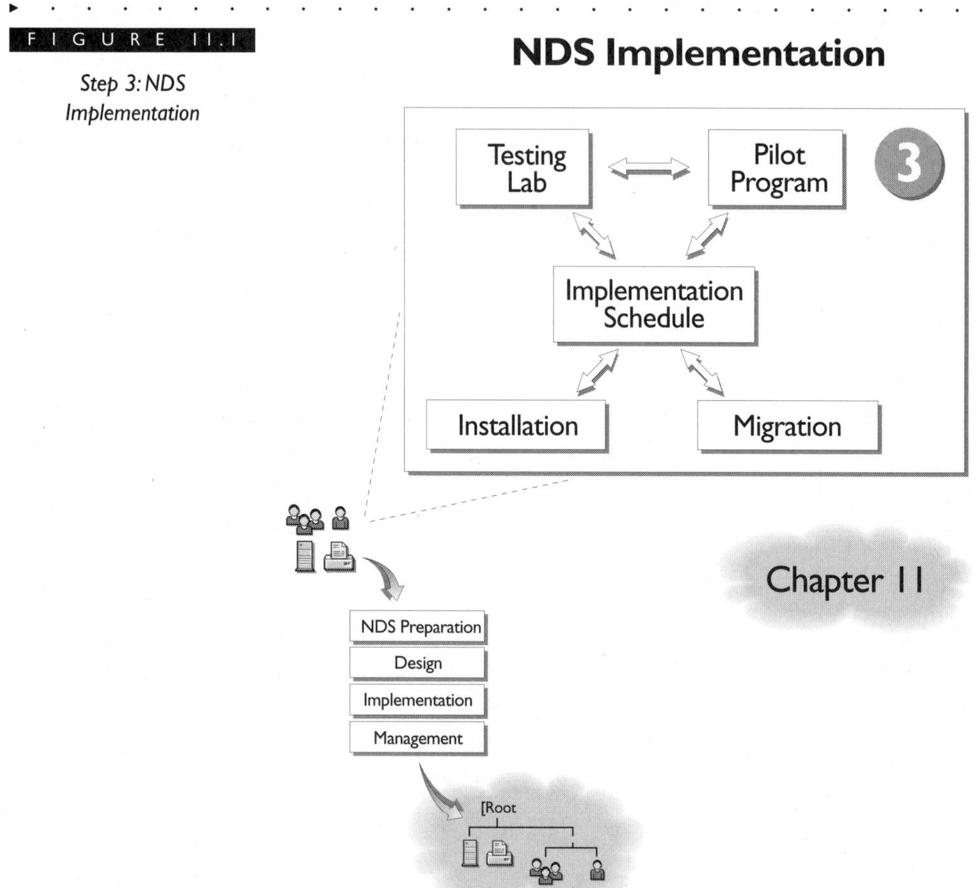

NDS implementation transcends all the other NDS design tasks, in that it gives you the opportunity to build your NDS tree. After you design your NDS tree, you must install the servers, build the tree, place the resources, and implement a User Environment Plan (UEP).

Data gathering is an important part of NDS implementation. For example, the following NDS design inputs should help you execute your NDS merging and partition management tasks: a company organizational chart, a physical network layout map, a network resources list, background information, and a workflow diagram.

Following are the four phases of NDS implementation:

- *Phase 1: Building the NDS Tree* — In Chapter 9, "NDS Tree Design," we learned how to create a preliminary NDS tree design. The top layers should be location based and the bottom layers should be function based. This layout optimizes your administrative approach, login scripts, Bindery Services, and container sizes. The design of the container structure should resemble the shape of a pyramid, with most of the containers at the bottom and fewer containers at the top. During the first phase of NDS implementation, you get an opportunity to build the design using NetWare Administrator.

- *Phase 2: Managing NDS Partitions* — During the installation of the first server in a NDS tree, the first partition is created for you (that is, the [Root] partition). Once your network servers are up and running, you can use NDS Manager to make additional partitions and to distribute them as replicas. For example, each geographic site should be contained in its own separate partition. In Chapter 10, "NDS Partitioning and Time Synchronization Design," we learned how to create, to move, and to merge partitions. We also learned how to add and to remove replicas, and how to change NDS replica types.

- *Phase 3: Merging NDS Trees* — In many cases, you may need to merge multiple NDS trees into a unified network (that is, a single tree) before you can perform the remaining implementation tasks. The process of merging two NDS trees is relatively simple. The implications of merging two NDS trees, however, can be dramatic. Therefore, careful planning and execution are critical. In the next section, "Merging NDS Trees," we will study detailed NDS merging considerations and step-by-step instructions.

- *Phase 4: Implementing a User Environment Plan* — Finally, you should implement a User Environment Plan (UEP) to manage how users will access NDS resources on your new network. Specifically, you should create ZENworks objects to manage the user's desktop environment, standardize the file system structure, implement network security measures, create login scripts for client accessibility, and provide access for mobile users.

In this chapter, we will learn how to merge separate NDS trees and explore ACME's full NDS rollout, including its testing lab, pilot program, and implementation schedule. Are you ready for action?

Merging NDS Trees

Merging NDS trees is one of the most traumatic NDS implementation phases. Therefore, you need to exercise both careful planning and an appropriate degree of caution. In NetWare 5.1, the merging of two trees is accomplished by using a menu-based server utility called DSMERGE. This utility enables you to combine multiple trees (two at a time) into a single, cohesive NDS network.

In this section, we will study the detailed steps of the NDS merge process. But first, we must discuss the design implications of combining two existing NDS trees.

Design Considerations for Merging NDS Trees

During the NDS merge process, you need to identify a *source* tree and a *target* tree. In Figure 11.2, UN-TREE represents the source tree and ACME-TREE is the target. You also need to identify a source server in the UN-TREE (for DSMERGing) and a target server in the ACME-TREE. (**Note:** It's imperative that each server contain a Master replica of its host [Root] partition.)

After the merge, the resulting NDS tree structure will probably look very different from the original structure. Therefore, you may experience a variety of naming problems in login scripts and workstation name contexts. Following are planning guidelines that help you minimize the negative impacts associated with merging two NDS trees:

FIGURE 11.2

Replica placement after merging NDS trees

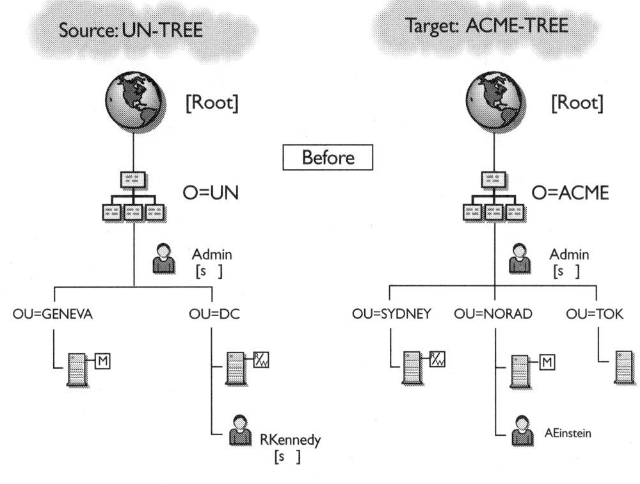

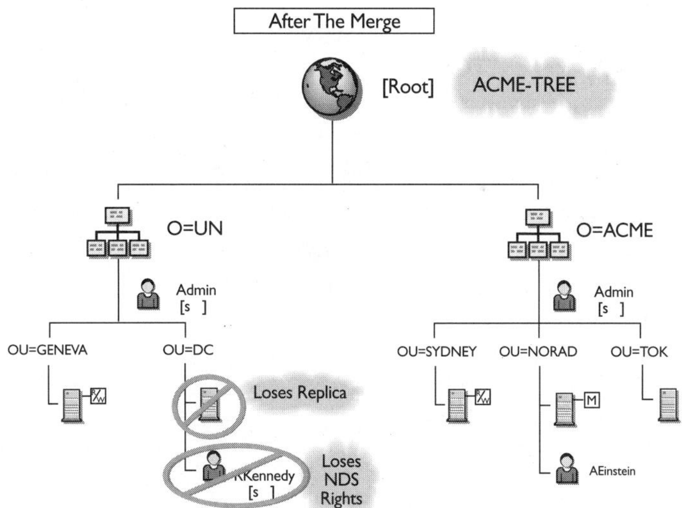

- Choose the source and target NDS trees carefully. Typically, the source tree should be the one with fewer objects directly under the [Root].

- Identify the full name and password for a User object with Supervisor [S] object rights at the [Root] of both the source tree and the target tree.

- Modify the source and target NDS trees so that they follow the same first-level container structure.
- At the time of the NDS merge, make sure that the names of the first-level containers in both trees are unique.

NDS Partitioning Considerations

During the merge process, the Master replica of the [Root] partition on the target server becomes the Master replica of the new, combined [Root] partition. Any servers in the target tree that held replicas of the old target tree [Root] partition are given a replica of the new [Root] partition.

In addition, the source server loses the Master replica of its old [Root] partition and is given a Read/Write replica of the new [Root] partition. Any servers in the source tree (except for the source server) that held a replica of the old source tree [Root] lose their replica, and they do not receive a replica of the new [Root] partition. Therefore, you need to manually distribute replicas of the new [Root] partition to any servers in the source tree (other than the source server) that need a replica of the new [Root] partition. (Refer to Figure 11.2.)

Finally, all first-level containers in the source tree [Root] partition become independent *partition roots* in the new tree. Although all servers in the source tree (except for the source server) that held a replica of the source tree [Root] partition lose their replica of the source tree [Root] partition, they gain replicas of the new first-level partitions in the new tree. Subordinate Reference replicas for the new partitions under the new [Root] are added to servers holding replicas of the new [Root].

Security Considerations

In addition to replica distribution changes, the NDS merge process also involves security implications. During the merge, the Access Control List (ACL) of the source tree [Root] is discarded, while the ACL of the target tree [Root] is maintained. The only source [Root] rights that are kept belong to the source tree User object that performed the merge (typically Admin).

Refer to Figure 11.2, Table 11.1, and Table 11.2 for an example of NDS merging security considerations. In the example, the source tree administrative user (Admin.UN) gains Supervisor [S] rights to the new [Root]—but all other source [Root] trustees lose their rights (such as `RKennedy.DC.UN`).

Before you begin merging the two trees, you need to create a plan to compensate for trustee rights that are automatically discarded during the merge. One solution, of course, is that prior to the merge, you can assign appropriate trustees the rights they need to containers below the [Root] in the source tree. Another solution is to grant these trustee rights immediately after the merge.

TABLE 11.1

Source and Target [Root] Trustee Lists before *the NDS Merge*

SOURCE TREE (UN-TREE)		TARGET TREE (ACME-TREE)	
Trustees of [Root]	Rights	Trustees of [Root]	Rights
Admin.UN	[S]	Admin.ACME	[S]
RKennedy.DC.UN	[S]	AEinstein.NORAD.ACME	[S]

TABLE 11.2

New [Root] Trustee List after *the NDS Merge*

MERGED TREE (ACME-TREE)	
Trustees of new [Root]	Rights
Admin.ACME	[S]
AEinstein.NORAD.ACME	[S]
Admin.UN	[S]

REAL WORLD

Study NDS merge security considerations carefully. Specifically, remember that during a merge, all first-level containers in the source tree [Root] partition become individual partition roots, and the source server that previously held the Master replica of the source tree [Root] partition gets a Read/Write replica of the new [Root] partition. Also, remember that the ACL of the source tree [Root] is discarded and the source tree administrator that performs the merge gets Supervisor [S] object rights to the new [Root].

Performing an NDS Merge

The NDS merge process is accomplished by using a NetWare 5.1 utility called *DSMERGE* (see Figure 11.3). This utility enables you to combine multiple trees (two at a time) into a single, cohesive NDS network. DSMERGE provides an important level of design flexibility by enabling network administrators to merge existing trees once the organization agrees on a single NDS design. As a result, distributed departments can implement NDS early and then merge into the parent tree at a later date. (**Note:** DSMERGE only works with NetWare 5.1 servers installed with NDS 7. It does not work with NDS 8.)

To merge two NDS trees, perform these four steps:

- *Step 1:* Merge Preparation
- *Step 2:* Merge Execution
- *Step 3:* Merge Confirmation
- *Step 4:* Merge Cleanup (Completion)

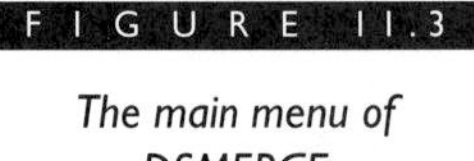
FIGURE 11.3

The main menu of DSMERGE

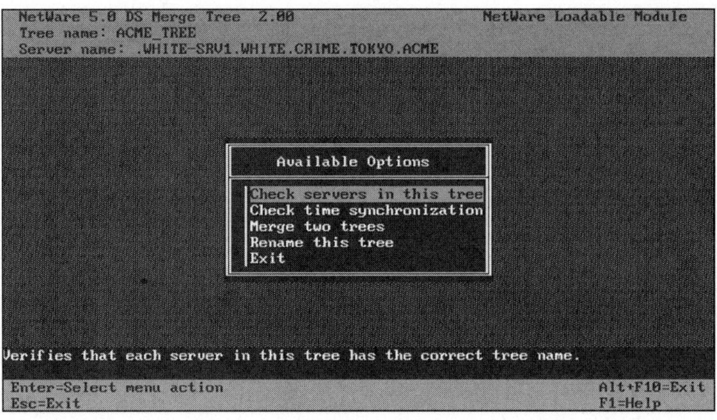

Step 1: Merge Preparation

Before merging two NDS trees, you need to perform a series of preparation tasks:

- *Identify the Appropriate Tools* — Before you begin, make sure you have access to the following NDS merging tools: an NDS backup utility (to back up NDS), TIMESYNC or NTP commands (to change time synchronization parameters), the Schema Manager component of NDS Manager (to confirm that the schemas are synchronized), the DSMERGE utility, NDS Manager or DSREPAIR (to confirm that the tree has been synchronized after the merge is completed), and NetWare Administrator (to customize the consolidated tree).

- *Back up the NDS Trees* — Next, you must back up both NDS trees. Even though the merge is theoretically protected from catastrophic failure by NetWare transaction tracking system (TTS), you should still perform a full backup of each NDS tree before beginning the merge. Also, be sure to verify your backups before you begin. As a result, you will be assured of having an up-to-date copy of each NDS tree, in case something goes wrong during the merge.

- *Synchronize the Schemas* — The preliminary check phase of DSMERGE helps ensure that the server running DSMERGE holds a replica of the [Root] partition. If it cannot find a replica of [Root], the operation aborts. It is imperative that both trees use the same schema. (The schema defines object classes and rules of containment.) If one tree contains a modified schema or if different versions of NDS are represented, use DSREPAIR to update the schemas before merging the trees. (**Note:** You may need to update the schema from the source NDS tree to the target NDS tree and from the target NDS tree to the source NDS tree.)

- *Establish Time Synchronization* — Finally, you must ensure that both trees are synchronized and that they reference the same time source. Once DSMERGE is loaded on the source server, you can initiate time synchronization, as shown in Figure 11.4. DSMERGE checks the time status of all servers participating in the DSMERGE, including the server name, NDS version, and time synchronization status. If there is a time delta between a NetWare 5.1 server and the local server running DSMERGE, the difference is shown onscreen in hours, minutes, and seconds.

FIGURE 11.4

The Time Synchronization Status screen in DSMERGE

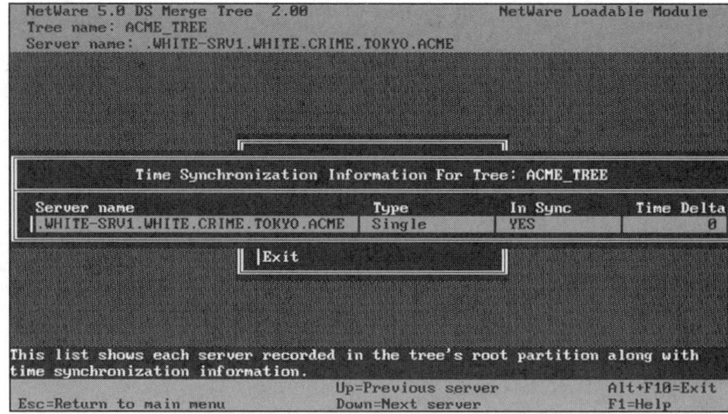

Step 2: Merge Execution

Once you have verified the status and synchronization of both the source and target NetWare 5.1 servers, you can follow these steps to perform the NDS merge:

1. At the source server console, enter the following:

```
DSMERGE
```

2. Then, to confirm that the source server's time is synchronized, select Check Time Synchronization.

3. Next, select Merge Two Trees.

4. Finally, to merge the two trees, select Yes.

After the DSMERGE process completes, you will have a single tree with a common [Root].

Step 3: Merge Confirmation

If you plan to perform additional partition operations after the merge, you will first need to confirm that the NDS tree is stable. One way to verify that the NDS tree is stable enough for additional partition activity is to confirm that the Replica State is "On" for all replicas on both source and target servers. You can accomplish this by using NDS Manager or DSREPAIR.

To view the replica status in NDS Manager, locate the source server in the NDS tree and then highlight it. On the right side of the screen, a list appears that contains the replicas on the designated server, as well as the status of each replica.

To view the Replica State of a server in DSREPAIR, perform the following steps:

1. At the source server, enter the following:

```
DSREPAIR
```

2. Next, select the Advanced Options menu.

3. Then select Replica and Partition Operations.

4. Finally, verify that the Replica State is "On."

REAL WORLD

If the state of the new partition doesn't go "On" in seven minutes or less, use the Schedule Immediate Sync option in DSREPAIR.

Step 4: Merge Cleanup (Completion)

Once the NDS merge is confirmed, you may need to perform one or more of the following tasks in order to finalize the new NDS tree structure:

- *Create the Final NDS Tree Structure* — To complete the NDS design, you may need to create, move, delete, or rename containers using NetWare Administrator. For more information, refer to Chapter 10, "NDS Partitioning and Time Synchronization Design."

- *Set up NDS Administration Rights*—During a merge, the source tree administrative object that performed the merge ends up with Supervisor [S] object rights to the [Root] of the new NDS tree. This trustee assignment may not be appropriate. Also, the other users in the source NDS tree who previously had rights to the [Root] of the source tree will not have such rights to the [Root] of the new tree. One method of handling this problem is to write down a list of the trustees of the source tree [Root] before the merge and then re-create those assignments to the new [Root] (if desired) after the merge. Another method is to grant trustees of the source tree's [Root] object rights to the containers immediately below the [Root] before the merge. Your organization's NDS administration style (that is, centralized or distributed) will influence the method you choose.

- *Correct Login Scripts*—After the merge, commands in login scripts may be invalid because resources are no longer in the same context. Edit and debug Container, Profile, and User login scripts, as needed.

- *Correct Bindery Services Commands*—After the merge, you may need to edit the AUTOEXEC.NCF file of each NDS server to correct errors in Bindery Services context naming.

- *Update Workstation Parameters*—After the merge, you may need to modify client parameters in order to identify the correct resources in their new context. For example, Name Context and Preferred Tree parameters will need to be changed. Consider creating an Alias object structure of the original tree as an interim solution to the name context challenge.

This completes Phase 3 of NDS implementation. NDS merging is one of the most critical and complex operations you will ever encounter as a network administrator. Now let's explore ACME's overall NDS rollout in a little more depth.

REAL WORLD

If you installed NDS 7 during NetWare 5.1 installation, you may want to upgrade to eDirectory Version 8 or later. To do so, you must first make sure that all users are logged out and all volumes are mounted. Next, insert the NetWare 5.1 Installation CD-ROM and run NWCONFIG from the server command line. Choose "Product Options" and then choose "Install NDS 8." Finally, enter the Administrator's distinguished name and password, and the installation program updates your server to the new eDirectory version.

ACME NDS Rollout

Once you have prepared, planned, and designed ACME's NDS tree, it is time to roll it out to the world. This can be accomplished by using the following roadmap:

- *ACME Testing Lab* — NDS implementation begins with five different experiments: hardware installation, NDS implementation, testing login scripts, testing applications, and testing backup and restore procedures. Then you will get an opportunity to practice NDS merging and partition management — all "offline."
- *ACME Pilot Program* — Next, you should create a bridge between the controlled testing lab and the uncontrolled production environment. Take it slowly.
- *ACME Implementation Schedule* — Finally, the heart and soul of NDS implementation is the *implementation schedule*. This ten-part matrix is your blueprint for ACME success.

That's NDS rollout in a nutshell. Let's take a closer look, starting with the ACME testing lab.

ACME Testing Lab

It all starts in the "offline" laboratory. The testing lab is a completely open environment where you can get comfortable and creative with NDS implementation. For example, you can perform the following tasks:

- Install NetWare 5.1 a bunch of times
- Design and build the ACME NDS tree
- Test the NDS compatibility of existing and new applications
- Merge multiple trees
- Manage NDS partitions and replicas
- Run login scripts
- Invent a new flavor of silicon-based ice cream

This kind of experience is invaluable — it can't be taught. The lessons you learn in the lab help you avoid major mistakes during the pilot and full-blown implementations. The lab experience allows you to learn how NetWare 5.1 operates within a subset of ACME. More importantly, the lab is a safe haven where you can experiment with strange modifications and view the impact of these changes on the NDS tree.

Your lab should consist of at least four nodes: two NetWare 5.1 servers and two workstations. The servers and adapter cards should be similar to the hardware that will be used in your network environment. If you are planning to upgrade your hardware, then use the new hardware in your lab environment. Each NetWare 5.1 server should exceed, if possible, the minimum hardware requirements recommended by Novell.

For the ACME site, lab testing is being handled at the NORAD facility in the Labs division. This facility evaluates all new software and hardware before deploying them in the production network. Figure 11.5 shows the ACME lab being used for testing NetWare 5.1 for the entire ACME tree installation.

FIGURE 11.5

The ACME testing lab

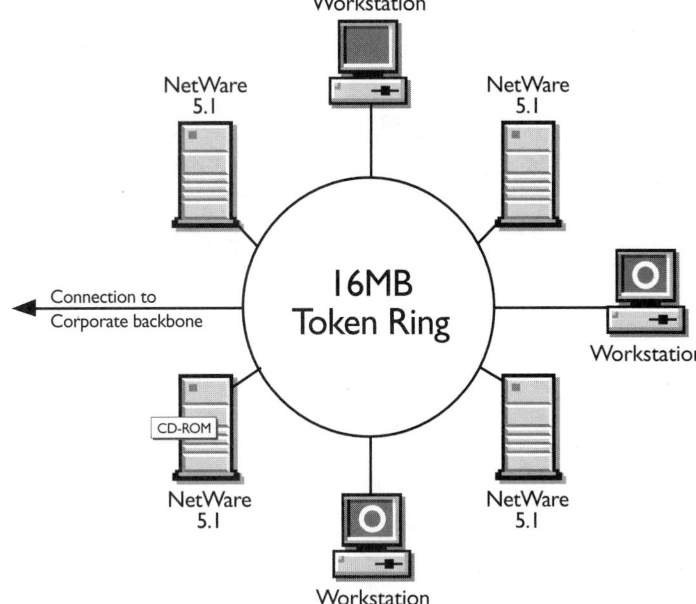

The ACME testing lab shown in Figure 11.5 has four dedicated NetWare 5.1 servers and three workstations for running the Novell and third-party utilities. Also, because the ACME network is primarily Token Ring, we have a Token Ring concentrator in the lab to connect the servers and workstations. All file servers have a CD-ROM drive, as well as sufficient disk and memory capacity. The lab ring also has a connection to the corporate backbone located in the Labs division of NORAD.

The purpose of any laboratory is to run experiments. ACME's testing lab is no different. ACME scientists are performing five interesting, new experiments even as we speak:

- *Experiment 1* — Hardware Installation
- *Experiment 2* — NDS Implementation
- *Experiment 3* — Testing Login Scripts
- *Experiment 4* — Testing Applications
- *Experiment 5* — Testing Backup and Restore Procedures

Once you have completed all of the testing lab experiments, you must take them into the real world. This involves a comprehensive pilot program.

ACME Pilot Program

Now you are almost ready for prime time. Before you can attack the ACME implementation head-on, you should consider testing your lab results on a small branch of the overall tree. The pilot program serves as a dress rehearsal before you move into full-scale migration.

In ACME's case, the pilot program will accomplish the following:

- Give the project team a chance to practice its implementation procedures
- Provide a live blueprint for full-scale client and server migration
- Provide more accurate feedback for application compatibility
- Give insight into how users react to NDS and the new logical network resources
- Gather valuable performance data for fine-tuning partitioning, replica, and time synchronization designs

We will start in the OU=LABS container because the scientists are more sympathetic to our experiments. In this case, we will migrate three pilot servers (LABS-SRV1, R&D-SRV1, and WHI-SRV1), two HP4SI printers, a print server (R&D-PS1), and all the administrative users under OU=LABS. This includes AEinstein, LDaVinci, CDarwin, MCurie, INewton, CBabbage, and Ada.

Refer to Task 9 of the ACME Implementation Matrix in Appendix D for more details. Speaking of schedules, let's stay on track and move forward to the center of NDS implementation—the schedule.

ACME Implementation Schedule

The ACME implementation schedule is a detailed blueprint for NDS rollout. It provides granular, measurable tasks that you can perform during ACME implementation. The main focus of the implementation schedule is the tasks and their associated subtasks. These become the focus of your Implementation Matrix (see Appendix D).

The focus of the schedule is a detailed time line with key milestones. The schedule helps you establish the proper timing and helps to organize all the NDS implementation tasks. The schedule also helps you track the status of the ACME project, and it can provide immediate feedback to your staff and management.

The Implementation Matrix (see Appendix D) consists primarily of a set of charts, each with a task description, its subtasks, guidelines, duration, start and end dates, percent completion, and task lead (person). If possible, the matrices should show the interdependencies of the tasks, measure progress, review work, and produce reports for management. Finally, be sure to update the matrices daily until the project is finished.

As you can see from the dates in Table D.10 of Appendix D, we've included a significant cushion in the rollout schedule. Even though the project theoretically takes only 21 weeks, the 21 weeks doesn't take into account scheduling conflicts, traveling, and Murphy's Laws. So, add another 25 percent to the total duration, and we should finish the ACME implementation on September 28, 2002. No sweat, now all we have to do is *just do it!*

Here is a quick overview of the ten tasks in ACME's implementation schedule:

- *Task 1* — Project Scope
- *Task 2* — Training
- *Task 3* — NDS Implementation
- *Task 4* — Security and Auditing
- *Task 5* — Client Migration
- *Task 6* — Server Migration
- *Task 7* — Printing Migration
- *Task 8* — Application Migration

- *Task 9* — Pilot Program
- *Task 10* — Rollout!

REAL WORLD

For a detailed example of ACME's implementation charts, task descriptions, responsible parties, and suggested NDS rollout timelines, study the schedules and matrices offered in Appendix D. This is a critical resource in planning your own NDS rollout.

Well, we finally made it! This completes Step 3 — NDS implementation.

More importantly, this completes Part II of this book, "NDS Design and Implementation" (Novell Course 575). In Part II, we expanded our NetWare 5.1 LAN into the realm of global NDS connectivity, and we mastered the first three steps in building a network: NDS preparation, NDS design, and NDS implementation.

In the first step, we gathered ACME data and built a project team. Then, in the second step, we constructed ACME's NDS tree with the help of naming standards, tree design guidelines, partitioning, time synchronization, and resource accessibility. Finally, in the third step, covered in this chapter, we built a testing lab and rolled out NDS using a ten-task implementation schedule.

Wow . . . Are we having fun yet?!

Have no fear, the remaining 11 chapters of this book are dedicated to keeping ACME running — NetWare Troubleshooting (Novell Course 580) and Networking Technologies (Novell Course 565). In Part III, "Service and Support" (Novell Course 580), we will experience a four-part boot camp in troubleshooting NICs, hard drives, workstations, and printing. In addition, we will build a troubleshooter bag full of tools and learn some preventative techniques for server fitness and network optimization.

It's time for "Service and Support" . . . *see ya there!!*

LAB EXERCISE 11.1: IMPLEMENTING ACME'S NDS DESIGN

Use the hints provided to find the 20 NDS implementation terms hidden in this word search puzzle. Omit any punctuation characters (such as blank spaces, hyphens, and so on) and spell out any numbers.

I	S	U	X	C	I	D	S	S	I	I	V	T	S	B	E
M	E	M	E	K	J	Z	Q	N	X	F	S	I	K	D	D
P	R	I	N	T	I	N	G	V	U	K	F	E	N	H	O
L	V	L	C	Y	A	U	V	P	L	L	Y	D	H	Z	L
E	E	Q	Y	H	T	E	S	T	I	N	G	L	A	B	R
M	R	U	I	H	Y	L	R	D	U	U	W	E	U	O	X
E	M	P	D	S	O	U	R	C	E	T	R	E	E	P	R
N	B	I	N	D	E	R	Y	S	E	R	V	I	C	E	S
T	R	A	I	N	I	N	G	R	D	L	T	R	O	I	F
A	S	T	C	Y	U	O	K	T	H	V	C	U	Z	Q	X
T	H	S	L	K	T	H	L	Y	C	L	E	A	N	U	P
I	B	Z	Z	T	U	T	R	K	I	L	X	U	L	G	K
O	B	C	K	D	T	P	J	J	S	P	I	N	M	Y	H
N	S	C	H	E	M	A	M	A	N	A	G	E	R	E	N
Z	O	F	F	L	I	N	E	T	E	S	T	I	N	G	Y
B	F	H	N	S	P	E	B	T	V	Q	A	X	J	T	F

Hints

1. NDS property that lists trustees of an object.
2. Important strategy that should be designed and implemented before a disaster occurs, rather than after.
3. A two-dimensional view of the 3-D NDS world.
4. The primary focus of Step 4 of the DSMERGE NDS tree merging process.
5. This type of migration is Task 5 in the implementation schedule.
6. Partition operation that involves splitting an existing one.
7. Process of executing planned NDS tasks.

8. Primary benefit provided by the testing lab.
9. This type of migration is Task 7 in the NDS Implementation schedule.
10. NDS Manager component that can be used to confirm that schemas are synchronized.
11. This type of migration is Task 6 in the NDS Implementation schedule.
12. This tree's Administrator wins in the battle for [S] object rights during an NDS tree merge.
13. Provides a non-production environment for testing hardware installation, NDS implementation, login scripts, network applications, and backup and restore procedures.
14. Critical network-related task that is often given inadequate attention and funding.
15. A plan for integrating User NDS access requirements during NDS Implementation.

See Appendix C for answers.

LAB EXERCISE 11.2: NDS IMPLEMENTATION

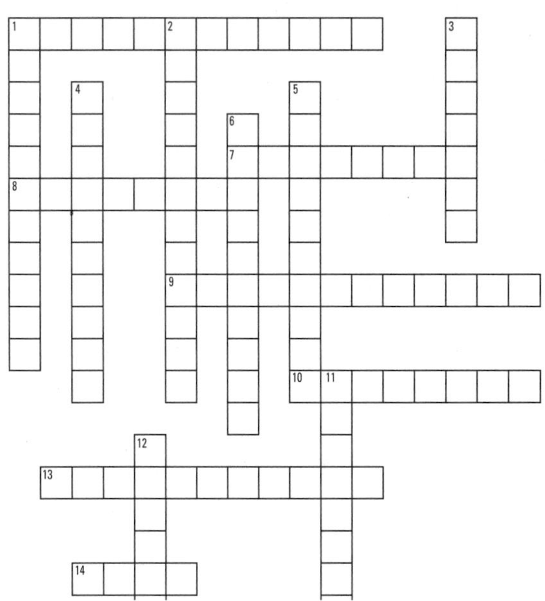

Across

1. Starts out with a small group
7. Fixing a broken tree
8. Copies of partitions
9. Step 3 of the DSMERGE NDS tree merging process
10. Task 4 of the NDS Implementation schedule
13. Where you indicate the Bindery Services context
14. Only partition created automatically

Down

1. The DSMERGE process starts here
2. Task 1 of the NDS Implementation schedule
3. Utility for combining trees
4. The final task in Step 4 of the DSMERGE NDS tree merging process
5. Pieces of the NDS tree

6. Windows-based utility for managing NDS partitions
11. Step 2 of the merge process
12. Final task in the implementation schedule

See Appendix C for answers.

PART III

Service and Support

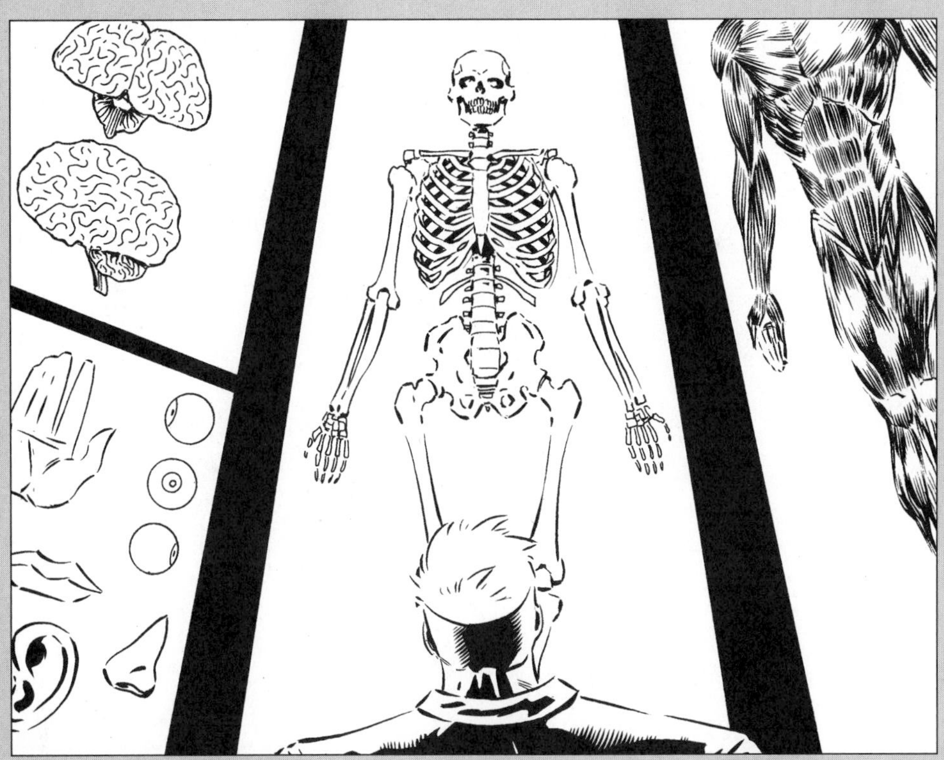

CHAPTER 12

Troubleshooting Fundamentals

As a network administrator, it is your responsibility to provide service and support for your users and your network equipment. In this chapter, *service and support* is defined as configuring and installing hardware and/or software and troubleshooting hardware and/or software problems for NetWare networks.

These service and support responsibilities include the following categories:

- Installing, configuring, and upgrading hardware (such as network boards, hard disks, and drive controllers)
- Installing, configuring, and upgrading server and other network software
- Troubleshooting network problems

The purpose of troubleshooting is to determine the cause of a problem and to implement a timely solution. A problem is not considered solved until the problem is no longer negatively impacting the user and the user is satisfied with the solution. The key to troubleshooting is developing the ability to break a problem into smaller parts and to discover the interrelationships between those parts. This ability helps you to efficiently isolate and resolve network problems.

The NetWare Troubleshooting Model

Novell's NetWare Troubleshooting Model is a useful tool for troubleshooting and resolving network problems. In this model, Step 1 involves utilizing quick-fix techniques (which often require little effort and minimal cost). If quick fixes do not work, you can move on to Step 2, where you gather more data (which may involve the use of diagnostic tools and network documentation). Once you have gathered sufficient data, you can move on to Step 3, where you develop a plan to isolate the problem and resolve it. After you have a plan in place, you can move on to Step 4, where you execute the plan and test the results. If the results prove unsatisfactory, you will need to further analyze the situation and create a new plan. If the results are acceptable, you can move on to Step 5, where you ensure user satisfaction. Finally, in Step 6, you record a detailed description of the problem and its solution in your documentation log.

To summarize, the six steps of the NetWare Troubleshooting Model are as follows (see Figure 12.1):

- Step 1: Try a Quick Fix
- Step 2: Gather Basic Information
- Step 3: Develop a Plan of Attack
- Step 4: Execute the Plan
- Step 5: Ensure User Satisfaction
- Step 6: Document the Solution

FIGURE 12.1

The six-step NetWare Troubleshooting Model

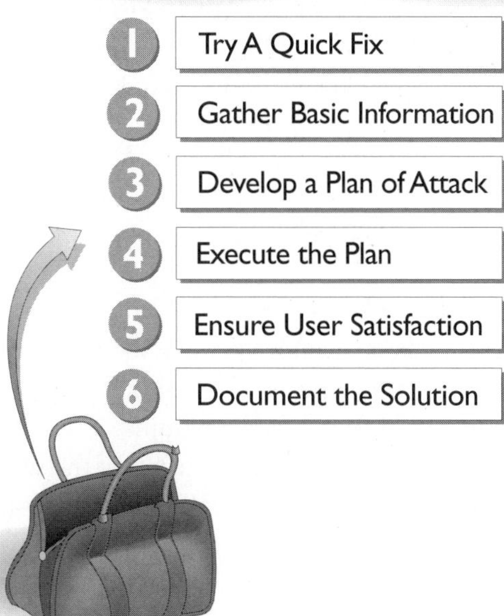

Step 1: Try a Quick Fix

As you gain experience with the NetWare troubleshooting process, you will begin to build a repertoire of common problems and their solutions. While the solution to some problems will be quite simple, the solution to others may be complex. In a complex case, you may find that you need to implement a temporary solution to restore service while working on a more complete solution.

Listed below are some quick fixes you can try before resorting to the remaining steps in the NetWare Troubleshooting Model:

- *Getting Started* — If hard disks are involved, be sure to back up the data and verify the backup before proceeding. Also, consider turning everything off and back on.

- *Eliminate User Error* — Next, ask yourself a simple question, "Who says it's broken?" All troubleshooting calls must come from someone. It's also helpful to understand the personalities and work habits of users, whenever possible. Many times, a user may exaggerate or misdiagnose a problem. The user may also leave out important details if the user feels that he or she has done something foolish or something that violates company policy. You should attempt to eliminate the possibility of user error by testing things yourself. If everything works fine, be sure to educate the user before you leave. This should help decrease follow-up calls.

- *Check the Inventory* — Be sure all the necessary hardware and software components are accounted for and configured correctly. For example, are all the cables plugged into the appropriate network components?

- *Simplify* — Simplify the system by removing unnecessary elements. For example, consider freeing up workstation memory and simplifying the operating environment by preventing the loading of device drivers and terminate-and-stay-resident programs (TSRs). On DOS and Windows 3.1 machines, you can prevent execution of the workstation's AUTOEXEC.BAT and CONFIG.SYS files by pressing F5 at startup.

  On Windows 95/98 workstations, you can load Windows in "safe mode" by pressing F8 at startup and then selecting option 3. (Safe mode starts Windows with no attached devices, no network support, and default settings.) Windows NT workstations present a startup menu, by default, with the following safe mode option: "Windows NT Workstation Version 4.00 [VGA mode]." Finally, you can remove expansion slot boards, one at a time, in an attempt to determine conflicts.

- *Software Anomalies* — When a software problem occurs, you will need to determine if any error messages are present, which version of the software is installed, known compatibility issues, and the availability of updates and/or patches. Both the Internet and the Novell Support Connection are good resources. (**Note:** Novell Technical Support will not handle your call if you have not applied all of the latest patches.) Before installing a new update or new patches, you should attempt to determine if there are any known problems associated with them. Check the accompanying README file and Novell Support Connection forums for important information. Even though installing an update or patches usually enhances performance, it may also cause new problems that didn't exist previously.
- *Insufficient Trustee Rights* — If one application runs successfully but another application does not, or if some users can run an application but others cannot — confirm that any user who is experiencing problems has been granted the appropriate trustee rights.

REAL WORLD

During Step 1 of the NetWare Troubleshooting Model, you may want to load a Windows 95/98 or Windows NT/2000 workstation in "simplified" mode. This is accomplished in Windows 95/98 by pressing F8 at startup and choosing any of the following options:

- Press 3 — Starts Windows 95/98 in safe mode with default settings, no network support, and no device drivers.
- Press 4 — Starts Windows 95/98 in safe mode with default settings, no device drivers, but still connected to the network.

Continued

Continued

- Press 5—Starts Windows 95/98 with line-by-line confirmation of every startup step.
- Press 6—Bounces you to the DOS prompt for manual startup.

Simplified startup is accomplished in the Windows NT environment by choosing the following option at startup:

- "Windows NT Workstation Version 4.00 [VGA mode]"

Step 2: Gather Basic Information

If quick fixes do not work, the next step is to collect relevant data. This occurs during the data-gathering phase of troubleshooting. During this phase, you should compile the following types of information:

- *List of Symptoms*—Develop a detailed list, including symptoms and affected users. Try to determine if the problem is unique to a single user, a particular group of users, or all network users. Also, attempt to ascertain when and under what conditions the symptoms occur.
- *Analyze Network Communications*—Determine if the problem is communications related (for example, if the problem only occurs during peak LAN utilization periods). You can use a protocol analyzer (such as LANalyzer for Windows) to track network bandwidth and to uncover communications-related anomalies.
- *Server Configuration Issues*—If a server is abending, Config Reader can be used to analyze information stored in CONFIG.TXT and to recommend a course of action. (**Note:** CONFIG.TXT must first be created by CONFIG.NLM, which can be downloaded from `support.novell.com`.)
- *Check Documentation*—In Step 6, we will discuss the importance of creating and maintaining good troubleshooting-related documentation. However, now, for Step 2, you will need to utilize this documentation to help isolate the problem and determine possible solutions. You can also use network logbooks to track current LAN usage against normal baseline values.

Be sure to document specific details about what users were doing at the time the problems occurred.

- *User Groups* — User groups, Usenet groups, and online forums are excellent sources of troubleshooting information. Two of the more popular network user groups are NetWare Users International (NUI) and Network Professional Association (NPA).

- *Diagnostic Tools* — Diagnostic tools provide information about your system that can help you isolate problems and solve them. Before choosing a diagnostic tool, be sure that it is suitable for your particular network configuration. Also, be sure that it has an efficient user interface, that it meets your reporting requirements, and that adequate technical support is available.

Step 3: Develop a Plan of Attack

After you have gathered all of the diagnostic data required, the next task is to use the information you gathered, along with background knowledge you have of the LAN, to determine whether the problem is a result of operating system, application software, equipment, or user error.

Once you have determined the source of the problem, your next step is to develop a troubleshooting plan of attack. The best approach typically includes a combination of intuition and methodology. First, you should use your intuition to identify the top two or three most likely causes of the problem (that is, hypotheses), as well as to determine how long it will take to fix or eliminate each cause. Potential costs to keep in mind include technician time, parts, and equipment downtime.

Then you will need to develop a logical plan of attack for testing each hypothesis. Different strategies include prioritizing each hypothesis based on its likeliness as a cause of the problem or first attacking any hypotheses that can be tested quickly. For example, consider a problem with three possible solutions: Hypothesis A requires 2 hours with a 70 percent chance of success; Hypothesis B requires 1.5 hours with a 25 percent chance of success; and Hypothesis C requires 15 minutes with a 5 percent chance of success. In this example, the best way to proceed would be C, A, and then B.

Step 4: Execute the Plan

Once you have developed your troubleshooting plan, the next step is to execute it. Step 4 utilizes the following scientific approach:

- Break your plan (or each hypothesis) into small, easily testable components. For example, if the problem is an interruption of network traffic between two nodes (A and B), you might want to consider the following:
    - Network card in Node A is bad.
    - The cable segment to the backbone is experiencing problems carrying the signal.
    - The router going to the backbone is experiencing problems routing the signal.
    - The backbone itself is bad.
    - The router between the backbone and the cable segment for Node B is experiencing problems routing the signal.
    - The cable segment for Node B is experiencing problems carrying the signal.
    - The network board for Node B is faulty.
- Test each component by changing only one thing at a time. (Otherwise, you won't know which change solved the problem.)
- After you have finished testing each component, document your results, return the component to its original state, and then move on to the next test.
- Use only reliable test equipment, software, and procedures. If you use a faulty utility disk, for example, you may become more confused than when you started.
- Use forward, backward, or binary chaining to eliminate possible network communications problems. Be sure to use reliable test equipment, diagnostics, and/or software procedures. (After all, you don't want to exacerbate the problem during the troubleshooting process.)

When using forward or backward chaining, be consistent in your approach. Do not start at one end, test, and then move back to the other end. Be systematic and controlled as you move from the source device to the destination device (forward chaining) or from the destination device to the source device (backward chaining) until the problem is located. Alternately, you can use binary chaining, which allows you to start half way between the source device and destination device, isolate the problem to one of the halves, divided the isolated segment in half, repeat the process with the two new halves, and so on.

- Watch for blindspots (which occur when the tester does not realize something that is obvious). If you suspect a blind spot, try consulting a trusted colleague, or take a break and think of something else.

- If the plan is unsuccessful, access additional resources, such as the Novell Support Connection Web site at `http://support.novell.com`.

Step 5: Ensure User Satisfaction

Even when you find and resolve a network problem, it is not actually fixed until the user (and/or the user's manager) is satisfied. Although some users will be happy just knowing the problem has been solved, others will want a detailed explanation of the problem and solution, and/or training on how the network should work versus how it currently is working.

Also, verification that a problem has truly been fixed can be dependent on the nature of the problem. Some solutions, for example, may have to be monitored for hours (or days) to ensure success.

Step 6: Document the Solution

Documentation is a critical but often overlooked step in the NetWare Trouble shooting Model. Although solving a problem is important, many network problems reoccur. This means that those who do not learn from history are destined to repeat it. Whenever you discover a solution to a problem, record the problem and solution in your Problem Resolution Log. Conversely, whenever a problem arises, one of the first sources you should consult is the Problem Resolution Log.

Following are the three main aspects of network documentation:

- *Network Components*—You should document where all your network hardware and software is installed and how they are configured. This information forms the foundation of your network documentation.
- *History and Users*—Next, you should track how the network is being used and important events that have occurred.
- *Resources*—Finally, you should generate a list of resources for troubleshooting help, such as bulletin board systems (BBSs), Web sites, and technical-support phone numbers.

Network Components

Network component records form the core of your troubleshooting documentation. You should keep track of where everything is, how many components there are, how they are related, and who uses them. For example, you should keep track of the following five types of components:

- *LAN Diagram*—Two types of useful network maps are logical maps and physical maps. *Logical maps* are topology overviews that focus on internetworking devices and connecting workstations. Their purpose is to establish the relationship between these devices and to show the flow of data. *Physical maps*, on the other hand, show a spatial representation of where various components are located. These detailed graphics should indicate the location of all servers, workstations, printers, bridges, gateways, repeaters, and wiring centers, as well as users and user groups. This information enables you to quickly locate, for example, a particular server or workstation.
- *LAN Inventory*—It's important to maintain an up-to-date record of hardware, software, and peripherals used with your network. You may want to purchase software that maintains such records (such as SupportSource 2000).

In addition, you will want to document the following information:

- *Servers* — Server documentation should include a detailed inventory of both production and test servers, including information such as location, manufacturer, model number, operating system, hard disks, LAN cards, and other peripherals.
- *Clients* — Client documentation should include the number of workstations and the type of network interface cards (NICs) the workstations use. Client documentation should also include each workstation's configuration, processor speed, RAM, and its role on the network.
- *Internetworking Devices* — Repeaters, concentrators, bridges, routers, and gateways should all be well-documented, including information such as vendor, model, location, and general connections.
- *Cabling Diagram* — You'll want to ensure that you have an accurate record of the type(s) of cabling used in your network and its physical layout. This can be invaluable when attempting to solve cabling problems.
- *Spares* — The spares inventory is one of the most critical types of network documentation. It tells you what options are available during Steps 2, 3, and 4 of the NetWare Troubleshooting Model. Some network administrators may wonder if a spares inventory is really needed if you a have a maintenance contract. The answer depends on what kind of contract you have and how patient your users are. Some contracts specify that the customer is responsible for maintaining the spares inventory. Also, if you have mission-critical services going through your network, it is unlikely your users will be patient, and, thus, you may need to maintain a large spares inventory.

- *Chronological Change Log* — This log documents network modifications, such as hardware additions and deletions, software upgrades, and configuration changes.

REAL WORLD

Networks grow and change, but all too often their physical maps are never updated. It only takes a few minutes to update a map when a change is made to a physical network, and this is time well spent. When a system starts to give you headaches, the minutes you spent updating the map will save you hours trying to find components.

If you're managing a large LAN, consider replacing the paneling in your office with white boards. This way you can draw the physical map on one wall and the logical map on the other. Every potential change can be updated immediately, and the components will be easily identifiable. This strategy also gives you a chance to play with colored markers.

History and Users

An accurate, detailed record of your LAN's history can help you solve current problems and prevent future catastrophes. One of the most important aspects of a LAN history is a solid understanding of the business environment and the users on the LAN. This area of network documentation focuses on four main concerns:

- *LAN Utilization* — LAN utilization information documents who the customers are and what services the LAN provides to them. It also outlines where LAN utilization problems have occurred in the past.
- *Change Order Log* — The basic goals of a Change Order Log are to maintain trend information on various systems and to document equipment repairs. This log adds accountability to changes made to the network. At a minimum, you may want to maintain a record of what has occurred over the past two years, including a description of problems and solutions, the location of problems (that is, the segment on which the situations occurred), and a record of incurred downtimes. You may also want to maintain a record of ongoing performance analysis for devices such as printers and routers.

- *General Business Model*—You should record the business purpose of your network, paying particular attention to how the network benefits the people who paid for it. When considering upgrades, they should be measured against this model. This is also a good place to record your company's mission statement, so you can ensure that the network is serving the organization's business interests as a whole.

- *User Data*—User data should include enough information to help you characterize different network users. For example, you may want to list usernames, a description of how each user utilizes the network, the servers they access, and training records. This documentation can be useful in helping you isolate problems and/or justifying equipment upgrades.

- *Baseline Information*—Maintaining baseline information can be useful for troubleshooting purposes. For example, you may want to maintain baseline statistics relating to CPU use, network traffic, bandwidth use, errors, and other information regarding how the network functions under normal conditions.

REAL WORLD

A good rule of troubleshooting is that there is no such thing as a coincidence. Often, changes made to solve one problem cause another problem to appear the next day. This is when the Change Order Log comes in. Always suspect the last changes made to a network as the causes of a new problem. The Change Order Log is an invaluable tool to help you zero in on high-probability suspects when trying to resolve a problem. Note, too, that the problem is sometimes the result of cumulative changes, not just the most recent change. Adding too many stations to an Ethernet LAN, for example, causes contention problems, but the resulting slow-down cannot be blamed on the last station added.

Resources

Resource documentation is usually relatively easy to maintain. The easiest way to store it is as ASCII data on a host file server, although this may not be the most useful method. For those with documentation flair, a database program or a spreadsheet can be employed for fast searching and sorting. You may also want to check out the inventory features available in the Novell ManageWise and ZEN works products. Regardless of how you store the resource list, be sure to update it carefully and to print a hard copy at least every other week (unless no changes have been made).

You'll want to keep track of the following two types of resources:

- *Technology Documentation* — Make sure you have access to important technical documentation before it is needed, including information about protocols, routing, and LAN architecture.
- *Technical Support* — It's important to maintain information relating to key technical-support contacts (including phone numbers and business hours) for the various products that you use. You'll also want to maintain a list of useful Internet Web sites and bulletin board numbers.

TIP

You should also ensure that serial numbers are included in your resource list. When you have a problem, tech support may require a serial number or license information. If the data is located on the same list as the phone numbers, then the matter can often be handled more quickly and easily than if you cannot find the information.

Another good reason to document problems and their solutions is that documentation can uncover troubleshooting patterns. For example, you may find that a batch of NICs is bad or that flaky power in one part of the building is damaging equipment. Being able to identify a pattern allows you to take *proactive* rather than *reactive* measures, therefore, avoiding network problems before they occur.

Implementing proactive strategies involves attempting to avoid or prepare for recurrence. Try these proactive strategies:

- If a component keeps burning out, either install a cooling fan or keep a supply of replacement parts on hand.

- Test the system on a regular basis, even if it is not experiencing problems. Make sure you use only up-to-date virus scanning and network performance-monitoring software. To ensure that tests are accurate, periodically introduce problems into the network in a controlled manner prior to testing. (**Note:** During such tests, consider using Config Reader to analyze the information.) Make sure that all team members are aware of the importance of this testing and that they properly document it.
- Maintain an up-to-date network map and floor plan to help spot potential problems.
- Keep handy copies of important Technical Information Documents (TIDs) and other vendor-supplied documentation.

Diagnostic Software

Diagnostic software can be useful for providing information about your network, as well as for isolating and solving problems. Various types of shareware, freeware, and commercial diagnostic packages are available at varying price and quality levels. Some programs, however, are incompatible with specific hardware and/or software configurations.

For example, Microsoft Diagnostics (MSD) is a fairly complete system diagnostic tool that is available for systems that use MS-DOS 6.2 and later. Similar information is available in Windows using the Device Manager tab under the System icon in the Control Panel. Windows also provides a System Information Tool that can be accessed by selecting Start ⇨ Accessories ⇨ System Tools ⇨ System Information.

Popular commercially available, third-party software applications include CheckIT, PC Doctor, and PC Clinic. Finally, shareware diagnostic utilities can be located at the `http://users.powernet.co.uk/sysserv/page146.html` Web site or by accessing `http://www.google.com` and searching for "shareware diagnostics."

Consider the following factors when evaluating diagnostic software for purchase:

- Compatibility with your particular hardware configuration
- Easy to use interface
- Satisfactory reporting capabilities
- Adequate and timely technical support

Some of the diagnostic tool capabilities you may require include the ability to furnish the following:

- Hardware and operating system information (which is useful for record-keeping purposes)
- Inventory of internal computer components, such as processor type, BIOS date, and amount of RAM
- Information needed for detecting and avoiding hardware incompatibilities, such as I/O addresses, memory addresses, and IRQs (hardware interrupts)
- System information relating to device drivers and TSRs (which is useful for determining software conflicts)
- Compatibility information associated with hardware and peripheral devices and with expansion boards you want to install.

You may need diagnostic tools that provide the following additional capabilities:

- View and edit complementary metal oxide semiconductor (CMOS) info-rmation. (This type of utility can be useful for protecting a computer's CMOS against battery loss and for restoring CMOS information to other machines with the same configuration. The latter capability is particularly useful in large networks that contain many nodes with identical configurations.)

- Generate system performance benchmarks (which enable you to evaluate your system and to compare your system to other systems)
- Run hardware diagnostic tests on components, such as hard disks, diskette drives, system boards, serial and parallel ports, and RAM.
- Supply performance enhancement capabilities, such as the following:
  - *Uninstall Utility* — Identifies and deletes files associated with Windows applications that are no longer needed
  - *Cleanup Utility* — Removes unnecessary files
  - *Memory Tune-up Utility* — Consolidates Windows memory fragments and increases the "largest memory block available"
- Provide compatibility with other diagnostic software.

NetWare Troubleshooting Tools

Following are three useful research tools that can be used in conjunction with the NetWare Troubleshooting Model:

- *SupportSource 2000* — SupportSource 2000 consists of technical databases that contain system board, hard drive, NIC, and I/O parameters. These third-party information databases (infobases) include diagrams and documentation covering jumper settings, memory configurations, connectors, and specifications for thousands of internal hardware components.
- *Novell Internet Services* — Novell information can be accessed via the Internet at the following sites: Novell's home Web site, the Novell Support Connection Web site, and Novell's FTP sites.
- *Novell Support Connection* — The *Novell Support Connection* CD is a technical infobase that provides a searchable engine for offline access to NetWare problems and solutions.

SupportSource 2000

SupportSource 2000 is an electronic-reference library product developed by EarthWeb Inc. This product, which is available by subscription in both CD-ROM and Web-based formats, can be used to find information on thousands of computer hardware-related questions. SupportSource 2000 provides a one-screen interface that contains data from technical information databases. As you can see in Figure 12.2, the database contents are divided into the following sections:

- Hard Drive Controller Cards
- Hard Drives
- Optical Drives
- Tape Drives
- Mainboards
- Data Communications Devices
- Telecommunications Devices
- Video Controller Cards
- Miscellaneous I/O Controller Cards
- Hardware Troubleshooting
- Database Management Systems
- Internet Technology
- Desktop Applications
- Distributed Applications
- Development Languages

- Networking
- Workstation Operating Systems

FIGURE 12.2

SupportSource 2000 main menu

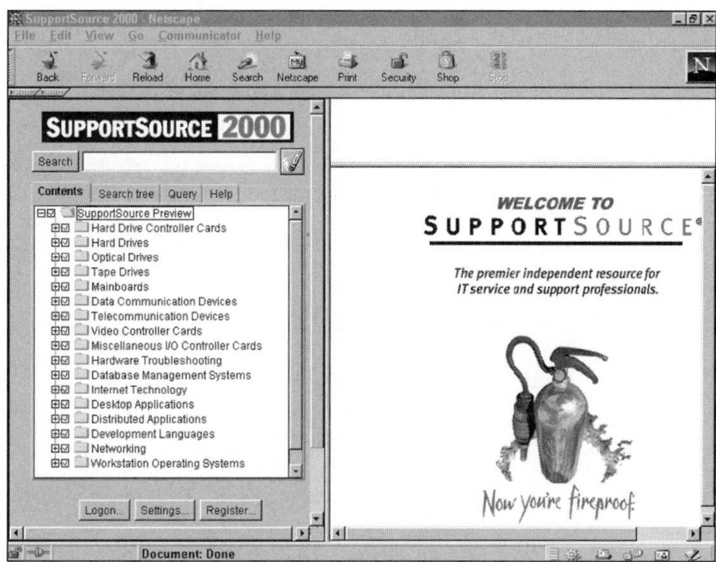

Each of these publications contains a large selection of useful background articles and reference pieces. For example, you might find a searchable annotated directory of manufacturers, a quick reference on setting node IDs, an appendix specifying cabling for various topologies, an article describing solutions to common disk problems, or a comprehensive searchable glossary of modems, hard disks, and networking terms.

Even though not every board is represented, SupportSource 2000 is still a useful tool for troubleshooting purposes. This product, which is updated quarterly, has the following requirements: Internet access and Internet Explorer 4.0 or Netscape 4.08 or later, with Java enabled.

The SupportSource 2000 interface contains three main frames:

- *The Search/Query Frame* — In this frame, you can navigate the contents (which are organized in the form of a data tree), enter database search terms, and perform queries using the Query Assistant.

- *The Document Selector Frame* — In this frame, you can view either the main document, a summary, or manufacturer information.
- *The Document Viewer Frame* — In this frame, you can scroll up or down to view the summary of or the entire body of a document that you have selected. For example, Figure 12.3 shows a document containing a diagram of a Fast Ethernet XL (3C905B-TX) network interface card (NIC).

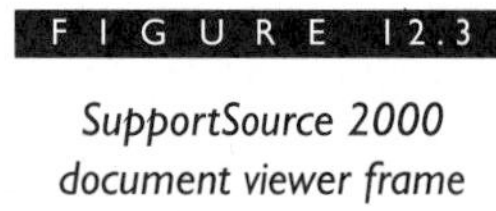

FIGURE 12.3

SupportSource 2000 document viewer frame

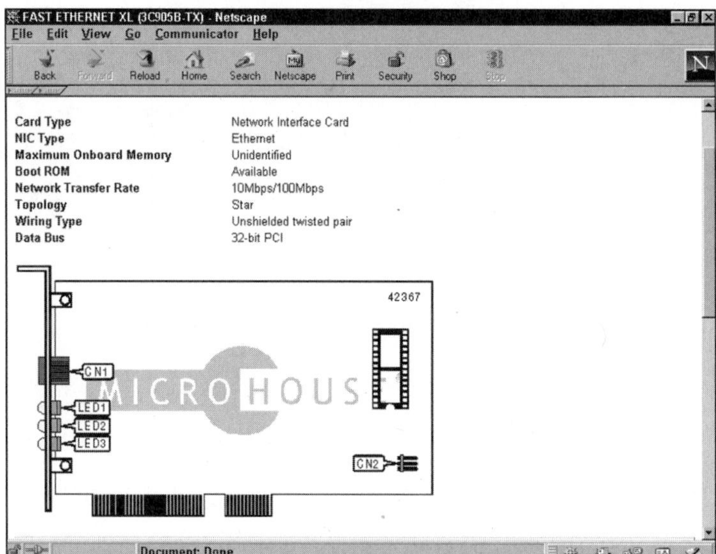

The SupportSource 2000 interface provides these search capabilities:

- *Browse the Data Tree* — Enables you to manually search for a document in the Data Tree.
- *Create a Query* — Allows you to manually enter a search statement in the Search/Query frame. You can then designate that the entire document, or only a portion of it, be searched. Be careful when using this option, as you are likely to wind up with far more information than you probably want. To solve this problem, you can use the Query Assistant to guide you through creating and executing a query. These forms provide valuable tools for "filtering" unwanted pieces of information.

- *Query Assistant* — Helps you construct a query. After you select the Query tab in the Search/Query frame to activate the search engine, the Query Assistant helps you select criteria for the search. An example is shown in Figure 12.4.

FIGURE 12.4

SupportSource 2000 Query Assistant

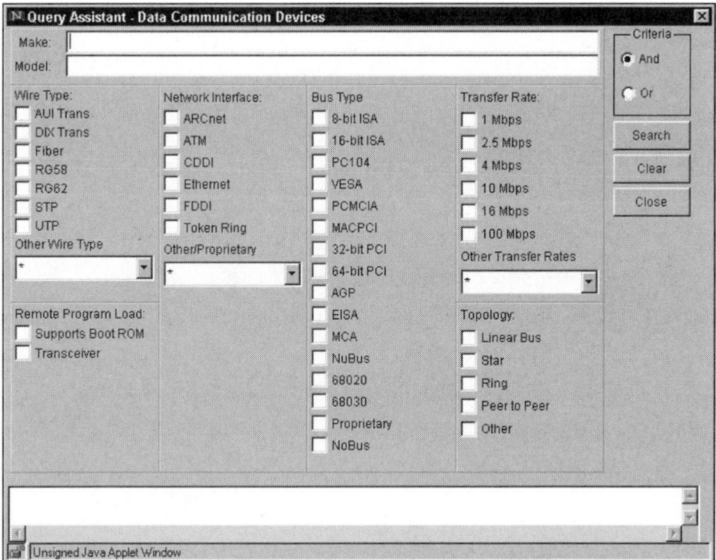

Novell Internet Services

Novell's Internet sites provide you with the technical information, resources, and contact information you need to help you manage and troubleshoot your network effectively. For example, these sites provide access to Novell company information, product information (including the *Novell Buyer's Guide*), press releases, and information about events and promotions. Other resources available include network services, technical support (including Technical Information Documents [TIDs], and hardware and software bulletins from Novell Labs), downloadable files (including files, patches, and fixes), and user forums. Finally, these Web sites list information about training and services, partners and developers, and Year 2000 issues.

To navigate Novell's Internet sites, you will need an Internet browser, such as Netscape Communicator or Microsoft Internet Explorer. You will also need reliable Internet access (using either a direct or dial-up modem connection) through an Internet Service Provider (ISP).

After you have installed and configured your browser, TCP/IP (if used), and communications parameters, you can access Novell Internet Services at the following sites:

- *Novell's Internet Support Connection Web site* (`http://support.novell.com`)—The Novell Support Connection site is an important source of Novell technical information. (Refer to the Novell Support Connection home page in Figure 12.5.) It contains much of the information found on the *Novell Support Connection* CD, including TIDs, manuals, an extensive library of downloadable files (including the most recent patches and drivers), and customer and partner options. This site also gives you access to the latest Novell product information, press releases, networking tips, technical bulletins from Novell Labs, and a complete set of AppNotes (available by subscription). Finally, it provides access to product support forums that allow you to post technical questions that are answered by system operators (SysOps) and other forum participants. (**Note:** This Web site contains the information that is most relevant to Novell Course 580, "Service and Support.")

- *Novell's Home Page* (`http://www.novell.com`)—Novell's home page provides Internet access to a wealth of technical information, including the following familiar categories: Products, Technical Support, Partners, Developers, Company Information, Training and Services, Promotions and Events, and File Downloads.

- *Novell's FTP Sites* (`ftp://ftp.novell.com`) *and* (`ftp://ftp.novell.de`)—Novell also provides anonymous access to two File Transfer Protocol (FTP) server sites. One is located in the United States (`ftp://ftp.novell.com`) and the other in Germany (`ftp://ftp.novell.de`). You can use your Web browser or a dedicated FTP client to access the FTP servers. Most publicly accessible FTP servers allow anonymous access. When you log into an anonymous FTP server, you will be prompted for a username and password. Proper Internet etiquette requires you to enter "anonymous" at the login prompt and your Internet e-mail address at the password prompt. This allows FTP server administrators to get some idea about the type of users who access their site.

FIGURE 12.5

The Novell Internet Support Connection home page

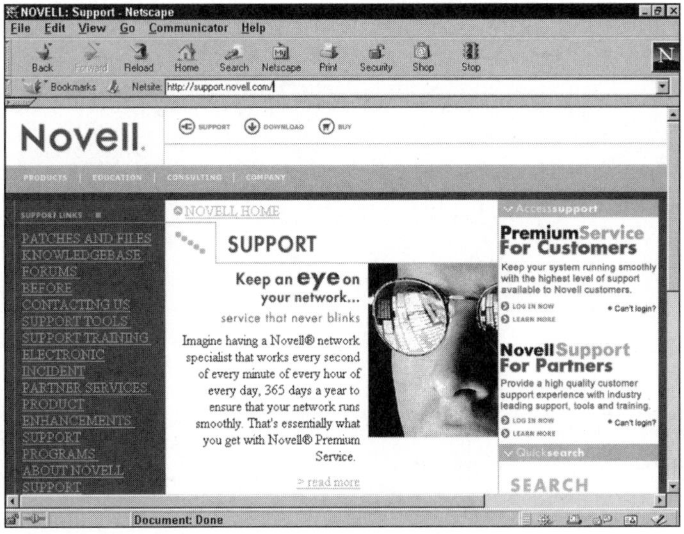

Novell Support Connection

The *Novell Support Connection* CD is an electronic infobase that contains the technical information you need to install, maintain, and troubleshoot NetWare networks. It also includes a powerful search engine called Folio Bound VIEWS. Using this engine, you can navigate through custom menus or perform a keyword search. You can also directly access files, patches, fixes, and software from the *Novell Support Connection* CD. Because it is a CD, however, the information contained is usually about a month behind what is currently available elsewhere.

Following are some of the types of searches you can perform using the *Novell Support Connection* CD (refer to Figure 12.6):

- Access a list of recent NetWare patches.
- Read a recent *Application Notes (AppNotes)* article on printing optimization.
- Find out if a Zenith Data Systems Model Z-241 will work with older versions of NetWare.
- Search for the term *Ethernet* in NetWare manuals.
- Find a local source for NetWare support.

- Find out where major Novell technical conferences are occurring around the world.
- Learn about the Novell Authorized Service Center program.
- Obtain information about Novell's certification programs, including CNE and Master CNE.
- Learn how to contact members of the Network Professional Association (NPA).

FIGURE 12.6

The Novell Support Connection *CD main menu*

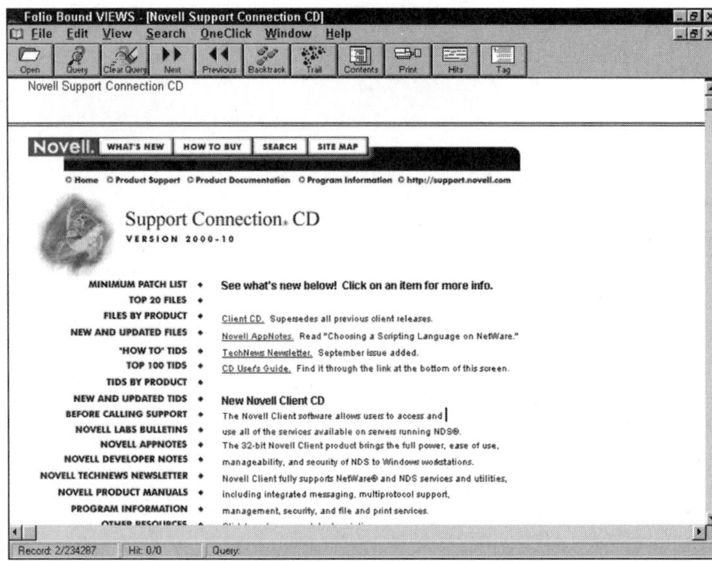

The *Novell Support Connection* CD contains several infobases that are organized according to their content. This organization helps you access valuable information in a hurry. Here's a list of what you can expect to find on the *Novell Support Connection* CD:

- *Network Systems Support* — Includes information on Novell operating systems, including NetWare 3.*x*, 4.*x*, 5.*x*, and intraNetWare. This is where most of the troubleshooting information resides.

- *GroupWare Support* — Includes information on Novell GroupWare products, including GroupWise.
- *Network TIDs* — Includes Technical Information Documents (TIDs) for NetWare operating system products. These documents have been authored by various Novell engineers and technicians, and they include a compilation of technical information from selected Novell support calls.
- *GroupWare TIDs* — Includes Novell GroupWare TIDs for GroupWise, SoftSolutions, and InForms products.
- *Novell Labs Bulletins* — Includes compatibility test results for various Novell and third-party hardware and software products. These tests are designed to certify Novell product compatibility with specific product configurations. These bulletins work in conjunction with other software testing reports to provide network administrators with third-party product compatibility information.
- *Novell Support Connection CD User's Guide* — Includes online documentation for optimizing your use of the *Novell Support Connection* CD.

The *Novell Support Connection* CD contains browsing and query windows that are similar to the windows in SupportSource. As you can see in Figure 12.6 earlier, the toolbar at the top of the main research screen contains 11 options for navigating, searching, and printing, and it allows one-click access to the tools and features you need the most. It can also be customized to fit your needs.

The *Novell Support Connection* CD engine also provides searching capabilities using folios and views. A *folio* is a record. For example, a description of NetWare 5 object types would be a folio. A *view* is a collection of folios. Because a view may not fit on a single screen, you may have to scroll through a view to display all of its component records.

The *Novell Support Connection* CD supports the following two types of searching:

- *Manual Navigation*—This is the most basic method of searching an infobase. You simply follow the book titles, topic headings, or icons to the information you need. Fortunately, the Folio search engine has been designed to make navigation simple and straightforward. This method is best for simple gross searches.

- *Query*—A Folio *query* is a more sophisticated method of searching for words or word patterns in an infobase. Using a query, you can perform text-based searches on an entire infobase or on selected portions only. As you can see in Figure 12.7, when you enter a query in the Query For box, a Results Map appears in the right pane, indicating the number of folios that contain the word(s) you are searching for. You can further refine folio queries by using a Boolean operator between two words or phrases. (A *phrase* consists of two or more words placed within quotation marks.) See Table 12.1 for a summary of common Boolean operators available in the Folio search engine. When you click OK, a Table of Contents (hit list) appears by default, listing each folio containing the word(s) you are searching for as well as the number of hits in that folio.

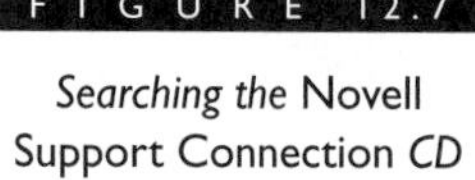
FIGURE 12.7

Searching the Novell Support Connection *CD*

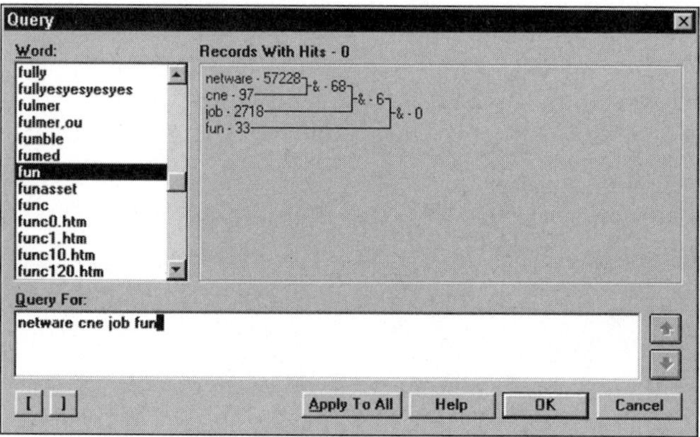

TABLE 12.1

Understanding Folio's Boolean Operators

TERM	OPERATOR	EXAMPLE	DESCRIPTION
AND	&	NetWare & CNE	This operator provide a list of records that contain *both* of the indicated words or phrases. In this example, we are searching for records that contain the words "CNE" *and* "NetWare." (**Note:** In a query, this operator accomplishes the same purpose as a space.)
OR	|	FDDI|ATM	This operator provides a list of records that contain *at least one* of the indicated words or phrases. In this example, we are searching for records containing the word "FDDI" *and/or* "ATM."
XOR	~	Token~Ring	This operator provides a list of records that contain *one* of the indicated words or phrases, *but not both*. In this example, we would locate records that contain the word "Token" or "Ring" *but not* "Token Ring."
NOT	^	NICS^Ethernet	This operator provides a list of records that contain *the first* word or phrase, *but not the second*. In this example, we would locate records that contain the word "NICs" *but not* "Ethernet." (**Note:** In a query, this operator is the inverse of the AND operator.)

Choosing the Appropriate Troubleshooting Tool

Refer to Table 12.2 for a comparison summary of the three troubleshooting tools we have discussed in this chapter: SupportSource 2000, Novell Internet Services, and the *Novell Support Connection* CD. Keep in mind that the same information is often available from multiple sources.

TABLE 12.2

Comparative Summary of NetWare Troubleshooting Tools

TOOL	ADVANTAGES	DISADVANTAGES
SupportSource 2000	Comprehensive central resource of hardware information. Excellent graphics. Both keyword and criteria searching.	Web-based subscription requires Internet access.
Novell Internet Services	Easy to use. Comprehensive. Provides up-to-date information. Two-way communication via newsgroups and mail lists.	Requires Internet access through an ISP.
Novell Support Connection CD	Easy to use. Unlimited usage for a one-time cost. Full-text database search engine. No modem required. Archive editions provide valuable resources.	Never entirely up-to-date. One-way communication.

LAB EXERCISE 12.1: TROUBLESHOOTING WITH NOVELL INTERNET SERVICES

Novell's Internet Services include the Novell corporate Web site, the Novell Support Connection Web site, and the Novell FTP site. In this exercise, we'll examine four real-world cases for using Novell's Internet Services. Therefore, to perform this exercise, you will need Internet access to various Novell Web sites.

Novell Internet Services — Case 1

Your (English-speaking) next-door neighbor just purchased a new Windows 95/98 workstation and needs the latest version of the Novell Client. Walk him through the steps for finding and downloading the appropriate file via the Internet so that he won't have to call you the next time he needs an updated copy of a file.

Novell Internet Services — Case 2

Rumors are circulating at the office about possible layoffs. You have checked the help wanted ads in the newspaper and noticed that many positions require a CNE. Access the Novell Education site on Novell's home page to get information on CNE certification requirements.

Novell Internet Services — Case 3

Your boss has asked if Novell offers pay-as-you-go technical support, and if so, whether the billing method is per minute or per incident. Access the Internet to find this information.

Novell Internet Services — Case 4

A colleague mentioned that she had seen a TID on the Web that discussed using DSREPAIR.NLM for weekly preventative maintenance tasks. Locate the TID.

See Appendix C for answers.

LAB EXERCISE 12.2: TROUBLESHOOTING WITH SUPPORTSOURCE 2000

SupportSource 2000 offers a set of technical databases containing system board, hard drive, network interface card, and I/O parameters. This third-party CD-ROM infobase includes diagrams and documentation covering jumper settings, memory configurations, connectors, and specifications for thousands of internal hardware components.

To perform this exercise, you will need Internet access to the SupportSource 2000 Web site.

Part I: Create a SupportSource 2000 Trial Account

To set up a seven-day trial account for SupportSource 2000, perform the following tasks:

1. Use a browser (such as Netscape Navigator or Internet Explorer) to access the SupportSource 2000 Web site at `http://www.supportsource.com`.
2. Click the link to create a trial account.
   a. At the bottom of the home page, click Subscribe.
   b. On the next screen, click "Click Here to Create a Trial Account."
3. Enter the required information and then click Send.
4. Click Accept to accept the terms and conditions in the user agreement.
5. Use the suggested username, enter a password, and then click Submit.
6. Review the "Product Preview and Known Limitations" information.
7. Click the "Click Here to Launch SupportSource 2000" link.
8. When the Logon window appears, enter your username and password.

Part II: Practice Using SupportSource 2000

When performing the following case studies, locate the information required and then document the steps you took and the reasoning for your decisions.

SupportSource 2000 — Case 1

A customer has requested that you install two 4MB SIMMs in Bank 0 of a Packard Bell 386SX computer. The system board has two unlabeled SIMM chip banks. Determine how to install the two 4MB SIMMs.

SupportSource 2000 — Case 2

A customer has a Micropolis 2112-15 Rev. 2 SCSI II drive. Determine where the jumper is located and how to set it to enable spindle synchronization.

TIP

Make sure you are adept at using SupportSource 2000 *before* you take the Service and Support exam! For example, you should be able to determine jumper settings for a particular NIC, Small Computer System Interface (SCSI) termination parameters, motherboard configurations, and the mean time between failure (MTBF) for a specified hard drive.

See Appendix C for answers.

LAB EXERCISE 12.3: CHOOSING THE APPROPRIATE TROUBLESHOOTING TOOL

Determine which of the following three tools in Table 12.3 can be used to find each type of information.

TABLE 12.3

Network Troubleshooting Tools

INFORMATION NEEDED	SUPPORTSOURCE 2000	NOVELL SUPPORT CONNECTION (INTERNET VERSION)	*NOVELL SUPPORT CONNECTION (CD-ROM VERSION)*
Application Notes			
Developer Notes			
Hard Drive Performance Specs			
I/O card Configuration Information			
Motherboard Memory Configurations			
NIC Jumper Settings			
Novell Labs			
Patches and Fixes			
Product Information			
Product Manuals			
Support Forums			
TIDs			

See Appendix C for answers.

LAB EXERCISE 12.4: NETWARE TROUBLESHOOTING

Use the hints provided to find the 20 troubleshooting fundamentals and tools terms hidden in this word search puzzle. Omit any punctuation characters (such as blank spaces, hyphens, and so on) and spell out any numbers.

Hints

1. Boolean operator that is represented by an "&".
2. Monthly publication for developers of NetWare applications.
3. A chunk of text and graphics that centers on a single purpose.
4. *Novell Support Connection* infobase that includes information on Novell GroupWare products, including GroupWise.
5. A picture of *how* data flows through your network.
6. Searching an infobase the hard way.
7. Boolean operator that is represented by an "^".
8. Boolean operator that is represented by a "|".
9. A picture of *where* data flows into your network.
10. *How To* documentation from Novell.

11. First step of the NetWare Troubleshooting Model.
12. Lounges for technical discussions.
13. An electronic reference library of infobases.
14. More of an art than a science.
15. Boolean operator that is represented by a "~".

See Appendix C for answers.

LAB EXERCISE 12.5: TROUBLESHOOTING FUNDAMENTALS AND TOOLS

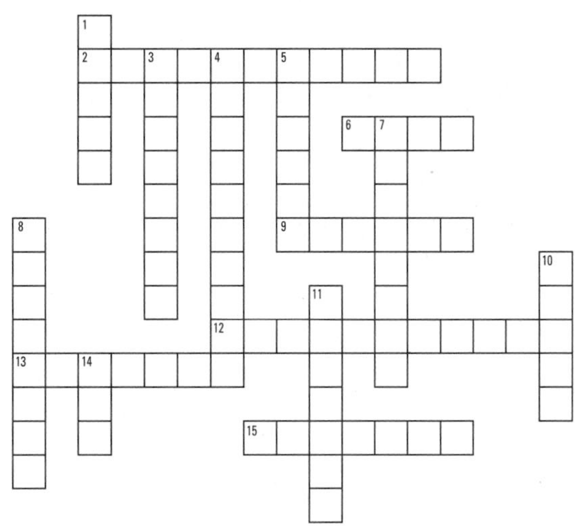

Across

2. Hardware problem-detection programs
6. A collection of folios
9. Forum moderators
12. Novell electronic products catalog
13. Software Band-Aids
15. Internet client interface

Down

1. Monthly source of tips and tricks
2. Internet client interface
3. Novell electronic products catalog
4. SupportSource 2000 "offline" delivery mechanism
5. Hardware problem-detection programs
6. Novell's is `www.novell.com`
7. A special type of searchable database
8. Item to search for
9. Test bulletin creators

10. Software Band-Aids
11. Easy way to search
12. Extra parts for emergencies
13. Forum moderators
14. Also known as Technical Information Document
15. A collection of folios

See Appendix C for answers.

CHAPTER 13

Troubleshooting NICs

An average conversation about network interface card (NIC) topology design can deteriorate quickly into an electronic Twilight Zone of IEEE 802 standards and interconnectivity buzzwords. More often than not, these specific elements are simply ingredients in a much larger, more important system. In Part IV of this book, "Networking Technologies," we will explore the conceptual technobabble that drives this network infrastructure.

For now, we are concerned with installing and troubleshooting the network. Fortunately for us, the networking world has settled on the following three major protocol/topology standards:

- Ethernet
- Token Ring
- FDDI

Before we dive into the troubleshooting fundamentals of NICs and cabling, we need to understand a little more about how these components work. We need to answer some fundamental questions: How do NICs and cabling connect to the server/workstation architecture? How are they arranged in specific topologies? What are the different types of NIC ports and how are they configured? And, finally, how do I deal with coaxial twisted-pair and fiber-optic cabling? After all, tin cans won't do you any good if the string is broken.

So, let's begin our discussion of the network infrastructure with an in-depth journey through NIC architecture and function.

Understanding NICs

Topology components form the framework of a network. They connect servers, workstations, and communications equipment (such as routers and gateways). Network topology components include server and workstation network interface cards (NICs), cabling, and supporting connectivity components (such as terminators, hubs, T-connectors, and transceivers).

In this chapter, we will discuss how to troubleshoot the three most popular topology architectures: Ethernet, token ring, and FDDI. But first, you will want to understand how the following topology components impact NIC troubleshooting:

- *Server/Workstation Architecture* — When choosing a NIC, it is important to know what type of PC bus architecture is used in the workstation or server. A *bus* is a common pathway or channel within a computer that connects two or more devices. An IBM-compatible computer contains several buses, including a processor bus (which provides a parallel data path between the CPU, memory, and peripheral buses), memory bus, I/O bus, and address bus.
- *Topologies* — To facilitate communication between computers, you must organize them in a specific layout, or *topology*. A topology defines the cabling layout and communication rules for a network.
- *NIC Ports* — A NIC serves as the electronic interface between the computer and the LAN cabling. The card includes an internal bus-specific edge connector and an external cabling port.
- *NIC Configuration* — Configuration information for your NIC may include some or all of the following parameters: IRQ (hardware interrupt), I/O address, memory address, and Direct Memory Access (DMA) support. If you install a manually configurable board, it is important to make sure that these parameters are set properly.
- *LAN Cabling* — Networks rely on cabling for connectivity, reliability, and speed. The three most common cabling types are coaxial, twisted pair, and fiber optic.

Internal communications focus on the server and workstation architecture and topology. External communications extend the internal bus to other machines with NIC ports, configurations, and LAN cabling. Refer to Figure 13.1 for an illustration of the two sides of LAN communications: internal and external.

FIGURE 13.1

Two sides of LAN communications

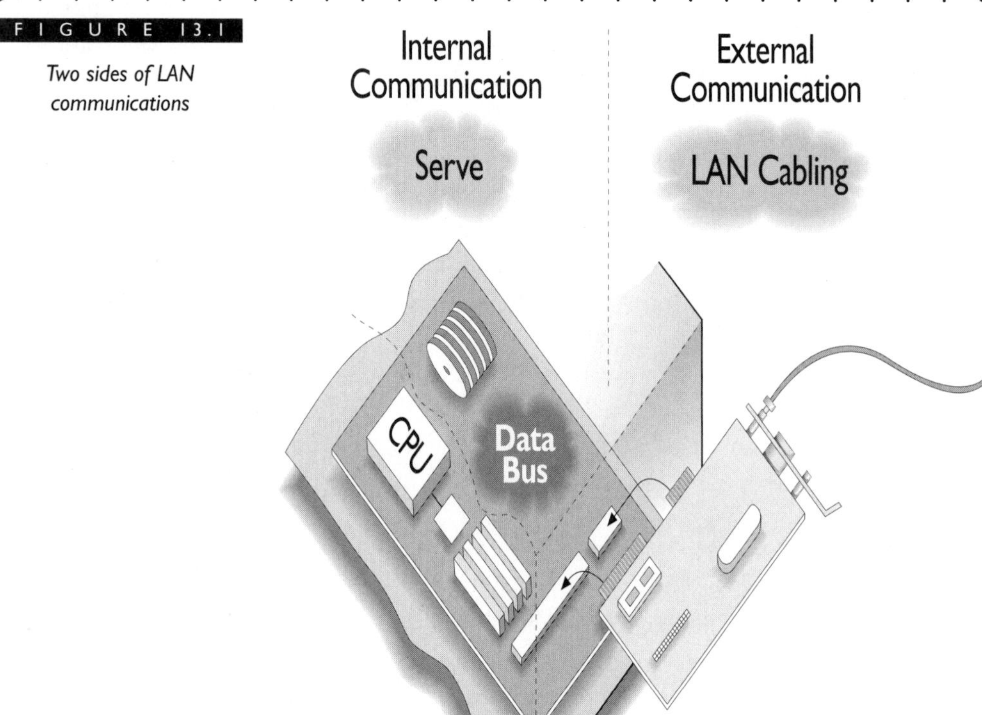

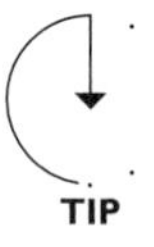
TIP

Here's an analogy that should help you and your friends better understand topology components and their fundamental processes. Think of the server and workstation as a city. Then think about how you move within and between cities. Within a city, for example, you're likely to take a bus. This is analogous to the bus inside a server or workstation. If you want to travel to another city, however, you're likely to take an airplane—NICs and cabling. So, the big question is: What's the transition point from the city to the airplane? You're right—the (air)port!

Now let's start our journey through NIC architecture at the server and workstation.

Server/Workstation Architecture

The transfer of data from the NIC to the server or workstation CPU occurs over an internal path called a *data bus*. The bus architecture of your network server or workstation can dramatically impact performance. To optimize and to troubleshoot the server or workstation architecture, you should understand the strengths and weaknesses of the following bus types (follow along in Figure 13.2):

- *Industry Standard Architecture (ISA)* — The original and still popular Industry Standard Architecture (ISA) bus was introduced with the IBM PC many years ago. The original ISA slots could only accommodate 8-bit data paths. When the 80286 CPU was introduced, the ISA standard was revised to allow for 8-bit or 16-bit transfers.

- *MicroChannel Architecture (MCA)* — IBM introduced MicroChannel Architecture (MCA) with their PS/2 product line. MCA is an improvement over ISA because it is much faster (32 megabits per second), more easily configurable, and provides better throughput. In addition, MCA uses a software configuration program to automate NIC and adapter settings. (**Note:** The 32-bit MCA slots only support MCA cards.)

- *Extended Industry Standard Architecture (EISA)* — Extended Industry Standard Architecture (EISA) cards use a 32-bit bus design and fit into a multilevel slot that appears similar to a 16-bit ISA slot. EISA slots can accommodate 16-bit and 8-bit ISA cards. This flexibility enables manufacturers to create faster EISA adapters for computers with single 8-bit, dual 16-bit, and tri-level 32-bit slots.

- *VESA Local Bus (VLB)* — The VESA Local Bus (VLB) was originally conceived as a low-cost I/O bus architecture designed to accelerate PC video performance. Like the EISA, MCA, and PCI buses, VLB supports bus mastering and burst transfers. These features, combined with a 32-bit bus width, enable video cards, network boards, and disk controllers to move data through a system much more quickly.

- *Peripheral Component Interconnect (PCI)* — Peripheral Component Interconnect (PCI) is a 32-bit to 64-bit bus that runs at 33 MHz and higher. PCI has a maximum data transfer rate of 524 megabits per second (Mbps). In addition, PCI includes a feature called *low-access latency,* which means that there is little time lapse between the time the CPU turns control over to the bus and the time the bus takes action.

- *Personal Computer Memory Card International Association (PCMCIA)* — PCMCIA cards are designed for notebooks and come in three different sizes: Type I, II, and III. Type I is used for memory devices, Type II for I/O devices (such as modems and LAN adapters), and Type III for hard drives. All three-card types use the same 68-pin connector to attach to the notebook data bus.

FIGURE 13.2

Internal server/ workstation architecture

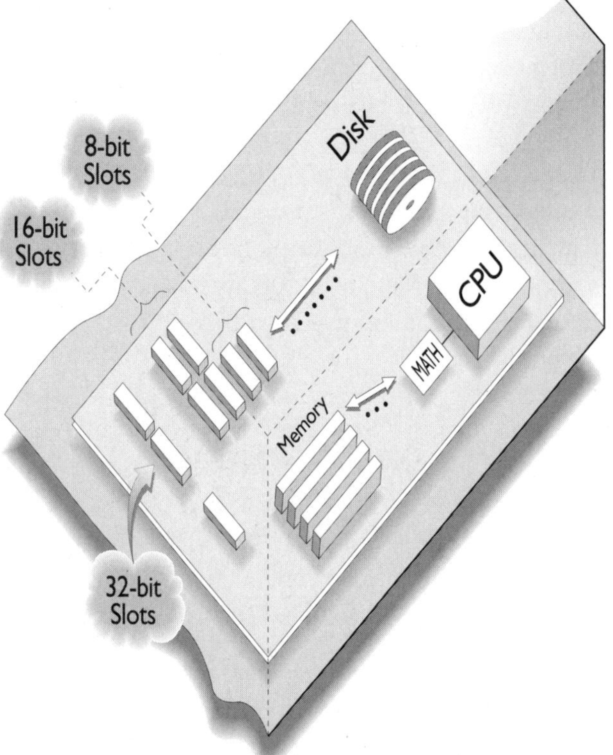

Refer to Table 13.1 for a quick comparison of the bus architectures (PCMCIA isn't a valid server architecture, so it isn't listed in the table). Now let's take a closer look.

TABLE 13.1

Server Bus Types

BUS TYPE	MAXIMUM SPEED	RELATIVE COST
ISA	8 Mbps	Low
MCA	32 Mbps	High
EISA	33 Mbps	Medium
VLB	132 Mbps	Low
PCI	133 Mbps to 524 Mbps	Low

TIP

Consider using bus mastering PCI NICs and hard drive controllers in your server so that incoming communications can be directly handled by the hard drive without interrupting the central CPU.

Topologies

Topology describes the geographic orientation and arrangement of networking components. *Protocol* refers to the set of rules and procedures that govern the transmission of messages over a physical networking medium. Together, protocols and topology are combined to create a networking standard (such as Ethernet, token ring, or FDDI).

The topology that you choose for your network determines the guidelines that should be used for installing NICs and cabling. File servers and workstations are arranged according to a variety of factors (such as speed, cost, reliability, distance, and load requirements). Each topology is ideally suited for a different combination of these factors, as exemplified by the following topology examples:

- *Bus* — Cheap and less reliable
- *Star* — Fast, expensive, large, and more reliable (see Figure 13.3)
- *Ring* — Fast, expensive, and reliable
- *Star-Ring* — Fast, cheap, and reliable

The star topology is the most popular among today's best networking standards. It is fast, reliable, and usually easy to maintain and troubleshoot. Refer to Table 13.2 for a summary of today's star-wired standards.

TABLE 13.2

Putting the Star Topology to Good Use

STANDARD	CENTRAL DEVICE	COMMENTS
Ethernet 10BaseT and 100BaseT	Concentrator	Star-wired Ethernet over twisted-pair or fiber-optic cabling. A great standard if wired in the correct star configuration with Category 5 twisted-pair cabling.
Token Ring	MSAU 8228	Multistation access unit (MSAU). Acronym varies depending on author and vintage. The 8228 portion of the name is IBM's term. This central device is not powered and does not provide signal regeneration.
	MSAU 8229	Same as 8228 but with signal regeneration.
	CAU/LAM	Controlled access unit and local access module. The CAU is SNMP enabled and powered. The LAM plugs into the CAU and merely adds more ports.
FDDI	Concentrator	Powered, acts as a repeater.

In a star-wired system, a central device controls workstations and servers. Each machine is connected to the device via its own cable. When laid out on a floor plan, this topology resembles a *hub-and-spoke system* (see Figure 13.3). In general, star topologies use the most cable but have the highest reliability. When a cable breaks, only the cable's host station will be affected, and unless it's the server, no one else will even notice.

FIGURE 13.3

Star topology

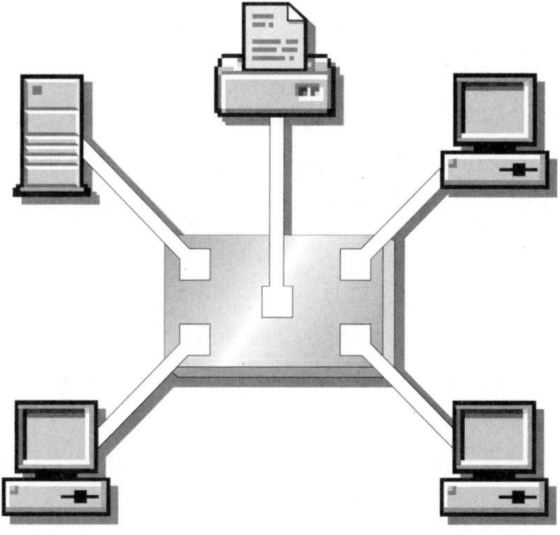

To extend the star topology, most central devices can be cabled together. The resulting topology is known as a *distributed star*. Oftentimes, the cable connecting the two hubs will be a little different than the cable connecting the workstations to the hubs. This difference might be for reasons of distance, reliability, or security. Remember, except for FDDI (which requires fiber), the media and the topology are independent.

In addition to the standard star-shaped topology, network designers can use a star-shaped ring. Instead of relying on a single twisted pair from station to station, you can take advantage of both twisted pairs within Category 3 and 5 twisted-pair cabling. In this configuration, the central Multistation Access Unit (Token Ring) accepts incoming signals on one of the two pairs and sends them back to the other pair. If a station is turned off, or if the cable is broken, then the central device bypasses that port.

Now that you understand the fundamentals of intracomputer and intercomputer communications, it's time to explore the components that make these communications work — NICs and cabling. We will begin by describing NIC ports, which are the cable-specific connection points between the internal NIC and external cabling. Next, we'll explore NIC configuration and then finish with a journey through coaxial, twisted-pair, and fiber-optic cabling. So, without any further ado, let's get on with the show.

NIC Ports

A NIC provides the electronic interface between a computer and LAN cabling. The card itself relies on two ports for connecting computer components to the network: an internal bus-specific edge connector to plug into the computer motherboard and an external cabling port that plugs directly into the LAN cabling. See Figure 13.4 for more information.

FIGURE 13.4

Typical NIC ports

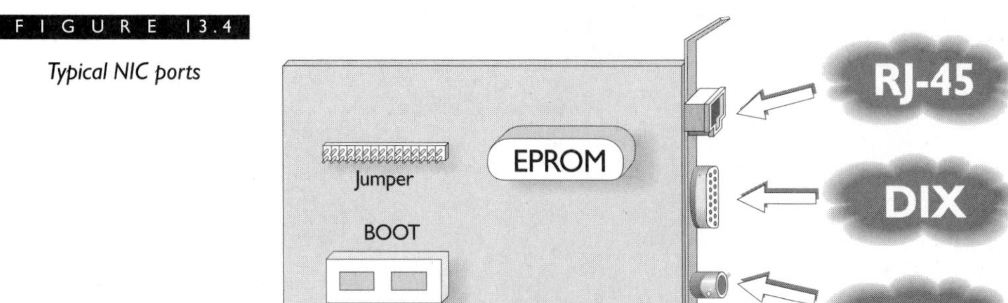

NIC ports support many different configurations, each port with its own purpose and function:

- *BNC*—The BNC connector was one of the first for network communications. There is some debate over what the acronym stands for: some authorities claim that it means *British Naval Connector*, whereas others insist that it stands for *Bayonet Nut Coupler*.

- *RJ-45*—In the business world, nearly all new cable installations use twisted-pair cabling with eight wires per cable. These eight wires are separated into four twisted pairs. The pairs are then terminated in an RJ-45 connector. This port looks much like the port attached to your home telephone except that it's a bit larger, with room for eight wires instead of four. By the way, your home telephone uses an RJ-11 port. RJ-45 ports are supported by the top two networking standards: Ethernet and Token Ring.

- *DIX* — DIX is an acronym for Digital, Intel, and Xerox, the companies that invented Ethernet. These early Ethernet connectors are D-shell shaped with 15 pins each (organized in two rows of seven and eight pins, respectively). The drop cable that plugs into this port looks a lot like your video connector except that it's a little longer and narrower.

- *AUI* — AUI stands for Attachment Unit Interface. When Xerox turned Ethernet over to the IEEE 802.3 standards committee, it was required to release its trademarks and patents to the public. At that point, it was no longer appropriate to name the connector after the three companies that sold most of the existing hardware. Other companies, such as Thomas-Conrad and Standard Micro Systems (SMC) objected to selling a part named after rival companies.

As you can see, a variety of NIC port types are available, and they are shared by many of the three network standards. Refer to Table 13.3 for a quick summary of the network standards and the ports and cabling that they use. Table 13.3 will serve as a good preview to the troubleshooting sections ahead.

TABLE 13.3
Understanding NIC Ports

STANDARD	NIC PORT	PRIMARY CABLE TYPE
Thick Ethernet	DIX	Thick coaxial
Thin Ethernet	BNC	Thin coaxial
Ethernet 10BaseT	RJ-45	Unshielded twisted pair and 100BaseT
Token Ring	AUI and RJ-45	Unshielded and Shielded twisted pair

The external port-cabling connection is an important connection. Be sure you understand these four port types before you start installing and troubleshooting topology components.

Furthermore, the NIC-motherboard connection is even more sophisticated. To be successful, the NIC must carve out its own niche in the forest of internal bus communications. As we saw earlier, the inside of most servers and workstations is a complex maze of bus channels and adapter slots. Let's take a closer look at how the NIC fits in.

NIC Configuration

Network servers and workstations employ a suite of internal configurations to control communication between internal memory, the NIC, hard drives, expansion cards, and the CPU. These configurations are controlled by the following four parameters:

- *IRQ* — Registers that define multiple channels of communication between internal components and the CPU. IRQs are used to allow multiple access to the CPU. (**Note:** It is important to configure a NIC with a unique, nonconflicting IRQ number.)
- *I/O* — The I/O address is a reserved spot in memory where a device can drop off its data for use by the CPU.
- *Memory Address* — Most PCs have a reserved memory range from 640K to 1MB. This range is used for video memory, expanded memory, paging, shadow RAM, and the storage of terminate-and-stay-resident memory programs (TSRs). NICs use the following address ranges in this area for communication buffers: CC00–CFFF and B000–B3FF.
- *Direct Memory Access (DMA)* — Direct Memory Access (DMA) is necessary when internal devices interact directly with server or workstation memory. Some devices (for example, disk controllers) that routinely move a significant amount of data are designed to write data straight to system memory without involving the CPU. The device then notifies the CPU where the data is. To facilitate this process, PCs have several DMA channels that open memory directly to such devices (such as NICs, hard disk controllers, and floppy drives).

In a simple configuration with few peripherals, it is often easy to avoid configuration conflicts because default NIC settings can be used. However, in a fully loaded workstation with multiple devices (such as serial and parallel ports, sound card, and modem), NIC configurations can be complex. Most NICs can be configured in one of the following ways: jumpers, DIP switches, plug-and-play, or software-enabled firmware. Refer to Table 13.4 for a list of some of today's standard configuration settings.

TABLE 13.4

Understanding NIC Configurations

DEVICE	INTERRUPT	I/O ADDRESS	MEMORY ADDRESS	DMA
System	0 (clock)	000–0FF (reserved)	F0000–FFFFF (BIOS)0	(refresh)
System keyboard	1			
System–special	2 (gateway)		E0000–EFFFF (reserved) purpose	
COM1 serial port	4	3F8–3FF		
LPT2 parallel port	5	278–27F		
Floppy disk	6	3F0–3F7		2 controller
LPT1 parallel port	7	378–37F		
Hard disk controller	14	1F0–1F8	C8000–C87FF	1
Game port		200–207		
EGA/VGA display			C0000–C7FFF B8000–BFFFF A0000–AFFFF	
Monochrome display			B0000–B7FFF	
Good choice for NIC1	3		CC000–CFFFF	3
Good choice for NIC2	5		DA000–DFFFF	4, 5, 6, or 7

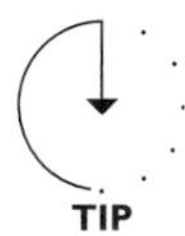

Most of today's computers are configured with two COM ports, in which case the second COM port (Interrupt 3) must be disabled before you install your NIC.

Software-enabled firmware enables you to configure internal NIC parameters using PC-based software. To install a software-enabled NIC, follow these three steps:

1. Install the NIC in the workstation/server.
2. Reboot the computer.
3. Launch the configuration software and customize all necessary parameters (such as IRQ, I/O address port, memory address, and/or DMA).

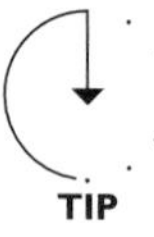

Study NIC configuration parameters and tools carefully. Specifically, understand the role of IRQ, I/O address port, memory address, and DMA in server and workstation communications. Finally, study the three installation steps for software-enabled NICs (that is, install the NIC, reboot, and launch the software).

LAN Cabling

Networks rely on cabling for connectivity, reliability, and speed. Typically, the LAN cabling type is driven by the topology standard: Ethernet primarily uses coaxial and UTP, ARCnet uses coaxial, token ring primarily uses STP and UTP, and FDDI uses fiber optic. Following are the four LAN cabling types that we will discuss in this section (see Figure 13.5):

- Coaxial
- Unshielded twisted pair (UTP)
- Shielded twisted pair (STP)
- Fiber optic

FIGURE 13.5

LAN cabling types

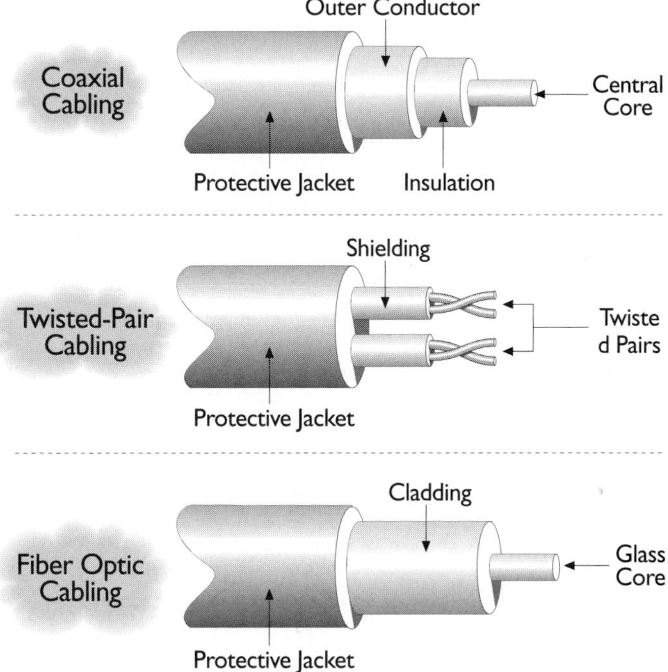

Coaxial Cabling

Coaxial cable (coax) is so named because it contains two conductors that are parallel to each other. The internal conductor is the central core (which is solid or stranded copper) and the external conductor is a copper mesh that forms a shield for electromagnetic interference (EMI) protection (see Figure 13.5).

Coaxial cabling is available in varying quality levels. The best quality consists of a stranded central core and tightly woven mesh, both of which are typically made of copper. Less desirable cabling uses aluminum instead of copper.

Coaxial cabling includes two characteristics that directly affect its network performance:

- *Gauge*—A measure of cabling thickness. Gauge is specified using radio grade (RG) measurements: the higher the RG number, the thinner the central core.
- *Impedance*—A measurement of cabling resistance to the flow of electrical current. This concerns the relationship of current to voltage in the coax cable, and impacts the distance that data signals can travel before they must be "regenerated."

Each topology standard has different requirements with respect to impedance: Thick Ethernet (RG-8 / 50 ohms), Thin Ethernet (RG-58 / 50 ohms), and ARCnet (RG-62 / 93 ohms). (**Note:** NICs, terminators, and the coaxial cabling must all have the same level of impedance.)

REAL WORLD

Many homes built in the 1970s and 1980s used aluminum wire rather than copper wire. Aluminum wire is much more susceptible to temperature differential than is copper wire. Changes in temperature can cause the aluminum electrical wiring to work loose from your home panel box. When this happens, sparking begins. All too often, sparking leads to fires. To protect yourself, check to see if you have aluminum wire. If you do, have an electrician show you how to safely tighten the wires yourself once or twice a year. If your home is served by a volunteer fire company, call the local chief and ask him or her to come over and show you what to do. Then make a donation.

Unshielded Twisted-Pair (UTP) Cabling

Twisted-pair cabling consists of two solid or stranded copper wires twisted together to decrease susceptibility to EMI (see Figure 13.5). Twisted-pair cabling comes in two varieties: unshielded twisted pair (UTP) and shielded twisted pair (STP).

Unshielded twisted-pair (UTP) cabling is less expensive to produce because it does not include a protective EMI copper shield. The quality of UTP is categorized according to its capability to handle voice or data transmissions:

- *Category 1* — Cable performance is intended for analog telephone and low-speed data communications.
- *Category 2* — Cable performance is intended for intermittent speeds, slower than 4 Mbps. This cable also works for any Category 1 application.
- *Category 3* — Cable performance is intended for high-speed data transmissions. This is the minimum data grade acceptable for 10 Mbps Ethernet networks. This cable supports transmission speeds of up to 16 Mbps.
- *Category 4* — Cable performance is intended for extended distance and/or high-speed LANs (roughly 20 Mbps).
- *Category 5* — Cable performance is intended for high-level, data-grade network applications. This is the highest category rating and supports 100 Mbps Ethernet implementations. It is also the recommended level for all UTP network installations.

Without protective shielding, UTP is susceptible to a variety of EMI sources, including incandescent lamps, electric motors, and computer power supplies. Ethernet networks can experience intermittent communication problems when Category 1, 2, or 3 UTP is used over extended distances or near strong sources of EMI.

Shielded Twisted-Pair (STP) Cabling

STP consists of the same copper wire core as UTP, but it has the added protection of a mesh shield (see Figure 13.5). The added shield protects STP against crosstalk and EMI, which provides higher transmission rates and greater reliability. The IBM Token Ring design uses STP cabling primarily (although some UTP standards also exist).

REAL WORLD

The low cost and flexibility of UTP makes it a tempting cabling choice, but don't base your decision solely on convenience. With UTP, EMI can jump up and bite you. Here's a case in point. A few years ago, I helped a school district troubleshoot a minor networking problem. Their headquarters was in an old elementary school, and they had wanted a LAN. When it came time to spring for cabling installation, they cut a few corners. They had noticed a few extra pairs of UTP running throughout the buildings—originally installed as extra phone lines. They installed an Ethernet LAN using the existing cabling and thought they'd save thousands of dollars.

What they didn't realize was that the cabling had been installed with voice in mind—not data! The big day arrived and their network came up without a hitch. Then, suddenly, at 9:00 a.m. sharp, it crashed. They couldn't isolate any major problems, so they brought it back up and continued working. Then, at 10:00 a.m., it happened again. For two and a half days, their network crashed every hour on the hour. They couldn't imagine what the problem was.

On the third day, they noticed the school bell. It was ringing every hour on the hour, starting at 9:00 a.m. It turned out that the bells' electrical system ran in the same conduit as their voice-grade UTP. Oops! It cost them more to retrofit the entire network than it would have cost to build it correctly at the start.

Let this be a lesson to you. If you're going to use UTP, don't use existing voice-grade phone wires. Install Category 5 cabling from scratch. Also, be sure to choose a cabling contractor who understands the importance and requirements of data-grade installation. It'll save you in the long run.

Fiber-Optic Cabling

Fiber-optic cabling consists of a fine optical fiber made from two types of glass: one for the inner core and one for the cladding (see Figure 13.5). The inner and outer cores have different indexes of refraction, which cause the light signal to bounce back and forth in a corkscrew path as it travels along the fiber cabling. A laser light emitting diode (LED) or injection laser diode (ILT) light signal travels from one end to another, bouncing off the inner cladding.

Most networks require 62.5-micron fiber. The advantage of this technology is that it relies on the properties and characteristics of light rather than electricity—which makes fiber-optic cabling immune to EMI.

Refer to Table 13.5 for a comparison of the advantages and disadvantages of coaxial, twisted-pair, and fiber-optic cabling.

TABLE 13.5

Advantages and Disadvantages of LAN Cabling Types

LAN CABLING	ADVANTAGES	DISADVANTAGES
Coaxial	Well understood technology	Moderately expensive
	Supports 10 Mbps	Incompatibility between different impedance types
	Supports great distances	Loose connectors cause intermittent problems
	Offers good EMI protection	
Twisted pair	Well-understood technology	Limited distance
	Inexpensive	Insecure
	Easy to install and maintain	Susceptible to strong sources of EMI
	Flexible configuration	
Fiber optic	Very high speeds	Very expensive
	Very reliable	Hard to install and maintain
	Immune to EMI	Easy to break
	Very secure	

This completes our journey through the basics of NIC architecture. In this section, we learned about the server and workstation architecture and how these machines are organized into LAN topologies. We learned about the ports and configurations of server NICs and the connectivity of central LAN cabling.

Now I hope you have a greater appreciation for the fundamentals of NIC configuration. In the remainder of this chapter, we will build on this baseline knowledge and explore troubleshooting techniques for the three main LAN standards:

- Ethernet
- Token Ring
- FDDI

Let's learn more about the diversity of NIC troubleshooting, starting with Ethernet.

Troubleshooting Ethernet

Ethernet is the most common network standard. Every major computer vendor supports Ethernet, including the three that developed it: Digital, Intel, and Xerox. This widespread support is one reason for its popularity. It also offers relatively high-speed throughput over a variety of cabling choices.

To categorize this diversity, we will explore the advantages and disadvantages of the following five IEEE Ethernet standards:

- *10Base5* — This standard, which is known as *Thick Ethernet*, offers 10 Mbps baseband signaling, with a 500-meter segment limit.
- *10Base2* — This standard, which is known as *Thin Ethernet*, offers 10 Mbps baseband signaling, with a 200-meter (actually 185 meter) segment limit.
- *10Base-T* — This standard, which is known as *Twisted-Pair Ethernet*, offers 10 Mbps baseband signaling over twisted-pair cabling, with a 100-meter segment limit. (You can also replace the *T* with an *F* to describe Ethernet over fiber-optic cabling.)
- *100Base-T* — This standard, which is known as *Fast -Ethernet*, offers 100 Mbps baseband signaling over twisted-pair cabling.
- *1000Base-T* — This standard, which is known as *Gigabit Ethernet*, offers 1000 Mbps baseband signaling over twisted-pair cabling.

Ethernet uses a contention-based protocol known as Carrier Sense Multiple Access with Collision Detection (CSMA/CD), which supports multiple workstation access to a shared cabling trunk. In this configuration, each workstation connects directly to the trunk and communicates with the LAN through an internal NIC.

When a station wants to transmit, it listens to the cable to determine if any other station is broadcasting. If not, it jumps in. Occasionally, a station will listen to the cable and determine that it's okay to jump in when, in reality, it isn't. A broadcast could be in progress, but the bits haven't traveled far enough for the second station to see them. When this happens, and two stations broadcast at once, a collision occurs. This whole scenario relies on the fact that Ethernet workstations broadcast their messages throughout the LAN. Follow along with Figure 13.6 as we send a message from Workstation B to Workstation A:

1. Workstation B has a message for Workstation A. Workstation B listens to the trunk and waits until all is clear. (This is called *carrier sensing.*)

2. When B detects that the trunk is clear, the workstation marks the message with a destination address (A) and sends it over the trunk. All of the other workstations continually monitor the trunk for a message with their address. (This is called *multiple access.*)

3. If Workstation A must send a message at the same time, it listens to the trunk but notices that a transmission is in progress. It waits. While A is waiting, it monitors a matching packet, accepts the message from B, and returns an acknowledgment of receipt. Problems occur when multiple workstations send messages simultaneously, resulting in collisions.

To deal with imminent collisions, the CSMA protocol has adopted a subprotocol called *Collision Detection* (CD). In the event of a collision, both transmitting stations back off and wait. Of course, if they waited exactly the same amount of time, they would collide again, so Ethernet has a random delay algorithm built into the CSMA/CD. It's called *binary exponential backoff* (BEB), which says "pick a random number between zero and two to the *n*th power, where *n* is the number of consecutive collisions." The first time, each station will choose a random number between zero and two. The next time, each station will choose a number between zero and four. By the tenth time, it will be a number between zero and 1,024. If there are ever 16 consecutive collisions, Ethernet gives up. In this rare instance, your user will see the following error message:

```
Error Sending on the Network
```

FIGURE 13.6

Understanding the Ethernet protocol

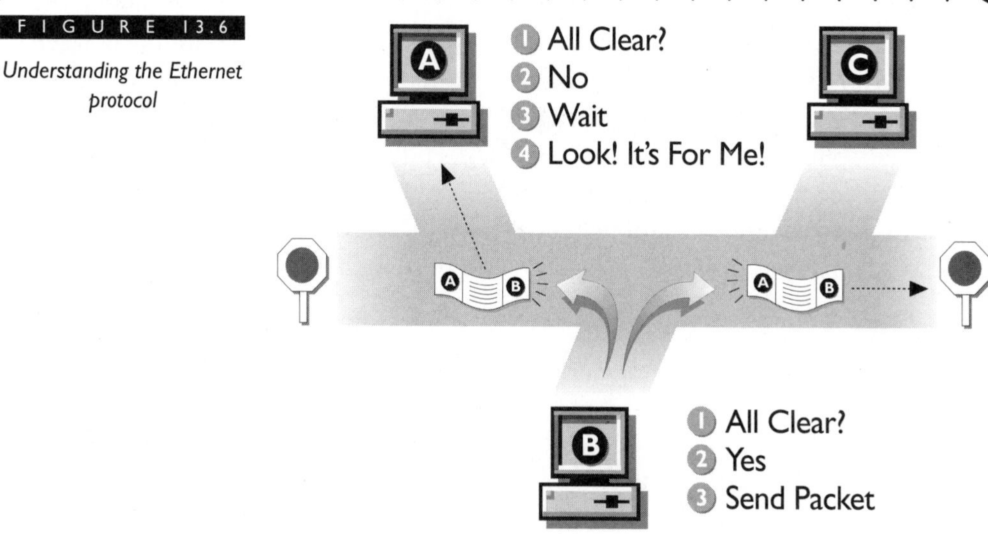

If the first station draws the random number zero, it will begin retransmitting right away. If the second station draws the number one, it will wait. However, when a station begins retransmitting, it first listens to see if any other station is already using the cable. If so, the station waits until the cable becomes available. Only if both stations draw the same random number or if a third station gets involved, will you have another collision.

The CSMA/CD logical Ethernet bus consists of one continuous length of coaxial cabling (that is, the trunk) with a terminating resistor (terminator) at each end. The Ethernet message travels along the bus in both directions, until it is picked up by a workstation NIC. If the message is missed or is not recognized, it reaches the end of the cabling and dissipates at the terminator. Ethernet supports two physical configurations of the logical bus: *bus* (Thick and Thin Ethernet) and *star* (Twisted-Pair Ethernet).

Refer to Table 13.6 for a summary of Ethernet's advantages and disadvantages.

TABLE 13.6

Ethernet Advantages and Disadvantages

ADVANTAGES	DISADVANTAGES
Relatively inexpensive.	Slows down with heavy loads because the CSMA/CD access method allows multiple access to a shared trunk.
High-speed transmissions (from 10 to 1000 Mbps).	Bus topology is difficult to troubleshoot. This is less of a problem in the 10Base-T star configuration.
Flexible cabling configuration (bus or star topologies).	
Easy to install.	
Supported well in the LAN and micro-to-mainframe environments.	

Thick Ethernet Cabling Rules

Thick Ethernet is the original Ethernet standard developed by Digital, Intel, and Xerox. It is also known as 10Base5, because it provides 10 Mbps throughput using baseband signaling over 500 meters of maximum cabling distance. The term Thick Ethernet became popular because it describes the thickness of the coaxial cabling (RG-8).

Although Thick Ethernet uses the same CSMA/CD protocol and bus topology as Thin Ethernet, it does so in a slightly different way. Thick Ethernet uses an external transceiver and a vampire clamp to attach to the thick bus trunk. The transceiver's independent box handles trunk communications and fastens directly to the Thick Ethernet cabling. The transceiver then attaches to a separate drop cable for communications to the NIC. Connectivity from the drop cable to the NIC is made through a 15-pin DIX port.

Refer to Figure 13.7 for a review of Thick Ethernet cabling rules.

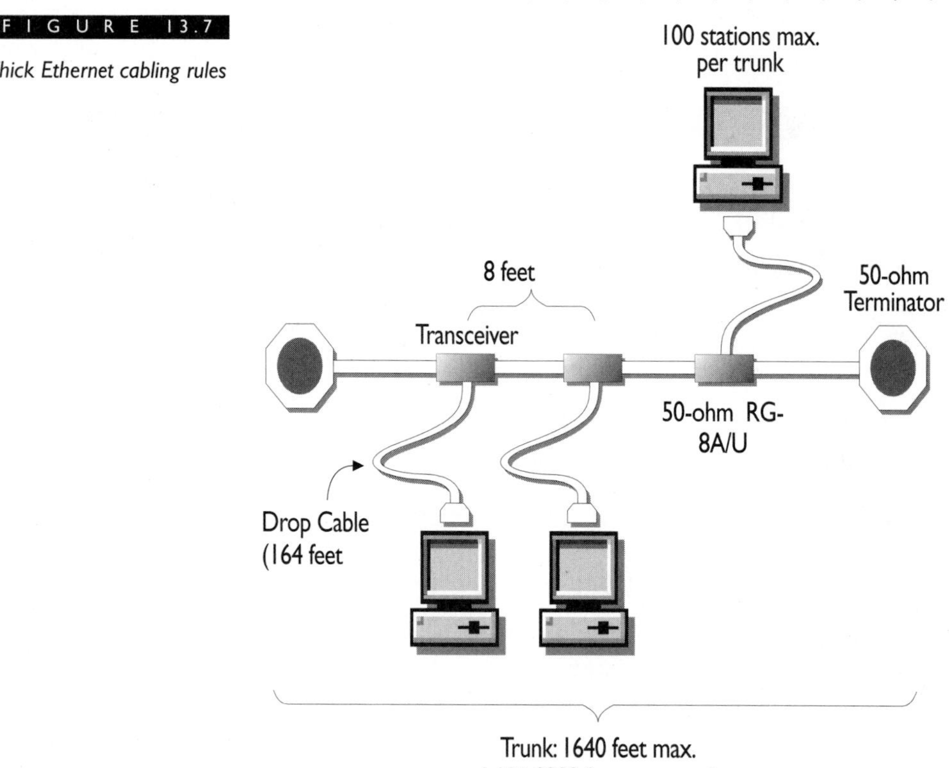

FIGURE 13.7

Thick Ethernet cabling rules

Thick Ethernet was designed for large, dispersed networks. Following is a summary of the cabling rules illustrated in Figure 13.7:

- The maximum length of the entire network can be 8,200 feet (2,500 meters), with each individual segment up to 1,640 feet (500 meters).
- You can have a maximum of five trunks connected by four repeaters. Only three of these trunks can be populated. This is known as the *5-4-3 Rule*.
- Each transceiver on the trunk must be separated by at least 8 feet (2.5 meters). Also, the drop cable cannot exceed 164 feet (50 meters). Drop cables do not have a minimum length.

- Thick Ethernet uses 50-ohm RG-8 or RG-11 coaxial cabling. It also requires a 50-ohm terminator on each end. Ensure that one (and only one) of the terminators is grounded.

Thin Ethernet Cabling Rules

The most significant difference between Thick and Thin Ethernet is the placement of the transceiver. With Thick Ethernet, the transceiver is external and is usually connected to the cable via a vampire clamp. With Thin Ethernet, the transceiver is a chip on the NIC. One disadvantage of the Thin Ethernet design is the proximity of the workstation to the trunk. Because most T-connectors are small, you have only a few inches of play between the NIC and the Ethernet trunk. This makes cabling cumbersome.

Refer to Figure 13.8 for a review of Thin Ethernet cabling rules.

FIGURE 13.8

Thin Ethernet cabling rules

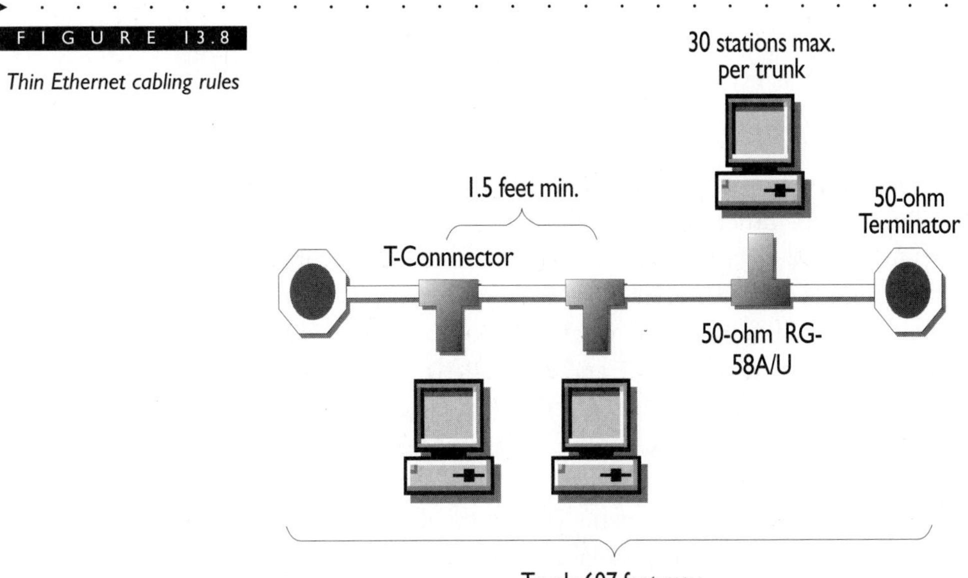

Thin Ethernet was designed for small networks. Following is a summary of the cabling rules illustrated in Figure 13.8:

- The maximum length of the total network cannot exceed 3,035 feet (925 meters). You can have a maximum of five trunks of up to 607 feet (185 meters), each connected by 4 routers. Only three of the trunks can be populated — with each supporting up to 30 devices. This is called the *5-4-3 Rule* (3 populated trunks connected by 4 routers, for a total of 5 trunks).
- Workstations must be at least 1.5 feet (0.5 meters) apart.
- Thin Ethernet uses 50-ohm RG-58 thin coaxial cabling and requires a 50-ohm terminator at each end of each trunk. One of the terminators must be grounded.
- The Signal Quality Error (SQE) test must be turned off if repeaters are used. This feature is present on some Thin Ethernet NICs.

Twisted-Pair Ethernet Cabling Rules

Twisted-pair Ethernet uses the same CSMA/CD protocol as the two Ethernet designs described earlier, but differs in its fundamental cabling scheme. This standard, simply known as 10Base-T, works in a physical star configuration, with each trunk of twisted-pair cabling terminated at a central concentrator. Two additional faster standards are 100Base-T and 1000Base-T.

The 10Base-T standard has several advantages, especially in larger networks. The centralized wiring concentrator makes the network more reliable and easier to manage. In addition, the hubs can have their own intelligence and route traffic around a defective cable segment. This eliminates the single point of failure found in bus topologies. Finally, 10Base-T supports the most popular type of LAN cabling: UTP.

Refer to Figure 13.9 for a review of Ethernet 10Base-T cabling rules.

FIGURE 13.9

Ethernet 10Base-T cabling rules

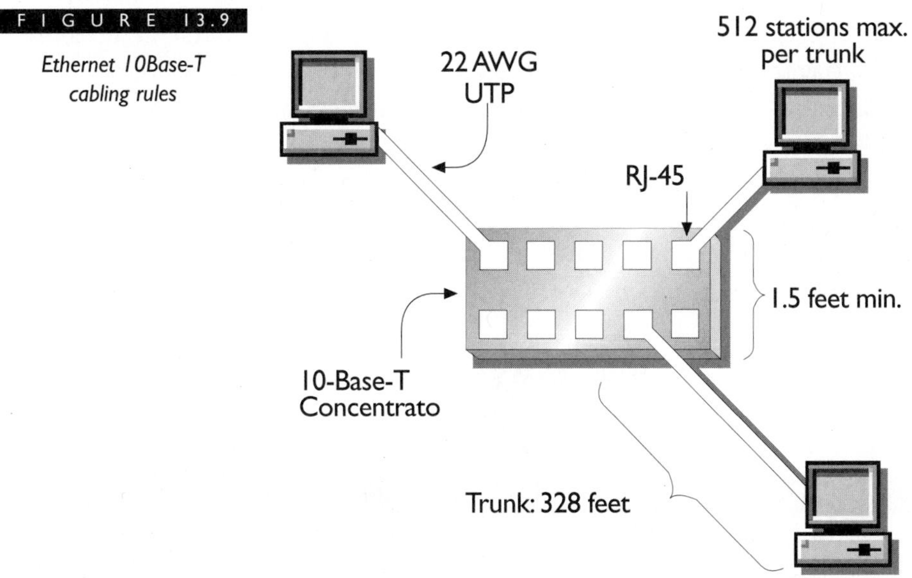

Ethernet 10Base-T is ideal for midsize and large networks with flexibility requirements. Following is a summary of the cabling rules illustrated in Figure 13.9:

- The maximum length of the total network is not a limiting factor; however, each workstation must be at least 2 feet (0.6 meters) and no more than 328 feet (100 meters) from a concentrator.

- As with all other Ethernet designs, 10Base-T must follow the 5-4-3 Rule, although it is actually a 5-4 Rule: any two workstations can have up to four concentrators between five linked segments. (The 3 in the 5-4-3 Rule applies to the number of populated segments in a bus scheme.) Expansion may be achieved by joining concentrators into two-level cascades. This configuration forms clusters of stars.

- You can have up to 512 nodes per segment, or a total of 1,024 workstations on the entire network. However, the total number of ports available on concentrators and the protocol limitation of Ethernet drop this number to less than 100.

- Ethernet 10Base-T uses 22-AWG UTP cabling. It requires at least Category 3 cabling, but Category 5 is recommended for reliability and future expansion. Each central end of the UTP segment is terminated with an RJ-45 port concentrator—workstation connections use straight-through pinouts, whereas concentrator connections use external crossover pinouts. (See the following Real World sidebar for more information.)

Refer to Table 13.7 for a summary of Thick, Thin, and Twisted-Pair Ethernet cabling rules.

TABLE 13.7

Summary of Ethernet Cabling Rules

RULE	THICK	THIN	TWISTED PAIR
Maximum nodes per segment	50	30	512
Maximum populated segments	3	3	1,024
Maximum number of repeaters	4	4	4
Maximum number of segments	5	5	1024
Maximum segment length	500 meters	185 meters	100 meters
Maximum total LAN length	2,500 meters	925 meters	N/A
Minimum cabling distances	3 meters	0.5 meters	0.6 meters

Advanced Ethernet Standards

In addition to the three Ethernet standards described earlier, the Institute of Electrical and Electronic Engineers (IEEE) has created four high-speed Ethernet alternatives:

- Fast Ethernet
- Gigabit Ethernet
- Switched Ethernet
- Full-Duplex Ethernet

REAL WORLD

10BaseT is very specific about how cables are constructed. Remember that twisted-pair cabling uses RJ-45 jacks, which have eight connectors or pins. They look the same as phone jacks, but are a little larger. Only four of these pins are used for Ethernet data—pins 1 and 2 for transmit, and pins 3 and 6 for receive. If you are going to create your own 10BaseT adapter cables, be sure to follow these pinouts:

- Pin 1 to pin 1, white/orange, transmit (+)
- Pin 2 to pin 2, orange/white, transmit (–)
- Pin 3 to pin 3, white/green, receive (+)
- Pin 6 to pin 6, green/white, receive (–)

However, if you are going to connect multiple concentrators to each other, you may need to create an external crossover cable. In this case, pin 1 is connected to pin 3, and pin 2 is connected to pin 6 on each side. Be sure to follow these UTP pinouts for concentrator-to-concentrator cables:

- Pin 1 to pin 3, white/orange, transmit (+), to receive (+)
- Pin 2 to pin 6, orange/white, transmit (–), to receive (–)
- Pin 3 to pin 1, white/green, receive (+), to transmit (+)
- Pin 6 to pin 2, green/white, receive (–), to transmit (–)

These pinouts describe the connections on either side of the cable. When creating RJ-45 cables, hold the connector with the notch down. Pin 1 is on the left side, pin 8 is on the right side. Fortunately, the wire pairs have similar color combinations. For example, the white wire with orange stripes is paired with the orange wire with white stripes. Have fun and remember to use steady hands.

Let's take a closer look.

Fast Ethernet

Fast Ethernet is an emerging standard adopted by the IEEE 802.3 subcommittee. It uses the standard CSMA/CD protocol supported by all existing Ethernet installations. In addition, it works over the twisted-pair pseudo-star topology design, which makes it compatible with the 15 million or so twisted-pair nodes already in existence. Because the packet structure is unchanged, Fast Ethernet supports all the network management tools already in place.

Fast Ethernet NICs are designed to operate at either 10 Mbps or 100 Mbps. This feature is called *auto negotiation*. All you have to do is change the concentrator and the card automatically switches to the appropriate capacity. If all cards can operate at 100 Mbps, then the hub runs at 100 Mbps. However, if one NIC slows things down, the hub switches to 10 Mbps operation, slowing everyone down. Newer, dual-speed hubs can provide both 10 Mbps and 100 Mbps ports in a single chassis.

Fast Ethernet has some cable-length limitations. The hub-to-hub distances are much more limited than they are for 10 Mbps Ethernet. You can only have two hubs between end stations, and the hubs must be connected by a 5-meter cable. Of course, you can use a fiber-optic connection between hubs and extend that distance to 400 meters. For this reason, most Fast Ethernet hubs are stackable, allowing anywhere from 8 to 100 ports or more in a single hub stack. Even though there are multiple hubs in the stack, the entire stack counts as a single repeater.

Fast Ethernet supports four standards:

- *100BaseTX*—Two-pair Category 5 UTP or STP (IEEE 802.3u)
- *100BaseT4*—Four-pair Category 3 through 5 UTP (IEEE 802.3u)
- *100BaseFX*—For fiber optics (IEEE 802.3u)
- *100BaseT2*—Two-pair Category 3 through 5 UTP (IEEE 802.3y)

Each cabling standard has different requirements with respect to UTP, STP, or fiber-optic media. These requirements are specific, and you must follow them closely. If you're interested in Fast Ethernet, but don't want to jump in yet, consider installing four pair of Category 5 UTP and purchasing as many Fast Ethernet NICs as you can afford. Then, later, you can replace your concentrator with a more expensive hub, and the in-place cabling will support three of the four Fast Ethernet standards. Refer to Table 13.8 for a summary of the Fast Ethernet cabling requirements.

TABLE 13.8

Fast Ethernet Cabling Requirements

FAST ETHERNET STANDARD	CATEGORY 3 UTP	CATEGORY 4 UTP	CATEGORY 5 UTP	FIBER OPTIC	TYPE STP I
100BaseTX			Two-pair		Two-pair
100BaseT4	Four-pair	Four-pair	Four-pair		
100BaseFX				One-pair	
100BaseT2	Two-pair	Two-pair	Two-pair		

You must always remember the following important rules when working with Fast Ethernet:

- No coaxial cables are allowed. Fast Ethernet only supports twisted-pair and fiber-optic media.
- The maximum length of a twisted-pair cable is 100 meters (328 feet).
- The maximum length of a multimode fiber-optic cable is 412 meters (1,351 feet).
- You cannot use multiconductor cable bundles, such as those used in wiring PBX and other telephone company equipment.
- Only two repeaters may be used in a single collision domain.

Gigabit Ethernet

The newest standard to emerge from the high-speed networking committee is Gigabit Ethernet—running at 1,000 Mbps! Here are the IEEE standards for this blazingly fast technology:

- *802.3z*—The 1000BaseX standard family for fiber-optic cable and short-haul copper media
- *802.3ab*—The 1000BaseT standard for Category 5 UTP

The 802.3z, 100BaseX standards use an encoding scheme known as 8B/10B, which was developed at IBM. Physical media-dependent standards in this family include the following:

- *1000BaseSX*—Specifies the rules for fiber-optic media
- *1000BaseLX*—Specification for fiber-optic media used in backbone applications
- *1000BaseCX*—Specification for copper media

Switched Ethernet

In a generic Ethernet environment, all devices fight for access to the cabling trunk. If the media is busy, all other devices wait until the trunk is free. Engineers reduced this problem slightly by introducing bridges, which split the total number of contending workstations into separate domains. Devices in one domain still contend with each other, but they don't interfere with devices in a different domain.

Although this is a step in the right direction, the solution itself generates new problems. When busy devices communicate across domains, the bridge might get more packets than it can handle. In this case, the bridge drops excessive packets and users lose their communications. Engineers solved this problem by building retransmission routines into upper-layer protocols. This in turn added traffic, which made the problem worse.

Switches were introduced to solve the problem of overloaded bridges. The switch's software causes it to learn the node address of all workstations on any port. Whenever the switch receives a packet, it sends the packet out the port that hosts the destination node ID. A switch with eight ports is capable of carrying on four separate "conversations," which might seem to imply that switches convert 10 Mbps Ethernet to 40 Mbps Ethernet. Unfortunately, it doesn't work out that way. In a client/server environment (such as NetWare), many workstations communicate with a few servers. This generates bottlenecks at the ports to which the servers are attached.

Full-Duplex Ethernet

With a switch in place, collisions may still happen because it is possible to drop packets if two or more stations are sending to the same receiver. This leads us to another solution: Full-Duplex Ethernet.

In twisted-pair cable, two of the pairs are idle. One is used for transmitting; the other is for receiving. When transmitting, the receive pair is monitored to detect collisions. In a switched environment, collisions are not possible. This simultaneous transmit-and-receive capability is known as *Full-Duplex Ethernet*.

To make use of this capability, the switched hub and all of the NICs must be built with the appropriate firmware. When Full-Duplex Ethernet is possible, the effective bandwidth is doubled. This, in conjunction with Fast Ethernet, can create mind-boggling throughput. Because of the high load this puts on the NICs, be sure to install bus-mastering adapters. As a matter of fact, you should use bus-mastering adapters whenever possible, even if you're not using Fast or Full-Duplex Ethernet.

This completes our discussion of Ethernet fundamentals, in which we have learned about protocols, topologies, cabling rules, and the future of *high-speed* Ethernet. I don't think we left a stone unturned. Now let's take a moment to explore Ethernet troubleshooting basics. Let's see what we can find.

Ethernet Troubleshooting Tips

When Ethernet trouble arises, always begin by asking some simple questions, such as (1) Is the cable plugged into the right card? (2) Is the concentrator power on? (3) Are you following established Ethernet cabling rules? By starting with these questions, which usually can be easily answered, you can quickly narrow down your options.

Next, you should perform a physical inventory of all Ethernet network components. Be sure that you follow established Ethernet cabling rules and that each component is connected to the right NIC or concentrator. Following are some Ethernet troubleshooting tips:

- *Check for Faulty Hardware*—A bad NIC or transceiver may cause an excessive number of bad packets to appear on the network. This is called *jabbering*. Use problem-isolation techniques to divide the network into smaller and smaller parts until the offending device is found. Follow these three steps: (1) Bring the network down, locate the midpoint of the cabling trunk, and insert two terminators; (2) Bring the network back up and analyze both halves to determine which half is still having the problem; (3) Repeat the process by moving to the midpoint of the bad half until the point of failure appears.

- *Check the Connecting Devices and Terminators* — Connecting devices such as T-connectors and vampire clamps are more likely to go bad than the cabling. Also, be sure that you are using 50-ohm components. Sometimes, for example, ARCnet and Ethernet co-axial terminators may get mixed.

- If only one workstation is having difficulty connecting to the network, check for a bad transceiver. A bad transceiver can also cause problems on the cable. You may need to swap out the workstation's NIC to isolate the problem, because Thin and Twisted-Pair Ethernet networks use internal transceivers.

- Use a Time Domain Reflectometer (TDR) to identify cable breaks and faulty terminators. This device sends a signal down the cable and listens for it to be reflected back. It then times the round trip and calculates the distance to the break.

- Use PING to track server and workstation communications. This DOS utility is included with the NetWare 5.1 Novell Client, and it can be loaded on workstations and used to track IP network communications. PING can be used to identify cable breaks by isolating noncommunicating computers on an IP network.

TIP

Study these Ethernet troubleshooting tips carefully. Specifically, learn the three-step process for isolating jabbering network components. Also, study the two Ethernet troubleshooting tools used to identify cable breaks and faulty terminators: Time Domain Reflectometer (TDR) and PING.

- If the workstation has a port-retry problem, or if the status link light does not light up when using UTP, the workstation may have a bad cable, an incorrectly configured NIC, and/or incorrect timing settings. Check or replace the cable and then verify the configuration with a diagnostic utility. Finally, check the UTP concentrator for a partitioned or disabled port.

- If the workstation displays a No Port Found error message when a port is installed, the workstation could have an I/O conflict or an incorrectly installed network board. Check the configuration of the NIC and potential conflicting devices, and then reinstall or replace the board.

- If the workstation experiences video distortion, or if it hangs while loading the LAN driver, the workstation may have a shared memory device conflict or a conflict between 8-bit shared RAM ports and 16-bit shared RAM ports. Replace the 8-bit shared memory device or remap it outside the C0000h to DFFFFh range.

There you have it. That's everything you ever wanted to know about Ethernet but were afraid to ask.

Ethernet is most network engineers' LAN standard of choice. Of course, it's not for everyone. Token Ring and FDDI are great options, as well. Let's continue our NIC Troubleshooting lessons with a closer look at these other two exceptional options, starting with Token Ring.

LAB EXERCISE 13.1: INSTALLING ETHERNET

Lab Exercises 13.1 through 13.5 have been built as a set, to be performed in order. In these exercises, you will learn how to install and troubleshoot Ethernet and Token Ring NICs and associated cabling connections.

By definition, the art of troubleshooting is very much a hands-on skill. Although you can learn many valuable techniques from a book such as this one, at some point, you'll need to practice what you've learned. If you don't have access to the appropriate hardware and software at this time, just use your imagination and follow along anyway!

In this first hands-on exercise, we're going to tackle Ethernet installation. As we discussed earlier in the chapter, Ethernet is the most common network standard. It offers relatively high-speed throughput over a variety of cable choices. It's a great choice in both the distributed LAN and centralized mainframe environments.

Thin and Thick Ethernet use a contention-based access method known as CSMA/CD, which relies on a shared trunk of cabling. The trunk is a single run of coax or twisted-pair cabling that extends throughout the topology of the LAN. Each workstation connects to the trunk directly and communicates with the LAN through an internal NIC.

You'll need the following hardware and software for this exercise:

- Two IBM-compatible computers
- Two Ethernet NICs with BNC and RJ-45 ports
- Two T-connectors
- Two 50-ohm terminators
- One Thin Ethernet cable
- Two 10BaseT cables
- One 10BaseT concentrator hub
- LAN drivers for the NICs

- PING utility (and associated files)
- Required IP client files

In this exercise, you will do the following:

1. Install an Ethernet connection using Thin Ethernet cable with BNC connectors.
2. Reinstall the Ethernet connection using 10BaseT cables with RJ-45 connectors connected to a central concentrator hub.
3. Test communications between the two computers using the PING utility.

As soon as you're ready, let's begin!

1. Configure the Ethernet NICs.
   - a. Choose two IBM-compatible computers. For convenience, place the two computers in proximity to each other, and then label one computer as a workstation and the other as a server. (Even though we're labeling one as a server, we're treating it like a workstation for the purpose of this exercise.)
   - b. Locate two Ethernet NICs containing BNC and RJ-45 ports. Ensure that you have the appropriate LAN drivers for the version of the NetWare Client that you plan to run. If you're not sure that you have the correct LAN drivers, you should surf to the NIC manufacturer's Web site and download the latest driver files. Alternately, you can call Novell Labs at 1-801-429-5544 for a list of drivers that have been certified as "Yes, Tested and Approved."

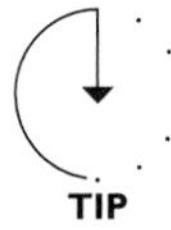
TIP

Always be sure you turn off the power on a computer before you add or remove boards. If you forget to turn off the power, you may find yourself purchasing a new board or computer that you hadn't planned on.

   c. Determine how to set the configurable parameters for each NIC. The parameters that typically need to be set on an Ethernet NIC are interrupt (IRQ), I/O port address, DMA, and connector type. Most Ethernet parameters can be defined using DIP switches or jumpers. Many of the newer Ethernet cards, however, have software-configurable firmware built into the card. If your NICs are software-configurable, be sure that the configuration disks that came with them are handy.

   d. Determine which settings are available on each computer. It's important that you choose NIC settings that do not conflict with settings used by existing hardware in the same computer. You'll need to use a shareware diagnostic utility to determine what hardware is already installed in each computer and how this hardware is configured. For instance, if you have a serial mouse installed on COM2, which uses IRQ 3, it will conflict with the default IRQ3 setting on some Ethernet boards, such as an NE2000.

   e. Set the configurable parameters for each NIC according to the manufacturer's instructions. Use unique settings for the IRQ, port address, DMA, and connector type settings.

2. Turn off both computers. Carefully insert one of the NICs into an empty expansion slot in each computer. Be sure that the board is seated firmly on the motherboard and that the mounting screw is used to ground the board.

3. Attach T-connectors, cable, and terminators. You'll notice that each T-connector has three arms: two that are identical and one that is different. The identical arms are used for attaching terminators or cable; the remaining arm is used to attach the T-connector to the back of the NIC.

   a. Attach a terminator to each T-connector. Attach a 50-ohm terminator on one of the identical arms, making sure to twist the terminator until it is locked in place, and then attach a 50-ohm terminator to the opposite end of the identical arm on the other T-connector.

   b. Attach the T-connectors to the cable. Attach the remaining identical arm on each T-connector to opposite ends of the Thin Ethernet cable.

c. Attach the computers via cable. Attach the remaining arm on each T-connector to the BNC connector on the corresponding NIC and then turn on both computers.

4. Test the connection.

   a. Locate the necessary files. As soon as you have completed the physical connection of the topology components, you're ready to test communications between the two computers. You can use the PING utility to perform this test, assuming that you also have access to the NetWare IP client connection files. Install the LAN Driver. Copy the appropriate LAN driver for each NIC into the C:\NWCLIENT directory on the corresponding computer.

   b. Load the NetWare IP connection files.

   c. Execute the PING utility. Run the PING utility on each computer by typing the following:

   ```
   PING
   ```

5. Switch to 10BaseT. 10BaseT differs from Ethernet in that it uses a star topology rather than a bus trunk. With 10BaseT, a NIC terminates each leg of the star using UTP with an RJ-45 connector. The other end of each leg is then connected to a concentrator hub in the center using an RJ-45 connector. Now that you've successfully connected the two computers using Thin Ethernet cable, let's try connecting the computers using 10BaseT.

   a. Turn off the two computers.

   b. Remove the T-connectors from both NICs.

   c. Reset both NICs to use the RJ-45 port for UTP cable.

   d. Plug one end of each 10BASE-T cable into one of the NICs. Next, take the free end of each cable and plug it into an available port on the concentrator.

   e. Turn on both computers.

Note: If you don't have a 10BaseT concentrator, you can use a crossover 10BaseT cable for connecting the two computers directly. See your cable vendor for details. In addition, you can use the D-shaped DIX connector on a NIC rather than the RJ-45 connector by connecting one end of the cable to the DIX connector and the other end to an external transceiver. You would then need to use a UTP cable to connect the transceiver to the concentrator.

f. Load the connection files and drivers.

g. Test the connection using the COMCHECK utility.

Congratulations! Now that you have successfully connected two computers using Thin Ethernet and 10BaseT cabling, let's experience some Ethernet troubleshooting problems — in Lab Exercise 13.2.

LAB EXERCISE 13.2: TROUBLESHOOTING ETHERNET

Network troubleshooting is often far more of an art than a science. An experienced network administrator, for instance, can often quickly diagnose a problem by checking for the most likely causes of the problem before embarking on a careful, systematic investigation of the problem.

Throughout this chapter, you will be provided with a set of scenarios that describe common network symptoms and, you will be given the opportunity to diagnose the cause of these problems, based on the limited information available. In each case, you will be asked to match the most likely cause of each problem with the symptoms.

A. Loose or unplugged T-connector

B. Violation of the 5-4-3 Rule

C. Network board set for the wrong connector type

D. Interrupt conflict

E. Misinterpretation of SQE (heartbeat) as signal jamming

F. Direct UTP connection with no concentrator

G. NIC not firmly seated in motherboard

H. Frame type mismatch

I. Incorrect terminator

J. Violation of Ethernet cable length rules

1. ___ One of the managers in the Finance Department just installed a modem in her computer and is now complaining that her network connection no longer works. She said that she checked the NE2000 network board and T-connector, and everything looks fine.

2. ___ One of your colleagues has just upgraded his network from NetWare 3.11 to NetWare 3.12. He said that, for some reason, none of the workstations will communicate with the server.

3. ___ One of the programmers at work decided to set up a small LAN at home. She purchased Ethernet NICs, Thin Ethernet cable, and T-connectors on her way home from work. When she got home, she realized that she had forgotten to purchase terminators. Her son suggested that she borrow terminators from a neighbor, who is always picking up computer parts at swap meets and garage sales. She tried screwing in the borrowed terminators, and they seemed to fit just fine. Unfortunately, the computers still wouldn't communicate.

4. ___ Your neighbor said that the new Ethernet LAN that was installed at his office doesn't work. He said that it has a maximum trunk length of 2,400 feet, consisting of five segments, connected by four repeaters, with approximately 25 nodes per segment.

5. ___ The MIS Manager moved a couple of spare computers into her office so that she could get up to speed on NetWare 4.1. She didn't want to plug into the regular 10BaseT network, so she just ran to the local computer super store and picked up a Thin Ethernet cable, a couple of T-connectors, and a couple of 50-ohm terminators so that she could connect the two computers directly. Even after she made sure that all of the physical connections seemed secure, she couldn't get the two computers to communicate.

6. ___ A couple of your users in a field sales office came into the office on Monday morning and found that they could no longer connect to the LAN. They said that they hope the paint fumes aren't affecting the equipment.

7. ___ Your nephew works a few hours a week in the computer lab at the local college. He said that as soon as they installed several new computers on the LAN, a number of the older ones stopped working.

8. ___ Your friend is an instructor at the local community college. She said that they just networked the computers in her classroom using Thin Ethernet. To save room, the computers were arranged at right angles to the front of the classroom, with each set of back-to-back computers separated by an aisle. She said that she knows they couldn't have exceeded the maximum cable lengths, because the computers are close together.

9. ___ One of your friends is taking a network class and decided to install a 10BaseT test system at home. Her system consists of a single server and workstation. She said that she has tried everything but just can't get the two computers to communicate. She said that she doesn't believe the cable connecting the two computers is the problem, because she purchased a standard, good quality, Category 5 cable in a factory-sealed package from a reputable vendor.

10. ___ One of the employees in the marketing department just installed a CD-ROM and a high-end sound card in his computer. He said that because of the design of the motherboard, he had a hard time trying to find a slot that the sound card would fit in. He said that it was a real pain having to move all of the cards around to find an arrangement that would fit. He said that it doesn't look like he has an interrupt or address conflict, but he still can't communicate with the network.

See Appendix C for answers.

Troubleshooting Token Ring

The token ring topology standard integrates the best characteristics of the other topology designs: it has the most reliable protocol (token passing) and the most trouble-free configuration (physical star).

Token ring uses a deterministic token-passing protocol. This civilized channel-access method ensures organized communications between workstations and servers on the network, one at a time. The token-passing protocol relies on a control signal called a *token*. A token is a 24-bit packet that circulates throughout the network, from NIC to NIC, in an orderly fashion. If a workstation wants to transmit a message, it seizes the token and gains complete control over the communications channel. This eliminates the possibility of signal collisions.

The token is created by the first initialized workstation. This special node, called the *active monitor* (or *ring monitor*), is responsible for ensuring the integrity of the token as it travels along the channel. If the token is damaged by line noise or a workstation crash, the active monitor waits seven seconds and then generates a new token. This level of fault tolerance, along with the civilized manner in which the token travels, makes token passing an excellent choice for large networks with medium-to-heavy load requirements.

Refer to Figure 13.10 for an illustration of the token-passing protocol scheme. In this scenario, the token circulates the ring 245 times a second and stops to visit each workstation along the way. The NIC that controls the token has exclusive access to the channel and may send a 2,048- or 4,096-byte message without any interference. To make this work, Token Ring NICs exist in one of four states: transmit, bypass, listen, and receive. Following is an explanation of the token-passing model illustrated in Figure 13.10:

1. Workstation A has a message for Workstation D. Workstation A enters into transmit mode and captures the free-flowing token.

2. Workstation A attaches its message to the token, marks it with a destination address, and sends the token along the network channel.

3. Workstation B is off, remaining in bypass mode, so the token continues straight through B's NIC and on to the next node.

4. Workstation C, in listen mode, notices the passing token and checks the destination address, but it doesn't find a match, so C sends the token back on its way.

5. Workstation D, also in listen mode, notices the token and checks the destination address. Now there's a match!

6. Workstation D switches into receive mode and copies the message into its memory. Remember, Workstation A still controls the token. To ensure continual communications, Workstation D must attach an acknowledgment to the token and send it back to A.

7. Once Workstation A receives the acknowledgment message from Workstation D, it releases the token and enters into listen mode.

FIGURE 13.10

Understanding the token-passing protocol

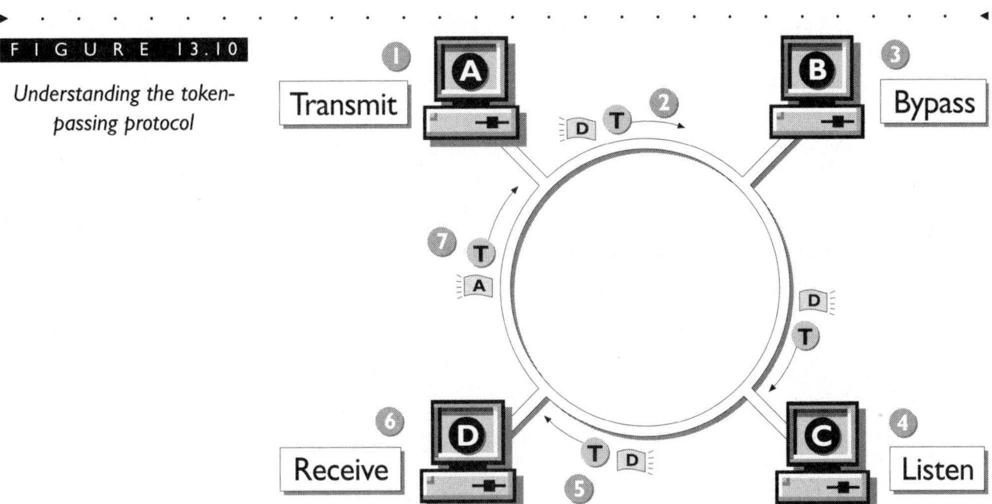

The token-passing protocol was designed to operate at 4 Mbps, but most of today's NICs can support speeds of up to 16 Mbps. The 16 Mbps design uses a special token-passing feature called Early Release Token Mechanism (ERTM).

Token ring operates over a logical ring, physical star topology and is designed to be self-healing in the event of a cable break or computer failure. The central point of the physical star configuration is a token ring hub called a *Multistation Access Unit (MSAU)*. Workstations and servers attach to the MSAU using special ring-in (RI) and ring-out (RO) ports.

Refer to Table 13.9 for a summary of token ring's advantages and disadvantages.

TABLE 13.9

Token Ring Advantages and Disadvantages

ADVANTAGES	DISADVANTAGES
Excellent throughput under high-load conditions	expensive, because of proprietary network components
Facilitates LAN-to-mainframe connections, especially in an IBM environment	Requires a high level of expertise for management and troubleshooting
Provides built-in troubleshooting mechanisms such as beaconing and auto-reconfiguration	
Supports STP and UTP cabling	
Best protocol (token passing), most reliable topology (star-ring), and a reasonably fast connectivity scheme (4 Mbps or 16 Mbps)	

Token Ring Cabling Rules

Token ring uses a token-passing protocol over a logical ring, physical star topology. The central point of each interconnected physical star is a token ring hub called an MSAU. As you can see in Figure 13.11, the MSAU attaches to distributed workstations and servers through special STP adapter cables. At the NIC end of the adapter cable is a 9-pin Attachment Unit Interface (AUI) connector. At the MSAU end is a specialized hermaphroditic connector.

The IBM 8228 MSAU is commonly known by its model number (8228). MSAUs usually have eight ports and are passive, nonintelligent hubs. MSAUs form a logical ring through special end connectors called ring-in (RI) and ring-out (RO) ports. The RO port from the first MSAU plugs into the RI port of its neighbor. The neighbor's RO port plugs into the next MSAU's RI port, until a ring of stars is created.

FIGURE 13.11

Token ring cabling rules

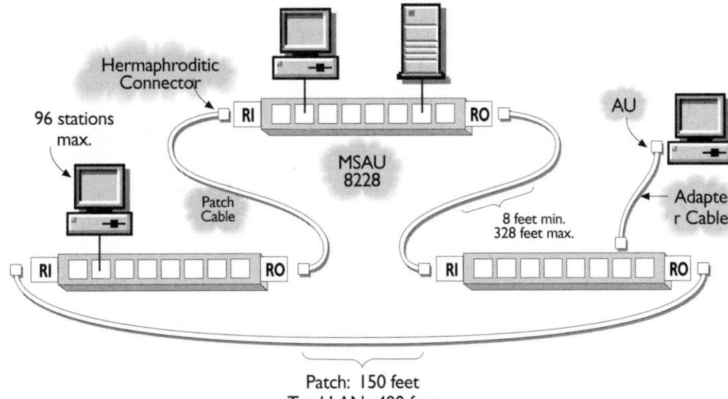

MSAU connections are made through patch cables and adapter cables. Patch cables connect MSAUs to each other, while adapter cables attach MSAUs to token ring NICs using a 15-pin AUI connector (see Figure 13.11 earlier). These cables are designed according to proprietary IBM Token Ring standards, which describe seven types of token ring cables. All cable is STP except for Type 3 (UTP) and Type 5 (fiber optics). Type 6 is the most popular specification for patch and adapter cables. Refer to Table 13.10 for a summary of Token Ring's cable types.

TABLE 13.10

Token Ring Twisted-Pair and Fiber-Optic Cable Types

TYPE	CHARACTERISTICS
Type 1	Braided cables shielded around two twisted pairs of 22-AWG wire. Type 1 is used for some patch cables and for inside-the-wall portions of adapter cables.
Type 2	Same as Type 1 but with the addition of four pairs of telephone-grade UTP. The intent was to lower building costs by combining telephone and data cables in one protective jacket.
Type 3	UTP Category 5. Type 3 cable must have at least two twists per foot to operate in the Token Ring environment.
Type 5	Fiber-optic cabling. Type 5 cable can be used as patch cables on the main ring path only.

Continued

TABLE 13.10

Token Ring Twisted-Pair and Fiber-Optic Cable Types (continued)

TYPE	CHARACTERISTICS
Type 6	Shielded twisted pair but with a higher signal loss per foot than Type 1. Type 6 cable is also much more flexible than Type 1. This cabling is used to attach workstations to the wall plate or where extra flexibility is needed. This is also the original cable type for patch and adapter cables.
Type 8	Special-use cable for data communications under carpeted floors. Type 8 cable has a special oval-shaped cable jacket. This cable type isn't a great solution because it has severe length restrictions and excessive data noise.
Type 9	A fire-retardant version of Type 6. Type 9 cable is required in open, plenum spaces.

Following is a summary of token ring cabling rules:

- The 8228 RI/RO ports enable each MSAU to create a logical ring. IBM Token Ring supports 260 devices on Type 1 or 2 cabling. The IEEE 802.5 specification supports 250 devices, but for practical purposes, you should limit your total token ring network to 96 stations and 12 MSAUs. This is the default for Type 6 cabling.
- Patch cables connect RI and RO ports of the star-wired MSAUs into logical rings. Originally, IBM Type 6 cable was used for patch cables, but other types of cable may now be used. Patch cables may be a maximum of 150 feet (45 meters) long and have a total ring size of 400 feet (120 meters). The minimum length is 8 feet (2.5 meters).
- Adapter cables connect workstations to MSAUs. On the NIC end, these cables use AUI connectors, and on the MSAU end, they use hermaphroditic connectors. Originally, IBM Type 6 cable was used for adapter cables, but other types of cable can now be used. The recommended maximum distance between the MSAU and workstation is 328 feet (100 meters).
- Token ring is now supported over UTP cabling. Today's MSAUs accept both Type 1 and Type 3 cabling, and the IEEE has created a specification called UTP/TR for 16 Mbps UTP token ring. The new specification includes the use of Category 5 UTP and has the advantage of less attenuation than Type 1 STP.

REAL WORLD

Token Ring over UTP cabling has become quite popular in LAN environments. Following are the UTP pinouts for creating a Token Ring RJ-45 connector. (**Note:** These specifications are for a straight-through cable.)

- Pin 1 to pin 1, brown/white, not used
- Pin 2 to pin 2, green/white, ground
- Pin 3 to pin 3, orange/white, transmit (+)
- Pin 4 to pin 4, blue/white, receive (+)
- Pin 5 to pin 5, white/blue, receive (–)
- Pin 6 to pin 6, white/orange, transmit (–)
- Pin 7 to pin 7, white/green, ground (signal)
- Pin 8 to pin 8, white/brown, not used

All in all, Token Ring is the ideal LAN standard (if you can afford it). In fact, one of the strongest advantages of Token Ring is its built-in network management and troubleshooting capabilities. Ready, set, go!

Token Ring Troubleshooting Tips

Token ring topology components provide various troubleshooting and maintenance tools that enhance your ability to solve networking problems. In this section, we will explore two token ring computer classifications and two self-healing features.

Token ring supports the following two computer classifications:

- *Active Monitor*—The active monitor is usually the first station turned on. It creates the token and ensures reliable data delivery. Every seven seconds, the active monitor sends out a frame to the next active device in the ring. The frame broadcasts the identity of the active monitor and requests that the device introduces itself to the next active device down the ring. This process continues until each machine is acquainted with its neighbors. This periodic token ring monitoring is essential in all troubleshooting efforts, especially those involved in isolating a failure domain.

- *Standby Monitor*—All other stations on the LAN are standby monitors, which can accept the active monitor role if the original active monitor becomes unavailable.

Token ring supports two self-healing features:

- *Beaconing*—When a station does not receive a message from its Nearest Active Upstream Neighbor (NAUN), it sends out a warning, otherwise known as a *beacon*. This beacon alerts every network device that a failure has occurred, and it begins to isolate the failure domain. Follow along in Figure 13.12. Assume that a fault occurs in the cabling between Stations 1 and 2. When Station 2 does not receive the expected seven-second greeting from Station 1, it complains by sending out a beacon. The beacon includes the address of Station 2, the address of Station 1, and the warning message. These addresses help to define the failure domain. That is, you can assume that the cable break occurred somewhere between Station 1 and Station 2. When a beacon occurs, the ring attempts to fix the problem without your intervention. This process of self-healing is called *auto-reconfiguration*.
- *Auto-Reconfiguration*—When a token ring station receives a problem alert from its NAUN, it initiates auto-reconfiguration. In the example in Figure 13.12, Station 2 recognizes a problem from Station 1. The internal NIC disconnects itself from the ring, performs internal diagnostics, and then connects itself back to the ring if it can do so safely. This process also occurs on the NAUN. If the two beaconing stations cannot solve the problem automatically, they send an error message to the network administrator identifying the failure domain.

FIGURE 13.12

Understanding beaconing

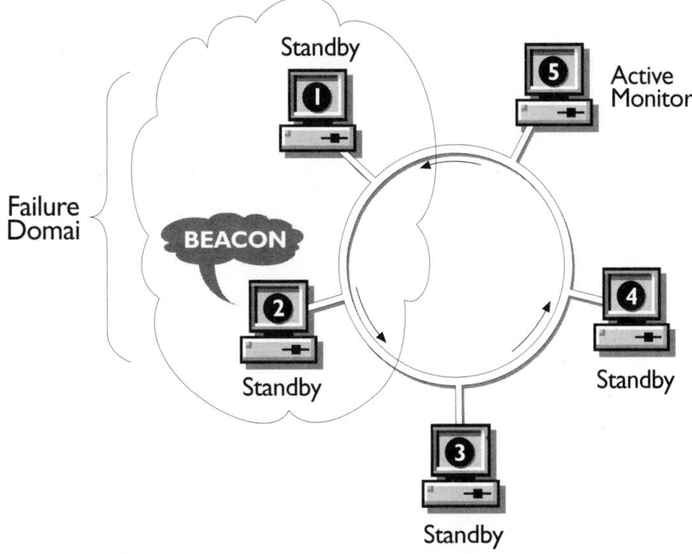

That does it for Token Ring. It is undoubtedly one of the strongest of all LAN standards. It integrates the best protocol with the most reliable topology and a reasonably fast cabling scheme. Of course, as we've learned, this great technology comes with a high price tag — in money and management expertise. If you're daring enough to tackle Token Ring, be sure to prepare yourself first. This is the best troubleshooting tip I can give you.

LAB EXERCISE 13.3: INSTALLING TOKEN RING

Welcome back to the hands-on portion of this chapter. As we learned earlier, Token Ring integrates the best characteristics of the other LAN standards. It has the most reliable protocol (token passing), the most trouble-free configuration (physical star), and a reasonably fast connectivity scheme (ring of hubs).

Once you choose to enter the Token Ring arena, you should stay with one particular manufacturer. Ethernet, on the other hand, is standardized sufficiently to allow for crossover from one manufacturer to another. The proprietary nature of Token Ring makes it expensive.

You'll need the following hardware and software for this exercise:

- Two IBM-compatible computers
- Two Token Ring NICs
- Two Token Ring adapter cables
- One MSAU
- LAN drivers for the NICs
- DOS 5.0 or later
- PING utility (and associated files)
- Required IP client files

In this exercise, you will do the following:

1. Install a Token Ring connection.
2. Test communications between the two computers using the COMCHECK utility.

As soon as you're ready, let's begin!

1. Configure the Token Ring NICs.

a. Choose two IBM-compatible computers. You can use the same two computers that you used in the "Lab Exercise 13.1: Installing Ethernet" and "Lab Exercise 13.2: Troubleshooting Ethernet" sections.

b. Load the DOS High Memory Manager in CONFIG.SYS and exclude the memory range required by the NIC. A common problem involving Token Ring workstations is RAM mismatch, which occurs when a memory manager allows other programs to use RAM that should be reserved for the NIC.

First, check that the two computers you are using contain DOS 5.0 or above. Next, use the instructions listed in the documentation that came with your Token Ring boards to load the DOS High Memory Manager in your CONFIG.SYS startup file and to exclude the block of addresses that are used by the NIC. (Although it's not necessary to load the DOS High Memory Manager on a Token Ring station, you'll find that it's done fairly often.)

Listed here is a sample of the lines that would appear in your CONFIG.SYS file. The actual address range would vary, however, depending on your NIC.

```
DEVICE=C:\DOS\HIMEM.SYS

DEVICE=C:\DOS\EMM386.EXE /FRAME=NONE /X=CC00-DFFF
```

c. Locate two Token Ring NICs. Be sure to use the type of board that corresponds to the type of computer you are using. Also, make sure you have the appropriate LAN drivers for the version of NetWare that you plan to run.

d. Determine how to set the configurable parameters for each NIC. IBM ISA Token Ring cards are set using DIP switches or software settings.

The parameters that can be set on a Token Ring NIC are interrupt (IRQ), data rate, primary/secondary, and ROM address.

e. Determine which settings are available on each computer. Choose NIC settings that do not conflict with settings used by existing hardware in the same computer.

f. Set the configurable parameters for each NIC according to the manufacturer's instructions. For example, if you're using a standard IBM 16/4 ISA Token Ring card, set these parameters:

- Use DIP switches 1 through 6 to set the ROM address. Be sure that the address you choose does not conflict with any other boards in the same computer.
- Use DIP switches 7 and 8 to set the IRQ. Be sure that the address you choose does not conflict with existing hardware in the same computer.
- Use DIP switch 9 to indicate whether the NIC is primary or secondary. Set the board to primary if you will have only one Token Ring board in this computer.
- Use switches 10 and 11 to indicate the shared RAM size. Novell recommends a shared RAM size of 16K.
- Use switch 12 to set the NIC speed. Be sure that all devices on the network are set at the same data rate. If possible, set both NICs to 16 Mbps.

2. Install the NICs. Turn off both computers. Carefully insert each of the NICs into an empty expansion slot in the corresponding computer.

3. Connect the computers to the MSAU.

a. Reset the ports on the MSAU using the reset tool. Some types of MSAUs do not need to be reset. If you are using a MSAU that needs to be reset, insert the tool until you hear a click.

b. Install the cables. Token Ring uses adapter cables (also called *lobe cables*) with large hermaphroditic ports to connect the NIC to the MSAU. Connect one end of each cable to a NIC and then connect the other end to the MSAU. You can use any available port on the MSAU except for those marked Ring In (RI) or Ring Out (RO). After you have connected the cables, turn on both computers.

4. Test the connection.

   a. Locate the necessary files. As soon as you have completed the physical connection of the topology components, you're ready to test communications between the two computers. You can use the PING utility to perform this test, assuming that you also have access to the NetWare IP client connection files. Install the LAN Driver. Copy the appropriate LAN driver for each NIC into the C:\NWCLIENT directory on the corresponding computer.

   b. Load the NetWare IP connection files.

   c. Execute the PING utility. Run the PING utility on each computer by typing the following:

   ```
   PING
   ```

Now that you have installed Token Ring NICs on your computers, you are ready to move on to the Token Ring troubleshooting problems in the next exercise.

LAB EXERCISE 13.4: TROUBLESHOOTING TOKEN RING

You are interviewing for a position as the top LAN administrator at a Fortune 100 firm. The interviewer explains that the company uses different network topologies in their various locations around the world. The first question he asks you on this subject is for your list of top ten troubleshooting solutions for a Token Ring network.

List the ten troubleshooting solutions that you gave him:

1. ______________________________
2. ______________________________
3. ______________________________
4. ______________________________
5. ______________________________
6. ______________________________
7. ______________________________
8. ______________________________
9. ______________________________
10. ______________________________

A list of possible answers can be found in Appendix C.

Troubleshooting FDDI

Fiber Distributed Data Interface (FDDI) uses fiber-optic cabling to send packets of information over light instead of electricity. It resembles token ring in many respects, including packet format, topology design, and protocol rules.

Like token ring, FDDI uses a token-passing protocol. When an FDDI station wants to transmit a packet, it waits for the token to arrive and then transmits its packet. Unlike token ring, an FDDI station attaches the token to the back of the packets. The next station downstream receives the packet and token combination and repeats it to the next neighbor. This is a fast and organized protocol, but it requires a tremendous amount of bandwidth. In addition, FDDI uses a timed token-rotation method to achieve high data rates of up to 100 Mbps.

FDDI uses a modified token ring topology that consists of two rings running in opposite directions (called *dual counter-rotating rings*). Stations downstream from the originating node read messages that are marked with their address. When a fault occurs, the stations immediately before and after the problem reroute the data they receive to the backup ring. They send it in the opposite direction, thereby reconstructing the broken ring (called *wrapping*).

In addition to FDDI over fiber optics, Asynchronous Transfer Mode (ATM) offers an excellent wide area network (WAN) backbone alternative. ATM is a packet-switching technology operating over existing UTP or fiber-optic cabling. Instead of variable length frames, ATM uses fixed length 53-byte cells to package network data. Primarily used for high-end clients, ATM supports complex multimedia applications with extremely high-speed communications (from 25 Mbps to 2,488 Mbps).

Refer to Table 13.11 for a summary of FDDI's advantages and disadvantages.

TABLE 13.11

FDDI Advantages and Disadvantages

ADVANTAGES	DISADVANTAGES
Fast (up to 100 Mbps).	FDDI network components are specialized and expensive.
Supports long cable distances (up to 200 km).	Substantial expertise is needed to install and maintain FDDI components.

Continued

TABLE 13.11

FDDI Advantages and Disadvantages (continued)

ADVANTAGES	DISADVANTAGES
Network management intelligence is built into all FDDI components.	
Fiber-optic cabling is a reliable and secure media that is immune to EMI.	
Fiber-optic cabling maintains ground isolation between buildings, which makes it an excellent WAN backbone solution.	

FDDI Cabling Rules

FDDI uses fiber-optic technology. These cables consist of a fine optical fiber made from two types of glass: one for the inner core and one for the outer core (called the *cladding*). Fiber-optic cabling is classified by the diameter of the core fiber. Most network components support one of the following three types of cable:

- *Single-Mode* — This is the most expensive, because of its exceptionally thin core (7 to 9 microns in diameter). Single-mode cable can carry signals extraordinary distances without repeaters, and it is used primarily for WAN communication and telecommunications. The thin fiber core limits attenuation, and therefore causes less propagation delay.
- *Step-Index Multimode* — This type was used mainly in early fiber installations. Step-index multimode cabling has been replaced almost exclusively by graded-index multimode.
- *Graded-Index Multimode* — This is the most popular type of fiber-optic cabling. It uses an enhanced cladding that reduces reflectance in the fiber core, making data transmission more efficient and increasing bandwidth. This cabling is typically built with a 62.5-micron fiber core.

To manage fiber-optic communication, FDDI supports the following two types of computer stations (follow along with Figure 13.13):

- *Class A* — These stations are attached to both of the dual counter-rotating rings. Class A connections are typically made from hub to hub to ensure network fault tolerance. Class A stations support a maximum network size of 100 km, with up to 500 nodes.
- *Class B* — These stations can connect to either ring at any time, but not to both. Class B connections are typically used for workstations and servers to ensure that computer failures are limited to specific FDDI hubs. Class B stations support a maximum network size of 200 km, with up to 1,000 nodes.

FIGURE 13.13

FDDI cabling rules

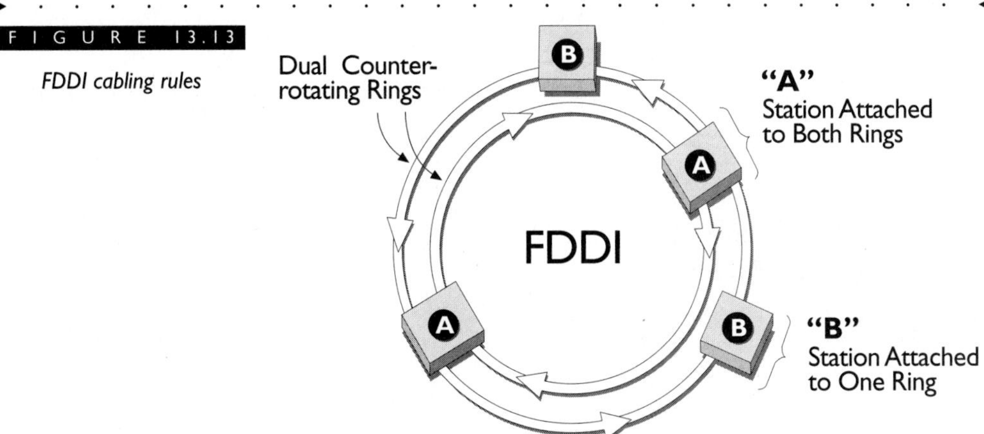

FDDI Troubleshooting Tips

FDDI troubleshooting requires more experience than Ethernet and token ring because it relies on sensitive photonic components and fiber-optic cabling. Following are some simple troubleshooting tips that will help you begin working with FDDI:

- The type of fiber-optic cabling chosen must match the total network size. Multimode fiber, for example, works best for distances up to 2 kilometers. Anything beyond that requires single-mode cabling.

- You can use an Optical Time Domain Reflectometer (OTDR) to test fiber-optic cabling. Also, never look into an active fiber-optic cable, because eye damage could result.
- A loss of optical power greater than 11 decibels is serious. Look for bad connectors, bad connections, or an open condition on the cable.
- Because data is transmitted as light using FDDI, dirty connectors can cause network communication problems. Periodically, clean FDDI connectors with a lint-free cloth dipped in alcohol.
- Plastic fiber-optic cable is available, but it is much less robust than glass cable. In addition, plastic fiber has more impurities than glass. Do not use plastic fiber-optic cabling for distances greater than 50 meters or if you require throughput over 10 Mbps.
- FDDI has a delay factor of as much as 4 milliseconds. This delay is inherent in the media and cannot be avoided. Therefore, consider implementing NetWare's Packet Burst Protocol when using FDDI.
- Because of the way FDDI translation bridges are configured, source routing is the preferred choice when using FDDI with NetWare.

Well, that does it for FDDI. And that completes our discussion of the three main LAN standards. To review, we have explored the NIC configuration and troubleshooting of the following LAN standards:

- *Ethernet*—Ethernet is the most popular of the three standards. In this chapter, we learned about Thin Ethernet, Thick Ethernet, and Ethernet 10BaseT. We explored some unique cabling setups and discovered the value of Fast and Switched Ethernet. Finally, we gained valuable Ethernet troubleshooting experience with respect to physical components, troubleshooting tools, workstation problems, and frame types.

- *Token Ring* — If Ethernet represents the average LAN, Token Ring is the most popular of three exceptional standards, and we learned just how exceptional Token Ring can be. After all, it uses the best protocol (token passing), most reliable topology (logical ring, physical star), and a reasonably fast cabling scheme (4 Mbps or 16 Mbps). And that's not all. We also learned about Token Ring monitoring, beaconing, and auto-reconfiguration.

- *FDDI* — The final standard brought us into the 21st century of networking — FDDI. Fiber-optic technology introduces a whole new way of transmitting data. It's faster, more reliable, and much more expensive. We learned about FDDI's token-passing protocol, dual counter-rotating ring, and three different cabling types.

My brain hurts . . . how about yours? That's okay, we'll fix it in Chapter 14, "Troubleshooting Hard Drives."

Sit back, relax, and enjoy the show!

LAB EXERCISE 13.5: MISCELLANEOUS TROUBLESHOOTING

You will need a network-knowledgeable coworker or friend for this exercise. In this exercise, you will each take turns creating real-life network hardware and cabling problems, and then have the other person troubleshoot the problem.

For this exercise, you will want to have a minimum of two computers and as many different types of network hardware and cabling as possible (that is, to support Ethernet, Token Ring, and so on). You will also need two telephones: one next to the two computers and one in a separate room.

This lab exercise has three troubleshooting levels. If you are new to network troubleshooting, you will probably want to start with the Beginning Level and work your way up to the Intermediate and Advanced Levels. If you are confident of your troubleshooting ability, you may want to go straight to the Advanced Level portion of this exercise.

Here are the three troubleshooting levels for this exercise:

1. *Beginning Level* — Create one hardware/cabling problem at a time, and have your partner troubleshoot it without any assistance from you.

2. *Intermediate Level* — Create several hardware problems at one time, and have your partner solve them without any assistance from you.

3. *Advanced Level* — Create several hardware problems at one time, and have your partner solve them over the phone. In other words, simulate a help-desk situation in which the person who created the problems is the customer and the person troubleshooting the problem is a help-desk technician at a remote site. Furthermore, in this scenario, the following conditions apply:

   - The customer has network hardware and/or cabling problems and has no idea what is causing the problems or how to solve them.

   - The customer has limited computer literacy and cannot tell one hardware and/or cabling component from another.

   - The customer is not allowed to lie, but does not have to volunteer any information.

- The help-desk technician must solve the problems over the phone without access to any of the equipment.
- Because the customer has limited computer literacy, all questions should be phrased in a manner that would be understood by an ordinary user.
- The help-desk technician should assume that the customer knows nothing about proper installation and troubleshooting techniques. This means that the technician should ensure that the customer does not injure himself or herself, or damage the equipment.

Be creative and have fun. If you run out of ideas, see Appendix C for some hints.

LAB EXERCISE 13.6: BUILDING ACME'S NETWORK

Use the hints provided to find the 20 NIC troubleshooting terms hidden in this word search puzzle. Omit any punctuation characters (such as blank spaces, hyphens, and so on) and spell out any numbers.

S	F	I	B	E	R	O	P	T	I	C	I	C	P
T	T	O	K	E	N	R	I	N	G	E	Y	F	M
R	H	A	S	I	A	L	S	E	Z	J	P	H	O
Y	I	O	R	S	D	C	F	Y	U	X	Y	D	B
N	N	V	L	A	R	C	O	M	N	V	U	L	P
N	E	H	A	T	N	F	P	N	K	F	U	R	Z
O	T	H	I	C	K	E	T	H	E	R	N	E	T
X	H	J	X	I	R	V	J	F	R	C	K	G	B
J	E	X	A	O	D	V	M	I	X	I	K	H	R
T	R	C	O	L	L	I	S	I	O	N	F	T	I
J	N	F	C	O	M	C	H	E	C	K	W	V	D
G	E	L	D	I	P	S	W	I	T	C	H	S	G
M	T	C	S	D	F	R	A	M	E	T	Y	P	E
Q	V	V	C	R	I	N	G	U	X	W	F	P	S

Hints

1. Used by lighthouses and troubled Token Ring workstations.
2. Split the total number of contending workstations into separate domains.
3. Ethernet, ARCnet, and cable TV have something in common.
4. Bring in the Ethernet tow trucks.
5. Novell utility that helps you isolate and identify cable breaks.
6. Hardware toggle used for setting configurable parameter.
7. An exciting 32-bit enhancement to ISA.
8. High-speed LAN communications over fiber-optic cabling.
9. Transmission technology based on photonics.
10. In NetWare 5, the default Ethernet one is 802.2.
11. Original IBM PC expansion bus architecture.

12. Wire bridge used to close a circuit and establish an electrical connection.
13. IBM Token Ring wiring hub (also known as 8228).
14. Link between internal and external LAN communications.
15. Hottest new bus standard for servers.
16. Deterministic topology for token-passing protocol.
17. Multiple nodes are connected to a central hub.
18. 10Base5 standard; uses RG-8 coaxial cabling.
19. 10Base2 standard; uses RG-58 coaxial cabling.
20. No one ever got fired for buying IBM.

See Appendix C for answers.

LAB EXERCISE 13.7: TROUBLESHOOTING NICS

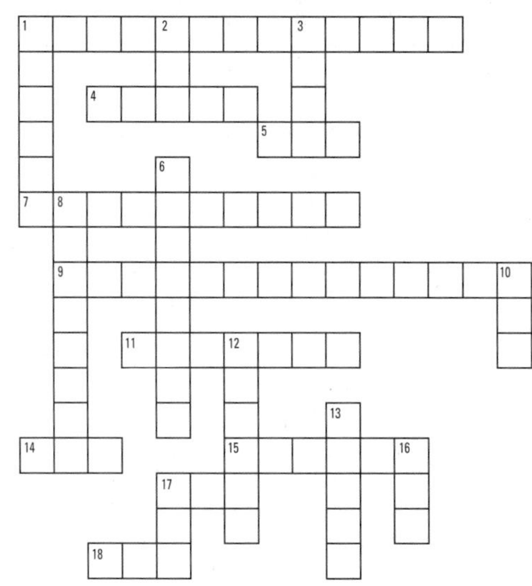

Across

1. In charge of the ring
4. Common connectivity medium
5. Thin Ethernet and ARCNet connector
7. "I'll be back!"
9. IBM's proprietary MSAU connector
11. Scary clamp
14. Cabling standard for IBM Type 1
15. Contention-based access method
17. Token Ring NIC connector
18. Baaaaaa for Token Ring

Down

1. Slow, but reliable LAN standard
2. Popular I/O bus architecture
3. Token Ring neighbor

6. Software marries hardware
8. Fast and cheap LAN standard
10. Moooooo for Token Ring
12. Notebook data bus architecture
13. Cable thickness measurement
16. Thick Ethernet connector
17. Doesn't dispense cash

See Appendix C for answers.

CHAPTER 14

Troubleshooting Hard Drives

This is your brain. This is your brain on NetWare. Any questions?

Like your brain, the server hard drive consists of five main components:

- The *platter* is the hard drive's frontal lobe. This is the magnetically encoded aluminum platter that forms the foundation of the hard drive. It's responsible for storing network data.
- The *track* consists of concentric circles inside a platter. These tracks are one of three components that help isolate specific pieces of data on the disk.
- The *cylinder* is a 3-D representation of all tracks on parallel platters at any given radius. Cylinders provide the 3-D capability of reading data from multiple platters. This is the second of three data-addressing components.
- The *sector* is the smallest logical unit on the disk and represents a pie-sliced cross section of tracks. It's the last data-addressing component.
- The *head* is the hard drive cerebellum. The hard drive head is a link to other regions on the network server disk. It reads and writes data from the disk and transfers it to the server via a disk controller.

Through your trials and tribulations as a NetWare troubleshooter, you'll find many problems begin and end with the server hard drive. In this chapter, we will explore basic hard drive principles, as well as installation, configuration, and troubleshooting issues. In summary, we'll study hard drive anatomy, various hard drive standards, five simple steps for hard drive setup, and some network storage alternatives (such as disk mirroring and duplexing, CD-ROM, and RAID).

So, without any further ado, let's begin our discussion of network storage troubleshooting with a lesson in hard drive anatomy.

Hard Drive Anatomy

Hard drives provide data storage and retrieval capabilities on your network. Because they are mechanical devices, they may experience problems from time to time. Therefore, it's important to be familiar with basic troubleshooting techniques.

A hard drive consists of one or more rigid platters sealed inside a protective container, along with associated read/write heads and electronics. (**Note:** The courseware assumes that you are using fixed, rather than removable, hard disks.) Hard drives also have platters, heads, tracks, cylinders, and sectors. (These five main components are discussed in-depth in the preceding introduction.)

The read/write *head* is the key link between physical data storage and the outside world. As you can see in Figure 14.1, each side of each platter has its own head. Much like how the human cerebellum is the brain's link to the outside world, the hard drive head transfers data to and from the server bus. When the disk controller requests a specific data address, the head sweeps across the platter and hovers above the appropriate track. (*Seek time* is a measure of how long this takes.) After a moment or so, the data rotates under the hovering head and is read into the disk controller. (*Drive latency* is a measure of how long the head hovers.)

FIGURE 14.1

Hard drive anatomy

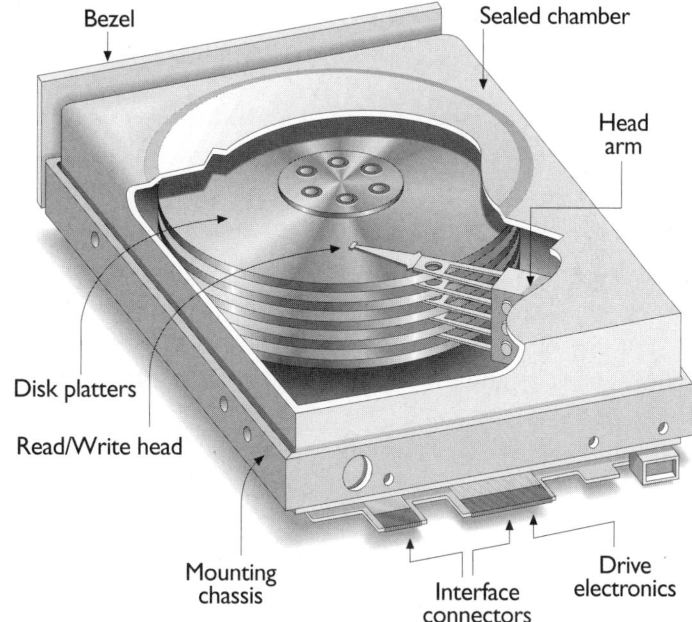

In addition to the components shown in Figure 14.1, a motor (called a *spindle motor*) rotates the platters within the disk. Some newer designs spin at up to 10,000 rpm. The read/write heads are held in place by a *head carriage,* which must be properly balanced. Finally, the *stepper motor actuator* (or the faster *voice coil actuator*) moves the heads to the correct position on the disk.

It's important to note that the head never touches the surface of the platter. High speeds in aerodynamics build a small air pocket between the platter and the head. If this air pocket breaks down, a head crash occurs. This contact often results in data loss, and if the crash is severe enough, it can damage the head, turning the entire disk into an expensive paperweight.

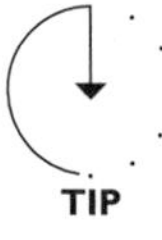

Server performance is tied closely to the speed of each internal read/write head. The most common measurement of drive performance is *access time,* which is a measurement of the time needed to get the data from the platter once it's been requested. Use the following formula to determine your drive's access time: access time = seek time + drive latency.

Before the server disk can be used to store user files, it must be partitioned and formatted. Hard disk partitioning prepares the platters for formatting. Formatting is the process of dividing the disk into tracks, sectors, cylinders, and ultimately laying down the operating system. As you will see later, NetWare partitioning and formatting is accomplished using the following server-based management utilities: INSTALL.NLM (NetWare 3 and NetWare 4) or NWCONFIG.NLM (NetWare 5.1).

Disk drives are often characterized by the type of interface they use. A *disk controller* serves as an interface between the computer motherboard and one or more hard drives. In this course, we are concerned with the following two types of hard drive interfaces:

- IDE
- SCSI

Let's start our hard drive anatomy discussion with IDE.

REAL WORLD

Skewing is another important hard drive troubleshooting concept. Most hard drive standards allow sectors to be skewed during a low-level format so that as the heads move from track to track, they start reading on the first sector in the next track. This enables the heads to move in a spiral pattern, which is much more efficient and reduces delays caused by rotational latency.

IDE

Integrated Device Electronics (IDE) is the most popular drive interface technology to date. Of course, that doesn't make it a perfect match for NetWare servers. It is, however, a huge improvement over older interfaces, such as ST-506 and Enhanced Small Device Interface (ESDI).

The IDE interface was created as a low-cost disk subsystem for AT-class motherboards. With this interface, the controller hardware is integrated with the disk drive. Performance benefits of using a built-in (that is, embedded) drive controller include a short data path and less electromagnetic interference. Another benefit is that only a single source of power is required.

A recent enhancement to IDE, called Enhanced IDE (EIDE), provides the following benefits:

- High-capacity addressing of AT Attachment (ATA) hard drives, which exceed the system BIOS limitation of 528MB
- Fast data-transfer rates (up to 16.6MB per second)
- Dual ATA host bus adapters that allow for support of up to four devices
- Support for peripherals other than hard disks

Understanding IDE

IDE drives use a master/slave strategy. The first task in drive setup is to ensure that the master/slave option is properly configured. If you have only one IDE drive in your server, it should be configured as *Single Drive Only.* If you have two IDE drives, the first drive (that is, the boot disk) should be set to *Master* and the second drive (that is, the one which is not a boot disk) should be set to *Slave*. EIDE technology is even more complicated, because it supports a maximum of two controllers with two IDE devices per controller, for a total of four hard drives.When choosing a CMOS Drive Type setting for your hard drive, always select the drive type whose key characteristics most closely match the one being installed. If you are installing an IDE hard drive in your server, you will most likely use Drive Type 47 (that is, user defined). When you specify Drive Type 47, you will be prompted to manually input the settings for hard drive parameters such as cylinders, heads, sectors, and capacity.

Because IDE uses an integrated drive technology, some of the jumpers and configuration settings are embedded in the hard drive, including the Digital Signal Processor (DSP) jumper for indicating the master/slave setting and the C/D jumper for designating C: and D: drives. The rest of the drive settings are configured on the IDE interface, including Base I/O Address, Base Memory Address, DMA Channel, and Interrupt.

Troubleshooting IDE

When IDE drives became generally available, they offered higher performance at a reasonable cost. Since then, they have become a favored solution for DOS and Windows-based workstations. Following is a list of IDE limitations, however, that make them a poor choice for NetWare servers:

- IDE does *not* support overlapped, multitasking input/output (I/O). In other words, once a command has been issued to an IDE drive, NetWare must wait until the command has been completed before issuing another command to any other disk. This is a severe limitation in a multitasking environment such as NetWare.

REAL WORLD

Most of today's computers autodetect IDE drives upon bootup.This is good news, because it means that you will never have to worry about programming CMOS.

- IDE does *not* support bus mastering. (Bus master adapters offload work from the CPU processor during data transfers. This can reduce CPU utilization by a ratio of as much as 7:1. Therefore, installing a bus master adapter in a server can have a dramatic effect on response time if CPU utilization is creating a bottleneck.)

- Older IDE controllers do *not* support tape or optical drives. Also, older IDE technology imposes a disk capacity limit of 528MB.

- IDE drives are not suitable for mirroring. (When you run IDE drives as a pair, the controller of the second drive is disabled. Both drives are then controlled by the built-in controller on the first drive — thereby creating a single point of failure.)

TIP

If given a troubleshooting scenario, you should be able to identify IDE hard drive limitations. Specifically, know that IDE does not support overlapped, multitasking I/O; bus mastering; or disk mirroring. Also, remember that IDE imposes a disk capacity limit of 528MB and that most disk configurations are set in a server's STARTUP.NCF file.

Following are some additional troubleshooting tips you should keep in mind when using IDE drives in NetWare servers:

- Do *not* low-level format IDE drives. (Doing so is fatal in most cases.) Unfortunately, you can accidentally do so in one of two ways: during NetWare installation or through use of third-party utilities. Both NetWare 2 and NetWare 3 installation programs offer low-level formatting options. Fortunately, newer IDE drive controllers often won't allow you to low-level format an IDE drive.

- When you load IDE disk drivers on a server, be sure to choose the correct interrupt and I/O settings. In most cases, the default interrupt is E (14 in decimal notation) and the default I/O port address is 1F0. For example, to use default settings with the IDEATA driver, add the following LOAD command to the server's STARTUP.NCF file:

```
LOAD IDEATA PORT=1F0 INT=E
```

- As we discussed earlier, IDE drives use a master/slave configuration. Typically, this jumper can be configured using one of three options: Single Drive Only, Master, or Slave. If you are installing a single drive in a server, designate it as *Single Drive Only.* If you are installing two drives in a server, designate the first drive (that is, the boot disk) as *Master* and the second drive (that is, the one that is not a boot disk) as *Slave.*

  Note: If a single drive is erroneously set to Slave (instead of to Single Drive Only), the following error message will be displayed:

  ```
  1782—disk controller failure
  ```

- On a server, be sure to load the correct IDE disk driver NLM. In NetWare 5.1, the new IDEATA.HAM driver is designed for all IDE interfaces. It also provides support for IDE CD-ROM drives. Loading an incorrect disk driver on a server will generate a variety of error messages.

This completes our discussion of IDE configuration and troubleshooting. Now let's explore a more ideal server storage standard: Small Computer System Interface, or SCSI.

LAB EXERCISE 14.1: TROUBLESHOOTING IDE HARD DRIVES

Now that you are a fledgling IDE master, let's test your troubleshooting skills with a few sample scenarios. Ready, set, learn!

- *Scenario 1:* When you boot your NetWare 5.1 server, you receive the following error message:

  ```
  Interrupt 496 is NOT supported and was ignored
  ```

  You immediately check your STARTUP.NCF file to look at the statement that loads the disk driver. It says the following:

  ```
  LOAD IDEATA PORT=E INT=1FO
  ```

  In the back of your mind, you seem to remember that E and 1F0 are the default values for IDE drives. You didn't expect to have an interrupt or address conflict with this machine when using default values. What do you think is causing the problem?

- *Scenario 2:* You have just installed a new IDE hard drive in your NetWare server. When you boot the computer, you receive the following error message:

  ```
  1782—disk controller failure
  ```

  What do you think is causing the problem?

- *Scenario 3:* You have just purchased new IDE hard disks and installed them in your server. Because you are a firm believer in Murphy's Law, you attempt to mirror the two disks but are unsuccessful. Both disks are the same model number and size. What do you think the problem is and how would you solve it?

- *Scenario 4:* Your IDE hard drive fails completely because of an enormous amount of reallocated blocks. When you check the Hot Fix Redirection statistic in MONITOR.NLM, it shows that no blocks have been redirected. What do you think happened and how would you solve the problem?

- *Scenario 5:* In an emergency, one of the computer technicians in your Boston office installed an old IDE hard disk from the spare parts inventory into the office's NetWare 5.1 server and decided to let NetWare format the drive. Why was this a bad idea?

See Appendix C for answers.

SCSI

Small Computer System Interface (SCSI) is a general system interface that supports storage components such as hard disks, CD-ROMs, tape backup drives, and so on. In a SCSI bus system, up to eight devices can be connected in a daisy-chain fashion, including one host bus adapter (HBA) and seven devices.

SCSI and its variations are fast becoming the interface of choice for NetWare servers, because none of the other interface standards can match SCSI speed and flexibility. One of the reasons SCSI drives have such great throughput is because they use parallel data communications, which is the same communications scheme used by motherboards, CPUs, and memory.

The basic specification for SCSI provides a 5MB per second (MBps) data transfer rate over an 8-bit wide bus. Lately, SCSI speed has been overshadowed by dramatic improvements in CPU speeds and bus transfer rates. As a result, the following SCSI advancements have emerged:

- *SCSI-II* — Improves overall data transfer rates (up to 10 MBps) by reducing command overhead and bus arbitration. This feature is somewhat analogous to packet bursting. *Fast Wide SCSI-II* widens the data path to 16 bits, to double or quadruple (up to 40 MBps) the maximum synchronous transfer rate. Naturally, these speeds require a properly matched HBA and hard drive.

- *SCSI-III* — Specifies an interface that can support up to 31 devices using a single HBA. A 32-bit wide data bus is used to achieve data transfer rates of up to 40 MBps SCSI-III is also known as *Ultra SCSI*.

- *Ultra2 SCSI* — Specifies an interface that supports data transfer rates of up to 80 MBps.

Understanding SCSI

One of the differences between SCSI and IDE is that every device on a SCSI bus is assigned an address. Addressing is important, because it enables a server's HBA to find the correct SCSI device when you request a data file.

SCSI drives and controllers fit together in a simple daisy-chain configuration. Once the components are in place, you will need to deal with two important considerations:

- *Termination*—Both ends of a SCSI bus must be terminated, just like an Ethernet bus. This is necessary to avoid signal reflectance. Termination can occur at the HBA or at a SCSI drive.
- *SCSI Addressing*—Each SCSI HBA can control up to eight devices (including itself). These devices are numbered from 0 to 7. It's important to verify that each SCSI device has its own unique address. In most cases, an HBA has a SCSI ID of 7. The other devices on the bus will be numbered from 0 (highest priority) to 6 (lowest priority). Depending on the hardware you are using, SCSI addresses can be set either through a hardware setting (that is, jumpers) or through software utilities that configure the ROM embedded into the card.

Let's learn more about these two critical SCSI configurations.

Termination Both ends of the SCSI bus must be terminated. This step is necessary to avoid signal reflectance—just like with the Ethernet bus. Termination can occur at the HBA or SCSI drive itself. It usually involves special jumper settings, but sometimes you may have to use an external terminating device.

As you can see in Figure 14.2, SCSI supports both internal and external devices. The exact placement of the terminators depends on the configuration you're using. Here's a quick summary:

- *Internal*—This is the simplest configuration. As you can see in Figure 14.2, there are two internal SCSI drives and one HBA. Terminators are activated at both ends of the bus—at the HBA and at Disk #1.
- *External*—This configuration is a little more complicated. If your SCSI drives are in an external cabinet, you may need to remove the termination from the individual disks and attach an external terminating device to the cabinet. With this method you won't have to remember which disk was terminated when you add additional drives to the same cabinet. As you can see in Figure 14.2, the HBA and external cabinet are terminated.

FIGURE 14.2

Comparing internal and external SCSI termination

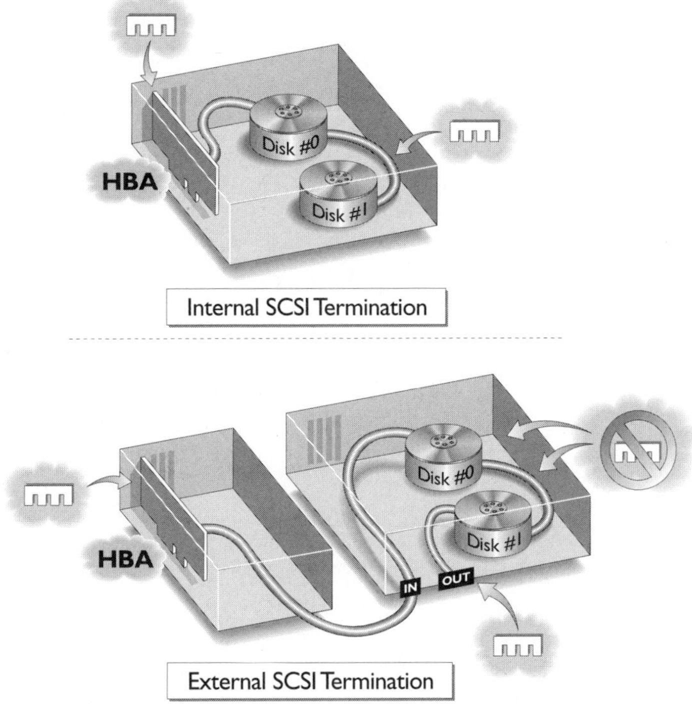

SCSI troubleshooting can become challenging when you mix internal and external disk configurations. Refer to the special example in Figure 14.3. In this graphic, Disks #0 and #1 are attached directly to the HBA inside the server and Disks #2 and #3 are placed in an external cabinet. In this case, the SCSI bus starts at the last internal drive (Disk #1) and ends at the external terminating port for the SCSI cabinet. As you can see in Figure 14.3, neither the HBA nor Disks #0, #2, or #3 are terminated.

FIGURE 14.3

Combining internal and external SCSI drives

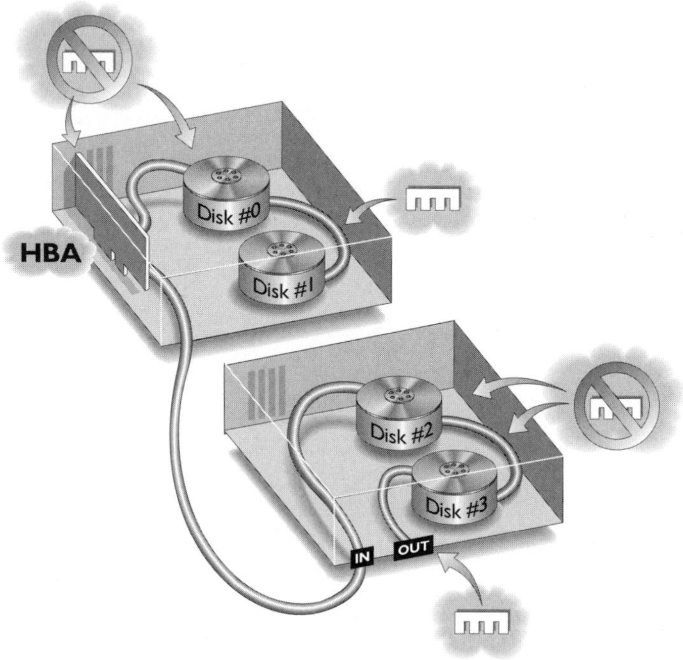

SCSI Addressing As we've just learned, each SCSI HBA can control up to eight devices (including itself). Therefore, the devices are numbered from 0 to 7. As a network administrator, you need to verify that each SCSI device has its own unique address. In most situations, the HBA has a SCSI ID of 7. All other devices on the bus will use numbers 0 (highest priority) through 6 (lowest priority).

SCSI addresses can be set either through a hardware setting (that is, jumpers) or through software utilities (such as an EISA configuration disk or a PS/2 reference disk). However, MicroChannel Architecture (MCA) computers implement SCSI addressing in the opposite direction. That is, number 6 is assigned to the highest priority device, and number 0 represents the lowest priority. Fortunately, MCA has one thing in common with the rest of the industry — the HBA is still assigned SCSI address number 7.

REAL WORLD

Some of today's newer SCSI drive-controller combinations work together to provide *active termination*. This feature provides automatic termination when required. This is a helpful feature for network administrators because active termination eliminates the need to add or remove physical terminators when you shuffle SCSI drives in the bus. Also, active termination ensures that the terminating power is handled correctly. Terminating power provides a stabilizing current for the data signals on the SCSI bus. In generic systems, terminating power can be supplied by the HBA or by the disks themselves. In active terminating systems, it's handled automatically.

In addition, some external SCSI devices have a built-in terminator that is activated automatically when the address is set to 0. This makes termination easy. Be sure to read your hardware documentation before you implement a termination and SCSI addressing scheme.

SCSI does not use CMOS drive table settings to communicate with a NetWare server. Instead, SCSI controllers supply their own BIOS information. This means that you need to set the CMOS Drive Type parameter for a SCSI drive to "Drive Type 0," "Not Installed," or "SCSI," unless the drive is controlled by the HBA. The SCSI controller's BIOS then takes care of the rest.

Jumper settings are extremely important for SCSI devices. Most of the jumper configurations are activated at the HBA. The two most important settings for SCSI drives are termination and SCSI addressing. As we learned earlier in this chapter, SCSI termination can occur at either the HBA or physical drive by setting a specific jumper. In some cases, this involves *active termination*, which analyses the bus to determine the presence of downstream devices. If the HBA or drive identifies more devices farther along the bus, it turns off the internal terminator. SCSI addressing is configured using three jumpers in a unique binary address.

Jumpers are also used to customize a variety of other drive parameters, including the following parameters:

- *Base I/O Address* — This parameter defines a location in RAM where data from the HBA will be placed for pickup by the CPU, and vice versa.

- *Interrupt* — This parameter distinguishes the hard drive controllers from other internal components.
- *Base BIOS Address* — Most SCSI cards need a specific address for BIOS communications. This parameter is only used, however, for controllers and HBAs that use onboard ROM BIOS, and it is only active when the onboard BIOS is enabled.
- *BIOS Enabled/Disabled* — This jumper allows you to disable the onboard BIOS. The default factory setting is "BIOS Enabled."
- *Direct Memory Access (DMA)* — Some SCSI controllers require their own DMA channel for access to server RAM.
- *Parity Enabled* — Most SCSI drives are shipped with this jumper set.

SCSI is the hard drive interface of choice for NetWare servers, and it is emphasized on the "Service & Support" exam. Study SCSI interface architecture. Understand the difference between SCSI, SCSI-II, and Fast Wide SCSI-II. Know that a SCSI HBA supports multiple devices in a daisy-chain configuration. Finally, study SCSI termination and addressing.

Troubleshooting SCSI

The complexity of SCSI architecture and termination can lead to some minor problems. Most of the problems stem from either improper termination or SCSI addressing. Following are some troubleshooting tips to keep in mind when using SCSI devices on a NetWare server:

- Because SCSI is a system interface rather than a simple drive interface, it requires termination configuration. Refer to the External SCSI Termination scenario in Figure 14.2. Also, you may run into problems if you forget to attach a terminator to the out port on the external cabinet or, even worse, if the external terminator malfunctions. To avoid these problems, you should routinely check terminations with an ohmmeter.

- Other problems are caused by duplicate SCSI addresses. Remember, each device (including the HBA and other drives) must have a unique address. As we discussed earlier, the HBA is usually assigned number 7, with other devices assigned addresses in descending priority, from 0 to 6. If your SCSI bus won't initialize, disconnect the external device chain and restart the server. When you start up a SCSI server, the HBA BIOS displays the device identifiers onscreen. This makes it easy for you to check internal and external SCSI addressing.

- Route SCSI cables with care. Tweaking a cable or routing it past power supplies or near metal for long distances can affect the impedance of SCSI cables and cause signal reflections. Placing devices too close together can cause significant reflections, resulting in data corruption. (**Note:** The minimum cable length between SCSI connectors is one foot, and the maximum distance between connectors on a SCSI cable is 0.5 meters [18 inches].)

- It's a bit trickier to load SCSI server disk drivers than IDE drivers, because no generic SCSI drivers work for all SCSI drives. In other words, each HBA has a manufacturer-specific driver that works best in its own environment. Be sure that you have the correct .CDM and .HAM device driver combination available before starting NetWare installation.

- As mentioned earlier in this chapter, the SCSI controller BIOS stores CMOS configurations. Sometimes, the BIOS can be activated by pressing Ctrl+A during bootup (such as with most Adaptec drives). If the BIOS is accidentally disabled with a jumper setting or the CMOS is set to override the BIOS, you will receive an error message.

This completes our detailed discussion of SCSI configuration and troubleshooting. Now that you know what IDE and SCSI hard drives look like, let's learn how to install them. After all, it's best to know how to put something together before you start taking it apart.

LAB EXERCISE 14.2: TROUBLESHOOTING SCSI HARD DRIVES

Now that you are quickly becoming a hard drive master, let's test your SCSI troubleshooting skills with a few sample scenarios.

- *Scenario 1:* You have just installed a SCSI hard disk in your server. When you attempt to boot the computer, you get the following message:

  ```
  Drive Not Ready—Error
  ```

  What do you think the problem is?

- *Scenario 2:* The network administrator in your Dallas office is out with the flu, so one of the college kids who works part time and who is anxious to get some network experience volunteered to install a new SCSI disk in the server. He said that he has a lot of experience installing SCSI devices on his home computer. (He lied.) He is anxious to fix the problem before anyone finds out. He said that when he boots the computer it alternately hangs or displays this message:

  ```
  Warning: Possible SCSI Bus Contention
  ```

  What do you tell him you think the problem is, and how would he solve it?

- *Scenario 3:* Your neighbor is taking Novell classes at the local community college and has decided that the best way to get some hands-on practice is to set up a small one-user network at home. He told you that he can't get the computer with the SCSI hard disk to boot as a NetWare server. He said that when he tries to boot, he receives the following error message:

  ```
  UNABLE TO FIND LOAD FILE SCSI
  ```

He said that he assumes that he's pointing to the wrong place on the hard disk. You ask him to read you the disk driver statement in his STARTUP. NCF file. It says the following:

```
LOAD SCSI PORT=1F0 INT=E
```

What do you tell him is the problem?

- *Scenario 4:* One of the technicians in your San Francisco office found an old HBA in the parts inventory and decided to try to create a temporary NetWare 5.1 server. He installed a 2GB SCSI hard disk, but it's only recognizing 1.07GB. What do you suspect the problem is, and how would you solve it?
- *Scenario 5:* Your wife's cousin, who is always annoying you with computer-related questions, called you and said that he just installed a third internal drive in his server and immediately began to experience all sorts of serious problems. He said that read/write performance has decreased dramatically and that the computer is beginning to experience data corruption. What are some of the things that you'd tell him to check?

See Appendix C for answers.

Hard Drive Setup

As an expert network troubleshooter, you will have plenty of opportunities to install NetWare server drives. Because this is the lifeline of your server data, you should be extra careful to follow the correct procedures. In this section, we will explore the five setup steps for both IDE and SCSI hard drives.

Following is a quick summary of the five hard drive setup steps:

- *Step 1: Physical Installation*—During Step 1, you configure the drive and controller with the correct I/O setting, interrupt, DMA channel, master/slave configuration, and physical SCSI address. These settings are defined using standard jumpers and/or DIP switches. Once the components have been configured, you can physically install them. Each drive interface type has specific rules governing physical installation.

- *Step 2: Drive Cabling*—In Step 2, you attach the hard drive cables. These cables provide a communications path between the server hard drive and controller. Each drive interface type uses a different type of cable, with varying numbers of parallel data channels.

- *Step 3: CMOS Configuration*—Once the physical components have been installed, you can move on to software setup. During Steps 3 through 5, you will define a special CMOS Drive Type and special formatting instructions. In Step 3, you configure the server's CMOS settings. These settings define key drive parameters, such as sectors, cylinders, heads, and capacity.

- *Step 4: DOS Partition Configuration*—In Step 4, you prepare the primary server hard disk for DOS and install the DOS operating system kernel. First, you will need to prepare the hard disk by performing a low-level format, if necessary. (This task is normally performed by the hard disk manufacturer.) Next, you must create a DOS partition and designate it as the active partition using the DOS FDISK.EXE utility. Finally, you will perform a high-level format of the DOS partition (and install the DOS operating system kernel) using the DOS FORMAT.COM utility.

- *Step 5: NetWare Partition Configuration*—Finally, in Step 5, you install the NetWare operating system. During this process, you typically create a NetWare partition on each server hard disk (if there's more than one) and then format the partition(s) by creating one or more NetWare volumes.

Let's take a closer look at these detailed hard drive setup procedures.

Step 1: Physical Installation

In general, three physical components create the link between NetWare and the server hard drive: a *disk driver* (to communicate with the internal HBA), the *HBA* (which communicates with the drive's embedded disk controller in an IDE configuration), and the *disk controller* (which tells the drive where the data is and how to get it).

The first step in hard drive installation involves drive configuration and physical installation. The first task in Step 1 is to customize specific hardware settings using controller and hard drive jumper settings. Once the jumpers have been set, you can move on to the second task in Step 1, where you physically install the controller and hard drive in the server. After they are in place, you can finish the installation by activating the appropriate server disk driver, for example, in the case of an IDE disk in a NetWare 4 server, with the LOAD ISADISK.DSK command. (See Table 14.1 in the section, "Step 3: CMOS Configuration," for further details.)

Step 2: Drive Cabling

Drive cabling provides the communications path between the drive controller and a physical hard drive. Each end of the ribbon cable has a special connector—one connector for the controller and one connector for the hard drive. Drive cabling is simplified by the appearance of a red or blue stripe. The stripe on the cable identifies pin number 1 on the connector. On the drive, pin number 1 should be identified by a small number 1 or a black square.

Each hard drive interface standard uses a different type of cable:

- *ST-506 and ESDI*—Use two ribbon cables: 20-pin for control and 34-pin for data (see Figure 14.4). Be sure that each end of each cable attaches to the appropriate port on the controller or the hard drive.

FIGURE 14.4

ST-506 and ESDI drive cabling

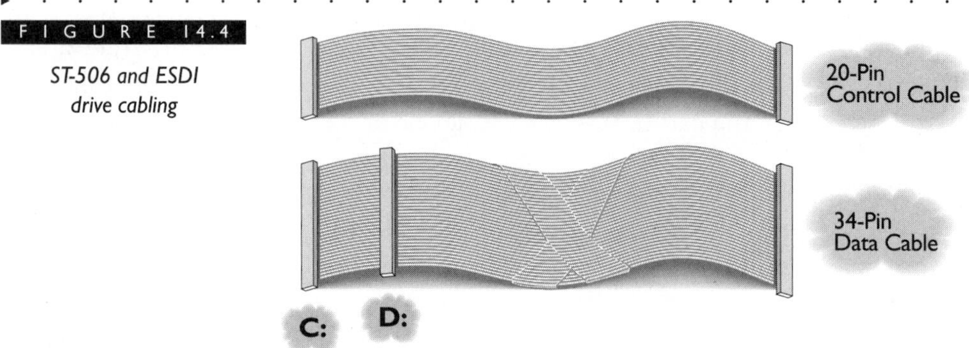

- *IDE* — Relies on one 40-pin ribbon cable for both data and control information (see Figure 14.5). IDE cabling also uses a colored stripe to designate pin number one. Notice the second connector part way down the cabling. This connector is typically used for the second drive. (**Note:** IDE cables have a maximum length of 0.5 meters [18 inches].)

FIGURE 14.5

IDE drive cabling

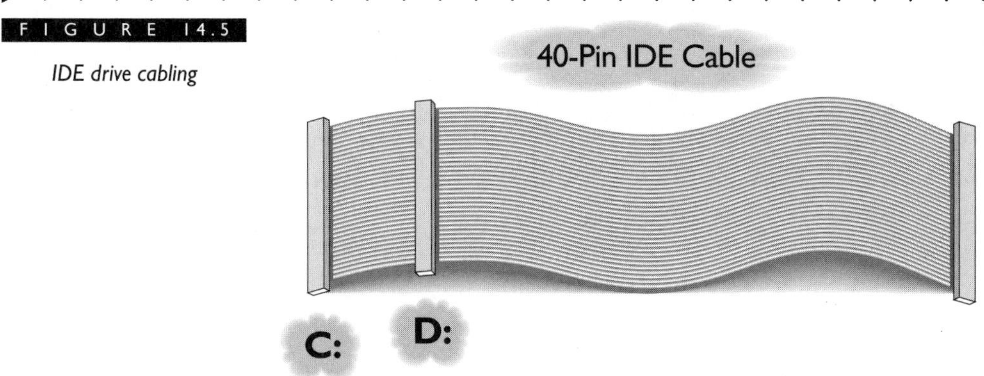

- *SCSI* — Uses one 50-pin or 68-pin cable for both data and control information (refer to Figure 14.6). SCSI connectors are slightly different than connectors used with other interfaces, because they are used as a system interface, rather than just a hard drive interface. SCSI cables can support many types of devices other than hard disks and CD-ROM drives.

When installing SCSI drives, be sure to use impedance-matched cables when connecting external devices. (**Note:** The maximum length between connectors on a SCSI cable is 0.5 meters [18 inches]. Fast SCSI-II uses a slightly larger data path via a slightly larger cable.)

FIGURE 14.6

SCSI drive cabling

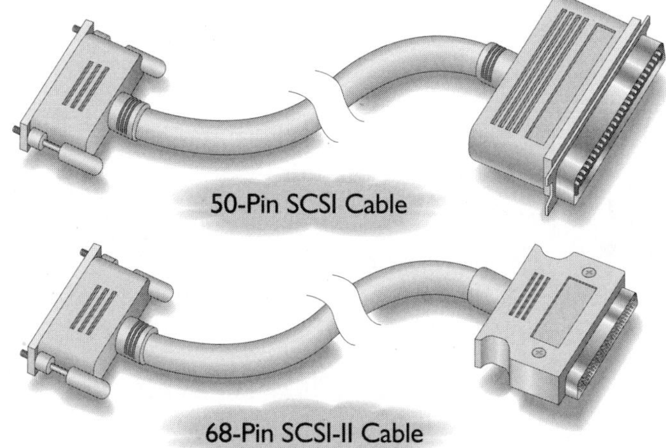

Well, that concludes our discussion of physical installation. So far, you have configured the jumper settings, installed the drive, loaded the disk driver, and connected the cables. Now it's time to prepare the server disk for NetWare. Disk preparation is actually a three-step process:

- *Step 3:* CMOS Configuration
- *Step 4:* DOS Partition Configuration
- *Step 5:* NetWare Partition Configuration

Step 3: CMOS Configuration

CMOS configuration is the easiest of the five hard drive setup steps. Many newer servers automatically detect a change when you boot them with a new hard drive installed, and they automatically update the hard drive parameters in CMOS for you. Older servers, however, require that you activate the CMOS setup screen manually.

Each interface standard has its own CMOS settings. For example, you will need to take special care when selecting the CMOS Drive Type setting for an ST-506 drive — that is, you must be sure to select a setting that does not exceed the actual number of cylinders or heads on the disk. With an ESDI drive, selecting a setting is a little simpler, because the CMOS information is taken from the ESDI controller's BIOS. For an IDE drive, select "Type 47" (user definable). SCSI drives don't use the server's CMOS. For a SCSI drive, select "Type 0," "Not Installed," or "SCSI."

Refer to Table 14.1 for a summary of the CMOS settings for each of the hard drive interface standards we have discussed. The table also includes a review of related jumper, disk drivers, and drive cabling configurations.

TABLE 14.1

Hard Drive Setup Summary

INTERFACE	JUMPERS	DISK DRIVER	DRIVE CABLING	CMOS
ST-506	Interrupt, I/O	ISADISK.DSK (NetWare 3 and NetWare 4); not supported by NetWare 5.1	20-pin cable (data) and 34-pin cable (control)	Depends on drive and drive type
ESDI	Interrupt, I/O and UMB Memory Address	ISADISK.DSK (NetWare 3 and NetWare 4); not supported by NetWare 5.1	20-pin cable (data) and 34-pin cable (control)	Type 1
IDE	Interrupt, I/O, master/slave, and C/D	IDE.DSK or ISADISK.DSK (NetWare 3 and NetWare 4); IDEATA.HAM (NetWare 5.1)	40-pin ribbon cable	Type 47 (that is, user defined)

TABLE 14.1

Hard Drive Setup Summary (continued)

INTERFACE	JUMPERS	DISK DRIVER	DRIVE CABLING	CMOS
EIDE	Interrupt, I/O, master/slave, and C/D	IDE.DSK or ISADISK.DSK (NetWare 3 and NetWare 4); IDEATA.HAM (NetWare 5.1)	40-pin ribbon cable	Type 47 (that is, user-defined)
SCSI	Interrupt, I/O, Base BIOS, DMA, termination, and SCSI addressing	Manufacturer specific	50-pin cable (SCSI-I, SCSI-II, 8-bit SCSI-III,and 8-bit Ultra2); 68-pin cable (Wide SCSI-II, 16-bit SCSI-III, and 16-bit Ultra2)	Type 0, Not Installed, or SCSI parameters in BIOS

Step 4: DOS Partition Configuration

In Step 4, you prepare the primary server hard disk for DOS and install the DOS operating system kernel. This involves up to three main tasks. First, you will need to prepare the hard disk by performing a low-level format, if necessary. (**Note:** This task is normally performed by the hard disk manufacturer.) Next, you must create a DOS partition and designate it as the active partition using the DOS FDISK.EXE utility. Finally, you will perform a high-level format of the DOS partition (and install the DOS operating system kernel) using the DOS FORMAT.COM utility. Following is some additional information involving these tasks:

- *Low-level Formatting*—Before you can store data on a hard disk, it must be low-level formatted. Hard disk manufacturers normally low-level format disks at the factory. The low-level formatting process configures drive parameters and magnetically marks cylinders and sectors on a disk. In addition, the process tests a disk's surface for reading and writing integrity and determines the interleave ratio that will be used. Only perform this procedure if appropriate. For example, *never* low-level format an IDE drive.

- *DOS Partitioning*—After you have low-level formatted the primary server hard disk (if necessary), you must create a DOS partition on it and designate it as the *active* partition using the DOS FDISK.EXE utility. (When a computer boots, one operating system takes control, even if two or three are present on the disk. The controlling operating system is identified as the one occupying the active partition. Interestingly, in the case of a NetWare server, the server is always first booted to the DOS operating system and then to the NetWare operating system. (The latter is done by executing the SERVER.EXE file from the DOS partition.) This means that the primary hard disk on a NetWare server needs to contain two partitions: a small, active DOS partition for booting and a larger NetWare partition for data storage, as shown in Figure 14.7).

FIGURE 14.7

Understanding drive partitioning

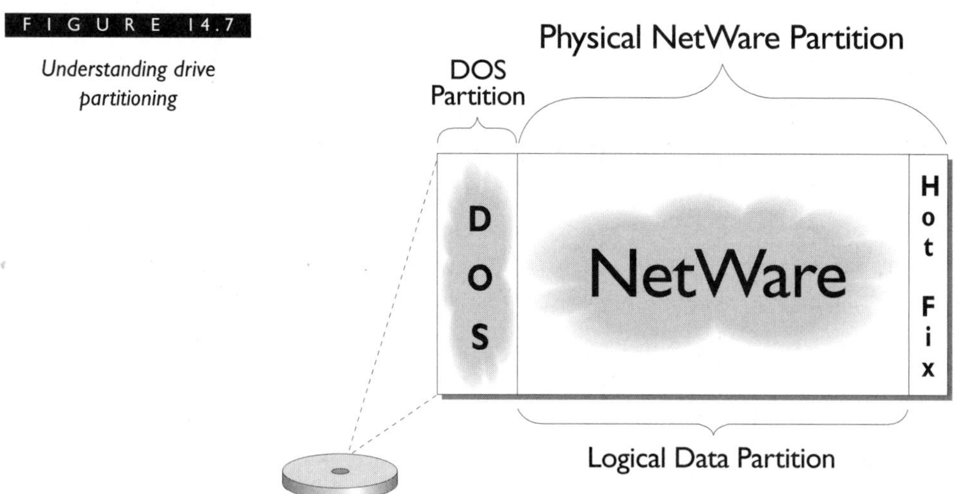

- *DOS Formatting*—After you create the DOS partition and make it active, the next step is to perform a high-level format of the DOS partition using the DOS FORMAT.COM *drive* /S command. (For example, FORMAT C: /S.) This command performs the following tasks:
  - Scans the disk and identifies bad sectors.
  - Creates the DOS boot sector.

- Creates the DOS File Allocation Table (FAT).
- Creates an empty root directory.
- Copies system boot files to the root directory. (This task would be skipped if you accidentally failed to use the /s parameter when issuing the DOS FORMAT command.)

Once you have configured the server's DOS partition, it's time to move on to the fifth and final step of hard drive setup—NetWare partition configuration. This step involves partition and volume creation via NetWare. Let's check it out.

REAL WORLD

The "real world" has a variety of low-level formatting options. CheckIt PRO has a built-in low-level formatting tool called CKTEST.EXE. In addition, SpinRite from Gibson Research is also capable of performing a low-level format on most standard drives. Finally, there's always the DOS stand-by—DEBUG.EXE. Most drive controller cards have their own low-level formatting code built in. DEBUG accesses this code and activates the low-level process. With most Modified Frequency Modulation (MFM), Run Length Limited (RLL), or ESDI controllers, you can accomplish this by running DEBUG.EXE at any DOS command line and then entering the following parameters:

```
g=c800:5
```

Step 5: NetWare Partition Configuration

In Step 5, you prepare the primary server disk for NetWare and install the NetWare operating system. During this process, you typically create a NetWare partition on each server hard disk (if there's more than one), then format the partition(s) by creating one or more volumes. (**Note:** If you want to create additional partitions and/or volumes after initial NetWare installation, use INSTALL.NLM (NetWare 3 and NetWare 4), NWCONFIG.NLM (NetWare 5.1), or the Installation/Upgrade program (NetWare 5.1).)

Following is some additional information involving these tasks:

- *NetWare Partitioning* — NetWare recognizes three types of partitions: primary DOS, extended DOS, and NetWare. NetWare 5.1 allows you to have multiple NetWare partitions on a single hard disk. Partitions for other operating systems, such as UNIX, are displayed as non-NetWare partitions. It's important to note that non-NetWare partitions cannot be mirrored using NetWare. As you can see in Figure 14.7, the NetWare partition takes up most of the server hard disk.
- *NetWare Volume Creation* — After you have created a NetWare partition on each server hard disk (if there's more than one), you can format the partition(s) by creating one or more *volumes*, which are the fundamental component of NetWare data storage. Keep this information in mind when creating:
  - A volume can be a subset of a NetWare partition, and each server can support up to 64 volumes.
  - A volume can occupy an entire NetWare partition or can span multiple NetWare partitions. As a matter of fact, a volume can span up to 32 hard drives. In this case, each piece of the volume on a different disk would be called a *segment*. Volume spanning is a great way to increase the size of a volume without having to reinstall NetWare, because segments can be added to an existing volume without bringing down the server. If you plan to span two or more hard drives with a single volume, however, be sure that you implement the NetWare disk duplexing feature, for fault-tolerance purposes.
  - A volume can consist of multiple NetWare partitions on a single hard drive (NetWare 5.1 only).

You can create NetWare partitions and volumes using any of the following three server-based utilities:

- *NetWare Installation Program* — During NetWare installation, you will be asked to create at least one NetWare partition and at least one NetWare volume. The default NetWare partition will occupy all available disk space and assign it to the default NetWare volume SYS:.
- *NWCONFIG* — As your network expands, you can add multiple storage devices and create new partitions and/or volumes after installation. Both partition and volume creation can be accessed from the Standard Disk Options menu of NWCONFIG. NWCONFIG also lets you mirror and delete NetWare partitions.
- *ServerMagic 3.0* — Several third-party utilities enable you to create NetWare partitions and volumes. ServerMagic 3.0 from PowerQuest is one of the most powerful utilities. You can access this utility from the server console by typing **SMAGIC** and then pressing Enter. ServerMagic 3.0 also lets you perform the following partition operations: create, copy, mirror, resize, move, hide, unhide, and delete.

Congratulations! You have successfully installed a server drive. It was as simple as 1-2-3-4-5. This completes the hard drive setup process. By now, you should feel pretty comfortable with the role of the server disk in the grand scheme of things. And you should feel pretty good about your ability to fix it if something goes wrong.

Throughout this chapter, we have focused on the skills needed to troubleshoot and set up server hard drives. But in this demanding world of high-performance graphics and multimedia, you will quickly discover that one hard drive isn't always enough. In these cases, you need options — you need network storage alternatives.

LAB EXERCISE 14.3: INSTALLING AN IDE HARD DRIVE

Now let's gain some valuable experience installing IDE hard drives. Read through the entire exercise before you get started.

For this exercise, you'll need the following:

- One IBM-compatible computer
- One IDE hard drive
- DOS installation disks (version 5.0 or higher)
- One blank floppy disk

In this exercise, you will do the following:

1. Prepare the IDE hard drive.
2. Install and configure the IDE controller board (if no IDE support is embedded on the system board).
3. Install and configure the IDE hard drive.
4. Partition and format the IDE hard drive.
5. Install DOS.

Perform the following tasks:

1. Prepare the IDE hard drive.
   a. Make backups of any old hard disks. Generate at least two full system backups of the information on existing hard disks, if there are any. (Be sure to verify that the data on these backups can be restored. All existing data on the hard disk will be destroyed during this exercise!)
   b. Create a boot disk.

- Use the FORMAT A: /S command to format a blank floppy as a bootable disk.
- Copy the DOS FDISK.EXE and FORMAT.COM files to the disk.

c. Record the CMOS values. As a precaution, run the CMOS setup utility and make a printout of the existing values on each screen. The CMOS setup utility is accessed differently on different computers. Some machines require a reference disk. Consult your computer documentation for further information.

d. Remove existing partition(s). Use the DOS FDISK utility to delete any existing partitions on the hard disk. (If your hard disk contains a NetWare partition, you need a copy of the FDISK utility from DOS 5.0 or higher to remove it. If an appropriate version of FDISK is not available, you need to reboot the computer as a server and remove the NetWare partition using INSTALL.NLM or NWCONFIG.NLM.)

e. Unplug the computer.

2. Install and configure the IDE controller board (if no support is embedded on the system board).

a. Configure the controller board.

- (Skip this step if IDE support is supplied by the system board.)
- Determine what parameters need to be set (such as IRQ, base I/O address, base memory address, and DMA channel) and how to set them. These values usually are set using DIP switches or jumpers on the board, although some newer plug-and-play computers are able to autoconfigure plug-and-play boards. Refer to an electronic reference library such as SupportSource or the documentation that came with the hard disk for more detailed information. Ensure that the values you select are unique and do not conflict with any of the other hardware in the computer.

b. Install the controller board. Ensure that the board is firmly seated in the expansion slot.

3. Install and configure the IDE hard drive.

a. Configure the IDE disk. Ensure that the disk is set as the master drive.

b. Install the IDE disk.

- First, install the IDE disk in the computer.
- Then connect the IDE cable to the controller board (or system board).
- Next, connect the free end of the IDE cable to the IDE disk.
- Finally, connect the four-pin connector on the power supply cable to the disk.

c. Boot the computer.

- Plug in the computer.
- Boot from the bootable disk that you made earlier. (You'll probably get an error message saying that the system does not recognize the new disk.)

d. Set the CMOS parameters for the disk (if required).

- If you must set the CMOS manually, do so at the CMOS setup screen. The CMOS setup screen is accessed differently on different computers. Some machines require a reference disk. Consult your hardware documentation for further information.
- Key in the disk type. If you do not know the correct disk type, you have two choices: attempt to determine the correct disk type based on the number of cylinders, heads, sectors, and the write precompensation value; or key in the values manually. If you attempt to choose the closest disk type, make sure that the disk type that you choose has a disk capacity that is less than or equal to the capacity of your disk (in megabytes). Don't forget that the numbering system for disk types is a function of the specific BIOS chip on your system board.

In other words, the set of parameters for Drive Type 10 on one machine may not be the same as the set of parameters for Drive Type 10 on another. If you are unable to determine a suitable drive type, you should select the user-definable type (which is usually Type 47). You will then be allowed to input each of the disk parameters manually.

4. Partition and format the IDE hard drive.

   a. Create the DOS partition.

   - Use the DOS FDISK utility located on the boot disk that you created earlier to create a DOS partition that occupies all available disk space.
   - Use the DOS FDISK utility to assign the new partition as the active partition.

   b. Format the DOS partition. Use the FORMAT utility located on the boot disk that you created earlier to format the hard disk and copy the system files to it. (**Hint:** Use the FORMAT C: /S command.)

5. Install DOS.

Install DOS according to the instructions that came with the operating system.

LAB EXERCISE 14.4: INSTALLING SCSI HARD DRIVES

In this exercise, you will simulate installing and configuring a SCSI hard disk and preparing it to be used as a NetWare server. Read through the entire exercise before starting.

For this exercise, you'll need the following:

- One IBM-compatible computer
- One SCSI hard disk
- DOS installation disks
- Blank floppy disk

In this exercise, you will do the following:

1. Prepare the hard drive.
2. Design a plan.
3. Install and configure the HBA, if necessary.
4. Install and configure the SCSI hard drive.
5. Partition and format the SCSI hard drive.
6. Install DOS.

Perform the following tasks:

1. Prepare the hard drive.
   a. Make backups of any old hard disks. Generate at least two full system backups of existing hard drives, if any. (Be sure to verify that the data on these backups can be restored. All existing data on the hard disk will be destroyed during this exercise!)

b. Create a boot disk.
   - Use the FORMAT A: /S command to format a blank floppy as a bootable disk.
   - Copy the DOS FDISK.EXE and FORMAT.COM files to the disk.

c. Record CMOS values. As a precaution, run the CMOS Setup utility and make a printout of the existing values. The CMOS Setup screen is accessed differently on different computers. Some machines require a reference disk. Consult your computer documentation for further information.

d. Remove existing partition(s). Use the DOS FDISK utility to delete any existing partitions on the hard disk.

2. Design a plan.

   a. Create a plan. The first step in installing a SCSI device is to generate a plan. The plan should include the following:
      - The physical layout of the system
      - The SCSI addresses you will use for the HBA and SCSI disk
      - An indication of where termination will be needed

   b. Unplug the computer.

3. Install and configure the HBA, if necessary. (Skip this step if support is built into the system board.)

   a. Configure the HBA. Determine which parameters need to be set and how to set them. These parameters may include BIOS address, BIOS enable/disable, DMA channel, interrupt number, port I/O address, SCSI ID number, and/or termination. If your HBA is software configurable, the configuration will be done after the hard disk is installed. See the documentation from the manufacturer for further information. Set the appropriate parameters and record your settings for future use.

   b. Install the HBA. Insert the HBA into an appropriate expansion slot and make sure that it is firmly seated.

4. Install and configure the SCSI hard drive.

a. Make sure that the termination is set properly on the hard drive itself (according to your plan).

b. Set the SCSI ID number for the hard drive (according to your plan).

c. Install the SCSI hard drive.

- First, install the SCSI hard disk.
- Then connect one end of the SCSI cable to the hard disk. (You will probably find that the connector is keyed to the pin block such that the connector can be inserted only one way.)
- Next, connect the free end of the SCSI cable to the HBA. (Some HBAs have an additional connector for a floppy disk drive. Consult the manufacturer's documentation to determine which connector is used for the hard disk.)
- Finally, connect the four-pin power supply cable to the SCSI disk.

d. Boot the computer.

- Plug in the computer.
- Boot from the bootable disk that you made earlier.

e. Set the CMOS parameters for the disk. (Skip this step if your computer identifies SCSI devices automatically.)

- Enter the CMOS setup screen. The CMOS setup screen is accessed differently on different computers. Some machines require a reference disk. Consult your hardware documentation for further information.
- Key in the disk type. Set the disk type to "None" or "Not Installed."
- Reboot the computer. Exit CMOS and reboot the computer using the boot disk you made earlier.

5. Partition and format the SCSI hard drive.

a. Create the DOS partition.

- Use the DOS FDISK utility located on the boot disk that you created earlier to create a 30MB DOS partition, and then assign it as the active partition. (Usually, you would create a DOS partition that would use all available disk space. In this case, you are leaving the remaining space for a NetWare partition, which is created during the NetWare installation process.)
- After you exit FDISK, you will need to reboot the computer using the boot disk that you made earlier.

b. Format the DOS partition.

- Use the FORMAT utility located on the boot disk that you created earlier to format the hard disk and to copy the system files to it. (**Hint:** Use the FORMAT C: /S command.)
- After you format the hard disk, remove the floppy disk from drive A: and reboot the computer from the computer's DOS partition.

6. Install DOS.

Install DOS according to the instructions that came with the operating system.

Network Storage Alternatives

The server drive is responsible for 50 to 75 percent of NetWare server functionality. Although the drive's importance cannot be debated, its storage capacity leaves something to be desired. Today's files are bigger than ever before, and user demands on server storage are increasing. Suddenly, 10GB or 20GB hard drives aren't big enough. In addition, mission-critical applications are putting a greater strain on the reliability of server drives. Alternative forms of server storage are becoming essential.

In addition to standard IDE and SCSI hard drives, NetWare supports a variety of network storage options. The following storage configurations can be used to enhance NetWare servers:

- *Disk Mirroring and Duplexing* — Mirroring and duplexing are system fault-tolerance strategies for protecting network storage in case of disk failure. Mirroring and duplexing represent two effective methods of reducing the chances of data loss and minimizing network down time. Duplexing results in performance improvements, as well.

- *CD-ROM* — CD-ROM optical technology can be used to extend the data storage capacity of your server by approximately 700MB. It is great for read-only documentation and resource data. We will explore how NetWare has integrated CD-ROM drives into NetWare servers later in this chapter.

- *Redundant Array of Inexpensive Drives (RAID)* — RAID is a set of solutions for data integrity and reliability, based on a series of redundant disks. This strategy expands the notion of disk mirroring and duplexing to include multiple drives, better throughput, and increased fault tolerance.

If you are going to be a successful network troubleshooter, you will need to have alternatives. Let's learn more about these three network storage alternatives.

REAL WORLD

Magneto-Optical (M-O) technology combines magnetism and laser optics to provide a storage medium ideal for certain applications. It can capture audio, video, text, and other data in an integrated form. In general, M-O combines the best features of hard disks and tape drives. Hard disks are faster than tape drives, but Digital Audio Tape (DAT) is less expensive per gigabyte. M-O technology is cheaper than hard drives and faster than tape.

Disk Mirroring and Duplexing

Disk mirroring and duplexing are two System Fault Tolerance (SFT) strategies for disk crash protection (see Figure 14.8). *Disk mirroring* duplicates the entire contents of one server disk on a second mirrored disk. If the first disk fails, the second disk automatically takes over. Disk mirroring is accomplished by attaching both drives to the same disk controller. This strategy is cheaper, but creates a single point of SFT vulnerability.

Disk duplexing solves this problem by duplicating the controller, controller cable, and power supply, as well as the disk (see Figure 14.8). In other words, all disk components in the entire channel are duplicated. Although this level of SFT is expensive, it offers a greater level of protection against disk crashes and network data loss. Disk duplexing also offers a performance feature called *split seeking*. Split seeking allows the system to read and write data to both disks at the same time, because duplexing mirrors the entire disk channel (disk, disk controller, cable, and so on).

The NetWare mirroring and duplexing features are configured using the INSTALL.NLM (NetWare 3 and NetWare 4) or NWCONFIG.NLM (NetWare 5.1) server utilities. Interestingly, both processes are referred to as "mirroring," since duplexing is simply mirroring along with additional hardware. Here are a few troubleshooting tips for disk mirroring and duplexing:

- The NetWare boot files on the DOS partition do *not* get mirrored. Thus, you will have to manually create the DOS partition on the second hard disk and copy the files there yourself. Also, you cannot mirror DOS, NetWare, and UNIX partitions together.

FIGURE 14.8

Disk mirroring and duplexing

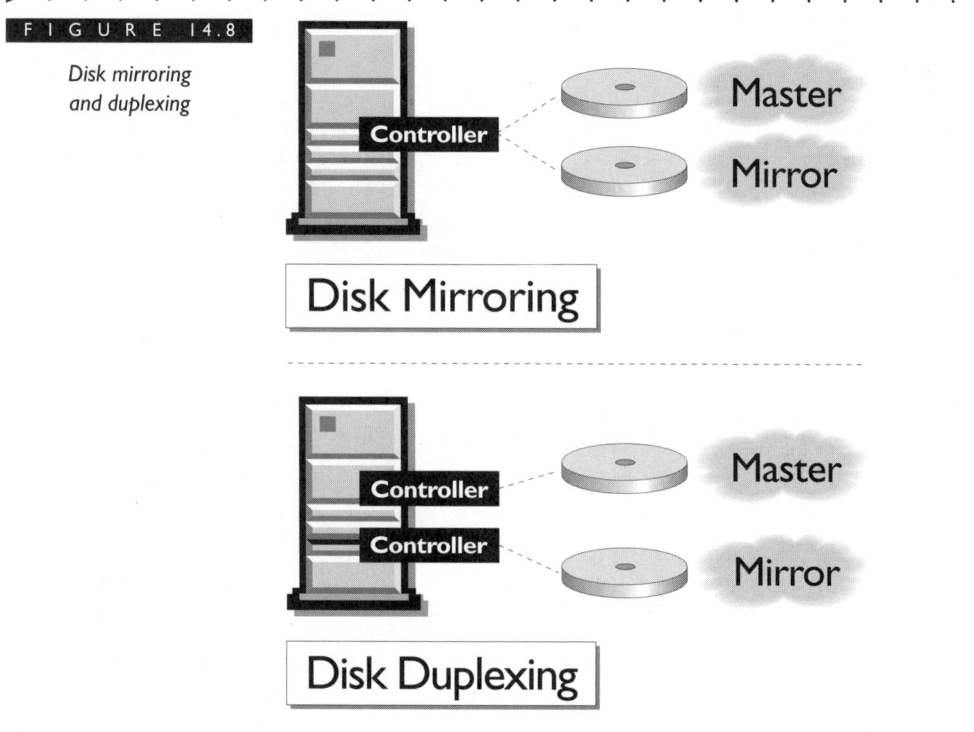

- Each device on a SCSI bus has a unique device code that is automatically derived by NetWare. The first two digits are the device driver ID number assigned to the manufacturer. The next two digits are the instance of that device driver on the system. The next two digits indicate the logical unit number, and the final two digits indicate the SCSI ID number. Keeping a record of these device codes for your hard disks will help you sort out any mirroring and duplexing problems that may occur.

- Always load disk drivers in the same order, preferably in controller or channel order. Load drivers for internal controllers first. Periodically check the status of your mirrored or duplexed drives using the MONITOR.NLM Volumes screen. Finally, check the error logs on each server.

- Mirroring and duplexing do not take the place of backups. You should perform system backups on a regular basis. Be sure to test restores, as well. In addition, make sure to duplex drives before you span them with a single volume.

- As we discussed earlier, IDE hard disks should not be mirrored because both hard disks are handled by the first hard drive's built-in controller (thus creating a single point of failure). IDE drives, however, can be duplexed.

TIP

It is best to mirror partitions that are the same size; however, they don't have to be. Remember, mirroring and duplexing involve logical partitions. If you have two different size physical drives, you can create logical partitions of the same size by manipulating the Hot Fix Redirection Area. Whatever you do, make sure duplex controllers use the same interface standard.

This completes our discussion of disk mirroring and duplexing. Remember, these are valuable strategies for increasing reliability and fault tolerance in your NetWare server drive. For some people, though, it's not enough. Many of today's network applications require the reliability of mirroring, but with a larger drive capacity. Remember, mirroring cuts your physical capacity in half. RAID, on the other hand, ensure the same level of reliability, but with greater hard drive capacity. But before we get into RAID, let's study CD-ROMs.

LAB EXERCISE 14.5: INSTALLING DISK MIRRORING

For this exercise, you'll need the following:

- A NetWare 3.12, NetWare 4, or NetWare 5.1 server
- Two SCSI (or IDE) hard drives

In this exercise you will do the following:

1. Make backups.
2. Install and configure a second hard drive.
3. Create a NetWare partition on the second hard drive.
4. Mirror the two partitions.

Perform the following tasks:

1. Make backups. Make at least two full backups of the data on both hard drives. All of the data on the new disk will be destroyed when you create a NetWare partition. The data on the existing drive may be destroyed if something goes wrong during the mirroring process.
2. Install and configure a second hard drive.
   a. Turn off the computer.
   b. Disconnect the power cord.
   c. Install and configure the second hard drive. See Exercise 15.3, "Installing an IDE Hard Drive," or Exercise 15.4, "Installing a SCSI Hard Drive," for further details.
   d. When you are done, reattach the computer's power cord and turn on the computer.

3. Create a NetWare partition on the second hard drive. The partition you create must be the same size (or larger) than the mounted partition containing the SYS: volume.

   a. Start the server. This can be done by executing the SERVER.EXE file at the DOS prompt.

   b. Execute the INSTALL.NLM or NWCONFIG NLM. Type one of the following commands at the console prompt:

      `LOAD INSTALL` (on a NetWare 3.*x* or 4.*x* server)

      `NWCONFIG` (on a NetWare 5.*x* server)

   c. Select Disk Options (NetWare 3.*x* and 4.*x*) or Standard Disk Options (NetWare 5.*x*).

   d. Choose one of the following:

      - Modify Disk Partitions and Hot Fix (on a NetWare 4.*x* and NetWare 5.*x* server)
      - Partition tables (on a NetWare 3.12 server)

   e. Select the new disk. You should see two physical disks listed. Choose the new disk, which should be listed as Device #1.

   f. Select the "Create NetWare (Disk) Partition" option.

   g. Indicate the size of the new partition. Indicate that all free space should be used for the new partition by pressing Esc. If you have large hard disks, you may want to restrict the partition size to 100MB, to ensure that the partition is not too large to be mirrored.

   h. Create the new partition. Indicate Yes when asked whether to create the partition.

   i. Return to the Disk Options screen. Press Esc.

4. Mirror the two partitions.

a. Choose one of the following:

- Mirror/Unmirror Disk Partitions (on a NetWare 4.*x* and NetWare 5.*x* server)
- Mirroring (on a NetWare 3.12 server)

b. Two disks should be listed. Each disk should have one of the following statuses:

- *Mirrored*: Indicates that the disk is part of a pair of disks that are consistent with each other.
- *Not Mirrored*: Indicates that the data on the disk is consistent with itself.
- *Out of Sync*: Indicates that some of the data on the disk is inconsistent with other data on the same disk.

c. Choose one of the following:

- Not Mirrored: Device 0 (on a NetWare 4.*x* and NetWare 5.*x* server)
- Not Mirrored: Non-Mirrored Partition #1 (on a NetWare 3.12 server)

d. The Mirrored Partitions box appears. The first disk is listed as synchronized with itself because no other disks are available.

e. Add the second disk.

- Press Insert.
- The Available Partitions box appears. Choose the second disk, which is the only available unmirrored partition, and then press Enter. (If the second disk is larger than the first disk, NetWare will display a warning and will allow you to change the partition size of the second partition.)

f. The disks are mirrored in the background.

- The Mirrored NetWare Partition box appears and both disks are listed. One disk is listed as synchronized and the other as unsynchronized.
- At this point, it may seem like nothing is happening, but if you look closely, you'll probably notice disk light activity. The disks are being mirrored in the background.

g. Return to the console prompt. Press Alt+Esc.

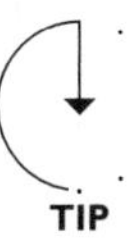
TIP

As long as you remain in the current NWCONFIG screen, the program will continue to indicate that the second disk is unsynchronized. To display the correct status, you need to exit the Mirrored NetWare Partition box and then return to it after the disks have been mirrored.

CD-ROM

CD-ROM optical technology is a great solution for storing large amounts of read-only data in a small physical space. To ensure compatibility, the International Organization for Standardization (ISO) developed a 9660 Standard called the High-Sierra Standard. Because virtually every major CD-ROM manufacturer follows this standard, it means that your server's CD-ROM drive should be capable of accessing data on any CD-ROM disk intended for PCs.

Besides offering large amounts of data in a small physical space, CD-ROM technology has many other advantages. First, it allows instant access to large volumes of data using keyword searches. Second, it uses lightweight media with low duplication costs. Third, this media cannot be damaged by magnetic fields. Finally, because it uses optical technology, CD-ROMs are more reliable than other magnetic storage media.

Keep the following tips in mind as you manage NetWare server CD-ROM drives:

- Some CD-ROM drives require a plastic container (or *caddy*) that helps protect the CD from damage. Caddies are inexpensive, so you should buy one for each CD-ROM. Also, CD-ROM drives are linked to the host computer by a SCSI bus, an IDE bus, or an ATAPI interface. Purchase the optimal configuration for your performance needs.

- Performance degradation can occur if you place a CD-ROM drive and a hard disk on the same SCSI HBA. Check with your hardware manufacturer for known incompatibilities.

- Avoid using parallel-to-SCSI adapters when networking CD-ROM drives. You can use this configuration, however, for initial installation procedures.

- Be sure to load the correct CD-ROM device drivers on your server. Also, when activating Novell's internal CD-ROM NLM, make sure you use the proper syntax. (**Note:** The following server commands can be used to view the volume name of attached CD-ROM devices: CD DEVICE LIST (NetWare 4.*x*), LIST DEVICES (NetWare 5.*x*), or VOLUMES.)

RAID

Generally speaking, Redundant Array of Inexpensive Disks (RAID) is any disk subsystem architecture that combines two or more standard physical drives into a single logical storage unit. This approach achieves two major goals: reliability (via data redundancy) and storage management (via increased capacity). Reliability is accomplished by writing files across multiple disks. RAID also includes a variety of parity and error-checking solutions.

RAID is a great solution if you need better reliability and more storage capacity. Six levels of RAID are currently available. Each level represents a different approach to redundant drives and has its own advantages and disadvantages. Note that these levels are independent standards. Level 0 is not the worst, nor is Level 5 the best. Each level has its own niche and drawbacks. Some levels were designed for the mainframe world, some are applicable to the NetWare environment, and others can be implemented on home PCs.

RAID is a great network storage alternative if you need high capacity, low cost, and built-in data redundancy. But the real trick is figuring out which RAID level is best for you. Refer to Table 14.2 for a comparison of the options.

By now, almost all of your 12 billion neurons are feeling the effects of hard drive troubleshooting. In this chapter, we explored hard drive anatomy, IDE and SCSI standards, and five simple steps for hard drive setup. But of course, it didn't end there. We also learned everything there is to know about alternative storage devices — mirroring, CD-ROM, and RAID.

So, where do we go from here? Well, now that we have the network infrastructure and server hard drive in place, it's time to shift our focus to workstations. After all, these distributed machines represent our network's connection to the outside world. Without them, the server would have nothing to do, and the infrastructure would have no reason to exist.

So, let's forge ahead into the next chapter where we will confront the challenging world of NetWare workstation troubleshooting.

TABLE 14.2

Understanding the Six Levels of RAID

FEATURE	LEVEL 0	LEVEL 1	LEVEL 2	LEVEL 3	LEVEL 4	LEVEL 5
Data striping	Block interleave	None	Bit interleave	Bit interleave	Block interleave	Block interleave
Error checking	None	Drive redundancy	Check sum	Parity checking	Parity checking	Distributed check data
Data strategy	System writes blocks of data to each disk in the array in succession.	Drives (and controllers) arepaired with each byte written to identical disks.	Data is written across each disk in succession, one bit at a time.	Typically consistsof four or five disks with one dedicated to parity information.	Single parity disk like RAID 3 but uses block data striping like RAID 0.	Block data striping and distributed check data error checking on all disks.
Advantages	Improved performance and larger volume size.	Simplicity, redundancy, and fast in "fault mode."	Fast parallel bit transfers.	Fast parallel bit transfers and more reliable than RAID 2.	Supports NetWareblocks, drives operate independently.	Supports NetWare blocks and provides virtual redundancy.
Disadvantages	No redundancy.	Expensive because it requires twice the disk space.	Supported only by mainframes; offers very slow writes.	Poor write performance because the parity disk must be accessed for every write.	Poor write performance because the parity disk must be accessed for every write. Entire array can go down with the failure of one controller.	Slow file transfers.
Use	Low-end RAID systems.	NetWare drive fault tolerance.	Mainframes.	For imple-mentations with many reads and few writes.	Most NetWare server environ-ments.	Some NetWare server environ-ments.

LAB EXERCISE 14.6: INSTALLING A CD-ROM AS A NETWARE VOLUME

For this exercise, you'll need the following:

- A NetWare 3.12, NetWare 4.*x*, or NetWare 5.*x* server
- One IDE or SCSI CD-ROM drive

In this exercise, you will do the following:

1. Prepare the server.
   a. Type the following at the server console to down the server:

      ```
      DOWN
      ```

   b. Type the following at the server console to exit to DOS (NetWare 4.*x* only):

      ```
      EXIT
      ```

   c. Turn off the computer.
   d. Remove the power cord.
2. Configure the CD-ROM. Determine which parameters need to be set (such as DMA, I/O address, IRQ, port address, SCSI ID, and/or termination) and how to set them. If your CD-ROM drive is software configurable, the configuration will occur after the CD-ROM is installed. See the manufacturer's documentation for further information.
3. Install the CD-ROM drive.
   a. First, connect the IDE or SCSI cable.
   b. Then install the drive.
   c. Next, attach the computer's power cord.
   d. Finally, turn on the computer.

4. Update the STARTUP.NCF file. You may need to add the following statement to the server's STARTUP.NCF boot file before mounting the CD-ROM:

   ```
   SET RESERVED BUFFERS BELOW 16 MEG=200
   ```

   Consult the manufacturer's documentation for further details. Don't forget to reboot the computer if you make this change after the server is up.

5. Start the server. Run SERVER.EXE at the DOS prompt to start the server. (This step may be done automatically by your server's AUTOEXEC.BAT file when you boot.)

6. Insert the CD-ROM that was included with this book in the CD-ROM drive.

7. Load the appropriate drivers.

   a. Load the appropriate IDE or SCSI disk driver. (This driver may already have been loaded automatically by your STARTUP.NCF if you have an existing SCSI hard drive.) See the manufacturer's documentation for further details. IDE CD-ROM drives require the IDEATA.HAM NLM.

   b. Load the appropriate SCSI HBA driver. This step should only be done if a SCSI HBA is being used. (This driver may have already been loaded automatically by your STARTUP.NCF file if you have an existing SCSI hard drive.) Refer to the documentation from the manufacturer for further details.

   c. For NetWare 3.12 servers, load the AFTER311 and NPA312 NLMs. This can be done by typing the following command at the server's console prompt:

      ```
      LOAD AFTER311
      LOAD NPA312
      ```

   d. Load the appropriate CD-ROM driver, if necessary. You may need to load a special CD-ROM driver for your CD-ROM drive, such as ASPICD.DSK or IDECD.CDM. Consult the documentation that came with the drive for more information.

8. Load the CD-ROM NLM and mount the CD-ROM as a volume. This can be done by typing the following command at the server console prompt:

```
LOAD CDROM
```

NetWare 3.*x* and 4.*x* CD-ROM console commands include the following:

```
CD DEVICE LIST
CD MOUNT
```

These commands are not required on NetWare 5.*x* servers because CD-ROMs are mounted automatically upon insertion and dismounted when ejected.

9. Log into the server. After you log into the server from a workstation, map a drive to the CD-ROM volume. (If you are using NetWare 4.*x* or NetWare 5.*x*, you might want to create a NetWare volume object for this CD-ROM so that it can be viewed in NDS. This is not required for accessing the CD-ROM, but it would make it easier for your users to locate the device.)

LAB EXERCISE 14.7: INSTALLING ACME HARD DRIVES AND CD-ROMS

Use the hints provided to find the 20 hard disk troubleshooting tools terms hidden in this word search puzzle. Omit any punctuation characters (such as blank spaces, hyphens, and so on) and spell out any numbers.

```
P A R I T Y C H E C K I N G K C O L B
X N C I D O H B A V Y V I O G T J F G
F B L O C K I N T E R L E A V E D F Y
H A U J D A I S Y C H A I N I N G C L
L S G S I X T Y F O U R R N F T T B X
D E K E M T R S M H U Q H S D F N R N
A I X E H A W D R I V E L A T E N C Y
T O U K W G S D I S K D R I V E R S I
A A C T I V E T E R M I N A T I O N B
S D Q I G V R P E Y G E C G R P U J P
T D W M Y J S O G R K T M U M B W D T
R R U E C K G E M S I J R B O I D B X
I E I H E D M A C H A N N E L I A M Q
P S Z W A T K H U T R Z G D Q O A F O
I S I M A G N E T O O P T I C A L M Q
N N M M P R D O S P A R T I T I O N M
G H C X X N R L T K L L G Q O M V X U
```

Hints

1. Provides auto-termination of SCSI devices
2. Identifies a unique path between the disk controller and the CPU
3. Unit of storage space on a NetWare volume
4. Uses blocks rather than bits for data striping
5. Controllers with an onboard CPU
6. 3-D tracks on parallel platters
7. One SCSI drive after another after another . . .
8. RAID Level 0
9. DOS utility that can be used for low-level formatting
10. Software interface between the drive and the server operating system
11. Hardware interface between the drive and the server data bus
12. Small on a server, large on a workstation
13. Control overhead in the SCSI world
14. Filename extension for disk drivers that are not supported in NetWare 5.1
15. Reading and writing with lasers
16. Most popular error detection scheme in RAID
17. Pie-shaped subdivision of a hard drive track
18. Time required for a read/write head to locate a specific track
19. Maximum number of volumes on a NetWare 5.1 server
20. Shifts starting sector of ESDI tracks to account for drive rotation

See Appendix C for answers.

LAB EXERCISE 14.8: TROUBLESHOOTING HARD DRIVES

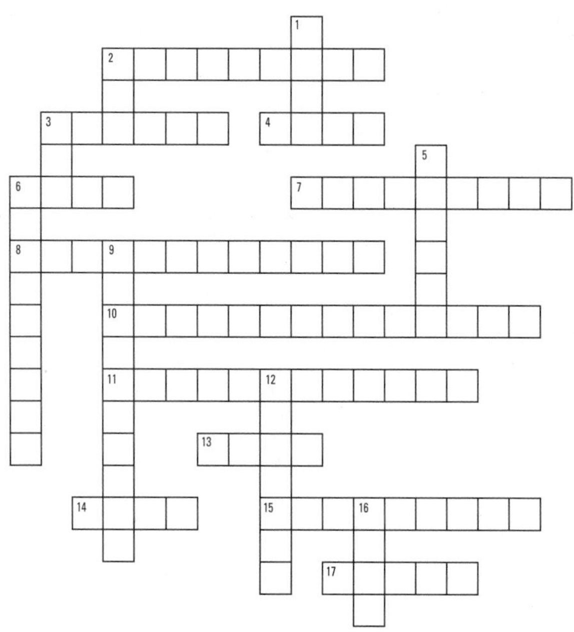

Across

2. RAID Level 1 with two controllers
3. Bad block reallocation feature
4. Hard drive read/write device
6. Bug spray or disk drive array
7. RAID Level 1 with a single controller
8. A variation on data striping
10. Control overhead in the SCSI world
11. Performance benefit of disk duplexing
13. Great drive technology; bad name
14. Complementary Metal Oxide Semiconductor
15. Dedicated channel to the CPU
17. 682MB of data in a small package

Down

1. The "new" IDE
2. Digital Audio Tape
3. SCSI Address 7
5. The result of NetWare formatting
6. Denotes Pin 1
9. Seek time plus drive latency
12. Also known as Ultra SCSI
16. The "new" ST-506

See Appendix C for answers.

CHAPTER 15

Troubleshooting Workstations

Sensation is your link to the outside world. Similarly, your network relies on sensory input from workstations for external and internal data. Without this data, there would be nothing for the server to do. In some strange way, workstations give the network a reason to live. In this chapter, we will study the following three workstation troubleshooting topics:

- *Novell Client Architecture* — The Novell Client architecture consists of four network senses performing four important tasks. First, the *LAN driver* is one of two components that work together to provide primitive communication between the local workstation and the centralized server. The other component, *communications protocol*, is the electronic road upon which all network communication travels. Next, the two intellectual senses (Requester and WOS), combine to make sure network messages are processed correctly at the workstation. The *Novell Client Requester* provides the services necessary to track network resources, to cache files, and to send automatic reconnection levels. Finally, the *Workstation Operating System (WOS) interface* completes the picture by serving as the interface layer between Windows 95/98/NT/2000 and the client services provided by NetWare.

- *Novell Client Troubleshooting Tools* — As you learned earlier, troubleshooting tools enable us to track internal and external server and workstation activity. The Novell Client provides a variety of troubleshooting tools to help you monitor all network communication and provide feedback concerning workstation performance. These tools include the Windows 95/98/NT/2000 Control Panel, the Novell Client Log, MODULES command, REGEDIT tools, and LANalyzer for Windows.

- *Novell Client Troubleshooting Model* — The Novell Client Troubleshooting Model can save you money, increase security, and enhance workstation performance. Using this five-step model, you can eliminate network communication obstacles. This is how it works: (1) list symptoms, (2) eliminate hardware issues, (3) eliminate LAN driver issues, (4) verify the Client version, and finally, (5) eliminate connection issues.

As you can see, there's much more to the Novell Client workstation than meets the eye. It's a complex collection of sensory devices and connectivity hardware—all of which makes troubleshooting workstations an incredible challenge.

To help simplify things, we will focus this workstation troubleshooting chapter on the two most prominent workstation operating systems: Windows 95/98 and Windows NT/2000. This means we won't be exploring the command-line environment of DOS or confusing ourselves with outdated Windows 3.1 problems.

Now let's start with a detailed overview of Novell's Client architecture and explore some troubleshooting tips along the way.

Novell Client Architecture

Novell offers client software for various workstation operating systems, including Windows 95/98, Windows NT/2000, Windows 3.*x*, DOS, Macintosh, UNIX, and OS/2. In this section, we will concentrate on Novell Client architecture, troubleshooting tools, and troubleshooting procedures for the Novell Client for Windows 95/98 and the Novell Client for Windows NT/2000.

Novell Client architecture consists of four client technologies organized into two functional categories: hardware (network interface card, or NIC) and software (workstation operating system, or WOS). See Figure 15.1.

Workstation hardware encompasses the first two client technologies—LAN drivers and communications protocols. Workstation hardware *is* responsible for physically connecting the workstation to the network and for providing a communications path to the server. It is *not* responsible for the content of the data, how the data is used on the workstation, or guaranteeing network privileges for access to any program or resource on the LAN. (These are the responsibilities of the workstation software.)

Workstation software encompasses the final two client technologies—the Novell Client Requester and WOS interface. The primary responsibilities of the workstation software are to create the content sent to and from the network, to format the data so that network resources can understand it, to help ensure that only authorized users access the network, and to control the flow of data within the workstation.

Refer to Table 15.1 for an overview of Windows 95/98 and Windows NT/2000 Novell Client architecture.

FIGURE 15.1

The detailed Novell Client architecture

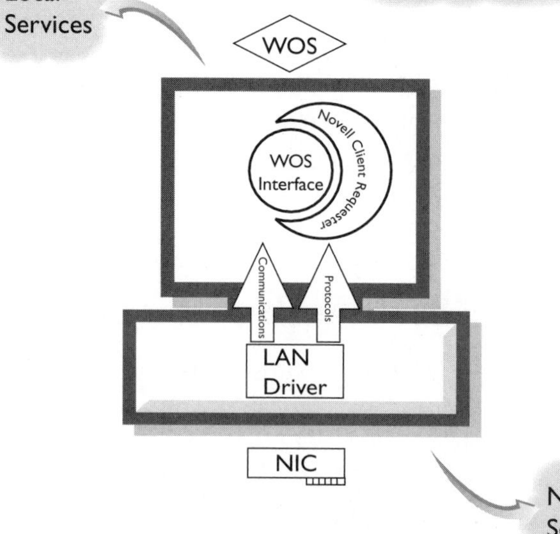

TABLE 15.1

Windows 95/98 and Windows NT/2000 Novell Client Architecture Overview

COMPONENT	DESCRIPTION
Workstation hardware	The Novell Client ensures that the Novell network provider is the primary network provider (or first on the list of network providers). The Novell Client supports TCP/IP, IPX/SPX, WinSock, named pipes, NetBIOS, and Simple Network Management Protocol (SNMP). The Novell Client can coexist with the Microsoft Client for Microsoft networks. The Novell Client provides full automatic reconnection to network files and resources.

TABLE 15.1

Windows 95/98 and Windows NT/2000 Novell Client Architecture Overview (continued)

COMPONENT	DESCRIPTION
Workstation software	The Novell Client is loaded by Windows 95/98 and Windows NT/2000 at startup. The Novell Client is fully integrated with the Windows Explorer and Network Neighborhood utilities. The Novell Client enables parameters to be managed using the System Policy Editor included with Windows 95/98 and Windows NT/2000. The Novell Client supports long filenames. The Novell Client enables a user to run login scripts from the desktop environment in Windows 95/98 or Windows NT/2000. The Novell Client supports the Automatic Client Upgrade (ACU) feature. The Novell Client supports the automatic installation of Windows 95/98 and the Novell Client for Windows 95/98 or Windows NT/2000 and the Novell Client for Windows NT/2000 — using the unattended install feature. The Novell Client allows simultaneous access to multiple NDS trees.

REAL WORLD

Carefully study the features and benefits of the Novell Client for Windows 95/98 and the Novell Client for Windows NT/2000 that are presented in Table 15.1. Specifically, recognize that the following features are unique to the Novell Client for Windows 95/98 and the Novell Client for Windows NT/2000: full automatic reconnection to network files and resources, Automatic Client Upgrade (ACU), and simultaneous access to multiple NDS trees. (**Note:** These features are not supported by the Microsoft Windows 95/98 Client or the Microsoft Windows NT/2000 Client.)

In this section, we will review the four client technologies that make up both the Novell Client for Windows 95/98 and the Novell Client for Windows NT/2000. Following is a preview of the four components presented in Figure 15.1:

- *LAN driver* — A LAN driver is used to translate communications between a workstation's NIC and a specific communications protocol. Both the Novell Client for Windows 95/98 and the Novell Client for Windows NT/2000 support Network Driver Interface Specification (NDIS) and Open Data-Link Interface (ODI) LAN driver architectures.

- *Communications Protocols* — Protocols determine the language used to move data across the network. In Windows 95/98 and Windows NT/2000, you have two choices: TCP/IP and IPX.

- *Novell Client Requester* — The Novell Client Requester provides the services required to track network resources, to cache files, and to set automatic reconnection levels. This is accomplished on Windows 95/98 and Windows NT/2000 workstations using the CLIENT32.NLM file.

- *WOS Interface* — The WOS interface exists at the heart of the Novell Client architecture. In Windows 95/98, the NetWare I/O Subsystem (NIOS) serves as an interface layer between the Windows 95/98 WOS and client services provided by NetWare. In Windows NT/2000 systems, these services are provided by a redirector/file system driver called NWFS.SYS.

Let's start near the bottom of Figure 15.1 with LAN drivers.

LAN Drivers

As you can see in Figure 15.1, the LAN driver sits near the bottom of the Novell Client architecture. Each physical NIC has its own specific LAN driver. The LAN driver accepts any type of packet, and then either sends the packet up to the communications protocol or down to the network cabling. The LAN driver is supported by a secondary interface called the *Link Support Layer* (LSL), which acts as a switchboard for routing packets between the LAN driver and the appropriate communications protocol. LSL identifies the packet and then passes it to the appropriate protocol. Together, the LAN driver and LSL handle all physical workstation communications.

Both the Novell Client for Windows 95/98 and the Novell Client for Windows NT/2000 support two different types of LAN drivers (see Figure 15.2):

- *Network Driver Interface Specification (NDIS)* — This is an internal interface found in Windows 95/98 and Windows NT/2000 that consists of a native Windows 95/98 or Windows NT/2000 driver and the VMLID.NLM support file.
- *Open Data Link Interface (ODI)* — This is Novell's own LAN driver standard. Both the Novell Client for Windows 95/98 and the Novell Client for Windows NT/2000 support the use of 32-bit ODI LAN drivers through the ODI NDIS support module (called ODINSUP). This enables you to access Microsoft networks using native Novell LAN drivers.

Communications Protocols

Communications protocols use a set of rules to determine the language used to move data across the network. Both Windows 95/98 and Windows NT/2000 workstations support two communications protocols: TCP/IP and IPX. Both of these protocol stacks receive data packets from the LAN driver and pass them to the Novell Client Requester (see Figure 15.1).

FIGURE 15.2

Novell Client LAN driver architecture

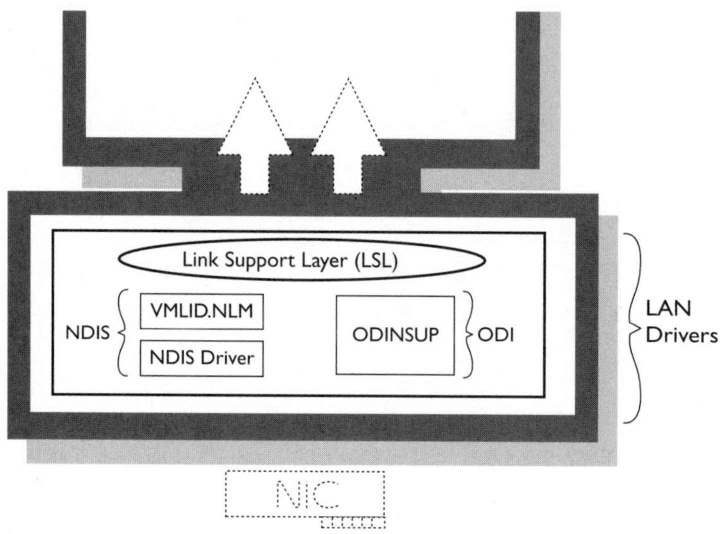

TCP/IP Protocol

TCP/IP is the Internet's main protocol suite and consists primarily of two components: the *Internet Protocol* (IP), which provides Network Layer routing, and the *Transmission Control Protocol* (TCP), which accepts messages from IP and packages them for Internet-based applications. With the introduction of NetWare 5.*x*, Windows 95/98 and Windows NT/2000 workstations can now take full advantage of their native TCP/IP capabilities.

Following is a brief list of some of the characteristics of the TCP/IP support available for the Novell Client for Windows 95/98 and the Novell Client for Windows NT/2000:

- TCP/IP is a suite of networking protocols that is used on a variety of UNIX workstations, minicomputers, and mainframes.

- TCP/IP provides a communications link between a server and the NIC installed in a workstation. When IP is loaded, any workstation program (including the Novell Client) can communicate with the network using native IP.

- TCP/IP is built into NetWare 5.1 and supports Transport Driver Interface (TDI-based) applications, WinSock applications, and NetBIOS applications.

IPX Protocol

The Novell Internetwork Package Exchange (IPX) protocol serves as the communications link between a Windows 95/98 or Windows NT/2000 workstation and older NetWare servers that are running NetWare version 2.2 through NetWare version 5.1. IPX is a proprietary Novell protocol that requires little user intervention and is easy to configure, administer, and troubleshoot.

Following is a brief list of the characteristics IPX offers the Novell Client for Windows 95/98 and the Novell Client for Windows Client for NT:

- IPX provides a communications link between a server and the NIC installed in a workstation. When IPX is loaded, any workstation program (including the Novell Client software) can communicate with the network using IPX.

- The NetWare "shell" and other applications access IPX to open and close IPX sockets. When a workstation receives an IPX packet, the protocol determines which socket the packet is addressed to and passes the packet to the program having that socket open.

- IPX determines the address of the network segment to which the workstation is physically connected.

- Microsoft provides an IPX-compatible protocol called NWLink that can be used by WinSock and NetBIOS applications.

That completes our exploration of workstation communication fundamentals. In these two sections, we have learned that LAN drivers and communication protocols provide a rudimentary interface between workstation hardware and the NetWare server.

Together, they handle communication functions with the internal NIC and direct packets to the appropriate workstation software.

These components do not, however, provide access to higher-level functions such as the Novell Client Requester and WOS interface. Let's continue with these two higher-level workstation components.

Novell Client Requester

The Novell Client Requester and WOS interface work together to provide the workstation with an intelligent view of the network. The Novell Client Requester performs network-specific functions and the WOS interface communicates directly with Windows 95/98 and Windows NT/2000.

As shown in Figure 15.1, the Novell Client Requester wraps around the heart of workstation software (that is, the WOS interface), and the Requester provides three key support services:

- Tracking network resources
- Caching files
- Setting automatic reconnection levels

In this capacity, the Novell Client Requester (CLIENT32.NLM) provides the following architectural advantages: modularity, memory swapping, DOS redirection, system optimization, and backward compatibility. All these advantages result in a fully backward-compatible client, where NETX shells and DOS Requester clients can run earlier Application Program Interfaces (APIs) without modification under the Novell Client for Windows 95/98 and the Novell Client for Windows NT/2000.

WOS Interface

The Novell Client offers two WOS interface solutions for Windows 95/98 and Windows NT/2000 workstations:

- *NetWare I/O Subsystem (NIOS)* — NIOS serves as an interface layer between Windows 95/98 workstations and the network.

- *NetWare File System Driver (NWFS)* — NWFS serves as an interface layer between Windows NT/2000 workstations and the network.

NetWare I/O Subsystem (NIOS)

NIOS is implemented on Windows 95/98 workstations as a virtual device driver called NIOS.VXD. Once loaded, this driver initiates a variety of other workstation-based NLM files using the Windows 95/98 Registry.

NIOS is the workstation equivalent of SERVER.EXE. It provides the loader software and module launcher that are used to load client modules and NLMs. Unlike SERVER.EXE (which has its own built-in memory manager), NIOS works with an extended memory manager that is automatically loaded with Windows 95/98. Once NIOS has access to the memory manager, it can dynamically allocate and deallocate client configuration settings. This offers the advantage of enabling you to implement client changes without having to reboot the workstation.

NetWare File System Driver (NWFS)

Unlike the Novell Client for Windows 95/98 (which is based on NIOS), NWFS is implemented as a redirector/file system driver called NWFS.SYS. As a result, this driver does not rely on other client modules for network connectivity. Instead, it utilizes the networking capability already integrated into Windows NT/2000 workstations.

At its most fundamental level, NWFS.SYS provides the internal tables and services required to track network resources, to cache files, and to set automatic reconnection levels. Because it is fully backward compatible with previous Novell client software, you can run older NetWare-aware applications using the Novell Client for Windows NT/2000.

NWFS also supports WinLogin. WinLogin is an integral part of Windows NT/2000 that provides a graphical user interface (GUI) for login support. As part of this implementation, Novell has written its own Graphical Identification and Authentication (GINA) module, called NWGINA.DLL. This new identification module performs all authentication and user interaction for Windows NT/2000 clients on a Novell network.

TIP

Carefully study the Novell Client architecture model in Figure 15.1 and its four main components. Be sure that you know the following definitions: *LSL* (acts as a switchboard to route packets between the LAN driver and communications protocol), *NIOS* (works with an extended memory manager to dynamically allocate and deallocate client settings), *NWFS.SYS* (provides the internal tables and services necessary to track network resources, to cache files, and to set automatic reconnection levels), and *NWGINA.DLL* (performs all authentication and user interactions for Windows NT/2000 clients on a Novell network). Finally, remember that NIOS is associated with Windows 95/98 workstations and NWFS is associated with Windows NT/2000 workstations.

This completes our journey through the four primary components of workstation connectivity. As we have learned so far, troubleshooting is especially difficult at the NetWare workstation because of user interference and application diversity. That's where you come in. As a NetWare troubleshooter, you make sure that the workstation's four primary senses are operating normally. You accomplish this by using two important troubleshooting strategies:

- Novell Client Troubleshooting Tools
- Novell Client Troubleshooting Model

I "sense" a new lesson coming on.

Novell Client Troubleshooting Tools

Both the Novell Client for Windows 95/98 and the Novell Client for Windows NT/2000 provide a variety of troubleshooting tools to help you monitor network communications and provide feedback concerning workstation performance. These tools also permit you to investigate problems associated with workstation connectivity and help you diagnose problems with routers and servers on an intranetwork.

In this section, we will explore five Novell Client troubleshooting tools:

- *Windows 95/98 and Windows NT/2000 Control Panel* — The Network dialog box in both the Windows 95/98 and Windows NT/2000 Control Panel enables you to configure network components such as protocols and the Novell Client for Windows 95/98 or the Novell Client for Windows NT/2000.
- *Novell Client Log File* — The NIOS.LOG file keeps a record of the NLMs that are loaded on a Windows 95/98 workstation. It also tracks diagnostic messages for troubleshooting purposes.
- *MODULES* — This DOS-based Novell Client command enables you to view a list of NLMs currently loaded on your Windows 95/98 or Windows NT/2000 workstation.
- *REGEDIT* — This native Windows tool enables you to view and edit settings in the Windows 95/98 Registry or the Windows NT/2000 Registry. It also enables you to identify client settings that have been changed from their default values.
- *LANalyzer* — Novell provides two LANalyzer agents for network protocol analysis and troubleshooting. The NetWare LANalyzer Agent in ManageWise is designed to enable a network administrator to analyze network traffic on all network segments from a single location. The LANalyzer for Windows product provides the same functions, but is a standalone application.

So far, we have just "touched" on a few of the features offered by these valuable client troubleshooting tools. Now let's take a long hard "look" at what these tools can do for NetWare troubleshooters.

Windows 95/98 and Windows NT/2000 Control Panel

The Network dialog box found in the Control Panel on both Windows 95/98 and Windows NT/2000 workstations enables you to configure a variety of network components, including the Novell Client, protocols, and LAN drivers. To access the Network dialog box, follow these three steps:

- *Step 1*—In the Windows 95/98 or Windows NT/2000 Control Panel, double-click the Network icon.
- *Step 2*—On the Configuration tab, highlight a specific network component from the list shown (see Figure 15.3). Each component is identified with one of three different icon types: Client (Novell NetWare or Microsoft), LAN adapter, or Protocol. For example, to select the Novell NetWare or Microsoft Client, click the small computer icon next to the desired client (as shown in Figure 15.3). To select a client LAN adapter, click the NIC icon associated with the correct manufacturer-specific client driver. To select a client protocol, click the appropriate wiring icon (as shown in Figure 15.4).
- *Step 3*—Click the Properties button to access the customized Settings screen for the highlighted component.

FIGURE 15.3

Troubleshooting the Novell Client using the Windows 95/98 Control Panel

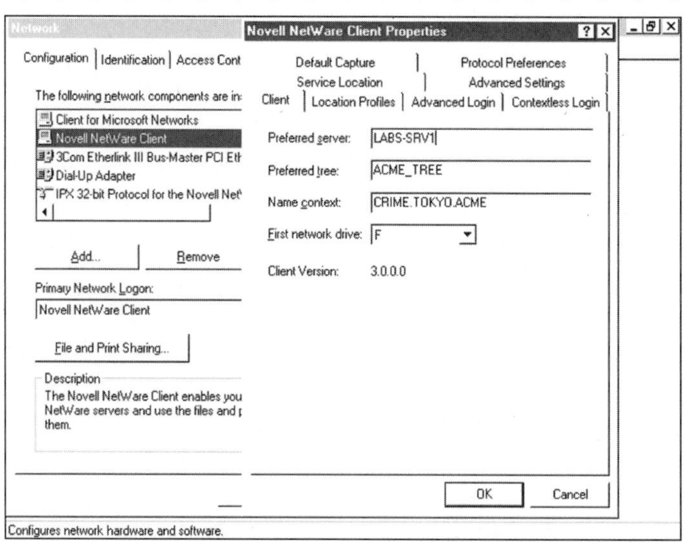

FIGURE 15.4

Troubleshooting the IPX protocol using the Windows 95/98 Control Panel

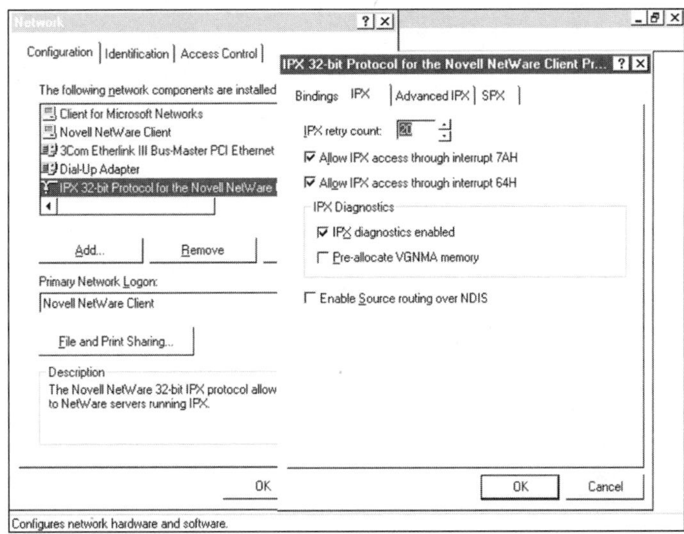

REAL WORLD

Practice troubleshooting Windows 95/98 and Windows NT/2000 workstations by exploring the Control Panel dialog box shown in Figure 15.3. Pay particular attention to the following tabs: Client (for client configurations), Advanced Settings, Protocol Preferences, and Advanced Login.

Novell Client Log File (NIOS.LOG)

The Novell Client log file (NIOS.LOG) keeps track of NLMs that are loaded on a Windows 95/98 workstation. It also tracks the properties that are used, as well as any diagnostic messages that are generated by NLMs.

Before you can view the log file, you will need to activate it using the Windows 95/98 SYSTEM.INI file. To do so, add the following line to the [386Enh] subsection:

```
NWEnablelogging=True
```

After you initiate this process, the Novell Client will create a NIOS.LOG file in the workstation's default Novell Client home directory (that is, C:\NOVELL\CLIENT32) or in a custom directory chosen by the network administrator. If the user encounters problems during the login process, you can check the log file for clues. For example, here are some of the types of problems that would be reported in this log:

- A client NLM did not load.
- IPX failed to bind successfully to the internal workstation NIC.
- All the NLMs loaded properly, but the Novell Client could not find a server.

If a workstation hangs during the boot process, you can view its NIOS.LOG file in one of two ways. The first method involves booting the workstation using the "Command Prompt Only" option. To do so, press F8 when you see the "Starting Windows 95/98" message and then use the DOS EDIT command to view the NIOS.LOG file in its default (or custom) location. The second method involves booting the workstation in "Safe Mode" and viewing the NIOS.LOG file using the Windows 95/98 Notepad utility (refer to Figure 15.5).

FIGURE 15.5

Using the Notepad utility to view the Novell Client log file

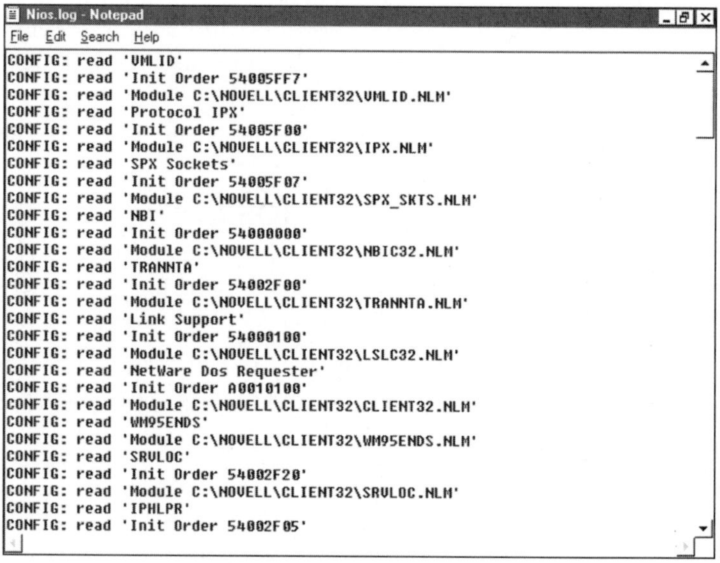

```
Nios.log - Notepad
File  Edit  Search  Help
CONFIG: read 'VMLID'
CONFIG: read 'Init Order 54005FF7'
CONFIG: read 'Module C:\NOVELL\CLIENT32\VMLID.NLM'
CONFIG: read 'Protocol IPX'
CONFIG: read 'Init Order 54005F00'
CONFIG: read 'Module C:\NOVELL\CLIENT32\IPX.NLM'
CONFIG: read 'SPX Sockets'
CONFIG: read 'Init Order 54005F07'
CONFIG: read 'Module C:\NOVELL\CLIENT32\SPX_SKTS.NLM'
CONFIG: read 'NBI'
CONFIG: read 'Init Order 54000000'
CONFIG: read 'Module C:\NOVELL\CLIENT32\NBIC32.NLM'
CONFIG: read 'TRANNTA'
CONFIG: read 'Init Order 54002F00'
CONFIG: read 'Module C:\NOVELL\CLIENT32\TRANNTA.NLM'
CONFIG: read 'Link Support'
CONFIG: read 'Init Order 54000100'
CONFIG: read 'Module C:\NOVELL\CLIENT32\LSLC32.NLM'
CONFIG: read 'NetWare Dos Requester'
CONFIG: read 'Init Order A0010100'
CONFIG: read 'Module C:\NOVELL\CLIENT32\CLIENT32.NLM'
CONFIG: read 'WM95ENDS'
CONFIG: read 'Module C:\NOVELL\CLIENT32\WM95ENDS.NLM'
CONFIG: read 'SRVLOC'
CONFIG: read 'Init Order 54002F20'
CONFIG: read 'Module C:\NOVELL\CLIENT32\SRVLOC.NLM'
CONFIG: read 'IPHLPR'
CONFIG: read 'Init Order 54002F05'
```

Once you have gained all the clues you can from the NIOS.LOG file, use the Network dialog box or any of the other tools in this chapter to solve the problem. Once the problem has been solved, consider disabling the Novell Client log file, because it will *slow down* workstation booting.

MODULES

The NetWare MODULES command displays a list of NLMs currently loaded on the workstation. To activate the MODULES command, simply type **MODULES** at the DOS command prompt. You can also redirect the MODULES list to an ASCII text file (CLIENT01.TXT, in this example) using the following syntax:

```
MODULES > CLIENT01.TXT
```

For troubleshooting purposes, you should run MODULES on both a problematic client and a workstation that is behaving normally—and then compare the results.

REGEDIT

Both Windows 95/98 and Windows NT/2000 rely on a special database called the Registry to store hardware and software settings. You can view and edit Novell Client settings by accessing the Registry via the Windows 95/98 or Windows NT/2000 Control Panel, or REGEDIT. (**Note:** Network administrators can cause serious system problems with the Registry if they are not experienced in editing it. Make sure to back up the Registry prior to editing.)

If you use the Control Panel method, any changes made to the Network dialog box will be stored in the Registry. REGEDIT, on the other hand, is a native Windows 95/98 and Windows NT/2000 tool that enables you to view and to edit Registry settings directly.

The Registry Editor uses a hierarchical tree structure similar to the Explorer feature found in Windows 95/98 and Windows NT/2000 (see Figure 15.6). To access REGEDIT, click Start ➪ Run, type **REGEDIT** in the Run dialog box, and then click OK. To access Novell Client configurations, simply double-click the following choices, in this order:

- *HKEY_LOCAL_MACHINE*—Identifies configuration settings for this workstation, including hardware, software, security, and the network.

- *Network*—Identifies configuration settings for the native Microsoft WinLogin utility and/or the Novell Client.
- *Novell*—Identifies configuration settings for the Novell Client for Windows 95/98 or the Novell Client for Windows NT/2000.
- *System Config*—Lists a variety of system configuration categories for Novell Client software, including installation options, language support, NetWare DOS Requester, protocols, and VMLID support for LAN drivers.

FIGURE 15.6

Troubleshooting the Windows 95/98 Registry with REGEDIT

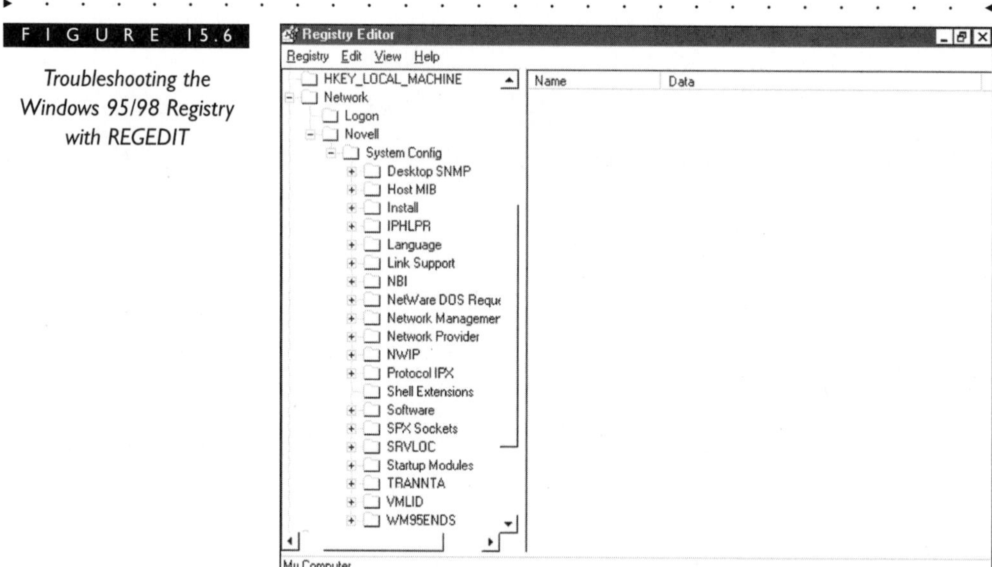

The System Config folder contains all your Registry-based Novell Client settings. Be very, very careful when you make changes to the Windows 95/98/NT Registry. Microsoft strongly recommends that you do not edit the Registry because it can result in loss of data, failure of a program, or even failure of the entire workstation system.

LANalyzer

Protocol analyzers are designed to help you analyze how your network is running and give you key feedback about traffic bottlenecks and other traffic problems. They also enable you to monitor network performance, to troubleshoot network errors, to optimize the LAN, and to plan for growth.

Protocol analyzers provide trend information by measuring specific variables, such as the number of CRC errors over time, network utilization statistics, and/or network overloads. Protocol analyzers come in two varieties: hardware/software analyzers and software-only analyzers. The major differences between the two are the speed at which they operate and the number of services they provide. For example, hardware/software analyzers are faster than software-only ones and are usually designed to handle a wider variety of different protocols. They also can typically transmit test traffic and receive data at the same time and can generate detailed analysis reports on the information they have gathered.

LANalyzer is a software protocol analysis tool available from Novell. Currently, two different versions of this product are available:

- *NetWare LANalyzer Agent* — This is a subcomponent of the Novell Manage Wise product. It is designed to enable a network administrator to analyze traffic on all network segments from a single location.
- *LANalyzer for Windows (LZFW)* — This is a standalone version of the NetWare LANalyzer Agent that performs the same functions, except that it performs the functions outside of the confines of ManageWise.

Both versions of LANalyzer include a diagnostic tool called the NetWare Expert. Other benefits of both versions include the capability to monitor network segments, to provide comprehensive information gathering, and, most importantly, to offer an inexpensive solution as compared to more full-featured hardware/software protocol analyzers.

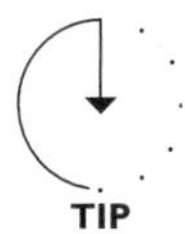
TIP

For more information on using LANalyzer for Windows as a NetWare troubleshooting and optimization tool, refer to the "LANalyzer for Windows" section in Chapter 17.

This completes our discussion of workstation architecture and troubleshooting. Now there is only one more lesson to go—the Novell Client Troubleshooting Model. This model will bring structure to your otherwise chaotic troubleshooting adventures.

Novell Client Troubleshooting Model

As a NetWare troubleshooter, it is important for you to stay in touch with your workstation's "sense." Novell Client troubleshooting is easy if you follow these powerful five steps (follow along with Figure 15.7):

- *Step 1:* List Symptoms
- *Step 2:* Eliminate Hardware Issues
- *Step 3:* Eliminate LAN Driver Issues
- *Step 4:* Verify the Novell Client Version
- *Step 5:* Eliminate Connection Issues

Step 1: List Symptoms

As we discussed in Chapter 12, data gathering occurs during Step 2 of the six-step NetWare Troubleshooting Model. We also discussed how to use diagnostic tools to analyze network communications, to check documentation, and to gain valuable help from the NUI and NPA user groups.

In this chapter, you need to apply your data-gathering skills to troubleshoot Novell Client problems. The first step in the Novell Client Troubleshooting Model is to list the symptoms of the problem.

FIGURE 15.7

The Novell Client Troubleshooting Model

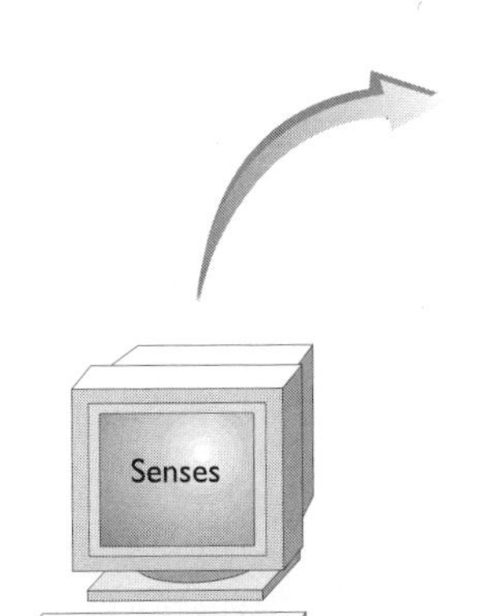

Step 2: Eliminate Hardware Issues

The next step in the Novell Client Troubleshooting Model is to eliminate hardware as a possible source of the problem. To do this, ask yourself the following questions:

- Is this Windows 95/98 or Windows NT/2000 workstation using a 486 processor or higher? (To determine this information, double-click the System icon in the Windows 95/98 or Windows NT/2000 Control Panel. The General tab of the System Properties page will display, by default. Note the processor value displayed in the bottom-right corner.)
- Does the workstation have enough RAM (16MB minimum for Windows 95/98 and 32MB minimum for Windows NT/2000)? (To determine this information, double-click the System icon in the Windows 95/98 or Windows NT/2000 Control Panel. The General tab of the System Properties page will display, by default. Note the total amount of installed RAM in the bottom-right corner, as shown in Figure 15.8.)

FIGURE 15.8

Checking workstation hardware in the Windows 95/98 Control Panel

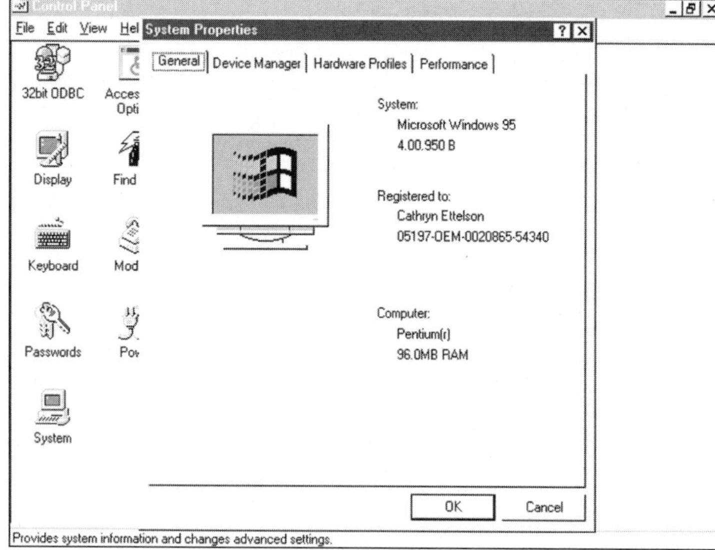

- Has any new hardware been installed since the last time the workstation worked properly?
- Is the same problem occurring on other workstations? If not, how are the other workstations different from this workstation (in other words, are there differences in hardware, software, and/or physical location)?
- Is this workstation being remote-booted?
- Is the Link Status indicator light green on all network boards, hubs, and other connectivity equipment between this workstation and the server?
- Is the network board or the Personal Computer Memory Card International Association (PCMCIA) adapter inserted properly? (To determine if the network board is working properly and if it is using the latest software, access the System icon within the Windows 95/98 or Windows NT/2000 Control Panel. Next, activate the Device Manager tab and double-click Network Adapters. Then highlight your adapter and click Properties.

Next, on the General tab, check the "Hardware Version" and "Device Status" fields, as shown in Figure 15.9. Finally, on the Resources tab, check resource settings and the Conflicting Device list.)

FIGURE 15.9

Checking workstation hardware status using the Windows 95/98 Control Panel

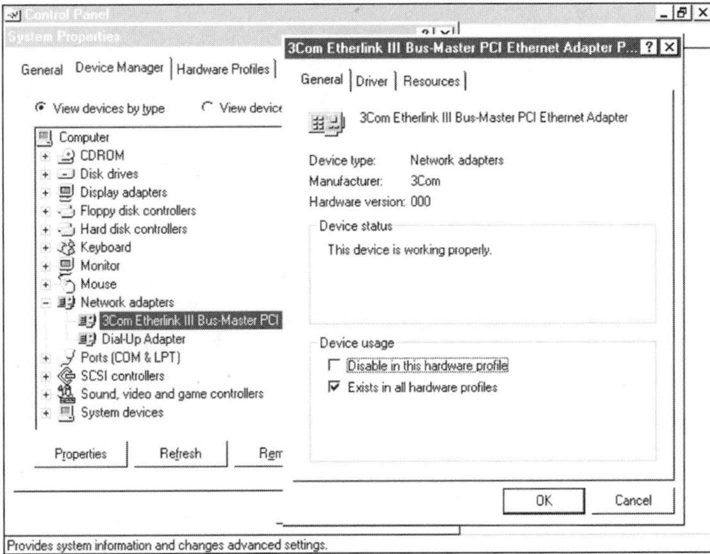

REAL WORLD

Practice troubleshooting the Novell Client by exploring the Device Manager in the System Properties section of the Windows 95/98 or Windows NT/2000 Control Panel. Pay particular attention to the workstation components that apply to networking, namely Network Adapters, Ports, and System Devices.

Once you have eliminated the workstation hardware issues, it's time to move on to LAN drivers themselves. After all, a LAN driver is a vital link between the internal NIC and client operating system. Let's take a closer look.

Step 3: Eliminate LAN Driver Issues

The workstation LAN driver links the internal NIC to the WOS. Therefore, you should ensure that each workstation has the correct manufacturer-specific driver loaded. To determine this information, use the NetWare MODULES command at the DOS prompt. You should also locate the LAN driver file and compare its date to the latest manufacturer-specific release:

- *ODI LAN Drivers* — Check the *.LAN driver file in the C:\Novell\CLIENT32 directory.

- *NDIS LAN Drivers* — Check the *.DOS driver file in the C:\Windows directory.

Once you have identified the date of your manufacturer-specific driver file, check it against the latest information available from the manufacturer's home page. And if that doesn't solve your problem, continue to Step 4 — verifying the Novell Client version.

Step 4: Verify the Novell Client Version

Both the Novell Client for Windows 95/98 and the Novell Client for Windows NT/2000 are included on the NetWare 5.1 *Novell Client* CD-ROM. You can also download these clients from the Novell Internet Support Connection Web site. If desired, you can then use the Automatic Client Upgrade (ACU) feature to automatically install or update client software when the user logs into the network.

Before installing the Novell Client software, follow these precautions:

- Save the Windows 95/98 or Windows NT/2000 Registry by executing the ERU.EXE (Emergency Recovery Utility) file, which is located in the \OTHER\MISC\ERU directory on the Windows 95/98 or Windows NT/2000 CD-ROM.

- Uninstall the Novell Client for Windows 95/98 (UNC32.EXE) or Windows NT/2000 (WNTUNC.EXE). These utilities remove key files and any special configuration changes made to the Windows 95/98 and Windows NT/2000 Registry.

The Uninstall utility does not, however, delete the client files placed on the workstation during the Novell Client for Windows 95/98 or Novell Client for Windows NT/2000 installations.

Once the Novell Client has been installed, you can check its current version using the Novell NetWare Client Properties page within the Network dialog box of the Windows 95/98 or Windows NT/2000 Control Panels. You should continue to ensure that you are using the latest version by periodically checking the file updates available on the Novell Internet Support Connection Web site.

Once you have eliminated hardware, LAN adapter, and Novell Client issues, there's only one possibility left — the network connection. Let's check it out.

Step 5: Eliminate Connection Issues

If you haven't solved the Novell Client problem by now, you are probably getting pretty desperate. At this point, you can accurately deduce that the problem isn't localized to your workstation. Chances are it has something to do with the network itself.

Novell offers two options for helping to eliminate client connection issues:

- *Windows 95/98 and Windows NT/2000 Control Panels* — Examine the connection-specific settings offered by the Network dialog box in the Windows 95/98 or Windows NT/2000 Control Panels. To do this, access the Novell NetWare Client Properties screen and check the Novell NetWare Client, Login, Default Capture, and Advanced Settings tabs. Next, consider checking the appropriate protocol properties and ensuring that bindings and addressing information are correct.
- *LANalyzer* — The NetWare LANalyzer Agent and LANalyzer for Windows (LZFW) products enable you to diagnose, isolate, and solve a variety of network-related problems.

Welcome to the end of the Novell Client Troubleshooting Model. If you still haven't solved your problem by traversing these five steps, you should consider moving to another network — just kidding! At this point, your problem could require more sophistication than is offered by this five-step model.

Consider returning to Chapter 12 and initiating the six-step NetWare troubleshooting model and/or using the *Novell Internet Connection*, which also is discussed in Chapter 12.

The bottom line is—there's a lot more to the NetWare workstation than meets the eye. It's a complex collection of user components and connectivity hardware. This makes troubleshooting workstations an incredible challenge. And, as we have learned in this chapter, you must have complete control of your faculties to pull it off.

So, where do we go from here? Well, we have one more troubleshooting component left—printing. So far, we have learned everything there is to know about troubleshooting NICs, hard drives, and workstation. Now we need something to tie them all together. We need printing output to help bring action into our otherwise dull and lifeless LAN.

LAB EXERCISE 15.1: TROUBLESHOOTING AN ACME WINDOWS 98 WORKSTATION

As you have learned in this chapter, your Novell Client uses built-in technology to link you to the NetWare 5.1 network. In this exercise, we will explore some quick things you can check if you are having problems connecting your Windows 98 workstation to your network.

The following hardware is required for this exercise:

- A NetWare 5.1 server
- A workstation running the NetWare 5.1 Novell Client for Windows 98

Good luck, and don't forget to use your enhanced workstation troubleshooting skills.

Part I: Network-Related Hardware Issues

1. Power off the computer.
2. Verify that the network board is installed properly.
3. Ensure that there are no loose cable connections.
4. Confirm that any termination, if necessary, has been performed properly.
5. Power on the computer.
6. Verify that the link status indicators are lit on all network boards, hubs, and other connectivity equipment between this workstation and the server.

Part II: Workstation Hardware Issues

1. Determine that the workstation is running an appropriate version of Windows 98, has an appropriate processor, and sufficient RAM.
   a. Open the Control panel.
      - Click Start.
      - Click Settings.
      - Click Control Panel.
   b. When the Control Panel folder opens, double-click the System icon.
   c. When the System Properties dialog box appears, the General tab is selected by default:
      - Verify that you're running Windows 98 or higher.
      - Confirm that the workstation is using a Pentium 90 MHz or higher processor.
      - Ensure that the workstation has at least 32MB of RAM.
2. Verify that the workstation has sufficient System Resources available.
   a. Click the Performance tab.
   b. When the Performance page appears, check the percentage of system resources free. You should also check that the workstation is configured to use virtual memory.
3. Determine if the network board is an appropriate version and if it is working properly.
   a. Click the Device Manager tab.
   b. When the Device Manager page appears, double-click Network Adapters.
   c. When the list of network adapters appears, click your network board to select it and then click Properties.

d. When the network board dialog box appears, the General tab should be selected by default:

- Verify that the hardware version of the network board is an appropriate version. (Check with the manufacturer of the network board for further information.)
- Check the Device Status section to make sure that it shows the following status:

  ```
  This device is working properly
  ```

- Click the Resources tab.

e. Follow these steps when the Resources page appears:

- Review the entries in the Resource Type/Setting list.
- Verify that the Conflicting Device List sections shows the following status:

  ```
  No Conflicts
  ```

- Click Cancel to return to the Device Manager page.

f. When the Device Manager page reappears, click Cancel to exit the System Properties dialog box.

g. When the Control panel folder reappears, select Close from the File menu to close it.

4. Determine if the workstation has sufficient hard disk space available.

a. On the workstation desktop, double-click the My Computer icon.

b. When the My Computer folder opens, right-click the icon representing your hard disk and then select Properties from the pop-up menu that appears.

c. When the hard disk Properties dialog box appears, the General tab is selected by default:
   - Ensure that there is an appropriate amount of free space available on your hard disk.
   - Click Cancel to close the hard disk Properties folder.

d. When the My Computer folder reappears, select Close from the File menu to close it.

Part III: LAN Driver Issues

1. Determine if an ODI or NDIS driver is installed.

   a. Open the Control panel folder.
      - Click Start.
      - Click Settings.
      - Click Control Panel.

   b. When the Control Panel folder opens, double-click the Network icon.

   c. When the Network dialog box appears, the Configuration tab is selected by default:
      - Click your network board.
      - Click Properties.

   d. When the network board dialog box appears, the Drive Type tab is selected by default:
      - Check to see what type of LAN driver is being used (ODI or NDIS).
      - Click the Bindings tab.

   e. Follow these steps when the Bindings page appears:
      - Determine which protocols are being used.
      - Click Cancel to return to the Configuration page.

f. When the Configuration page reappears, click Cancel to close the Network dialog box.

g. When the Control Panel dialog box reappears, select Close from the File menu to close it.

2. Determine which LAN drivers are being loaded.

a. Display a DOS prompt.

- Click Start.
- Click Programs.
- Click MS-DOS Prompt.

b. Type the following at the DOS prompt and press Enter:

```
MODULES
```

c. Determine which LAN drivers are being loaded from the onscreen list.

d. Exit MS-DOS. To exit, type the following at the DOS prompt and press Enter:

```
EXIT
```

3. If the workstation is using an ODI driver, determine if it is the latest version.

a. Launch Windows Explorer.

- Click Start.
- Click Programs.
- Click Windows Explorer.

b. Follow these steps when the Windows Explorer screen appears:

- Double-click Novell.
- Double-click Client32.
- Locate the appropriate *.LAN driver file.
- Check the date of the *.LAN driver file.

c. Select Close from the File menu to exit the Windows Explorer utility.

4. If the workstation is using an NDIS driver, determine if it is the latest version.
   a. Launch Windows Explorer.
      - Click Start.
      - Click Programs.
      - Click Windows Explorer.
   b. Follow these steps when the Windows Explorer screen appears:
      - Double-click Windows.
      - Locate the appropriate *.DOS driver file.
      - Check the date of the *DOS driver file.
   c. Select Close from the File menu to exit the Windows Explorer utility.

Part IV: Novell Client Issues

1. Determine the version of the Novell Client using the Registry Editor.
   a. Click Start and then click Run.
   b. When the Run dialog box appears, type the following in the Open field and click OK:

      ```
      REGEDIT
      ```
   c. Follow these steps when the Registry Editor window appears:
      - Double-click HKEY_LOCAL_MACHINE.
      - Double-click Network.
      - Double-click Novell.
      - Double-click System Config.
      - Double-click Install.
      - Click Client Version to display its contents in the right pane.

   d. Determine the Client version by examining the values of the following parameters in the right pane:
      - Major Version
      - Minor Version
      - Revision
      - Level
   e. Select Exit from the Registry menu to exit the Registry Editor.

2. Determine the version of the Novell Client using the Control Panel.
   a. Open the Control Panel folder.
      - Click Start.
      - Click Settings.
      - Click Control Panel.
   b. When the Control Panel folder opens, double-click the Network icon.
   c. When the Network dialog box appears, the Configuration tab is selected by default:
      - Click Novell NetWare Client.
      - Click Properties.
   d. Follow these steps when the Novell Client Configuration dialog box appears:
      - Click the various tabs to examine the settings on each page for incorrect information.
      - Click Cancel to return to the Network dialog box.
   e. When the Network dialog box reappears, click Cancel to close it.
   f. When the Control Panel reappears, select Close from the File menu to close it.

3. Determine if there is a more current version of the Novell Client available on the Web.

   a. Launch your Web browser.

   b. Access the following Web site:

      `http://support.novell.com`

   c. Click File Finder.

   d. Click Download Novell Clients.

   e. In the "Client – Network" section, review the available Novell Client versions to determine if a more recent version is available.

4. Download a more current version of the Novell Client, if applicable.

   a. Click the URL for the appropriate Windows 98 client.

   b. Follow these steps when the next screen appears:

      - Read the onscreen information.
      - Click "Proceed to Download."

   c. Follow these steps when the next screen appears:

      - Review the default information carefully. (If you fail to review the information, you may be surprised to find yourself on mailing lists you hadn't planned on.)
      - Complete the required information.
      - Click Connect.

   d. Depending on the client version you selected, a U.S. Export Restriction screen may appear:

      - Read the onscreen information.
      - Click Accept to accept the terms and conditions listed.

   e. Follow these steps when the next screen appears:

      - Review the onscreen options.

- Click Readme to display the Readme file and then press the Backspace button in your browser to return to the preceding screen
- In the Full File section, click the appropriate button (either Inside U.S. or Outside U.S.).

f. Wait while the updated Novell Client file downloads.

g. Exit your browser

5. Install the new version of the Novell Client on your workstation.

Part V: Connection Issues

1. Enable the NetWare Client log file.

a. Click Start and then click Run.

b. When the Run dialog box appears, type the following in the Open field and click OK:

```
SYSEDIT
```

c. Follow these steps when the System Configuration Editor window appears:

- Click the WINDOWS\SYSTEM.INI file to select it.
- Add the following line to the [386Enh] subsection:

```
NWEnablelogging=True
```

- Select Save from the File menu to save the file.
- Select Exit from the File menu to exit the System Configuration Editor.

d. Log off the network.

e. Log into the network.

f. Using the text editor of your choice (such as the Windows Notepad utility), open the NetWare Client log file and review the information regarding your login. (The file is called C:\NOVELL\CLIENT32\NIOS.LOG.)

2. Examine the Novell Client settings using the *N* icon in the System Tray.

   a. Right-click the *N* icon in the System Tray. (It's located, by default, at the right end of the Windows taskbar.)

   b. Select Novell Client32 Properties from the pop-up menu that appears.

   c. When the Novell Client Configuration dialog box appears, the Client tab is selected by default:

      - Note the value in the Client Version field.
      - Click the various tabs to examine the settings on each page for incorrect information.
      - Click Cancel to close the Novell Client Configuration dialog box.

LAB EXERCISE 15.2: FIXING ACME WORKSTATIONS

Use the hints provided to find the 20 workstation troubleshooting-tools terms hidden in this word search puzzle. Omit any punctuation characters (such as blank spaces, hyphens, and so on) and spell out any numbers.

Hints

1. Focus of Step 5 in the Workstation Troubleshooting Model.
2. One method for saving the Windows 95/98 and Windows NT Registry.
3. WinLogin Graphical Identification and Authentication module.
4. Focus of Step 2 in the Workstation Troubleshooting Model.
5. Root key of the Windows Registry that holds configuration settings for the local workstation, including hardware, software, security, and the network.
6. Novell provides two of these agents for network protocol analysis and troubleshooting.
7. Standalone version of the agents described in Hint 6.
8. Benefit of the Novell Client Requester.

9. Novell Client DOS-based command that enables you to view a list of NLMs that are currently loaded on a Windows 95/98/NT workstation.
10. Interface that consists of a native Windows 95/98/NT driver and a VLIMD. NLM support file.
11. Simultaneous access to multiple ones of these is supported by the Novell Client.
12. Protocol that provides application programs with a set for commands for requesting the lower-level services required to conduct sessions between network nodes.
13. Hardware that provides fundamental communications between the local Workstation Operating System (WOS) and the NetWare server.
14. File that maintains a record of the NLMs loaded on a Windows 95/98 workstation, as well as tracking diagnostic messages for troubleshooting assistance.
15. Microsoft IPX-compatible protocol called NWLink that can be used by WinSock and NetBIOS applications.
16. NIC architecture that enables multiple LAN drivers and protocols to be used with a single NIC.
17. Support module that enables you to use Microsoft networking with native Novell LAN drivers.
18. Dangerous way to edit the Windows 95/98 and Windows NT Registry.
19. Important Windows 95/98 and Windows NT database that is used to store hardware and software settings.
20. Novell utility that is used to uninstall the Novell Client for Windows 95/98 (or Novell Client for Windows NT) and that removes key files and the additions made to the Windows NT Registry.

See Appendix C for answers.

LAB EXERCISE 15.3: TROUBLESHOOTING WORKSTATIONS

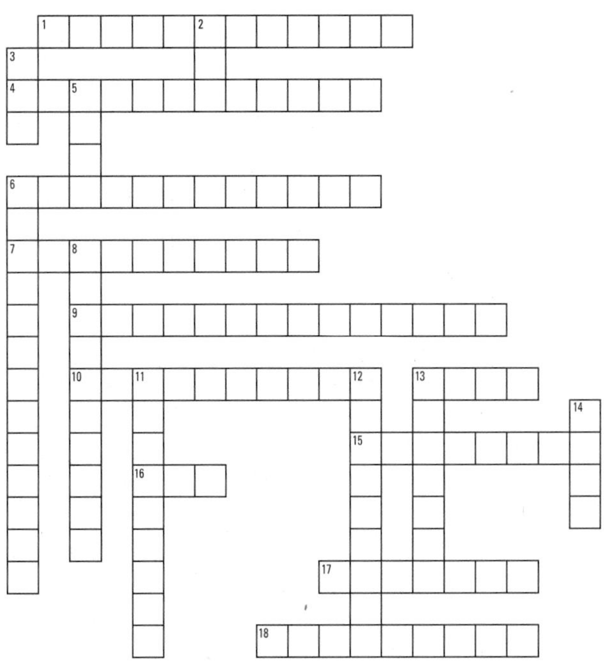

Across

1. Implemented as CLIENT32.NLM
4. Safe way to change Windows 95/98/NT settings
6. Step 1 of the Workstation Troubleshooting Model
7. NETBIOS-based protocol supported by the Novell Client
9. Novell Client Requester benefit
10. Focus of Step 3 in the Workstation Troubleshooting Model
13. Interface layer between Windows NT workstations and the network
15. Windows mode used for troubleshooting
16. Proprietary NetWare protocol
17. NIOS virtual device driver implementation
18. Native NT GINA

Down

2. Acts as a switchboard
3. Automated client install
5. Main component of the Novell Client for Windows 95/98
6. File naming convention supported by the Novell Client
8. Another Novell Client Requester benefit
11. Novell's GINA module
12. Windows configuration file for activating NIOS.LOG
13. Main component of the Novell Client for Windows NT
14. NetWare "shell"

See Appendix C for answers.

CHAPTER 16

Troubleshooting Printing

Printing is the foundation of your network's muscular system. Printing works together with your network's cabling, workstations, and server disks to provide form and function. Ultimately, all your users' electronic bits have to find their way to a printer. Fortunately, NetWare employs two powerful printing systems to make this dream a reality: Queue-based and NDPS. NetWare queue-based printing consists of three main components:

- *Print Queue*
- *Print Server*
- *Printer*

When set up correctly, these three components create a well-orchestrated printing system — you click a button on the workstation and a piece of paper comes out of the printer down the hall. So, how can you possibly satisfy the lofty expectations of your users while maintaining a rock-solid NetWare printing architecture? That's one of the greatest mysteries of all.

In this chapter, we will explore the fundamentals of NetWare printing from a troubleshooter's point of view. We will gain valuable insight into users' expectations and discover some life-saving troubleshooting tips for print queues, print servers, and printers. And, to make your life even more exciting, we'll do it from two totally different points of view:

- *Novell Distributed Print Services (NDPS)* — This is the next-generation printing architecture offered by NetWare 5.*x*. It replaces the older, queue-based printing architecture included with previous versions of NetWare.
- *Queue-Based Printing* — This is the old way of doing things. Queue-based printing offers NetWare doctors with a simpler, less sophisticated alternative to NDPS. Queue-based printing is available in all versions of NetWare.

First, we will review the fundamental architecture of NDPS and then offer some comprehensive troubleshooting flowcharts. Then, when you have mastered NDPS, we will move onto queue-based printing. In the second half of this chapter, we will review the basic architecture of queue-based systems and offer some in-depth troubleshooting help.

Let's get started with a review of NDPS.

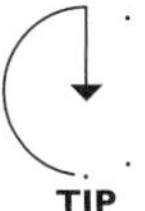
TIP

In the first half of this chapter, we're going to focus on the NetWare 5.x platform because that's the foundation of NDPS printing. Then, in the second half of the chapter, we're going to switch to NetWare 3 and NetWare 4. After all, that's where queue-based printing was born.

NDPS Printing Overview

Novell Distributed Print Services (NDPS) is the result of a joint development effort by Novell, Hewlett-Packard, and Xerox. Although it was created to replace the queue-based printing architecture found in earlier versions of NetWare, it can also be used to service existing print queues, if desired.

NDPS was designed to handle the increasing complexity of today's large networks—specifically, to help network administrators manage printing devices in any type of network environment, ranging in size from small workgroups to enterprise-wide systems. NDPS was also designed with Novell Directory Services (NDS) in mind. Benefits of NDPS include improved overall network performance, fewer network printing problems, reduced administration costs, and less management time.

Some of the main features offered by NDPS include the following:

- Plug and print support, including automatic print driver download and installation
- Greater control with the help of bi-directional communications
- NDS integration
- Configurable event notification and multiple printer configurations
- Network traffic reduction
- Enhanced client support (for Windows 3.*x*, Windows 95/98, and Windows NT/2000 clients)
- Backward compatibility

NDPS Printing Architecture

NDPS printing architecture was designed to ensure the scalability of the NetWare 5.1 printing environment and to allow users to print to a variety of network devices — ranging from simple dot-matrix printers to laser printers and large-scale production devices.

Figure 16.1 illustrates the major components of the NDPS architecture. As you can see, NetWare 5.1 printing consists of three support components and the Printer Agent (PA):

- *Printer Agent* — This is the heart of NetWare 5.1 NDPS printing. The Printer Agent combines the functions previously performed by a printer, print queue, print server, and spooler into one intelligent, simplified entity.
- *NDPS Manager* — The NDPS Manager is a logical entity used to create and manage Printer Agents. It is represented as an object in the NDS tree.
- *NDPS Gateway* — NDPS gateways enable you to support *non-native* printing environments. Non-native printing environments include non-NDPS-aware printers and print systems that require jobs to be placed in queues. NDPS currently supports two gateways: the Novell Gateway and Third-Party Gateways. Furthermore, the Novell Gateway consists of a Print Device Subsystem (PDS) and a Port Handler (PH) component.
- *NDPS Broker* — When NDPS is installed, the installation utility ensures that a Broker object is loaded on your network and provides three network support services not previously available in NetWare. Although these services are invisible, you must be aware of them in case the Broker decides to take a vacation. The three NDPS support services are Service Registry Services (SRS), Event Notification Services (ENS), and Resource Management Services (RMS).

Now let's take a closer look at each of these four NDPS components and learn how they combine to create a robust network printing system.

FIGURE 16.1

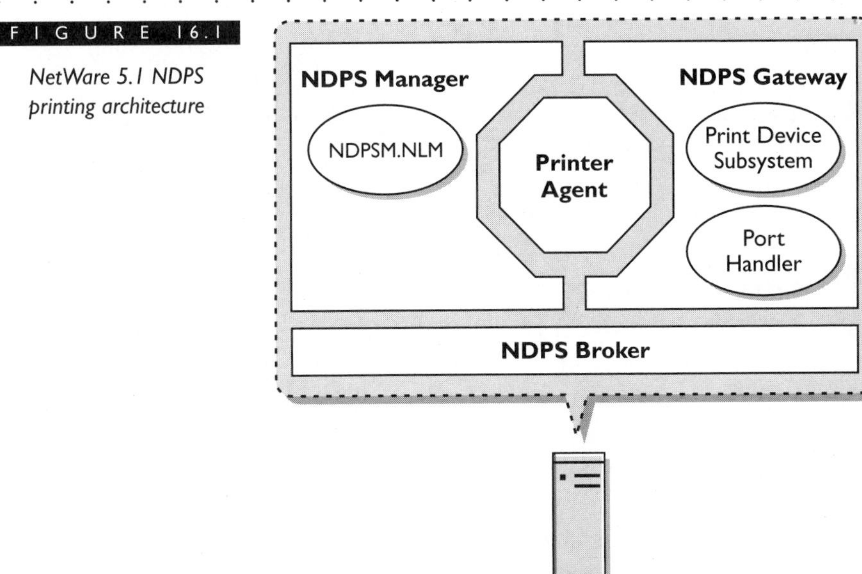

NetWare 5.1 NDPS printing architecture

NDPS Printer Agent

Printer Agents combine the functionality previously provided by queue-based print queues, printers, and print servers into one intelligent, integrated entity. With NDPS, each printer has a one-to-one relationship with a Printer Agent. This means that no Printer Agent can represent more than one printer. A Printer Agent can represent either a Public Access or Controlled Access printer (both of which are discussed later in this chapter).

A Printer Agent can exist as *software* (running on a NetWare 5.1 server and controlling a printer attached directly to the network, to a server, or to a workstation) or *firmware* (embedded within a network-attached printer). In either case, a Printer Agent provides the following NDPS services:

- It manages print job processing and many operations performed by the physical printer.
- It answers queries from network clients concerning print jobs, documents, or printer attributes.

- It generates event notification for job completion, errors, printing problems, or changes in the status of a print job, document, or printer.
- It ensures the scalability of the printing environment, enabling you to print to a variety of devices in a local area network (LAN), wide area network (WAN), or enterprise environment.

NDPS Manager

An NDPS Manager is a logical NDS object that is used to create and manage Printer Agents. You must create an NDPS Manager object before creating server-based Printer Agents. The good news is that a single NDPS Manager can control an unlimited number of Printer Agents. A good rule of thumb is to create an NDPS Manager object for each server that has NDPS printers assigned to it.

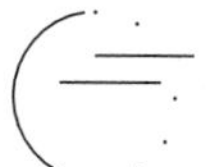
NOTE

Only one NDPS Manager is allowed per server.

The NDPS Manager software runs on a NetWare 5.1 server as NDPSM.NLM. This NLM carries out instructions provided by the NDPS Manager object and can be loaded in one of two ways: manually at the server console or automatically with AUTOEXEC.NCF.

Although you can perform some configuration and management tasks directly through the NDPS Manager console interface, NetWare Administrator is a much better tool for performing these tasks. Refer to Figure 16.2 for a quick look at configuring the NDPS Manager using NetWare Administrator.

NDPS Gateways

An NDPS Gateway is a software bridge that directly links Printer Agents to NDPS printers. It accomplishes this by translating NDPS commands into device-specific language that the physical printer can understand. This is possible because gateways are configured to know the specific type (make and model) of printer being used.

You must select and configure an NDPS Gateway whenever you create a Printer Agent.

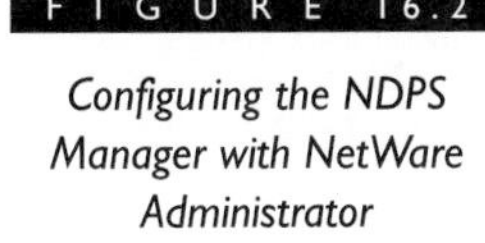

FIGURE 16.2

Configuring the NDPS Manager with NetWare Administrator

NDPS currently supports two types of gateways:

- *Novell Gateway* — This gateway consists of a Print Device Subsystem (PDS) and a Port Handler (PH) component. The gateway supports local and remote printers including those using NPRINTER or queues. Check out the Novell Gateway shown in Figure 16.3. In addition, the Novell Gateway provides support for RP mode-enabled IPX printers and/or LPR mode-enabled IP printers. LPR printers use a UNIX-based printing protocol in IP environments.

- *Third-Party Gateways* — These alternative gateways perform the same types of tasks as the Novell Gateway, but are customized by printer manufacturers to support their own network-attached devices.

FIGURE 16.3

Understanding the Novell NDPS Gateway

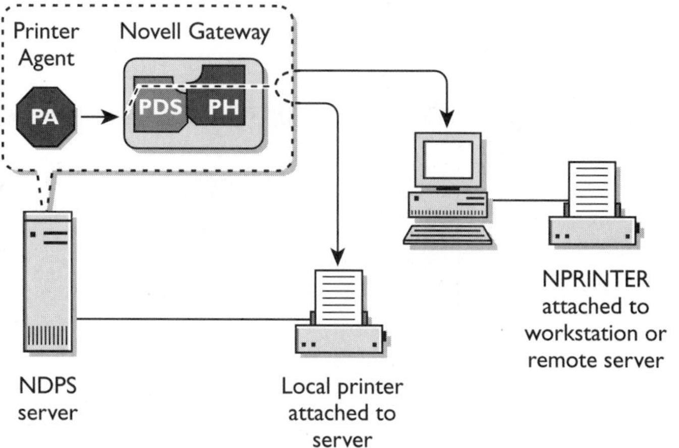

REAL WORLD

While NDPS supports most current JetDirect cards, some older cards that meet the following criteria must be upgraded or replaced:

- If the model number of the JetDirect card is between J2337A and J2550A, the flash memory must be upgraded by installing new SIMMs.
- Any card with a model number before J2337A must be replaced.
- If the model number is greater than J2550A, the firmware revision should be greater than A.03.0. If it is not, the flash memory must be upgraded.

Check the Hewlett-Packard Web site (`hp.com`) for more information.

NDPS Broker

An NDPS Broker is a special management component that is composed of two complementary parts: an NDS leaf object (NDPS Broker) and a server-based NLM (BROKER.NLM). Together, these components provide three important services to the NetWare 5.1 printing architecture:

- *Service Registry Services (SRS)*—NDPS Service Registry Services (SRS) allow Public Access printers to advertise themselves so that troubleshooters and users can find them. This service maintains information about device type, device name, device address, and device-specific data—such as the printer manufacturer and model number.
- *Event Notification Services (ENS)*—NDPS Event Notification Services (ENS) is a *middleman* between event consumers (users) and event suppliers (printers). Users register with ENS by identifying the types of events about which they want to be notified. Similarly, printers register with ENS by identifying the kinds of events they're capable of reporting. You can configure ENS to send event notifications to two different types of people: operators (non-job owners) and users (job owners). Check out Figure 16.4 for an illustration of the different ENS delivery methods.
- *Resource Management Services (RMS)*—NDPS Resource Management Services (RMS) is a central repository for printing resources. RMS allows you to install NDPS drivers, banners, and definition files in a central location and then automatically download them to clients, printers, and anyone else who needs them. RMS supports adding, listing, and replacing NDPS resources—including Windows-based printer drivers, Novell Printer Definition (NPD) files, banners, and fonts. In addition, RMS offers a number of brokering benefits, including improved resource sharing, more manageable resource distribution and updating, plug-and-print support, and centralized print driver downloading. In short, RMS greatly simplifies your life as a NetWare 5.1 CNE.

REAL WORLD

The open architecture of NDPS enables third parties to develop additional ENS delivery methods. By default, NDPS is enabled to work with the industry-standard Simple Network Management Protocol (SNMP). This way developers can build NDPS Event Notification directly into their network management systems.

FIGURE 16.4

Understanding NDPS Event Notification Services (ENS)

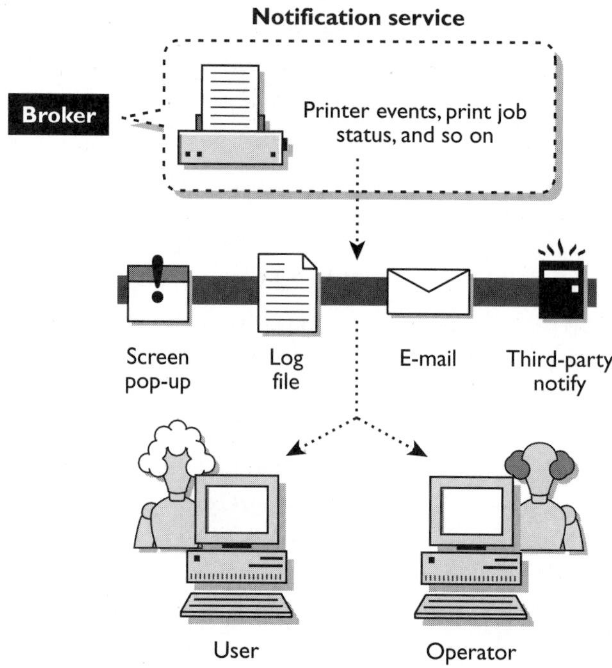

When NDPS is initially installed on a network, the setup tool ensures that an NDPS Broker object is created. After that, an additional NDPS Brokerobject is automatically created only if you install NDPS on a server that is more than three hops away from the nearest existing Broker.

Fortunately, you do not have to worry about activating an NDPS Broker, because it is automatically loaded on a server when NDPS is initialized. After it is loaded, the NDPS Broker logs into the NDS tree and authenticates itself to the server.

NDPS Printer Types

A network printer that is managed by NDPS can be connected to the network in one of three ways: as a *network-attached printer* (attached directly to the network cable), a *remote printer* (attached to a workstation or remote file server using special software provided by NDPS), or a *local printer* (attached directly to the NDPS server).

Regardless of the way you attach an NDPS printer, it must be defined as one of the following two types:

- *Public Access Printer* — A Public Access printer is available for public use. In other words, anyone on the network can use the printer without any restrictions. Following are important points to remember about Public Access printers: they have no corresponding NDS object, they can provide true plug-and-print capabilities, they afford low security, they allow little administrative support, and they support limited job event notification.
- *Controlled Access Printer* — A Controlled Access printer, on the other hand, is represented by an NDPS Printer object in the NDS tree. Because of this, you can use NDS rights assignments (via NetWare Administrator) to restrict access, change printer values, or set up event notification. A Controlled Access printer provides the following advantages over a Public Access printer: it offers a full range of security, event notification, and status notification options; it can be configured with a full range of printer configurations; and it provides simple or automatic client installation.

Refer to Table 16.1 for a summary of the most important differences between Public Access and Controlled Access printers.

TABLE 16.1

Comparing Controlled Access and Public Access Printers in NDPS

FEATURE	PUBLIC ACCESS PRINTERS	CONTROLLED ACCESS PRINTERS
NDS object	No	Yes
Security	Low	High
Configuration	Limited	Full range
NetWare Administrator support	Via the Tools menu or through the NDPS Manager object associated with the Printer Agent	As an NDS object
Event notification	Limited	Full range
Plug-and-print	Yes	Yes
Automatic client installation	Yes	Yes
Printer accessibility (by default)	All network users	User objects in the same container as the NDPS Printer object

REAL WORLD

Printers can also be classified according to how and where the printing software is loaded: *Autoload* printers are attached directly to print servers (where the printing software resides), whereas *Manual Load* printers connect to remote workstations and rely on auxiliary printing software. When you create a Controlled Access printer, NDS rights are automatically granted to all users in the printer's context. Other users do not have access until appropriate NDS rights are granted by you — the network administrator.

In the "NDPS Printing Overview" section, we have been unraveling one of the strongest features offered by NetWare 5.1 — NDPS printing. So far, you have honed your muscle tone by uncovering the fundamental architecture of NDPS. You can't stop now. Let's continue with a brief overview of NDPS printing setup.

NDPS Printing Setup

As you recall, NDPS has three main elements:

- *NDPS Broker* — Provides support services from the NetWare 5.1 server
- *NDPS Manager* — Creates and manages Printer Agents
- *NDPS Printer Agent* — Combines the functions previously performed by a printer, print queue, print server, and spooler into one intelligent, simplified entity

Believe it or not, NDPS printing setup is as simple as 1–2–3. First, you must establish NDPS Services on your NetWare 5.1 file server with the LOAD BROKER console command. This authenticates the NDPS Broker and activates NetWare 5.1 printing.

Once the Broker is in place, you must create an NDPS Manager. The NDPS Manager provides a platform for Printer Agents that reside on your server. This is all accomplished using NDPSM.NLM. Once the Manager is in place, it's time to begin creating NDPS printers by using Printer Agents. NDPS supports either Public

Access or Controlled Access printers. Unfortunately, there always seems to be a Step 4. In this case, it involves workstations and users. Before you can use your new NDPS printing system, you must install printers on each workstation. Fortunately, NetWare 5.1 supports both automatic and manual installation processes.

Here's a quick preview of the NetWare 5.1 NDPS printing setup process:

- *Step 1:* Install NDPS on the Server.
- *Step 2:* Create an NDPS Manager.
- *Step 3:* Create NDPS Printer Agents.
- *Step 4:* Install NDPS Printers on Workstations.

If you build it, they will come . . . and print!

Step 1: Install NDPS on the Server

Before you can use NetWare 5.1 NDPS, you must determine which setup strategy you want to use. You can either upgrade your current queue-based printing resources to NDPS or create a completely new NDPS printing system from the ground up. If you want to upgrade your existing printing environment with all its current printing objects and users intact, you'll need to use the Novell Upgrade Wizard.

On the other hand, it's safer and cleaner to create a new NDPS printing system from the ground up. Regardless of the strategy you use, NDPS will not disable your current printing system. The good news is that your users can continue to print just as they always have, until you decide to disable queue-based printing. This can be done gradually or all at once.

In this overview, we will use the "ground up" methodology. That means we're going to start with a clean slate and build the NDPS objects from scratch.

In Step 1, we're going to start at the NDPS server. During server installation, you can choose between a Typical or Custom installation method. It's important to understand that either installation you use for the NetWare 5.1 server will have significant consequences on NDPS printing setup. In addition, you should understand the rights required for configuring NDPS and when and where NDPS Brokers are created.

Here are some important aspects of NDPS printing setup — Step 1:

- *Typical Versus Custom Install* — If you select the Typical server installation method, NetWare 5.1 automatically installs NDPS and copies the RMS resource database to the SYS:NDPS/RESDIR directory. However, if you select the Custom server installation method, NetWare 5.1 offers you the option of placing the RMS resource database on this server, or another one. In general, you'll want a resource database enabled for each NDPS Broker that you create.
- *Rights Requirements* — To install NetWare 5.1 and NDPS on a given server, you must have certain NDS and file system rights.
- *Creating the NDPS Broker* — The first time NDPS is installed in a Directory tree, an NDPS Broker object is automatically created in the container where the Server object resides. Then when NDPS is subsequently installed on other servers in the same Directory tree, certain conditions affect where, and whether or not, additional Brokers are created.

The NDPS setup process begins with an NDPS Broker. This is a key service provider for NetWare 5.1 file servers. Regardless of how it happens, the important point is that an NDPS Broker object has been created in the Directory tree and loaded on your server. Now it's time to move on to Step 2.

Step 2: Create an NDPS Manager

Once your NDPS Broker is in place, you must create a centralized NDPS Manager. The NDPS Manager is used to control server-based Printer Agents similar to the way PSERVER was used to manage printing resources on queue-based servers. In short, you must create an NDPS Manager on each server that directly supports NDPS printers.

The good news is that a single NDPS Manager can control an unlimited number of Printer Agents. The best rule of thumb is to create an NDPS Manager object for each server that will host NDPS printers. Also, be sure that each server-based local printer sits on the same server as its host NDPS Manager.

To create an NDPS Manager in NetWare Administrator, perform the following four tasks:

- *Home Container* — In NetWare Administrator, select the container where you want the NDPS Manager object to reside. Select Create from the Object menu and then highlight NDPS Manager from the New Object dialog box. Finally, type a name of your choice in the NDPS Manager Name field (see Figure 16.5).
- *Host Server* — Browse for the host server where you want this NDPS Manager to reside. This can be any server in the current Directory tree on which you have installed an NDPS Broker. Keep in mind that any printer you designate as a local printer must be attached directly to this host server. Finally, the NDPS Manager will store its database on a volume on this server (see Figure 16.5).
- *Database Volume* — You'll need to identify a volume for hosting the NDPS Manager database. This can be any volume residing on the host server (see Figure 16.5).
- *Administrator* — Once you've identified the Manager's host server and database volume, mark Define Additional Properties and then click Create. At this point, the NDPS Manager Details dialog appears. Specify an Administrator User object for the Manager and then click Create (see Figure 16.5).

NDPS Manager runs on the NetWare 5.1 server as NDPSM.NLM. This NetWare Loadable Module carries out instructions provided by the NDPS Manager object. Once this object has been created using the tasks just discussed, it's time to load it. This is accomplished using a simple server console command:

```
LOAD NDPSM.NLM <NDPS Manager Distinguished Name>
```

For example, you might try the following line:

```
LOAD NDPSM.NLM NDPSMGR01.LABS.NORAD.ACME
```

FIGURE 16.5

Creating an NDPS Manager in NetWare Administrator

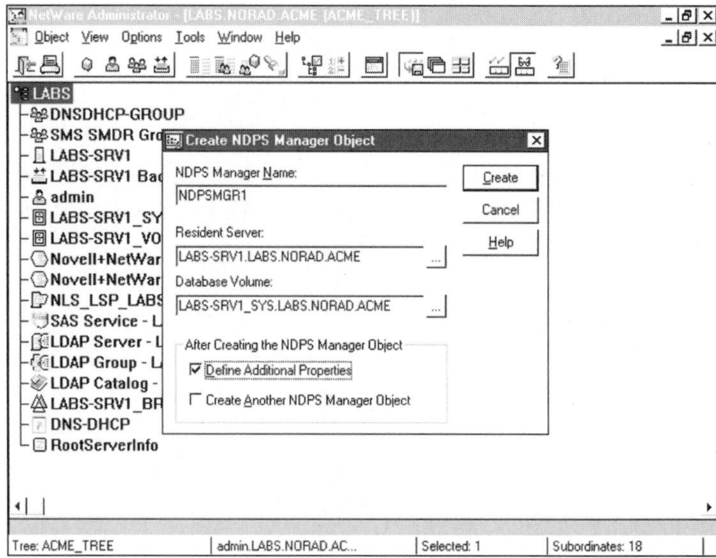

You can type this line manually at the NetWare 5.1 server console, or automate the process using AUTOEXEC.NCF. Either way, you must activate the NDPS Manager before its Printer Agents can be created. If you forget this final task, and move onto Step 3 in haste, NetWare 5.1 will automatically prompt you to load the NDPS Manager.

Step 3: Create NDPS Printer Agents

The Printer Agent is the heart of NetWare 5.1 NDPS printing. Before a printer can be incorporated into NDPS, it must be represented by a Printer Agent. For simplicity's sake, a Printer Agent has a one-to-one relationship with each printer. This means that no Printer Agent can represent more than one printer, and no printer can be represented by more than one Printer Agent.

Once you've activated your NDPS Manager, you can create NDPS Printer Agents in a variety of ways:

- *NetWare Administrator* — This NDS-aware tool enables you to create Public Access printers from the Manager object or Controlled Access printers as separate printer objects. We'll explore these two activities in just a moment.

- *Novell Upgrade Wizard*—You can upgrade your queue-based printers to NDPS using this upgrade utility.
- *NDPSM.NLM*—You can create NDPS printers at the server console using the NDPS Manager NLM. Simply load the NDPSM menu utility, and press Insert to create a new Printer Agent. This server-based tool even includes a Printer Configuration screen.
- *Third-Party Gateways*—Some Third-Party Gateways will automatically create Printer Agents when they find manufacturer-specific printers on the network.

As a network administrator, you should use NetWare Administrator to create Public Access and Controlled Access printers. To create a Public Access printer, you must ensure that it has a guardian Printer Agent. Ironically, the Printer Agent is created and identified during the process of printer creation. To create a Controlled Access printer, you must first create an NDPS Printer object in the Directory tree (see Figure 16.6). Then associate the printer with its own Printer Agent, and identify a host NDPS Manager.

FIGURE 16.6

Creating a Controlled Access Printer object in NetWare Administrator

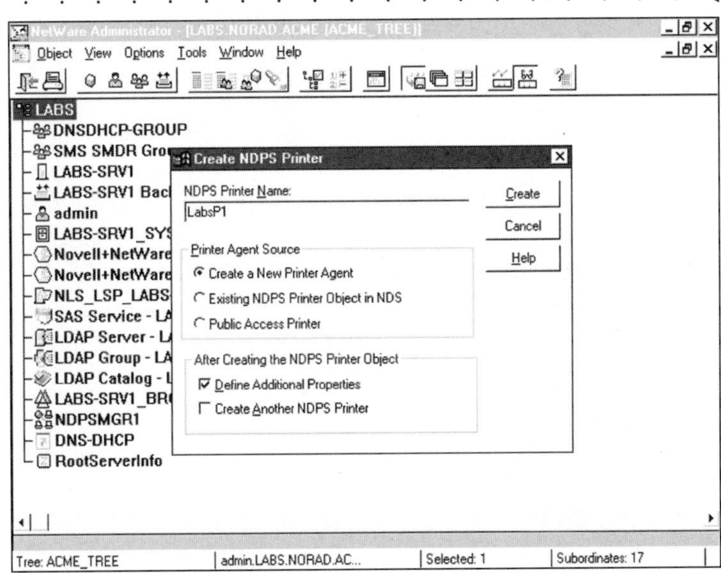

That completes the core steps of NDPS printing setup. Now you should be printing . . . sort of. Actually the server is printing, but the users aren't! To open up NDPS printing to all your users (and make it truly productive), you will need to install printing services on each workstation. Fortunately, NDPS allows you to do this automatically.

Step 4: Install NDPS Printers on Workstations

Before your users can take full advantage of NDPS, each workstation must be using the Novell Client that ships with NetWare 5.1. The Novell Client supports Windows 3.1, Windows 95/98, and Windows NT/2000 workstations.

The NDPS components of the Novell Client require approximately 800K of RAM. If you select the *Custom* install option, be sure you have enabled NDPS. Once you have enabled NDPS at the workstation, it's time to add printers. This can be accomplished automatically (good) or manually (work):

- *Automatic NDPS Workstation Installation* — Although NDPS allows users to download and install printers on their workstations manually, it also allows you to designate certain printers to be downloaded and installed automatically (see Figure 16.7). You can designate a printer to be installed automatically by using the Remote Printer Management (RPM) feature in NetWare Administrator. Once you have designated a printer for automatic installation, it magically appears on the workstation's Installed Printers list next time the user logs in.

- *Manual NDPS Workstation Installation* — Of course, if the automatic installation doesn't work, there's always the "old-fashioned way." If you want to live dangerously, you can choose to *manually* install NDPS printers on user workstations. This is accomplished using the Novell Printer Manager tool. Also keep in mind that you can use the Windows Add Printers Wizard in the Windows Printers folder to install NDPS printers on Windows 95/98 and Windows NT/2000 workstations.

Congratulations! You have passed the first test. You have successfully built a NetWare 5.1 NDPS printing system.

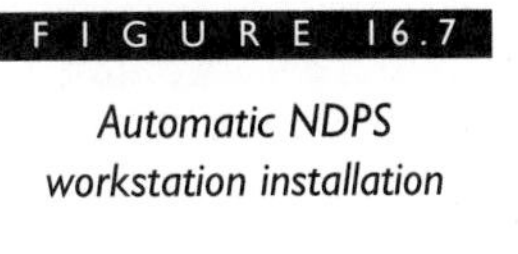
FIGURE 16.7

Automatic NDPS workstation installation

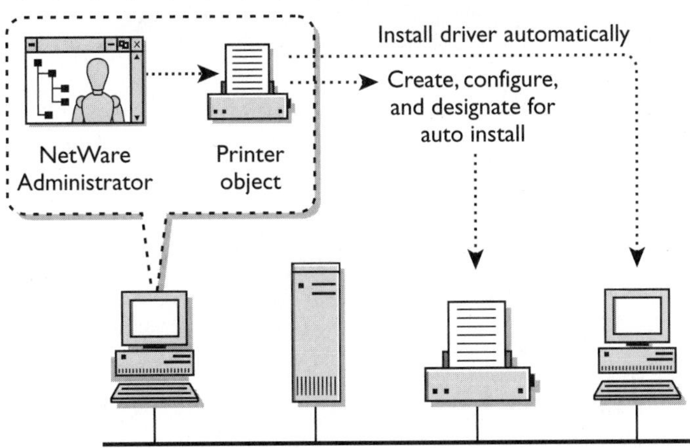

From NetWare Administrator, an administrator can create and configure Printer objects and designate printers to be automatically installed on user workstations.

Now comes the fun part—fixing it! This is where you get to flex your muscles as a NetWare 5.1 troubleshooter. NDPS Printing Troubleshooting is your life. More than any other network resource, printing services require constant attention. You'll need to learn how to fix Brokers, Managers, Printer Agents, and printers. Fortunately, the next section, "Troubleshooting NDPS Printing," provides seven powerful flowcharts for just this type of emergency.

Check it out.

LAB EXERCISE 16.1: SETTING UP NDPS PRINTING IN THE CRIME FIGHTING DIVISION OF ACME

Welcome back to ACME! In this first NDPS lab exercise we will build an NDPS printing system for the Crime Fighting division in Tokyo. Specifically, we will create three NDPS printing components on the CRIME-SRV1 server in the CRIME. TOKYO.ACME organizational unit.

First, we will activate server-based NDPS printing with the creation of an NDPS Broker. Fortunately, this step occurs automatically during NetWare 5.1 server installation. Second, we will create an NDPS Manager to support multiple Printer Agents. And third, we will create a Public Access printer and convert it to a Controlled Access printer object using NetWare Administrator.

Here's a quick preview:

- *Step 1:* Verify NDPS Broker activation.
- *Step 2:* Create and Load an NDPS Manager.
- *Step 3:* Create an NDPS Printer Agent and Public Access printer.
- *Step 4:* Configure the workstations in the CRIME container to use the CrimePA1 Public Access printer.
- *Step 5:* Test the CrimePA1 printer configuration on your workstation.
- *Step 6:* Convert the Public Access printer to a Controlled Access printer object.
- *Step 7:* Configure Admin's workstation to use the CrimeP1 Controlled Access printer.
- *Step 8:* Test the CrimeP1 printer configuration on Admin's workstation.
- *Step 9:* Configure the new Controlled Access Printer object.

Those are all of the detailed steps of NDPS setup and configuration. To accomplish this ACME exercise, you need the following network hardware:

- A NetWare 5.1 server
- A workstation running either the NetWare 5.1 Client for Windows 95 or NetWare 5.1 Client for Windows NT/2000
- A printer physically attached to your server (not your workstation). Also, you'll need to determine the following information for your printer: printer type, gateway type, and printer driver.

In this exercise, you will need the *NetWare 5.1 Client* CD-ROM if you don't have the NetWare 5.1 NDPS client software installed on your workstation. (**Note:** You cannot use the Novell client found on the *ZENworks* CD-ROM for this exercise.)

Let's get started.

1. Verify NDPS Broker activation.

  a. Be sure that your printer is powered on. If it isn't, follow these steps:

  - Do a normal shutdown/power off of your NetWare 5.1 server.
  - Be sure that the printer has paper.
  - Turn the printer on and make sure it's online.
  - Power on your server. Wait until the NetWare 5.1 operating system is finished loading on your server.

  b. You'll need to verify that an NDPS Broker was created and activated when you built the CRIME-SRV1 server in Chapter 1. On your CRIME-SRV1 server console, press Alt+Esc until the NDPS Broker screen appears.

  c. Verify that the following three services are running:

  - Service Registry Services (SRS)
  - Event Notification Services (ENS)
  - Resource Management Services (RMS)

d. If the NDPS Broker is not running, use Alt+Esc to find the server console prompt. Once there, type the following and then press Enter:

```
LOAD BROKER.NLM
```

2. Create and Load an NDPS Manager.

a. On your workstation, log into the tree as Admin, if you haven't already done so.

b. Launch the NetWare Administrator utility.

c. Right-click the CRIME container and then choose Create from the pop-up menu that appears.

d. When the New Object dialog box appears, scroll down and select NDPS Manager and then click OK.

If NDPS Manager is not listed as an option, it probably means that the NDPS client service is not installed on your workstation. If so, you'll need to do a custom reinstall of the NetWare 5.1 Client using the *NetWare 5.1 Client* CD-ROM. (Do not install the Novell Client that is included on the *ZENworks* CD-ROM.) During the installation, don't forget to configure both the IP and IPX protocols. Also, make sure that you mark the Novell Distributed Print Services checkbox on the Novell Client for Windows 95/98 Custom Options screen.

e. Follow these steps after the Create NDPS Manager Object dialog box appears:

- Enter the following in the NDPS Manager Name field:

  ```
  NDPSMGR1
  ```

- Click the Browse button to the right of the Resident Server field. Select CRIME-SRV1 and then click OK.
- Click the Browse button to the right of the Database Volume field. Click CRIME-SRV1_SYS.CRIME.TOKYO.ACME and then click OK.
- Click Create to create the NDPS Manager object.

f. Once the NDPSMGR1object has been created, you must activate it at the server. I recommend that you add the LOAD statement to the server's AUTOEXEC.NCF file so that it will automatically load each time the server is booted. Here's how it works:

- At the server console, press Alt+Esc until you get to a console prompt.
- At the console prompt, type the following and then press Enter:

```
EDIT AUTOEXEC.NCF
```

- Insert the following command at the bottom of the file:

```
LOAD NDPSM.NLM .NDPSMGR1.CRIME.TOKYO.ACME
```

- Press Esc to save the file.
- Select Yes and press Enter when asked if you want to save SYS:SYSTEM\AUTOEXEC.NCF.
- Press Esc to exit the screen that gives you the opportunity to edit another file.
- Select Yes and press Enter when asked whether to exit the EDIT utility.

g. Next, you'll need to load the NDPS Manager manually on the server (so that you don't have to reboot the server to execute the command you just added to the AUTOEXEC.NCF file). To do so, type the following at the server console prompt and then press Enter:

```
LOAD NDPSM.NLM .NDPSMGR1.CRIME.TOKYO.ACME
```

The server responds with a blank Printer Agent List screen. Now it's time to fill it in.

3. Create an NDPS Printer Agent and Public Access printer.

a. Return to your workstation. In NetWare Administrator, double-click the NDPSMGR1 object you just created.

b. The Identification page for the NDPS Manager object appears by default. After the Identification page appears, follow these steps:

- Ensure that the Version field has a version number in it.

- Confirm that the Net Address field lists the network address for your server.
- Verify that the Status section indicates that the NDPS Manager is active.
- Click the Printer Agent List tab.

c. When the Printer Agent List page appears, click New.

d. Follow these steps after the Create Printer Agent dialog box appears:

- Type the following in the "Printer Agent (PA)" Name field:

  `CrimePA1`

- Ensure that the NDPS Manager you created earlier is listed in the NDPS Manager Name field.
- Select the appropriate gateway in the Gateway Type field. (**Note:** In most cases, you should select the Novell Printer Gateway even if your printer manufacturer is listed. For more details, refer to the documentation that comes with NetWare 5.1.)
- Click OK.

e. Follow these steps after the Configure Novell PDS for Printer Agent "CrimePA1" dialog box appears:

- In the Printer Type list box, select the appropriate printer driver for your printer.
- In the Port Handler Type field, ensure that Novell Port Handler is selected.
- Click OK.

f. Follow these steps after the first Configure Port Handler for Printer Agent "CrimePA1" dialog box appears:

- In the Connection Type section, mark the "Local (Physical Connection to Server)" radio button.

- In the Port Type section, ensure that the LPT1 radio box is marked (assuming that your printer is attached to the LPT1: port on your server).
- Click Next.

g. When the second Configure Port Handler for Printer Agent "CrimePA1" dialog box appears, do the following:

- In the Controller Type field, ensure that Auto Select is listed.
- In the Interrupts section, verify that the "None (Polled Mode)" radio button is marked.
- Click Finish.

h. Wait for the Printer Agent to load.

i. Follow these steps after the Select Printer Drivers dialog box appears:

- Click the tab corresponding to your workstation platform.
- Select the appropriate printer driver for your printer.
- Click Continue.

j. Follow these steps after the Information dialog box appears:

- Review the print drivers to be installed.
- Click OK.

k. Follow these steps after the Printer Agent List page reappears:

- Ensure that the status of the CrimePA1 printer agent is listed as Idle.
- Click Cancel.

4. Configure the workstations in the CRIME container to use the CrimePA1 Public Access printer.

a. Click Tools in the menu bar to display the Tools menu and then select NDPS Remote Printer Management.

b. Follow these steps after the NDPS Remote Printer Management dialog box appears:
   - Mark the "Show the Results Window on Windows Workstations" checkbox.
   - Click the Add button under the "Printers to Install to Workstations" field.

c. Follow these steps after the Available Printers Options dialog box appears:
   - Click CrimePA1.
   - Click OK.

d. When the NDPS Remote Printer Management dialog box reappears, click OK to save your changes.

5. Test the CrimePA1 printer configuration on your workstation.

   a. Log back into the tree as Admin and then follow these steps:
      - Click Start in the Windows taskbar.
      - Click Shut Down.
      - When the Shut Down Windows dialog box appears, ensure that the "Close All Programs and Log on as a Different User" radio button is marked and then click Yes.
      - Log into the tree as the Admin user.
      - Wait while NDPS modifies your printer setup. Eventually, the NDPS Remote Printer Management dialog box will display a message advising you that Printer CrimePA1 is installed. Click Close to acknowledge the message.

   b. Launch NetWare Administrator.

   c. Click Object in the menu bar to display the Object menu and then click Print Setup.

d. Follow these steps after the Print Setup dialog box appears:

  - In the Printer section, open the pull-down box in the Name field and select CrimePA1.
  - Click OK.

e. Click the Printer icon in the toolbar.

f. Follow these steps after the Print dialog box appears:

  - Ensure that CrimePA1 is listed in the Printer field.
  - Click OK.

g. A printout of your NDS tree should appear on your printer. If this happens, congratulations — you are now the proud owner of a new Public Access printer.

6. Convert the Public Access printer to a Controlled Access printer object.

a. Click Tools in the menu bar to display the Tools menu and then select NDPS Remote Printer Management.

b. When the NDPS Remote Printer Management dialog box appears, click the Add button under the Printers to Remove From Workstations field.

c. Follow these steps after the Available Printers Options dialog box appears:

  - Click CrimePA1
  - Click OK.

d. Follow these steps after the NDPS Remote Printer Management dialog box reappears:

  - You'll notice that CrimePA1 has disappeared from the Printers to Install to Workstations field and has appeared in the Printers to Remove from Workstations field.
  - Click OK to save your changes.

   e. Next, we will convert the Public Access printer into a more secure Controlled Access device. This is accomplished at your client workstation. In NetWare Administrator, right-click the CRIME.TOKYO.ACME container and select Create from the pop-up menu that appears.

   f. When the New Object dialog box appears, double-click NDPS Printer.

   g. Follow these steps after the Create NDPS Printer dialog box appears:

      - Type **CrimeP1** in the NDPS Printer Name field.
      - In the Printer Agent Source section, click the Public Access Printer radio button.
      - Click Create.

   h. A Warning dialog box appears, advising you that converting a Public Access printer to an NDPS Printer object will require every client installation of this printer to be reinstalled. Click OK to acknowledge the warning.

   i. When the Select Printer Agent dialog box appears, ensure that CrimePA1 is selected and then click OK.

   j. Wait while NDPS creates the NDPS Printer object.

   k. The new Controlled Access Printer object will magically appear in ACME's NDS tree. Yeah!

7. Configure your workstation to use the CrimeP1 Controlled Access Printer.

   a. Click Tools in the menu bar to display the Tools menu and then select NDPS Remote Printer Management.

   b. When the NDPS Remote Printer Management dialog box appears, click the Add button under the Printers to Install to Workstations field.

   c. Follow these steps after the Available Printers Options dialog box appears:

      - Click CrimeP1.CRIME.TOKYO.ACME
      - Click OK.

d. Follow these steps after the NDPS Remote Printer Management dialog box reappears:

- CrimeP1.CRIME.TOKYO.ACME should be listed in the Printers to Install on Workstations field.
- CrimePA1 should be listed in the "Printers to Remove from Workstations" field. (You configured this field in an earlier step.)
- Click OK to save your changes.

8. Test the CrimeP1 printer configuration on your workstation.

a. Log back into the tree as Admin and then follow these steps:

- Click Start in the Windows taskbar.
- Click Shut Down.
- When the Shut Down Windows dialog box appears, ensure that the "Close All Programs and Log on as a Different User" radio button is marked and then click Yes.
- Log into the tree as the Admin user.
- Wait while NDPS modifies your printer setup. Eventually, the NDPS Remote Printer Management dialog box will display a message advising you that Printer CrimeP1.CRIME.TOKYO.ACME is installed and CrimePA1 is removed. Click Close to acknowledge the message.

b. Launch NetWare Administrator.

c. Click Object in the menu bar to display the Object menu and then click Print Setup.

d. Follow these steps after the Print Setup dialog box appears:

- In the Printer section, open the pull-down box in the Name field and select CrimeP1.CRIME.TOKYO.ACME.
- Click OK.

e. Click the Printer icon in the toolbar.

f. Follow these steps after the Print dialog box appears:

- Ensure that CrimeP1.CRIME.TOKYO.ACME is listed in the Printer field.
- Click OK.

g. A printout of your NDS tree should appear on your printer. If this happens, you're almost finished.

9. Configure the new Controlled Access Printer object.

a. Finally, you should configure the new CrimeP1 object with additional security restrictions and pop-up notification. First, double-click the CrimeP1 NDPS Printer object in NetWare Administrator.

b. When the "NDPS Printer: CrimeP1" dialog box appears, click the Access Control tab.

c. Follow these steps after the Access Control page appears:

- By default, Admin is assigned as a Manager, Operator, and Print User. Also, the printer's home container (CRIME.TOKYO.ACME) is designated as a Printer User. This means that everyone in the CRIME container can use the new printer. Let's restrict access to the Admin user.
- In the Role field, click Users.
- In the Current Users field, click CRIME.TOKYO.ACME.
- Click Delete.

d. In case something goes wrong with the new Controlled Access printer, you may want to notify the CrimeP1 Manager with a pop-up notification message. Follow these steps to activate this NetWare 5.1 feature:

- Click Managers in the Role field.
- Click Admin.CRIME.TOKYO.ACME in the Current Managers field.
- Click Notification.
- If your printer driver allows you to (some may not), set up notification parameters.

e. Click OK to save your changes.

Troubleshooting NDPS Printing

NDPS printing problems are often due to a combination of unrealistic user expectations, traffic overloads, and technical breakdowns. In this section, we will discuss some time-proven techniques for isolating and solving NDPS printing problems.

The centerpiece of NDPS printing troubleshooting consists of seven flowcharts that help you isolate problematic components and then take corrective action. These flowcharts should quickly become an integral part of your NetWare troubleshooting arsenal:

- *Chart A: Getting Started*—It all begins with a few simple questions and some basic quick fixes. If that doesn't solve your problem, you must determine your printing environment and move on to Chart B.
- *Chart B: Narrowing Your Focus*—Next, you should try a quick test by sending the print job to the same printer from another workstation. If that doesn't work, you should move on to Chart F. On the other hand, if other users can successfully access the printer, you should take a closer look at this specific workstation. Your next move depends on the workstation platform you're using: non-Windows problems are covered in Chart C and Windows-based problems are covered in Chart D.
- *Chart C: Non-Windows Workstation Problems*—Non-Windows workstations offer little flexibility in the arena of NDPS troubleshooting. At this point, you're stuck with a few fundamental solutions or a quick jump to Chart G.
- *Chart D: Windows Workstation Problems*—On the other hand, Windows-based workstations offer tremendous flexibility in NDPS troubleshooting. First, you should check the status of the printer in the Windows Control Panel to determine what Windows sees. If Windows is working properly, you'll need to focus on the Printer object itself: Is it an NDPS object or queue-based object? If it's an NDPS Printer object, you need to move on to Chart E. Queue-based objects are handled in a slightly different way—see Chart G.

- *Chart E: Testing NDPS Printing Flow* — If you weren't able to solve the problem by trying a few quick fixes or exploring workstation-based solutions, you may want to test the NDPS printing flow. In Chart E, we'll walk through the three steps of NDPS testing: pausing the output of the printer, sending or resending a test file, and checking the Job List in NetWare Administrator. Then we'll offer some valuable solutions based on whether the job appeared in the NDPS Printer List or not. This testing process often provides a successful solution to your NDPS printing problems.

- *Chart F: Printing Problems Affecting Everyone* — Flowcharts F and G offer general NDPS solutions for printing problems affecting everyone or those in an NDPS/queue mixed environment. In Chart F, we'll explore a variety of different printing problems and offer general solutions. Hopefully, this will successfully end your NDPS printing dilemma.

- *Chart G: Printing Problems in a Mixed Environment* — Chart G offers specific solutions for doctors working in an NDPS/queue mixed environment. First, you must determine which mixed configuration you are using: non-NDPS clients printing to NDPS printers or NDPS clients printing to queue-based printers. As I'm sure you can imagine, the first configuration offers much more troubleshooting flexibility. This is because the Printer object itself is NDPS-aware. In either case, we hope to end your NDPS printing dilemma here!

Wow, that's a lot of flowcharting! The good news is these seven flowcharts were developed by a group of very smart troubleshooters working with some very troublesome printers. So, let's start our NDPS flowcharting experience at the beginning . . . with a few simple questions.

Chart A: Getting Started

Chart A begins your NDPS flowcharting expedition with a simple question and some quick fixes. This first great NDPS troubleshooting flowchart is displayed in Figure 16.8.

FIGURE 16.8

Chart A: Getting Started

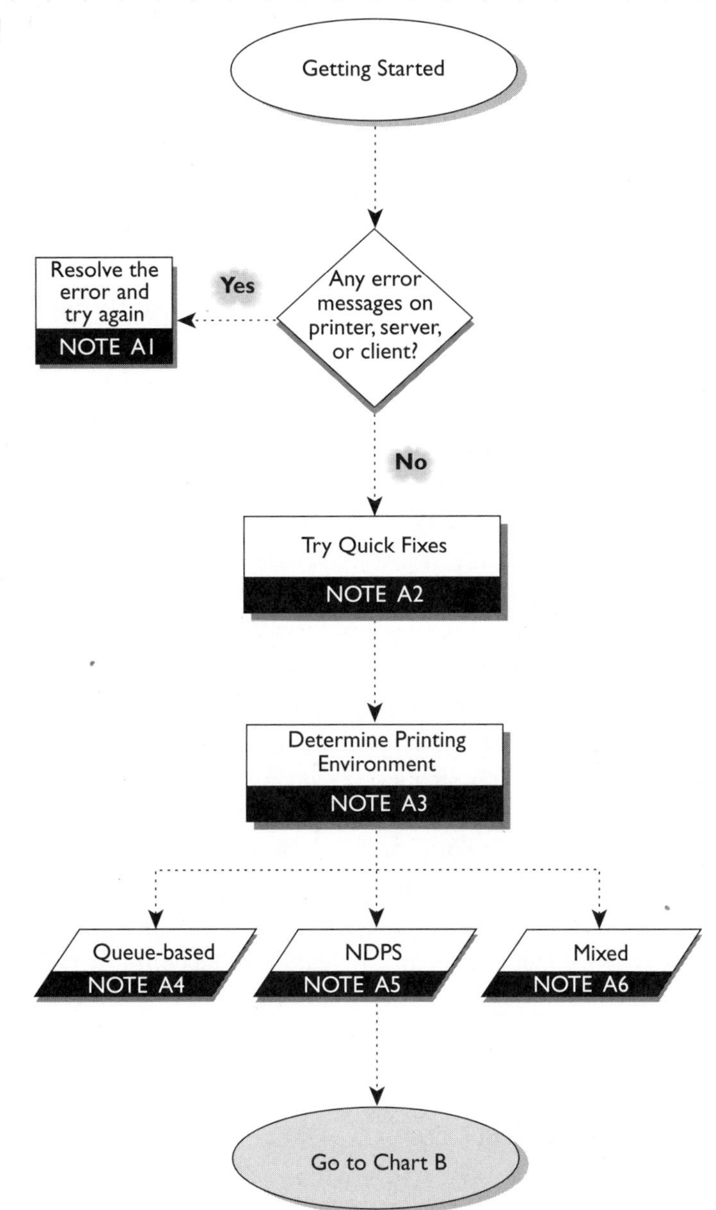

Chart A begins by asking if there are "Any error messages on printer, server, or client?" If messages are displayed, you should resolve the errors using documentation and/or past experience. If not, you should try some quick fixes. Follow along with Figure 16.8 as you review the following Getting Started notes:

- *Note A1: Resolve the Error and Try Again* — Most NDPS printing problems return an error message to the printer itself, to the file server, and/or to the client that is attempting to print. If an error message says that the client could not connect to the Printer Agent, check to see if the NDPS Manager or NDPS Broker is *down*. You should also consider checking available disk space on the spooling volume. If a client receives a message that the print job was rejected, the spooling volume may be full, and, therefore, unable to accept additional jobs.
- *Note A2: Try Quick Fixes* — Many times, NDPS printing problems occur because of simple or temporary conditions. If a problem is affecting a number of workstations, try these quick fixes: in the Novell Printer Manager, check "Printer Information" for NDPS error messages and then check the printer's Job List to ensure that the print job is getting to the spooling area and that the spooling volume is not full. Also, check the physical printer for error messages and error conditions (such as beeps or LCD panel lights), turn the printer off and back on, and check the printer cabling.
- *Note A3: Determine Printing Environment* — If error message resolution and quick fixes do not solve your NDPS printing problem, you should determine whether you are using a pure NDPS environment, pure queue-based environment, or a mixed NDPS/queue environment.
- *Note A4: Pure Queue-Based Printing Environment* — If your users submit print jobs to NetWare queues and then the jobs are sent to the printer through PSERVER.NLM, you are using queue-based printing. For more troubleshooting help, consult the "Troubleshooting Queue-Based Printing" section later in this chapter.

- *Note A5: Pure NDPS Printing Environment* — If your users are running Novell Client 2.2 or higher, and are submitting print jobs through NDPS Printer Agents, you are using NDPS. For more help solving your NDPS printing problems, continue on to Chart B.
- *Note A6: Mixed NDPS/Queue Printing Environment* — For backward-compatibility purposes, NetWare 5.1 offers support for both NDPS and queue-based printing in a mixed environment. This occurs in one of two configurations: non-NDPS clients printing to NDPS printers or NDPS clients printing to queue-based printers.

TIP

Study the quick fixes in Chart A carefully and be able to suggest some quick fixes if given a complex printing scenario. Specifically, focus on the following quick fixes: check the printer's Job List to ensure that the job is being spooled, check "Printer Information" in Novell Printer Manager, turn the printer off and back on, and check the printer cabling.

Chart B: Narrowing Your Focus

In Chart B, you should begin narrowing your NDPS troubleshooting focus by trying out a simple test (see Figure 16.9).

As you can see in Figure 16.9, Chart B begins with a simple test — sending the problematic print job to the same NDPS printer, but from other workstations. This test enables you to narrow your troubleshooting focus to either the workstation or the NDPS printer. If other users can access the printer successfully, then the workstation must be the problem. However, if no one can access the printer, then the printer is the problem.

- *Workstation Problem* — First, you should determine if the workstation has ever accessed this particular printer successfully. If so, you will need to determine which workstation platform you are using and move on to the appropriate chart — Chart C: Non-Windows Workstation Problems) or Chart D: Windows Workstation Problems. If not, you should check the printer setup and configuration options at the workstation.

FIGURE 16.9

Chart B: Narrowing Your Focus

Start Here
Send job to the same printer from other workstations
Can other users access this printer successfully?
No
Has printing ever worked with current configuration?
No
Check to make sure that the printer setup and configuration is correct
Yes
Go to Chart F
Yes
Has this workstation used this printer before?
No
Check to make sure that the printer setup and configuration is correct
Yes
Which workstation platform are you using?
Non-Windows
DOS, MAC, UNIX, Non-NDPS
Go to Chart C
Windows
WINDOWS 95/98 NT, v3.1
Go to Chart D

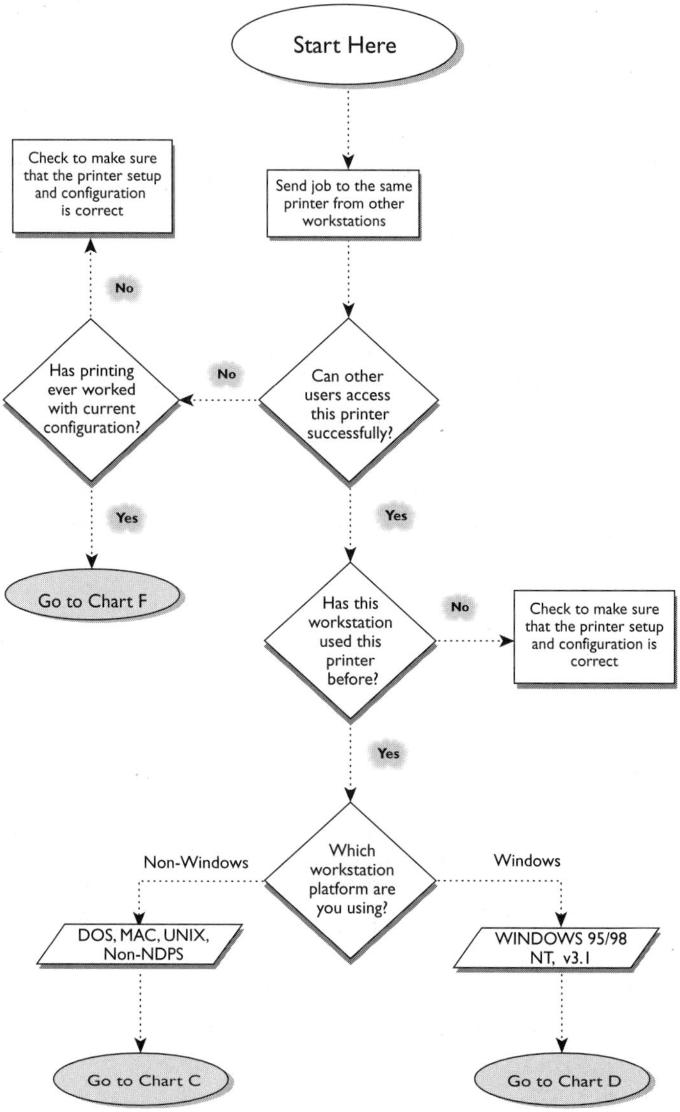

- *NDPS Printer Problem* — First, you should concentrate on the current printer configuration. If this is the first time this particular configuration has had a problem, you should consider some of the general troubleshooting solutions in Chart F. Otherwise, check to see if the printer configuration is incorrect.

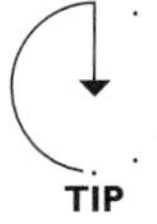

Study Chart B. Be sure that you are able to match printing troubleshooting descriptions with the following causes: problems affecting everyone, printer setup and configuration problems, Windows workstation problems, and/or non-Windows workstation problems.

Chart C: Non-Windows Workstation Problems

If you narrow your NDPS troubleshooting problems to non-Windows workstations, you will need to explore the solutions offered in Chart C (see Figure 16.10).

FIGURE 16.10

Chart C: Non-Windows Workstation Problems

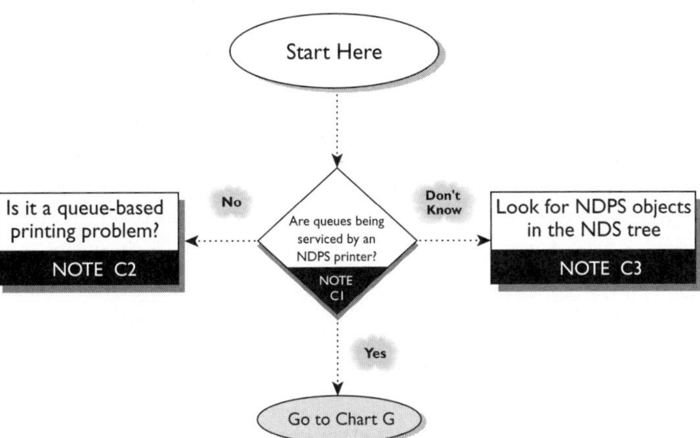

As you can see in Figure 16.10, Chart C starts with one simple question: "Are queues being serviced by an NDPS printer?" As you recall, non-Windows workstations can't access NDPS Printer Agents. Therefore, they must send jobs off to NetWare queues. As you can see, this question has three simple answers: No, Yes, and Don't Know.

Refer to Figure 16.10 as you review the following Chart C notes:

- *Note C1: Are Queues Being Serviced by an NDPS Printer?*— Non-Windows workstations do not support NDPS. This means that your DOS, Macintosh, OS/2, and UNIX clients must print to NetWare print queues. Once a print job finds its way to a print queue, it can then be sent to a queue-based printer (using PSERVER.NLM) or an NDPS printer (using a Printer Agent).

- *Note C2: It Is a Queue-Based Printing Problem*— If non-Windows clients are submitting jobs to a print queue that is being serviced by PSERVER.NLM, the printing environment is queue-based. For help with queue-based printing problems, refer to the "Troubleshooting Queue-Based Printing" section later in this chapter.

- *Note C3: Look for NDPS Objects in the NDS Tree*— If no NDPS printing objects are defined, determine if a Print Server object exists. If an NDPS Printer object is defined, check its configuration to see if it is set up to emulate a print server and service jobs from the appropriate queue.

Chart D: Windows Workstation Problems

If you narrow your NDPS troubleshooting focus to Windows-based workstations, you will need to explore the solutions offered in Chart D (see Figure 16.11).

As you can see in Figure 16.11, Chart D focuses on the printer status displayed in the Windows Control Panel. If the status indicates a problem, then the printer may be set for working offline. If the status is fine, you will need to determine which network object the printer is servicing. Refer to Figure 16.11 as you review the following Chart D notes:

- *Note D1: Check the Status of the Printer in the Windows Control Panel*— Printing from a Windows-based workstation introduces several complexities that may or may not be related to the NDPS printer or NetWare WAN. You can find and resolve some of these problems using the Windows Control Panel. As you might expect, Windows 95/98 and Windows NT workstations offer a great deal more reporting status details than Windows 3.1 clients.

FIGURE 16.11

Chart D: Windows Workstation Problems

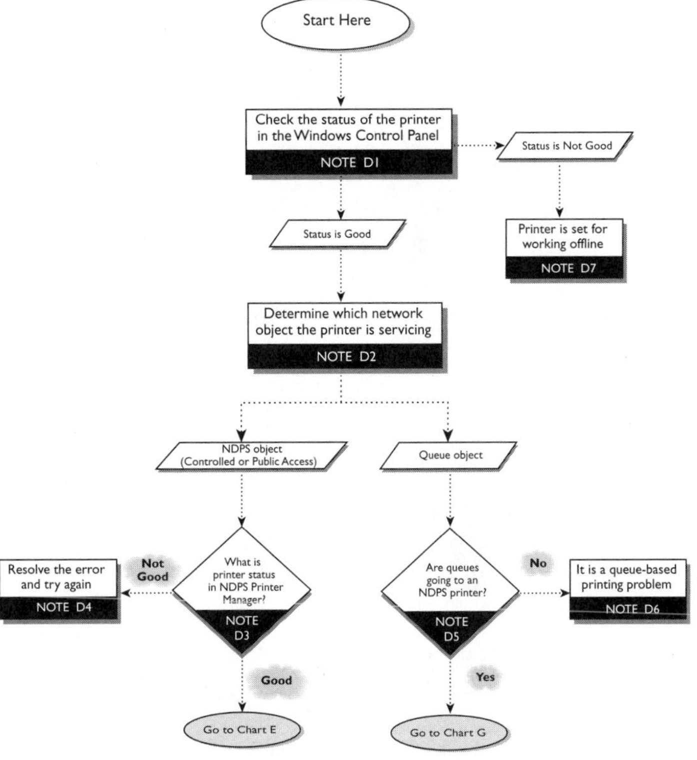

- *Note D2: Determine Which Network Object the Printer Is Servicing*—If the printer status in the Windows Control Panel is fine, then you will need to determine where the print jobs are being redirected. On Windows 95/98 and Windows NT workstations, you can determine the port redirection status by following these simple steps: (1) Select Start and choose Printers from the Settings menu, (2) Highlight the appropriate printer and select File and Properties, and (3) Click Details.

- *Note D3: What Is the Printer Status in NDPS Printer Manager?*—If you have determined that your Windows-based workstation is sending jobs to an NDPS Printer object, you should check the printer status in NDPS Printer Manager.

- *Note D4: Resolve the Error and Try Again*—If the printer status in NDPS Printer Manager indicates a problem, then you should interrogate the printer and/or server for error messages. If error messages are present, consult the appropriate documentation for possible solutions.

- *Note D5: Are Queues Going to an NDPS Printer?*—If your Windows-based workstation is printing to a Print Queue object, you will need to determine whether the print jobs will go to an NDPS or queue-based printer.

- *Note D6: It Is a Queue-Based Printing Problem*—If Windows-based clients are submitting jobs to a Print Queue object that forwards them to a queue-based printer, you are using a queue-based printing system. For more troubleshooting help in this environment, refer to the "Troubleshooting Queue-Based Printing" section later in this chapter.

- *Note D7: Printer Is Set for Working Offline*—If the printer status in the Windows Control Panel indicates a problem, then there might be a problem with the Windows software itself. Under certain circumstances, the printer might be set for working offline. If you cannot set the printer to online, Windows may have lost communication with the network printing system.

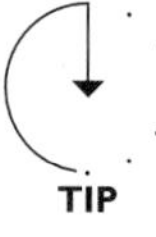
TIP

Study the printer status in the Windows Control Panel and be able to suggest possible solutions if problems are indicated (for example, that the printer is set to work offline or the Windows software is malfunctioning). Also, note that NDPS can still have problems even if the printer status is fine (such as the job having been sent to the wrong printer).

Chart E: Testing NDPS Printing Flow

Chart E offers a simple three-step test for identifying problematic components in the NDPS printing flow. Refer to Figure 16.12 for a flowchart overview.

As you can see from Figure 16.12, the NDPS troubleshooting test begins with three simple steps:

- *Step 1: Pause Output of the NDPS Printer*—It all begins by pausing output of the printer so you can determine where the print job stalls.

FIGURE 16.12

Chart E: Testing NDPS Printing Flow

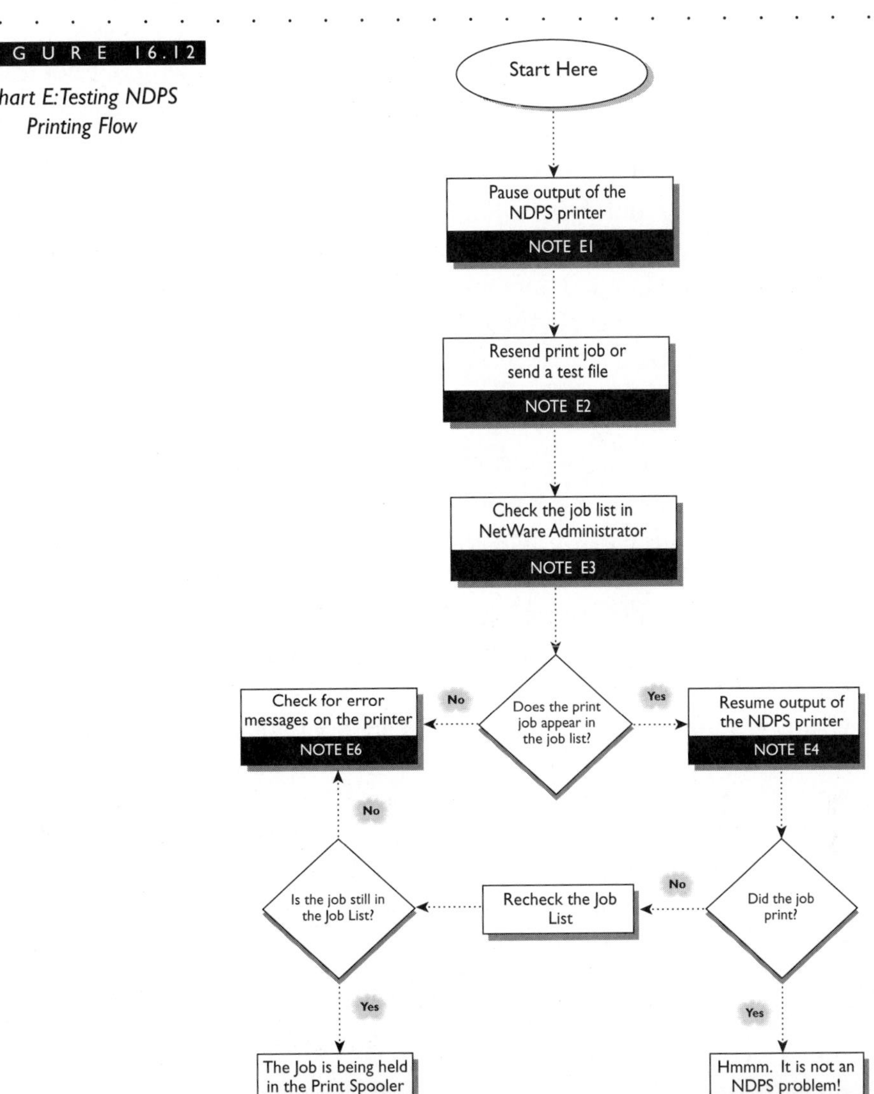

- *Step 2: Resend Print Job or Send a Test File*—You can either resend the problematic print job or send a printer-ready test file using the drag-and-drop method from the Windows 95/98/NT/2000 Explorer.

- *Step 3: Check the Job List in NetWare Administrator* — You can check the printer Job List in NetWare Administrator to determine whether or not it arrived at the printer.

Once the job is sent off into the NDPS ether, you must determine where it stalls. If the print job appears in the NDPS Printer Job List, then you should resume output of the printer and watch what happens. If the job prints, it's magic. If not, you should recheck the Job List and hunt for error messages. At this point, chances are good that the job is being held in the Print Spooler for some unknown reason. So, let's test the NDPS printing flow. Refer to Figure 16.12 as you review the following Chart E notes:

- *Note E1: Pause Output of the NDPS Printer* — Our NDPS troubleshooting test begins by pausing output of the printer. To pause printer output for an NDPS Controlled Access printer, double-click the NDPS Printer object in NetWare Administrator. The Details page should appear. Next, click Pause Output. To pause printer output for an NDPS Public Access printer, switch to the NDPSM.NLM screen at the server console and select the Printer Agent you are interested in. Press Enter to continue. Then select Status ⇨ Control and press Enter. Finally, select Pause Output and press Enter.

- *Note E2: Resend Print Job or Send a Test File* — To isolate the nature of the NDPS printing problem, you should send test print files to your paused printer from Windows using the drag-and-drop method. This method avoids problems that might be caused by an application or print driver and allows you to focus on network- and printer-specific issues. You can print any *printer-ready* file using the Windows 95/98 or Windows NT Explorer utility or the Windows 3.1 File Manager by selecting the file list and dragging it to the icon in the main NDPS Printer Manager window. A *printer-ready* file is specifically formatted in a language the printer understands such as PostScript, Printer Command Language (PCL), or ASCII.

- *Note E3: Check the Job List in NetWare Administrator*—Once you have paused the NDPS printer and sent the test file, you must check NetWare Administrator to ensure that the print job found its way to the spooling area. You can view the Job List for an NDPS Controlled Access printer within NetWare Administrator. You can also check the Job List of a Public Access printer using NDPSM.NLM at the server console or from the client using Novell Printer Manager.

- *Note E4: Resume Output of the NDPS Printer*—If the test file finds its way to the spooling area, it will appear in the NDPS Job List. At this point, you should consider resuming output of the NDPS printer and determining if the job actually prints.

- *Note E5: Hmmm. It Is Not an NDPS Problem!*—If the test job prints, then there is no authoritative explanation as to why it did not print the first time.

- *Note E6: Check for Error Messages on the Printer*—If the test file does not appear in the Job List, then something is wrong with the NDPS data flow from the client to the spooling area. First, check for error messages on the printer, the client, and the server. Use the information provided and appropriate documentation to solve the problem and then try again.

- *Note E7: The Job Is Being Held in the Print Spooler*—If your test file appears in the Job List but does not print, it is being held in the Print Spooler. If so, check for job holds, delays, and priority settings. For example, if a user is printing from a lower priority print queue, the user's print jobs might seem as if they are on hold, even though they are not. If this is the case, consider changing the priority of the print queue so that the jobs print.

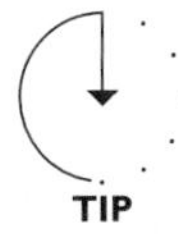

Study the drag-and-drop method of printing a file in Windows. Know the three printer-ready file formats (PostScript, PCL, and ASCII). Also, learn how to check the Job List of a Controlled Access printer (in NetWare Administrator) and a Public Access printer (using NDPSM.NLM at the server console).

Chart F: Printing Problems Affecting Everyone

As you can see in Figure 16.13, Chart F is a compilation of the previous five charts. It is a launching point for a variety of NDPS and queue-based solutions offered by the flowcharts in this chapter.

FIGURE 16.13

Chart F: Printing Problems Affecting Everyone

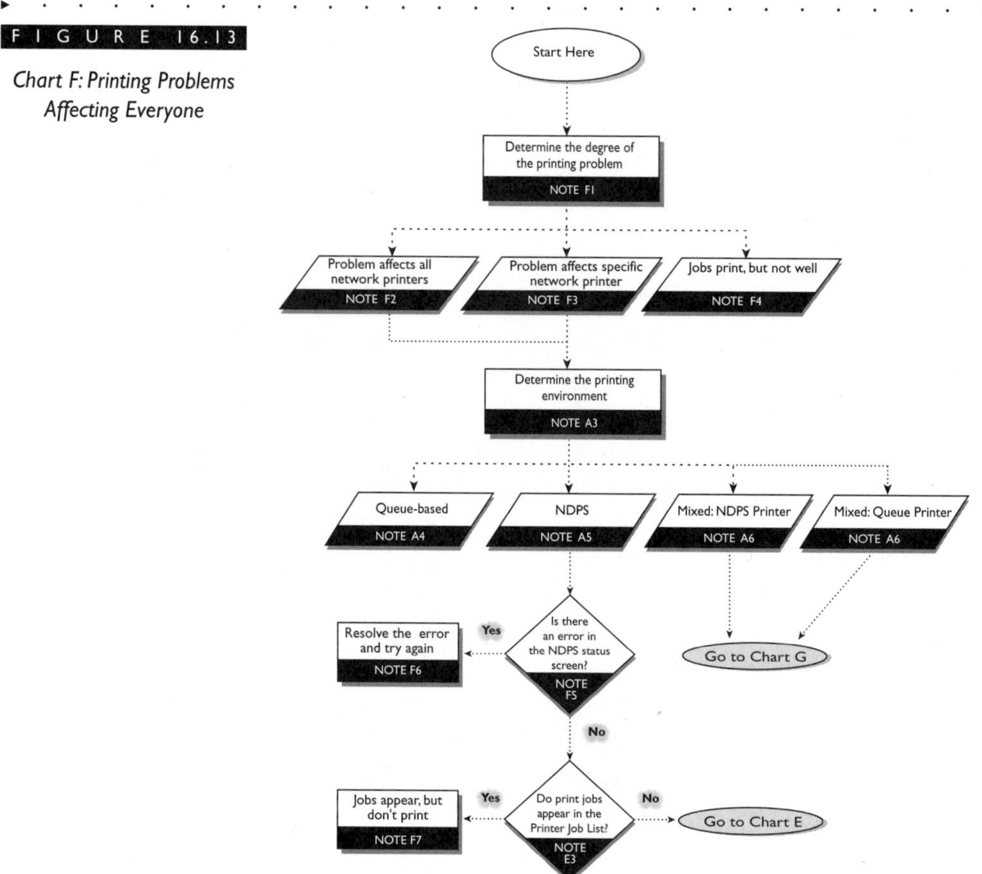

As you can see in Figure 16.13, Chart F starts with the following three degrees of NDPS printing problems:

- Problems that affect all network printers.

- Problems that affect specific network printers.
- Jobs that print, but don't print well.

If your problem affects all or specific network printers, you will need to determine which printing environment you are using. Just like in Chart A, three (or four, in this case) configurations are possible:

- Pure queue-based
- Pure NDPS
- Mixed with an NDPS printer
- Mixed with a queue-based printer

If you're using a pure queue-based printing system, you should refer to the section entitled "Troubleshooting Queue-Based Printing" later in the chapter. If you're using a mixed NDPS/queue printing system, jump to Chart G. However, if you're using a pure NDPS printing system, you should continue with Flowchart F by checking the NDPS Status screen and printer Job List. Refer to Figure 16.13 as you review the following Chart F notes:

- *Note F1: Determine the Degree of the Printing Problem* — To start the NDPS compilation flowchart, you will need to determine the degree of the printing problem. First, determine if print jobs are printing at all. If they are printing, but not well, consult Note F4. If no jobs are printing, determine whether the problem affects all network printers or only a specific printer.
- *Note F2: Problem Affects All Network Printers* — If you cannot print from any network printer, the problem is universal (network-wide), in which case the cause of the problem could be that the printing system is disabled; that the necessary NDPS or queue-based NLMs are not loaded; or that the server is in a critical state because of problems with memory, disk space, or LAN connections.

- *Note F3: Problem Affects Specific Network Printer*—If the printing problem is limited to a particular printer, the problem has two possible causes: the physical printer itself is malfunctioning or the printer is configured incorrectly.
- *Note F4: Jobs Print, but Not Well*—If you are not satisfied with the way your network print jobs are performing, there may be two possible symptoms: slow printing or job corruption.
- *Note F5: Is There an Error in the NDPS Status Screen?*—To check the Status screen of an NDPS printer, access NetWare Administrator. Find the NDPS Printer object and view the Printer Control page. Click Printer Information and select Information. The Printer Information dialog shows the current status of the printer and details about it.
- *Note F6: Resolve the Error and Try Again*—If an error appears in the NDPS Status screen, you can check NetWare documentation or other flowcharts in this section for possible solutions. You can also investigate the grayed out and unavailable options for clues about a possible problem or solution.
- *Note F7: Jobs Appear, but Don't Print!*—If NDPS print jobs appear in the Printer Job list but do not print, perform any or all of the following solutions: ensure that no holds or delays exist, ensure that the printer is configured properly, and check the status of the NDPS Gateway, if one is being used.

Chart G: Printing Problems in a Mixed Environment

The final NDPS troubleshooting flowchart explores problems that occur in a mixed NDPS/queue printing environment (see Figure 16.14).

As you can see in Figure 16.14, a mixed printing environment can be achieved in two ways:

- *Non-NDPS Client to NDPS Printer*—In this configuration, non-NDPS clients print to NetWare queues, which then forward the jobs to Printer Agents and ultimately on to NDPS printers. Troubleshooting in this environment focuses on the Printer Agent Job List and print job spooling. In both these instances, you need to make sure that the queue is forwarding print jobs to the correct NDPS Printer Agent.

FIGURE 16.14

Chart G: Printing Problems in a Mixed Environment

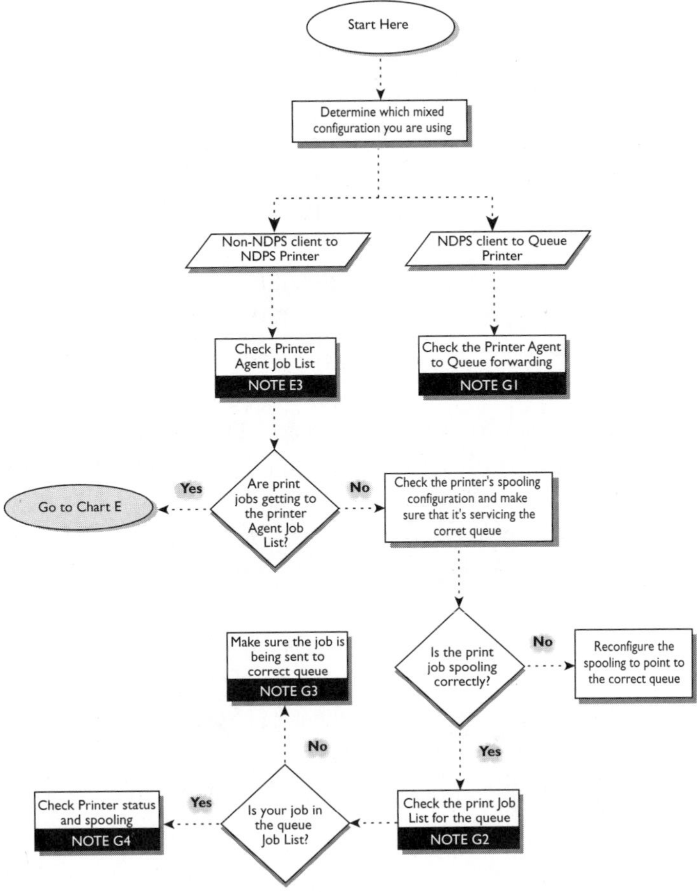

- *NDPS Client to Queue Printer* — In this configuration, the NDPS-aware client prints to its own NDPS Printer Agent which then forwards the job to a NetWare queue and ultimately to a queue-based printer. In this environment, you must make sure that the NDPS Printer Agent is forwarding the jobs to the correct NetWare queue.

Refer to Figure 16.14 as you review the following Chart G notes:

- *Note G1: Check the Printer Agent to Queue Forwarding*—If you are having a problem with your NDPS clients printing to queue-based printers, chances are it has to do with how the NDPS Printer Agent is forwarding print jobs to the NetWare queue. You can check Printer Agent job forwarding by accessing the Details page of the NDPS Printer object in NetWare Administrator.
- *Note G2: Check the Print Job List for the Queue*—If your non-NDPS clients are having a problem printing to NDPS printers, the problem probably has something to do with the Printer Agent or queue job spooling. You can collect data about job spooling by checking the Print Queue object's Job List. In order for a print job to find its way to an NDPS printer from non-NDPS clients, it must appear (if only temporarily) in the Print Queue object Job List.
- *Note G3: Make Sure Job Is Being Sent to Correct Queue*—Many applications are not designed for network printing. If you are having a problem with your user's job finding its way to an NDPS printer, make sure that the workstation is captured to the correct print queue.
- *Note G4: Check Printer Status and Spooling*—If you navigate your way all the way through Chart G and find that the print job is in the queue list, but it is not printing, then your problem may be something as simple as a misconfiguration between your NetWare print queue and NDPS printer.

Troubleshooting Common NDPS Printing Problems

Now that you have mastered the NDPS troubleshooting flowcharts, let's take a moment to explore some common NDPS printing problems. While troubleshooting, you may encounter any of the following issues:

- *Installing a Remote Printer*—You must create a Printer Agent to represent a printer that is running in NPRINTER mode. This is required for printers that are (1) attached to a workstation or remote file server, or (2) attached directly to the network, but no third-party NDPS Gateway is available. A Printer Agent configured in this mode emulates a legacy printer server, and no longer requires PSERVER.NLM.

- *Configuring an NDPS Printer to Service a Queue*—Before an NDPS printer can service a legacy print queue, it must be installed as a Controlled Access printer. You cannot configure a Public Access printer to service legacy print queues. To configure an NDPS printer to service a queue, use the Printer Control button of NetWare Administrator. Next, click Jobs and choose Spooling Configuration. Finally, add the queue name to the Service Jobs from NetWare Queues field.

- *Installing NDPS 2.0 after NetWare 5.x Is Installed*—NDPS 2.0 is installed as part of the NetWare 5.*x* Typical installation (see Chapter 1). If NDPS is not installed during server installation, you must decide if it is better to reinstall NetWare 5.*x* or follow the NDPS 2.0 After Installation procedure.

- *Preventing Installation of Printers to Unwanted Workstations*—NDPS Printers might be installed to unwanted workstations if multiple printers are automatically created in the same container. This is because every NDPS printer in a given container is automatically installed for all workstations in the container. The only workaround involves the Printer Policy feature in ZENworks. Printer policies can be created as part of a Windows 95/98 or NT/2000 workstation package that pushes NDPS printers according to User or Group membership.

- *Determining When to Use the Novell Gateway*—As a general rule, you should use the Novell Gateway when your printer manufacturer does not provide a specific third-party NDPS Gateway. Specifically, use the Novell Gateway in any of the following circumstances: the printer is attached directly to the file server, the printer is attached to a workstation running NPRINTER, the printer is using a JetDirect card running in RPRINTER mode, or the printer manufacturer has not created an NDPS Gateway of its own. Keep in mind, Novell does not guarantee that its Gateway works with all printer types.

Wow! That was fun. I bet you didn't think NDPS troubleshooting could be so complex. And you probably don't ever want to see another flowchart in your life! As we discovered in this section, printing problems are caused by a combination of unrealistic user expectations, traffic overload, and technical breakdown.

NDPS is only the first piece of a much larger, more complex puzzle. In the remainder of this chapter, we will journey through the legacy queue-based printing system by exploring its basic architecture and discovering a *single* queue-based troubleshooting flowchart. So, let's begin our second lesson in NetWare printing troubleshooting with a review of the queue-based printing architecture. I think you'll find it refreshingly simple.

LAB EXERCISE 16.2: TROUBLESHOOTING NDPS PRINTING PROBLEMS

Match the appropriate NDPS printing solution with each of the following troubleshooting problems.

A. Resolve the error and try again.
B. Test the NDPS printing flow.
C. Check the Job List.
D. Determine which mixed printing configuration you are using.
E. It must be a queue-based printing problem.

1. ____ NetWare queues are not being serviced by an NDPS printer.
2. ____ The Printer Agent forwarding is not working correctly.
3. ____ Error messages appear on the printer, server, and/or client.
4. ____ Jobs from a non-NDPS client aren't getting to the Printer Agent Job List.
5. ____ Job spooling is configured correctly, but non-NDPS print jobs still aren't printing.
6. ____ NetWare queues are being serviced by NDPS printers.
7. ____ The Status of your NDPS printer in Printer Manager is "Not Good."
8. ____ The Status of your NDPS printer in Printer Manager is "Good."
9. ____ PSERVER.NLM is not loaded correctly.
10. ____ The third step in testing NDPS printing flow.

See Appendix C for answers.

Troubleshooting Queue-Based Printing

Earlier we learned that queue-based printing is a fairly simple process—you click a button on the workstation and a piece of paper comes out of the printer down the hall. Yet printing is the most common troubleshooting topic on Novell's support hotline. Why? In the remainder of this chapter, you're going to learn some time-proven techniques for isolating printing problems. After you've identified the culprit, you can then implement a variety of troubleshooting solutions.

Queue-based printing is used in NetWare 3 and NetWare 4. It is also available in NetWare 5.1 as an alternative to NDPS. To set up a NetWare 5.1 queue-based printing environment, you will need to create the following three types of NDS printing objects (as shown in Figure 16.15):

- *Print Queue*—A shared directory on the file server that stores print jobs as they arrive from user workstations.
- *Print Server*—Tracks print job priority and directs print jobs from print queues to network printers.
- *Printer*—An NDS object that corresponds to a local or remote printing device.

FIGURE 16.15

Understanding NetWare 5.1 queue-based printing

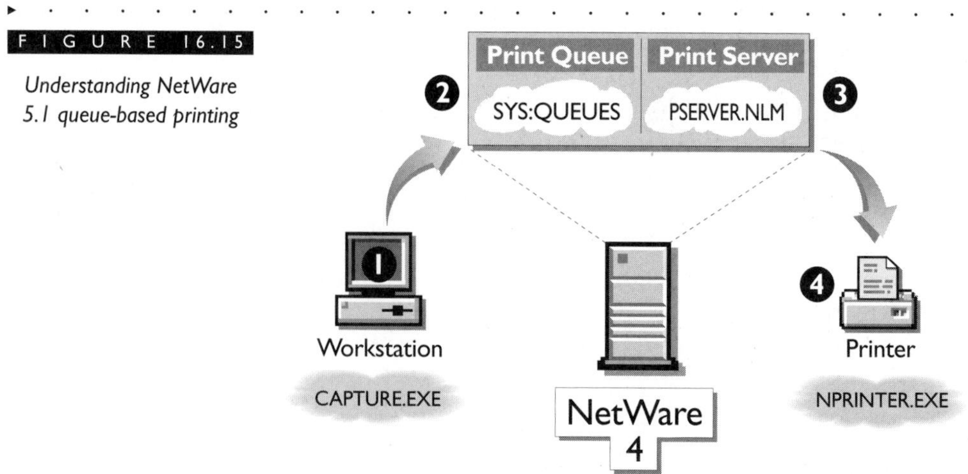

In NetWare 3, printing setup is accomplished using the PCONSOLE utility. This DOS-based tool enables you to create print queues, print servers, and printers on a server-by-server basis. Once you've created these elements, you can activate printing with PSERVER.

NetWare 4 uses PCONSOLE as well, but it also includes an advanced PCONSOLE feature called Quick Setup. This feature consists of one simple form—an automated PCONSOLE object creation form. In addition, NetWare 4 and 5.*x* include a Windows-based printing setup tool called NetWare Administrator, which allows you to create printing objects as though they were any other physical resource. Then you use built-in management features to activate the printing objects.

Once queue-based printing has been activated, user jobs are captured to central print queues and then forwarded to appropriate printers by the print server. This system is fairly fragile, and includes many possible breakdown points. In this section, we will study the queue-based printing troubleshooting flowchart and focus on four main components: workstation, print server, print queue, and printer.

Queue-Based Printing Troubleshooting Flowchart

The centerpiece of queue-based printing troubleshooting is a *single* flowchart that helps you isolate the problematic component (see Figure 16.16). This flowchart enables you to solve queue-based printing problems with the following two stages:

- *Stage 1:* Identify the problematic component.
- *Stage 2:* Implement the solution.

The queue-based printing troubleshooting flowchart in Figure 16.16 guides you through the following three gates in Stage 1 (identifying the problematic printing component):

- *Gate 1: Troubleshoot Printing Setup*—The adventure begins with a question, "Did Printing Ever Work"? If not, you can assume the problem is in the printing setup. If so, move on to Gate 2.
- *Gate 2: Printing Quick Fixes*—Begin with a variety of quick fixes, just in case the problem is trivial. If none of them solves your printing problem, then move on to the final gate.

FIGURE 16.16

The queue-based printing troubleshooting flowchart

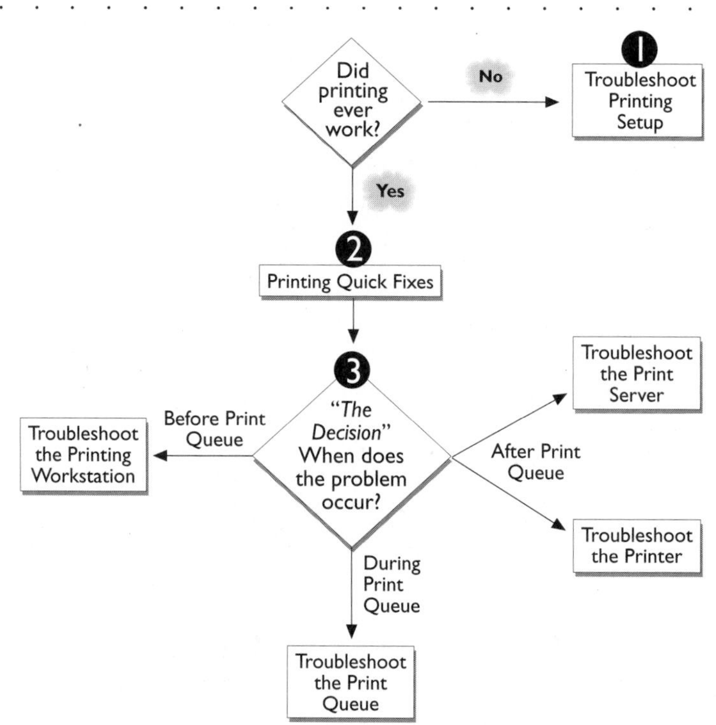

- *Gate 3: "The Decision" When Does the Problem Occur?*—Finally, determine if the problem occurred before, during, or after the job arrived at the print queue. If the problem occurred before the job entered the print queue, it is the workstation's fault. However, if it occurred after the job left the print queue, it can be either the print server's or printer's fault. Finally, many problems actually occur inside the print queue.

Gate 1: Troubleshoot Printing Setup

If queue-based printing never worked on this network, you can assume that something is wrong with the printing setup process. Following is a list of possible solutions:

- Retrace the four steps of the queue-based printing setup process to ensure that all three printing objects have been linked correctly. Verify that the print queue is assigned to the printer and the printer is assigned to the print server.

- Install the most recent printing software. These files can be found in compressed form at Novell's Internet Connection Web site (`support.novell.com`). (You should search on the keyword "Printing.")
- Confirm that the file server has enough disk space to hold the print jobs assigned to its print queue. Remember, print jobs can get quite large and may temporarily occupy hundreds of megabytes of disk space. To solve this problem, you may want to consider configuring queue directories to "Purge Immediately Upon Deletion."
- Shorten your print queue names to avoid confusion.
- Ensure that CAPTURE, NPRINT, and local applications are sending output to the correct LPT: port. Test the hardware by temporarily attaching a local printer directly to the workstation. For Windows 95/98 and Windows NT/2000, check your printer status in the Windows Control Panel to make sure the UNC path to the printer is correct.

Gate 2: Printing Quick Fixes

If the problem does not stem from the queue-based printing setup, then it must exist at one of the four sites along the printing journey. But before you begin troubleshooting all four of the queue-based printing components, you should try one or more of the following quick fixes:

- Check the cabling between the printer and workstation or server. If you are using a direct printer, ensure that the LAN connection is operating properly. Finally, check the printer cover (to see if it is properly closed) and the paper feed (for jams).
- Turn the printer off and back on.
- Check the workstation printer redirection. You may also want to test the local port with a temporary local printer.
- Check printing forms to ensure that they have been mounted correctly at the printer and print server.

- Gather information from file server console messages and the error log. Look for error messages on the printer LCD panel. If the problem is with the physical printer, you can reference error codes in its documentation.

Gate 3: "The Decision" When Does the Problem Occur?

The final gate in the queue-based printing troubleshooting flowchart is the most critical one. The following instructions enable you to identify the problematic component (workstation, print queue, print server, or printer):

- *Workstation* — Stop all print jobs from leaving the troubled print queue by setting the "Allow Service by Current Print Servers" option to NO. Then send a test job to the print queue using CAPTURE or any of the queue-based printing tools. Finally, view the print queue Job List in PCONSOLE (NetWare 3) or NetWare Administrator (NetWare 4 and NetWare 5.*x*). If the test job is not in the queue, you can assume that the problem is with the printing workstation. Refer to the "Troubleshooting the Printing Workstation" section later in this chapter.

- *Print Queue* — If the test job appears in the print queue, view its Status. If the Status shifts from "Adding" to "Ready," you can assume that the job arrived in one piece. Ensure that the job is not corrupted by sending it to another print queue and/or printer. Next, release the print queue and allow the job to print. If its Status does not switch to Active, and the job never leaves the queue, you can assume that the problem is with the print queue. Refer to the "Troubleshooting the Print Queue" section later in this chapter.

- *Print Server* — If the print job switches to Active but does not print, you could have a problem with the print server or printer. View Print Server Status in NetWare Administrator and make sure that the server is servicing the job. If not, you have a problem with the print server. Refer to the "Troubleshooting the Print Server" section later in this chapter.

- *Printer* — If the test print job finds its way to the print queue, is serviced by the print server, but never prints, you can suspect the printer. If all else fails, refer to the "Troubleshooting the Printer" section later in this chapter.

Troubleshooting the Printing Workstation

The workstation is responsible for redirecting print jobs from local applications to a centralized print queue. This function is accomplished through NetWare-aware applications, capturing, and/or queue-based printing tools, such as PCONSOLE or NetWare Administrator.

Workstation problems are characterized by any of the following symptoms: the printing problem is specific to a single workstation; the print job does not arrive at the print queue or arrives in a corrupted form; the print job arrives at the print queue, but the job status remains in the "Adding" or "Hold" mode; or the print job arrives at the printer, but merges with another print job.

Following are some time-proven workstation printing solutions:

- Determine if local printing works by attaching a local printer directly to the workstation and printing from the command line or Windows. Also, check the workstation's CAPTURE settings and verify that local applications are NetWare-aware. For Windows 95/98 and Windows NT/2000, check your printer status in the Windows Control Panel to make sure the UNC path to the printer is correct.

- Increase the buffer size to a combined maximum of 255 bytes by using PRINT HEADER and PRINT TAIL statements in NET.CFG or by using the Advanced Settings tab of the Novell Client Properties dialog box.

- Simplify printer redirection for users by configuring it as a menu-driven option. Be sure that your users know which queue is associated with which printer.

- If large graphic files are being printed with premature page breaks, lengthen or disable the Time Out setting in the job definition. Also, the TAB parameter usually exchanges the ASCII tab character (09) for eight spaces, which can cause output problems.

- A print job cannot be completed if the NetWare volume containing the print queue does not have enough free disk space. In NetWare 3.12, that is the SYS: volume. In NetWare 4 and NetWare 5.*x*, you can alleviate this problem by off-loading the QUEUES directory to an empty volume (or a volume with a large amount of available space). In addition, you may want to consider configuring queue directories to "Purge Immediately Upon Deletion."

- Overnight print jobs that are generated using CAPTURE can be lost if your backup system clears all connections at midnight. This can have disastrous results if print jobs are deleted from the print queue. To avoid this problem, use the /KEEP switch with CAPTURE to preserve print jobs after the connection is lost.

Troubleshooting the Print Queue

A *print queue* is a subdirectory on the file server that stores incoming print jobs on a first-come, first-served basis. Print queues also redirect jobs to specific printers. Print queue problems are characterized by any of the following symptoms: the print job was sent uncorrupted, but it is corrupted in the print queue; the print server abends (abnormal ends) when accessing the print queue; or printing occurs sporadically.

Following are some time-proven print queue solutions:

- Most queue problems are caused by running out of volume space. If you do not have enough disk space to spool incoming jobs, the following error message will appear: `WARNING—CANNOT CREATE SPOOL FILE`. Use NetWare Administrator to verify space problems. In NetWare 3.12, you do not have much of a choice; you will have to off-load files from the SYS: volume to make more room on the volume. In NetWare 4 and NetWare 5.*x*, you can move the QUEUES directory to an empty volume (or a volume with a large amount of free space). Finally, you may want to consider configuring queue directories to "Purge Immediately Upon Deletion."

- The second most common print queue problem is corruption. If captured jobs do not appear in print queues, they may be corrupted. Use the CAPTURE /SH command to verify where jobs are sent. Then monitor Current Job Entries in PCONSOLE or NetWare Administrator to make sure they arrive at the print queue. To fix a corrupted print queue, delete the print queue definition, redefine it, and reassign the print queue to a printer.

- An out-of-date NetWare shell or Novell Client can also cause unpredictable queue errors, especially if you are using IPX.COM with NetWare 3 or NetWare 4. Be sure to install the latest copies of workstation connectivity software, printer drivers, and NetWare utilities from `support.novell.com`.

Troubleshooting the Print Server

The *print server* is a logical process that controls print queues and shuffles jobs to corresponding network printers. In NetWare 3.12, print server functionality is provided by PSERVER.NLM at the file server and/or by PSERVER.EXE on a dedicated workstation. In NetWare 4 and NetWare 5.*x*, print server functionality is restricted to the file server only, via PSERVER.NLM.

Print server problems are characterized by any of the following symptoms: the print job status in the print queue switches to "Active," but the print job is never printed; or the print job leaves the print queue, but is never printed.

Following are some time-proven print server solutions:

- Most print server problems occur during initialization. This involves PSERVER.NLM and PSERVER.EXE (NetWare 3.12 only). Be sure to download the latest versions of these programs from Novell's Support Connection Web site (`support.novell.com`).

- Many times, the availability of print server RAM can dramatically affect performance and reliability. An inadequate amount of RAM will cause the following error messages to appear when you load PSERVER.NLM: `Not Enough Free Buffers` and `Unable to Create Display Portal`.

- Another common print server problem stems from a corrupted definition. This problem is manifested as slow or erratic printing, or an unexpected password prompt, when loading the PSERVER module. You can correct these problems by deleting the existing print server definitions and re-creating them.

- Remember that modifications made to the print server definition do not take effect until the print server is brought down and reinitialized. The safest method to bring down the print server is to deactivate it in PCONSOLE or NetWare Administrator before you unload the module.

- If your network is using the IPX protocol, PCONSOLE will rely on an SPX connection for distributing printing management data. Whenever you use the Print Server Status/Control option in PCONSOLE, NetWare activates SPX connectivity. This type of connection, however, may have trouble crossing routers. If so, increment the SPX TIME OUT and IPX RETRY values in NET.CFG to alleviate the problem.

- To have your print server reboot automatically after an interruption, use the utilities in the NETERR.ZIP file found on Novell's Support Connection Web site (`support.novell.com`). Search on the keyword "Printing."

- PSERVER.EXE, combined with DOS and the NetWare shell, requires approximately 512K of conventional memory. Each additional printer requires 10K more.

Troubleshooting the Printer

The printer represents the final destination of the queue-based printing system. Printer problems are characterized by any of the following symptoms: the print job passes uncorrupted through the print queue, but it never prints or is corrupted when it prints; the print job prints properly when a different printer is attached to the same port; the Print Job Status shifts from "Ready" to "Active," but is never printed; or the print job contains dropped or random characters.

Following are some time-proven printer solutions:

- If print jobs arrive at the print queue but never print, look for physical problems at the printer. Verify that the printer is turned on and is not offline. Check for loose cables, jammed paper, or an empty toner cartridge. Use the printer's own self-test facility to verify that it is functioning properly. Finally, check the printer for electrical problems caused by paper static.

- Remote printing enables you to distribute shared printers on non-dedicated workstations throughout the network. To do so, you will need to activate the appropriate software (that is, RPRINTER.EXE, NPRINTER.EXE, or NPRINTER Manager) on each workstation that has a network printer attached.

- If you reboot a remote printing workstation to reestablish a lost connection, you might get a message that the remote printer is still in use. Because RPRINTER uses SPX connectivity, it requires 30 seconds to time out. If you increase the SPX ABORT TIME OUT and/or IPX RETRY COUNTS, the delay may be significantly longer.
- Use RPRINTER in Polled mode when you are working with Windows 3.1 or if you are experiencing persistent port conflicts. Although an interrupt configuration is faster, printing using the Polled mode setting typically provides a trouble-free alternative.
- Consider the advantages and disadvantages of serial and parallel communications when choosing network printers. On the one hand, serial printing supports greater distances and provides a more reliable printing path. On the other hand, parallel printing is much faster and more easily configured. Refer to Table 16.2 for a comparison of serial and parallel printers.
- When using a PostScript cartridge on an Hewlett-Packard LaserJet or similar printer, make sure the cartridge is completely installed in the bay. If the cartridge is not operating properly, the PostScript language will not be available and incoming print jobs will be garbled.
- Use the NO BANNER (/NB) and NO TABS (/NT) parameters for all PostScript print jobs in Byte Stream mode. Sending a NetWare banner can cause the PostScript printer to see the job as a PCL file. Similarly, disable form feeds with the /NFF parameter.
- When PRINTDEF is used to create PostScript Printer-Definition Files (PDFs), you may experience problems if the modes are larger than the default header size of 64 bytes. In this case, you may need to increase the PRINT HEADER value in NET.CFG or in the Advanced Settings tab of the Novell Client Properties dialog box on a Windows 95/98 or Windows NT/2000 workstation.

TABLE 16.2

Serial Versus Parallel Printers

SERIAL PRINTERS	PARALLEL PRINTERS
Slower than parallel.	Four to six times faster than serial.
50 feet standard maximum distance. Some cables are guaranteed up to 500 feet.	10 feet maximum distance. Some cables are guaranteed for up to 150 feet; however, these special cables have a lower impedance value.
Uses parity for error checking, which can reduce speed by 10 to 25 percent.	Limited error checking, but relatively error free.
Installer sets interrupt XON/XOFF parity, bits-per-second rate, data bits, and stop bits. Added complexity because logical print server and physical printer configurations must match.	The interrupt must be set by the installer for parallel ports.
Compatibility may be a problem.	Universally compatible.

Congratulations! You've made it through the minefield of network printing troubleshooting. Printing is your LAN's quintessential productivity tool. It works with NICs, hard drives, and workstations to provide form and function to your network.

The goal of printing is to provide a hard copy outlet for your network's electronic bits. In this chapter, we learned how NetWare employs two powerful printing systems to make this dream a reality — NDPS and queue-based printing. And in review, NetWare queue-based printing consists of the following three main components:

- *Print Queue*
- *Print Server*
- *Printer*

What's left? You've mastered the four main lessons of network troubleshooting. You've earned a bag full of valuable troubleshooting tools. You've even learned the NetWare Troubleshooting Model. There's only one lesson left . . . *Fitness!*

LAB EXERCISE 16.3: TROUBLESHOOTING QUEUE-BASED PRINTING PROBLEMS

Match the appropriate queue-based printing component with each of the following troubleshooting problems.

A. Workstation
B. Print Queue
C. Print Server
D. Printer

1. ____ The print job leaves the print queue, but it is never printed.
2. ____ The print job was sent uncorrupted, but is corrupted in the print queue.
3. ____ The print job passes uncorrupted through the print queue, but it never prints or is corrupted when it prints.
4. ____ The print job contains dropped characters or random errors.
5. ____ The print server abends when accessing the print queue.
6. ____ The print job status in the print queue goes to Active, but the print job is never printed.
7. ____ The print job passes uncorrupted through the print queue, but arrived corrupted at a remote printer.
8. ____ Printing occurs sporadically.
9. ____ The print job status goes to Active or leaves the print queue, but is never printed.
10. ____ The print job prints properly when a different printer is attached to the same printer port.

See Appendix C for answers.

LAB EXERCISE 16.4: FIXING ACME PRINTING PROBLEMS

Use the hints provided to find the 20 printing terms hidden in this word search puzzle. Omit any punctuation characters (such as blank spaces, hyphens, and so on) and spell out any numbers.

Hints

1. Legacy process for redirecting print jobs from a local workstation port to a network printer.
2. More secure than Public Access printers.
3. Computer containing print queues.
4. Printers that use a UNIX-based printing protocol in IP environments.
5. NDPS feature that enables network administrators to administer all printing devices from a single location using NetWare Administrator.

6. Provides a software bridge between NDPS and legacy local and remote printers, including those using NPRINTER or queue-based technology.
7. Type of user who maintains a printer on a day-to-day basis by managing print jobs and setting configuration defaults.
8. Menu utility for managing the queue-based printing environment.
9. Used to avoid interrupt conflicts.
10. Printing component that ensures that the PDS can communicate with a physical printer, regardless of what type of interface is used.
11. Page Description Language for high quality printers.
12. Printing component that combines the functions previously performed by a printer, print queue, print server, and spooler into one intelligent, simplified entity.
13. Converts print jobs to the correct printer format.
14. Bridge between NDPS clients and legacy printers.
15. Workstation utility for managing NDPS printing tasks.
16. File stored in the print queue directory while waiting to be printed.
17. Legacy printing object used for managing printers and print queues.
18. Setting up NetWare 4 printing in a hurry.
19. Printer not directly attached to the print server.
20. Enables Public Access printers to advertise themselves so that network administrators and users can find them.

See Appendix C for answers.

LAB EXERCISE 16.5: TROUBLESHOOTING PRINTING

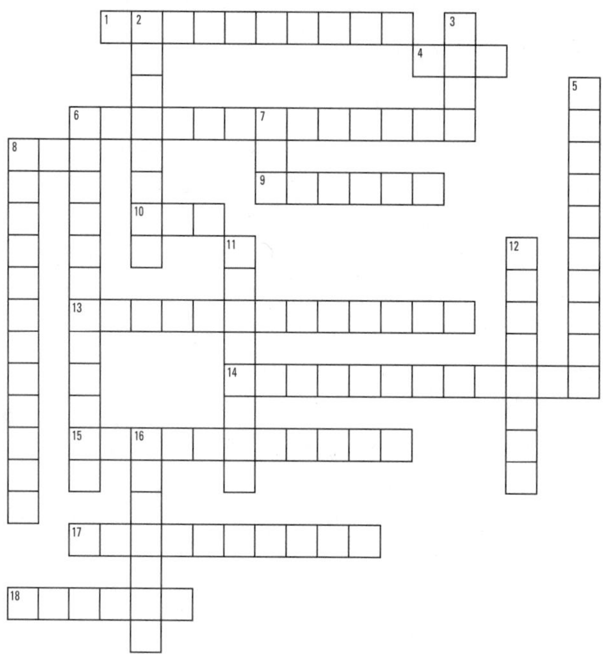

Across

1. Network directory that stores print jobs
4. Queries a printer in its native language
6. Loose or damaged ones cause printing problems
8. Language used for Hewlett-Packard LaserJet printers
9. NetWare 3 parent directory for print queues
10. Middleman between users and printers
13. Printer attached directly to the cable
14. Printer attached directly to the print server
15. Manages Printer Agents
17. NPRINTER loaded by the network administrator
18. NetWare 4 parent directory for print queues

Down

2. NetWare 3 remote printing utility
3. New NetWare 5.1 printing architecture
5. Provides SRS, ENS, and RMS support services
6. Relies on automatic hardware detection
7. Central repository for printing resources
8. Less secure than Controlled Access printers
11. NPRINTER loaded by print server
12. Rock solid until you add users
16. Peripheral device for producing printed material

See Appendix C for answers.

CHAPTER 17

Troubleshooting the Server and the Network

Congratulations, you are a network troubleshooter! In the previous five troubleshooting chapters, you learned how to use the NetWare Troubleshooting Model, gained a variety of troubleshooting tools, and mastered the four main network components — NICs, hard drives, workstations, and printing.

This chapter is about fitness. The American Academy of Physical Education defines fitness as this:

The ability to carry out daily tasks with vigor and alertness, without undue fatigue and with ample energy. To engage in leisure-time pursuits and to meet the above-average physical stresses encountered in emergency situations.

As a network troubleshooter, you will need to promote fitness within your LAN and WAN. This means monitoring the health and activity of your server and network components. This final troubleshooting chapter focuses on the troubleshooting of both servers and the network itself:

- *Server Troubleshooting* — Server troubleshooting involves maintaining current software, troubleshooting server crashes, and building a disaster recovery plan.
- *Network Troubleshooting* — Network troubleshooting targets connectivity hardware problems (relating to NICs, cabling, and so on) and performance bottlenecks.

Let's start with a comprehensive lesson in server fitness.

Server Troubleshooting

NetWare servers are vital components in your network because they house shared resources and control network management and security. In this first section, we will explore three aspects of server troubleshooting:

- Maintaining current software
- Troubleshooting server crashes
- Recovering from disaster

It all begins by maintaining fresh software. If you keep the server updated with patches and new drivers, the chances of a crash diminish. Furthermore, new software adds greater functionality and increases server performance. If these measures don't work, you'll experience a server crash — they're unavoidable. The best things you can do in the event of a server crash are to recognize the warning signs and take immediate action. Taking these steps is usually enough to restore server health. Sometimes, however, they're not. In those cases, you will need an established disaster recovery plan to get back on your feet.

Maintaining Current Software

If a server seems to be experiencing problems, one of the first troubleshooting steps you should perform is to determine if the server is running the latest version of operating system patches, device drivers, and NLMs.

Novell provides three types of operating system patches for known server problems:

- *Dynamic* — Dynamic patches are implemented as .NLM files that can be loaded and unloaded while the server is running. Unloading a dynamic patch restores the operating system to its original, unpatched state.

- *Semistatic* — Semistatic patches can be loaded while the server is up and running, but they cannot be unloaded without restarting the server. To remove a semistatic patch, simply restart the server without loading the patch.

- *Static* — Static patches are implemented using a DOS executable that modifies the SERVER.EXE file. Once a static patch is applied, the effects are permanent. Therefore, you should always make a backup of SERVER.EXE before applying a static patch.

You can install patches individually or via a Support Pack. A Support Pack includes all updates to the products included in a NetWare operating system version as of a certain date. The advantage of installing a Support Pack, rather than individual patches, is that the updated files in a Support Pack have been tested both individually and as a complete suite. To install a Support Pack, use NWCONFIG.NLM (NetWare 5.*x*) or INSTALL.NLM (NetWare 4.11).

To install a dynamic patch on a NetWare 3.12 server, you must first load the Patch Manager, which is implemented as PATCHMAN.NLM. This utility tracks all official NetWare patches and can be found in the same file as the patches. To load a dynamic patch automatically on a NetWare 3.12 server, place the appropriate LOAD statement in the server's AUTOEXEC.NCF configuration file. To view a list of loaded patches at the server console, type **PATCHES** and then press Enter.

Novell uses a specific naming convention for operating system patch files. The following are examples of operating system patch files that follow the official Novell naming convention: 312PTD.EXE (NetWare 3.12), 410PT8.EXE (NetWare 4.1), and IWSP5B.EXE (intraNetWare). The first three digits refer to the operating system version; the next two characters stand for the type of patch (for example, PT stands for *passed test* and SP stands for *support pack*); and finally, the last character is the revision number or letter.

Use the following procedure to install service packs and patches on a NetWare 4.11 or NetWare 5.1 server:

1. Back up all volumes on your server.
2. Obtain the latest service pack from the *Novell Support Connection* CD or the Novell Support Connection Web site.
3. Create a temporary directory on one of the server's volumes.
4. Expand the service pack by entering the filename at the DOS prompt. For example

   ```
   IWSP5B
   ```

5. Enter one of the following console commands:

   LOAD INSTALL (NetWare 4.11), or

   NWCONFIG (NetWare 5.1.x)

6. Select Product Options.

7. Choose "Install a Product Not Listed."

8. Press F3, then specify the complete path to the temporary directory you created in Step 3.

9. Follow the instructions.

10. Restart the server.

Refer to the README file included with patches and updates for information about applying software updates to your NetWare 3.12 server.

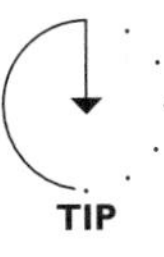

Study the three types of NetWare patches carefully. Remember that dynamic patches can be loaded and unloaded while the server is running; semistatic patches can be loaded while the server is running, but they cannot be unloaded without restarting the server; and static patches modify the operating system permanently. Know that all patches in a Support Pack are automatically loaded when you install the pack. Remember that PATCHMAN.NLM is the Patch Manager for NetWare 3.12 servers and that the PATCHES command enables you to view all loaded patches. Finally, be sure that you understand the naming convention used for NetWare patch files.

It is also important to ensure that your server is running the latest version of various device drivers. Device drivers are software programs that form the interface between NetWare and hardware resources, such as storage devices or network boards. Three important types of server device drivers include *LAN drivers* (for server NICs), *disk drivers* (for server storage devices), and *NWPA drivers* (new driver architecture for server storage devices). (**Note:** NetWare 5.1 does not support disk drivers with a .DSK filename extension found in earlier versions of NetWare.)

Finally, it is important to ensure that your server is running the latest version of various NLMs. NLMs can typically be loaded and unloaded while the server is running without affecting the NetWare operating system. System NLMs are stored in the SYS:SYSTEM directory, by default. Other NLMs are stored elsewhere. The latest versions of these server programs are available on the *Novell Support Connection* (Internet site or CD-ROM).

Troubleshooting Server Crashes

A server crash occurs when the NetWare operating system or server hardware unexpectedly stops working. Following are the two main types of server crashes:

- *Server Abends*—Abend stands for *abnormal end*. A server abend occurs when internal server activity stops abruptly. It is typically caused by a server process or condition that threatens the integrity of internal data.
- *Server Lockups*—A server lockup occurs when internal processing ends for no apparent reason. Lockups differ from abends in that all input/output (I/O) is frozen and no error message appears. Server lockups can be caused by a variety of problems, such as a hardware malfunction or an NLM thread that dominates the CPU and refuses to relinquish control.

In this chapter, we will explore the architecture of server crashes and learn how to troubleshoot server abends and lockups.

Understanding Server Crashes

The NetWare operating system continually monitors the status of various server activities in order to ensure proper operation. If NetWare detects a condition that threatens the integrity of its internal data, it abruptly halts the active process and displays an abend message on the server console screen.

Abends may be detected by the internal CPU or by NetWare itself. Following are three types of NetWare abends:

- *Interrupt*—When the server CPU detects an error, the processor can interrupt program execution by issuing an interrupt or exception. An interrupt is generated by an external device that needs attention.
- *Exception*—An exception is caused by the processor responding to a condition it detected while executing an instruction. Exceptions are classified as faults, traps, or aborts. The most common type of NetWare exception is the Non-Maskable Interrupt (NMI).

- *Consistency Check*—Consistency checks continually validate critical disk, memory, and communications processes. If a consistency check fails, it indicates a serious error and some degree of memory corruption. A consistency check error can be caused by a corrupted operating system file, outdated drivers or NLMs, bad packets from a client, or an internal hardware failure.

When a NetWare 4.11 or above server experiences an abend, the abend messages and additional information are written to the ABEND.LOG file. Depending upon several SET parameters, the server may immediately restart or will restart after a preset amount of time has passed. By default, NetWare determines the source of the abend, suspends the process, restores the process to a safe state, or brings the server down.

Table 17.1 describes abend-related SET parameters in NetWare 4.11 and above.

TABLE 17.1

Abend-Related SET Parameters

PARAMETER	DEFAULT	VALUES
AUTO RESTART AFTER ABEND	1	0: Do not recover. 1: Suspend crashed process and remain running or force a delayed restart. 2: Force a delayed restart for all abends. 3: Force an immediate restart for all abends (NetWare 5.x only).
AUTO RESTART AFTER ABEND DELAY TIME	2	The number of minutes to wait before restarting the server after an abend. Values can range from 2 to 60 minutes.
CPU HOG TIMEOUT AMOUNT	60	The number of seconds to wait before suspending a process that has taken control of the server CPU(s). Values can range from 0 (disabled) to 3,600 seconds.

Refer to the sample NetWare abend message in Figure 17.1 while reviewing the following descriptions:

- *Line 1: Date and Time* — Indicates the date and time at which the system halted.
- *Line 2: Abend Message String* — Includes the text of the abend message. This information can help you determine whether the error was detected by the CPU or the operating system. In this case (Figure 17.1), it's a CPU error.
- *Line 3: Operating System Version* — Identifies the version of NetWare that was running on the server at the time of the abend.
- *Line 4: Running Process* — Identifies which process was running at the time of the abend. This process may or may not have caused the abend.
- *Line 5: Stack* — The hexadecimal bytes displayed on the abend screen represent part of the CPU's stack from the current process. All three lines of the stack dump may be useful to Novell Technical Support in diagnosing the cause of the problem.
- *Line 6: Executing NLM* — The name of the NLM that was being executed when the error occurred.
- *Line 7: Server Action* — Displays the action that will be taken by the server upon error detection.
- *Line 8: OS Version and State* — Displays the operating system version and the server's current operating state.
- *Line 9: Console Prompt* — Indicates the number of threads that have been stopped since the server was last rebooted, displayed in angle brackets next to the console prompt.

FIGURE 17.1

Analyzing abend messages

```
(1) System halted Saturday, February 19, 2000 2:56:28 PDT
(2) Abend: Page Fault Processor Exception (Error code 00000002)
(3)     OS version: Novell NetWare 4.11 August 22, 1996
(4)     Running Process: Abendemo Process
(5)     Stack: C1 82 01 F1 85 95 11 F8 08 00 00 00 00 00 00 00
               28 8F 2C 01 10 40 2C 01 01 00 00 00 F3 99 11 F8
               10 00 00 00 10 BF 2C 01 0C BF 2C 01 B4 BF 2C 01
(6) Additional Information:
        The CPU encountered a problem executing code in
        ABENDEMO.NLM. The problem may be in that module or in
        data passed to that module by another NLM.
(7) The running process will be suspended.
(8) 2-19-00   2:56:28 pm:    SERVER-4.11-4631
        Warning! Server LABS-SRV1 experienced a critical error.
        offending process was suspended or recovered. However,
        services hosted by this server may have been affeced.
(9) LABS-SRV1<1>:
```

Abends are the most common type of server crash, and they provide a clear troubleshooting path. Server lockups, on the other hand, are a bit harder to diagnose and troubleshoot. A server lockup occurs when internal processing ends for no apparent reason. Lockups differ from abends in that all I/O is frozen and no error message appears. Most server lockups fall into one of two categories: full server lockup or partial server lockup.

When a *full server lockup* occurs, no processes are allowed to run, users are unable to log in, and all current connections are dropped. In addition, the server console keyboard is frozen. *Partial server lockups* freeze only the current server screen. Users may still be allowed to log in and some NLMs continue to work.

A server lockup may be caused by a variety of different problems. For example, one possible cause is an NLM thread that becomes caught in a tight loop and fails to relinquish control of the server CPU. This type of server lockup can be related to either a hardware or software problem and can be controlled with the CPU Hog Timeout SET parameter. Another possible cause is a process that locks up resources by blocking access to them. Finally, server lockups can be caused by the same types of problems that cause server abends: corrupted operating system files, corrupted or outdated drivers, bad packets, or simple hardware failures.

If a server crashes and no abend or other error message displays, press Ctrl+Alt+Esc to access the Hung Server console screen. Select "Down the File Server and Exit to DOS" and then restart the server.

To help diagnose the cause of a server abend, you may be instructed by Novell Technical Support to generate a memory image file and to send it to them. The memory image is a byte-for-byte representation of the NetWare server's memory at the time of the abend. Normally, the abend error console gives you the opportunity to create a memory image file. However, you may encounter an error that causes you to "force" a memory image copy. This can be accomplished in one of three ways:

- *Abend Console*—The abend console will automatically prompt you to copy the memory image to a designated DOS drive. In NetWare 4.*x* and later, the following two SET parameters must be configured for the memory image copy to work: Auto Restart After Abend = 0 and Developer Option = On.
- *NetWare Debugger*—If the NetWare server is running, press Left-Shift + Right-Shift + Alt + Esc in order to load the NetWare Debugger. From the Debugger console, enter **.c** to start the diagnostic image copy. When the copy is finished, press *G* to enable NetWare to continue or press *Q* to exit to DOS.
- *Forced NMI*—You can force the NetWare Debugger to load by issuing a Non-Maskable Interrupt (NMI) using an approved method from the server manufacturer.

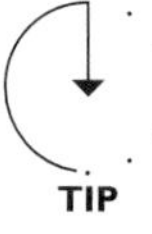
TIP

An abbreviated version of the server memory image containing only the most vital components is automatically placed in the ABEND.LOG file. The total size of the memory image file is roughly equal to the size of server memory.

Once you have created the memory image file, you must choose one of four destination storage media for it: floppy disk, hard drive, network drive, and/or parallel port (to an external hard drive. If you choose a floppy drive letter, the abend console prompts you for formatted 1.44MB disks. This destination medium should be used as a last resort because bad sectors on a single disk can make an image unreadable. A local DOS hard disk is a much better choice. In this case, the default image filename is COREDUMP.IMG. You can also copy the image to a NetWare drive using the IMGCOPY.NLM utility bundled with NetWare.

The ultimate level of memory image fault tolerance and performance can be accomplished using the network drive method (it is five times faster than other methods). To use this method, the server must meet the following minimum configuration: two NIC cards installed, at least one client driver loaded in DOS conventional memory, and NETALIVE.NLM running in server memory.

Diagnosing Server Crashes

You can use the following five steps to troubleshoot server crashes and eliminate some of the most obvious causes:

- *Step 1: Gather Information* — When faced with a critical server problem, you should gather as much information as you can, including error messages, complete hardware configurations, and disk and LAN driver information. You should also gather a list of the following: current NLMs and NCF files, the most recent changes made to the system, and all events that occurred prior to the crash. To help you gather this information, Novell provides an NLM called CONFIG.NLM, which creates a text file called CONFIG.TXT in the SYS:SYSTEM directory. This text file contains a list of all modules that were loaded on the server at the time it was run. It also tracks the contents of all NetWare and DOS startup files.

- *Step 2: Identify Probable Causes* — Next, identify probable causes by asking a variety of questions, such as the following: When did the abend problem begin? Did it coincide with any other activity? Is the server running the latest version of patches, drivers, and NLMs? Do the server error logs shed any light? After you have asked yourself any pertinent questions, restart the server and check the System Error log and Volume Error log. Also, check the ABEND.LOG file for NetWare 4.11 and above servers.

- *Step 3: Test Possible Solutions* — Once you have gathered all the relevant information, you should begin formulating hypotheses. The first thing you can try is applying current patches, drivers, and NLMs. Next, you may want to consider replacing suspect components, such as NICs, memory chips, and/or hard drive controllers. (**Note:** You can isolate suspect components more easily by removing other hardware temporarily.)

- *Step 4: Use Debugging Tools* — If you have not been able to gather enough information to form conclusions about the abend or lockup, consider the use of additional debugging tools (such as MONITOR.NLM) and network analyzers (such as LANalyzer for Windows).
- *Step 5: Resolve the Problem and Document the Solution* — Once you have identified the cause of the server crash, you can implement the solution. Finally, be sure to document both the problem and its solution.

In general, server crashes can be dangerous. Fortunately, you can resolve them quickly and painlessly with just a bit of preparation and guidance. Here's an important troubleshooting rule to remember:

The severity of a server disaster is directly related to your ability to recover from it.

Recovering from Disaster

In the event that you cannot recover from a server crash, you will need a reliable disaster recovery plan to fall back on. This plan should include recovery tools, procedures, and third-party solutions. Following are three vital components of a NetWare disaster recovery plan:

- VREPAIR for volumes
- DSREPAIR for NDS
- ODR for NetWare

VREPAIR is an NLM that corrects minor data structure errors on a volume. DSREPAIR performs a similar operation on NetWare NDS databases. These utilities can only solve relatively minor problems. For really serious disaster recovery, you should consider third-party solutions such as ODR for NetWare and other professional data recovery services.

Let's take a closer look.

TIP

Before using VREPAIR (to recover from file system errors) or DSREPAIR (to recover from NDS disasters), you should create multiple backups and verify them carefully.

VREPAIR for Volumes

The VREPAIR NLM is designed to correct minor data structure errors on a volume. Like other system NLMs, VREPAIR is loaded from the SYS:SYSTEM directory, by default, unless otherwise instructed. VREPAIR can repair one dismounted volume, while other NetWare volumes are functioning. One way to repair the SYS: volume is to load VREPAIR from the DOS partition. Alternately, you can load VREPAIR from the SYS: volume, press Alt+Esc, dismount the SYS: volume, and then run VREPAIR.

Following are some problems that VREPAIR may be able to solve:

- A hardware failure that either prevents a volume from mounting or causes a disk read error.
- A volume that was corrupted by a power failure.
- A server that displays memory errors and is unable to mount a volume after a name space is added. If this happens, you must either add more memory to the server or use VREPAIR to remove the newly added name space.
- A volume containing a name space that needs to be removed.
- A volume containing bad blocks.

To run VREPAIR, you must first make sure that the target volume is dismounted. If this is the SYS: volume, confirm that VREPAIR.NLM is on the DOS partition. You can then use the SEARCH ADD command to create a console path. Whatever you do, make sure you warn users on the volume to close their files before you dismount the volume. You can do this by using the BROADCAST or SEND console commands.

Once you have dismounted the appropriate volume, follow these simple steps for repairing it:

1. Load the VREPAIR NLM by typing the following at the server console:

```
LOAD VREPAIR
```

2. Check the VREPAIR options and change them if necessary by selecting Set VREPAIR Options.

3. Select "Repair a Volume" from the Options menu. When the list appears, select the appropriate volume.

4. If you are using a NetWare 4 or above server, the Current Error Settings screen appears. Change the current settings, if necessary.

5. Choose the appropriate option to continue with the repair.

6. A screen appears listing total errors and current error settings. If VREPAIR seems to be finding a large number of errors, press F1 to change the setting to "Not Pause on Errors."

7. Press any key to return to the Options menu. Then choose the appropriate option to exit.

8. Mount the repaired volume.

If a damaged volume contains one or more name spaces, you will need to load the appropriate NLM(s) to retain the name space(s) during the VREPAIR process. They are V_LONG.NLM for Windows 95/98 or Windows NT, V_MAC.NLM for Macintosh, and/or V_OS2.NLM for OS/2.

DSREPAIR for NDS

NetWare Versions 4 and above include the DSREPAIR.NLM utility, which repairs errors in the NDS database and resolves inconsistencies related to time and replica synchronization. Figure 17.2 shows the main menu of DSREPAIR and both synchronization options.

The Advanced Options menu in DSREPAIR enables you to set advanced repair configurations, such as Log File Management, Pause on Errors, Validation, Scheme of Rebuilding, Remote Server ID List, and Scheduling. Following is a list of NDS corruption symptoms that DSREPAIR may be able to solve:

- Users cannot create, delete, or modify objects, even though they have sufficient rights.

- Users cannot log into the NDS tree with the correct username and password.
- Unknown objects appear in the NDS tree and do not disappear after all servers are synchronized.
- Administrators cannot create, merge, or modify partitions.

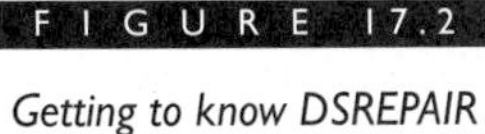

Getting to know DSREPAIR

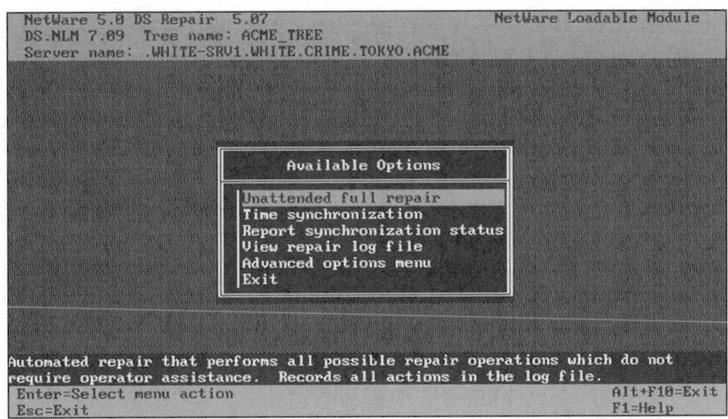

To load DSREPAIR, type the following command at the file server console: **LOAD DSREPAIR**. You can also use the –U option, which loads DSREPAIR, performs volume repairs, and then automatically exits upon completion. After the DSREPAIR process is complete, you can review the DSREPAIR.LOG file in the SYS:SYSTEM directory.

ODR for NetWare

OnTrack Data Recovery for NetWare (ODR for NetWare) is a third-party data recovery and protection utility that resolves data loss and server crash problems. It consists of three utilities: NetFile4, NetScan4, and NetDisk4. Together, these tools enable you to perform the following tasks:

- Recover files from a downed server. The files may be recovered to another active server through a workstation connection, to a DOS partition, or to floppy disks.

- Rebuild the file structure within a server volume. In addition, ODR enables you to examine, modify, and save any sector on a server device.
- Perform media analysis without destroying data that is already on the server hard disk. Defective sectors will be redirected to Hot Fix so that NetWare will not attempt to store data in those sectors.

ODR for NetWare consists of three utilities: NetFile5, NetScan5, and NetDisk5. *NetFile5* is a file recovery tool and editor that lets you access files on a corrupted NetWare volume. You can use this utility to save one or more files from a NetWare volume to DOS-formatted diskettes, a DOS partition, or another NetWare server. *NetScan5* is designed to examine and nondestructively repair NetWare structural errors within a volume. In addition, data in defective blocks can be redirected to more stable areas of the volume. Finally, *NetDisk5* is a sector editor that lets you examine and modify the data in any sector of a hard disk or optical drive. It can access data from a file server even if DOS and NetWare are no longer recognizable.

ODR for NetWare enables you to create a set of emergency disks that can be used to boot the server in case of serious SYS: volume or DOS partition corruption. These disks contain SERVER.EXE, STARTUP.NCF (stored as STARTUP.OFF), CLIB.NLM, STREAMS.NLM, and any applicable device drivers.

If OnTrack's recovery solutions don't solve your problem, consider other third-party professional services. Skilled recovery engineers are generally able to recover any data that is still physically recorded on the drive. For example, in the event of a head crash, data may be recovered from other areas not affected by the crash. This process usually involves sending your damaged drive to a company that specializes in disaster recovery.

Most disaster-recovery companies also offer on-site services at an extremely high additional charge. Professional data recovery can be quite costly. If the data is not valuable, this may not be the best option. You can expect to spend roughly $4,000 for recovery of data from a NetWare server. Typical turnaround time is two to five days. Of course, in comparison to the value of your data, this might be a minor cost and inconvenience. Companies providing data recovery services include Data Recovery Labs, Data Rescue, OnTrack, Precise Data Recovery Services, and Total Recall.

Regardless of the disaster recovery option you choose, it's best if you have a reliable suite of backup tapes readily available. Backup is really your best defense against drive-related disasters.

This completes our lesson in server troubleshooting. So, what have we learned? First, we learned to appreciate that *an ounce of prevention is greater than a pound of cure*. This strategy is implemented by maintaining the freshest server software available, which means eliminating out-of-date components and replacing them with the most recent patches, device drivers, and NLMs.

Now let's extend our fitness lesson to include the network as a whole. In the next section, we will explore network-wide bottlenecks and some great protocol analysis tools, namely LANalyzer for Windows.

Network Troubleshooting

Network troubleshooting encompasses more than just file servers. It extends to all other network components, including NICs, cabling, and workstations. In this section, we will cover two topics:

- *Bottlenecks* — A bottleneck is a source of delay and, thus, represents a weakness in the network channel. Identifying and solving network bottlenecks increases both productivity and user satisfaction.

- *Protocol Analyzers* — Protocol analyzers enable you to monitor network performance, troubleshoot network errors, optimize the network, and plan for growth. A popular protocol analyzer is Novell's *LANalyzer for Windows* (LZFW) product. This software-based analysis tool gathers, sorts, and reports data about how your network is running.

Troubleshooting Bottlenecks

Network bottlenecks slow us down. If the disk is full, you cannot print. If the printer's down, you cannot access saved files. As a network troubleshooter, you need to be able to quickly identify bottlenecks and take steps to resolve them.

Most networks experience bottlenecks in four areas:

- Disk I/O
- Network I/O
- CPU
- Bus I/O

As you can see, bottlenecks don't discriminate — they can occur anywhere. This makes troubleshooting bottlenecks an even greater challenge. In addition, bottlenecks are interdependent, which means that a problem in any of these four components can bring the entire network to its knees. Let's take a closer look.

REAL WORLD

NetWare provides two utilities to analyze, manage, and troubleshoot performance bottlenecks: NetWare Management Portal and MONITOR.

The NetWare Management Portal enables you to manage NetWare servers from any location on your network through a Web browser. Specifically, it allows you to check server processes and resources, view the status of memory usage, and view information regarding processor data and hardware resources.

MONITOR is a console-based NLM that enables you to view server statistics, access server RAM, monitor processor utilization, set server parameter values, and print server settings to a file.

Disk I/O Bottlenecks

The server disk is probably the most active component in the network. It stores the central network operating system (NOS) and participates in almost every activity from file sharing to printing. This is a great place to start your bottleneck explorations.

The best way to determine if you have a disk I/O bottleneck is to load MONITOR.NLM at the server and check the number of Dirty Cache Buffers. Also consider monitoring current disk requests. If these numbers are growing at a constant rate, you may have a disk I/O problem. Finally, on some machines, the disk light is a great indicator of overwork. You should be concerned if it's continually flashing.

An obvious way to increase disk performance is to utilize faster disks. Using many smaller disks to replace one large one can also improve the speed of the disk subsystem. As we learned in Chapter 14, RAID offers dramatic improvements in speed because of data striping and simultaneous disk requests. Upgrading to a fast disk controller can also alleviate disk I/O bottlenecks. Consider Fast SCSI II or Wide SCSI II for central servers. Check out Chapter 14 for more on Disk I/O bottlenecks.

Network I/O Bottlenecks

Next, check the communications path between users and the central server. Many times congestion and LAN traffic can adversely affect network performance.

Probably the best way to identify network I/O problems is through the LAN/WAN Information screen in MONITOR.NLM. If any of the following statistics are rapidly climbing, you may have a network I/O bottleneck (NetWare 5.1 statistics are shown in parentheses):

- Send packet too big (transmit failed, packet too big)
- Receive packet overflow count (adapter overflow condition)
- Receive packet too big count (receive failed, packet too big)
- Send packet miscellaneous errors (transmit failed, miscellaneous errors)
- No ECB available
- Packet receive buffers (receive discarded, no available buffers)
- Receive packet miscellaneous errors (receive failed, miscellaneous error)

The best way to solve network I/O bottlenecks is to upgrade the server NIC. Consider 32-bit bus mastering and/or Peripheral-Component Interconnect (PCI). In addition, you may want to split the LAN channel into multiple segments by adding NICs to the server. Of course, at some point, the high level of network I/O will overload the server processor or disk. In this case, you may consider adding bridges or routers to externally segment the LAN. In either case, the goal is to minimize traffic overload.

CPU Bottlenecks

With today's fast CPU technology, processor performance is rarely an issue. Most Pentium III processors (and above) perform at sufficient speeds to handle network requests. Remember, the server is only handling 5 percent of the network's overall processing. Of course, this doesn't mean the server CPU is immune from bottleneck problems. If you're using an older CPU with a slow clock speed (below 500 MHz), you may run into problems. Also, CPU-intensive applications may create bottlenecks of their own. If CPU upgrading isn't an option, consider using bus-mastering NICs and disk controllers. These devices communicate directly with each other and don't bother the CPU for simple I/O tasks. This leaves the CPU free for all the important work.

The best way to identify CPU bottlenecks is with the Processor Utilization screen in MONITOR.NLM. Not only does it allow you to track CPU load, it identifies specific internal resources. As a result, you can determine if it's the CPU or an NLM that is causing the problem.

Bus I/O Bottlenecks

Bus I/O bottlenecks are related to server CPU problems. As a matter of fact, it's difficult to distinguish between the two in many cases. Bus mastering I/O devices contend with cache systems for access to main memory, but they run much slower than the CPU. Therefore, most high-performance servers are manufactured to overcome this problem by allowing I/O devices and the CPU to access memory simultaneously. If your server is not engineered to do this, consider upgrading to a model that is. This is especially important if you have many users and an active server disk.

This completes our lesson on network bottlenecks. The most important thing to remember is that the LAN is only as strong as its weakest component. Use MONITOR.NLM and other protocol analysis tools to track disk, network, CPU, and bus bottlenecks. This strategy goes a long way in helping you achieve holistic LAN fitness. Now let's take a much closer look at one of the most powerful network troubleshooting tools — LANalyzer for Windows.

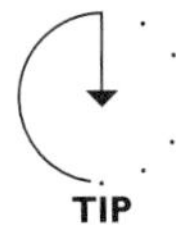

TIP

Study the four types of network bottlenecks listed in this lesson. Specifically, be able to identify which type of bottleneck is causing a specific network problem: disk I/O (high number of Dirty Cache Buffers or Current Disk Requests), network I/O (climbing receive packet overflow count or receive packet too big count), CPU (slow applications), and/or bus I/O (slow network communications). Finally, learn everything you can about bus mastering and remember that it can solve both network I/O and bus I/O bottlenecks.

Using LANalyzer for Windows

LZFW is a popular software-based protocol analysis tool for NetWare systems. It gathers, sorts, and reports data about how your LAN is running. The good news is that LZFW doesn't require a high degree of technical knowledge in order to use it. It runs within a simple Microsoft Windows interface and provides numerous details within a single main screen (see Figure 17.3). Subsequent screens provide even more detail in a graphical or text-based format.

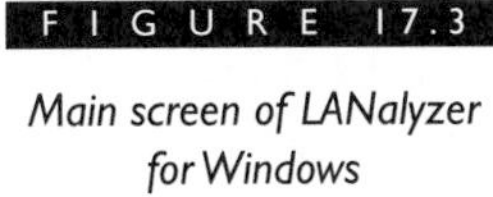

FIGURE 17.3

Main screen of LANalyzer for Windows

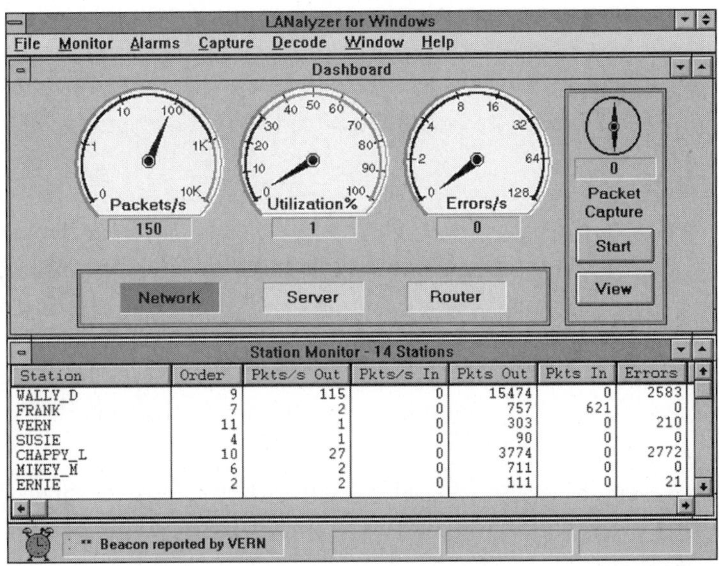

Following are some of the main features offered by LANalyzer for Windows:

- *Monitor Real-Time Activity* — You can see how your network is performing by using the dashboard gauges, alarm indicators, and detail windows. In addition, the Station Monitor provides information about traffic and errors for each station on the LAN. The Ring Monitor screen provides special information for Token Ring networks.
- *Identify Trends* — A built-in baselining tool enables you to graph network activity over time. Parameters include transmitted packets, transmitted kilobytes, network errors, and utilization percentage.
- *Create Reports* — A built-in report generator enables you to track network performance, plan future growth, and justify expenditures. You can generate printed reports on Station Monitor data, Ring Monitor data, and Alarm Logs. You can also print detailed graphs showing trend data.
- *Troubleshoot Problems* — Built-in alarm indicators notify you of unusual activity. When you double-click an alarm indicator, LZFW displays information about the network activity that caused the alarm. In many cases, this leads to interactive help — through the NetWare Expert. Yes, there's a little Nerd living inside your computer.
- *Diagnose Network Problems* — LZFW can identify an enormous variety of network problems, including defective NICs, improper Ethernet configurations, crosstalk, defective hubs, broken UTP cabling, faulty drivers, routing inefficiency, address conflicts, and invalid addressing.

All of this troubleshooting functionality is accomplished with a single Windows-based application running on a NetWare workstation. LZFW works directly with LAN cabling and analyzes all packets as they traverse the network. As a matter of fact, the workstation doesn't even need to be attached to a file server. It just needs an internal 16-bit NIC and promiscuous drivers. Pentium computers and 32-bit NICs work best for LZFW.

Now that you understand what LZFW can do, let's take a closer look at how it does it. Network troubleshooting is accomplished in a three-step process:

- *Step 1*: Baselining
- *Step 2*: Thresholds
- *Step 3*: Network Alarms

During Step 1, you capture trend data for a minimum of one month. This information isolates bandwidth, kilobytes, packets, and errors. After a baseline has been established for normal conditions, you can customize alarm thresholds—that's Step 2. When the network experiences unusual spikes in any of these components, the alarms activate and identify potential problems. During Step 3, you zero in on these problems and resolve them.

Step 1: Baselining

A baseline is a simple measurement of your network's typical performance. This information is gathered over time and can be plotted on trend graphs (see Figure 17.4). These trend graphs create the foundation of your fitness program.

FIGURE 17.4

Step 1: Baselining

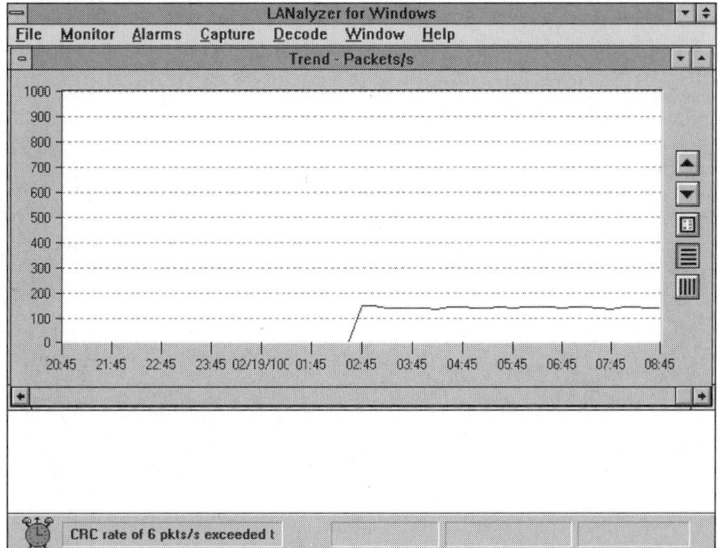

LZFW can capture trend data for six months. A minimum of one month's data should be used to establish a baseline. Longer periods can be analyzed by periodically exporting trends to a spreadsheet. LZFW provides four baseline measurements:

- *Utilization %*—Commonly called *bandwidth*, this measures the usage of the cabling system and should not be confused with utilization of the file server.
- *Kilobytes/Second*—This reports the throughput on the cabling system.
- *Packets/Second*—This reports the count of traffic packets. These packets can be generated by user applications. They can be requests for data or administrative SAP and RIP traffic.
- *Errors/Second*—This reports the number of general errors on the network. More than one error per second is considered a problem.

As with most components on your network, these four trends are interrelated. Often, you will see their values increasing and decreasing together. To complete your baseline, you should track the most active users, servers, and routers on your network. This will indicate basic network load balance for future planning.

Once you have established an accurate baseline, it's time to set alarm thresholds for anomalous conditions.

Step 2: Thresholds

Thresholds enable you to customize LZFW monitoring. You should set these values high enough so that normal peak activity does not trigger an alarm. Although LZFW has built-in defaults, you should alter thresholds according to baseline data. Figure 17.5 shows the default threshold screen in LZFW. Use these simple guidelines to get the most out of network alarms:

- *Packets/s*—Should be set at 5 percent to 10 percent over normal peak activity.
- *Utilization %*—Should be set at 5 percent above normal peak activity.

- *Broadcasts/s* — Should be set at 10 and adjusted upward as utilization increases.
- *Fragments/s* — Should be set at 15 and adjusted upward as utilization increases.
- *CRC Errors/s* — Should be initially set at 5.
- *Server Overloads/min* — Should be initially set at 5.
- *Advanced Alarms* — These signal events that should never occur on the network; therefore, you shouldn't build in any threshold tolerance for them.

As you can see in Figure 17.5, all the alarms are enabled. This means that they will go off at the first instance of the event.

FIGURE 17.5

Step 2: Thresholds

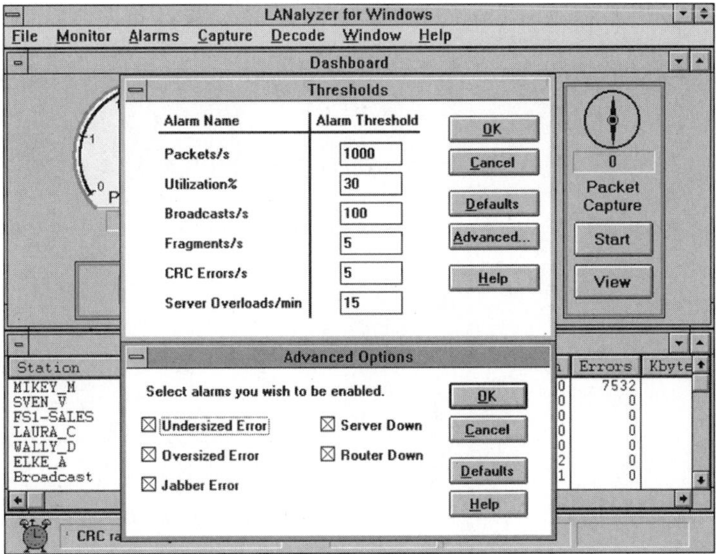

So, how do alarms work? Once a network condition exceeds the alarm threshold, an LZFW alarm is activated. This alarm notifies you that something bad is happening to the network. That's when you jump into action.

Step 3: Network Alarms

Once you have established a baseline and used it to build alarm thresholds, all you have to do is wait. Sometime, someday, an LZFW value will exceed the alarm threshold. At this point, four things will happen (see Figure 17.6):

- The Network Alarm indicator changes from green to red.
- LZFW sounds the alarm and draws attention to the workstation.
- The Alarm Clock appears in the lower left-hand corner of the Station Monitor.
- A scrolling message appears onscreen, describing the condition.

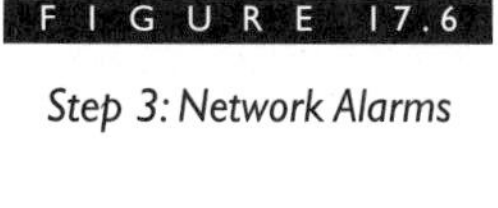

FIGURE 17.6

Step 3: Network Alarms

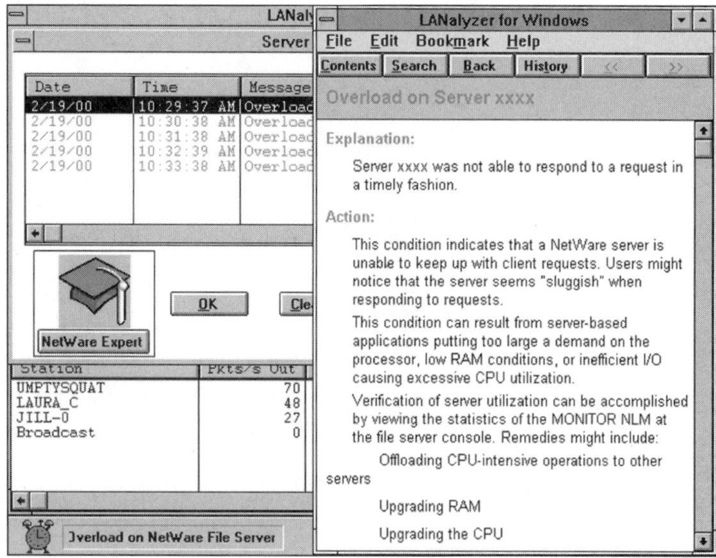

Once you recognize an alarm condition, double-click the offending alarm indicator and activate the Network Alarm screen. This screen shows the date and time of the alarm and a descriptive message. It also includes the NetWare Expert, an AI database full of solutions. The Network Expert can further analyze the alarm condition for you and provide possible solutions.

Let's take a closer look at some of the most common LZFW alarms:

- *CRC/Alignment Errors* — Indicate that a bad packet has been sent. The packet has a faulty Frame Check Sequence (FCS) or does not divide evenly by eight. Cabling problems normally cause this. Check the cable with a Time Domain Reflectometer (TDR). If it's okay, check cable routing and connection points, such as punch-down blocks and hubs.

- *Fragment Errors* — Occur when packets on the network are smaller than the 64-byte minimum and have a faulty FCS. Fragment errors are caused by collisions and normally bless Ethernet LANs. A serious condition can develop when the number of fragment errors is higher than a small percentage of the total number of packets. If fragmentation becomes a problem, consider redesigning the network using bridges and routers to filter out this overloaded condition. If the condition occurs when the network load is low, it probably means that a NIC or transceiver has failed.

- *Oversized Packets* — They are longer than 1,514 bytes but have a good FCS. This is an advanced alarm and, therefore, activated upon the first instance. If oversized packets are traversing the LAN, consider replacing the offending NIC or checking cable terminations.

- *Undersized Packets* — They are shorter than 64 bytes with a good FCS. Undersized packets differ from fragmentation in that they maintain reliable data integrity. Once again, this is an advanced alarm and should be handled immediately. If you are experiencing multiple short packets, consider replacing the NIC driver of the offending workstation.

- *Jabber Errors* — Occur when the network transports oversized packets with a faulty FCS. Jabbering is also an advanced alarm and, therefore, activated upon the first instance. Jabbering can cause many related problems because of packet collisions. Like oversized packets, consider replacing the offending NIC or checking cable terminations.
- *Overloaded Server* — Occurs when more than 15 packets are delayed per minute. Delays occur when the server cannot respond to a request in a timely fashion. If the server overload alarm is activated, consult the NetWare Expert for more details. It will probably tell you to offload CPU-intensive operations, upgrade server RAM, upgrade the CPU, or increase disk drives and NIC I/O channels.
- *Overloaded Network* — Normally occurs when the network cabling system cannot handle the number of kilobytes being transmitted from workstations and servers. If users are experiencing severe slow-downs or duplicate client requests, you may have an overloaded network. LZFW provides the following four alarms relating to network overload: Utilization %, Broadcast rate, Packets/second, and Error rate. If any of these alarms are activated, you should react to the problem immediately. The best way to deal with overloaded networks is to isolate the offending workstations. You can identify which ones are making the most NCP requests by sorting stations by the Packet Out column.

This completes our discussion of LZFW. As you can see, this is a powerful ally for your network troubleshooting program. In this chapter, we explored NetWare fitness from the server and network's point of view. We've gained some valuable insight into server protection and network troubleshooting.

This also completes our exhaustive journey through Novell Course 580, "NetWare Service & Support." Throughout this journey, we have gained increasing appreciation for the complexity of network troubleshooting: the skeleton NICs and cabling, central server hard drive, distributed workstations, and NDPS printing flowcharts.

What a wild ride!

Now that you are armed with some of the most comprehensive troubleshooting knowledge available, just be careful what you do with it!

LAB EXERCISE 17.1: FIXING THE ACME SERVERS AND NETWORK

Use the hints provided to find the 20 network management terms hidden in this word search puzzle. Omit any punctuation characters (such as blank spaces, hyphens, and so on) and spell out any numbers.

S	E	R	V	E	R	L	O	C	K	U	P	D	Q	M	Q
U	T	J	D	L	B	N	I	O	O	C	E	O	I	E	J
P	B	A	S	E	L	I	N	I	N	G	B	R	R	Y	T
P	C	B	T	V	Q	N	V	A	I	I	I	F	Y	Z	P
O	S	B	K	I	S	Z	X	B	F	J	T	A	B	E	X
R	C	E	C	D	C	T	Z	R	G	U	W	Z	L	X	Y
T	F	R	A	G	M	E	N	T	A	T	I	O	N	C	F
P	R	O	T	O	C	O	L	A	N	A	L	Y	Z	E	R
A	D	X	S	E	M	I	S	T	A	T	I	C	H	P	V
C	Y	W	F	X	T	T	R	B	U	B	N	E	R	T	C
K	N	E	T	W	O	R	K	E	X	P	E	R	T	I	L
P	A	S	S	E	D	T	E	S	T	H	E	N	N	O	U
R	M	O	N	I	T	O	R	N	L	M	T	K	D	N	J
P	I	F	Q	G	M	O	C	R	V	J	B	Q	Q	E	E
A	C	R	Y	L	O	G	E	Q	V	B	U	S	Q	O	V

Hints

1. When the server abruptly halts the active process and displays a message on the server console.
2. The process of documenting network performance characteristics under normal conditions for future reference.
3. A type of patch that can be loaded and unloaded while the server is running.
4. These can be classified as faults, traps, or aborts.
5. This occurs when network packets are less than 64 bytes and have a faulty FCS.
6. This occurs with oversized packets that have a faulty FCS.

7. Utility used for checking high utilization, memory issues, and resource conflicts.
8. LANalyzer for Windows database that indicates the type of error and recommends a solution.
9. Patches that handle the first problems found and solved for a given NetWare version.
10. Tool that provides trend information by measuring specific variables over time.
11. Patches that can be loaded, but not unloaded, while the server is running.
12. This type of problem may be caused by an NLM thread that becomes caught in a tight loop and does not relinquish control of the CPU.
13. The name for the 30 hexadecimal bytes displayed at the bottom of the abend screen that represent part of the CPU stack from the current process.
14. A type of patch that is applied once and whose effects are permanent.
15. This includes all patches needed to update a given version of NetWare.

See Appendix C for answers.

LAB EXERCISE 17.2: TROUBLESHOOTING THE SERVER

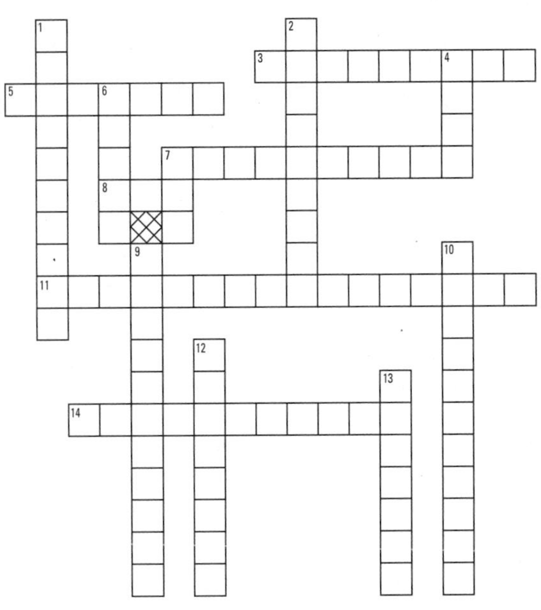

Across

3. Communications channel transmission capacity
5. NetWare 3.1*x* volume repair utility
7. Standing in the way of progress
8. A bottleneck category
11. A crisis plan
14. Core dump

Down

1. LANalyzer cutoff points
2. Novell protocol analyzer software
4. A second bottleneck category
6. Software fix
7. A third bottleneck category

9. NetWare patch manager tool
10. Types include abends and lockups
12. NetWare NDS repair tool
13. A fourth bottleneck category

See Appendix C for answers.

PART IV

Networking Technologies

CHAPTER 18

The OSI Model

What is a network (choose one)?

A. An open-work structure of twine with periodic intersections

B. A buzzword used in cyberspace

C. An exceedingly average collection of television broadcast stations

D. A collection of distributed, intelligent machines that share data and services through interconnected lines of communication

The correct answer is *D*. The key concept for understanding computer networks is *sharing*. Sharing is the foundation of networking technologies from the Physical Layer of the OSI model (transmission media and devices) to the Application Layer (X.500 and network services). These rules provide the framework for data transfer and interconnectivity.

Welcome to the world of networking. In this final part of *Novell's CNE Study Guide for NetWare 5.1*, we will explore the past, present, and future of networking technologies. You'll probably learn more about networking than you ever wanted to know, but study hard, because this is your springboard to an exciting future. Because this course was primarily written to be independent from Novell products, it provides an excellent perspective on many networking industry concepts.

Now let's start at the beginning, with the three faces of networking.

Understanding Computer Networking

Computer networking relies on strict rules regarding transmission media, protocols, and services. These rules are organized into the following three categories (see Figure 18.1):

- *Network Models* — These models classify networks by size, distance, and structure. The three network models discussed in this section are local area networks (LANs), metropolitan area networks (MANs), and wide area networks (WANs).

- *Network Management*—These management categories determine the rules for managing LANs and WANs, including configuration, fault tolerance, performance, security, and accounting.
- *Network Elements*—These elements define the pathway and protocols for electronic communications. Elements in this category control how messages travel from Point A to Point B using network services, protocols, and transmission media. Network elements are further organized according to the OSI model.

FIGURE 18.1

Three categories of computer networking

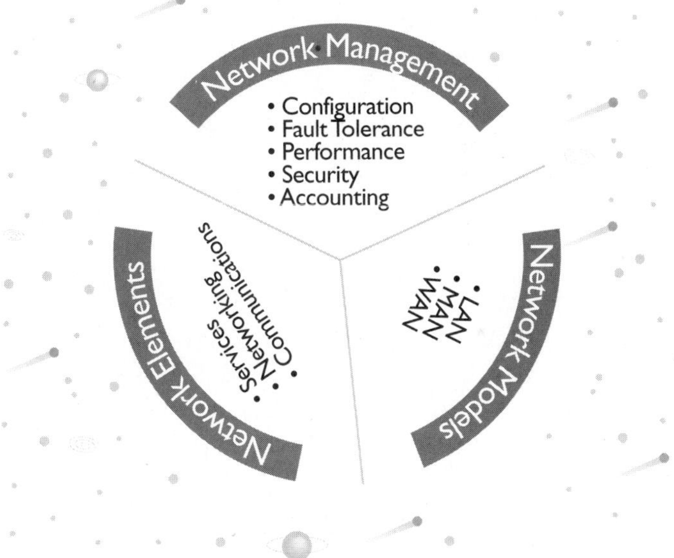

Network Models

For network administrators, network models represent the simplest of the three categories of networking. As we learned earlier, network models are used to classify networks by size, distance, and structure. These models help us understand the relationships among centralized, distributed, and collaborative computing systems. In a *centralized* computing system, a central computer (such as a mainframe) provides all computational and data storage capabilities, with terminals simply acting as remote input/output devices. In a *distributed* computing system, both servers and workstations have their own processing capability, with each task being assigned to a single computer. A *collaborative* computing system (also known as a *cooperative processing* system) is a type of distributed system where two or more computers can share the same task, as needed. Computing systems can also be classified as a *client/server* computing system (where applications are divided into a front end for user input and a back end for providing the requested service), a *client/network* computing system (where computers access network services without logging into a specific service provider), or as a *peer-to-peer* computing system (where computers access network services directly from each other).

Following are the three fundamental classifications of network models:

- Local area networks (LANs)
- Metropolitan area networks (MANs)
- Wide area networks (WANs)

A LAN links a small group of functionally similar workstations within a local geographic area, such as a series of adjacent cubicles or offices on the same floor. Once a network expands to include diverse organizations within a metropolitan area, it becomes a MAN. Finally, a WAN is simply a "LAN of LANs." WANs can expand the boundaries of networking to a global (or even galactic) scale.

Let's take a closer look at these three network models.

Local Area Networks (LANs)

A LAN combines computer hardware and transmission media in a relatively small geographic area, typically not exceeding tens of kilometers. These systems are usually contained within a single department, building, or campus and often employ a single (typically bounded) transmission media type. While LANs are generally characterized by comparatively high-speed communications, MANs and WANs typically rely on unbound communications media, which equates to much slower speeds.

As you can see in Figure 18.2, LANs occupy a relatively small area. Generally, they include a relatively small number of machines, and all components connect directly to the communications media.

FIGURE 18.2

A local area network (LAN)

More than any other network model, LANs must successfully balance network hardware with network software. LAN hardware gives the system its processing, communications, system fault tolerance, and most importantly, connectivity. LAN software provides a system with productivity, user interface, network management, and most importantly, user transparency. The two most important components in a LAN are the file server(s) (hardware) and network operating system (software).

Metropolitan Area Networks (MANs)

A MAN is larger than a LAN and, as its name implies, covers the area of a single city. MANs rarely extend beyond 100 km and frequently comprise a combination of different hardware and transmission media. In addition, they have somewhat slower data communication rates than do LANs, in part, because of their reliance on unbound media over great distances.

The most important characteristic of MANs is their diversity. They are typically used when you need to connect dissimilar systems within a single metropolis. As you can see in Figure 18.3, we've connected bank, home, and work LANs into a single MAN.

FIGURE 18.3

A metropolitan area network (MAN)

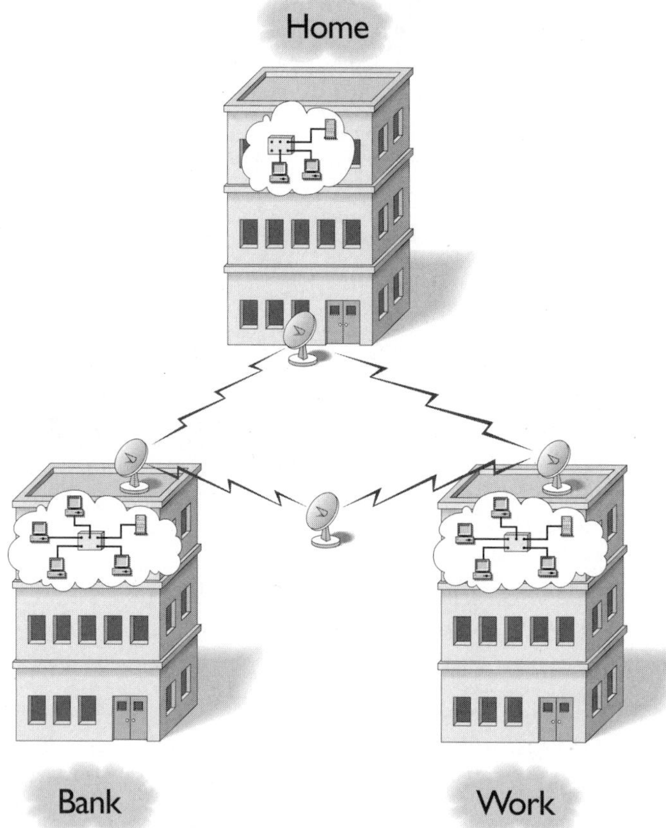

Two of the most important considerations associated with MANs are security and standardization. Security is important because information is being shared between dissimilar systems. Many users are still wary of MAN computing because of the sensitivity of their data. Standardization is necessary to ensure reliable data communications. Pretty soon, we'll all be enjoying the benefits of metropolitan area networking — such as cyber-universities and banking through your television.

Wide Area Networks (WANs)

A wide area network is simply a "LAN of LANs." WANs connect LANs that may be on opposite sides of a building, across the country, or around the world. Of the three network models, WANs, which often use telephone or satellite communications, are characterized by the slowest data communication rates and by covering the longest distances. Another benefit of WANs is that they can connect different types of networks together. For example, you can connect a centralized computing system (mainframe) with a distributed LAN. These connections frequently are made through a special type of device called a *gateway*.

As you can see in Figure 18.4, our WAN connects LANs from around the world.

FIGURE 18.4

A wide area network (WAN)

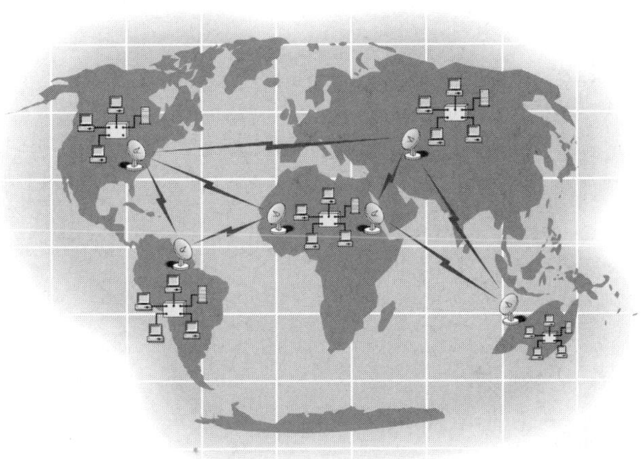

There are two special types of WANs:

- *Enterprise WANs* — An enterprise WAN connects an entire organization, including all LANs at various sites. This term is used for large, widespread organizations, such as corporations, universities, and governments. Even though the LANs may be in different parts of the country (or the world), they must all belong to a single company or institution. For example, the WAN in Figure 18.4 could represent Novell sales offices or branches of a global university.

- *Global WANs*—A global WAN can connect diverse locations, organizations, and institutions throughout the world. One of the most well-known examples of a global WAN is the Internet. A global WAN can be public or private. The Internet, for example, is a public global network, which means that anyone can attach to it from anywhere in the world. Private WANs are also available. For example, Novell and AT&T have signed an agreement to build a private global WAN. So, what will you get for your money? Stronger security, better management, and guaranteed connectivity. This private new WAN should provide an attractive solution for many organizations that fear the openness of the Internet.

As more networks are connected together, the current classifications may begin to disappear. Technological progress is expected to result in the development of a single computer networking infrastructure. Faster and cheaper data communications will transcend the need for LANs, MANs, and WANs. Who knows? We may end up with a single global LAN.

Network Management

A network manager's role is probably both the most excruciating and the most rewarding role involved in networks. While designers and installers move on to other systems, other designs, and new frontiers, you remain behind to manage the network on a daily basis.

Network management success hinges on three characteristics: network knowledge, management skills, and fire containment. You must fully understand the intricacies of your system, as well as being knowledgeable about networking upgrades, enhancements, and technical improvements that are available. You must also be sensitive to user issues and concerns; open to alternative configurations; and continually be in touch with the evolving relationships among users, groups, applications, and security. Finally, as a network administrator, you must develop precautionary guidelines for handling network crashes and create an effective procedure for calmly and rationally dealing with everyday system "brush fires."

If you dedicate a small amount of your daily time to developing the following management skills, your reign as a network administrator can be a long and fulfilling one:

- *Configuration Management*—Includes keeping track of changes to your network setup. This responsibility requires you to maintain a detailed record of historical, current, and proposed network configurations.

- *Fault Management*—Means "never having to say you're sorry." With adequate system fault tolerance and backup systems in place, you'll always have a contingency plan in case something goes wrong.

- *Performance Management*—A proactive strategy for collecting and interpreting performance measurements. Once this data has been gathered, you can attempt to enhance it through protocol and server optimization.

- *Security Management*—Used to minimize network risks. Security management protects data and equipment from internal and external intruders.

- *Accounting Management*—is the collection, interpretation, and use of network cost information. It involves budgets, cost allocation, charge-back systems, and planning for future growth.

So, that's what it means to be a network manager. Are you still interested? I knew you would be. So, let's take a brief peek at your future by exploring each of these five responsibilities, starting with configuration management.

Configuration Management

Configuration management starts with network documentation. Unfortunately, few areas of networking are as neglected as documentation. Good documentation helps you stay on top of your network. After all, as soon as you get your network working, things will probably change almost immediately. The only constant in networking is variation and transition. You should focus on the following areas as you develop your configuration management documentation:

- *Network Management Systems*—Help you gather and track the configuration data you need for documentation purposes

- *Documentation Elements*—Include the network, history and users, and resources

- *Change Order Management*—A method for tracking changes to the network and documentation elements

Let's take a closer look at these three critical aspects of configuration management.

Network Management Systems Network documentation can be a full-time job, so you'll need help gathering all your data. A network management system is a set of programs that integrate many management functions under a single interface. Many systems include problem detection and reporting capabilities. Along with fault management, a management system will often be capable of creating baseline data for making comparisons and for charting trends.

Network management systems may consist of software only, with some hardware requirements specified, or they may be implemented as a combination of hardware and software. Management systems are in transition right now. Management utility vendors are moving toward integrated management suites, which in turn are being integrated with infrastructure management programs, such as Hewlett-Packard's OpenView and Novell's ManageWise products. While ManageWise's forté is the world of NetWare, it is also quite capable of managing networks other than Novell's.

Documentation Elements Good network documentation incorporates a plethora of LAN/WAN statistics; far more than you can keep in the back of your mind. Even if you did memorize everything about the network, new team members and outside contractors would be unaware of these important facts.

Here are the three main aspects of network documentation:

- *The Network*—Information about the network represents the core of your documentation and provides details about several different aspects of both the physical and logical network. For example, you need to keep track of where everything is, how many components there are, how the components are related, and who uses them. Specifically, you must keep track of the following five components: physical maps, clients, servers, internetworking devices, and spares.

- *History and Users*—History teaches us much about the present and the future. A detailed and accurate record of a LAN's history can help you solve current problems and prevent future catastrophes. Nothing has more of an effect on current and future catastrophes than users. One of the most important aspects of LAN history is a full understanding of your business environment and the users who utilize it. A record of your company's purpose, its relationship to the LAN technology, and details about the business enterprise as a whole can serve you well in solving business-related problems. This area of network documentation focuses on three main concerns: LAN utilization, a general business model, and user data.

- *Resources*—Your network documentation should also include resources for configuration management. Network resource documentation can be organized into four categories: client data, special situations, networking concepts, and product knowledge. Such resources include vendor sales, BBS and tech support hotlines, fax-back numbers, a list of reliable consultants, frequently used telephone numbers, Web sites, and other technical support resources available within (and outside) your company. Resource documentation is usually easy to keep and maintain. You may find that the easiest way to store it is to create one or more ASCII files on a host file server.

Refer back to Chapter 12 for more information on network documentation elements. Now let's check out the third and final configuration management topic: change order management.

Change Order Management Change order management is an important aspect of configuration management. It involves keeping track of what you're doing to the network and the documentation. As a result, a Change Order Log forms the centerpiece of change order management.

Unfortunately, the process of maintaining a Change Order Log has become a lost art in most organizations. In many mainframe environments, however, maintaining a Change Order Log has been a standard procedure for many years. In these environments, it is simply unheard of to leave the office without recording what you did and why you did it.

The basic goals of a Change Order Log are to record trend information for systems and to monitor how problems (such as malfunctioning hardware) were fixed. It adds accountability to changes made to the network. Although the process of maintaining a Change Order Log never quite caught on in most LAN environments, you may find that it (along with regular system backups) may save your job when things go wrong.

Refer to Table 18.1 for the detailed elements of a sample Change Order Log.

TABLE 18.1

Elements of a Change Order Log

ITEM	COMMENTS
What	Start with a basic description of the change. This should be a quick description of the nature and scope of the work. It need not contain detailed information about all the steps performed.
Who	Indicate who did the work. If a problem results from a change, you may need to identify the person who made the change.
Why	Make a note of what motivated the change. Perhaps the goal was to eliminate a problem or to improve performance.
Where	Identify which components were involved. If a problem is detected on the network at a later date, you will need to know which components were changed or swapped, as well as their physical location.
When	Note when the work started and when it was completed. This information provides the scope for important changes.

This completes our discussion of configuration management. Do yourself a favor and pay close attention to your network configuration. More importantly, document it. Now let's take a look at the second network management topic: fault management.

Fault Management

To paraphrase a popular bumper sticker: Stuff Happens! Unfortunately, network "stuff" happens all too often. How well you handle yourself and the network at these times will set you apart from the crowd as a great network administrator. When you expertly manage the stuff that happens, you will be considered a champion proactive manager.

Fault management involves establishing systems and procedures to handle problems in a calm, organized manner. Three important skills are required for fault management: knowing how to identify faults quickly, knowing how to assign priorities to problems, and knowing how to respond to and fix problems. Here's what you'll need:

- *System Fault Tolerance (SFT)* — System fault tolerance (SFT) involves online redundancy. SFT hardware and/or software solutions are available from various vendors for many types of network equipment, such as power supplies, hard drives, disk controllers, memory, and total file server systems. When an SFT-protected device experiences the failure of one of its components, an online spare takes over quickly enough to maintain uninterrupted service. Your users probably won't even notice. SFT is ideal for keeping critical components running, thereby ensuring reliable network service. Remember, however, that no level of SFT can take the place of timely (and reliable) data backups.

- *Backup Systems* — It is amazing how many networks are not adequately protected by timely, reliable data backups. No matter how much SFT you've built into your network, these backups are still an absolute necessity.

- *Cable Testers* — Cable testers are electrical tools that are used to evaluate the electrical properties of a network segment. To use a cable tester, you must know the exact specifications for your network wiring system. For example, on a 10Base5 segment, the data travels at a rate of about 0.77 times the speed of light, which is the speed of propagation. Also, each segment must be terminated with two 50-ohm resistors, which results in 25 ohms of resistance when measured on the cable as a whole. A cable tester can be used to determine if the cable meets these specifications.

- *Data Recovery Tools* — Although NetWare has some excellent disk management and recovery features built into the operating system, you may sometimes need extra help from third-party data recovery tools and/or services.

REAL WORLD

Lost data can have a dramatic effect on the present and future success of your organization. Here are some sobering statistics about data loss:

- The average company will lose 2 to 3 percent of its gross annual sales within eight days of a sustained computer outage.
- The average company that sustains a computer outage lasting longer than ten days will never fully recover. Half of these companies will be out of business within five years.
- The chances of surviving a disaster affecting a corporate data processing center are less than 7 in 100. The chances of experiencing such a disaster are 1 in 100.

Performance Management

When users are asked how fast a network should be, they always answer, "Just a little faster." Users measure network performance in response time — how fast can they log in, launch an application, and print a report. How well a network performs is based partly on identifying bottlenecks. Managing network performance means creating baseline reports of errors and throughput, looking at program response times, estimating future needs, and finding ways to keep users satisfied. Several tools and techniques are available to help us with these tasks.

Following is a brief description of some of the most useful performance-management protocol-analysis tools:

- *LANalyzer for Windows (LZFW)* — Novell's LANalyzer for Windows (LZFW) is a software-based protocol analyzer that enables you to monitor and record the frames and packets being sent on a network. LZFW is capable of reading and interpreting information for NetWare, TCP/IP, AppleTalk, ODI, and other protocols, which we'll discuss in depth in upcoming chapters. LZFW works with the ODI protocol stack and can run on most network interface cards. Refer to Chapter 17 for more details on performance management using LZFW.

- *LANalyzer from NCC*—LANalyzer from Network Communications Corporation (NCC) was one of the first available protocol analyzers. Novell developed it but later sold it to NCC. It uses custom-developed software that requires specialized network interface cards. LANalyzer from NCC can record data and decode frames sent on the segment to which the device is attached, measure bandwidth utilization, and filter data selectively by address or protocol. It can also test the physical media for errors. LANalyzer's traffic-generation capabilities are especially useful. For example, a skilled operator can make the LANalyzer generate a certain level of traffic and then measure the number of errors the line experiences.

- *Sniffer*—Network General's Sniffer product is a high-end hardware-based network analysis tool that is able to read and decode a wide array of protocols. This high-priced performance management tool is a combination of analytical software and specialized adapters all in one.

Now that you have your network performing at optimal levels, it's time to shift your focus to security management.

Security Management

Security management protects your network from external and internal threats. Believe it or not, some of the most dangerous threats are internal and unintentional. Intentional harm also happens, although not as often. It usually sneaks in through vulnerable spots in the network. Security management involves implementing procedures to protect against both accidental and intentional harm. In the realm of computer security, three basic levels of threat exist:

- *Operational Security*—Operational security governs user behavior toward organizational resources, particularly computer data. Even the tightest physical and logical security can be rendered useless by an authorized user's careless behavior. Operational security standards can be designed by the personnel department and/or the networking group, but it is up to your users to implement them properly. For example, you can designate the types of documents that may be printed, document disposal procedures, and the type of data that is allowed to be copied and taken home. Good operational security is ensured only by proper training and user cooperation.

- *Physical Security* — Many people incorrectly believe that NetWare security is so good that you don't need to worry about physical security. If an intruder gains access to your server keyboard, however, he or she can cause much damage. Today's CPUs are so small and compact that intruders can even walk off with them. You should consider hiding your server in a secure, well-ventilated room; marking all machines with silent alarms; and implementing standard procedures for repairing and removing equipment.
- *Logical Security* — Logical security involves passwords, file system rights, server console privileges, and restrictions on network use.

That is security management in a nutshell. Remember, data is valuable, and that's where accounting management comes in.

Accounting Management

Accounting management involves tracking usage of network resources, discerning which parties use which resources, and charting trends. Accounting management helps you accomplish several tasks. First, you can find out how much of a network's total capacity is being used, which lets you plan for the future growth. Second, you can see who is doing what. Perhaps one department's use of disk space is increasing, while another's is relatively flat in terms of storage requirements. This information can have a profound effect on requests for additional funds for new disks. Finally, regardless of who is charged what, accounting data yields good information about how a network is being used and which resources are justifiable.

Most major network architectures have facilities for implementing network accounting. The data collected may include connect time, disk storage, CPU time, packets sent and received, WAN time use, specific programs accessed, and more. New third-party programs have emerged that enable you to assign costs to various network services, such as application usage, and then track the service's cost. In general, accounting management can help you with the following:

- *Budget and Cost Allocation* — When a budget is put together, the networking group submits its requirements for the coming fiscal year. Granted, some expenditures can be estimated without historical accounting data, but cost allocation can be most fairly estimated by referring to past use of resources.

- *Charge-Back Systems*—In some organizations, the network group is on its own and is not allocated a budget, per se. Instead, the group must fend for itself by charging for its services, as though it were an outside vendor. Implementing an accounting system in this architecture enables you to charge fairly for the general use of the network. Some third-party metering and auditing programs can print charge-back reports and invoices, which saves you time.
- *Unplanned Purchases*—Budgets are estimates. They estimate needs for a given fiscal period, but these estimates don't always cover unexpected failures or additions. Someone must pay for the added expense. Accounting management enables you to look at a given purchase and either charge the party who used it the most or fairly distribute the cost among the various network service users, based upon their usage statistics.
- *Planning for Growth*—Accounting also can help to quantify network service used and demanded. The nonfinancial uses for accounting data are limited only by your own creativity.

This completes our discussion of network management. Next, we will dive into the center of computer networking by discussing network elements.

Network Elements

Network elements represent the framework of LANs and WANs. These elements include physical cabling, data signals, LAN protocols, and network services. Network elements are further organized by the OSI model (discussed in the next section, "The OSI Model"). Following is a list of the three main network elements (refer to Figure 18.5):

- *Communications (What)*—The communications pathway is the road on which a network message travels. Service requesters and service providers communicate with each other over this framework. In addition, a third classification acts as both a client and a server. It is called a *peer.* Physical communications deal with transmission media, devices, network structures, and data signals. Logical communications expand on this framework by providing media access methods, physical addressing, frame synchronization, flow control, and error checking. In Chapter 19, we will explore the principles of physical and logical communications in great depth.

- *Networking (How)* — The communications medium provides a pathway for the message, but it doesn't guarantee that the two machines will understand each other. Networking protocols provide two primary functions: internetworking and transportation. *Internetworking* defines the rules for moving data from Point A to Point B. These rules cover the network path, logical addressing, switching, routing, and network control. *Transportation* enhances internetworking by organizing datagrams into segments and delivering them reliably to service requesters. Networking transportation consists of service addressing and transport control. In Chapters 20 and 21, we will explore networking protocols (such as TCP/IP and IPX) in great depth.

- *Services (Who)* — Network services are the "things networks can do." Using a combination of hardware and software, network computers provide you with a variety of services, including data storage and retrieval, printing, communications, and messaging. Network services has two main service elements: service providers (servers) and service requesters (clients). In Chapter 22, we will explore the details of network services (including the four most popular implementations: SNA, Digital Network Architecture [DNA], AppleTalk, and Directory Services).

FIGURE 18.5

Understanding network elements

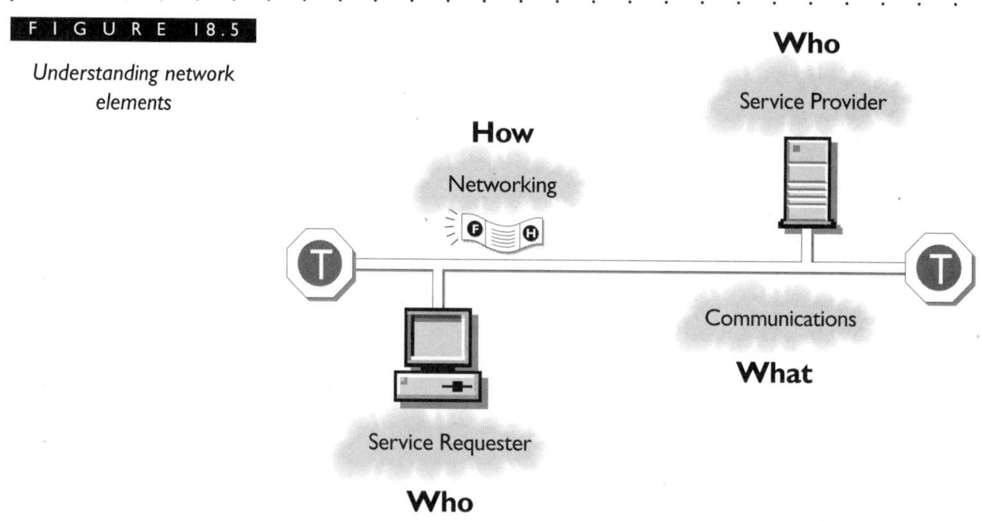

The OSI Model

The wealth of technologies encompassing computer networking have been classified and organized by function into a seven-layer architecture called the *OSI model* (also known as the Open Systems Interconnection Reference Model, or OSI Reference Model). This sophisticated map, which was developed by the International Standards Organization (ISO), lays down a framework for communication between network elements.

The OSI model has become a standard through which all networking standards operate, including NetWare IPX/SPX, TCP/IP, Systems Network Architecture (SNA), and AppleTalk. It also sets the standards for communications syntax and grammar. Without these rules, no common reference point for connectivity between diverse platforms would exist. This level of interoperability between different products and technologies is the primary function of the OSI model.

In this section, we will preview the OSI model's seven-layer architecture and introduce its three functional segments: communications, networking, and services. Then, in the next four chapters, we will drill down into each segment and explore various technologies, standards, and implementations.

OSI Model Architecture

The task of handling communication between two completely different computer platforms may seem a little overwhelming, but it becomes easier to manage if you break down the task into subtasks. The OSI model relies on a seven-layer framework that divides the process of networking into unique and functional subtasks. Each layer performs its role independently from the others, but in coordination with the overall goal of communications translation.

As you can see in Figure 18.6, the OSI model starts at the Physical Layer (Layer 1) and works its way up to the Application Layer (Layer 7). As the networking message travels up and down the OSI model, each layer manipulates it in a specific way.

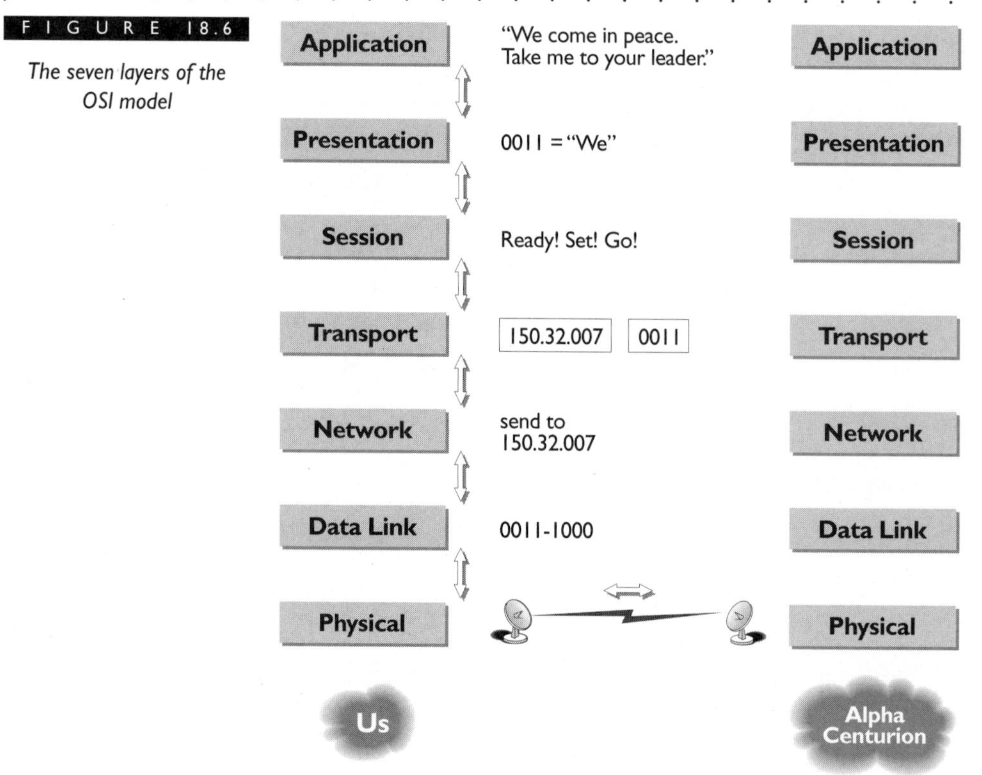

FIGURE 18.6

The seven layers of the OSI model

Following is a brief communications summary of the function of each layer of the OSI model (follow along in Figure 18.6):

- *Physical Layer*—The first step is for both computing platforms to agree on a common communications medium. The Physical Layer defines the basic electronic format of the message and communicates using units of information called *bits*.
- *Data Link Layer*—Next, the computers organize the physical zeros and ones into words. The Data Link Layer establishes a syntax and grammar for the message and uses units of information called *frames*.
- *Network Layer*—Next, the system must find a way for the message to travel from one computer to the other (also known as *routing*). The Network Layer routes units of information called *datagrams*.

- *Transport Layer*—Before the source machine can send the message, it must package it with correct coordinates and details about how to translate the data. The Transport Layer uses *segments* to ensure end-to-end reliability.
- *Session Layer*—Finally, the two computers open the lines of communication and exchange information as *messages*. The Session Layer controls the dialog between communicating systems.
- *Presentation Layer*—Once the receiving machine accepts the message, it must translate it into a native format for processing. At the Presentation Layer, the message is converted into a format that the receiving computer can understand.
- *Application Layer*—The Application Layer provides access to the network's shared services.

As you can see in Figure 18.6, communication between layers in the OSI model occurs vertically. The only layer that makes actual contact with any other device is the Physical Layer. This is how the zeros and ones are exchanged. Interlayer communications occur within the OSI model using *headers* (the administrative information added to the front of the packet) and *footers* (the administrative information added to the back of the packet).

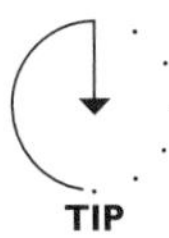

Mnemonics can be used to remember the order of the OSI model's seven layers. Some of my favorites include "Please Do Not Throw Sausage Pizza Away" and "Please Do Not Take Sales People's Advice." In the reverse order, try these: "All People Seem To Need Data Processing" and "All People Should Try Nice Dreams Periodically."

We will study OSI technologies, protocols, and implementations using the following three functional segments (see Figure 18.7):

- *Communications*—The bottom Physical Layer and Data Link Layer are responsible for defining the electronic communications pathway and formatting the message.

- *Networking* — The middle Networking Layer and Transport Layer are responsible for routing messages reliably from sending devices to one or more receivers.

- *Services* — The top Session Layer, Presentation Layer, and Application Layer are responsible for managing the lines of communications and coupling messages with appropriate network services.

FIGURE 18.7

Network elements and the OSI model

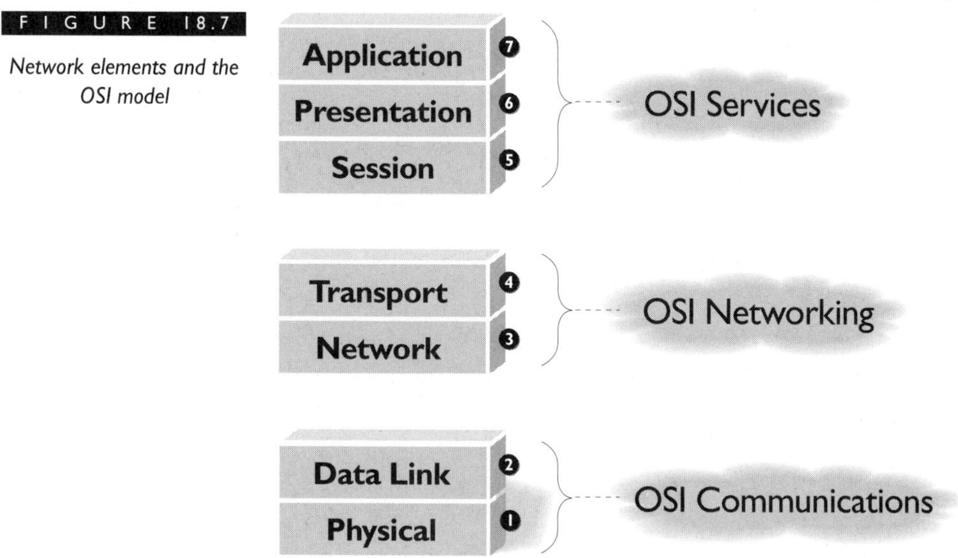

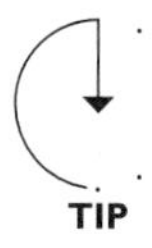

Study the architecture of the OSI model carefully. Specifically, learn the primary function of each of the seven layers: Physical (electronic communication of bits), Data Link (formatting bits into frames), Network (routing datagrams), Transport (reliable end-to-end delivery of segments), Session (dialog control of messages), Presentation (translation of messages), and Application (delivery of messages to appropriate network services).

OSI Communications: The Bottom Layers

The first functional segment involves the bottom two layers of the OSI model:

- Physical Layer
- Data Link Layer

The Physical Layer defines the pathway for electronic communications. The Data Link Layer organizes the physical bits into logical words. Let's take a closer look.

Physical Layer

The Physical Layer handles low-level rules for transmitting bits. This layer encodes or decodes bits, and sends or receives the stream of data. The Physical Layer defines the following:

- Electrical properties
- Transmission media
- Transmission devices
- Physical topology
- Data signaling
- Data synchronization
- Data bandwidth

Electrical properties define rules for how a message travels over *transmission media,* which then create bound or unbound pathways for the transmission of bits. *Transmission devices* provide midpoints and functionality to the transmission media. They are the raw implementation tools. *Physical topologies* provide form and function. They are defined by connection types and geographic arrangements of network nodes.

Data signaling encompasses coding and timing rules for digital and analog communications. These rules govern how data is encoded at the sender and decoded at the receiver. *Data synchronization* defines one of two states for an electronic message: asynchronous or synchronous. Finally, *data bandwidth* defines the capacity of transmission media, which determines the communications methodology and transmission speed. Most LANs use baseband communications, whereas WANs operate in the broadband arena.

Data Link Layer

The Data Link Layer organizes physical bits into logical groups called frames. A *frame* is a contiguous series of bits grouped together as a unit of data. The Data Link Layer also detects, and sometimes corrects, errors. It controls data flow and identifies computers on the network through physical addressing. The Data Link Layer is organized into two sublayers:

- Media Access Control (MAC)
- Logical Link Control (LLC)

The MAC sublayer defines media access protocols and physical addressing. *Media access protocols* define how the network functions, not how it looks. These protocols use logical topologies and communication rules. Examples include contention, token passing, and polling protocols. Next, *physical addressing* provides a physical identification scheme for network devices.

The LLC sublayer governs frame synchronization, Data Link flow control, and error checking. *Frame synchronization* enhances bit synchronization by coordinating frame transmissions. Just as with data synchronization, frame synchronization uses asynchronous or synchronous communications. *Flow control* regulates how much data the receiving station can handle. Finally, *error checking* is concerned with the integrity of the data frame.

That's it for the bottom layers of the OSI model. Figure 18.8 summarizes OSI Communications. Notice the functions that occur at each layer. We will explore each of these functions in greater depth in Chapter 19.

The bottom two layers of the OSI model manifest themselves in the following communication implementations: SONET/SDH, SLIP/PPP, IEEE 802 series, FDDI, and frame relay.

FIGURE 18.8

Overview of OSI Communications

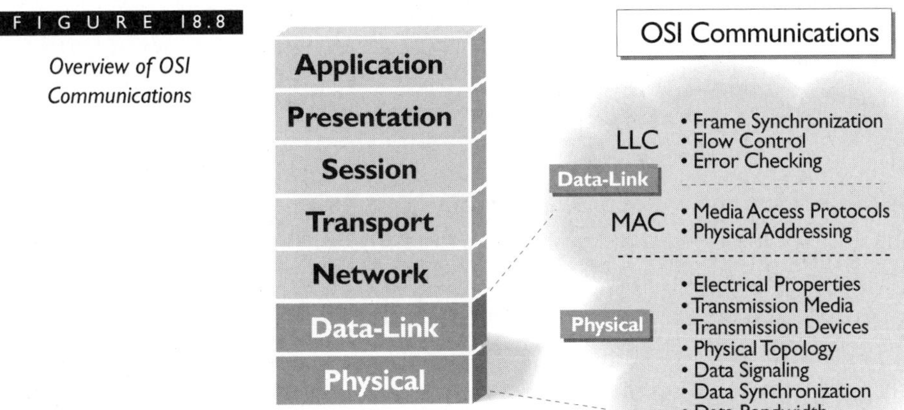

OSI Networking: The Middle Layers

The next two layers of the OSI model are concerned with getting the frames from Point A to Point B, all in one piece. Remember that each layer of the OSI model performs its role independent of the other layers. Therefore, OSI Networking is not concerned with what a message looks like or the electronic path it takes. This part of the model is concerned only with getting a message where it's going. This networking function is handled by two layers:

- Network Layer
- Transport Layer

The Network Layer handles internetworking and routing. This is the primary layer for moving data from Point A to Point B. The Transport Layer supports this function by organizing datagrams into segments and reliably delivering them to upper-layer services. Let's take a closer look.

Network Layer

The Network Layer is concerned primarily with moving data from Network A to Network B. Specifically, the Network Layer has the following four functions:

- Logical addressing

- Switching
- Routing
- Network control

Logical addressing helps determine a logical path during internetwork communications and combines with physical addressing to seek out destination devices. *Switching* strategies enable datagrams to move across a network in different ways, although the ultimate path is controlled by routing. *Routing* uses two strategies (route discovery and selection) to move datagrams across LANs and WANs. Finally, *network control* provides flow control, sequencing, and translation.

Transport Layer

The Transport Layer organizes datagrams into segments and provides reliable end-to-end delivery to upper-layer services. If segments are not delivered to the destination correctly by the Network Layer, transport functions come to the rescue. The OSI Transport Layer consists of the following components:

- Service addressing
- Segmentation
- Transport control

Service addressing provides a doorway to upper-layer services. The Transport Layer uses connection IDs, ports, and sockets to ensure that messages find the correct destination service. *Segmentation* is a housekeeping task that packages messages into acceptable sizes. Finally, *transport control* provides error checking and flow control.

That's it for the middle layers of the OSI model. Figure 18.9 summarizes OSI Networking. Notice the functions that occur at each layer. We will explore each of these functions in greater depth in Chapter 20.

The middle two layers of the OSI model manifest themselves in the following networking implementations: Internet TCP/IP, NetWare IPX/SPX, ATM/SMDS, ISDN/B-ISDN, and X.25.

FIGURE 18.9
Overview of OSI Networking

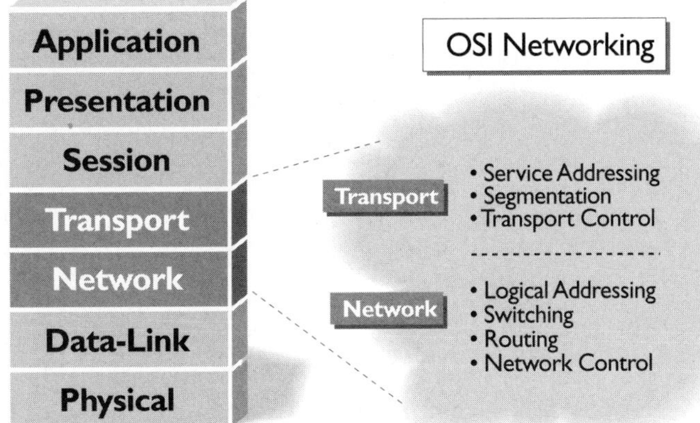

OSI Services: The Top Layers

The third functional segment involves the top three layers of the OSI model:

- Session Layer
- Presentation Layer
- Application Layer

The Session Layer opens a dialog between the sender and receiver. This is the control center for ongoing communications. The Presentation Layer helps translate the message if it uses a different syntax or if encryption is involved. Finally, the Application Layer is the message. Let's take a closer look.

Session Layer

The Session Layer controls the lines of communications by opening and closing networking dialogs. This layer often helps network services find each other and connect using the following three steps:

- *Step 1:* Connection Establishment
- *Step 2:* Data Transfer
- *Step 3:* Connection Release

Connection establishment initiates the dialog between two systems using networking protocols (to find a dialog path) and communications media (to send messages back and forth). During the *data transfer* step, the Session Layer manages the dialog and ensures reliable conversations through simplex, half-duplex, or duplex transmissions. Finally, *connection release* ends the dialog and closes the connection.

Once the session dialog has been opened and data transfer has begun, we can move our focus to the Presentation Layer.

Presentation Layer

The Presentation Layer is the OSI model translator. It transforms the message into a mutually agreed-upon format. At this point in the model, the dialog is open and data transfer has begun, but before the Application Layer can read the message, it must be translated and decrypted. The Presentation Layer has two main tasks:

- Translation
- Encryption

Translation is the Presentation Layer's main purpose. Translation is needed when two systems that speak different languages try to communicate. Translation can occur in any of the following ways: bit order, byte order, character code, and/or file syntax. *Encryption* adds security for sensitive data and operating systems. One example is public/private key-pair and authentication in NetWare 5.1.

Application Layer

The Application Layer is at the top of the OSI model. It uses special networking protocols to provide file, print, message, application, and database services. The Application Layer performs the following two important tasks:

- Service advertisement
- Service availability

Service advertisement enables other systems (and users) to know what services are available. Providers use active or passive techniques to define the scope of their network services. *Service availability* provides access to a network service once the requester has chosen one. Service availability can be provided using OS call interception, remote operation, and/or collaborative computing.

That's it for the top layers of the OSI model. Figure 18.10 summarizes OSI Services. Notice the functions that occur at each layer. We will explore each of these functions in greater depth at the end of the book in Chapter 22.

FIGURE 18.10

Overview of OSI Services

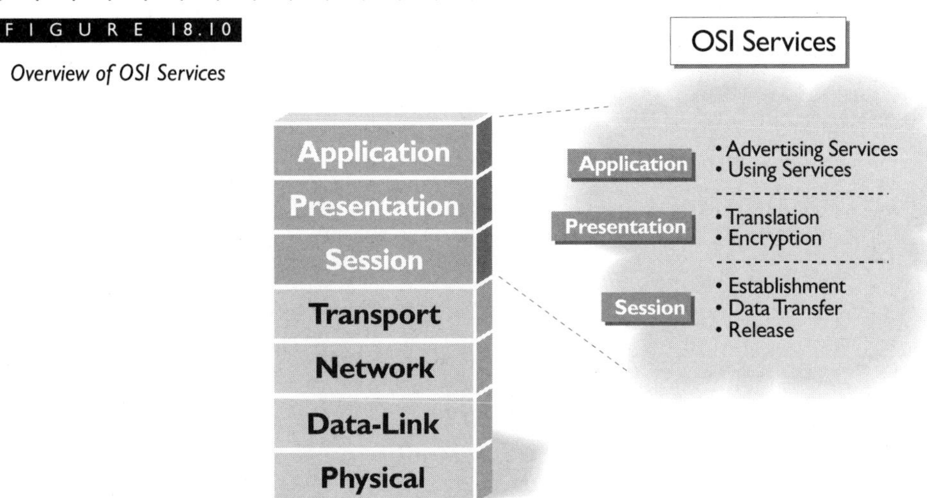

The top three layers of the OSI model manifest themselves in numerous service implementations, including the following: SNA, DNA, AppleTalk, X.500, and Lightweight Directory Access Protocol (LDAP).

This completes our summary of OSI Communications, Networking, and Services. In this section, we've learned the details of the OSI model and were introduced to its seven layers. Remember, this is just an introduction. We'll learn a lot more about the OSI model in the next four chapters.

But there's more to computer networking than the OSI model. In this chapter, we learned that networking consists of three main components:

- Network models
- Network management
- Network elements

Network elements may be the core of networking, but we can't overlook the importance of models or management. Network models enable us to classify networks according to size and function. LANs, MANs, and WANs give us insight into the relationships among distributed networking systems. Similarly, network management helps us deal with important relationships within our own network. As a network administrator, network management will be one of your most important responsibilities.

So, even though we're going to spend most of our time learning about network elements, you'll want to keep network models and network management in mind, as well. They will help you keep things in perspective.

This completes our preview chapter. Now you're ready to journey into the center of computer networking. Of course, you won't be alone. You'll have me as your trusted guide, and the 3-D OSI map will show us the way.

In the next four chapters, we're going to explore every nook and cranny of OSI Communications, Networking, and Services. This is a monumental journey for the future of human communications, and judging from our past, we could use a few monuments. So, without any further ado . . .

Warp speed ahead!

LAB EXERCISE 18.1: INTRODUCTION TO THE OSI

Match each of the numbered items with the OSI model layer with which it is associated.

A. Physical
B. Data Link
C. Network
D. Transport
E. Session
F. Presentation
G. Application

1. ____ Encryption
2. ____ Physical addressing
3. ____ User interface
4. ____ Routing
5. ____ Connection release
6. ____ Coaxial cable
7. ____ Logical addressing
8. ____ Data compression
9. ____ LLC sublayer
10. ____ Network services
11. ____ Data signals
12. ____ Data transfer
13. ____ Data sequencing
14. ____ Service advertisement
15. ____ Dialog synchronization
16. ____ Frame synchronization
17. ____ Segmentation
18. ____ Translation
19. ____ Internetworking
20. ____ Reliable delivery of datagrams
21. ____ Token Ring
22. ____ RS232 serial communications
23. ____ Establishing a dialog
24. ____ Gateways
25. ____ Network structures

See Appendix C for answers.

LAB EXERCISE 18.2: UNDERSTANDING COMPUTER

Use the hints provided to find the 20 networking terms hidden in this word search puzzle. Omit any punctuation characters (such as blank spaces, hyphens, and so on) and spell out any numbers.

P	P	N	E	T	W	O	R	K	M	O	D	E	L	S	O	G	V
E	E	E	W	D	D	I	S	T	R	I	B	U	T	E	D	K	V
R	E	T	O	O	F	O	E	I	M	R	M	M	D	J	O	A	P
F	R	W	G	S	B	A	C	K	U	P	S	Y	S	T	E	M	S
O	C	O	N	F	I	G	U	R	A	T	I	O	N	Q	N	D	D
R	O	R	P	P	F	Z	R	L	N	G	H	Y	K	V	H	Y	S
M	M	K	C	D	A	C	I	R	T	U	X	R	D	U	F	M	B
A	M	L	L	H	H	A	T	V	D	X	P	U	G	V	O	F	Q
N	U	A	Y	L	S	V	Y	K	C	A	B	E	G	R	A	H	C
C	N	E	T	W	O	R	K	S	E	R	V	I	C	E	S	E	H
E	I	Q	B	I	X	Z	M	S	T	N	C	N	Y	J	N	A	A
I	C	S	S	T	B	K	I	M	P	A	Z	L	Y	T	F	D	N
Y	A	I	E	L	U	G	G	P	Y	F	O	J	R	R	C	E	G
U	T	A	C	C	O	U	N	T	I	N	G	A	H	F	B	R	E
S	I	E	V	L	I	S	W	W	D	M	L	K	D	G	W	F	O
Y	O	E	C	V	P	V	S	Y	R	I	T	P	U	C	D	C	R
B	N	R	P	Y	O	Y	R	O	Z	U	Y	D	H	K	H	D	D
R	S	J	W	X	N	G	N	E	T	W	O	R	K	I	N	G	E
O	J	K	P	W	O	M	D	M	S	Y	I	G	F	G	K	I	R

Hints

1. Network management area that deals with the collection and interpretation of network cost information.
2. Murphy's Law insurance.
3. Computing model where a central mainframe handles 100 percent of the overall processing load.

4. Management aspect of Configuration Management that involves keeping track of what you're doing to the network and documentation.
5. Type of accounting system that is useful for a department that must fend for itself by charging for its services, as though it were an outside vendor.
6. Bottom two layers of the OSI model (*what* computers use for network data transmission).
7. Management area whose primary goal is to maintain a detailed record of historical, current, and proposed network configurations.
8. Computing model where the central server handles relatively little of the overall processing load.
9. Network management area that deals with diagnosing, testing, and repairing network failures.
10. Added to the back of a packet at each level of the OSI model.
11. Added to the front of a packet at each level of the OSI model.
12. A collection of distributed, intelligent machines that share data and services through interconnected lines of communication.
13. Classifies networks by size, distance, and structure.
14. Common ones include file services, print services, and messaging.
15. Middle two layers of the OSI model (*how* computers communicate).
16. Famous Reference Model.
17. A service requester or provider.
18. Network management area that involves attempting to improve the speed and efficiency of the network.
19. Network management area that includes any action necessary to protect your network data and equipment.
20. Top three layers of the OSI model (*who* requests and provides the network data).

See Appendix C for answers.

LAB EXERCISE 18.3: THE OSI MODEL

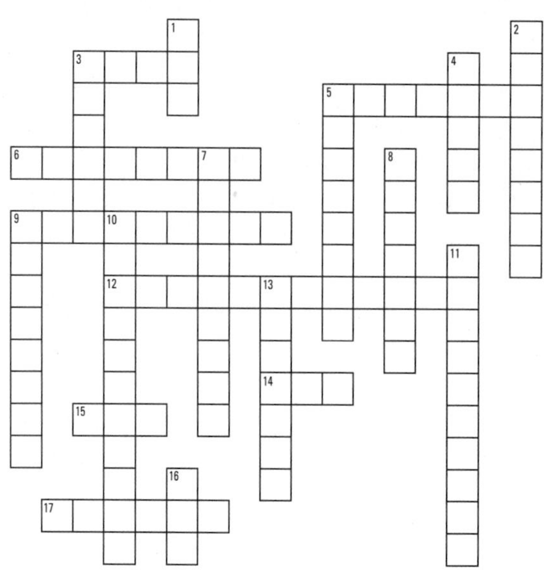

Across

3. Messages at the Physical Layer
5. Messages at the Network layer
6. Messages at the Transport Layer
9. Packets at the Network Layer
12. Layer 6 of the OSI model
14. A LAN of LANs
15. Your domain as a CNE
17. A large, interorganizational WAN

Down

1. Developers of the OSI model
2. Packets at the Session Layer
3. Expense estimate
4. Number of layers in the OSI model
5. Layer 1 of the OSI model
7. Layer 4 of the OSI model

8. Layer 5 of the OSI model
9. Layer 2 of the OSI model
10. Layer 7 of the OSI model
11. A WAN within a single organization
13. Layer 3 of the OSI model
16. A metropolitan group of LANs

See Appendix C for answers.

CHAPTER 19

The OSI Model — Bottom Layers

Welcome to the first functional domain of computer networking!

This region deals with networking communications. It covers the bottom two layers of the 3-D Open Systems Interconnection (OSI) reference map. As we learned in Chapter 18, network elements are the third phase of networking. They define the *what, how,* and *who* of networking technologies. In the communications domain, we will explore the *what.*

From the beginning of time, communications has been the goal of networking. Computers communicate with each other through a variety of media including coax, twisted-pair, and fiber optics. These media also use different data signaling methods and transmission devices. Communications forms the pavement of our information superhighway.

According to the OSI map (see Figure 19.1), the following are the bottom two functional layers:

- The Physical Layer
- The Data Link Layer

FIGURE 19.1

Understanding OSI Communications

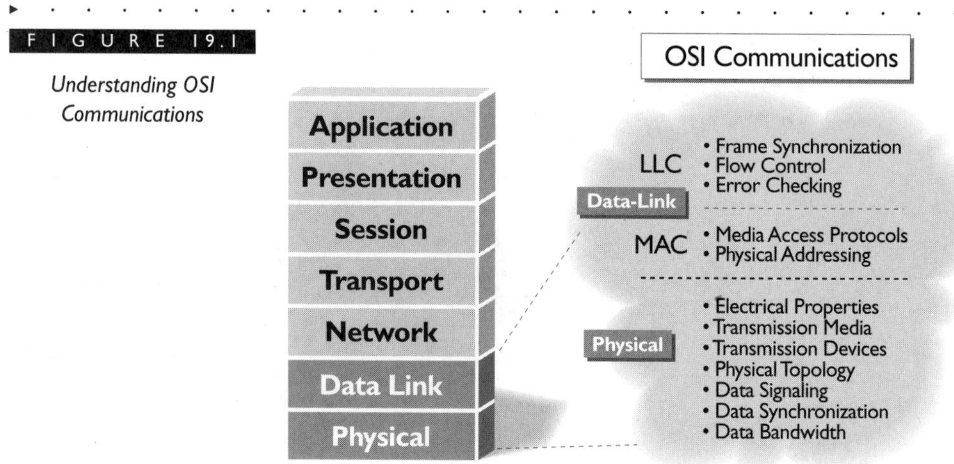

The *Physical Layer* defines a communications pathway for networking messages. This pathway includes the transmission media and devices, physical topology, and data signaling required for silicon chitchat. Once the pathway has been established, the bits are organized into a data frame. The *Data Link Layer* handles this responsibility through two critical sublayers — Media-Access Control (MAC) and Logical-Link Control (LLC). The MAC sublayer defines a channel access method and a physical addressing scheme, whereas that LLC sublayer provides flow control and error checking.

Let's begin our exciting communications journey by exploring the first two layers of the OSI Model — the Physical and Data Link Layers. Don't worry, we'll cover the other five layers in Chapters 20, 21, and22.

The Physical Layer

The Physical Layer of the OSI model defines rules for transmitting bits. This includes the rules for physical network structures, mechanical and electrical specifications for using the transmission medium, and bit transmission encoding and timing rules. The Physical Layer encompasses the following seven networking technologies:

- *Electrical Properties* — Define rules for how networking data travels over transmission media.
- *Transmission Media* — Creates cable or wireless pathways for the transmission of bits.
- *Transmission Devices* — Communication components that control the data as it travels over transmission media.
- *Physical Topology* — Provides form and function to a network. Physical topologies are defined by different connection methods and by different physical arrangements of networking nodes. Common topology choices include bus, star, ring, and cellular.

- *Data Signaling*—Encompasses coding and timing rules for digital and analog communications. These rules govern how service requesters and network hosts receive data bits.
- *Data Synchronization*—Defines one of two states for an electronic message: asynchronous or synchronous.
- *Data Bandwidth*—Capacity of transmission media. Data bandwidth determines the communications methodology and the transmission speed. Most LANs use baseband communications, whereas WANs use broadband transmissions.

This is going to be a long and exciting journey, and I can't think of a better place to start than at the beginning—electrical properties.

Electrical Properties

It is important to be familiar with the effects of the following electrical properties and to be familiar with how these electrical properties influence network communication:

- *Resistance*—This is the opposition your cable offers to the passage of direct current (DC). The net effect of resistance is a drop in the voltage of electricity that is traveling through a wire.
- *Impedance*—This is the same as resistance, except that it measures opposition to alternating current (AC) rather than to DC. Impedance and resistance both are measured in *ohms* (denoted by the Greek omega symbol, Ω). DC signals travel through a wire's core; high-frequency AC signals travel on a wire's surface. And because most modern LANs run at high frequencies (5 MHz and higher), using bigger wires does not offer better throughput.

- *Capacitance*—This is the measure of an object's capacity to hold a charge. Refer to Figure 19.2, which shows a graph of electrical potential over time, where most digital communications appear as even squares. As capacitance increases, the nice square waves start to look like ocean waves. This rounding effect can result in data errors. Fortunately, most LAN components (such as cables, outlets, and patch panels) are usually designed to have as little capacitance as possible.

- *Noise*—This is another electrical property that can alter the square wave of digital communications. In general, noise is a common term for radio frequency interference (RFI) and/or electromagnetic interference (EMI). In Figure 19.2, noise causes the square communications wave to become fuzzy, which can alter the signal enough to create data errors. Noise can be caused by fluorescent lights, electrical equipment, arc welders, transformers, lightning, the power company, and anything else that creates a significant electrical field.

- *Attenuation*—This is the reduction of signal strength as electric currents pass through cable. Attenuation is the result of capacitance, resistance, impedance, or other characteristics of a wire. Typically, attenuation is measured in decibels per thousand feet (dB/Kft). In Figure 19.2, you will notice that the signal degrades over time.

- *Crosstalk*—Current creates a magnetic field around cable. Other wires nearby then absorb some of that magnetic field, creating a reverse current. Because the current that leaks from one pair of wires into another is not the data itself, crosstalk is simply an advanced form of noise.

- *Propagation*—The nominal velocity of propagation (NVP) is a measure of how fast data can travel over a particular type of cable. LAN cabling typically has an NVP between 0.78 and 0.95. This means that data travels through cabling at 78 percent to 95 percent the speed of light (that is, of the speed of light in a vacuum). Networking propagation impacts both speed and cabling distance requirements.

FIGURE 19.2

Fundamentals of electrical properties

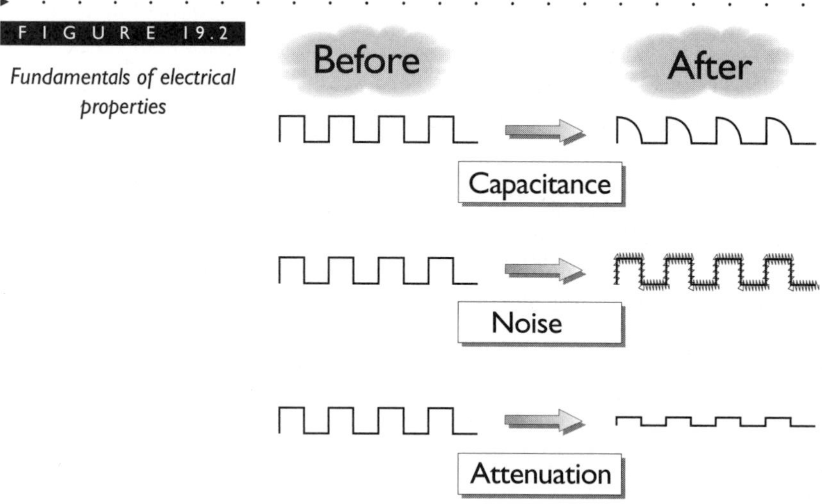

So, there you have it—that's electricity in a nutshell. Don't you feel smarter already? You should, because your brain relies on the same electrical principles that we just discussed. Now that you understand the fundamentals of electronic communications, let's take a closer look at the paths over which they travel. Let's explore the second technology of the Physical Layer—transmission media.

Transmission Media

Transmission media provide the physical path through which data and electric currents flow. At the Physical Layer, network data is represented as binary zeros and ones. As you can see in Figure 19.3, the electromagnetic (EM) spectrum defines electronic communication vehicles from power and telephone lines to gamma rays. These vehicles provide a wide range of communications solutions.

Transmission media are organized into two categories:

- *Cable Media*—Cable transmission media consist of a central conductor surrounded by a physical jacket. This configuration offers advantages in security, reliability, and speed—which makes cable media ideal for LANs. Following are the four primary cable media available for network communications: unshielded twisted-pair (UTP), shielded twisted-pair (STP), coaxial, and fiber optics.

FIGURE 19.3

The electromagnetic spectrum

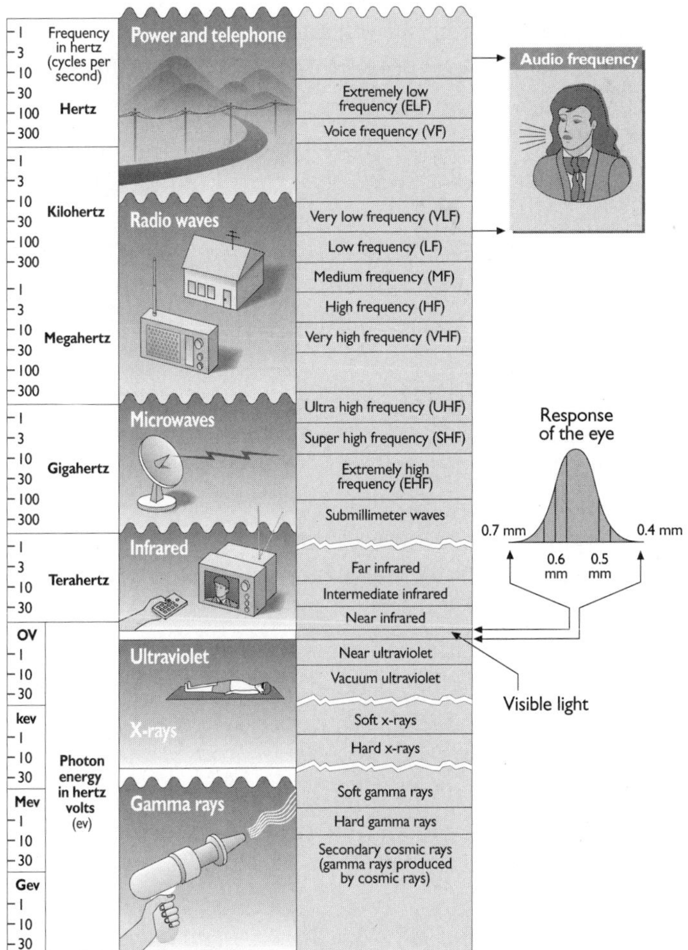

- *Wireless Media* — Wireless transmission media extend beyond the limiting confines of cabling. They provide an excellent communications alternative for WANs. The inherent lack of physical restrictions provides larger bandwidth, as well as wide-area capabilities. These properties make it possible for geographically diverse LANs to communicate with one another on a real-time basis. Following are three primary wireless media available for network communications: radio waves, microwave, and infrared.

Each transmission medium discussed in this section has certain characteristics that distinguish it from the other transmission media. For example, UTP is easy to install, but highly susceptible to EMI. In contrast, fiber optics is difficult to install, but immune to EMI. Therefore, UTP works best in small, clean environments, whereas fiber optics is a better solution for large, noisy networks. As you consider the advantages and disadvantages of each transmission medium, focus on the following five factors:

- *Cost* — The medium you choose will directly affect your network's performance — so you will need to balance performance against cost.
- *Ease of Installation* — Ease of installation affects cost and performance. Complex cabling installations cost more and will experience performance problems if the installation was not performed properly.
- *Capacity* — The capacity of a particular transmission medium is often stated in terms of bandwidth, which is the range of frequencies supported in cycles per second (Hz). Bandwidth measurements are subjective because a medium's capacity varies with changes in distance and also varies depending upon the signaling techniques used. Therefore, we will measure capacity in bits per second (bps). This is a better measurement because it factors in all electrical properties.
- *Attenuation* — Similarly, attenuation is important because it defines the distance limitations of a network, given its capacity.
- *Immunity from EMI* — Electromagnetic interference (EMI) can have a profound effect on network reliability because it has a negative effect on network data as it travels along the medium.

Now let's begin our in-depth comparison with the first of four cable media: unshielded twisted-pair.

Unshielded Twisted-Pair (UTP)

Unshielded twisted-pair (UTP) cabling consists of two or more insulated copper wires twisted around each other. UTP typically uses 22–26 gauge copper in an insulated jacket (see Figure 19.4). Note that UTP is not shielded against EMI. That's what the twists are for: Twisting reduces crosstalk, but it does not protect the cable from EMI like STP does.

FIGURE 19.4

Unshielded twisted-pair cabling

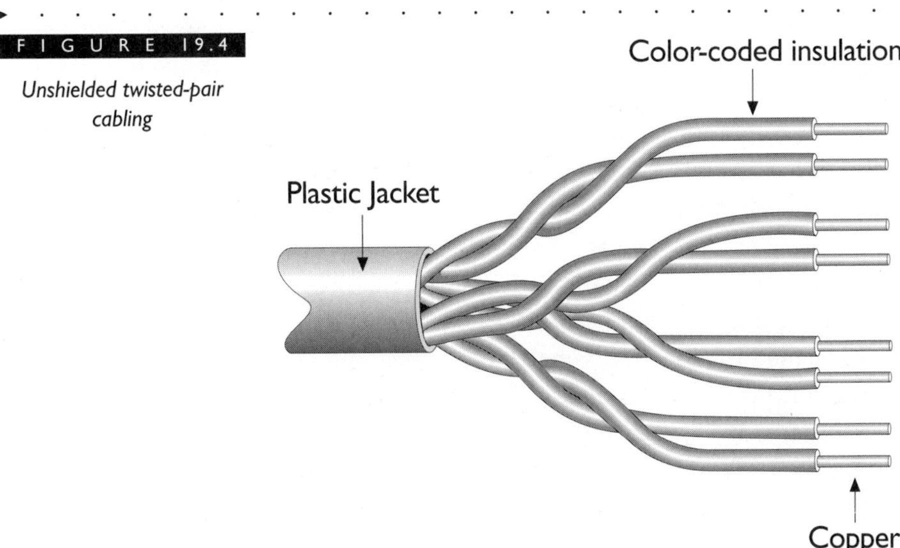

UTP cabling comes in two types: voice grade and data grade. Most common implementations use voice-grade cable, which is not good enough for LAN communications. So, to standardize UTP installations, the Electrical Industry Association (EIA) created the following category labeling scheme for five qualities of twisted-pair cable:

- *Categories 1 and 2*—Voice-grade UTP that supports very low-speed data communications (4 Mbps).
- *Category 3*—Commonly used for most contemporary computer networks. Typically supports speeds in the 10 Mbps to 16 Mbps range, although 100 Mbps is possible.
- *Category 4*—Data-grade UTP that supports 19 Mbps.

- *Category 5* — Commonly used for most contemporary high-speed computer networks. Category 5 includes some enhancements (such as having the most twists per foot and a higher-grade insulator) to improve transmission media performance. Category 5 installations also require compatible equipment and more exacting installation techniques. This type of UTP cabling supports speeds in the 1000 Mbps range.

UTP is extremely low in cost compared with other transmission media. It continues to be mass-produced for telecommunications and has become a popular computer network medium. Although some network integrators use existing spare wires that are located in the wall for network implementation, this is not a good idea, especially if the cabling grade is lower than Category 3. Most of today's UTP installations require brand-new Category 5 cabling.

UTP is installed in much the same way as typical phone systems. It all starts at the workstation. The user's machine has a UTP NIC installed with an RJ-45 connector. A patch cable carries the signal from the workstation to an RJ-45 jack installed on the wall. The wall jack connects the UTP cable drop to one side of a 66-port *punchdown block*. The opposite side of the punchdown block is wired to a *patch panel*. This patch panel provides multiple ports that connect to other workstations, the server, or network connectivity devices (such as 10BaseT hubs). All in all, UTP installation equipment is inexpensive, easy to use, and widely available because it borrows from telephone technology.

UTP's capacity depends on the quality of cabling used. Although it generally supports data transfer rates from 1 Mbps to 100 Mbps, 10 Mbps seems to be the most common transmission rate in use today, as defined by Ethernet 10BaseT. For more information on this standard and other 100 Mbps options, refer to Chapter 13.

With all of its advantages, UTP does have some shortcomings — mostly in the areas of attenuation and immunity from EMI. All copper wire suffers from rapid attenuation when used as a communications medium. Current technology restricts UTP's effective range to only a few hundred meters. In addition, the unshielded nature of UTP makes it susceptible to EMI. This is probably the most restrictive disadvantage. Also, external devices can be used to intercept signals and eavesdrop, thus breaching your network's security.

In summary, UTP is a relatively inexpensive, mature medium that can be easily installed, managed, and reconfigured. Unfortunately, it is limited to a few hundred feet, and is highly susceptible to EMI and eavesdropping.

Shielded Twisted-Pair (STP)

To reduce twisted-pair sensitivity to electrical noise, shielding is added just under the outer jacket. This copper-braided shield is connected to electrical ground through a drain wire. Any RFI or EMI is then captured and dissipated harmlessly into the ground. Some more expensive cables even add shielding around each pair to prevent crosstalk between pairs (see Figure 19.5).

FIGURE 19.5

Shielded twisted-pair cabling

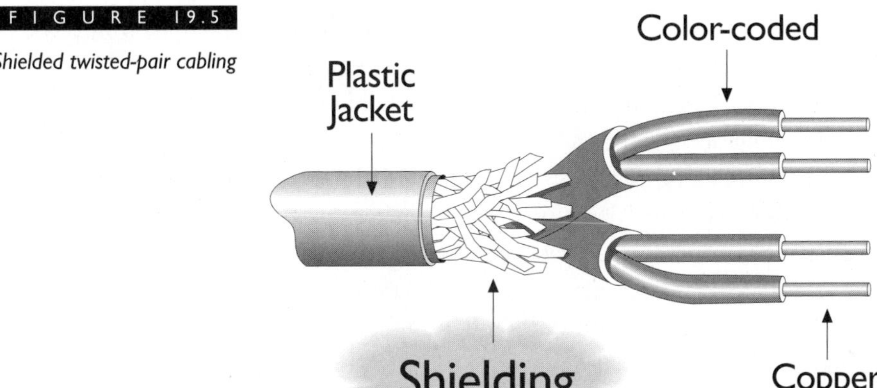

Various transmission media specifications from Apple Computer and IBM use STP cable. For example, IBM employs a type specification for different qualities and configurations of STP. This type specification is the foundation of IBM's popular Token Ring networking standard (see Chapter 13). Here's how it goes:

- *Type 1* — Two pairs of 22 gauge solid conductor wire with Mylar foil shield around each pair and an overall copper-braided shield.
- *Type 2* — Two Type 1 data pairs plus four 22 gauge voice-grade UTP in a single jacket.

- *Type 6*—Two pairs of 26 gauge stranded wires shielded like Type 1. Used for patch panels.
- *Type 7*—One shielded pair of 22 gauge solid conductor wires.
- *Type 9*—Two pairs of 26 gauge solid conductor wires shielded like Type 1.

The problem with STP is that it's relatively expensive, mostly because Apple and IBM still maintain proprietary standards. Of course, you can manufacture your own cables and bring down the cost considerably. STP currently costs more than UTP, but it is less expensive than thick coax or fiber-optic cabling. Similarly, STP is more difficult to install than UTP. STP requires an electric ground and proprietary connectors. You can use standardized or preconfigured cables to simplify the process, but this strategy adds tremendously to your cost.

You'll run into additional installation problems if you use Type 2 STP cabling. This cable is a classic engineer's solution to an electrician's problem. Type 2 cabling has two shielded pairs for Token Ring data and four unshielded pairs for your phone, all in the same jacket. This usually doesn't present a problem because the data patch panels and voice patch panels are located at opposite sides of the phone closet. The panels are arranged this way to avoid confusion between the two systems.

The good news is that STP supports much higher speeds because of the reduction of outside EMI. As a matter of fact, STP can operate at 500 Mbps at 100 meters. Unfortunately, most standards don't support data rates higher than 155 Mbps, and today's most common STP standard (Token Ring) provides relatively slow speeds—16 Mbps.

Attenuation is still a problem with STP because it operates on the same electrical principles as UTP. The only difference is that shielding provides better resistance to EMI, which does increase STP's capacity and distance tolerance, but not substantially. As a matter of fact, most STP LANs are still limited to a few hundred feet.

In summary, STP is a mature and stable standard that offers greater capacity and reliability than UTP. Unfortunately, it's more expensive, harder to install, and limited to relatively short distances. Technically, STP is superior to UTP, but practically speaking, it's just not as easy to work with. Refer to Table 19.1 for a comparison of UTP and STP.

TABLE 19.1

Comparison of UTP and STP Transmission Media

MEDIA	COST	EASE OF INSTALLATION	CAPACITY	ATTENUATION	IMMUNITY FROM EMI
UTP	Extremely low	Very simple	1 to 100 Mbps; 10 Mbps is most common	High; restricted to hundreds of meters	Low
STP	Moderate	Simple to moderate	1 to 155 Mbps; 16 Mbps is most common	High; restricted to hundreds of meters	Moderately low

Coaxial

Coaxial cabling is made of two conductors that share a common axis—hence, the name *coax*. Typically, the center conductor is made of stiff solid copper, which the second conductor surrounds as a wire mesh. As you can see in Figure 19.6, the two conductors are separated by insulation. Finally, a tough plastic tube forms the cover of the cable.

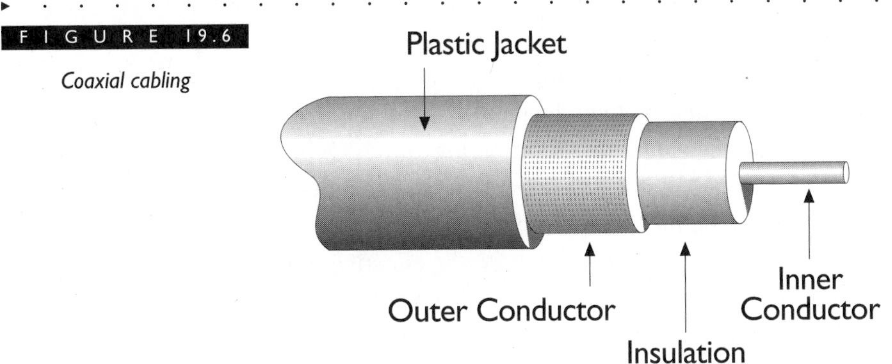

FIGURE 19.6

Coaxial cabling

Today's computer networks use a variety of coaxial cabling standards. Most of these standards define specific characteristics, such as impedance and size. Following are some common network (and nonnetwork) coaxial standards:

- 50-ohm RG-8 or RG-11 is used for Thick Ethernet LANs.

- 50-ohm RG-58 is used for Thin Ethernet LANs.
- 75-ohm RG-59 is used for cable TV.
- 93-ohm RG-62 is used for ARCNet LANs.

Be sure you use the correct coaxial cabling standard for your LAN. Many of your network's transmission devices expect a specific size cable working within a certain impedance range. A cable mismatch can cause a variety of problems, including a network crash, and such a mismatch is much easier to do than it sounds because all the cables look alike.

Coaxial cabling is relatively low in cost, although the cost increases with the diameter and composition of the conductors. Thin coaxial cabling, for example, costs less than STP or Category 5 UTP. Thick coaxial, in contrast, is more expensive than all cable transmission media, except fiber optics. Coaxial LANs frequently are installed in a bus topology that requires terminators and T-connectors (see Chapter 13). Thick coaxial LANs further complicate installation by introducing external transceivers and vampire clamps. Both of these devices wrap a metal ring around the cable and make electrical connections to the shield and center conductor. One of the benefits of this design is that it supports the flexibility of drop cables.

In theory, coaxial cabling has a much larger capacity than twisted-pair cabling. Unfortunately, current technology does not take advantage of the increased bandwidth. Most of today's coaxial LANs run at around 10 Mbps. Note that the bandwidth potential of coaxial cable increases with the diameter of the inner conductor. In addition, coaxial cabling suffers from high attenuation, but less so than twisted-pair cabling. With current LAN technology, the effective range of coaxial cabling is in the thousands of meters (not hundreds). Finally, coaxial cabling offers better immunity from EMI than does twisted-pair cabling, partly because of the second conductor's shielding effect. Furthermore, coaxial's EMI resistance is enhanced with the addition of a grounded terminator.

In summary, coaxial cabling is a well understood medium that supports relatively high bandwidths and offers better immunity to EMI than twisted-pair cabling. It's also relatively easy to install, unless you use vampire clamps and thicker cabling. On the downside, coaxial cabling is more expensive than twisted-pair cabling, and it suffers from moderately high attenuation. But all in all, coaxial is a great alternative for networking because it is designed for data transmissions. Refer to Table 19.2 in the next section for a comparison of coaxial to fiber-optic cabling. Speaking of which, let's take a look at the final cable medium — fiber optics. It is a whole new ballgame.

Fiber Optics

Fiber-optic technology is the future of network cabling. It relies on a completely new technology — photonics. Photonics uses the properties of light instead of electricity to transmit data; therefore, it's completely immune to EMI.

The secret of fiber-optic technology is really quite simple (see Figure 19.7). Each fiber consists of two pieces of glass: an inner core and an outer core (or *cladding*). Data travels as impulses of light through the inner core. When the signal tries to escape, the cladding reflects it back. This technology works because the cladding has a different index of refraction. Think of the cladding as a cylindrical mirror surrounding the inner core.

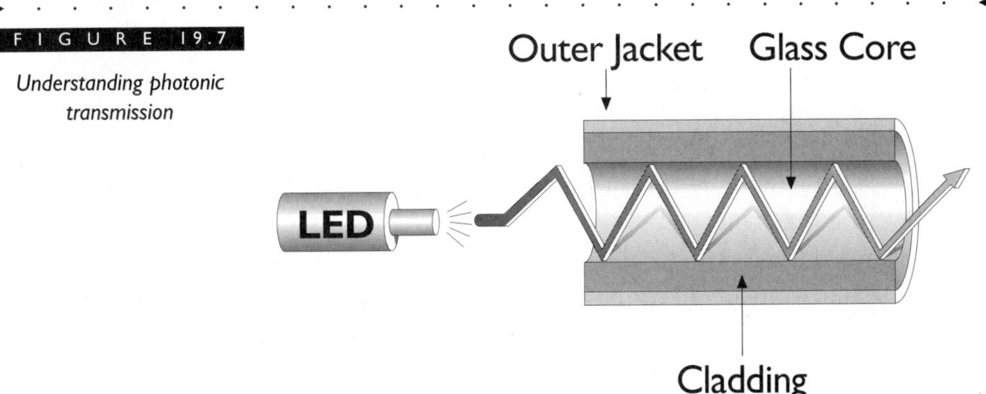

FIGURE 19.7 *Understanding photonic transmission*

Figure 19.8 shows the possible configurations of a fiber-optic cable. Between the plastic sheath and the plastic jacket, there can either be liquid gel or strength wires. In a *loose configuration*, a gel surrounds the fiber. In a *tight configuration*, strength wires surround it.

FIGURE 19.8

Fiber-optic cabling

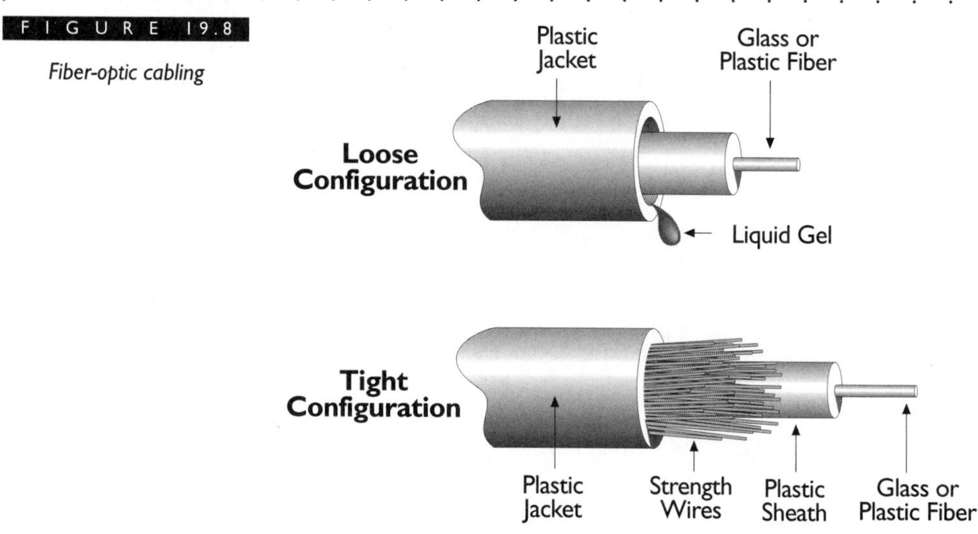

Fiber-optic cables can be composed of a single jacketed strand, but multiple strands are often bundled together because they're more lightweight than copper wires. Some fiber-optic cables also have metallic kevlar wire to increase their cable strength. This makes them ideal for limited-space environments and more force can be used in pulling the cable. Optical fibers may be single-mode or multimode in nature. *Single-mode* fiber has been optimized to allow only one light path. *Multimode* fibers, in contrast, allow multiple paths. By bending the light at different rates, multimode fibers enable the signal's parts to arrive simultaneously, and they appear to be a single pulse to the receiver. This is made possible by the coherent nature of lasers. That is, they generate single-frequency light.

In general, single-mode fiber has a higher capacity, but it costs more to produce and use than multimode. Here is a list of today's most popular fiber-optic cabling, starting with the most popular type:

- 62.5-micron core/125-micron cladding multimode
- 8.3-micron core/125-micron cladding single-mode
- 50-micron core/125-micron cladding multimode
- 100-micron core/140-micron cladding multimode

Bulk fibers and connectors have been relatively expensive compared to copper media, but these costs are falling rapidly. Even so, that's not where most of the costs are anyway. The real hidden cost of fiber-optic cabling is in installation and supporting equipment. Fiber-optic networks have developed a reputation for being hard to install, fragile, and expensive. To an extent, these perceptions are true. It seems like just a few years ago that it took 19 minutes and $1,000 in tooling to terminate a fiber-optic cable. Over the past few years, however, fiber-optic components have become less expensive and much easier to use. As a matter of fact, some of today's highest-quality components use snap-on connectors.

Most fiber-optic workstation connections use two ports: incoming and outgoing. The interfaces are connected directly to fiber cables that are terminated with mechanical connectors. The opposite ends of the cables are attached to a connection (splice center) or hub. Somewhere along the line, electronic computer signals are translated into light pulses and back again via fiber-optic modems.

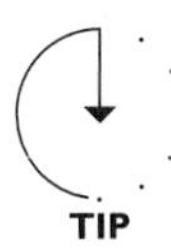
TIP

Fiber-optic light pulses are generated by light emitting diodes (LEDs) on multimode fiber or by injection laser diodes (ILDs) on single-mode fiber. They are converted back to electronic signals by avalanche photo diodes (APDs) or by P instrinsic N diodes.

The greatest advantage of fiber optics is in its capacity. Optical fibers support extremely high bandwidths because they rely on the high-frequency photon properties of light rather than electricity. Current technologies allow data rates from 10 Mbps (10BaseF) to more than 2 Gbps (that's gigabits!). The actual data rate you get depends on the fiber composition, the mode you're using, and the wavelength. The most common LAN implementation uses glass multimode fiber and 850 nm wavelength LEDs. This configuration can sustain a transmission rate of 100 Mbps at a distance of approximately 19 km.

However, fiber-optic cabling has some disadvantages. For starters, it's relatively expensive and not well understood. Furthermore, fiber-optic connections require high-precision manufacturing, and the cabling is relatively complex to configure and install. Refer to Table 19.2 for a comparison of coaxial and fiber-optic cabling.

TABLE 19.2

Comparison of Coaxial and Fiber-Optic Cabling

MEDIA	COST	EASE OF INSTALLATION	CAPACITY	ATTENUATION	IMMUNITY FROM EMI
Coaxial	Low to moderate	Simple	1 Mbps to 1 Gbps; 10 Mbps is most common	Moderate; cabling supports thousands of meters	Moderate
Fiber Optics	Moderate to high	Difficult	10 Mbps to 2 Gbps; 100 Mbps is most common	Low; extends many kilometers	Very high

This completes our discussion of cable media. Now let's expand our horizons into the WAN arena by exploring some wireless transmission media. Here's a list of the three technologies we'll discuss next:

- Radio wave
- Microwave
- Infrared

Refer to Figure 19.3 to see where these technologies fit in the EM spectrum. As you can see, they each support progressively higher frequencies, which is advantageous for data communications. Let's start with radio waves.

Radio Waves

Radio frequencies fall between 10 KHz and 1 GHz (gigahertz) on the EM spectrum (see Figure 19.3). Most of this area is regulated in the United States by the Federal Communications Commission (FCC) and in Canada by the Canadian Radio-television and Telecommunications Commission (CRTC). Obtaining a license for a specific frequency range can take a long time and cost much money. For this reason, many network designers like to operate in the unregulated bands:

- 902–928 MHz

- 2.4 GHz (also applies internationally)
- 5.72–5.85 GHz

TIP

A *band* is a contiguous group of frequencies that, because of convenience or technical details, is used for a single purpose (or treated like a single frequency). The preceding list contains three unregulated radio-wave bands.

Unlicensed frequencies are highly desirable because few restrictions are placed upon them. Error-free transmissions, however, are impossible to guarantee in uncontrolled frequency bands. Also, competition for these unregulated frequencies is increasing rapidly. As a result, most radio-wave network devices operate at regulated power levels (under 1 watt in the United States), which minimizes interference with other signals and limits multiuser interference to a relatively small area.

Radio waves can be broadcast omnidirectionally or fine-tuned for directional use. The antenna and transceiver you use determine the frequency and power of your radio frequency (RF) signal. Figure 19.9 shows some typical antennae: an omnidirectional radio tower, a half-wave dipole, a random length wire, and a yagi beam.

FIGURE 19.9

Radio-wave antenna types

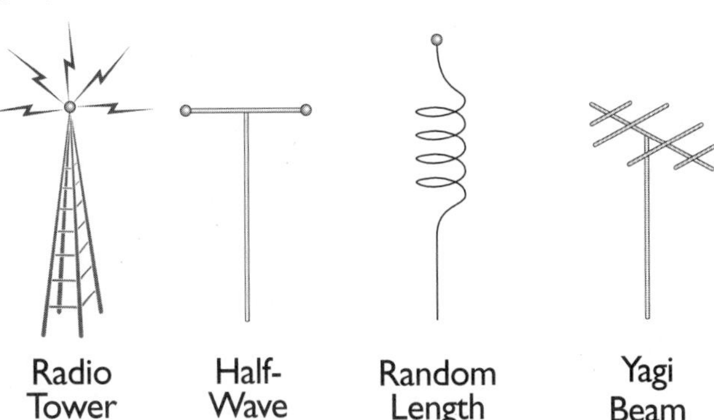

Global WANs use omnidirectional shortwaves to propagate beyond the horizon, whereas local LANs use directional very high frequency (VHF) or ultra-high frequency (UHF) transmissions. Radio-wave transmissions fall into three categories:

- Low-power, single-frequency transmissions
- High-power, single-frequency transmissions
- Spread-spectrum transmissions

Low-Power, Single-Frequency Radios As the name implies, this technology uses only one frequency to send data over low-power devices. This option is often used in short-distance, open environments; therefore, low-power, single-frequency radio is best for local directional WAN implementations. Typical products operate at 5.7 Mbps across a maximum of 25 meters. Although these systems may operate within the entire RF range, computer networks typically use the higher gigahertz (GHz) ranges because they offer higher transmission rates.

Low-power systems are generally less expensive than other wireless technologies. However, sophisticated transceivers or antennae can boost the price. Ease of installation also depends on the combination of transceiver and antenna used. Most systems come with antennae and other equipment preconfigured, which makes them easy to install. More sophisticated systems, including those designed for point-to-point use, must be installed by trained radio technicians.

So, at what speed do these systems work? Commercially available systems range from less than 1 Mbps to 10 Mbps. For the most part, attenuation depends on the radio frequency power level. Because low-power, single-frequency radios use little power by definition, they usually suffer from extreme attenuation. This problem explains the short distance limitations of these radio signals. Finally, single-frequency signals are highly susceptible to EMI. This is especially true in the lower bandwidths, where consumer devices (such as garage door openers) and electric motors operate. These signals also are vulnerable to eavesdropping, external interference, and jamming.

In summary, low-power, single-frequency radios are moderately priced and relatively simple to install. In addition, stations can be stationary or mobile, which adds valuable flexibility. On the downside, all radio-wave devices may require frequency licensing and approved equipment. In addition, they only support low speeds and are highly susceptible to EMI.

High-Power, Single-Frequency Radios These devices are identical to low-power, single-frequency radios, except that they use more power, which means that high-power, single-frequency radios can operate over much longer distances than their low-power cousins. Depending on the modulation technique, they may require an unobstructed line-of-sight path or may be bounced off the Earth's atmosphere (with shortwave radio). This flexibility makes high-power systems ideal for mobile transmissions.

Like their low-power cousins, high-power systems operate within the entire RF range. Computer networks typically use the higher gigahertz ranges because they offer higher transmission rates, but they cost a little more, too. Although radio transceivers are relatively inexpensive, the antenna towers and high-output equipment can make this a moderately expensive solution. But you get what you pay for: High-power radio operates at relatively high speeds (1 Mbps to 10 Mbps) and resists attenuation very well. As a matter of fact, on a clear night, a 50,000-watt transmitter can connect New York and Chicago. Wow!

On the downside, high-power, single-frequency radio systems are complex and difficult to install. Poorly implemented radios can cause spurious signals, signal power loss, or low transmittal rates, and that's not all. These systems are highly susceptible to EMI, external interference, and eavesdropping. In this case, more power isn't always better.

Spread-Spectrum Radio Spread-spectrum systems were developed by the military to be highly resistant to jamming and eavesdropping. Unlike the more common single-frequency systems, spread-spectrum radios use one of two modulation schemes to transmit data using more than one frequency at a time:

- *Direct-Sequence Modulation*—Spreads groups of data chips across a subset of radio frequencies. The receiver knows which frequencies are valid and deciphers the signal by collecting only the valid data. Other signals and noise are simply discarded. Although an eavesdropper could intercept the spread-spectrum signal, it would be difficult to reconstruct it without the valid frequencies and a chip-encoding scheme. Current 900 MHz direct-sequence systems offer transmission rates from 2 Mbps to 6 Mbps. This system is the more common of the two systems.

- *Frequency Hopping*—These systems send a short burst of data on a single frequency and then switch to another frequency for the next burst. Both the transmitter and receiver must agree on the frequencies to be used and the timing of the bursts. Most systems use a complicated frequency switching scheme and multiple frequency bands to improve performance.

Theoretically, spread-spectrum systems can use the whole RF range, although most commercially available systems use the 902 MHz to 928 MHz band to avoid FCC licensing. Some newer systems are migrating to the 2.4 GHz range. Most commercial systems are moderately priced and come with preconfigured transceivers and antennae, which makes spread-spectrum systems a simple plug-and-play solution. Like their single-frequency cousins, spread-spectrum radios suffer from high attenuation because they typically use low-power devices (due to FCC regulations).

In summary, spread-spectrum radio is a highly secure and more reliable alternative to other radio-wave standards. They are easily installed with preconfigured systems and offer comparable data transfer rates (2 Mbps to 6 Mbps). On the downside, they may require frequency licensing and approved equipment, are moderately expensive, and suffer from relatively high attenuation.

This completes our discussion of wireless radio-wave transmissions. Refer to Table 19.3 for a comparison of these three strategies. As you can see, it's a tricky technology, but it offers many advantages for WAN communications.

Microwave

Microwave communications extend beyond radio waves into the upper gigahertz band of the EM spectrum (refer to Figure 19.3 earlier). A higher frequency means better throughput and better performance. Since their invention, microwave has been a better wireless WAN medium than radio. Microwave data communications systems can be implemented in one of two places:

- Terrestrial microwave (on Earth)
- Satellite microwave (in outer space)

TABLE 19.3

Comparison of Radio-Wave Transmission Media

MEDIA	COST	EASE OF INSTALLATION	CAPACITY	ATTENUATION	IMMUNITY FROM EMI	FREQUENCY RANGE
Low power, single frequency	Moderate (depends on equipment)	Simple	1 to 10 Mbps	High	Extremely low	Entire RF; high GHz is most common
High power, single–frequency	Moderately expensive	Difficult	1 to 10 Mbps	Low	Extremely low	Entire RF; high GHz is most common
Spread spectrum	Moderate (depends on equipment)	Simple to moderate	2 to 6 Mbps	High	Moderate	Entire RF; 902–928 MHz (in U.S.) and 2.4 GHz (internationally) are most common

Terrestrial microwave systems are cheaper, but their ranges are usually limited to a few miles. Satellite systems, in contrast, are the only choice for many global WAN implementations because they provide almost instantaneous access to any point on Earth. Let's take a closer look at each of these microwave solutions.

Terrestrial Microwave Terrestrial microwave systems use directional parabolic dish antennae mounted on buildings or on stand-alone towers. Because these dishes use very narrow directional beams, the sender and receiver must be in the same line of sight. Long-distance telephone companies, for example, use special antennae, focused transmitters, and microwave towers mounted on hills several miles apart. One of today's most popular long-distance companies (MCI, or Microwave Communications, Inc.) was founded on this technology.

Terrestrial microwave systems usually operate in the low gigahertz range—typically between 6 GHz to 11 GHz or between 21 GHz to 23 GHz. Equipment costs depend mostly on the operating signal strength and frequency. Short-distance systems (hundreds of meters) are relatively inexpensive, but long-distance solutions (kilometers) can be pricey.

So, how do they work? Because microwave lengths do not use contiguous cable, they may cross inhospitable terrain much more easily than cable-based solutions. Typically, microwave lengths are used to connect separate buildings where cable installation would be troublesome or more expensive; however, they require licensed frequencies and special equipment. The good news is that some smaller-scale terrestrial solutions can use small dishes with centrally placed omnidirectional hubs. These hubs can create a backbone throughout a building (see Figure 19.10).

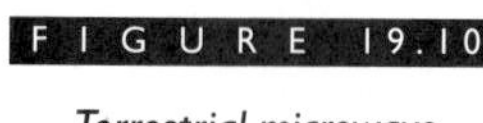

FIGURE 19.10

Terrestrial microwave

In general, line-of-sight systems are difficult to install because they require exacting adjustments (that is, trial and error), which can be a problem if you don't have a clear line of sight between two transmitters. If you don't have a clear line of sight, you may want to consider satellite microwave or radio. Like radio waves, microwave capacity depends on frequency. Single-frequency systems typically range from less than 1 Mbps up to 10 Mbps. Similarly, attenuation varies according to signal frequency and antenna size. Higher frequency systems are susceptible to weather interference over long distances, but across short distances they're not bothered at all. Finally, microwave lengths are susceptible to external interference, jamming, and eavesdropping.

In summary, terrestrial microwave provides a relatively high-capacity wireless solution for short WAN lengths over inhospitable terrain. Its price varies from inexpensive to expensive, depending on the effective range. Unfortunately, microwave is highly susceptible to atmospheric conditions and general EMI, and microwave systems are difficult to install because of line-of-sight requirements.

Satellite Microwave Like terrestrial microwave, satellite systems use low gigahertz frequencies. They also rely on parabolic sending and receiving antennae. The main difference between the two forms of microwave transmissions is the location of antennae. With satellite microwave transmission, one antenna is on Earth (Earth uplink and downlink station) and the other antenna is 22,300 miles up in space (geosynchronous orbiting). Earth-based uplink and downlink stations (also called Master Earth Stations) receive signals from the geosynchronous satellite and send them to LANs over conventional cable media (see Figure 19.11). Satellite transmissions require roughly the same time and expense to cross countries or oceans as it takes to cross a few kilometers. For this reason, satellite systems are best when used for large global WANs.

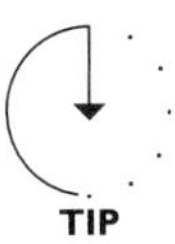
TIP

Because of the extreme distance that a signal must travel, satellite transmissions are subject to relatively long delays, called *propagation delays*. These delays may range from 500 milliseconds to more than 5 seconds. Although this is a problem for most real-time computer applications, satellite transmissions enable you to reach the most remote areas of the world (and space).

FIGURE 19.11

Satellite microwave

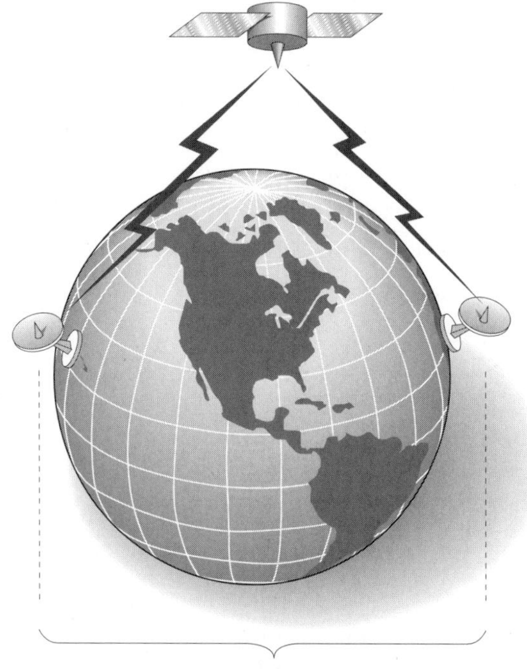

Like microwaves, satellite links usually operate in the low gigahertz range (11 GHz to 14 GHz). Satellite installation, in general, requires extremely complicated space technology, whereas Earth stations are more "down to earth." In either case, equipment costs are high, and you'll need to rent time on the satellite from AT&T, Hughes, Network Systems, or Scientific-Atlanta, just to name a few.

So, what do you get for all this money? Data communications over great distances at relatively average speeds—less than 1 Mbps to 10 Mbps. Attenuation is not much of a problem for satellite transmissions, but because satellite communications rely on general microwave signals, EMI, interference, jamming, and eavesdropping can be a problem.

In summary, satellite microwave communications provide relatively high bandwidths over enormous distances. They can support narrow- or wide-beam paths and offer great flexible mobility. On the downside, this medium choice is expensive and requires modern space technology. In addition, installation is complex, and it suffers from noticeable propagation delays. Finally, satellite systems, like their microwave cousins, are highly susceptible to external interference, jamming, and eavesdropping. All in all, satellite microwave transmission is a cool technology and is certainly the current state of global WAN communications; however, with the advent of internetwork connectivity and "cloud" protocols, such as frame relay and ATM, satellite microwave transmission may be on the way out for computer networks.

This completes our overview discussion of microwave communications. Refer to Table 19.4 for a comparison of terrestrial and satellite microwave transmission media. As you can see, they are two very different solutions for local and global wireless communications.

Infrared

Welcome to light waves. As we learned earlier, the properties of light provide a great pathway for data communications. Infrared links use light emitting diodes (LEDs), injection laser diodes (ILDs), or photo diodes to exchange data among networking nodes. Transmitted signals may be picked up by line-of-sight receivers or omnidirectional broadcast antennae; however, the light is not capable of penetrating walls or other opaque objects and is diluted by strong light sources. For these reasons, infrared is most useful in small or open indoor environments. In general, infrared communications operate in the terahertz (THz) electromagnetic band and, therefore, provide excellent throughput and performance.

As we said earlier, infrared communication supports two types of transmission:

- Point-to-point transmission
- Broadcast transmission

Point-to-point transmissions are tightly focused and provide much higher transmission rates. Broadcast infrared, on the other hand, provides better flexibility and good transmission distances. Let's take a closer look.

Point-to-Point Infrared Point-to-point infrared (IR) systems use tightly focused beams of light directed at specific targets. This strategy reduces the effects of attenuation and the possibility of eavesdropping. Two types of commercial point-to-point IR systems are available: low-power LED and laser systems. Low-power LED systems are commonly used for TV remote controls, remote control mice, and notebook computer communications. Laser systems, on the other hand, use much more power and offer higher transmission rates between buildings.

TABLE 19.4

Comparison of Microwave Transmission Media

MEDIA	COST	EASE OF INSTALLATION	CAPACITY	ATTENUATION	IMMUNITY FROM EMI	FREQUENCY RANGE
Terrestrial Microwave	Moderate to high (depends on equipment)	Difficult	1–10 Mbps	Variable (based on strength, frequency, and atmospheric conditions)	Low	Low GHz; 6 to11 GHz, or 21 to 23 GHz is most common
Satellite Microwave	High	Extremely difficult	1–10 Mbps	Variable (based on strength, frequency, and atmospheric conditions); supports global distances	Low	Low GHz; 11 to14 GHz is most common

Infrared transmitters typically operate in the lowest range of light frequencies (approximately 100 GHz to 1,000 THz). Low-power systems are inexpensive, but laser-based high-speed systems can be extremely costly. As we learned in the section on microwave systems, tightly focused line-of-sight systems require exact installation and precise maintenance. Also, you must be careful when working with high-power lasers because they can burn or damage your eyes. In terms of capacity, the Infrared Data Association (IRDA) is attempting to standardize low-power and point-to-point transmissions at 115 Kbps. Laser systems, however, offer much more realistic data transfer rates—up to 16 Mbps.

Infrared attenuation depends on light intensity, light purity, and atmospheric conditions. Depending on the conditions, reliable infrared data transmissions may be limited to several meters, or they may carry the signal a few kilometers. The good news is that all infrared transmissions are totally immune to EMI. As a result, they are fairly resistant to eavesdropping and jamming. Unfortunately, some intense light conditions (fluorescent lighting, for example) can cause problems with the data signal.

In summary, point-to-point infrared systems offer high transmission rates at a relatively low cost. They resist all forms of EMI and eavesdropping, but they are susceptible to high-intensity light and certain atmospheric conditions. On the downside, point-to-point systems require strict line-of-sight paths and exact positioning, which makes installation troublesome and costly.

Broadcast Infrared Broadcast infrared relaxes the focus of the beam in order to diffuse it, in other words, to broadcast the signal over a wide area. As you can see in Figure 19.12, one broadcast transceiver may communicate with multiple devices throughout a room. With broadcast infrared, it is much easier to line up transceivers, and receiving devices can be moved around much more easily; however, this also means that the signal can be intercepted.

Broadcast infrared systems operate in the same frequency range as point-to-point systems. In addition, their cost is highly dependent on the type of light filtering materials required. Unlike point-to-point systems, however, broadcast infrared is easy to install because of the diffused nature of its signal path. In addition, reconfiguration is relatively simple because devices may be located anywhere in the room. Unfortunately, broadcast infrared equipment provides slower data rates because of the diffused signal—less than 1 Mbps. In addition, attenuation is a problem because of light impurity and atmospheric conditions. However, the effects of semiopaque obstructions are less troublesome because devices may be relocated.

FIGURE 19.12

Broadcast infrared

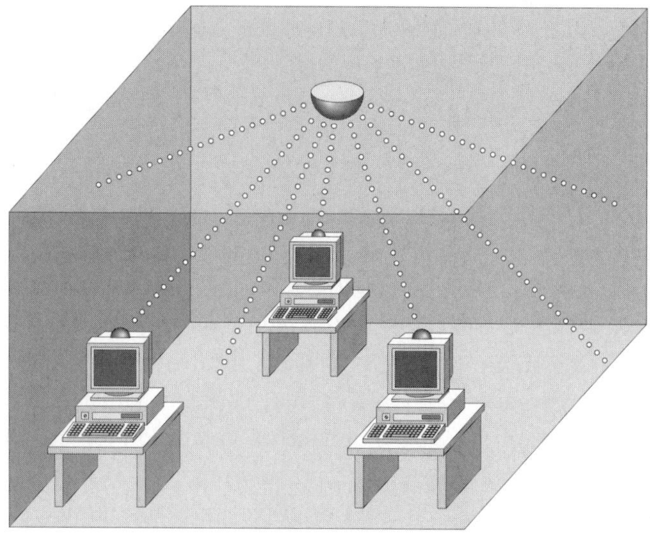

In summary, broadcast infrared is a great alternative to point-to-point systems because of the signal's flexible path. It shares all the same advantages and disadvantages of other infrared solutions, except that its capacity is dramatically reduced (less than 1 Mbps) because of signal loss caused by diffusion. Refer to Table 19.5 for a comparison of the two infrared transmission media.

This completes our discussion of wireless WAN media. In this section, we learned about how radio waves, microwaves, and infrared signals can be used to extend networking communications beyond land boundaries. Wireless media are flexible and relatively fast. On the downside, they're complex, expensive, and sometimes difficult to install.

So, with cable and wireless transmission media under our belts, let's complete this section with a look at how they can be combined to create public and private networks. After all, many times it doesn't pay to reinvent the wheel.

Public and Private Networks

In many cases, your network can benefit from existing WAN infrastructures. Many existing public and private networks are available so that you don't have to install transmission media from scratch. Although it's generally a good idea to build your own LAN, it's not a cost-effective solution for every organization. Imagine if you had offices in New York and San Francisco — would it make sense to run your own cable across the country or to launch your own satellite?

TABLE 19.5

Comparison of Infrared Transmission Media

MEDIA	COST	EASE OF INSTALLATION	CAPACITY	ATTENUATION	IMMUNITY FROM EMI	FREQUENCY RANGE
Point- to-Point Infrared	Low to moderate	Moderate to difficult	1–16 Mbps	Variable (based on light intensity, purity, and atmospheric conditions)	High	100 GHz–1000 THz
Broadcast Infrared	Low	Simple	1 Mbps	Variable (based on light intensity, purity, and atmospheric conditions)	Moderate	100 GHz–1000 THz

Instead, a group of public and private concerns have established networks that you can use. Here are two of the most popular networks:

- Public Switched Telephone Network (PSTN)
- Internet

Perhaps the most common of these networks is the *Public Switched Telephone Network* (PSTN). Almost every country has a PSTN, although many (especially in third-world countries) aren't reliable. The conglomeration of these PSTNs makes up the largest network on Earth.

Because many of these networks were developed at the same time, the details of national telephone networks differ on a country-by-country basis, although most of them use transmission media we've already discussed and have some features in common. In this discussion, we'll look at the U.S. telephone network and see how a typical PSTN operates.

Since the 1984 AT&T divestiture, the U.S. PSTN is divided into several distinct parts, each owned and controlled by a different party (see Figure 19.13):

- *Subscriber Wiring and Equipment* — Sometimes called CPE (for consumer premises equipment), this is the wire and equipment from the point where the local telephone company's cables are grounded, protected, and connected. This point is called the *demarcation point*, *network interface*, *point of presence* (POP), or *demarc*. Subscriber wiring is almost always UTP ending in RJ-11, RJ-14, or RJ-15 jacks. Before divestiture, all subscriber wiring was owned by AT&T and leased to customers. Today, almost all subscriber equipment and cabling is owned and maintained by the user organization.
- *Local Loops* — This is the proverbial last mile of UTP or fiber-optic cable. Local loops connect the demarc at the customer site with the local telephone company central office (CO). Each CO interconnects client sites with signaling, switching, filtering, and DC power supply equipment that is used to initiate an electronic circuit. The local loop is owned and maintained by the local telephone company, which is typically either a Regional Bell Operating Company (RBOC) or a GTE affiliate.

- *Trunk Lines*—These connect COs together over great distances and link them to long-distance carriers. This function originally was accomplished using UTP, but today trunk lines are made of fiber-optic cable or microwave links. They are also owned and maintained by local telephone companies.

- *Long-Distance Carrier Facilities*—These are groups of COs and switching offices that rely on a complex network of high-capacity long-distance carriers to provide transmission access to virtually any location in the world. These long-distance carrier facilities often are a mixture of high-bandwidth coaxial cable, fiber-optic cable, microwave, and satellite links. These carriers typically are owned by independent organizations, such as AT&T, Sprint, and MCI.

FIGURE 19.13

The Public Switched Telephone Network (PSTN)

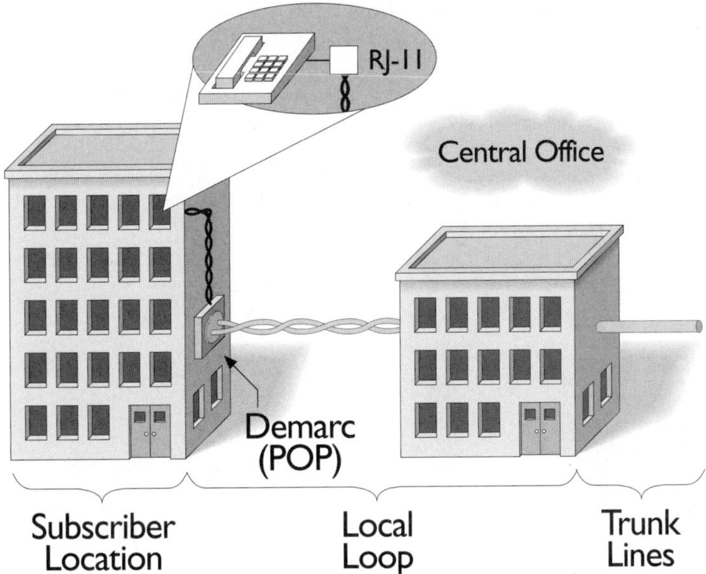

PSTNs sell their capacity through a series of services or service classes that include dial-up lines (called POTS, for plain, old telephone service), dedicated lease lines (for example, T-1, T-3, and E-1), and new sophisticated services, such as Synchronous Optical Network (SONET), Integrated Services Digital Network (ISDN), and Asynchronous Transfer Mode (ATM). Each of these services uses just a portion of the overall PSTN. Media and installation costs, therefore, may be spread among many users to reduce expense.

When you lease a T-1 line from New York to Los Angeles, for example, you're using 1.544 Mbps of data transport rather than a physical line. Your long-distance carrier will multiplex the data along with voice calls and other leased lines to increase efficiency. Refer to Figure 19.14 for a graphic summary of various PSTN services.

FIGURE 19.14

PSTN services

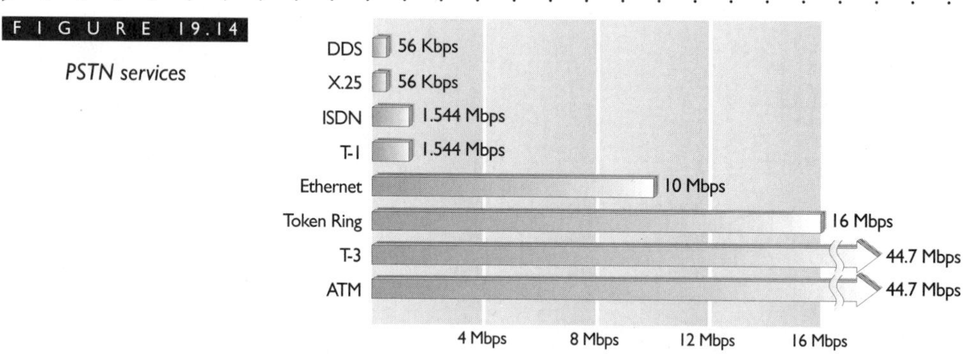

In addition to networks owned by public and private companies, there is at least one other system not owned or controlled by anybody—it's a cooperative venture. This network is the *Internet*—a community of government agencies, educational institutions, and private organizations from more than 100 nations that share transmission media and computer facilities. No one really owns the Internet, and anyone can use its facilities.

Well, that does it. *Whew!* That was quite a handful. As you can see, diverse transmission media are available for networking communications. Whether they're cable or wireless, public or private, transmission media provide a physical path for the exchange of information. This is also the beginning of our OSI journey.

REAL WORLD

Many ways exist for accessing the Internet. The two most popular are direct access and gateway access. *Direct access* requires a Thick Ethernet NIC, the TCP/IP protocol suite, and an Internet address. These components can be difficult to acquire and configure for the average user. *Gateway access* provides a much more user-friendly doorway to the Internet. Various asynchronous and WAN gateways exist through which you can connect to the Internet by using a modem or existing LAN connection. World Wire, for example, provides unlimited access to the Internet as part of its regular online service.

In addition, the usually cryptic Internet interface has recently undergone a radical facelift. The World Wide Web (WWW) is a graphical portion of the Internet that provides simple searching and data-retrieval capabilities. It's almost as simple as flipping through TV channels—and almost as fun. To use it, you'll need a Web browser, such as Microsoft's Internet Explorer or Netscape's Communicator. Come visit me on the Web. It's fun; I guarantee it!

LAB EXERCISE 19.1: TRANSMISSION MEDIA

Match each of the following advantages and disadvantages with the corresponding type of transmission media.

A. Unshielded twisted-pair cable
B. Shielded twisted-pair cable
C. Coaxial cable
D. Fiber-optic cable
E. Low-power, single-frequency radio wave
F. High-power, single-frequency radio wave
G. Spread-spectrum radio wave
H. Terrestrial microwave
I. Satellite microwave
J. Point-to-point infrared
K. Broadcast infrared

1. ____ Wireless medium that does not require exact positioning and is ideal for locally mobile devices.
2. ____ Cable medium that uses relatively sturdy cable and that experiences a moderate rate of attenuation.
3. ____ Wireless medium that requires strict line-of-sight paths and exact positioning.
4. ____ Cable medium that is immune to interference or eavesdropping from outside the cable.
5. ____ Wireless medium that typically offers relatively low transmission rates (less than 1 Mbps) and is susceptible to high-intensity light and atmospheric conditions.
6. ____ Wireless medium that involves moderate cost and relatively simple installation, but is extremely susceptible to external interference, jamming, and eavesdropping within the signal's effective range.
7. ____ Wireless medium that is moderately expensive to install and that must be installed carefully with complex tuning equipment.
8. ____ Cable medium that is moderately susceptible to EMI (under extreme conditions) and eavesdropping.
9. ____ Cable medium that is inexpensive, easy to install, and widely available.

10. ____ Wireless medium with a relatively low rate of attenuation.
11. ____ Wireless medium that requires expensive modern space technology and for which communication costs are independent of distance.
12. ____ Wireless medium for which high transmission rates are possible but have not been developed for over 16 Mbps.
13. ____ Cable medium that is more expensive and harder to install (when connectors are not preinstalled) than UTP and coaxial cable and whose most common transmission rate in use today is 16 Mbps.
14. ____ Cable medium whose connections require high-precision manufacturing and complex installation.
15. ____ Wireless medium that requires extremely complex and costly installation.
16. ____ Wireless medium that is easily installable with preconfigured systems and whose bandwidth is restricted only by frequency availability.
17. ____ Wireless medium that requires complex installation, especially when direct line of sight is unavailable.
18. ____ Wireless medium for which signals are partially or fully constrained to the intended area by walls or other objects.
19. ____ Wireless medium that is subject to noticeable propagation delays.
20. ____ Cable medium that is unsuitable for very high-speed (greater than 500 Mbps) data transmission and is not currently used for data rates higher than 155 Mbps.
21. ____ Cable medium for which the basic technology and standards are mature and stable and that supports data transfer rates of 1 to 100 Mbps up to 100 meters, with 10 Mbps as the most common transmission rate.
22. ____ Wireless medium for which costs vary from inexpensive to expensive, depending on the effective range, but that is potentially much less expensive than cable in difficult or congested areas.
23. ____ Wireless medium that offers high immunity from EMI and eavesdropping.
24. ____ Cable medium for which low attenuation rates are possible (measured in kilometers).
25. ____ Wireless medium for which no intervening ground facilities are required between transmission points, even between continents.

See Appendix C for answers.

Transmission Devices

Now that you understand the types of transmission media, we need to study the devices that enable them to communicate. A network path relies on transmission devices to provide basic communication services and interconnectivity. Without these devices, network packets would have nowhere to go.

In this section, we will extend the Physical Layer to cover three types of transmission devices:

- *Communications Devices* — Support basic data communications principles. These devices include modems, multiplexers, and channel service unit/digital service units (CSU/DSU).
- *Network Devices* — The infrastructure of today's LANs. They connect cable and wireless transmission media into organized communication networks. These devices include media connectors, network interface boards, repeaters, and hubs.
- *Internetwork Devices* — Extend LANs into the realm of WANs. These devices include bridges, routers, and gateways.

Now let's explore all these transmission devices in three categories. The goal here is to learn how transmission media are connected into LANs and WANs. Let's start with communications devices.

Communications Devices

Communications devices provide basic data communications functions. They transmit, translate, and transform data into signals that can be used in the digital world. In this section, we will look at the three most common communications devices:

- Modems
- Multiplexers
- CSU/DSU

Modems Modems are necessary because computers and transmission media speak different languages. Computers speak in digital zeros and ones, whereas most transmission media speak in analog. For digital computers to communicate over analog media, they need a translation device. That's where a modem comes in. As you can see in Figure 19.15, the modem actually performs two distinct tasks: modulation and demodulation. During modulation, the modem translates digital information into an analog waveform. Next, the data travels along the medium to the destination device, where the analog wave is demodulated into digital zeros and ones.

FIGURE 19.15

How modems work

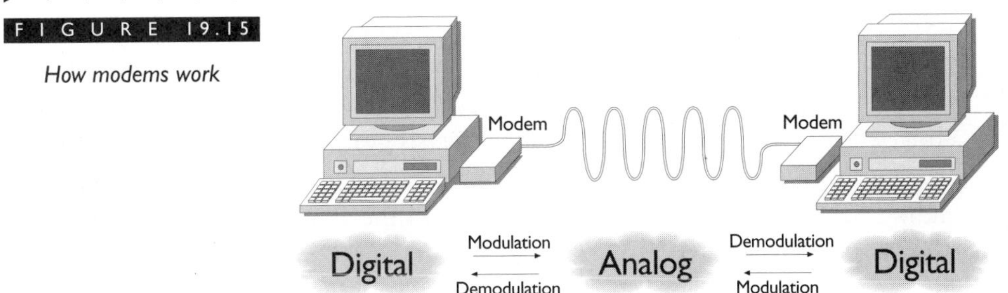

Modems extend networking communications by connecting two digital computers via PSTN or microwave communications. Modem speeds are typically measured in baud (or, loosely, bits per second). Today's faster modems can support speeds up to 56,000 bps (compressed) or 33,000 (uncompressed). Later in this section, we'll learn about CSU/DSU devices that provide speeds in excess of 56,000 bps by using special PSTN lines.

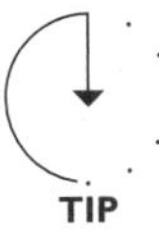

TIP

The networking industry has invented two translation devices related to modems: codecs and null modem cables. A *Codec* (which is short for coder-decoder) is a modem-like transmission device that provides the opposite conversion—from analog to digital. A *null modem cable* provides simple communications over relatively short distances (within tens of meters). This cable connects the transmit circuit from one workstation to the receive circuit of another. In some ways, this special cable emulates the role of a modem. As a matter of fact, some people call them *virtual* modems.

Multiplexers Multiplexers enable you to send multiple signals across single transmission medium. Multiplexing (or *muxing*) refers to the process of funneling multiple data connections into one circuit for transport across a single medium. An excellent example of multiplexing can be found in TV cabling. If you think about it for a moment, you have 100 or more channels arriving through one piece of coaxial cabling. Your cable box or VCR demultiplexes the signal and separates the channels.

Multiplexers are based on the idea that it is inherently good to make full use of a scarce resource. In this case, the scarce resource is the link between two networks. We'll take a deeper look at multiplexing later in this chapter.

CSU/DSU Modems enable you to connect digital computers to analog transmission media. But what if the transmission medium is also digital, such as a leased line or a T-1 circuit? In these cases, you don't need to convert the data with a modem. Instead, you should use a channel service unit (CSU) and digital service unit (DSU) combination. The CSU portion takes care of line management, such as grounding and loopback testing. The DSU formats the data into the correct frame type and provides an interface standard to your computer's RS-232 serial port. In addition, CSU/DSUs protect you and other public network users from electrical noise or unsafe electric voltages on the WAN media. Note that most WAN providers require that you lease the CSU/DSU device from them. This ensures system-wide continuity and safety.

This completes our discussion of communications devices. Each of these components provides a specific function in getting network messages from Point A to Point B. Now let's take a closer look at some other transmission devices that provide network and internetwork connectivity.

Network Devices

Network transmission devices connect individual workstations and servers into a synergistic LAN. These devices start as simple connectors and evolve in complexity and sophistication. Along with transmission media, these devices are the foundation of the bottom two layers of the OSI model. In this section, we'll explore four network transmission devices:

- Media connectors
- Network interface boards

- Repeaters
- Hubs

Media Connectors Transmission media connectors attach directly to the medium itself and serve as the physical interface between cabling and network nodes. Each medium has its own standards governing the construction of these devices. Figure 19.16 shows some common media connectors and the cabling they use.

FIGURE 19.16

Media connector types

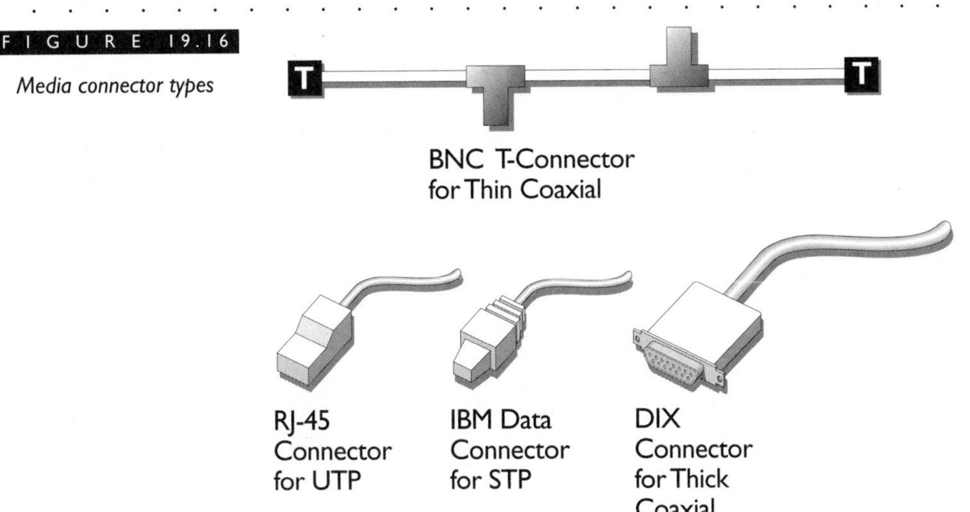

Network Interface Boards Just as media connectors work with LAN cabling, network interface boards talk to your computer. Technically, these devices include all the physical and logical intelligence your computer needs to communicate over the LAN. A network interface board typically is a logic card that connects to your machine's data bus. It can, however, be built into the motherboard, operate as software on a generic hardware port, or attach to existing parallel adapters. This board goes by many different names, such as network interface card (NIC), LAN board, LAN host adapter, and so on. The bottom line is that network interface boards are the critical link between your workstation's internal communications and the external network.

No matter which LAN standard you choose, you'll need a network interface board to match your transmission media. Refer to Chapter 13 for a detailed discussion of the four most popular standards: Ethernet, Token Ring, ARCnet, and FDDI. Now let's expand our network with repeaters and hubs.

Repeaters As the name implies, repeaters repeat network data. In general, repeaters operate at the electronic level and contain no real intelligence. A repeater accepts weak signals, electrically regenerates them, and then sends the messages on their way.

Repeaters are used most often to increase a network size by connecting multiple segments. The trunk of an Ethernet bus, for example, is limited to 607 feet. To extend the network beyond this technical restriction would require a repeater. The repeater effectively doubles the network size by connecting two 607-foot segments.

Theoretically, you could connect an unlimited number of segments using repeaters, but you'll find that many LAN standards have built-in repeater limitations. Ethernet, for example, uses the 5-4-3 rule — five segments can be connected using four repeaters, but only three of them can be populated by workstations or servers. There are two types of repeaters: amplifiers and signal-regenerating repeaters:

- *Amplifiers* — Amplifiers regenerate all incoming electromagnetic waves, including undesirable noise. They aren't smart enough to tell the difference between data and EMI. Also, as the number of amplifiers increases, the quality of the signal decreases. This is not a great option for digital networks.

- *Signal-Regenerating Repeaters* — These repeaters strip the data out of the transmission signal, reconstruct it, and then send it on its way. The new signal is an exact duplicate of the original, boosted to its original strength. This technology filters out harmful noise. Signal regeneration usually is preferable; however, it requires more time and logic than simple amplification.

Most repeaters have two ports. A multiport repeater is used to connect several cable segments together, further extending a network's size. Although repeaters enable you to increase the size of your network, they don't provide any LAN structure. That's what hubs are for.

Hubs Technically speaking, a hub is simply a multiport repeater. In addition to regenerating network data, hubs add form and function to the layout of the LAN. In many topologies, the hub is the central component of the network transmission media (see Figure 19.17).

FIGURE 19.17

The hub!

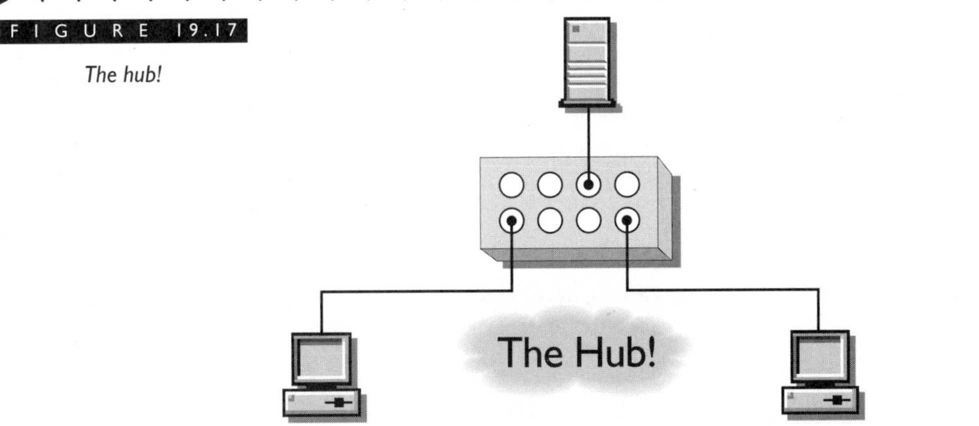

Here's a quick look at the three most popular hubs:

- *Passive Hub*—This is a simple signal splitter. Passive hubs don't perform any signal regeneration. For this reason, they lower the maximum cabling distance. For example, a passive UTP hub decreases the maximum segment length from 300 meters to 150 meters. Even worse, passive ARCnet hubs drop the maximum segment length from 2,000 feet to 100 feet. Wow!
- *Active Hub*—These are more actively involved in regenerating network signals than are passive hubs. This technology extends the maximum cable length. Unfortunately, some active hubs are amplifiers and not signal regenerators, which means that they amplify EMI, as well as data. Another drawback is their lack of intelligence. All computers connected to an active hub will receive all signals from all other computers—in a broadcast fashion. If what you're after are switching capabilities, you need to purchase a switch.

- *Intelligent Hub*—This is an active hub that includes built-in remote management software. Most intelligent hubs implement the Simple Network Management Protocol (SNMP) in order to provide remote management and real-time status reporting capabilities. More on SNMP later.

Intelligent hubs represent the highest evolution of network transmission devices. We've come a long way from simple media connectors. As a matter of fact, some of these hubs border on the functions of internetwork transmission devices. The key difference is that hubs are restricted to local networks. If you want to extend into the WAN arena, you'll need bridges, routers, and gateways. Let's take a closer look.

REAL WORLD

Stackable hubs are the latest innovation in hub design. Stackable hubs allow you to start off with a 12-port hub and add additional ports by stacking more hubs on top of the original one. These hubs are then interconnected using a special backbone cable. The beauty is that the whole stack of hubs act like a single repeater, which enables you to use multiple hubs without exceeding the maximum number of allowed repeaters. This is especially important if you are using Fast Ethernet devices.

Internetwork Devices

A LAN links a small group of functionally similar workstations within a local geographic area (for example, a series of adjacent cubicles or offices on the same floor). Once your network expands to include other floors or even other LANs, it ceases to be "local" and becomes a WAN. To connect multiple LANs into a WAN, you need flexible advanced internetwork transmission devices, such as the following devices:

- Bridges
- Switches

- Routers
- Gateways

These four internetwork devices have incrementally increasing intelligence. If you map them against the OSI model, you'll see what I mean—check them out in Figure 19.18. As you can see, *repeaters* have little intelligence and only operate at the Physical Layer. *Bridges* and *switches* offer a little more intelligence by analyzing physical address information. *Routers* are a little better because they use physical and logical addresses—at the Network Layer. Finally, *gateways* are the most intelligent because they can translate upper-layer network protocols. (**Note:** Another device, called a *brouter,* can provide both Data Link and Network Layer functionality. A brouter routes packets containing Network Layer data or acts as a bridge if only MAC information resides in the packet.)

FIGURE 19.18

Transmission devices and the OSI model

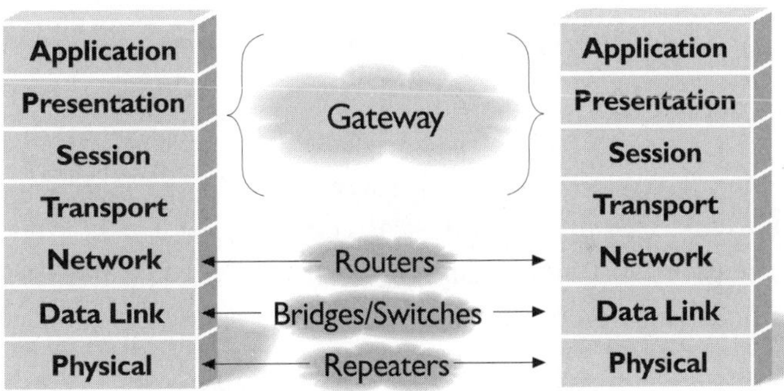

Now let's take a closer look at each of these four internetwork transmission devices.

Bridges Like repeaters, bridges extend the maximum distance of your network by connecting separate segments together. However, unlike repeaters, bridges act intelligently. How do they work? Simple. Bridges analyze network packets from multiple segments and determine who gets through and who doesn't. This is all based on the physical address.

Check out Figure 19.19. In the figure, Workstation 100 sends a message to Workstation 101. The bridge recognizes the communication as intrasegment and, therefore, prohibits it from traveling to Segment B. This strategy effectively separates communications on the two segments, which reduces traffic load. In contrast, if Workstation 190 sends a message to 101, the bridge recognizes it as intersegment and broadcasts the message to both segments. Ultimately, Workstation 101 recognizes the physical address on both packets and picks them up.

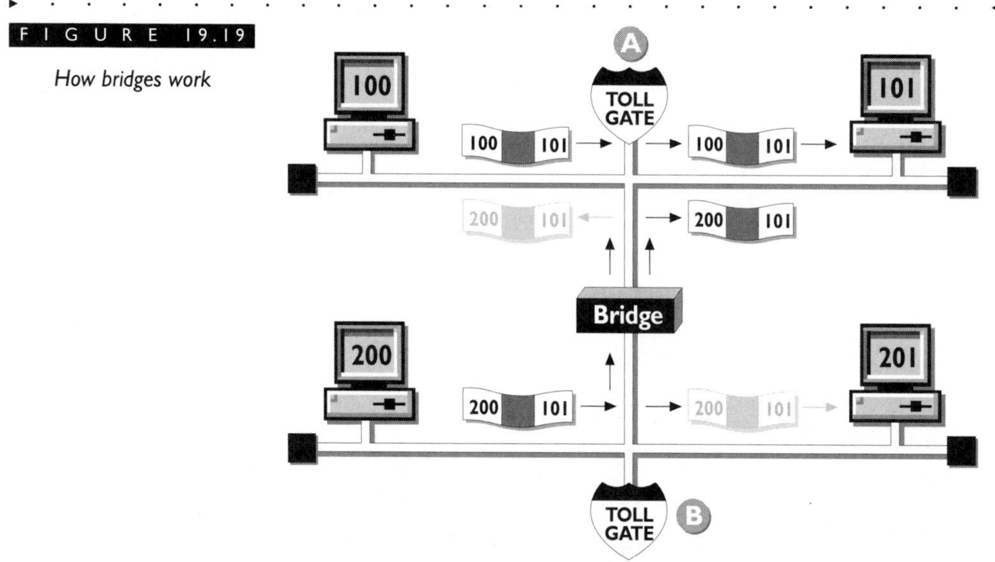

FIGURE 19.19

How bridges work

Bridges can only use physical addresses, which is limiting, especially if your internetwork has more than two or three segments. In these cases, you'll need the additional intelligence of a switch.

Switches A switch is a bridge with a PhD. Switches are multiport devices that provide high-speed forwarding of frames. There are circuit switches and packet switches. A *circuit switch* connects the sender and receiver over a virtual circuit that is dedicated for the duration of their conversation. This is how telephone company switches operate. A *packet switch* divides a conversation into small units called *packets* and forwards each individual packet through the network. Each packet may take a different physical path to reach its destination. The receiving system reassembles the packets based on their sequence numbers. See Chapter 20 for more information.

In Figure 19.20, we can see that a switch looks like a multiport bridge, only it's on steroids! Each device has its own switch port. Unlike bridges, which forward frames to all of the nodes on a given segment, a switch receives a frame on one port and forwards it only to the destination device's port.

FIGURE 19.20

How switches work

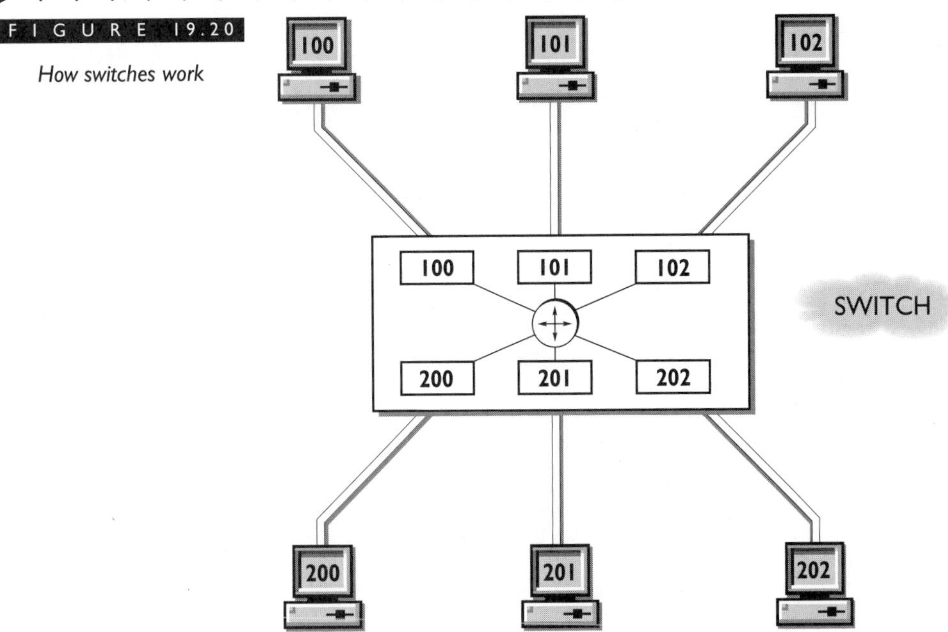

Switches and bridges don't provide enough intelligence for today's complex WANS. Instead, most network administrators long for the added intelligence of logical addressing and optimal path calculations. Welcome to the world of routers!

Routers Routers are more intelligent than bridges. Instead of being limited to the physical address, routers can use both physical and logical addressing, which allows you to break your internetwork into logical subnets.

Check out Figure 19.21. In this figure, our internetwork consists of five subnets (A–E). If we used bridges to attach the subnets, messages would be broadcast throughout the WAN and cause a great deal of traffic. Routers, on the other hand, can more accurately and efficiently calculate the optimal path. Let's say we want to send a message from Workstation 100 to Workstation 300. In this case, the packet goes directly to Router AB, which recognizes it for Segment C. This is accomplished using an internal routing table (see Chapter 20 for more information). Router AB changes the logical address and sends it off to Router BC. This router then forwards the packet to the correct segment. In this example, subnets D and E are untouched, and the packet travels a minimum path instead of being broadcast throughout the WAN.

FIGURE 19.21

How routers work

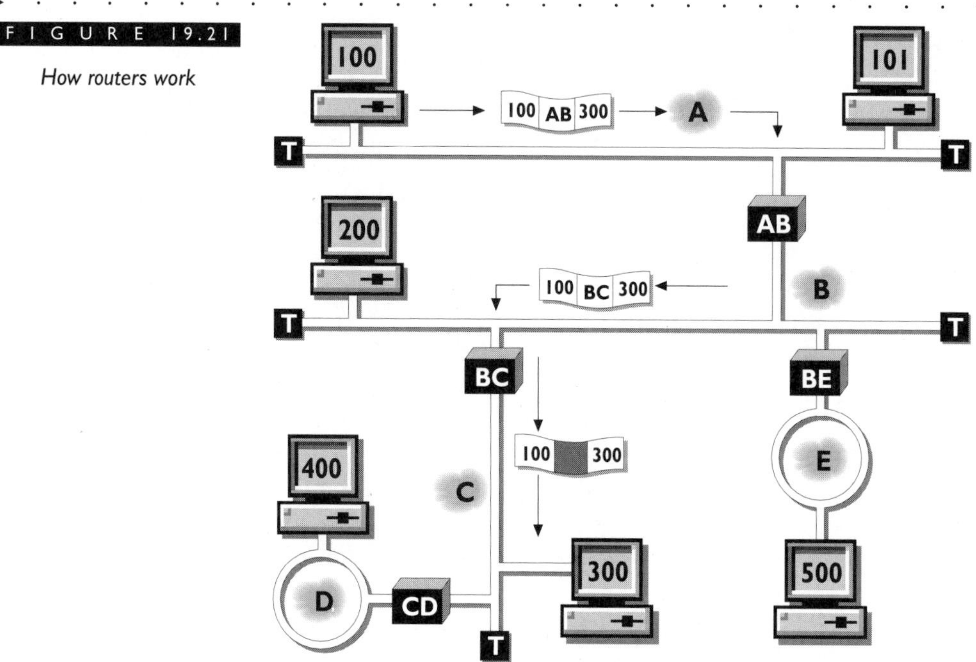

All of this magic relies on the function of both the physical and logical addresses. The physical address is programmed onto each workstation's NIC by the manufacturer. This is sometimes referred to as the *node address* (see Chapter 13). The *logical address*, on the other hand, operates at the Network Layer and breaks up our internetwork into five subnets. The logical address is created by network administrators during initialization of the server or router. Be sure you keep track of your internetwork's physical and logical addresses. Documentation is a great place to start.

If your internetwork contains completely dissimilar devices (such as servers and mainframes), you'll need a protocol translation device. Now's the time to learn about gateways.

Gateways Gateways represent the pinnacle of internetwork transmission devices. As we learned earlier, they operate at the upper four layers of the OSI Reference Model. As a matter of fact, they perform more software translation than anything. Routing capabilities built into the gateway device do the packet routing.

Gateways are required when network messages travel between two entirely different systems. A classic example is the exchange of data between centralized and distributed CPUs. For example, a Systems Application Architecture (SAA) gateway is required for conversations between NetWare LANs and centralized IBM mainframes (see Chapter 22). For these two systems to communicate, the gateway must read the network address, reconfigure the packet protocols from IPX to SNA, translate the operating software, and in most cases, completely rewrite the data alphabet. Wow, that's a lot of work! Good thing you don't have to do it.

Well, that does it for transmission devices. I hope you have a new appreciation for how hard it is to mold transmission media into functional LANs and WANs. Of course, it's all worth it, because when you're finished, the network takes on such an awe-inspiring shape. Of course, the shape you choose relies on three important components:

- Physical topology
- Media-access protocol
- Networking standard

Physical Topology

Physical topology establishes the geographic arrangement of networking devices. Topologies are fundamentally driven by two network connection types: *point-to-point* (a direct link between two devices) and *multipoint* (a link between three or more devices attached to a central CPU or hub).

Physical topologies that are used in LANs and WANs include the following:

- *Bus*—The physical bus topology is the simplest of the network designs. It typically consists of one continuous length of cabling (called a *trunk* or *backbone*), with a terminating resistor *(terminator)* at each end. All nodes on the bus topology have equal access to the trunk.
- *Ring*—The physical ring topology is a circular loop of point-to-point links. Each device connects directly to the ring or indirectly through an interface device or drop cable. Messages travel around the ring from node to node in a very organized manner. Each workstation checks the messages for a matching destination address. If the address does not match, the node simply regenerates the message and sends it on its way. If the address matches, the node accepts the message and sends a reply to the originating sender.

- *Star*—The physical star topology uses a central controlling hub with dedicated legs pointing in all directions (like points of a star). Each network device has a dedicated multipoint link to the central hub. This strategy prevents collisions and keeps the lines of communication free of network traffic. Star topologies are somewhat difficult to install because each device requires its own dedicated segment.

- *Mesh*—The mesh physical topology is the only true point-to-point design. It uses a dedicated link between every device on the network. This design is not practical in most situations because of its excessive waste of transmission media.

- *Cellular*—The cellular physical topology combines wireless point-to-point and multipoint designs to divide a geographic area into cells. Each cell represents the portion of the total network area in which a specific connection operates. Devices within the cell communicate with a central station or hub. Hubs are then interconnected to route data between cells.

Each physical topology design has advantages and disadvantages when it comes to ease of installation, ease of reconfiguration, troubleshooting capabilities, and reliability. Refer to Table 19.6 for a comparison of these five designs.

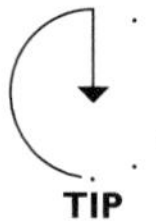
TIP

For more detailed information regarding the physical architecture and operation of bus, ring, and star topologies, refer to the Ethernet and Token Ring discussions in Chapter 13.

Data Signaling

Computer systems represent data using a binary digital alphabet consisting of zero (0) and one (1). Conversely, communications rely on the analog properties of electricity to transfer data over distances. Network data communications between computers can be accomplished using digital or analog signaling as follows:

- *Digital Signaling*—Data is represented using discrete bits of electrical current.

- *Analog Signaling*—Data is represented as properties of an electromagnetic waveform.

TABLE 19.6

Comparison of Five Physical Topologies

PHYSICAL TOPOLOGY	EASE OF INSTALLATION	RECONFIGURATION	TROUBLESHOOTING CAPABILITIES	RELIABILITY
Bus	Easy—less media	Difficult	Poor	Low; single break causes network crash
Ring	Hard—more media	Difficult	Good	Low; single break causes network crash
Star	Hard—more media	Simple	Good	High; single break affects only one node
Mesh	Very hard—too much media	Difficult	Good	High; single break affects only one node
Cellular	Easy—wireless media	Simple	Good	Low; hub failure affects entire cell

In the next sections, we will need to explore both digital and analog signaling methods in order to fully grasp the configuration of complex transmission devices (such as switches and routers).

Digital Signaling

Digital systems represent data using one of two states. The two states can be indicated in a variety of ways, such as on/off, high/low, or 1/0. Digital signals send bits of data using these discrete values. As the signal level jumps from one point to another, it is measured during a bit interval. As you can see in Figure 19.22, the presence or absence of a pulse determines the bit value at each interval. The pulse has a rather boxy look because the digital wave is restricted to two states: on (1) or off (0).

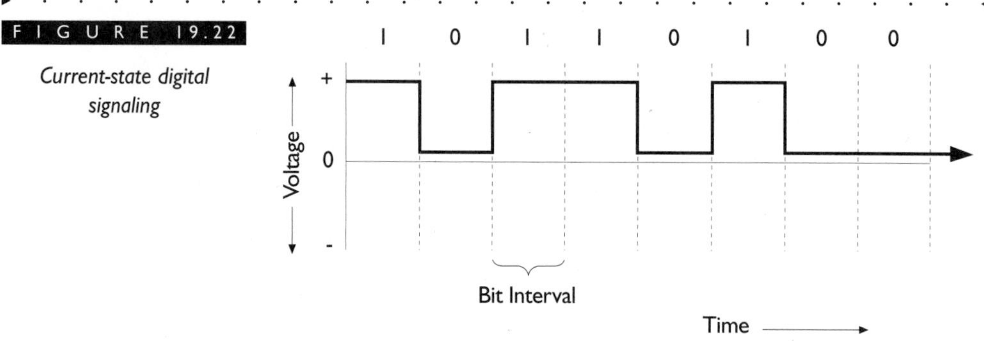

FIGURE 19.22

Current-state digital signaling

Digital devices use one of the following signaling schemes to determine the structure of data bytes:

- Current-state
- State transition

Current-State Current-state encoding schemes measure the presence or absence of a state or signal characteristic. For example, electronic NICs represent data by the presence or absence of a certain voltage level. Fiber optics represent data by turning a light source on or off. In either case, the bytes look similar to the one shown in Figure 19.22. As you can see, the presence of a positive voltage level indicates a one, and the absence of voltage indicates a zero.

As you can see in Figure 19.22, everything relies on the bit interval. The sending and receiving devices must be synchronized so that they use the same time slots. The following digital signal encoding schemes use current-state technology:

- *Unipolar*—In unipolar schemes, either a positive or a negative voltage represents the data. For example, +3V may be a zero and 0V may be a one, or –3V may be a zero and 0V may be a one.
- *Polar*—In polar schemes, both positive and negative voltages are used. For example, +3V may be a zero and –3V may be a one.
- *Return-to-Zero (RZ)*—This current-state scheme relies on a midbit transition. That is, the signal moves from positive or negative value to zero midway through the bit interval. A positive transition to zero is a zero, and a negative transition to zero is a one.
- *Biphase*—Biphase schemes also require a midbit transition. In a typical biphase scheme, a high-to-low midbit transition represents a zero, and a low-to-high midbit transition represents a one. A popular biphase encoding scheme called Manchester is used in Ethernet LANs.

State Transition The transition between two states can also be used to encode data on the digital signal. For example, instead of measuring the absolute voltage during the bit interval, you can keep track of what happens at the point of transition (see Figure 19.23). Let's say that no transition represents a zero, and any positive or negative transition represents a one. As you can see in the figure, the first and second bit intervals have no transition between them, so the first bit is a zero. In contrast, the second and third intervals have a transition between them, so the second bit is a one. Go ahead and follow along the rest of the byte.

FIGURE 19.23

State transition digital signaling

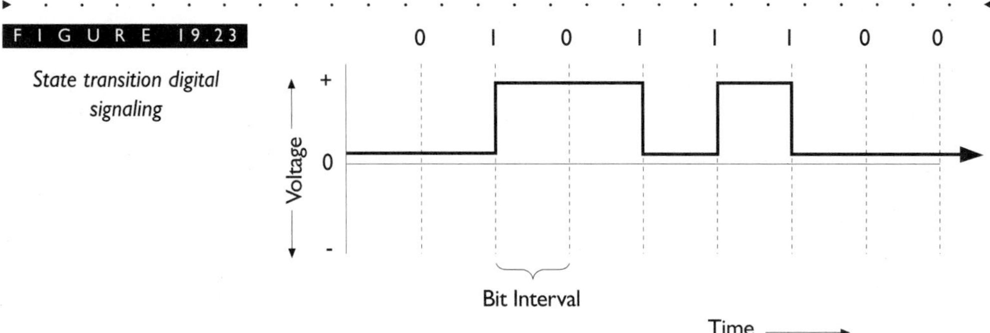

State transition encoding schemes are a bit trickier because they use a moving target; however, they are more reliable than current-state schemes because the transition allows the sender and receiver to stay in sync at all times. The following digital signal encoding schemes use state transition technology:

- *Alternate Mark Inversion (AMI)* — This is a typical bipolar encoding scheme in which the digital signal varies among three levels: positive, zero, and negative. A one is represented by a transition from high to low or low to high, whereas zero is distinguished as any stable voltage at the beginning of the bit interval.
- *Non-Return-to-Zero (NRZ)* — In these schemes, the signal never returns to zero. Binary encoding is determined by the presence or absence of a transition at the beginning of the bit interval. A one is represented by a transition, a zero with no transition.
- *Differential Manchester* — This is a biphase encoding scheme similar to Manchester, but it uses state transition instead of current-state encoding. Differential Manchester relies on a transition at the beginning of the bit interval. A transition represents a zero, and no transition represents a one. Differential Manchester encoding is used in Token Ring LANs.
- *Biphase Space (FM-0)* — This is another biphase encoding scheme similar to Differential Manchester. This time, however, a transition at the beginning of an interval represents a one, and no transition is a zero. This is the simplest of the state transition encoding schemes and can be seen in Figure 19.23.

Overall, digital signals work well with binary data. They're not as easily compatible with analog transition media, but they are more compatible with the data itself. Digital equipment is usually simpler and cheaper because it speaks the same language as the data. In addition, there is usually less error from noise and interference because binary states are more forgiving. The amplitude of most noise is small compared to the amplitude of the signal. On the downside, digital communications suffer more attenuation than analog because the signal is so complex.

Well, that's enough digital conversation. Now for something more familiar—analog signaling.

Analog Signaling

Analog signaling is ideal for data communications because it uses the common sine wave shown in Figure 19.24. This graph is quite different from the boxy-looking digital graph. Analog waves are measured according to the following three key characteristics:

- *Amplitude*—Amplitude represents the strength of the analog signal. Amplitude is commonly expressed in volts (for electrical potential), amps (for electrical current), watts (for electrical power), and/or decibels (for the ratio between the power of two signals). To carry digital data over analog media, networks use *amplitude shift keying* (ASK) to encode data by comparing the signal's amplitude against a given threshold (in many cases, 0.6V). If the amplitude exceeds the threshold, it is a one; if not, it is a zero.

- *Frequency*—Frequency is a count of the number of cycles that a wave completes within a given period (time frame). Frequency is typically measured in hertz (Hz), or cycles per second. Some networking devices encode binary data by varying the signal's frequency. This method is called *frequency shift keying* (FSK), which uses a high frequency to represent a one and a lower frequency to represent a zero.

- *Phase*—The phase of an analog signal refers to the relative state of the wave when timing begins. For example, the wave in Figure 19.24 crosses the zero voltage line exactly at time interval zero. If another wave came along and crossed the zero voltage line half a cycle later, it would be 180 degrees out of phase. This scheme is based on a full cycle of 360 degrees.

Some network devices are capable of encoding digital data on an analog waveform by alternating its phase. This feature is called *phase shift keying* (PSK).

FIGURE 19.24

The analog waveform

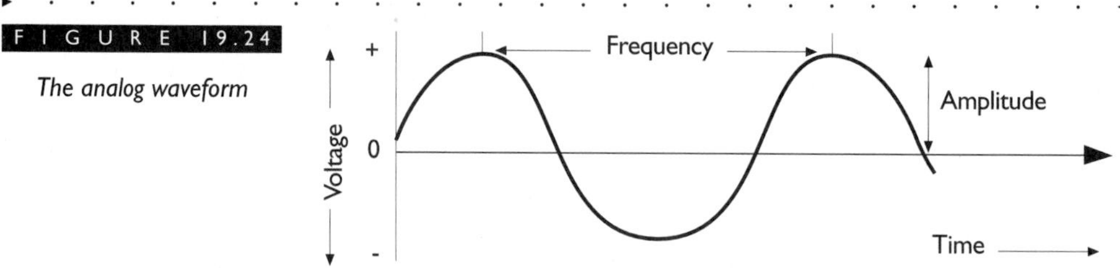

There you have it. That's everything you wanted to know about analog signaling but were afraid to ask. In summary, analog devices are much more media friendly than digital devices. They represent digital data by altering certain wave characteristics, such as amplitude, frequency, or phase. In general, they support much greater distances than do digital signals. Unfortunately, analog signals are highly susceptible to EMI noise and outside interference. Overall, it's a great signaling method for modems and long-distance communications.

Data Synchronization

In our data signaling discussion, we learned that binary information can be encoded onto digital or analog signals. Both schemes rely on the existence of distinct bit intervals, which allow the sender and receiver to agree on where the data is in the transmission stream. In fact, all data transmissions require some form of data synchronization. Following are the two most popular types of data synchronization:

- *Asynchronous* — Means *untimed*. When asynchronous systems communicate, they do so on an unscheduled, as-needed basis. When no data is being transmitted, no signals or state changes occur. However, when it is time to start the transmission, the sending device broadcasts a single start bit (or state change) before transmitting data. The receiving device then starts its internal clock and measures bit intervals according to a preestablished pattern. This continues until a stop bit is received.

- *Synchronous*—Means *timed*. For this reason, synchronous clocks are always turned on, and the receiving station is forever awaiting a data byte. This is a much more efficient strategy because no control overhead is necessary. Instead, the sender and receiver agree on timing intervals before transmissions start. Critical clocking information can be exchanged in three ways: guaranteed state change (embeds clocking into the data signal), separate clock signals (relies on a separate channel for clock timing), or oversampling (receiver samples the signal at ten times the data rate).

This completes our exploration of data synchronization. Let's review our journey so far. We looked at the differences between digital and analog signals. We learned about binary encoding schemes and the use of critical bit intervals. Then synchronization helped us understand how the bit interval is managed. Now the final Physical Layer section, "Data Bandwidth," will help us understand how these data signals interact with transmission media.

Data Bandwidth

Data bandwidth is related to transmission speed, but not in the way you might think. It doesn't determine the actual speed of your transmissions. Rather, it determines how much data you can fit on a single cable. Earlier, we defined bandwidth as the range of frequencies supported by any given medium. This range of frequencies can be segregated into multiple channels, just like lanes of a highway. A four-lane road, for example, will support many more cars at higher speeds than a two-lane road, especially during rush hour. In this scenario, the speed of the cars hasn't increased, but their capability to travel faster has increased.

Sometimes when traffic gets really bad, we install a carpool lane. This dedicated channel for special users guarantees high speeds even in the highest traffic situations. Similarly, you can create dedicated channels for priority high-speed data transmissions. Let's say you have a fiber-optic transmission medium capable of 100 Mbps. You could split that medium into six channels, one traveling at 50 Mbps and five operating at 10 Mbps. This process, called *multiplexing*, can use two technologies:

- *Baseband*—This approach uses a transmission medium's entire capacity for a single channel. The channel can use either analog or digital signaling, but digital is much more common (see Figure 19.25).

- *Broadband* — This approach divides a medium into multiple channels. As you can see in Figure 19.25, each channel operates at a different frequency. Broadband systems always use analog signaling.

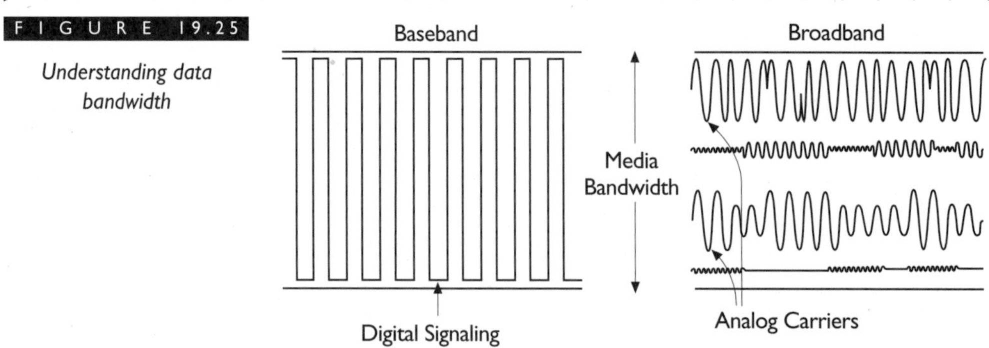

FIGURE 19.25

Understanding data bandwidth

Let's take a closer look at how each of these data bandwidth technologies work.

Baseband Transmissions

As we just learned, baseband transmissions use the entire medium's capacity for a single channel. This technology relies on the discrete properties of digital signaling. Although baseband channels can support only one signal at a time, multiple conversations can be combined using multiplexing. If you remember from our earlier discussion, multiplexing enables multiple devices to communicate simultaneously over a single transmission medium. A network device called a *mux* performs multiplexing and demultiplexing.

In the baseband world, multiplexing is accomplished using two strategies:

- *Time Division Multiplexing (TDM)* — Divides a single channel into short time slots. In this system, each conversation gets exclusive access to the entire channel for a predetermined period of time. When a conversation's time is up, the next conversation takes over. This process continues until all conversations have had their turn, and then it starts over again. This technique can be used on baseband systems or within an individual channel of a broadband system. Conventional TDM systems are sometimes called *synchronous TDM* because the time divisions are fixed when the muxes are set up. The time slots are always the same length and are assigned in the same order. This approach is inefficient if many time slots are left unused.

- *Statistical Time-Division Multiplexing (STDM)*—Solves the inefficiencies of conventional TDM by allocating time slots dynamically to active devices on a first-come, first-served basis. This system also supports time-slot prioritization. STDMs are ingenious devices that add intelligence and load balancing to the tedious work usually done by conventional TDMs. As a matter of fact, these systems are so good that they allow bandwidth borrowing—carpooling for the network.

One of the most common TDM implementations is T-1. T-1 lines use a time-slot approach for multiplexing voice and data, which allows you to combine the capabilities of 24 individual 64 Kbps PSTN lines into one 1.544 Mbps digital channel. Baseband transmissions provide excellent throughput because the digital signal occupies the entire channel. Most of today's high-speed computer networks operate over baseband systems.

Broadband Transmissions

Broadband systems divide the medium's bandwidth into multiple analog channels. Each channel uses a separate frequency. This multiplexing technique is known as *Frequency Division Multiplexing* (FDM). FDM relies on a special mux that creates distinct broadband carrier signals with different frequencies. Data travels over each carrier and is removed at the other end. This is probably the best bandwidth technology for long-distance WAN communications.

REAL WORLD

One of the most common implementations of broadband transmission is cable TV. Think about it. A single coaxial cable comes into your house carrying more than 100 different channels, each operating at a different frequency. When you use your remote control to switch from Channel 3 to 4, the TV focuses on a different carrier signal.

That completes our comprehensive coverage of the OSI Physical Layer. Wow, what a journey! In this section, we've explored the Physical Layer of network communications from every conceivable angle. We started with the four structural components of communications: electrical properties, transmission media, transmission devices, and physical topology. Next, our journey took us inside the path of communications, where we found data signaling, data synchronization, and data bandwidth. These are the nuts and bolts of Physical Layer transmissions.

Now it's time to organize all of our Physical Layer bits into Data Link frames.

The Data Link Layer

Welcome to the Data Link Layer! This is the first point of logical organization in the OSI reference model.

The Data Link Layer organizes electronic bits into logical groups called *frames*. Each frame is a contiguous series of bits grouped together as a discrete unit of data. Framing enables the network to organize bits into a logical unit and to transmit them to the correct computer.

Data Link framing is accomplished by two sublayers:

- *MAC (Media-Access Control)* — Defines media-access protocols and physical addressing.
- *LLC (Logical-Link Control)* — Governs frame synchronization, Data Link flow control, and error checking.

Let's take a closer look at each of these two OSI Data Link sublayers, starting with Media-Access Control.

MAC (Media-Access Control)

The overall purpose of the Data Link Layer is to package physical bits for reliable delivery. The MAC sublayer defines media-access protocols and physical addressing. *Media-access protocols* define how the network functions, not how it looks. These protocols use logical topologies and communication rules. *Physical addressing* then provides a physical identification scheme for network devices.

In this section, we will study three media-access protocols:

- *Contention Media-Access Protocol*—Relatively simple and straightforward. All devices on the network compete for a single channel.
- *Token-Passing Media-Access Protocol*—Much more civilized. In this system, network communications relies on the possession of a special control frame called the token.
- *Polling Media-Access Protocol*—Relies on a central controlling node for all network communications. Nobody can speak unless the boss says so.

In social terms, contention is survival of the fittest, token-passing is democracy, and polling is a dictatorship. Let's check them out.

Contention Media-Access Protocol

The contention protocol relies on a shared trunk of cabling. The trunk is a single run of coax or UTP cabling that extends throughout the topology of the LAN. Each workstation connects to the trunk directly and communicates with the LAN through an internal NIC. Whenever a station wants to transmit, it listens to the cable to determine if any other station is broadcasting. If no other station is broadcasting, it jumps in. Occasionally, a station will listen to the cable and determine that it's okay to jump in when, in reality, it isn't. When this happens, a collision occurs. By definition, collisions are bad.

Follow along with Figure 19.26 as we send a message from Workstation B to Workstation A:

1. Workstation B has a message for Workstation A. Workstation B listens to the trunk and waits until all is clear (this is called *carrier sensing*).
2. When B detects that the trunk is clear, the workstation marks the message with a destination address (A) and sends it over the trunk. All the other workstations continually monitor the trunk for a message with their address (called *multiple access*).

3. If Workstation A must send a message at the same time, it listens to the trunk but notices that a broadcast is in progress. It waits. While A is waiting, it monitors a matching packet, accepts the message from B, and returns an acknowledgment of receipt. Problems occur when multiple workstations send messages simultaneously, resulting in collisions.

FIGURE 19.26

Contention media-access protocol

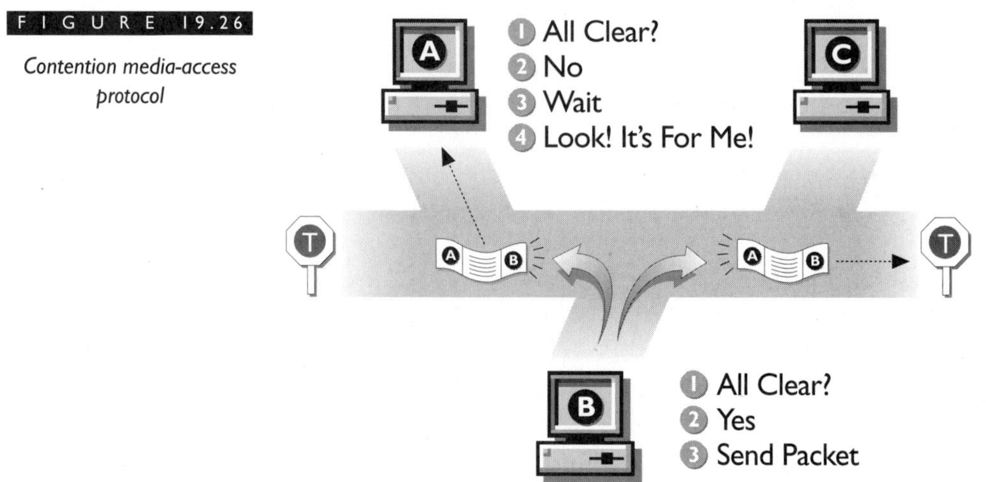

To deal with imminent collisions, contention-based protocols have adopted one of two solutions:

- *CSMA/CD*—Stands for Carrier Sense Multiple Access with Collision Detection. In the event of a collision, both transmitting stations back off and wait. Of course, if they waited exactly the same amount of time, they would collide again, so CSMA/CD builds in a random delay algorithm to make sure they don't collide. This is the protocol of choice for Ethernet LANs.
- *CSMA/CA*—Stands for Carrier Sense Multiple Access with Collision Avoidance. This system uses time slicing for channel access. This protocol avoids collisions altogether. Although it sounds like a much more civilized scheme, it takes too much time and, therefore, degrades network performance. CSMA/CA is the protocol of choice for Apple LocalTalk networks.

In summary, contention protocols enable immediate and complete control of the media as long as no other network device has access. In addition, the software is relatively simple to produce and involves little overhead. On the downside, access times are not predictable because of imminent collisions and retransmission. As a matter of fact, things get worse geometrically with the addition of new devices. Later in this section, Table 19.7 provides a comparative summary of the contention protocol and other media-access protocols.

Token-Passing Media-Access Protocol

The token-passing protocol relies on a control signal called the token. A token is a 24-bit packet that circulates throughout the network from NIC to NIC in an orderly fashion. If a workstation wants to transmit a message, it must first seize the token. At that point, it has complete control over the communications channel. The existence of only one token eliminates the possibility of signal collisions.

This organized approach makes transmission rates predictable. The token-passing protocol is said to be a *deterministic protocol*, in contrast to the contention protocol, which is a *probabilistic protocol*. So, how does it work? Refer to Figure 19.27 and follow these simple steps in order to learn how it works:

1. Workstation A has a message for Workstation D. Workstation A enters into transmit mode and captures the free-flowing token.

2. Workstation A attaches its message to the token, marks it with a destination address, and then sends the token along the network channel.

3. Workstation B is off, remaining in bypass mode, so the token continues straight through B's NIC and onto the next node.

4. Workstation C, in listen mode, notices the passing token and checks the destination address, but it doesn't find a match, so C sends the token back on its way.

5. Workstation D, also in listen mode, notices the token and checks the destination address. Now there's a match!

6. Workstation D switches into receive mode and copies the message into its memory. Remember, Workstation A still controls the token. To ensure continual communications, Workstation D must attach an acknowledgment back to the token and send it back to A.

7. Once Workstation A receives the acknowledgment message from Workstation D, it releases the token and enters into listen mode.

FIGURE 19.27

Token-passing media-access protocol

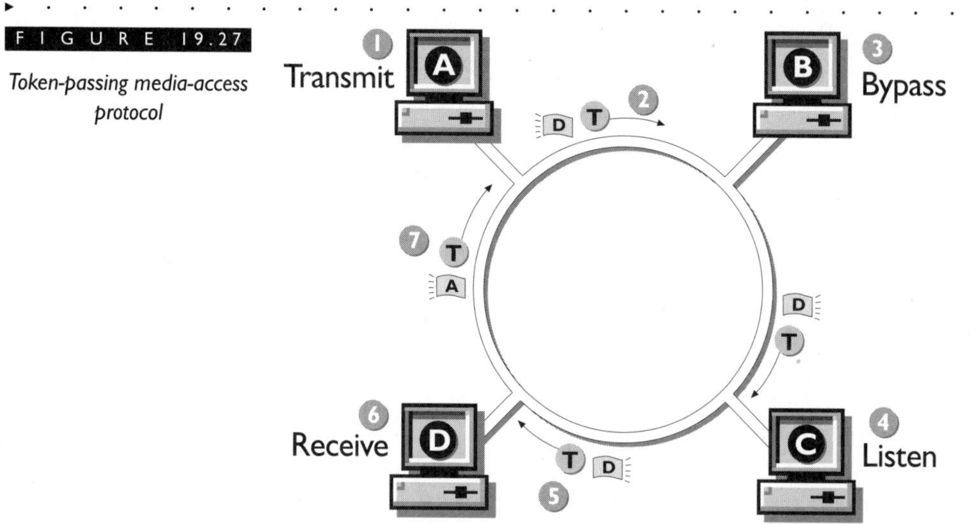

In summary, the token-passing protocol offers predictable, deterministic transmissions, which reduces collisions and, therefore, provides a high level of throughput, especially in high-load conditions. Performance is enhanced further by the addition of prioritization mechanisms. On the downside, the token-passing protocol requires complicated, intelligent devices that can be expensive and difficult to install. Also, network management requirements can make reconfiguration time consuming. Refer to Table 19.7 for a comparative summary of the token-passing protocol and other protocols.

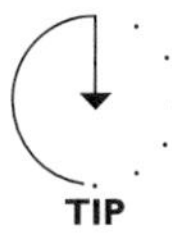

If you compare the performance of contention and token-passing networks, you find some interesting results. In high-load environments, token-passing networks provide much better throughput because they avoid collisions. In low-load environments, contention networks outperform token-passing networks because devices have immediate access to the channel. So, which environment do you live in?

Polling Media-Access Protocol

The polling media-access protocol relies on a central controlling device as a media-access administrator. This machine is sometimes called the controller, primary, or master. The central node polls each workstation (secondary) to determine whether there is a message to be sent. When a sending node is ready, the primary reserves the channel and the message is sent. Built-in rules determine how much data each secondary can transmit once it has been polled.

Polling typically is used in centralized systems because it relies on the intelligence and dexterity of a central controlling node. Most centralized systems have such a node available. In addition, polling systems are ideal for time-sensitive systems such as industry automation equipment.

In summary, polling networks provide predictable deterministic transmissions. The central controlling node can implement priority schemes and/or alternating time slices. In addition, polling enables complete use of the medium's capacity because it eliminates collisions. Unfortunately, polling has many built-in delays, especially if your node is at the low end of the totem pole. Also, because polling sends numerous notices and acknowledgements back and forth, it wastes much bandwidth.

Table 19.7 shows a comparative summary of the three media-access protocols discussed in this section.

Now that you understand how data signals get onto transmission media, let's learn where they go once they get there (also known as *physical addressing*).

TABLE 19.7

Comparative Summary of Media-Access Protocols

CONSIDERATION	CONTENTION	TOKEN-PASSING	POLLING
Channel access	Probabilistic	Deterministic	Deterministic
Prioritization	No	Yes	Yes
High-load performance	Slow	Fast	Medium
Low-load performance	Fast	Slow	Medium
Controlling overhead	None	Much	Too much

Physical Addressing

Network addressing provides critical routing information to transmission devices as packets traverse a network. Following are three hierarchical addresses that provide physical and logical information as data travels up the OSI model from the Physical Layer to the Application Layer:

- *Physical Address* — Operates at the Data Link Layer. Each data frame must include a unique 12-digit hexadecimal ID that represents the destination workstation NIC. This ID is hard-coded into each individual NIC.
- *Logical Address* — Operates at the Network Layer. Routers use this address to identify the destination network.
- *Service Address* — Operates at the Transport Layer. Finally, each data frame must include a service address to identify the destination upper-layer application.

Well, that does it for the MAC sublayer. Now let's turn our attention away from the physical aspects of Data Link transmission to the more logical administrative tasks. The second Data Link sublayer, Logical-Link Control, handles all the control functions needed to maintain your network link, including frame synchronization, flow control, and error checking.

Logical-Link Control (LLC)

The LLC sublayer governs the following three administrative technologies:

- *Frame Synchronization*—Enhances data synchronization by coordinating frame transmissions. As with data synchronization, frame synchronization uses *asynchronous* or *synchronous* communications, as well as a third form called *isochronous*.
- *Flow Control*—Regulates how much data the receiving station can handle.
- *Error Checking*—Concerned with the integrity of the data frame.

Each of these tasks is critical for maintaining node-to-node links. Furthermore, these administrative functions can contribute to the overall health of your network. Without them, transmissions would be reckless and out of control. Let's take a closer look.

Frame Synchronization

At the Physical Layer, asynchronous and synchronous data synchronization enables computers to identify bit intervals. At the Data Link Layer, these same data synchronization techniques are used to identify frame boundaries.

Asynchronous devices send each frame separately using the asynchronous data synchronization method. Each frame begins with a start bit, ends with a stop bit, and is transmitted with complete disregard for the timing of other transmissions because senders and receivers maintain their own internal clocks. *Synchronous* transmissions, in contrast, rely on the sender and receiver having synchronized clocks. This synchronization is accomplished with a special control character (known as SYNC) or with a separate dedicated clock channel.

Isochronous is a relatively new method of frame synchronization. It incorporates the advantages of both asynchronous and synchronous methods. Isochronous transmissions use a constant fixed-frequency transmission clock provided by the network. This is advantageous because all network machines rely on a third-party objective time provider, thus eliminating the excessive overhead of the asynchronous method and the expensive equipment required for the synchronous approach.

You should be aware of which frame synchronization method your network uses because depending upon which method you use, it can add considerable overhead and, therefore, waste capacity. Refer to Table 19.8 for a comparative summary of the three frame synchronization methods. After you've finished, move on to the second Data Link LLC technology—flow control.

TABLE 19.8

Comparison of Data Link Frame Synchronization

CONSIDERATION	ASYNCHRONOUS	SYNCHRONOUS	ISOCHRONOUS
Overhead	High	Low	Low
Complexity	Simple	Complex	Complex
Transmission speed	Slow	Fast	Moderate
Error checking	Parity	CRC	CRC

Data Link Flow Control

Data Link flow control regulates how much data can be broadcast on a given channel at one time. Networks are typically made up of devices with different transmission speeds, storage capacities, and processing capabilities. Most networks support two types of flow control:

- *Window Flow Control*—Window flow control establishes a window of opportunity for data transmissions. Typically, a special buffer is created that allows only a certain amount of data in a given period of time. This buffer can be fixed or dynamic. In static window flow control, the buffer is fixed in size. The sender must fill all the buffers, number them, and then send them one at a time. The receiver sends back an acknowledgment when it's time for the next buffer. This procedure is pretty inflexible and, many times, inefficient. To solve this problem, some networks use dynamic window flow control. In this scheme, the size of the buffer varies according to the receiver's capabilities.

- *Guaranteed Rate Flow Control*—Guaranteed rate flow control is similar to the static window scheme in that data flows at a fixed rate.

  But, unlike window flow control, guaranteed rate rules are established before transmissions are ever sent. The sender and receiver agree upon an acceptable transmission rate, which is maintained for the entire conversation.

That completes the second piece of Data Link LLC administration. So far, the sender and receiver have agreed on a synchronizing method and data rate. Now it's time to determine an error-checking scheme.

Data Link Error Checking

Network communications support three levels of error checking. Each method operates at increasingly higher layers of the OSI model. Together they ensure reliable end-to-end communications.

The first error checking function operates at the Data Link Layer, using a complex cyclic redundancy check (CRC) calculation. CRC ensures the integrity of a packet by calculating a 16-bit or 32-bit number based on the contents of the packet. If any of the contents change, the CRC value also changes. This number is calculated by the sender and placed in the CRC Data Link field. The receiver performs the same computation on the other end. If the CRC value matches, all is well and an acknowledgment is sent back to the sender. If the CRC value does not match, the receiver responds with a negative acknowledgment (NAK).

Congratulations! You have survived the onslaught of Physical and Data Link communications infrastructure. So far in this chapter, we have learned how logical rules can assist the physical transmission characteristics of network communications and provide form to an otherwise hectic world of zeroes and ones.

Now let's spend a moment learning how Physical and Data Link theories come to life (that is, Bottom Layer Implementations).

REAL WORLD

As we've just learned, LLC administration is responsible for frame synchronization, flow control, and error checking. In the world of networking, these Data Link functions are organized into the following three types of connection services:

- *Unacknowledged Connectionless Services* — Send and receive frames with no flow control, no error checking, or packet sequence control. It's a free-for-all — just raw speed.
- *Connection-Oriented Services* — Provide strict rules for flow control, error checking, and packet sequence. This is all accomplished with the help of acknowledgments. This system is structured and methodical.
- *Acknowledged Connectionless Services* — Use acknowledgments to furnish flow control and error checking between point-to-point transmissions. This system is a compromise.

Each type of Data Link implementation requires a different level of connection services. For example, automated teller machines require connection-oriented services because the transmission is so important. The good news is that you don't choose the Data Link connection service. It's chosen for you. Most of today's networking applications are based on one of these three standards.

Bottom Layer Implementations

So far, we have studied the theoretical technologies underlying OSI communications. Of course, all the theories in the world aren't going to mean anything if we can't bring them to life. That's what implementations are for. OSI communications implementations bring Physical and Data Link theories to life.

There are two notable implementations at the Physical Layer:

- Serial Line Interface Protocol (SLIP)
- Synchronous Optical Network (SONET) and Synchronous Digital Hierarchy (SDH)

Furthermore, we will explore four notable implementations at the Data Link Layer:

- PPP
- FDDI
- Frame relay
- IEEE 802 series

In the following sections, we will explore these six implementations from the inside out. Now you get to apply all of those conceptual models you've been struggling through in this chapter. So, without any further ado, let's start at the Physical Layer.

Physical Layer Implementations

The following notable implementations operate at the Physical Layer of the OSI model (see Figure 19.28):

- *Serial Line Interface Protocol (SLIP)*—SLIP provides dial-up telephone connections using the IP protocol. SLIP is a WAN implementation at the Physical Layer that connects LANs to WANs or modems to other modems. SLIP was the first of two protocols developed to provide IP dial-up connectivity (the other protocol, Point-to-Point Protocol, or PPP, is more complex). SLIP uses a peer-to-peer relationship between a remote IP node and the Internet host. The dial-in host is located on a network and must have access to the Internet.

- *SONET and SDH*—Bell Labs introduced Synchronous Optical Network (SONET) in 1984, and the American National Standards Institute (ANSI) quickly accepted it. By the end of 1988, the Consultative Committee for International Telegraphy and Telephony (CCITT), a subgroup of the International Telecommunications Union (ITU), published a similar set of standards called Synchronous Digital Hierarchy (SDH).

SONET and SDH are optical implementations that take advantage of the bandwidth and high reliability of fiber optics over point-to-point connections. In addition, they use time-division multiplexing (TDM) over a mesh or ring physical topology. SONET and SDH are the physical foundations of various high-level implementations, including FDDI, Switched Multimegabit Data Service (SMDS), and Asynchronous Transfer Mode (ATM).

FIGURE 19.28

Physical Layer implementations

Application
Presentation
Session
Transport
Network
Data Link
Physical
SLIP
SONET/SDH

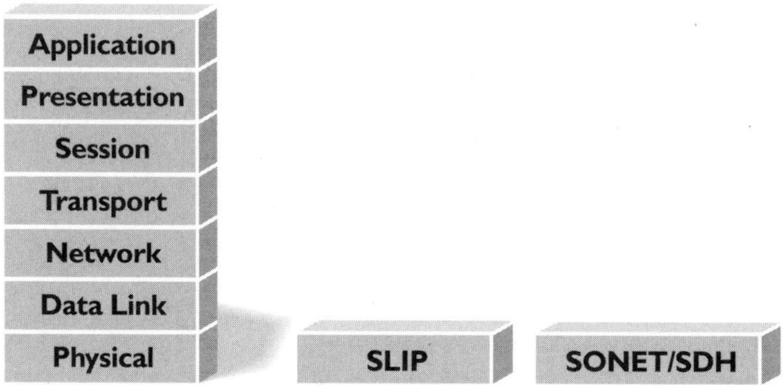

Refer to Table 19.9 for a feature summary of these Physical Layer implementations.

TABLE 19.9

A Feature Summary of Physical Layer Implementations

IMPLEMENTATION	CONNECTION TYPE	PHYSICAL TOPOLOGY	DATA BANDWIDTH
SLIP	Point-to-point	Peer-to-Peer	
SONET and SDH	Point-to-point	Mesh or ring	Baseband with TDM

Data Link Layer Implementations

The following four notable implementations operate at both the Physical Layer and Data Link Layer of the OSI model (see Figure 19.29):

- *PPP*—The Point-to-Point Protocol (PPP) is the successor to SLIP. It was designed by the Internet Engineering Task Force (IETF) to be an improvement over SLIP and to provide a variety of Data Link functions, including dynamic IP addressing, support for multiple protocols on the same link, password login, and error checking.

- *FDDI*—The Fiber Distributed Data Interface (FDDI) was developed in 1986 by ANSI's X3T9.5 Committee to describe a protocol standard for high-speed optical communications. FDDI provides 100 Mbps data transmissions over fiber-optic cabling using a protocol similar to IEEE 802.5 (token ring). FDDI's performance exceeds 802.5 because it takes advantage of the high bandwidth and EMI immunity of fiber-optic cabling. In addition, pressure to provide support for twisted-pair media has led to the development of a copper-based version of FDDI called *Copper Distributed Data Interface* (CDDI).

FIGURE 19.29

Physical and Data Link Layer implementations

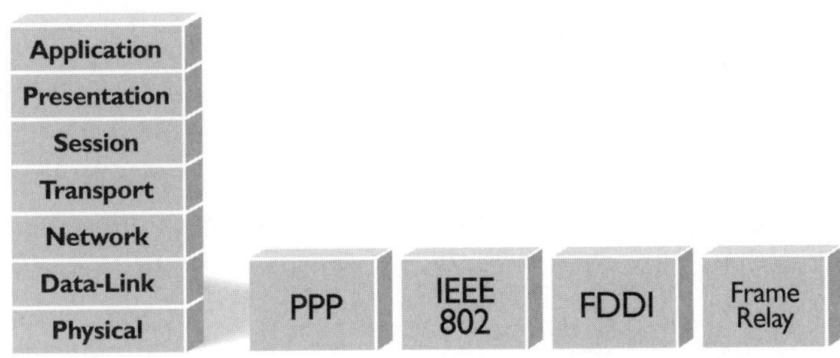

- *Frame Relay* — Frame relay was developed to address packet switching communications over Public Switched Telephone Networks (PSTNs). Although frame relay operates only at the Physical Layer and Data Link Layer, it is related to X.25 (which operates at the Network Layer). At the Physical Layer, frame relay supports point-to-point communications across a hybrid mesh topology. It relies on packet switching for bit organization. At the Data Link Layer, frame relay supports flow control and error checking. Interestingly, it can detect errors, but not recover from them. Frame relay is commonly offered at capacities ranging from 56 Kbps to 1.544 Mbps.

- *IEEE 802 Series* — The IEEE 802 series currently includes 12 protocols that provide a variety of critical Physical Layer and Data Link Layer network functions. These protocols are described in depth in the next section.

Refer to Table 19.10 for a feature summary of three of the four Data Link Layer implementations described in this section.

IEEE 802 Series

In 1985, the Institute of Electrical and Electronic Engineers (IEEE) published a series of Physical and Data Link standards through the Project 802 Committee. ANSI quickly adopted these standards, and the International Standards Organization (ISO) has also revised and reissued the standards as the 8802 protocols. The IEEE 802 series currently consists of 12 standards, numbered 802.1 through 802.12. All of these standards operate at the Physical Layer and Data Link Layer, except 802.1 and 802.10 (which extend into upper layers).

Following is a brief description of each of the 12 IEEE 802 series protocols:

- *IEEE 802.1* — This protocol identifies network management and internetworking technologies in the top layers of the OSI model.

- *IEEE 802.2* — This protocol is also known as Logical-Link Control (LLC), which adds administrative information to the following MAC packets: 802.3, 802.4, 802.5, and 802.6.

TABLE 19.10

A Feature Summary of Data Link Layer Implementations

IMPLEMENTATION	CONNECTION TYPE	PHYSICAL TOPOLOGY	DATA SIGNALING	DATA BANDWIDTH	MEDIA-ACCESS PROTOCOL	LLC
PPP	Point-to-point					Error checking
FDDI	Ring of stars	Dual ring	State transition	Baseband	Token-passing	
Frame relay	Point-to-point	Hybrid mesh				Flow control and error checking

- *IEEE 802.3* — This protocol is commonly referred to as the Ethernet protocol. IEEE 802.3 extends beyond the original Ethernet standard by providing more variety at the Physical Layer and Data Link Layer, including different signaling modes, media types, physical topologies, and data rates. A variety of IEEE 802.3 standards have emerged: 10Base5 (Thick Ethernet), 10Base2 (Thin Ethernet), and 10BaseT. In addition, IEEE 802.3u Fast Ethernet employs twisted-pair or fiber-optic media at 100 Mbps, the standard Carrier Sense Multiple Access with Collision Detection (CSMA/CD) MAC protocol, and the hierarchical star topology made popular by 10BaseT. Finally, IEEE 802.3z and 802.3ab specifications define 1000Base-T Gigabit Ethernet.

- *IEEE 802.4* — This protocol was created to satisfy the LAN needs of factory and industrial automation. The 802.4 subcommittee was active from 1984 until 1988. During that time, the subcommittee defined a standard that uses a bus topology, a token-passing media-access protocol, baseband and broadband media, and a 75-ohm CATV-type cable or optical fiber.

- *IEEE 802.5* — This protocol is commonly referred to as token ring. IEEE 802.5 uses a token-passing media-access method and Differential Manchester encoding to provide data rates of 1 Mbps, 4 Mbps, or 16 Mbps. This standard differs from IBM's Token Ring specification in two respects: It does not specify a particular transmission medium (IBM uses STP) or physical topology (IBM uses a ring).

- *IEEE 802.6* — This protocol is a reliable high-speed Physical Layer and Data Link Layer implementation for metropolitan area networks (MANs). The committee's solution was a technology called *Distributed Queue Dual Bus* (DQDB), which uses a fiber-based, dual-bus topology that may be looped for fault tolerance. Each bus is unidirectional and the two buses operate in opposite directions.

- *IEEE 802.7*—This protocol defines a standard for integrating video and digital networks.
- *IEEE 802.8*—This protocol defines a Fiber Optic Technical Advisory Group to work with 802 working groups on fiber-optic solutions for IEEE 802.3, 802.4, and 802.5 implementations. In addition, this group is working on standards for fiber-optic installation and training documentation.
- *IEEE 802.9*—This protocol defines an isochronous version of Ethernet known as *IsoEnet*. This standard provides 16 Mbps data transmission by combining one asynchronous 10 Mbps channel with 96 individual 64 Kbps dedicated channels over UTP.
- *IEEE 802.10*—This protocol defines standards for LAN security, encryption, management, and OSI compliance.
- *IEEE 802.11*—This protocol defines standards for wireless network communications.
- *IEEE 802.12*—This protocol defines a successor to 802.3 called 100 VG-AnyLAN. This standard has a rated speed of up to 100 Mbps over Category 3 UTP (voice-grade) cabling. Unfortunately, 100 VG-AnyLAN does not support standard 10BaseT Ethernet concentrators. Instead, you must connect your workstation to a special hub that provides channel access, based on the priority of the data.

Refer to Table 19.11 for a feature summary of the most notable IEEE 802 series protocols.

TABLE 19.11

A Feature Summary of IEEE 802 Series Protocols

IMPLEMENTATION	CONNECTION TYPE	PHYSICAL TOPOLOGY	DATA SIGNALING	DATA SYNCHRONIZATION	DATA BANDWIDTH	MEDIA-ACCESS PROTOCOL
IEEE 802.3 and 802.3u	Multipoint	Bus	State transition	Synchronous	Baseband (except 10Broad-36)	Contention
IEEE 802.4	Multipoint	Bus	State transition	Synchronous	Baseband	Token-passing
IEEE 802.5	Multipoint	Ring of stars	State transition	Synchronous	Baseband	Token-passing
IEEE 802.6	Point-to-point	Ring			Baseband	
IEEE 802.11		Cellular				Contention
IEEE 802.12	Multipoint	Star	State transition	Synchronous	Baseband	Contention

Wow—You did it!

This completes our comprehensive journey through the bottom two layers of computer networking. It certainly has been a knowledge-packed trip. Think about how much your brain has grown since you began reading this chapter.

So, what's next? Well, provided that your brain isn't Jell-O by now, we can continue our trek into the networking and services domains of OSI. See you in the next chapter.

LAB EXERCISE 19.2: GETTING TO KNOW THE BOTTOM LAYERS

Use the hints provided to find the 20 communications terms hidden in the word search puzzle. Omit any punctuation characters (such as blank spaces, hyphens, and so on) and spell out any numbers.

S	L	I	P	B	N	J	T	W	X	Y	C	A	J	E	Y	C	E
Y	O	L	C	R	Q	R	F	L	H	G	N	S	A	R	G	M	B
N	G	Q	A	L	F	O	R	A	M	T	C	D	N	M	L	Q	M
C	I	R	A	I	S	C	J	T	F	R	T	E	M	M	P	Y	H
H	C	X	Y	D	X	J	K	Y	J	K	F	X	P	M	T	X	U
R	A	S	M	C	C	A	B	L	E	M	E	D	I	A	G	D	U
O	L	L	T	P	O	P	O	L	L	I	N	G	K	E	M	J	E
N	A	O	J	A	S	Y	N	C	H	R	O	N	O	U	S	T	C
O	D	I	G	I	T	A	L	S	I	G	N	A	L	I	N	G	V
U	D	S	L	D	B	T	O	K	E	N	P	A	S	S	I	N	G
S	R	S	L	Y	E	U	D	B	E	O	D	U	R	P	O	D	D
D	E	T	W	R	A	M	I	M	C	R	V	N	F	N	O	C	J
V	S	N	S	I	F	R	A	M	E	R	E	L	A	Y	V	G	Y
Q	S	V	R	E	T	U	O	R	B	R	O	A	D	B	A	N	D
M	T	U	T	Q	U	C	M	I	C	R	O	W	A	V	E	O	F
H	I	V	C	W	Z	N	H	E	M	V	J	T	N	O	Z	Q	Y
G	C	G	V	C	U	R	R	E	N	T	S	T	A	T	E	B	Y
D	Q	H	J	T	M	W	K	I	S	B	V	W	A	Z	E	S	M

Hints

1. Typical bipolar encoding scheme in which the digital signal varies among three levels: positive, zero, and negative. A one is represented by a transition from high to low or low to high, and zero is distinguished as any stable voltage at the beginning of the bit interval.
2. Data synchronization with "start" and "stop" bits.

3. A contiguous group of frequencies that, because of convenience or technical details, are used for a single purpose (or treated like a single frequency).
4. Data bandwidth for analog communications and your cable TV.
5. A "well-behaved" router; sounds like a Green Bay sausage.
6. Coaxial and fiber-optic cabling have this in common.
7. Ethernet and cable TV have this in common.
8. Polar and RZ have this in common.
9. Where the subscriber's wiring meets the phone company.
10. If only the world was "black and white."
11. WAN implementation that relies on PSTN for reliable point-to-point packet delivery.
12. Addressing at the Network Layer.
13. "Transmit that data or your goose will be cooked!"
14. Relies on a central controlling node for network communications.
15. Where the CO and long-distance carrier meet.
16. Dial-up access to IP networks; operates at the Physical Layer.
17. Baseband multiplexing on a first-come, first-served basis.
18. Multiport devices that provide high-speed forwarding of frames.
19. Means "with clock."
20. A common deterministic media-access protocol.

See Appendix C for answers.

LAB EXERCISE 19.3: THE OSI MODEL — BOTTOM LAYERS

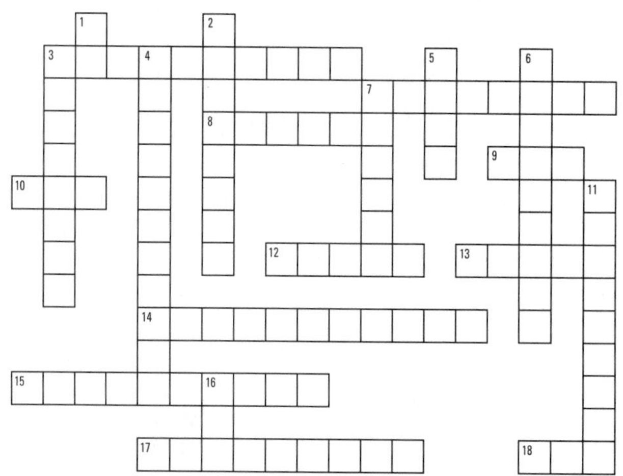

Across

3. A "free-for-all" media-access protocol
7. Data bandwidth for digital communications
8. Transmission device at the Network Layer
9. ANSI standard for photonic communications
10. Center of the star
12. Digital to analog and back
13. A backward modem
14. Loss of signal strength over distance
15. Light pulses on hair-like pieces of glass
17. Analog signal strength
18. A more EMI-resistant version of UTP

Down

1. Local telephone company central office
2. TV remote-control technology
3. Networking over your car phone
4. One of three types of bound media
5. The largest network in the world

6. "Range of frequencies"
7. Transmission device at the Data Link Layer
11. From demarc to CO
16. Data Link implementation of SLIP

See Appendix C for answers.

CHAPTER 20

The OSI Model—Middle Layers

Welcome to the second functional domain of computer networking!

This region deals with OSI Networking communications, which covers the middle two layers of the 3-D OSI Reference Map. As we learned in Chapter 18, network elements are the third phase of networking. They define the *what, how,* and *who* of networking technologies. In the OSI Networking domain, we will explore the *how.*

In the previous chapter, we learned that network communications provide the electronic pathway that computers use to communicate with each other. We learned about physical cabling, data signals, and LAN standards.

Now, in this chapter, we're concerned with getting the frames from Point A to Point B, all in one piece. *Networking* represents the rules of the road. It defines protocols that instruct different machines on how to speak to each other. Today's most popular networking protocols include IPX/SPX, TCP/IP, and AppleTalk (for Macintosh computers).

According to the OSI Reference Map (see Figure 20.1), the middle two functional layers are the following:

- The Network Layer
- The Transport Layer

FIGURE 20.1

Understanding OSI Networking

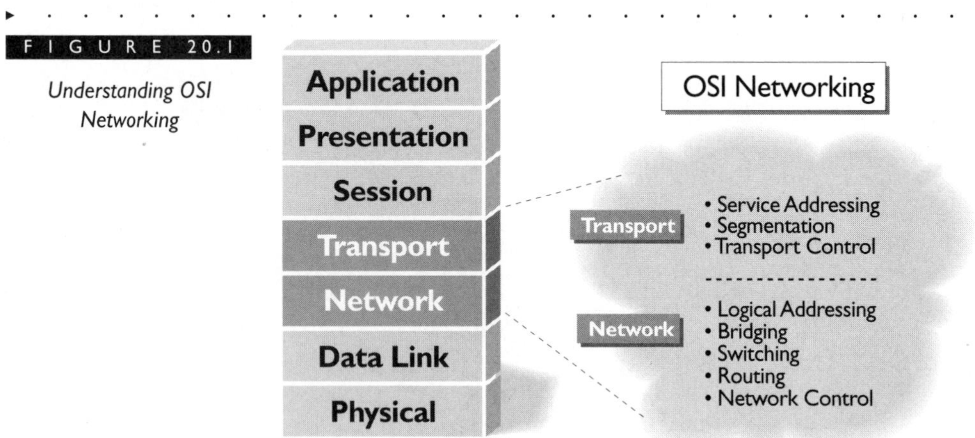

The *Network Layer* provides a logical pathway for LAN-to-LAN communications. It includes logical addressing, bridging, switching, routing, and network control functions. Without the Network Layer, LANs would be isolated islands of information. The *Transport Layer* supports WAN communications by providing service addressing, segmentation, and transport control. The primary purpose of the Transport Layer is to organize datagrams into segments and deliver them reliably to the correct upper-layer services.

Let's begin our exciting networking journey by exploring the first layer of the Networking domain—the Network Layer.

The Network Layer

The Network Layer of the OSI model is primarily responsible for moving data from source devices, through the network infrastructure, to destination devices. This is accomplished using the following five capabilities:

- *Logical Addressing*—This is a Network Layer addressing scheme that determines the logical path during internetwork communications. Logical addressing combines with physical addressing (at the Data Link Layer) to identify destination network segments.
- *Network Control*—This is a category of Network Layer administration that ensures flow control, sequencing, and translation. Specifically, network control manages bottlenecks and reassembles datagrams in the correct order.
- *Bridging*—This is a Data Link Layer packet-routing technology that filters network traffic based on the Media Access Control (MAC) address. Bridging works together with switching and routing to ensure reliable network trafficking.
- *Switching*—This is a Data Link Layer packet-routing technology that provides a choice of architectures for end-to-end packet delivery (such as circuit, message, and packet).

- *Routing*—This is the primary Network Layer technology that routes OSI model messages via two important steps: route discovery and route selection. During *route discovery,* the network builds a Routing Information Table (RIT) and lists all possible paths to reach a given destination. Once routers have discovered these paths, they use *route selection* to choose the optimum one.

Let's start our exploration of OSI Network Layer functionality with a lesson in logical addressing.

Logical Addressing

Network addressing provides critical routing information to transmission devices as packets traverse the network. Following are three hierarchical types of addresses that provide physical and logical information as data travels up the OSI model from the Physical Layer to the Application Layer:

- *Physical Address*—This operates at the Data Link Layer. Each data frame must include a unique 12-digit hexadecimal ID that represents the destination workstation NIC.
- *Logical Address*—This operates at the Network Layer. This address is used by routers to identify the destination network.
- *Service Address*—This operates at the Transport Layer. Each data frame must include a service address to identify the destination upper-layer application.

In Figure 20.2, suppose workstation 7654321 prints to a queue on file server 1234567. To accomplish this, the workstation must send a packet with three pieces of information: the logical address (ABC, to identify the correct network), the physical address (1234567, to identify the correct server), and the service address (B Printing, to identify the correct service).

FIGURE 20.2

Logical addressing at the Network Layer

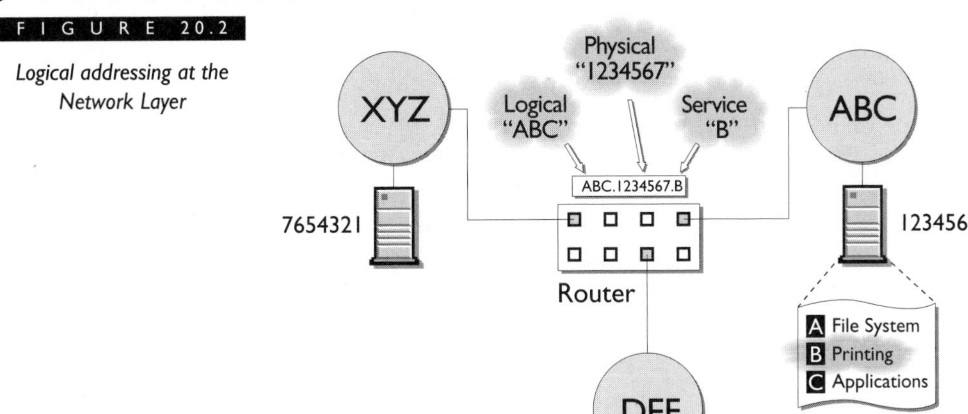

On a NetWare 5.1 network, physical, logical, and service addressing are handled by distinctly different devices and services. The *physical address* is burned into the NIC by the manufacturer at the factory. The *logical address* is defined by the BIND statement during server startup (for example, `BIND IPX to 3C5X9 NET=ABC`). Finally, the *service address* identifies unique network services (such as file, system, printing, and applications) with the core NetWare 5.1 operating system.

Network Control

Network control defines a suite of Network Layer administrative tasks that support internetworking and routing. These tasks include the following:

- *Network Flow Control*—This monitors the amount of data that follows any specific path in the network. With network flow control, transmission speeds and network reliability can change from one moment to the next, based on the amount of traffic being generated by all senders and receivers throughout the system. Using internal administrative mechanisms, the Network Layer can control the amount of data sent on a given route and provide alternate paths for certain packets. This function is sometimes called *congestion control*.

- *Network Sequencing* — This reorders packets at the destination device to ensure that the message is reassembled in the correct order. Network sequencing uses internal address information to piece packets back together. This type of Network Layer administration is required for packet-switching networks, where datagrams routinely arrive out of order. It may also be required for large virtual-circuit networks. As you can see in Figure 20.3, network sequencing uses two pieces of information: Datagram ID (which identifies pieces from the same packet) and sequence number (which provides ordering information for different datagrams within the same packet).

- *Network Error Checking* — This detects packet delivery errors and requests retransmission, if necessary. Network Layer error checking is concerned primarily with packet loss, duplicate packets, and altered data. Some Network Layer implementations may use internal error-checking algorithms for transmission reliability, but most of them operate at the Transport Layer and Data Link Layer.

FIGURE 20.3

Network sequencing

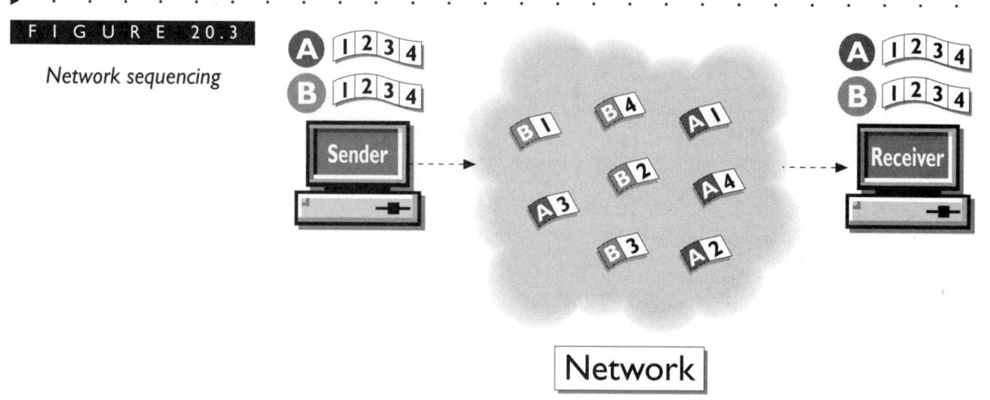

Let's review. So far, we've defined the physical network path from Point A to Point B by using various technologies at the Physical and Data Link Layers. Next, logical addressing enabled us to focus on a specific LAN segment. This is where bridges, switches, and routers come into play. In the next three sections, we will explore these critical internetworking devices in great depth. Have fun!

Bridging

Bridges reduce network utilization by filtering traffic on network segments. Bridges use the six-byte hexadecimal MAC addresses of NICs to make packet-forwarding decisions. The primary function of a bridge is to contain local intrasegment traffic and forward only intersegment packets.

Following is a list of bridging activities:

- Bridges maximize available network bandwidth.
- Bridges base packet-forwarding decisions on MAC addresses only, not on upper-layer protocol information. In other words, the operation of a bridge is completely independent of upper-layer protocols such as IPX/SPX or TCP/IP.
- Bridges operate at the Data Link Layer.
- Bridges can increase the maximum diameter of a network because they also act as repeaters.
- Bridging design encourages use of the *80/20 rule*. Simply stated, at least 80 percent of a network's total traffic should be intrasegment (contained on a single segment), and no more than 20 percent should be intersegment (forwarded by a bridge). To comply with the 80/20 rule, you must carefully examine the devices that are connected to your network (such as servers and shared printers) and determine who accesses these resources most frequently.

In the scenario offered in Figure 20.4, suppose that Workstation 100 sends a message to Workstation 101. The bridge would recognize the communication as intrasegment and prohibit it from traveling to Segment B. This strategy effectively separates communications on the two segments, which reduces traffic load. In contrast, if Workstation 200 sends a message to Workstation 101, the bridge would recognize it as intersegment and broadcast the message on both segments. Ultimately, Workstation 101 would recognize the physical address of both packets and pick them up.

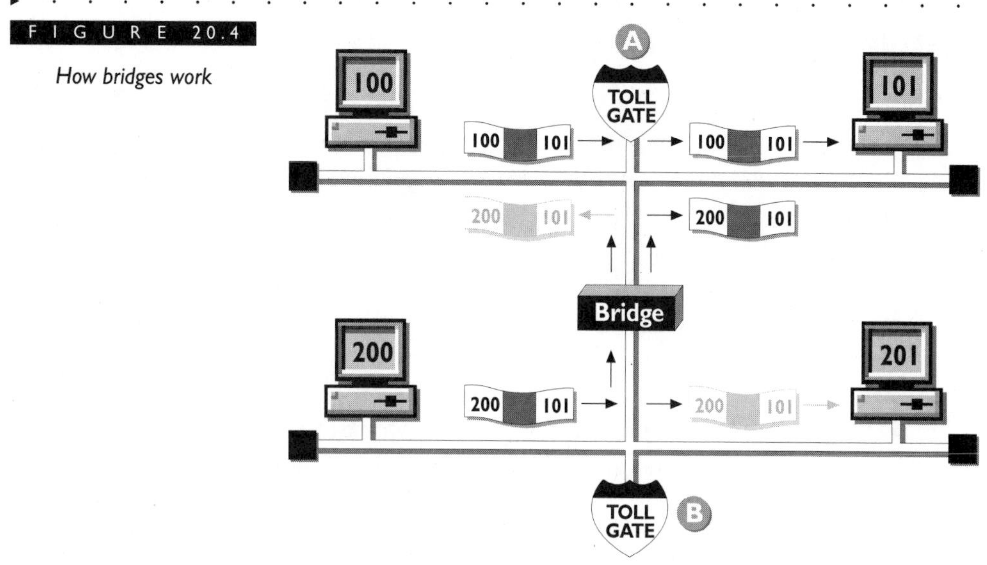

FIGURE 20.4
How bridges work

Following are two of the most popular types of bridges:

- *Transparent Bridges (Also Known As Learning Bridges)* — Transparent bridges are widely deployed and easy to implement because they have minimal installation and setup requirements. These bridges learn the location of network devices by examining the source MAC address field and providing transparent forwarding services. Transparent bridges are based on the IEEE 802.1d Spanning Tree Protocol (STP), which enables network administrators to configure redundant paths between network segments.
- *Source-Routing Bridges* — Source-routing bridges are typically used in IBM Token Ring networks. Like transparent bridges, a source-routing bridge forwards frames from one cable segment to another. The manner in which they perform this task is significantly different, however. Unlike transparent bridges, source-routing devices do not maintain a filtering database. Instead, each device maintains its own dynamic table of routes and transmits this information in the MAC headers of the frame.

Transparent Bridging

Upon initial startup, transparent bridges forward *all* packets to all segments (other than the segment where the transmission originated). Over time, each bridge builds a filtering database that associates each device's MAC address with a port on the bridge. Manufacturers insert permanent broadcast and multicast entries into this database to meet protocol specifications. Network administrators are also allowed to make changes manually. A one-to-one relationship exists between the number of entries in the filtering database and every device using the network. This is required so that the database can keep track of every broadcast and multicast address that is forwarded between segments. This is called a *flat addressing scheme*. Once the bridge learns the address of all network devices, it will only forward intersegment traffic.

In the following sections, we will explore the five operational states of bridge ports and learn how transparent bridges decide which packets get forwarded. Next, we will learn how filtering databases are created and maintained. Then we will study how the Spanning Tree Protocol helps avoid *bridging loops*. Finally, we will expand our general understanding of bridge operations with a quick look at what happens when network topologies change.

Transparent Bridge Port States

Bridges connect two or more network segments by way of *bridge ports*. These ports provide the same functionality as an NIC. A bridge port normally exhibits one of the following five different states:

- *State 1: Disabled*—This identifies a port that has been switched off. A disabled bridge port will not learn of or forward packets.
- *State 2: Blocking*—This is *standby mode*. A bridge port in the blocking state responds only to bridge protocol frames addressed to the bridge's multicast address. This is the state of all bridge ports during the initialization process. In addition, this is the state of all Backup Bridges that have been configured in a redundant pair of bridges.
- *State 3: Listening*—A bridge port in the listening state is counting down (by way of a timer) in preparation for the learning and forwarding states. During this time, no entries are made to the filtering database and no packets are forwarded.

- *State 4: Learning*—A bridge port temporarily enters the learning state for a predetermined amount of time before finally reaching the forwarding state. This is done to reduce the risk of *bridging loops,* which occur when two bridges forward a frame back and forth between two segments. In this state, a bridge will place as many entries into the filtering database as possible until it reaches the forwarding state.

- *State 5: Forwarding*—This identifies a functioning bridge port. In this active state, the bridge can learn device addresses and forward frames.

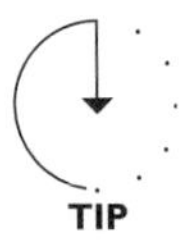

TIP

According to the IEEE 802.1d Spanning Tree Protocol, bridge ports progress from State 1 through State 5 during reconfiguration.

A virtual worker, known as a *port relay entity*, lives inside each transparent bridge. The relay entity is responsible for deciding whether or not a frame should be forwarded. To make this decision, our virtual worker uses the following criteria:

- According to the filtering database, the destination device is connected to a remote segment.

- The frame contains data for the LLC or higher-layer protocols.

- The cyclic redundancy check (CRC) is valid.

- The frame is not a control frame addressed to the bridge.

The process of receiving a frame, storing it temporarily to examine the destination address, and then forwarding the frame is called *store-and-forward operation*. This means that a bridge receives an entire frame, validates the CRC, and then makes the frame forwarding decision. The amount of time required by a bridge to perform this process is known as the *latency period*. Because bridged networks use variable-sized frames, the latency period is directly proportional to the size of a frame.

So, that's how the bridge ports know *when* to ignore, learn, or forward MAC frames. But the real trick is deciding *who* gets through. That's the responsibility of the filtering database. Let's take a closer look at it.

REAL WORLD

By verifying a frame's CRC, bridges prevent damaged frames from being forwarded. This helps to keep malformed frames, such as *runts* (undersized) and *giants* (oversized), from clogging up the network and causing mass hysteria.

Building a Filtering Database

Figure 20.5 shows the beginning of building a filtering database. In this scenario, suppose bridge B1 is connected to three cable segments—labeled S1, S2, and S3. The bridge has just been powered on for the first time. When Station A wants to transmit a frame to Station D, it builds a frame and enters Station D's physical address in the destination address field of the MAC header. It also enters its own physical address in the source address field and calculates the cyclic redundancy check (CRC) value.

FIGURE 20.5

Building a filtering database

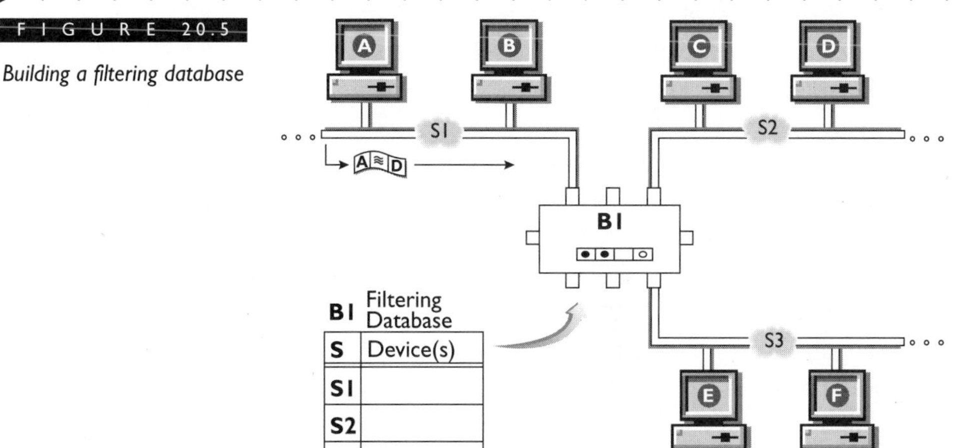

Station A's NIC transmits the frame's bits to cable segment S1. Bridge B1 receives the frame along with all other devices connected to segment S1 and copies the bits into memory. Next, the bridge reads the source address value contained in the MAC header and places an entry in its filtering database that associates Station A's physical address with cable segment S1. Thus, the bridge has learned where Station A is located. Figure 20.6 shows the initial contents of the filtering database—Step 1.

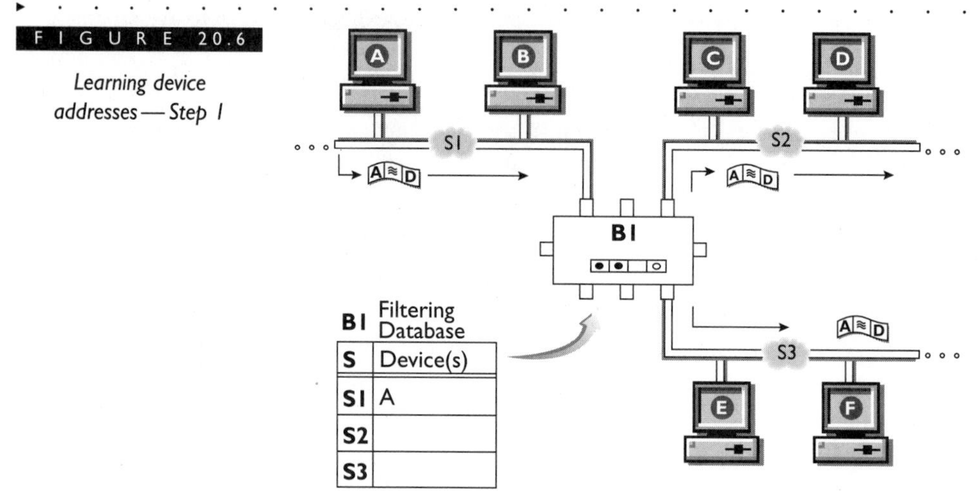

FIGURE 20.6

Learning device addresses — Step 1

Because the bridge has not yet determined where Station D is located, it forwards the frame to segments S2 and S3 and hopes that the destination device will be located on one of these segments. When a reply is transmitted from Station D to Station A, the process is essentially reversed. Station D places Station A's physical address in the destination address field of the frame's MAC header, as well as its own address in the source address field. The CRC is calculated and the frame's bits are transmitted to segment S2.

Finally, the bridge reads the source address value and places an entry in its filtering database that associates Station D's physical address with cable segment S2. The bridge now knows where Station D is located. Figure 20.7 shows the growing contents of the filtering database — Step 2. Because the filtering database contains an entry for Station A, the bridge forwards the frame to cable segment S1 only. If there were no entry for Station A in the database, the frame would be forwarded to segments S1 and S3.

You might be wondering what the bridge does when a frame does not need to be forwarded. Figure 20.8 shows a frame transmission from Station C to Station D. First, Station C places Station D's physical address in the destination address field of the frame's MAC header, as well as its own address in the source address field. The CRC is calculated and the frame's bits are transmitted to segment S2. The bridge reads the source address value and places an entry in its filtering database that associates Station C's physical address with cable segment S2. The bridge now knows where Station C is located.

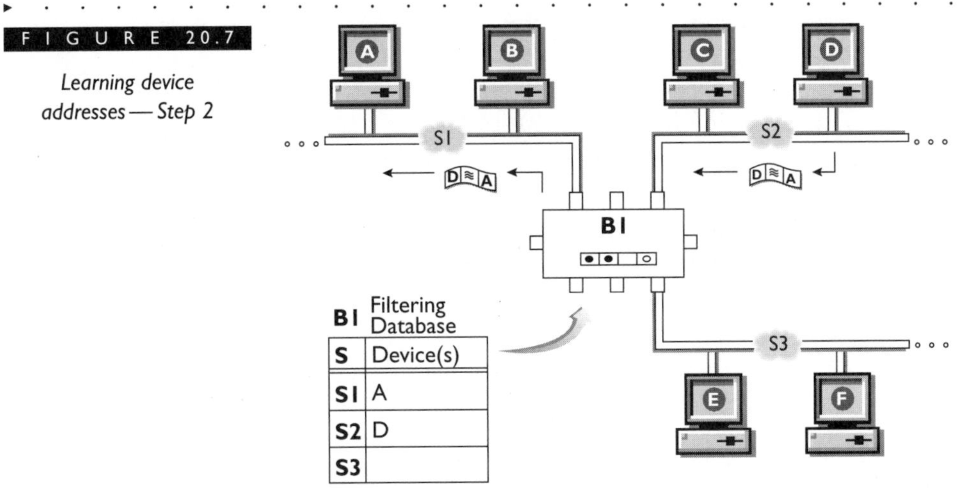

FIGURE 20.7

Learning device addresses — Step 2

Next, the bridge reads the destination address value and examines its filtering database to determine if the frame should be forwarded. Because the database indicates that Station C and Station D are on the same segment, the bridge recognizes this as intrasegment bridging and discards the frame. Once all device addresses have been learned, our bridge can filter traffic as it was intended to.

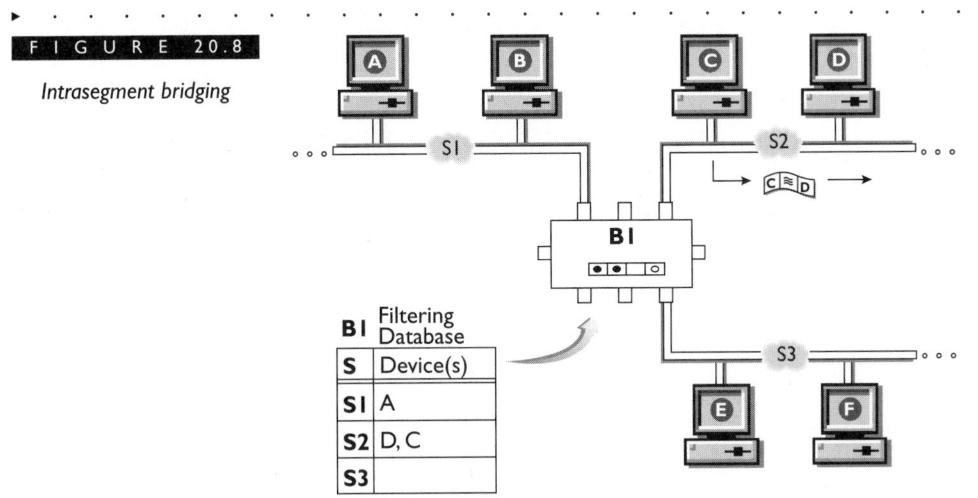

FIGURE 20.8

Intrasegment bridging

REAL WORLD

The performance of a bridge is rated according to its ability to filter and forward frames (in packets per second). Most bridges can filter somewhere between 10,000 to 12,000 packets per second and forward between 6,000 to 8,000 packets per second. This is a little slower than the data rate of most network protocols. For example, the maximum theoretical data rate of Ethernet is 14,688 packets per second.

Very good! Now let's examine how to use bridges to create redundant paths across our network while avoiding bridging loops.

Spanning Tree Protocol

For redundancy purposes, most network segments will have two or more connecting bridges. While this is a good idea from a reliability perspective, it can lead to bridging loops (also known as *broadcast storms*). Bridging loops occur when two redundant bridges forward a frame back and forth between themselves and the frame does not reach the correct destination segment.

Figure 20.9 illustrates the evolution of a bridging loop. In this configuration, two redundant bridges, B1 and B2, are connected to segments S1 and S2. Station A has transmitted a frame to Station B and both bridges have added an entry for Station A to their respective filtering databases. Even though both bridges have similar performance characteristics, they each forward the frame to segment S2 at slightly different times. In this scenario, bridge B1 is slightly faster in forwarding the frame to segment S2.

Bridge B2, however, does not know that the frame it receives on segment S2 is the one that was forwarded by bridge B1. Instead, it concludes that Station A (the frame's source) must have been physically relocated to segment S2. It updates its filtering database, and forwards the frame to segment S1. When bridge B1 receives the frame, it reads Station A's physical address (from the source address field), determines that Station A has moved to segment S2, and updates its filtering database to reflect the change. The result is a continuous bridging loop.

FIGURE 20.9

Evolution of a bridging loop

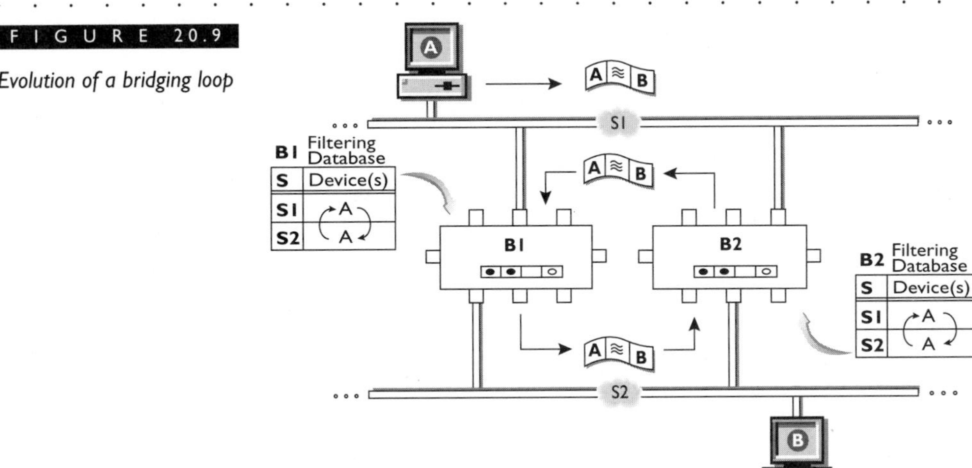

The IEEE 802.1d Spanning Tree Protocol (STP) was designed to manage multiple redundant bridges and eliminate bridging loops. The 802.1d Protocol uses pairs of redundant bridges that are configured in a primary and secondary arrangement. The primary bridge is called the *Designated Bridge* and it operates in learning or forwarding mode. The secondary bridge is called the *Backup Bridge* and it operates in standby mode.

The Spanning Tree Protocol provides the following capabilities (see the STP hierarchical structure in Figure 20.10):

- Dynamic path configuration between redundant bridges
- Dynamic failure detection and reconfiguration
- Elimination of bridging loops

The bridge residing at the top of the 802.1d hierarchy is called the *Root Bridge*. The Root Bridge transmits periodic configuration messages that are forwarded by all Designated Bridges. Interbridge communications use a special packet called a *Bridge Protocol Data Unit* (BPDU). Bridges send BPDU packets to dynamically select the Root Bridge and to communicate between the Root Bridge and Designated/Backup Bridges.

FIGURE 20.10

Spanning Tree Protocol hierarchy

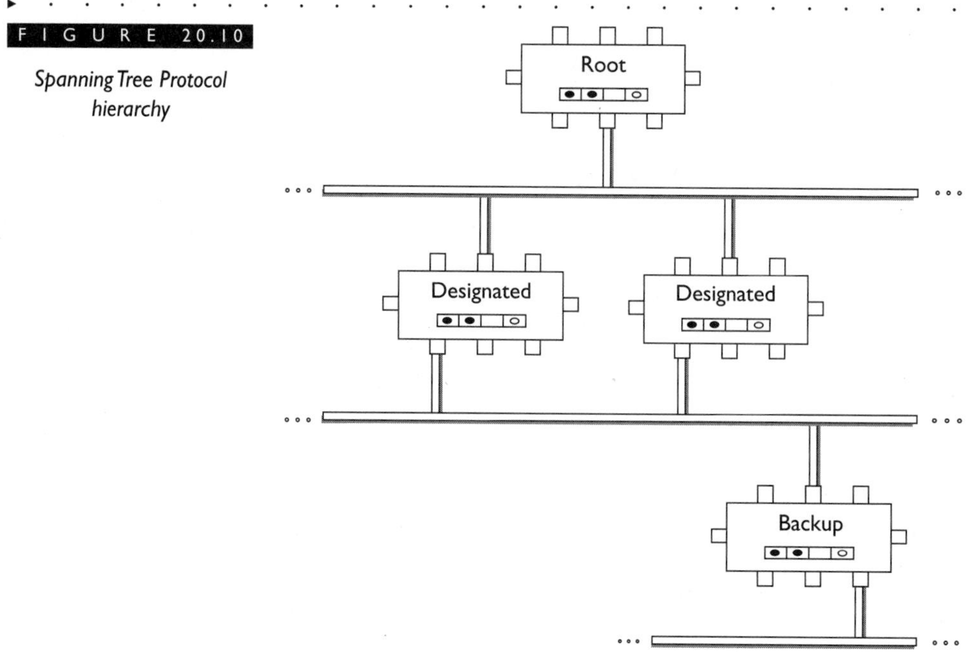

Each bridge is identified by a unique *Bridge ID number*. The bridge with the lowest ID number is the Root Bridge. A bridge ID consists of eight bytes. The network administrator configures the first two (most-significant) bytes, while the last six (least-significant) bytes represent the physical address of the bridge port network interface.

The 802.1d protocol allows only one Root Bridge per network. When selecting the Root Bridge, choose a high-performance device that is physically located at the center of the network cable system. By doing so you help to minimize the time required by bridges during reconfiguration. The Root Bridge is determined as soon as you initialize a network using the Spanning Tree Protocol. Each bridge broadcasts a BPDU frame on all of its ports. The BPDU broadcast frame consists of the fields shown graphically in Figure 20.11 and explained in detail in Table 20.1.

FIGURE 20.11

BPDU broadcast frame format

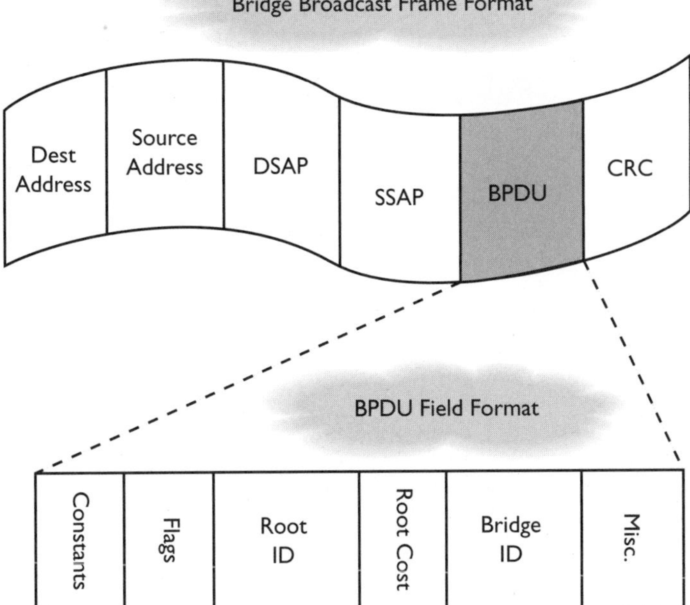

TABLE 20.1

Understanding the BPDU Broadcast Frame Format

BPDU FIELD	BPDU SUBFIELD	DESCRIPTION
Constants (1 or 2 Bytes)	Protocol Identifier=0	Permanent data that encompasses 2 bytes
	Version=0	Permanent data that encompasses 1 byte
	Message Type=0	Permanent data that encompasses 1 byte
Flags (1 Byte)	TCN	Topology Change Notification
	TCA	Topology Change Acknowledgment
Root ID (8 Bytes)	Root ID	Root Bridge ID
Port Cost (4 Bytes)	Port Cost	Cost of the preferred path to the Root Bridge

Continued

TABLE 20.1

Understanding the BPDU Broadcast Frame Format (continued)

BPDU FIELD	BPDU SUBFIELD	DESCRIPTION
Bridge ID (8 Bytes)	Bridge ID	Transmitting bridge's ID
Miscellaneous (2 Bytes)	Port ID	If two bridges that wish to become the Root Bridge have the same bridge ID, this field is used as a tiebreaker.
	Message Age	Elapsed time since the last configuration message.
	Max Age	Maximum age for a message before it is discarded.
	Hello Time	Elapsed time since the last configuration message from the Root Bridge.
	Forward Delay	Delay timer value used when transitioning between bridge port states during a topology reconfiguration.

To determine the Root Bridge, each bridge broadcasts a BPDU frame announcing itself as the Root Bridge. The frame contains the bridge's ID in both the Bridge ID and Root ID fields of the BPDU. The Control field in the frame's LLC header contains a message that informs each bridge to copy all of the BPDUs that it receives.

When a bridge receives a BPDU with a lower Root ID value than its own, it stops broadcasting BPDUs. Next, it begins to forward the BPDU with the lower Root ID and places its own ID in the Bridge ID field.

Let's say that B1 gets to be the Root Bridge because it possesses the lowest bridge ID value. In addition, bridge B2 becomes the backup for B1 because it is connected in parallel with the Root Bridge. As such, B2 will put both of its ports into the blocking state. Refer to Figure 20.12 for an illustration of this configuration.

Bridge B1 will now follow the Spanning Tree Protocol guidelines and transmit BPDUs on both of its ports at the IEEE recommended interval of two seconds. Bridge B2—the Backup Bridge whose ports are in the blocking state—will process all incoming BPDUs but will not learn or forward. Once the Root Bridge has been selected, the designated routes to each cable segment must be determined. BPDUs are transmitted from the Root Bridge and received by other bridges through their root port—the port closest to the Root Bridge.

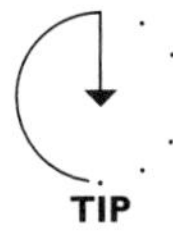

All BPDU frames should be transmitted to a preassigned multicast address. All bridges respond to frames addressed to the multicast address. Each individual bridge will also respond to its own physical (MAC) address or addresses.

Network Topology Change

A network topology change occurs when a bridge or cable segment fails. Figure 20.12 shows a failure in bridge B3, which is the Designated Bridge between cable segments S3 and S4. The Backup Bridge, B4, has placed its ports into the blocking state but is still receiving BPDU frames that have been transmitted on cable segment S4. After enough time has elapsed and bridge B4 has not received any BPDU frames from bridge B3, it determines that bridge B3 has malfunctioned.

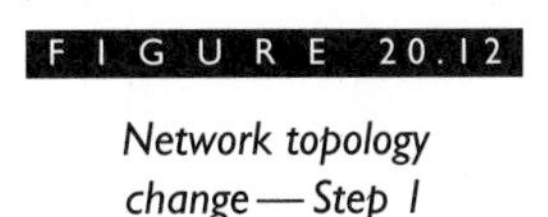

FIGURE 20.12

Network topology change — Step 1

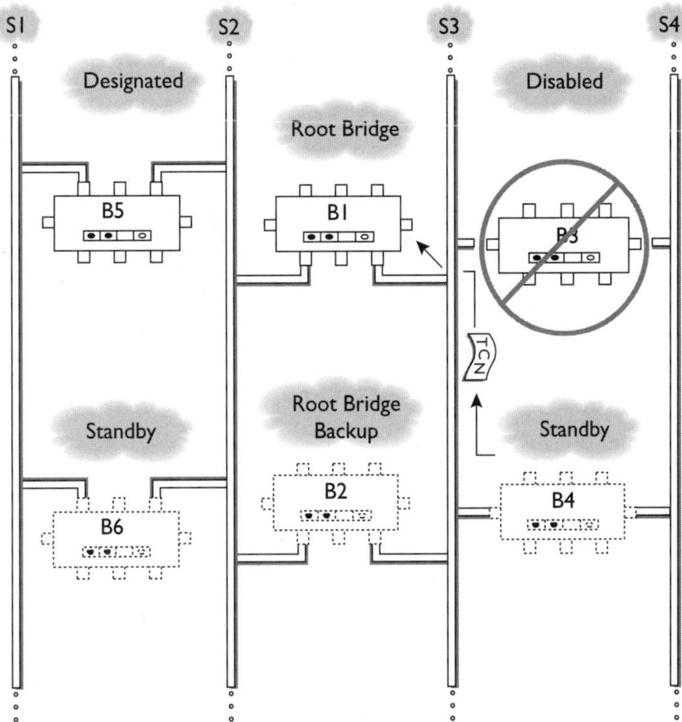

To initiate a reconfiguration, bridge B4 transmits a *Topology Change Notification (TCN)* BPDU frame through its Root port. Once the Root Bridge has been determined, subordinate bridges only transmit BPDU frames on their root ports during a topology change.

Once the upstream Designated Bridge has acknowledged the receipt of the TCN, bridge B4 will stop transmitting Topology Change Notification BPDU frames. This process is repeated until the Root Bridge acknowledges receipt of the TCN. Figure 20.13 shows the next step in the topology change process. The Root Bridge (B1) has received the TCN. At this point, B1 sets the *Topology Change Acknowledgment (TCA)* bit in the BPDU frames that it transmits every two seconds (as previously described).

FIGURE 20.13

Network topology change — Step 2

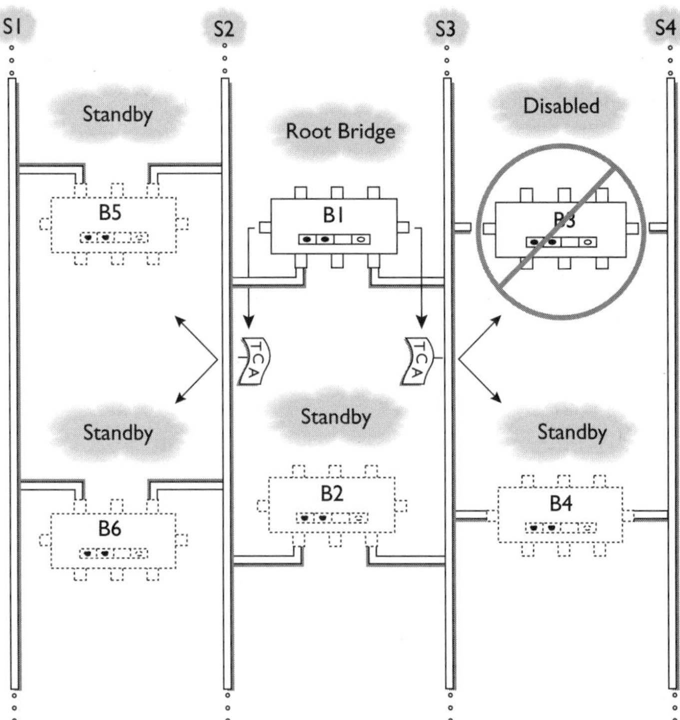

When a subordinate bridge receives a BPDU frame with the TCA bit set, it halts all frame forwarding, erases the nonpermanent contents of its filtering database, and places its ports into the blocking state.

Eventually, all of the bridges on the network (other than the Root Bridge) will place their ports into the blocking state. They remain in this state for a time period specified by the forward delay value contained in the BPDU frames, which are transmitted by the Root Bridge.

Once the forward delay value has expired, the process of determining Designated Bridges is repeated (as discussed previously). In Figure 20.14, bridge B4 has become the Designated Bridge between segments S3 and S4 (replacing B3, which was the Designated Bridge previously). During this process, all bridge ports cycle from the blocking state to the forwarding state.

FIGURE 20.14

Network topology change—Step 3

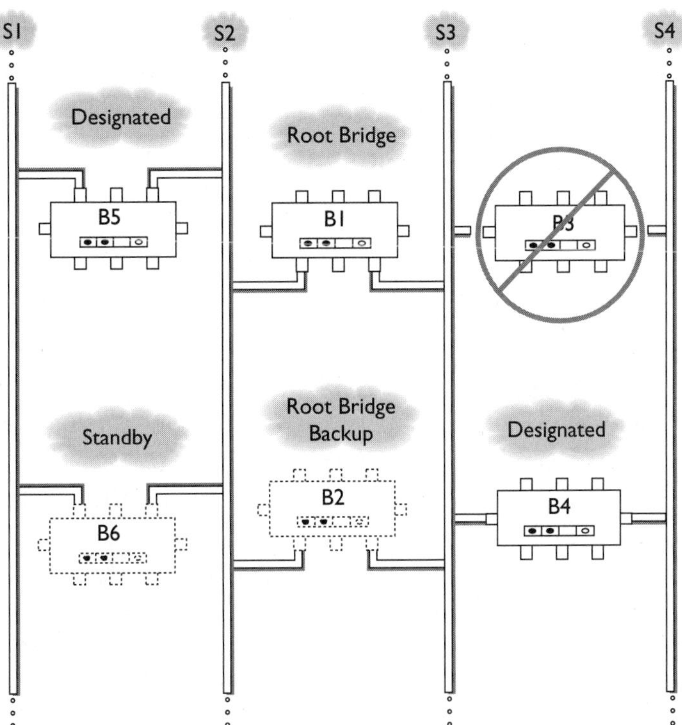

This completes our lesson in transparent bridging, the most popular bridging method in use today. Next, we will expand our Networking Layer journey into the realm of switches. But before we do, let's take a quick look at the second cousin of transparent bridging—source-routing bridges.

REAL WORLD

In an ideal bridged network, a frame should never have to pass through more than two bridges. Additionally, a frame should never have to pass through more than three bridges after a topology change.

Source-Routing Bridging

Following is a list of differences between transparent and source-routing bridges:

- Source-routing bridges do not maintain a filtering database.
- Source-routing bridges only respond to frames that contain source-routing header information.
- The end devices in a source-routing environment maintain a dynamic table that contains complete network-reachability information. This table is called the *route table*.

In a simple example, Computer A transmits a frame to Computer B through source-routing bridge B1. To do so, Computer A examines its route table, locates an entry for Computer B, and transmits a frame. The frame's source-routing header includes all the information required by bridge B1 to forward the frame to the correct cable segment.

The process used by end devices to build a route table is called *route determination*. Before a device can transmit a frame, it must first transmit a Hello frame to the destination device. Source-routing bridges along the way add route information to the source-routing header. The header expands as the Hello frame travels from ring to ring.

Upon receiving the Hello frame, the destination device responds with a frame that contains all the route information required by the two devices. It also sets the *Address Recognized Indicator (ARI)* bit in the source-routing header. This bit informs the Hello frame's sender that the destination device was successfully located. Both devices then update their route tables accordingly.

REAL WORLD

You may have figured out that there's quite a difference in the computational power required by transparent and source-routing bridges. The sophistication of transparent bridging places much more processing responsibility on the bridge itself, whereas source-routing bridging requires more processing by the end devices.

Switching

Switches are multiport devices that provide high-speed forwarding of frames. Network Layer routers are capable of the following three types of switching:

- *Circuit Switching*—Circuit switching connects the sender and receiver by a single path during the duration of the conversation. Once a connection is established, a dedicated path exists between both ends until the connection is terminated. Circuit switching provides a dedicated transmission channel with a guaranteed data rate. As a result, there is virtually no channel access delay after the circuit has been established. However, this level of dedicated connectivity is an inefficient use of the communications media.

- *Message Switching*—Message switching does not establish a dedicated path between the two stations. Instead, conversations are divided into messages. Each message is packaged with its own destination address and then transmitted from router to router through the internetwork. Each router receives the message, briefly stores it, and then transmits it to the next device. This type of network is sometimes called a *store-and-forward* WAN. Because of its store-and-forward nature, message switching does not support real-time connectivity.

- *Packet Switching*—Packet switching combines the advantages of circuit and message switching. Packet switching breaks datagrams into small parts called *packets*. Each packet is constructed with source and destination addresses that enable it to work its way through the internetwork and find its destination.

Datagram packet switching is similar to message switching in that each datagram (message) has various paths to choose from (see Figure 20.15). On the other hand, *virtual-circuit packet switching* relies on a logical connection between the sender and receiver. This connection is formed when the devices exchange messages at the outset of a conversation.

FIGURE 20.15

Datagram packet switching

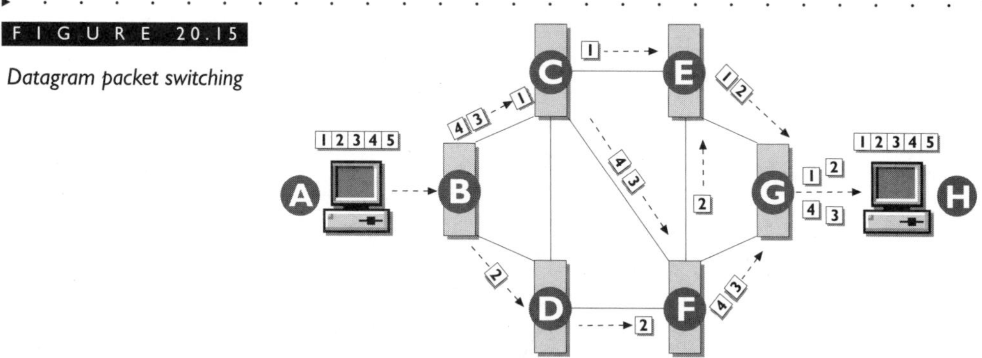

Refer to Table 20.2 for a comparative summary of these three switching techniques.

TABLE 20.2

Feature Summary of Network Layer Switching Techniques

FACTORS	CIRCUIT SWITCHING	MESSAGE SWITCHING	PACKET SWITCHING
Bandwidth utilization	Poor	Good	Very good
Speed	Fast	Slow	Very fast
Reliability	High	High	Fair
Cost effectiveness	No	No	Yes
Options	Dedicated network path	Prioritization and load balancing	Datagram and virtual circuits

This completes our discussion of Network Layer switching. Now let's examine how switching hubs put the *zip* back into networks that suffer from poor performance.

Switching Hubs

Switching hubs eliminate packet collisions on switched Ethernet networks by segmenting the bus into virtual switched legs. To accomplish this, switching hubs maintain a table of the physical addresses of all connected devices. Unlike a traditional hub (which transmits frames to all of the devices attached to a cable segment), a switching hub forwards frames only to the appropriate destination device's port. Ethernet switches are available in 10 Mbps or 100 Mbps configurations.

Another performance advantage of a switched hub is its ability to concurrently forward frames between multiple ports. It is also possible to connect a cable segment that is populated with multiple devices to a single switch port. In this case, individual collision domains are created, where each switch port represents a separate collision domain. This further enhances network performance by isolating collisions to a subset of the network devices.

Figure 20.16 shows a typical switching hub configuration. As you can see in the figure, network devices attach to the individual switch ports via separate cable segments.

Most switching hubs use one of the following two methods to forward frames:

- *Store-and-Forward*—Store-and-forward switches copy an entire frame into memory, verify the CRC, and then transmit the frame to the correct switch port. This introduces an average latency of about 1,200 microseconds. One advantage of the store-and-forward method is that the integrity of each frame is verified before being retransmitted.

- *Cut-Through*—Cut-through switches attempt to increase performance by reading only the destination address field of a frame's MAC header before forwarding it to the correct port. This technique reduces latency to an average of 40 microseconds. Because cut-through switches do not read the entire frame and verify its CRC, bad frames are forwarded.

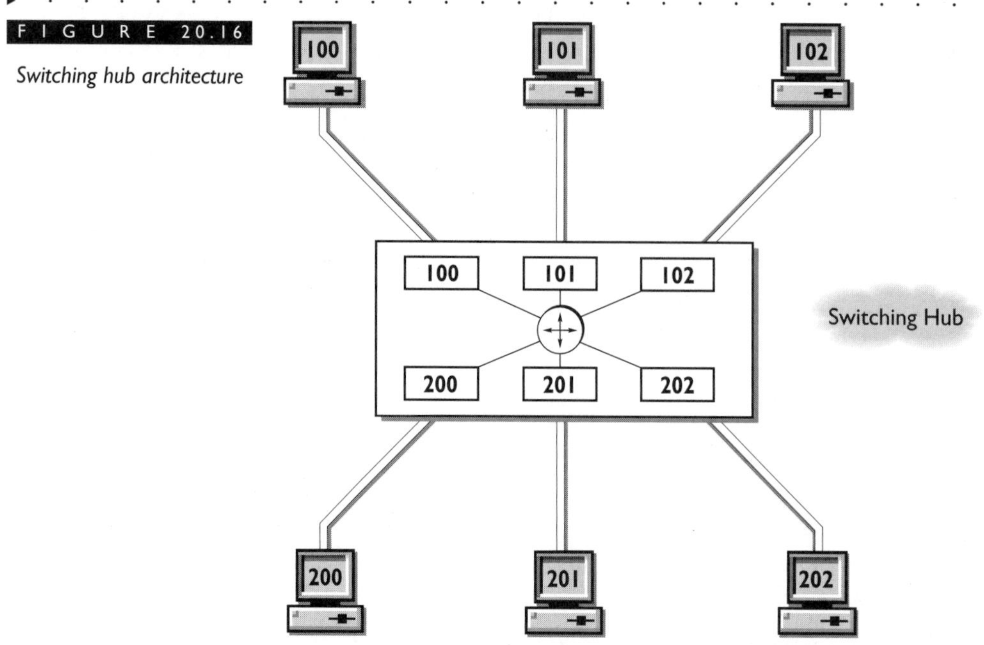

FIGURE 20.16

Switching hub architecture

By definition, switched networks have a problem scaling beyond several dozen segments because of excess broadcast traffic and switch latency. Virtual LANs (VLANs) group logical devices together into virtual collision domains. By using this technique, broadcasts and other traffic are isolated to devices in the VLAN. VLANs can be created at either the Data Link Layer or Network Layer.

- *Data Link VLANs*—Data Link Layer VLANs are configured by network administrators. The devices in a VLAN should be grouped according to the way they are accessed, just as in a bridged environment. All frames in a Data Link Layer VLAN are switched according to physical device addresses.
- *Network Layer VLANs*—Network Layer VLANs require more intelligent switches because they rely on Network Layer protocol information used by TCP/IP, IPX/SPX, and other protocol suites. VLANs created at the Network Layer divide a network into subnetworks that use specific protocols. Inside a virtual subnet, frames are switched according to physical addresses, and the switching hub routes inter-VLAN traffic by using Network Layer intelligence.

Token Ring Switching

Currently, most switched networks are built using Ethernet or Fast Ethernet components. However, store-and-forward and cut-through switching techniques may also be applied to token-ring based networks. Following are some switching advantages that are inherent in the token ring protocol:

- Token ring switches are drop-in replacements for standard multistation access units such as the IBM 8228.
- Token ring switches enhance network performance.
- Token ring switches reduce the number of hops that a frame must traverse in large-scale network implementations.
- Token ring switches are capable of full-duplex operation.

These are all great features, but Token Ring switching lacks comprehensive analysis tools. As a network administrator, you must make a choice between the benefits of switching and legacy network analysis tools. Or, you can implement a much more robust OSI Networking methodology — routing.

Routing

Routers are more intelligent than bridges and switches. They use both physical and logical addressing to divide an internetwork into subnets.

Refer to Figure 20.17 for a sample routing scenario. Suppose the internetwork consists of five subnets (A through E). In this example, Workstation 100 sends a message to Workstation 300. First, the packet travels directly to router AB, which recognizes that it is for Segment C. This is accomplished using an internal routing table. Router AB changes the logical address and sends the packet to router BC. Router BC then forwards the packet to the correct segment. In this example, Subnets D and E are untouched, and the packet travels a minimum path instead of being broadcast throughout the network.

FIGURE 20.17

How routers work

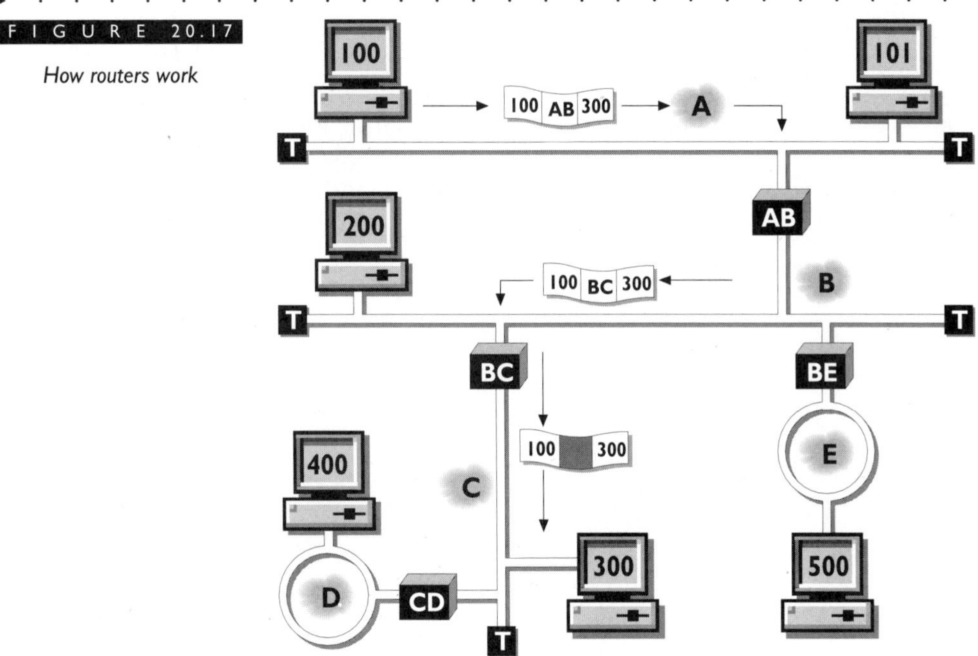

Routing uses the following two-step process in order to enable intermediate network devices to make intelligent decisions about how a packet should travel from Point A to Point B:

- *Step 1:* Route Discovery
- *Step 2:* Route Selection

Step 1: Route Discovery

During route discovery, the internal Routing Information Protocol (RIP) builds a *Routing Information Table (RIT)* for each router that lists all possible paths from the host router to a given destination. Each router builds its own table and continues to modify it as needed. Every RIT is made up of the following three important components:

- *Network Addresses* — Each table contains all known network addresses. These values are discovered by using RIP broadcasting techniques.

- *Next Hop to Reach the Destination LAN*—Each corresponding network address is identified by the intermediate routers between the device and the destination LAN. This hop count parameter enables the router to determine the minimum number of hops from LAN to LAN.

- *Cost to Reach the Destination LAN*—Cost information is calculated for each route between the device and the destination network. Specific routing algorithms are used to factor in hop count, tick count (the amount of time required to reach the destination network), and relative expenses (which are user-definable values based on the amount of money or other criteria required to use a specific path).

So, what does the router do with this information? Remember the primary function of the RIT is route discovery. After the information has been gathered, you can use it to determine an optimal path—that's route selection. But before you move on to Step 2, let's explore the two most popular route discovery methods: distance-vector and link-state.

Distance-Vector Route Discovery

Distance-vector routers compile and send RITs to all routers on their segment. Each router builds its own table, which it updates constantly. One problem with this method is overhead. Because the internetwork is often large and complex, each RIT can get quite large. Also, routers only update neighbor RITs, which means RITs must pass through the entire internetwork from router to router. This process is slow and generates a lot of overhead. In addition, route reachability decisions are based primarily on secondhand information.

Distance-vector protocols are easy to implement and work well in LAN environments. However, these broadcast-heavy protocols can quickly degrade network performance in bandwidth-starved WAN applications, and they introduce unnecessary hop count limitations. Common distance-vector Network Layer protocols include the Internet Protocol (IP), IPX RIP, and AppleTalk Routing Table Maintenance Protocol (RTMP).

Another disadvantage of distance-vector routing protocols is the amount of time required to propagate information to all routers on a network—this is known as the *convergence problem*. When a network reconfiguration occurs, every router must recalculate its entire RIT. In addition, the phenomenon known as *count to infinity* can completely isolate one or more network segments.

Link-State Route Discovery

Link-state route discovery relies on global broadcasts. Each router identifies its own segment by broadcasting a Link-State Packet (LSP) to all routers on the internetwork. This initial message contains information about the networks that the router is directly attached to and is commonly known as *flooding*. This way, each router can initially build a complete RIT based primarily on firsthand information, which is updated only when changes occur. Each router broadcasts changes to the global RIT and other routers modify their own tables. This strategy ensures accurate RITs, but broadcasts changes only. In addition, change information is not broadcast back to the network where the information was obtained.

Link-state routing protocols determine route reachability information based on the lowest hop count. In addition, most link-state protocols are flexible in terms of the metrics they use to determine the best path to a destination network, and may take into consideration parameters such as line speed, line quality, and so on. Common link-state Network Layer protocols include Open Shortest Path First (OSPF), Novell's Link Services Protocol (NLSP), and OSI's Intermediate Systems-to-Intermediate Systems (IS-IS).

In summary, distance-vector routing protocols work well in most LAN applications. Link-state protocols excel in WAN applications and on bandwidth-starved LANs. Link-state protocols quickly converge on topology changes and do not suffer from count to infinity problems. The only real disadvantages of link-state protocols are slightly more processing overhead in routers and a more complicated installation procedure for the network administrator.

Once the router has built an RIT, you should have a complete list of all hops between your network and the destination network. These paths also are valued according to time and cost information. With this data, you are ready to make a choice. That's Step 2: route selection.

Step 2: Route Selection

Once a router has built its RIT, it can use cost information to calculate an optimal path to the destination device. Route selection supports these two approaches:

- *Dynamic* — Route selection uses internal routing algorithms to continually gather cost information. Every packet is assigned a route, depending on the latest discovery cost.

Multiple paths may be used to send packets between two devices, depending on the changing nature of the network. In addition, route selections are made at every router in the network.

- *Static*—Route selection is based on a predetermined path. Every packet must follow this path, and every router must make selection decisions based on the path.

Routing Management

The following routing management issues must be controlled in order to maintain an efficiently functioning network:

- Count to infinity
- Load balancing
- Nonroutable protocols

Let's learn more about these routing management issues.

Count-to-Infinity Problem

The count-to-infinity problem is inherent in distance-vector routing protocols. Essentially, two or more routers can get out of sync and provide each other with invalid network reachability information. The most common cause is a "Ping-Pong" scenario similar to the bridging loop concept discussed earlier. Figure 20.18 illustrates this problem.

In this example, Routers R1, R2, and R3 are connected to Networks A, B, C, and D, respectively. We are assuming that the cost associated with each router is one, which means that the cost to reach a given network is equal to the hop count (the number of routers crossed on the way to the destination). Based on information obtained during RIP broadcasts, Router R1 determines that it is three hops away from Network D. Router R2 determines that it is two hops away from Network D and Router R3 determines that it is one hop from Network D.

FIGURE 20.18

Counting to infinity

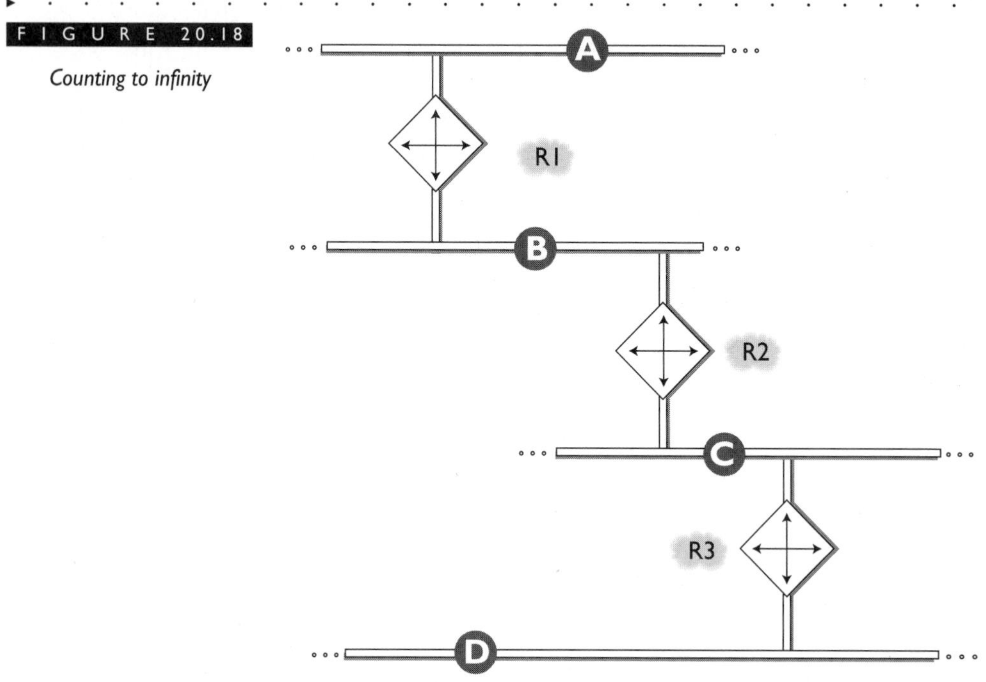

If a failure occurs in Router R3 or on Network C, Router R2 must update its RIT. Where does this new information come from?—Router R1's RIP broadcasts. Router R3 is no longer broadcasting RIP updates, so R1 only hears broadcasts from Router R1. Router R1 informs R2 that it is three hops away from Network D, so R2 calculates a cost of four to reach Network D.

Router R2 now broadcasts a hop count of four to reach Network D in all of its RIP updates. Upon hearing this, Router R1 updates its RIT with a hop count value of five for Network D. In the next RIP broadcast from Router R1, R2 updates its RIT with the new information and now believes that the cost to reach Network D is six. This Ping-Pong scenario will continue until the routers reach a cost of infinity. In most Network Layer protocol implementations a cost of 16 indicates an unreachable or infinite route.

The following two algorithms can be employed to minimize the count-to-infinity problem:

- *Split-Horizon Algorithm*—The split-horizon algorithm prevents a router from advertising route reachability information back to the network where the information was originally obtained.

- *Split-Horizon with Poison-Reverse Algorithm*—The split-horizon with poison-reverse algorithm requires that routers advertise route reachability information back to the network where the information was originally obtained. However, the router advertises to these networks with a cost of 16 (infinity), which effectively prevents other routers from attempting to reach those networks through the advertising router.

Load Balancing

In many cases, there may be multiple routes available to reach a given destination network. If this scenario exists, a technique called *load balancing* is used to allow a router to utilize multiple paths to a single destination network.

Load balancing can be implemented by both distance-vector and link-state routing protocols. When determining the routes in a load-balanced configuration, routers may either sequentially or randomly select available routes. By implementing load balancing, routing protocols can make more efficient use of network bandwidth.

Nonroutable Protocols

Some protocols cannot be routed. This is because they were designed to operate in stand-alone network environments and do not provide Network Layer functionality. Following are some examples of nonroutable protocols:

- *Systems Network Architecture (SNA)*—All routes in an IBM SNA network are static. A lookup table is used to help locate a device's destination address, which is then converted to a local address format by a front-end processor. Newer SNA protocol implementations (such as Advanced Peer-to-Peer Networking, or APPN) include dynamic routing capabilities.

- *Network Basic Input/Output System (NetBIOS)* — NetBIOS is a Session Layer protocol that establishes, maintains, and terminates the dialog between communicating devices on a LAN. No Network Layer information is provided, relegating NetBIOS to LAN-only applications.

- *NetBIOS Extended User Interface (NetBEUI)* — NetBEUI is an extension of NetBIOS designed by IBM for use in its LAN Manager network operating system. It is only intended for use on LANs.

- *Local Area Transport (LAT)* — LAT was designed by Digital Equipment Corporation (DEC) as a protocol to help LAN-based terminal servers interface with host systems in DECnet networks.

Well, there you have it — bridging, switching, and routing in a nutshell. Remember, these three Network Layer technologies help electronic messages find their way from Point A to Point B over LANs and WANs. And, they do it with increasing levels of sophistication and intelligence. Now let's take a moment to compare the advantages and disadvantages of these three cousins.

Comparing Bridges, Switches, and Routers

In most networks, routers are used in conjunction with bridges and switches. In this configuration, bridges and switches increase performance in the local LAN by filtering intersegment traffic. In addition, routers perform intelligent path selection between separate networks using common upper-layer protocols (such as TCP/IP).

Devices called *brouters* can provide both Data Link Layer and Network Layer functionality. A brouter will route packets containing Network Layer data or act as a bridge if only MAC information resides in the packet.

Following are advantages of routers (as compared to bridges and switches):

- Routers understand the entire internetwork and make path selection decisions based on the best information available at the time.

- Routers that implement link-state routing protocols are quick to converge on topology changes. Bridged networks require considerably more time to converge on these changes.

- Routers can usually perform the packet fragmentation and reassembly tasks necessary to communicate across networks consisting of disparate Physical Layer and Data Link Layer protocols. A bridge can only discard frames that are too large.
- Routers perform congestion control and can route packets through multiple physical paths, based on bandwidth and service availability.
- Routers can filter traffic and create independent collision and broadcast domains.
- Routers can connect networks consisting of unlike Physical Layer and Data Link Layer protocols (such as Ethernet-to-Token Ring protocols).

Following are advantages of bridges and switches (as compared to routers):

- Bridges and switches are easy to install and configure.
- Bridges cost less than routers and introduce less latency in communications.
- Bridges are protocol-independent. They use only physical address information.

This completes our journey through the Network Layer of computer networking. So far in this chapter, we have learned about logical addressing, network control, bridging, switching, and routing.

Each of these important functions aids us tremendously on our journey from the Physical Layer up to the OSI Application Layer. Logical addressing helps us isolate specific sending and receiving devices. Then bridging and switching provide us with a variety of different paths through the network. But routing is probably the most important task at the Network Layer. Routing relies on discovery tables and selection intelligence to choose an optimal path from Point A to Point B. Proper routing ensures the most efficient use of our communications channel.

Now it's time to move on to the second OSI Networking function—the Transport Layer.

The Transport Layer

The Transport Layer of the OSI model organizes packets into segments and reliably delivers them to upper-layer services. The Transport Layer consists of the following components:

- *Service Addressing*—As we learned earlier, network communications rely on three different addresses: physical (Data Link Layer), logical (Network Layer), and service (Transport Layer). Service addresses (or ports) identify upper-layer network services. The Transport Layer uses two methods to keep track of service-oriented conversations: connection identifier and transaction identifier. *Connection identifiers* rely on a conversation-method address called a connection ID, port, or socket. *Transaction identifiers* break conversations into smaller units. Instead of tracking the entire conversation, transaction IDs are assigned to each request.

- *Segmentation*—Transport Layer segmentation accomplishes two administrative tasks: grouping Network Layer packets into larger segments for delivery to upper-layer services and breaking down large upper-layer messages into smaller packets for delivery to the Network Layer.

- *Transport Control*—Transport control performs the remainder of the Transport Layer functions: error checking and flow control. Transport *error checking* ensures that the message arrives at the destination station. Transport *flow control* builds on earlier flow control techniques by negotiating window sizes.

Middle Layer Implementations

So far, we have studied the theoretical technologies underlying OSI Networking. Of course, all of the theories in the world aren't going to mean anything if we can't bring them to life. That's what implementations are for. OSI Networking implementations bring Network and Transport theories to life.

The Network Layer has the following three notable implementations:

- Asynchronous Transfer Mode (ATM)
- X.25
- Switched Multimegabit Data Service (SMDS)

Furthermore, we will explore the following three notable implementations at the Network and Transport Layers:

- NetWare IPX/SPX
- Internet TCP/IP
- ISDN and B-ISDN

In this section, we will explore these seven implementations from the inside out. Now you get to apply all of those conceptual models you've been struggling through in this chapter. So, without any further ado, let's start at the Network Layer.

Network Layer Implementations

Following are three notable implementations that operate at the Network Layer of the OSI model (see Figure 20.19):

- *Asynchronous Transfer Mode (ATM)*—Asynchronous Transfer Mode (ATM) is an emerging broadband ISDN standard that uses cell-relay technology. Although ATM is entering the marketplace as a WAN protocol, it is usually considered a LAN, MAN, or WAN implementation. ATM performs Network Layer activities on top of various Physical Layer protocols such as SONET/SDH and FDDI. From a functional perspective, ATM uses its own isochronous frame synchronization and error checking at the Data Link Layer. At the Network Layer, ATM uses a variation of packet switching. ATM packets are fixed-sized cells (53-bytes) that follow a virtual circuit. Route selection is performed using a static algorithm. In summary, ATM provides high-speed data delivery across existing optical networks.

- *X.25* — Recommendation X.25 is a strict Network Layer implementation of packet switching. It was developed in 1974 by CCITT as an alternative to existing packet-switching networks by Datapac, TYMNET, and Telenet. Although X.25 operates at the Network Layer, the standard relies on other implementations at the Physical Layer and Data Link Layer. These standards are organized into three levels: Level I (X.21), Level II (LAPB), and Level III (X.25). X.25 packet switching supports both permanent virtual circuits (PVCs) and switched virtual circuits (SVCs). In summary, X.25 is a popular and powerful WAN communications standard.
- *Switched Multimegabit Data Service (SMDS)* — Switched Multimegabit Data Service (SMDS) technology was developed in 1991 as a technical requirement by Bell Communications Research. Although SMDS is an emerging technology, industry analysts consider it a precursor to ATM. SMDS combines the advantages of ATM (it organizes packets into fixed-size cells) and X.25 (it uses packet switching across virtual circuits).

FIGURE 20.19

Network Layer implementations

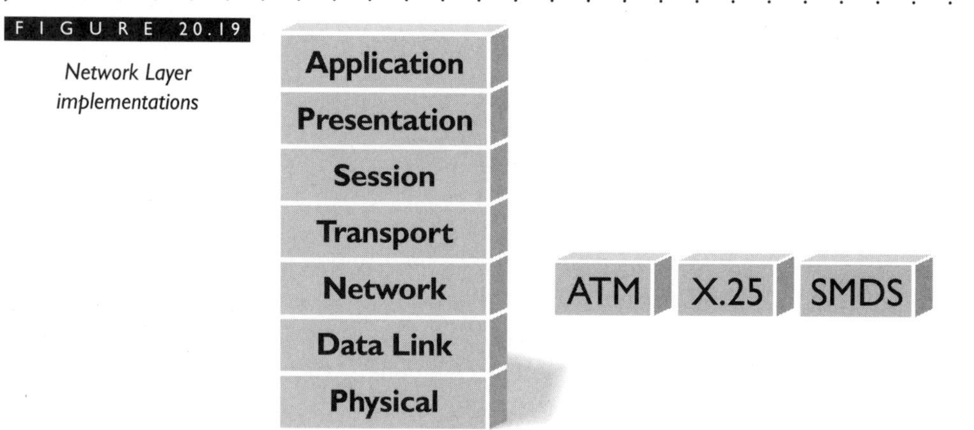

Refer to Table 20.3 for a comparative summary of these three Network Layer implementations.

TABLE 20.3

Feature Summary of Network Layer Implementations

IMPLEMENTATION	LOGICAL ADDRESSING	ROUTE SWITCHING	SELECTION	NETWORK CONTROL
ATM		Virtual-circuit packet switching	Static	
X.25	Channel addressing	Virtual-circuit packet switching		Flow control and error checking
SMDS		Virtual-circuit packet switching		

Transport Layer Implementations

Following are four notable implementations that operate at both the Network Layer and Transport Layer of the OSI model (see Figure 20.20):

- *NetWare IPX/SPX*—Early versions of NetWare used protocols named *IPX* (which operates at the Network Layer) and *SPX* (which operates at the Transport Layer). Upper-layer Novell services are protocol independent and provide a complete suite of NetWare file, print, and messaging applications. We will explore NetWare IPX/SPX in great depth in Chapter 21, "Middle Layer Protocol Families."

- *Internet TCP/IP*—The foundation of the Internet protocol suite consists of *IP* (which operates at the Network Layer) and *TCP* (which operates at the Transport Layer). Upper-layer services are provided through a complete suite of Internet applications. We will explore Internet TCP/IP in great depth in Chapter 21, "Middle Layer Protocol Families."

- *ISDN and B-ISDN*— Integrated Services Digital Network (ISDN) and B-ISDN (a broadband version of the same implementation) are a set of international standards initiated by the Consultative Committee for International Telegraphy and Telephony (CCITT) (now called the International Telecommunications Union, or ITU) that provide a standardized approach to integrating voice and data transmissions over digital telephone networks. B-ISDN enhances this technology further by using fiber-optic technology. The biggest challenge to ISDN is that it requires the conversion of telephone devices from analog to digital. To accomplish this goal, ISDN uses time-division multiplexing at the Physical Layer. It provides physical addressing at the MAC sublayer and frame sequencing at the LLC sublayer of the OSI Data Link Layer. Through ISDN, users can access digital communication channels using packet-switched or circuit-switched connections.

FIGURE 20.20

Network and Transport Layer implementations

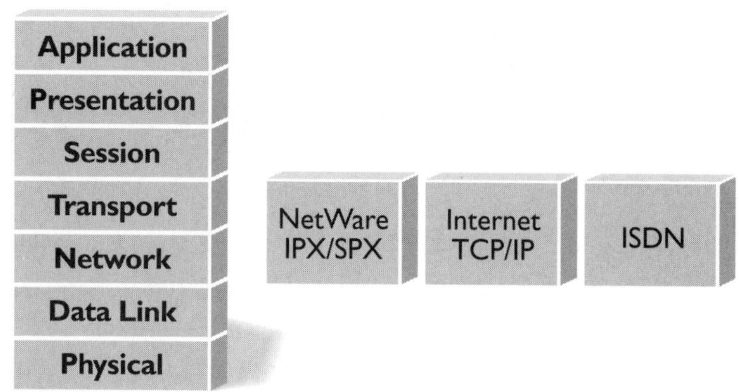

Congratulations!

This completes our "theoretical" journey through the middle two layers of computer networking. It certainly has been a knowledge-packed trip. But this is only the beginning of OSI Networking technologies. The real fun is in the following two Network and Transport Layer implementations:

- NetWare IPX/SPX
- Internet TCP/IP

In the next chapter, we will apply all of our newly acquired OSI knowledge to the two most powerful LAN/WAN networking protocols. Hold onto your hat, because this is going to be a great trip!

LAB EXERCISE 20.1: GETTING TO KNOW THE MIDDLE LAYERS

Use the hints provided to find the 20 networking terms hidden in this word search puzzle. Omit any punctuation characters (such as blank spaces, hyphens, and so on) and spell out any numbers.

R	O	U	T	E	S	E	L	E	C	T	I	O	N	S	J
I	A	C	O	N	N	E	C	T	I	O	N	I	D	I	N
T	N	Q	G	B	M	K	C	K	B	I	Y	Y	W	K	Z
O	S	E	G	M	E	N	T	A	T	I	O	N	G	Z	F
K	O	P	P	V	J	X	D	L	J	W	R	O	A	E	E
E	U	E	L	O	A	D	B	A	L	A	N	C	I	N	G
N	R	X	K	I	T	F	U	C	A	G	V	Z	N	Y	V
R	C	O	U	N	T	T	O	I	N	F	I	N	I	T	Y
I	E	J	I	B	P	H	O	R	Q	K	L	V	Y	P	R
N	R	S	L	K	O	Y	O	T	W	J	L	K	Z	D	I
G	O	R	C	A	R	N	O	R	Z	A	Q	V	Y	B	P
G	U	E	B	R	T	U	V	Y	I	E	R	N	Q	M	U
J	T	J	S	A	C	M	L	E	Z	Z	A	D	D	L	I
G	I	F	Y	Q	O	X	A	J	D	M	O	S	I	I	Q
E	N	E	P	I	S	D	N	F	I	E	Y	N	V	N	V
P	G	L	O	R	T	N	O	C	W	O	L	F	E	Y	G

Hints

1. Emerging broadband ISDN standard that uses cell-relay technology.
2. Identifies all segments that share a common conversation.
3. A distance-vector routing problem caused by invalid network reachability information.
4. Error checking by a bridge's port relay entity.
5. Route selection that uses internal routing algorithms to continually gather cost information.
6. Negotiates window sizes at the OSI Transport Layer.

7. "Active State" for a functioning bridge port.
8. Standardized approach for integrating voice and data transmissions over digital phone networks.
9. A DEC protocol that helps LAN-based terminal servers interface with host systems.
10. Allows a router to utilize multiple paths to a single destination network.
11. Numerical representation of the preferred path to the Root Bridge in a BPDU broadcast frame.
12. Lists all possible paths from the host router to a given destination using the Router Information Protocol.
13. Network Layer process for choosing the optimal path.
14. Transport Layer housekeeping task that packages messages into acceptable sizes.
15. An IBM non-routable protocol that relies on static lookup tables.
16. IBM Token Ring bridges that maintain their own dynamic tables of routers and transmit them in MAC headers.
17. A routing algorithm that prevents the router from advertising route reachability information back to the network where the information was originally obtained.
18. A special BPDU frame sent through the Root port to initiate a bridge reconfiguration.
19. Enhanced switches that reduce the number of hops that a frame must traverse in large-scale network implementations.
20. A logical grouping of network devices into a virtual collision domain.

See Appendix C for answers.

LAB EXERCISE 20.2: THE OSI MODEL — MIDDLE LAYERS

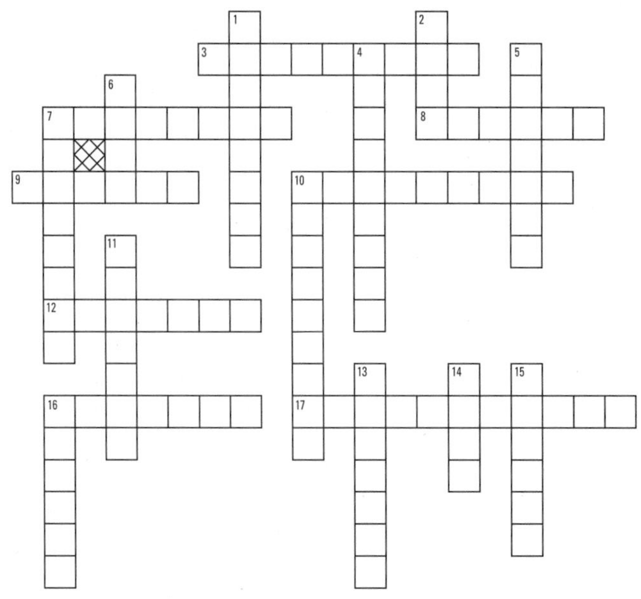

Across

3. Elapsed time since the last Root configuration message
7. Routes packets based on Data Link Layer and Network Layer information
8. Circuit, message, and packet routing at the Data Link Layer
9. Intelligent connection device that operates at the Network Layer
10. Counting down in preparation of bridge forwarding
12. A Session Layer protocol for LAN-only applications
16. Addressing at the Transport Layer
17. Learning bridges with minimal installation requirements

Down

1. "Rally" time for a bridge port
2. A compromise between ATM and X.25
4. OSI layer that provides reliable WAN communications
5. Decision time for a transparent bridge

6. The bridge at the top of the 802.1d hierarchy
7. A bridge port is in this state when it is “standing by”
10. Route discovery that relies on global broadcasts
11. OSI layer that provides logical LAN-to-LAN routing
13. Connection device that operates at the upper layers
14. A special packet for interbridge communications
15. LAN connection device that operates at the Data Link Layer
16. Route selection based on a predetermined path

See Appendix C for answers.

CHAPTER 21

Middle Layer Protocol Families

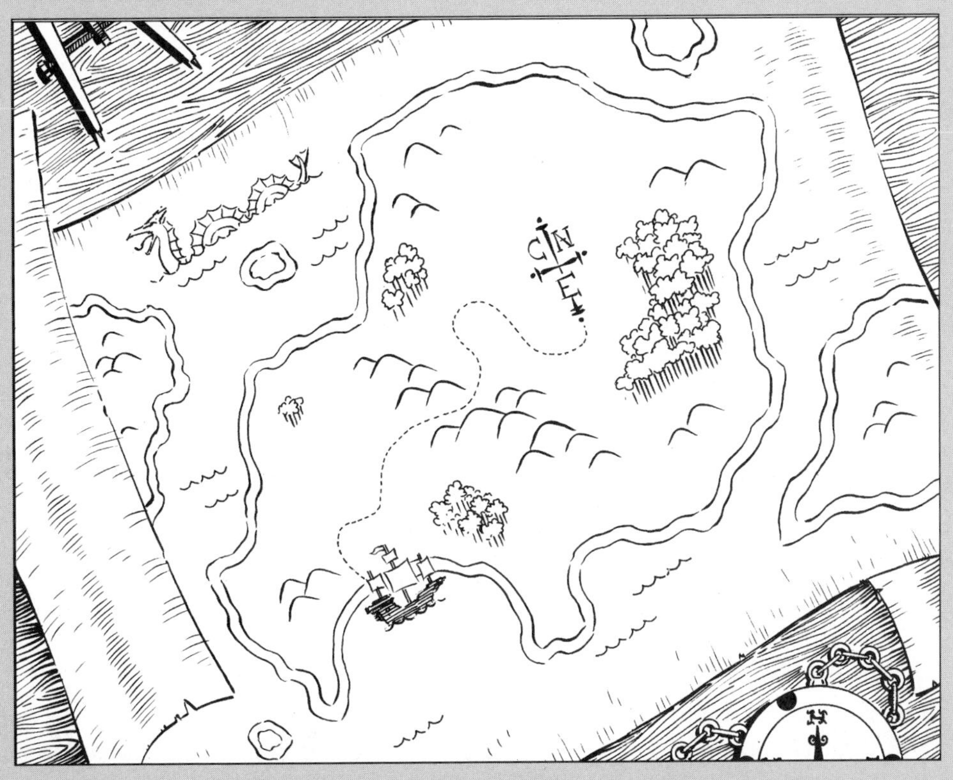

Welcome to the "Real World."

In the previous chapter, we learned how theoretical OSI networking capabilities provide a logical, reliable pathway for network communications. During that discussion, you explored addressing, bridging, switching, routing, and administrative control at the Network and Transport Layers of the OSI Reference Model.

Now in this chapter, we will apply these OSI theories to some "Real World" networking protocols. Specifically, we will explore two functional protocol families:

- *Internet Protocols*—The foundation of the Internet protocol suite consists of the *Internet Protocol* (IP), which operates at the Network Layer; and the *Transmission Control Protocol* (TCP), which operates at the Transport Layer. Top-layer services are provided through a complete suite of Internet applications. In this chapter, we will explore Middle and Top Layer Internet protocols, as well as three important networking functions: IP addressing, subnetting, and supernetting.

- *NetWare Protocols*—Earlier versions of NetWare were based on *Internetwork Packet Exchange* (IPX), which operates at the Network Layer; and *Sequenced Packet Exchange* (SPX), which operates at the Transport Layer. Top-layer services are provided through a complete suite of file, print, and messaging applications. In this chapter, we will explore Middle and Top Layer NetWare protocols, including the WAN-based NetWare Link Services Protocol (NLSP).

Let's begin our OSI networking implementation discussion with Middle Layer Internet protocols.

Middle Layer Internet Protocols

The Internet protocol suite was developed in the 1970s by and for the United States Department of Defense (DoD) and various research organizations. In the early years, the Internet was called Advanced Research Projects Agency Network (ARPAnet) and provided packet-switched network connectivity among government agencies, universities, and research institutions. ARPAnet was the first major internetwork to provide communications between a wide range of dissimilar devices. Up to that point, large WANs were primarily proprietary systems (for example, IBM's SNA and Digital Equipment Corporation's DNA).

The foundation of the Internet protocol suite consists of *IP* (also known as IPv4), which operates at the Network Layer, and *TCP*, which operates at the Transport Layer (see Figure 21.1). Other Middle Layer support protocols include IPv6, User Datagram Protocol (UDP), Router Information Protocol (RIP), and Open Shortest Path First (OSPF).

REAL WORLD

The Internet protocol suite is organized into three functional groups:

- *Internet Protocols* — These protocols help move data through and between networks, thus connecting diverse senders and receivers. They are the foundation of the Internet suite and correspond roughly with the OSI Network Layer. The two most popular Internet protocols are IP and Internet Control Message Protocol (ICMP).
- *Host-to-Host Protocols* — These protocols deliver data to and receive data from peer protocols in other network systems. These implementations correspond roughly to the OSI Transport Layer. The most popular host-to-host protocols are TCP and UDP.
- *Process Protocols* — These protocols provide user application services and correspond roughly to the upper three layers of the OSI model. The most popular process protocols are FTP, Telnet, Simple Mail Transfer Protocol (SMTP), and NFS.

IPv4

IP (also known as IPv4) is the main Internet protocol. IP is a connectionless packet-switched Network Layer implementation that performs logical addressing and dynamic route selection. In addition, IP uses established datagram sequencing technologies to fragment packets into smaller parts and to reassemble them at an intermediate station (usually a router) or at their destination.

FIGURE 21.1

Mapping Internet TCP/IP to the OSI model

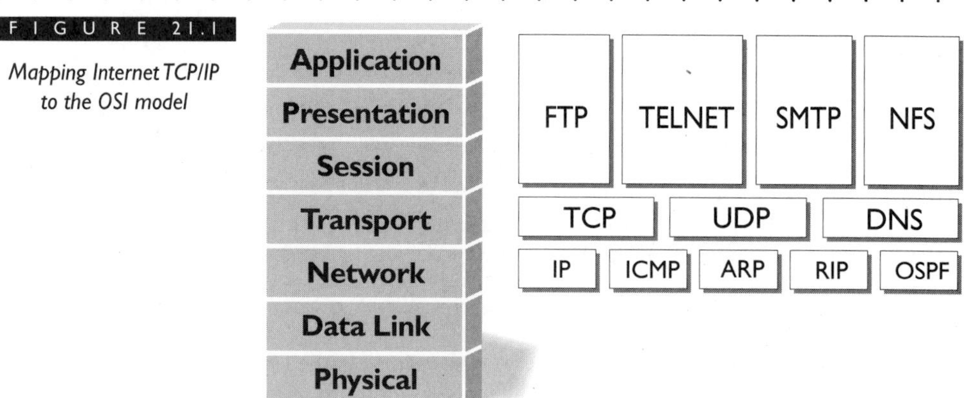

Depending on the network structure, several paths may be available between the sender and receiver. IP moves datagrams through the internetwork one hop at a time by referencing dynamic Routing Information Tables (RITs) at each hop. Each router along the way makes a decision about a datagram's next hop, based on the logical network and physical device addresses. IP network control functions are provided by the ICMP support protocol. Distance-vector or link-state route discovery is provided by the RIP and OSPF support protocols, respectively.

Figure 21.2 shows the contents of an IP packet.

IPv6 (IPng)

To support large-scale Internet access in the coming years, a new version of IP has been introduced — known as *IPv6* or *IPng* (that is, *IP next generation*). IPv6 provides significant improvements over traditional IP, including the following:

- *Expanded Address Space* — IPv6 supports 128-bit addresses.
- *Anycast Address* — A new kind of address that allows a packet to be delivered to any one of a given set of devices.
- *Header Format Simplification* — Headers have been modified to increase efficiency.
- *Improved Option Support* — Optional IP header components use improved encoding, which helps to increase packet forwarding efficiency.

FIGURE 21.2

IPv4 packet format

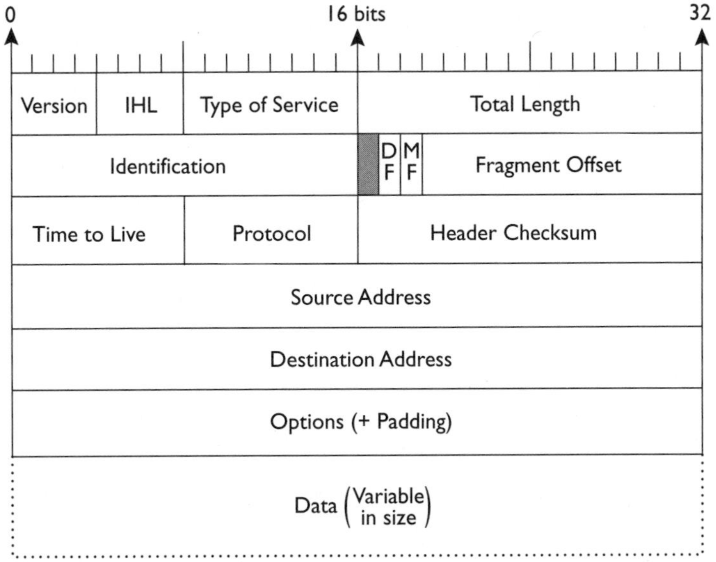

0 16 bits 32

Version | IHL | Type of Service | Total Length
Identification | DF | MF | Fragment Offset
Time to Live | Protocol | Header Checksum
Source Address
Destination Address
Options (+ Padding)
Data (Variable in size)

Legend	
IHL	IP Header Length
DF	Don't Fragment
MF	More Fragments

- *Quality-of-Service Features* — Packets can now specify the type of service required. This is useful for time-sensitive data, such as audio and video.
- *Authentication and Privacy* — IPv6 now includes authentication, integrity checking, and security services.

TCP

Transmission Control Protocol (TCP) is the main Internet Transport Layer protocol. TCP accepts messages of any length from an upper-layer service and provides full-duplex, connection-oriented transport. At the most basic level, TCP accepts large messages and breaks them into segments for IP. Because IP is connectionless, TCP must provide sequenced synchronization for each segment. TCP accomplishes this task by assigning sequence numbers at the byte level. Finally, TCP acknowledgments enhance error checking at the Transport Layer.

Figure 21.3 shows the format of a TCP header.

FIGURE 21.3

TCP header format

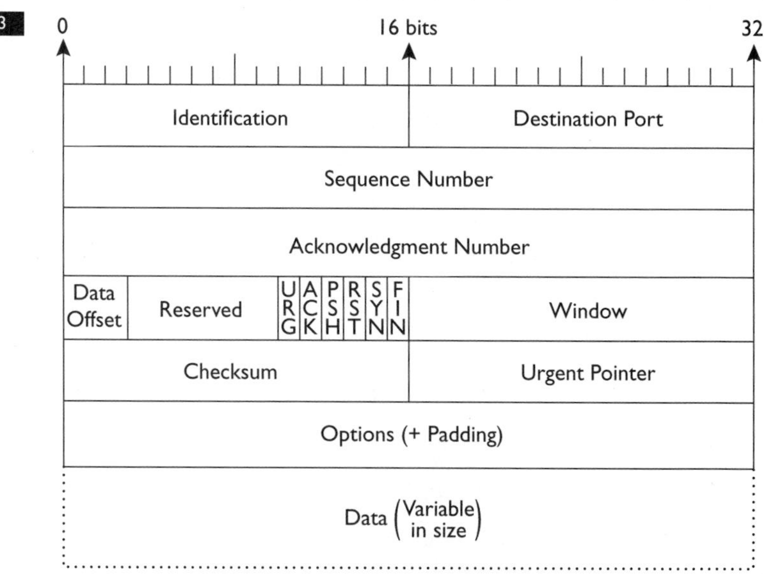

Legend	
URG	Urgent
ACK	Acknowledgment
PSH	Push
RST	Reset
SYN	Syncronize
FIN	Finish

UDP

User Datagram Protocol (UDP) is closely related to TCP in that it provides Transport Layer services. UDP, however, is not connection-oriented and does not acknowledge data receipt. It simply accepts and transports datagrams. This simplicity enables UDP to transfer data much faster (although more unreliably).

RIP

Large IP networks are typically subdivided into logical subnetworks that are referred to as *autonomous systems*. Each autonomous system (AS) is considered to be a fully functional entity by an outside network authority.

Following are two external protocols that handle communications between multiple autonomous systems:

- *Exterior Gateway Protocol (EGP)*—EGP is an older, link-state protocol that cannot scale to large IP network environments.
- *Border Gateway Protocol (BGP)*—BGP is an enhanced version of EGP, designed for inter-domain applications and large-scale deployment.

Similarly, a number of internal protocols manage routing within an autonomous system. These protocols are called Interior Gateway Protocols (IGPs). Following are two of the most popular IGPs:

- *Routing Information Protocol (RIP)*—RIP is a distance-vector-based routing protocol. RIP routers periodically broadcast the contents of their RITs to determine the route with the lowest cost. Cost is usually equal to the hop count and may range in value from 1 to 16, where an entry with a cost of 16 indicates an unreachable destination network.
- *Open Shortest Path First (OSPF)*—OSPF uses the Hello protocol to establish and maintain dialogs between neighboring routers on a given network segment.

An enhanced version of RIP, called RIP II, has been introduced. It provides support for the following added features: authentication, subnet masks (this increases the total number of subnetworks and hosts available on the network), next hop addresses, and multicast packets.

OSPF

As we mentioned earlier, OSPF uses the Hello protocol to establish and to maintain dialogs between neighboring routers on a given network segment. Routers periodically transmit multicast Hello packets that enable neighboring routers to identify one another. This process is similar to the Ping-Pong communication system used by NLSP routers (discussed later in this chapter).

The Hello packet contains the following information:

- OSPF router data (including its address and subnet mask)
- The identity of neighboring routers
- Hello packet transmission interval
- The identity of the Designated Router (DR) and the Backup Designated Router (BDR)

The OSPF router with the highest priority value becomes the DR. Remaining routers arbitrate to determine which will become the BDR. If a new router comes online with a higher priority value, either the DR or the BDR will deactivate and the new device will assume the appropriate role. When the DR fails, the BDR is promoted to DR and a new BDR is elected, based on its priority value.

In addition, each OSPF router maintains a link-state database that represents a router map of the entire internetwork. Once the DR and BDR have been elected and each router is aware of its neighbor list, all routers create and synchronize their link-state databases with the DR and the BDR.

That completes our brief discussion of Middle Layer Internet protocols. Now let's take a closer look at how IP and TCP work together to ensure reliable end-to-end networking communications. In the next few sections, we will explore IP addressing, subnetting, and supernetting.

IP Addressing

Logical IP addressing uses a combination of Data Link Layer physical addressing and Network Layer logical addressing. The logical IP address consists of a 32-bit, dotted-decimal value that contains both network and host address components.

The sample IP address in Figure 21.4 contains 4 bytes (or octets) that represent two key data units:

- *Network Address* — Identifies the network segment. This address varies from 1 to 3 bytes. In Figure 21.4, the IP network address component is 132.132. Following IP addressing convention, the IP network address in this example can be written as 132.132.0.0.
- *Host Address* — Sometimes referred to as node or station address, this 1-byte to 3-byte field represents the physical machine. In Figure 21.4, the host address component is 87.176. Following IP addressing convention, the IP host address in this example can be written as 0.0.87.176. Most IP implementations do not allow a host address of 0 (because it is not supported by all systems) or 255 (because it is reserved for broadcasts). Also, be aware that a host address ending in 0 could be confused for a network address.

FIGURE 21.4

IP address architecture

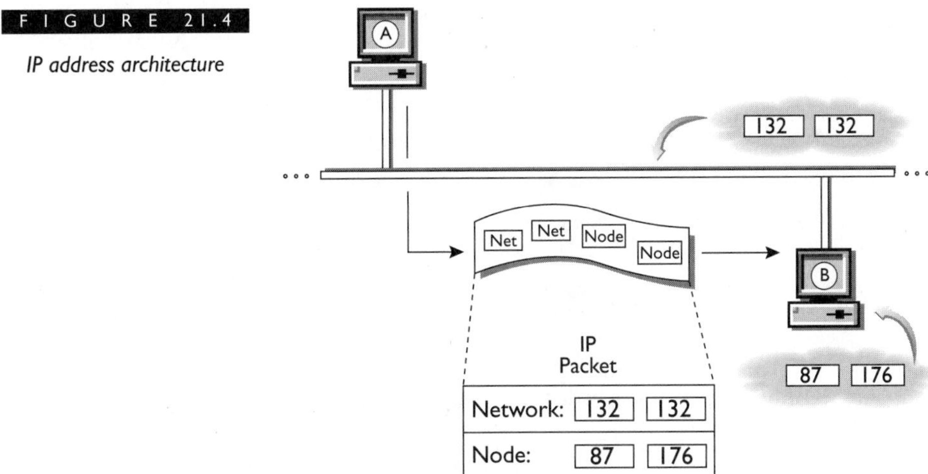

It is fairly common to express IP addresses in binary (base 2) format. This is especially helpful when implementing or decoding addresses on subnetworks. For example, the IP address 132.132.87.176 would look like this in binary format:

```
10000100.10000100.01010111.10110000
```

Each bit represents a value ranging from 128 (left-most position) to 1 (right-most position). For example, the decimal number 132 is 10000100 in binary. Use the following method to determine the value:

```
1 * 128 = 128
0 * 64  =   0
0 * 32  =   0
0 * 16  =   0
0 *  8  =   0
1 *  4  =   4
0 *  2  =   0
0 *  1  =   0
          ===
          132
```

Using this scheme, IP can identify any network using one of the following five classes (see Figure 21.5):

- *Class A Addresses* — These addresses are used for systems with a small number of networks and a large number of hosts. The first octet represents the IP network address, while the remaining three octets represent the node address. Class A addresses use a first octet value in the range of 0 to 127. There are 216 possible Class A networks, each supporting up to 16,777,216 hosts.

- *Class B Addresses* — These addresses provide equal support for networks and hosts. The first two octets represent the IP network address, while the remaining two octets represent the node address. Class B addresses use a first octet value in the range of 128 to 191. This class is the most common for universities and commercial organizations. There are 16,384 possible Class B networks, each supporting up to 65,534 hosts.

- *Class C Addresses* — These addresses are used by systems with a large number of networks and a small number of hosts. The first three octets represent the IP network address, while the remaining octet represents the node address. Class C addresses use a first octet value in the range of 192 to 223. There are 2,097,152 possible Class C networks, each supporting up to 255 hosts.

- *Class D Addresses* — These are multicast addresses that send data to specific multiple hosts simultaneously. Class D addresses use a first octet value in the range of 224 to 239.

- *Class E Addresses* — These addresses are reserved for experimental research and development. Class E addresses use a first octet value in the range of 240 to 255. The class E address 255.255.255.255 represents a broadcast.

FIGURE 21.5

Understanding IP address classes

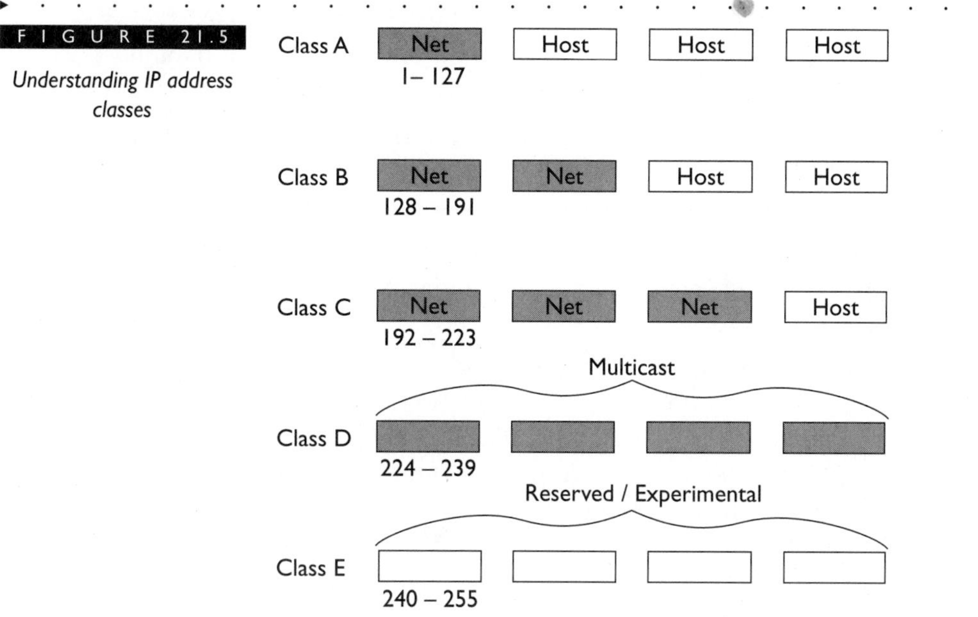

REAL WORLD

Several IP addresses have been reserved for special uses, including the following addresses:

- *Network 0.0.0.0*—Routers use this notation to express the default route.
- *Network 127.0.0.0*—This is referred to as the loopback address. The address 127.0.0.1 is often used to refer to the local host.
- *Addresses with all network bits set to 0*—This is used to refer to a host on a given network. For example, the address 0.0.1.10 could be used to refer to host 1.10 on the local network.
- *Addresses with all host bits set to 0*—This is used to refer to the IP Network segment address (such as 132.132.0.0 in our previous example).
- *Addresses with all network or host bits set to 1*—This indicates a packet intended for all hosts within a specific network segment or throughout the WAN.
- *Network 255.255.255.255*—This indicates a broadcast intended for all hosts on the local network.

When it is time to connect your organization's network to the Internet, you will need to obtain a registered IP address. Network Solutions, Inc. (formerly InterNIC) is responsible for managing the assignment of registered IP addresses. In addition, a new, nonprofit organization called the American Registry for Internet Numbers (ARIN) has been formed to administer IP address assignments (`www.arin.net`).

Both ARIN and InterNIC are responsible for North America, South America, South Africa, and the Caribbean. The Reseaux IP Europeans (RIPE) (`www.ripe.net`) and Asia Pacific Network Information Center (APNIC) (`www.apnic.net`) are responsible for Europe and the Pacific Rim, respectively.

So, what can you do if you have lots of networks and only one network address? Fortunately, TCP/IP allows you to divide an IP network into logical subnets. Let's take a closer look.

Subnetting

Subnetting enables network administrators to extend an IP address by breaking up the internal network address into "sub" nets. With this scheme, external Internet devices cannot access internal devices directly, but they are aware that a network has been subnetted. Refer to Figure 21.6 for an illustration of iACME subnetting. In this figure, ACME's network (known as iACME) has been internally subdivided into six logical subnets.

FIGURE 21.6

Building internal iACME subnets

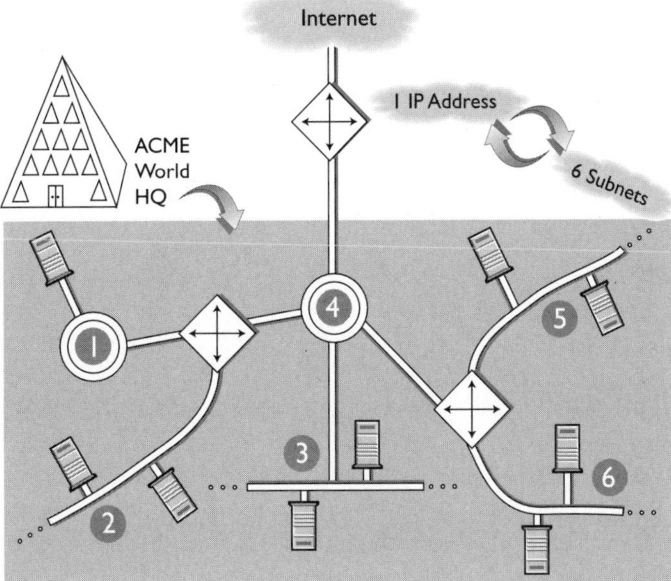

Following are some advantages of IP subnetting:

- *Optimize bandwidth utilization* — Subnets separate your network into individual collision domains, thus reducing network congestion.
- *Minimize broadcast traffic* — Subnets reduce the amount of network-wide broadcast traffic by isolating broadcasts to local subnets. This reduces the CPU overhead in all network devices.

- *Isolate failure domains* — By dividing a network into logical subnets, network device failures on one subnet do not typically affect devices located on other subnets.
- *Enhance security* — Because broadcast traffic is isolated to individual subnets, sensitive address and routing information is not made available everywhere on a network. In addition, the routers that are used to separate subnets can implement packet filtering to prevent access to certain services.

Creating Subnets

In this section, we will explore a variety of subnetting scenarios to help you grasp the immense value of this sophisticated IP address expansion scheme. But first, let's walk through the three steps of subnet construction. To create a valid IP subnet mask and assign new host addresses, follow these three steps:

- *Step 1:* Determine the Number of Subnets.
- *Step 2:* Define the Required Subnet Mask.
- *Step 3:* Assign New Host Addresses.

Let's take a closer look.

Step 1: Determine the Number of Subnets

A conventional IP address consists of 32 bits. Subnetting requires that we borrow host bits and assign them to internal subnets. Subnetting is easiest when you begin with a Class A or Class B address. In such a case, you would have either 24 or 16 host bits to work with, respectively.

In the case of Class C addresses (where there are only eight host bits to work with), subnetting can be difficult. The number of subnets available can be calculated according to the following formula:

$$2^n - 2$$

In the preceding formula, *n* is the number of bits used for subnets. The reason you need to subtract two from the possible number of subnets is because subnet addresses consisting of all ones or all zeros are not allowed.

Step 2: Define the Required Subnet Mask

A subnet mask is required to inform routers and hosts that the default address bit assignments defined by IP address classes have been overridden. In Figure 21.7, a Class A network number (110.0.0.0) has been subnetted by redefining the meaning of the first *host* octet (which is the second octet in the address). In this scenario, the entire second octet (8 bits) has been reassigned for subnetting, leaving the remaining two octets for hosts.

FIGURE 21.7

Creating a subnet mask for ACME

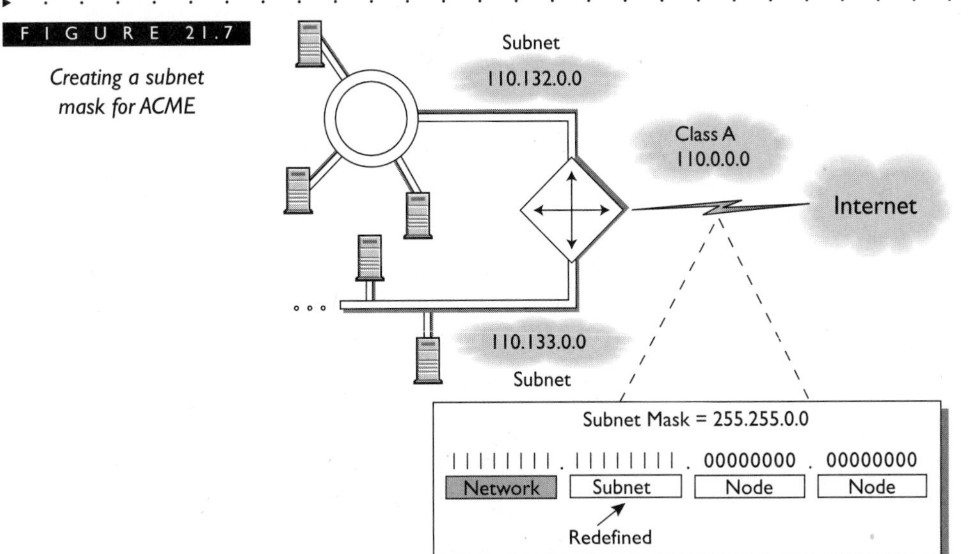

The default mask for a Class A network is 255.0.0.0. In this case, the first octet represents the network portion of the address and the remaining three octets represent the individual hosts. By overriding the default mask and creating a subnet mask of 255.255.0.0, you will effectively inform all routers and hosts on the network that the first two octets of the TCP/IP address contain network information and the remaining octets contain host information.

Step 3: Assign New Host Addresses

Finally, the subnet mask is logically ANDed with the IP address to determine each host's subnet number, thereby assigning new addresses to internal network devices. Any bit in the mask that is set to 1 represents a network bit, and any bit set to 0 represents a host bit. In Boolean algebra, when you AND a 1 bit with another bit, the result of the operation is equal to the value of the other bit.

For example, 1 AND 0 equals 0, whereas 1 AND 1 equals 1. By setting the network bits in the subnet mask to 1, a router can effectively filter out the host bits (which it does not use) and be left with only the bits that represent logical network addresses.

When you implement subnetting, you are changing the meaning of IP addresses from two components (network and host) to three components (network, subnet, and host). Let's look at some Class A, B, and C scenarios that represent a variety of subnetting implementations at ACME.

Class B Subnets

Consider the Class B subnet example shown in Figure 21.8. In this scenario, the IS department has decided to use the entire third octet of their Class B address (132.132.0.0) to represent subnetworks. The default mask for a Class B network is 255.255.0.0. To meet the new subnetting requirements, all routers and hosts will be configured with a subnet mask value of 255.255.255.0. This informs all of the devices on the network that the third octet represents subnet bits.

FIGURE 21.8

Creating a Class B subnet mask

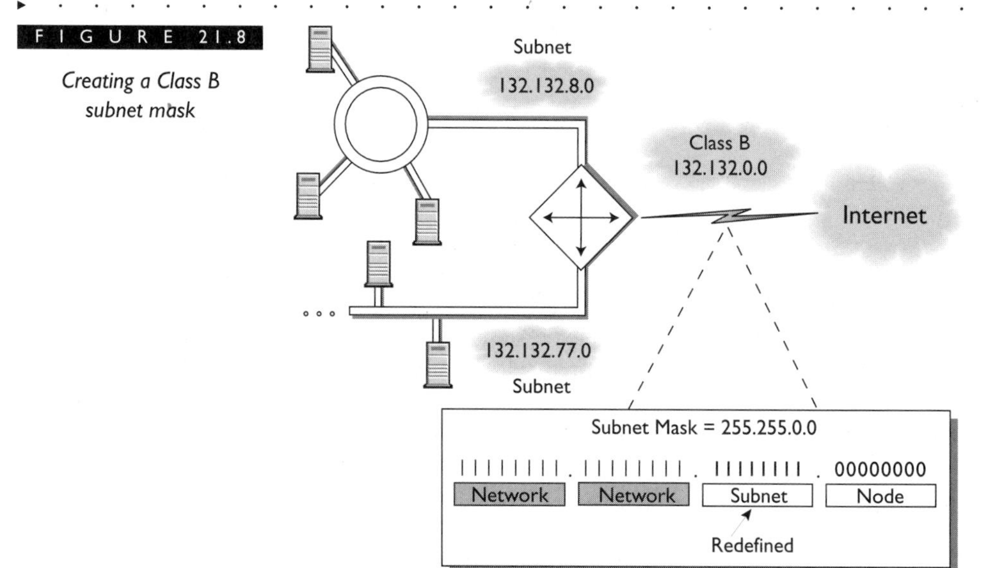

In this example, each IP address has the following meaning:

- *Network*—The first two octets represent the IP network number (132.132.0.0), as assigned by InterNIC. All hosts on the network use the same network number.
- *Subnet*—The third octet represents the subnet number. All hosts on a given subnet will share the same value.
- *Host*—The fourth octet contains a unique host number.

Class C Partial Octet Subnets

It is also possible to create subnets by dividing an address on non-octet boundaries (known as *partial octets*). For example, Class C addresses do not support entire octet subnetting because only one host octet is available. In this case, you must borrow partial bits from the host octet.

Consider the scenario illustrated in Figure 21.9. The first attempt at subnetting assigned a mask of 255.255.255.255, which left no bits available for host addressing. This is not allowed. The second attempt reserves the first three bits of the fourth octet for subnets. The resulting subnet mask has a value of 255.255.255.224. By borrowing three bits we can define up to six ($2^3 - 2 = 6$) subnetworks.

FIGURE 21.9

Using partial octets to create a subnet mask

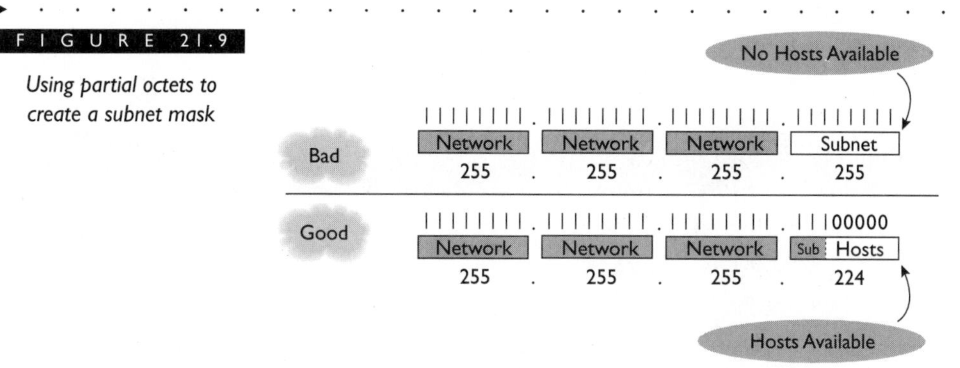

Table 21.1 indicates the subnet mask values for various partial octet subnetting schemes.

TABLE 21.1

Common Subnet Masks

NUMBER OF SUBNET BITS	CLASS A	CLASS B	CLASS C
0 (Default Mask)	255.0.0.0	255.255.0.0	255.255.255.0
1	255.128.0.0	255.255.128.0	255.255.255.128
2	255.192.0.0	255.255.192.0	255.255.255.192
3	255.224.0.0	255.255.224.0	255.255.255.224
4	255.240.0.0	255.255.240.0	255.255.255.240
5	255.248.0.0	255.255.248.0	255.255.255.248 (Only allows seven hosts per subnet.)
6	255.252.0.0	255.255.252.0	255.255.255.252 (Only allows three hosts per subnet.)
7	255.254.0.0	255.255.254.0	255.255.255.254 (Only allows one host per subnet.)
8	255.255.0.0	255.255.255.0	Can't be used because 255.255.255.255 is reserved for broadcasts.

In some cases it is not practical to implement Class C subnetting because of the limited number of Host bits. In this case, Table 21.2 illustrates the breakdown of Class C partial octet subnetting.

TABLE 21.2

Class C Partial Subnetting

NUMBER OF SUBNET BITS	MASK VALUE (BINARY)	MASK VALUE (DECIMAL)	SUBNETS	HOSTS PER SUBNET
1	10000000	128	2	128
2	11000000	192	4	64
3	11100000	224	8	32
4	11110000	240	16	16
5	11111000	248	32	8
6	11111100	252	64	4
7	11111110	254	128	2

Class A Partial Octet Subnets

In this final scenario, we'll explore a Class A partial octet subnetting scheme. In this example, ACME has been assigned a Class A network address of 98.0.0.0. The IS department has decided that the first three bits of the second octet shall be used for subnetting. Figure 21.10 shows how the IP address bits will be used within our organization, as well as the binary and decimal representations of our subnet mask components.

FIGURE 21.10

Using a three-bit subnet mask

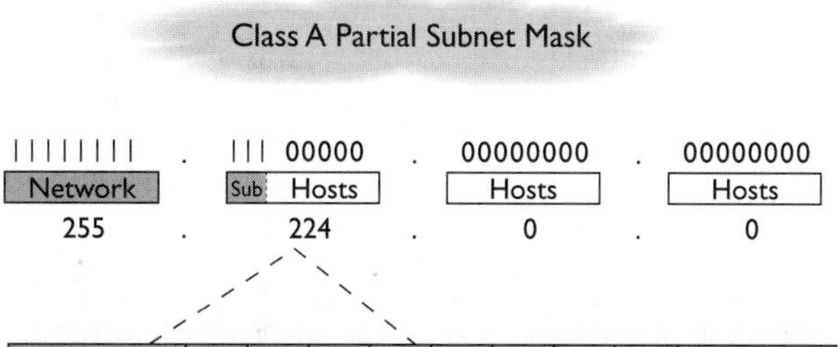

Class A Partial Subnet Mask

11111111 . 111 00000 . 00000000 . 00000000

Network | Sub Hosts | Hosts | Hosts

255 . 224 . 0 . 0

Binary	2^7	2^6	2^5	2^4	2^3	2^2	2^1	2^0	Binary Equivalent
Decimal	128	64	32	16	8	4	2	1	
255	1	1	1	1	1	1	1	1	11111111
224	1	1	1	0	0	0	0	0	11100000

Following are the possible combinations of the three subnet bits in Figure 21.10:

```
000  100
001  101
010  110
011  111
```

We have already learned that subnet numbers can't consist of all 0 bits or all 1 bits, so we throw out the first (000) and last (111) combinations. This leaves us with six (23 – 2 = 6) possible subnets. To determine the actual subnet values, you have to take into account the rest of the bits in the second octet. Fortunately, they have all been conveniently masked to 0. So, here are the subnet numbers in binary and decimal format:

```
00100000 = subnet 32
01000000 = subnet 64
01100000 = subnet 96
10000000 = subnet 128
10100000 = subnet 160
11000000 = subnet 192
```

In our example, ACME was assigned a Class A address of 98.0.0.0. Our first subnet is number 32. The range of host addresses on subnet 32 is 98.32.0.1 to 98.62.255.255. For subnet 96 it's 98.96.0.1 to 98.126.255.255.

In summary, keep the following rules in mind when assigning addresses on a subnetted network:

- Every address must be unique.
- All devices on the same cable segment must use the same network and subnet numbers.
- The Node bits may not be set to a value containing all 0 or all 1 bits.
- Plan for growth.

Now that we've learned how to create a variety of subnet schemes, let's take a quick look at some growth planning and design criteria. After all, you don't want to *sub*net when you should *super*net.

Subnet Planning and Design

Following are some key issues to consider when you're planning on growing your IP network through subnetting:

- How many subnets are required immediately?

- How will network growth affect the required number of subnets down the road?
- How many hosts are required on each subnet?
- How will network growth affect the number of hosts on any given subnet?

One of the biggest problems with subnetting is that you can get locked into your plan quite easily. If you need to eventually increase the number of subnets, you could be facing a massive amount of reworking. All of your subnet masks and addresses would need to be reassigned. In a large network environment, this could be an impossible task.

To address this issue, RFC 1209 provides some guidelines that, if followed carefully, could save you hours of work. The general concept provided by RFC 1209 is that Subnet bits should be assigned from left to right, while Host bits should be assigned from right to left.

In the final scenario, we determined the subnet numbers for a 3-bit mask (224). When determining the subnet numbers we simply counted from 001 to 110. What if we assigned the subnets in the following order?

```
10000000 = subnet 128

01000000 = subnet 64

11000000 = subnet 192

00100000 = subnet 32

10100000 = subnet 160

01100000 = subnet 96
```

By using this numbering scheme, we can assign the first three subnets without impacting the third subnet bit. This allows us to alter the subnet mask to four bits or more at a later time without needing to reassign IP addresses to network devices. Accordingly, node address assignments would be made in the following order:

```
For subnet 128    10000001 (12910)
                  to
                  10011110 (15810)
```

```
For subnet 64        01000001 (6510)
                     to
                     01011110 (9410)
```

The primary goal here is to leave an unused buffer area between the Subnet and Node bits so that we can alter our subnet mask at a later time without a lot of fuss. Subnet bits grow from left to right and Host bits grow from right to left. At some point, they will meet and you will no longer be able to maintain a buffer zone.

To determine a device's subnet number when dealing with partial octet subnetting, you have to use the Boolean AND operator. Following is an example of a Class C address that has been subnetted using the first three bits of the fourth octet:

```
Class C Network:      192.128.64.0
Subnet Mask:          255.255.255.224
Host Address:         192.128.64.129


Binary Host Address: 11000000.10000000.01000000.10000001
Binary Subnet Mask:  11111111.11111111.11111111.11100000
AND                  ===================================
                     11000000.10000000.01000000.10000000
```

After performing the AND operation, the resulting bits represent the network number (11000000.10000000.01000000 = 192.128.64) and the subnet number (100). We then pad the Subnet bits with the remaining five masked bits to obtain the actual subnet number (10000000 = 128).

Finally, to determine the Host bits, subtract the subnet number (128) from the fourth octet's original value (129) and you are left with 1. This means that you have just decoded the address of Host number 1 on subnet 128 of network 192.128.64.0.

That's all there is to it! As you learned in this section, IP subnetting provides an excellent method for stretching your single IP address over hundreds (or thousands) of internal network devices. Now let's take a look at another IP addressing expansion scheme called supernetting.

REAL WORLD

A real benefit of subnetting on a complete octet is the fact that the numeric value you see specified in that octet is the device's actual subnet number. When subnetting on partial octets, you must know the subnet mask value and then perform the AND operation before determining the subnet number. In real life you will quickly become familiar with your organization's subnetting scheme and deciphering subnet numbers will become a breeze.

Supernetting

Supernetting is the opposite of subnetting — that is, supernets *combine* multiple Class C addresses into one supernet address. Supernetting enables you to extend the usable life of 32-bit IP addressing by providing a larger number of hosts per logical network. Supernetting is also known as *address aggregation.*

The following conditions are required to supernet multiple IP addresses:

- Multiple, consecutive Class C IP addresses.
- The first address' third octet value must be evenly divisible by 2.

In contrast to a traditional subnet mask, the "supernet" subnet mask borrows network bits to increase the total number of available hosts. For example, the default Class C subnet mask is 255.255.255.0. This mask indicates that the first three octets (24 bits) represent the network portion of the address, while the remaining octet (8 bits) represents the host portion. If you alter the mask to a 23-bit subnet mask (255.255.254.0), you will end up with an extra bit for hosts (9 bits). This doubles the total number of available hosts (from 256 to 512 devices).

Refer to Figure 21.11 for a supernetting scenario where the Class C addresses 201.41.18.0 and 201.41.19.0 have been combined into a supernet. Routers on this network will advertise the first Class C address (201.41.18.0) along with a subnet mask modifier of "/23" — which indicates the number of bits in the subnet mask. Next, receiving routers will interpret the address and the 23-bit mask and determine that two contiguous Class C network addresses have been combined into a supernet. Network 201.41.18.0 will represent supernet 0 and network 201.41.19.0 will represent supernet 1.

FIGURE 21.11

Building supernets

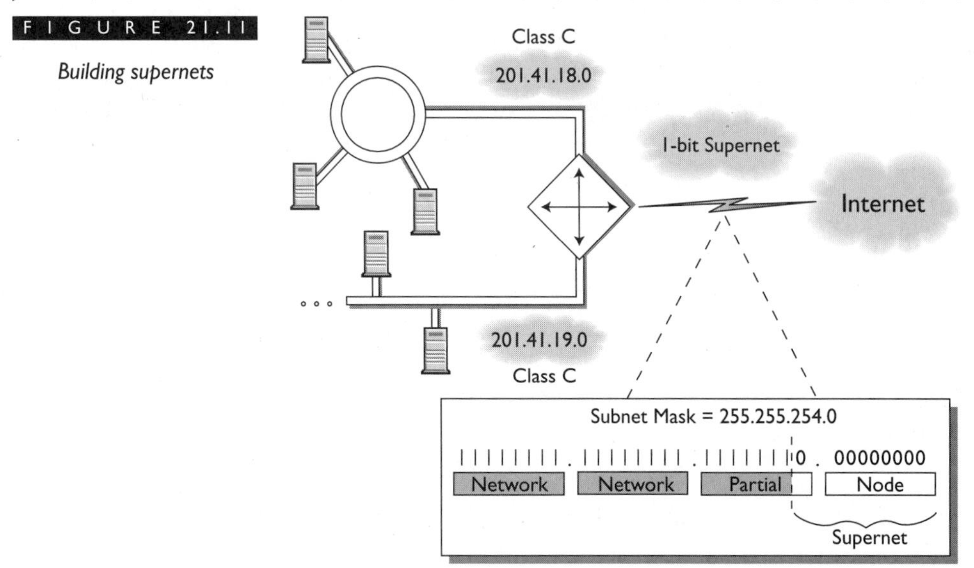

In order for routers to understand supernetting, they must support the Classless Inter-Domain Routing (CIDR) protocol. This protocol allows devices to specify nonstandard masks (such as those required by supernetting). An example of an IP address that uses CIDR is 220.12.78.0/23. In this case, the "/23" informs network devices that the left-most 23 bits represent the subnet mask.

With CIDR, combined supernet addresses are combined under a single mask and advertised as one address block. This helps to reduce the amount of route reachability information that must be exchanged between intermediate devices.

Furthermore, you can create even larger supernets if you have more than two contiguous Class C addresses available. Table 21.3 illustrates the total number of hosts that can be supported by combining multiple Class C IP addresses.

TABLE 21.3

Building Large Supernets

NUMBER OF SUPERNET BITS	7	6	5	4	3	2	1	0
Subnet Mask	128	192	224	240	248	252	254	255
Contiguous Class C Addresses	128	64	32	16	8	4	2	0
Possible Number of Hosts		> 8192 < 16,384	> 4,096 < 8,192	> 2,048 < 4,096	> 1,024 < 2,048	> 512 < 1,024	> 256 < 512	< 256

That completes our adventure through IP addressing, subnetting, and supernetting. Fortunately, you rarely have to pay attention to these tedious details. IP addressing is made transparent with the help of various IP management protocols, such as DNS and DHCP. Speaking of which, let's extend our Internet protocol lesson into the Top Layers and explore DNS, DHCP, NFS, FTP, TELNET, SMTP, SNMP, and HTTP.

Top-Layer Internet Protocols

The foundation of the Internet protocol suite consists of *IP*, which operates at the Network Layer, and *TCP*, which operates at the Transport Layer (see Figure 21.1, earlier in this chapter). Top-layer services are provided through a complete suite of Internet applications, including the Domain Name System (DNS), Dynamic Host Configuration Protocol (DHCP), Network File System (NFS), File Transfer Protocol (FTP), TELNET, Simple Mail Transfer Protocol (SMTP), Simple Network Management Protocol (SNMP), and Hypertext Transfer Protocol (HTTP).

Domain Name System (DNS)

The Domain Name System (DNS) is a distributed database that matches computer names to device IP addresses. In this section, we will cover two important DNS concepts:

- *DNS Hierarchy* — The DNS Hierarchy (also called the *Domain Name Space*) specifies a host's location in the global Internet tree. This tree consists of top-level *domains* and more precise partitions called *zones*.
- *DNS Name Services* — This is the functional DNS component that maps a host's name to a computer's IP address. This service has *Master* (or Primary) and *Replica* (or Secondary) servers, and clients called *resolvers*.

DNS Hierarchy

The *DNS Hierarchy* organizes IP hosts into a logical upside-down tree (refer to Figure 21.12). In this figure, each node in the tree represents a domain. The end leaves of the tree are individual host machines on the Internet (such as SRV1 located in the NORAD zone in the figure).

An absolute (or fully qualified) DNS domain name is constructed by listing all domains on the path from the end device to the root. A period is used to delimit the labels in the domain name. For example, in Figure 21.12, the absolute domain name for the host SRV1 in NORAD is represented as the following:

```
SRV1.NORAD.ACME.COM.
```

In this case, the interior nodes of the DNS tree (such as .COM and .ACME) do not represent network devices. Instead, they represent logical divisions of the DNS name space.

As you can see in Figure 21.12, many of the top-level domains have already been established by InterNIC, the Internet governing body. These predefined domains help organize the vast Internet into functional zones (see Table 21.4).

FIGURE 21.12

DNS tree architecture

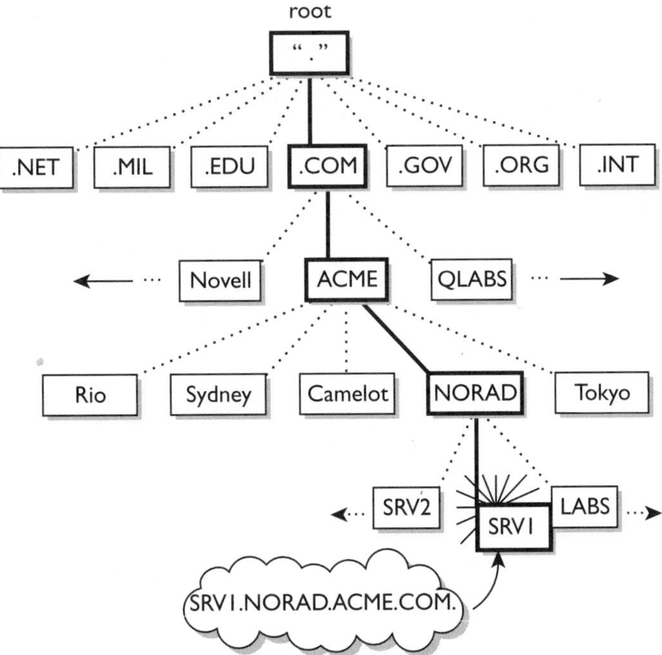

REAL WORLD

To master the subtle differences between DNS and NDS naming, you should memorize the following rules:

- DNS domain names can be up to 255 characters.
- Each domain within the absolute name can be up to 63 characters, provided that the total length doesn't exceed 255 characters.
- DNS domain names are not case sensitive.
- All absolute DNS domain names should end in a trailing period; however, the period can be omitted.
- You can use relative DNS domain naming by specifying the path from your current position to the root. (This naming scheme is analogous to relative NDS naming.)

TABLE 21.4

Predefined Domains at the Top of the NDS Tree

DOMAIN	FUNCTION
.COM	Commercial organizations. This is the most popular domain used by today's high-profile Internet organizations.
.EDU	Educational institutions. Many universities, colleges, schools, educational service organizations and consortia register here. More recently, a decision has been made to limit further registrations to only four-year colleges and universities. Primary schools, secondary schools, and two-year colleges are now registered in the Country domains.
.UK	A new two-letter country code. The ISO-3166 Committee has determined that each country should be represented by a specific two-letter country code. For example, .UK represents Great Britain, .AU represents Australia, .US represents the United States, .DE represents Germany, and .CA represents Canada.
.GOV	Government agencies. This domain is reserved for U.S. Federal Government agencies.
.INT	International organizations. This domain is reserved for organizations that have been established by international treaties.
.MIL	Military. This domain is reserved for U.S. military services.
.NET	Networking entities. This domain represents computers of network providers (such as NIC and NOC computers).
.ORG	Miscellaneous organizations. This domain is an open-book for organizations that do not fit into any of the previous domain categories.

The DNS Hierarchy can be further subdivided into partitions called *zones* (or subdomains). Zones begin at a specific domain and extend downward until they reach either a terminating host or another subzone. For example, the shaded area in Figure 21.13 represents the ACME.COM. zone. Furthermore, any private network (such as ACME.COM.) can implement its own domain names within a specific zone. However, you must be sanctioned by the InterNIC to connect your zone to a public network such as the Internet.

DNS supports three different zone types:

- *Standard Zones* — A standard DNS zone contains records that resolve domain names into IP addresses. Most of today's Internet devices are addressed using standard DNS zoning rules.

FIGURE 21.13

The ACME.COM. DNS zone

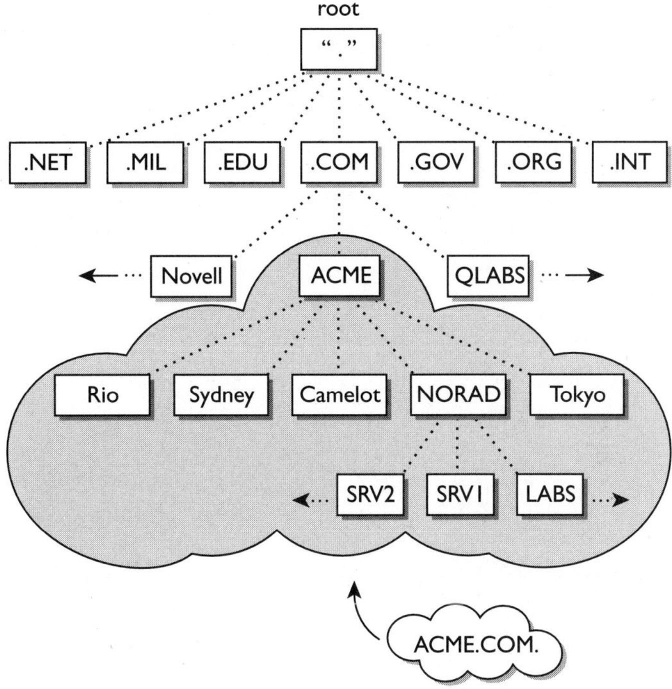

- *IN-ADDR.ARPA Zones* — The IN-ADDR.ARPA zone type works in the reverse of standard zones (hence they are sometimes called "reverse zones"). This type of zone provides mappings of IP addresses to domain names. IN-ADDR.ARPA zones use a format that is slightly different than standard zones. For example, the 192.168.1.0 network address would be represented as 1.168.192.IN-ADDR.ARPA (in reverse).
- *IP6.INT Zones* — The ever-increasing use of the Internet, along with the limited number of available IP addresses, is driving the development of a new IP addressing scheme known as IPv6. Devices using this scheme in a subdomain of the Internet are part of an IP6.INT zone type.

REAL WORLD

Prior to DNS, all hosts connected to the Internet had to periodically download host name and address information to keep their databases current. This was a problem for two reasons. First, the information was only as current as the last time it was updated. Second, as the Internet grew, the amount of information needing to be regularly downloaded by each host was eating up valuable network bandwidth.

DNS Name Services

DNS Name Services map host names to IP addresses. These name services rely on a server-client architecture. In this model, clients (resolvers) query one or more servers for host address information. If the DNS server does not have the information a client needs, it relays the request to another name server up or down the DNS Hierarchy.

The names and IP addresses of all hosts in a DNS zone are maintained on a single server called the *Master server.* The information contained on the Master server is called the *authoritative database* for that zone. This database includes the following information:

- Names and addresses of all IP hosts within the zone.
- Names of all subzones and addresses of the DNS servers for those zones.
- Addresses and DNS servers for the *root* domain and all other zones within the tree. These addresses are necessary to link your domain to the existing DNS Hierarchy.

In Figure 21.14, I have set up the SRV1.NORAD.ACME.COM. server as the Master DNS server for the NORAD.ACME.COM. zone. All updates to the DNS database for the zone are made on this server.

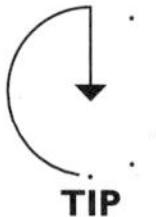

It's a good idea to keep the Master DNS server within your local zone; however, it's not required. By rule, the DNS server for NORAD. ACME.COM. can be located anywhere in the DNS Hierarchy.

FIGURE 21.14

Using Master and Replica DNS servers

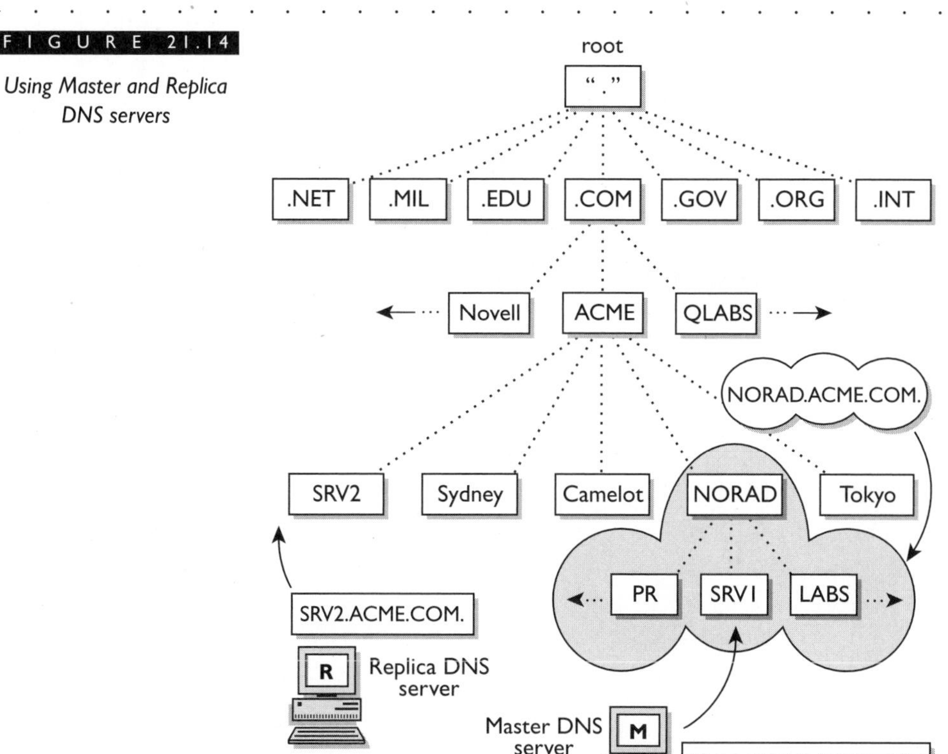

What happens if the Master DNS server goes down? Fortunately, DNS supports a backup naming server called a *Replica server* (also known as the *Secondary server*). Replica DNS servers provide redundancy and load balancing for DNS naming within a zone. This backup periodically downloads a copy of the DNS database from the Master server. It's important to note that updates to the zone database are only made at the Master server and then distributed to the Replica server when the Replica server requests a copy. This process is known as a *zone transfer*.

In Figure 21.14, I have configured SRV2.ACME.COM. as the Replica DNS server for the NORAD.ACME.COM. zone. As I'm sure you've noticed, the Replica DNS server is located outside its home zone. Once again, a DNS name server can be located anywhere in the Hierarchy. While it's a good idea to keep Master DNS servers inside the zone, you should distribute Replica DNS servers in geographically remote locations. Remember, we're trying to achieve redundancy and load balancing. A remote Replica server can service queries originating from outside the zone and provide a redundancy in case the local link goes down.

REAL WORLD

Master DNS servers can also function as Replica DNS servers for other zones. This way, if you're short on DNS name servers, you can service local and remote zones from the same machine.

So, how do DNS servers resolve IP addresses? The process is actually quite similar to the way you might find a telephone number for someone who lives in a remote city. Let's say, for example, you live in NORAD and want to call somebody in Tokyo. First, you would call your local operator to obtain the country code and the number for directory information in Japan. Then you would call directory information in Japan and get the local number for Tokyo. Then you would call Tokyo and query for your friend by name.

Imagine if your workstation was located in the LABS division of NORAD within ACME. From your DNS client (resolver), you want to access a device in the QLABS. COM. zone. Here's how your local DNS server would resolve the destination IP address (follow along in Figure 21.15):

- *Point 1* — To find a machine named JANE in the QLABS.COM. zone, you must first ask your local DNS server if it has a cached entry for JANE. If not, your local Master server will relay the request to the *root* server.
- *Point 2* — Your local Master DNS server asks the *root* DNS server for the location of the .COM server. At this point, you'll begin resolving JANE's IP address from the top down.
- *Point 3* — Next, the .COM server finds the IP address of the Master server in the QLABS.COM. zone and sends it to your local server.

- *Point 4* — Once your request finds its way to the Master DNS server in the QLABS.COM. zone, you'll be able to resolve the specific IP address for JANE. This address will then be relayed back to our local Master DNS server (Point 1) by backtracking through all the servers (or routers) that it took to get there.

FIGURE 21.15

DNS address resolution for JANE.QLABS.COM.

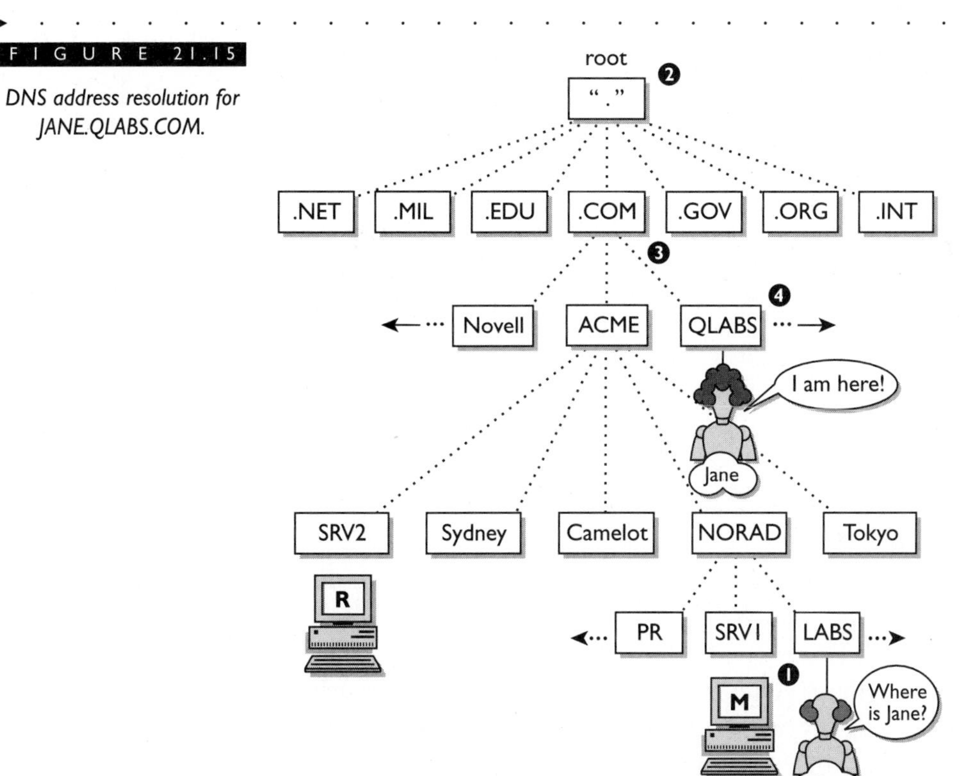

DNS can help your users resolve complex IP addresses without having to understand the details of IP address resolution. This dramatically reduces your TCP/IP management load. Now let's continue our Top-Layer Internet protocol journey with DHCP.

DHCP

The *Dynamic Host Configuration Protocol* (DHCP) was created to reduce the labor associated with the assignment and maintenance of IP addresses. DHCP uses a client/server model consisting of DHCP servers and appropriate operating-system-specific client software.

Administrators configure a DHCP server to host a pool of available IP addresses. These addresses are then dynamically assigned to requesting clients. By pooling available addresses, it is possible to provide IP services when more hosts are available than addresses. However, once all available addresses have been assigned, subsequent requests will be denied. DHCP allows IP addresses to be assigned in the following manner:

- *Automatic Allocation* — Permanent IP address assignments to hosts.
- *Dynamic Allocation* — Temporary IP address assignments to hosts, based on a first-come, first-served algorithm.
- *Manual Allocation* — Requires that the system administrator specify which host will be assigned to a given IP address.

NFS

The *Network File System* (NFS) was developed by Sun Microsystems and is the name most often associated with a family of standards that comprise Sun's Open Network Computing (ONC) platform. NFS allows users of dissimilar computers and operating systems to access shared information using the local computer environment. A related protocol, XDR (eXternal Data Representation), operates at the Presentation Layer and encodes data in a machine-independent format, thus providing a conduit for heterogeneous connectivity.

FTP

File Transfer Protocol (FTP) enables a user to transfer files between two networked computers. It also provides a variety of login, directory inspection, file manipulation, command execution, and other upper-layer services. In addition, FTP can be used to move files between dissimilar operating systems using TCP.

Telnet

Telnet is the remote terminal emulation protocol. Telnet enables users to access host-based applications from personal computers that act as dumb terminals. In its simplest form, Telnet software enables a computer to emulate a terminal, and like FTP, it can provide connectivity between dissimilar systems.

SMTP

The *Simple Mail Transfer Protocol* (SMTP) is an electronic mail routing standard that uses TCP and IP to route mail messages between network hosts. SMTP gateways are used to exchange electronic-mail messages between proprietary systems such as Lotus Notes, Novell's GroupWise, Microsoft Exchange, and so on. SMTP does not provide a local-mail user interface, however.

SNMP

The *Simple Network Management Protocol* (SNMP) is a client/server protocol that defines agents and management consoles. An SNMP agent is a software program embedded in a network device, such as a NIC or a router. This agent maintains a small database called a management information base (MIB). SNMP management consoles can send a query to an agent requesting read-only or read-write access to the agent's MIB.

HTTP

The *HyperText Transfer Protocol* (HTTP) is the client/server protocol that drives the World Wide Web (WWW). HTTP servers send requested information to users utilizing client browsers such as Netscape Communicator or Microsoft Internet Explorer. Users can view text, graphics, audio, video, and other multimedia content by connecting through a local Internet Service Provider (ISP).

Refer to Table 21.5 for a feature summary of these top-layer Internet implementations.

TABLE 21.5

Feature Summary of Internet Top-Layer Implementations

IMPLEMENTATION	SESSION ADMINISTRATION	TRANSLATION	SERVICE USE	NETWORK SERVICE
DNS				Address-to-name resolution
DHCP				Automated address assignment service
NFS			Remote operation	File services
FTP				Nontransparent file transfer services
Telnet	Connection establishment, half-duplex data transfer, and connection release terminal emulation	Byte order and character code	Remote operation	
SMTP				Message services
SNMP				Network management services
HTTP				World Wide Web service

This completes our discussion of the Internet protocol family. These numerous protocols are the foundation of today's global Internet network. You probably interact with them every day, but until now, you didn't fully understand how they work together.

Now let's zero in on the LAN and WAN protocols that NetWare uses to route packets between senders and receivers.

NetWare Protocols

Novell's Internetwork Packet Exchange (IPX) and Sequenced Packet Exchange (SPX) are the primary Middle Layer protocols for routing NetWare file, print, message, application, and database services. NetWare is based on a server-centric architecture in which clients (workstations) make requests of servers. These requests are then handled by upper-layer services. (**Note:** The NetWare 5.1 operating system also includes native support for the TCP/IP protocol.)

As shown in Figure 21.16, original NetWare consists of numerous protocols that operate at various levels throughout the OSI model. The two most prominent OSI networking implementations are IPX (at the Network Layer) and SPX (at the Transport Layer). In addition, IPX is supported at the Network Layer by Routing Information Protocol (RIP) and NetWare Link Services Protocol (NLSP).

IPX/SPX are supported at the bottom layers by several Physical and Data Link standards, including Multiple Link Interface Driver (MLID) and Link Support Layer (LSL). Finally, at the upper layers, IPX/SPX routes messages to NetWare Core Protocol (NCP) and Service Advertising Protocol (SAP) for processing.

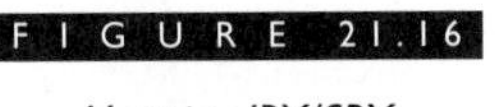
FIGURE 21.16

Mapping IPX/SPX to the OSI model

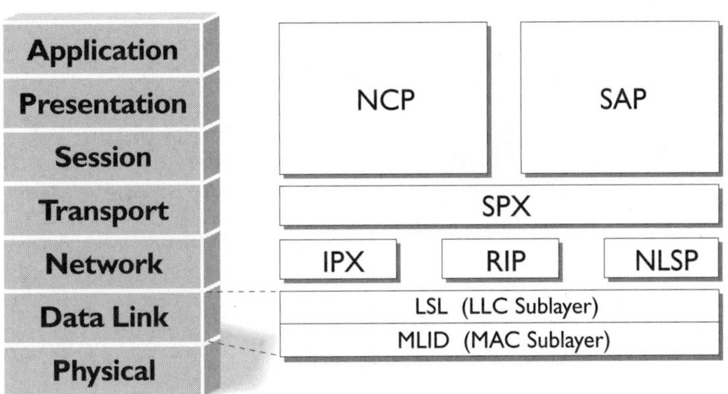

Internetwork Packet Exchange (IPX)

IPX is a connectionless datagram protocol that operates at the Network Layer of the OSI model. As a Network Layer implementation, IPX performs logical network addressing and internetwork routing functions. It relies upon the underlying hardware's physical address for node addressing and for upper-layer service addresses for the ultimate packet destination.

IPX uses its own dynamic route selection algorithm, but it relies on RIP for distance-vector route discovery. In addition, IPX's reliability has been enhanced by the introduction of a new link-state route discovery protocol called NetWare Link Services Protocol (NLSP).

Together, IPX and SPX utilize several layers of addressing to deliver data across a network (see Figure 21.17):

- *Network Address* — An IPX network address is a 4-byte number consisting of eight hexadecimal characters. This address identifies a logical network and is used to route packets through an IPX internetwork. The addresses 00000000, FFFFFFFE, and FFFFFFFF are reserved. IPX network address assignments are made when IPX is bound to a NIC in a NetWare server. This is accomplished by using the following command (or something similar) at the file server console: `BIND IPX NE2000 NET=12345678`. In this example, IPX is bound to an NE2000 NIC and assigned an IPX network address of 12345678. In Figure 21.17, 12345678 is the network address.

- *Internal Network Address* — In addition to an IPX network address, all NetWare servers running IPX/SPX are identified by an internal IPX network address. This address is also a 4-byte (eight hexadecimal digit) number with the same restrictions as previously described. All packets addressed to the internal network specify a node address of 000000000001. In Figure 21.17, DADDEE1is the internal network address.

- *Physical Node Address* — A node address is the 6-byte (12 hexadecimal digit) hardware address assigned to each NIC by its manufacturer. In Figure 21.17, 000000000001 is the node address.

- *Socket Number* — An IPX socket number determines a packet's ultimate destination process (such as NCP, SPX, or RIP).

FIGURE 21.17

IPX/SPX address architecture

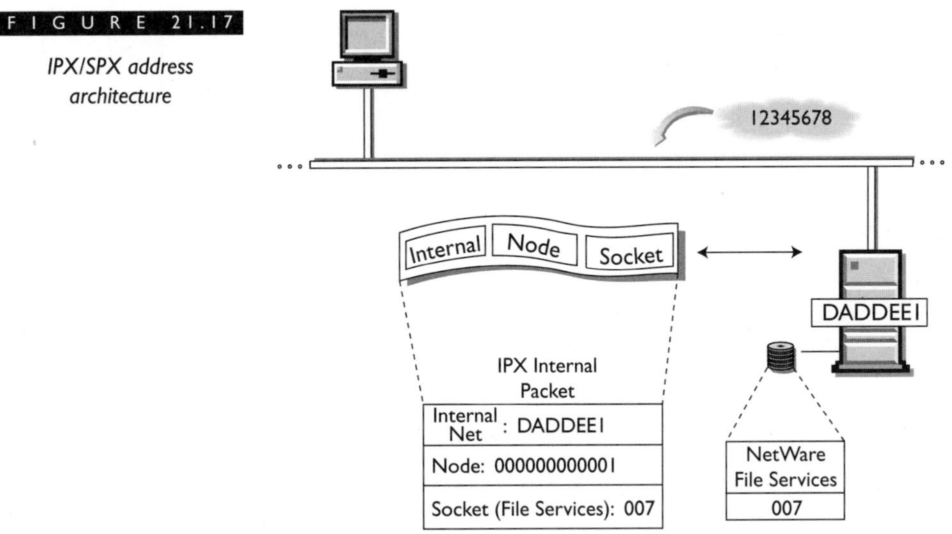

Now that you understand the purpose of IPX, let's take a closer look at its packet format (shown in Figure 21.18). Because IPX is a connectionless protocol, you will not find any fields related to a particular conversation between two devices. An interesting item to note about IPX packets is that the physical addresses of the source and destination devices are repeated in the packet itself. This is in addition to the addresses that are included in the frame's MAC header. For this reason, the IPX/SPX protocol suite does not include an address resolution protocol such as TCP/IP's ARP or AppleTalk's AARP.

Sequenced Packet Exchange (SPX)

SPX operates primarily at the Transport Layer to provide reliable delivery of Network Layer datagrams. SPX uses connection ID addressing, segmentation, end-to-end flow control, and error checking.

When NetWare servers are running IPX/SPX, many of their services rely on SPX for reliable packet delivery. These services include the Remote Management Facility, remote printing, dedicated print servers, and the NetWare for Systems Application Architecture (SAA) gateway.

FIGURE 21.18

IPX packet format

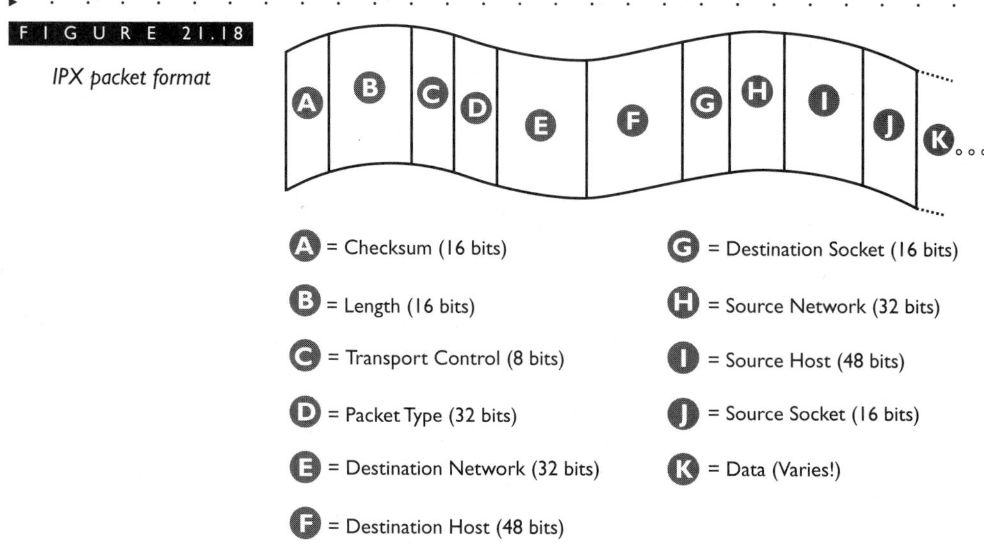

Figure 21.19 shows the format of an SPX packet. SPX's connection-oriented operation requires the addition of connection ID, sequence, and acknowledgment fields. Only communications that require guaranteed delivery use SPX because of the overhead involved in connection-oriented administration. SPX can perform segmentation, reassembly, and segment sequencing tasks as required by underlying Network, Data Link, and Physical Layer protocols.

FIGURE 21.19

SPX packet format

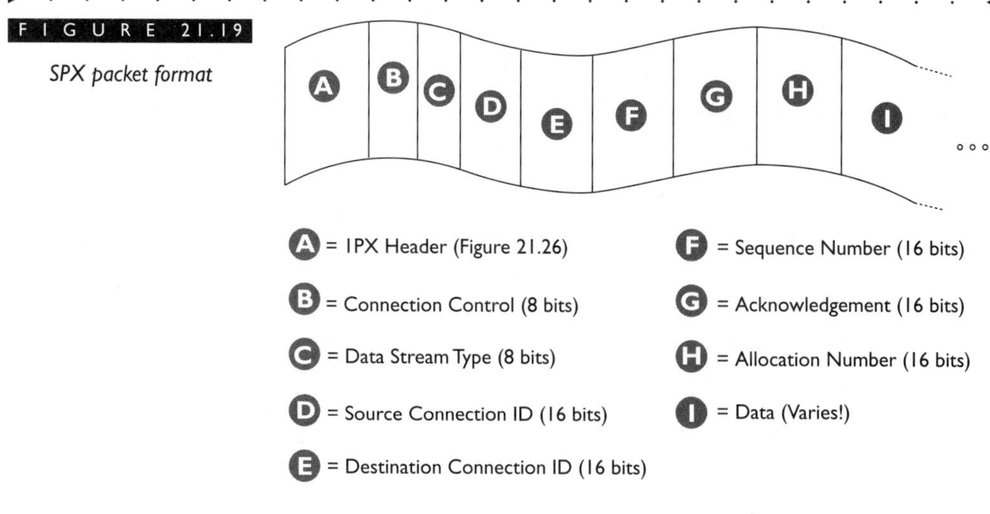

This completes our discussion of IPX and SPX protocols in the Middle Layers of the OSI model. Now let's explore some additional Middle and Top Layer NetWare-based protocols — namely RIP, SAP, and NCP.

Routing Information Protocol (RIP)

RIP works in conjunction with IPX to perform route selection and route discovery. RIP packets are broadcast by IPX routers during initialization and network reconfiguration. Also, if a route table request is received from another router, an IPX router will respond by transmitting the entire contents of its route table to the requesting device.

As a distance-vector protocol, RIP requires that IPX routers broadcast a packet containing the entire contents of their route tables at 60-second intervals. Finally, when an IPX router is taken down, it will broadcast its route table and specify an unreachable number of hops (16) for all of its destination routes.

RIP uses the following five-step process to discover optimal routes (follow along with Figure 21.20):

1. First, a RIP router broadcasts the contents of its route table, which includes information about all of its local routes (that is, networks that the router is physically connected to).

2. Next, the RIP router broadcasts a route request packet requesting that all the other IPX routers broadcast the contents of their route tables.

3. The neighboring routers then reply by broadcasting the entire contents of their route tables.

4. The initial RIP router then gathers all of the route reachability information and builds its own route table.

5. Finally, the router broadcasts the contents of its route table to all RIP routers that it has discovered. The information contained in this broadcast will be subject to any filtering required by the split horizon algorithm.

Refer to Table 21.6 for a feature summary of NetWare's Middle Layer IPX/SPX protocols.

FIGURE 21.20

IPX RIP route discovery process

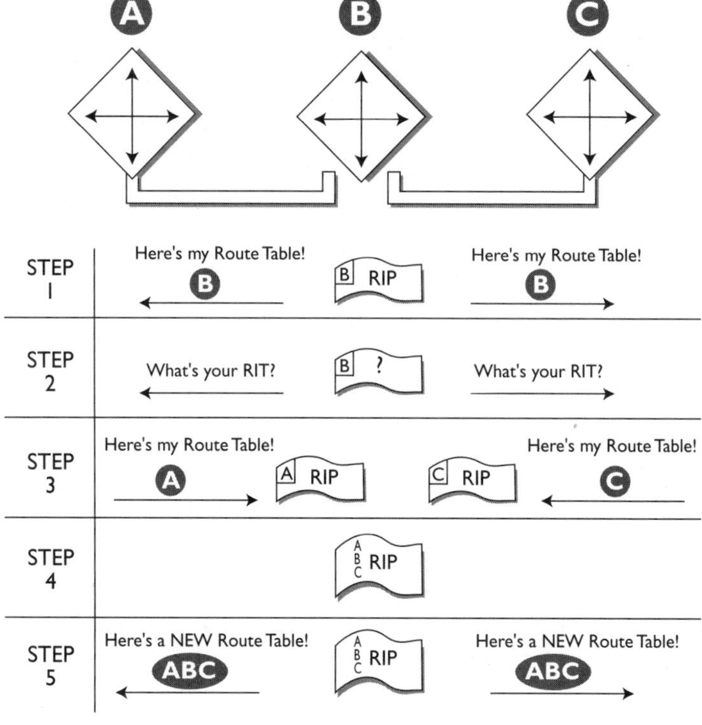

TABLE 21.6

Feature Summary of NetWare's Middle Layer IPX/SPX Protocols

IMPLEMENTATIONS	ADDRESSING	ROUTING	NETWORK CONTROL	SEGMENTATION	TRANSPORT CONTROL
IPX	Logical addressing	Dynamic route selection	Connectionless		
SPX	Connection ID service addressing			Division and combination segment sequencing	Error checking ing and end-to-end flow control
RIP		Distance-vector route discovery			

Service Advertising Protocol (SAP)

SAP is used to provide service availability information to the network. NetWare 3 servers are required to use only SAP, while NetWare 4 and NetWare 5 servers use SAP and NDS to locate services on the network. Furthermore, NetWare 5 servers running TCP/IP can use the SLP protocol for locating services. Some common NetWare IPX/SPX services that require SAP include filing, printing, and remote access.

Information from these broadcasts is gathered by SAP agents and stored in a Server Information Table (SIT). Clients either contact a nearby SAP agent to learn about service availability or receive SAP packets that are broadcast on the network by various servers. Each SAP agent periodically broadcasts the entire contents of its SIT to the network. This technique enables service availability information to propagate across the network in a similar manner to the way in which route reachability information is propagated. SAP supports the following three packet types:

- *Periodic SAP Information Broadcasts* — Each server transmits a SAP broadcast packet every 60 seconds.
- *SAP Service Queries* — This packet is used by clients who are looking for a particular service.
- *SAP Service Responses* — These packets are sent in response to SAP Service Query packets. SAP specifies the General Service response for broadcasts and the Nearest Service response for replies to service inquiries.

To learn about the services available on an IPX network, SAP routers perform a similar five-step discovery procedure. First, a SAP router advertises its own local services, if available. Next, it broadcasts a SAP Service Query packet, seeking to obtain a list of available services. Neighboring routers and servers then respond with the contents of their SIT, and the initial router stores the information in its SIT. Finally, the router includes the new service availability information in its next SAP broadcast.

REAL WORLD

The periodic broadcast techniques used by SAP work fine for most LAN applications. However, the techniques present numerous problems in large WAN environments. Fortunately, NetWare allows you to configure SAP filtering on IPX routers to minimize the impact of SAP broadcast traffic on WAN performance.

Because each service type is identified by a unique ID number, it is possible to prevent print server and other SAP types from propagating through a WAN. Simply determine the services that need to be available on either side of a WAN connection and implement the appropriate SAP filters.

NetWare Core Protocol (NCP)

NCP contains numerous function calls that support a variety of network services. At the Session Layer, NCP is responsible for data transfer. At the Presentation Layer, NCP handles character code and file syntax translation. Finally, at the Application Layer, NCP handles OS Redirector and Collaborate service use. (**Note:** NetWare 3 and NetWare 4 require IPX/SPX access to NCP, while NetWare 5 can be configured to make NCP calls via IPX/SPX or TCP/IP.)

In addition, NCP is supported at the bottom layers by two communications protocols:

- *Multiple Link Interface Driver (MLID)* — This protocol is a NIC interface driver that operates at the MAC Layer. Because an MLID is not linked directly to an individual protocol stack, it can support multiple upper-layer services simultaneously.
- *Link Support Layer (LSL)* — This is an interface between the MLID driver and various upper-layer protocol stacks. It operates at the LLC sublayer of the Data Link Layer in the OSI model.

As we learned in this section, RIP and SAP work great in small LANs. However, they bog down in large WANs. Fortunately, NetWare offers the NLSP solution for these larger implementations. Let's take a closer look.

NetWare Link Services Protocol (NLSP)

NLSP is Novell's link-state Network Layer protocol. It is typically used to replace RIP/SAP in WAN or large LAN environments. NLSP is modeled after a specific ISO standard called Intermediate System-to-Intermediate System (IS-IS). It consumes less network bandwidth than RIP/SAP, converges on topology changes more quickly, can scale to complex internetworks, and supports load balancing.

NLSP routers use several databases to manage Network Layer functions. The adjacency databases keep track of adjacency routers, the link-state databases track links, and a forwarding database tracks routing paths.

Following is the four-step process for NLSP route discovery:

- *Step 1*: Adjacency Database
- *Step 2*: Elect a Designated Router (DR)
- *Step 3*: Create a Pseudonode
- *Step 4*: Build an Internetwork Map

Let's take a closer look.

Step 1: Adjacency Database

The first step in the NLSP discovery process requires that adjacent NLSP routers on a network learn about each other's presence through the exchange of Hello packets. This exchange allows the routers to establish bidirectional communications (which is required by NLSP). Figure 21.21 shows the Hello packet exchange between two NLSP routers.

In Figure 21.21, router A has just been powered on. It exchanges Hello packets with neighboring routers, including router B. This periodic Hello packet exchange is used to maintain contact between routers and ensure the accuracy of route reachability information. The Hello packets include information about each router's operational status, direct routes, and priority value.

FIGURE 21.21

Hello packet exchange in Step 1 of NLSP route discovery

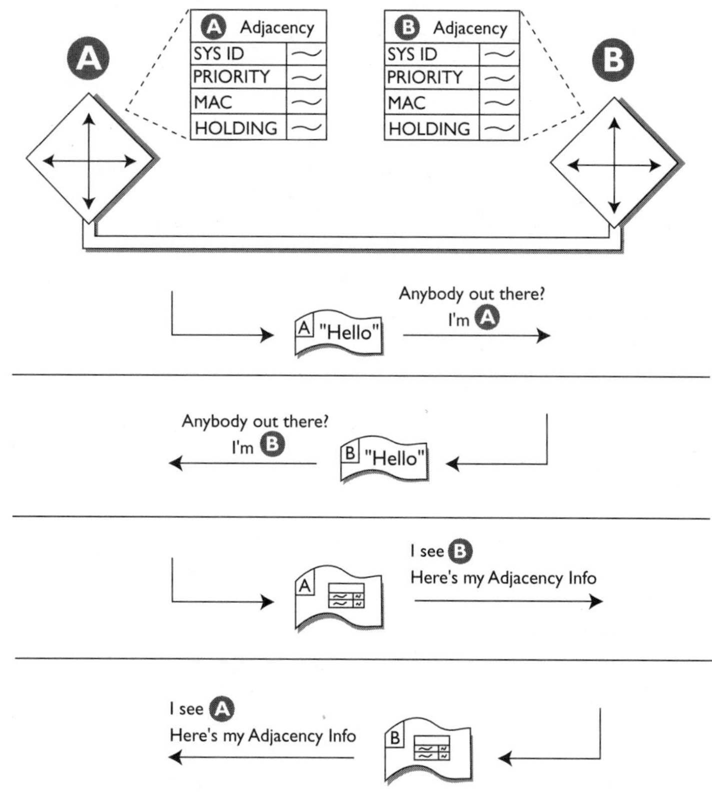

When two NLSP routers discover each other, they each update internal *adjacency databases* with the following information:

- *System Identification (ID)* — This is the internal IPX address of the source NLSP router.
- *Priority* — A field whose value is used to determine a given network's DR.
- *Physical Address* — The adjacent router's MAC address.
- *Holding Time* — Specifies the Hello packet interval. If a Hello packet is not received from the adjacent router before the interval expires, the router is considered to be down.

Step 2: Elect a Designated Router (DR)

In Step 2, a designated router (DR) is selected for each logical network. The DR is elected based on the highest priority value in each adjacency database. If two routers have been configured with the same priority value, the router whose physical address value is larger becomes the DR.

When the DR is elected, it adds "20" to its priority value, thus minimizing the chances that the DR will need to be reelected. The DR is responsible for creating a pseudonode, which oversees database synchronization, and receives and interprets IPX RIP/SAP router information.

Step 3: Create a Pseudonode

Once the DR is elected, NLSP must define the network's topology. To enable NLSP to function correctly, all routers on the network must possess identical link-state databases. Before the link-state database can be created, the DR must create a *pseudonode* (that is, a virtual network device that all NLSP routers connect to).

Each router believes that it is connected to a single pseudonode. In turn, the pseudonode believes that it is connected to all routers on the network. This architecture reduces the size of each router's adjacency database, because the information only has to be kept for one pseudonode, rather than for every node on the network.

Figure 21.22 shows a simple bus network and how it is represented physically, actually, and logically—with a pseudonode in place.

In our example, the Actual Adjacencies map requires that each router manage three neighbors in its link-state packet. However, the logical map (with a pseudonode) requires that each router maintain only one neighbor in its link-state packet.

On behalf of the pseudonode, the DR maintains a link-state packet (LSP), which includes all the pseudonode's router links. Once an NLSP router has connected to the pseudonode, it exchanges link-state database information with all other routers on the network by transmitting LSPs that contain the following required router information: direct links, available services, router name, and network number.

Once the router sends the first LSP, it floods the LSPs to all connected networks. Each NLSP router on these networks receives the LSPs and updates its link-state database accordingly. Upon completion of this process, all routers should possess identical link-state databases.

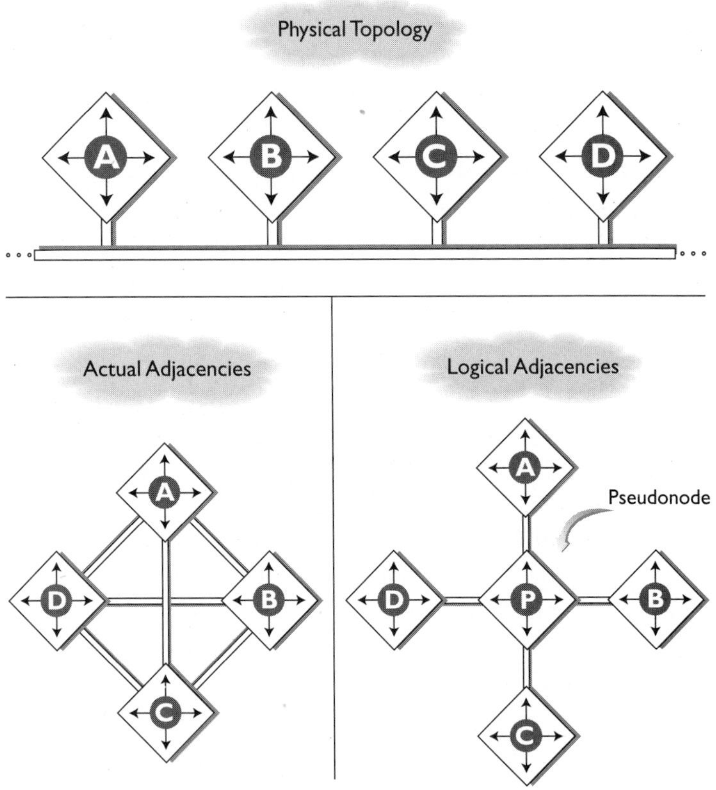

FIGURE 21.22

Creating a pseudonode in NLSP discovery Step 3

Physical Topology

Actual Adjacencies

Logical Adjacencies

Pseudonode

Step 4: Build an Internetwork Map

In the final step, NLSP builds a complete internetwork map using a *forwarding database*. This database identifies the best path for reaching any available destination network. The forwarding database includes information that is similar to the information used by RIP for network path selection, but differs in the following ways:

- The forwarding and link-state databases are maintained separately. This means that an NLSP router does not need to recalculate before flooding can occur.

- The contents of the forwarding database are determined by a calculation performed on the link-state database.

- Route selection is based on a metric called *cost*, not hops or ticks. The cost value for each router is assigned by the network administrator. The best route is the one with the lowest cost. Interfaces may be assigned a cost value in the range of 1 to 63.
- The forwarding database can contain up to eight redundant, equal-cost routes for any destination network. The database is recalculated when a change is made to the link-state database.

NLSP uses the Shortest Path First (SPF) Hold-Down Interval to prevent continuous recalculations. This interval determines the minimum amount of time required between recalculations.

NLSP Synchronization

Once all NLSP routers have learned the best possible routes, they can manage synchronization traffic efficiently. At this point, the DR must oversee the synchronization of all routers and notify all routers when a topology change occurs.

Figure 21.23 illustrates the three-step NLSP synchronization process:

- *Step 1* — Every 30 seconds (by default), the DR transmits a Complete Sequence Number Packet (CSNP) to all of the routers it represents. This packet contains a summary of the DR's link-state database, not its entire contents.
- *Step 2* — Routers that receive the CSNP compare its contents with their local link-state databases. If new information is contained in the CSNP, the receiving router transmits a Partial Sequence Number Packet (PSNP) to the DR requesting the complete information (Step 2a in Figure 21.23). The DR then responds by transmitting an LSP to all of the routers it represents (Step 2b in Figure 21.23).
- *Step 3* — If some of the information contained in the CSNP is old, the receiving router marks it and then floods the correct information to all routers on the internetwork.

FIGURE 21.23

NLSP synchronization

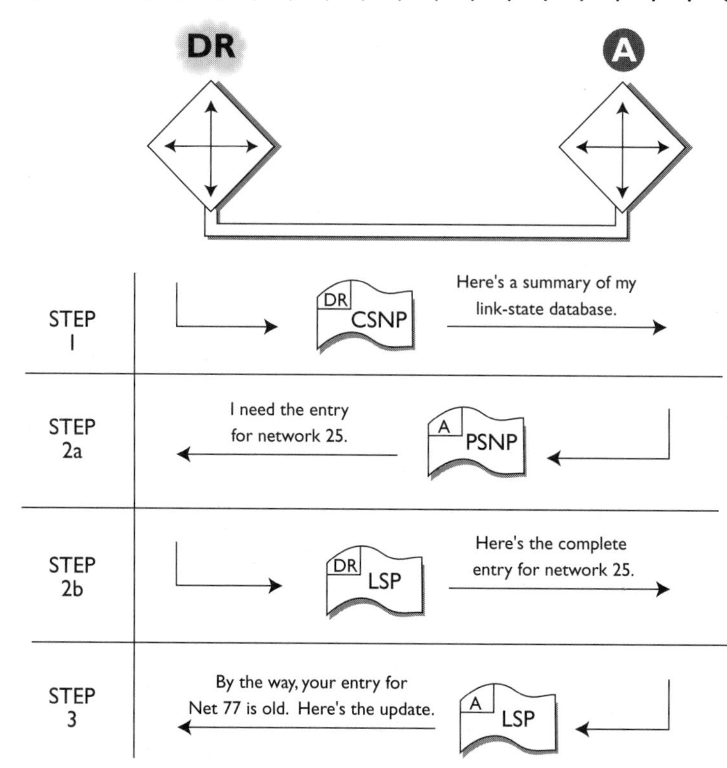

This completes our discussion of NetWare protocols. As we learned, NetWare offers a full-service networking solution that encompasses all seven layers of the OSI model. In summary, NetWare is a highly complex operating system that hides most of its functionality from the user. This level of transparency has a great deal to do with NetWare's popularity. Of course, user transparency comes with a cost — your hard work and network management dedication.

Congratulations! You survived the Internet and NetWare protocol family reunion.

This completes our "Real World" journey through the middle two layers of computer networking. Specifically, this completes our in-depth discussion of Internet and NetWare protocol technologies. In this chapter, we learned that TCP/IP is the foundation of the global Internet. In addition, we discovered three critical networking functions: IP addressing, subnetting, and supernetting. Then we studied the original foundation of NetWare (IPX/SPX), and we explored a number of Middle and Top Layer NetWare protocols, including the WAN-based NetWare Link Services Protocol (NLSP).

In the final chapter of this book, we will conclude the OSI journey with a detailed lesson in Session, Presentation, and Application Layer technologies. I bet you can't wait!

LAB EXERCISE 21.1: GETTING TO KNOW INTERNET AND NETWARE PROTOCOLS

Use the hints provided to find the 20 Middle Layer protocol terms hidden in this word search puzzle. Omit any punctuation characters (such as blank spaces, hyphens, and so on) and spell out any numbers.

R	W	B	M	C	I	D	R	E	S	O	L	V	E	R	S
N	S	S	U	N	L	P	D	I	S	O	E	J	T	E	U
Q	F	K	O	Q	N	A	X	T	P	S	J	W	E	P	B
G	F	X	E	Q	M	A	S	T	E	R	V	V	N	L	N
H	O	S	T	M	L	S	V	S	P	P	O	X	L	I	E
T	R	A	F	F	I	C	M	P	C	Q	P	P	E	C	T
T	W	P	R	A	D	N	B	E	P	T	A	N	T	A	M
P	A	U	T	H	E	N	T	I	C	A	T	I	O	N	A
C	R	Z	Q	S	U	B	N	E	T	T	I	N	G	Z	S
S	D	E	E	V	I	F	Q	O	R	Y	H	Y	K	L	K
D	I	T	C	C	E	Y	X	P	O	N	C	A	J	P	G
S	N	T	K	I	L	X	R	Z	V	V	A	D	P	T	I
L	G	T	Y	N	I	R	X	W	D	G	Q	L	Q	C	S

Hints

1. Internet protocol that combines physical and logical addresses to create a complete Internet address.
2. A new Internet protocol feature included with IPv6.
3. A special supernetting protocol that allows devices to specify nonstandard address masks.
4. IP address class that supports systems with a large number of networks and a small number of hosts.
5. This type of database uses NLSP to identify the best path to reach any available destination network.
6. Sometimes referred to as a node or station address, this field represents each physical machine on an IP network.

7. The client/server protocol that handles graphical communications between Internet servers and client browsers, such as Netscape.
8. Works with IP at the Network Layer to provide error control information.
9. IPX address that defines communications within a server or network device.
10. A NetWare connectionless datagram protocol that operates at the Network Layer of the OSI model.
11. Names and IP addresses of all hosts in a DNS zone are maintained on this server.
12. The NetWare NIC driver that operates at the MAC Layer of the OSI Reference Model.
13. Type of server that provides redundancy and load balancing for DNS naming within a particular zone.
14. DNS clients that query one or more servers for host address information.
15. Network Layer distance-vector route discovery protocol that uses a hop count to determine cost.
16. The "old" way to advertise network services. Has been replaced by TCP/IP's SLP protocol.
17. Establishes rules for routers and hosts to follow regarding address bit assignments.
18. Technique to expand IP addresses within an organization so that they are not visible to external hosts.
19. Internet protocol that enables users to access host-based applications from PCs that act as dumb terminals.
20. This is minimized by logical subnetting.

See Appendix C for answers.

LAB EXERCISE 21.2: MIDDLE LAYER PROTOCOL FAMILIES

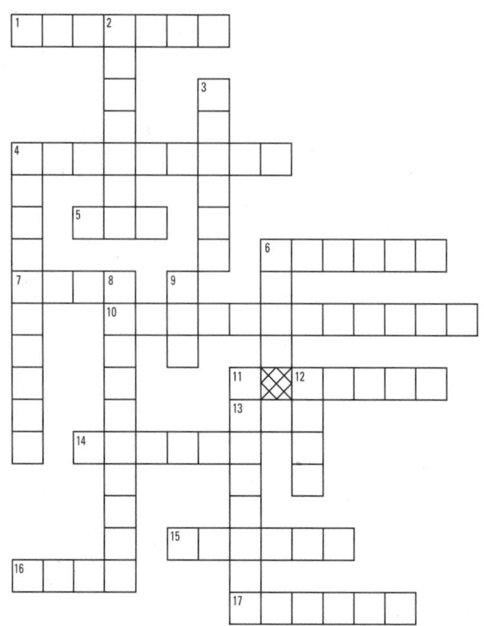

Across

1. Internet in the early years
4. Internal NLSP databases that get updated during discovery
5. Upper-layer file transfer protocol
6. Equal address support for networks and hosts
7. Is typically used to replace RIP/SAP in WAN environments
10. Opposite of subnetting
12. Each IP address consists of four
13. Application Layer platform-independent file sharing protocol
14. Determines an IPX packet's ultimate destination process
15. DHCP allocation method whereby you determine IP addresses
16. DNS partition
17. IP addressing for a large number of hosts

Down

2. Addressing to any one of a given set of devices
3. Format of IP addresses
4. Logical subnet divisions of a large IP network
6. A summary of a designated router's link-state database
8. Virtual NLSP network device
9. NetWare connection-oriented Transport Layer protocol
11. Manages IP address registration in North America
12. Network Layer link-state route discovery protocol

See Appendix C for answers.

CHAPTER 22

The OSI Model — Top Layers

Welcome to the third and final functional domain of computer networking! This region deals with OSI network services—the top three layers of our OSI 3-D map. As we learned in Chapter 18, network elements are the third phase of networking. They define the *what, how,* and *who* of networking technologies. In the Services domain, we will explore the *who.*

In Chapter 20, we learned that OSI Networking routes packets as they traverse the computer LAN or WAN. We learned about bridging, routing protocols, switching, and transport administration. Now, in this chapter, we will explore the "final frontier" of computer networking. *Services* represent the ultimate applications and functionality of networks. In simple terms, this is the goal of client/server network communications.

According to the OSI map (see Figure 22.1), these are the top three functional layers:

- The Session Layer
- The Presentation Layer
- The Application Layer

FIGURE 22.1

Understanding OSI Services

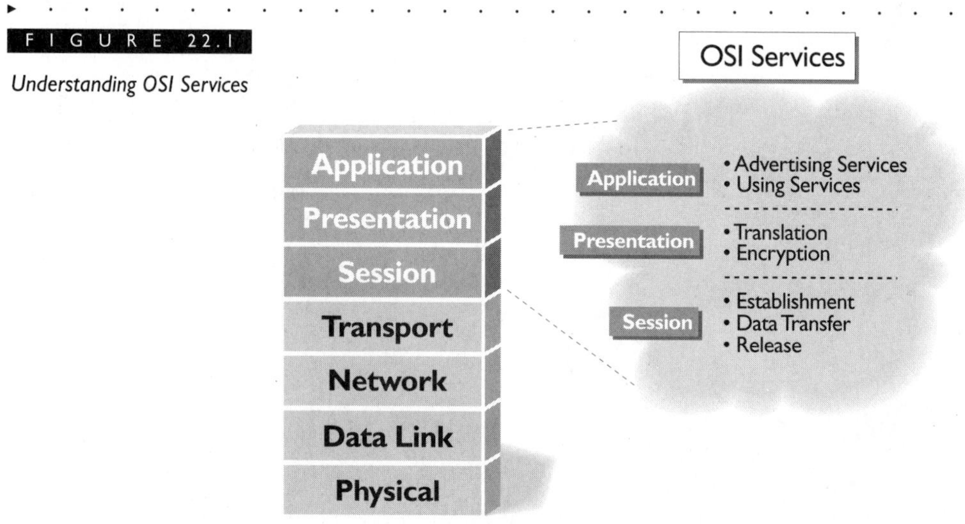

The *Session Layer* opens a dialog between a sender and a receiver. It also continually monitors conversations and ensures that everyone is getting along. The Session Layer does all this by using three simple steps: connection establishment, data transfer, and connection release. Once the Session dialog has been established and data transfer has begun, the system moves its focus to the *Presentation Layer*, which transforms data into a mutually agreed-upon format that each application can understand. The Presentation Layer also compresses large data and encrypts sensitive information. Translation is involved when two computers speaking different languages open a dialog.

This brings us to the pinnacle of the OSI journey: the *Application Layer.* The Application Layer uses specific networking applications to provide file, print, message, application, and database services. It controls how these services are advertised and made available.

Let's begin our final networking journey by exploring the first layer of the Services domain—the Session Layer.

The Session Layer

The Session Layer is the first of the three top OSI layers that focus on network applications and services. The Session Layer opens and controls networking dialogs during the following three steps:

- *Step 1:* Connection Establishment
- *Step 2:* Data Transfer
- *Step 3:* Connection Release

As the name implies, *connection establishment* initiates the dialog between two systems. It uses networking protocols to find a dialog path and communications media to send messages back and forth (that's data transfer). During *data transfer*, the Session Layer manages the dialog and ensures reliable conversations through simplex, half-duplex, or full-duplex transmissions. Finally, *connection release* ends the dialog and closes the connection. Incidentally, connection release can be either planned or accidental.

Let's take a closer look at these steps and try to understand how networking messages find their way to the correct service.

Step 1: Connection Establishment

During Step 1, the sender and receiver recognize each other and agree to communicate. Connection establishment includes all the subtasks necessary to initiate communications. Often these subtasks include the following steps:

- Verifying user login names and passwords.
- Establishing connection ID numbers. This function relies on the Transport Layer to identify the correct service addresses.
- Agreeing on which services are required and for what duration. This usually occurs early in the conversation.
- Determining which entity will begin the conversation.
- Coordinating acknowledgment numbering and retransmission procedures. This is Session Layer error checking.

Once these tasks have been accomplished and the connection has been opened, data transfer can begin. That's Step 2.

Step 2: Data Transfer

During Step 2, the actual transfer of data occurs. Data transfer tasks manage Session Layer messages and ensure productive conversations. Data transfer occurs through a specific dialog, which is an established connection between two network entities currently engaged in data transfer. Dialogs can occur in one of three ways:

- *Simplex Conversation*—One device is allowed to transmit, and all other devices receive (see Figure 22.2). With simplex conversations, the channel's full bandwidth is always available for signals traveling from the sender to the receiver. On a simplex channel, the transmitting device cannot receive information, and the receiving devices cannot transmit. Simplex data transfers have many advantages, including inexpensive hardware, no channel contention, broad area coverage, and a large target audience. Unfortunately, they only allow one-way communication, which severely limits the data communications applications of simplex dialog. Currently, commercial broadcast radio and television stations are the most popular simplex conversations.

- *Half-Duplex Conversation*—Each device can transmit and receive, but not at the same time (see Figure 22.2). With half-duplex conversations, the channel's full bandwidth is available to the transmitting device, but it can't receive while it's transmitting. On the upside, half-duplex dialogs require only one channel for both transmission and reception, and they support bidirectional communications. Unfortunately, only one unit can transmit at a time, and the hardware is more expensive than simplex conversation hardware. Also, the channel is not used efficiently during direction changes. Some of the most popular half-duplex implementations include citizens band radio and some LAN standards.
- *Full-Duplex Conversation*—Full-duplex communications allow every device to transmit and receive at the same time (see Figure 22.2). Many full-duplex systems require every device to have two transmission channels, one for transmit and one for receive. An excellent example of full-duplex dialogs device is the telephone. Even though full-duplex conversations have inherent advantages (both ends can transmit at the same time), costs are associated with it. The hardware is more expensive than half-duplex and full-duplex hardware, it requires more transmission media than half-duplex and full-duplex conversations, and most point-to-point implementations reach a limited target audience.

In addition to dialog control and data transfer, Step 2 performs two reliability tasks: acknowledgment and resumption. In coordination with the OSI Data Link Layer, the Session Layer is responsible for acknowledgments (or negative acknowledgments) during data transfer. This reliability feature ensures that lower-layer protocols keep track of which messages belong to which upper-layer service. In addition, part of the Session Layer's error-checking algorithm calls for the resumption of interrupted communications.

FIGURE 22.2

Step 2: Data Transfer methods

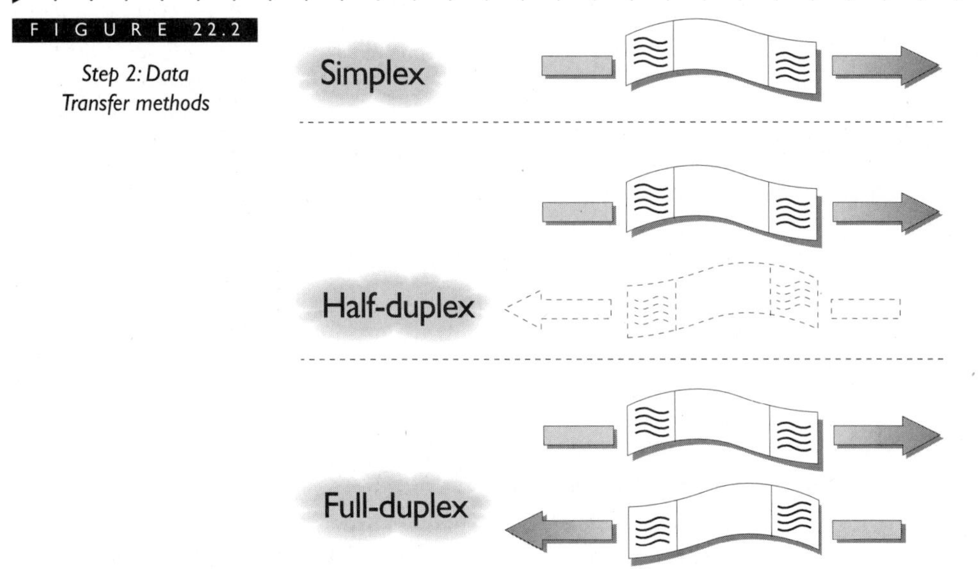

Data transfer continues throughout the life of the conversation. Once communications have ended, the connection must be released. That's Step 3.

Step 3: Connection Release

After data transfer is complete, the connection must be released to make room for future conversations. This process can be planned or accidental. Planned connection release usually is accomplished by agreement between the two systems, similar to both parties saying "good-bye" to end a telephone conversation. Accidental connection release usually is caused by a physical anomaly—that is, an obvious loss of connection.

Lower layer protocols recognize a loss of connection when they do not receive the acknowledgments or negative acknowledgments they expect. It is their responsibility to inform the Session Layer that the connection has been lost. In this case, Session Layer error checking resumes the interrupted dialog or restarts the communication using a new conversation. Either way, accidental connection release is resolved by the Session Layer.

This completes the first layer of the OSI Services domain. Once the networking connection has been established and data transfer has begun, focus shifts to the Presentation Layer.

The Presentation Layer

The Presentation Layer is responsible for transforming data into a format that is mutually agreed upon by the sender and receiver. *Translation* is the Presentation Layer's main task. It is required when two dissimilar computer systems exchange data. In addition to translation, this layer can also encrypt/decrypt data and compress/expand data.

Following are four translation technologies provided by the Presentation Layer:

- *Bit-Order*—At the most basic level, computers that want to communicate must agree on how many bits represent a complete character. Some use 4 bits *(nibble)*, some use 7 or 8 *(byte)*, and others use 16 or 32 *(quad)*. In addition, the sender and receiver must agree on how to read the message (that is, from left to right or right to left).

- *Byte-Order*—Once the sender and receiver agree on a bit-level translation scheme, they must determine in which order a series of bytes will be read. For example, byte-order translation determines how the two computers will represent complex numbers requiring more than one byte (that is, using the little endian or big endian method).

- *Character-Code*—Character-code translation converts bits and bytes into a language that users can understand. Some of the most popular schemes include ASCII (see Figure 22.3), Shift-JIS, EBCDIC, and Unicode.

- *File-Syntax*—The final translation scheme organizes data files into the file syntax or format required by the operating system. File-syntax translation deals with issues including organization, boundaries, naming, access security, and storage.

FIGURE 22.3

ASCII translation table

First Three Bit Positions (columns) / Last Four Bit Positions (rows)

	000	001	010	011	100	101	110	111
0000	NUL	DLE	SP	0	@	P	`	p
0001	SOH	DC1	!	1	A	Q	a	q
0010	STX	DC2	"	2	B	R	b	r
0011	ETX	DC3	#	3	C	S	c	s
0100	EOT	DC4	$	4	D	T	d	t
0101	ENQ	NAK	%	5	E	U	e	u
0110	ACK	SYN	&	6	F	V	f	v
0111	BEL	ETB	'	7	G	W	g	w
1000	BS	CAN	(	8	H	X	h	x
1001	HT	EM	)	9	I	Y	i	y
1010	LF	SUB	*	:	J	Z	j	z
1011	VT	ESC	•	;	K	[	k	{
1100	FF	FS	,	<	L	\	l	|
1101	CR	GS	–	=	M	]	m	}
1110	SO	RS	+	>	N	^	n	~
1111	SI	US	/	?	O	-	o	DEL

Encryption is the second major task that is handled by the Presentation Layer. This involves operating system security and protecting sensitive data. Most software encryption systems rely on two keys: public and private. *Private key* encryption schemes use only one key for both sending and receiving. *Public key* methods, in contrast, use two keys — where one of the keys encrypts the data and the other decrypts it.

This completes our discussion of the Presentation Layer. As I'm sure you can imagine, this layer is an important component in the OSI Services domain. Without Presentation Layer translation, computers would be speaking technobabble, and without encryption, the wrong people might gain access to your data.

Now it's time to move on to the pinnacle of OSI Networking — the Application Layer.

The Application Layer

While the six lower layers in the OSI model provide generic support for network services, the Application Layer sits at the top of the OSI model and deals with providing specific network services. This involves the following:

- Service advertisement
- Service availability

The Application Layer uses special networking protocols to provide file, print, message, application, and database services. *Service advertisement* lets other systems (and users) know what services are available. Providers use active or passive techniques to define the scope of their network services. *Service availability* is the next step. Once a service has been advertised, it must be made available. Service availability can be accomplished in several ways, including OS Call Interception, remote operation, and/or collaborative computing.

Let's start our discussion with service advertisement.

Service Advertisement

Service advertisement lets people (and computers) know which services are available. Network servers can use one of two different techniques for sending out their menu:

- *Active*—Active service advertisement relies on the eagerness of centralized servers. With this Application Layer scheme, each server sends out periodic messages to announce its availability. In addition, the service menu includes Transport Layer addresses to each application. Workstations then poll the servers and build tables of currently available services. When a user is ready to print, for example, his or her client knows exactly which printers are available and who is servicing them. NetWare IPX/SPX, for example, uses the Service Advertising Protocol (SAP) to broadcast available services every minute.

- *Passive* — Passive service advertisement, in contrast, relies on a centralized directory. Servers register their services with a single directory and provide routing instructions and addressing. When a user wants to print, his or her client simply looks up the service in the central table. NetWare 5.1, for example, includes a sophisticated service advertisement scheme called the Service Location Protocol (SLP). Novell's implementation of SLP creates more management overhead than the traditional SAP, but decreases unneeded network channel congestion. These features are typical of passive service advertisement schemes as compared to active schemes.

Whichever service advertisement method you choose, be sure your clients are aware of each server's services. Once a service has been advertised, it must be made available to the workstation's local operating system. This is the final task performed at the Application Layer.

Service Availability

Before a network service can be used, it must make itself available to the user's local operating system. Following are the most popular service availability methods:

- *OS Call Interception* — Each service availability method differs in the client's and server's awareness of each other. At one extreme, OS Call Interception relies on a completely unaware client. That is, the local operating system is completely unaware of the network and goes about its business uninterrupted. When the user requests a network file, a special client shell intercepts the message and routes it to the server. As far as the client knows, everything's being handled locally.

- *Remote Operation* — At the other extreme, remote operation relies on a completely unaware server. In this case, the server is completely unaware of the client and goes about its business uninterrupted. When a remote user sends in a request, the server processes it as if it were local. This is the method of choice for Remote Procedure Call (RPC) applications and operating systems that support terminal emulation. (**Note:** UNIX NFS uses this method.)

- *Collaborative Computing*—Collaborative computing is the best of both worlds. In this service availability scheme, the server and the client both are fully aware of each other and don't mind working together. As a matter of fact, they collaborate on all local and network requests.

Congratulations! You have made it to the top of the OSI Reference Model.

Once the networking conversation has been opened, the message has been translated, and the services have been made available, you are done. So, what do you get for all your trouble? Good question. One of five network services. Let's take a closer look.

Network Services

Network services represent the ultimate goal of networking. If it wasn't for services, there would be no need for physical communications, transmission devices, routing, error checking, or translation. In this lesson, we will review the following five network services:

- File services
- Print services
- Message services
- Application services
- Database services

File services include file transfer and storage, data migration, file-update synchronization, and archiving. These features are the most popular reasons for networking. *Print services* provide shared access to valuable printing devices. *Message services* facilitate e-mail, manage integrated e-mail and voice mail, and coordinate object-oriented applications. *Application services* enable you to centralize high-profile applications. Finally, *Database services* involve the coordination of distributed data and replication.

Although no one networking system can provide all these network services, NetWare comes close. NetWare provides file, print, and database services right out of the box, and application and messaging services can be added relatively easily. Let's take a closer look at these five features.

File Services

In most networks, the central networking machine is the file server (see Figure 22.4). Therefore, file services are the most popular of all network services. In addition to serving files, networks can rapidly transmit documents, share storage hardware more efficiently, manage multiple copies of the same file, and backup critical data. In general, file services perform read, write, access control, and data management functions for a variety of computer storage media.

FIGURE 22.4

Understanding file services

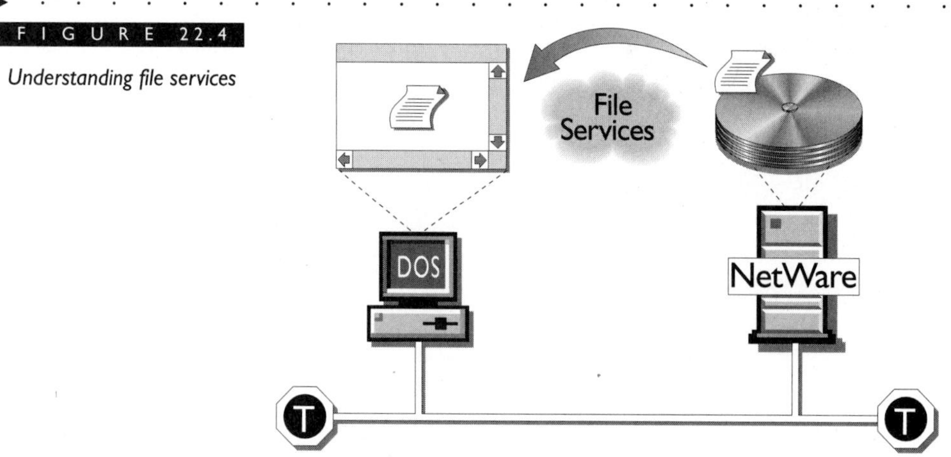

File service functions include:

- *File Transfer*—File transfer refers to any service that saves, retrieves, or moves files from a network client. File transfers can be performed with relative ease regardless of file size, distance, and often even the local operating system. This service not only increases an organization's efficiency, but it also provides access to data information that previously was inaccessible.

- *File Storage*—The demands of network file services put a heavy load on centralized storage devices. You learned in Chapter 14 that a variety of network storage devices exist, including hard drives and CD-ROM drives. In general, three types of devices can be used for network file storage (see Figure 22.5): *online* storage devices (immediately available to the computer), *offline* storage devices (data is not immediately available to the computer), and *near-line* storage devices (provide an excellent compromise between online and offline storage).

- *Data Migration*—Data migration is the process of moving information from one storage medium to another, as shown in Figure 22.5. As data ages and is used less often, for example, it can be moved from expensive online hard drives to less expensive and durable offline storage media. NetWare 5.1's High-Capacity Storage System (HCSS) extends the storage capacity of a NetWare server by integrating an optical disk library or jukebox into your WAN.

- *File-Update Synchronization*—File-update synchronization is an elegant solution for today's ever-growing mobile workplace. File-update synchronization solves the problem of unsynchronized local and remote computers by comparing the time and date stamp between corresponding files. It may also keep track of who has a specific file and if intermediary changes have been made. Using this information, synchronization protocols can automatically update all file locations with the latest version.

- *File Archiving*—File archiving creates important duplicate copies of mission critical data on magnetic tape or other offline storage media. NetWare's Storage Management Services (SMS), for example, handles archiving automatically and at predefined intervals.

Network file services are probably the most important things your network will ever do for you. Take care of the server, and make sure it's handling files correctly.

FIGURE 22.5

Understanding data migration

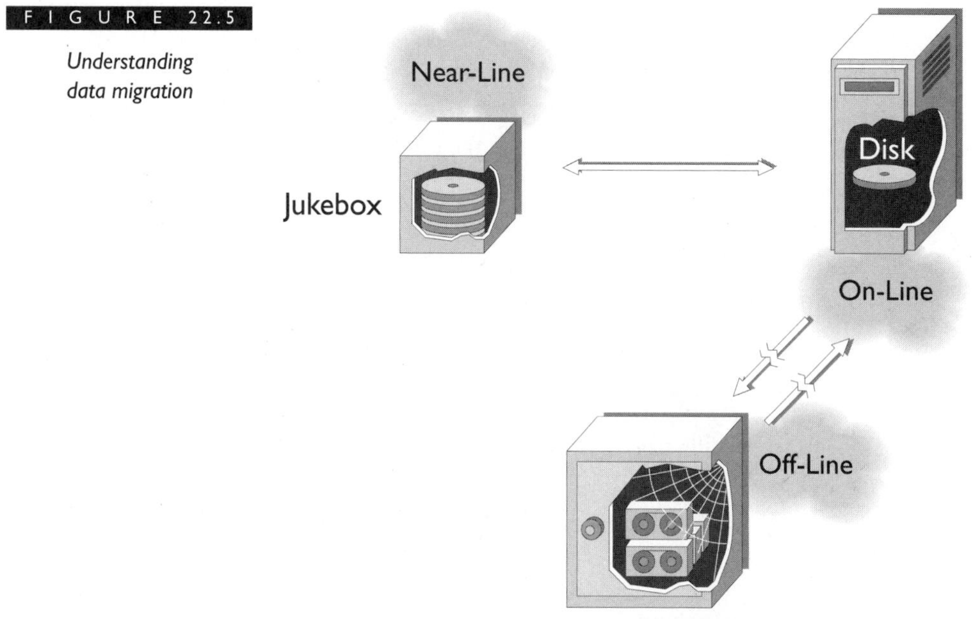

Print Services

Networks were originally conceived as a simple way to share file resources, but users quickly realized that they could share printers, as well. Now advanced print services and network faxing capabilities are beginning to dominate network services. Print services accept print job requests, interpret print job formats, process printer configurations, manage print queues, and interact with networkable printers and fax equipment.

Following is a brief list of the capabilities of network printers and fax machines:

- *Provide Multiple Access* — Most modern printers provide multiple ports or interfaces, although the number of interfaces is generally relatively small. Typically, only two or three computers may be connected directly to each printer. In contrast, a network connection requires only one interface — to the NIC. NetWare print queues and print servers then allow many computers to send data to a shared printer.

- *Eliminate Distance Constraints* — Printer ports are often based on cable interface specifications that limit the distance between the printer and attached computers. Network cable systems enable devices to be spread out across much greater distances.
- *Queuing* — Because shared printers support simultaneous requests from multiple users, bottlenecks can become a problem. Queuing solves this problem by temporarily capturing print jobs on a first-come, first-served basis (see Figure 22.6).
- *Sharing Specialized Equipment* — Some printers are designed for special use, such as high-speed output, large-format paper, or color printing. Shared network printing enables you to centralize these special devices.
- *Network Faxing* — This service enables users to send and receive faxes using special network hardware and software, which reduces the time and paper handling normally involved in traditional fax transmissions.

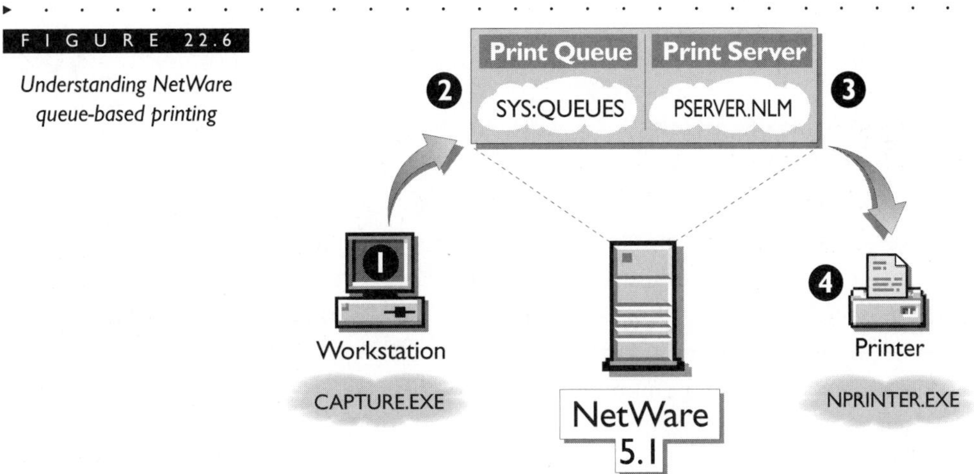

FIGURE 22.6

Understanding NetWare queue-based printing

That does it for network print services. As you can see, shared printing is just as important as file serving. Sometimes it's even more important, depending on the level of paperwork in your office. Speaking of the office, let's take a look at electronic staff meetings: message services.

Message Services

Messaging involves any application capable of storage access and message delivery. Messages can include binary data, graphics, digitized video, and/or voice. Message services go beyond the basic storage of these network components—they control interactions among computer users, applications, and documents. With message services, network workstations can pass computer-generated notes between users, integrate e-mail with voice systems, route and share data using workflow management software, and organize user information through directory services.

Message services are organized into two major categories:

- E-mail
- Workgroup applications

Application Services

Application services can enhance networks by providing shared access to specialized servers. These specialized servers use specialized hardware and software to increase speed, data integrity, and security. Application servers enable you to increase a network's capabilities without upgrading every computer on the LAN. Private branch exchanges (PBXs) and client/server database systems are examples of specialized application servers.

A PBX is a specialized computer that provides telephone-switching services. In NetWare, a special technology called *Telephony Services Application Programming Interface* (TSAPI) is used to connect a PBX to a network. CallWare, for example, provides enhanced telephony application services by extending this model to include a special operating system. In general, network application services can provide organizations with relatively inexpensive upgrade paths.

Database Services

Network database services provide centralized data storage and retrieval to NetWare clients. These systems are typically client/server oriented, meaning that both the client and server participate in database processing. Depending on the design goal of the system, the client is given a portion of the task and works closely with the server in processing requests.

In general, network database services perform the following tasks:

- Optimize the computers that store, search, and retrieve database records
- Control where data is stored geographically
- Organize data logically between organizational departments
- Provide data security
- Reduce database client access time

There you have it: That's network services in a nutshell. Even though you can count them on one hand, these five services encompass all the things a network can do. Now let's learn how they are implemented in the "real world" by IBM, DEC, Apple Computers, and others.

Top Layer Implementations

So far, we have studied the theoretical technologies underlying OSI Services. Of course, all the theories in the world aren't going to mean anything if we can't bring them to life. That's what implementations are for. The following five standards operate at the top three layers of the OSI Reference Model (see Figure 22.7):

- Systems Network Architecture (SNA)
- Digital Network Architecture (DNA)
- AppleTalk

- X.500
- Lightweight Directory Access Protocol (LDAP)

FIGURE 22.7

OSI Services implementations and the OSI model

OSI Layer	SNA	DNA	AppleTalk
Application	DIA	FTAM	AppleShare
Presentation	CICS	Session Control	AFP
Session			ASP
Transport	VTAM	NSP	ATP
Network	NCP	CLNS	DDP
Data Link	Token Ring	Ethernet v.2	LocalTalk
Physical			

As a matter of fact, the first three standards listed above operate at *all* seven layers of the OSI Reference Model. IBM's *Systems Network Architecture* (SNA) includes its own seven layers that loosely follow the OSI model (see Figure 22.7). DEC's *Digital Network Architecture* (DNA) is much more cooperative than SNA and follows the OSI model exactly. DEC worked closely with the ISO when early in the development of this reference model. Finally, *AppleTalk* is Apple's proprietary network implementation. It, too, provides a more accurate mapping to the OSI model.

So, let's start our final OSI lesson with the SNA reference model.

Systems Network Architecture (SNA)

SNA is IBM's proprietary networking solution. As an architecture, SNA does not define a single stack of protocols. Instead, SNA describes the general characteristics of computer hardware and software. In its initial release, SNA supported only hierarchically organized networks with hosts, communication controllers, cluster controllers, and terminals. This concept was updated in 1984 to support newer technology, including distributed processing, internetworking, network management, and many other advanced features. This new peer-to-peer SNA solution, called *Advanced Peer-to-Peer Networking* (APPN), exploits the computer processing power distributed throughout the network in the form of diverse mainframe, minicomputer, and PC systems.

In 1987 IBM announced a subgrouping of SNA called *Systems Application Architecture* (SAA). The Common Communication Support (CCS) of SAA incorporated only specific portions of SNA—LU6.2 and PU2.1, to be precise. These products are the strategic foundation of IBM's networking future. SNA and the OSI model have a great relationship primarily because SNA was the most popular networking model when OSI was conceived. As you can see in Figure 22.8, SNA also has seven layers:

- *Physical Control*—Concerned with electrical, mechanical, and procedural characteristics of the physical media and its interfaces. This layer is directly analogous to the OSI Physical Layer.
- *Data Link Control*—Similar to the OSI Data Link Layer. SNA defines the SDLC protocol for implementation of communication links on peer-to-peer networks.
- *Path Control*—Includes many of the functions of the OSI Network Layer. Some of its most popular features include routing, datagram sequencing, and flow control.
- *Transmission Control*—Provides a reliable end-to-end connection just like the OSI Transport Layer. The SNA Transmission Control Layer also provides encryption services (a function usually reserved for the OSI Presentation Layer).
- *Data Flow Control*—Corresponds roughly to the OSI Session Layer. This layer controls conversation requests and responses. It also determines whose turn it is to talk, group messages, and interrupt data flow on request.
- *Presentation Services*—Specifies data translation algorithms just like the OSI Presentation Layer. This layer also coordinates resource sharing and synchronizes operations.

- *Network-Addressable Unit (NAU) Services* — The pinnacle of our SNA journey. Just like the OSI Application Layer, this mountaintop provides application services in the form of distributed processing and/or management. A good example of an NAU transaction service is *SNA Distribution Services* (SNADS), which provide a distribution system for use by SNA applications.

FIGURE 22.8

SNA and the OSI model

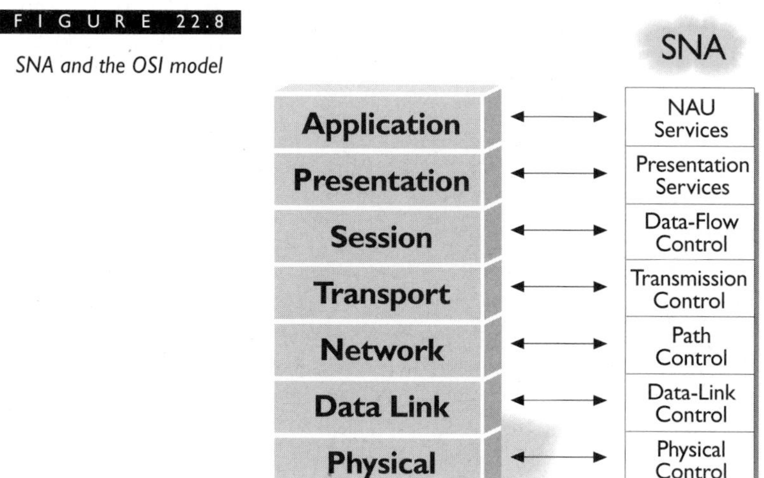

That describes the foundation of SNA architecture. Now let's explore SNA components and layer-specific implementations.

SNA Components

Because SNA is designed to integrate IBM and IBM-compatible products, the architecture relies on various units called *nodes*. Nodes work together to provide key services to the overall network. Following is a summary of the top three SNA components (see Figure 22.9):

- *Host Nodes (PU Type 5)* — These include mainframes and mid-range systems. A host node controls a domain that includes one or more subareas, each with subordinate nodes and peripherals. As you can see in Figure 22.9, the host node has central control over all other components. Incidentally, SNA networks typically include multiple host nodes, which in turn allow access from any terminal throughout the system.

- *Communications Controller Nodes (PU Type 4)* — These are hardware devices that route and control the flow of data in a hierarchical network. These nodes are sometimes called *front-end processors.* As you can see in Figure 22.9, the communications controller is a central connectivity point between the host node and distributed peripherals.
- *Peripheral Nodes (Type 2)* — These include the many different client devices we can use to access SNA networks, for example, cluster controllers, terminals, and printers.

FIGURE 22.9

Understanding SNA components

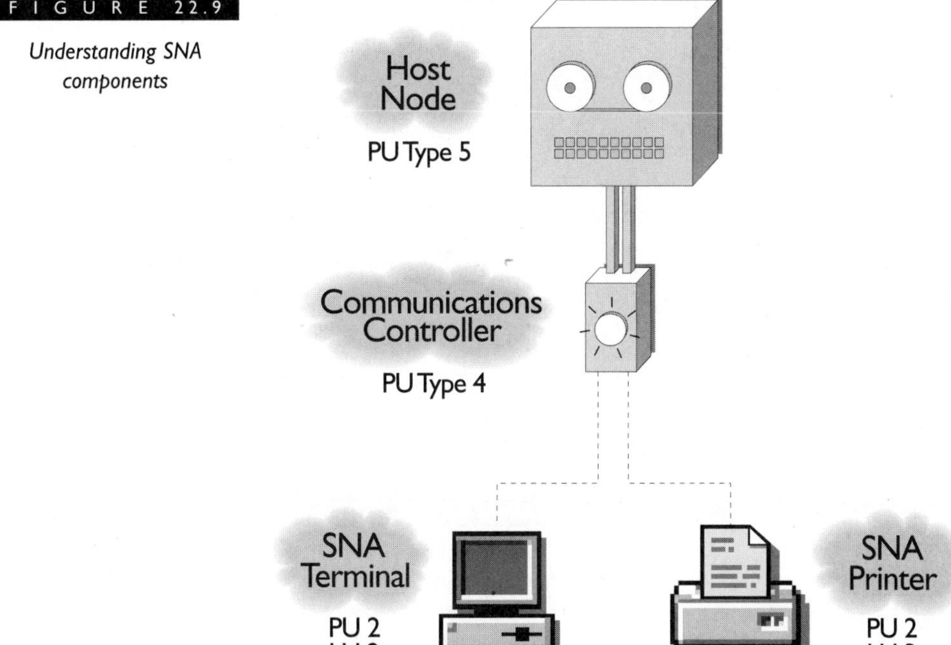

To interconnect these different nodes, SNA relies on a complex classification scheme for physical, logical, and control units. *Physical units* (PUs) are combinations of hardware, firmware, and software that manage and monitor the resources of a node. *Logical units* (LUs) support physical devices by providing connection points to internodal communications. Finally, *control points* are specialized management tools that enable certain PUs to control network data flow (specifically Type 5 and 2.1 PUs). Type 5 control points operate a System Services Control Point (SSCP) program that manages users throughout the network. Similarly, Type 2.1 control points offer the same functionality but on a much smaller scale.

Refer to Tables 22.1 and 22.2 for a complete description of SNA Physical and Logical Units. Remember, these are simple classifications that help you understand the function of SNA nodes.

TABLE 22.1

Getting to Know SNA Physical Units

TYPE	DESCRIPTION
PU Type 1	Terminal nodes
PU Type 2	Terminals, printers, cluster controllers, or other peripherals that can communicate only with a mainframe
PU Type 2.1	Minicomputers, cluster controllers, gateway devices, and occasionally workstations that can communicate with a mainframe or other peer-to-peer Type 2.1 devices
PU Type 4	Communication controllers that link host mainframes and cluster controllers or other PU Type 2 devices
PU Type 5	Host computers

TABLE 22.2

Getting to Know SNA Logical Units

TYPE	DESCRIPTION
LU Type 0	General-purpose logical units that are used in program-to-program communications. Although LU Type 0 devices use a relatively old standard, they are still quite common. This specification is currently being replaced by LU Type 6.2.
LU Type 1	Batch-type terminals, card readers, and printers, such as IBM 3077 and 3277 devices.
LU Type 2	Strictly terminals, such as the IBM 3270.

TABLE 22.2
Getting to Know SNA Logical Units (continued)

TYPE	DESCRIPTION
LU Type 3	Batch-type terminals, card readers, and printers, such as IBM 3270 printers. This is the printing equivalent of the LU Type 1 terminal.
LU Type 4	Older peer-to-peer connections, such as IBM 5250 printers.
LU Type 6	Customer Information Control System (CICS) peer-to-peer connectivity. This specification also defines Information Management System (IMS) communications between mainframes.
LU Type 6.1	Same as LU Type 6.
LU Type 6.2	The new SNA peer-to-peer standard. In conjunction with PU Type 2.1, this is the logical foundation of the new Advanced Peer-To-Peer Networking (APPN) specification.
LU Type 7	IBM 5277 display stations.

This completes our general discussion of SNA components. Once again, refer to Figure 22.9 for a graphical view of these physical, logical, and control components. Now let's take a closer look at the protocols these nodes use to communicate. As you may recall from Figure 22.8, SNA maps pretty closely to the seven-layer OSI model. We'll start our discussion at the bottom two layers.

SNA and OSI Communications

At the bottom two layers (Physical and Data Link), SNA relies on two key implementations: Token Ring and Synchronous Data Link Control (SDLC) (see Figure 22.10). These protocols provide the communications foundation of SNA connectivity. Let's take a closer look:

- *Token Ring*—IBM's LAN specification that was used as a model for IEEE 802.5. As you learned in Chapters 14 and 20, Token Ring specifies a logical ring, physical star topology. It uses the token-passing media access method to provide data rates of 4 Mbps and/or 16 Mbps. At the Physical Layer, Token Ring relies on STP or UTP cabling and uses proprietary IBM data connectors. Token Ring is the preferred communications standard for IBM LANs and WANs.

- *SDLC*—Uses specific hardware to interface with dedicated leased or dial-up telephone lines. It can support point-to-point or multipoint connections. SDLC uses the polling channel access method and synchronous frame synchronization. It can provide half-duplex and full-duplex connections. SDLC also generates its own specific control messages in addition to adding Data Link Layer headers to incoming packets.

FIGURE 22.10

SNA and OSI Communications

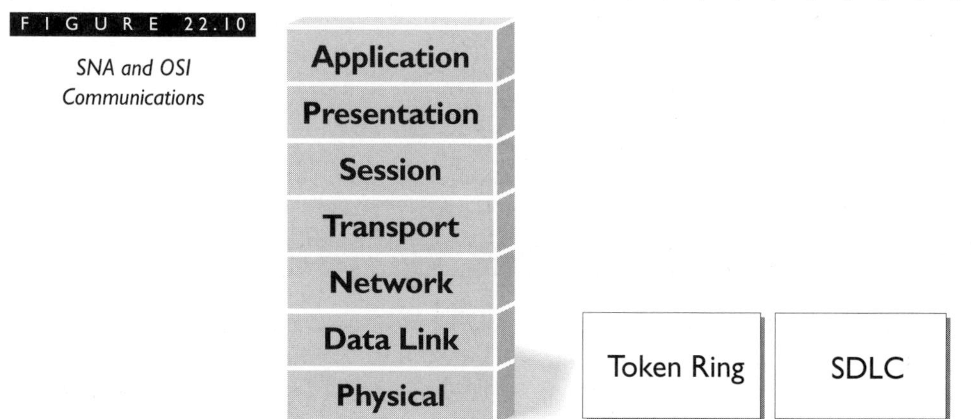

SNA and OSI Networking

At the middle layers (Network and Transport), SNA relies on the Network Control Program (NCP) for network routing. The Virtual Telecommunications Access Method (VTAM) provides Transport Layer service addressing, segmentation, and flow control. NCP and VTAM work together to route SNA messages between Type 2, 4, and 5 devices. APPN is a relatively new architecture that provides a peer-to-peer alternative at the Network and Transport Layers (see Figure 22.11). Let's take a closer look:

- *Network Control Program (NCP)*—Handles PU Type 4 communication controller activities and SNA routing functions. It was designed to operate front-end processors, but it now performs logical network addressing, static route selection, and some polling.

- *Virtual Telecommunications Access Method (VTAM)*—Controls the flow of data throughout SNA networks. It provides single domain, multiple domain, and interconnected network capability. At the Transport Layer, VTAM performs connection ID service addressing, segment synchronization, and end-to-end flow control. It also handles some Session Layer activities, such as connection establishment, data transfer, and connection release. VTAM and SSCP are considered synonymous terms, although this is not entirely true. VTAM is the program product, and SSCP is the main software within it.

- *Advanced Peer-to-Peer Networking (APPN)*—Performs Network and Transport Layer functions for connectivity between PU Type 2.1 devices only (no mainframes). It relies on APPC for logical connection points and provides route discovery, directory services, and windowed flow control. Think of it as a peer-to-peer alternative to NCP and VTAM.

FIGURE 22.11

SNA and OSI Networking

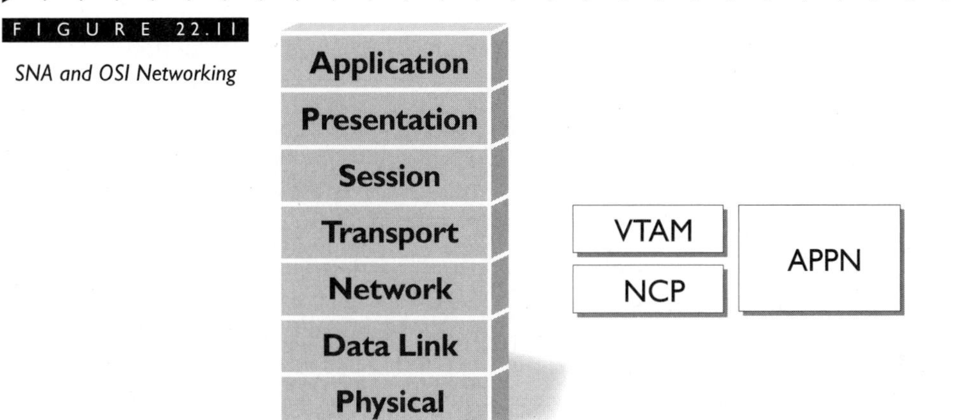

SNA and OSI Services

At the upper layers (Session, Presentation, and Application), SNA provides its own suite of service applications. These applications provide services ranging from document interchange to distributed data management.

Figure 22.12 illustrates the six most popular SNA services:

- *Advanced Program-to-Program Communication (APPC)* — Works in conjunction with APPN to provide logical connectivity between non-mainframe peers (PU Type 2.1 devices). APPC uses connection ID service addressing, segment synchronization, and half-duplex dialog control. It also performs a few upper-layer services, such as connection establishment, data transfer, and connection release.

- *Customer Information Control System (CICS)* — Supports transaction processing applications by generalizing I/O commands for use on the network. Software developers use CICS commands to build applications that carry out transactions on local and remote systems. Chances are that you used CICS at the checkout counter the last time you bought new sneakers. From the OSI point of view, CICS provides half-duplex data transfer, connection establishment, connection release, and file-syntax translation. From a programming point of view, CICS provides terminal-to-application communications, distributed file access, security, multitasking, storage management, transaction tracking and recovery, transaction reversal, and a graceful recovery facility.

- *Information Management System (IMS)* — Similar to CICS in that it's a transaction processing product. But unlike CICS, IMS is composed of two products: the IMS Transaction Manager and the IMS Database Manager. Using these products, IMS enables multiple applications to share databases and provide message-switching capabilities. Once again, it uses half-duplex data transfer, connection establishment, connection release, and file-syntax translation.

- *Document Interchange Architecture (DIA)* — One of three SNA Application Layer services that provide file services by allowing the exchange of documents between diverse computer systems. At its most basic level, DIA relies on file storage, retrieval, and transfer.

- *SNA Distribution Services (SNADS)* — One of three SNA Application Layer services that handles messaging.

- *Distributed Data Management (DDM)*—One of three SNA Application Layer services that provides transparent remote file access to SNA service requesters. It performs this function using the OS Call Interception service availability method. DDM receives file requests from applications and executes them through the local OS or through a DDM server across the network.

FIGURE 22.12

SNA and OSI Services

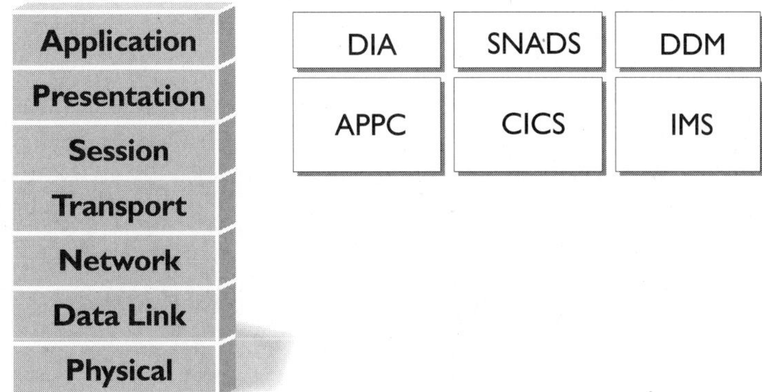

This completes our discussion of SNA and the OSI model. To summarize, SNA is a complete proprietary network architecture designed and supported by IBM that predates the OSI model. Now let's turn our attention to another seven-layer proprietary model: DNA.

Digital Network Architecture (DNA)

DNA is Digital Equipment Corporation's (DEC) Digital Network Architecture. Released in 1974, DNA is now in its fifth iteration (referred to as Phase V). Products that implement DNA are referred to as DECNet products. The term DECNet is used loosely to describe the family of products that operate within the DNA model. Like SNA, DNA has evolved over the years to reflect changes in networking technologies. Most recently, DNA has refocused on supporting ISO standards in direct cooperation with the OSI model.

DNA maps better with OSI Communications, Networking, and Services than do any of the other proprietary standards. Let's take a closer look.

DNA and OSI Communications

At the bottom two layers (Physical and Data Link), DNA relies on mostly non-proprietary protocols. As you can see in Figure 22.13, DNA uses Ethernet v. 2, HDLC, and DDCMP to provide low-level connectivity. The final protocol is the only proprietary one.

- *Ethernet v.2* — The second generation of the Ethernet specification. Version 2 was developed jointly by DEC, Intel, and Xerox. Like IEEE 802.3, this standard uses the CSMA/CD MAC protocol and Manchester digital encoding, and it operates over coaxial cabling. The main differences between Ethernet v.2 and IEEE 802.3 are in the frame typing that each uses and in v.2's reliance on a Signal Quality Error (SQE) heartbeat for NIC monitoring.
- *High-Level Data Link Control (HDLC)* — A variation of IBM's SDLC that supports both asynchronous and synchronous frame synchronization. It operates primarily at the LLC sublayer of the OSI's Data Link Layer and provides certain types of flow control and error checking.
- *Digital Data Communications Message Protocol (DDCMP)* — Designed in 1974 for WAN links. Like HDLC, it operates with synchronous or asynchronous transmissions. It can also be used with full- or half-duplex point-to-point or multipoint configurations. DDCMP also operates at the LLC sublayer and provides connection-oriented error checking and flow control.

DNA and OSI Networking

At the middle layers (Network and Transport), DNA provides connectionless or connection-oriented network routing. In either case, two specific Transport Layer protocols provide reliable error-checking and flow-control functions. As you can see in Figure 22.14, DNA performs OSI Networking through the following implementations:

- *Connectionless Network Service (CLNS)* — Operates primarily at the Network Layer and provides logical network addressing, link-state route discovery, and both static and dynamic route selection. Although DNA can support both connectionless and connection-oriented routing, Phase V typically uses CLNS. CLNS is further supported by ISO 8473 (for data transmission), ISO 9542 (for simple routing), and ISO 10589 (for packet delivery).

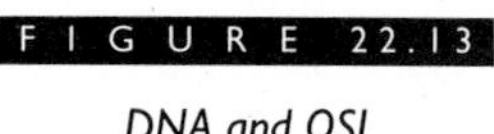

DNA and OSI Communications

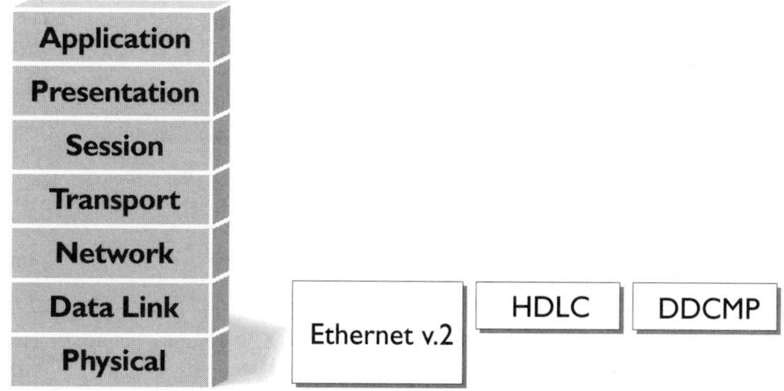

- *Connection-Oriented Network Service (CONS)* — Also operates at the Network Layer, providing logical network addressing, distance-vector route discovery, and both static and dynamic route selection. The main difference between CLNS and CONS is that CONS handles these tasks more reliably because connections are guaranteed. To accomplish all of this, CONS relies on ISO 8208 and ISO 8878 for X.25 packet switching and connectivity.
- *ISO 8073* — Is a generic OSI Transport Layer specification. ISO 8073 performs connection ID service addressing, segment synchronization, and Transport Layer error checking.
- *Network Services Protocol (NSP)* — A proprietary Transport Layer solution that offers connection-oriented flow-controlled service through full-duplex channels. NSP supports Network Layer implementations by tracking packets and making sure that they arrive safely. NSP also performs connection ID service addressing and segment synchronization.

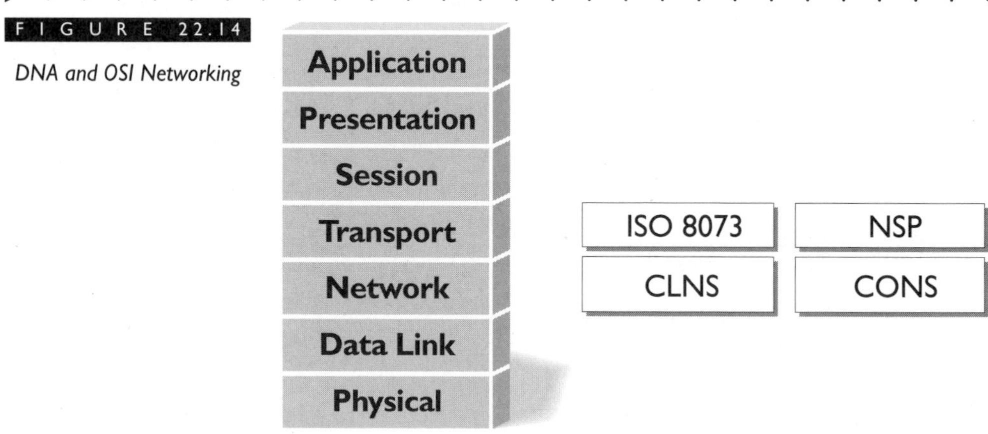

FIGURE 22.14

DNA and OSI Networking

DNA and OSI Services

At the upper layers (Session, Presentation, and Application), DNA provides its own suite of service applications. These applications include services ranging from file storage to messaging. Following is a brief description of the seven most popular DNA services (see Figure 22.15):

- *Session Control*—A proprietary DNA architecture that operates at the Session and Presentation Layers. At the most fundamental level, session control provides an interface between upper-layer applications and the lower-layer transport protocols. It handles address-to-name resolution, protocol stack selection, connection ID service addressing, and Session Layer dialog control—that is, connection establishment, data transfer, and connection release.

- *ISO 8327*—A generic OSI Session Layer protocol. It performs half-duplex data transfer, connection establishment, and connection release. ISO 8327 organizes data transfer by synchronizing packets according to major and minor bookmarks. These bookmarks enable dialogs to be reset to any synchronization point. Incidentally, ISO 8237 bookmarks are sometimes called synchronization tokens.

- *ASN.1 (Abstract Syntax Notation Character Code Translation Scheme)*— Uses Basic Encoding Rules (BER) to translate to and from ASN.1 notations. Think of this protocol as a common denominator for Presentation Layer DNA translation.

- *A Generic File Transfer, Access and Management (FTAM) protocol*—A DNA application that provides file transfer and management capabilities in coordination with DAP (Data Access Protocol). DAP enhances FTAM by providing file retrieval, storage creation, deletion, and renaming functions. It also supports heterogeneous file systems and allows multiple access to the same remote file. FTAM and DAP also support database indexing.

- *A Generic Network Virtual Terminal Service (NVTS)*—A DNA application that provides terminal emulation through remote operation service availability. Using NVTS, data can be translated from the local terminal format to the network format before it's transmitted to the host. This process ensures that heterogeneous systems can communicate effortlessly.

- *X.400*—An international standard for messaging. This DNA application relies on a family of products, called DEC MAILbus products, which use the X.400 recommendation to interact with other X.400 implementations on a large internetwork.

- *X.500*—An international standard for naming services. DNA uses X.500 with its own naming services to provide address-to-name resolution and directory services. This allows DNA machines to exist in a large hierarchical management system.

This completes our discussion of DNA and the OSI model. To summarize, DNA is a completely proprietary network architecture designed and supported by DEC. Even though DNA is a proprietary standard, it relies primarily on nonproprietary implementations from the seven-layer OSI model. For this reason, our DNA discussion also serves as an OSI review.

FIGURE 22.15

DNA and OSI Services

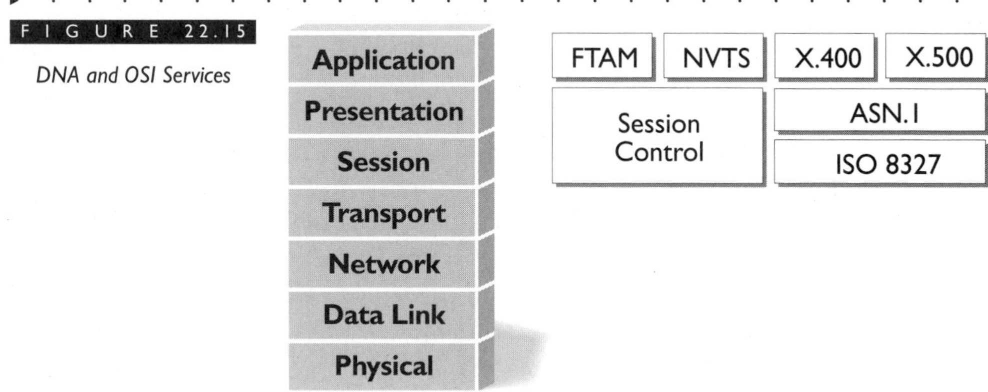

AppleTalk

Apple Computer, Inc., began development of the AppleTalk protocol suite in 1983. At that point in networking history, SNA and DNA were dominating standards. Apple Computer decided to diverge from the established standards and develop its own networking solution, and thus, AppleTalk was born. AppleTalk provides connectivity for a variety of computer systems, including IBM PCs running MS-DOS, IBM mainframes, DEC VAX hosts, and various UNIX computers. To do all of this, Apple extended its original network specifications to embrace wide-area networking. This new enhancement, called AppleTalk Phase II, was introduced in 1989.

Refer to Table 22.3 for a feature comparison of AppleTalk Phase I and Phase II. As you can see from the table, Phase II extends AppleTalk's capability into large complex internetworks.

TABLE 22.3

Feature Comparison of AppleTalk Phase I and Phase II

FEATURE	PHASE I	PHASE II
Maximum zones per segment	1	255
Addressing	Physical only (node ID)	Logical and physical

TABLE 22.3
Feature Comparison of AppleTalk Phase I and Phase II (continued)

FEATURE	PHASE I	PHASE II
Maximum nodes per network	254	16,000,000
Link-access protocols supported	LocalTalk and Ethernet	LocalTalk, Ethernet, and Token Ring
Split-horizon routing	No	Yes

AppleTalk and OSI Communications

At the bottom two layers (Physical and Data Link), AppleTalk relies on its own proprietary implementation: LocalTalk. AppleTalk also supports two IEEE variations of LocalTalk: EtherTalk and TokenTalk (see Figure 22.16). These three connectivity solutions are the foundation of Macintosh networking:

- *LocalTalk*—Technically referred to as the LocalTalk Link Access Protocol (LLAP). LocalTalk operates at both the Physical and Data Link Layers. It uses the CSMA/CA media access control across STP cabling. At the Physical Layer, LocalTalk calls for multipoint connection types across a bus topology using state-transition digital signaling. LocalTalk relies on synchronous bit synchronization. At the MAC sublayer, it uses physical node addressing for contention access to a bus topology. AppleTalk also provides synchronous frame synchronization and Data Link level flow control and error checking at the MAC sublayer.

- *EtherTalk*—Also known as the EtherTalk Link Access Protocol (ELAP). EtherTalk is a hybrid of AppleTalk and the IEEE 802.3 Ethernet specification. In EtherTalk, all communication services are provided by built-in Ethernet cards in the Macintosh devices.

- *TokenTalk*—Also known as the TokenTalk Link Access Protocol (TLAP). TokenTalk is an integrated hybrid of AppleTalk and IEEE 802.5 Token Ring. In TokenTalk, IEEE 802.5 provides all the bottom-layer communication functionality.

FIGURE 22.16

AppleTalk and OSI Communications

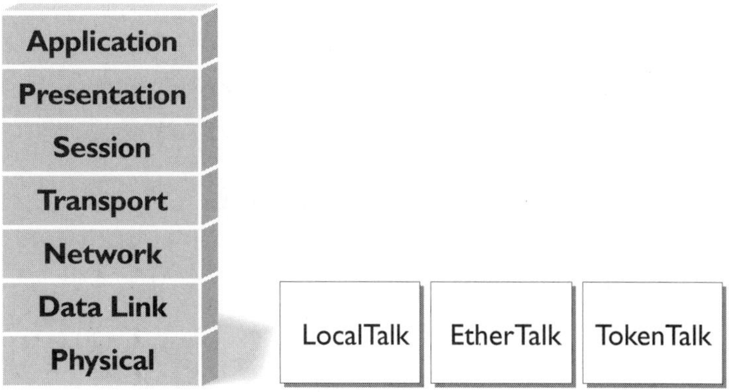

AppleTalk and OSI Networking

At the middle two layers (Network and Transport), AppleTalk relies on four powerful networking protocols. Two of them handle routing, and the other two provide Transport Layer management functions. These protocols work together to route AppleTalk messages between distributed Macintosh computers (see Figure 22.17):

- *Datagram Delivery Protocol (DDP)* — The primary Network Layer implementation for AppleTalk. DDP provides connectionless routing between multiple AppleTalk services. Like any other Network Layer protocol, DDP uses the complete address to route packets through the Internet. This complete address consists of a Network Layer logical number and a Data Link Layer physical address. Because LocalTalk uses its own physical addressing scheme, a translation method must be used when you work with EtherTalk or TokenTalk. This address translation task is handled by the AppleTalk Address Resolution Protocol (AARP). In its most basic form, DDP provides logical networking addressing and dynamic route selection. Optimal paths are chosen based on numbers from Routing Information Tables (RITs). These tables are maintained by RTMP.

- *Routing Table Maintenance Program (RTMP)* — Performs route discovery functions to create and maintain Network Layer RITs. RTMP uses a distance-vector routing algorithm similar to RIP.

- *AppleTalk Transaction Protocol (ATP)* — Operates at the Transport Layer and performs transaction ID service addressing, segment synchronization, and Transport Layer error checking. Unlike most Transport Layer protocols, however, ATP is based on the concept of a transaction rather than on simply moving a stream of data across a reliable connection. In the AppleTalk world, a transaction is defined as a request followed by a reply. Data is transmitted when the sender receives an acknowledgment within a given period of time. ATP and DDP work together to perform the majority of AppleTalk's networking functions.
- *Name Binding Protocol (NBP)* — An address resolution protocol operating at the Transport Layer. NBP's primary job is to translate physical device IDs into user-friendly node names. These node names can then be used by upper-layer services to simplify access to AppleTalk entities, such as file servers and printers.

FIGURE 22.17

AppleTalk and OSI Networking

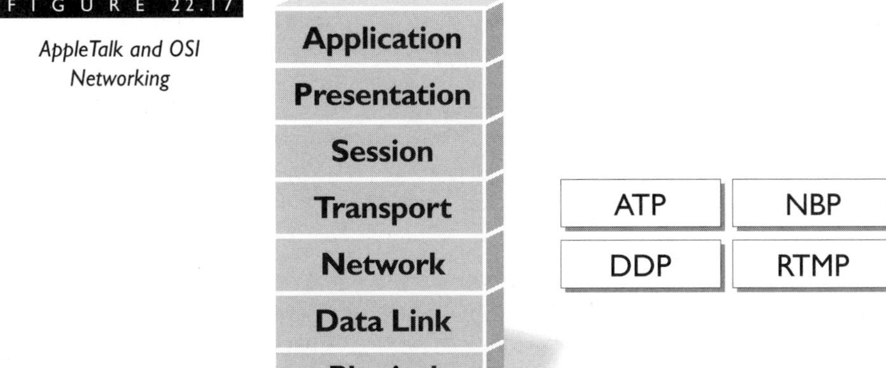

AppleTalk and OSI Services

OSI Services are where AppleTalk shines. At the upper layers (Session, Presentation, and Application), AppleTalk consists of numerous services and applications (see Figure 22.18). The most exciting of these applications is AppleShare, which consists of three primary components that provide file, print, and interconnectivity services. But before we can reach AppleShare, we need to pass through five intermediate protocols:

- *Standard AppleTalk Session Protocol (ASP)* — Performs traditional Session Layer functions for AppleTalk networks (that is, connection establishment, data transfer, and connection release). ASP also performs some higher-level Transport Layer functions, including segment synchronization and end-to-end flow control.
- *AppleTalk Data Stream Protocol (ADSP)* — Considered a Session Layer protocol because it can establish and release logical relationships between two AppleTalk nodes. ADSP can also perform segment synchronization and sliding window flow control at the Transport Layer — obviously, a multitalented implementation. ADSP provides a full-duplexed, flow-controlled connection-oriented service that runs on DDP. Unlike ATP, ADSP is not transaction based. It uses a connection ID scheme and byte stream rather than transactions. As a result of this and other differences, ADSP is better suited for low-bandwidth channels than is the ATP/ASP combination.
- *Printer Access Protocol (PAP)* — Similar to ASP in that it performs generic Session Layer functions. However, PAP was designed to optimize print service connectivity. For this reason, ASP is better for file requests, and PAP is better for printing requests.

TIP

PAP is a much more generic protocol than its name implies. It offers a few Session Layer advantages over ASP. Namely, PAP allows either the service requester or service provider to initiate a session. In contrast, ASP forces service requesters to get things started. Then again, ASP can use multiple ATP transactions to reduce overhead on large data transfers, which is not the case with PAP.

- *Zone Information Protocol (ZIP)* — Uses zones to logically organize service provider names on large internetworks so that users can narrow in on the type or location of servers they're interested in. Using ZIP, AppleTalk limits the number of providers presented to users at one time.

- *AppleTalk Filing Protocol (AFP)*—Facilitates AppleTalk file services by translating native local commands into an acceptable network format. To accomplish this goal, AFP relies on file-syntax translation at the Presentation Layer. AFP also verifies and encrypts login names and passwords for file access security.
- *AppleShare (AppleTalk's Application Layer Suite)*—Includes three programs: AppleShare File Server, AppleShare Print Server, and AppleShare PC. AppleShare File Server is Apple's network operating system (NOS). It uses AFP to provide shared access to centralized network files. Just like NetWare, AppleShare enables users to log in and access resources using a multilayered security model. AppleShare Print Server uses PAP to provide network print sharing. Like NetWare, AppleShare sends data to print queues and redirects jobs to local or remote printers. Finally, AppleShare PC allows DOS workstations to enter the Apple universe. AppleShare PC supports a variety of third-party Ethernet and Token Ring NICs.

FIGURE 22.18

AppleTalk and OSI Services

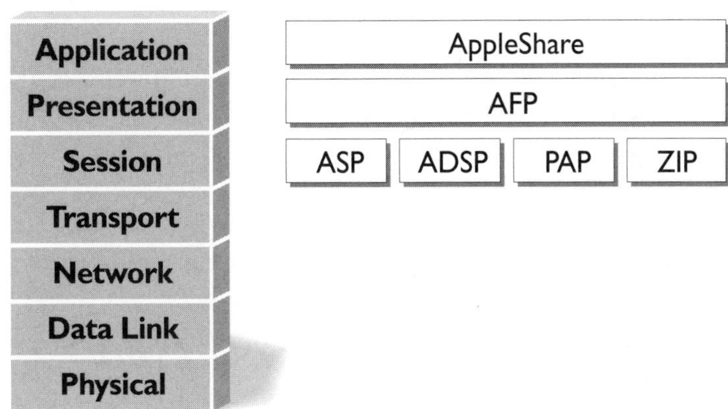

This completes our discussion of AppleTalk and its seven-layer implementations. As you've learned, there are many support protocols for networking and one main protocol for OSI Services: AppleShare. Now let's complete our final OSI lesson with a comprehensive overview of X.500 and LDAP.

X.500

X.500 organizes network resources (such as users and servers) into a globally accessible *Directory.* The X.500 specification establishes guidelines for representing, accessing, and using information stored in a directory database. In fact, Novell Directory Services (NDS) is Novell's implementation of the following X.500 features:

- *Scalability* — Large databases can be subdivided into smaller Directory System Agents (DSAs). A DSA can represent either a single organization or multiple organizations, and its contents may be distributed across multiple Directory servers. NDS calls them *partitions.*
- *Replication* — This feature allows the Directory database, or portions thereof, to be replicated on backup Directory servers located throughout the network.
- *Synchronization* — Because X.500 must manage a loosely coupled, distributed database, each server must be able to synchronize its database contents with other servers. Directory database updates may be made either at the original master database (master-shadow arrangement) or at any writable replica (peer-to-peer mechanism). In either case, X.500 propagates Directory database change information to all servers holding replicas of the database or a DSA.

The X.500 Directory is represented by a Directory Information Tree (DIT) and Directory Information Base (DIB). The DIB consists of objects (or nodes) and their associated properties and values. Intermediate objects act as containers that aid in organizing the DIT. Leaf objects represent individual network entities, such as servers, printers, and so on. Refer to Figure 22.19 for an illustration of the X.500 Directory architecture.

The rules that determine the type of information that may be stored in the DIB are held in the Directory's *schema.* Each object in an X.500 DIT has a unique name that is referred to as its distinguished name (DN) (that is, complete name). Each object may also be referred to by a relative distinguished name (RDN) (that is, partial name).

FIGURE 22.19

X.500 Directory architecture

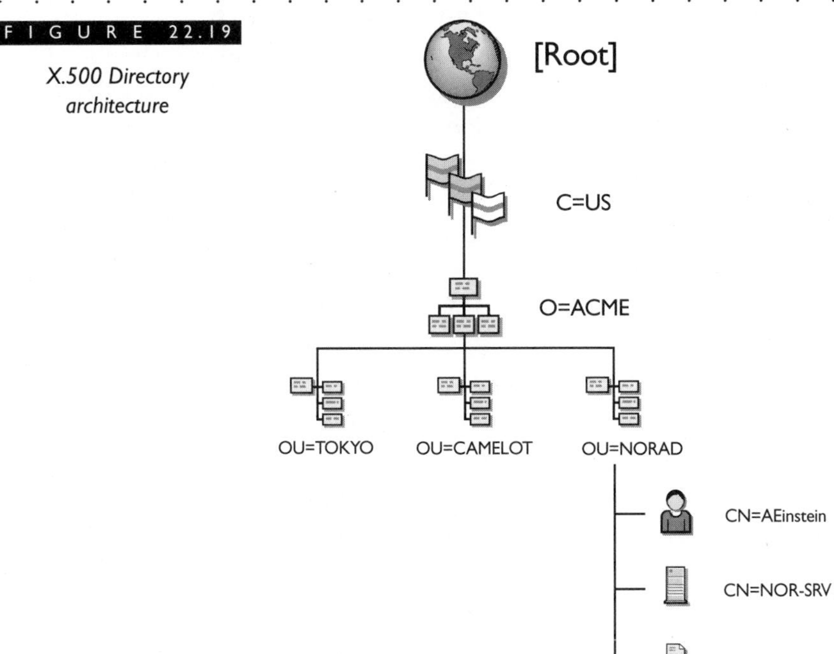

Directory database access is managed by a DSA running on a local server. Users access the database through a Directory User Agent (DUA). DUAs are available in command-line, forms-based, and browser-style interfaces. DSAs and DUAs communicate with each other using the Directory Access Protocol (DAP). Furthermore, DSAs may communicate with one another using the Directory System Protocol (DSP), Directory Information Shadowing Protocol (DISP), or the Directory Operational Binding Management Protocol (DOP).

Following are three ports defined for DUA-to-DSA communications:

- *Read* — Supplies read, compare, and abandon functions
- *Search* — Provides list and searching functions
- *Modify* — Allows for the addition, removal, and modification of database entries

Lightweight Directory Access Protocol (LDAP)

The Lightweight Directory Access Protocol (LDAP) is designed to provide clients with access to information stored in an X.500 Directory. It is *not* a Directory Service, but rather, a protocol for accessing Directories. It is used when simple read/write interactive access to the Directory is required and is specifically targeted at simple management and browser applications.

LDAP can use the services of TCP or any other connection-oriented, reliable Transport Layer protocol. LDAP clients transmit queries to LDAP servers who perform Directory database lookups on the clients' behalf. LDAP is described in RFC 1777.

In addition to LDAP, the Connectionless Lightweight Directory Access Protocol (CLDAP) is an extension of LDAP designed for simplified lookups consisting of only a small number of read requests directed to a single device.

Congratulations! You made it. You have successfully traversed the entire NetWare 5.1 CNE program (or at least, most of it). In this comprehensive study guide, we have covered the following four courses:

- *Novell Course 570* — In the first three chapters of Part I, "NetWare 5.1 Advanced Administration," we built on the NetWare 5.1 Administration course with a plethora of advanced CNE tasks, including installation, IP services, and Internet infrastructure. Then in Chapters 4 through 6, we explored three advanced management arenas: advanced server management, advanced NDS management, and advanced security management. Finally, in Chapter 7, we completed our examination of Novell Course 570 with a comprehensive look at NetWare 5.1 Optimization.

- *Novell Course 575* — In Part II, "NDS Design and Implementation," we expanded our NetWare 5.1 LAN into the realm of global NDS connectivity. As a NetWare 5.1 CNE, we mastered the first three steps of network construction: NDS preparation, NDS design, and NDS implementation. In Step 1 (Chapter 8), we gathered ACME data and built a project team. Then in Step 2 (Chapters 9 and 10), we constructed ACME's NDS tree with the help of naming standards, tree design guidelines, partitioning, and time synchronization. Finally, in Step 3 (Chapter 11), we implemented the new global tree with a comprehensive implementation schedule.

- *Novell Course 580*—In Part III, "NetWare Service and Support," we discovered that networks are alive. In Chapter 12, we explored all aspects of NetWare troubleshooting fundamentals, including the NetWare troubleshooting model and a variety of tools (such as SupportSource 2000 and Novell Internet Services). Then in Chapters 13 through 16, we honed critical troubleshooting skills with respect to NICs, hard drives, workstations, and printing. In each chapter, we focused on how these components fit into the network model and how to keep them alive. We ended our study of Novell Course 580 with some detailed tips on keeping the network fit and healthy in Chapter 17, "Troubleshooting the Server and the Network."

- *Novell Course 565*—In Part IV, "Networking Technologies," we explored the three adventurous domains of computer networking: OSI Communications, OSI Networking, and OSI Services. Our lessons in the Communications domain (Chapter 19) taught us a great deal about how networking works. We learned seven Physical Layer secrets and helped build frames using Data Link technologies. Next, the Networking domain (Chapters 20 and 21) provided valuable lessons in routing and Transport Layer management. In addition, we used various route discovery and selection mechanisms to traverse the WAN. Finally, we learned all there is to know about NetWare IPX/SPX and Internet TCP/IP—two of the most successful implementations in the Networking domain. Finally, our adventure brought us to the pinnacle of computer networking—OSI Services (Chapter 22). We studied three difficult layers (Session, Presentation, and Application) to discover the secrets of OSI network services: file, print, message, application, and database. We finally explored five Top Layer implementations: SNA, DNA, AppleTalk, X.500, and LDAP.

Wow, what a journey! You should be proud of yourself. You are the final piece in ACME's globe-trotting puzzle. You will save the world with NetWare 5.1. Your mission—*should you choose to accept it*—is to pass the NetWare 5.1 CNE exams. You will need courage, an NDS tree, Novell Internet Services, the OSI model, and this book. If you succeed, you will save the world and become a CNE!

All in a day's work . . . .

Well, that does it! The End . . . Finito . . . Kaput. Everything you wanted to know about NetWare 5.1, but were afraid to ask. I hope you've had as much fun reading this book as I've had writing it. It's been a long and winding road—a life changer. Thanks for spending the last 1,200 pages with me, and I bid you a fond farewell in the only way I know how:

"Cheerio!"

"Happy, Happy—Joy, Joy!"

"Hasta la vista!"

"Ta Ta for Now!"

"Grooovy Baby!"

"So long and thanks for all the fish!"

"May the force be with you . . ."

LAB EXERCISE 22.1: GETTING TO KNOW THE TOP LAYERS

Use the hints provided to find the 20 OSI Services terms hidden in this word search puzzle. Omit any punctuation characters (such as blank spaces, hyphens, and so on) and spell out any numbers.

Hints

1. Upper-layer protocol that facilitates file sharing by translating local commands into an acceptable network format.
2. A combined Transport and Session Layer protocol; is the version of SNA that was the first to allow peer-to-peer communications between logical units that did not involve a mainframe host.
3. Provides DOS computers with access to AppleTalk file and printing services.

4. Specialized servers that balance the convenience of local processing with the increased speed, data integrity, and security of centralized processing.
5. This Network and Transport Layer architecture is SNA's latest peer-to-peer implementation.
6. Commercial pilot rating or Apple's main Transport Layer implementation.
7. Upper-layer protocol that supports transaction processing applications by generalizing input and output commands for use on a network.
8. Network Layer protocol that provides logical network addressing, link-state route discover, and both dynamic and static route selection.
9. Provides X.25-type packet switching for DNA at the Network Layer.
10. Involves the coordination of distributed data and replication.
11. A byte-oriented, Data Link Layer synchronous protocol that is the primary Data Link component of DECnet.
12. Network Layer protocol that provides connectionless routing between two AppleTalk sockets.
13. Established connection between two network entities that are currently engaged in data transfer.
14. Digital Equipment Corporation's network architecture that operates at all seven layers of the OSI model.
15. Includes archiving, data storage and migration, file transfer, and file-update synchronization.
16. Application Layer generic file transfer, access, and management protocol.
17. Mainframe or midrange computer that controls an SNA domain.
18. Facilitates e-mail, manages integrated e-mail and voice mail, and coordinates object-oriented applications.
19. Combination of hardware, firmware, and software that manage and monitor the resources of a node.
20. A combined Network and Transport Layer protocol that uses a distance-vector routing algorithm similar to RIP.

See Appendix C for answers.

LAB EXERCISE 22.2: THE OSI MODEL — TOP LAYERS

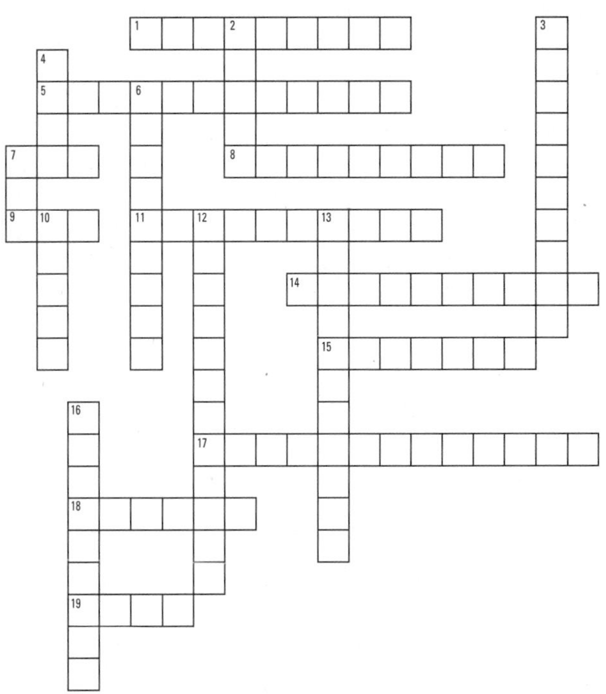

Across

1. Apple's Token Ring implementation
5. Manages messages and ensures reliable conversations
7. Provides routing and gateway functionality in SNA networks
8. Uses CSMA/CA media access across shielded twisted-pair cabling
9. Session Layer protocol designed to optimize print service functions
11. Scrambling data to prevent unauthorized access
14. Communications technique used by walkie-talkies
15. Communications technique used by broadcast radio
17. Provides shared access to valuable printing devices
18. IBM mainframe character code set
19. Apple Session Layer protocol

Down

2. Message transfer and storage application
3. Communications technique used for telephones
4. Advancement over the SDLC Data Link protocol
6. Apple's proprietary protocol suite for network communications
7. Used to assign user-friendly names to printer addresses
10. Character code set used for PCs
12. Used to manage and control data flow to the network
13. Necessary when two computers speak different languages
16. Apple's Ethernet implementation

See Appendix C for answers.

APPENDIX A

NetWare 5.1 Certification: A World of Knowledge

In a world where people and businesses and organizations and governments and nations are being connected and sharing information at a dizzying rate, Novell's primary goal is to be the infrastructure that connects people and services together all over the world.

To help fulfill this goal, Novell Education provides quality education programs and products to help create a strong support base of trained networking professionals. By itself, the Novell Education department isn't nearly large enough to provide high-quality training to the vast number of people who will require it. Therefore, Novell Education has developed training partnerships throughout the world to provide authorized training. In addition, Novell Education has created certification programs to help ensure that the standard for networking skills is maintained at a high level.

Today, Novell has more than 1,500 authorized education partners worldwide, including colleges, universities, professional training centers, e-Learning companies, and so on.

This appendix describes Novell Education and the CNA/CNE program. It also provides some practical tips for finding alternatives to formal classes, taking take the test, and where to go from here. Specifically, we're going to learn how Novell Education and NetWare 5.1 will help you build your own on-ramp to the global Web — also known as a whole new "World of Knowledge."

Novell Certification

Every year, Novell certifies thousands of professionals around the world to manage and support its information technology (IT) products. Whether you are a network administrator, systems integrator, or other networking professional, you'll undoubtedly find that Novell offers one or more network certifications to meet your needs. If you want to learn more about the various types of certifications available, you should check out the information at `http://www.novell.com/education/certinfo/`.

NetWare 5.1 CNA Certification

If you are new to the Novell certification process, you may find that the NetWare 5.1 CNA certification is the right one for you. This certification track consists of *one* course and *one* exam. Table A.1 lists the latest course and associated exam number that were valid as of the writing of this study guide.

TABLE A.1

NetWare 5.1 CNA Exam Requirements

COURSE NUMBER	COURSE TITLE	EXAM NUMBER
Course 560	NetWare 5.1 Administration	Exam 50-653

NetWare 5.1 CNE Certification

If you're looking for a more comprehensive certification, you may find that the NetWare 5.1 CNE certification is the right one for you. This certification track consists of *six* courses and *six* required exams. (You'll notice that one of the required courses, Course 560, is also a requirement for the CNA certification.) Five of the courses are pre-selected for you. You'll also be asked to select one of four electives. Table A.2 lists the latest courses and exam numbers that were valid as of the writing of this book.

TABLE A.2

NetWare 5.1 CNE Exam Requirements

COURSE NUMBER	COURSE TITLE	EXAM NUMBER
Course 560	NetWare 5.1 Administration v2.0	Exam 50-653
Course 565	Networking Technologies v1.0	Exam 50-632
Course 570	NetWare 5.1 Advanced Administration v2.0	Exam 50-654
Course 575	NDS Design and Implementation, v2.0	Exam 50-659
Course 580	Service and Support v2.0	Exam 50-635

Continued

TABLE A.2

NetWare 5.1 CNE Exam Requirements (continued)

COURSE NUMBER	COURSE TITLE	EXAM NUMBER
	Electives: Select *one* of the following:	
Course 350	GroupWise 5.5 System Administration	Exam 50-633
Course 555	Integrating NetWare & Windows NT	Exam 50-644
Course 606	TCP/IP for Networking Professionals	Exam 50-649
Course 730	Management Using ManageWise 2.6	Exam 50-641
Course 770	Internet Security Management with Border Manager Enterprise Edition 3.5 v1.02	Exam 50-650
Course 780	Desktop Management with ZENworks	Exam 50-656
Course 990	Oracle Database Operator for NetWare	Exam 50-436

While you are working toward your certification, it's very important that you always have access to an up-to-date version of the *certification track* relating to the certification you are interested in. If you plan to obtain a NetWare 5.1 CNA certification, check out the CNA Certification Track at `http://www.novell.com/education/certinfo/cna/`. If you are interested in the NetWare 5.1 CNE certification, check out the various CNE Certification Tracks at `http://www.novell.com/education/certinfo/cne/`.

Continuing Education Requirements

Like other networking technology, Novell products are constantly being updated and enhanced. Because of this, you will eventually find that the Novell product related to your certification has become obsolete. When this happens, you will typically have approximately 12 to 18 months to re-certify by taking an exam on the new product. If you fail to do so, your existing certification may be invalidated.

Exam Preparation

You can obtain most Novell certifications by simply signing a Novell Education Certification Agreement and passing the required exams. Neither the CNA or CNE certifications require you to attend formal training classes.

Preparation Methods

There are many ways to prepare for an exam, including: formal Novell-authorized classroom training, CNA/CNE Study Guides from Novell Press, Clarke Notes books from Novell Press, Novell Student Kits, on-line training from CyberStateU.com (an official Novell Online Training Provider), computer-based training, videos, and practice exams. No matter which method(s) you choose, it is critical that you gain a thorough understanding of the technical concepts, as well as a firm grasp of the hands-on material.

Study Hints

As you prepare for the CNA and CNE exams, be sure that you tailor your study habits toward the testing objectives. The exam questions are based on the testing objectives listed and cross-referenced in Appendix B of this book. Also, be sure that you know the course material *well*. You'll find that some exam questions rely on *memorization* of facts, while others require you to actually *apply* the knowledge that you've acquired.

Here are a few more study hints that should help you prepare for the CNA and CNE exams:

- Remember that exam questions may be presented in a variety of different formats including single-answer multiple choice, multiple-answer multiple choice, true/false, fill-in-the-blank, and drag-and-drop. You may also get a number of simulation (performance-based) questions and exhibit-related questions (especially in the exams for Novell Courses 570, 575, and 580). In simulation situations, you may be asked to perform a number of sequential tasks. Unfortunately, you may find that the simulator is not programmed to allow your favorite method of performing a certain task—so it's always wise to be familiar with alternative methods. Be prepared!

- You will probably find that the "Service & Support" exam emphasizes use of the SupportSource 2000 troubleshooting tool. In other words, you may be presented with numerous scenarios that require you to manually navigate the SupportSource 2000 application to locate the answers to specific questions and/or to solve particular problems. Therefore, be sure to practice using this tool prior to taking the exam.
- After you've read this entire study guide, go back and take a second look at the Real World and Tip icon references. If you don't have a high degree of confidence, read the book again and spend additional time practicing the hands-on lab exercises.
- Interestingly, you may occasionally find exam questions that do not appear to be in the official Novell course material. This is unfortunate, but cannot be avoided. If this occurs, your best bet is to use your overall knowledge of the subject to architect the correct answer(s).

The Exam

Okay. You've finished the course, you've studied this book, you've spent hours in the lab or on your own network practicing hands-on tasks. Now, you're ready to show your stuff, and prove that you have the baseline of knowledge required to take on network administrator duties in the real world. You're ready to take the exam and become a CNA (or alternately, take your first step toward becoming a CNE).

Registering for the Exam

In the United States and Canada, Novell exams are administered by one of two professional testing organizations: Prometric or Virtual University Enterprises (VUE). If you take a Novell-authorized course, your instructor will probably be able to give you information about where to take the exam locally.

Otherwise, to find a location that administers this exam, simply call one of the following numbers:

- Novell Education, at 1-800-233-EDUC (toll-free in Canada and the U.S.) or 1-801-861-3382.
- Prometric, at 1-800-RED-TEST or 1-800-RED-EXAM (both toll-free in Canada and the U.S.) or 1-952-820-5706.
- Virtual University Enterprises (VUE), at 1-800-TEST-CNE (toll-free in Canada and the U.S.), or 1-952-995-8970.

Outside of the USA and Canada, contact your local Novell office, or a local Prometric office or VUE office.

When you call the testing organization, you'll be asked to provide the following information: your testing ID (which is your Social Security Number if you are in the United States), name, organization, address, telephone number, exam title, exam number, and method of payment (credit card is recommended).

The standard fee for the exam at the time of this writing is $100. When you register for the exam, write down the name of the testing center, the address, phone number, driving directions to the testing center, the exam date/time, as well as the final date/time you can call to reschedule or cancel the exam without penalty. Also, confirm that the exam number you have requested is the correct one, as well as the exam format (form or adaptive), the time limit, and the total number of questions.

What Is the Exam Like?

The NetWare 5.1 Administration exam, like all Novell exams, is computer-based. In other words, you take the exam by answering questions on the computer. However, unlike more traditional exams, the NetWare 5.1 Administrator exam is also performance-based. This means that instead of just asking you to regurgitate facts, the exam also requires you to apply your knowledge to solve problems. For example, the exam may include scenarios describing network problems or tasks (such as adding a user with specific properties). In those cases, you'll need to use simulations of NetWare utilities to complete the tasks or solve the problems.

The exam is closed-book and is graded on a pass/fail basis. You will not be allowed to take any notes into or out of the exam room, although the testing center should provide you with two pieces of paper and a pencil (or the equivalent) for temporary notes.

"Form" Exams

The exam format, number of questions, and time limit will vary, depending on when you take the exam. Novell changes these parameters from time to time. If you take the exam early in a product's life cycle, you'll probably be given a "Form" exam. Form exams offer a fixed number of questions (and simulations) in a specific time period — such as 67 questions (including simulations) in 90 minutes.

"Adaptive" Exams

"Adaptive" exams, on the other hand, offer questions of varying difficulty based on your last answer. In other words, the exam begins with a fairly easy question. If you answer it correctly, the next question is slightly more difficult. If you answer that one correctly, the next question is even more difficult. If you answer a question incorrectly, on the other hand, the next question is slightly easier. If you miss that one, too, the next will be easier yet, until you get one right (or reach the maximum number of questions allowed).

Adaptive exams allow less time than form exams, because they include less questions — typically 15-25 questions in 30, 45, or 60 minutes. The number of questions you'll be asked varies, depending on your level of knowledge. If you answer all the questions correctly, you'll be presented with the minimum number of questions. If you answer any questions incorrectly, you'll be asked one or more additional questions — up to the maximum allowed.

Hints for Taking the Exam

Once you've completed your in-depth studies, it's time to take the test. Here are some hints you may find helpful while taking a Novell certification exam:

- Show up early and bring two appropriate forms of ID (one must have a picture and one must have a signature). Leave everything else in your car trunk or at home. (You will not be allowed to bring study materials into the exam room.)

- When you sit down at the computer, take a deep breath and try to relax. Try not to hyperventilate. (It will only make you dizzy.) The good news is that you'll probably find that taking exams usually tends to get a bit less nerve-wracking after you've taken several of them.

- If this is your first certification exam, you may want to take the (sample) orientation exam before you take the real one, to get a general feel for how the exam process works. (On the sample exam, don't worry about getting the answers right—just concentrate on understanding the exam process itself.)

- Before you begin the actual exam, re-confirm the time limit, total number of questions, and whether questions must be answered sequentially, or if you can skip around and go back to previous questions. Also, make sure that the information on the opening screen is correct (such as your name, your testing ID, the exam title, and the exam number.). If any of the information is incorrect—do not begin the exam! (Instead, discuss the matter with the exam administrator.)

- Keep track of the time. Don't be concerned, however, if a particularly complex question takes 5 minutes, because you will probably be able to answer other questions in 30 seconds or less. Don't panic if most of the early questions seem to be long and complex. If so, the later questions will hopefully be shorter and simpler.

- You'll be given something to write on during the exam (such as a pencil and paper, dry erase board and marker, laminated paper and grease pencil, and so on). Although you will not be able to leave the building with it—you may find that it comes in quite handy during the exam. As soon as you begin the exam, you may want to take a moment and write down those things you have memorized that you don't want to forget. Also, during the exam, you may want to write down anything important you see in an exam question that you think might help you later on.

- Read each question *carefully*. Don't glance at key words in a question and assume that you understand the question. (This is a very common mistake.) For example, some questions may ask you to indicate which statements are *not* correct.

- Remember that exam questions may be presented in a variety of different formats including single-answer multiple choice, multiple-answer multiple choice, true/false, fill-in-the-blank, and drag-and-drop. You may also get a number of simulation (performance-based) questions and exhibit-related questions. In simulation situations, you may be asked to perform several sequential tasks.

- In most form exams, you're not allowed to skip ahead or go back—so be sure of your answer before you move on. If you simply do not know the correct answer, start by eliminating the answers that appear to be the most unlikely. Then review each remaining answer to see if you can find anything subtle that would make it incorrect. Do not simply pick the answer that leaps out as the "obvious" correct answer—because it may be a trick!

- In questions that require multiple answers, be sure that you select the correct number of choices.

- In any situation where multiple screens are involved (such as simulations and those that include exhibits), use Alt+Tab to toggle between the screens and/or "tile" the windows to see more information on the screen at one time.

- Be careful about typographical errors.

- Don't "waste" mouse clicks on simulator questions. Plan ahead.

- These exams were developed by Novell Education. Therefore, it's generally best to give the answer found in the courseware, rather than, for example, relying on information found in some obscure Technical Information Document (TID) you found on the Web.

- When you finish the exam, be sure that you obtain the exam results printout from the exam administrator. It will list information such as the passing exam score required, your score, whether you passed, and any topics that you missed questions on. It will not, however, tell you which questions you missed.

If you fail the exam, take heart. You can take it again. In fact, you can take it again as many times as it takes to pass the exam (or until your checkbook runs dry, whichever comes first). Be aware that there may be a mandatory waiting period imposed, however, between each exam attempt. (Check with the testing center that you registered with for further details.) Because of the way the exam is designed, questions are drawn from a large database. Therefore, you may not get the same exam questions twice, no matter how often you take the exam.

Checking Your Certification Status

To receive your official certification status, you must sign a Novell Education Certification Agreement and complete any exam requirements. The certification agreement contains the usual legal jargon you might expect with such certification. Among other things, it grants you permission to use the trademarked name "CNA" on your resume or other advertising, as long as you use the name in connection with providing network administration services on a NetWare 5.1 network. It also reminds you that if the network administration services you offer don't live up to Novell's high standards of quality, Novell can require you to meet those standards within "a commercially reasonable time."

If you'd like to check your new or existing certification status, you can do so at `http://www.novell.com/education/community/`. At this site, you can

- Update your personal information, such as name, address, phone, fax, e-mail address, and so on.
- View a list of certifications that you have already been awarded.
- Verify the exams that you have already completed.

This site requires a username and password, so you'll need to contact Novell CNA (or CNE) Administration if you don't know what those are.

For More Information

And, of course, you can always get more information about Novell products and services by surfing over to any of the Web sites described in Table A.3. Keep in mind that Novell changes its Web sites frequently, and thus, URLs may change over time. If this happens, simply browse to the Novell home page and perform a "search" for the topic you're interested in. Remember, we're here for you and *we care!*

TABLE A.3

For More Information

TYPE OF INFORMATION	WEB SITE URL
Novell Education	http://www.novell.com/education/
Novell Education Contact Information (Phone Numbers)	http://www.novell.com/education/about/contacts.html
Novell Education Feedback (E-mail Addresses)	http://www.novell.com/education/about/feedback.html
Novell Certification Information	http://www.novell.com/education/certinfo/
Certification Headline News	http://www.novell.com/education/certinfo/ certnews.html
Novell CNA Program Information	http://www.novell.com/education/cna/
Novell CNE Program Information	http://www.novell.com/education/cne/
Novell Certification Brochure	http://www.novell.com/education/certinfo/certbroc.pdf
Novell Certification Explorer	http://www.novell.com/education/certinfo/explorer.html
Continuing Certification Requirements	http://www.novell.com/education/certinfo/cneccr.html
Novell Training Options	http://www.novell.com/education/training/index.html

TABLE A.3

For More Information (continued)

TYPE OF INFORMATION	WEB SITE URL
Novell Authorized Training Locator	http://www.novell.com/education/locator/
Novell Press	http://www.novell.com/books
Hungry Minds	http://www.hungryminds.com
CyberStateU.com (an official Novell Online Training Provider)	http://www.cyberstateu.com
Novell Education Certification Agreement	http://www.novell.com/education/certinfo/certagrm.html
Novell Testing Information	http://www.novell.com/education/testinfo/
CNENET (for current CNEs; requires username and PIN)	http://cnenet.novell.com/
Novell Education Personal Status Information (for current CNAs and CNEs; requires username and PIN)	http://www.novell.com/education/community/
Novell, Inc.	http://www.novell.com/
NetWare 5.1 Home Page	http://www.novell.com/products/netware/
Novell Online Documentation	http://www.novell.com/documentation/
Novell Technical Support	http://support.novell.com/

APPENDIX B

CNE Cross-Reference to Novell Course Objectives

Following is a list of the Novell-authorized test objectives required for four of the six NetWare 5.1 CNE courses. Novell Education uses these objectives to write authorized courseware and to develop certification exams. In order to become a NetWare 5.1 CNE, you must become intimately familiar with every objective in the following courses:

- *Novell Education Course 560*—NetWare 5.1 Administration
- *Novell Education Course 570*—NetWare 5.1 Advanced Administration
- *Novell Education Course 575*—NDS Design and Implementation
- *Novell Education Course 580*—Service and Support
- *Novell Education Course 565*—Networking Technologies

Novell's CNE Study Guide for NetWare 5.1 enables you to learn the objectives for Courses 570, 575, 580, and 565. Objectives for Novell Course 560 are covered in the pre-requisite book, *Novell's CNA Study Guide for NetWare 5.1*.

In this appendix, I will present you with specific page number cross-references for each Novell-authorized testing objective. My goal is to clarify the relationship between this book and your Novell-authorized education—and to point you in the right direction.

Have fun and good luck!

Novell Education Course 570: NetWare 5.1 Advanced Administration

Your CNE education continues with NetWare 5.1 Advanced Administration. In this course, we will build on NetWare 5.1 Administration with a plethora of advanced CNE tasks, including Installation, NetWare IP Services, and NetWare Internet Infrastructure. Then, we'll explore three advanced management arenas – advanced server management, advanced NDS management, and advanced security management. Finally, we'll complete Novell Course 570 with a comprehensive look at NetWare 5.1 Optimization.

It's time to learn, and this is a great place to start.

Section 1: Installing NetWare 5.1 and NLS, and Determining Which Management Tools to Use

1. Install NetWare 5.1: **4-58.**
2. Describe NLS: **59-62.**
3. Install NLS: **62-73.**
4. Perform license management tasks: **62-73.**
5. Determine which network administration tools to use: **4-58.**

Section 2: Using the Server Console to Control and Manage a NetWare Server

1. Identify NetWare operating system components: **208-214.**
2. Execute commands at the server console: **214-215.**
3. Identify how to load and unload NLMs: **216-217.**
4. Identify server configuration files: **217-219.**
5. Use server script files to automate console commands: **217-219.**
6. Determine requirements for Java application support on the NetWare server: **224-228.**
7. Define and configure the NetWare GUI: **228-235.**
8. Identify administrative tasks performed with ConsoleOne: **236-244.**
9. Identify how to remotely manage the console: **219-223.**
10. Define methods for prote.cting your server: **223-224.**

Section 3: Building a TCP/IP Network Using NetWare 5.1

1. Configure a DHCP server: **104-130, 131-147.**
2. Create a private network with NAT: **90-93.**
3. Configure a DNS server: **104-130, 148-164.**
4. Configure dynamic DNS: **148-164.**
5. Configure SLP: **93-103.**

Section 4: Building an Internet Infrastructure with NetWare 5.1

1. Describe and configure NetWare Enterprise Web Server: **171-185.**
2. Describe and configure NetWare FTP Server: **186-189.**
3. Describe and configure NetWare News Server: **191-193.**
4. Describe and configure NetWare MultiMedia Server: **194-196.**
5. Describe and configure NetWare Web Search Server: **196-199.**
6. Describe the benefits of using WebSphere: **199-202.**

Section 5: Managing Novell Certificate Server

1. Describe public key cryptography: **297-300.**
2. Describe Novell Certificate Server: **301-307.**
3. Perform Novell Certificate Server tasks: **307-314.**

Section 6: Setting Up a Novell Storage Service (NSS) System

1. Define NSS and its components: **245-246.**

2. Describe the NSS architecture: **246-250**.

3. List the advantages and disadvantages of using NSS: **245-246**.

4. Implement NSS: **250-253**.

5. Manage storage groups and NSS volumes: **253-254**.

Section 7: Managing and Optimizing the NetWare 5.1 Platform

1. Use NetWare Management Portal: **337-339**.

2. Define NetWare 5.1 memory management: **320-323**.

3. Describe and manage virtual memory: **323-326**.

4. Describe and manage NetWare applications: **340-341**.

5. Describe and manage protected address performance: **326-329**.

6. Evaluate MONITOR screen statistics: **329-332**.

7. Identify how to monitor and modify cache performance: **332-335**.

8. Identify server buffer and packet parameters: **335-337, 348-353**.

9. Identify methods for optimizing disk space: **341-347**.

Section 8: Maintaining Novell Directory Services

1. Identify the benefits of NDS eDirectory: **270-271**.

2. Define NDS replication and synchronization: **272-277**.

3. Identify basic administration procedures for the NDS database: **278-280**.

4. Troubleshoot NDS database inconsistencies: **281**.

5. Identify NDS repair procedures: **281-288.**

6. Recovering from a crashed SYS volume: **289-290.**

Section 9: Migrating to IP from IPX

1. Configure the Compatibility Mode Driver (CMD): **87-90.**

2. Configure CMD to provide Migration Agent and backbone support: **87-90.**

3. Identify IPX to IP migration strategies: **78-87.**

Section 10: Backing Up Servers and Workstations

1. Explain backup strategies: **254-258.**

2. Back up data with NWBACK32: **258-262.**

3. Restore data with NWBACK32: **258-262.**

Novell Education Course 575: NDS Design and Implementation

With NDS comes great responsibility! Gone are the days when you could yank NetWare out of the box and slam it into a server over lunch. Now you must fully understand the "purpose" of your WAN before installing the very first server. The good news is Novell Education has developed a special design course just for you.

In this course, we will master the first three steps of network construction – namely, NDS preparation, NDS design, and NDS implementation. In the first step, we will gather ACME data and build a project team. Then, in Step 2, we will construct ACME's NDS tree with the help of naming standards, tree design guidelines, partitioning, time synchronization, and resource accessibility. Finally, in Step 3, we'll execute the plan with a comprehensive NDS implementation schedule.

This is one of the trickiest tests of them all. *Study hard!*

Section 1: Preparing for NDS Design

1. Describe basic NDS concepts: 400-417.
2. Describe why NDS design is important to the success of a network: 362-364.
3. Explain the roles needed to complete an NDS design: 373-377.
4. Explain the major tasks in an NDS design cycle: 364-373.
5. Explain NDS design implications for merging two companys' trees: 378-393.

Section 2: Creating an NDS Structure

1. Create a naming standards document: 418-426.
2. Design the upper layers of an NDS tree: 426-444.
3. Draft the lower layers of an NDS tree: 445.
4. Finalize the design of the lower layers of an NDS tree: 446-450.

Section 3: Determining a Partition and Replica Strategy

1. Explain NDS partitioning and replication: 467-474.
2. Determine a partition and replica strategy: 475-487.

Section 4: Planning the User Environment

1. Create a user accessibility needs analysis document: 451-452.
2. Create an accessibility guidelines document: 452-453.
3. Create an administrative strategies document: 454-459.

Section 5: Planning a Time Synchronization Strategy

1. Explain why time must be synchronized on the network: 494.
2. Set up time synchronization: 495-502.
3. Plan a time synchronization strategy: 502-507.

Section 6: Implementing an NDS Design

1. Merge NDS trees: 514-525.
2. Create, modify, and manage partitions and replicas: 488-494.
3. Modify the NDS tree: 525-530.
4. Implement a User Environment Plan: 525-530.

Novell Education Course 580: Service and Support

Welcome to NetWare Service & Support — an exciting "hands on" troubleshooting course.

In this course, we will learn how to troubleshoot four different network components: NICs and cabling, hard drives, workstations, and printing. In addition, we'll acquire a variety of valuable troubleshooting tools and learn some preventative server fitness and network optimization.

This course gives you a chance to prove your worth.

Section 1: Using a Systematic Troubleshooting Process

1. Use the 6-step Network Troubleshooting Model to solve problems: 538-551.
2. Use system diagnostic software to troubleshoot problems: 551-553.
3. Document your network to avoid or prepare for recurrence: 545-551.

Section 2: Using Electronic Research Tools When Troubleshooting

1. Find troubleshooting information with Novell Internet Services: 557-563.
2. Find troubleshooting information with SupportSource 2000: 553-557.
3. Choose the appropriate research tool: 563-564.

Section 3: Installing and Troubleshooting Cables and Network Boards

1. Describe network cabling types: 586-591.
2. Configure and install network boards: 574-591.
3. Support a Token Ring network: 616-628.
4. Support an Ethernet network: 592-615.
5. Support an FDDI network: 629-635.
6. Support an ATM network: 629-635.

Section 4: Installing and Troubleshooting Network Storage Devices

1. Describe basic hard disk principles: 642-659.
2. Install a SCSI hard disk: 660-677.
3. Install an IDE hard disk: 660-677.
4. Install and configure a CD as a NetWare volume: 686-691.
5. Prepare a hard disk for use: 665-677.
6. Create a NetWare Storage System: 665-677.

7. Set up disk mirroring and duplexing: **679-685.**

8. Troubleshooting common SCSI and IDE disk problems: **649-650, 658-659.**

Section 5: Troubleshooting Novell Client Problems

1. Describe the Novell Client for Windows 98: **700-708.**

2. Troubleshoot the Novell Client on a Windows 98 workstation: **708-732.**

3. Describe the Novell Client for Windows NT: **700-708.**

4. Troubleshoot the Novell Client on a Windows NT workstation: **708-732.**

Section 6: Troubleshooting Network Printing Problems

1. Explain NDPS, its components, and printer types: **737-767.**

2. Use general troubleshooting principles to solve NDPS printing problems: **767-787.**

3. Troubleshoot common NDPS printing problems: **767-787.**

4. Explain queue-based printing, its components, and processes: **788-789.**

5. Troubleshoot queue-based network printing problems: **789-792.**

6. Troubleshoot queue-based printing problems at the workstation: **793-794.**

7. Troubleshoot queue-based printing problems at the print queue: **794-795.**

8. Troubleshoot queue-based printing problems at the print server: **795-796.**

9. Troubleshoot queue-based printing problems at the remote workstation: **796-798.**

10. Troubleshoot queue-based printing problems at the printer: **796-798.**

Section 7: Troubleshooting Server and Network Problems

1. Install the newest server software: **807-809.**
2. Resolve server abends and lockups: **810-816.**
3. Create a memory image to resolve server abends and lockups: **813-815.**
4. Troubleshoot performance bottlenecks: **821-825.**
5. Use LANalyzer to diagnose performance problems: **825-832.**
6. Explain disaster recovery options: **816-820.**

Novell Education Course 565: Networking Technologies

Welcome to the World of Computer Networking—an exciting "hands off" journey through acronyms and communications theory.

In Networking Technologies, we will venture into a "hands off" conceptual course that surveys the entire world of computer networking, from the OSI model to IP routing to IBM's SNA gateway (and everything in between). First, we'll begin with a brief introduction to the OSI model and we'll learn about its three primary functions: communications, networking, and services. Then, we'll explore each of these functions in excruciating depth.

This is the last of five required CNE courses. Good luck, and enjoy the show!

Networking Technologies Volume I

Section 1: Introducing Computer Networking

1. Define *computer networking*: **840-841.**
2. Contrast the features of the computing models: **841-846.**
3. Compare *local area network* (LAN) and *wide area network* (WAN): **841-846.**

4 Identify the three basic networking elements, and describe the roles of clients, servers, peers, transmission media, and protocols in delivering network services: **855-856.**

Section 2: Network Services

1. Identify the functions and features of the five basic network services: **1071-1072.**

2. Determine when network file services should be implemented: **1072-1074.**

3. Determine when network print services should be implemented: **1074-1075.**

4. Determine when network message services should be implemented: **1076.**

5. Determine when network application services should be implemented: **1076.**

6. Determine when and how network database services should be implemented: **1077.**

7. Identify how the delivery of individual network services is affected by centralized and distributed network architectures: **841-842.**

Section 3: Transmission Media

1. Define the term *transmission media* as it relates to computer networks: **880-882.**

2. Identify the appropriate transmission media to meet a stated business need: **882-911.**

Section 4: Connectivity Devices

1. Identify the general functions of connectivity devices in computer networks and computer internetworks: **912.**

2. Identify the appropriate network connectivity devices: **912-918.**

3. Identify the appropriate the internetwork connectivity devices: **918-923.**

Section 5: Network Protocols and Models

1. Identify why rules are needed in computer networks: 857-860.

2. Identify the seven layers of the OSI reference model and how the layers interact: 857-860.

3. Identify the relationship between the OSI reference model and computer network protocols: 861-867, 934-940.

Section 6: The OSI Physical Layer

1. Identify the basic purpose of the OSI Physical Layer: 877-878.

2. List the characteristics of the two common connection types used in computer networks: 878-880.

3. List the characteristics of the five common physical topologies used in computer networks: 923-925.

4. Identify the difference between digital and analog signals: 924-930.

5. List the ways a digital signal can be manipulated to represent data: 926-929.

6. List the ways an analog signal can be manipulated to represent data: 929-930.

7. Identify the ways that bit synchronization can be achieved: 930-931.

8. Identify the two bandwidth use methods and explain how multiplexing can be used in each: 931-934.

Section 7: The OSI Data Link Layer

1. Identify the basic purpose of the OSI Data Link Layer: 934.

2. Identify the characteristics of the two logical topologies: 934.

3. Identify the characteristics of the three media access methods: 934-940.

4. Identify the nature and uses of the addresses defined and managed at the Data Link Layer: **940.**

5. Identify the characteristics of the three transmission synchronization techniques that can be used at the Data Link Layer: **941-942.**

6. Identify the characteristics of the connection services that can be implemented at the Data Link Layer: **942-944.**

Section 8: The OSI Network Layer

1. Identify the basic purpose of the OSI Network Layer: **959-962.**

2. Identify the uses of the addresses defined at the Network Layer: **962-963.**

3. Identify the characteristics of the three switching methods: **981-985.**

4. Identify the characteristics of the two route discovery methods: **986-988.**

5. Identify the characteristics of the two route selection methods: **988-989.**

6. Identify the characteristics of the connection services that can be implemented at the Network Layer: **963-964.**

7. Identify the basic purpose of gateway services: **992-993, 922-923.**

Section 9: The OSI Transport Layer

1. Identify the basic purpose of the OSI Transport Layer: **994.**

2. Identify the two address/name resolution methods and list the characteristics of each: **994.**

3. Identify the addresses used at the Transport Layer and list the characteristics of each: **994.**

4. Identify the primary functions of segment development: **994.**

5. Identify the connection services used at the Transport Layer and list the characteristics of each: **997-999.**

Section 10: The OSI Session Layer

1. Identify the basic purpose of the OSI Session Layer: **1063-1064.**

2. Identify the characteristics of the three dialog control methods: **1064-1067.**

3. Identify the characteristics of the three elements of session administration: **1064-1067.**

Section 11: The OSI Presentation Layer

1. Identify the basic purpose of the OSI Presentation Layer: **1067.**

2. Identify the characteristics of the translation methods that can be implemented at the Presentation Layer: **1067-1068.**

3. Identify the characteristics of the encryption methods that can be used at the Presentation Layer: **1067-1068.**

Section 12: The OSI Application Layer

1. Identify the basic purpose of the OSI Application Layer: **1069.**

2. Identify the characteristics of the two service advertisement methods that can be used at the Application Layer: **1069-1070.**

3. Identify the characteristics of the service use methods that can be implemented at the Application Layer: **1070-1071.**

Networking Technologies Volume 2

Section 1: Computer Networks and the OSI Model

1. Explain why networking protocols are important: **857-860.**

2. Outline the major tasks of each of the layers of the OSI reference model: **858-859.**

3. Contrast the characteristics and uses of the physical and logical topologies that are used in computer networks: **861-867**.

4. Map the functions of the network interface boards, repeaters, active hubs, intelligent or switching hubs, bridges, routers and gateways to the appropriate OSI layers: **861-867, 912-913**.

Section 2: Lower Layer Protocols

1. Identify the function of the IEEE 802.x standards in computer networks: **948-953**.

2. Identify the media access procedures, transmission media, connectivity devices, and basic design rules of the IEEE 802.3 standard and Ethernet: **950**.

3. Identify the media access procedures, transmission media, connectivity devices, and basic design rules of the IEEE 802.3u standard and Fast Ethernet: **950**.

4. Identify the media access procedures, transmission media, connectivity devices, and basic design rules of the IEEE 802.5 standard and Token Ring: **950**.

5. Identify the media access procedures, transmission media, connectivity devices, and basic design rules of FDDI: **947-949**.

6. Identify the Wide Area Network (WAN) protocols SLIP, PPP, X.25, frame relay, ISDN, and ATM: **944-948**.

Section 3: Bridging, Switching, and Routing

1. List the reasons connectivity devices are needed on LANs and WANs: **914-918**.

2. Distinguish between Ethernet and token ring repeaters: **916-917**.

3. List three benefits of bridging and three types of bridges: **965-966.**

4. Explain transparent bridge operation: **967-979.**

5. Configure a spanning tree network: **972-977.**

6. Explain source-routing bridge operation: **980-981.**

7. Explain the use of switching hubs: **983-984.**

8. Identify the benefits of using token ring switches: **985.**

9. Identify and describe distance vector and link state dynamic routing protocols: **987-991.**

10. Identify the characteristics of nonroutable protocols, and name a method for dealing with a nonroutable protocol: **991-992.**

11. Identify different kinds of combination devices: **992-993.**

12. Decide when to use bridges, switches, and routers: **992-993.**

Section 4: IP Addressing

1. Define the IP address structure: **1012-1014.**

2. Identify network classes: **1014-1015.**

3. Obtain a registered IP address: **1016.**

4. Register a domain name: **1016.**

5. Assign addresses to hosts: **1030-1037.**

6. Describe the function of host names, host tables, and DNS: **1030-1037.**

Section 5: Creating Subnets

1. Explain the purpose of subnets: **1017-1018.**
2. Define a subnet mask: **1018-1020.**
3. Describe how subnet masks are used: **1018-1020.**
4. Assign subnet addresses: **1020-1024.**
5. Create subnet masks and assign subnet addresses for a sample company: **1020-1027.**

Section 6: Creating Supernets

1. Describe the purpose of supernets: **1027-1029.**
2. Identify the IP address criteria used for supernets: **1027-1029.**
3. Describe routing considerations when creating supernets: **1027-1029.**

Section 7:TCP/IP Protocol Stack

1. Identify the components of the TCP/IP protocol suite as they relate to the OSI and DoD models: **1006-1012.**
2. Describe distance vector routing with IP: **987-991.**
3. Describe link state routing with IP: **987-991.**
4. Determine which protocol from the TCP/IP protocol suite should be implemented to provide a needed functional or correct an error condition in your network: **1006-1012, 1029-1040.**
5. Identify the uses of protocol analyzers in managing a TCP/IP network: **825-832.**
6. Describe IPv6: **1008-1009.**

Section 8: IPX Protocol Stack

1. Describe the purpose of internetwork Packet Exchange (IPX) and Sequenced Packet Exchange (SPX): **1041-1045.**

2. Identify and describe the components and characteristics of IPX addresses: **1041-1045.**

3. Identify the components of the IPX/SPX protocol suite as they relate to the OSI model: **1041.**

4. Describe the IPX routing protocols RIP and SAP: **1045-1047.**

5. Describe link state routing with IPX NLSP and compare RIP/SAP, NLSP, and OSPF functionality: **1049-1055.**

6. Identify other IPX network services and what they do: **1048.**

7. Explain the benefits of protocol analyzers in managing an IPX/SPX network: **825-832.**

Section 9: Directory Services

1. List the features of X.500: **1098-1099.**

2. List the features of LDAP: **1100-1102.**

APPENDIX C

Solutions to Exercises and Puzzles

Chapter 1: NetWare 5.1 Installation

Lab Exercise 1.3: Getting Started (Word Search)

N	O	N	P	R	O	D	U	C	T	I	O	N	N	R	I
S	F	N	L	S	E	N	V	E	L	O	P	E	N	M	B
S	E	C	U	R	E	R	M	L	A	A	T	A	N	E	A
E	Y	X	S	D	I	S	O	L	A	T	E	D	S	T	T
R	S	E	Z	I	M	O	T	S	U	C	D	Y	H	V	C
V	D	O	S	P	A	R	T	I	T	I	O	N	B	K	H
E	M	A	N	G	K	D	R	Q	O	W	V	G	Y	E	N
R	E	G	I	O	N	A	L	S	E	T	T	I	N	G	S
I	B	F	O	E	W	S	K	V	X	J	B	F	F	I	J
D	X	I	G	R	S	W	D	T	E	T	I	J	V	M	M
N	C	C	U	P	R	U	Z	B	C	Q	K	I	Z	H	D
U	J	U	L	H	I	V	P	V	N	R	T	X	A	E	O
M	C	G	T	I	P	J	D	Z	C	N	F	I	N	V	B
B	R	B	T	U	V	Q	B	C	F	F	C	E	S	S	V
E	K	K	L	O	V	S	Z	N	J	I	V	L	N	H	V
R	S	Z	B	H	Q	V	B	X	X	P	F	L	Q	W	G

1. AUTOEXEC.NCF
2. Batch
3. CLA
4. Customize
5. DOS Partition
6. Isolated
7. MLA
8. NLS Envelope

9. Non-Production
10. NSS
11. Regional settings
12. Secure
13. Server ID number
14. TTS
15. VLA

Lab Exercise 1.4: NetWare 5.1 Installation (Crossword)

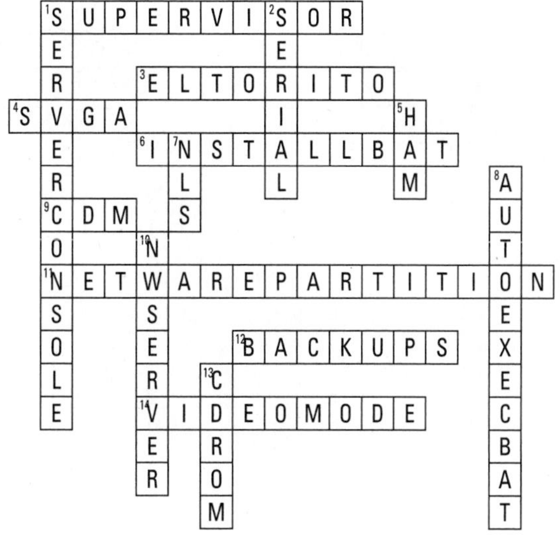

Chapter 2: NetWare 5.1 IP Services

Lab Exercise 2.4: Migrating to IP and DNS/DHCP (Word Search)

A	O	N	Z	O	N	E	T	R	A	N	S	F	E	R	H	V
P	N	R	E	L	A	Y	A	G	E	N	T	C	P	U	K	S
P	L	A	M	I	O	B	O	O	T	P	H	V	H	I	W	T
C	I	S	U	B	N	E	T	P	O	O	L	K	F	E	G	W
H	N	M	V	T	M	P	L	O	C	A	L	I	T	Y	M	O
D	O	M	A	I	N	N	A	M	E	S	P	A	C	E	H	A
H	D	N	S	S	E	R	V	E	R	X	W	P	C	A	H	Q
C	O	M	P	A	T	I	B	I	L	I	T	Y	M	O	D	E
P	T	C	K	C	Z	E	P	K	S	T	M	I	B	U	O	E
S	I	U	I	C	D	Q	R	B	H	S	X	R	F	H	Q	K
E	P	T	G	R	U	H	X	K	P	N	G	C	X	D	L	H
R	G	W	M	L	Z	C	R	M	C	I	L	D	Z	H	W	Y
V	H	F	U	B	Q	P	M	S	V	P	Q	P	W	Y	S	H
E	J	I	L	B	N	U	T	L	X	I	H	J	K	P	O	Q
R	L	M	I	G	R	A	T	I	O	N	A	G	E	N	T	I
H	H	N	C	B	U	Q	D	H	T	D	I	R	Q	N	R	T

1. BOOTP
2. Compatibility Mode
3. DHCP
4. DHCP Server
5. DNIPINST
6. DNS
7. DNS Server
8. Domain Name Space
9. IPX
10. Locality

11. Master
12. Migration Agent
13. Relay Agent
14. Replica
15. SAR
16. Schema
17. SLP
18. Subnet Pool
19. TCP
20. Zone Transfer

Lab Exercise 2.5: NetWare 5.1 IP Services (Crossword)

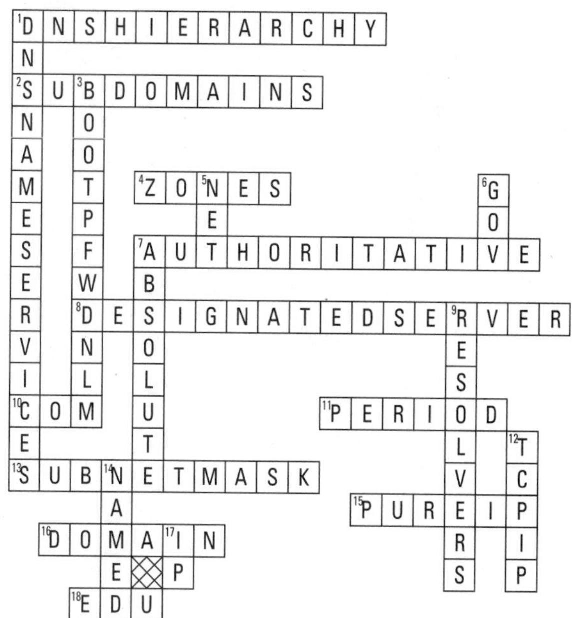

Chapter 3: NetWare 5.1 Internet Infrastructure

Lab Exercise 3.1: The NetWare Web (Word Search)

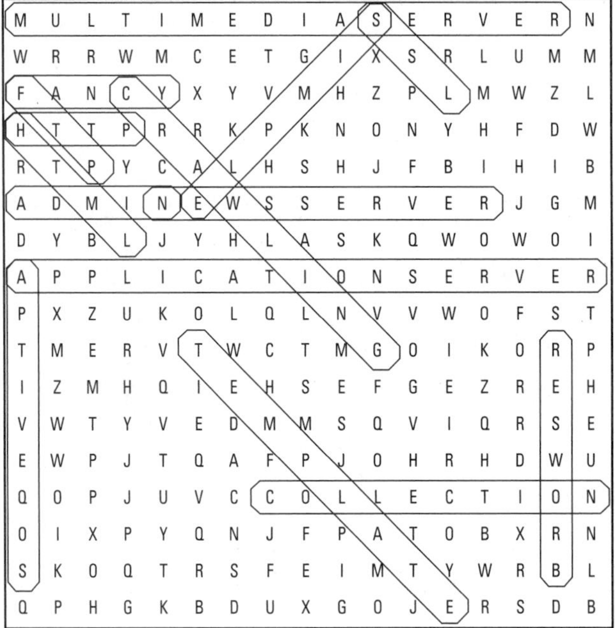

1. Adaptive QoS
2. Admin
3. Application Server
4. Browsers
5. Collection
6. Crawling

7. Fancy
8. FTP
9. HTML
10. HTTP
11. Multimedia Server
12. News Server
13. Simple
14. SSL
15. Template

Lab Exercise 3.2: NetWare 5.1 Internet Infrastructure (Crossword)

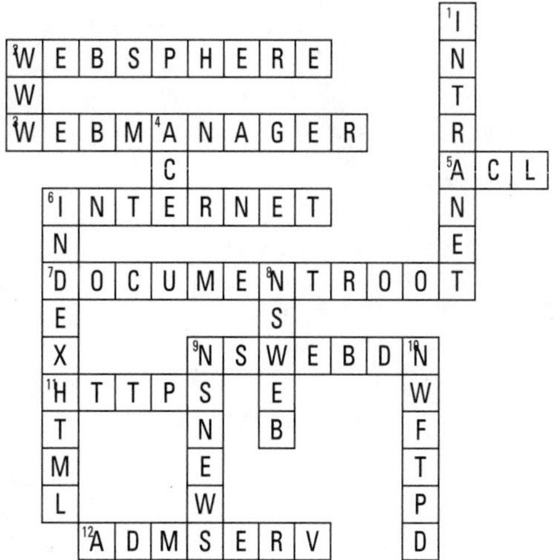

Chapter 4: NetWare 5.1 Advanced Server Management

Lab Exercise 4.3: The NetWare 5.1 Server (Word Search)

Q	D	D	C	D	H	C	T	U	C	T	R	O	H	S	H	Q
R	H	N	M	L	O	A	D	B	A	L	A	N	C	I	N	G
T	S	U	G	Y	T	R	E	F	R	E	S	H	R	S	G	W
Q	A	P	P	L	E	T	V	I	E	W	E	R	F	R	T	E
D	L	L	T	Q	Q	C	E	V	E	D	P	Q	H	E	H	J
Y	P	F	I	J	M	B	Q	C	U	K	G	I	M	M	E	G
N	J	A	V	A	A	P	P	L	I	C	A	T	I	O	N	T
A	A	A	U	M	O	N	I	T	O	R	N	L	M	T	E	G
M	V	M	V	W	Y	N	P	J	M	Q	H	D	U	E	T	X
I	A	D	E	A	G	S	N	H	G	G	F	L	K	C	W	O
C	C	K	K	S	A	S	E	V	P	S	H	R	D	O	O	T
A	L	J	P	H	P	P	T	R	I	T	D	O	K	N	R	I
L	A	H	T	M	L	A	P	B	V	P	J	W	O	S	K	F
L	S	R	N	X	W	R	C	L	P	E	E	Y	E	O	F	B
Y	S	X	S	W	V	F	U	E	E	F	R	M	T	L	S	N
O	E	M	J	P	R	E	E	M	P	T	I	O	N	E	V	E

1. Applet Viewer
2. Dynamically
3. HTML
4. Java Applet
5. Java Application
6. Java Class
7. Load Balancing
8. LRU
9. MONITOR.NLM

10. MPK
11. My Server
12. My World
13. Name Space
14. Preemption
15. Refresh
16. Remote Console
17. Scheduling
18. Shortcut
19. The Network
20. VESA

Lab Exercise 4.4: NetWare 5.1 Advanced Server Management (Crossword)

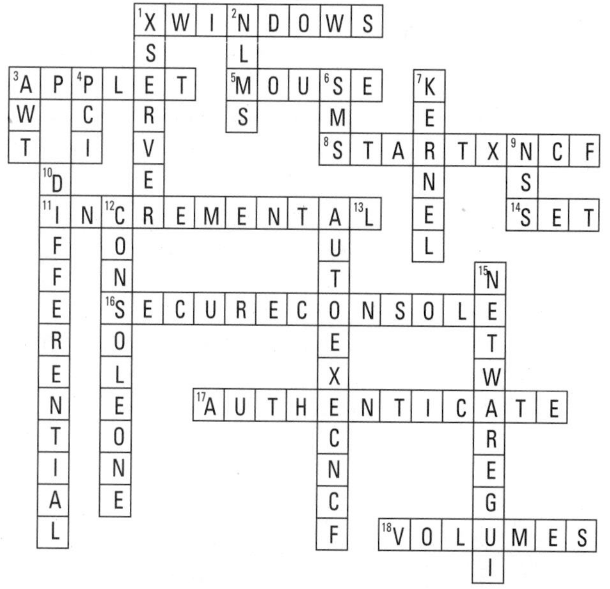

Chapter 5: Advanced NDS Management

Lab Exercise 5.1: Maintaining the NDS Tree (Word Search)

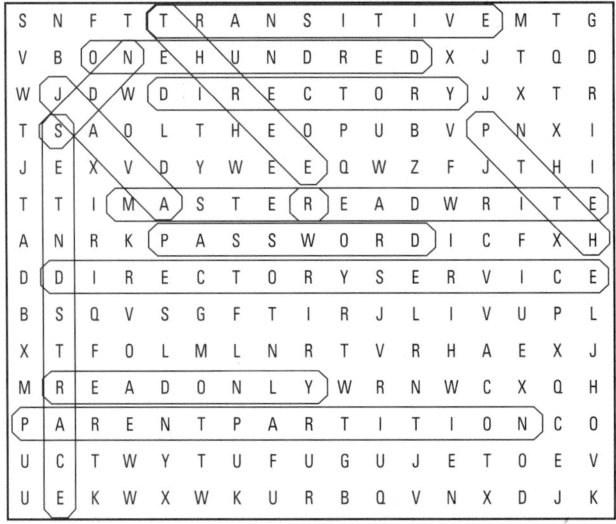

1. Directory
2. Directory Service
3. HTTP
4. Java
5. LDAP
6. Master
7. NDS
8. One Hundred

9. Parent Partition
10. Password
11. Read-Only
12. Read/Write
13. SET NDS TRACE
14. Three
15. Transitive

Lab Exercise 5.2: Advanced NDS Management (Crossword)

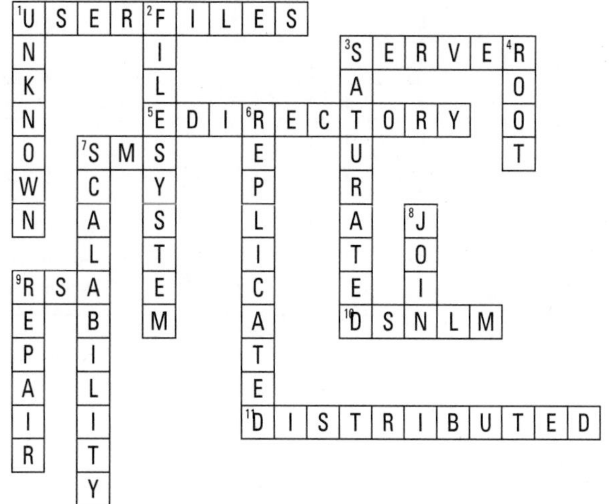

Chapter 6: NetWare 5.1 Advanced Security Management

Lab Exercise 6.1: Novell Certificate Server (Word Search)

C	E	N	C	R	Y	P	T	I	O	N	S	H	E	M
O	G	B	I	S	X	B	F	T	H	U	U	X	W	N
N	N	M	L	C	R	E	D	F	R	O	P	I	N	N
S	P	U	B	L	I	C	K	E	Y	O	E	A	I	Y
O	R	C	R	Y	P	T	O	G	R	A	P	H	Y	S
L	I	F	E	S	P	A	N	T	X	Y	D	M	H	P
E	V	G	T	G	J	J	G	K	E	Y	P	A	I	R
O	A	U	T	H	E	N	T	I	C	A	T	I	O	N
N	T	R	U	S	T	E	D	R	O	O	T	J	K	F
E	E	K	A	H	S	D	N	A	H	B	E	V	S	M
H	K	G	J	B	I	J	I	J	W	B	J	F	T	L
J	E	Y	N	L	X	W	F	K	H	J	K	D	K	N
N	Y	Y	K	D	H	L	E	M	K	T	I	X	T	X

1. Authentication
2. ConsoleOne
3. Cryptography
4. CSR
5. DER
6. Encryption
7. Export
8. Handshake

9. Import
10. Key Pair
11. Life Span
12. NICI
13. Private Key
14. Public Key
15. Trusted Root

Lab Exercise 6.2: Advanced Security Management (Crossword)

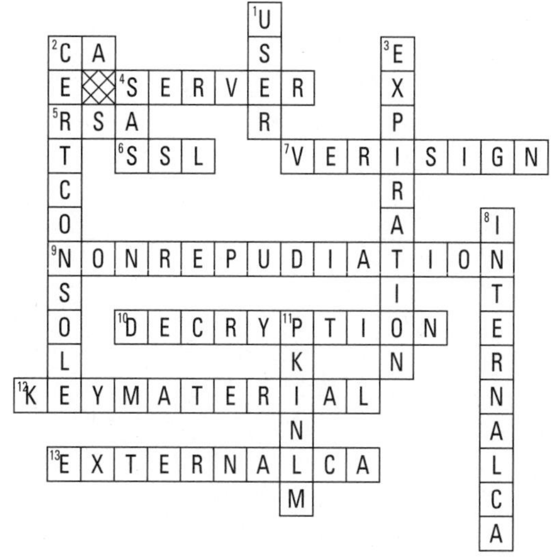

Chapter 7: NetWare 5.1 Optimization

Lab Exercise 7.1: Monitoring and Optimizing the Server (Word Search)

F	R	E	E	G	C	Q	L	P	E	H	V	T	V	E	U	J	X	Q
I	G	J	N	A	U	T	O	E	X	E	C	N	C	F	W	Q	Q	I
L	B	Q	C	O	M	P	R	E	S	S	I	O	N	R	A	T	I	O
E	D	H	O	F	Q	D	N	G	P	K	K	I	Z	C	E	X	X	M
C	E	I	P	W	J	B	Z	A	M	A	X	I	M	U	M	V	S	D
A	S	E	R	V	I	C	E	P	R	O	C	E	S	S	E	S	W	X
C	V	B	B	T	W	E	N	T	Y	M	Y	K	R	B	H	Q	A	S
H	R	C	H	B	Y	N	T	S	R	U	B	T	E	K	C	A	P	Q
I	Q	W	D	N	H	S	W	V	O	Y	W	S	N	T	N	E	F	J
N	N	C	D	V	J	A	G	Z	Q	I	C	M	J	X	K	I	I	B
G	A	R	B	A	G	E	C	O	L	L	E	C	T	I	O	N	L	P
E	S	I	V	Q	W	H	C	D	D	S	M	W	F	Q	H	O	E	E
Y	Z	Q	Y	W	O	J	S	T	A	R	T	U	P	N	C	F	C	D
D	Z	K	T	W	B	H	C	D	X	M	O	X	D	K	B	M	O	C
Q	K	E	R	N	E	L	A	D	D	R	E	S	S	L	S	U	C	O
F	Z	A	L	T	K	C	T	G	I	A	X	I	E	Q	G	E	C	O
R	H	P	I	Q	W	P	M	G	F	L	Z	V	V	U	T	N	T	G
J	L	V	I	R	T	U	A	L	M	E	M	O	R	Y	J	X	F	N

1. AUTOEXEC.NCF
2. Block Size
3. Cache
4. Compression Ratio
5. Dirty
6. File Caching
7. Free
8. Garbage Collection
9. Kernel Address
10. Maximum

11. One
12. Packet
13. Packet Burst
14. Page
15. PRB
16. Service Processes
17. STARTUP.NCF
18. Swap File
19. Twenty
20. Virtual Memory

Lab Exercise 7.2: NetWare 5.1 Optimization (Crossword)

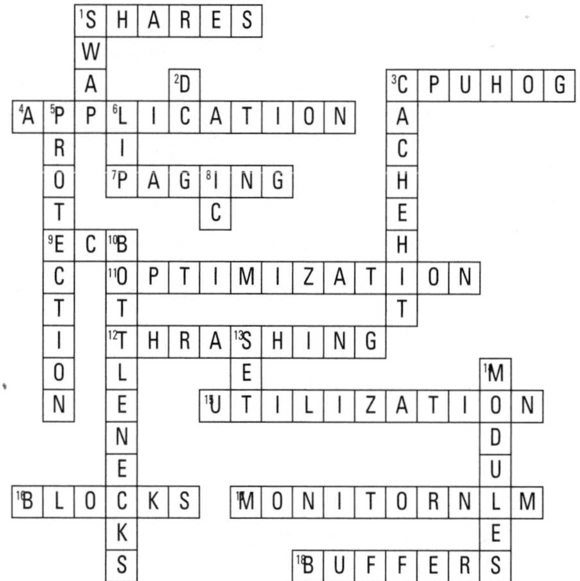

Chapter 8: NDS Preparation

Lab Exercise 8.1: Building the ACME Team (Word Search)

P	R	O	J	E	C	T	S	C	O	P	E	O	M	D	X	S	L
I	E	R	N	Y	U	O	B	F	B	G	D	V	S	I	S	A	T
L	S	G	D	A	T	A	G	A	T	H	E	R	I	N	G	Z	Q
O	O	A	S	L	U	H	B	H	P	R	S	H	O	A	D	Z	R
T	U	N	D	S	P	R	E	P	A	R	A	T	I	O	N	X	R
P	R	I	V	C	F	T	A	P	M	P	Z	J	N	K	G	U	X
R	C	Z	I	C	L	D	S	T	R	U	C	T	U	R	E	D	I
O	E	A	N	W	O	R	K	F	L	O	W	K	M	P	U	H	S
G	L	T	E	B	V	C	O	N	N	E	C	T	I	V	I	T	Y
R	I	I	L	P	R	O	J	E	C	T	T	E	A	M	B	U	Q
A	S	O	A	Q	K	D	F	O	M	N	H	R	S	D	A	V	H
M	T	N	D	E	S	I	G	N	I	N	P	U	T	S	X	D	H
R	S	A	L	J	H	L	A	C	I	N	H	C	E	T	A	B	C
S	C	L	S	Q	Q	V	H	U	U	R	X	J	W	M	V	B	T

1. Connectivity
2. Data Gathering
3. Design Inputs
4. NDS
5. NDS Preparation
6. Organizational
7. Pilot Program
8. Project Scope
9. Project Team
10. Resource Lists
11. SDLC
12. Structured
13. Technical
14. The Process
15. Workflow

Lab Exercise 8.2: NDS Preparation (Crossword)

1 I	N	2 C	R	E	M	E	3 N	T	A	4 L							
		A					D			I							
		M			5 T	E	S	T	I	N	G	L	A	B			
6 C		P					T			E							
H		U					R		7 W	A	N	L	A	Y	O	U	T
8 R	E	S	O	U	R	C	E	S	⊠	R							
O		M					E		9 A		10 M						
N		A							C		A						
I		11 P	R	O	J	E	C	T	M	A	N	A	G	E	R		
C		S							E		A						
L											G						
E							12 N	D	S	D	E	S	I	G	N		
13 S	P	I	14 R	A	L						M						
			O								E						
			L								N						
15 N	D	S	E	X	P	E	R	T			T						
			S														

Chapter 9: NDS Tree Design

Lab Exercise 9.1: Understanding NDS Objects (Matching)

Part I

1. L
2. C
3. L
4. L
5. C

6. L

7. L

8. L

9. L

10. C

Part II

1. Container (Organizational Unit)

2. Leaf

3. Leaf

4. Leaf

5. Container (Organization)

6. Leaf

7. Container (Country or Organizational Unit)

8. Leaf

9. Container (Organizational Unit)

10. Leaf

Lab Exercise 9.2: Designing the ACME NDS Tree (Word Search)

R	M	R	J	P	I	I	U	E	F	L	M	K	D	F
D	A	O	B	J	E	C	T	C	O	N	T	E	S	T
S	C	R	B	T	Y	P	E	L	E	S	S	N	U	Q
X	P	G	B	I	W	A	N	L	I	N	K	S	O	Z
T	P	A	B	O	L	R	E	M	O	T	E	P	T	V
N	T	N	Q	K	R	E	G	I	O	N	A	L	I	B
W	D	I	S	T	I	N	G	U	I	S	H	E	D	U
H	W	Z	C	O	N	T	E	X	T	L	E	S	S	G
J	A	A	H	W	W	K	Y	Z	V	R	J	Q	T	P
V	N	T	E	G	P	R	O	P	E	R	T	I	E	S
U	J	I	M	U	H	O	Y	U	E	Y	N	H	G	R
N	V	O	A	D	Q	F	N	K	I	F	D	H	O	K
C	E	N	T	R	A	L	I	Z	E	D	U	F	J	T
Z	E	H	F	U	N	C	T	I	O	N	A	L	S	B

1. Centralized
2. Contextless
3. Distinguished
4. Functional
5. Mobile
6. Object Context
7. Organization
8. Parent
9. Properties
10. Regional
11. Remote
12. Schema
13. Typeful
14. Typeless
15. WAN Links

Lab Exercise 9.3: NDS Tree Design (Crossword)

```
   G E O G R A P H Y
       B   O
       J   O R G C H A R T
       E   T         L
       C       L     I
 C O N T A I N E R   A
 O   A         A     S   F
 M   M         D         L E A F
 M   E         I         A
 O   C U R R E N T C O N T E X T
 N   O         G
 N   N   P R O P E R T Y
 A   T   Y     E
 M   E   R     R
 E   X   A     I
     T   M   C O U N T R Y
         I     D
         D
```

Numbered entries: 1 GEOGRAPHY, 2 OBJECT, 3 ROOT, 4 ORGCHART, 5 ALIAS, 6 LEADINGPERIOD, 7 CONTAINER / COMMONNAME, 8 NAMECONTEXT, 9 FLAT, 10 LEAF, 11 CURRENTCONTEXT, 12 PROPERTY / PYRAMID, 13 COUNTRY

Chapter 10: NDS Partitioning and Time Synchronization Design

Lab Exercise 10.1: Designing ACME's NDS Partitions (Word Search)

T	I	M	E	S	Y	N	C	N	L	M	U	E	P	O
N	E	T	W	O	R	K	T	I	M	E	M	M	A	V
A	X	N	W	T	M	N	L	M	E	V	T	L	R	E
M	N	X	R	E	P	L	I	C	A	L	I	S	T	R
E	E	Q	G	E	N	L	V	U	K	I	U	L	I	L
R	E	E	F	Q	L	T	C	N	S	M	I	V	T	A
E	W	B	U	G	J	Q	Y	X	I	Y	I	Q	I	P
S	Y	N	C	H	R	O	N	I	Z	A	T	I	O	N
O	A	Q	M	W	K	N	B	Z	E	D	S	L	N	R
L	E	C	N	A	R	E	L	O	T	T	L	U	A	F
U	T	S	I	L	D	E	R	U	G	I	F	N	O	C
T	C	T	R	E	F	E	R	E	N	C	E	W	A	R
I	I	I	U	K	D	I	D	G	U	D	D	G	X	N
O	R	N	O	I	T	A	C	I	L	P	E	R	O	J
N	I	I	B	B	F	B	T	O	B	V	S	Q	Y	L

1. Configured List
2. Fault Tolerance
3. Name Resolution
4. Network Time
5. Overlap
6. Partition
7. Polling
8. Reference

9. Replica List
10. Replication
11. Synchronization
12. Ten
13. TIMESYNC.NLM
14. Twenty
15. WTM.NLM

Lab Exercise 10.2: NDS Partitioning and Time Synchronization Design (Crossword)

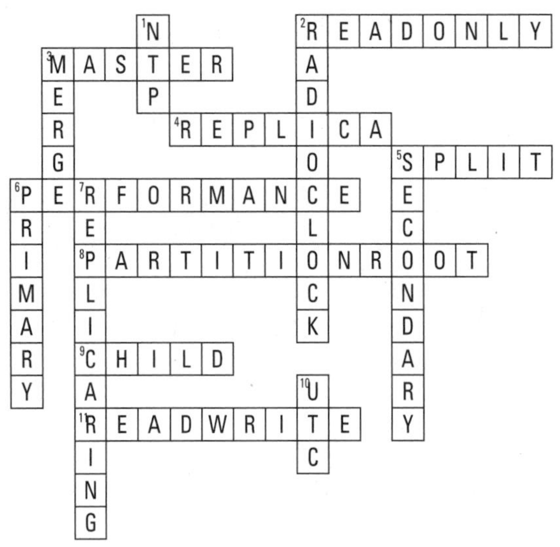

Chapter 11: NDS Implementation

Lab Exercise 11.1: Implementing ACME's NDS Design (Word Search)

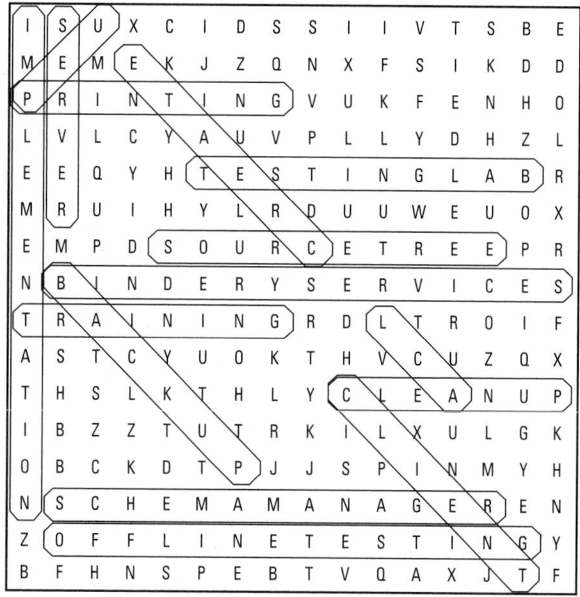

1. ACL
2. Backup
3. Bindery Services
4. Cleanup
5. Client

6. Create
7. Implementation
8. Off-Line Testing
9. Printing
10. Schema Manager
11. Server
12. Source Tree
13. Testing Lab
14. Training
15. UEP

Lab Exercise 11.2: NDS Implementation (Crossword)

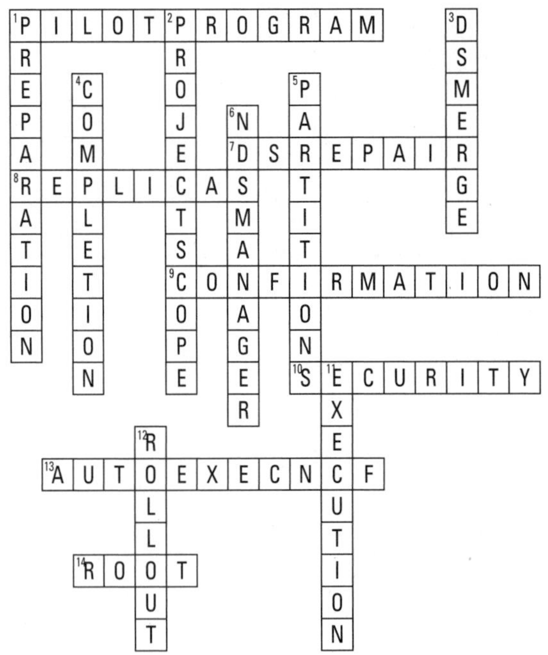

Chapter 12: Troubleshooting Fundamentals and Tools

Lab Exercise 12.1: Troubleshooting with Novell Internet Services

Note: As you begin to work with the *Novell Support Connection* CD, you will undoubtedly discover that it provides multiple menu routes to the same information. Because of this, you may find that the steps you use to locate the information required in these exercises are different than the possible solutions listed in this appendix.

Novell Internet Services — Case #1

Answer: (See steps listed below.)
Possible solution:

1. Access the Novell Support Connection Web site at `http://support.novell.com`.
2. When the Support page appears, click Patches & Files under the Support Links heading in the left column.
3. When the Patches & Files page appears, click Novell Downloadable Software Index under the Related Links heading at the bottom of the left column.
4. When the Novell Software Downloads (English Downloads) page appears, click Clients under the Subject Links heading in the left column.
5. When the Clients list appears, click Client 3.3 for Windows 95/98 English in the center column.

6. When the Client 3.3 for Windows 95/98 English Product Description page appears, click Proceed to Download in the center column.

7. When the Client 3.3 for Windows 95/98 English Lead Collection (that is, registration form) page appears, fill out the form in the center column, then click Connect. (**Note:** A red field name indicates a required field.)

8. When the U.S. Export Restriction Notice page appears, click Accept to agree to its terms and conditions.

9. When the Download Links page appears, click Download Now.

10. When the Save As... dialog appears, specify a location and click Save.

11. The file will then be downloaded to the location you specified.

Novell Internet Services — Case #2
Answer: (See steps listed below.)
Possible solution:

1. Access the Novell corporate home page at `http://www.novell.com`.

2. Select Education near the middle of the main page.

3. When the Education page appears, click Certifications under the Education Links heading in the left column.

4. When the Novell Professional Certifications page appears, scroll down the page, then click on the Certified Novell Engineer (CNE) link in the middle column.

5. When the CNE Certification page appears, click the What Does It Take to Become A CNE link near the top of the middle column.

Novell Internet Services — Case #3

Answer: Pay-as-you-go telephone support is not available directly from Novell on a per-incident or per-minute basis. Package plans are available, however.

Possible solution:

1. Access the Novell corporate home page at `http://www.novell.com`.
2. Click Support at the top of the main page.
3. When the Support page appears, click Support Programs under the Support Links heading in the left column.
4. When the Support Programs page appears, scroll down, then click Tell Me More under the Premium Service section in the middle column.
5. When the Premium Service page appears, click the Features Chart link corresponding to your geographic area in the left column. (For example, if you are located in Europe, you would click the EMEA Feature Chart link under the Europe, Middle East, Africa heading on the left.)
6. When the Overview of Premium Services page appears, you'll notice that a number of different pre-paid service package options are listed. None of them, however, provide telephone support on a (per-minute or per-incident) pay-as-you-go basis.

Novell Internet Services — Case #4

Answer: (See steps listed below.)

Possible solution:

1. Access the Novell Support Connection Web site at `http://support.novell.com`.
2. When the Support page appears, click Knowledgebase under the Support Links heading in the left column.

3. In the Search field titled "Enter a Word, Phrase, or Technical Information Document Number", enter DSREPAIR Maintenance Procedures, then click Search Now.

4. When the Search Results page appears, click the NDS Health Check Procedures link in the center column. (It is dated 29 Sep 2000.)

Lab Exercise 12.2: Troubleshooting with SupportSource 2000

Note: You must create a SupportSource 2000 trial account using the directions in Part I of this lab exercise before you can perform the remaining tasks in the exercise.

SupportSource 2000 — Case #1

1. Log into the SupportSource 2000 web site.

2. Click the Query tab.

3. Double-click Mainboards (since SIMMs are installed on the system board).

4. When a search criteria screen appears:

   a. In the Make field, enter **Packard Bell** (since it is the manufacturer of the system board).

   b. In the Model field, enter **386SX** (since it is the only listing that matches the system board's model).

   c. Click search.

5. When a screen appears listing the search results:

   a. In the left column, click the plus (+) to the left of Mainboards to expand the list.

   b. Double-click the appropriate system board.

6. A diagram of the system board will appear, as well as various types of information about the board.

SupportSource 2000 — Case #2

1. Click the Query tab.

2. Double-click Hard Drives.

3. When a search criteria screen appears:

    a. In the Make field, enter **Micropolis**.

    b. In the Model field, enter **2112-15 Rev. 2**.

    c. In the Interface field, select SCSI-2 from the dropdown list.

    d. Click Search.

4. When a screen appears listing the search results:

    a. In the left column, click the plus (+) to the left of Hard Disks to expand the list.

    b. Double-click the appropriate hard disk. (**Note:** You'll notice that the answer to the jumper setting is located near the bottom of the tables.)

5. A diagram of the hard disk will appear, as well as various types of information about the board. Scroll down to the Connections Table. Locate the SPINDLE SYNC CONNECTOR J2 assignment and take note of the location of the jumpers.

Lab Exercise 12.3: Choosing the Appropriate Troubleshooting Tool

TABLE C12.1

Network Troubleshooting Tools

INFORMATION NEEDED	SUPPORT SOURCE 2000	NOVELL SUPPORT CONNECTION (INTERNET VERSION)	NOVELL SUPPORT CONNECTION (CD-ROM VERSION)
Application Notes		X	X
Developer Notes		X	X
Hard Drive Performance Specs	X		
I/O card Configuration Information	X		
Motherboard Memory Configurations	X		
NIC Jumper Settings	X		
Novell Labs		X	X
Patches and Fixes		X	X
Product Information	X	X	X
Product Manuals		X	X
Support Forums		X	
TIDS		X	X

Lab Exercise 12.4: NetWare Troubleshooting (Word Search)

Q	U	I	C	K	F	I	X	E	S	M	O	R	P	Q	Y	X	D
S	U	P	P	O	R	T	S	O	U	R	C	E	W	F	P	S	E
U	R	H	L	B	I	G	V	B	R	P	R	A	J	M	A	I	V
P	L	I	T	N	L	T	Q	R	V	F	N	L	N	H	Y	F	E
P	O	I	F	T	Q	S	W	G	V	N	P	Y	D	M	P	Q	L
O	G	R	O	U	P	W	A	R	E	S	U	P	P	O	R	T	O
R	I	M	L	X	G	D	P	H	Y	S	I	C	A	L	M	A	P
T	C	T	R	O	U	B	L	E	S	H	O	O	T	I	N	G	E
F	A	M	O	W	H	K	N	H	R	T	D	E	N	B	G	W	R
O	L	M	A	N	U	A	L	N	A	V	I	G	A	T	I	O	N
R	M	O	C	N	G	X	F	N	G	L	R	G	S	F	P	W	O
U	A	P	R	O	D	U	C	T	M	A	N	U	A	L	S	V	T
M	P	W	R	N	N	M	L	Y	J	X	P	K	S	W	R	K	E
S	D	S	F	X	S	V	P	T	D	B	Y	F	P	L	L	W	S

1. AND
2. Developer Notes
3. Folio
4. GroupWare Support
5. Logical Map
6. Manual Navigation
7. NOT
8. OR
9. Physical Map
10. Product Manuals
11. Quick Fixes
12. Support Forums
13. SupportSource
14. Troubleshooting
15. XOR

Lab Exercise 12.5: Troubleshooting Fundamentals and Tools (Crossword)

		[1]C														
		[2]D	I	[3]A	G	[4]N	O	[5]S	T	I	C	S				
		R		P		O		P								
		O		P		V		A		[6]V	[7]I	E	W			
		M		N		E		R			N					
				O		L		E			F					
[8]H				T		L		[9]S	Y	S	O	P	S			
O				E		L					B					[10]Q
M				S		A			[11]K		A					U
E						[12]B	U	Y	E	R	S	G	U	I	D	E
[13]P	A	[14]T	C	H	E	S			Y		E					R
A		I							W							Y
G		D					[15]B	R	O	W	S	E	R			
E									R							
									D							

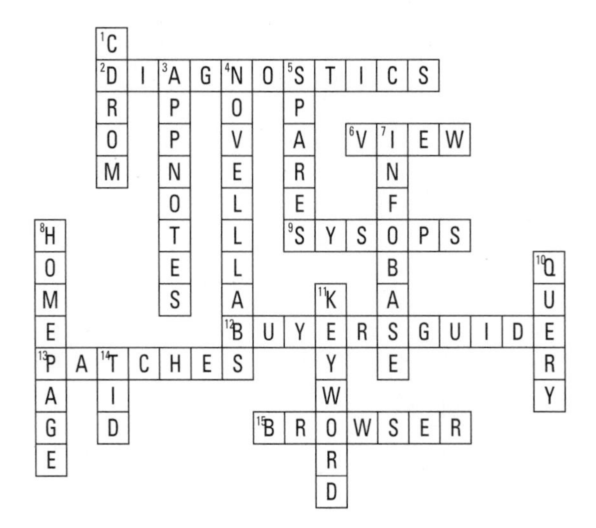

Chapter 13: Troubleshooting NICs

Lab Exercise 13.2: Troubleshooting Ethernet

1. D (Both the modem and the NIC may be using Interrupt 3. Both COM2 and NE2000 NICs use Interrupt 3, by default. If she happens to have installed her modem on COM2, and is using the default interrupt for both the modem and the NIC, an interrupt conflict would occur.)

2. H (The default Ethernet frame type for NetWare 3.11 is 802.3, whereas the default Ethernet frame type for NetWare 3.12 is 802.2. The frame type used by the workstations and servers must match in order for them to recognize each other.)

3. I (They may be ARCNet terminators—you can't tell the ohm rating of a terminator just by looking at it.)

4. B (The 5-4-3 rule for thin Ethernet states that you can have a maximum of 5 Ethernet segments, separated by 4 repeaters, with only 3 of the segments populated by workstations or servers. In this case, all five of the segments were populated by workstations or servers.)

5. C (He probably forgot to reset the connector type on the NIC from RJ-45 to BNC.)

6. A (The T-connector was probably loosened or unplugged when the painters moved the furniture.)

7. E (Some older cards and repeaters in a mixed Ethernet environment will misinterpret the SQE heartbeat that is broadcast by some of the newer cards as signal jamming. This, in turn, will cause the workstations to continually back off, and not transmit any data.)

8. J (The cable lengths may be too short instead of too long. The minimum thin Ethernet cable length between BNC connectors is 1.5 feet)

9. F (You need to use a special cable if you want to connect the computers directly instead of through a hub)

10. G (If he had to move boards around a lot to get the sound card to fit, he may not have seated all of them properly.)

Lab Exercise 13.4: Troubleshooting Token Ring

1. Speed mismatch between Token Ring NICs

2. Adapter cable attached to MSAU Ring In or Ring Out port

3. NIC addresses not excluded from use by memory manager

4. IBM LAN Support not being loaded if communication required with an IBM host
5. Prioritization set incorrectly
6. Duplicate node addresses (if set manually)
7. IRQ conflict
8. ROM address conflict
9. Shared memory conflict
10. Primary/second switch set incorrectly
11. Outdated LAN driver
12. Faulty MSAU or MSAU port
13. Other problems with non-8228 MSAUs, such as faulty fuses or power problems
14. I/O settings mismatch between the client software (NET.CFG) and NIC
15. Faulty network board
16. NIC not seated properly
17. Incorrect cable type
18. Incorrect attachments of patch cables and adapter cables
19. Faulty cable
20. Break in the daisy-chained MSAUs
21. Faulty connectors
22. Interference problems when using UTP

23. Exceeding maximum cable lengths for type of cable being used
24. Problems caused by mixing MSAUs from different vendors
25. The Type 3 media filter, if connecting to a 4 Mbps twisted pair network

Lab Exercise 13.5: Miscellaneous Troubleshooting

Some of the type of network hardware/cabling problems that you may want to simulate are:

1. Interrupt conflict
2. I/O address conflict
3. Connector parameter set wrong (for example, set to BNC instead of RJ-45)
4. Terminator(s) missing
5. Wrong speed setting on a Token Ring NIC
6. Patch cable not plugged into MSAU
7. Patch cable plugged into Ring Out instead of Ring In port
8. No cable plugged into the NIC
9. NIC card not firmly seated
10. 16-bit board in an 8-bit slot
11. Computer or display turned off or not plugged in
12. Two ARCnet cards with the same node address
13. Link Driver section in NET.CFG that doesn't match the NIC

14. O's (as in opposite) and I's (as in interrupt) instead of zeros and ones in NET.CFG

15. Section heading indented in NET.CFG

16. Wrong frame type (for example, Ethernet 803.2 instead of 802.2)

17. Wrong cable type (for example, RG-62 A/U being used for Ethernet)

18. NICs in two computers set up for incompatible cables

19. Defective cable

20. Defective (or loose) cable connector

Lab Exercise 13.6: Building ACME's Network (Word Search)

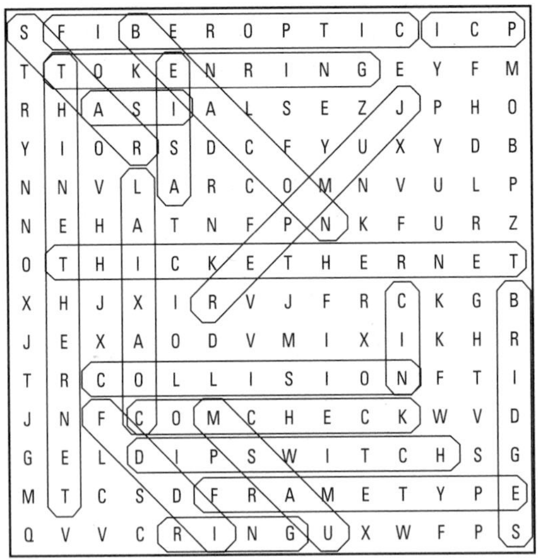

1. Beacon
2. Bridges
3. Coaxial
4. Collision

5. COMCHECK
6. Dip Switch
7. EISA
8. FDDI
9. Fiber Optic
10. Frame Type
11. ISA
12. Jumper
13. MSAU
14. NIC
15. PCI
16. Ring
17. Star
18. Thick Ethernet
19. Thin Ethernet
20. Token Ring

Lab Exercise 13.7: Troubleshooting NICs (Crossword)

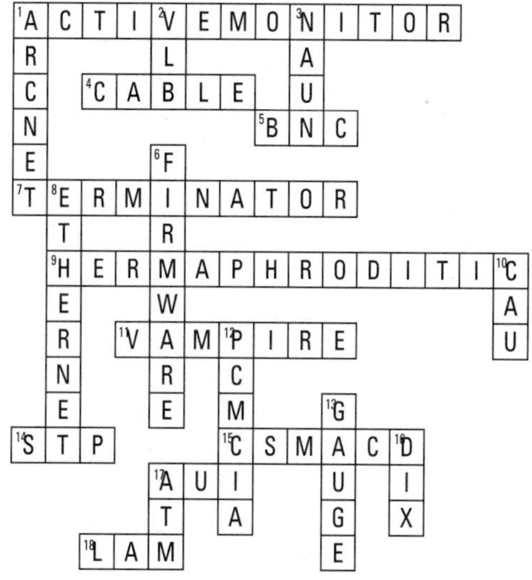

Chapter 14: Troubleshooting Hard Drives

Lab Exercise 14.1: Troubleshooting IDE Hard Drives

1. You have accidentally reversed the default values for the interrupt and port address. The statement should read:

   ```
   LOAD ISADISK PORT=1F0 INT=E
   ```

2. You have inadvertently set the Master/Slave setting for your only disk drive to Slave.

3. IDE hard disks cannot be mirrored. You can solve the problem by placing the second hard disk on its own channel and using duplexing instead of mirroring.

4. IDE hard drives do own defect reallocation internally, which fools the NetWare Hot Fix feature. Because of this, you never really know how many bad blocks you have. The best way to solve this problem is to purchase a third-party utility that tracks re-allocated blocks instead of attempting to rely on the statistics in MONITOR.NLM.

5. He would be doing a low-level format of the hard disk instead of a high-level one.

Lab Exercise 14.2: Troubleshooting SCSI Hard Drives

1. The BIOS must be enabled on your HBA in order for your SCSI disk to be bootable. Determine how to set the configurable parameters for your HBA (using jumpers or software configuration), then reset the HBA BIOS setting from "Disabled" to "Enabled." Refer to the manufacturer's documentation for further details.

2. You suspect that the HBA and SCSI hard disk both have the same SCSI ID number assigned. You suggest that he try setting the SCSI ID number for the hard disk to 0 and the one for the HBA to 7.

3. Novell does not provide a generic disk driver called SCSI.DSK, since SCSI disk drivers are manufacturer-specific. You suggest that he consult the documentation that came with the hard disk, or the manufacturer of the hard disk, for information on which disk driver to use.

4. The problem is probably caused by using an old HBA that only supports 1GB. The solution is to purchase a new HBA that will support a larger capacity SCSI disk.

5. It's very important to route SCSI cables with care. He needs to ensure that the hard drives are not seated too close together and that he's not running cables past the power supply.

Lab Exercise 14.7: Installing ACME Hard Drives and CD-ROMs (Word Search)

P	A	R	I	T	Y	C	H	E	C	K	I	N	G	K	C	O	L	B
X	N	C	I	D	O	H	B	A	V	Y	V	I	O	G	T	J	F	G
F	B	L	O	C	K	I	N	T	E	R	L	E	A	V	E	D	F	Y
H	A	U	J	D	A	I	S	Y	C	H	A	I	N	I	N	G	C	L
L	S	G	S	I	X	T	Y	F	O	U	R	R	N	F	T	T	B	X
D	E	K	E	M	T	R	S	M	H	U	Q	H	S	D	F	N	R	N
A	I	X	E	H	A	W	D	R	I	V	E	L	A	T	E	N	C	Y
T	O	U	K	W	G	S	D	I	S	K	D	R	I	V	E	R	S	I
A	A	C	T	I	V	E	T	E	R	M	I	N	A	T	I	O	N	B
S	D	Q	I	G	V	R	P	E	Y	G	E	C	G	R	P	U	J	P
T	D	W	M	Y	J	S	O	G	R	K	T	M	U	M	B	W	D	T
R	R	U	E	C	K	G	E	M	S	I	J	R	B	O	I	D	B	X
I	E	I	H	E	D	M	A	C	H	A	N	N	E	L	I	A	M	Q
P	S	Z	W	A	T	K	H	U	T	R	Z	G	D	Q	O	A	F	O
I	S	I	M	A	G	N	E	T	O	O	P	T	I	C	A	L	M	Q
N	N	M	M	P	R	D	O	S	P	A	R	T	I	T	I	O	N	M
G	H	C	X	X	N	R	L	T	K	L	L	G	Q	O	M	V	X	U

1. Active Termination
2. Base I/O Address
3. Block
4. Block Interleave
5. Bus Mastering
6. Cylinder
7. Daisy-Chaining
8. Data Striping
9. Debug
10. Disk Driver
11. DMA Channel

12. DOS Partition
13. Drive Latency
14. DSK
15. Magneto-Optical
16. Parity Checking
17. Sector
18. Seek Time
19. Sixty-Four
20. Skewing

Lab Exercise 14.8: Troubleshooting Hard Drives (Crossword)

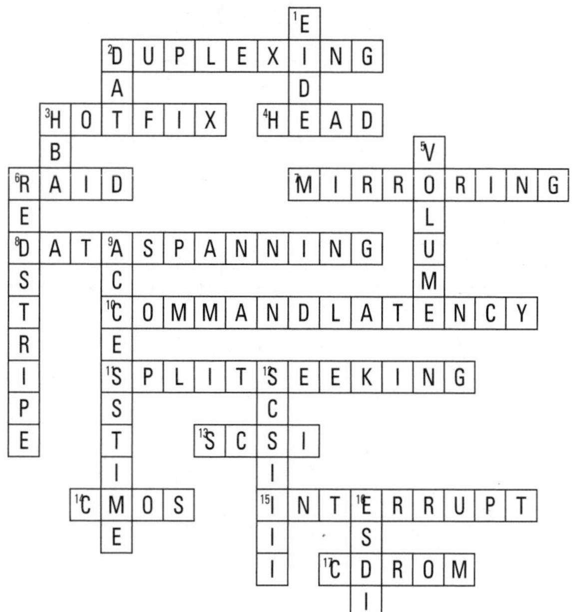

Chapter 15: Troubleshooting Workstations

Lab Exercise 15.2: Fixing ACME Workstations (Word Search)

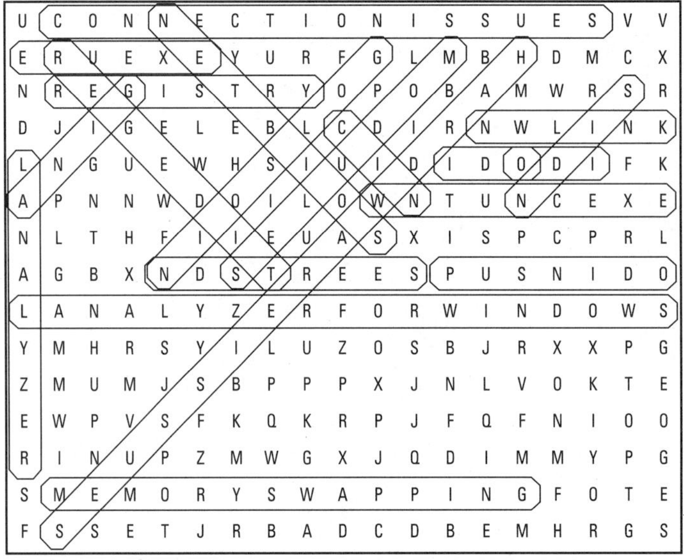

1. Connection Issues
2. ERU.EXE
3. GINA
4. Hardware Issues
5. LANalyzer
6. LANalyzer For Windows
7. Memory Swapping
8. MODULES
9. NDIS
10. NDS Trees
11. NetBIOS

12. NIC
13. NIOS.LOG
14. NWLink
15. ODI
16. ODI
17. ODINSUP
18. REGEDIT
19. Registry
20. WNTUNC.EXE

Lab Exercise 15.3: Troubleshooting Workstations (Crossword)

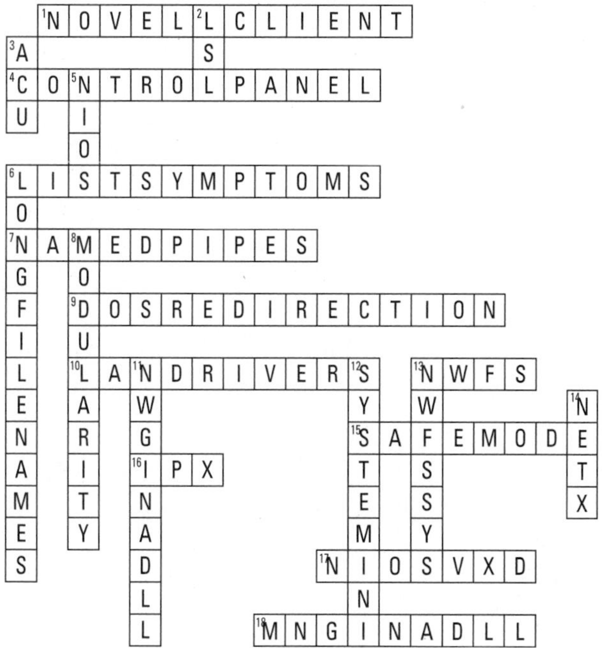

Chapter 16: Troubleshooting Printing

Lab Exercise 16.2: Troubleshooting NDPS Printing Problems (Matching)

1. E
2. D
3. A
4. B
5. C
6. D
7. A
8. B
9. E
10. C

Lab Exercise 16.3: Troubleshooting Queue-Based Printing Problems (Matching)

1. C
2. B
3. D
4. A
5. B
6. C
7. A
8. B
9. A
10. D

Lab Exercise 16.4: Fixing ACME Printing Problems (Word Search)

F	V	E	S	Y	R	E	V	I	R	D	R	E	T	N	I	R	P	H
I	J	D	B	F	Y	H	T	N	E	G	A	R	E	T	N	I	R	P
C	A	O	C	M	V	X	H	J	B	D	H	V	O	T	Y	F	I	O
M	C	M	X	N	D	S	I	N	T	E	G	R	A	T	I	O	N	R
T	T	D	X	B	X	U	H	K	P	T	O	I	U	O	M	X	T	T
H	Q	E	N	Q	P	W	C	H	B	Q	U	F	H	N	T	U	E	H
D	U	L	D	X	W	U	U	W	Y	V	D	B	N	F	E	T	R	A
F	I	L	E	S	E	R	V	E	R	B	R	P	X	O	P	Q	M	N
O	C	O	N	T	R	O	L	L	E	D	A	C	C	E	S	S	A	D
I	K	P	R	I	N	T	E	R	G	A	T	E	W	A	Y	O	N	L
M	S	E	C	R	E	V	R	E	S	T	N	I	R	P	D	Q	A	E
S	E	R	S	O	N	S	J	D	C	A	P	T	U	R	I	N	G	R
H	T	A	R	T	N	R	E	M	O	T	E	P	R	I	N	T	E	R
Z	U	T	I	P	O	S	T	S	C	R	I	P	T	N	N	R	R	R
J	P	O	M	X	L	N	O	V	E	L	L	G	A	T	E	W	A	Y
Y	U	R	N	F	E	D	C	L	A	P	N	V	B	J	O	O	B	N
C	O	A	H	D	R	Z	J	E	E	Y	G	T	V	O	U	K	J	U
K	B	L	E	B	K	V	Q	R	P	C	M	W	A	B	C	I	B	O

1. Capturing
2. Controlled Access
3. File Server
4. LPR
5. NDS Integration
6. Novell Gateway
7. Operator
8 PCONSOLE
9. Polled Mode

10. Port Handler
11. Postscript
12. Print Job
13. Print Server
14. Printer Agent
15. Printer Driver
16. Printer Gateway
17. Printer Manager
18. Quick Setup
19. Remote Printer
20. SRS

Lab Exercise 16.5: Troubleshooting Printing (Crossword)

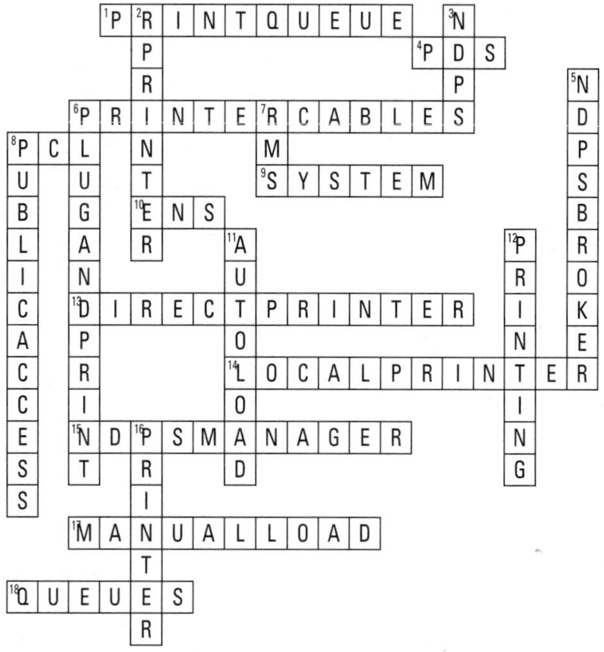

Chapter 17: Troubleshooting the Server and the Network

Lab Exercise 17.1: Fixing the ACME Servers and Network (Word Search)

S	E	R	V	E	R	L	O	C	K	U	P	D	Q	M	Q
U	T	J	D	L	B	N	I	O	O	C	E	O	I	E	J
P	B	A	S	E	L	I	N	I	N	G	B	R	R	Y	T
P	C	B	T	V	Q	N	V	A	I	I	I	F	Y	Z	P
O	S	B	K	I	S	Z	X	B	F	J	T	A	B	E	X
R	C	E	C	D	C	T	Z	R	G	U	W	Z	L	X	Y
T	F	R	A	G	M	E	N	T	A	T	I	O	N	C	F
P	R	O	T	O	C	O	L	A	N	A	L	I	Z	E	R
A	D	X	S	E	M	I	S	T	A	T	I	C	H	P	V
C	Y	W	F	X	T	T	R	B	U	B	N	E	R	T	C
K	N	E	T	W	O	R	K	E	X	P	E	R	T	I	L
P	A	S	S	E	D	T	E	S	T	H	E	N	N	O	U
R	M	O	N	I	T	O	R	N	L	M	T	K	D	N	J
P	I	F	Q	G	M	O	C	R	V	J	B	Q	Q	E	E
A	C	R	Y	L	O	G	E	Q	V	B	U	S	Q	O	V

1. ABEND
2. Baselining
3. Dynamic
4. Exception
5. Fragmentation
6. Jabber
7. MONITOR.NLM
8. Network Expert
9. Passed Test
10. Protocol Analyzer
11. Semi-static
12. Server Lockup

13. Stack
14. Static
15. Support Pack

Lab Exercise 17.2: Troubleshooting the Server and the Network (Crossword)

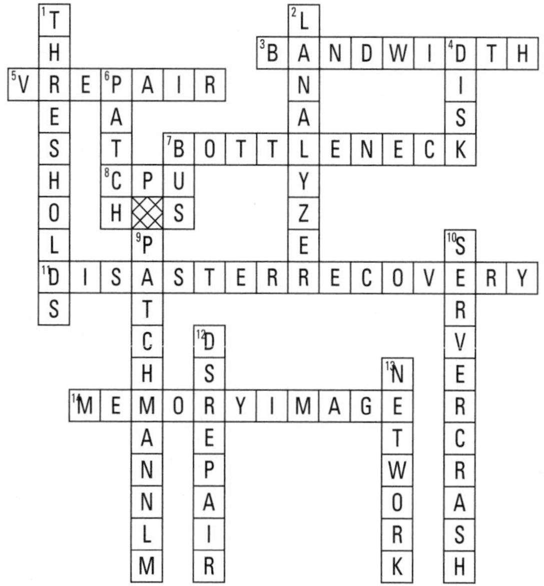

Chapter 18: The OSI Model

Lab Exercise 18.1: Introduction to the OSI Reference Model (Matching)

1. Presentation

2. Data-Link

3. Application

4. Network
5. Session
6. Physical
7. Network
8. Presentation
9. Data-Link
10. Application
11. Physical
12. Session
13. Network
14. Application
15. Session
16. Data-Link
17. Transport
18. Presentation
19. Network
20. Transport
21. Data-Link
22. Physical

23. Session

24. Network

25. Physical

Lab Exercise 18.2: Understanding Computer Networking (Word Search)

P	P	N	E	T	W	O	R	K	M	O	D	E	L	S	O	G	V
E	E	E	W	D	D	I	S	T	R	I	B	U	T	E	D	K	V
R	E	T	O	O	F	O	E	I	M	R	M	M	D	J	O	A	P
F	R	W	G	S	B	A	C	K	U	P	S	Y	S	T	E	M	S
O	C	O	N	F	I	G	U	R	A	T	I	O	N	Q	N	D	D
R	O	R	P	P	F	Z	R	L	N	G	H	Y	K	V	H	Y	S
M	M	K	C	D	A	C	I	R	T	U	X	R	D	U	F	M	B
A	M	L	L	H	H	A	T	V	D	X	P	U	G	V	O	F	Q
N	U	A	Y	L	S	V	Y	K	C	A	B	E	G	R	A	H	C
C	N	E	T	W	O	R	K	S	E	R	V	I	C	E	S	E	H
E	I	Q	B	I	X	Z	M	S	T	N	C	N	Y	J	N	A	A
I	C	S	S	T	B	K	I	M	P	A	Z	L	Y	T	F	D	N
Y	A	I	E	L	U	G	G	P	Y	F	O	J	R	R	C	E	G
U	T	A	C	C	O	U	N	T	I	N	G	A	H	F	B	R	E
S	I	E	V	L	I	S	W	W	D	M	L	K	D	G	W	F	O
Y	O	E	C	V	P	V	S	Y	R	I	T	P	U	C	D	C	R
B	N	R	P	Y	O	Y	R	O	Z	U	Y	D	H	K	H	D	D
R	S	J	W	X	N	G	N	E	T	W	O	R	K	I	N	G	E
O	J	K	P	W	O	M	D	M	S	Y	I	G	F	G	K	I	R

1. Accounting
2. Backup Systems
3. Centralized
4. Change Order
5. Charge-Back
6. Communications
7. Configuration

8. Distributed
9. Fault
10. Footer
11. Header
12. Network
13. Network Models
14. Network Services
15. Networking
16. OSI
17. Peer
18. Performance
19. Security
20. Services

Lab Exercise 18.3: The OSI Model (Crossword)

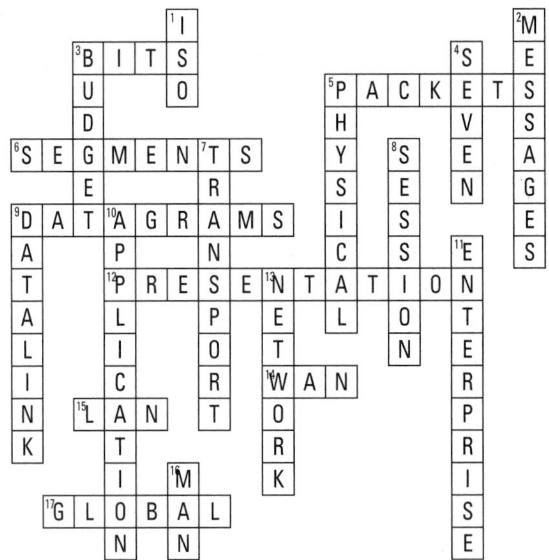

Chapter 19: The OSI Model — Bottom Layers

Lab Exercise 19.1: Transmission Media (Matching)

1. K
2. C
3. J
4. D
5. K
6. E
7. F
8. C
9. A
10. F
11. I
12. J
13. B
14. D

15. I

16. G

17. H

18. E

19. I

20. B

21. A

22. H

23. G

24. D

25. I

Lab Exercise 19.2: Getting to Know the Bottom Layers (Word Search)

S	L	I	P	B	N	J	T	W	X	Y	C	A	J	E	Y	C	E
Y	O	L	C	R	Q	R	F	L	H	G	N	S	A	R	G	M	B
N	G	Q	A	L	F	O	R	A	M	T	C	D	N	M	L	Q	M
C	I	R	A	I	S	C	J	T	F	R	T	E	M	M	P	Y	H
H	C	X	Y	D	X	J	K	Y	J	K	F	X	P	M	T	X	U
R	A	S	M	C	C	A	B	L	E	M	E	D	I	A	G	D	U
O	L	L	T	P	O	P	O	L	L	I	N	G	K	E	M	J	E
N	A	O	J	A	S	Y	N	C	H	R	O	N	O	U	S	T	C
O	D	I	G	I	T	A	L	S	I	G	N	A	L	I	N	G	V
U	D	S	L	D	B	T	O	K	E	N	P	A	S	S	I	N	G
S	R	S	L	Y	E	U	D	B	E	O	D	U	R	P	O	D	D
D	E	T	W	R	A	M	I	M	C	R	V	N	F	N	O	C	J
V	S	N	S	I	F	R	A	M	E	R	E	L	A	Y	V	G	Y
Q	S	V	R	E	T	U	O	R	B	R	O	A	D	B	A	N	D
M	T	U	T	Q	U	C	M	I	C	R	O	W	A	V	E	O	F
H	I	V	C	W	Z	N	H	E	M	V	J	T	N	O	Z	Q	Y
G	C	G	V	C	U	R	R	E	N	T	S	T	A	T	E	B	Y
D	Q	H	J	T	M	W	K	I	S	B	V	W	A	Z	E	S	M

1. AMI
2. Asynchronous
3. Band
4. Broadband
5. Brouter
6. Cable Media
7. Coaxial
8. Current State
9. Demarc
10. Digital Signaling
11. Frame Relay
12. Logical Address
13. Microwave
14. Polling

15. POP
16. SLIP
17. StatTDM
18. Switches
19. Synchronous
20. Token Passing

Lab Exercise 19.3: The OSI Model — Bottom Layers (Crossword)

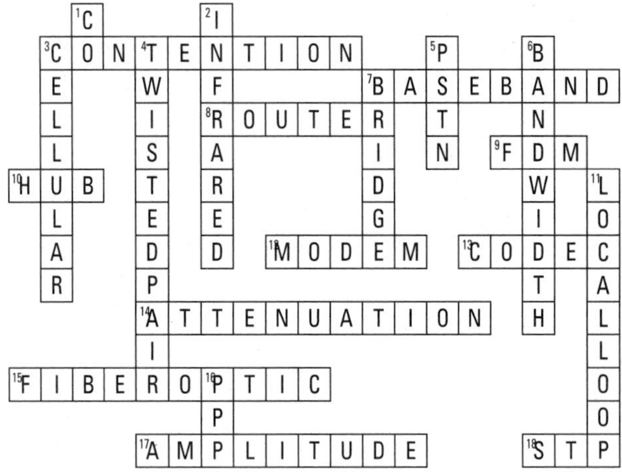

Chapter 20: The OSI Model — Middle Layers

Lab Exercise 20.1: Getting to Know the Middle Layers (Word Search)

R	O	U	T	E	S	E	L	E	C	T	I	O	N	S	J
I	A	C	O	N	N	E	C	T	I	O	N	I	D	I	N
T	N	Q	G	B	M	K	C	K	B	I	Y	Y	W	K	Z
O	S	E	G	M	E	N	T	A	T	I	O	N	G	Z	F
K	O	P	P	V	J	X	D	L	J	W	R	O	A	E	E
E	U	E	L	O	A	D	B	A	L	A	N	C	I	N	G
N	R	X	K	I	T	F	U	C	A	G	V	Z	N	Y	V
R	C	O	U	N	T	T	O	I	N	F	I	N	I	T	Y
I	E	J	I	B	P	H	O	R	Q	K	L	V	Y	P	R
N	R	S	L	K	O	Y	O	T	W	J	L	K	Z	D	I
G	O	R	C	A	R	N	O	R	Z	A	Q	V	Y	B	P
G	U	E	B	R	T	U	V	Y	I	E	R	N	Q	M	U
J	T	J	S	A	C	M	L	E	Z	Z	A	D	D	L	I
G	I	F	Y	Q	O	X	A	J	D	M	O	S	I	J	Q
E	N	E	P	I	S	D	N	F	I	E	Y	N	V	N	V
P	G	L	O	R	T	N	O	C	W	O	L	F	E	Y	G

1. ATM
2. Connection ID
3. Count To Infinity
4. CRC
5. Dynamic
6. Flow Control
7. Forwarding
8. ISDN
9. LAT
10. Load Balancing
11. Port Cost
12. RIT

13. Route Selection
14. Segmentation
15. SNA
16. Source Routing
17. Split Horizon
18. TCN
19. Token Ring
20. VLAN

Lab Exercise 20.2: The OSI Model — Middle Layers (Crossword)

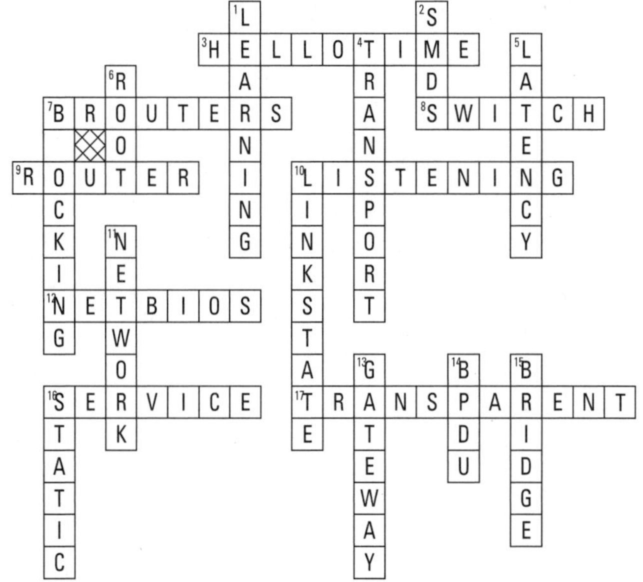

Chapter 21: Middle Layer Protocol Families

Lab Exercise 21.1: Getting to Know Internet and NetWare Protocols (Word Search)

```
R W B M C I D R E S O L V E R S
N S S U N L P D I S O E J T E U
Q F K O Q N A X T P S J W E P B
G F X E Q M A S T E R V V N L N
H O S T M L S V S P P O X L I E
T R A F F I C M P C Q P F E C T
T W P R A D N B E P T A N T A M
P A U T H E N T I C A T I O N A
C R Z Q S U B N E T T I N G Z S
S D E E V I F Q O R Y H Y K L K
D I T C C E Y X P O N C A J P G
S N T K I L X R Z V V A D P T I
L G T Y N I R X W D G Q L Q C S
```

1. ARP
2. Authentication
3. CIDR
4. Class C
5. Forwarding
6. Host
7. HTTP
8. ICMP
9. Internal
10. IPX
11. Master

12. MLID
13. Replica
14. Resolvers
15. RIP
16. SAP
17. Subnet Mask
18. Subnetting
19. Telnet
20. Traffic

Lab Exercise 21.2: Middle Layer Protocol Families (Crossword)

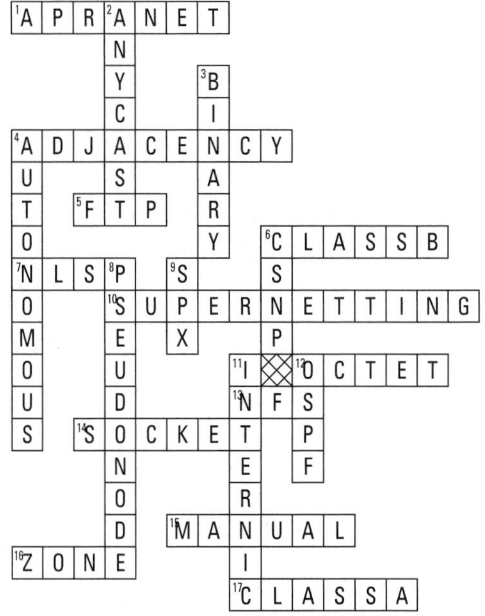

Chapter 22: The OSI Model — Top Layers

Lab Exercise 22.1: Getting to Know the Top Layers (Word Search)

D	I	A	L	O	G	Z	G	T	W	I	M	U	X	V	Y	D	N	I
A	N	X	K	Q	K	Q	P	D	C	K	D	L	O	C	H	T	W	O
T	M	A	T	F	I	L	E	S	E	R	V	I	C	E	S	O	C	O
A	P	P	L	E	S	H	A	R	E	A	T	P	W	U	X	Q	C	A
B	H	Y	D	Q	S	Y	W	C	F	P	P	M	L	I	E	S	K	E
A	Y	R	F	D	D	C	M	P	Y	P	H	P	P	O	I	S	G	M
S	S	K	E	C	P	V	I	F	N	N	O	C	C	X	U	H	H	D
E	I	F	I	Q	S	N	O	C	L	N	S	S	P	V	E	C	A	Q
S	C	B	Y	B	Q	B	I	C	P	I	T	B	K	H	I	E	C	O
E	A	P	P	L	I	C	A	T	I	O	N	S	E	R	V	E	R	S
R	L	Y	F	M	Z	B	W	N	P	E	O	A	B	V	L	M	E	Y
V	U	S	W	K	K	H	X	M	Q	F	D	M	X	E	O	T	H	U
I	N	O	M	E	S	S	A	G	E	S	E	R	V	I	C	E	S	L
C	I	K	D	X	Q	D	H	R	P	T	D	D	V	T	G	W	Q	J
E	T	P	N	Q	U	J	G	Q	O	V	R	X	B	S	I	M	H	Q
S	U	R	D	Y	P	H	M	S	E	K	X	Y	W	C	O	G	S	U

1. AFP
2. APPC
3. AppleShare
4. Application Servers
5. APPN
6. ATP
7. CICS
8. CLNS
9. CONS
10. Database Services
11. DDCMP
12. DDP

13. Dialog
14. DNA
15. File Services
16. FTAM
17. Host Node
18. Message Services
19. Physical Unit
20. RTMP

Lab Exercise 22.2: The OSI Model — Top Layers

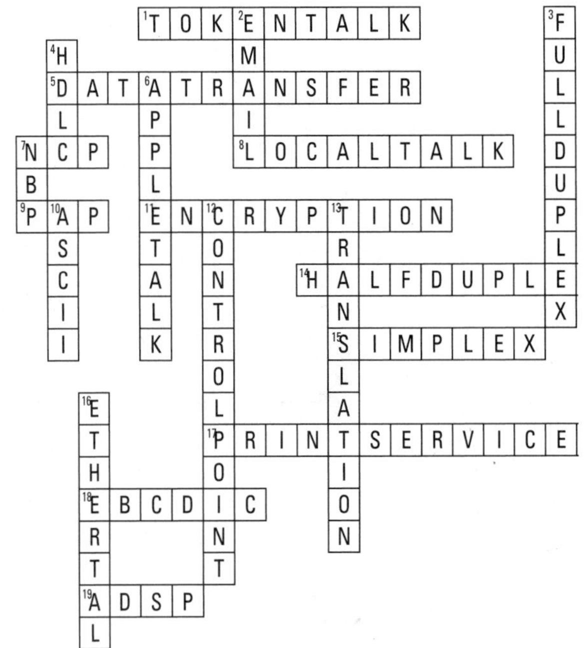

APPENDIX D

Just Do It! ACME Implementation Matrix

As a CNE, you come highly recommended. Your mission—*should you choose to accept it*—is to build the ACME WAN and NDS tree. You will need courage, design experience, NDS know-how, and this appendix. If you succeed, you will save the world and become a CNE! All in a day's work.

Actually, you have a daunting task ahead of you. A project of this magnitude requires sharp thinking and a very organized approach. All the fancy footwork and LAN lexicon in the world isn't going to help you if you don't have a game plan. That's where this appendix comes in—it's your ACME game plan. As you learned in Chapter 11, saving the world falls into four simple steps:

- Step 1: NDS Preparation
- Step 2: NDS Design
- Step 3: NDS Implementation
- Step 4: NDS Management

Welcome to Step 3 . . . this is Prime Time!

The ACME Implementation Matrix is where all the action is. It is the center of attention, a blueprint for success—another road map for saving the world. More important, it's your friend.

Make one, learn it, use it!!

The Implementation Matrix should provide detailed, measurable tasks that you can perform during the life of the ACME implementation. The main focus of this matrix is the tasks and their associated subtasks. You should also include a detailed timeline with key milestones. In addition, the schedule will establish the proper timing and help to organize all the NDS implementation tasks.

The schedule also helps you track the status of the project, and can provide immediate feedback to your staff and management. A well-planned implementation schedule will not only help you manage and track the status of the NetWare 5.1

project, but it can be used to set deadlines for each task. Let's be honest; these things can go on forever.

The Implementation Matrix consists primarily of a set of charts — each with a task description, a list of its subtasks, guidelines, duration, start and end dates, percent completion, and task lead (team member). If possible, the schedule should also show the interdependencies of the tasks, measure the progress, review the work, and produce reports for management. Finally, be sure to update the chart daily, weekly, and monthly — until the project is finished.

Here's a quick preview of the ten tasks in ACME's Implementation Matrix:

- *Task 1* — Project Scope
- *Task 2* — Training
- *Task 3* — NDS Implementation
- *Task 4* — Security and Auditing
- *Task 5* — Client Migration
- *Task 6* — Server Migration
- *Task 7* — Printing Migration
- *Task 8* — Application Migration
- *Task 9* — Pilot Program
- *Task 10* — Rollout!

Now, let's build ACME's Implementation Matrix together. We will discuss each task in depth, and create a task-oriented timing chart. Remember, these charts are the road maps for ACME's success.

Please take them very seriously — we have!

Task I — Project Scope

It all starts with the *Project Scope*. This establishes the boundaries of ACME's NDS implementation. This is strictly a planning stage — it doesn't involve any action. It does, however, continue throughout the first half of the project.

You must continually assess the scope of your implementation and make subtle adjustments as needed. This involves scheduling, task orientation, documentation, and acceptance testing. ACME's Project Scope Implementation Matrix is shown in Table D.1. But, before we explore this first schedule, let's review some of its key components:

- *Task and Subtask* — A detailed description of each task and its associated subtasks, usually in outline form.
- *Duration* — The actual time it takes to complete the task. The duration is calculated according to an eight-hour workday and five-day workweek, and is always less than the difference between the start and end dates. This is because of organizational concerns, scheduling conflicts, and Murphy's Laws.
- *Start Date* — When the task begins, according to the calendar. This shows interdependencies between tasks because some tasks start after others. But most are staggered (that is, they happen at the same time).
- *End Date* — When the task finishes. This is usually greater than the start date plus duration.
- *%Complete* — An ongoing meter of task progress.
- *Person* — Whoever is in charge of the task and accountable for the schedule.

Table D.1 is a template for all ten of your Implementation Matrices. Fill in the information as needed.

TABLE D.1

ACME's Project Scope Matrix

TASK	SUBTASK	DURATION	START DATE	END DATE	%COMPLETE	PERSON
Main Task: Project Scope		**12 weeks**	**1/1/02**			
1.1 Determine Milestones						
1.2 Determine Critical Path						
1.3 Determine Success Factors						
1.4 Risk Analysis						
1.5 Establish Reporting and Tracking						
1.6 Documentation						
1.7 Acceptance Testing						

Task 2 — Training

"Knowledge is nourishment for the mind."

This has never been more obvious than with ACME and NDS implementation. Do not skimp on training. This is one of the most critical tasks in the entire process. Like project scope, training occurs throughout the life of the project. As a matter of fact, training occurs before, during, and after the ACME implementation.

Because some of the later tasks are dependent on training, we will start this task first — on January 1, 2002. During the training phase, you need to train your administrators, users, and the project team. The training task also involves lab testing.

Here are some excellent sources for NetWare 5.1 training:

- *Novell Authorized Education Centers* — Numerous courses are available for NetWare 5.1 alone. Surf the Web to `www.novell.com/education`.
- *Colleges and Universities* — Many formal institutions now offer certified NetWare 5.1 training courses.
- *Novell Press books* — *Novell's CNA Study Guide for NetWare 5.1* and *Novell's CNE Study Guide for NetWare 5.1* are just a few of the titles you'll find useful. Surf the Web to `www.novell.com/education/books`.
- *Novell Application Notes* — Novell's monthly technical journal for network design, implementation, administration, and integration. Check them out on CD-ROMs #2 and #3 in this book.

Refer to Table D.2 for ACME's Training Matrix.

TABLE D.2

ACME's Training Matrix

TASK	SUBTASK	DURATION	START DATE	END DATE	%COMPLETE	PERSON
Main Task: Training		**20 weeks**	**1/1/02**			
2.1 Determine Training Needs						
2.2 Determine Training Strategies						

TABLE D.2

ACME's Training Matrix (continued)

TASK	SUBTASK	DURATION	START DATE	END DATE	%COMPLETE	PERSON
Main Task: Training		**20 weeks**	**1/1/02**			
2.3 Obtain Training						
2.4 Set Up the Lab						

Task 3 — NDS Implementation

NDS implementation transcends all the other tasks in the sense that it occurs continually. Once you have designed the NDS tree (see Chapter 9), you must install the servers (see Chapter 1), and finally, put the resources in place and manage the tree. This is where we build on the NDS Merging and Partition/Replica Management duties we learned earlier in Chapter 11.

Following are some estimated time frames for each of ACME's NDS implementation subtasks:

1. *Create NDS Naming Standard* — 4 days
2. *Design NDS Tree* — 2 days
3. *Design and Implement Partitions and Replicas* — 3 days
4. *Design and Implement Time Synchronization* — 2 days
5. *Develop NDS Accessibility Plan* — 7 days

Remember, these aren't consecutive calendar days — they are actual durations. The real calendar time will be much longer. Refer to Chapters 9 and 10 for an in-depth discussion of these subtasks. For now, refer to Table D.3 for ACME's NDS Implementation Matrix. Notice that it occurs one month after training begins. You'll have to learn this stuff before you can schedule it.

TABLE D.3

ACME's NDS Implementation Matrix

TASK	SUBTASK	DURATION	START DATE	END DATE	%COMPLETE	PERSON
Main Task: NDS Implementation		**5 weeks**	**2/1/02**			
3.1 Create NDS Naming Standard (4 days)	3.1.1 Identify Existing Standards					
	3.1.2 Create NDS Naming Documents					
	3.1.3 Deliver NDS Naming Documents					
3.2 Design NDS Tree (2 days)	3.2.1 Gather Corporate Documents					
	3.2.2 Review WAN Maps					
	3.2.3 Review Campus Maps					
	3.2.4 Design Top of Tree					
	3.2.5 Review Organization					
	3.2.6 Review Resource List					
	3.2.7 Design Bottom of Tree					
	3.2.8 Place Resources in Containers					
	3.2.9 Design Considera-tions					

TABLE D.3

ACME's NDS Implementation Matrix (continued)

TASK	SUBTASK	DURATION	START DATE	END DATE	%COMPLETE	PERSON
Main Task: NDS Implementation		**5 weeks**	**2/1/02**			
3.2 Design NDS Tree (2 days) *(continued)*	3.2.9.1 Administration					
	3.2.9.2 Partitioning					
	3.2.9.3 Login Scripts					
	3.2.9.4 Bindery Services					
	3.2.9.5 Test NDS Tree Design					
3.3 Design and Implement Partitions and Replicas (3 days)	3.3.1 Review WAN Map					
	3.3.2 Partition Top of Tree					
	3.3.3 Build Replica Strategy					
	3.3.3.1 Replicate Locality					
	3.3.3.2 Replicate for Fault Tolerance					

Continued

TABLE D.3

ACME's NDS Implementation Matrix (continued)

TASK	SUBTASK	DURATION	START DATE	END DATE	%COMPLETE	PERSON
Main Task: NDS Implementation		**5 weeks**	**2/1/02**			
3.3 Design and Implement Partitions and Replicas (3 days) *(continued)*	3.3.4 Partition Bottom as Needed					
	3.3.5 Develop Partition and Replica Guidelines					
	3.3.6 Test Partitions and Replica Strategy					
3.4 Design and Implement Time Synchronization (2 days)	3.4.1 Evaluate Time Synchronization Options					
	3.4.1.1 Single-Reference (Default)					
	3.4.1.2 Time Provider Group					
	3.4.2 Choose Options Based on WAN					
	3.4.3 Evaluate Time Synchronization Communications					

TABLE D.3

ACME's NDS Implementation Matrix (continued)

TASK	SUBTASK	DURATION	START DATE	END DATE	%COMPLETE	PERSON
Main Task: NDS Implementation		**5 weeks**	**2/1/02**			
3.4 Design and Implement Time Synchronization (2 days) *(continued)*	3.4.3.1 Service Advertising Protocol (SAP)					
	3.4.3.2 Configured List					
	3.4.4 Develop Time Synchronization Strategy					
	3.4.5 Test Time Synchronization Strategy					
3.5 Build NDS Accessibility Plan (7 days)	3.5.1 Analyze Existing Login Scripts					
	3.5.2 Move System Login Script to Container Login Script					
	3.5.3 Test Login Scripts					
	3.5.3.1 Container Login Scripts					

Continued

TABLE D.3

ACME's NDS Implementation Matrix (continued)

TASK	SUBTASK	DURATION	START DATE	END DATE	%COMPLETE	PERSON
Main Task: NDS Implementation		**5 weeks**	**2/1/02**			
3.5 Build NDS Accessibility Plan (7 days) *(continued)*	3.5.3.2 Profile Login Scripts					
	3.5.4 Develop Mobile User Strategy					
	3.5.5 Test Mobile User Access					
	3.5.6 Deliver Accessibility Plan					

Task 4 — Security and Auditing

Security and Auditing are very important parts of the NDS implementation. Once you've established the tree guidelines, you'll need to concentrate on securing it. See *Novell's CNA Study Guide for NetWare 5.1* for more details.

Note that migrating users don't have to worry about file system security — it should already be in place. You should, however, test it first. Refer to Table D.4 for ACME's Security and Auditing Matrix.

TABLE D.4

ACME Security and Auditing Matrix

TASK	SUBTASK	DURATION	START DATE	END DATE	%COMPLETE	PERSON
Main Task: Security and Auditing		**1 week**	**3/1/02**			
4.1 Design Server Security	4.1.1 Set Server Settings					
	4.2 Create NDS Security					
	4.2.1 Object Security					
	4.2.2 Property Security					
	4.2.3 Develop NDS Security Strategy					
	4.2.4 Test Security Strategy					
4.3 Design File System Security	4.3.1 Develop File System Strategy					
	4.3.2 Test File System Strategy					
4.4 Build Auditing System	4.4.1 Define Audit Procedures					
	4.4.2 Under-stand Audit Utilities					

Continued

TABLE D.4

ACME Security and Auditing Matrix (continued)

TASK	SUBTASK	DURATION	START DATE	END DATE	%COMPLETE	PERSON
Main Task: Security and Auditing		**1 week**	**3/1/02**			
4.4 Build Auditing System *(continued)*	4.4.3 Develop Audit Strategy					
	4.4.4 Test Audit Strategy					

The next two tasks represent the *Big Two* of the implementation tasks: Client Migration and Server Migration. After all, users depend on NetWare 5.1 clients and the NDS tree depends on NetWare 5.1 servers.

Let's take a closer look.

Task 5 — Client Migration

Client Migration is the first of two critical implementation tasks: Client Migration and Server Migration. In Chapter 1, we discovered how to install NDS client/server resources. Now let's take a moment to learn NetWare 5.1's five-step Client Migration strategy:

- *Step 1* — Assess Existing Network Clients
- *Step 2* — Determine Migration Strategy
- *Step 3* — Share New Client Software with Administrators
- *Step 4* — User Training
- *Step 5* — Upgrade Clients

Step 1: Assess Existing Network Clients

During the first step of client migration, you'll need to assess the current state of clients throughout your network. Survey the client operating systems (including version numbers) and determine whether they are compatible with NDS and NetWare 5.1. If most of your users are using the NETx shell for connectivity, you will need to upgrade them to the new Novell Client. This step usually precedes server migration because the newer shells support connectivity to both NetWare 3.12, NetWare 4.11, and NetWare 5.1.

Finally, assess each user's level of networking expertise. Determine the impact of new Client software on their daily routine. The most important goal of this step is to gain an appreciation for the client diversity within your network. One of your most important tasks as a CNE is to standardize connectivity throughout the WAN.

Step 2: Determine Migration Strategy

The next step is to determine your overall client migration strategy. This involves a number of client compatibility issues from protocol to performance. Here are a few things to think about when developing a client migration strategy:

- *Protocols* — List all the protocols needed for each workstation.
- *Workstation management* — Will you manage workstations using SNMP tools? These tools provide information to network administrators about workstations connected to the WAN. If SNMP is necessary, be sure to include the appropriate Novell Client SNMP extensions.
- *Security* — If you plan on using RSA encryption or NetWare-enhanced security, be sure to include the appropriate Novell Client extensions.
- *Backward compatibility* — Will the workstation connect to bindery-based servers? Do applications running at this workstation require NETx compatibility? If so, be sure to include the appropriate Novell Client extensions.
- *Performance* — If the workstation requires enhanced performance, consider including parameters for Large Internet Packets (LIP) or packet bursting.

Once you've addressed all these issues, you can start to formulate a client migration strategy. During the migration or installation of the new Client software, test different methods for the best efficiency. Try running the setup utility over the network or from a batch file at your workstation.

Also consider an automated strategy for upgrades from the server. For example, when the user logs into a NetWare 5.1 server, the automated program could download the required programs to the user's workstation—this is called *Automatic Client Upgrade* (ACU). Finally, consider upgrading other system software for the workstation while you're there. For example, you could take this opportunity to upgrade the workstations to the latest version of Windows or perform other necessary upgrades.

Step 3: Share New Client Software with Administrators

Once you have determined what your client migration strategy will be, be sure to share the results with distributed administrators. If you have a lab, train the administrators on migrating typical workstation configurations. In the case of Client 16, this means you'll need to prepare some sample INSTALL.CFG files. Also assign administrators to upgrade their own workstations to get them familiar with the different client architecture.

This brings me to an important point. During client migration, consider moving the entire client team and other IS staff members to the new software first. This will enable them to become familiar with the technology. Then, when you migrate the users, your administrators will already have personal experience with the system. Once the administrators are comfortable with the new client migration strategy, you're well on your way to NetWare 5.1 *Nirvana*.

Step 4: User Training

Now it's time to review Step 1 again. Go back to your user assessment and break the users into three different categories: Really Smart, Average, and Clueless. Based on these different levels, you can customize a user training strategy. *Really Smart* users can be left alone while *Average* and *Clueless* clients require a great deal more attention. Also consider the workstation as the main point of network interface for users. Sometimes training doesn't stop with Novell Client connectivity. Most of the time you'll need to review some basic Windows 95/98 topics before they understand the concepts of logging in or name context. Be careful, though—you're beginning to waiver outside the realms of your CNE responsibility.

During the training process, consider all types of training—e-mail messages, paper handouts, quick-reference cards, classroom training, and on-line courses. Once you have trained your users, you're ready for Step 5.

Step 5: Upgrade Clients

Schedule the migration of your workstations during a period that is long enough to migrate a given selected set of users. You may need to schedule this process during a weekend. Obviously, the more people involved in the migration, the faster it will go.

The client team should plan for about 15 minutes per workstation to complete the installation of the latest client software. The team should also combine all necessary changes into a single visit to each workstation. Earlier in this study guide, we learned there are a variety of different client types supported by NetWare 5.1, including Windows 95/98, Windows 3.1, DOS, OS/2, Windows NT/2000, UNIX, and Macintosh.

Refer to Table D.5 for ACME's Client Migration Matrix. You will need a little training to get the client migration started, so you'll see that we're waiting a month after the training time line. This process could start at the same time as NDS implementation, because the Novell Client supports NetWare 3.12, NetWare 4.11, and NetWare 5.1.

It's a great place to start.

So, how long will it take? Consider the following calculation for ACME:

2,000 workstations × 15 minutes per workstation = 30,000 minutes
30,000 minutes = 500 hours = 62.5 workdays = 12.5 weeks

Even though we've calculated a duration of 12.5 weeks, it could take up to 4 calendar months to visit every workstation.

TABLE D.5

ACME's Client Migration Matrix

TASK	SUBTASK	DURATION	START DATE	END DATE	%COMPLETE	PERSON
Main task: Client Migration		**12 weeks**	**2/1/02**			
5.1 Functional testing for each desktop						
5.2 Evaluate Client Migration Options						
5.3 Determine Client Migration Strategy						
5.4 Test Client Migration Strategy						

Task 6 — Server Migration

The second of the *Big Two* implementation tasks focuses on the NetWare 5.1 server. This is the Big Kahuna! The server houses NDS, stores the users' files, and provides a gateway to the cyber-frontier. For all these reasons, you should take great care in server migration.

The Server Team should consider the following functions in preparing for the migration of each NetWare 5.1 server:

1. Apply the corporate NDS Naming Standard while the objects are still in the bindery. NDS does not support different object types having the same name. By contrast, the binderies in previous versions of NetWare do support different object types with the same name. For example, in NetWare 3, a Group object called HP4SI and a print queue called HP4SI have the same name because they are different object types.

In NetWare 5.1, you cannot have any leaf object with the same name in the same container. This conflict must be resolved before the migration of the server to NetWare 5.1. If there is a duplicate, the migration utilities will not migrate the second occurrence of a duplicate object name. A Novell utility called DUPBIND (found on the Novell Internet Support Connection Web site) displays the duplicate object names in the binderies so that they can be changed before a migration begins.

2. Clean up the binderies and delete users and other objects that are no longer in use. Take this opportunity to remove security and access privileges that are no longer required. The SECURITY.EXE program in NetWare 3 will help you find and expose the detailed security information for each of the objects in the bindery. Users that have left the company or are no longer using that server should be removed.

3. Make a complete backup of your servers before beginning a migration. Some companies have individuals in an Operations group who are responsible for backups. The server team should work with this group to ensure that a recent backup has been performed on any server that is about to be migrated.

4. Run the BINDFIX utility in NetWare 3 to remove any objects that are corrupted in the bindery.

5. If you are migrating multiple NetWare 2 or NetWare 3 servers into a single NetWare 5.1 server, the server team should check for users with accounts on the multiple servers. Migrating multiple servers and duplicate users will present you with several challenges during migration to NetWare 5.1. First, the Novell Upgrade Wizard prompts you to change the username on the second and subsequent servers. Second, the Wizard will merge the User objects that have the same name into a single NDS object with cumulative rights. This may not be what you had intended.

6. If each of the multiple NetWare 2 or NetWare 3 servers are migrated into different containers in the NDS tree (OUs), the duplicate username will be migrated to each individual container with the same name, but a different context. In most cases, you do not want to manage the same user twice in the tree.

7. Delete old files and applications from the file system. This will free up disk space for other purposes. You may discover many old, unused, and duplicated applications that are wasting disk space.

8. If you are using IPX over Ethernet, ensure that your network uses the NetWare 5.1 default Ethernet frame type of 802.2. Although NetWare 5.1 will support both the 802.3 raw and IEEE 802.2 frame types, 802.2 provides automatic check-summing of packets to ensure greater communication reliability and is the preferred standard.

Refer to Table D.6 for ACME's Server Migration Matrix. This is the most time-consuming aspect of NDS implementation, because it involves most of the other implementation tasks. At ACME, we will be migrating a total of 52 servers, 3 of which will be part of the earlier pilot program—leaving us with 49 servers. It takes about 1.5 days per server, once you know what you're doing. So, here's the math:

49 servers × 1.5 days = 74 days = 15 weeks

Also, notice that the server migration starts 1.5 months after the client migration. This is because of two factors. First, the NDS implementation must be completed before we can begin (4 weeks after 2/1/02). Second, we have to wait for the procedures from the pilot program (15 days more). That puts us at 3/15/02.

TABLE D.6

ACME's Server Migration Matrix

TASK	SUBTASK	DURATION	START DATE	END DATE	%COMPLETE	PERSON
Main Task: Server Migration		**15 weeks**	**3/15/02**			
6.1 Evaluate In-Place Upgrade Wizard						
6.2 Evaluate Across-the-Wire Migration Utility						
6.3 Determine Strategy for Server Migrations						
6.4 Perform Mock Migration in the Lab						
6.5 Test Server Migration Strategy						
6.6 Develop Backup and Restore Strategy						
6.7 Build Server Migration Blueprint						

Task 7 — Printing Migration

The ACME Printing Team is responsible for designing the printing strategies for NetWare 5.1. All the print software and hardware should be tested for compatibility. This includes connections greater than 250 users. The printing strategies should also encompass printing in a mixed environment — NetWare 3 and NetWare 4 queue-based printing, and NetWare 5.1 NDPS.

Refer to Table D.7 for ACME's Printing Migration Matrix. This process depends entirely on the server migration tasks. Printing implementation takes roughly 2 hours per server:

52 servers × 2 hours per server = 104 hours = 13 days = 2.5 weeks

We will begin implementing printing with the very first pilot server; therefore, this process starts on 3/1/02.

TABLE D.7

ACME's Printing Migration Matrix

TASK	SUBTASK	DURATION	START DATE	END DATE	%COMPLETE	PERSON
Main Task: Printing Migration		**5 weeks**	**3/1/02**			
7.1 Identify Existing Printing Environment						
7.2 Evaluate Proposed Printing Layout						
7.3 Evaluate Direct Print Cards and Printers						
7.4 Determine Printing Migration Strategy						
7.5 Test Printing Migration Strategy						

Task 8 — Application Migration

The Application Project Team is responsible for performing compatibility testing for applications running on both NetWare 5.1 servers and clients. There are several issues to deal with during the compatibility testing, including:

- Bindery-based software programs
- NDS-aware applications
- Connections greater than 250 users
- Novell Client compatibility

This group is also responsible for the migration and implementation of existing applications into the new NetWare 5.1 production environment. Not all applications must be tested for compatibility — primarily because NetWare 3 and NetWare 4 have been around for a few years and also because mainstream applications are already known to be completely compatible. Applications written by internal staff, however, should be tested.

Installing shared network applications is easier, but the process still has many drawbacks. For example, you must install an icon on each user's desktop, you might have to visit each geographically separated workstation, you may assume more complex support responsibilities, and you must continually maintain desktop settings — including icons, drive mappings, and so on.

NetWare 5.1 and Z.E.N.works solve all these problems with the Novell Application Launcher (NAL). This special workstation management tool enables you to distribute network-based applications to users' workstations and manage the applications as objects in the NDS tree. Users then access the applications assigned to them using the Application Launcher Window or Application Explorer.

In addition, NAL implements solutions such as fault tolerance and load-balancing to guarantee that users always have access to the applications they need. Furthermore, if the user deletes application .DLL files from his or her hard disk, NAL automatically detects the missing files and restores them when the user attempts to launch the application.

So, what can NAL do for you? Here's a list:

- NAL provides multilevel folders to hierarchically order Application objects in the NDS tree.
- NAL automatically grants file rights to users so that they can access the applications assigned to them.
- NAL automatically grants NT Supervisor rights to the Admin user so that Admin can handle advanced Registry settings in Windows NT.
- NAL provides an application-suspension configuration to allow you to schedule a time when application access will terminate.
- NAL provides the snAppShot utility, which can be used to capture a workstation's configuration before and after an application is installed.

Refer to Table D.8 for ACME's Application Migration Matrix. Note that the actual migration of the applications occurs during the server migration phase—the duration of which is included in the 15-week estimate for Task 6.

In this section, we will estimate the duration of compatibility pretesting. This task also occurs before client and server migration. It takes roughly 1 day to test each application, and ACME has 24 different applications. Therefore, compatibility pretesting will take approximately five weeks. We'd better start as soon as we can. **Note:** The client migration may overlap with application pretesting.

TABLE D.8

ACME's Application Migration Matrix

TASK	SUBTASK	DURATION	START DATE	END DATE	%COMPLETE	PERSON
Main Task: Application Migration		**5 weeks**	**2/1/02**			
8.1 Identify all Applications						

TABLE D.8

ACME's Application Migration Matrix (continued)

TASK	SUBTASK	DURATION	START DATE	END DATE	%COMPLETE	PERSON
Main Task: Application Migration		**5 weeks**	**2/1/02**			
8.2 Analyze Internally-Written Applications	8.2.1 Install					
	8.2.2 Test on a Desktop					
	8.2.3 Test on Server					
	8.2.4 Test Printing					
	8.2.5 Document Compatibility					
8.3 Deliver Applications into Production						

Task 9 — Pilot Program

The Pilot Program is a very important precursor to server migration. It allows you to test the implementation procedures on a few "live" production servers. The goal here is to establish procedures and blueprints for the remainder of the server migrations.

It usually takes twice as much time to perform a pilot migration as a regular migration. This is because you're working on your first couple of servers and you're documenting every step. This means that it will take us two weeks to adequately migrate the three Labs pilot servers.

Refer to Table D.9 for ACME's Pilot Program Matrix.

TABLE D.9

ACME's Pilot Program Matrix

TASK	SUBTASK	DURATION	START DATE	END DATE	%COMPLETE	PERSON
Main Task: Pilot Program		**2 weeks**	**3/1/02**			
9.1 Pilot Preparation	9.1.1 Clean Up (Objects and Files)					
	9.1.2 Apply Naming Standards on all NetWare Servers					
	9.1.3 Run BINDFIX					
	9.14 Back Up Servers					
9.2 Pilot Installation or Migration	9.2.1 Upgrade Server to NetWare 5.1					
	9.2.2 Test Server (Production-like)					
	9.2.3 Document any Problems					
	9.2.4 Modify Procedures Based on Results					

TABLE D.9

ACME's Pilot Program Matrix (continued)

TASK	SUBTASK	DURATION	START DATE	END DATE	%COMPLETE	PERSON
Main Task: Pilot Program		**2 weeks**	**3/1/02**			
9.3 Acceptance Testing	9.3.1 Provide Daily Support to User					

Task 10 — Rollout!

Well, we finally made it!

This is the last leg of a very exhausting race. The Rollout Matrix is an overview of the entire project. In includes project scope, training, NDS, resource migration, and the pilot program.

As you can see in Table D.10, we've included a significant cushion in the Rollout Matrix. Even though the project will theoretically only take 21 weeks, it doesn't factor in scheduling conflicts, traveling, and Murphy's Laws. So, add another 25 percent to the total duration, and we should finish the ACME implementation on September 28, 2002. No sweat, now all we have to do is-just do it!

Ready, set, rollout.

TABLE D.10

ACME's Final Rollout Matrix

TASK	SUBTASK	DURATION	START DATE	END DATE	%COMPLETE	PERSON
Main Task: Rollout		**21 weeks**	**2/1/02**	**9/28/02**		
10.1 Just Do It!						

Wow, that's a lot of work! I can feel a very large "workquake" approaching. We're going to be very busy over the next eight months. It's a good thing we're attacking this ACME WAN together.

This completes Step 3. As you can see, NDS implementation centers on the Implementation Matrix. It is truly a road map for ACME success.

APPENDIX E

Help! For More Information

Whenever a product becomes as popular and as widely used as NetWare, an entire support industry crops up around it. If you are looking for more information about NetWare 5.1, you're in luck. There are a wide variety of places you can go for help, advice, information, or even just camaraderie.

NetWare 5.1 information is as local as your bookstore or local user group, and as international as the Internet forums that focus on Novell products. It can be as informal as articles in a magazine, or as structured as a college course. Best of all, it's easy to tap into most of these resources, wherever you may happen to be on the planet.

There is no point in trudging along through problems by yourself, when there is such a vast array of helpful people and tools at your fingertips.

This appendix describes the following ways you can get more information or technical support for NetWare 5.1. With a little digging, you can probably turn up even more resources, but these will get you started:

- General Novell product information
- The *Novell Buyer's Guide*
- NetWare 5.1 manuals
- Novell information on the Internet
- Novell Technical Support
- *Novell Support Connection*
- DeveloperNet (Novell's developer support)
- *Novell Application Notes*
- NetWare Users International (NUI)
- Network Professional Association (NPA)
- Novell Press books and other publications

General Novell Product Information

The main Novell information number, 1-800-NETWARE, can be your inroad to all types of information about Novell and its products. By calling this number, you can obtain information about Novell products, the locations of your nearest resellers, pricing information, and so on.

The Novell Buyer's Guide

If you are responsible for helping find networking solutions for your organization, you may want to get a copy of the *Novell Buyer's Guide*. This guide is a complete book on everything you could possibly want to buy from Novell.

The *Novell Buyer's Guide* explains all the products Novell is currently offering, complete with rundowns on the technical specifications, features, and benefits of those products. The *Novell Buyer's Guide* is available in a variety of formats, too. It is also available on-line through Novell's Web site on the Internet (`www.novell.com/info/bg/howtobuy.html`).

The *Novell Buyer's Guide* is also included on the *Novell Support Connection* CD-ROMs (formerly NSEPro) which are included on CD-ROMs #2 and #3 in the back of this book. If you prefer the written version, you can order the *Novell Buyer's Guide* by calling one of the following phone numbers (which are all toll-free in Canada and the USA):

- 1-800-NETWARE
- 1-800-544-4446
- 1-800-346-6855

There may be a small charge to purchase the printed version of the *Novell Buyer's Guide*.

NetWare 5.1 Manuals

NetWare 5.1 manuals are the complete reference guides to the features and workings of NetWare 5.1. In your NetWare 5.1 package, you should have received one or two printed manuals (just enough to get you started), plus a CD-ROM containing the full set of manuals on-line.

If you install the on-line documentation on your server, you'll be able to access the manuals from any workstation on the network that has an HTML browser installed, such as Netscape Navigator. If you have a laptop computer, you may want to install the on-line documentation on it, so that you can carry the entire set around with you.

If you really like having printed documentation, you can order the full printed set of manuals from Novell.

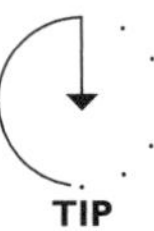
TIP

The only manual that is not included in the printed set is the *System Messages* manual. Believe me, you don't want to see how big that book would be if it were printed.

To order the printed manuals for NetWare 5.1, you can use the order form that came in your NetWare 5.1 box, or call one of the following phone numbers:

- 1-800-336-3892 (toll-free in Canada and the USA)
- 1-512-834-6905

Novell on the Internet

A tremendous amount of information about Novell and NetWare products (both official and unofficial) is on the Internet. Officially, you can obtain the latest information about Novell from Novell's home page on the Internet, as well as from the Novell forums on CompuServe. Unofficially, there are several active user forums that deal specifically with Novell products.

Novell's on-line forums offer you access to a wide variety of information and files dealing with NetWare 5.1 and other Novell products (such as GroupWise, LAN

Workplace, intraNetWare, and ManageWise). You can receive information such as technical advice from SysOps (system operators) and other users, updated files and drivers, and the latest patches and workarounds for known problems in Novell products.

Novell's on-line site also provides a database of technical information from the Novell Technical Support department, as well as information about programs such as Novell Education classes and NetWare Users International (NUI). In addition, you can find marketing and sales information about the various products that Novell produces.

Novell's Internet and CompuServe sites are very dynamic, well-done, and packed with information. They are frequently updated with new information about products, education programs, promotions, and the like.

Novell's Internet site is managed by Novell employees and by SysOps who have extensive knowledge about NetWare 5.1. Public forums can be quite active, with many knowledgeable users offering advice to those who experience problems.

To get technical help with a problem, post a public message and address the message to the SysOps. (Don't send the SysOps a personal e-mail message asking for help — the public forums are the approved avenue for help.)

To access the Novell forums on CompuServe, you need a CompuServe account. There is no additional monthly fee for using the Novell forums, although you are charged the connection fee (on an hourly rate) for accessing the service. To get to the Novell forums, use GO NETWIRE. There, you will find information for new users, telling you how the forums are set up, how to get technical help, and so on. Finally, you can also get to the Novell site on the Microsoft Network by using GO NETWIRE.

If you have a connection to the Internet, you can access Novell's Internet site in one of the following ways:

- World Wide Web: `http://www.novell.com`
- Gopher: `gopher.novell.com`
- File Transfer Protocol (FTP): anonymous FTP to `ftp.novell.com`

REAL WORLD

Users in Europe should replace `.com` with `.de`

Novell Technical Support

If you encounter a problem with your network that you can't solve on your own, there are several places you can go for immediate technical help.

Try some of the following resources:

- Try calling your reseller or consultant.
- Go on-line, and check out the Technical Support areas of Novell's Internet site. There, you will find postings and databases of problems and solutions. Hopefully, someone else will have already found and solved your problem for you.
- While you're on-line, see if anyone in the on-line forums or Usenet forums knows about the problem or can offer a solution. The knowledge of people in those forums is broad and deep. Don't hesitate to take advantage of it, and don't forget to return the favor if you know some tidbit that might help others.
- Call Novell Technical Support. You may want to reserve this as a last resort, simply because Novell Technical Support charges a fee for each incident. (An "incident" may involve more than one phone call, if necessary). The fee depends on the product for which you're requesting support.

When you call Technical Support, make sure you have all the necessary information ready (such as the version of NetWare and any utility or application you're using, the type of hardware you're using, network or node addresses and hardware settings for any workstations or other machines being affected, and so on). You'll also need a major credit card.

To get to Novell's Technical Support, call 1-800-858-4000 (or 1-801-861-4000 outside of the U.S. and Canada).

Novell Support Connection

A subscription to the *Novell Support Connection*, formerly known as the *Novell Support Encyclopedia Professional Volume* (NSEPro), can update you every month with the latest technical information about Novell products. The *Novell Support Connection* CD-ROMs contain technical information such as:

- Novell Technical Information Documents (TIDs)
- Novell Labs hardware and software test bulletins
- On-line product manuals
- *Novell Application Notes*
- *Novell Developer Notes*
- Patches, fixes, and drivers
- The *Novell Buyer's Guide*
- Novell corporate information (such as event calendars and press releases)

The *Novell Support Connection* CD-ROMs includes Folio information-retrieval software that allows you to access and search easily through the *Novell Support Connection* information from your workstation using DOS, Macintosh, or Microsoft Windows.

To subscribe to the *Novell Support Connection*, contact your Novell Authorized Reseller or Novell directly at 1-800-377-4136 (in the United States and Canada) or 1-303-297-2725.

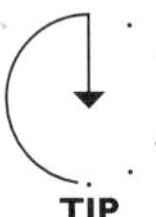
TIP

For more information on using the Novell Support Connection as a NetWare troubleshooting tool, consult Chapter 13 of this book. Note: the latest full version of the *Novell Support Connection* is included on CD-ROMs #2 and #3 in this book.

DeveloperNet Novell's Developer Support

If you or others in your organization develop applications that must run on a NetWare 5.1 network, you can tap into a special information resource created just for developers.

DeveloperNet is a support program specifically for professional developers who create applications designed to run on NetWare. Subscription fees for joining DeveloperNet vary, depending on the subscription level and options you choose. If you are a developer, some of the benefits you can receive by joining DeveloperNet include:

- The *Novell SDK (Software Development Kit)* CD-ROM, which contains development tools you can use to create and test your application
- The *DeveloperNet Handbook*
- Special technical support geared specifically toward developers
- *Novell Developer Notes*, a bimonthly publication from the Novell Research department that covers software-development topics for NetWare products
- Discounts on various events, products, and Novell Press books

For more information, to apply for membership, or to order an SDK, call 1-800-REDWORD (in the USA or Canada) or 1-801-861-5281. You can also contact the program administrator via e-mail at `devprog@novell.com`.

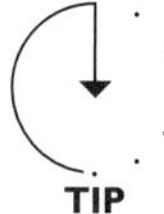

More information about DeveloperNet is available on-line on CompuServe (GO NETWIRE) or on the World Wide Web. On the Web, you can connect to the DeveloperNet information through Novell's home site, at `http://www.novell.com`**, or you can go directly to the DeveloperNet information at** `http://developer.novell.com`**. Both addresses get you to the same place.**

Novell Application Notes

Novell's Research department produces a monthly publication called the *Novell Application Notes*. Each issue of the *Novell Application Notes* contains research reports and articles on a wide range of topics. The articles delve into topics such as network design, implementation, administration, and integration.

A year's subscription costs $110 ($129 outside the United States), which includes access to the *Novell Application Notes* in their electronic form on CompuServe.

To order a subscription, call 1-800-377-4136 or 1-303-297-2725. You can also fax an order to 1-303-294-0930.

NetWare Users International (NUI)

NetWare Users International (NUI) is a nonprofit association for networking professionals. With more than 250 affiliated groups worldwide, NUI provides a forum for networking professionals to meet face-to-face, to learn from each other, to trade recommendations, or just to share "war stories."

By joining the NetWare user group in your area, you can take advantage of the following benefits:

- Local user groups that hold regularly scheduled meetings.
- *Novell Connection*, a bimonthly magazine that provides feature articles on new technologies, network management tips, product reviews, NUI news, and other helpful information.

- A discount on Novell Press books through the *Novell Connection* magazine and also at NUI shows.
- NUInet, NUI's home page on the World Wide Web (available through Novell's home site, under "Programs," or directly at `www.novell.com/community/nui`), which provides NetWare 3, NetWare 4, and NetWare 5 technical information, a calendar of NUI events, and links to local user group home pages.
- Regional NUI conferences, held in different major cities throughout the year (with a 15 percent discount for members).

The best news is, there's usually no fee or only a very low fee for joining an NUI user group.

For more information or to join an NUI user group, call 1-800-228-4NUI or send a fax to 1-801-228-4577.

For a free subscription to *Novell Connection*, fax your name, address, and request for a subscription to 1-801-228-4576. You can also mail NUI a request at:

Novell Connection
P.O. Box 1928
Orem, UT 84059-1928
USA

REAL WORLD

You don't even have to officially join NUI to get a subscription to ***NetWare Connection***, but don't let that stop you from joining. "Networking" with other NetWare 5.1 administrators can help you in ways you probably can't even think of yet.

Network Professional Association (NPA)

If you've achieved (or are working toward) your CNA or CNE certification, you may want to join the Network Professional Association (NPA), formerly called CNEPA. The NPA is an organization for network computing professionals. Its goal is to keep its members current with the latest technology and information in the industry.

If you're a certified CNE, you can join the NPA as a full member. If you're a CNA, or if you've started the certification process, but aren't finished yet, you can join as an associate member. Associate members have all the benefits of full membership, except that they cannot vote or hold offices in the NPA.

When you join the NPA you can enjoy the following benefits:

- Local NPA chapters (more than 100 worldwide) hold regularly scheduled meetings that include presentations and hands-on demonstrations of the latest technology
- *Network News*, a monthly publication that offers technical tips for working with NetWare networks, NPA news, classified ads for positions, and articles aimed at helping CNEs make the most of their careers
- Discounts on NPA Satellite Labs (satellite broadcasts of presentations)
- Product discounts from vendors
- Hands-On Technology Labs (educational forums at major trade shows and other locations as sponsored by local NPA chapters)
- Discount or free admission to major trade shows and conferences

Membership in NPA costs $150 per year. For more information or to join NPA, call 1-801-379-0330.

Novell Press Books and Other Publications

Every year, more and more books are being published about NetWare and about networking in general. Whatever topic you can think up, someone's probably written a book about it.

Novell Press itself has an extensive selection of books written about NetWare and other Novell products. For an up-to-date Novell Press catalog, you can send an e-mail to Novell Press at `novellpress@novell.com`.

You can also peruse the selection of books on-line. From Novell's main Internet site (`http://www.novell.com`), you can get to the Novell Press area (located under "Programs"). You can also get to the same location by going directly to `www.novell.com/education/books`

In addition to books, there are a wide variety of magazines that are geared specifically toward networking and general computing professionals, such as *Network News*, *Novell Connection* (from NUI), *LAN Times*, *PCWeek*, and so on.

APPENDIX F

What's On the CD ROM

This appendix includes information and installation instructions for the contents of the two CD-ROMs included with this book. The CD-ROMs contain the following information:

Disc 1

- NetWare 5.1 Operating System — 3-User Demo

Disc 2

- Client Software (including ZENworks Starter Pack)

NetWare 5.1 Operating System — 3-User Version

The *NetWare 5.1 Operating System* CD-ROM (Disc 1) that comes with this book contains a 3-user version of NetWare 5.1 with the NetWare 5.1 license embedded in the NetWare 5.1 code. No separate license disk is required to install this software. During installation, the license loads itself from the CD-ROM. Additionally, this software has no expiration date, so you can install it at any time.

NetWare 5.1 Minimum Requirements

Here are the minimum requirements for server hardware in order to run NetWare 5.1:

- Server-class PC with a Pentium processor
- VGA display adapter
- 64MB of RAM
- 600MB available disk space (50MB for the boot partition, 550MB for the NetWare partition)
- Network board

- CD-ROM drive
- PS/2 or serial mouse recommended

Installing NetWare 5.1

The following steps guide you through the installation of NetWare 5.1 on your system:

1. Create a 50MB DOS boot partition.
2. Install a CD-ROM drive and drivers according to your hardware vendor's instructions.
3. Insert the NetWare 5.1 Operating System CD-ROM (Disc 1) and type **INSTALL**.
4. Accept the License Agreement.
5. Choose the server language, if prompted.
6. Select New Server.
7. Confirm computer settings.
8. When prompted for the License Diskette, select the license located in the \LICENSE directory on the NetWare 5.1 Operating System CD-ROM. *Please note that there is no separate license diskette.*
9. Complete the installation by following the onscreen instructions.

Client Software

Disk 2 of the CD-ROM set contains the Client Software from Novell, which includes the Zenworks Starter Pack.

Installing Client Software

Follow these steps to install the Client Software:

1. On a computer running Windows, insert the Client Software CD-ROM (Disc 2) and run WINSETUP.EXE.
2. Select a language for the installation.
3. Select a platform for the installation.
4. Select the software to install.
5. Complete the installation by following the onscreen instructions.

Index

D

G

H

I

J

K

L

M

Continued

Continued

O

P

R

Continued

S

T

U

V

W

Continued

X

Z

NOTES

NOTES

NOTES

NOTES

NOTES

NOTES

MORE BOOKS FROM NOVELL PRESS™

Certification:

Novell's CNE® Study Set for NetWare® 5	0-7645-4554-X	US $174.99 / CAN $262.99
Novell's CNE® Study Guide for NetWare® 5	0-7645-4543-4	US $ 99.99 / CAN $139.99
Novell's CNE® Update to NetWare® 5 Study Guide	0-7645-4559-0	US $ 49.99 / CAN $ 69.99
Novell's CNE® Clarke Notes™ for NetWare® 5 Administration: Course 560	0-7645-4577-9	US $ 24.99 / CAN $ 37.99
Novell's CNE® Clarke Notes™ Update to NetWare® 5: Course 529	0-7645-4575-2	US $ 24.99 / CAN $ 37.99
Novell's CNA℠ Study Guide for NetWare® 5	0-7645-4542-6	US $ 74.99 / CAN $105.99
Novell's CNE® Study Set for IntranetWare/NetWare® 4.11	0-7645-4533-7	US $148.99 / CAN $208.99
Novell's CNE® Study Guide for IntranetWare/NetWare® 4.11	0-7645-4512-4	US $ 89.99 / CAN $124.99
Novell's CNA℠ Study Guide for IntranetWare/NetWare® 4.11	0-7645-4513-2	US $ 69.99 / CAN $ 96.99
Novell's CNE® Study Guide for Core Technologies	0-7645-4501-9	US $ 74.99 / CAN $104.99
Novell's Certified Internet Business Strategist℠ Study Guide	0-7645-4549-3	US $ 39.99 / CAN $ 56.99
Novell's Certified Web Designer℠ Study Guide	0-7645-4548-5	US $ 49.99 / CAN $ 69.99

NetWare:

Novell's NetWare® 5 Resource Kit	0-7645-4545-0	US $ 99.99 / CAN $149.99
Novell's Guide to NetWare® 5 Networks	0-7645-4544-2	US $ 74.99 / CAN $105.99
Novell's NetWare® 5 Administrator's Handbook	0-7645-4546-9	US $ 39.99 / CAN $ 56.99
Novell's Guide to Troubleshooting NetWare® 5	0-7645-4558-2	US $ 49.99 / CAN $ 69.99
Novell's NetWare® 5 Basics	0-7645-4563-9	US $ 29.99 / CAN $ 44.99
Novell's Guide to Integrating NetWare® 5 and NT	0-7645-4580-9	US $ 44.99 / CAN $ 67.99
Novell's Guide to NetWare® 5 and TCP/IP	0-7645-4564-7	US $ 49.99 / CAN $ 69.99
Novell's Guide to IntranetWare Networks	0-7645-4516-7	US $ 59.99 / CAN $ 84.99
Novell's IntranetWare Administrator's Handbook	0-7645-4517-5	US $ 39.99 / CAN $ 54.99
Novell's Introduction to intraNetWare	0-7645-4530-2	US $ 39.99 / CAN $ 56.99
Novell's Guide to Integrating intraNetWare and NT	0-7645-4523-X	US $ 44.99 / CAN $ 67.99
Novell's Guide to TCP/IP and IntranetWare	0-7645-4532-9	US $ 49.99 / CAN $ 69.99
Novell's Guide to NetWare® for Small Business 4.11	0-7645-4504-3	US $ 34.99 / CAN $ 49.99
Novell's Guide to NetWare® 4.1 Networks	1-56884-736-X	US $ 59.99 / CAN $ 84.99
Novell's NetWare® 4.1 Administrator's Handbook	1-56884-737-8	US $ 29.99 / CAN $ 42.99
Novell's Guide to Integrating NetWare® and TCP/IP	1-56884-818-8	US $ 44.99 / CAN $ 62.99
Novell's Guide to NetWare® Printing	0-7645-4514-0	US $ 44.99 / CAN $ 62.99

Novell Directory Services® (NDS):

Novell's Guide to Troubleshooting NDS™	0-7645-4579-5	US $ 44.99 / CAN $ 67.99
Novell's NDS™ Developer's Guide	0-7645-4557-4	US $ 59.99 / CAN $ 84.99
NDS™ for NT	0-7645-4551-5	US $ 39.99 / CAN $ 56.99

Available wherever books are sold or call 1-800-762-2974 to order today.
Outside the U.S. call 1-317-572-3993.

www.novell.com/books • www.idgbooks.com

ManageWise:

Novell's ManageWise® Administrator's Handbook	1-56884-817-X	US $ 29.99 / CAN $ 42.99

GroupWise:

Novell's GroupWise® 5.5 Administrator's Guide	0-7645-4556-6	US $ 44.99 / CAN $ 63.99
Novell's GroupWise® 5.5 User's Handbook	0-7645-4552-3	US $ 24.99 / CAN $ 35.99
Novell's GroupWise® 5 Administrator's Guide	0-7645-4521-3	US $ 44.99 / CAN $ 62.99
Novell's GroupWise® 5 User's Handbook	0-7645-4509-4	US $ 24.99 / CAN $ 34.99
Novell's GroupWise® 4 User's Guide	0-7645-4502-7	US $ 19.99 / CAN $ 27.99

Border Manager:

Novell's BorderManager™ Administrator's Handbook	0-7645-4565-5	US $ 34.99 / CAN $ 52.99
Novell's Guide to BorderManager™	0-7645-4540-X	US $ 49.99 / CAN $ 69.99

ZENworks:

Novell's ZENworks™ Administrator's Handbook	0-7645-4561-2	US $ 39.99 / CAN $ 59.99

Internet/Intranets:

Novell's Internet Plumbing Handbook	0-7645-4537-X	US $ 34.99 / CAN $ 48.99
Novell's Guide to Web Site Management 0-7645-4529-9	US	$ 59.99 / CAN $ 84.99
Novell's Guide to Internet Access Solutions	0-7645-4515-9	US $ 39.99 / CAN $ 56.99
Novell's Guide to Creating IntranetWare Intranets	0-7645-4531-0	US $ 39.99 / CAN $ 54.99
Novell's The Web at Work: Publishing Within and Beyond the Corporation	0-7645-4519-1	US $ 29.99 / CAN $ 42.99

Networking Connections/Network Management:

Novell's Guide to Troubleshooting TCP/IP	0-7645-4562-0	US $ 59.99 / CAN $ 89.99
Novell's Guide to LAN/WAN Analysis: IPX/SPX™	0-7645-4508-6	US $ 59.99 / CAN $ 84.99
Novell's Guide to Resolving Critical Server Issues	0-7645-4550-7	US $ 59.99 / CAN $ 84.99

General Reference:

Novell's Guide to Networking Hardware	0-7645-4553-1	US $ 69.99 / CAN $ 98.99
Novell's Encyclopedia of Networking	0-7645-4511-6	US $ 69.99 / CAN $ 96.99
Novell's Dictionary of Networking	0-7645-4528-0	US $ 24.99 / CAN $ 34.99
Novell's Introduction to Networking	0-7645-4525-6	US $ 19.99 / CAN $ 27.99

Available wherever books are sold or call 1-800-762-2974 to order today.
Outside the U.S. call 1-317-572-3993.

www.novell.com/books • www.idgbooks.com

Hungry Minds, Inc.
End-User License Agreement

READ THIS. You should carefully read these terms and conditions before opening the software packet(s) included with this book ("Book"). This is a license agreement ("Agreement") between you and Hungry Minds, Inc. ("HMI"). By opening the accompanying software packet(s), you acknowledge that you have read and accept the following terms and conditions. If you do not agree and do not want to be bound by such terms and conditions, promptly return the Book and the unopened software packet(s) to the place you obtained them for a full refund.

1. **License Grant.** HMI grants to you (either an individual or entity) a nonexclusive license to use one copy of the enclosed software program(s) (collectively, the "Software") solely for your own personal or business purposes on a single computer (whether a standard computer or a workstation component of a multi-user network). The Software is in use on a computer when it is loaded into temporary memory (RAM) or installed into permanent memory (hard disk, CD-ROM, or other storage device). HMI reserves all rights not expressly granted herein.

2. **Ownership.** HMI is the owner of all right, title, and interest, including copyright, in and to the compilation of the Software recorded on the disk(s) or CD-ROM ("Software Media"). Copyright to the individual programs recorded on the Software Media is owned by the author or other authorized copyright owner of each program. Ownership of the Software and all proprietary rights relating thereto remain with HMI and its licensers.

3. **Restrictions On Use and Transfer.**

   (a) You may only (i) make one copy of the Software for backup or archival purposes, or (ii) transfer the Software to a single hard disk, provided that you keep the original for backup or archival purposes. You may not (i) rent or lease the Software, (ii) copy or reproduce the Software through a LAN or other network system or through any computer subscriber system or bulletin-board system, or (iii) modify, adapt, or create derivative works based on the Software.

(b) You may not reverse engineer, decompile, or disassemble the Software. You may transfer the Software and user documentation on a permanent basis, provided that the transferee agrees to accept the terms and conditions of this Agreement and you retain no copies. If the Software is an update or has been updated, any transfer must include the most recent update and all prior versions.

4. **Restrictions on Use of Individual Programs.** You must follow the individual requirements and restrictions detailed for each individual program in Appendix X of this Book. These limitations are also contained in the individual license agreements recorded on the Software Media. These limitations may include a requirement that after using the program for a specified period of time, the user must pay a registration fee or discontinue use. By opening the Software packet(s), you will be agreeing to abide by the licenses and restrictions for these individual programs that are detailed in Appendix X and on the Software Media. None of the material on this Software Media or listed in this Book may ever be redistributed, in original or modified form, for commercial purposes.

5. **Limited Warranty.**

(a) HMI warrants that the Software and Software Media are free from defects in materials and workmanship under normal use for a period of sixty (60) days from the date of purchase of this Book. If HMI receives notification within the warranty period of defects in materials or workmanship, HMI will replace the defective Software Media.

(b) **HMI AND THE AUTHOR OF THE BOOK DISCLAIM ALL OTHER WARRANTIES, EXPRESS OR IMPLIED, INCLUDING WITHOUT LIMITATION IMPLIED WARRANTIES OF MERCHANTABILITY AND FITNESS FOR A PARTICULAR PURPOSE, WITH RESPECT TO THE SOFTWARE, THE PROGRAMS, THE SOURCE CODE CONTAINED THEREIN, AND/OR THE TECHNIQUES DESCRIBED IN THIS BOOK. HMI DOES NOT WARRANT THAT THE FUNCTIONS CONTAINED IN THE SOFTWARE WILL MEET YOUR REQUIREMENTS OR THAT THE OPERATION OF THE SOFTWARE WILL BE ERROR FREE.**

(c) This limited warranty gives you specific legal rights, and you may have other rights that vary from jurisdiction to jurisdiction.

6. **Remedies.**

(a) HMI's entire liability and your exclusive remedy for defects in materials and workmanship shall be limited to replacement of the Software Media, which may be returned to HMI with a copy of your receipt at the following address: Software Media Fulfillment Department, Attn.: *Novell's CNE Study Guide for Netware 5.1,* Hungry Minds, Inc., 10475 Crosspoint Blvd., Indianapolis, IN 46256, or call 1-800-762-2974. Please allow four to six weeks for delivery. This Limited Warranty is void if failure of the Software Media has resulted from accident, abuse, or misapplication. Any replacement Software Media will be warranted for the remainder of the original warranty period or thirty (30) days, whichever is longer.

(b) In no event shall HMI or the author be liable for any damages whatsoever (including without limitation damages for loss of business profits, business interruption, loss of business information, or any other pecuniary loss) arising from the use of or inability to use the Book or the Software, even if HMI has been advised of the possibility of such damages.

(c) Because some jurisdictions do not allow the exclusion or limitation of liability for consequential or incidental damages, the above limitation or exclusion may not apply to you.

7. **U.S. Government Restricted Rights.** Use, duplication, or disclosure of the Software for or on behalf of the United States of America, its agencies and/or instrumentalities (the "U.S. Government") is subject to restrictions as stated in paragraph (c)(1)(ii) of the Rights in Technical Data and Computer Software clause of DFARS 252.227-7013, or subparagraphs (c) (1) and (2) of the Commercial Computer Software - Restricted Rights clause at FAR 52.227-19, and in similar clauses in the NASA FAR supplement, as applicable.

8. **General.** This Agreement constitutes the entire understanding of the parties and revokes and supersedes all prior agreements, oral or written, between them and may not be modified or amended except in a writing signed by both parties hereto that specifically refers to this Agreement. This Agreement shall take precedence over any other documents that may be in conflict herewith. If any one or more provisions contained in this Agreement are held by any court or tribunal to be invalid, illegal, or otherwise unenforceable, each and every other provision shall remain in full force and effect.

CD-ROM Installation Instructions

For complete contents and descriptions of the software included on the two CD-ROMs that accompany Novell's CNE Study Guide for NetWare 5.1, please see Appendix F, "What's On the CD-ROM." Detailed installation instructions and system requirements are also provided for all included programs.

To install the software on any of the two CD-ROMs included with this book with Windows 95, 98, or NT 4.0, follow these steps:

1. Place the desired CD-ROM disc in your CD-ROM drive.

2. Click the Start button and select Run.

3. Type the letter of your CD-ROM drive with a colon and backslash (for instance, D:\) and the directory name that contains the program you wish to run, followed by the name of the appropriate executable installation file. For example, to install the Visio Solution Pack for NDS (Disc 3), you would type the following:

   ```
   D:\nds\setup.exe
   ```

4. Click OK and follow the onscreen installation instructions.